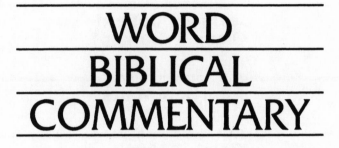

WORD
BIBLICAL
COMMENTARY

WORD

BIBLICAL

COMMENTARY

Volume 20

Psalms 51-100

MARVIN E. TATE

THOMAS NELSON
Since 1798

NASHVILLE   DALLAS   MEXICO CITY   RIO DE JANEIRO

Word Biblical Commentary
PSALMS 51-100
Copyright © 2000 by Thomas Nelson, Inc.

Library of Congress Cataloging-in-Publication Data
Main entry under title:

Word biblical commentary.

    Includes bibliographies.
    1. Bible—Commentaries—Collected works.
BS491.2.W67   220.7 '7   81–71768
ISBN 0–8499-0219-3 (vol.20) AACR2

Printed in Mexico

The author's own translation of the text appears in italic type under the heading " Translation," as well as in brief Scripture quotations in the body of the commentary, except where otherwise indicated.

ISBN: 978-0-8499-0219-2

14 15 16 17 18 EPAC 15 14 13 12 11

For Julia

Contents

Author's Preface

It hardly needs to be said that for the preparation of this commentary I am indebted to a host of previous commentators on the Psalms. The reader will recognize my dependence on the textual notes in the works of Charles Augustus and Emilie Grace Briggs (ICC, 2 volumes, 1906) and Hermann Gunkel's *Die Psalmen* (1926). No commentary yet published equals the scope and quality of the textual work in these two, dated though they are.

Those who use Louis Jacquet's massive compendium of the interpretation of the Psalms in his three-volume work, *Les Psaumes et le coeur de l'homme*, may disagree with the previous statement. Jacquet's work has been called the "best all-round commentary in any language" (C. Stuhlmueller, *Psalms* 2, 224), which may be correct, but his textual notes do not usually go much beyond those of Briggs and Gunkel.

Among more recent commentaries, that of Kraus is easily the most outstanding and I have made constant use of it. The English translation of Kraus appeared in the late stages of the preparation of my work. When the references in the pages which follow are only to Kraus by name, followed by a volume number and a page number, they are the fifth German edition of 1978 (the volume numbers in the Kraus references are actually superfluous since the pagination is continuous from volume one to volume two). When the English edition is referred to, I use the English titles followed by the page numbers, except that the title may be omitted where the reference is clear.

Artur Weiser's commentary has also been a constant companion. We may grow weary of his overemphasis on the covenant festival, but his profound piety and theological insights are treasures of great worth. As with most interpreters of the Psalms today, I suppose, I have had continual recourse to Mitchell Dahood's three-volume commentary in the Anchor Bible. Most of us probably will decide to reject Dahood's readings with considerable frequency, but he cannot be ignored. He is one of the innovative scholars of our time, forcing us to justify our own readings, even if only to repudiate his. The freshness of his approach, not to mention his audacity, has stimulated new readings. He has been one of the pioneer gadflies in contemporary study of Hebrew poetry (d. 1982). This list could go on at some length, but I will bring it to a close with a word of appreciation for the fine working commentary of A. A. Anderson (New Century Bible, 2 volumes). The commentaries listed in the bibliography at the beginning of this volume are referred to only by author and page number.

Translation of the Psalms is an enduring challenge. I have struggled long and hard on my translations in this commentary, but I know very well that they are often deficient and, I fear, downright wrong in some places. No one comes to the English translation of the Bible without utilizing the centuries-long tradition of such translation. It would be foolish to attempt to translate *de novo*, without the help of the major collegiate English versions. The reader will be aware of my constant use of the major translations. I have tried to note my dependence in numerous cases, but the text would be far too cluttered to note it in every case. The translations are intended to express the meaning of the Hebrew text of the psalms for study purposes. I am not a poet, and I ask the reader to avoid judging my efforts in terms of artistry and liturgical beauty. The biblical translations in this book are my own unless noted to be otherwise. Commonly known biblical statements are quoted at times, however, without annotation.

The verse references in the Psalms are all to the Hebrew text, unless noted otherwise. This will cause some inconvenience for the English reader, since the verse numbers frequently differ by one or two numbers between the Hebrew and the English (mostly because of the titles used with many psalms and counted as the first verse in numerous cases). The adjustment, however, is not difficult for the reader and the inconvenience is better than having the text cluttered with hundreds of double references.

My approach to the meter in the Hebrew poetry of the psalms is reflected in the meter, or unit, system found in the right-hand margin of the translations. I have attempted to follow the pattern set by Peter Craigie in his volume in this commentary on Pss 1–50 (for his explanation, see pp. 36–39 of his commentary). The system is not marked by great precision and is "essentially descriptive of the phenomenon of line length or relative line lengths" (Craigie, 38).

After considerable indecision, I have decided to use the familiar word "colon" for the component parallel lines of the Hebrew verses, rather than "line," "stich," or "verset." The colons are properly poetic line-halves, line-thirds, or line-fourths (infrequent, and the verse division is probably incorrect where it occurs). For the most part, I have avoided the use of the poetic terms "stanza" or "strophe."

I have been for some years the "missing tooth" between the work of Peter Craigie on Pss 1–50 and Leslie C. Allen on Pss 101–150. I join with many others in regret for the untimely death of Peter Craigie. He was a fine younger scholar, whose substantial contributions to biblical scholarship were cut off in midstream. The publishers and editors of this commentary have shown almost incredible patience with me as I have crawled along behind the two volumes already in print. John D. W. Watts, the OT editor, has been a constant source of patient encouragement and help. I am sure that I have caused him to spend a considerable amount of time explaining my tardiness to the general editors and to representatives of the publisher.

I owe a debt of gratitude to all my colleagues at The Southern Baptist Theological Seminary and especially for the support and permission given to be free from some other responsibilities by Provost G. Willis Bennett and Dean Larry L. McSwain of the School of Theology. My colleagues Page H. Kelley and Thomas G. Smothers have been kind enough to assist me with matters pertaining to Hebrew and Semitics on numerous occasions. The key to the Hebrew text of the psalms prepared by my senior colleague John Joseph Owens has saved me much time and energy and preserved me from many errors that I might have made.

I have been assisted in the work on some psalms by several people who have been graduate students. Carol Grizzard helped me for almost a year, and I am especially grateful to her. Others who gave me assistance over shorter periods of time are: Forrest Cornelius, Dwight Stinnett, and David Fleming.

Peter Craigie wrote of his objective in the preface to his commentary on Pss 1–50 that:

a surfeit of knowledge in the *minutiae* may lead to confusion as surely as shortage. I have sought to find a middle path in this book, drawing on the wealth of information now at our disposal, but in the end trying to clarify the meaning of each psalm in the modern world.

In my own way, that is what I have hoped to do in this volume. If I am able to help readers of the Psalms to read them with even a modest degree of improved understanding and enhanced appreciation, I will be satisfied.

Marvin E. Tate

Louisville, August 1990

Editorial Preface

The launching of the *Word Biblical Commentary* brings to fulfillment an enterprise of several years' planning. The publishers and the members of the editorial board met in 1977 to explore the possibility of a new commentary on the books of the Bible that would incorporate several distinctive features. Prospective readers of these volumes are entitled to know what such features were intended to be; whether the aims of the commentary have been fully achieved time alone will tell.

First, we have tried to cast a wide net to include as contributors a number of scholars from around the world who not only share our aims, but are in the main engaged in the ministry of teaching in university, college, and seminary. They represent a rich diversity of denominational allegiance. The broad stance of our contributors can rightly be called evangelical, and this term is to be understood in its positive, historic sense of a commitment to Scripture as divine revelation, and to the truth and power of the Christian gospel.

Then, the commentaries in our series are all commissioned and written for the purpose of inclusion in the *Word Biblical Commentary*. Unlike several of our distinguished counterparts in the field of commentary writing, there are no translated works, originally written in a non-English language. Also, our commentators were asked to prepare their own rendering of the original biblical text and to use those languages as the basis of their own comments and exegesis. What may be claimed as distinctive with this series is that it is based on the biblical languages, yet it seeks to make the technical and scholarly approach to a theological understanding of Scripture understandable by—and useful to—the fledgling student, the working minister, and colleagues in the guild of professional scholars and teachers as well.

Finally, a word must be said about the format of the series. The layout, in clearly defined sections, has been consciously devised to assist readers at different levels. Those wishing to learn about the textual witnesses on which the translation is offered are invited to consult the section headed *Notes*. If the readers' concern is with the state of modern scholarship on any given portion of Scripture, they should turn to the sections of *Bibliography* and *Form/Structure/Setting*. For a clear exposition of the passage's meaning and its relevance to the ongoing biblical revelation, the *Comment* and concluding *Explanation* are designed expressly to meet that need. There is therefore something for everyone who may pick up and use these volumes.

If these aims come anywhere near realization, the intention of the editors will have been met, and the labor of our team of contributors rewarded.

General Editors: *David A. Hubbard*
Glenn W. Barker †
Old Testament: *John D. W. Watts*
New Testament: *Ralph P. Martin*

Abbreviations

1. Periodicals, Reference Works, and Serials

AB	Anchor Bible
AJSL	*American Journal of Semitic Languages and Literature*
ANET	J. B. Pritchard (ed.), *Ancient Near Eastern Texts*
AOAT	Alter Orient und Altes Testament
AOT	*Altorientalische Texte zum Alten Testament*
ASTI	*Annual of the Swedish Theological Institute*
ATANT	Abhandlungen zur Theologie des Alten und Neuen Testaments
ATD	Das Alte Testament Deutsch
AusBR	*Australian Biblical Review*
AUSS	*Andrews University Seminary Studies*
BA	*Biblical Archaeologist*
BAR	*Biblical Archaeology Review*
BASOR	*Bulletin of the American Schools of Oriental Research*
BDB	F. Brown, S. R. Driver, and C. A. Briggs, *Hebrew and English Lexicon of the Old Testament* (Oxford: Clarendon, 1907)
BeO	*Bibbia e oriente*
*BHK*³	R. Kittel, *Biblia hebraica*³
BHS	*Biblia herbraica stuttgartensia*
BHT	Beiträge zur historischen Theologie
Bib	*Biblica*
BibLeb	*Bibel und Leben*
BibOr	Biblica et orientalia
BJRL	*Bulletin of the John Rylands University Library of Manchester*
BK	*Bibel und Kirche*
BMik	*Beth Mikra*
BN	*Biblische Notizen*
BSOAS	*Bulletin of the School of Oriental (and African) Studies*
BTB	*Biblical Theology Bulletin*
BWANT	Beiträge zur Wissenschaft vom Alten und Neuen Testament
BZ	*Biblische Zeitschrift*
BZAW	Beihefte zur ZAW
CAD	*The Assyrian Dictionary of the Oriental Institute of the University of Chicago*
CBC	Cambridge Biblical Commentary
CBQ	*Catholic Biblical Quarterly*
CJT	*Canadian Journal of Theology*
CML	*Canaanite Myths and Legends* (G. R. Driver, 2nd ed. J. C. L. Gibson)
ConB	Coniectanea Biblica
CPIP	A. R. Johnson, *The Cultic Prophet and Israel's Psalmody*
CTA	A. Herdner, *Corpus des tablettes en cunéiformes alphabétiques*
CTM	*Concordia Theological Monthly*

DOTT	D. W. Thomas (ed.), *Documents from Old Testament Times*
EstBib	*Estudios bíblicos*
ET	English translation
ETL	*Ephemerides theologicae lovanienses*
EvT	*Evangelische Theologie*
ExpTim	*The Expository Times*
FOTL	Forms of Old Testament Literature
FreibZ	*Freiburger Zeitschrift für Philosophie und Theologie*
FRLANT	Forschungen zur Religion und Literatur des Alten und Neuen Testaments
GKC	*Gesenius' Hebrew Grammar*, ed. E. Kautzsch, tr. A. E. Cowley
HAT	Handbuch zum Alten Testament
HBT	*Horizons in Biblical Theology*
HeyJ	*Heythrop Journal*
HKAT	Handkommentar zum Alten Testament
HOTTP	*Preliminary and Interim Report on the Hebrew Old Testament Text Project*, vol. 3. Stuttgart: United Bible Societies, 1977.
HSM	Harvard Semitic Monographs
HTR	*Harvard Theological Review*
HUCA	*Hebrew Union College Annual*
IB	*Interpreter's Bible*
ICC	International Critical Commentary
IDB	G. A. Buttrick (ed.), *Interpreter's Dictionary of the Bible*
IDBSup	Supplementary volume to *IDB*
IEJ	*Israel Exploration Journal*
Int	*Interpretation*
ITQ	*Irish Theological Quarterly*
JANES	*Journal of the Ancient Near Eastern Society of Columbia University*
JAOS	*Journal of the American Oriental Society*
JBL	*Journal of Biblical Literature*
JBL MS	Journal of Biblical Literature Manuscript Series
JCS	*Journal of Cuneiform Studies*
JETS	*Journal of the Evangelical Theological Society*
JNES	*Journal of Near Eastern Studies*
JNWSL	*Journal of Northwest Semitic Languages*
JQR	*Jewish Quarterly Review*
JRT	*Journal of Religious Thought*
JSOT	*Journal for the Study of the Old Testament*
JSOT SS	JSOT Supplementary Series
JSS	*Journal of Semitic Studies*
JTS	*Journal of Theological Studies*
KB	L. Koehler and W. Baumgartner, *Lexicon in Veteris Testamenti libros*

NCB	New Century Bible (new ed.)
NewslUgSt	*Newsletter for Ugaritic Studies*
NovT	*Novum Testamentum*
NTS	*New Testament Studies*
OTL	Old Testament Library
OTS	Oudtestamentische Studien
PEQ	*Palestine Exploration Quarterly*
PIW	S. Mowinckel, *The Psalms in Israel's Worship*
PRU	*Le Palais royal d'Ugarit*
RB	*Revue biblique*
RevExp	*Review and Expositor*
RevistB	*Revista biblica*
RevQ	*Revue de Qumrân*
RHPR	*Revue d'histoire et de philosophie religieuses*
RHR	*Revue de l'histoire des religions*
RIH	*Ras Ibn Hani*
RivB	*Rivista biblica*
RSP	*Ras Shamra Parallels,* ed. L. Fisher
RSR	*Recherches de science religieuse*
SANT	Studien zum Alten und Neuen Testament
SB	Sources bibliques
SBLDS	SBL Dissertation Series
SBLMS	SBL Monograph Series
SBM	Stuttgarter biblische Monographien
SBS	Stuttgarter Bibelstudien
SBT	Studies in Biblical Theology
SEÅ	*Svensk exegetisk årsbok*
Sem	*Semitica*
SJT	*Scottish Journal of Theology*
SR	*Studies in Religion/Sciences religieuses*
TDOT	Theological Dictionary of the Old Testament
THAT	*Theologisches Handwörterbuch zum AT*, ed. E. Jenni and C. Westermann, 2 vols.
ThLZ	*Theologische Literaturzeitung*
TOTC	Tyndale Old Testament Commentary
ThQ	*Theologische Quartalschrift*
TRev	*Theologische Revue*
TRP	D. W. Thomas, *The Text of the Revised Psalter*
TRu	*Theologische Rundschau*
TS	*Theological Studies*
TSK	*Theologische Studien und Kritiken*
TToday	*Theology Today*
TTZ	*Trierer theologische Zeitschrift*
TynB	*Tyndale Bulletin*
TZ	*Theologische Zeitschrift*
UF	*Ugaritische Forschungen*
UT	C. H. Gordon, *Ugaritic Textbook*

VCaro	*Verbum caro*
VD	*Verbum domini*
VF	*Verkündigung und Forschung*
VT	*Vetus Testamentum*
VTSup	Vetus Testamentum, Supplements
WBC	Word Biblical Commentary
WMANT	Wissenschaftliche Monographien zum Alten und Neuen Testament
WO	*Die Welt des Orients*
WTJ	*Westminster Theological Journal*
WUS	J. Aistleitner, *Wörterbuch der ugaritischen Sprache*
ZAW	*Zeitschrift für die* alttestamentliche Wissenschaft
ZDMG	*Zeitschrift der deutschen morgenländischen Gesellschaft*
ZNW	*Zeitschrift für die neutestamentliche Wissenschaft*
ZTK	*Zeitschrift für Theologie und Kirche*

2. Biblical and Ancient References

A. *General*

ἀ	Aquila
G	Greek Old Testament
G^A	Codex Alexandrinus
G^B	Codex Vaticanus
G^L	Lucian's recension
G^O	Hexaplaric recension
G^S	Codex Sinaiticus
K	*Kethiv,* consonantal Hebrew text of OT
L	Latin Old Testament
MT	Masoretic Text
Q	*Qere,* Masoretic vocalized Hebrew text of OT
σ′ or Symm	Symmachus
Syh	Syrohexaplaric text
θ	Theodotian

B. *Biblical and Apocryphal Books*

OLD TESTAMENT

Gen	Genesis	1 Chr	1 Chronicles
Exod	Exodus	2 Chr	2 Chronicles
Lev	Leviticus	Ezra	Ezra
Num	Numbers	Neh	Nehemiah
Deut	Deuteronomy	Esth	Esther
Josh	Joshua	Job	Job
Judg	Judges	Ps(s)	Psalms
Ruth	Ruth	Prov	Proverbs
1 Sam	1 Samuel	Eccl	Ecclesiates
2 Sam	2 Samuel	Cant	Song of Solomon
1 Kgs	1 Kings	Isa	Isaiah
2 Kgs	2 Kings	Jer	Jeremiah

Lam	Lamentations	Mic	Micah
Ezek	Ezekiel	Nah	Nahum
Dan	Daniel	Hab	Habakkuk
Hos	Hosea	Zeph	Zephaniah
Joel	Joel	Hag	Haggai
Amos	Amos	Zech	Zechariah
Obad	Obadiah	Mal	Malachi
Jonah	Jonah		

NEW TESTAMENT

Matt	Matthew	1 Tim	1 Timothy
Mark	Mark	2 Tim	2 Timothy
Luke	Luke	Titus	Titus
John	John	Philem	Philemon
Acts	Acts	Heb	Hebrews
Rom	Romans	Jas	James
1 Cor	1 Corinthians	1 Peter	1 Peter
2 Cor	2 Corinthians	2 Peter	2 Peter
Gal	Galatians	1 John	1 John
Eph	Ephesians	2 John	2 John
Phil	Philippians	3 John	3 John
Col	Colossians	Jude	Jude
1 Thess	1 Thessalonians	Rev	Revelation
2 Thess	2 Thessalonians		

APOCRYPHA

1 Kgdms	1 Kingdoms	1 Macc	1 Maccabees
2 Kgdms	2 Kingdoms	2 Macc	2 Maccabees
3 Kgdms	3 Kingdoms	3 Macc	3 Maccabees
4 Kgdms	4 Kingdoms	4 Macc	4 Maccabees
Add Esth	Additions to Esther	Pr Azar	Prayer of Azariah
Bar	Baruch	Pr Man	Prayer of
Bel	Bel and the Dragon		Manasseh
1 Esd	1 Esdras	Sir	Sirach
2 Esd	2 Esdras	Sus	Susanna
4 Ezra	4 Ezra	Tob	Tobit
Jdt	Judith	Wis	Wisdom of
Ep Jer	Epistle of Jeremy		Solomon

C.   *Rabbinic and Other References*

Ber.	Berakot
Bik.	Bikkurim
C	Cairo Geniza
Jub.	Jubilees
Ros. Has.	Ros Hassana
RS	Ras Shamra
Sop.	Soperim
Tg	Targum

D. *Dead Sea Scrolls and Related Texts*

CD	Cairo (Genizah text of the) Damascus (Document)
Hev	Nahal Hever texts
Mas	Masada texts
Mird	Khirbet Mird texts
Mur	Wadi Murabbaᶜat texts
P	Pesher (commentary)
Q	Qumran
1Q, 2Q, 3Q, etc.	Numbered caves of Qumran, yielding written material; followed by abbreviation of biblical or apocryphal book
QL	Qumran literature
1QapGen	*Genesis Apocryphon* of Qumran Cave 1
1QH	*Hôdāyôt* (*Thanksgiving Hymns*) from Qumran Cave 1
1QIsaᵃˑᵇ	First or second copy of Isaiah from Qumran Cave 1
1QpHab	*Pesher on Habakkuk* from Qumran Cave 1
1QM	*Milhāmāh* (*War Scroll*)
1QS	*Serek hayyahad* (*Rule of the Community, Manual of Discipline*)
1QSa	Appendix A (*Rule of the Congregation*) to 1QS
1QSb	Appendix B (*Blessings*) to 1QS
3Q15	Copper Scroll from Qumran Cave 3
4QFlor	*Florilegium* (or *Eschatological Midrashim*) from Qumran Cave 4
4QMess ar	Aramaic "Messianic" text from Qumran Cave 4
4QPrNab	Prayer of Nabonidus from Qumran Cave 4
4QPsᵃ, etc.	Fragmentary texts with verses from various psalms from Qumran Cave 4
4QTestim	*Testimonia* text from Qumran Cave 4
4QTLevi	*Testament of Levi* from Qumran Cave 4
4QPhyl	Phylacteries from Qumran Cave 4
11QPsApᵃ	Text which includes Ps 91:1–6 from Qumran Cave 11
11QPsᵃ	Psalms scroll from Qumran Cave 11
11QMelch	*Melchizedek* text from Qumran Cave 11
11QtgJob	*Targum of Job* from Qumran Cave 11

3. Translations

ASV	American Standard Version
AV	Authorized Version
JB	Jerusalem Bible
KJV	King James Version
NAB	New American Bible
NASV	New American Standard Version
NEB	New English Bible
NIV	New International Version

NJB	New Jerusalem Bible
NJV	New Jewish Publication Society Version of the Holy Scriptures
NRSV	New Revised Standard Version
REB	Revised English Bible
RSV	Revised Standard Version
TEV	Today's English Version

4. Grammatical and Other Abbreviations

c.	*circa*, about
chap(s).	chapter(s)
const.	construct
ed(s).	editor(s), edited by
EVV	English versions
fem.	feminine
FS	Festschrift
Heb.	Hebrew
impf.	imperfect
impv.	imperative
inf.	infinitive
J	the Yahwistic source
LXX	Septuagint
masc.	masculine
ms(s)	manuscript(s)
n.s.	new series
NT	New Testament
OT	Old Testament
P	the Priestly source
perf.	perfect
pl.	plural
prep.	preposition
sing.	singular
Ugar.	Ugaritic
UP	University Press
Vg	Vulgate
1 c.s.	common singular
1 c.p.	common plural
x	times
>	becomes
=	equals

Main Bibliography

1. Commentaries on Psalms

Alexander, J. A. *The Psalms.* 3 vols. New York: Baker and Scribner, 1850. **Allen, L. C.** *Psalms 101–150.* WBC 21. Waco, TX: Word Books, 1983. **Anderson, A. A.** *Psalms.* 2 vols. NCB. London: Oliphants, 1972. **Barnes, A.** *Notes on the Old Testament: Psalms.* 3 vols. 1869; repr. Grand Rapids, MI: Baker Book House, 1950. **Barnes, W. E.** *The Psalms.* 2 vols. Westminster Commentaries. London: Methuen & Co., 1931. **Bäthgen, F.** *Die Psalmen.* Göttingen: Vandenhoeck & Ruprecht, 1904. **Beaucamp, E.** *Le Psautier.* Sources Bibliques. 2 vols. Paris: Gabalta, 1976, 1979. **Briggs, C. A.** and **Briggs, E. G.** *A Critical and Exegetical Commentary on the Book of Psalms.* 2 vols. ICC. Edinburgh: T & T Clark, 1906. **Buttenwieser, M.** *The Psalms.* The Library of Biblical Studies. Prolegomenon by N. M. Sarna. 1938; repr. New York: KTAV Publishing House, 1969. **Cheyne, T. K.** *The Book of Psalms* London: Kegan Paul, Trench & Co., 1888. **Cohen, A.** *The Psalms: Hebrew Text, English Translation with an Introduction and Commentary.* London: Soncino Press, 1985. **Craigie, P. C.** *Psalms 1–50.* WBC 19. Waco, TX: Word Books, 1983. **Dahood, M.** *Psalms I:1–50; Psalms II:51–100; Psalms III:101–150.* AB 16, 17, 17a. Garden City, NY: Doubleday, 1966, 1968, 1970. **Deissler, A.** *Die Psalmen.* 3 vols. Düsseldorf: Patmos-Verlag, Teil 1, 1971⁴; Teil 2, 1969²; Teil 3, 1967². **Delitzsch, F.** *Biblical Commentary on the Psalms.* Tr. F. Bolton. 3 vols. 2nd ed. 1867; repr. Grand Rapids, MI: Eerdmans, 1952. **Duhm, B.** *Die Psalmen.* Kurzer HKAT. Tübingen: Mohr (Siebeck), 1899, 1922². **Durham, J. I.** *Psalms.* The Broadman Bible Commentary 4. Nashville: Broadman Press, 1971. **Eaton, J. H.** *Psalms.* Torch Bible Paperbacks. London: SCM Press, 1967. **Eerdmans, B. D.** *The Hebrew Book of Psalms.* Leiden: Brill, 1947. **Ehrlich, A. B.** *Die Psalmen Neu übersetzt und erklärt.* Berlin: M. Poppelauer, 1905. **Gerstenberger, E. S.** *Psalms Part 1, with an Introduction to Cultic Poetry.* FOTL 14. Grand Rapids, MI: Eerdmans, 1988. **Gross, H.** and **Reinelt, H.** *Das Buch der Psalmen.* Geistliche Schriftlesung 9. 2 vols. Düsseldorf: Patmos Verlag, 1982². **Gunkel, H.** *Die Psalmen.* HKAT. Göttingen: Vandenhoeck & Ruprecht, 1929⁴, 1968⁵. **Jacquet, L.** *Les Psaumes et le coeur de l'homme. Etude textuelle, littéraire et doctrinale.* 3 vols. Gembloux: J. Duculot, 1975, 1977, 1979. **Kidner, D.** *Psalms.* 2 vols. London: Inter-Varsity Press, 1973, 1975. **Kirkpatrick, A. F.** *The Book of Psalms.* 1902; repr. Cambridge: Cambridge UP, 1951. **Kissane, E. J.** *The Book of Psalms.* 2 vols. Dublin: Browne & Nolan, 1953, 1954. **Kittel, R.** *Die Psalmen übersetzt und erklärt.* Leipzig: Deichert-Scholl, 1929⁵·⁶. **Knight, G. A. F.** *Psalms.* The Daily Study Bible Series. 2 vols. Philadelphia: Westminster Press, 1982. **Kraus, H.-J.** *Psalmen.* BKAT 15.1; 15.2. 5 Auflage. Neukirchen-Vluyn: Neukirchener Verlag, 1978. ———. *Psalms 1–59: A Commentary.* Tr. H. C. Oswald (from 5th ed. of *Psalmen*). Minneapolis: Augsburg, 1988. ———. *Psalms 60–150: A Commentary.* Tr. H. C. Oswald (from 5th ed. of *Psalmen*). Minneapolis: Augsburg, 1989. **Lamparter, H.** *Das Buch der Psalmen.* Die Botschaft des Alten Testament 14. 2 vols. Stuttgart: Calver Verlag, 1958¹, 1959¹. **Leslie, E. A.** *Psalms: Translated and Interpreted in the Light of Hebrew Worship.* Nashville: Abingdon Press, 1949. **Leupold. H. C.** *Exposition of the Psalms.* 1959; repr. Grand Rapids, MI: Baker Book House, 1969. **Loretz, O.** *Die Psalmen,* II. Beitrag der Ugarit-Texte zum Verständnis von Kolometrie und Textologie der Psalmen. Psalm 90–150. AOAT 207/2. Neukirchen-Vluyn: Neukirchener Verlag, 1979. **Maillot, A.** and **Lelièvre, A.** *Les Psaumes.* 3 vols. Geneve: Labor et fides, 1961, 1966, 1969. **McCullough, W. S.** and **Taylor W. R.** "The Book of Psalms." *IB.* Nashville: Abingdon Press, 1955. 4:3–763. **Oesterley, W. O. E.** *The Psalms.* London: SPCK, 1939, 1959. **Perowne, J. J. S.** *The Book of Psalms.* 4th ed. 1 vol. 1878; repr. Grand Rapids,

MI: Zondervan, 1976. **Podechard, E.** *Le Psautier.* 2 vols. Lyon: Facultés Catholiques, 1949, 1954. **Rogerson, J. W.** and **McKay, J. W.** *Psalms 1–50; Psalms 51–150.* CBC. Cambridge: Cambridge UP, 1977. **Sabourin, L.** *The Psalms: Their Origin and Meaning.* Enlarged, updated ed. New York: Alba House, 1974. **Schmidt, H.** *Die Psalmen.* HAT 15. Tübingen: Mohr (Siebeck), 1934. **Spurgeon, C. H.** *The Treasury of David.* 3 vols. (originally 6 vols., 1874–92). Grand Rapids, MI: Zondervan, 1966. **Stuhlmueller, C.** *Psalms.* Old Testament Message: A Biblical-Theological Commentary, 21, 22. Wilmington, DE: Glazier, 1983. **Weiser, A.** *The Psalms: A Commentary.* Tr. H. Hartwell. ATD 14/15, 5th ed. 1959. OTL. Philadelphia: Westminster Press, 1962.

2. Text, Versions, and Textual Studies

Bardtke, H. "Liber Psalmorum." In *Biblia Hebraica Stuttgartensia,* ed. K. Elliger and W. Rudolph. Stuttgart: Württembergische Bibelanstalt, 1969. **Barnes, W. E.** *The Peshitta Psalter according to the West Syrian Text.* Cambridge: Cambridge UP, 1904. **Colunga, A.** and **Turrado, L.** *Biblica Sacra Iuxta Vulgatam Clementinam,* Nova Editio. Quarto Editio. 1953; repr. Madrid: Biblioteca de Autores Cristianos, 1965. **Rahlfs, A.** *Psalmi cum Odis.* Septuaginta: Vetus Testamentum Graecum/Societatis Scientiarum Gottingensis 10. Göttingen: Vandenhoeck & Ruprecht, 1931. ———. *Septuaginta.* Vol. II, Libri poetici et prophetici. Editio Quinta. Stuttgart: Privilegiente Württembergische Bibelanstatt, 1952.

3. Linguistic Tools

Barthelemy, D. et al. *Preliminary and Interim Report on the Hebrew Old Testament Text Project* 3, *Poetical Books.* Stuttgart: United Bible Societies, 1977. **Brown, F., Driver, S. R.,** and **Briggs, C. A.** *A Hebrew and English Lexicon of the Old Testament with an Appendix Containing the Biblical Aramaic.* Oxford: Clarendon Press, 1906. **Gesenius, F. W.** *Hebrew Grammar.* Rev. E. Kautzsch. 2nd English ed., ed. and tr. A. E. Cowley. 1910; repr. Oxford: Clarendon Press, 1957. **Jastrow, M.** *A Dictionary of the Targumim, the Talmud Bahbli and Yerushalmi and the Midrashic Literature.* London, New York: Trubner, 1903. **Joüon, P.** *Grammaire de l'hébreu biblique.* 2nd ed. Rome: Institut Biblique Pontifical, 1947. **Köhler, L.** and **Baumgartner, W.** *Lexicon in Veteris Testamenti libros.* 2nd ed. Leiden: Brill, 1958. **Liddell, H. G.** and **Scott, R.** *A Greek-English Lexicon.* Rev. H. S. Jones and R. McKenzie. 9th ed. Oxford: Clarendon Press, 1940. **Waltke, B.** and **O'Connor, M.** *An Introduction to Biblical Hebrew Syntax.* Winona Lake, IN: Eisenbrauns, 1990. **Williams, R. J.** *Hebrew Syntax: An Outline.* 2nd ed. 1976; repr. Toronto: University of Toronto Press, 1984.

4. Major Monographs and Studies

Aejmelaeus, A. *The Traditional Prayer in the Psalms.* BZAW 167. Berlin: de Gruyter, 1986. **Albertz, A.** *Persönliche Frömmigkeit und offizielle Religion.* Calwer Theologische Monographs 9. Stuttgart: Calwer, 1978. **Alter, R.** *The Art of Biblical Poetry.* New York: Basic Books, 1985. **Auffret, P.** *La Sagesse à Bati sa Maison; Études de structure littéraires dans l'Ancien Testament et spécialement dans les Psaumes.* Orbis Biblicus et Orientalis 49. Göttingen: Vandenhoeck & Ruprecht, 1982. **Barth, C.** *Die Erretung vom Tode in den individuellen Klage- und Dankliedern des AT.* Zollikon: Evangelischer Verlag, 1947. **Baumann, E.** "Struktur-Untersuchungen im Psalter. 2." *ZAW* 62 (1949/50) 115–52. **Beaucamp, E.** "Structure strophique des Psaumes." *RSR* 56 (1968) 199–223. **Becker, J.** *Israel deutet seine Psalmen: Urform und Neuinterpretation in den Psalmen.* SBS 18. Stuttgart: Verlag Katholisches Bibelwerk, 1966. **Bellinger, W. H., Jr.** *Psalms: Reading and Studying the Books of Praises.* Peabody, MA:

Hendrickson Publishers, 1990. **Beyerlin, W.** *Die Rettung der Bedrängten in dem Feindpsalmen der Einzelnen.* FRLANT 99. Göttingen: Vandenhoeck & Ruprecht, 1970. **Birkeland, H.** *The Evildoers in the Book of Psalms.* Oslo: Jacob Dybwad, 1955. **Broyles, C. C.** *The Conflict of Faith and Experience in the Psalms.* JSOT SS 52. Sheffield: JSOT Press, 1989. **Brueggemann, W.** *Israel's Praise: Doxology against Idolatry and Ideology.* Philadelphia: Fortress Press, 1988. **Childs, B. S.** "Psalm Titles and Midrashic Exegesis." *JSS* 16 (1971) 137–50. **Clines, D. J. A.** "Psalm Research Since 1955: 1. The Psalms and the Cult." *TynB* 17 (1966) 103–26. ————. "Psalm Research Since 1955: 2. The Literary Genres." *TynB* 20 (1969) 105–25. **Cross, F. M.** *Canaanite Myth and Hebrew Epic.* Cambridge: Harvard UP, 1973. **Crüsemann, F.** *Studien zur Formgeschichte von Hymnus und Danklied in Israel.* WMANT 32. Neukirchen-Vluyn: Neukirchener Verlag, 1969. **Culley, R. C.** *Oral Formulaic Language in the Biblical Psalms.* Toronto: University of Toronto Press, 1967. **Day, J.** *God's Conflict with the Dragon and the Sea: Echoes of a Canaanite Myth in the Old Testament.* Cambridge: Cambridge UP, 1985. **Delekat, L.** *Asylie und Schutzorakel am Zionheiligtum: Eine Untersuchung zur den privaten Feindpsalmen.* Leiden: Brill, 1967. **Delekat, L.** "Probleme der Psalmenüberschriften." *ZAW* 76 (1964) 280–97. **Eaton, J. H.** *Kingship and the Psalms.* SBT 2.32. London: SCM Press, 1976. **Eissfeldt, O.** *The Old Testament: An Introduction.* Tr. P. R. Ackroyd. Oxford: Basil Blackwell, 1965. **Fohrer, G.** *Introduction to the Old Testament.* Tr. D. Green. Nashville: Abingdon Press, 1968. **Freedman, D. N.** *Pottery, Poetry, and Prophecy: Studies in Early Hebrew Poetry.* Winona Lake, IN: Eisenbrauns, 1980. **Gerstenberger, E. S.** *Der bittende Mensch.* WMANT 51. Neukirchen-Vluyn: Neukirchener Verlag, 1980. ————. "Lyrical Literature." In *The Old Testament and Its Modern Interpreters,* ed. D. A. Knight and G. M. Tucker. Chico, CA: Scholars Press; Philadelphia: Fortress Press, 1985. 409–44. ————. *Psalms.* Old Testament, Form Criticism, ed. J. H. Hayes. Trinity University Monograph Series in Religion 2. San Antonio: Trinity UP, 1974. **Goulder, M. D.** *The Psalms of the Sons of Korah.* JSOT Sup 20. Sheffield: JSOT Press, 1982. **Gunkel, H.** and **Begrich, J.** *Einleitung in die Psalmen.* 2nd ed. Ed. J. Begrich. Göttingen: Vandenhoeck & Ruprecht, 1933. **Howard, D. M., Jr.** *The Structure of Psalms 93–100.* Ph.D. diss. University of Michigan, 1986. Ann Arbor: UMI, 1988. **Jeremias, J.** *Kultprophetie und Gerichtsverkündigung in der späten Königszeit Israels.* WMANT 35. Neukirchen-Vluyn: Neukirchener Verlag, 1970. **Johnson, A. R.** *The Cultic Prophet in Ancient Israel.* 2nd ed. Cardiff: University of Wales Press, 1962. ————. *The Cultic Prophet and Israel's Psalmody.* Cardiff: University of Wales Press, 1979. **Keel-Leu, O.** *The Symbolism of the Biblical World: Ancient Near Eastern Iconography and the Book of Psalms.* Tr. T. J. Hallett. New York: Crossroad Books, Seabury Press, 1972, 1978. **Kloos, C.** *Yhwh's Combat with the Sea.* Amsterdam: G. A. van Oorschot; Leiden: Brill, 1986. **Kraus, H.-J.** *Theology of the Psalms.* Tr. K. Crim. Minneapolis: Augsburg, 1979, 1986. ————. *Worship in Israel: A Cultic History of the Old Testament.* Tr. G. Buswell. Oxford: Basil Blackwell, 1966. **Kugel, J. L.** *The Idea of Biblical Poetry: Parallelism and Its History.* New Haven: Yale UP, 1981. **Michel, D.** *Tempora und Satzstellung in den Psalmen.* Abhandlungen zur evangelischen Theologie 1. Bonn: H. Bouvier, 1960. **Miller, P. D., Jr.** *Interpreting the Psalms.* Philadelphia: Fortress Press, 1986. ————. "Psalms and Inscriptions." VTSup 32 (1980), Congress Volume, ed. J. A. Emerton, 311–32. **Mowinckel, S.** *Psalmenstudien.* Bd. 1–6. Oslo: Kristiana, 1921–24. ————. *The Psalms in Israel's Worship.* 2 vols. Tr. D. R. Ap-Thomas. Oxford: Basil Blackwell, 1962. **Nasuti, H. P.** *Tradition History and the Psalms of Asaph.* Ph.D. diss. Yale University, 1983. Ann Arbor: UMI, 1985. **Ollenburger, B. C.** *Zion the City of the Great King.* JSOT Sup 41. Sheffield: JSOT Press, 1987. **Reventlow, H. G.** *Gebet im Alten Testament.* Stuttgart: W. Kohlhammer, 1986. **Robertson, D. A.** *Linguistic Evidence in Dating Early Hebrew Poetry.* SBLDS 3. Missoula, MT: Scholars Press, 1972. **Sanders, J. A.** *The Dead Sea Psalms Scroll.* Ithaca, NY: Cornell UP, 1967. **Sawyer, J. F. A.** "An Analysis of the Context and Meaning of the Psalm-Headings." *Transactions of Glasgow University Oriental Society* 22 (1967–68) 26–38. **Schildenberger, J.** "Bemerkungen zum Strophenbau der Psalmen." *Estudios Eclesiasticos* 34 (1960) 673–87. **Seybold, K.** "Toward an Understanding of the

Formation of Historical Titles in the Book of Psalms." *ZAW* 91 (1979) 350–80. **Thomas, D. W.** *The Text of the Revised Psalter.* London: SPCK, 1963. **Watson, W. G. E.** *Classical Hebrew Poetry.* 2nd ed. Sheffield: JSOT Press, 1986. **Watters, W. R.** *Formula Criticism and the Poetry of the Old Testament.* BZAW 138. Berlin: de Gruyter, 1976. **Watts, J. W.** *Psalms in Narrative Contexts of the Hebrew Bible.* Ph.D. diss. Yale University, 1990. **Westermann, C.** *Praise and Lament in the Psalms.* Tr. K. R. Crim and R. N. Soulen. Atlanta: John Knox Press, 1981. ———. *The Living Psalms.* Tr. J. R. Porter. Grand Rapids, MI: Eerdmans, 1984, 1989. **Widengren, G.** *The Accadian and Hebrew Psalms of Lamentation as Religious Documents.* Stockholm: Atkiebolaget Thule, 1937. **Wilson, G. H.** *The Editing of the Hebrew Psalter.* SBLDS 76. Chico, CA: Scholars Press, 1985.

Introduction

Following the lead of Leslie C. Allen in *Psalms 101–150* of the WBC, the reader is referred to the introduction to the Psalter by Peter C. Craigie in *Psalms 1–50*. His introduction is easily readable but covers the major subject matters and is still relatively up to date, though published in 1983. Excellent introductions are readily available in other commentaries, special studies, and introductions to the OT. Among the introductions to the OT, the older works of S. R. Driver and Otto Eissfeldt should not be overlooked.

The Psalms are fairly frequently divided as in this series of commentaries (1–50; 51–100; 101–150), but it is rather artificial and less than desirable for an understanding of the present Psalter, which is divided into five books: Pss 1–41, 42–72, 73–89, 90–106, and 107–150. Obviously, Ps 51 with which the present commentary begins is well inside the collections in Book II, which begins with a series of psalms attributed by title to the "sons of Korah" (42–43, 44, 45, 46, 47, 48, and 49 = seven psalms). These psalms are followed by the isolated Asaphite Ps 50.

Ps 51 begins a run of Davidic psalms which extend through Ps 71 (reading 70 and 71 together; 71 has no title in MT). This series is interrupted by Pss 66 and 67, which are nonattributed but titled. Ps 72 is attributed to Solomon (one of two such psalms; the other is Ps 127) but ends with the statement: "The prayers of David son of Jesse are ended," which may be intended in the present arrangement to include all of Books I and II, bringing the non-Davidic psalms under Davidic authority.

The significance of the collection of psalms in Book II has received little attention from commentators but is worthy of more consideration than it has been given and more than I can attempt to do here. The collections in Book II probably originated in later pre-exilic or exilic times (note Gerstenberger, 29, who places Pss 42–49 in later pre-exilic times and Pss 51–72 in the exilic period). This dating refers to the collections, of course, not to individual psalms. In general terms, the later pre-exilic and exilic contexts seem to match well the content of these psalms. The heart of Book II is found in Pss 51–64. Anyone who has worked through these psalms knows that they deal with great pain and agony of soul. Ps 51 is the only true confession of sin in the Psalter of any length, and it is a powerful one.

The psalms which follow in Pss 51–64 are dominated by the language of lamentation, complaint, and petition. They reflect a society either under or threatened by oppression, fierce foes, or corruption, and in the more urgent need of divine intervention and help. The terrible petitions regarding enemies in Pss 58 and 59 are likely to reflect a minority of people who are oppressed and persecuted by those among whom they live. The speaker in Ps 57:5 says:

> I am in the midst of lions;
>   I lie among ravenous beasts—
> men whose teeth are spears and arrows,
>   whose tongues are sharp swords. (NIV)

The experience of a people defeated, deported, and economically deprived, as in the exile, is compatible with these psalms. This may also accord with the most extensive run of historical references in titles in the Psalter (Pss 51, 52, 56, 57, 58, 59, 60, 63). All of these historical notes relate to crisis situations in the career of David according to the biblical accounts. They are probably later scribal Davidizations of the psalms, and one can hardly doubt that the trials of the Davidic monarchy in later times are behind them.

But this is not the whole story. The psalms on either side of the central core of Pss 51–64 are not uniform in content, but generally they accentuate praise or vows of praise. In particular, two aspects of pre-exilic Judah are emphasized: Zion, the dwelling place of Yahweh, and the Davidic monarchy. Pss 42–50 focus on Zion and express confidence in Yahweh's presence there and his commitment to the city:

> From Zion, perfect in beauty,
>   God shines forth.
> Our God comes and will not be silent;
>   a fire devours before him,
>   and around him a tempest rages. (Ps 50:2–3, NIV)

From Zion Yahweh speaks to all the peoples of the world and from there he will summon and gather his dispersed people (e.g., Pss 49:2–3; 50:1–6).

At the other end of the Book II is the prayer for the king in Ps 72. In the scribal traditions this psalm was probably understood as a prayer of David for Solomon and his reign. David left much unfinished work for Solomon to do, according to the biblical traditions (1 Kgs 1–2; and recall David's careful preparations for the building of a temple in Jerusalem by Solomon). In this tradition, David is presented as carefully transferring his blessings, authority, and responsibilities to Solomon. Ps 72 sets forth the ideals of Israelite monarchy and in a subtle way prays for a new "Solomon" to actualize the Davidic ideals; the "prayers of David are finished" and the people wait for "Solomon." An old era has ended, but the new has not yet begun.

Book III begins with the affirmation that "Truly God is good to Israel" (Ps 73:1; the change from "to Israel" to "to the upright" should not be made). The reader knows right away that this thesis is going to be tested severely in this section of the Psalter, both in terms of individual faith and in terms of the nation Israel. Ps 73 in its present form is a positive testimony of faith, but the speaker has come from the brink of spiritual disaster (73:1–3, 13–14). The problem has been the prosperity of the wicked and the suffering of the righteous: Why does God, who is supposed to be good to Israel, allow the sinners to do so well?

Ps 73 is followed immediately by a communal lament in Ps 74, which lays before Yahweh the terrible work of foes who have wrecked and ruined his holy place, and who scoff and revile his name. In a similar way, Ps 79 sets before Yahweh the ruin and bloodshed wrought by the nations that have defiled his holy temple and taken over his inheritance, though they are nations who do not "know" him or call on his name (74:6). They have "devoured Jacob and laid waste his habitation" (74:7, NRSV). The Shepherd of Israel is implored to inspect and restore his wonderful vine, transplanted from Egypt to ground he cleared for it, where it took deep root and filled the land with its great size and luxurious growth (Ps 80). The vine and its vineyard are now ravaged and at the mercy of passersby and vagrants. These communal laments almost certainly reflect the destruction of Jerusalem in 587 B.C.E. and its aftermath. So we are on sound ground in assigning a date for Book III to the exilic period, or more probably to the post-exilic period (as in Gerstenberger, 29), reflecting rites of lamentation and penitential liturgies of the exilic and post-exilic periods.

In Book III, the monarchy does not seem to provide much, if any, basis of hope for the future. The book closes with the lengthy poem in Ps 89, which struggles with the terrible problem of Yahweh's failure to keep his promises, taken on oath, to David and to his dynasty:

> Lord, where is your steadfast love [חסדיך] of old,
>   which by your faithfulness you swore to David?
>   (Ps 89:50, NRSV)

The pain of failed monarchy is exacerbated by the review of the "riddle" of Israel's history in Ps 78, which culminates with Yahweh's choice of Judah and "his servant David," and of "Mount Zion, which he loves" (Ps 78:68–71).

The future hope of Israel rests with Israel's Shepherd himself. He must restore and revive his people, who now live "forsaken among the dead," as the speaker in Ps 88 puts it in terms of personal experience. Ps 82 seems to be a key psalm in this section with its portrayal of Yahweh risen in the divine assembly to pronounce a sentence of judgment on the gods who have failed to establish justice and right order on earth. At the end of Ps 82, Yahweh is called upon with acclamation to rise in judgment of the earth and claim his patrimony in all nations. The kings have failed, and the gods have been sentenced to death; Yahweh must do it alone, but the question hangs in the air: Will he? Will he do any better than the gods he has banished to die like mortal humanity?

In the commentary which follows on Pss 90–100 I have tried to put forward a modest argument for Book IV of the Psalter as a Moses-book, which has the exodus and wilderness traditions in mind. I suggest this approach for at least Pss 90–100. I am not prepared to argue very much for Pss 101–106, except to say that the two Davidic psalms in this section (101, 103) may point to a basis of faith in the Moses traditions followed by Davidic traditions. The Davidic umbrella is extended to Ps 102 by 101 and to 104 by 103 (G. Wilson, *The Editing of the Hebrew Psalter*, 180, 217-19). Pss 105 and 106 have a thematic unity in that they are both reviews of the history of Israel with Yahweh. They are also joined by the linguistic features of the use of "hallelujah" (הללו יה) at the end of 104, at the end of 105, and at the beginning and end of 106, and the use of the verb form הודן ("praise/give thanks") in 105:1 and 106:1. Pss 103 and 104 are also connected by the inclusion "Bless Yahweh O my soul" (Pss 103:1, 2, 22; 104:1, 35).

The Mosaic theme is introduced in Ps 105 with a review of Yahweh's saving acts in the history of Israel during the time of Moses, who is referred to by name as the "servant" of Yahweh in 105:26. Moses is also referred to by name in 106:16, 23, 32. Therefore, I suspect that there has been a reversal of authority in this section of the Psalter and that actually the Davidic psalms are now brought under the umbrella of Mosaic authority.

The setting of Book IV is rather explicitly given at the end of Ps 106:

> Save us, O Lord our God,
>> and gather us from the nations,
> that we may give thanks [לְהֹדוֹת] to your holy name
>> and glory in your praise. (v 47, NIV)

This can hardly mean anything else but a post-exilic setting for this collection of psalms (Gerstenberger, 29). These are psalms which represent the struggle for faith by people who have suffered long-deferred hope and have become very aware of both the wrath of God and the fragility and transience of human life (Pss 90–91). The enormous time spans through which God works focuses a brilliant light on the weakness and mortality of human beings.

Faith is not lost in these psalms, however. At the heart of Book IV are the repeated affirmations of the divine kingship of Yahweh (Pss 93, 95–99). Yahweh is the "Great god, the Great King above all gods" (Ps 95:3), who is coming to judge the world (96:13; 98:9). The Davidic monarchy is over; the sons of David are all dead, but Yahweh reigns as King:

> Say among the nations, "The Lord reigns."
>> The world is firmly established, it cannot be moved;
>> he will judge the peoples with equity. (Ps 96:10, NIV)

Those who worship may sing a new song of joy and victory about Yahweh and his works (Pss 96:1; 98:1).

These psalms seek to ground faith in the pre-monarchical, Moses traditions. It was Moses who proclaimed the divine kingship of Yahweh, according to the biblical traditions (Exod 15:18), and it was under the leadership of Moses that Yahweh demonstrated his marvelous power and saving works. It was also in the wilderness that Israelite disobedience and rebelliousness incurred the divine wrath (Ps 95:8–11) and the exodus generation was denied entry into the "rest" of Yahweh. A new generation, far removed in time from the Moses generation, but only a step away in matters of life and faith, is encouraged not to harden their hearts and not to put Yahweh to the test, as the exodus generation did at Meribah (95:8–9). The way of wisdom is to know that whoever is disciplined and taught by Yahweh will be blessed and enter into the judgment which is founded on righteousness (94:12–15). The way is not easy, but those who still desire to serve Yahweh can sing new songs and summon the whole earth to

> Raise a shout to Yahweh . . .
> Serve Yahweh with gladness;
> Come before him with joyful songs.
> Acknowledge that Yahweh, he is God.
> He made us, and we are indeed
> his people and the flock he shepherds.
>> (Ps 100:1–3)

Psalms 51-100

A Confession of Sin and Prayer
for Forgiveness   (51:1–21)

Bibliography

Auffret, P. "Note sûr la structure littéraire de Ps LI 1–19." *VT* 26 (1976) 142–47. **Caquot, A.** "Purification et expiration selon le psaume LI." *RHR* 1969 (1966) 133–54. **Condron, K.** "The Biblical Doctrine of Original Sin." *ITQ* 34 (1967) 20–36. **Dalglish, E. R.** *Psalm Fifty-One in the Light of Ancient Near Eastern Patternism.* Leiden: Brill, 1962. **Eichrodt, W.** *Theology of the Old Testament.* Tr. J. A. Baker. Philadelphia: Westminster Press, 1961. **Goldingay, J.** "Psalm 51:16a (English 51:14)." *CBQ* 40 (1978) 388–90. ————. *Songs from a Strange Land: Psalms 42–51.* Downers Grove, IL: Inter-Varsity Press, 1978. **Knierim, R.** *Die Hauptbegriffe für Sünde im Alten Testament.* Gütersloh: Mohn, 1965. **Köhler, L. H.** *Old Testament Theology.* Tr. A. S. Todd. Philadelphia: Westminster Press, 1957. **Kselman, J. S.** "A Note on Ps. 51:6." *CBQ* 39 (1977) 251–53. **Johnson, A. R.** *The Cultic Prophet and Israel's Psalmody.* 412–31. **Neve, L.** "Realized Eschatology in Psalm 51." *ExpTim* 80 (1969) 264–66. **Ridderbos, N. H.** "Psalm 51:5–6." In *Studia Biblica et Semitica, Theodoro Christiano dedicata.* Wageningen: Veenman & Zonen, 1966. 299–312. **Stöbe, H. J.** *'Gott, sei mir Sünder gnädig': Eine Auslegung des 51. Psalms.* Biblische Studien 20. Neukirchen: Neukirchener Verlag, 1958. **Terrien, S. L.** *The Elusive Presence: Toward a New Biblical Theology.* San Francisco: Harper & Row, 1978. ————. *The Psalms and Their Meaning for Today.* Indianapolis: Bobbs-Merrill, 1952. **Youngblood, R.** "A New Look at Three Old Testament Roots for 'Sin.'" In *Biblical and Near Eastern Studies.* FS W. S. LaSor, ed. G. A. Tuttle. Grand Rapids, MI: Eerdmans, 1978. **Zink, J. K.** "Uncleanness and Sin: A Study of Job XIV and Psalm LI 7." *VT* 17 (1967) 354–61.

Translation

1–2 For the leader;[a] a Davidic psalm;[b] when the prophet Nathan came to
him after he [David] had gone (in) to[c] Bathsheba,

3 (1) *Have mercy on me, O God, according to your loyal-love,*[a]   (3+3)
according to your abundant mercy blot out my acts of rebellion.[b]

4 (2) *Wash away*[a] *[the guilt of] my waywardness,*[b]   (3+2)
and cleanse me from my sin.[c]

5 (3) *For I know well my rebellious acts,*[a]   (3+3)
and my sin is ever before me.

6 (4) *Against none other than you*[a] *have I sinned,*   (3+3+3+2[3])
before your eyes I did that which is evil.
And so[b] *you are in the right when you speak,*[c]
(and) blameless in giving judgment.[d]

7 (5) *Indeed,*[a] *I was born in waywardness,*   (3+3)
and my mother conceived me in sin,

8 (6) *though*[a] *you wanted faithfulness*[b] *even in the womb,*[c]   (3+3)
and while in the uterus[d] *you caused me to know wisdom.*

9 (7) *Remove [the guilt of] my sin*[a] *with hyssop*[b] *so that I will be
clean indeed,*   (3+3)
wash me so that I will be whiter than snow.

10 (8) *Cause me to hear*^a *joy and gladness;*   (3+3)
       let the bones you crushed rejoice.

11 (9) *Hide your face from my sins,*   (3+3)
       and all [the guilt of] my wayward acts blot out.

12 (10) *Create for me a clean heart, O God,*   (4+4)
       and renew a steadfast spirit in me.

13 (11) *Do not banish me from your presence,*   (3[4]+4)
       and your holy spirit do not take from me.

14 (12) *Restore to me the joy of your salvation,*   (3+3)
       and let a willing spirit empower me.

15 (13) *(Then) I will teach your ways*^a *to the rebellious,*   (3+3)
       and to sinners, who [then] may return to you.^b

16 (14) *Deliver me from blood-guilt,*^a *O God,*   (3+2+3)
       O God of my salvation;^b
       [then] my tongue will sing out your righteousness.

17 (15)   *O Lord, open my lips,*   (3+3)
       so my mouth can voice your praise.

18 (16) *For you would not be pleased with a sacrifice,*^a   (3+1+3)
       or I would give it,^b
       (nor) would you want a whole-offering.

19 (17)   *The sacrifices of God*^a *are a broken spirit,*   (3+2+3)
       a broken and contrite heart;^b
       [these], O God, you will not reject.^c

20 (18) *In your good will make Zion prosper;*   (3+3)
       rebuild^a *the walls of Jerusalem.*

21 (19) *Then you will be pleased*^a *with right sacrifices,*   (3+2+3)
       offerings whole and complete,^b
       then bulls can be offered^c *on your altar.*

Notes

1–2.a. The term למנצח is found at the beginning of 55 psalms and in Hab 3:19. The occurrences of the term are mostly in the first part of the Psalter: 19 times in Book I and 26 times in Book II, but only 7 times in Book III and only 3 times after Ps 88 (109, 139, 140). The KJV reads, "to the chief musician"; RSV has "to the choirmaster"; JB has "For the choirmaster"; NAB, NJV, and REB have "for the leader"; NIV has "for the director of music." Dalglish (*Psalm Fifty-One*, 56, 234–38) takes a different approach and translates it "for stringed rendition." In Vol. 1 of this commentary, P. C. Craigie uses "musical director," while L. C. Allen in Vol. 3 reads "director's" for Ps 109 and "director's collection" for Pss 139; 140.

The word מנצח is usually assumed to be a piel participle from the root נצח, "to shine, beam," and thus "to be preeminent/distinguished." This line of meaning easily results in "leader/director/victor" (Jerome) or the like. However, the root also carries the idea of "endurance/everlastingness," which is reflected in the noun נצח and the expression לנצח ("forever"). The LXX seems to reflect the second line of meaning with the translation εἰς τὸ τέλος ("until/for/regarding the end"). L. Delekat (*ZAW* 76 [1964] 283–90) takes his cue from LXX and argues that למנצח was a response with the meaning "for evermore," which marked the end of the recitation of psalms. According to him, after the exile the expression was no longer understood as a response and was reinterpreted as "excellent one" or "victorious one" (note the νικῆσαι in the Greek text of Hab 3:19), identified as David or as some other person(s) associated with the psalm (A. A. Anderson, 48, notes that I. Engnell believed that למנצח was the North Israelite equivalent of לדוד, "to David," which was used in Jerusalem; see Kraus, I, 25).

As noted above Dalglish relates למנצח to a root נצח which is taken to mean "to perform on stringed instruments" and similar to נגן, "play a stringed instrument/make music." He argues for the meanings of "for the director of strings" and "for stringed rendition." S. Mowinckel (*PIW*, II, 212) argues that the meaning involved in the participle with the preposition ל would be about the aim or method of performance of an action rather than about the acting person. Taking the basic meaning of the verb to mean "to shine" or "to give light," he argues that the meaning of למנצח was to recite the psalm involved to such music as would make Yahweh's face "shine" (with pleasure and favor) upon the worshiper. The meaning of the psalm heading would be "for the merciful disposition (of Yahweh)" or "to dispose (Yahweh) to mercy." He notes that the Targum renders the terms as "for praise." Similarly, Eaton (16) prefers "for propitiation."

Eerdmans (54–61) stresses the contexts in which the verb is used of Levites controlling or directing laborers (e.g., 2 Chr 2:1; Ezra 3:8,9) and argues that the original idea was that of striking a musical note, such as twanging a string of a stringed instrument, so that the carriers of the Ark could keep in step (1Chr 15:21), or that laborers in general could keep in rhythm and time in their work. Those who twanged the strings would know when to pluck them (or to use other instruments) by reciting a psalm in unison. Thus Eerdmans argues that the basic meaning was "to have authority" (noting against Mowinckel, that הָאִיר פָּנִים is the usual expression for "to make the face shine": Num 6:23; Pss 31:17; 67:2; 80:4, 8, 20; 119:135) and in the developed meaning it denoted "leader," in the sense of the one who had authority to select appropriate poems for recitation on different occasions.

No one really knows what this term meant, and it probably had different meanings at different times (see J. F. A. Sawyer, *Transactions of Glasgow University Oriental Society* 22 [1967–68] 26–38, esp. 27). I have chosen the tradional "for the leader" on the basis that (1) the meaning of מנצח is that of a leader or an official responsible for the selection and recitation of a psalm (Sawyer [36] argues that למנצח means "to be recited by the official in charge"), and (2) there seems to be no more persuasive option (note the comment of Kidner, I, 40). It seems highly probable that at some stage the preposition connoted attribution and designated a psalm from a known collection (see Briggs I, *LXXII–LXXIV*; Kraus, I, 27; Jacquet, I, 253).

1–2.b. The much discussed לדוד ("to/for/belonging to/by/about David") has received a succinct but very competent treatment by P. C. Craigie in Vol. 1 (33–35) of this commentary, and the work need not be repeated here. I have adopted the translation "Davidic" or "Davidic psalm" as an English expression which has an equivalent ambiguity to the Hebrew expression.

1–2.c. The euphemistic meaning of sexual intercourse ("go into/come into") is understood.

3.a. The slight ms evidence for the plural of חסד (see *BHS*) can be disregarded, though the plural forms a better parallel with רחמיך ("your mercies"). LXX indicates that הַגָּדֹל is supposed: "according to your great mercy." For the translation of חסד as "loyal-love," see *Comment* below.

3.b. Translation of פשעי is traditionally "my transgressions." The translation above is that of Goldingay (*CBQ* 40 [1978] 388–90) who argues that "transgression" has lost much of its theological meaning in contemporary usage. See *Comment*.

4.a. The *qere* reads הֶרֶב, apocopated hiphil imperative of רבה; *kethiv* may be read as הַרְבֵּה, hiphil infinitive absolute, used adverbially (Dalglish, *Psalm Fifty-One*, 64–65). The "away" is an effort to reflect the adverbial force.

4.b, c. Goldingay's suggestion of "waywardness" for עון (usually read as "iniquity") has been adopted. However, the traditional "sin" has been retained for חַטָּאת. Goldingay (*Songs*, 154) suggests "failure," which is certainly involved, but the English "sin" is still well understood in contemporary English and has a range of meaning comparable to the Hebrew concept. See *Comment*.

5.a. LXX reads singular for the Hebrew plural פשעי, as also in v 3, which is probably an interpretation of the Hebrew plurals as abstract and parallel to "my sin," though LXX uses plural in v 11 (Dalglish, *Psalm Fifty-One*, 63). Dahood proposes to read אוני for אני ("I") as a plural participle of אנה ("to meet/face") and translates, "My rebellious acts that face me I know too well," arguing that the object–subject–verb order is rare (GKC, 142). However, his proposal involves too much change for too little gain to be convincing.

6.a. The masculine singular noun בַד "separation," plus ל, means to be in a state of separation or by oneself. Elsewhere with God as the subject, see 71:16; 72:18; 83:18; 86:10; 136:4; 148:13.

6.b. The much discussed לְמַעַן should not be read here as expressing purpose ("in order that/so that") but as expressing result or consequence, which is supported by a considerable number of examples: Pss 30:12; 68:23; Exod 11:9; Lev 20:3; Deut 29:18; 1 Kgs 8:41; 2 Kgs 13:23; 22:17; Prov 2:20; Isa 44:9; Hos 8:4; Amos 2:7; Joel 3:6; Ezek 21:15, 28. Some of these examples are moot, but there are enough to establish the usage. See Buttenwieser, 193; Dahood, II, 4; Kissane, 227; Eerdmans, 273; N. H. Ridderbos, "Psalm 51:5–6," *Studia Biblica et Semitica*, 307–9; H. A. Brongers, "Die Partikel לְמַעַן in der biblisch-hebraischen Sprache," *Oudtestamentische Studiën* 18 (1973) 88–89. See *Comment*.

6.c, d. The qal infinitive construct of דבר is found only here. Several Heb. mss, LXX, σ´, Vg, and Rom 3:4 read or suppose בְּדָבְרֶיךָ, pl. of the noun דָּבָר = "your words (of judgment)." A similar treatment of בְּשָׁפְטֶךָ (MT, qal inf. const.) is found in some Heb. mss ("in your judgments"), but LXX takes as passive or middle, "when you are judged/when you enter into judgment." The unique qal inf. of דבר may have been chosen for the sake of harmony (so Delitzsch, II, 157).

7.a. and 8.a. These attempts to express the force of the הֵן (traditionally, "behold") used at the beginning of each verse. The assumption is that הֵן is being used in both verses as a conjunction with deictic force. See C. J. Labuschagne, "The Particles הֵן and הִנֵּה," *Oudtestamentische Studiën* 18 (1973) 1–14; note the "Whereas it is deep-seated truth that Thou dost desire" of A. R. Johnson, *CPIP*, 425.

8.b. More commonly, "truth." For discussion of אֱמֶת ("faithfulness"), see A. Jepsen, *TDOT*, I, 309–16. Jepsen (313) argues that "reliability" is the most comprehensive expression for the idea of אֱמֶת. See *Comment*.

8.c, d. The meanings of both בַּטֻּחוֹת, translated "womb," and of בְּסָתֻם, translated as "uterus," are both highly uncertain. The first appears to be a fem. plural noun, perhaps from טוּחַ, "overspread/coat/besmear" (BDB), or from טִיחַ, "plaster/coating." The only other occurrence is Job 38:36, where the meaning "cloud-layers" (dark hidden places) is sometimes given, though traditional interpretations understand it as "heart" or "kidneys," with reference to the innermost part of a human being. The parallel שֶׂכְוִי in Job 38:36b is also much disputed. The interpretation of שֶׂכְוִי as "heart" (from שָׂכָה, "look/see") and by extension "reflection/thought" fits the context in Job badly (see R. Gordis, *The Book of Job: Commentary, New Translation and Special Studies* [New York: Jewish Theological Seminary of America, 1978], 452–53). Another approach is to link שֶׂכְוִי with *Souchi*, the Coptic name of the god Mercury and to assume that תֻּחוֹת represents the Egyptian *Thot*, the god of wisdom (see M. H. Pope, *Job*, AB 15 [New York: Doubleday, 1965], 256–57). Gordis argues that טֻחוֹת is the *ibis ethiopica*, a bird which symbolized *Thot*, and that שֶׂכְוִי is the cock or rooster associated with forecasting rain and heralding the dawn. However, the idea of birds does not fit the context in Ps 51:8. Dahood links טֻחוֹת with the Egyptian *Thot*, but argues that the meaning is that of the "cleverness" which is associated with *Thot*, and used with a pejorative connotation. Dahood reads the parallel סָתֻם as "secret lore," on the basis of Ezek 28:3, "Look, you are wiser than Daniel, and no secret lore [סָתֻם] is too hidden for you." This seems to be a reasonable way of understanding the meanings of טֻחוֹת and סָתֻם, but the results fit badly in Ps 51:8. To make the meanings fit, Dahood is forced to treat the ב on טֻחוֹת and סָתֻם as comparative and to read the verb תּוֹדִיעֵנִי as an imperative request: "Since you indeed prefer truth to cleverness and secret love,/Teach me Wisdom!" This is not very convincing.

The translation above is postulated on the assumption that vv 7 and 8 should be read together. The birth and conception language of v 7 indicates that the covered, hidden place connoted by טֻחוֹת and the "stopped up" or "shut up" place denoted by סָתֻם (apparently a qal passive participle of סָתַם, note Dan 12:9) both refer to the womb and to the fetus which is caused to know wisdom even before birth. See *Comment*. All interpretations of these words should be considered as tentative. An alternative approach to 8b would be to read סָתֻם as a construct with "wisdom" (בְּסָתֻם חָכְמָה): "and you instructed me in the secret(s) of wisdom." This may receive some support from the Syriac reading, "But you have desired equity, and the hidden things of your wisdom you have made known to me." Also, LXX, ἰδοὺ γὰρ ἀλήθειαν ἠγάπησας τὰ ἄδηλα καὶ τὰ κρύφια τῆς σοφίας σου ἐδήλωσάς μοι ("For look, you love truth, [and] the secret and hidden things of your wisdom you have revealed to me").

9.a. The verb חטא appears a few times in piel (and hithpael) forms with the meaning "to purify from sin," or more literally "to unsin" or "to de-sin" (so Dahood, II, 5, but long before by John Donne, as noted by Perowne, 419; cf. Lev 8:15; 14:49, 52; Num 19:19; Ezek 43:20, 22, 23; 45:18).

9.b. "Hyssop" (אֵזוֹב) probably refers to a small bush known technically as *Origanum Maru L*, the Syrian marjoram (J. C. Trever, *IDB*, E–J, 669–70). In 1 Kgs 4:33 it refers to a small bush which grows out of a wall.

10.a. The חַשְׁמִיעֵנִי, "cause me to hear," has been rather frequently amended to חָשְׁבִּיעֵנִי ("satisfy me") with the Syriac version, but MT need not be changed.

15.a. Syriac has "your way" (sing.), but most Heb. mss, LXX, and Vg read as in MT. Cf. Ps 32:8.

15.b. So Johnson, *CPIP*, 413; see GKC, 155f.

16.a. Gunkel emends מִדָּמִים ("from bloods") to מִדֳּמָם, "from silence [of death]" and is followed by

Oesterley. Dahood repoints it as דָּמִים and relates it to a verb דמם, which he assumes can mean "to weep," based on Ugaritic usage. He suggests that the noun has come to signify the "place of tears par excellence" (cf. Matt 8:12) and translates, "the tears of death." The verb נצל appears very rarely with a plea for forgiveness (cf. 39:9; 79:9); it usually refers to rescue from enemies or from deathlike situations. There is no mention of violent acts elsewhere in the psalm which would incur blood-guilt. However, such literal acts are not required for the use of "bloods" in the sense of "blood-guilt" (see *Comment*). For the use of "blood" in the singular and plural, see A. R. Johnson, *The Vitality of the Individual in the Thought of Ancient Israel* (Cardiff: University of Wales Press, 1949), 72. The use of the plural with נצל would seem to imply violent or premature death (as, e.g., Gen 4:10–11; Lev 20:9, 11–13; 2 Sam 3:28; 16:8; Ps 9:13; Isa 1:15; Mic 3:10; 7:2); though נצל is not used elsewhere directly with "blood," either singular or plural, but it is used indirectly in Ezek 3:17–19; 33:7–9. For examples of blood-guilt, see Exod 22:1–2; Deut 19:10; 22:8; Hos 12:15 [14]. However, the line between "bloodshed" and "blood-guilt" is not clearly drawn in some passages.

16.b. "O God of my salvation" is sometimes treated as an addition on metrical grounds (e.g., Kraus); A. A. Anderson calls it a "later (although fitting) addition." Such changes should not normally be made on the exceedingly tenuous basis of meter. In this case, the three colons of v 16 correspond to the three colons of v 19 to form a subunit in the psalm (see *Form/Structure/Setting*).

18.a. LXX reads MT לֹא as לוּ and changes the expression from negative to positive:

ὅτι εἰ ἠθέλησας θυσίαν ἔδωκα ἄν
'ολοκαυτώματα οὐκ εὐδοκήσεις

"For if you desire sacrifice, I would have given it;
whole-offerings you do not desire."

Dalglish (*Psalm Fifty-One*, 189) argues that the כי as "for" is awkward, and since v 18 does not seem to be the statement for v 17, he reads the כי as intensive: "Yea, thou delightest not in sacrifice" (cf. Hos 6:6). However, it seems equally probable that the text assumes that the reader/hearer's repertoire of understanding includes the recognition that joyful freedom of the tongue and mouth to praise God was expected as a result of the acceptance of a sacrifice as a sign of forgiveness. Conventionally, accepted sacrifice would open the mouths of worshipers to praise God (note 1 Kgs 18:39; Pss 20:4–6; 66:13–16). This text, however, affirms that the expected consequence of sacrifice (i.e., praise) does not result.

18.b. Some commentators and translators relate וְאֶתֵּנָה to 18b rather than to 18a: "and were I to give" (so Gunkel; Kraus; Schmidt; Weiser; Dalglish, *Psalm Fifty-One*, 50, 71, 191; RSV; NEB; JB; NAB). The balance of the colons is improved by this procedure, but it is unnecessary. Unbalanced colons are common in Hebrew poetry. Dahood argues for a tricolon (three colons) in the verse, with an emphatic *waw* and reading the first part of the verse as contingent (vocalizing the לֹא, "not," as לוּא, with כי = "for should"): "For should you be pleased, a sacrifice indeed would I offer." However, this seems too contrived. If a tricolon is desired, it can be gotten by assuming that זבח ("sacrifice") is understood as being repeated with "I indeed would give" (a 3+2+3 verse); see Buttenwieser, 193. For the treatment of אתנה as an apodosis rather than as a protasis, see GKC, 108f.

19.a. Following MT. The change to "my sacrifice" (זִבְחִי) seems to have better agreement with רוּחַ ("spirit") and has the support of some commentators (e.g., Gunkel, Kraus, Dalglish, *Psalm Fifty-One*, 194). It may also have the support of LXX (which reads θυσία τῷ θεῷ, "sacrifice to God") and is followed by some translations (e.g., JB, NEB, NAB). Dahood proposes to read אלהים as superlative and translates as "the finest sacrifices" (also, Goldingay, *Songs*, 171, "a godly sacrifice"). See *Comment*.

19.b. Syriac omits *waw* before וְדִכֶּה and a number of commentators omit נִשְׁבָּר (e.g., Gunkel) on the grounds of dittography. However, the formation of the verse matches that of v 16 and should probably be retained regardless of how it got into its present form (see n. 16.b.).

19.c. LXX and Syriac read לא תבזה as 3rd masc sg, "he will not reject." Dahood insists on reading the imperfect with imperative force, which seems unlikely.

20.a. The imperfect is treated as having imperative force in this context (so, e.g., Dahood). LXX seems to read תִּבָּנֶה as niphal with "walls" as the subject ("and let the walls of Jerusalem be built / rebuilt"). The meaning of the verb as "build" or "rebuild" depends on the context. NIV adopts the ambiguous "build up the walls."

21.a. Dalglish (*Psalm Fifty-One*, 201) argues from the continuation of the petition in v 21 that the verbs are jussive: "then mayest thou delight . . . then may they offer bulls . . ." He argues for a uniform pattern with 20b. However, the presence of the double אז ("then") in 21 seems to signal a fulfilled type of condition, following such usage of אז as those in Ps 19:14; Prov 3:21–23; Job 11:14–15; 13:20; Isa 35:4–6.

21.b. Lit., "whole-offering [עולה, traditionally 'burnt-offering'] and whole-offering [כליל]." The two words are usually regarded as an explanatory addition, though Dahood argues that they should be retained because each colon of v 21 is introduced by אז and has 4 beats and 11 syllables in each part—though it seems to me that the syllable count should be 10+10.

21.c. Lit. either "bulls will go up on your altar" (qal), or "bulls will be caused to go up on your altar" (hiphil). The latter is the more probable.

Form/Structure/Setting

This is the best known of the seven traditional penitential psalms (6; 32; 38; 51; 102; 130; 143). However, the psalm is not easily classified in the usual form-critical categories. It is usually placed in the general classification of the laments of the individual (for discussion of this kind of psalm, see C. Westermann, *Praise and Lament*, 181–94; B. W. Anderson, *Out of the Depths: The Psalms Speak for Us Today*, rev. ed. [Philadelphia: Westminster Press, 1983], 73–105). However, such characteristic features as complaint about enemies and prayer for their defeat and/or punishment is missing, as well as any protestation of innocence on the part of the speaker in the psalm (cf. Pss 7:4–5; 17:2–5), and there is no motivational appeal to God for action (cf. 22:10–11). On the other hand, there is a full confession of sin which is without parallel in any other biblical psalm (though such confession in the past is recalled in 32:5; also note 38:19; 41:5; 69:6; 130:1–8; cf. the confessional prayer of Ezra in Ezra 9:6–15, which is communal in nature; also Num 14:13–23; Isa 6:1–13; Neh 1:4–11; Job 42:1–6; Dan 9:4–19). The paucity in the Psalms of the confession of sin and pleading for forgiveness is striking. B. W. Anderson (*Out of the Depths*, 93–102) treats the "Psalms of Penitence" (6; 32; 38; 51; 102; 130; 143) as a subcategory of individual laments and suggests that they differ in that they tend to internalize the problem of evil (94) and argues that "they agree on the fact that there is no human ground for *claiming* God's grace (*hesed*)" (99). Anderson (*Out of the Depths*, 95) also argues that the confession in 51:3–7 serves as the complaint element of the lament. Westermann (*Praise and Lament*, 185) contends that in such prayers as that found in Ps 51 (he cites 27:9) "the complaint lies hidden in the petition," assuming that in later Israelite religion there was a gradual curtailment of the direct complaint to and against God and an increase in petition, with the element of complaint tending to disappear (186). Thus in a broad sense, Ps 51 may be called an individual lament, but it is more specifically an individual confession of sin and a prayer for forgiveness (cf. Kraus, I, 58–59).

The title at the head of the psalm associates it with David and his confrontation with the prophet Nathan after committing adultery with Bathsheba and arranging for the death of her husband, Uriah (2 Sam 11–12). Davidic authorship has been claimed for the psalm on the basis of the title and the historical note attached to it. The general appropriateness of the psalm for the situation of David in 2 Sam 12 is obvious. However, such a claim rests on uncertain grounds, and as is true of all the psalms, authorship is not clearly established. The titles, which appear on many psalms (116 in the Hebrew text), are generally accepted as later additions—though how late or how early and by whom they were added are questions which lack precise answers. It is probable that all the components of the titles do not date from the same time but were added at different stages of use. The ascription "to David" (לדוד) does not necessarily indicate authorship in the literary sense (see note 1.b. above). The historical notes attached to some psalms are more likely exegetical constructs by scribal interpreters than separate historical traditions. The last two verses of the psalm (20–21) are almost certainly from a time later than David, though their Davidic origin has been defended (e.g., Delitzsch). Of course, vv 20–21 could be a supplement to an earlier primary psalm in 3–19, and there is nothing in the primary psalm which makes it impossible to assume Davidic authorship. On the other hand, there is nothing which is completely persuasive for such a conclusion. A. R. Johnson (*CPIP*, 414–31) argues that the historical note in the title referring the psalm to David's experiences in 2 Sam 12:1–5 is not reliable and that a more appropriate context for the psalm was David's sojourn at Mahanaim beyond the Jordan after leaving Jerusalem behind in control of his rebellious son, Absalom, and his associates (2 Sam 17:24–29). In particular he thinks of the anxious period in the city gate after David had been persuaded not to go out personally to meet Absalom with armed force and while he waited for news of the battle between his troops and those of Absalom (2 Sam 18:1–33). This is an interesting thesis, which illustrates the way the scribal interpreters who supplied the historical note probably worked, and which is no more historically reliable than theirs!

It has been widely assumed that the psalm belongs to the period after the fall of Jerusalem in 597 B.C.E. based on vv 20–21, which (as noted above) may be a later addition and no reliable evidence of the date for the primary psalm. Stronger evidence is supplied by the fact that individual prayers of confession are more common in the later literature of Israel's history, though not absent in earlier accounts (note Achan in Josh 8:20–21; David in 2 Sam 12:13). For references, see above, and note the powerful Prayer of Manasseh in the Apocrypha. Verbal and conceptual parallels between Ps 51 and Jeremiah, Ezekiel, and Isa 40–66 have been used to argue for a general context of later Israel. Dalglish (*Psalm Fifty-One*, 224–25) supplies the following chart for parallels with the prophetic writings:

Ps 51:3	Isa 43:7
4	Isa 43:25; 44:22; Jer 2:22; 4:14
5f	Isa 59:12–13; Isa 65:5–7
6	Isa 42:44; 25:12; 66:4
7	Ezek 16:2–4; Jer 2:11; Isa 43:27
9	Ezek 36:25; Isa 1:18
10	Ezek 37
11	Isa 59:2; Ezek 39:23–24
12	Jer 31:33–34; Exod 36:26; cf. Ezek 11:19; Jer 32:29; Isa 51:7
13	Jer 23:39; 33:25; Isa 63:10, 11b.
16	Ezek 3:18–20; 33:6, 8, 9; Isa 61:10–11
18	Hos 6:6; Amos 6:21, 22
19	Isa 57:15b; 61:1b; 66:2b

Note also the similarity of attitude toward sacrifice (vv 16–19) with Amos 5:21, 22; Hos 6:6; Isa 1:11–13, 16; Jer 6:20; 7:22; 14:22, as well as the "clean heart" and "steadfast spirit" (v 12) with Jer 24:7; 31:33, 32:39; 36:26. The "holy spirit" appears elsewhere in the OT only in Isa 63:10, 11 (cf. Isa 63:14). These parallels (and other similar ones) can be interpreted to argue that Ps 51 reflects the thought of the prophets from Amos into the post-exilic period (see Johnson, 414–16). However, the evidence is not as strong as it may seem, because it is quite probable that both the prophetic literature and Ps 51 reflect common traditions which antedate both, and those in Ps 51 could be earlier than those in the prophetic writings.

Dalglish (*Psalm Fifty-One*, 223–32) argues for the probability of a date for the psalm in the time of Josiah (c. 640–609 B.C.E.). The supplement at the end (vv 20–21) would have been added after 597 B.C.E. to re-interpret the prayer in vv 16–19 and to allow the exiles to make a Davidic confession their own. Thus in this interpretation a pre-exilic individual psalm was adapted for communal use by a liturgical supplement (Dalglish, *Psalm Fifty-One*, 201–8; note a similar process reflected in 130:7–8).

Nothing seems to be fully decisive about the date and origin of Ps 51. It could go back to the direct experience of David and/or to his authorship. On the other hand, it probably does not. The weight of literary parallels with later literature tilts the conclusion toward a date well down in the monarchy. The writer may have been a cult prophet (a secondary proposal of A. R. Johnson, *CPIP*, 418), who "faced with the imminent prospect of death and thus an end to all his [*sic*] professional activities, recognizes how far he himself has strayed from the path which he has been wont to urge upon others." This would fit well with concern about being banished from the presence of Yahweh and deprived of the empowering presence of the divine spirit—especially important for a prophet. However, it is equally probable that the writer was a priest and professional psalm writer. We should not assume that the language of the psalms *necessarily* represents the direct personal experience of their writers. All good poets and hymn writers have the ability to enter into the experience of human life in such ways as to seem extremely personal and with language which evokes positive identification and response from many different hearers and readers. Further, it is certainly not improbable that the writer of Ps 51 deliberately designed it with David in mind. It was and is an appropriate prayer for David—and for all the other "Davids" who have followed him in history.

How is the speaker in the psalm to be identified? Of course the traditional interpretation has identified the speaker as David during one of the great crises of his career. Dalglish (*Psalm Fifty-One*, 226) argues that while the book is probably not from David, it is "a royal penitential psalm spoken by or for the king." J. H. Eaton (*Kingship and the Psalms*, SBT 2nd series 32 [Naperville, IL: Allenson, 1975], 71–72, 177–81) also presents a case for a king as the speaker. He maintains that emphasis on the spirit of God in 51:12–14 "points beyond an ordinary Israelite, and in fact to the king" (71; also Dalglish, *Psalm Fifty-One*, 228). He thinks that the appeal to God's faithfulness and love in v 3, the appeal to God's righteousness in 16, and the expression "God of my salvation" all point to a kingly personal covenant with God. The role of the king as teacher and admonisher is recognized in v 15 (cf. Eaton, *Kingship and the Psalms*, 181–82), and it is assumed that the psalm would have been appropriate for an annual rite of atonement led by the king in pre-exilic Israel (72, 177). Dalglish (*Psalm Fifty-One*, 227) suggests that the "bloodshed"/"blood-guilt" of v 16 is appropriate to the judgment on Manasseh in 2 Kgs 24:3 (". . . for he filled Jerusalem with innocent blood; and the LORD would not pardon"). The kingly office was a representative one, and Dalglish argues that "unrequited blood" must have been "like a Damo-clean sword" which threatened the life of the nation during the reign of Josiah.

The interpretation of the speaker as the king is an attractive one, and, if it is correct, the scribes who supplied the superscription rightly understood the psalm. The penitence of kings is well established both in and outside the OT (besides David, note Ahab in 1 Kgs 22:27–29; Josiah in 2 Kgs 22:11–13; 23:21–25, and the Prayer of Manasseh referred to above; for reference to nonbiblical literature see the works of Dalglish and Eaton, *passim*). The probability of atonement rites is high. However, confessions of sin and prayers for forgiveness were not restricted to kings. Prophets, priests, and lay persons in small-group rituals were not excluded.

It is very doubtful that we should conclude that abiding possession of the spirit was a sole prerogative of kings (note Num 11:25, 29). If this were the case, the absence of the spirit from the royal psalms would be odd. While the spirit is associated with the ideal of kingship (Isa 11:2), it is markedly lacking in descriptions of reigning kings in OT accounts (Neve, *ExpTim* 80 [1969] 266) and is associated with prophets. Further, it is difficult to believe that Josiah or any other king would have advocated the attitude toward sacrifice found in 51:18–19. Other interpretations of vv 11 and 14 are quite possible (see *Comment*). As noted above, the kingship characteristics of the psalm may be the result of the author consciously writing with David in mind; placing, as it were, the psalm in the mouth of David.

The difficulty of attaining precision in determining the condition and identity of the speaker points toward a composition for cultic usage. Evocative generalization is characteristic of such writings, intended for repeated use by various individuals and groups. The background of cultic purification rituals which seems to be supposed (especially the "with hyssop" in 9) adds further support to this conclusion, as does the re-interpretation of the original psalm in vv 20, 21. Of course, cultic composition and use do not rule out profound spiritual experience or make the psalm merely the product of an "office." Cultic message and spiritual depth are not necessarily antithetical. It is well to remember that most of the great hymns and anthems of the Church were written by professional hymn writers.

It is quite possible that the primary psalm in 51:3–19 was used in a ritual of repentance and healing for a sick person and was designed for recitation in a private sickroom, aided perhaps by a priest (for the elaboration of such ceremonies, see K. Seybold, *Das Gebet*, and more briefly in K. Seybold and U. B. Müller, *Sickness and Healing*, Biblical Encounter Series [Nashville: Abingdon Press, 1981], 43–56—though Seybold [*Das Gebet*, 63–64] is not sure that Ps 51 belongs to such rituals). In a somewhat similar manner, E. S. Gerstenberger (*Der bittende Mensch*) has argued that individual laments were used in familial contexts for persons

threatened by a wide range of afflictions and troubles. A ritual expert—a liturgist, but not a priest—participated with the needy person in rites of healing and
restoration. The individual was never ill or otherwise threatened alone, because
the group to which the ill person belonged was involved in the condition of the
sufferer. The penitential psalms would seem to fit such contexts (see the proposed
"setting" for Ps 6 by Gerstenberger, *Psalms: Part 1,* FOTL 14 [Grand Rapids:
Eerdmans, 1988], 62).

Commentators have not found Ps 51 easy to outline. Weiser notes what he judges
to be a lack of "homogeneous construction" and attributes this to the molding of
its outward form by "the distress of the life of prayer out of which the psalm has
arisen" (401). Auffret (*VT* 26 [1976] 142–47) and A. R. Ceresko ("The Function of
Chiasmus in Hebrew Poetry," *CBQ* 40 [1978] 6) support a major division in the
psalm between vv 11 and 12, marked at the beginning and end by the verb מְחֵה, "blot
out" (in vv 3 and 11). However, Auffret thinks that there is also a relationship
between v 10 and v 19 (note the use of the verb דכה, "crushed," in each verse). Also
v 10 fits well with v 14 (שָׂשׂוֹן, "joy," is in both verses), and indeed it relates well to the
restoration theme in vv 12–16. On the other hand, the use of חטא, "sin" in v 11
relates well to vv 4, 5, 6, 7 and 9, and עון, "iniquity/waywardness" relates to vv 4 and
7. Thus an interlocking structure like the following makes good sense: 3–9, 11 and
12, 19–10. The conclusion in vv 20–21 lies outside the primary psalm. The first
major division can be subdivided as follows:

Prayer for forgiveness	vv 3–4
Confession of sin	vv 5–6b
Rightness of divine judgment	vv 6cd
Confession of sinfulness	vv 7–8
Prayer for forgiveness	vv 9, 11

The second division divides as follows:

Prayer for restoration	vv 10, 12–14
Vow to teach sinners	v 15
Prayer for the ability to praise	vv 16–19

Vv 20–21 form an addendum.

Comment

Superscription (51:1–2). See the *Notes* above for discussion of v 1. The historical
note in v 2 relates the psalm to the events recounted in 2 Sam 11–12. While it is
linguistically possible to read the second verb בוא ("come/go") of a visit by Nathan
to Bathsheba (after the birth of her child?) it is much more probable that the
reference is to David's sexual intercourse with Bathsheba described in 2 Sam 11:4.
The verse is concerned to set the psalm in the context of Nathan's confrontation
with David after the arranged death of Uriah and the birth of a child to Bathsheba
(2 Sam 12:1–14). Scribal interpreters judged the psalm to be appropriate as a
statement of confession for David's sin and a petition for forgiveness. There are, of
course, a number of verbal and content parallels between the psalm and the

account of David's confession and restoration (Dalglish, *Psalm Fifty-One*, 15–16). David's confession to Nathan, "I have sinned against Yahweh," fits well with the "against you alone I have sinned" (Ps 51:6). The "I have done what is evil in your eyes" of 51:6 matches the "to do the evil in his eyes" of 2 Sam 12:9. The use of חטא ("sin") in seven verses of Ps 51 (4, 5, 6, 7, 9, 11, 15) corresponds to the use of the same verb in David's confession in 2 Sam 12:13 ("I have sinned against Yahweh"). The "blood-guilt"/"bloodshed" of 51:16 correlates with the murder of Uriah and other bloody incidents in the career of David. Also, the absence of enemies in Ps 51 fits the context of David in 2 Sam 11–12, where the actions have to do with David and Yahweh; enemies are present only in a minor way in the military campaign led by Joab (Miller, *Interpreting the Psalms*, 54).

However, these parallels do not establish Davidic authorship of the psalm. The language of the psalm is general and not specific. The basic nature of the superscriptions and historical notes points toward scribal interpretation more than toward composition. The historical note is a way of saying that the understanding of the psalm is helped when it is read in a particular context. The question of literary composition is largely irrelevant (Miller, *Intrepreting the Psalms*, 53), but the authority of the psalm as a Davidic psalm is enhanced by the historical note.

Prayer for forgiveness (51:3–4). The suppliant prays to God for mercy and cleansing from sin. As in the case of 32:1–2, the vocabulary of sin and forgiveness is prominent. The חָנֵּנִי, "be merciful to me," expresses the desire for favorable and beneficent action, usually involving the response of a superior to an inferior (e.g., 2 Sam 12:22; Job 19:21; 33:24; Pss 4:2; 56:2; 57:2; see also חֵן, "favor" or "mercy," in Gen 6:8; 30:27; Pss 45:2; 84:11; etc.). The prayer is for mercy and unmerited favor from God.

The suppliant desires mercy in accord with God's חֶסֶד and his רַחֲמִים. חסד is a word which has varied nuances of meaning and is very difficult to translate into English (See K. D. Sakenfeld, *The Meaning of Hesed in the Hebrew Bible: A New Inquiry*, HSM 17 [Missoula, MT: Scholars Press, 1978] and *Faithfulness in Action: Loyalty in Biblical Perspective* [Philadelphia: Fortress Press, 1985]). In general, חסד refers to the obligation assumed by one person to act on behalf of another, who is usually dependent on the aid of the first and helpless to function adequately without it. God's willingness to deliver is a central focus in a number of psalms (e.g., 31:17; 94:18; 107:8, 15, 21, 31; 109:26; 143:12), and divine protection is also involved (32:10; 36:11). The relationship of חסד to forgiveness is found in 85:8 and 90:14, two communal laments in which the people pray for restoration and removal of the divine wrath (also 25:7; 103:6–8, 10–14). Thus in Ps 51 the suppliant appeals for mercy on the basis of God's willingly assumed and continued obligation (his "loyal-love") to act for the removal of anything, including guilt, which threatens the welfare of an individual (or people) for whom he is responsible. Of course, the suppliant has no power to command such mercy, but it can be asked for on the basis of the confession and prayer which follows. Sakenfeld (*The Meaning of Hesed*, 227–30) notes that apart from Pss 51, 106, and 130, the relationship of the recipients of the divine חסד to God is generally one of trust and hope; e.g., 32:10b, "steadfast love surrounds him who trusts in Yahweh"; 130:7, "O Israel, hope in Yahweh, for with Yahweh there is steadfast love." Thus a latent confidence undergirds the appeal in 51:1.

The word רחמים ("compassion") is an absolute plural intensive of the word רֶחֶם, "womb." The form suggests the idea of the feelings of a mother toward her baby (cf. Isa 47:5–7). The word may also mean "bowels" in several references (e.g., Gen 43:30; 1 Kgs 3:26; Isa 63:15: "the sound of your bowels and your רחמים") and refer to the seat of emotions. The reference is to God's compassionate mercy, which is רב, "great" or "abundant," a word which intensifies the compassion in a quantitative way (as also in 69:17; note that רב is used with חסד a few times elsewhere: 5:7; 69:13; 106:7, 45; Isa 63:7). The use of חסד and רחמים together as a word pair (e.g., Hos 2:21; Jer 16:5; Pss 25:6; 40:12; 69:17; 103:4; Dan 1:9) tends to emphasize the mercy element of חסד. It should be recognized that 3a reflects formulaic liturgical usage, as is demonstrated by its relatedness to Exod 34:6–7 and to the expression "praise Yahweh . . . for his steadfast love endures forever," which appears in one form or another some forty-two times (1 Chr 16:34, 41; Jer 33:11; Ps 100:5; etc.—twenty-five times in Ps 136; Sakenfeld, *The Meaning of Hesed*, 227, 111–39, 165–68).

The מָחָה used in 3b means "to blot out" or "to obliterate" and is the first of three verbs expressing vigorous action in the petitions for forgiveness. The מָחָה is used in the sense of "wipe off" (Prov 30:20; Isa 25:8; 2 Kgs 21:13) or "obliterate" a name, a remembrance, or a written curse (Deut 9:14; Exod 17:14; Num 5:23; Ps 109:13). The use in Ps 51 may be metaphoric in a general sense, as in Isa 44:22:

> I have swept away [מחה] your transgressions like a cloud,
> and your sins like mist . . .

However, it is likely that the idea of erasing from a written scroll or tablet is in mind. Several places in the OT refer to deeds and/or names of people being written on a scroll or book, as is Ps 69:28:

> Let them be blotted out [מחה] of the book of the living,
> let them not be enrolled among the righteous.

(See also Exod 32:32, 33; Isa 4:3; Mal 3:16; Neh 13:13; Dan 7:10; Luke 10:20; Phil 4:3; Heb 12:23; Rev 3:5; 13:8; 17:8; 20:12, 15; 21:27; *Jub.* 30.20, 22; 36.10; *1 Enoch* 47.3; 108.3.) A reference to a "tablet of one's sin" is found in Babylonian usage, as well as the prayer "may the tablet of my sins be broken" (Dalglish, *Psalm Fifty-One*, 86–88). The idea of breaking a tablet is applied to a contract in the Code of Hammurabi (Dalglish, *Psalm Fifty-One*, 37) and to the cancellation of a debt by "washing off" the tablet; cf. Num 5:23: "The priest shall write these curses . . . and wipe them off [מחה] into the water of bitterness." The idea of blotting out from a scroll or written record is considered to be so strong by Weiser that he proposes to add "from the book of guilt" after "blot out" (402).

The second verb used in the petitions for forgiveness is כבס in 4a, used with הרבה ("thoroughly," see *Notes*). כבס seems to be derived from the domestic practice of washing clothes (Exod 19:10, 14; Lev 13:6, 34; 2 Sam 19:24) and does not refer, primarily at least, to bathing (for which רחץ is used, Num 19:19; Perowne, 414, notes that the Greek verbs πλύνω = כבס and λούω = רחץ have the same distinction). The usage for washing clothes accords with the basic meaning of the verb, which is "to tread" or "to pummel," since clothes were washed by beating or treading them in water. However, כבס is also used with a metaphoric sense (Jer 2:22; 4:14; Mal 3:2). Jer 2:22 is vivid.

> Though you wash yourself [תְּכַבְּסִי] with lye
> and use much soap
> the stain of your guilt is still before me.

Thus the suppliant desires to be cleansed from sin with the thoroughness used in washing dirty clothes.

The third verb for forgiveness (טהר) is found in 4b ("and cleanse me from my sin"). This verb is used of a physical cleansing: dross from metal (Mal 3:3); clouds from the heaven (Job 37:21); from disease (2 Kgs 5:10, 12–14); unclean things from the temple (2 Chr 29:15, 16; Ezek 31:45). Apart from these references, however, the verb is used of cleansing or purity in a ritual sense (Lev 11:32; 12:7, 8; etc.). The ritual associations are certainly in view here, but probably not to the extent supposed by Leslie when he translates, "And declare me clean of my sin" (399). Dalglish (*Psalm Fifty-One*, 91, 94) notes that in the case of כבס the sense is not "wash sin from me" but "wash me." We should see the same emphasis in 4b: "Wash *me* thoroughly from my iniquity and cleanse *me* from my sin," or, as in the translations above, "Wash away *my* waywardness." In the OT generally, uncleanness is essentially that which disqualifies from participation in ritual and excludes the worshiper from the presence of God. However, no clear distinction can be made between purely ritual and moral cleanness or uncleanness, and none should be attempted here.

The three verbs for forgiveness are matched by three prime words for sin in vv 3–4. The first of these is פֶּשַׁע, which has been defined in a theological sense as "willful, self-assertive defiance of God" (Dalglish, *Psalm Fifty-One*, 88). L. Köhler (*OT Theology*, 170) declares that the word means ". . . rebellion. It is the disobedience, παρακοή, of Rom 5:19." Numerous references demonstrate the idea of revolt carried by the verb (e.g., 1 Kgs 12:19; 2 Kgs 3:4–5; Hos 9:1; Isa 1:2; Amos 3:14). However, R. Knierim (*Die Hauptbegriffe für Sünde im Alten Testament*, 178) thinks the most appropriate expression for the root idea is "to break with" or "to do wrong." The word represents a rather formalized overall concept of many-sided types of wrongdoing, which vary in different contexts. Ronald Youngblood ("Three Old Testament Roots for 'Sin,'" 201–5) argues that one nuance of פשע is that of "deviating" or "straying." He cites a number of OT references, including Amos 2:4, "For three transgressions [פשעי] of Judah, and for four, I will not revoke the punishment . . . their lies have led them astray [root תעה or טעה], after which their fathers walked." Also Isa 59:13a, 15b: ". . . transgressing [פשע], and denying Yahweh, and turning away [root סוג] from following our God . . . and he who turns aside from evil makes himself a prey"; Hos 7:13a, ". . . they have strayed [root נדד] from me . . . they have rebelled [פשעו] against me!" (and parallel in 7:14d, "they rebel [root נסור] against me").

The second word for sin in v 4 is עָוֹן, which is commonly assumed to derive from the root idea of bending or twisting. However, S. R. Driver (*Notes on the Hebrew Text and the Topography of the Books of Samuel*, 2nd ed. [Oxford: Clarendon Press, 1913], 170, n. 2) has argued that two roots, distinct in Arabic, have been confused in

Hebrew (also Dalglish, *Psalm Fifty-One*, 91–92). One root means "to bend" and the other "to err, go astray." Driver argues that עון in the OT is properly "error" or "deviation from the right track." He cites the versions of Isa 19:14 (where LXX has πνεῦμα πλανήσεως, "spirit of error," for MT רוח עועים) and Prov 12:8. Youngblood ("Three OT Roots for 'Sin,'" 204) thinks that "err from the road" is a primary meaning of עון and cites numerous passages in which it is found in the context with "way," "turns to/from," "walks," and "turn aside" or the like: e.g., Lam 3:9, "He has blocked my ways . . . he has made my paths crooked [עוה]"; 2 Sam 22:22a, 24b, "I have kept the ways of Yahweh. . . . I have kept myself from iniquity [עון]; Jer 14:10, "They have loved to wander [נוע], they have not restrained their feet . . . he will remember their iniquity [עון] and punish their sins [חטאת]." Thus the "way-wardness" of the translation above cannot be far off the mark.

On the other hand, the idea of bending or twisting seems to appear in some contexts: e.g., Ps 38:7, "I am utterly bowed down [עוה] and prostrate"; Isa 21:3, "I am bowed down from hearing"; Isa 24:1, "and he will twist [עוה] its surface [that of the land or the earth] and scatter its inhabitants." Thus the word can be understood with either sense. Actually, the idea of bending or twisting is not very different from the idea of deviation or error. L. Köhler (*OT Theology*, 169) argues that עון "designates a sin that originates in wrong intention and contrasts with חטא and פשע." This approach is reflected also in S. Terrien (*The Psalms*, 171), who writes that "'iniquity' designates a state of distortion, bending, or twisting, which vitiates the whole outlook and therefore the subsequent behavior. . . . It is the disintegration of heart and volition." But one can argue on the basis of OT contexts that חטאת and פשע also carry the ideas of guilt and "state of distortion"—the "disintegration of heart and volition" is characteristic of sin generally, regardless of the word used. In the case of עון, it is especially important to observe that regardless of the root idea adopted, the word refers to deliberate action rather than to innate or accidental wrongdoing.

The third word for sin is חַטָּאָה, commonly translated as "sin." This form of חטא occurs some 155 times in the OT and, along with other forms, is part of the most used complex of words for sin (over 400 times). The root idea of "missing the mark" is often cited, especially using Judg 20:16b, "everyone could sling a stone at a hair, and not miss [חטא]" (also Prov 8:36; 19:2; Job 5:24). The idea of failure is frequently attached to the word. However, it is important to remember that the failure involved is the result of choice or of a clear act of will (A. A. Anderson, 393), although the verb and noun do appear in a few references to unwilling sins, primarily of a cultic nature (e.g., Lev 4:2–3; 5:15–16; Num 15:27–28). Köhler qualifies his treatment of חטא as "failure" by arguing that it is concerned with the violation of commands and prohibitions (*OT Theology*, 169). He pushes his analysis so far as to contend that פשע is less concerned with the violation of "objective commands" than חטא, being essentially concerned with the "revolt of the human will against the divine will" (170). He calls פשע "the OT's most profound word for sin" (also S. J. De Vries, *IDB*, 4, 361). But numerous uses of חטא occur without any explicit reference to commandments or instruction, as is the case with the much less frequently used פשע. At least in Hos 8:1 and Ezek 18:22, 28, 30, 31, פשע appears where instruction and commandments are clearly in the context. *Any attempt to find greater profundity in one of these three major words for sin than in another seems to be poorly supported.* After extensive discussion of the root ideas of פּשׁע, עון, and חטא, Dalglish (*Psalm Fifty-One*, 93) concludes that "although their conceptual motif may differ, there is no great difference of any importance in the use. . . ." (See also the excursus by Knierim (*Die Hauptbegriffe*, 229–35) on the connection of פּשׁע, עון, and חטא). Youngblood ("Three OT Roots for 'Sin,'" 205) refers to the interpretation of the various roots and concludes that "sin is comprehensively viewed in the Old Testament as the deliberate act of veering off the road that God wants us to travel."

Confession of sin (51:5–6b). The confession begins with a forthright statement of personal knowledge in 5a. The force of the "I know" is increased by the addition of the separate personal pronoun. The "I know" should be understood in a personal sense of knowing rather than in the sense of "I acknowledge" or "I confess." The parallel in 5b is equally strong: "my sin [*or*, sinfulness] is ever before me." This expression certainly conveys a sense of continual awareness rather than an occasional consciousness and most probably also the idea of continuing tension because of fear and shame (cf. 32:3–5; 38:18). The "courage to deal impartially" with oneself is a necessary characteristic for true confession.

The heart of the confession is found in 6a: "Against you, you only, I have sinned." Some commentators (see the summaries in Perowne, 415; Gunkel, 222) have noted the absence of any confession of sin against other human beings and have assumed that such awareness is missing from the confession. But other OT passages make it clear that from an early time in Israel sins against persons were believed to be sins against God (Kraus, 543); see 2 Sam 12:9, 10, 13; Gen 39:9; Prov 14:31; 17:5. Violation of the commandments of God is construed as sin against God himself (Kraus, 544; Weiser, 403).

The parallel statement in 6b is also emphatic: "And I have done evil in your sight." The expression "evil in your [or his] sight" is the opposite of "what is right [יָשָׁר] or good [טוֹב] in the eyes of Yahweh" (e.g., Deut 6:18; 12:8, 25, 28). Basically, רַע, "evil," refers to whatever is bad, disagreeable, or unpleasant and may or may not have a specific ethical sense (e.g., worthless or corrupt: 2 Kgs 2:19; Prov 20:14; 25:19; Jer 24:2; Matt 6:23; 7:17; displeasing, ugly, or sad: Gen 21:11–12; 28:8; 41:19–20; Neh 2:3; Eccl 7:3; painful or injurious: Gen 26:29; 31:7; Deut 26:6; 28:35; 2 Sam 12:18; Prov 11:15; Rev 16:21).

The rightness of divine judgment (51:6cd). The לְמַעַן of v 6c has stimulated a great deal of somewhat perplexed discussion because it most often expresses "in order that" rather than result ("so that"). The idea of purpose results in the translation "in order that you may be in the right [*or*, justified] when you speak and blameless when you judge." Such a translation produces an extraordinary tension between 6ab and 6c: "I have sinned against you . . . in order that you may be justified. . . ." Some interpreters have accepted this tension and chosen to understand the verse in the sense of "I sinned to the glory of God," especially in a Pauline sense (e.g., Perowne, Kirkpatrick, Weiser, Dalglish [*Psalm Fifty-One*, 109–13], Goldingay [*Songs*, 158]). Weiser cites Rom 11:32–33, "God has consigned all men to disobedience, that he may have mercy upon all," though he also argues that "these thoughts on God's ultimate purpose being made manifest by sin" (405) do not alleviate man's responsibility or the seriousness of sin (cf. Rom 6:15). Appeal is also made to Rom 3:3–5 where Paul quotes 6c (in its Greek form) and says "But if our wickedness serves to show the justice of God, what shall we say?" Kirkpartick (290) sums up this approach: "Probably . . . we are meant to understand that man's sin brings out into a clearer light the justice and holiness of God, who pronounces sentence upon it."

Another approach to 6c is to assume that the reference goes back to v 5, with v 6ab treated as a parenthesis, or else to conjecture that something like "I confess this so that . . ." has dropped out (so Dalglish, A. A. Anderson, etc.). This interpretation lends itself to the treatment of 6c as an element borrowed from the so-called "doxology of judgment," in which the sinner acknowledges the rightness of divine punishment and glorifies the acts of God's judgment (see Kraus, 544; G. von Rad, *Old Testament Theology,* tr. D. M. G. Stalker [New York: Harper, 1962] 1:357–59). The best example is Joshua's counsel to Achan, "My son, give glory to the LORD God of Israel, and render praise to him; and tell me now what you have done" (Josh 7:19). In the "doxology of judgment" the guilty persons confess and praise God by confirming the rightness of a divine judgment.

These difficult explanations are avoided by reading למען as an expression of consequence or result (so Buttenwieser, 193; Kissane, 227; Eerdmans, 273; Dahood, II, 4; N. H. Ridderbos, "Psalm 51:5–6," 307–9). Actually, examples of the use of למען for consequence or result are fairly numerous. For example, Perowne cites 30:12; Exod 11:9; Deut 29:18; Isa 44:9; Hos 8:4; Dahood cites Ps 68:23 and Prov 2:20. Some of the examples are moot, but the number can be increased: 1 Kgs 8:41; 2 Kgs 13:23; 22:17; Amos 2:7; Joel 3:6; Ezek 21:15, 28 (see H. A. Brongers, "Die Partikel לְמַעַן in der biblisch-hebraischen Sprache," *Oudtestamentische Studiën* 18 (1973) 88–89). This approach avoids the theologizing required by the purpose clause and still allows v 6c to reflect an element of the "doxology of judgment."

Rom 3:4 follows the LXX and takes the זכה, "blameless," in v 6d as "to be victorious/prevail" in accord with its Aramaic sense. However, the limited usage of the word in the MT (only eight times) points toward the ideas of acquittal or favorable judgment, and seems to reflect legal usage (Dalglish, *Psalm Fifty-One,* 112–13; Dahood II, 4: "No one can bring a legitimate claim against you"). If the idea of "prevail" is adopted, it should be understood as "prevailing in judgment," and thus "blameless."

Confession of sinfulness (51:7–8). The counterpart of v 6 is formed by v 7 and extends the acute present sense of sin into the past. The suppliant's sinful condition is not merely of recent vintage. The whole of life is involved in the confession of sin: "Indeed I was born in waywardness, and my mother conceived me in sin." Thus the sin confessed in the present extends back to the very beginnings of the speaker's life.

This verse has been especially popular with Christian expositors, who have used it in connection with the doctrine of original sin (see Dalglish, *Psalm Fifty-One,* 118–23; Zink, *VT* 17 [1967] 354–61). Some interpreters have understood the sin involved as that of sexual passion or sexual intercourse, and perhaps even adultery on the part of the mother. Attention is focused on יחם, "to be hot/rut/conceive." Delitzsch (157) flirts with the attraction of this view when he says that the verb "hints at the beast-like element in the act of coition," though he does not adopt it. This interpretation is augmented by the widespread interpretation of the "knowledge of good and evil" in Gen 3 as sexual intercourse and by references that declare sexual acts, bodily discharges, and birth to be ritually unclean (Exod 21:9; Lev 12; 15; etc.). A modern Jewish scholar, Y. Kaufmann (*The Religion of Israel, from Its Beginnings to the Babylonian Exile,* tr. M. Greenberg [Chicago: University of Chicago Press, 1969], 293–94), illustrates this approach when he argues that sexual desire is the archetypical sin in Gen 3, "the characteristic mark of the evil impulse." Procreation becomes not a blessing (as in Gen 1:28), but the result of sin. "The sexual act . . . is the child of sin. Offspring was given to man only after he had sinned and became subject to death. . . . The race was born from sin." Kaufmann applies this interpretation to Ps 51:5, "Man was created by grace, but is born through sin." More recently Caquot (*RHR* 1969 [1966] 144–45) interprets v 5 as applying to Jerusalem as the "mother" of the Israelites. He suggests that the background is found in the sexual symbolism used in Hos 2:6–9; Ezek 16:3; 23:25 (also note Isa 50:1; 64:1–8; Jer 50:1–12). He notes that the coarseness of the verb with its bestial application would be appropriate if sinful and adulterous Jerusalem is in mind.

However, this influential interpretation is dubious. That sexual desire is the "archetypal sin" of Gen 3 is very doubtful (see commentaries). Dalglish points out that "nowhere in the Old Testament is the legitimate act of coition referred to as sinful" (*Psalm Fifty-One*, 119). Such passages as Gen 1:28; 9:1, 7; 29:31; 30:22, 23; Ruth 4:13; Job 10:8–12; Ps 139:13–16 make it extremely difficult to maintain any inherent sinfulness in sexual intercourse, conception, and birth. Admittedly, the verb is used elsewhere of animals (Gen 30:38, 39, 41; 31:10; the more common verb is הרה) and one can understand Delitzsch's "hint." But it occurs only six times, and too much should not be built on such limited usage. Caquot's case for Jerusalem is possible, but far from certain. Regardless of the identity of the mother, her sexual passion is not the central focus of the confession. *The suppliant is not confessing a mother's sin.* The emphasis is on personal sinfulness: "For my acts of rebellion, I know indeed . . . against you, you only, I have sinned."

The passage is more commonly understood today as a confession of the essential human condition of the speaker. "One is a sinner simply as a result of one's natural human descent" (W. Eichrodt, *Theology of the Old Testament*, I, 268). Closely related to this approach is what may be called the social view. "It is the tragedy of man that he is born into a world full of sin" (Weiser, 405; also A. A. Anderson, 395). No particular sinfulness of the mother or the process of conception is involved. The emphasis is on the sin of the speaker, who admits that sin has been "no freak event" (Kidner, 190), but goes back to the roots of personal existence (see Ps 58:3). Thus the psalm reflects acceptance of the understanding that human life always involves sin and guilt (see Gen 8:21; Job 14:4; 15:14–16; 25:4; Ps 143:2; John 3:6; Kraus, 544).

J. K. Zink has taken up the interpretations of various Jewish commentators and argued that 51:5 and Job 14:4 should be understood in the sense of ritual uncleanness. This approach links these verses to laws on uncleanness and purification after sexual intercourse (Lev 15:18). Zink (*VT* 17 [1967] 360) points out that the Levitical laws frequently use "sin" and "uncleanness" as synonyms and argues that "iniquity" and "sin" in 51:7 should be understood in the same way (note the "cleanse me" in v 2). Thus the confession is concerned with a birth that occurred in the "sinful" state of disqualification from participation in ritual worship.

The best interpretation seems to be the second discussed above. However, the background of ritual impurity enhances the force of the confession and properly deserves attention. Further, the verse may indeed have been understood with Jerusalem as the mother after the re-interpretation of the psalm by the addition of vv 18–19. A purely ritual basis (as proposed by Zink) is too restricted for the comprehensive confession of sin. Such ritual uncleanness would be, after all, unavoidable on the part of every person (and could be used as an excuse). This is hardly adequate for the emphatically personal confession of rebellion and sin in vv 5–6. It is hardly probable that the ritual uncleanness of the worshiper's mother at conception and childbirth would be continually before the speaker or that he or she should declare "against you, you only, I have sinned." The main point is the comprehensive nature of the suppliant's *own* sin.

The meaning of v 8 eludes all assurance. The long notes 8.c and 8.d above attempt to set forth a modest rationale for the translation adopted. The interpretation is influenced (a) by linking v 8 with v 7 (v 8 is a continuation of the confession in v 7), and (b) by the Talmudic tradition (*Nid.* 30b; noted by Dalglish, *Psalm Fifty-One,* 124–25) that *torah* was taught to an embryonic person, though it was all forgotten at birth. The involvement of Yahweh with the formation of the fetus seems to be well established in such passages as Ps 139:13–18; Job 10:10–12; Eccl 11:5; Ps 22:9–10; 2 Macc 7:22–23; Wis 7:1–3; see also the Egyptian Hymn of Aton. If this interpretation is correct, the verse means that the suppliant does not claim to be simply a victim of circumstance (v 7) but confesses that no time in his or her existence as a human being has been without the gifting of divine truth and wisdom. Thus the verse serves to strengthen the rightness of God's judgment of the speaker's sin in v 6b. The verse is far too uncertain, however, for much confidence in any interpretation.

A wide range of meaning characterizes both אֱמֶת, "truth," and חָכְמָה, "wisdom," in the OT (for אמת see A. Jepson, *TDOT,* I, 309–16; for חכמה see J. L. Crenshaw, *IDBSup,* 952–56). Jepsen (313) finds that "reliability" is the most comprehensive expression of the idea of אמת. The concept involves relationship, pertains to speech and actions, and represents characteristics that have to be demonstrated. Our word "truth" tends to convey meaning that is too abstract and too self-evident. In Exod 18:4, Jethro urges Moses to "choose [תחזה, "look for/scrutinize"] able men for all the people, such as fear God, men who are trustworthy [אמת] and who hate a bribe" (cf. Deut 1:13). Joseph must test the words of his brothers before he can know that they are אמת (Gen 42:16). God is pleased when אמת is present because it is so often absent. "Truth" is the essential quality of reliability which is necessary for a proper relationship with God. "Yahweh is near . . . to all who call upon him in truth [אמת]" (also 1 Kgs 2:4; Hos 4:1–2; Jer 4:2; Pss 15:2; 86:11; Isa 38:3; Zech 7:9; Ezek 18:8).

A fully satisfactory definition of "wisdom" is elusive, having been summarized as "the art of succeeding in life, practical knowledge of laws governing the world, based on experience . . . ability to cope; right deed or word for the moment; an intellectual tradition" (Crenshaw, *IDBSup,* 952). In general, it is the coping ability to deal with those skills, temptations, responsibilities, and sufferings which are common to human life in ways that enhance the performance of healthy and successful living. Such performance involves the "fear of Yahweh" (e.g., Prov 1:7; 9:10; Job 28:28; Ps 111:10), which can be roughly defined as reverence toward God and thus willingness to obey the divine will. Perhaps the best passage from the wisdom literature to complement Ps 51 is Prov 28:13–14:

He who conceals his transgressions will not prosper,
but he who confesses and forsakes them will obtain mercy.
Blessed is the man who fears the LORD always;
but he who hardens his heart will fall into calamity. (RSV)

"Wisdom" in this context refers to the abiding endowment of human beings by God (Exod 36:2; Eccl 2:26; Prov 2:6; 14:33), which empowers them with the ability to cope with life in healthy and constructive ways. It has its origin before birth, according to Ps 51:8.

Prayer for forgiveness (51:9, 11). A respectable exegetical tradition contends for a continuation of positive statements in vv 9–10, reading them as expressions of confidence in what God will do (e.g., LXX, Jerome, Perowne, Kirkpatrick, Kidner). But it seems better to read the verbs with jussive or imperative force, and this is strengthened by the literary analysis which links v 9 with v 11, where the imperative is used. It is also strengthened by the emphatic position of ואטהר ("and I will be clean indeed," see Dahood). The prayer is literally to be "un-sinned with hyssop." The verb חטא appears a few times in piel (and hithpael) with the meaning "to purify from sin" or more literally "to unsin" or "to de-sin" (so Dahood, II, 5, but long before by John Donne, see Perowne, 419; also Lev 8:18; 14:49, 52; Num 19:19; Ezek 43:20, 22, 23; 45:18).

For "hyssop" (אזוב) see note 9.b. A hyssop bush was used to sprinkle blood on the doorposts at Passover (Exod 12:22), in rituals for cleansing of a leper (Lev 14:4, 6, 49, 51, 52), and in the purification of a person defiled by contact with a corpse (Num 19:6, 18). Thus the verb reflects a background of cleansing rituals, though the use here may be strongly metaphorical.

The second point of v 9 ("wash me so that I will be whiter than snow") uses the symbolism of whiteness for forgiveness (Dalglish, *Psalm Fifty-One*, 136). Snow does fall in Palestine, though not frequently. Note the contrast between the scarlet of sin and the whiteness of forgiveness in Isa 1:18. Blackness and dark sackcloth are associated with lamentation, sickness, and mourning (Isa 1:3; Ps 35:13, 14; Rev 6:12; also Exod 4:6; Num 11:10; 2 Kgs 5:27; Lam 4:17; Dan 7:9). To be whiter than snow is to be completely clean and prepared for the divine presence.

The prayer continues in v 11, where Yahweh is asked to hide his face from sin and blot out the guilt of waywardness. The hiding of the divine face (in the sense of turning it away?) is a graphic metaphor for forgiving action. In some contexts, God hides his face in displeasure and withdrawal of favor (e.g., 13:2; 27:9; 102:3; 143:7), but here the speaker prays that God will turn his face away from sin. For a treatment of God's hiding his face, see S. E. Balentine, *The Hidden God: The Hiding of the Face of God in the Old Testament* (Oxford: Oxford UP, 1983). See also Pss 22:25; 27:9; 69:17, 18a, 19a; 88:15; 102:3; 143:7. The background of the expression relating to God's hiding his face seems to be rooted in the idea of a deity turning away in rejection and separation from a suppliant. Balentine (44) points out that "hide the face" was a part of the common religious language of the ancient Near East. The prayer in v 11 is for God to separate himself in a gracious self-alienation from the suppliant's sins—a startling concept of forgiveness. The "blot out" in the parallel colon of v 11 draws attention back to the same words in v 3.

Prayer for restoration (51:10, 12–14). The first prayer of the second major part of the psalm begins with a request that the suppliant may again hear the joy and gladness of a healthy life, probably with reference to a return to festal gladness with other worshipers (cf. Pss 42:5; 68:6; 105:43; Jer 31:7; Zeph 3:17). Some commentators think in terms of an oracle of forgiveness spoken to the suppliant by a priest (see Dalglish, *Psalm Fifty-One*, 138–41; Weiser, 406; A. A. Anderson, I, 397, with attention to Pss 38:14–16; 130:5–6; 143:7, 8a; 1 Sam 9:27; Joel 2:17–19).

The "crushed bones" of v 10b may refer to an illness which has made the suppliant acutely aware of personal sinfulness, or it may refer to mental and spiritual distress caused by guilt. The word "bones" (עֶצֶם) occurs with ideas of health and well-being (e.g., Ps 34:21; Job 20:11; Prov 15:30; Isa 66:14) as well as with ideas of sickness or woe (e.g., Pss 6:3; 32:2; 38:4; Job 30:30; 38:4); the plural is used as a collective term for the limbs of the body (Judg 19:29; Pss 31:10–11; 32:3; Job 33:19). The "bones you crushed" may be only a strong statement of overpowering spiritual remorse, though this could certainly involve psychosomatic elements in most biblical contexts. In any case, the speaker is confident that God could make the crushed bones "rejoice" (גִּיל). The NEB catches the spirit of v 10b, "Let the bones dance which thou hast broken."

In v 12, the suppliant prays for a restoration of "heart" (לֵב) and "spirit" (רוּחַ). The לב (and לבב) was regarded as the volitional center of a person's being (see H. W. Wolff, *Anthropology of the Old Testament* [Philadelphia: Fortress Press, 1974], 40–58). The intellectual and rational function that we normally ascribe to the mind was located in the heart according to biblical language (Deut 29:4; Isa 6:10; Prov 15:14; Job 8:10; Ps 90:12). Wolff (47) warns against the "false impression that biblical man is determined more by feeling than by reason." The heart has the capacity for perception, reason, wisdom, and it is the source of the will. It can also represent the person as such (e.g., 22:15; Jer 23:16).

The spirit of a person has much the same meaning as heart, and indeed seems to be a synonym in v 12 (A. A. Anderson, I, 398; for רוּחַ, see F. Baumgärtel, "Spirit in the OT," *TDNT,* VI, 359–67; Wolff, 32–39). רוח refers to moving air in a meteorological sense (as in Gen 3:8; 8:1; ?Isa 7:4) and in a physical sense to breath (Gen 7:22; Job 9:18; 19:17; etc.). It is the animating factor in mankind and in animals (e.g., Gen 6:17; 17:15; Ezek 37:6; 8:10, 14). Idols lack the vital force of spirit (Hab 2:19). רוח is also the center of emotions, intellectual functions, and the will (Gen 41:8; Isa 54:6; Prov 14:24; 18:14; Deut 34:9; Dan 6:4; Ezek 28:3; etc.). Yahweh's רוח can repre-sent his creative power (Ps 33:6) and is the endowment which he gives to persons for special actions (Judg 3:10; 14:6; 1 Sam 10:6; 11:6; Isa 11:2; 42:1; Joel 2:28).

In v 12, the suppliant prays for a "clean heart" and a "steadfast spirit." The נכון (niphal participle from כון) means "to be firmly established" (used of heart in Pss 57:8; 78:37; 112:7). The idea is that of consistency and loyalty. Is "spirit" here the spirit of the worshiper or the spirit of God? The usual translation of בְּקִרְבִּי is "within me," and the expression is taken to refer to the establishment of a steadfast inner disposition for the suppliant. However, it should be noticed that בקרבי can mean "over" or "on" when used as a ballast variant for בְּ with spirit (Isa 63:11c; 19:14; cf. 29:10; Ezek 36:27; cf. 37:14), name (Exod 23:21), blood (Deut 21:8), and signs (Exod 10:1). See H. J. van Dijk, "A Neglected Connotation of Three Hebrew Verbs," *VT* 18 (1968) 16–30. The most frequent idea associated with the spirit of God is that it comes upon or is poured on a person rather than being put into the inner being. "The communication of the Lord's Spirit is not a kind of surgical operation, but a rather dynamic event: the prophet and the other men of God are overwhelmed by its onrush" (van Dijk, 19). Thus it is quite probable that the spirit in v 12 is God's steadfast and firmly reliable spirit, which is given to those who serve him.

The verb "create" in v 12a is the well-known בָּרָא, which always has God as the subject (in qal and niphal forms) and has accusatives which represent the products of the divine actions (see K. H. Bernhardt, G. P. Botterweck, H. Ringgren, *TDOT*, II, 242–49). In OT usage, the verb refers to divine action which "brings forth something new and astonishing" (W. Eichrodt, *Theology of the Old Testament*, II, 104; note Exod 34:10; Isa 48:6–8; Jer 31:22). There is, however, no need to conclude that בָּרָא denotes *creatio ex nihilo* (creation out of nothing in a strict sense). The divine activity results in a new order of existence, a new arrangement, or a new emergence of something shaped by the divine power and will. While the prayer in v 12 is not for *creatio ex nihilo*, it is a bold one for a transformation which could be accomplished only by divine power and a work on the order of the first creation of the world (Gunkel, 224; Kraus, 546; cf. 2 Cor 5:17). "None but God can create either a new heart or a new earth" (Spurgeon, 405).

The verb in v 12b is הַדֵּשׁ, which should be translated in the sense of its regular meaning (in piel and hithpael) as "to renew" (Kidner, 192; e.g., Ps 104:30; Isa 61:4; Lam 5:21; Job 10:17 may be an exception). The renewal of spiritual endowment is made possible by the creation of a clean heart.

V 13 continues the plea for restoration with the urgent request that God not banish the suppliant from the divine presence. Those denied the presence of God (lit. "from before your face") lose a source of joy, and indeed of life itself (Ps 42:1–4; 2 Kgs 13:23; Jer 23:39). The suppliant does not want to be like Cain (Gen 4:14, 16), or David (1 Sam 26:20), or Saul (1 Sam 16:14), and be driven from a vital experience of worship.

"Your holy spirit" (רוח קדשׁך) is an unusual expression that is found elsewhere in the MT only in Isa 63:10, 11 (cf. Wis 9:17); though "your good spirit" is in Neh 9:20 (cf. "an evil spirit," 1 Sam 16:14; "spirit of wisdom," 1 Sam 11:2). Various connotations emerge when "spirit" is associated with God. The spirit is sometimes God's creative power (see 33:6; also Job 33:4; Jdt 16:14; Wis 1:7). The life-giving power of the divine spirit is a form of creation (Ps 104:27–30; Job 34:14–15; Ezek 37:9–14). A few texts link רוח so clearly with God that the operation of the spirit is equivalent to the action of God, and the spirit seems identical with the personality of God in some cases. The transcendent realm of God is spirit and not flesh.

> The Egyptians are men, and not God,
>   and their horses are flesh, and not spirit (Isa 31:3, RSV)

See also Isa 34:16 and the operation of the spirit with the mind of Yahweh in Isa 40:13 (cf. John 4:24).

Isa 63:11–14 is of particular interest in the case of "holy spirit." The holy spirit of Yahweh is parallel with his "glorious arm," which was with Moses through the exodus experiences (cf. Isa 40:10; 51:9). The spirit of Yahweh gave them "rest," meaning "rest" in the promised land from attacks by their enemies (Josh 21:44; 23:1; Deut 12:10). Note that "his holy spirit" is parallel with the "angel of his presence" in Isa 63:9 (though the text is sometimes emended to read "it was no messenger or angel, but his presence which saved them"—a reading which would enhance the linkage between spirit and the presence of Yahweh). Israel's rebellion against Yahweh has "grieved his holy spirit." "The spirit is depicted as personal—no mere power or influence, but the object of a possible personal relationship" (G. W. H. Lampe, "Holy Spirit," *IDB*, II, 629). Thus the appeal in Ps 51:11 seems to be for a continuing experience of the creative, life-giving, and empowering presence of

God himself. One cannot experience the presence of God when his holy spirit is taken away.

What is the significance of the qualifying idea of "holy" (קדשׁ)? The biblical ideas of holiness are elusive and involve a wide semantic range (see K. G. Kuhn and O. Procksch, *TDNT*, I, 88–115; J. Muilenburg, "Holiness," *IDB*, II, 616–25). Muilenburg defines it as "the 'given' undergirding and pervading all religion; the distinctive mark and signature of the divine" (616). The root idea seems to be that of separation; in a theological sense, it is that which is separated or set apart or belonging to deity or associated with the divine. Holiness is especially evident whenever the divine presence is perceived (e.g., Exod 3:2–3; 19:18; Isa 6). "Wherever God's presence is felt these men [*sic*] encounter the wonder and mystery of holiness" (Muilenburg, 617). The range of meaning in the OT is so extensive that Muilenburg uses twelve "associations" of terms with holiness in his attempt to comprehend it, and says that the list could be extended: fire (very pervasive, also in the NT, e.g., Matt 3:11, Acts 2:1–4), jealousy, wrath, fear, remoteness ("the radical cleavage between the human and the divine"), cleanness, majesty, uniqueness, wonderful, great, exalted, and living God. Awe and dread are characteristic of the awareness of the holy, the *mysterium tremendum,* the perception of "an undefined and uncanny energy . . . of the imponderable and incomprehensible, an inarticulate feeling of an inviolable potency outside and beyond" (Muilenburg, 616).

The human correlate of the holiness of God is the fear of God. However, the fear of God is not a terror which drains away the vitality of the divine-human relationship. The fear of God and the awareness of the holy presence has "a mysterious power of attraction which is converted into wonder, obedience, self-surrender, and enthusiasm" (Eichrodt, *Theology of the Old Testament,* II, 270). Thus God's holy Spirit is his awe-inspiring, empowering, and joy-provoking presence. Perhaps no other word in the entire biblical vocabulary is so characteristic of the divine as "holy."

The reference to the "holy spirit" of God inevitably raises questions about the relationship to the "Holy Spirit" of Christian theology. Any interpretation of the "holy spirit" in Ps 51 and Isa 63 in terms of the developed understandings of the Holy Spirit in the NT and in Christian thought would be anachronistic. On the other hand, the Holy Spirit is the Spirit of God, as in the OT. The infrequent use of "holy spirit" in MT should not be allowed to obscure the fact that its substance is rather common in OT passages that deal with רוח. In a profound sense, there is but "One Spirit."

The suppliant's prayer for restoration continues in v 14 with an appeal for the return of "the joy of your salvation." The joyful awareness of God's saving presence had been lost and was lacking from the relationship disrupted by sin. (For "joy," שָׂשׂוֹן, see v 10; with the idea of "salvation," see, e.g., Pss 9:14; 13:5; 21:2; 35:9; 40:16; though none of these use שָׂשׂוֹן or יֶשַׁע; יְשׁוּעָה and תְּשׁוּעָה are used, though note the verb שׂושׂ in Pss 35:9; 40:17. יֶשַׁע, יְשׁוּעָה, and תְּשׁוּעָה all seem to have the same meaning.) The meaning of the words for "salvation" is derived from the verb יֶשַׁע, "to give width/freedom to," thus "to help," "to deliver," and so "help" or "deliverance." As is the case with other comprehensive biblical terms, the range of meaning is quite wide. The nouns, especially, "comprehend a totality which includes not only deliverance or help but also the ensuing state of salvation, though it is impossible to differentiate the ante and post, the cause and effect, since that act and the intended cause cannot be separated" (G. Fohrer, *TDNT,* VII, 974). The verb is used frequently in the psalter for the invoking and receiving of the help of Yahweh, especially with regard to enemies who are attacking a suppliant (e.g., 3:2; 7:2; 12:2; 18:3, 28; 28:9; 55:17; 86:2; for the nouns see, e.g., 14:7; 53:7; 18:47, 51; 24:5; 27:1; 71:15; 79:9). The physical and the spiritual merge in the concept of "salvation." A few references refer to the comprehensive help and deliverance which God gives (e.g., Deut 32:15; Isa 17:10; Ezek 34:22; Pss 78:22; 132:16). In Ps 51, deliverance from illness may be involved, but surely the major point of the request in v 12 is an appeal for a joyful freedom from the consequences of guilt, even though the use of ישׁע in verb or noun forms with the forgiveness of sin is rare in the OT. Ezek 36:29 is especially significant: "I will save you from all your uncleanness [טמאותיכם]," followed in the parallel line with a promise of abundant grain and the absence of famine.

The second part of the plea in v 14 is for a "willing spirit" to sustain the suppliant in the new condition for which he or she prays. The word נְדִיבָה is a feminine ad-jectival form derived from נדב, which carries the idea of "willing/voluntary," and "generous," though its most basic idea is "to urge" or "to impel." In some contexts, the meaning is "noble one" or "prince" (e.g., Num 21:18; 1 Sam 2:8; Pss 47:9; 83:11). The thrust of meaning in v 12 may be similar to that in Exod 35:5, 22: "Take from among you an offering to the LORD; whoever is of a generous [נְדִיב] heart, let him bring the LORD's offering. . . . So they came, both men and women; all who were of a willing [נְדִיב] heart . . ." (RSV). The ideas of an enthusiast and volunteer are suggested by the word (Kidner, 192). However, the idea of "noble" or "princely" can be defended (supported by LXX's ἡγεμονικός, the "guiding" of a prince or governor). So S. Terrien (*Elusive Presence,* 325): "A knight is not a knave. He helps and respects others with the ease, elegance, and style of a prince. The new being is a moral aristocrat, not of birth but of service. Freedom to be oneself implies the power to serve willingly." Perhaps the two ideas complement one another (cf. 1 Sam 32:8) though it is doubtful that a somewhat romantic idealization of knighthood would have been intended by the psalmist.

The question of the nature of the spirit in v 14 arises. Is this the holy spirit of God (v 11)? Or a new spirit in man? Dahood (II, 7) argues that the suffix on "salvation" in 14a does double duty and translates 14b as "by your generous spirit sustain me." Certainly, the suffix could have double duty, and the verb "sustain" (סמך) tends to support the understanding of the spirit as that of God because of its usage for the divine work of support and help (e.g., Pss 37:17, 24; 54:6; 71:6; 119:116; 145:14). The LXX reading of "your guiding spirit" also supports this interpretation. Neve argues that the presence of the holy spirit in 13b should be understood in terms of moral guidance rather than of communion with God (*ExpTim* 80 [1969] 265). He thinks that the pattern of thought in vv 9–13 is found in Ezek 36:25–27; 39:29. Cleansing from sin is anticipated in Ezek 36:25, while v 26 (note the similarity with 51:10) has the promise of a new heart and a new spirit, and v 27 tells of the guidance in obedience to be provided by the internalized spirit; in Ezek 39:29, Yahweh will not hide his face anymore (cf. Ps 51:11) after he pours out his spirit on Israel. If this is correct, it would strengthen the interpretation of רוח in v 14b as the guiding spirit of God (note also the guiding function of the "good spirit" of God in Ps 143:10). Thus it is probable that רוח in vv 12, 13, and 14 refers to the spirit of God in each case.

Vow to teach sinners (51:15). The purpose for restoring forgiveness and charismatic endowment is followed by a commitment to teaching and praise. The suppliant promises to teach rebellious sinners the "ways" of God. The etymology of דֶּרֶךְ ("way") is not certain (see Ps 1:1; G. Sauer, *THAT*, I, 457–59; J. Bergman et al., *TDOT*, III, 270–93), but it is the most common word in the OT for the ideas of "road/way/street" or "path" (though several other words are also used). In a physical sense, דֶּרֶךְ can mean "road" (e.g., Gen 38:14; Deut 2:27; Josh 2:7; Ezek 21:21). In a metaphorical sense it can mean the course of life and the conduct characteristic of it. When used of God, it can mean either the divine course of action (e.g., noun in Deut 8:2; Isa 55:8–9; Nah 1:3; Pss 103:7; 145:17; verb in Amos 4:13; Mic 1:3; Hab 3:15) or the behavior which God requires of human beings in terms of his will and commandments (e.g., Exod 32:8; Gen 18:19; Deut 5:33; 11:28; Isa 48:17; Pss 25:4; 32:8) or ways approved by God (Isa 53:6; Jer 10:2). "Your ways" in v 15 may certainly include the ways God intends for the guidance of his people as expressed in commandments and teachings. In the context, however, the ways of God in dealing with sinners must be included. Instruction in God's gracious, forgiving restoration of sinners would be an integral part of the teaching.

Prayer for the ability to praise God (51:16–19). These verses resume the prayer in vv 10, 12–14. V 16 begins with the controversial expression, "Deliver me from blood-guilt/bloodshed" (see note 16.a. above). On the surface, at least, neither blood-guilt nor bloodshed seems to fit the context in Ps 51. References to enemies or violence are missing from the psalm. The use of "bloods" could, of course, be the result of the composition of the psalm with David in mind (see above; and note the concern of David for the removal of blood-guilt in 2 Sam 3:28–29; 1 Kgs 2:31–33; also 2 Sam 16:7, 8). A better approach may be along the line of "bloods" as a figurative expression which does not require reference to actual bloodshed or even to "bloodthirstiness" (see the study by N. A. Van Uchelen, "אַנְשֵׁי דָמִים in the Psalms," *Oudtestamentische Studiën* 15 [1969], 205–12). See Prov 12:6; 29:10; Pss 5:7; 26:9–10; 55:22, 24; Lev 19:19 (cf. Ezek 22:6–12; also Acts 20:26–27).

Perhaps the best interpretation in 51:16 is that of "deadly guilt"—guilt for which one could be held responsible unto death (as in Ezek 3:17–19; 33:7–9; the prophet is made answerable for the "blood"—life/death—of his people; cf. Pss 9:13; 30:10). This meaning fits well with the emphasis on the inadequacy of sacrifice in v 18. The murderer cannot be ransomed except by his or her own blood, according to Num 35:30–34 (because bloodshed pollutes the land). Also, see the discussion below of sin with a "high hand" in Num 15:30. Thus the guilt confessed in Ps 51 reaches its climax in the deadly guilt of v 16. No actual bloodshed may be involved at all, but the guilt is too great for normal means of atonement. God must deliver and loose the tongue, lips, and mouth to sing out praise of the divine power and grace.

The verb רָנַן in v 16c indicates a joyful expression, an exuberant cry (Dahood, "loudly cry"; NAB, "my tongue shall revel"; cf. Pss 5:12; 67:5; 90:14; etc.). The "righteousness" (צְדָקָה; also צֶדֶק) of God is a word with polyvalent meaning. A forensic element is present in a number of places, where Yahweh functions as a judge to set matters right and to uphold the justice of his ways (Pss 9:5, 9; 50:6; 96:13; 99:4; Isa 58:2; Jer 11:20). This meaning cannot be ruled out of v 16c entirely (note v 4bc). However, the context of praise and testimony suggests that it should be understood here in a salvific sense (Pss 22:32; 31:8; 69:28; 103:17; 143:1, 11, etc.; Dalglish, *Psalm Fifty-One*, 181). The sense is that of Ps 40:10–11.

I have told the glad news of deliverance [צֶדֶק]
>   in the great congregation. . . .
> I have not hid thy saving help [צִדְקָתְךָ] within my heart
> I have spoken. . . . (RSV)

Righteousness with this emphasis is understood as God's willing intervention to deliver and/or to give victory on behalf of his people. These are his "saving" deeds and judgments, his "power which brings salvation to you" (see G. Klein, *IDBSup*, 750; E. R. Achtemeier, *IDB*, IV, 87).

The prayer continues in v 17 with an appeal to God to open the speaker's lips and to allow his or her mouth to declare the praise of God. Two ideas are conveyed. First, the suppliant prays to be released from the restrictive results of guilt, the condition of "one whose conscience has shamed him into silence" (Kidner, 193) and who has been cut off from freedom to worship (cf. Ezek 16:13). God's forgiveness would break the seal of guilt and give new joy (cf. 30:11–13; Ezek 3:26–27; 33:22). Second, the prayer is for an empowerment of speaking ability in order to teach and give testimony, which cannot be done adequately without divine help (cf. Jer 1:4–10). A somewhat parallel idea is that of God putting a new song in the mouth of one who has been delivered (40:4; also, Balaam's ass in Num 22:28; cf. Dan 10:16; Jer 1:9).

Vv 18 and 19 continue the prayer by giving a reason for it. These verses also correspond to the opening plea for mercy and forgiveness in vv 3–4. The merciful action of God will not be received on the basis of sacrifice alone. The sacrifice sure to be accepted is that of a broken and contrite heart. Indeed, according to v 18, God is not receptive to sacrifices in the usual sense. The verbs חפץ and רצה both mean "to take pleasure in" or "to accept" (חפץ has already appeared in v 8 and will again in v 21; חפץ is related to sacrifices in Ps 40:7, Isa 1:11; רצה in Ps 119:108; Jer 14:12; Lev 1:3; etc.). Two common words for animal sacrifices are used (זֶבַח andעוֹלָה). The first generally refers to a sacrifice in which the flesh of the animal is eaten by the worshipers, and the second to a sacrifice entirely consumed on the altar (see J. Milgrom, *IDBSup*, 763–71). The suppliant declares a willingness to give sacrifices if God would be willing to accept; however, God is not willing.

The nature of the statement in v 18 has given rise to considerable discussion. Is this statement designed as an absolute rejection of animal sacrifices? Is the intent to say that God will not accept a sacrifice at all? Some interpreters have linked this statement with a number of passages that express a secondary or negative evaluation of sacrifices (Pss 40:7; 50:13–14; 69:31–32; Prov 27:3; Isa 1:11–17; Jer 7:21–23; Hos 6:6; Amos 5:21–24, 25; Mic 6:6–8). These statements can be read as emerging from groups, especially prophets, which categorically rejected sacrifice as an essential part of worship. If this is the case, the speaker in Ps 51 seems to be repudiating the concept of animal sacrifice.

However, other writers are concerned with the difficulties of such a sweeping view and assume that a total rejection of sacrificial rites is not intended (see Dalglish, *Psalm Fifty-One*, 192–94; H. H. Rowley, "The Meaning of Sacrifice in the Old Testament," in *From Moses to Qumran: Studies in the Old Testament* [New York: Association Press, 1963], 67–107). Variant interpretations are possible along this line. We may adopt the view that the confession in the psalm involves sin of such a nature as to exclude the effective use of sacrifice. Appeal can be made to the sin with a "high hand" for which no ritual atonement is provided (Num 15:30). The high-handed sins may be those committed because they express the sinner's real nature, "arising out of the essential purpose of his heart" (Rowley, 94), not sins primarily of a ritual nature. Sins such as adultery or murder are not provided for in sacrificial instructions, and the execution of the adulterer or the murderer is required. If Ps 51 was composed with David in mind (which is certainly possible), the writer may have had the nonsacrificial situation of David in view (note that in 2 Sam 12:13 forgiveness is given to David without mention of sacrifice, on the basis of his confession). If this is the case, v 18 is postulated on the assumption that the sin confessed is beyond ritual atonement.

Another approach is simply to assume that the absolute statement in v 18 actually has a relative meaning. "Though the expression of condemnation is unconditional it should be taken in a relative sense" (Vaux, R. de, *Ancient Israel : Its Life and Institutions,* tr. J. McHugh [New York: McGraw-Hill, 1961] 454). The contexts of the prophetic critiques make it difficult to assume absolute opposition to sacrificial ritual (Rowley, "The Meaning of Sacrifice," 83–100). In some cases, at least, the force of the sayings is comparative, rather than absolute; as in Hos 6:6, "For I desire steadfast love and not sacrifice, and knowledge of God more than burnt offerings" (reading the מִן in v 6b as comparative rather than privative, and assuming that v 6a has the same force) and in 1 Sam 15:22: "Behold, to obey is better than sacrifice, and to hearken is better than the fat of rams" (again reading מִן as comparative). It should be recognized that both Hos 6:6 and 1 Sam 15:22— as well as Prov 21:3—are forms of the so-called better-proverbs, which may appear without the טוב element (see G. S. Ogden, "The 'Better'-Proverbs (TOB-Spruch), Rhetorical Criticism, and Qoheleth," *JBL* 96 [1977] 493). Taken in this way, v 18 is a powerful statement of the subordination of sacrifice to confession and those personal qualities that are acceptable to God and necessary for forgiveness. The verse leaves no room for any automatic effectiveness for forgiveness by ritual means. Further, sacrifices were intended to correlate with the appropriate spiritual condition of the worshiper and in turn to strengthen right attitudes and patterns of behavior (Rowley, "The Meaning of Sacrifice," 86). Rowley (*Worship in Ancient Israel: Its Forms and Meaning* [Philadelphia: Fortress Press, 1967] 136–38) suggests that the recitation of psalms like 51 helped to make worshipers aware of the significance of confession and the spiritual condition necessary for forgiveness.

The suppliant is sure that the sacrifices of a "broken spirit" and a "contrite heart" would be acceptable to God (v 19). The reading, "My sacrifice, O God, is a broken spirit" has its attractive aspects and conveys the idea that the worshiper turns away from burnt offerings and the like to present a personal spiritual condition as a sacrifice to God. But it is better to let the verse stand as a generalizing statement regarding the absolutely acceptable sacrifice. The worshiper who offers this sacrifice, accompanied by burnt offerings or not, can be sure of divine acceptance (Ps 34:19; Isa 57:15; 61:1). The "broken spirit" (cf. Pss 34:19; 147:3; Prov 15:4, 13; Jer 23:9) and "contrite heart" (lit. "crushed," דכה—used for bones in v 10; cf. Pss 38:9; 90:3; Isa 3:15; 53:5) describe the condition of profound contrition and awe experienced by a sinful person who becomes aware of the divine presence (cf. Isa 6; Job 42:1–6). "The sacrifice that God demands is a sacrifice of man's self-will and self-importance; in other words, it is the surrender of man's own self to God" (Weiser, 410; Rom 12:1).

Addendum (51:20–21). The last two verses of the psalm were added by a later reviser who wanted to interpret the psalm in terms of Israel's corporate experience and also to correct any absolutely anticultic interpretation of vv 18–19. The form is that of a prayer for the restoration of Jerusalem so that sacrifices could be made on the altar in the temple. God is asked to "do good to Zion" in his "good pleasure" (רָצוֹן, which means "will" when used of God, Pss 40:9; 103:21; 143:10; Ezek 10:11, and of men, Dan 8:4; 11:3, 16, 36; Neh 9:24; Esth 1:8; 9:5). However, it can also be used of God with the nuance of "favor" or "grace" (Pss 5:12; 30:6, 8; 89:18; 106:4; Prov 8:35; 12:2; 18:22), and in this verse it should be understood as something like "in your gracious will."

God is asked to "do good" (הֵיטִיבָה, hiphil imperative cohortative from יטב) to Zion (cf. Ps 125:4; Jer 18:10, 11; 32:40, 41; Job 24:21; Josh 24:20). In some passages the imperative form of the verb has the connotation of "change" or "make better" (see Jer 7:3; 18:11; 26:13; 35:15, all references to changes of behavior). Possibly, the use of the verb in v 20 carries the nuance of a change in God's action toward Zion, i.e., a change from judgment to restoration, and this is supported by v 20b: "rebuild the walls of Jerusalem." The verb בָּנָה means either "build" or "rebuild" according to the context. In this case, it probably means "rebuild" and expresses the exilic Israelite hope for the restoration of Jerusalem (cf. Isa 26:1; 33:20; 62:6–7; Jer 31:38; Pss 102:13, 16; 147:2).

The adverb "then" (אָז) is repeated twice in v 21, in emphatic positions, and has a temporal quality. The redactor probably interpreted the psalm as applying to Israel during the time of the exile. The unsuitable nature of sacrificial ritual in v 18 is taken as relative and as referring to the period shortly before and during the exile. Whenever God restores Jerusalem and renews its worship, sacrifices on the altar there will be acceptable to him again. "Righteous sacrifices" (זבחי־צדק; cf. 4:6; Deut 33:19) may mean legitimate and proper sacrifices, i.e., according to appropriate ritual prescriptions (see Dahood, II, 10; D. W. Thomas, *TRP*, 19, "sacrifices in their appointed seasons"), or sacrifices that are appropriate because they are offered in the right spirit and right relationship with God (cf. Kraus, I, 170–71). Perhaps the best interpretation is that of sacrifices that will be "rightfully due" because they will be an appropriate response to what God will do (B. A. Levine, *In the Presence of the Lord: A Study of Cult and Some Cultic Terms in Ancient Israel* [Leiden: Brill, 1974], 135–37).

"Whole-burnt-offering" (כָּלִיל) is apparently a synonym of עוֹלָה ("burnt-offering"; 1 Sam 7:9; cf. Lev 6:22; Deut 33:10). The root idea is that of wholeness and completeness (Dalglish, *Psalm Fifty-One*, 191; Milgrom, 769) and thus a sacrifice not eaten at all by the worshiper. פָּרִים, "young bulls," is used frequently in the OT in sacrificial contexts. These animals were prime sacrificial victims (note the priority given to them in such references as Num 28:11, 12; 29:2, 3–5, 12–16).

While this interpretation of the addendum seems to be essentially correct, A. R. Johnson (*CPIP*, 430–31) provides an appropriate caveat against reading vv 20–21 as a rather crude addition to tone down the language of the primary psalm and to involve no more than a return to traditional sacrifices offered along ritually correct lines:

When the redactor refers to "sacrifices of the right kind" (lit. "sacrifices of righteousness"), it is far more likely that he or she has in mind sacrifices which will be offered, not merely along lines which are right according to cultic law even though the Hebrew certainly permits such a conclusion, but primarily in what Yahweh will find to be the right spirit and thus truly symbolic of the worshiper's complete dedication; and thus he is promising that, if only Yahweh will consent to the rebuilding of Jerusalem, He can be sure that sacrifices will be offered with penitent and obedient hearts and so may approve of their being renewed.

These are words of wisdom.

Explanation

The first part of this psalm focuses on *confession of sin.* Genuine confession has two fundamental aspects. First, it must be directed to God, accepting the rightness of his judgment and his power to cleanse and forgive. Such confession presupposes full dependence on God and a gracious nature on his part. It also presupposes the divine power to cleanse from guilt. Human guilt may become so pervasive as to block the sinner away from forgiveness unless there is the will to turn to the Divine Presence and seek cleansing. Guilt may be so strong that cleansing seems impossible from any source. The courage to lay claim to the grace of God is imperative. "Have mercy on me, O God, according to your loyal-love."

Second, confession places on the sinner the necessity, often painful, of honest confrontation with his or her own sin (vv 5–8). More than a passing mood of reflection is involved. "I know my transgressions and my sin is before me always." "This is not the fleeting mood of a depressed conscience, but the clear knowledge of a person who, shocked by that knowledge, has become conscious of his or her responsibility . . . and sees things as they really are" (Weiser, 403). Confession which has this quality constitutes the inner essence of sacrifice acceptable to God (vv 18–19).

True confession encloses the multiple dimensions of guilt. Guilt is personal: "I know my transgression." Guilt is social and extends back along the entire trail of life: "I was born in iniquity, and my mother conceived me in sin." The threads of human existence are woven through intricate and interlocking patterns from conception till death. The sensitive conscience accepts the absence of purity, but does not despair because of it. Guilt arises from sin against God, even when the transgression may have seemingly involved only other human beings or the world in which we live. It can be a shocking revelation to discover that what we considered to be sins against others are really sins against God: "Against you, you only, I have sinned." But this revelation is the key that unlocks the real secret of wisdom, for the essence of wisdom is the "fear of the Lord."

The second part of the psalm focuses on *restoration.* The sinner cannot be self-restored. A divine work of re-creation and endowment is essential. Forgiveness involves a creative work: "Create in me a pure heart." This is not a creative work in the sense of creation-out-of-nothing, but a creative work in the sense of bringing order and peace where chaos and hopeless turbulence were before. As in Gen 1, light is created to overcome darkness; days emerge from what had been endless night; life emerges where there had been only surging matter; purpose and blessing are given to human beings, themselves created into an order of life that had not existed before; the ceaseless roaring of the primeval sea gives way to the ordered world, and God and man pause for a sabbath to celebrate its completion. The creative work of God is the prelude to his blessing. "Therefore, if anyone is in Christ, he is a new creation; the old has gone, the new has come" (2 Cor 5:17, NIV; cf. Gal 6:15; John 3:3, 6; 1 Pet 1:23).

The spirit of God empowers the creative work of forgiveness (cf. Gen 1:2; Ps 104:30). A threefold presence of the spirit is prayed for in Ps 51. I have argued for the interpretation that the spirit in all three references (vv 12, 13, and 14) refers primarily to the spirit of God. However, no sharp division should be drawn between the qualities ascribed *to* the spirit and the qualities effected *by* the spirit in human beings. The "steadfast spirit" of God produces a "firmly rooted, enduring power in man" (S. Terrien, *The Psalms*, 176). The "holy spirit" is the animating Presence which activates the will of the human being with whom it abides to seek the divine will. The "willing spirit" is that aspect of the divine Presence which endows with the freedom to serve willingly and is a mark of deliverance from the bondage of guilt. The spirit of God "imparts in the creature some holiness of the divine; the energy of God himself transforms the unstable, fluctuating, self-centered human animal into a steadfast and willing servant" (Terrien, 176; also *Elusive Presence*, 324–25).

Restoration naturally leads to ministry. The worshiper makes a commitment to teach transgressors and sinners the "ways" of God (v 15). The psalm expresses the powerful urge to minister which is stirred into life by confession and divine forgiveness. Testimony and praise flow from the new creation and the presence of the spirit. Confession and forgiveness are always necessary as a prelude to mission. However, confession without mission is abortive and ends in an apathetic spiritual state.

The confidence of the worshiper is placed in that which God will certainly accept, "a broken and contrite heart" (vv 18–19). We should avoid the conclusion that these verses point to a repudiation of cultic worship and that they encourage a kind of spirituality wholly detached from sacrifices. Rather the point is that burnt offerings or other sacrifices which God will accept must express the sacrificial reality of the "crushed" heart of the worshiper. It is possible that one use of this psalm was for recitation at the time of sacrificial offerings. The psalm expresses the real meaning of sacrifice: confession, forgiveness, ministry, total dependence on a merciful God, and a joyful new life that emerges from that process. The depressing awareness of personal sinfulness can result in a debilitating frustration and despair. The sinner needs to know that there is a grace and power which frees "from the fear of failure, from a perverse sense of inferiority or superiority, and above all, from the insidious suspicion that life is a boredom or a fruitless, insane, and sometimes sadistic adventure" (Terrien, *The Psalms*, 180). Shakespeare's Macbeth desired "some sweet oblivious antidote" which would "cleanse the stuff'd bosom of that perilous stuff which weighs upon the heart." The antidote is the broken spirit and the contrite heart offered to God.

The last two verses of the psalm are probably an addition added to give a new interpretation (see *Comment*). However, they should not be dismissed as theologically worthless on this basis. They express a very important corrective of any tendency to interpret the original psalm in hyper-personal and individual-istic ways. The personal experience of the original psalm must not be under-stood as negating the significance of corporate worship. The context for the most personal and private religious experience is usually *in* the context of the worshiping community. In turn, the worshiping community must be nurtured by personal spiritual life like that expressed in the original psalm. Neither can thrive without the other.

The Divine Judgment of a Mean and Powerful Person   (52:1–11)

Bibliography

Jeremias, J. *Kultprophetie.* 120. **Scharf, A.** "Quaedam Commentationes in Ps. 52, 7." *VD* 38 (1960) 213–22. **Schedl, C.** "*hesed 'ed* in Psalm 52 (51)." *BZ,* n.f. (1961) 259–60.

Translation

1–2   For the leader;[a] a Davidic[b] *maskil;*[c] when Doeg the Edomite came and told Saul, "David came to Ahimelech's house."[d]

3 (1)   *Why brag about evil, you hero!*[a]   (3+3)
    —God's loyal-love does not cease[b]—

4 (2)   *(Why) does your tongue plot destruction,*[a]   (3+2+2)
    like a sharpened razor, you con-man![b]

5 (3)   *You love evil more than good,*   (3+3)
    a lie, more than speaking the truth. SELAH.[a]

6 (4)   *You love every cruel word,*[a]   (3+2[3])
    (and) a deceitful tongue,

7 (5)   *Therefore*[a] *God will ruin you completely.*[b]   (3+3+3)
    He will snatch you up[c] *and tear you away from your tent,*
    he will root you out from the land of the living. SELAH.

8 (6)   *And the righteous will see it with awe,*[a]   (3+2)
    but then they will laugh at him (saying):

9 (7)   *"Look at the man who did not make God his stronghold!*   (4+3+2)
    He trusted in his great wealth,
    he tried to be strong[a] *by being destructive."*[b]

10 (8)   *But I am like an olive tree which thrives in God's house;*   (4+3+2)
    I trust in God's loyal-love,
    (which lasts) forever and ever.[a]

11 (9)   *I will forever declare praise for what you have done!*   (3+3+2)
    I will proclaim[a] *your name that is so good*
    in the presence of those loyal to you.[b]

Notes

1–2.a, b. see n. 51:1–2.a, b.

1–2.c. The term מַשְׂכִּיל is found in the superscriptions of Pss 32, 42, 44, 45, 52–55, 74, 78, 88, 89, 142, and in 47:8. The meaning is uncertain (see Craigie, n. 32:1.a.). The meanings usually suggested are (1) a skilled composition, or an "efficacious song" (one which is effective); (2) a psalm of understanding (wisdom); (3) a didactic psalm; (4) a meditation. Perhaps the best clue to the meaning of the term is found in 2 Chr 30:22, where a group of Levites spoken to by Hezekiah are designated as הַמַּשְׂכִּלִים שֵׂכֶל־טוֹב לַיהוה, "those having understanding of a good understanding as to Yahweh." The context indicates that they are concerned with singing and praise in worship. This seems to strengthen the conclusion that *maskil* has reference to a collection of psalms (or a subsection) composed for use in worship by a group of *maskilim*, priests skilled in music and festival worship, especially in confession before Yahweh (note the מְתוֹדִים of 2 Chr 30:22; cf. Lev 5:5; 16:21; 26:40; Dan 9:4, 20; etc.). It is even possible that the collection was made during the time of Hezekiah.

1–2.d. The historical note refers to the chief of Saul's herdsmen (1 Sam 21:7), who informed Saul that David had gone to Nob and received food, spiritual encouragement, and Goliath's sword from Ahimelech, the priest (1 Sam 21:1–9; 22:9–10). The result was the massacre of the priests at Nob by Doeg, after the warriors of Saul refused to obey his order. The scribal interpreters who supplied the historical note probably thought of David as the speaker, directing his remarks to Doeg, possibly to Saul, though the psalm does not fit either very well.

3.a. הַגִּבּוֹר, "the mighty man"/"hero," is sometimes changed to הַגֶּבֶר, "the man," as in v 9 (e.g., Gunkel, Kraus), but this is probably incorrect; the sense here is ironic or sarcastic, as also is גֶּבֶר in v 9 (see Dahood).

3.b. Lit., "the loyal-love of God all the day" (חֶסֶד אֵל כָּל־הַיּוֹם). RSV reflects a frequently accepted change of the text, supported by the Syriac text, of assuming a transposition to חֶסֶד אֵל from אֶל חֶסֶד and assuming that חֶסֶד should be understood as חָסִיד ("godly/loyal one"), resulting in the translation: "Why do you boast of wickedness . . . of mischief done against the godly? All the day you are plotting . . ." NEB has ". . . all against God's loyal servant (עַל חֶסֶד אֵל)," linking "all the day" with "plotting destruction" in v 4 (also JB and NAB). Dahood translates "O devoted of El," vocalizing as חֲסַד אֵל and understanding the expression as sarcastic. C. Schedl (*BZ*, n.f. [1961] 259–60) takes the חֶסֶד as a verbal form (probably piel infinitive absolute used in place of a finite verb) meaning "to scorn/revile": "reviling God all day long." Cf. NIV, "you who are a disgrace in the eyes of God." The LXX has ἀνομίαν for חֶסֶד אֵל ("lawlessness/mischief"), probably equal to חָמָס, "violence/wrongdoing." The option chosen above simply stays with MT and takes the words as a statement of God's loyal-love set over against the boasting of destructive action by the person addressed.

4.a. It is possible that here הַוּוֹת means "threats" or "intimidation." See A. A. Anderson, I, 404.

4.b. Lit., "one who does deceit/treachery." Elsewhere in Ps 101:7.

5.a. *Selah* (סֶלָה) is a scribal notation appearing in many psalms (71 times, plus 3 times in Habakkuk). The exact meaning is unsure, but it almost certainly indicated a pause in the reading of the text, despite ancient Jewish traditions that it meant "forever" or "everlasting." The question of what the pause was for is much more difficult and has generated a plethora of answers (for convenient summaries and references, see Craigie, 76–77; A. A. Anderson, I, 48–49; M. D. Goulder, *The Psalms of the Sons of Korah*, JSOT SS 20 [Sheffield: JSOT Press, 1982], 102–4). The suggestions include bowing in prayer or prostration, probably with the recitation of liturgical sayings such as "forever," "Yahweh is good," or "for his loyal-love endures forever," or a shout of "Hallelujah," or some other appropriate expression. A refrain may have been sung or chanted, or the previous verse repeated, perhaps with a choir or the congregation joining the cantor. Goulder has argued for the meaning of a "cantillation" or "recitative," in which the relevant section of a major tradition in Israel's history would be recalled in prayer or in story (e.g., the cantillation of Josh 24 would be appropriate after Ps 44:8). We should remain open to the likelihood that the selah-pause was flexible, used in different ways in different psalms and on different occasions. In some psalms, the *selah* seems to mark off sections of the psalms into acceptable outlines; in others this does not seem to work well. The function of the *selah* as a poetic intensifier, at least in some cases, should be allowed. For the role of intensification in Hebrew poetry, see R. Alter, *The Art of Biblical Poetry* (New York: Basic Books, 1985), 62–84. Fairly frequently, the *selah*-pause seems to come just before a climactic statement or between such statements.

6.a. Lit., "words of swallowing" (דִּבְרֵי בָלַע). The suggestion to read בְּלִיַּעַל, "belial" or "things of Belial" (cf. 41:8; 101:3) is not very convincing (for בליעל, see Allen, n. 101:3.a.). Dahood proposes to read everything after the verb as a construct chain (pointing בַּלַּע as בֶּלַע, [masculine noun, "swallowing"]) and translates: "You love all the words of your destructive deceitful tongue!" He argues that "tongue" forms an inclusion with "your tongue" in v 4 and requires no suffix (see also Dahood, I, 88–89). This may be essentially correct, with the reading being as follows:

> You love all devouring words,
>   (the words) of your deceitful tongue.

7.a. Reflecting the גַם, which usually means "also," but here seems to have the force of "therefore" = לָכֵן, as in the announcements of disaster in prophetic judgment speeches. Cf. Isa 66:4; Ezek 16:43; Mal 2:9.

7.b. לָנֶצַח is frequently translated "forever," with the idea of perpetuity. But the meaning here seems to be "completely" or "finished." The destruction will be so complete that any reconstruction is excluded. Cf. Kissane, "pull thee down utterly."

7.c. MT reads from חתה, "snatch up," as the snatching up of hot coals (Isa 30:14). Aquila, Jerome, and Targum indicate יחתך from חתת ("to demolish/shatter"), which would give a somewhat easier sequence in the colon. Gunkel reads the verb as jussive, giving expression to a curse. This is adopted by Dahood, who identifies it with Ugaritic gm, "aloud, with a loud voice" and translates, "With a crash may El demolish you . . ." Dahood's elaborate arguments for reading the verb יחתך as "unchild you" and the verb וְשֵׁרֶשְׁךָ as "snatch your sons" seem unnecessary and rather far-fetched.

8.a. Lit., "and they will fear." The wordplay between וְיִרְאוּ, "and they will see," and וְיִירָאוּ, "and they will fear," should not be lost by following the Syriac and reading וְיִשְׂמְחוּ, "and they will rejoice," as sometimes proposed (BHS), though the reading is certainly easier (cf. Isa 30:2).

9.a. MT has qal imperfect of עזז, "be strong." It is sometimes suggested that the verb should be derived from עוז, "take refuge." The meaning "trust" or "rely on" is acceptable, but "prevail" (cf. 9:20) or "boast" or "be strong" is best here.

9.b. MT could be read as "in his desire," but it is better to retain the meaning of "destruction" as in v 4. The emendation to בהונו (see BHS), "in his wealth," is unnecessary. Cf. Dahood.

10.a. The unending nature of God's love is a better understanding than that of the worshiper's unceasing trust. Dahood assumes an enclitic mem on אלהים and translates, "the love of the eternal and everlasting God."

11.a. The Hebrew קוה usually means "to wait for" or "to hope," and this may be the meaning here: "In your name I will hope, for your name is good" (NIV; also JB). RSV and others assume וְאֲחַוֶּה, "and I will proclaim." However, the emendation may not be necessary since קוה seems to mean "call" or "cry" in some cases (see 19:4; 37:9; 40:2; Job 17:13), and I have adopted this meaning.

11.b. The term חָסִיד appears some 24 times in the Psalter, and only a few times elsewhere (e.g., Mic 7:2). The word is closely related to חֶסֶד, "loyal-love" (see Comment on 51:3). The verb does not appear in the OT except in the hithpael form in 1 Sam 22:26/Ps 18:25. The word appears three times in plural form in the books of Maccabees (1 Macc 2:42; 7:12–13; 2 Macc 14:6), a time or two in the psalm literature from Qumran (11Qpsa 154, 155), and is the subject of some attention in rabbinic literature. Despite the scanty evidence, various scholars have attributed the collection and canonization of the prophetic writings, the roots of the Essene and Pharisaic movements, and the authorship of Daniel and other apocalyptic writings to the hasidim (חסידים; see J. J. Collins, The Apocalyptic Vision of the Book of Daniel [Missoula, MT: Scholars Press, 1977], 201–5). The later hasidim appear to have been a scribal group or party, more or less organized, that emerged before and during the Maccabean revolt, and who found the methods and leadership of Judas Maccabee at least temporarily acceptable. It is most unlikely, however, that the hasidim in Psalms belonged to any party or formally organized group, though at times the category of hasid may have been more identifiable than at others.

The word itself is probably a derivative from an old passive qatil form, analogous to נָשִׂיא ("elected chief/deputy"), פָּקִיד ("commissioner/examiner/overseer"), נָבִיא ("prophet/spokesman"), and מָשִׁיחַ ("anointed/messiah") in which originally passive forms have acquired a stative or active meaning (see K. D. Sakenfeld, The Meaning of Hesed in the Hebrew Bible: A New Inquiry, HSM 17 [Missoula, MT: Scholars Press, 1978], 241). In general terms, it means one who is motivated by חסד ("loyal-love") and who responds with devotion and faithfulness. The view of A. R. Johnson, consistently advocated for more than thirty years (see CPIP, 23, n. 3; with reference to Interpretationes ad Vetus Testamentum Pertinentes S. Mowinckel, ed. A. S. Kapelrud, 1955, 100–112) is that the nearest English equivalent to חָסִיד is "devotee" or "votary" (and in some contexts, "one who is devout"). Johnson is almost certainly correct in a technical sense. However, "devotee" and "votary" have occult nuances in contemporary English usage that are not very appropriate for some OT contexts. Therefore, the translation adopted in this commentary is usually "loyal ones" or "the faithful"; hopefully this carries some of the ideas of enduring loyalty, devotion, love, and obedience and accords with my choice of "loyal-love" for חֶסֶד.

The contextual meaning of any word is most important. Nelson Glueck, (*Hesed in the Bible*, tr. A. Gottschalk [Cincinnati: Hebrew Union College Press, 1967] 66–69) defines חָסִיד in three categories: (1) as the opposite of the sinner; the חָסִיד relies on God, practices justice, shows loyalty, and orders his or her life according to divinely given commandments (see 37:28; 97:10; 1 Sam 2:9; Prov 11:17); (2) as those who are identical with the honest and the just (see 18:25–26; 2 Sam 22:26; Micah 7:2; Prov 2:8; Isa 57:1); (3) as those who are identical with the faithful (see Prov 20:6, where אִישׁ חֶסֶד is parallel to אִישׁ אֱמוּנִים, "a faithful man"; Pss 12:1; 31:25; cf. Jer 3:12). Sakenfeld (*The Meaning of Hesed*, 243) says that the plural of חָסִיד connotes three different groups of people: (1) in a broad sense, all Israel, all the people who have received Yahweh's *hesed* (see 50:5; 79:2; 148:14; 149:1); (2) the faithful and/or upright in Israel, a subgroup who remain loyal to Yahweh and live accordingly (e.g., 37:28–29; 31:23; 97:10–11; 85:8–9; Prov 2:8); (3) priests who seem to be identified as חֲסִידִים in Ps 132:9, 16 (quoted in 2 Chr 2:47), as is Levi in Deut 33:8, based on LXX and a Qumran reading yielding:

> Give to Levi your *urim*
> To your man of *hesed* your *thummin*.

(see Sakenfeld, 244; cf. NAB, NEB, NIV). Perhaps, the use of חָסִיד for religious functionaries is the most basic usage, a usage which would accord well with the meaning of "devotee" or "votary." The meaning was broadened, of course, eventually to become "a simple adjective meaning faithful or upright" (Sakenfeld, 245) and "loyal."

Form/Structure/Setting

This psalm does not seem to fit any regular form-critical category (Kraus, *Psalms 1–59*, 509–10). Gunkel links it with the individual laments and argues for a design similar to Ps 58. H. Schmidt classifies it as a thanksgiving psalm on the basis of v 11. The best approach, however, is to read the psalm in terms of the language of prophetic judgment speech to an individual (A. A. Anderson, I, 403; Kraus, I, 551–52; cf. C. Westermann, *Basic Forms of Prophetic Speech*, tr. H. C. White [Philadelphia: Westminster Press, 1967], 137–68; K. Koch, *The Growth of the Biblical Tradition: The Form-Critical Method*, tr. S. M. Cuppitt from 2nd German ed. [New York: Scribner, 1969], 210–13; W. E. March, "Prophecy," in *Old Testament Form Criticism*, ed. J. H. Hayes [San Antonio: Trinity UP, 1974], 157–62). Kraus suggests that the closest parallel is Isa 22:15–19 (also see Jer 20:3–6; 28:12–16). The judgment speech is abbreviated and lacks some elements and formulaic expressions commonly found (especially, "Thus says Yahweh"). Judgment speeches have two basic parts: (1) an accusation and (2) a prediction (or announcement) of judgmental disaster. The use of accusing questions of reproach is found in some prophetic judgment speeches (note 2 Kgs 1:3, 6, 16; Jer 22:15). The oracle in Ps 52 is found in vv 3–9 and contains the following components:

Accusing questions,	vv 3–4
Accusation, or indication of situation,	vv 5–6
Announcement of judgment,	vv 7–9
The judgment of God,	vv 7
The response of the righteous,	vv 8–9

The speaker in vv 10–11 uses the language of thanksgiving, including a *toda*-formula in v 11 (so Kraus; F. Crüsemann, *Studien zur Formgeschichte,* 275). Westermann (*Basic Forms,* 155) notes that the statements of announcement or prediction of judgment sometimes have a strong element of contrast between the judgment and Yahweh's intention for the judged party—an intention thwarted by the deeds described in the accusation. Such an element is not explicitly stated in 52:7–9, but it is implied and vv 10–12 serve as a substitute for it.

As in the case of most of the psalms, any attempt to be definitive and specific about the setting from which the psalm emerged and/or in which it was used is very elusive and tentative. The superscription relates the psalm to David and places it in the context of his flight from Saul (see 1 Sam 21:1–8; 22:6–19). The scribal interpreters who provided the superscription were probably thinking of David as the speaker, making a second address to Doeg (the first is in 1 Sam 22:22–23) and pronouncing judgment on him, though it is possible that Saul was thought of as the person addressed. The scribes probably took for granted that David was the speaker and found a suitable context in the Davidic accounts, taking a cue from the *gibbor* ("mighty man/giant/hero") in the first line and assuming that Doeg was one of the *gibborim* associated with Saul (note 1 Sam 14:52). However, the character of Doeg does not fit the psalm in a very exact manner. According to 1 Samuel he was no liar, at the most only an informer, who told Saul the truth. The wealth referred to in v 9 could be inferred from Doeg's status as chief herdsman of Saul, but it seems odd. The massacre at Nob is not alluded to in the psalm, and the reference to the "house of God" in v 10 does not fit the Davidic context. Such details probably did not bother the scribal interpreters; it was sufficient that the psalm as a whole was deemed appropriate for such a temple lurker (1 Sam 21:8), informer, and executioner as Doeg. The language of the psalms is usually more formulaic than specific.

If the Davidic context for the psalm is not accepted, it is impossible to be specific about alternatives (which should not be taken as support for the Davidic solution). The most probable understanding would seem to be one relating the psalm to internal conflict between cultic prophets or priests who have been attacked (and perhaps persecuted) by temple personnel who are opposed to them. One immediately thinks of a prophet like Jeremiah—or of Amos. In any case, the psalm is likely to reflect internal conflict and corruption in the cultic establishment. A date is impossible to determine, but because evidence for conflict in the post-exilic temple is clear, a date after 515 B.C.E. would be reasonable.

Comment

Accusing questions (52:3–4). The speech begins with an abrupt question directed toward a "hero," who boasts of his evil ways. The question confronts him with his self-glorification in wickedness and with his disregard for the continual presence of God's loyal-love. He is a "big shot" (Durham), who brags about his power and unconcern for the divine presence (cf. Pss 53:2; 73:3–12; Luke 12:16–21). His tongue plots destructive actions in the community with the deadly effectiveness of a sharpened razor. He is a "doer of deceit" (עֹשֵׂה רְמִיָּה) or "con-man" (cf. Ps 101:7), whose perverted sense of values is disruptive and threatening to those who oppose him or stand in his way.

The accusation (52:5–6). The person under judgment has inverted values, rejecting that which is good in preference for that which is harmful. The lie is loved more than the reliable and constructive word of righteousness. The person addressed does not desire the ways of goodness and righteousness. "Love" here means to prefer or to take pleasure in something (cf. Pss 11:5, 7; 109:17; Prov 20:13; 21:17; etc.). The rebuked person loves cruel words, hurtful and malicious talk. The description is of a person absorbed in his or her evil ways—in love with them and prepared to leave all else for them. The "good" (or "goodness") of v 5 is generally that which is beneficial and not harmful. "Good" also means that something is suited for its purpose (C. Westermann, *Creation*, trans. J. J. Scullion [Philadelphia: Fortress Press, 1974], 61). In theological contexts, "goodness" refers to what God intends (Gen 1:31): "What is good is good in the eyes of God: *God* looks at his work and *he* says of it that all is very good" (ibid., 61). "Goodness" is that which evokes praise; that which is beautiful and not harmful and ugly. The evil (רע) is the opposite. It evokes complaint, misery, and pain.

The announcement of judgment (52:7–9). The prediction of judgment is expressed in severe but simple words: the boaster's present security, built on self-glorification, lying, and destructiveness, will be swept away with terrible finality; ruined (or demolished) like a house that is wrecked; snatched up like the quick moving of fire from a hearth (see Isa 30:14); and torn away from the tent. The "tent" probably refers to the dwelling place of the addressee (cf. Ps 132:3; Job 18:14) rather than to the temple. However, Weiser argues for the possibility of the tent as God's abode (cf. Ps 78:60) and for understanding the removal from it as expulsion from the faithful community, an expulsion which would precede the death experience of being uprooted from the "land of the living." In any case, the judgment will be complete and will result in sudden and drastic change of fortunes for the "hero" (cf. Ps 73:18–20).

The second part of the prediction of judgment deals with the response of the righteous (vv 8–9). At first, the righteous will be astounded when they see what God will do. But then their fear will turn to delight and find expression in laughter and praise. Perhaps the speaker has in mind the righteous joining in the laughter of God himself at the foolish ways of the wicked (cf. Pss 2:4; 37:13; 59:8; Prov 1:26). The laughter is intended as a response to the perception of God's work in transforming the circumstances of an arrogant and oppressive person (cf. Ps 126:2; Prov 8:30–31; Job 38:7), rather than as a mere gloating over the fall of an enemy. The movement from rejoicing at the judgment of God to the gloating which marks a spirit of vengeance is, of course, easy to make. Thus Prov 24:17–18 (cf. Job 31:29) is a healthy counterpart: "Do not gloat when your enemy falls . . . or Yahweh will see and disapprove."

A. A. Anderson (I, 406) suggests that vv 8–9 reflect the form of a mocking song or saying (see O. Eissfeldt, *The Old Testament*, 92–94; cf. Num 21:27–30; Isa 14:4–20). A major feature of such composition is the vivid contrast between former glory and present dishonored powerlessness (note the contrast motif in the prophetic judgment speeches referred to above in *Form/Structure/Setting*). The pride before is measured by the pitiful state that follows. The "hero" (*gibbor*) of v 3 has become a mere *geber,* an ordinary man (v 9), who exemplifies the person who refuses to make God a personal stronghold and trusts rather in wealth and in the ability to plan and promote harmful schemes. Spurgeon remarks (427), "Wherever we see to-day a man great in sin and substance, we shall do well to anticipate his end, and view this verse as the divine *in memoriam.*"

A *thanksgiving* (52:10–11). The speaker's trust in God's loyal-love has made him or her "like a thriving [green] olive tree in the house of God." The gray-green, fruit-bearing olive tree provides a rich metaphor (cf. Pss 92:13–15; 1:3; Jer 11:16). The olive tree was very important for the economy of ancient Israel. The land of Israel is described as "a land of wheat and barley, of vines and fig trees and pomegranates, a land of olive trees and honey" (Deut 8:8; also 2 Kgs 18:32). The olive is an evergreen that may bear fruit (usually in alternate years) for centuries. Even if the main trunk dies, shoots grow up to prolong its existence (see Ps 128:3). It grows well in the Mediterranean climate, needing some seven months of sunshine and heat. However, since some frost helps productivity, the central highlands of Palestine (especially on lower slopes and valleys) were very fruitful. The olive was used in various ways: as food and as a source of fat in cooking (cf. 1 Kgs 17:12; other types of fat were hard to preserve but olive oil kept well), for hygienic and medicinal purposes (such as for soap and for ointments; cf. Isa 1:6), for cosmetic uses (cf. Eccl 9:7–8), for lamp oil (necessary for culture, since most study had to be done at night), and for liturgical uses (e.g., Exod 29:40; Num 48:5). The export of olive oil (1 Kgs 5:11 // 2 Chr 2:14–15; Ezra 3:7) was an important element in the economy of Israel.

There is little reason to doubt (as some do) that olive trees actually grew in the area of the temple on Mount Zion. Cypress and olive trees grow in the Dome of the Rock area of Jerusalem today. Trees were common in temple areas throughout the ancient Near East, symbols of life, fertility, and power (see O. Keel, *The Symbolism of the Biblical World,* 135–36, 354; cf. Ps 104:16). The temple trees were living reminders of God's invisible, mysterious blessing which was operative in them and in his people. Incidentally, a tree-based economy was more stable than one based on grain crops in the Palestinian area, because trees can survive drought (cf. Jacob and the movement to Egypt for grain).

The closing verse of the psalm (v 11) contains a formulaic vow to praise God for what he has done and to proclaim his good name in the presence of his faithful worshipers. This verse seems to reflect a ceremony of thanksgiving ("in the presence of those loyal to you"), which sometimes, at least, must have involved a sacrifice and a shared meal with family members, friends, and others (see Pss 7:18; 22:23–27; 26:12; 54:8; 66:13–15; 116:12–14, 17–19). Hymnic/thanksgiving elements are found in this verse (e.g., כִּי־עָשִׂיתָ, "for you have done it"); see also Pss 22:32; 54:8; 100:5; 106:1; 107:1; 135:3; 136:1; Isa 38:15; Jer 33:11.

Explanation

The main intention of the psalm is to affirm faith in God's ability and willingness to deal with the powerful, wicked people who confront the faithful. The faithful have a "wholesome saving strength and vitality" (Weiser) which flows through their relationship with God. The message is a warning to the wicked, who try to disregard God and oppress his people. Two things are emphasized: the inglorious fall of the mighty, which the righteous will see and know to be the work of God, and the stability and long-lived fruitfulness of the faithful, who are like olive trees in the house of God. The words of 1 John 4:4 can be used to sum up the message of the psalm (though the context is different): "For he who is in you is greater than he who is in the world"—and it is important to note that the "you" in this verse is *plural*, because it is often preached as applying to individuals. The God who is in the midst of his faithful ones is greater than any power that is in the world.

Judgment on Fools Who Try to Ignore God   (53:1–7)

Bibliography

Bennett, R. A. "Wisdom Motifs in Ps. 14:53—*nabal* and *esah*." *BASOR* 220 (1975) 15–21. **Jeremias, J.** *Kultprophetie.* 110–20.

Translation

1	For the leader;[a] according to *mahalath*;[b] a Davidic *maskil*,[c]	
2 (1)	*The fool says in his heart,*	(3+2+3+2)
	"There is no God."	
	They are corrupt; they do vile deeds;[a]	
	no one does good.	
3 (2)	*God*[a] *looks down from heaven*	(3+2+3+2)
	on the children of humanity,	
	to see if anyone is acting wisely,	
	(to see) if there is anyone who seeks after God.	
4 (3)	*They have all been faithless*[a] *and all are impure;*[b]	(4+2+2)
	no one does good—	
	no, not even one.	
5 (4)	*Why don't the evildoers know*[a]*—*	(3+3+3)
	those who devour my people as those who eat bread,[b]	
	(and) who do not call on God?	
6 (5)	*So*[a] *they were overcome with fear,*[b]	(3+2+4+3)
	—there where they had not been afraid,[c]*—*	
	for God scattered your besiegers' bones;[d]	
	you put them to shame,[e] *for God despised them.*	
7 (6)	*Let Israel's salvation*[a] *be given from Zion!*	(4+4+4)
	When God restores the fortunes of his people,	
	Jacob will rejoice and Israel will be glad.	

Notes

1.a. See n. 51:1–2.a.

1.b. A term of uncertain meaning, which occurs again in the title of Ps 88 (with *leʿannoth*, "to afflict" or "to humble," or "for reciting antiphonally") but does not appear with Ps 14. The term is usually thought to be the name of a tune (or perhaps an instrument). LXX transliterates; but some Greek texts and Jerome (see *BHS*) have as χορεία = מחלת, "a round dance" (cf. 130:2; 149:3; 150:4), probably thinking of some type of cultic dancing and singing (Kraus, I, 22). S. Mowinckel (*PIW*, II, 210) thinks that the expression על מחלת refers to flute playing in rites of lamentation. *Mahalath* is used twice as a feminine proper name (Gen 28:9; 2 Chr 11:18) and is very nearly the same as the word for sickness or disease (מַחֲלָה). Sickness fits well with Ps 88, but not well with Ps 53.

1.c. See n. 52:1–2.c.

2.a. Ps 14 has עֲלִילָה "deed"; less forceful than עָוֶל "evil deed."

3.a. Note the use of אלהים for יהוה.

4.a. From סוג, "to turn back/prove faithless." Ps 14:3 has סור, "to turn aside"; or possibly from סרר, "to rebel/be stubborn" (so Dahood). The words seem to be synonyms.

4.b. The word נאלחו is found elsewhere only in 14:3 and Job 15:16. In Arabic, the word refers to tainted or soured milk. It is used here in a moral sense, of course.

5.a. Several translations are possible (see Perowne, Gunkel); e.g., "Have those who work evil no understanding?" (RSV); "Haven't they learned anything from experience?"; "Will the evildoers never learn . . . ?" (NIV); NEB has, "Shall they not rue it, these evildoers who devour my people . . . ?" NEB may be influenced by LXX (which seems to reflect יִדְעוּ, "Shall they not experience . . . ?") but is probably more influenced by the suggestion that ידע is equal here to the Arabic cognate *waduʿa*, which means "was still/submissive" and sometimes has the sense of "humiliated/punished" (D. W. Thomas, *TRP*, 5).

5.b. Following RSV, NAB, NIV, and others; the evildoers devour the people as naturally as eating daily food. Some commentators (Gunkel, Schmidt, Oesterley) assume that the evildoers are priests who eat the sacrificial bread of God without "calling on his name" (reading שָׁם from the following verse as שָׁמוֹ). Cf. Lev 21:6, 8, 17, 22; Num 28:2. Another interpretation is to assume that the eating of bread refers to the normal life of the evildoers who go on with their lives content to ignore God. In any case the emendations proposed by Gunkel and others are not likely to be correct. Dahood's "the grain of God they did not harvest" (reading קרא as "harvest") also seems improbable (see Craigie, n. 14:4.b.).

6.a. See n. 66:6.c.

6.b. See Craigie, n. 14:5.a.

6.c. Ps 14:5 has כי אלהים בדור צדיק "for God is with the generation of the righteous" or "for God is in the assembly of the righteous." The meaning of פחד לא־היה in 53:6 can be "where there was no cause to fear," but the context seems to favor the idea that they (the besiegers) had not been afraid before being overcome by dread from divine attack.

6.d. RSV has "the bones of the ungodly," apparently following LXX's ἀνθρωπαρέσκων, "men-pleasers," which may indicate Heb. חָנֵף "profane/irreligious/apostate." Thus JB has "the apostate." MT should be retained in this context. Ps 14:6 has עֲצַת־עָנִי תָבִישׁוּ כִּי יְהוָה מַחְסֵהוּ, "the counsel of the poor they would put to shame (reject), but [*or,* for] Yahweh is his refuge." The meaning of each psalm is altered by the differences between vv 5–6 of Ps 14 and v 6 of Ps 53.

6.e. The *Translation* assumes that the subject is the collective whole of the Israelites addressed in the psalm and the object is the besieger(s) in the previous verse. However, the verb can be read as meaning that the subject is put to shame (hiphil of בוש; Briggs, I, 111; note Pss 44:7; 119:31, 116; Jer 2:26; 6:15; 46:24). In this case the meaning of the verse would be that Israelites had never learned to trust God to scatter their attackers and were chagrined when he did.

7.a. The plural form (singular in Ps 14:7) adds intensity to the idea; or else Dahood is correct in arguing that the *-ot* ending is actually a fem. sing. absolute following the Phoenician pattern.

Form/Structure/Setting

Ps 53 is a different version of the same psalm found in Ps 14. The variants between the psalms seem minor except in two regards. Ps 53 uses *Elohim* instead of *Yahweh* in four cases, a usage that is common in Pss 42–83. Second, major differences occur in 53:6, and an additional verse is found in Ps 14:6. The two texts can be translated as follows:

14:5b, 6
For God (is) with the generation of the righteous.
The counsel of the poor you would put to shame,
but Yahweh is his refuge.

53:6bc
For God scattered your besieger's bones;
you put them to shame, for God despised them.

Both psalms belong to the general genre of prophetic speech. J. Jeremias has classified Pss 12, 14, and 75 as prophetic judgment proclamations by cultic prophets in the late pre-exilic period (followed in part by Kraus et al.), a conclusion which may well be correct. It is interesting to note that Pss 11, 12, 13, and 14 can be taken together as a kind of prophetic liturgy. The same could be said for Pss 52 and 53. Not enough attention has been paid to the placement of psalms in the Psalter and their interrelations.

The genre of prophetic judgment speech has two basic features: (1) a lament by the speaker regarding personal and social conditions, and (2) a citation of or reference to speech by Yahweh (Ps 12:6; see also Hab 1:2–17; 2:6–19; 3:1–16). Jeremias (*Kultprophetie*, 114–15) argues that these two main features are found in Ps 14:1–4 and 5–7. They are also present in Ps 53, with the intervention of Yahweh expressed as an event which has already happened in 53:6.

Ps 53 should not be treated as merely the product of editorial changes or textual corruption, as is often the case in modern commentaries. Each psalm has its own message, and the redactions should be respected. In the case of Ps 53, it can be argued (at least) that vv 5–6 have given the psalm a new genre, or, better, a variant of the genre suggested above for Ps 14. Ps 14 may be read as referring to evildoers in Israel (though v 7 certainly encourages one to think of Israel in a hostile world) and of God's judgment of them. In Ps 53 the situation is that of Israel having been recently under siege and of the powerful intervention of God against foreigners who try to devour his people. Thus, the genre seems more nearly that of prophetic mocking speech or taunt (see O. Eissfeldt, *The Old Testament*, 91–98 and the discussion of Ps 52). Examples of such speech can be found in Num 21:27–30; Ezek 28:2–10, 12–19; Isa 14:4–20. Thus the fools in Ps 53 who disdain God are not Israelites but foreigners who disregard Yahweh. They "do not call on God [Yahweh]" (v 5). The fools are foreigners, and the addressees of the psalm appear to emerge in v 6 as Israelites who need to hear the message of judgment on foreign fools who seek to ignore Yahweh's will and power.

The psalm can be divided into three parts. Vv 2–5 form a prophetic complaint about the fools who disregard Yahweh. The complaint ends with a despairing question in v 5. A description of the results of the intervention of Yahweh is found in v 6. The last verse expresses a strong wish for the restoration and well-being of the prophet's people, with saving deliverance coming forth from Zion.

Comment

Superscription (53:1). See *Notes* above.

A prophetic complaint (53:2–5). A prophetic speaker laments the abominable behavior of human beings who ignore the reality of God and his power. The "fool" is characterized by corrupt actions—opposite to those of the wise, who do good and seek to do the will of God (cf. Ps 74:18b and Isa 32:5–6b). The fool, of course, is not a person who is simple-minded by nature. Fools are persons who deliberately choose stubborn and pernicious behavior. The paradigmatic figure of the fool (נבל) in the OT is Nabal in the account of his conflict with David (1 Sam 25:1–44). R. A. Bennett (*BASOR* 220 [1975] 15–21) has argued that Ps 14–53 is a commentary on *nabal* ("fool"). He traces the usage of *nabal* in the OT and finds that in its earlier use, especially, it connotes sacrilege, behavior involving serious abuse, and is characteristic of an outcast (note Gen 34:2; Josh 7:15; Judg 19:23; 20:6, 10; Deut 22:21; 1 Sam 13:11). The earlier references tend to involve sexual behavior which threatens the well-being of individuals and the community (for example, communal stability is to the fore in Prov 30:21–23). The prophets indict the whole nation of Israel in regard to *nabal*-behavior; e.g., Isa 9:15–17, "the prophet who teaches lies . . . those who lead this people astray . . . everyone is godless [חנֵף, "profane"] and an evildoer [מרע] and every mouth speaks folly [נבלה]" (cf. Jer 17:11, Nah 3:6).

Generally, a *nabal* is a person whose behavior is disruptive and disintegrative of family, community, and nation. It is worthwhile to note that in Ps 53, the "evildoers" [פעלי און] are linked with the *nabal*, whose behavior is so vile, corrupt, and destructive. The fools formulate their judgments in their hearts (or minds). They may not speak of their decisions with their lips, but they act out of the volitional center of their lives. The description of a completely corrupt society is similar to those found elsewhere (see Ps 12:2–3; Isa 59:4; 64:7; Jer 8:6; Mic 7:1–7). In Ps 14, the behavior is intended as characteristic of Israelites, but it seems probable in Ps 53 that the reference is to the actions of those who are the enemies of Israel and Yahweh. They are those "who consume my people" (v 5)— the prophet's people. The enemies are fools not only because of what they do and say, but also because they disregard the punishment from Yahweh that is sure to come.

A prophetic taunt (53:5–6). The evildoers who seek to destroy "my people" (the people of Yahweh) are those who do not "call on God"; i.e., they have no regard or reverence for God; they try to act as "practical atheists"—ignoring the divine presence and power. V 6 provides a picture of the sudden dread and destructive confusion which falls on those who attack the people of Yahweh. It is possible that some historical incident is alluded to; commentators regularly recall the overthrow of Sennacherib's army (2 Kgs 18:13–37). In any case, the enemy is overwhelmed by overpowering fear, which results in their bones being scattered on the battlefield or around the city walls, to remain there in the sun and the rain (cf. Ps 141:7; Ezek 6:5; 37:1–6; Jer 8:1–2). The enemy soldiers suffer a shameful rout because God despises them. The self-destruction of enemies from dread and panic is fairly common in OT accounts (e.g., Josh 10:10; Judg 7:19–23; 1 Sam 14:20; 2 Kgs 7:3–8; Ezek 38:21–23), and similar descriptions are found in prophetic oracles against foreign nations (e.g., Isa 13:7–8, 13–14; 29:5–8; Jer 48:40–43; also Pss 46:6–7; 48:5–8; Isa 29:5–8; Ezek 38:21–23). The words of v 6 bring to mind a major feature of Yahweh-war in the OT in that the decisive action is that of Yahweh and is not dependent on the strength and power of the Israelites. The panic and fear which Yahweh could spread among the enemy forces were far more deadly than the weapons of the Israelites.

Prayer for saving deliverance (53:7). The psalm ends with a strong wish that the salvation of Yahweh would come forth from Zion, the place of Yahweh's presence (e.g., Pss 20:3; 128:5; 134:3) and from which he comes to help and to bless. Commentators have noted the awkwardness of this verse in Ps 14 and frequently suggested that it is a liturgical addition reflecting the condition of the exiles in Babylon. The verse fits much better with Ps 53, however, if the interpretation of vv 5–6 suggested above is correct. But this does not necessarily mean that Ps 14 is an adaptation of Ps 53. Each psalm is to be interpreted in its own form and context.

Explanation

The first part of Ps 53, regardless of its original usage, carries the same message as Ps 14. The fool, whether Israelite or foreigner, demonstrates folly by assuming that there is no effective presence of God. "In his heart," refers to the volitional center of one's being. It is here that the affirmation is made that "there is no God." Such a judgment seeks to ignore the fact that the vile and corrupt ways of human beings are under the scrutiny of the one who "looks down from heaven" (see Gen 6:5) and makes a mockery of the inveterate aspirations of humankind to act as if there were no God (see Rom 3:9–10).

Ps 53 shifts the emphasis from Israelites who ignore their God and devour one another (Ps 14) without regard for the divine will to foreigners who are fools enough to think that they can destroy the people of Yahweh. The psalm expresses both confidence and longing for the divine intervention which will bring to an end the corrupt and godless domination of the world. Yahweh is the great judge who will reduce to impotence the powerful rebellions of humankind. Let the fools on earth take notice.

As noted above, the atheism in the statement "there is no God" is unlikely to be a theoretical atheism, which was rare in the ancient world. Peter Craigie (126–27) has given this subject excellent treatment in the *Explanation* section of Pss 9–10. He argues that "the practical or functional atheists . . . are the most dangerous species of human being," because their character and behavior are determined by rejecting the concepts of morality and justice postulated on commitment to God, or on any ultimate basis. However, an even more dangerous species of human being may be the person who affirms God but who allows no impact of that affirmation on the actual reality of living—or else attempts to use faith affirmations for ungodly ends. The course of religious history is replete with fools who have said "There is no God" and with even greater fools who have said "Lord, Lord," but who have refused to do the will of God (cf. Matt 7:21–23). The divine judgment for them is "I never knew you; depart from me, you evildoers." This psalm (with its mate, Ps 14) affirms God's lordship over human destiny and seeks to encourage faithfulness by the genuine people of God.

Prayer and Assurance in the
Name of God   (54:1–9)

Bibliography

Becker, J. *Israel deutet seine Psalmen.* 64–65. **Beyerlin, W.** *Die Rettung der Bedrängten.* 23–24. **Hubbard, R. L., Jr.** *Dynamics and Legal Language in Conflict Psalms.* Ann Arbor, MI: UMI, 1984. 105–19. **Johnson, A. R.** *CPIP.* 359–64.

Translation

1–2   For the leader;[a] with instrumental music;[b] a Davidic *maskil;*[c] when the
      Ziphites went and said to Saul, "Is not[d] David hiding among us?"

3(1) *O God,*[a] *save me by your name,*	(3+3)
and defend me by your might,	
4(2) *O God, hear my prayer;*	(3+3)
give ear to the words of my mouth,	
5(3) *For strangers*[a] *have risen against me*	(3+3+3)
and the ruthless seek my life;[b]	
those who have no regard for God.[c] SELAH.	
6(4) *Give attention,*[a] *O God, my helper!*	(3+3)
O Lord,[b] *sustainer of my life.*[c]	
7(5) *Let the evil recoil*[a] *onto my slanderers;*[b]	(3+3)
in your true faithfulness[c] *silence them.*	
8(6) *Freely*[a] *would I sacrifice to you;*	(3+4)
thankfully praise your name, O Yahweh,[b] *for it is good.*	
9(7) *It*[a] *delivers me from all distress,*	
and my eye looks (in triumph)[b] *over my foes!*	(3+3)

Notes

1–2.a. See n. 51:1–2.a.

1–2.b. Found with Pss 4, 6, 54, 61 (with על-), 67, and 76. Mowinckel (*PIW*, II, 210) notes that בנגינת always appears after למנצח ("for the leader"), and thus is apparently an instruction for the leader in the recitation of the psalm. The term is usually understood to refer to the music of stringed instruments (see 1 Sam 16:16–18; 18:10; 19:9; 2 Kgs 3:15; Isa 38:20; Ezek 33:32; Ps 68:26; Lam 3:14; 5:14).

1–2.c. See n. 52:1–2.

1–2.d. Dahood is probably correct to argue that the הלא here is equal to הנה, "behold, look"; also BDB, 520a, etc. However, the meaning would be substantially the same.

3.a. *Elohim* in Pss 42–83 stands for *Yahweh* in most cases.

5.a. Often read זדים, "insolent men," after 86:14, some Hebrew mss, and Targum. Dahood notes the parallelism of זרים and עריצים ("ruthless/terrible persons") in Isa 25:2, 3, 5; 29:5, according to LXX and 1QIsaᵃ. See *Form/Structure/Setting.*

5.b. Lit. "my *nephesh,*" traditionally translated as "my soul." The word נפש pertains to that which breathes and is alive. Its range of meaning is illustrated by the series of words used by BDB to express its basic meaning: "soul, living being, life, self, person, desire, appetite, emotion and passion." Fairly frequently the word means "I" or "me," and it could be translated "me" in 54:5, though "my life" seems better. Unfortunately the fine term "soul" has been severely damaged in theological traditions and has to be used with caution. The "soul" has often been thought to be part of the human person which is immortal and separate from the body and the self. Properly speaking, the "soul" of man is "the concrete human self in all of its relations" (D. Moody, *The Word of Truth* [Grand Rapids: Eerdmans, 1981], 487, also 170–87).

5.c. Lit. "they have not set God before them." Dahood notes this rather strange expression and proposes that לְנֶגְדָּם be read as לנגדי־ם "my Leader" (with enclitic *mem*) used of God. His conjecture makes it necessary to translate לֹא שָׂמוּ as "they are not aware," and does not commend itself. Cf. 16:8; 119:30.

6.a. The הִנֵּה is used here to introduce a request (see A. R. Johnson, *CPIP*, 360) with the force of the expression: "Look, so-and-so, do this for me." Johnson translates as "prithee."

6.b. The translation "my Lord" is adopted here, but the meaning "the Lord (of all)" may be correct (see O. Eissfeldt, *TDOT*, I, 59–72).

6.c. It is usual to consider the pl. בסמכי ("among/with the supporters of. . . .") as intensive expressing the superlative ("the sustainer par excellence") or the class of supporters to which God belongs in the sense of a basic characteristic (not simply as one among others). The בְּ is usually considered as *beth essentiae* (GKC, 119i). It may, however, be emphatic and used simply to strengthen the superlative quality of the plural (Dahood, Johnson, *CPIP*, 360, n. 3).

7.a. Reading with *kethiv* and Targum as יָשׁוּב or יָשׁוֹב. *Qere*, LXX, and σ´ read as hiphil imperfect יָשִׁיב. Syriac and Jerome reflect imperative הָשִׁיבָה "Turn back the evil on my foes." On the other hand, if God is understood as subject, the *qere* is better.

7.b. See n. 56:3.a.

7.c. For אֱמֶת, "truth," see 25:5; 51:6. Gunkel proposes בחמתך "in your wrath," but this is unnecessary. Dahood reads "in his fidelity," but the changes proposed are too extensive.

8.a. The בִּנְדָבָה is read here as an adverbial accusative, signifying the voluntariness of the action. The alternative is to read, "with a freewill offering . . ." (RSV). The verb is in a nodal imperfect, expressing strong willingness.

8.b. The name "Yahweh" lengthens the line and is sometimes treated as an intrusion which should be omitted for metrical reasons (so Kraus). However, metrical considerations should not be allowed to dominate meaning—regardless of how the word got into the psalm. Whether from the original poet or a later redactor or scribe, the presence of the name Yahweh serves to emphasize the Name theology in the psalm. It makes unmistakable the identity of the God addressed in vv 3 and 4.

9.a. The subject of the verb may be either Yahweh or his name (cf. v 6).

9.b. Lit. "and my eye looked at my enemies," but the nuance is that of rejoicing or gloating over the defeat of foes (see Johnson, *CPIP*, 190, n. 5). I take the כִּי in 9a as emphatic, which also applies to 9b.

Form/Structure/Setting

Ps 54 belongs to the general category of the individual laments, though vv 8–9 could suggest a thanksgiving of a persecuted person who praises the name of God and is prepared to offer sacrifice. However, it seems best to treat v 9 as expressing a change of mood like that found in several psalms of lament (see Pss 3:7; 6:9; 10:16–18; 13:5–6; 22:22–23; 28:6–7; 56:11–14; see C. Westermann, *Praise and Lament*, 79–81). Whether these transitions were the result of some cultic act external to the worshiper, such as a word from a priest, or whether the psalms were designed to bring the one praying them to a point of faith and confidence is uncertain (see Craigie's discussion of Ps 6:9–11). Westermann (80–81) points out that the "heard petition" is a major component of the psalms of individual lament. Such laments move into thanksgiving (Westermann's "declarative praise") and no longer represent mere petition. It is also possible to understand v 9 as expressing certainty of victory in the future, in which case the worshiper anticipates deliverance. V 8 strengthens the petition in vv 6–7 and is really not a thanksgiving for help already received. Mowinckel (*PIW*, I, 219–20) places this psalm in a group which he calls "protective psalms," because they express prayer to Yahweh for protection against imminent danger. Mowinckel argues that such psalms have more confidence and assurance of getting help than do the psalms of lamentation. Kraus places Ps 54 in the broad category of "prayer songs," under the Hebrew תפלה (I, 49–54; *Psalms 1–59*, 47–56), but with petition and complaint predominating.

The situation reflected in the psalm is that of a worshiper who is under strong attack from ruthless opponents (v 5). The "strangers" of v 5 suggests the possibility of a prayer of a king for deliverance from foreign foes (e.g., Dahood). This could be the case and the psalm be treated as a king's prayer (see Johnson, *CPIP*, 359–64). However, it is not certain that "strangers" refers to foreign enemies (see below). Kraus is among those who think the psalm is appropriate for a persecuted worshiper, probably a poor person who has fled to the temple area for refuge and awaits God's judgment with confidence (also Beyerlin, *Die Rettung der Bedrängten*, 23; Hubbard, *Dynamics*, 107–8). Hubbard stresses the legal language in the psalm, used, however, in the context of a dynamic process dependent on Yahweh. Mowinckel (I, 217) suggests that the "I" in such psalms as this is an individual speaking for the congregation. J. Becker (*Israels deutet seine Psalmen*, 64–65) argues that Ps 54 belongs to a group of psalms that were originally individual laments but were reworked and given a new interpretation in the post-exilic period as psalms of the community. The "I" of the individual lament has become "Israel." He contends that the following psalms show signs of such re-interpretation: 9, 10, 22, 40, 45, 54, 56, 59, 66, 68, 69, 85, 93, 102, 107, 108, and 118 (see also his *Wege der Psalmen exegese* [Stuttgart: Katholisches Bibelwerk, 1975]). In the case of Ps 54, Becker argues that the major clue is the *zarim* (זרים, "strangers/foreigners") of v 5, which he thinks would be more appropriate as *zedim* (זדים, "insolent/arrogant persons") with the verb "rise up against me" (see note 5.a.). According to Becker, the change was deliberate, and not a matter of textual corruption. He considers especially instructive the use of first person in Isa 25:1–5 and Ps 44:5, 7 (Becker, 23). An alternative explanation for the change to a first person speaker is that the compositions in question assume an alternation of speakers (see Craigie, *Form/Structure/Setting* on Ps 44). However, this would negate the possibility of a change of meaning in the present form from an earlier form. A major flaw in Becker's thesis is the probability that the "I" in the laments always represented the community or group to one degree or another. It is unlikely that the speakers in very many psalms voice purely personal concerns.

Any attempt to date a psalm like this is probably a futile effort. Some commentators argue for rather late post-exilic dating (e.g. Oesterley, Buttenwieser). With more reason, Kraus suggests that the "theology of the name" in the psalm points to a post-Deuteronomic dating. A more precise suggestion is probably not wise.

The structure of the psalm is not complicated. A superscription with a historical note is found in vv 1–2. Vv 3–4 contain a prayer for help. V 5 is a description of the speaker's troubles. A prayer for the judgment of the suppliant's foes appears in vv 6–7. A vow to offer sacrifice (v 8) and a statement of assurance (v 9) conclude the poem.

Comment

Superscription (54:1–2). The historical note in v 2 relates the psalm to an incident in the career of David, apparently to 1 Sam 23:19. The association of the psalm with this incident probably arose from a wordplay between v 3 ("and ruthless ones *seek my life*") and 1 Sam 23:15 ("And David was afraid because Saul had come out to *seek his life*"). The Ziphites lived in a hill town southeast of Hebron (see also 1 Sam 26:1).

Prayer for help (54:3–4). The prayer uses the vocative form in addressing God, which is characteristic of the laments. The distinctive element here is the prayer for deliverance by the name of Yahweh. The prayer presupposes a theology of the Name, which is an expression of the presence of God (for discussion see G. von Rad, *Old Testament Theology,* tr. D. M. G. Stalker [New York: Harper, 1962], I, 179–87; T. N. D. Mettinger, *The Dethronement of Sabaoth: Studies in the Shem and Kabod Theologies,* trans. F. H. Cryer, ConB, Old Testament Series 18 [Lund: Gleerup, 1982], 38–79). The Name carried something of the essential nature and power of God. To invoke his name was to invoke his presence. The Name theology is especially evident in the Deuteronomic writings. The Israelites were to worship at the place chosen by Yahweh where he would "put his name" (see Deut 12:5, 11, 21, passim; also Exod 20:24). The use of the Name to protect both the transcendence and presence of Yahweh is especially present in the Solomonic address to the people and prayer at the dedication of the temple (1 Kgs 8:1–66). Yahweh is repeatedly affirmed to be in heaven, but his powerful presence is invoked because his name is in the temple (see R. E. Clements, *God and Temple* [Philadelphia: Fortress Press, 1965], 90–99; for an overview of "name" in the Psalter, see H.-J. Kraus, *Theology of the Psalms,* trans. K. Crim [Minneapolis: Augsburg, 1979/86], 17–31).

The verb "save" (ישע) carries the idea of "help/deliver/rescue," probably going back to a root idea of "to be wide/broad," and thus in the causative form it conveys the idea of "to make room" or "to free from constricting circumstances." Either God or man can be the subject of the verb (e.g., in 2 Kgs 16:7 Ahaz asks the king of Assyria to "save" him). The divine ability to save, of course, greatly exceeds that of human power. Weiser (415) remarks that "the worshiper confides in the superior power of God at a time when he [*sic*] has nothing to expect from the power of man." The suppliant wants God to hear the prayer and respond to it. The exact nature of the divine response desired is not specified, but in the context it seems likely that victory over the threats of enemies is the main point (v 9).

The second line of v 3 uses the verb דין ("defend/judge"), which carries ideas associated with legal settings. However, it also occurs in contexts dealing with victory in battle (see Gen 49:16–17; Ps 110:6). Claus Westermann (*Elements of Old Testament Theology,* tr. D. W. Stott [Atlanta: John Knox Press, 1978/82], 36–40) has surveyed the meaning of God's saving action in the OT and comes to the conclusion that "*God's saving has comprehensive significance*" (40) and stresses that, while there are major differentiations between God's saving in the OT and his saving in the NT, "God is the savior both in the Old and in the New Testament" (40). The comprehensive and indispensable saving works of God are of central significance in both Testaments.

Description of trouble (54:5). The "strangers" of the MT may denote foreigners and suggest the interpretation of the psalm as a prayer by a king. But Becker's argument (see above) that the psalm is the prayer of an Israelite in the post-exilic period speaking as the embodiment of Israel about the "strangers" or foreign people who threaten the nation should not be overlooked. If the word is used metaphorically, the reference is to those members of the suppliant's own community who are not true members of the Yahweh-community (Weiser). They are ruthless persons: "who have no regard for Yahweh." If this is the case, they have made themselves outsiders by their behavior. V 5c is a key statement in the psalm: "those who have no regard for God." Yahweh does not have his proper place with these people. They arrogantly seek to ignore the will of the God who matters.

Prayer for judgment (54:6–7). V 6 is used to enhance the forcefulness of the request in v 7. Since Yahweh is the suppliant's helper and sustainer, let him allow the evil designed for the suppliant to recoil on the enemies. In so doing, Yahweh will demonstrate his faithfulness (or "truth") to those who depend upon him. Kraus notes that v 7 touches on the problematic subject of the act-consequence relationship, i.e., the extent to which an act, good or evil, activates power inherent in the deed itself which sooner or later returns the appropriate consequence onto the doer (for discussion see G. von Rad, *Wisdom in Israel* [Nashville: Abingdon Press, 1972], 128–37; *Old Testament Theology,* tr. D. M. G. Stalker [New York: Harper, 1962], 384–86; Pss 57:7; 141:10.) The discussion in this area owes much to the provocative article of K. Koch, "Gibt es ein Vergeltungsdogma in Alten Testament?"; ET in *Theodicy in the Old Testament,* ed. J. L. Crenshaw [Philadelphia: Fortress Press, 1983], 57–87. The *kethiv* reading adopted in the *Translation* (see note 7.a.) reflects more of a built-in-consequence approach than does the reading in the margin, which is a causative and assumes that God is the subject of the verb: "Turn back the evil on my foes." However, the second color makes it clear that the action requested is not exclusively inherent in the evil itself; the speaker does not ask for the automatic function of a system. God is asked to silence the foes; both the permissive will and the active will of God are involved.

Vow and statement of assurance (54:8–9). The suppliant anticipates the time when a sacrifice of thanksgiving and praise to the Name of Yahweh will be willingly made. The reference to a sacrifice freely or willingly made turns away from any sense of a legal requirement or of any kind of magical use of sacrifice (see Exod 46:12; Ezra 3:5; 2 Chr 31:14). The verb (ידה) conveys the idea of expressing the praise of Yahweh's name in the form of thanksgiving. The speaker looks forward to a joyful thanksgiving sacrifice and for an occasion to affirm the goodness of Yahweh's name (for the thank-offering ceremony see Pss 22:25–26; 40:6–10; 50:14; 61:9; 116:12–19). The psalm concludes with a strong statement of deliverance and victory (v 9), which to some degree, at least, is already happening. The speaker anticipates as already having occurred a triumphal looking at the discomfiture of the enemies (cf. Pss 58:11; 59:11; 92:12).

Explanation

The major stress in the psalm is clearly on the powerful and effective Name of Yahweh. Yahweh may seem absent from the world, but those who invoke his Name with faith and courage will discover the reality of his awesome presence. Those who forget his Name and seek to disregard his will may experience the terrible recoil of their own wickedness, a recoil which is sustained by divine power. The message of the psalm is clear enough: the Name of Yahweh will not fail the suppliant in a time of crisis. The enemies will not prevail. Yahweh will make a necessary connection between act and consequence, and the power of ruthless foes will be turned back against themselves.

Weiser (416–17) finds the psalm severely marred by the worshiper's unwillingness to give himself up to God and to be willing to accept and patiently endure suffering. He complains about "human self-will and man's low instincts of vindictiveness and gloating" in the psalm and concludes that the prayer is "unable to exercise a liberating influence; for it does not lead on to the uttermost depths of ultimate truth." Weiser is correct to say that the prayer is subject to the judgment of Christ, as indeed the entire OT is, but he surely asks too much from these brief verses out of the traditions of ancient Israel. It is enough to let them bear their message of the powerful name of Yahweh and their defiance of those human beings who disregard God and seem so often to do so well. In a world which sometimes seems to be one big lie, this psalm declares that the "truth" (v 7) of God will triumph (v 9). We know that there is more to be said beyond this psalm, but let it say what it has to say without too quickly bringing it under the perspective of the Cross. There is a time for judgment, and there is a time for forgiveness.

The Complaint of a Citizen of a Vile City Betrayed by a Friend   *(55:1–24)*

Bibliography

Dahood, M. "A Sea of Troubles: Notes on Psalms 55:3–4 and 140:10–11." *CBQ* 41 (1979) 604–7. ————. "Philological Observations on Five Bib Texts." *Bib* 63 (1982) 390–94.

Translation

1   For the leader; [a] with instrumental music; [b] a Davidic *maskil.* [c]

2(1)   *Give ear, O God, to my prayer,*   (3+3)
      and do not ignore [a] *my plea for favor.*

³⁽²⁾   *Give attention to me—and answer me;*   (3+2)
      *my complaint has me at my wits' end.*ᵃ
      *I am distraught*ᵇ
⁴⁽³⁾   *from the voice of the enemy,*   (3+3+3+2)
      *from the threat*ᵃ *of the wicked;*
      *for they move*ᵇ *evil over on me,*
      *and hunt me down*ᶜ *in wrath.*
⁵⁽⁴⁾   *My heart races in my breast;*   (3+4)
      *the terrors of death*ᵃ *have fallen upon me.*
⁶⁽⁵⁾   *Fear and trembling have invaded me;*   (3+2)
      *horror*ᵃ *overwhelms me;*
⁷⁽⁶⁾   *So I say,*   (1+3+2)
      "Oh, that I had wings like a dove!
      I could fly away and be at rest.
⁸⁽⁷⁾   *Indeed, I could flee far away,*   (3+2)
      *and live*ᵃ *in the wilderness.* SELAH.
⁹⁽⁸⁾   *I could hurry to a shelter for myself*   (3+3)
      *from the wind of a furious storm."*ᵃ
¹⁰⁽⁹⁾ *Destroy (them),*ᵃ *O Lord!*
      *Confound their speech,*ᵇ   (2+2+2+2)
      for I see Violence and Strife in the city;
¹¹⁽¹⁰⁾   *day and night they make rounds*ᵃ *on its walls;*   (3+2)
      Evil and Trouble are within it.
¹²⁽¹¹⁾   *Destruction*ᵃ *is there;*   (2+3)
      *Oppression*ᵇ *and Deceit never leave its public square.*
¹³⁽¹²⁾*For it is not*ᵃ *an enemy who taunts me—*   (3+1+3+2)
      *I could bear that.*ᵇ
      The one who hates me has not vaunted himself against me—
      I could hide from him!
¹⁴⁽¹³⁾*But it is you, one like myself,*ᵃ   (3+2)
      *My buddy,*ᵇ *my close friend—*
¹⁵⁽¹⁴⁾   *together, we had sweet fellowship,*ᵃ   (4+4)
      *as we walked in the crowd*ᵇ *at the house of God.*
¹⁶⁽¹⁵⁾*Let death surprise*ᵃ *them!*   (3+3+3)
      Let them go down to Sheol alive,
      *for Wickedness is at home*ᵇ *in them.*ᶜ
¹⁷⁽¹⁶⁾*As for me, I call*ᵃ *to God,*   (3+2)
      and Yahweh will save me.
¹⁸⁽¹⁷⁾   *Evening, morning, and noon,*   (3+2+2)
      I complain and moan,
      *and he will hear*ᵃ *my voice!*
¹⁹⁽¹⁸⁾*He will redeem*ᵃ *my life in well-being*ᵇ   (3+2[3]+3)
      *from the battle*ᶜ *against me,*
      *when many*ᵈ *oppose me.*ᵉ
²⁰⁽¹⁹⁾*God will hear (me) and he will answer them*ᵃ*—*   (3+2+4+3)
      *(God) enthroned from of old,*ᵇ SELAH.
      *(God) who does not change,*ᶜ*—*
      (he will answer) those who have no fear of God.

21(20) *He has stretched out his hands against those at peace with him;* [a]   (3+2)
    he has profaned his covenant.

22(21) *His speech is smoother than cream,* [a]   (3+2+3+2)
    but his heart is war!
    His words are more soothing than oil,
    but they are drawn swords! [b]

23(22) *Cast your lot in life* [a] *on Yahweh*   (3+2+4)
    and he will sustain you;
    he will not let the righteous be shaken [b] *forever.*

24(23) *And you, O God,*   (2+3+3+3)
    you will make them go down to the pit of corruption [a]—
    those murderous [b] *and treacherous men;*
    they will not live out half their days.
    But as for me, I trust in you.

Notes

1.a. See n. 51:1–2.a.

1.b. See n. 54:1–2.b.

1.c. See n. 52:1–2.c.

2.a. The hithpael of עלם, "conceal oneself," has here the force of "ignore" or "withhold help" as in Deut 22:4, "You shall not see your brother's ass or his ox fallen down by the way, and withhold your help from them [lit. "and hide yourself from them"]." See also Pss 10:1; Isa 58:7; Job 42:3; cf. Job 38:2.

3.a. The meaning of the verb אָרִיד is uncertain. It is frequently assumed to be from a root רוד which is understood from Arabic to mean "to wander to and fro" or "to be restless" (see also Gen 27:40). LXX reads ἐλυπήθην, "to give pain to/to grieve," probably suggesting Heb. רעע, "to be in a bad or evil condition" (Jerome and Vg seem to agree with LXX). D. W. Thomas (*TRP*, 10) reads אֶרֹּד, "I am beaten down" from רדד (also Kraus). In his commentary, Dahood takes the verb as an aphel masc. sing. impv. from ירד, "to go down," and translates "descend at my complaint." In a later study (*Bib* 63 [1982] 390–94) he argues for the less probable reading of אָרִיד as from ארה, "to pluck/grasp," yielding the translation, "grasp my hand in my anxiety."

RSV has בְּשִׂיחִי as "by my trouble"; others have "by my complaint"—about the dangerous situation depicted in the following verses. The word is usually associated with speaking in one form or another; see v 18. NEB has "for my cares give me no peace."

3.b. BDB assumes that אָהִימָה is from הום or הים, which means "to murmur, be driven about, distracted." The form is cohortative, which gives it "a modal force not easy in the context" (Briggs; see n. 57:5.b.). LXX has ἐταράχθην, and Vg *conturbatus*, "troubled" or "disturbed." Several commentators suggest reading from המה, "to growl, groan," vocalizing אֶהֱמָיָה as in 77:4 or אֶהֱמֶה as in v 18. The verb is contained in v 3 but rather clearly applies to what follows in v 4.

4.a. The word עָקַת appears only here in the MT and its meaning is uncertain. It may be from Aramaic עוק, "to press" (equal to Heb צוק) and thus "to oppress" (see root עוק in Amos 2:13, and derivative noun in Ps 66:11). KB (730) suggests that the construct form here means "pressure," perhaps an Aramaism for Heb. צרה (Kraus). The change to מִזַּעֲקַת (so Oesterley, discussed in Gunkel), "from the cry of the wicked," is not likely (see Briggs). NEB, "at the shrill clamour of the wicked enemies," reflects the understanding of the word from Arabic as meaning "cry" (see Thomas, *TRP*, 20). In his commentary Dahood takes עקת from Ugar. 'q ("eyeball") and translates "the stare" (adopted by NIV). In a later study (*CBQ* 41 [1979] 604–7), he takes a different approach and argues for two broken construct chains in 55:4. He explains עקת as a 1st person singular of the verb עוק ("to press/compress," repointing to עֲקֹתִי) and translates as "constrained by the presence of the wicked." In the second case, he divides ימישׁו (from מוש, "totter/shake/slip") into יָם, "sea" and the hiphil verb ישׁו (derived from נשׁה, "to stretch out/spread out") and parses יָם as a construct of אָוֶן ("trouble/evil") with the כ as emphatic: "Indeed they spread as a sea of troubles over me."

4.b. Kraus thinks that יָמִישׁו is not likely in this sentence and prefers the LXX's ἐξέκλιναν, which may reflect ישׁו from נשׁה ("to stretch out/extend"). Dahood and NEB translate the verb as "heap (on)" (see n. 4.a. above for another approach taken by Dahood; also see Dahood on 140:11; NEB has "tipped upon"). The verb מוֹט means "to totter/shake/slip," and though the hiphil appears only here and in 140:11 there seems to be no reason to reject the meaning of "cause to move." "They bring down on me" is a possible meaning in v 4 (Kissane; NIV).

4.c. The verb שָׂטַם is usually understood to mean "bear a grudge/cherish animosity against" and so RSV, "they cherish enmity against me." However, N. H. Tur-Sinai, *The Book of Job* (265), argues for the meaning "and he hunteth me" in Job 16:9. M. H. Pope, *Job* (AB 15, 114), translates in Job 16:9 as "rages against me." E. Dhorme, (*A Commentary on the Book of Job*, tr. H. Knight [London: Nelson, 1967], 234), argues for the idea of "pursue" or "persecute" in Job 16:9 and Ps 55:4. NAB has "and with fury they persecute me." NEB and NIV both use "revile me." The contexts seem to indicate an active condition. Dahood (I, 237) thinks "slander" is best.

5.a. Possibly the expression should be a superlative, "deadly terrors"; so Thomas, *TRP*, 20. It is also possible that מָוֶת is the result of dittography and should be omitted (so Briggs, Gunkel, Oesterley).

6.a. LXX has "darkness." פַּלָּצוּת occurs only three times elsewhere in MT (Isa 21:4; Job 7:18; 21:6) and the verb is found once (Job 9:6). It may mean "shuddering" in one or two contexts and perhaps here.

8.a. The verb is לִין, which normally means "to remain for a night," but some usage seems to indicate it can be another word for "to live" (e.g., Ruth 1:16; Prov 15:31). NIV has "stay in"; Dahood, "it would settle." Perhaps we could translate "and bivouac in the wilderness."

9.a. סָעָה is found only here and its precise meaning is uncertain. BDB assumes on basis of Syriac and Arabic stems that the basic idea is "rushing" and thus "rushing wind." LXX has ἀπὸ ὀλιγοψυχίας καὶ καταιγίδος, "from faint-heartedness and tempestuousness," which may reflect מֵרוּחַ צְעָרָה וְסָעַר. Some commentators suspect dittography and delete סָעָה, reading מֵרוּחַ סְעָרָה, "from the wind (or roar) of the storm" (e.g., Kraus). NEB has "from wind and storm," apparently מֵרוּחַ מִסְעָר. Dahood relates סעה to Ugaritic sᶜt and translates "sweeping." The meaning is probably something like "raging" or "sweeping"—metaphorical in nature, of course.

10.a. RSV adds "their plans" after the verb, following Targum. A. A. Anderson suggests that the two verbs of v 10 be coordinated (cf. GKC, 120d) and rendered "Confuse completely, O Lord, their speech." It is doubtful, however, that בלע means "confuse, confound, frustrate" (BDB, 118; KB, 131). The word seems to refer consistently to "swallowing" and thus to destroying or removal (see J. Schupphaus, *TDOT*, II, 136–9). If the verbs are coordinated, as Anderson suggests, the translation could be "O Lord, confuse (and) confound their speech!" Kraus (following Gunkel) reads מִסְעָר ("from the storm") from the previous verse with בלע pointed as בֶּלַע ("swallowing = destruction") and translates "from the destructive storm." However, he finds it necessary to replace אֲדֹנָי ("O Lord") with גְּרֹנָם ("their neck, throat") and then repoint פַּלַּג ("confound") as פֶּלֶג, ("channel") as of a stream, with reference to their speech (also, Kissane). With Gunkel, Kraus seems to assume the continuation of the picture of a bird, which flies for refuge from the destructive storm which comes from the throat of the foes. However, the emendations required are too extensive to be convincing. NEB has "from blasts of calumny," apparently reading בלע as בֶּלַע, "calumny" (see KB, 131).

10.b. Lit. "split their tongue." Dahood repoints פַּלַּג לְשׁוֹנָם as פֶּלֶג לְשׁוֹנָם, lit. "the cleft of their tongue" and makes it the direct object of בַּלַּע: "Destroy, O Lord, their forked tongue!" It does not seem necessary, however, to insist on such a literal meaning of פלג as Dahood does here.

11.a. The subject of the verb is not stated. The reference can be to "Violence and Strife" in v 10, or it could be to the evildoers. The picture could be that of besiegers prowling about the walls looking for a weak point. But the ironic idea of "Violence and Strife" as watchmen on the city walls is more probable. The city is "protected" by deadly watchmen and "Evil and Trouble" live in it with Violence and Strife.

12.a. See n. 52:4.a.

12.b. The word תֹּךְ is found also in Pss 10:6 and 72:14. LXX has τόκος, "interest on money," both here and in 72:14. The word probably has to do with varied sorts of injustice and injury.

13.a. LXX seems to suggest לוֹ for MT לֹא, reading "If an enemy . . ." as in NAB.

13.b. No object is expressed for the verb, but there is no need to supply one; cf. 51:18.

14.a. Lit. "a man according to my value (or rank)." The idea of rank is likely to be secondary to that of similarity of mind and interests. NIV has "like myself." NAB has "my other self," and NEB has "a man of my own sort."

14.b. The word seems to refer to a close or intimate friend; i.e., "buddy." LXX reads "guide" (so also KJV), as אַלּוּף, II, used in references like Exod 15:15; Zech 9:7.

15.a. The word סוֹד may refer to the confidential talk or the plans of a group (e.g., Pss 64:3; 83:4; Prov 11:13). It may also refer to a group of people who meet and share a close relationship (Pss 89:8; 111:1; Jer 6:11; 15:17; Job 19:19; Gen 49:6). The group may be a happy one (as in Jer 15:17) or it may be evil in nature (Ps 64:3). L. Köhler (*Hebrew Man,* tr. P. R. Ackroyd [Nashville: Abingdon Press, 1957], 84–91) gives an interesting projection of the סוֹד in terms of village life and suggests that it could apply to the gathering of the adult men in the gate area after the evening meal for exchange of news, conversation, and wisdom sayings. The complexity of the word is illustrated by the use of 12 different words in the Greek texts for the 21 uses of the noun in MT (M. Saebo, *TDOT,* II, 147). The LXX has ἐδέσματα, which could represent צֵיד, "food" shared in companionship, but it may be only a translation to get the force of סוֹד.

15.b. רָגַשׁ appears only here, but as רִגְשָׁה in Ps 64:3 and in verb form in 2:1. Both BDB and KB assume that the basic idea is "to be in tumult." But its use with סוֹד in Pss 2:1; 55:14; 64:3 points to the idea of gathering together or assembling (see Briggs, I, 17–18; Dahood, I, 7). The idea of "crowd" or "throng," in this case a crowd gathered for a festal occasion, seems best. The attachment of נהלך ברגש to the next verse is suggested by some (e.g., Gunkel and Kraus). רגש is then read as רַגַע or רַגָּשׁ and נהלך is read as יַהֲלֹכוּ or יְהַלְכוּ, "Let them go quickly [*or,* with quaking] to (their death)," assuming that the curse begins.

16.a. *Kethiv* has a pl. noun meaning "desolations" from שָׁו. *Qere* is more probable: יַשִּׁי מָוֶת (= יַשִּׁיא מָוֶת). Briggs reads the verb as hiphil imp. defective from נשׁא, "beguile" (also Perowne). Gunkel derives the verb from שׁאא, "devastate/ruin." Dahood argues for a root ישׁה or ושׁה from which is derived תּוּשִׁיָּה, which he contends means "victory" or "success" (also, M. Pope, *Job,* AB 15, 90; Job 12:16a), and thus translates "May death overcome them." The ideas of "beguile" and therefore "surprise" seem best, particularly in a context of premature, and thus unexpected, death (cf. 89:22).

16.b. Lit. "in their living place." מָגוּר is a "sojourning place" or "living place" (Job 18:19; Ps 119:54; Ezek 20:38). The RSV, "let them go away in terror," represents an unnecessary emendation (עברד במגור בקרבם), nor should במגורם be omitted (so Buttenwieser, 720, with Syriac).

16.c. Perhaps the בקרבם should be deleted as an explanatory gloss which seems to overload the line.

17.a. The tense of the imperfect and the verbs which follow is uncertain. Dahood argues for past action, and says that his judgment is confirmed by the use of the *waw* consecutive in the expression "and so hear my voice" in 18c. The context of the psalm, however, makes past action difficult to assume for all the verbs in 16–19; cf. 2–6, 23. Leslie McFall (*The Enigma of the Hebrew Verbal System* [Sheffield: Almond Press, 1982], 18), cites וישמע in Ps 55:18 [17] as one of some 30 examples of the *waw* consecutive with imperfect as having future tense. It should be added, however, that he thinks there are some 14,202 cases of past tense (see Appendix 1, Table 2). Cf. Ps 64:8–10. After a present time situation, a following *wayyqtl* form represents a sequential or explanatory situation in the same time frame (B. K. Waltke and M. O'Connor, *An Introduction to Biblical Hebrew Syntax* [Winona Lake, IN: Rivenbraun, 1990], 559 [33, 3, 3c], who cite Ps 3:5 among their examples). If this pattern is followed, the verbs could be persistent present tense in every case in vv 17–18, including the *wayyqtl* form in 18c. However, it seems more likely to me that future tense is intended in 17b (why the complaint if Yahweh already saves?) and that the *wayyqtl* form in 18c follows as an explanatory statement for 17b. The parallelism is: 17a and 18ab; 17b and 18c. The future saving action of Yahweh is given further explanation in v 19.

18.a. See n. 17.a.

19.a. The perfect form of פדה is eased by LXX's future tense which may read יִפְדֶּה; Syriac = adjective, פָּדֶה, "redeem." But MT may be retained, with the perfect read as future, or, perhaps, a perfect of resolve: "He is going to redeem my life . . ." (cf. Waltke and O'Connor, *Biblical Hebrew Syntax,* 489).

19.b. שָׁלוֹם has a wide range of meaning and the English "peace" is too restricted. Perhaps the best idea here is "victory"; cf. Jer 43:12; also Ps 29:11. Dahood's change to piel inf. const. ("making payment") from שׁלם, "to pay compensation," is not necessary, nor is his repointing פדה as a participle, "the Ransomer."

19.c. The word קְרָב means "war" or "battle" (from the verbal idea of approaching with hostile intent), cf. v 21; 68:30; 78:9; 144:1; Job 38:23; Zech 14:3. LXX reflects מקרבים, "from those drawing near," or perhaps qal inf. const. from קרב. Gunkel and Kraus prefer כִּי קְרָבִים לִי רֹבִים "for the archers are drawing near to me," assuming that רֹבֶה in Gen 21:20 means "archer." NEB has "when they beset me like archers," probably from מקרבים לי כרבים. Dahood changes to קָרַב, "he (El) drew near," but without good reason.

19.d. The prep. -בְּ may be for emphasis (Dahood, Anderson) or *beth essentiae* (cf. GKC, 119i).

19.e. עִמָּדִי, "with me," occurs in contexts of hostile intent; e.g., Gen 20:9; Job 10:17; 13:19 (with רִיב, also Exod 17:2; Job 23:6; 31:13). Syriac probably reads בְּרָבִים, "in controversies."

20.a. MT reads "and he will answer them." LXX, Vg, and Jerome assume piel from ענה (יַעֲנֵם), "he will humble them," and this is commonly adopted. However, MT may be correct. The normal sequence with "hear" is "answer," and the "answer" here may assume that God will answer them judicially; i.e., in judgment (see Delitzsch). Thus the meaning may be essentially the same. The *waw* on יֹשֵׁב is explanatory and emphatic.

20.b. Gunkel, Kraus, Thomas (*TRP*, 21), and NEB follow the interpretation that there is a reference here to Arabic tribes from the East. Thomas reads יִשְׁמָעֵאל וִיעֲנֵ[י]ם, "Ishmael and the tribes of the desert" (also NEB). Gunkel and Kraus read יִשְׁמָעֵאל וְיַעְלָם, "Ishmael and Jaalam" (or Jalam, see Gen 36:5, 14, 18; 1 Chr 1:35). But this is too conjectural and not supported by the versions. For the idea of God enthroned from of old, see 9:7; 29:10; 74:12; Deut 33:27; Hab 1:12.

20.c. The meaning is uncertain. חֲלִיפוֹת can mean "a change of garment" (Gen 45:22) or "relays" (1 Kgs 5:28[14]); in Job 14:14 it may mean "relief" or "reward" (see N. H. Tur-Sinai, *The Book of Job* [Jerusalem: Kiryath-Sepher, 1957], 236–39; Pope, 102), while in 1QM 16.10 the word is used in the military sense of "reserve" (A. A. Anderson). An Arabic root suggests "covenant/oath," and "faithfulness" in keeping such, a reading reflected in NEB: "who have no respect for an oath." RSV has "because they keep no law." The Greek translations suggest the idea of "exchange" or "barter." Kraus and Schmidt think the meaning here is that of unwillingness to exchange prisoners of war. Another line of interpretation is to refer to lack of change on the part of those who have no fear of God. The idea then can be (1) that they have suffered no setbacks in life nor received appropriate retribution for their deeds, or (2) that they are people who never intend to change their behavior; they are set in their ways. NAB has "for improvement is not in them," and apparently understands "change" in the sense of a modification of bad behavior. JB has "no change of heart for them"; NIV reads "men who never change their ways." Dahood notes correctly that לָמוֹ may mean "for him" in some contexts (see GKC, 103f, n. 3) and reads with reference to God, "in him there is no variation," and comments, "Unlike the Canaanite deities, the Primeval One of Israel is not a capricious God." I assume that God is the subject.

21.a. For שָׁלוֹם in this sense, see Ps 41:10; Jer 20:10; 38:22; cf. Pss 7:5; 69:23. The plural may indicate that the worshiper belonged to a circle which was victimized by the action of an unfaithful member. The emendation to sing. "his friend" is accepted by some (Briggs, Gunkel, Kraus). LXX reads with reference to God, probably reading בשלמיו as בְּשַׁלֵּם, "in retribution": "He (God) has reached out his hand in retribution." Dahood reads "his closest ally" and interprets as a reference to the psalmist himself, understanding the plural as an example of intensity or perhaps an old genitive ending with a sing. suffix.

22.a. MT apparently reads, "The creamy things (words?) of his mouth were smooth." מַחְמָאֹת appears only here and seems to be a fem. plural noun (construct). The usual word is חֶמְאָה, "cream, butter, curds." Some ms evidence (see *BHS*) points to the reading מֵחֶמְאָה or more probably מַחֲמָאוֹת (see Dahood), "more than cream." LXX indicates פָּנָיו, "his face," which is better with the pl. verb than "his mouth."

22.b. The word פְּתִחוֹת appears only here (for figurative use of verb forms, see Ezek 21:33 [28]; Ps 37:14; cf. Pss 52:2; 59:8) but appears to mean something like "drawn swords/knives." LXX has "javelins" or "darts."

23.a. יְהָבְךָ is found only here. The word appears in the Talmud with the meaning of "burden" or "lot." LXX has "care" or "anxiety" (τὴν μέριμνάν σου). It is probably derived from a root יהב meaning "to give/provide/permit," and thus, "what he has given you," or "your lot in life" (see BDB, 396, and Dahood; the latter, however, reads as qal participle "your Benefactor").

23.b. See v 4 for the verb, which means to move or shake in a way that threatens to be destructive. Cf. 46:2, "though the mountains be moved into the heart of the seas"; also, Pss 10:6; 15:5; 16:8; 21:8; 30:7; 62:3, 7; 82:5; 93:1; etc.

24.a. The word שַׁחַת can mean "pit," along with בְּאֵר, giving rise to the translation "pit of the grave" or "the lowest pit." However, LXX has "pit of destruction [*or*, ruin]," and it is likely that some such meaning is the case for שַׁחַת here. M. Pope (*Job*, AB 15, 72–74) translates in Job 9:31 as "filth," with reference to the putrescent character of the netherworld, particularly the loathsome quality of its watery nature. Dahood prefers "sludgy Pit."

24.b. See Ps 51:16 for דָמִים, "bloods."

Form/Structure/Setting

In general terms this psalm is a lament of an individual, though (as in the case of Ps 54) it has strong statements of assurance and exhortation which move it somewhat toward the thanksgiving genre. Mowinckel (*PIW,* I, 219) places the psalm among the national psalms of lamentation; "I"-psalms which are in reality national (9–10; 13; 31; 35; 42–43; 55; 56; 59; 69; 94; 102; 109; 142), in which the king or leader speaks on behalf of the whole community. An argument for the psalm as the prayer of a king is made by J. H. Eaton (*Kingship,* 74–75).

Dahood follows a suggestion of Gunkel (238) that the psalm was composed by an Israelite resident in a pagan city. The betrayer who is denounced in vv 13–15 would be a fellow Jew with whom the worshiper had made a trip or pilgrimage to Jerusalem. If this is the case, the psalm possibly shares a common viewpoint with Ps 42 and may belong to the exilic period (so Deissler, II, 52). In a similar manner, B. D. Eerdmans thinks of the psalm as the hymn of an Israelite who was away from home and in great terror in a city which he could not leave (285).

The evidence is too scanty and unfocused to support, or decisively refute, any of these views. It is best to adopt a more general position, like that of Kraus who classifies the psalm as a prayer song of an individual (note the תפלה in v 2, and see Ps 54) who is undergoing intolerable strain because of evil and dangerous conditions, and especially because of the betrayal of a former friend (vv 13–15, 21–22).

The title ascribes the psalm to David, and it has been commonly supposed to refer to David's relationship with Ahithophel during the rebellion of Absalom. However, the circumstances in the psalm do not fit well with the narratives which refer to Ahithophel. For example, the prayer of David in 2 Sam 15:31 has a different tone from that of the psalm, and the psalm supposes that the speaker is in the city, while in 2 Sam 15:30 David only knew of the treachery of Ahithophel after he left Jerusalem (see discussion of Perowne and Kirkpatrick).

Vv 7–8 suggest a relationship to Jer 9:1–2, and occasionally Jeremiah is suggested as the author, or else the one who provided inspiration for the psalm. The treacherous friend of v 13 would be Pashhur, who beat Jeremiah and put him in stocks (Jer 20:1–6). The conditions in the city, as described in the psalm, are similar to the descriptions in Jer 29:5–6. However, there is no reason to think that Pashhur's relationship with Jeremiah was the kind described in the psalm. The descriptive language is not unlike more than one example of prophetic preaching and probably is drawn from common literary traditions. Thus the date and the identity of the psalm and the people in it elude specific determination.

Gunkel and others argue that the psalm is composed of two separate parts (2–19b, 23; 19c–22, 24). Kraus divides into 2–19a and 19b–24. Jacquet divides as follows, with some transposition of verses:

Appeal to Yahweh	2–10b
Angry complaint	10cd–15; 21–23
Petition for divine intervention	17–20 (with v 16)
Final statement	24

The shift of subject matter can be accounted for by (1) the nature of such laments/prayers and (2) the portrayal of the emotional stress of the worshiper. The psalm is held together by a common theme of the trouble brought by the treacherous actions of a friend. Also, note the use of the verb מוש ("move/shake") in vv 4 and 23, a wordplay which links the first part of the psalm with the second, which is also true of ירד ("go down") in vv 16 and 24.

The text is difficult and all translations represent a considerable number of rather subjective judgments (Dahood is a dissenter to the common opinion and finds this psalm to be a happy hunting ground). The variations in the major English translations reveal the presence of problems. The *Translation* should be considered tentative in a good many cases.

The "jagged, hectic character" (Eaton, *Kingship*, 74) of the psalm's content is not always easy to follow. The following outline is used in the *Comment* section:

Superscription	1
Address to God	2–3b
Complaint	3c–6
A wish to escape	7–9
Prayer and complaint	10–12
Betrayal by a friend	13–15
Prayer for judgment	16
Testimony of confidence in the faithfulness of God	17–20
The unfaithful friend	21–22
Words of encouragement	23–24

Comment

Superscription (55:1). For the expressions in the title, see *Notes*.

Address to God (55:2–3b). The suppliant pleads with intense language for a hearing by God. For details of the language, see the *Notes*. Notice the emphasis on God's not hiding himself from the situation of the worshiper (see note 2.a.). The verb carries the idea of ignoring or "staying in the dark" regarding a situation; e.g., Deut 22:4. For the strong imperative "give attention," see Pss 5:3; 17:1; 61:2; 146:7.

Complaint (55:3c–6). The vivid language conveys an impression of almost intolerable strain. The source of such great distress is the threats and persecution of the wicked. The enemies are human beings, but the description of them has an eerie, nightmarish quality, in which they take on the character of demons and the dread reality of the terrors of death (see Ps 88:4). The suppliant is overcome with shuddering horror (v 6). The enemy is unidentified, beyond being the wicked (v 4).

A wish to escape (55:7–9). In the midst of great distress the suppliant wishes for the wings of a dove to fly away and be at rest. The choice of a dove is probably due to the practice of doves nesting in the clefts of hard-to-reach precipices, above and beyond the "storm" of confusion and turmoil in the city (for the dove, see Cant 2:14; Jer 48:28). The "wilderness" (מדבר) has different connotations in biblical texts. In general, the "wilderness" was the area between fertile settled areas and the true desert. Wilderness areas are arid or semiarid and are not suited for permanent settlements or crops, but such areas can be used as pasture land for small stock (see S. Talmon, "Wilderness," *IDBSup*, 946–49; 1 Sam 17:28; Ps 65:13; Jer 23:10; Joel 2:22). Thus "wilderness" (מדבר) is a technical term for pastures or semiwild areas adjacent to permanent or semipermanent settlements. People are scarce in a wilderness area ("in which there is no man," Job 38:26). Like Jeremiah (Jer 9:1), the speaker in vv 7–9 thinks that simple living accommodations in the wilderness would be a place of rest from the raging disorder of the city. The suppliant would hurry to such a place like a traveler who is caught in a sudden wilderness storm and rushes for shelter.

Prayer and complaint (55:10–12). V 10 opens with a passionate request for divine action against the wicked people of the city. In v 10, there may be an allusion to the story of the Tower of Babel and the confusion of languages (Gen 11:5–9). The words of the suppliant suggest that similar action of confusion and destruction is in mind (cf. 2 Sam 15:31). The vile condition of the city is cited to affirm the justification of the drastic requests. The poet personifies the sevenfold evil characteristics of the city: Violence, Strife, Evil, Trouble, Destruction, Oppression, and Deceit. Violence and Strife are ironically described as city watchmen who make their sounds on the walls (v 11). Oppression and Deceit never leave the public square (רחוב), the broad open space in a town, usually near the gate, where social, business, and legal affairs were conducted. Such "broad ways" might also be courtyards before a temple or palace. The city is continually in the hands of people who embody the elements of wickedness and violence.

Some interpreters are quite sure that the city is Jerusalem. Thus Leslie (333) says, "The city can be only Jerusalem" (following Buttenwieser, dating the psalm to c. 312 B.C.E. when Jerusalem was conquered by Ptolemy). Such confidence is not justified. As noted above, the poet may have had a foreign city in mind, in which a faithful Israelite was living. The historical identity of the city is not determinative for the message of the psalm. For somewhat similar descriptions of social degeneration, see Isa 1:21–23; Mic 7:1–6; Hab 1:2–6.

Betrayal by a friend (55:13–15). The suppliant's distress is greatly increased because of the unfaithfulness of a trusted friend. The taunts of an enemy would be expected and could be borne with relative ease. In v 13 the enemy is said to be a former close friend, who had shared fellowship with the suppliant in the temple during the happy times of the festivals (v 15). The language is too general for any specific identification, and vv 14–15 represent a common element of distress in human affairs.

Prayer for judgment (55:16). The text shifts from singular to plural, not uncommon for imprecations (see Dahood, I, 34–35, 134, who refers to: Pss 7:2–3; 17:11–12, 13–14; 35:7–8; 109:5–6). The plural adds to the impassioned nature of the language. The prayer is for a swift and surprising judgment of death: "Let them go down to Sheol alive"—which recalls the fate of Korah and his family (Num 16:31–35). The words convey a picture of sudden judgment and death (see Prov 1:12; Isa 5:14; Ps 52:7). Let them perish as quickly as if the earth opened up and swallowed them into Sheol (the realm of the dead).

Testimony of the faithfulness of God (55:17–20). In contrast to the enemies, who do not fear God (v 20), the suppliant proclaims confidence in God's willingness to hear and to respond. The testimony has the appearance of being a public one, probably in the temple. The suppliant prays three times a day (cf. Dan 6:10; Acts 10:9, 30)—at set times? The speaker declares confidence in the eternal God, who does not change (v 20), and who will save, and in divine action which will put such people as the suppliant in an unassailable condition of well-being (v 19).

The unfaithful friend (55:21–22). The main point of the second description of the unfaithful friend seems to be that he has profaned his covenant. It is normal to translate the verb "profaned" (חלל) as "violated" a covenant, which is surely correct in terms of modern English. However, it is doubtful that the verb ever loses all its theological nuances. The root idea of חלל appears to be "untie/loosen" (see W. Dommershausen, *TDOT*, IV, 409–10), but in OT usage the principle idea is the opposite of holy; to profane is to make not-holy. All covenants have a holy quality; they lay on the makers an obligation which is in a sense "holy," even if they are what we would describe as secular. This is true especially of covenants that are confirmed by oath. The oath either directly or indirectly calls upon the deity to see that the penalty for violation is paid (see M. Weinfeld, *TDOT*, II, 260; A. A. Anderson, I, 418). To profane a covenant is to make it common, and thus to loosen the commitment of the maker and place it at his or her disposal (note the use of חלל in Deut 20:6: a man has planted a vineyard, but "has not made profane [חלל] its fruit [i.e., has not been able to use it for himself] but another will profane [חלל] its fruit"; for other uses of the verb with covenant, see Ps 89:32–35; Mal 2:10).

The covenant is not identified in the context. Those commentators who read a reference to Arabic tribes (see *Notes*), think of a covenant which binds together the members of a tribal group (e.g., Kraus). A violation of such a covenant was a grave offense. However, the covenant here may be a personal one (see 1 Sam 18:3), and the verse may reflect the pain and hurt of personal betrayal, common among the righteous. Perhaps the covenant here is paradigmatic of covenants in general. The highly descriptive language of v 22 emphasizes the severity of the offense. "The face of a murderer has hidden itself behind a mask of friendly words" (Kraus, 564). "His words were butter-slick, yet *war* was in his mind. His speech was oil-smooth, yet each word was a glittering naked sword" (Durham, 283).

Words of encouragement (55:23–24). The suppliant is encouraged (perhaps by himself) to continue to have faith in Yahweh (another usage of *Yahweh* in this Elohistic section of the Psalter). Kraus (*Psalms 1–59*, 522) argues that v 23 is an oracle of encouragement and salvation offered to the oppressed person. In any case, assurance is given to the speaker that Yahweh will sustain and protect. The message puts the suppliant among the righteous, who will not be "shaken." The word יהב ("lot," or more commonly "burden") has the idea of that which is given—the appointed lot of one's life (NEB, "your fortunes"); cf. Pss 16:5–6; 73:26; 119:57; 142:6 for somewhat similar ideas. If this verse is not taken as a message of encouragement for the suppliant, two other approaches are possible: (1) the verse is a testimony of the speaker to others, exhorting them to have faith (note, however, that the personal address in the verse is singular); (2) the verse can be treated as the taunting speech of the enemy in v 22 (so Jacquet); cf. Pss 22:9; 37:5.

In v 24, the speaker expresses to God assurance that he, God, will not allow the enemies to live out their lives in their blood-guilty and deceitful ways. The suppliant is confident that God will punish them with dreadful premature death— the terrors of which now threaten to overcome him/her (v 5). For premature death, see Pss 37:35–38; 109:8; Job 20:4–11; 21:7–13; 36:13–14; Isa 38:1–3, 10, 12. Premature death is considered generally in the OT as a great evil, the opposite of death "in a good old age" (Gen 15:15; 25:8; Job 5:26; L. R. Bailey, Sr., *Biblical Perspectives on Death* [Philadelphia: Fortress Press, 1979], 48–52).

Explanation

This psalm is marked by vivid descriptions of the troubles which beset a worshiper. The agony of the suppliant (vv 5–6) is rooted in three conditons: (1) persecution and danger (v 4); (2) the social conditions of the city in which the speaker lives (vv 10c–12); (3) the unfaithfulness of a close friend who should have given support. Perhaps the contemporary reader will identify most readily with the description of the city—a city where Violence and Strife guard the walls while vile wickedness flourishes inside. The city is not named, but it can be any city in the world—the city where I live or where you live. Many will say, "I know that city, because I live in it."

It is possible that this may be a psalm of an alien, an Israelite living in a foreign city, separated from the life in the homeland. In a sense, we all become aliens in the city, even if it is our home (so J. Ellul, *The Meaning of the City* [Eerdmans, 1970], 55). Every city is full of resident aliens. The city (or town or village; the size matters little) is a place where friends desert one another, where the bitterness of unfaithfulness poisons the inner sources of life, and where oppression and deceit never leave its public square. The loss of loyal and enduring friendship characterizes much of life in the city. Anonymity and immunization against close personal relationships is common (see H. Cox, *The Secular City* [New York: Macmillan, 1965], 38–49).

Two reactions in the psalm are worthy of special note. The first is the impulse to flee away from the city, which seems so fearful and painful (vv 7–9). This is the escapist impulse, known to all who read the words of the psalm. The wilderness lures the city dweller. It seems to offer shelter, peace, and contentment denied in urban surroundings. The seeming simplicity of the wilderness offers a refuge from the tangled complexities of urban life. Flight seems to offer so much that at times it becomes almost irresistible (on the psychology of flight, see P. Tournier, *The Healing of Persons* [New York: Harper & Row, 1965], 95–109). The wilderness, of course, is quite deceptive, as it may be the place of dire human needs and of death. Perhaps it is well to remember that the wilderness is never in itself a goal in biblical traditions but is a transition place for the passage of the people of God to some other place. The Land of Promise lies beyond the wilderness.

The second reaction is found in the message of encouragement in v 23. The suppliant is urged to cast upon Yahweh his or her lot-in-life—that which is given. Yahweh will provide for such a person, though not necessarily deliver, and not necessarily provide a way out or remove all the enemies and change all the bad situations, but he will provide the strength and resources to deal with life as it comes. The promise is that he will sustain. The verb "cast on" (v 23) suggests that God will take us as we are, in the context in which we live, wherever it is and whatever the circumstances. The final words of the psalm (v 24) indicate that the suppliant is willing to accept the word of encouragement.

The fierceness of the prayer in the verses which precede the statements of trust is somewhat of a shock to our spiritual sensitivities (see Weiser's comments, 420–21, "he is once more dominated by sentiments of vindictiveness and retaliation which contend for victory with his professions of trust in God"). For a discussion of such prayers and attitudes toward enemies, see the *Explanation* of Ps 58. The realism of these psalms is a reminder of the anguish of life for so many in the cities of the world. We look for a city "built as a city should be" (Ps 122:3), one with good foundations "whose architect and builder is God" (Heb 11:10), but in the meantime we live by faith in vile cities where Violence and Strife are the watchmen on the walls and Oppression and Deceit do business in the public square.

Excursus: Enemies in the Psalms

Bibliography

Anderson, G. W. "Enemies and Evildoers in Psalms." *BJRL* 48 (1965) 16–29. **Barth, C.** *Introduction to the Psalms.* Tr. R. A. Wilson. New York: Scribner's Sons, 1966. 43–48. **Beyerlin, W.** *Die Rettung der Bedrängten.* **Birkeland, H.** *The Evildoers in the Book of Psalms.* (A major revision of his views in *Die Feinde des Individuums in israelitriechen Psalmenliteratur.* Olso, 1933.) **Delekat, L.** *Asylie und Schutzorakel am Zionheiligtum.* **Gunkel, H.** and **Begrich, J.** *Einleitung in die Psalmen.* 196–211. **Keel, O.** *Feinde und Gottesleugner: Studien zum Image der Widersacher in den Individualpsalmen.* SBM 7. Stuttgart: Katholisches bibelwerk, 1969. ———. *The Symbolism of the Biblical World.* 78–109, 291–306. **Kraus, H.-J.** *Psalms 1–59: A Commentary.* 95–99. ———. *Theology of the Psalms.* Tr. K. Crim. Minneapolis: Augsburg, 1986. 125–36. **Mowinckel, S.** *Psalmenstudien I: Awan und die individuellen Klage Psalmen.* Kristiania (Oslo): Jacob Dybwad, 1921; for Mowinckel's revised views, see *PIW,* II, n. 28, 250–51. **Ruppert, L.** *Der leiden der Gerechte und seine Feinde: eine Wortfelduntersuchung.* Würzburg: Echter Verlag, 1973. **Schmidt, H.** *Das Gebet der Angeklagten im Alten Testament.* BZAW 49. Giesson: Alfred Topelmann, 1928 (a shorter form is found in *Old Testament Essays,* SOTSMS [Oxford and London: Charles Griffin and Co., 1927], 143–55). **Westermann, C.** *Praise and Lament.* 188–94.

One prominent feature in the psalms is the presence of foes or enemies. They appear in royal psalms (2:2, 8, 10; 18:38–39, 47–48; 21:9; 45:5; 72:11; 89:24, 43; 110:1, 5; 132:18; 144:2) as well as in communal laments (44:11, 14–15; 74:4–8; 79:1–3, 7; 80:7, 13–14; 83:2–8) and individual laments (5:9; 6:7; 7:13; 9:5; 10:7; 13:2, 4; 22:6–8, 12–13, 17–18; 27:2–3; 28:3; 31:4; 35:7–8, 11–16, 19–21; 38:11–12, 19–20; 42:3, 9–10; 43:2; 52:2–4; 55:12–14, 20–21; 56:6; 69:9; 88:8; 102:8; 109:2–5, 20, 25; 119:42, 69; 140:4–5). They oppress, threaten, strike, pursue, speak, and act treacherously against individuals, the nation, and God. Their behavior has such characteristics as exalting themselves (Ps 13:3), making themselves great (Lam 1:9), jeering and reviling (Ps 74:10, 18; Lam 1:21; Ezek 36:2). They may be described with the metaphors of lions (Pss 7:3; 10:9; 17:12;

22:14; 35:17) who are "eager to tear in pieces" (Ps 17:12), or as bulls (Ps 22:13) or howling dogs (Pss 22:17, 21; 59:7–8, 15).

Several words are used to describe the enemies. They are אוֹיְבִים ("enemies"), קָמִים ("adversaries"), צָרִים ("foes"), מְרֵעִים ("causers of evil"), רְשָׁעִים ("wicked ones"), מַשְׂנְאִים ("haters"), רֹדְפִים ("pursuers"), פֹּעֲלֵי אָוֶן ("evildoers"), אַנְשֵׁי דָמִים ("men of blood"), מִרְמָה אִישׁ ("men of deceit"), and בֹּגְדִים ("treacherous ones"). These terms have a strong emotional content but are not sufficiently explicit to provide much help in determining who or what the enemies are. In fact, enemies are seldom identified explicitly (a series of nations appears in Ps 83 and the Babylonian captors torment the exiles in Ps 137) and so there has been much speculation as to who they are. The enemies seem easier to identify in royal psalms and communal laments than in the individual laments, though even in these there is often uncertainty.

In the royal psalms the enemies are enemies of the nation, and thus foreigners. Ps 2:2 speaks of "the kings of the earth" plotting against Yahweh and his anointed king. In Pss 89:24; 110:1, 5; and 132:18, Yahweh promises the king victory over enemies and rival kings, while Pss 18:38–39, 46–47 and 21:9 have royal thanksgivings for the subduing of foes. Sometimes foreign enemies can be raised by Yahweh against the king, as Ps 89:43 attests. Not all of these alien foes can be readily equated with specific historical assailants, but their nature as military opponents is not usually questioned.

The foes in communal laments are also usually best understood as foreign foes. Ps 83:3–9 depicts Israel's neighbors conspiring against her to destroy her entirely, and in 44:11–12 they have scattered her people among the nations. In Pss 74:3–4, 7 and 79:1 enemies have despoiled the holy places of Israel, and they mock those whom they have defeated (cf. Pss 44:14–15; 74:10; 79:10; 80:7). These national enemies are not only Israel's but Yahweh's as well (74:4, 23; 83:3, 6), although their victories may be due to the anger of Yahweh against his chosen people (Ps 60).

In the individual laments the situation is much less clear. The enemies plan violence against their victims (11:5) and set traps and snares for them (Pss 7:16; 31:5; 35:7–8; 57:7; 64:4; 140:5). They use deceit and false witness to injure their prey (5:6; 12:2; 27:12; 35:11; 69:4). Their accusations (7:3–5) and mockery (22:6; 39:8) demoralize the lamenter to the point of death (102:11; 109:23). At times the enemies pretend friendship with the one they hate (41:7; 55:22; 144:8). Their hostility can be described as war (35:1–3). Although "the nations" may appear in these psalms (9:16; 59:9), the evil of the enemies in the individual laments seems more personal than national.

The enemies in the individual lament are characterized in two ways: by their actions and by their words. Unlike the harm done in the communal laments, the danger in the individual laments is more of a threat than an actuality. In the former psalms, the invaders have destroyed the nation (44:11–15), and defiled her holy places (74:3–4); in addition, charges of plots and accusations of more than physical harm may be made.

The actions of the enemies in the individual laments tend to involve conspiracy and planning. The enemies plot and threaten (31:14; 56:6–7) and prepare traps for their victim (31:5; 140:5), whose life they seek (35:4; 38:13; 40:15; 54:5). They draw near and encircle the speaker (22:13–17; 27:2–3). They hate (69:5) and pursue their prey (7:2), attacking with what seems to be military force (56:2; 7:13–14). In their zeal against the one they hate, they seem like animals (17:11–12; 22:13, 17).

The words of the enemies sometimes seem harder for the oppressed to bear than overt actions. The suppliants are bowed down by the weight of curses directed at them (10:7; 31:19; 59:13). The misfortune of a suppliant causes them to rejoice (13:5; 22:18; 35:15–21, 26; 38:17) and to mock and gloat (22:8; 42:11; 69:9; 89:52; 102:9; 119:42). The victim is overwhelmed by their words and deeds to the point that no resistance is possible (69:2–5; 109:23–25). The speaker may appear totally alone with no supportive community in a time of suffering, so it appears that even those who do not join the enemies in their threats and mockery give tacit consent to their attacks.

The identity of the enemies in the individual laments has been the subject of investigation, discussion, and disagreement by many scholars in the field. Some hold that the enemies are foreigners and some argue for Israelites, while others emphasize their larger-than-life nature and powers. H. Birkeland contends that the enemies in these psalms are identical with those in the communal laments: foreign political enemies (*Evildoers in the Book of Psalms,* 9). He looks at communal laments that are indisputably nationalistic (Pss 44, 60, 79, 80, 83, 124, 125) and compares them to a group of individual laments that describe the enemies in the same terms (18, 20, 21, 61, 73, 89, 144). This leads him to conclude that the individual laments deal with foreign enemies and that the speaker, even when not so identified, is a king. Thus the individual laments differ from the communal laments only in that in the first case the speaker is a king who represents the community and in the second it is the community itself.

C. Westermann disagrees sharply with this view, believing that "the enemy in the lament of the individual is totally different from the enemy in the lament of the people" (*Praise and Lament,* 193). Westermann stresses that the suffering individual never seems to be speaking on behalf of a group and that the danger is more of a threat than actual. He also points out that, unlike the enemies in the communal lament, those in the individual lament are members of the same community as the one they torment (41:7; 55:13–15, 22; 144:8, 11), and this precludes the possibility that they are foreign attackers. Westermann thinks that the enemies are not a political party but simply people bound by their contempt for the distressed person. They no longer take Yahweh seriously (Ps 73) and mock the speaker for his or her enduring faithfulness to him (194).

H. Schmidt regards the enemies as Israelites as well. He sees the psalmist's problem as often involving illness, which the enemies interpret as indicating divine displeasure at the afflicted one's sin. This attitude on their part is the false accusation of which the lamenter complains (Pss 69:5–8; 109:2). The individual laments are taken as prayers of the falsely accused, and in some cases were intended for use in the ancient rite of incubation, i.e., sleeping, or passing the night at a sanctuary, near the presence of Deity, and awaiting some sort of divine visitation. In all of these, the falsely accused person seeks deliverance and vindication from the attacks of enemies.

The relationship of enemies to illness has received major attention by scholars in the interpretation of the psalms. S. Mowinckel (*Psalmenstudien* I) argued that nearly all the individual psalms of lamentation are psalms of illness (see also, *PIW,* II, 1–30). The enemies are those who are considered to have brought about the illness, or who take advantage of the illness to attack the sick person and to make the illness fatal. At least some of the individual psalms of lamentation were intended to be used at ceremonies for cleansing from illness, with thanksgiving psalms offered up after the healing. Mowinckel emphasized the ability of enemies to produce and worsen sickness by means of evil curses and potent words of magic.

In this regard, Mowinckel gave attention to the expression פעלי און ("workers of iniquity" or "evildoers") and argued that און connotes "power" in an evil, anti-social sense; the negative counterpart of און ("vigor/wealth") (*Psalmenstudien,* I, 29–32). און refers to "the operative, evil-power, pregnant with disaster and everything connected with it" (*PIW,* II, 7). Thus in Ps 41, Mowinckel notes that the speaker complains: "My enemies speak evil of me: When will he die and his name perish?" (v 6). Those who visit speak "lying words" (שוא ידבר) and collect און in their hearts, hovering about the sick person while they whisper together and desire ways to make the situation worse (vv 7–8; see Craigie's treatment of Pss 38 and 41). Mowinckel suggests that this involved forms of sorcery and that the פֹּעֲלֵי אָוֶן ("evildoers") are "people who by means of potent curses and other words and magic have brought upon a person impurity, weakness, illness or some other disaster. . . ." (*PIW*, II, 7). Thus the enemies need not be known to the sick person, having used powerful cursing words against the person and produced a disasterous situation. In his later work, Mowinckel (*PIW*, II, 3) is careful to emphasize that פֹּעֲלֵי אָוֶן need not refer to a special class of sorcerers (or witches), though there are always those who are willing to practice sorcery for money or are accepted as such because they are different. But any person might use such trouble-producing things as: evil words, calumnies, abusive terms, threats, bad wishes, cultic words of other religions, potent ceremonies, and manipulations. These were the stock and trade of the פֹּעֲלֵי אָוֶן, professional or otherwise, who enhanced their hostility with occult power.

Mowinckel's argument with regard to the enemies of individuals, or similar approaches, has received a measure of acceptance in modified forms. For example, O. Keel emphasizes the demonic and the role of the powers of both good and evil in the matter of the enemies of the individual (*The Symbolism of the Biblical World*, 78–100). He suggests (85) that ordinary human enemies of individuals are depicted in the psalms with the roles of demons and magicians in Mesopotamian prayers. Destructive forces are embodied in enemies, individual and national. The powers of chaos and death can manifest themselves in the invasion of hostile people (108; cf. Pss 60:3–6; 74:23; 65:8; 89:10–11; also Jer 51:34, where the king of Babylon is said to devour Jerusalem like a dragon or chaos monster, תַּנִּין—cf. Isa 27:1; 51:9; Ezek 29:3; 32:2; Job 7:12; Ps 74:13; J. Day, *God's Conflict with the Dragon and the Sea* [Cambridge: Cambridge UP, 1985], 109–13, 120–40).

H.-J. Kraus (*Theology of the Psalms*, 131, 135) judges the translation "evildoers" for אָוֶן פֹּעֲלֵי to be weak. אָוֶן is "the dark counterpole to צֶדֶק "righteousness" and the פֹּעֲלֵי אָוֶן is the evil counterpart of the פֹּעֵל צֶדֶק ("doer of righteousness"). The evildoers (and wicked, רְשָׁעִים) are "doers of uncanny deeds" (135). He finds indications of magic in the curses of Pss 10:7; 2:9; 14:4. The enemies are at times in league with mythical powers such as the "cords of Sheol," the "snares of death," and the "torrents of perdition" (Ps 18:5, 6). The tumult of the people is juxtaposed with the roaring of the primeval sea in Ps 65:8. The hostile primeval powers of Sheol and death are constantly at war with Yahweh, his people, and his purposes, seeking to cause separation between God and those who are in need of his help (133). Thus the enemies, in some cases at least, are the agents of mythical powers; primeval powers that bring chaos and destruction: "All opponents who rise up against Yahweh, his anointed, his people, and his servant are powers of Sheol and forces of death. The foes of the individual are human, but their nature and work are surrounded by an eerie darkness that has come from the mythological tradition" (134).

Kraus adds that the borrowing from mythological tradition "does not create myths, but it uses mythical metaphors to depict the reality of that which exceeds human understanding." The powers of Sheol always intend to separate those who trust in God from him; they emerge from the realm (Sheol), which is the "diametrical opposite of the life that has its source in Yahweh (Ps 36:10)" (135). See also, H. Ringgren, *The Faith of the Psalmists* (Philadelphia: Fortress Press, 1963) 43–46.

Each of these hypotheses has its merits, and there is no need to choose one to the exclusion of the others. G. W. Anderson points out that the descriptions of the enemies betray a certain "conventional monotony" that is in keeping with their liturgical nature ("Enemies and Evildoers in the Book of Psalms"). The laments were intended to be used in different situations and consequently had to use language general enough to be applicable in all of them. We need not suppose that each lament arose from and was intended only for use on one occasion. On the other hand, the descriptions of enemies in the various psalms have enough in common to make them applicable to different contexts, though they do not correspond in every particular. Anderson (29) concludes: "We must, then, allow for a wide range of interpretation, taking in the assaults of national enemies, the bane of illness in a national leader or private individual, the potent word of slander or derision, and a variety of cultic acts and situations." This is surely correct, but we should add to Anderson's fine summary the function of human foes as the agents of mythical powers of Sheol and chaos.

Old Testament scholars have not yet given sufficient attention to the social setting of the psalms and to sociological analysis of the enemies referred to in them. E. S. Gerstenberger (*Psalms*, I, 30–34) has made a start in this direction. He notes that research on group life has shown that all human aggregations (family, community, institution, ethnic entity, nation) which have some inner coherence try to define their boundaries so as to divide between in-group and out-group affairs. Outsiders are frequently viewed as enemies, sometimes as possessing the qualities of devils and demons. We must allow for much of the division of the world in the psalms into friend and foe as reflecting the in-group versus out-group dynamics of human social entities, small and large. The complaints against enemies doubtless reflect concern for group survival, and, in some cases, group dominance. O. Keel (*The Symbolism of the Biblical World*, 78) remarks that "The view which a particular group or culture holds of its enemies is crucial to the understanding of that group or culture," which brings to mind the common saying that "a man (or, a woman) is known by his (her) enemies."

The emergence of enemies, or perceived enemies at least, seems to be inherent in human societies. This is probably especially true in class-dominated activities where economic, political, and military interests exploit and marginalize the poorer and more vulnerable people (for Israel, cf. Amos 2:6–8; 5:11–12; Isa 5:8–10; Neh 5:1–13). To what extent do the complaints and petitions in the Psalms represent the situation of the marginalized poor of Israel? The answer is surely that they do in some cases at least; e.g., Ps 10. However, the matter of enemies does not seem to be confined to the poor and exploited classes. Acute concern about enemies—again real or perceived—is prevalent in every socioeconomic stratum. Sometimes, at least, the people of wealth and power seem to worry more about enemies than do the poor; perhaps they have reason to do so. This is a matter which needs further investigation.

Trust in God and Fear No Person   *(56:1–14)*

Bibliography

Becker, J. *Israel deutet seine Psalmen.* 64. **Beyerlin, W.** *Die Rettung der Bedrängten.* 25–26. **Driver, G. R.** "Thou tellst my wanderings." *JTS* 21 (1970), 402–3. **Johnson, A. R.** *CPIP.* 331–40.

Translation

1   For the leader;[a] according to *jonath-elem-rehoqim;*[b] a Davidic *miktam;*[c] when the Philistines seized him at Gath.

2 (1) *Have mercy on me,*[a] *O God, for people hound*[b] *me;*   (4+3)
       all day long they press the attack[c] *against me.*

3 (2) *They hound me, my slanderers* [a] *do, all day long—*   (3+3)
      Oh, how many fight me![b]

4 (3) *O Most High,*[a] *when I am afraid I put my trust in you.*   (2[3]+3)

5 (4) *By God's help* [a] *I will be able to praise* [a] *his word;*   (3+3+3)
      in God I trust; I am not afraid!
      What can mortals [b] *do to me?*

6 (5)   *All day long they twist* [a] *my words,*   (3+3)
      all their schemes are aimed at me for evil.[b]

7 (6)   *They plot,*[a] *they lurk about;*[a]   (3+2+3)
      they watch my heels [b]
      as they wait, hoping to take my life.[c]

8 (7) *For (their) evil—*
      Will there be liberation for them?[a]   (2+2+4)
      Bring these people [b] *down in your wrath,*[c] *O God.*

9 (8) *You must have kept a record of my misery;* [a]   (3+3+2)
      put my tears in your bottle [b]*—*
      Is that in your reckoning?[c]

10 (9) *If that is true,*[a] *my enemies will turn back*   (4+2+4)
      on the day when [b] *I call;*
      by this [b] *I will know that God is for me.*

11 (10) *By God's (help)* [a] *I will be able to praise a word* [b]*—* (3+3)
      by Yahweh's (help) [a] *I will be able to praise a word!*[b]

12 (11)   *In God I trust; I am not afraid.*   (3+3)
      What can human beings do to me?

13 (12) *I have bound myself*[a] *with vows to you, O God;*   (3+3)
      I am ready to make thank-offerings [b] *to you.*

14 (13)   *Surely* [a] *you will deliver me from death—* (3+3+3+2)
      Have you not kept my feet from stumbling?[b]*—*
      to let me go on walking before God
      in the light of life.

Notes

1.a. See n. 51:1.a.

1.b. The literal meaning could be "according to a silent dove (or dove of speechlessness) of distant ones." The reading "dove of distant terebinths" is obtained by pointing אֵלֶם as אֵלִם (defective for אֵלִים, taken as pl. of אֵלָה, a species of big tree, like an oak). LXX reads as "concerning the people removed far from the sanctuary (holy one/things)." The Targum paraphrases as "concerning the community of Israel likened to a silent dove when they are far from their cities and repeat and praise the Lord of the universe" (Cohen, 177). Apparently, both the LXX and Targum interpret the "dove" (*jonah*) as alluding to the people of Israel, and the LXX treats the אֵלֶם as "gods" (אֵלִים), freely understood as "holy ones/things/sanctuary." Mowinckel (*PIW*, II, 213–14) translates "over [עַל] the dove to the distant gods" and argues that the statement alludes to a purificatory rite in which a dove was dipped into water with the blood of a sacrifice and then released "into the open field" (see Lev 14:1–5; cf. Lev 1:14–15; 5:6–10)—the idea being that the sins of the person involved were sent off to the supernatural beings/gods/demons in the distant areas of the desert outside the "world." Eerdmans (66) argues that the dove was a carrier pigeon, belonging to the temple, released by a pious Israelite in a distant place to carry his tears (v 9) back to the temple in Jerusalem in a skin bottle (cf. Pss 68:14; 84:4). The psalm was one to be recited while the carrier pigeon was freed. Such conjectures are not very convincing, and the best guess is that the expression refers to some sort of tune or recitative pattern for use with the psalm. The reference to a dove in 55:7 may be intended to link Ps 56 to Ps 55 in some way (Kidner).

1.c.   The term *miktam* occurs in the superscriptions of Pss 16, 56, 57, 58, 59, and 60. It rather obviously marks a small collection of psalms (see G. H. Wilson, "Editorial Divisions in the Hebrew Psalter," *VT* 34 [1984], 342–43; also, his *The Editing of the Hebrew Psalter,* 158–62), though it is difficult to determine any common features among them other than that they are all psalms of distress and crisis, in which the speaker moves to confidence and assurance that enemies will receive appropriate consequences for their deeds. The meaning of *miktam* is uncertain. See the discussion by Craigie, n. 16:1.a., who argues that it is most likely to mean "inscribed," in an enduring manner, such as inscribed on a stone pillar (see Kraus, *Psalms 1–59,* 24–25). It is possible that the expression connotes "written for public use." There is also the good possibility that the *miktam* psalms are a small collection, probably derived from a larger collection, of "letter prayers," thought of by the scribal redactors (and perhaps originally composed as such) as letters or inscriptions written to God. The use of "letter prayers" seems to have been fairly common in ancient Near Eastern practice (see W. Hallo, "The Royal Correspondence of Larsa: A Sumerian Prototype for the Prayer of Hezekiah," in *Kramer Anniversary Volume: Cuneiform Studies,* FS S. N. Kramer, ed. B. L. Eichler et al. [Kevelaer: Butzon & Bercker, 1976], 209–24; briefly in "Sumerian Literature—Background to the Bible," *Bible Review* 4 [1988] 36–37). The prayer of Hezekiah in Isa 38:9 is called a מִכְתָּב, translated "writing/poem/canticle," but which means "letter" in later Hebrew (e.g., 2 Chr 21:12). The LXX translation of *miktam* as στηλογραφία, "inscription (on a stele)," lends support to the conclusion that there was a Hebrew root כתם ("inscribe/write a letter"), closely related to כתב ("write"). See Craigie, 154, n. 1.a. For "Davidic," see n. 51:1–2.b.

2.a.   See 51:3.

2.b.   The verb שָׁאַף can mean "to crush/trample upon" or "to gasp/pant after" (Job 7:2). The latter seems most appropriate in this context. NIV has "hotly pursue"; JB has "harry me." Dahood's "hound me" is adopted.

2.c.   Cf. NIV. Lit. "all the day a fighter presses me."

3.a.   Gunkel and Dahood are correct in understanding שׁרֹרָי as "my slanderers" or "my defamers." Cf. Pss 5:9; 27:11; 54:7; 59:11. Some prefer the idea of "watchers" or "ambushers"; Weiser has "who lie in wait for me"; NEB, "my watchful foes."

3.b.   Taking כִּי as exclamatory (see Dahood).

4.a.   The מָרוֹם is a problem, which has been given varied solutions. RSV follows a long line of exegesis and treats it as an adverbial accusative, "for many fight against me proudly." Other exegetes treat it as a designation of Yahweh (see Dahood and A. A. Anderson). A. R. Johnson (*CPIP*, 334, n. 1) reads literally "smiting from above," understanding haplography and an original מִמָּרוֹם (cf. *BHS*), with a "reference to those who are beating up their victim as he lies prostrate at their feet." NEB and JB alter the word into an imperative ("appear on high" and "raise me up"). For מרום as a designation of God, see Ps 92:9 and possibly 75:6; cf. Mic 6:6. Another way of interpreting this passage is to read לִי as "to my help"; thus, "for many fight for me (in) the heights"—referring to angels (see *HOTTP*, 263). The choice made in the *Translation* treats the word as a vocative, matching the "O God" in v 2, and shifts it to the beginning of v 4 for a better metrical balance. This is the choice of NRSV.

5.a.   A. R. Johnson (*CPIP*, 334, n. 2) argues that the construction here is equal to "through God I praise His 'Word.'" The praise is possible because of divine aid or guidance, equal to the use of דרשׁ in seeking divine aid or guidance; cf. 2 Kgs 1:16; 1 Chr 10:13–14; 2 Chr 34:26; Ezek 14:7.

5.b.   "Flesh" (בשׂר) is a variant for אנושׁ, "human," in v 2 and אדם, "human beings," in v 12. NEB and NIV have "mortal men." See *Comment*.

6.a.   עצב more frequently means "to hurt/grieve," but in a few cases means "to intertwine/shape/twist." See KB, 725.

6.b.   It is possible that לְרָע ("for evil/hurt") belongs at the beginning of v 7, as in Kraus. But the colons are well balanced in MT.

7.a.   The verbs in this colon receive varied interpretations. BDB (158) takes יגורו from גור (גרה), "to stir up strife." But it is more probable that the root means "to gather together" for ambush or conspiracy (thus Jerome, *congregabuntur* = יגד > גדד, "to troop together"). Cf. Gunkel and others; Pss 59:4; 94:21; 140:3; Isa 54:15.

The second verb may be read as hiphil (*kethiv*) or as qal (*qere*) with the meanings of "hide" or "lurk/spy" in either case.

7.b.   Perhaps the more lit. "heels" is better here than "steps" (RSV), because it fits better the picture of watching from concealment, "the heels being the part exposed to any person coming from behind, or to an enemy lying like a serpent in the path" (Perowne, 446).

7.c. Johnson (*CPIP*, 334) expresses the eager anticipation in קוּה with "as they wait eagerly for me" (NIV, "eager to take my life"). כַּאֲשֶׁר here means "as" (see Perowne, 448).

8.a. The meaning of this colon is uncertain. RSV has "so recompense them for their crime," reflecting acceptance of a frequently suggested emendation of פַּלֵּט, "escape/deliver" to פַּלֵּס, "weigh out/recompense." The *Translation* follows the assumption that the first half of the verse is a bitter question expecting the answer "No." פַּלֵּט is taken as an infinitive meaning "to save, salvation" (see *HOTTP*, 263–64). However, Dahood could be correct with his "from their malice deliver us," reading פַּלֵּט as imperative and לָמוֹ as "for us" rather than "for them/him" (II, 44; I, 173). LXX indicates אָוֶן is taken as noun meaning "nothing": "For you will on no account save them." Johnson (*CPIP*, 334) proposes עַל־לֹא־אָוֶן on the ground of haplography and reads as an idiomatic way of saying, "for peace's sake [meaning 'to put an end to trouble'] grant deliverance from them," reading לְ with the force of "from."

8.b. Heb. עַמִּים, "peoples/nations." See *Comment*.

8.c. "Your" is not expressed in MT, but no suffix is required with names of parts of the body (אַף is lit. "nose"); so Dahood; cf. Lam 2:3; Job 40:24; Prov 26:6.

9.a. The *Translation* reflects the meaning of "lamentation" or "grief" for נֹדִי from נוּד, "to move to and fro, show grief"; see Ps 69:21; Job 2:11; 42:11; Jer 22:10. However, נוּד in Gen 4:16 is commonly taken in the sense of "wander" or "fleeing" (cf. 4:14), and translations read "my wandering you have counted" or with KJV, "Thou tellst my wanderings." The verb is read with precative force and is a very emphatic construction.

9.b. The conventional "bottle" is used, but the word refers to a skin bottle used for water, milk, or wine (Josh 9:4, 13; Judg 4:19; also Job 14:17; Hos 13:12). Some versions seem to reflect בְּנֶגְדְּךָ (see *BHS*), "in front of, before you."

9.c. The MT reads literally "Is it not in your book/scroll?" The word סִפְרָה may be understood as "your scroll of remembrance" (Mal 3:16) or "reckoning." On the other hand, it may be understood as an explanation or alternative to "in your bottle," with the meaning, "Actually, in your book/on your scroll" (see Johnson, *CPIP*, 337, n. 4; *TRP*, 265).

10.a. The adverb אָז is understood in the sense of indicating the fulfillment of a condition = "if" or "when this has been done" (BDB, 23).

10.b. Reading זֶה, "this," with the force of "then" (so Dahood, "then I will know that God is for me"; see his discussion). NIV, "By this I will know that God is for me." Also, Kraus, I, 565.

11.a. Lit. "in God" and "in Yahweh."

11.b. Johnson (*CPIP*, 337) translates, "I have to thank God for a 'Word' . . ." (see n. 5.a.), understanding "word" as a prophetic "word" or message to a follower of Yahweh. It is more common to assume that the possessive "his word" (or "whose word") is understood. The translation has been left as literal (see *Comment*).

13.a. Lit. "upon me, O God, (are) your vows"; meaning, "I accept responsibility for vows I made to you." The Heb. נֶדֶר may mean either a vow or a sacrifice made to fulfill a vow, such as a votive sacrifice (see Pss 22:26; 50:14; Deut 12:11, 17, 26; 2 Sam 15:8). In most instances in the OT, a vow is a promise to give something to God.

13.b. תּוֹדֹת can mean either "thankful praise" (cf. Dahood, "my vows with praises"; KJV) or "thank-offerings" (as in RSV, JB, NEB, NAB, NIV).

14.a. Reading the כִּי as emphatic with precative perfect (as in Buttenwieser). Dahood reads, "Would that you rescue me from Death. . . ."

14.b. As in the case of 9.c. above, there seem to be two approaches to the interpretation of this expression. The *Translation* treats it as a parenthetical element of the text. The other option is to treat the expression as an explanatory gloss on the preceding expression: "Is that not to keep my feet from stumbling?" Johnson (*CPIP*, 338, n. 2) does not treat these words as a gloss, as he does in v 9, arguing that the parallelism requires them in the text. However, they are parenthetical in any case.

Form/Structure/Setting

Gunkel classified this psalm as a lament of an individual, but others have chosen alternative genres. Mowinckel puts it with a series of "I"-psalms that

belong to the general category of national psalms of lamentation (*PIW*, I, 219). The
LXX title supports Mowinckel, "For the people removed far from the sanctuary,"
and indicates that the psalm was considered to refer to the nation (as in the
Targum: "Concerning the congregation of Israel, which is compared to a silent
dove at the time when they are far from their cities, and turned again and
praised the Lord of the world"). H. Schmidt (followed by Leslie) argues that the
psalm is the prayer of one who has been falsely accused and who is beset by
enemies. Weiser calls it a lament but suggests that it was designed for recitation
in public worship after a prayer had been answered, but before the thank-
offering (v 13) was made. He understands the lament and petition to have been
spoken before the time of the psalm's recitation (422), which seems unlikely.
Kraus puts Ps 56 rather generally among the broad category of prayer psalms of
an individual (566/525; cf. Ps 54), recognizing elements of petition, description
of distress, vow making, and thanksgiving.

These comments show that attempts to identify the nature of the speaker in
the psalm and its setting vary widely. Older critical commentators thought in
terms of an individual dated sometime between the fall of Jerusalem in 587 B.C.E.
and the Maccabean period of the second century B.C.E. (e.g., Briggs, Buttenwieser,
Gunkel). In this interpretation the speaker voices a national prayer in a struggle
against the "people" or the "nations" of v 8, though the psalm may have originally
been that of an individual. Perhaps emending עַמִּים, "peoples" to עֲזִים, "violent ones/
mighty ones" (so Schmidt, 108) would permit the psalm to be understood in the
context of party strife in the nation. Dahood argues that the psalm is a pre-exilic
lament of a king (so also, Johnson, *CPIP*, 336). But the "democratization" common in the psalms could mean that, while the speaker was originally a king, or at
least the metaphors are drawn in part from the sphere of kingship (so Kraus),
the present psalm is intended for individual use as a prayer in any suitable time
of trouble.

However, the psalm may be a prayer designed for an individual without ever
having been either a national prayer or a royal lamentation (Durham, 284). The
scribal writer of the historical note in the superscription interpreted the psalm in
the context of the career of David, and this may be an accurate reflection of the
nature of the psalm, i.e., written with a situation in mind which shared common
elements with that of David in 1 Sam 21:10–15 and 30:6 (cf. Deissler, 55). That is
to say, David's kingship provided the model, the story context, for either the
original design of the psalm or its interpretation—or both. J. H. Eaton refers to a
process of "thoughtful comparison with the situation of King David" (*Kingship*,
29; the reference is to the superscription of Ps 3). The language is that of
kingship, but it has sufficient ambiguity to allow it to become meaningful for any
reader. For the process of the democratization of the royal psalms for nonroyal
use, see Mowinckel, *PIW*, I, 78–80; H. Gunkel and J. Begrich, *Einleitung*, 147–49;
I. Engnell, *A Rigid Scrutiny: Critical Essays on the Old Testament*, tr. J. T. Willis
(Nashville: Vanderbilt UP, 1969), 104–5.

The text of the psalm is difficult to read. The *Notes* above and the variations
among translations provide evidence of the severity of the problems involved.
The verse structure seems ragged in places, and interpretations have to be tentative.
The *Translation* reflects an understanding of the psalm as the presentation of a

suppliant who expresses strong faith but who has not yet experienced the fulfillment of the requests made in prayer. The speaker walks a middle way between the pole of assurance and the pole of deep complaint and bitter petition, one with confidence in the intervention of God, but who has not yet experienced deliverance. The suppliant is ready to pay vows made and celebrate with thankofferings (v 13), but death is still a real possibility (v 14).

The psalm can be divided into two parts of almost equal length: vv 2–8 and vv 9–14. Both sections are gathered around central core statements which express strong trust in God rather than in human strength: vv 4–5 and vv 11–12. The first section is bracketed by petitions in v 2 and v 8, and the language seems more conventional than that of the lament genre. The second section is constructed of a complaint/petition in vv 9–10, a core of faith in vv 11–12, and an anticipatory waiting on God in vv 13–14. The mood of the second section seems somewhat more tentative and less assured than that of the first section.

Comment

Superscription (56:1). The historical note refers to an incident from the career of David which happened at Gath. The reference may arise, in part at least, from a wordplay on the root הלל ("to praise") in the psalm (vv 5, 11) and the verb "to act like a madman," (יתהלל) in 1 Sam 21:14 (13). Also, see the same verb for "fear" in Ps 56:4, 5, 12 and 1 Sam 21:13 (12). The text in 1 Sam 21 does not actually say that the Philistines held David as a prisoner at Gath, but the context, along with the mention of his escape in 22:1 (note the play on מלט 1 Sam 22:1 and פלט in Ps 56:8), allowed for the conclusion in the superscription. The reading of גדי in v 9 as "wanderings/flight" may also have been deemed appropriate for David when he made his desperate trip to Gath.

Plea for mercy and complaint (56:2–3). The suppliant cries for a merciful response from God because of the hounding, slanderous attacks of enemies. The anguished cry to God for mercy is a characteristic feature of the laments (Pss 4:2; 6:3; 26:11; 27:7; 51:3; 86:16; passim). The designation of those who hound the suppliant as "men" (אנוש) should not be overlooked. Though the word אנוש seems to have carried the original meaning of "to be weak," too much should not be made of a contrast with אדם (v 12) and an emphasis on the mortal, weak condition of human beings. אנוש is used quite generally for human beings and does not differ markedly from other terms for humanity (see F. Maas, *TDOT*, I, 345–48). Nevertheless, the usage here alerts the reader to the fundamental nature of the enemies, who belong to the human realm of things and who will not prevail against God. They are "man" and not God.

Statements of trust and praise (56:4–5). The speaker deals with fear by turning to trust in God. Praise is directed toward the word of God (v 5), which is not further defined (cf. v 11). The reference may be to the promises of God in a general sense, or it may indicate an expected oracle of salvation (cf. Ps 130:5). The form of the text favors the idea of seeking divine aid or guidance in the form of a specific response from God (see note 5.a.). A favorable response from God is anticipated and the speaker is prepared to offer praise because of the condition that mortal human beings cannot overcome one who trusts in God. The word "flesh" (בשׂר) emphasizes the mortal nature of human beings versus the qualitatively different nature of God. The "flesh" conveys the idea of human nature, with nuances of creatureliness, earthly nature, weakness, transitoriness, and dependence on God: "All flesh is grass, and all its beauty is like the flower of the field. The grass withers, the flower fades, when the breath of Yahweh blows upon it" (Isa 40:6–7, RSV). Hezekiah declared about Sennacherib, the king of Assyria: "With him is an arm of flesh [i.e., human power]; but with us is the LORD our God" (2 Chr 32:8, RSV; also see Jer 17:5). The affirmation that Yahweh is superior to all human flesh is rather common in the OT (see N. P. Bratsiotis, *TDOT*, II, 330–32).

Complaint about enemies (54:6–7). The enemies twist the words of the suppliant as they scheme together with evil intent, plotting and lurking about hoping for any opportunity for mischief. Vv 6–7 suggest domestic difficulties of a king or other leader whose enemies are eagerly seeking any opportunity to kill—probably through rebellion or a coup of some kind. The enemies constantly plot for the harm of the speaker; they lurk about, watching every movement, "like men lurking in ambush to watch an approaching wayfarer so that they may fall upon him with murderous intent" (Johnson, *CPIP*, 332).

Petition for judgment (56:8). The use of the plural "peoples/nations" in v 8 is unusual and can be used to argue that the enemies are foreigners attacking the king and his nation. Johnson (*CPIP*, 334, n. 6) argues that the emphatic position of the word before the verb means "actual nations," suggesting that the reference not necessarily be construed as referring to the great powers such as Egypt, Assyria, or Babylon, but to nearby peoples such as Edom, Moab, Ammon, and Syria, or to the persistent unrest of the Philistines and others of the coastal plain. On the other hand, the plural of עם is used of a people ruled by a king in Esth 1:11, 16 (cf. Pss 1:5; 18:48; 144:20); these seem to be the only direct references, but the plural is used in a singular or collective sense in such references as Gen 17:14; Exod 30:33, 38; Lev 7:20, 21; 21:1, 4, 14, 15; Ezek 18:18. Thus it is not necessary to assume that the plural עמים refers to foreign nations, though it may have been read in that way, especially in post-exilic communities. It is possible that "peoples" should be construed in a broader sense of judgment on evil people, foreign and domestic—as by Kirkpatrick, who suggests the "desire for a general judgment of the world" (381). Durham (284) suggests the collective kindred of the psalmist's enemies.

Prayer to be remembered by God (56:9–10). The interpretation reflected in the *Translation* is that the speaker expresses an assurance that his or her condition has been recorded in the divine records, though there is no overt response yet from God. Thus the imperative petition follows: "Put my tears in your bottle." Dahood allows for a full precative perfect and reads: "Write down my lament yourself"—and he may be correct; I have attempted to allow for the force of the perfect followed by imperative in a slightly different manner. The use of the idea of "tears in your skin bottle" is strange; there seems to be no evidence for a "tear-bottle" as such. Apparently the idea is that the speaker's tears of lament be preserved with care similar to that given to water, wine, or milk. Of course, this is especially meaningful in dry climates where fluids must be treated with great care lest they be lost and unavailable when needed. Two wordplays or puns seem to be present in this verse. The *nod* (נוד) of the "misery/wanderings" is matched by the *no'd* (נאד) of the "skin bottle," and the ספר\הספר ("count/record"—"reckoning/scroll-book") plays on the background idea of a divine "scroll of remembrance"—God's book about the behavior of the righteous; see Ps 69:29; Exod 32:32, 33; Isa 4:3; 65:6; Job 14:17; 19:23; Mal 3:16; Dan 7:10; Rev 20:12; 21:27. The desired divine response is spelled out in v 10.

Trust and praise (56:11–12). These verses are essentially the same as vv 4–5 and form a kind of refrain or core set of statements. A loose chiastic linkage seems to join vv 4–5 with vv 11–12.

> A   I will praise his word, v 5   A'   I will praise a word, v 11
> B   I trust God, v 4   B'   I trust God, v 12

In addition, there is a chiasm between v 4 and v 12:

> v 4   When I am afraid   A   I trust you   B
> v 12 I trust in God   B'   I am not afraid   A'

The rhetorical question "What can mortals/human beings do to me?"—expecting the answer "nothing"—closes both sections. Note the very similar expressions to vv 4–5 and 11–12 in Ps 118:6–8.

The "word" without the pronoun "his" in v 11 may not be significant (see *Notes* above). However, it may signal expectancy on the part of the speaker for an overt response on the part of God, either in a message or action (דבר can mean "message/communication/promise" or "action/response"). The appearance of the name Yahweh in v 11 is striking in an Elohistic psalm. It is hardly accidental and should not be changed.

Ready with vows and thank-offerings (56:13–14). The suppliant accepts responsibility for and readiness to fulfill vows made to God. The vows would be fulfilled with praise and thank-offerings. Such offerings were times for the testimonies of those healed or delivered from distress to those assembled (probably family and friends) for the occasion (cf. Pss 22:23–32; 32:6–11; 40:10–11; 51:15–17; 116:17–19). The speaker has been saved from premature death thus far ("my feet from being pushed"—into the underworld of Sheol) and is confident that God will continue to deliver so that he or she can continue to walk in "the light of life"—equivalent to "the Lord of the Living" (see Dahood, I, 222–23; A. R. Johnson, *The Vitality of the Individual in the Thought of Ancient Israel*, 2nd ed. [Cardiff: University of Wales Press, 1964], 105–6). The suppliant, like the person in Ps 16:11, wants to continue on "the path of life" and escape the gloomy darkness of Sheol.

Explanation

Fear and faith struggle together in this psalm. But faith seems dominant, and the psalm's message is one of confidence in God. The crucial points for the message of the psalm are in vv 4–5 and 11–12: "By God's help I will be able."

Trust in God, when activated and confirmed by a word from God, is more powerful than the evil actions of human beings. The spirit of the psalm is like that of Moses speaking to the Israelites in a time of terrible danger from the Egyptians: "Fear not, stand firm, and see the salvation of the Lord, which he will work for you today" (Exod 14:13, RSV). And of Isaiah:

> Woe to those who go down to Egypt for help and rely on horses. . . .
> but do not look to the Holy One of Israel. . . .
> The Egyptians are men and not God;
>   and their horses are flesh, and not spirit.
> When the Lord stretches out his hand,
>   the helper will stumble, and he who is helped will fall,
> And they will all perish together. (Isa 31:1, 3, RSV)

And Jeremiah: "Cursed is the man who trusts in man and makes flesh his arm" (17:5, RSV).

The message of the psalm is reflected in the bold affirmation of the Apostle Paul: "If God is for us, who can be against us?" (Rom 8:31; see also Ps 118:6–9). NT readers will find a new dimension of v 13 in John 8:12: "I am the light of the world. Whoever follows me will never walk in darkness, but will have the light of life" (NRSV).

A Prayer for God to Rise Up in Glory   (57:1–12)

Bibliography

Auffret, P. "Note sur la structure littéraire du Psaume LVII," *Sem* 27 (1977) 59–73. **Baumann, E.** "Struktur-Untersuchungen im Psalter. 1." *ZAW* 61 (1945–48) 173–76. **Beyerlin, W.** *Die Rettung der Bedrängten.* 129–37. **McKay, J. W.** "My Glory—A Mantle of Praise," *SJT* 31 (1978) 167–72.

Translation

1   For the leader;[a] *al-tashheth;*[b] a Davidic *miktam;*[c] when he fled from Saul into the cave.[d]

2 (1) *Have mercy on me,*[a] *O God,*[b] *Have mercy on me;*   (3+3+3)
         for I[c] *have sought refuge with you,*
         in the shadow of your wings I take refuge,
         until Destruction[d] *passes by.*
3 (2) *I call to God, the Most High One,*[a]   (3+3)
         to the God who will fulfill his purpose for me.[b]

4 (3)	*He will send*ᵃ *from heaven and save me;*	(3+2+4)
	*he will challenge*ᵇ *whoever hounds me;*ᶜ Selah	
	*God will send forth his loyal-love and faithfulness.*ᵈ	
5 (4)	*O my soul!*ᵃ	(1+3+3+3)
	*among lions I must lie down,*ᵇ	
	*(among) man-eaters,*ᶜ	
	whose teeth are spears and arrows,	
	and whose tongues are sharp swords.	
6 (5)	*Rise up*ᵃ *over the heavens, O God,*	(3+3)
	Over all the earth be your glory!	
7 (6)	*They set a net for my feet,*	(3+2+3+2)
	*my soul is bowed down,*ᵃ	
	*they dig a pit in front of me*ᵇ—	
	*(but) they will fall in it!*ᶜ Selah	
8 (7)	*Firmly fixed is my heart,*	(2+1+2+2)
	O God,	
	firmly fixed is my heart;	
	*I am ready to sing and chant praise.*ᵃ	
9 (8)	*Awake!*	(3+4)
	*O my glory,*ᵃ	
	Awake!	
	*With the lute and harp,*ᵇ	
	*I am ready to wake up Dawn!*ᶜ	
10 (9)	*I would thankfully praise*ᵃ *you among the peoples, O my Lord,*	(3+2)
	I would chant your praise among the nations!	
11 (10)	*For great*ᵃ	(1+2+2)
	to the heavens is your loyal-love	
	and to the skies is your faithfulness.	
12 (11)	*Rise up over the heavens, O God;*	(3+3)
	over all the earth be your glory!	

Notes

1.a. See n. 51:1–2.a.

1.b. This expression is also in the superscriptions of 58, 59, and 75. The translation is not certain: "do not destroy/do not let it destroy" or possibly "No-Destruction." It is usually taken as the opening words of a song, indicating that the following psalm should be sung to the song's tune. A bit of support for this may come from Isa 65:8, where "do not destroy" may be a popular saying and possibly a phrase from a vintage song. David's "destroy him not" in 1 Sam 26:9 and Moses' "destroy not your people" in Deut 9:26 should also be noted. The verb שׁחת carries a connotation of ruining or spoliation, as well as defacing and mutilating (note Deut 20:19). In the case of 1 Sam 26:9, David's concern seems to be that Saul's body not be violated or defiled.

1.c. See n. 56:1.c.

1.d. The allusion is probably to 1 Sam 22:1, though reference to the cave incident at Engedi according to 1 Sam 24 is possible also.

2.a. See 6:3; 51:3; 56:2.

2.b. *Elohim* in this part of the Psalter is usually equal to *Yahweh*.

2.c. Lit. "my soul/life" = "myself" = "I" (נַפְשִׁי). The verb חסיה is qal perfect 3rd fem. sing. from חסה, with the original *yodh* preserved, "seek refuge."

2.d. See 52:4; 55:12; also 38:13; 93:3; 94:20. The word means "ruin" or "destruction," or related ideas according to context. The *Translation* treats the word as personified; see *Comment* on personification in vv 4, 9.

3.a. The אלהים עליון is a variation of "Yahweh Most High" (see 7:18) and אל עליון, "El Elyon." For עליון see 46:5; 47:3; 73:11; 78:17; 82:6; etc.

3.b. Lit. "to the God who fulfills/completes regarding me." The basic idea of גמר is "to bring to an end/complete." LXX seems to reflect the verb גמל, "to deal bountifully/repay" and could yield the translation "My Benefactor," which would be an appropriate parallel to the first colon. Dahood (I, 45; II, 51) argues for the root meaning of גמר as "avenge" and thus "the one who avenges me," or "Avenger El" in this context—or better "El who Avenges for me."

4.a. The object of the verb is in the third colon: Loyal-Love and Faithfulness.

4.b. MT has חרף, piel perfect of חָרַף, "to reproach/rebuke/taint." The verb is used elsewhere only with human beings as the subject. However, here God is the subject. Dahood reads חָרֵף, piel infinitive, governed by the preposition "from" attached to "heavens": "from the taunts of those who hound me." NEB's "frustrate my persecutors" represents the argument that חרף can mean "to confuse / disorder" (see KB, 335). The *Translation* reflects the work of Roland de Vaux in "Single Combat in the Old Testament" (in *The Bible and the Ancient Near East* [Garden City, NY: Doubleday, 1971], 123, 127), who argues that חרף in piel is used to express "I challenge" in 1 Sam 17:25, 36, 45 and "to stimulate/provoke" in 2 Sam 21:21 (note also Judg 8:15; 2 Kgs 19:23 = Isa 37:23; Zeph 2:8-10; 1 Sam 11:2). The verb carries the connotations of defiance, provocation, and contempt. I take the perfect as expressing future tense, which is set by the imperfect ישלח ("he will send") in 4a (the perfect functions as if prefixed with a simple *waw* conjunction).

4.c. See n. 56:2.b.

4.d. For "loyal-love," see n. 51:3.a. For "faithfulness" ("truth"), see *Comment* on 51:6, 8. This colon follows the *selah*, and some interpreters think of it as an additional comment added to the psalm. If so, the נפשי, "my life," at the beginning of v 5 probably stood at the end of the 2nd colon of v 4: "from the taunting [חרף] of those who seek (or hound) my life" (see Gunkel, Schmidt, Kraus). But the expressive חרף שאפי forms a short pivot colon between the long colons in 4a and 4c. There is no need for the drastic revision of the verse as advocated by Kraus (*Psalms 1–59*, 529, n. 3c). See *Comment*.

5.a. I read this verse as having a form of the pivot pattern; in this case נפשי is an anacrusis. See n. 11.a.

5.b. The *Translation* follows the interpretation of the cohortative form of the verb as a complaint ("I must lie down . . ."); the cohortative has the sense of external compulsion (GKC, 108a). It is possible that we should read as determination or assurance: "I will lie down. . . ."

5.c. "Man-eaters" is NEB's vivid rendering of להטים בני־אדם. The verb להט has been understood traditionally as "to set on fire" or "flaming," thus "fiery ones," "fire-breathers," or the like. But the better meaning here is "devour/consume" (see KB, 474). Dahood has "raging for human prey"; JB, "greedy for human prey." NIV follows LXX and attaches "sons of mankind" ("men") to the next colon, "men whose teeth are. . . ."

6.a. This translation assumes that the language is that associated with theophanic thought. The strong imperative seeks to persuade God to manifest his power and glory over the earth. "Be exalted" is too static; as is Dahood's proposal that רומה be understood as a substantive, receiving its suffix from "your glory," and meaning "your stature [*or*, height] is above the heavens."

7.a. The verb כפף usually appears with a transitive meaning, which would be: "he has bowed down my soul." However, an indefinite subject can be assumed: "one has bowed down my soul" = "my soul is bowed down" (Perowne, 454). Dahood reads consonantal כפף as "noose/snare," ("a noose for my neck [נפשי]"), parallel with "net." But the pivot pattern indicates that "my soul is bowed" is a suspended expression between two short framing lines. Cf. v 11.

7.b. Dahood wants to translate lit. "for my face," with the idea that a pit is dug for the person to fall into face down.

7.c. The context indicates that the perfect form of the verb (נפלו) should be read as future. More properly, perhaps, the durative present tense of the perfect extends into subsequent action.

8.a. The verbs שיר and זמר form a word pair in both Hebrew and Ugaritic. See Dahood, II, 54; see Pss 21:14; 27:6; 105:2; 1 Chr 16:9.

9.a. Frequently changed to "my liver," כְּבֵדִי (Gunkel, Dahood); cf. Pss 7:6; 16:9; see Craigie on 7:6; 16:9; and McKay *SJT* 31 (1978) 167–72. For "my glory," see *Comment*.

9.b. Usually taken as the object of the second "awake," but the pivot pattern in this verse indicates that "my glory" is the object of both verbs (cf. vv 2a, 8a). Note also the article on "lute." נבל and כנור ("lute and harp") form a word pair; e.g., Pss 81:3; 108:3; 150:3; 1 Kgs 10:11; 1 Chr 13:8; 15:16, 28. Apparently, the two words refer to two different types of stringed instruments widely used in the ancient Near East (see O. Keel, *The Symbolism of the Biblical World*, 346–49).

9.c. "Dawn" is personified. See *Comment*.

10.a. An attempt to translate the hiphil of ידה, which varies between "to thank" and "to praise" (see C. Westermann, *Praise and Lament in the Psalms*, 25–30; F. Crüsemann, *Studien zur Formgeschichte von Hymnus and Danklied in Israel* [Neukirchen: Neukirchener Verlag, 1969], 279–82). Crüsemann argues that the German *danken*, "to thank," is more basic than *loben*, or *preisen*, "to praise" (contra Westermann) in most cases. The expressional framework is usually, "I thank you, because you have. . . ." But Westermann's declarative praise comes out to be much the same thing. Dahood is probably correct in assuming that the suffix "you" in this verse is dative rather than accusative, meaning that the sense is: "I will give thanks to you among the peoples." The praise is sung and chanted *to* God (note Crüsemann, 281), but such thankful praise is not private in most cases. Others are listening; so it becomes testimony as others overhear the worshiper voicing praise and thanks to God. The praise of God to others is supported by the panel parallel in 10b.

11.a. This verse seems to have the pivot pattern prevalent in this psalm, except that the central word comes before the bicolon (an anacrusis), as in Amos 2:9:

ואשמיד	And I will destroy
פריו ממעל	his fruit from above
ושרשיו מתחת	and his roots from beneath.

The arrangement in v 11 is

כי־גדל	For great
עד־שמים חסדך	to heaven is your love
ועד־שחקים אמתך	and to clouds your truth.

Form/Structure/Setting

As is the case with Ps 56, Ps 57 is usually classified as an individual lament (following Gunkel, Kraus, et al.). However, the psalm only partially fits in that category. Kraus puts it in his broad classification of prayer songs (*Gebetslieder*), which it undoubtedly is, but such a broad classification offers little help. The strong elements of confidence throughout the psalm move it away from lament toward thanksgiving and praise. The suppliant speaks as one already in the sanctuary, under the protection of God (v 2), who is prepared to give thanksgiving-praise to God among the peoples and nations (v. 10) and to affirm that the loyal-love of God is as great as the heavens (v 11). As in 56, the psalm stops the action, as it were, between the lament proper (vv 2–5) and the full thanksgiving which looks back on the conditions of lament that are safely past. The speaker is ready to give thankful praise, in fact vows to do so, but the situation has not yet been changed from one of lament to praise.

The unity of the psalm should not be questioned and no attempt should be made to treat it as two psalms (as, e.g., Briggs), despite the fact that 57:8–12 is found in Ps 108:2–6 (with some differences) and that v 11 is similar to Ps 36:6. Since Ps 108 seems to be a mosaic of parts found elsewhere (vv 7–14 are found in Ps 60:7–14), it is possible that Ps 57 is the source of the material there. However, it is equally probable that both psalms use material drawn from a common repertoire out of the traditions of the pre-exilic temple in Jerusalem (Beyerlin, *Die Rettung der Bedrängten*, 130). The unity of the psalm is suggested by Auffret *Sem* 27 [1977] 59–73), who argues that the repetition of v 6 in v 12 at least points to a redactional unity. He also argues that the psalm is characterized in all its major parts by the use of the "pivot word pattern" of poetic style (utilizing Dahood, III, 439 ["double-duty modifier"]; W. G. E. Watson, "The Pivot Pattern in Hebrew, Ugaritic and Akkadian Poetry," *ZAW* 88 [1976] 239–53). The pattern refers to the use of a word (such as a divine name or title) or expression suspended between two fairly short colons and modifying both at the same time. E.g., in v 8:

נכון לבי	Firmly fixed is my heart
אלהים	O God
נכון לבי	Firmly fixed is my heart.

Jer 2:15:

עליו ישאגו	Over which roar
כפרים	lions
נתנו קולם	they growl loudly.

The structure of the pivot-pattern is most often ab c ab. The pivot word(s) may be placed before or after the two lines; e.g., Amos 2:9:

ואשמיד	I will destroy
פריו ממעל	his fruit from above
ושרשו מתחת	and his roots from beneath.

Ps 57 begins with a traditional prayer for mercy in v 2 and moves quickly to assurance of God's response in vv 3–4. The center section of the psalm is marked by the two *selah*'s: the first, at the end of 4b, serves to intensify the statement in 4c; the second is at the end of v 7, following the emphatic "they will fall in it!" Vv 8–11 contain energetic statements of confidence and a vow to praise God, whose loyal-love and faithfulness tower up to the heavens (v 11). V 12 repeats the refrain in v 6 to close the psalm.

The identity of speakers in the psalms is a perennial problem, and Ps 57 is no exception. The psalm is properly related closely to 56, in location in the Psalter, in language (note 56:2 and 57:2), in thought, and in form. In both psalms, the original writer(s) may have had a king in mind. The king is being harassed by vicious enemies, probably internal rather than foreign, and prays to God with both anxiety and assurance. The superscription links the psalm with David's experience of hiding in a cave from Saul. The reference is probably to David in the cave of Adullam (1 Sam 22:1), though his adventure in the cave in the wilderness of Engedi (1 Sam 24) is possible. The psalm is appropriate for reflection on David's dangerous early career: "We can sense the same realistic but adventurous spirit, spurred instead of cowed by danger, in the psalm as in the story" (Kidner, 205). The psalm has been democratized in interpretation, however (see *Form/Structure/Setting* of Ps 56), and can be read by any person who struggles with dangers which threaten to overwhelm. As in the case of many of the individual laments, allowance should be made for their use in family or group rituals as well as in the temple. The speaker is not *necessarily* a king.

Comment

Superscription (57:1). The expression *al-tashheth,* "do not destroy," is also found in the titles of Pss 58; 59; 75. It may be linked to Deut 9:26: "And I [Moses] prayed to the LORD, "O LORD, God, destroy not [אל תשחת] thy people." So Dahood, who argues that the liturgist responsible for the psalm heading interpreted the psalm as a lament of a king or religious leader. However, the reference is too general for such specific identifications. Delitzsch notes also 1 Sam 26:9 and Isa 65:8. Indeed, the Isa 65:8 reference may provide the key for the obscure expression:

> As the wine is found in the cluster,
> and they say, "Do not destroy it
> for there is a blessing in it,"
> so will I do for my servants' sake.

The "do not destroy it" expression seems to have been a popular saying or proverb which reflected the idea of a vineyard keeper refusing to destroy grapevines when the first clusters of grapes were bad. The vines still had the blessing of life in them and a potential for future production. Like the vines, Israel had brought forth grapes worthy of destruction, but Yahweh would not destroy Israel because she still contained a blessing (cf. Isa 28:23–28). If this is the case, the expression is appropriate for the psalms to which it was applied (cf. Mowinckel, *PIW*, II, 215).

Prayer for saving mercy (57:2–4). The suppliant asks God for a merciful response, because he/she has taken refuge under the protective care of God. The use of the root חנן ("have mercy") in a context like this probably carries a connotation of loyalty on the part of the suppliant as well as that of request for a gracious response (A. A. Anderson, I, 405). The prayer is designed to put a claim on God to protect the one who has taken asylum under the divine protection. The reference to "the shadow of your wings" probably represents more than a mere metaphorical reference to the protective care of God (see Pss 17:8; 36:8; 63:8; also see 61:5; 91:1, 4). The metaphor certainly suggests the protective care of a bird for its young (note Deut 32:10–11), under whose wings the young seek refuge when danger threatens (see Craigie, 292). However, it is very likely that there is a more direct reference to the symbolism of the cherub wings so strongly associated with the temple in Jerusalem (see 1 Kgs 6:23–28; 8:6–7). Those interpreters who stress the reflection of the asylum function of the temple in the psalms are prone to point to the outstretched wings of the cherubim over the Ark in the Holy of Holies and the safety of the temple area for those who are falsely accused and/or persecuted (e.g., Beyerlin, Kraus, Schmidt). Perhaps the refugee could see the wings of the cherubim in the Holy of Holies of the temple. If there is an allusion to the cherubim in the expression "under the shadow of your wings," it refers to the outspread wings which were conceptualized as bearing the throne of God (1 Sam 4:4; 2 Sam 6:2; 2 Kgs 19:15; Isa 37:16; Lev 16:21; Pss 80:1; 99:1). The cherubim in the temple were models of the heavenly creatures used by God for various purposes, including the support of his heavenly throne (see M. Haran, "The Ark and the Cherubim: Their Symbolic Significance in Biblical Ritual," *IEJ* 9 [1959] 30–38, 89–94; *Temple and Temple Service in Ancient Israel* [Oxford: Clarendon Press, 1978], 246–59). The biblical cherubim are depicted as having different functions. The reference to Yahweh riding upon a cherub in 2 Sam. 22:11 // Ps 18:11, in the context of a saving theophany, is of major significance for Ps 57 (see Dahood, I, 107–8; cf. Hab 3:3–4). The allusion almost surely includes the idea of a divine bird or flying creature with a great wingspan and the power to protect whatever is under its wings (note Exod 19:4; Deut 32:11).

The second part of the prayer (vv 3–4) expresses the confidence of the suppliant in the Most High God, who will challenge the enemies to combat and who is going to send forth his love and faithfulness to bring the suppliant to safety. Perhaps, the divine attendants should be personified here as Loyal-Love and Faithfulness (or Truth). See Pss 51:3, 8 for discussion of these words; see also Pss 23:6; 40:12; 43:3; 85:11; cf. 25:21; 87:37; 89:15. If metaphorical personification is present, it is an adaptation of the concept of two attendants who accompanied a god or a dignitary, such as a king (see Dahood, I, 148, 24; II, 51). If this is the case, the divine servants will come and help the suppliant in a difficult situation. The verb (גמר) in v 3 implies finishing or bringing to an end (see Ps 7:10) and avenging in some contexts.

A complaint and petition (57:5–7). The speaker expresses complaint about great danger in v 5. The enemies are compared to man-eating lions, who wait to spring on their prey with vicious teeth. The metaphor of threatening animals representing enemies is found in several individual laments (e.g., Pss 7:3; 10:9; 17:12; 22:13-14, 17, 22). The suppliant is forced to lie down (assumedly for sleep) in the midst of those who would tear one to pieces—with words at least ("whose tongues are sharp swords"). The lying down suggests something like an accused person who flees to the sanctuary of Yahweh in order to be tested and freed from the charges and attacks of accusers, perhaps spending the night with the accusers and waiting for some kind of divine verdict with the coming of the dawn (so H. Schmidt; similarly Kraus, Beyerlin). The imagery would fit some sort of night vigil (see Pss 5:4; 17:3; Johnson, *CPIP*, 197, 244–45, 251–54), but such a context is not required. The figure of speech can be a simple one of rest at night.

The writer of the psalm may have had a king in mind (like Solomon in 1 Kgs 3:11, or David in such situations as indicated by the title). Of course, in a democratized interpretation the language became almost completely metaphorical and depicted the day-by-day harassment by the enemies of a worshiper. Craigie (200), commenting on 22:13–19, writes, "The words evoke the abject terror of one who is powerless, but surrounded, with no avenue of escape; those who look upon him in his miserable estate assume the proportion of beasts (in the language of poetry)."

In v 6, God is exhorted to rise up above the heavens in a great demonstration of his glory. Weiser, Kraus, et al., are correct in understanding this as the language of a theopł any/epiphany (see Pss 18:8–16; 50:1–3; 68:2–5; 82:8; 97:2–5). What did the suppliant expect to happen? What did the poet have in mind? Unfortunately, the present stage of research into the history of Israelite religion does not seem to permit a definitive answer. Was the theophanic experience purely a visionary one? Were there ritual components to portray the divine presence, such as fire, the sound of the *shophar*-trumpet, and the smoke in the temple representing the column of clouds which symbolized the divine presence? Was the divine presence signaled by music and singing, perhaps accompanied by cult acclamations and chants? Was the rising of the sun on festival days considered to be a symbolic enactment of the theophany? Was the theophany a word-event in which the worshipers were brought to experience the reality of the divine presence by the recitation of psalms and other spoken/written material—especially if such recitations occurred in the sanctity of a holy place in which the worshiper was powerfully conditioned for the actualization of a theophanic experience (for example, representing the actuality of the Sinai theophany, as in Exod 19 and 24)? Was the theophanic presence perceived in actions by priests, proclamations of the divine name, victories in battle, healings from disease, and the like? Probably, all these elements and more were woven into the theophanic expectations and experiences of Israelite worship (see J. Jeremias, "Theophany in the OT," *IDBSup*, 896–98, for a summary discussion and citation of the major literature). In any case, the prayer expresses the desire for a saving manifestation of glory and power of the divine presence in the heavens and over the earth.

The speaker returns to complaint in v 7 and laments of being bowed down like a captive before enemies. The enemies have set traps for the speaker's feet and a pit "for my face," perhaps, as Dahood argues, so that speaker might fall face first into it. The danger is great, but v 7d expresses confidence in the act-consequence process: the diggers will fall into their own hole! This is obviously a form of the "He who digs a pit will fall into it" thought about retribution (see Prov 1:18–19; 26:27; 28:10; ; Eccl 10:8; Ps 141:10). See *Comment* on Ps 54:7; also Pss 7:16; 9:16–17; 37:7–8.

Affirmation, readiness to praise, and vow of thanksgiving (57:8–11). The speaker feels an internal steadfastness of heart/mind, which is true and loyal to God (contrast Ps 78:37; see Pss 51:12; 112:7–8; 118:2), and eagerly anticipates the coming of dawn and the thanksgiving he or she is prepared to give. The self-exhortation in v 9 encourages the worshiper to awake and to use musical instruments to usher in the dawn. The "my glory" in v 9 is probably the God-given faculty of worth and praise, that aspect of human personhood which responds to God. McKay (*SJT* 31 [1978] 171) defines it as "the capacity to receive a divinely imparted glory and to glorify God in return." Of course, the "my glory" is equal to "myself," as in the case of "my soul" or "my liver." However, the expression should not be reduced to mere "self." Weiser (428) comments, "The worshiper's whole being is filled with the thought of God; and this state of mind is his 'glory,' which is spread over him like the resplendent majesty of God." Thus the speaker's "glory" is a sense of personal worth and ability to praise God.

Some translations treat the "dawn" in v 9c as a reference to time, as in kjv: "I myself will awake early" (see Perowne, 454). But it is more likely that the word is personified and reflects a dual background of understanding. First, a Canaanite god of dawn, actually one of a pair of gods, Shachar and Shalim (Dawn and Dusk), were associated with the celebration of rejuvenation and fertility (see Theodor H. Gaster, *Thespis* [Garden City, NY: Doubleday, 1961], 406–39). These gods were among the "gracious gods," associated with good vintage and harvest, with love, and life. For Shachar, see also Isa 14:12, הֵילֵל בֶּן־שָׁחַר, "O shining one, son of dawn," traditionally translated as "Lucifer, son of the morning," and incorrectly associated with a supposed fall of Satan from heaven. Second, the expectation of intervening help from Yahweh is put in the context of the dawn and the morning in some OT texts (see Pss 46:6; 90:14; 143:8)—so much so that it is sometimes argued that the morning was the time for divine help, though this should not be overemphasized (see C. Barth, *TDOT*, II, 227–28). The concepts of dawn and morning convey ideas of the new, the different, and the future in contrast to the day and night behind them. The time itself, however, was not the reason for saving action, as Barth comments: "It was primarily the new presence of Yahweh in a theophany and in an oracle which made the morning the time more than any other when the oppressed and 'Israel' expected help." Thus the speaker is ready to rouse the dawn (Dawn) out of night with music and praise. Leslie (356) describes the speaker as "one with a vibrant sense of spiritual release and a deep sense of religious security."

We could take v 10 as reflecting a large congregation of people, suitable for a king, who have gathered and who can hear the thankful praise of the speaker. In this case, the people have come to a festival in Jerusalem from many different places (cf. Acts 2). This interpretation follows even if we translate the verbs as "I will thank . . . I will praise." I have read the verbs as modal imperfects, expressing "the hyperbole of a joyful heart" (McCullough, 301). With enthusiastic joy of anticipation, the speaker is ready to sing God's praise to the peoples and nations of the whole world. In hymnic fashion (note the "for," כִּי), v 11 expresses the greatness of the loyal-love (חֶסֶד) and faithfulness (אֱמֶת) of God (on these words see *Comment* on v 4 above). "The Divine mercy and truth are so extensive as to be a connecting link between heaven and earth, and all mankind should unite in praise of God in recognition of the blessing" (Cohen, 182).

A final petition (57:12). This verse repeats v 6 (except that there is no article on "heavens," as in v 6) and may be intended as the response of the hearer/reader of the psalm, who is urged to join with the suppliant's prayer in v 6 for a theophanic manifestation of the glory of God. If this is correct, the suppliant's prayer ends with v 11; v 12 is the reader's prayer. Vv 11 and 12 combine to plead with God to manifest over heaven and earth his loyal-love and faithfulness, which tower up to the heavens in their greatness (cf. Isa 6:1; see O. Keel, *The Symbolism of the Biblical World*, 171–72; Dahood, II, 53).

Explanation

Weiser (428) comments that the suppliant in this psalm is presented as one who stands before God *simultaneously* possessing and expecting. The suppliant knows that he or she is in deadly peril from the scourge of attacks from enemies, but there is no panic or sense of being at the brink of despair and defeat because of the conviction that God will cause the wicked dealings of the enemies to come back on them for their own destruction. The speaker eagerly anticipates the "dawn" when there will be some kind of theophanic experience which will demonstrate the will and glory of God, because he or she has nothing to fear from the rising up of God in glory.

The psalm emphasizes the divine, heavenly realm as the source of help for faithful worshipers, whether they are kings or peasants. In this psalm God is referred to twenty-two times by name or pronoun in eleven verses. The references to "heavens" in vv 4, 6, 11, 12 emphasize the resources of the divine realm which are available for the faithful on earth. In this regard, it may be noted that the psalm brings together the multipartite world of ancient thought. A bipartite view of the universe is prevalent in the OT (though others are found). The "heavens and the earth" in Gen 1:1 is the union of two separate cosmic realms according to R. Knierim ("Cosmos and History in Israel's Theology," *HBT* 3 [1981] 76). The formulaic expression "heavens and earth" seems to carry both the idea of the bipolar nature of creation and its oneness. The interaction of these two fundamentally different realms of creation is reflected in Ps 57. Earth is the living space for human beings, and heaven is the living space for God, the locus of his heavenly temple and throne (see Pss 11:4; 18:7) and of his cosmic dominion. However, God moves into the realm of earth and manifests his glorious presence, especially through his acts of salvation. His temple or sanctuary on earth is an extension of the heavenly realm (Knierim, 79). God's presence and will on earth are contested and distorted, especially through those human actions which are reflected so vividly in the psalms of lament. But in the heavenly realm, his will is supreme (see Ps 82; Matt 2:6; 3:2). God's created order may be threatened, especially by the wicked and violent actions of human beings (see Jer 4:19–22). Therefore it was appropriate for the Israelite worshiper to pray that the glory of God be "over all the earth"; i.e., that he would actualize his will and authority throughout the living space of humanity: "Thy will be done on earth as it is in heaven."

Ps 57 is regularly used in some Christian churches on Easter morning, and it is appropriate for such use. The Easter period is one in which we celebrate the message: "Christ the Lord is risen today!" and because of this we are "strengthened with all power, according to his [God's] glorious might" and we are delivered from "the dominion of darkness and transferred . . . to the kingdom of the beloved Son" (Col 1:8–11, RSV). But we also wait with expectancy for the coming of the Lord ("until he comes," 1 Cor 11:26), for the awaking of the great dawn when the fullness of God's glory will be so manifest on the earth that "all flesh shall see it together" (Isa 40:5) and acknowledge that "every knee should bow, in heaven and on earth and under the earth, and every tongue confess that Jesus Christ is Lord, to the glory of God the Father" (Phil 2:10–11, RSV; cf. also 1 Pet 5:8). Let us join with ancient suppliants in praying that God will rise up in glory over the heavens and the earth. As with the speaker in Ps 57, we can hardly wait to start the celebration. Indeed, we are already singing.

Judgment Speech and Prayer *(58:1–12)*

Bibliography

Althmann, R. "Psalm 58:10 in the Light of Ebla." *Bib* 64 (1983) 122–24. **Bonhoeffer, D.** "A Bonhoeffer Sermon," tr. D. Bloesch. *TToday* 38 (1982) 465–71. **Jeremias, J.** *Kultprophetie.* 120–25. **Seybold, K.** "Psalm LVIII, Ein Lösungsversuch." *VT* 30 (1980) 56–66.

Translation

1   For the leader;[a] *al tashheth*,[b] a Davidic *miktam*.[c]

2 (1)   *Do you really speak justly, You "Mighty Ones"?* [a]   (4+3)
       do you judge people [b] *with equity?*

3 (2)   *No, in your heart* [a] *you do evil;*   (3+4)
       preparing the way [b] *in the land for the violence of your hands.*

4 (3)   *Such wicked ones are loathsome* [a] *from birth;*   (3+4)
       wayward liars [b] *from the womb.*

5 (4)   *Their venom is like snake venom;*   (3+4)
       they are like a cobra [a] *that has stopped its ears;*

6 (5)   *that will not hear the voice of snake-charmers—*   (4+3)
       who are skilled weavers of spells! [a]

7 (6)   *O God, smash* [a] *their teeth in their mouth;*   (4+4)
       break off (their) lion-fangs, [b] *O Yahweh.*

8 (7)   *Let their strength drain away* [a] *like water that flows away;* (4+4)
       let them shoot their arrows without force; [b]

9 (8)   *Let them be like a snail* [a] *which melts as it goes;*   (4+4)
       like an aborted fetus which never saw the sun.

10 (9) *Before their* [a] *pots can feel (the heat of) a thorn bush,*   (4+3)
       let him (God) sweep them away alive as in the fury of a storm. [b]

11 (10) *The righteous will rejoice because they see (their) vindication;* [a] (4+4)
       they will wash their feet in the blood of the wicked; [b]

12 (11) *People will say:*   (2+3+4)
       "Surely there is a reward for the righteous;
       surely there is a God who judges [a] *on the earth!"*

Notes

1.a. See n. 51:1–2.a.
1.b. See n. 57:1.b.
1.c. See n. 56:1.c.
2.a. MT has אֵלֶם, which apparently means "silence" or "muteness," and the verse would be read, "Do you indeed speak righteousness in silence?" or perhaps, "Do you really speak a mute righteousness?" or "Indeed, is the righteousness you should speak mute in your mouth?"—meaning(?) that those addressed (judges) pronounce sentences in such ways as to negate the effectiveness of the justice they are supposed to establish: "They are *dumb* when they ought to speak, or afterwards they

are said to be *deaf* when they ought to hear" (Perowne, 455). The most probable reading is אֵלִים or אִלֶם
with reference to gods or angels ("mighty ones") who were delegated responsibilities for maintaining
the proper order on earth (see Ps 82; A. A. Anderson, Mowinckel, *PIW*, I, 148; Gunkel, Kraus). Rogerson
and McKay, in a manner similar to Gunkel (249), suggest that the image here is sarcastic; "they lord it
like gods over the righteous," but their injustice is far from godlike (NAB, "Do you indeed like gods
pronounce justice . . ."). However, the term could be understood as "mighty ones" (those with
divine characteristics) with reference to leaders or judges (see Ps 82; cf. Exod 21:6; 22:7, 8); LXX and
Jerome read אֻלָם = אֵלֶם, "but/indeed/truly," though Aquila read as MT. Kimchi (see Cohen) read
אֵלֶם (from the root "bind") as a "company"—"Do you indeed speak as a righteous company
(should)?"—and KJV uses "congregation," but such usage is not found elsewhere in MT. The option
adopted in the *Translation* is to read either as אֵלִם, "gods/mighty men/leaders," or as אֵלִים (defective
form of אֵילִים), "rams," used metaphorically for "Mighty Ones," "leaders," or "authorities" (so Dahood,
I, 9–10; II, 57; BDB, 18a).

2.b. Lit., "sons of mankind" = "human beings." It is possible that בְּנֵי־אָדָם should be treated as
vocative, "O human beings," as it probably is in the LXX (Delitzsch, II, 205, argues that it must be an
accusative objective rather than the vocative, which would be בְּנֵי־אִישׁ, as in Ps 4:3; but the בְּנֵי־אָדָם can
be read as vocative in Ps 90:3; cf. בֶּן־אָדָם in Ezek 2:1, passim).

3.a. Syriac suggests כֻּלְּכֶם, "all of you," for "in your heart," which is easier but probably incorrect. It
is possible that the expression should be understood as willingness to commit evil deeds, since the
"heart" is the mind and the center of volition (so NAB, "Nay, you willingly commit crimes"). The
meaning taken here is that of meditating on or planning for crimes, which is explained in the second
line.

3.b. The verb פָּלַס is frequently taken in the sense of "weigh out/mete/deal out" and so, as in RSV,
"Your hands deal out violence on the earth." Another option is to take פָּלַס as meaning "look at, watch"
(see KB, 764; cf. Prov 4:26; 5:6, 21); so NEB, "and survey the violence that you have done on earth"
(also NAB). The best option is to understand פָּלַס in the sense "break through" or "prepare," especially
of a road (see KB, 764; Ps 78:50; Isa 26:7). The evil deeds done in their hearts prepare the way for the
violence of their hands. This seems to be the basic meaning regardless of the exact reading of the
verbs. Cf. Mic 2:1.

4.a. Following Dahood; see KB, 253; Job 19:17; M. Pope, *Job*, AB 15, 132.

4.b. LXX has "they speak lies," but MT need not be changed; nor is it necessary to follow Gunkel
and Kraus and take the verb with what precedes: ". . . they err from the womb, they speak lies from
their birth." NAB, "astray from birth have the liars gone"; NEB, "liars, no sooner born than they go astray."

5.a. The exact identity of the snake intended here is uncertain. A cobra or adder of some type
seems likely. A dangerous snake is required by the context.

6.a. See Dahood; NEB, NAB, et al.; KB, 273. The plural participle מְחֻכָּם (חכם), "learned/skilled,"
appears elsewhere only in Prov 30:24.

7.a. LXX reads, "God has broken . . . ," indicating a perfect rather than an imperative verb, and
also reads vv 7–10 as statements of confidence. But MT seems preferable, with imprecatory statements. Cf. 3:7; 124:6–7.

7.b. The etymology of מַלְתָּעוֹת is uncertain. Usually taken as מְתַלְּעוֹת, "jaw bones" or "jaw teeth," as
in Joel 1:6; Job 29:17; Prov 30:14. See Dahood.

8.a. The verb is niphal imperfect indicative or jussive of מאס, usually considered to be a variation
of מסס, "to dissolve, melt." Cf. Job 7:5; Pope, *Job*, AB 15, 56, translates "oozes."

8.b. A difficult colon subject to different interpretations. Kraus follows Gunkel and reads כְּמוֹ חָצִיר דָּרֶךְ and
understands the verb מלל in the sense of "wither": "withered like grass along the pathway"; cf. RSV, "like
grass let them be trodden down and wither." So also NEB, D. W. Thomas (*TRP*, 22), as כְּמוֹ חָצִיר יָדֵךְ יִתְמֹלָלוּ,
reading ידך = דכה, "crushed, pounded": "may they wither like trodden grass"; also JB. MT, however, may
yield a meaning like that given in the *Translation* provided דרך is understood in the sense of stretching the bow to shoot arrows. כְּמוֹ יִתְמֹלָלוּ may have either of two meanings, "as if they were headless"
(מלל in the sense of "circumcise, cut off"; cf. Josh 5:2; Gen 17:11; NAB, "headless shafts") or "as if they
were without force" (מלל in the sense of "wither, fade, languish"; see *HOTTP*, 269). The latter is
adopted.

9.a. שַׁבְּלוּל occurs only here. S. R. Driver (see Anderson) argues for the meaning "miscarriage,"
which is reflected in NEB's "like an abortive birth that melts away," parallel to the "aborted fetus" in
the next line.

10.a. The text is eased in the context by a 3rd masc. pl. suffix (see *BHS*): "their pots." MT has "your
pots."

10.b. A difficult verse; even Dahood refuses to attempt a translation! NEB follows S. R. Driver (see n. 9.a.) and D. W. Thomas (*TRP*, 22) and reads כְּמוֹ חֹחַ כְּמוֹ חָרוּל יְשָׂעֵם (for MT יִשָׂעָרֶנּוּ כְּמוֹ־חָרוֹן): "All unaware, may they be rooted up like a thorn-bush, like weeds which a man angrily clears away." Kraus also adopts חֹחַ, "thorn," and חָרוּל, "weed," along with assuming that יְבִינוּ is a transposition of יָנוּבוּ, "grow up/thrive." The change of the verb in the first line can be assumed without any changes in the second line: "Before your thorns grow on the bush, while it is still green, he will sweep it away as if it were dried" (see PIR, 270). The translation above is only another conjecture. See *Comment.* חָרוֹן is taken as the "burning anger" or "fury" of a storm (cf. 88:17–18). R. Althmann (*Bib* 64 [1983] 122–24) follows a suggestion of M. Dahood that the two כְּמוֹ forms be read as a contraction of a Sumerian-Eblaite *ma-wu*, "water," plus the preposition כְּ, resulting in

> like running water, like raging water
> He will sweep him away.

The storm imagery is probably correct, but it seems possible without the importation of an Eblaite word.

11.a. Better than the usual "vengeance." See Dahood (who uses "victory") and the references cited, and George E. Mendenhall (*The Tenth Generation: The Origins of the Biblical Tradition* [Baltimore: Johns Hopkins UP, 1973], 69–104), who argues that the meaning transmitted by נקם is best expressed as "defensive or punitive vindication." Cf Ps 18:47.

11.b. Dahood argues, with some persuasiveness, that the בְּ should be understood as "of"; "he will wash his feet *of* the blood of the wicked" = "he will wash from his feet the blood of the wicked." Also, Sabourin, 300; Dahood, III, 391–93.

12.a. The use of the plural participle with *Elohim* is unusual. LXX has κρίνων αὐτούς = שֹׁפְטָם, "who judges them" (either the wicked or the righteous), and may be correct. A plural verb is sometimes used with *Elohim* (as in 2 Sam 7:23). Possibly we should read, "there is divine judgment on the earth," thinking more in terms of systems of retribution and act-consequences rather than direct action by God.

Form/Structure/Setting

Form-critically, this psalm is most often classified as a lament of the communal type (see A. A. Anderson, 429; Leslie, 230). Leslie describes it as "a congrega-tional lament over tyranny which is suffered by human beings" (also Mowinckel, *PIW*, I, 196, 200, 202, 221). In general terms, this is correct. However, more specifically, Ps 58 is more like prophetic judgment speech (see *Form/Structure/ Setting* of Ps 52). It most probably stems from the preaching of cult prophets or prophetic-like persons (see Jeremias, *Kultprophetie*, 120–25) during the festivals and possibly other times of public worship. The psalm is a vehement denunciation of the corruption of leaders and judges and an equally vehement call for their judgment. It concludes with an affirmation of the justice of God. The details of the context reflected in the psalm are too obscure for any certainty, but in general, the psalm is probably derived from preaching of cultic prophets in pre-exilic sanctuaries such as Amos at Bethel (Amos 7:10–17). For major discussions of cultic prophecy in the Psalms, see A. R. Johnson (*CPIP*) and J. Jeremias (*Kultprophetie*).

Klaus Seybold (*VT* 30 [1980] 56–66) argues for an original psalm consisting of vv 2–3, 5, 8–10, 12, with vv 4, 6, 7, 11 resulting from a secondary redaction at a later time. The original psalm was a judgment speech of God against divine beings ("gods" or "mighty ones" in v 2) who had failed in their responsibilities to establish justice and order in human affairs (cf. Ps 82). In this view, the redaction reinterprets the psalm in terms of human beings who are wicked leaders and judges. Seybold thinks that the additions reflect strong emotions, stemming out of painful conditions, lacking a more theoretical, wisdom-like quality. The result is a series of "absurdities" in the present text, according to Seybold. He may be correct about a redactional process in which an original psalm was re-interpreted, which would account for the ambiguity in v 2. However, it seems prudent to allow the redactor more skill than does Seybold. The "absurdities" are probably more ours than the redactor's.

The psalm can be divided into the following sections:

vv 2–3	Arraignment of unjust leaders
vv 4–6	The nature of the wicked
vv 7–10	Prayer for judgment
vv 11–12	Assurance of the righteous

Comment

Arraignment of unjust leaders (58:2–3). The uncertainties of v 2 make exegesis of these verses precarious, but if the translation and notes above are correct, the leaders are addressed by a speaker with sarcastic rhetorical questions which imply the answer "No." For the use of such questions, see Pss 52:3; 62:4. The background of the address to the אלים, "mighty ones/gods," in v 2 is that reflected in Deut 32:8–9 and Ps 82, which is the concept of the apportioned assignment of divine beings, or angels, to support and establish justice among the people to whom they were assigned. In Ps 82, the divine beings are put under the judgment of Yahweh because of their failure to maintain justice for the weak and dependent people of their realms (see *Comment*, Ps 82). The actual functions of the divine beings were exercised, of course, by human agents: kings, leaders, judges. It is clear in Ps 58 that immoral leaders are attacked and that they are the אלים, "mighty ones/gods," of v 2a. Thus the expression is sarcastic, addressing leaders who are supposed to function as agents of divine beings (probably claiming divine ordination for their powers) but who are in reality רשעים, "wicked ones" (v 4), whose true nature is described emphatically in v 3. There is probably an intended contrast between the "Mighty Ones" and the "sons of mankind" (translated "people" above). The leaders have the means and the responsibility to care for the common people, who have little defense against the oppression of those who have power. The Mighty Ones plot evil in their minds ("hearts") and then carry it out in the land (v 3; cf. Ps 36:5), as in Mic 2:1:

> Woe to those who desire wickedness
>   and work evil upon their beds!
> When the morning dawns, they perform it,
>   because it is in the power of their hand. (rsv)

The condemnation of unjust judgments and the evasion of the responsibility for justice on the part of leaders is a rather common subject in the prophetic literature: e.g., Amos 5:7; 6:12; Isa 1:23; 5:23; 10:1–4; Mic 3:11; Jer 5:26–29.

The nature of the wicked (58:4–6). The wicked (רשעים) is a frequent term in the Psalter (the root word in one form or another appears some ninety-two times, more than in any other book in the OT). The basic idea of the word seems to go back to legal traditions and to apply to someone in a community who was judged guilty of a charge. In its primary usage, the word does not refer to general wrongdoing but to individual cases. However, the usage of רשע in the psalms is varied and generalized in terms of character and behavior. The range of meaning spreads from guilt to wrongdoing, to sinful behavior, and to godlessness. "Wicked" is the linguistic counterpart of "righteous" (see discussion of Ps 52:8). Whatever the righteous *are*, the wicked *are not*, and vice versa. The descriptive language associated with the wicked in the psalms gives an understanding of what is involved in wicked character and behavior:

They speak peace with their neighbors, but are evil in heart	Ps 28:3
Parallel with "evil-doers" (Ps 59:3)	Pss 28:3; 92:8; 101:8; 141:9–10.
"Their right hand is full of bribes" contrasted with a person of integrity in	Ps 26:4–5, 9–10; Ps 26:1–3, 11–12.
They are "unjust and cruel"	Ps 71:4
They are arrogant and scornful	Pss 1:1; 119:51; 73:3; 75:5
They practice oppression and "love violence"	Pss 11:5; 55:3; 94:3–6
They lie and bear false witness	Pss 5:7; 12:3; 26:4

Ps 36:2–5 provides a definitive description of the wicked:

Transgression speaks to the wicked
    deep in his heart;
there is no fear of God
    before his eyes.
For he flatters himself in his own eyes
    that his inequity cannot be found out and hated.
The words of his mouth are mischief and deceit;
    he has ceased to act wisely and do good.
He plots mischief while on his bed;
    he sets himself in a way that is not good;
    he spurns not evil. (RSV, see also, 10:1–11)

(See Craigie's comments, 291–92).

In general, the wicked person was any person who, if carefully examined and tried, would be judged guilty of violations of both the norms of the human society in which he or she lived and of disregard for the will of God. The wicked are always guilty. (For discussion, see C. van Leeuwen, *THAT*, II, 813–18; K. H. Richards, *A Form and Traditio-Historical Study of RŠ^c (Wicked)* [Ph.D. diss., Claremont Graduate School, 1970]; H.-J. Kraus, *Theology of the Psalms*, 129–31, 154–55; L. Köhler, *Old Testament Theology*, tr. A. S. Todd [Philadelphia: Westminster Press, 1957], 171).

The description of the wicked in vv 4–6 is that of the class to which the Mighty Ones belong. At least, this seems more probable than to assume that the wicked are the result and/or the agents of the unjust activity of the Mighty Ones. The

Mighty Ones are wicked in the totality of their existence (see Ps 51:7), loath-some, wayward lions from birth. Their words and deeds are as poisonous as the venom of the deadly cobra (v 5). In addition, they are so congenitally wicked that they are like a *deaf* cobra, which cannot be charmed to permit the removal of its venom. "The rulers and judges are so corrupt that no amount of pleading, however just and right, can dissuade them from their iniquitous behavior" (Dahood, II, 60). The hyperbole of the language drives home the point of the deadly and incorrigible nature of the Mighty Ones. They are truly wicked—and unfortunately we know them well.

Prayer for judgment (58:7–10). The prayer is composed of a series of extremely forceful statements. The intensity of the statements was probably intended to reach a climax in v 10. Unfortunately the translation and meaning of v 10 are very uncertain, and no significant exegetical emphasis should be put on it. Using the figure of the lion, the speaker prays that God will break the teeth of the wicked (v 7, i.e., destroy their effectiveness for doing harm. The prayer for reduction to impotent strength is given four figures of speech in vv 8–9: (1) that their strength would drain away like the quick disappearance of water in a dry wadi; (2) that they would dissipate their strength like a warrior who shoots arrows ineffectively—without force (arrows are too expensive to waste in aimless shoot-ing); (3) that they dissolve like a snail—which according to popular opinion melted in the slimy trail which was left in its track; (4) that they be like an aborted fetus, i.e., that they have nonexistence as normal human beings. V 10 seems to be a request that the wicked Mighty Ones be swept away as in a furious storm—quicker than the heat of a burning thorn bush can reach a cooking pot (a dry thorn bush would provide almost instantaneous heat).

The maledictions in vv 8–10 belong to the category of a curse whose execution is the responsibility of a deity. The technical terms of cursing are not present, but the language of the prayer contains the kind of vehement and violent expressions found in curses, e.g., the breaking or rendering ineffective of weapons (see D. R. Hillers, *Treaty-Curses and the Old Testament Prophets*, BibOr 16 [Rome: Pontifical Biblical Institute, 1964], 60; Jer 49:35; 51:56; Ezek 39:3; etc.) and the aborted birth (see Job 3:16). As is the case generally in the prayers of the Psalter, the worshiper does not curse the enemies directly, but calls on God to activate the appropriate consequences of their actions.

Assurance of the righteous (58:11–12). For the term "the righteous," see Ps 52:8. Note the contrast between the "righteous" and the "wicked" described in vv 4–6 (also note that the "justly" in v 2 is צֶדֶק, "rightness/righteousness"). The righ-teous are assured that they will rejoice at their vindication and deliverance from the power of the Mighty Ones. V 11b is a very harsh statement, unless Dahood is correct (see note 11.b.). However, the statement should be understood as a hyperbolic idiomatic expression which should not be pressed for a literal mean-ing. The point is that there are harsh judgments on earth which set things right; let the wicked beware (cf. Rev 18:20). The world is not totally dominated by Mighty Ones, whose sinister ways stem from the evil in their hearts. There is a God who will not indefinitely tolerate the cobra-like ways of those who falsely act like gods (or act for false gods). The righteous can expect a "reward" (v 12), literally, "a fruit," the "fruit" of vindication and victory (for פְּרִי, "fruit," see Ps 104:13; Isa 3:10; Prov 11:30; Gal 5:22). The double אַךְ in v 12 ("surely/nevertheless") provides a strong emphasis on something contrary to what had been said or expected (note Ps 23:6, and see the discussion of Ps 73:1). The victory of the righteous and the judgment of God are assured, but they contravene normal human expectations. Let the "mighty ones" take note.

Explanation

This psalm has the character of a prophetic judgment speech, as noted in the *Form/Structure/Setting* section above. However, it also contains a prayer in vv 7–10 which is typical of the petitions in the laments and asks for divine judgments of a drastic nature. The major question which arises from this psalm is that of the seemingly harsh and vindictive attitude expressed toward enemies. God is asked to carry out terrible judgments on the foes of the speakers in the psalms. Besides this psalm, Pss 59, 69:23–25, 109, and 137 are well known for expressing hope in the destruction of foes, but there are also other passages containing petitions aimed at violent ends for enemies, e.g., Pss 5:11; 10:15; 17:13; 54:7; 55:10 (according to A. Aejmelaeus, *The Traditional Prayer in the Psalms*, 43, there are some forty imperative petitions which ask for injury to or destruction of enemies). These statements are disturbing to the sensitive conscience and have received considerable theological attention. The remarks which follow are aimed at providing a modest rationale for dealing with such psalm elements.

In the appropriation of this language into the life of faith it is well to begin with a framework of understanding rather than with an apology in the sense of an effort to explain away the disturbing elements. Those who take the Bible seriously know that its writings are very realistically human; the realities of life are confronted without blinking or shrinking back. The psalms contain "honest-to-God" language which expresses the actual feelings of human beings in ordinary life, devoid of some sort of supposed (and false) spiritual idealism. They confront us with our full humanity and the true nature of the world in which we live. The petitions about enemies give "freedom of expression to those raw edges in our life that do not easily submit to the religious conviction we profess on good days" (W. Brueggemann, *The Message of the Psalms: A Theological Commentary* [Minneapolis: Augsburg, 1984], 85).

The significance of expressing anger and hurt *to* God should be evaluated positively. Fear, hurt, anger, and the desire for revenge are elements in our lives as human beings. We gain nothing by denying the real nature of our experiences. Forgiveness of enemies is not easy, but it is facilitated by the acknowledgment to God of our hurt and anger. When bitterness and pain are poured out to God, the way may be cleared for a fresh vision of reality and new trust in God. These psalms help to purify us of feelings of rage, and also of dereliction and abandonment. They lead toward a catharsis of faith and a renewal of the soul. They also help us to realize that there is no place or condition of life where God is not.

Further, in most cases, the language about enemies is directed to God rather than to the enemies (there are some exceptions, e.g., Ps 52), and the suppliants ask for God to take direct action or to activate the act-consequence process of retribution. The speakers do not ask for the power to take things into their own hands and to be able personally to punish their foes, and permission is never granted for them to do so. Brueggemann (85) has stressed that this points to submission in faith to the divine presence and relinquishment of personal retribution. The petitions in the psalms thrust their readers toward a faith in Yahweh and his avowed will to set things right and deal with destructive people:

> Vengeance [vindication, נָקָם] and retribution belong to me. . . . For Yahweh will judge [vindicate, יָדִין] his people and he will have compassion [יִתְנֶחָם] on his servants, for he sees that their power is gone and only prisoners and abandoned ones remain (Deut 32:35–36; also see v 41; Ps 94:1; Rom 12:1).

Yahweh is not an indifferent God, who turns away from the terrible evils of humanity; he is the defender of the poor and oppressed, the comforter of those who hurt and mourn. He is a God who hears and saves. "The raw speech of rage can be submitted to Yahweh because there is reason for confidence that Yahweh takes it seriously and will act" (Brueggemann, 85). The psalms do not allow for the personal possession of retribution; it must be surrendered to God: "whoever entrusts revenge to God dismisses any thought of ever taking revenge himself" (Bonhoeffer, *TToday* 38 [1982] 469).

The imprecatory elements in the psalms are also evocative, challenging the reader to identify with oppressed and suffering people, even though the reader may be quite comfortable. The psalms which deal with enemies invite those of us who read and hear them to enter into them on *behalf of others,* if not for ourselves. The language of these psalms evokes in us an awareness of the terrible wickedness that is in the world. They may not be our prayers, at the moment at least, but they are the prayers of our sisters and brothers who are trampled down by persons and powers beyond their control. The long Christian interpretation of the imprecatory psalm as the prayers of Christ on behalf of the poor and needy may be of real value in this regard. An ancient Christian tradition treats the psalms as both *about* Christ and as prayers *of* Christ (and, of course, in some cases as prayers addressed *to* Christ, identified with the deity addressed in the psalms). In this mode of interpretation, Augustine (c. A.D. 400) said of Ps 31:

> So then Christ is speaking here in the prophet. I say it boldly, Christ is speaking. He is going to say some things in this psalm which it would seem cannot possibly fit Christ, either as our glorious head in heaven—let alone as the eternal Word of God—or even as having the form of a servant, the form which he took of the Virgin. And yet it is Christ speaking, because Christ lives in Christ's members. . . . So it can be Christ speaking after all, because in Christ the Church speaks, and in the Church Christ speaks, the body in the head and the head in the body.

(The translation is that of E. Hill, *Nine Sermons of Saint Augustine on the Psalms* [London: Longmans, Green & Co., 1958], 111). Dietrich Bonhoeffer revived this old approach to the psalms in this century, by arguing that the psalms should be understood, in part at least, as the prayers of Christ. Bonhoeffer asked, "Who prays the Psalms? David (Solomon, Asaph, etc.) prays, Christ prays, we pray. We—that is, first of all the entire community in which alone the vast richness of the Psalter can be prayed" (D. Bonhoeffer, *Psalms: Prayer Book of the Bible*, tr. J. H. Burtness [Minneapolis: Augsburg, 1970], 21). How is it possible for us to do this? Bonhoeffer answers:

> How is it possible for a man and Jesus Christ to pray the Psalter together? It is the incarnate Son of God, who has borne every human weakness in his own flesh, who here pours out the heart of all humanity before God and who stands in our place and prays for us. He has known torment and pain, guilt and death [and enemies] more deeply than we. Therefore it is the prayer of human nature assumed by him which comes here before God. It is really our prayer, but since he knows us better than we know ourselves and since he himself was true man for our sakes, it is also really his prayer, and it can become our prayer only because it was his prayer. (Ibid., 20–21)

(For a full analysis of Bonhoeffer's approach, see M. Kuske, *The Old Testament as the Book of Christ: An Appraisal of Bonhoeffer's Interpretation*, tr. S. T. Kimbrough, Jr. [Philadelphia: Westminster Press, 1976]). This approach should not be taken as a simple Christianizing of the psalms or as assuming that they speak directly of Christ. The question concerns an interpretative stance, a faith context for reading the psalms.

Such a faith stance involves spiritual risk. The imprecatory psalms are likely to convict us of our own guilt. When we ask for divine judgment on our enemies, we are liable to an identity switch: We are often the enemies! How often have we and our kind been the just recipients of the judgments in the supplications to God in the Psalms! The imprecatory psalms may evoke in us who read them an awareness of our own violent sins and our hate, of our own need for confession, and for repentance. It may come as a shock to realize that despite our profession of Christ-like love of foes, our real attitude is more attuned to Ps 58 (and others like it). John Bright (*The Authority of the Old Testament* [Nashville: Abingdon Press, 1967]) has stressed that the OT makes us aware of our "B.C. perspective." Bright (206) explains that he does not mean by this a historical epoch which ended with the birth of Christ. Rather,

> it is a condition of living. It is a condition of standing, whether through ignorance or by decision, outside, or not fully subject to, the messianic kingdom of Christ. It is the condition of those who have never heard the gospel or who, having heard it, have refused it in favor of some "salvation" more congenial to their way of thinking. As far as such men [sic] know, or can believe, no Messiah (Christ) has ever come.

Bright writes of the speaker in Ps 137 that he is a man [sic] committed to God, "yet who is estranged from God's spirit" (238). The speaker's longing (for Jerusalem, for home and well-being) can only be filled by God, but his anger must surely be judged by God. "He is a man yearning for some gospel, some good news of God's intervention, yet a man to whom the gospel must come as a strange thing. We know this man well: there is more than a little of him in most of us." So it is.

Finally, it is important to recognize that the language of enemies in the psalms indicates that they transcend the capacities of ordinary foes in human society.

The enemies embody the "principalities and powers" with which we contend; they are beyond "flesh and blood" (Eph 6:12), encompassing the "world rulers of this present darkness" and the "spiritual hosts of wickedness in heavenly places" (see Kraus, *Theology of the Psalms*, 125–36, and *Excursus:* "The Nature of Enemies in the Psalms"). These powers, embodied in foes of varied sorts, clash with both God and his people; they confront both Yahweh and faithful Israelites with "eerie, demonic attributes," and they seek to cause "separation between God and the poor, the just, and the sick," "to sever the bonds that unite Yahweh and his servants" (Kraus, 133). The imprecatory psalms serve to "unmask" these powers and their destructive ways (the term "unmasking" is from W. Wink, *Unmasking the Powers: The Invisible Forces that Determine Human Existence* [Philadelphia: Fortress Press, 1986]). When the powers which try to rule the earth are unmasked, their strength drains away. They shoot arrows, but they land harmlessly. The "Mighty Ones" are, after all, only wicked human beings who have either allowed themselves to be used by the powers, or have deliberately chosen to make common cause with the "rulers of darkness" which invade and bedevil our lives. With psalms like 58, we rip their masks away and their power melts away.

> And tho this world with devils filled,
> should threaten to undo us,
> we will not fear, for he hath willed
> his truth to triumph thro' us.
> The Prince of Darkness grim,
> we tremble not for him;
> his rage we can endure.
> For lo, his doom is sure;
> one little word shall fell him.
>
> Martin Luther, A.D. 1529

Enemies Who Are Like Hungry Prowling Dogs   (59:1–18)

Bibliography

Becker, J. *Israel deutet seine Psalmen.* 59–60. **Goldingay, J.** "Repetition and Variations in the Psalms." *JQR* 68 (1977) 148–49. **Hubbard, R. L., Jr.** *Dynamistic and Legal Language in Conflict Psalms* (Ph.D. diss. Claremont Graduate School, 1980). Ann Arbor, MI: UMI, 1984. 119–49.

Translation

1   For the leader;[a] *al-tashheth:*[b] a Davidic *miktam:*[c] when Saul sent (men) and they watched David's house in order to kill him.

2 (1) *Deliver me from my enemies, O my God;*[a]   (3+2)
       make me inaccessible[b] *to those who rise up against me.*

3 (2) *Deliver me from evildoers,*[a]   (3+3)
       and from murderers save me.[b]

4 (3) *For see how they lie in wait for me!*   (3+3)
       Mean people plot against me,[a]
       but for no offense of mine and no sin of mine, O Yahweh.[b]

5 (4) *There is no waywardness (on my part),*   (3+3)
       but they run and prepare to attack —
       Rouse yourself to meet me and see (for yourself)!

6 (5) *For you are Yahweh, God of Hosts,*[a]   (3+2+3+3)
       O God of Israel,
       up now, to punish all the nations;
       show no mercy to all evil deceivers![b] SELAH

7 (6) *They howl like dogs which return at evening*[a]   (4+2)
       and prowl around a town.

8 (7) *See how they slaver*[a] *at the mouth;*   (3+2+2)
       swords come from their lips![b]
       For (they think), "Who will hear?"

9 (8) *But you, O Yahweh, will laugh at them;*   (3+3)
       You will scoff at all those nations.

10 (9) *O my Strength,*[a] *I will watch*[b] *for you;*   (3+2)
        for you, O God, are my bulwark.

11 (10) *My God will come to meet me with his loyal-love;*[a]   (3+3)
        God will cause me to look in triumph o'er my foes![b]

12 (11) *Don't kill them (outright),*[a] *lest my people forget;*   (3+3+2)
        send them staggering[b] *by your might,*[c] *and bring them down,*[d]
        O my Lord, our Shield.[e]

13 (12) *(For) the sin of their mouths (and) the words of their lips* (2+3)
        let them be snared by their arrogance,
        (and) for the curses and lies they utter.

14 (13) *In wrath put an end to them;*   (2+2+4+2)
        put an end to them so that they are no more,
        and let them know to the ends of the earth[a]
        that God rules over Jacob. SELAH

15 (14) *They howl like dogs which return at evening*   (4+2)
        and prowl around a town.[a]

16 (15) *They roam about*[a] *for prey;*   (3+3)
        unless they are satisfied, they may stay all night![b]

17 (16) *But I will sing of your strength;*   (3+3+3+3)
        I will sing in the morning of your loyal-love,
        for you are my bulwark,
        and a refuge in my time of trouble.

18 (17) *O my Strength,*[a] *I will sing praise*[b] *to you;*   (3+2+2)
        for you, O God, are my bulwark;
        O my God of loyal-love![c]

Notes

1.a. See n. 51:1–2.a.

1.b. See n. 57:1.b.

1.c. See n. 56:1.c.

2.a. LXX and Syriac have "O God," which may indicate an original "O Yahweh," as indicated by a few Heb. mss. Note "Yahweh" in vv 4, 6, and 9.

2.b. More literally "Set me up high (from those rising against me)." The imperfect form following an imperative is a stylistic variation; see Dahood, I, 65–66. The word appears in noun form in vv 10, 17, 18.

3.a. See Ps 53:5, and *Excursus:* "The Nature of Enemies in the Psalms."

3.b. Lit. "men of bloods." See Ps 51:16. This verse has the ABBA pattern, usually obscured by the translation in English.

4.a. It is unlikely that עֻזִּים should be read עֻזִּים, "with strength" (cf. Briggs, II, 55). Some commentators prefer to read יָגוֹדוּ (for יָגוּרוּ, "stir up strife") from גדד "to attack," with some support from LXX, ἐπέθεντο, "have set upon or attacked." See Ps 56:7.

4.b. יהוה may not have been in the original poem, but now functions as an inclusion with "O God of Israel" in v 6.

6.a. The term "God of Hosts" occurs much less frequently than "Yahweh of hosts," though it occurs more than 20 times (versus over 200 times for "Yahweh of hosts"). See Ps 24:10. The absolute form אלהים צבאות occurs elsewhere in Pss 80:4, 19; 84:8; the other references being constructs, אלהי צבאות. It has been rather common to assume that אלהים was added to an original יהוה צבאות and should be deleted (e.g., Kirkpatrick, Kraus). However, this approach has to assume that יהוה was either retained in the text or added by a later redaction, which seems hardly likely. The אלהים may be emended to אלהי to conform to most references; but Dahood may be correct in understanding a construct chain with an interposed enclitic *mem*, or the term may be explained by analogy with "Yahweh-hosts" (Perowne, 467). The deletion of "God of Israel" (e.g., Briggs, Gunkel, Kraus) appears unnecessary in view of the use of "Yahweh, God of hosts, God of Israel" elsewhere; e.g., Jer 35:17; 38:17; 44:7. The "O God of Israel" expression functions here, also, as an inclusion with "O Yahweh" in v 4. See *Notes* and *Comment* on Ps 80.

6.b. This phrase (בגדי און) is found only here, and is probably a fusion of the פעלי און in v 3 with בגדי, "treacherous ones/deceivers," perhaps a shortened form of כל בגדי פעלי און, "all the treacherous workers of evil" (so Briggs). LXX uses the same expression here as in v 3. The basic meaning of בגד is "faithlessness" or "to act treacherously." For the idea of "faithless to a relationship" see 25:3; 78:57; Hos 5:7; Mal 2:11. בגדים sometimes alternates with רשעים, "wicked" (e.g., Prov 2:22; 11:5–8; 21:18), in contrast with the righteous who strive to live in peace with the divine order.

7.a. Thomas (*TRP*, 22) suggests "go to and fro" from שוב in sense of Arabic *saba*, "to run about, wander." So NEB. Dahood proposes a by-form of ישׁב, "to sit, wait," and so: "They wait till evening," referring to the practice of wild dogs or jackals staying in their dens during the day and going forth at dusk to search for food. However, the common idea of "return" is adequate. Perhaps we should translate המה here as "snarl." Briggs and Eerdmans link the verbs ישׁובו and יהמו and translate: "Again and again they snarl."

8.a. "Slaver" or "foam" with Gunkel, Weiser, Kraus. Others take the verb נבע, "to pour forth," as referring to sound coming from the mouth: RSV, "bellowing with their mouths"; NAB, "though they bay with their mouths." Kirkpatrick, Briggs, and Dahood think that the simile changes in this verse from the dogs to a description of the speech of the wicked. Dahood retains "belch," as in Ps 94:4; Prov 15:28, and argues that the object is "swords" in the next line. Also, NIV: "See what they spew from their mouths—they spew out swords from their lips."

8.b. Reading ב as "from." See Dahood, II, 69; III, 391–92. NAB, "blasphemies on their lips."

10.a. MT has "his strength I will keep for you" or "his strength I will watch for you," which is difficult to understand in the context. Eerdmans proposes to read שמר in the sense of "leave to" or "transfer to for safekeeping" as in Job 2:6 [perhaps also Gen 2:15; Exod 22:7] and translates, "I leave thee his strength . . . ," with the sense of leaving the power of an enemy for God to deal with (cf. Perowne, 467). This is not a common meaning of שמר, however, and the interpretation seems forced. Most commonly the עזו is emended to עזי, "my strength," with v 18, LXX, Targum,

Vg, and some Heb. mss. When read with reference to God, this becomes "O my Strength." It is possible that עֻזּ should be read as "refuge" (cf. KB, 693).

10.b. RSV follows Syriac and changes אֶשְׁמֹרָה ("I will protect" or "I will watch") to אֲזַמְּרָה or אָשִׁירָה, "I will sing praises to thee." A. A. Anderson suggests that MT is a later modification· of the verb in keeping with the use of שָׁמַר in the title. Dahood (II, 70) proposes that עֻזּוֹ preserves the archaic nominative ending and should be read as "a fortress." However, he then finds it necessary to read אֵלֶיךָ as אֵלִיכִי, "My God is a fortress (indeed)," with כִּי read as emphatic.

11.a. Following the *kethiv*, which could be: "My God—his love will go before me"; *qere* reads אֱלֹהֵי חַסְדִּי = "God of my loyal-love" or, "my loving (or gracious) God" (see v 18). LXX has "My God, his mercy will go before me. . . ." The verb קָדַם can mean "to meet" or "to march in front" (see 68:26). The supposition of a combat idea in this verse would favor a "going before," but a theophanic idea (so Weiser) favors a "meeting me" or "coming to help."

11.b. Perhaps "slanderers"; see Dahood on Ps 54:7.

12.a. The negative is sometimes omitted, yielding a positive request: "Kill them, but my people forget." It is possible that אַל could be read as an asseverative particle, "Do indeed kill them" (Anderson, I, 439). The versions, however, support the negative, and the statement is usually understood as a request that the enemy not be destroyed too suddenly in order that the people not overlook the action and too easily forget. Kirkpatrick (336) comments, "What he desires is that they may not be destroyed outright by some signal catastrophe, but visibly punished as a living example, until at last their own wickedness proves their destruction." Cf. Exod 9:15, 16; 1 Sam 17:46. The supposed tension with v 14 should not be forced—Kirkpatrick (336) remarks that "burning indignation does not study logical consistency."

12.b. A vivid interpretation of the verb (נוע) from Dahood. The verb can mean "to scatter," "cause to wander about," or "to waver/totter." Thus, NIV has "make them wander about"; NJV, "make wanderers of them"; JB, "harry them."

12.c. The word חַיִל could refer to military force: "by your army" (e.g., Delitzsch, Kirkpatrick, Briggs). However, it can refer to power and/or wealth in a more general sense. Dahood reads חֵיל as חֵיל, "rampart/bastion," and the בְּ as "from": "Send them staggering from your bastion."

12.d. The meaning is probably "bring them down to Sheol (realm of the dead)," though the idea of a humiliating defeat should not be excluded; NEB, "bring them to ruin"; NJV, "bring them low."

12.e. "Shield" is used figuratively for God's protection against the assaults of enemies (cf. Pss 3:3; 18:2; 28:7; 33:20; 84:9). LXX and Syriac have the 1st person singular suffix: "my shield." NEB's "Deliver them, O Lord, to be destroyed" seems to assume a form like מַגְּנֵמוֹ from מגן, "to deliver up/hand over." Cf. Kissane, I, 255.

14.a. Dahood reads, "That they might know that God rules from Jacob to the edges of the earth," which necessitates reading בְּ as "from." With מָשַׁל, however, בְּ normally means "over."

15.a. See v 7.

16.a. The qal form in the *kethiv* is better here than the *qere's* hiphil, which is required in v 12b.

16.b. MT reads from לִין, "to spend the night." The versions seem to be based on לוּן, "to murmur," thus "to growl/howl/whine": NIV, "and howl if not satisfied"; NJV, "and whine if not satisfied." Either reading is adequate—and unpleasant enough! Dahood has "they retire not," following Syriac; KJV has "grudge," which is based on לוּן, "murmur against." Kidner (I, 214) favors "growl" or "whine."

18.a. See n. 10.a.

18.b. See v 10.

18.c. See *Comment* on 51:3 and n. 51:3.a.

Form/Structure/Setting

This psalm, described by Briggs (II, 50) as "exceedingly difficult," is a lament in terms of traditional form-critical categories. The content is predominantly personal, but seems to have communal elements in vv 6, 9, and 12–14. It is quite possible that an original individual lament was adapted to be a collective lament for national use. Becker (*Israel deutet seine Psalmen,* 60) suggests that vv 6ab, 9b, 12, and 14 show redactional changes of this type. It is possible that "nations" in vv 6 and 9 is a deliberate change of שׁוֹבְנָאִים ("proud/arrogant ones") in the original psalm to גוים, "nations." However, if the speaker in the psalm is thought of as a king, the two elements fit together (see scholars who take a strong kingship approach; e.g., Mowinckel, *PIW*, I, 226; J. H. Eaton, *Kingship*, 47). Dahood (II, 66) argues that the speaker is presented as a king who complains about domestic enemies who attack him like a pack of hungry dogs (vv 7, 8, 15, 16) and about foreign foes who are preparing to attack the nation (vv 5, 6, 9, 12, 14). Indeed, this seems to be the best reading of the psalm in its present form. However, its use by ordinary Israelite worshipers, especially in small-group rituals, should not be discounted. Individual prayers in later literature contain sections relating to the nation (e.g., see the prayers in the Book of Tobit), and such double engagement is likely to have been a part of the piety of Israelites at a much earlier time. Thus it is probable that we have a prayer originally designed for a king attacked by vicious domestic enemies and threatened by foreign foes, which was expressed in traditional language. This prayer was later read and heard by nonroyal worshipers who found themselves under fierce and deceitful attack. The reference to the nations would have been meaningful for post-exilic communities under the domination of foreign powers.

Any attempt at locating a precise date or context founders on a lack of information and the complex nature of the psalm. If the psalm is primarily the prayer of a king, it is reasonable to think of a pre-exilic setting during some time of stress and danger. The title puts the psalm in the broad category of Davidic psalms, and the historical note places it in David's career before his accession to power. Kidner (211) argues that the present form of the psalm must be dated after David's assumption of power as king because the speaker refers to "my people" (v 12) and the world-wide repercussions of a defeat of the speaker's enemies (v 14). However, the superscription is best understood as an indication of how the psalm was read at one (later) stage of its history. It is possible, of course, that the psalm was composed by later scribal psalm-writers as they meditated on David and his career. It is more probable, however, that it was an earlier psalm read in such a scribal context as being appropriate for David during his flight from Saul (as recorded in 1 Sam 19 and 24)—regardless of some anachronistic features. The word parallels between the psalm and 1 Sam 19:11 and 24 are of some interest (see Stuhlmueller, I, 275):

Watch:	in the title in a hostile sense; in a positive sense in v 10 of the psalm.
Morning:	in Ps 59:17 and in 1 Sam 19:11–12; Saul sent messengers to kill David in the morning.
Innocence:	in Ps 59:4–5 and 1 Sam 19:4; 24:10–12.
Seeing:	in sense of "seeing" in order to act in victory: Ps 59:5, 11 and 1 Sam 19:15; Saul sent messengers "to see David," saying, "Bring him up to me in the bed"; also 1 Sam 24:11.
Dogs:	Ps 59:7–8, 15–16 and 1 Sam 24:14; also see 2 Sam 9:8 and 16:9, related to enemies of David.
Ambush:	Ps 59:4 and 1 Sam 24:11 (though a different verb is used).
Blood:	Ps 59:3 and 1 Sam 19:5; note 2 Sam 16:7–8.

Such word parallels provided the basis for a Davidic reading of Ps 59 in an exegetical process which frequently "forgot" historical context and temporal sequence.

The complex nature of the text makes it difficult to find a clear structural outline in the psalm. Weiser divides it into two parts, marked by a refrain (vv 10, 18), with each part subdivided by another refrain (vv 7, 15). Jacquet also divides into two parts: an appeal for help in vv 2–9, and a request for the repression of enemies in vv 10–17, with v 18 as a liturgical addition. Kraus divides: vv 2–3, an appeal to Yahweh; vv 4–5a, description of distress and statement of innocence; vv 5b–6, appeal for the judging intervention of God; vv 7–8, lament over the doings of the enemies; vv 9–11, statements of trust; vv 12–14, judgment wishes of the suppliant; vv 15–16, variation of v 7 and further description of the distress; v 17, a thanksgiving vow; and v 18, a statement of trust which is related to vv 10–11. Stuhlmueller (I, 275) has the following arrangement:

vv 2–6	12–14	Call for help, lament and prayer
vv 7–8	15–16	Refrain about dogs—one's enemies
vv 9–11	17–18	Refrain about confidence in God.

In the case of this psalm, the *selah* divisions seem to work quite well as a broad outline and are followed in the *Comment.* The selah at the end of v 6 gives a satisfactory unit of prayer and complaint and merges the two types of enemies, domestic and foreign. The *selah* at the end of v 14 results in a section which describes the enemies, expresses confidence, and prays for judgment. This division has the merit of beginning a section with vv 7–8, which correspond to vv 15–16 of the third division. Thus the *selah* arrangement provides a reasonable working basis for reading the psalm (with some literary merit) and is rather obviously intended to blend the two types of enemies into one prayer of David.

Comment

Superscription (59:1). See *Notes* and *Form/Structure/Setting* above.

Petitions and complaint (59:2–6). The complaint relates to enemies who are described with seven descriptive expressions: those who rise up to attack (v 2b), evildoers (3a), murderers (3b), those who lie in ambush (4a), mighty men (Ps 18:18) who conspire against the suppliant (4b), those who run to prepare to attack (5a), and those who are evil deceivers (6d). Repeatedly, the suppliant prays for deliverance and help. In v 2b, the prayer is for the speaker to be put in a place which is inaccessible to those who rise up to attack (the verb is שׂגב used three times in noun form in vv 10, 17, 18). "Deliver me" is used rather often in laments: see Pss 25:20; 31:3, 16 (2, 15); 39:9 (8); 51:16 (14); 107:6. The causative form of the verb נצל carries the idea of deliverance from trouble of various kinds (A. A. Anderson, II, 751).

The speaker complains that the attacks of the enemies are without cause (vv 4–5). The protestation of innocence serves as a motivation for divine action: "Rouse yourself to meet me and see for yourself" (v 5b), and again in v 6b: "Up, now [*or,* 'awake'], to punish [lit. 'to visit'] all the nations." Yahweh, God of Hosts and the God of Israel, is urged to become active and involved. The verbs "rouse" and "get up/awake" express the idea of coming from sleep or other forms of inactivity into action. They were undoubtedly derived ultimately from cultic "wake-up calls" such as those used by the worshipers of Baal (see 1 Kgs 18:27; Kraus, I, 582; see also Ps 44:24; Isa 51:9; cf. Isa 26:19; 52:1; Judg 5:12). However, in the present context they are only strong supplications addressed to God with the intention of spurring him on to acts of deliverance (cf. Pss 7:7; 35:23; 44:24).

The prayer for the punishment of all the nations in v 6 extends and incorporates the personal complaint and prayer of vv 2–5 into one of national scope. The "nations" (גוים) is a term for non-Israelite peoples. The force of vv 6 and 9 is similar to the appeal to Yahweh as judge of the peoples in Ps 7:9: "O Yahweh, who judges the peoples, give me justice" (cf. 18:48; 144:2). The last colon of v 6 is, however, general in nature and implores Yahweh to show no mercy to any evil, treacherous people—from whatever source they come, foreign or domestic (cf. Ps 25:3).

Description of the enemies, confidence of the suppliant, and petitions for judgment (59:7–14). The enemies are described as being like howling dogs which prowl about a town at night, slavering at the mouth, growling and biting as if they had swords for teeth. Dogs were not always considered bad in the ancient world. Sometimes they were highly valued, even worshiped, and kept as companions (note the dog which follows Tobias in Tob 5:16; 11:4). The little dogs that ate the "crumbs that fall from their master's table" are likely to have been pets (Matt 15:27; Mark 7:28). More commonly, however, references to dogs are contemptuous or express self-abasement (1 Sam 17:43; 2 Sam 9:8) or disdain for others. (See 1 Sam 24:15; 2 Sam 16:9; P. K. McCarter, *1 Samuel,* AB 8, 384–85, notes that the emphasis seems to be on insignificance more than on disparagement, though the latter is obvious in 2 Sam 16:9. McCarter also notes that "dog" and "dead dog" are terms of self-disparagement or contempt in Akkadian letters, Amarna tablets, and the Lachish letters; see also his *2 Samuel,* AB 9, 261.) "Dog" is used to designate the wicked in Isa 56:10–11 (also, see Phil 3:2; Rev 22:15). In Deut 23:19 (18) the term "hire of a dog" is commonly taken to refer to money gained from male prostitution. As in Ps 22:16, the "dogs" in Ps 59 refer to enemies, who pose a threat to the communities they invade. O. Keel, *The Symbolism of the Biblical World,* 85–87, even argues that the dogs in Ps 59 are considered to be demon-possessed. Kirkpatrick's comment (334) is colorful:

> He compares his enemies to a troop of savage and hungry dogs (xxii.16) . . . in the day-time sleeping in the sun or slinking lazily about, but as night comes on collecting together, and traversing the streets in search of food, howling dismally.

The worshiper defies the threat of such enemies with bold statements of confidence and assurance in vv 9–11. Yahweh will laugh at the efforts of the enemies to harm one who is faithful to him. For the scornful laughter of God over the efforts of enemies to challenge his power and sovereignty see also

Pss 2:4; 37:13. God is declared to be a bulwark for the worshiper, and the divine strength (עז) will match the strength of those who conspire against the threatened person. The meaning of "I will watch for you" in v 10 is not entirely clear. One may think with Weiser of the expectation of the imminent appearance of God in some sort of theophanic occasion, an epiphany of God before the congregation. On the other hand, the suppliant may be waiting for any suitable divine response against the enemies. In any case, the speaker is confident of being met by a loyal and powerful God who will give victory over the foes (v 11).

The prayer for the punishment of the enemies in vv 12–14 begins with the request that they not be killed outright, "lest my people forget" (the words of a king?). The speaker prays that God will strike the foes a mighty blow and send them staggering down to Sheol (v 12), to put an end to them so that they are no more (v 14a). The people forget so easily; a sudden destruction would not establish itself effectively in their memories. A. A. Anderson (I, 439) comments that "they would be living witnesses to the reality of God's retribution"—while they stagger down to the realm of the dead!

V 13 seems to carry the idea of the act-consequence, a self-producing concept of retribution with the petition that the enemies be taken captive (caught or trapped) by their own arrogant pride (see *Comment* on 57:7). The speaker asks that the judgment of God will be such that Yahweh's ("God" in v 14) rulership over Jacob will become known world-wide (cf. 1 Sam 17:46). Jacob in this context is most probably understood as Israel (see Pss 22:24; 53:7; 114:1; "the God of Jacob" is found several times, e.g., Pss 20:2; 75:10; 76:7; 81:2, 5; 94:7; 146:5).

Description of enemies and vow of praise (59:15–18). The description of the enemies as howling dogs in vv 15–16 repeats the description in vv 7–8, but with variation in v 16. The disturbing and destructive nature of the dogs is emphasized (see *Comment* on vv 7–8), for they roam at night looking for food and prey. There is a possibility that v 16 should be read ironically; i.e., though the dogs prowl about unpleasantly, they roam about unsatisfied—able only to growl and whine! (see note 16.b.). If this interpretation is followed, the translation should be more like:

> But they roam about for food,
> and if they are not satisfied, they may whine!

In this case, the dangerous dogs of v 8 only whine for food in v 16. However the verse is read, the speaker vows to praise God for his loyal-love and strength. The speaker has a "bulwark" and a place of refuge in the present time of trouble. The howling of roaming dogs will be more than matched by praise sung out at morning time: "Howl on, you prowling dogs, I have a refuge, a sure retreat, where you cannot reach me, and from my safe place, I will watch you stagger down to hell!" The "watching" for God in v 10 is fulfilled in the singing of praise in v 18 (note the change of verbs). (For the morning as a time of divine help and deliverance, see Pss 5:4; 30:6; 46:6; 49:15; 90:14; 92:3; 130:6; 143:8; Isa 33:2; etc.) Morning likely reflects both cultic and metaphorical meaning. The morning was the time when prophets preached their messages and priests gave oracles, a time of sacrifice and rites of worship. Metaphorically, the morning was the time when night and watching and waiting were over and a new day was at hand.

Explanation

Though institutional and cultic settings for this psalm are strongly advocated (see Hubbard, *Dynamistic and Legal Language in Conflict Psalms*), its distinctive quality seems to be literary, with its strong descriptions of enemies as prowling dogs. The content of the psalm reminds us that we have not escaped the problem of enemies and their evil work in human society. The "dogs" prowl about in our communities and towns as they did in the ancient world—"dogs" which embody the devouring, malignant persons and forces in human affairs.

Like ancient Israelite communities, we too are dependent on Yahweh for deliverance. As Hubbard (144) argues, this psalm seems to reflect a breakdown of both legal and moral processes (he calls them "dynamistic processes"): "Law no longer mediates justice nor does the dynamic automatically connect acts and consequences." The perversion and corruption will grind on unless Yahweh is willing to intervene. Of course, the psalm brings to the fore the matter of attitude toward enemies in the harshly worded petitions for divine judgment (see *Explanation* of Ps 58). The enemies are dealt with in the context of faith in Yahweh's supreme judgeship and the refuge and "bulwark" which he provides for those who put their faith in him. Ps 59 points to trust in the saving power of God, whose laughter and derision (v 9) are more than a match for the evildoers who, like hungry dogs, prey on people.

> A mighty fortress is our God;
> A bulwark never failing.
> Our helper he, amid the flood
> Of mortal ills prevailing . . .
> Martin Luther

It is fitting that the last word of Ps 59 is "loyal-love" (חֶסֶד), a word which conveys the faithful commitment of Yahweh to the deliverance and protection of his people (see K. D. Sakenfeld, *Faithfulness in Action: Loyalty in Biblical Perspective* [Philadelphia: Fortress Press, 1985], esp. 83–100). God is a high tower, a sure retreat: "my God of loyal-love" (or "my loyal God"); cf. Pss 5:7; 13:5; 17:7; 32:10; 31:7–8; 40:11; 57:3; 143:12.

Human Help Is Futile; God's Help Would Be Sufficient (60:1–14)

Bibliography

Johnson, A. R. *CPIP.* 165–75; **Kellermann, U.** "Erwägungen zum historichen Ort von Psalm LX." *VT* 28 (1978) 56–65. **North, C. R.** "אֶלְזָה אֲחַלְּקָה שְׁכֶם, (Psa LX 8 // Psa cviii 8)." *VT* 17 (1967) 242–43. **Ogden, G. S.** "Psalm 60: Its Rhetoric, Form, and Function." *JSOT* 31 (1985) 83–94. **Yaron, R.** "The Meaning of *Zanah*." *VT* 13 (1963) 237–39.

Translation

1–2   For the leader;[a] *ʿal-shushan ʿeduth;*[b] a Davidic *miktam* for teaching;[c]
      when he fought[d] Aram-Naharaim and Aram-Zobah, and Joab re-
      turned and struck down twelve thousand Edomites in the Valley of
      Salt.[e]

3 (1)   *O God, who*[a] *has spurned*[b] *us, who has breached our defenses*[c]   (3+3)
        though you are angry, turn back to us![d]—

4 (2)   *You who made the land quake; ripped it open!*[a]   (3+3)
        Heal[b] *its fissures, for it has split apart!*[c]

5 (3)   *You who made your people suffer hard times;*[a]   (3+3)
        who gave us wine to drink that made us reel;[b]

6 (4)   *You who put up a banner*[a] *for those who fear you—*   (4+2)
        only to let them flee[b] *before the bowmen!*[c] SELAH

7 (5)   *So that*[a] *those dear to you may be rescued,*   (3+3)
        save (us) by your right hand and answer us![b]

8 (6)   *God made a holy promise:*[a]   (3+3+3)
        "I will exult[b] *(and) divide up Shechem,*
        and measure off the Valley of Succoth.

9 (7)   *Gilead is mine, and Manasseh too;*   (2+3+2)
        Ephraim is a helmet for my head;[a]
        Judah is my staff;

10 (8) *Moab is my washpot;*[a]   (3+3+3)
        I will throw my shoe[b] *over Edom—*
        Philistia, shout because of me!"[c]

11 (9) *Who can take me to the siege-proof city?*[a]   (3+3)
        Who can lead[b] *me to Edom?*

12 (10) *Is it not you, O God, though you spurned us*[a]—*?*   (3+3)
        Will you not go forth, O God, with our forces?

13 (11) *Give us relief from distress;*[a]   (3+3)
        for human aid is futile!

14 (12) *With God we could gain success;*[a]   (3+3)
        he could tread down our foes!

Notes

1–2.a. See n. 51:1–2.a.

1–2.b. Usually understood lit. as "lily of testimony." The expression is probably the name of a tune or other musical direction for the recitation of the psalm. The same expression is used with variations in the titles of Pss 45, 69, and 80. S. Mowinckel (*PIW,* II, 214) suggests that the words refer to a rite in which oracles/revelation/omens were received from the way lilies did or did not bloom (citing the blossoming of Aaron's rod Num 17:21–25 [EVV 6–10]). Mowinckel speculates that the four psalms involved may have been sung over lilies in expectation of a sign of a divine response. L. Delekat ("Probleme der Psalmenüberschriften," *ZAW* 76 [1964] 294–95) attempts to relate the expression to the contents of the four psalms by using the LXX reading of "for those who shall be changed," assuming שנים + שׁ + על (from, שׁנה "change") and suggesting that the psalms are for those "whose situation changes for the worse." Delekat suggests that the expression in 45:1 belongs to Ps 44, where it would be appropriate. If the expression does refer to a melody, the word "lily" may refer to love, especially to the female in sexual relations (see Cant 6:3; 4:5, and note that Ps 45 is a song for a royal wedding). The word עֵדוּת is found also in the title of Ps 80. Eerdmans (67) assumes that the word means "covenant" (see also Kidner, I, 42), and since he assumes that Pss 60 and 80 refer to tribes of North Israel he infers that the word indicates a song which extends the covenant to all the tribes of Israel. Mowinckel (ibid.), as noted above, takes the word in the sense of "revelation" or "oracle," which may point in the right direction. The word עֵדוּת can mean "exhortation/reminder" (KB, 683), and in a context like Ps 119:88 is equivalent to "teaching" or "instruction." LXX in 60:1 seems to take עֵדוּת as עוֹד, "yet, again"—"those that shall yet be changed."

1–2.c. For "Davidic *miktam*," see n. 56:1.c. The expression "for teaching" (לְלַמֵּד) has been supposed to refer to a psalm to be learned by heart, which is improbable since all the psalms were recited from memory. S. Mowinckel (*PIW*, II, 217) thinks ללמד was not a liturgical term, but meant "to prod" or "to goad on," with the meaning of encouraging the people (as David did the sons of Judah to fight in 2 Sam 1:18), or to "goad on" Yahweh to get him to intervene for his people. The option of encouraging and informing the people is more probable.

1–2.d. LXX reads "when he burned Mesopotamia and Syria," taking the verb from יצת rather than נצה.

1–2.e. See *Comment*.

3.a. With Johnson (*CPIP*, 166, n. 2), taking the construction as coordinate relative clauses with the relative particle omitted (GKC, 155f).

3.b. Keeping the traditional translation of זנח as "cast off/reject/spurn," rather than as "angry" with Yaron ("The Meaning of *Zanah*," 230) and Dahood.

3.c. The verb פרץ carries ideas of breaking down a wall (80:13; 89:41), of breaking out (106:29), and of a breach or gap (106:23). The best parallel here is probably 2 Sam 5:20, where the idea is that of breaking through the ranks of a military force.

3.d. The polel imperfect of שוב can mean to "restore fully," as in 23:3 (see A. R. Johnson, *CPIP*, 166, n. 2). However, in this context the meaning seems to be "turn back from your anger to us." A. Aejmelaeus (*The Traditional Prayer in the Psalms*, 34–37) has demonstrated that שוב in some contexts, with God as the subject, carries the meaning of "return from battle," or from the execution of punishment, or "return from anger." See Num 10:35; Pss 7:7–8, 12–13; 18:38; 85:5–6; 90:7–9, 11; Exod 32:12; Deut 13:18; Josh 7:26; 2 Kgs 23:26; Jonah 3:9. LXX reads "and you had pity on us," apparently reading the verb as equivalent to רחם or חנן. Johnson reads as a question: "Will thou in thine anger forsake us completely?"—with the first verb having concessive force and the polel of שוב meaning "completely," used with intransitive force as in Jer 8:5 (following Dahood), with ל meaning "from." NEB has "and rebuked us cruelly." NAB ("Rally us!") assumes a battle scene and a plea for God's help when the ranks of Israel's defenders have been broken.

4.a. The verb פצם appears only here. The probable meaning refers to the opening of fissures in the ground as the result of an earthquake. Dahood prefers "and it went to pieces." LXX, however, understands the word to mean "throw into confusion" or "disturb."

4.b. The reading is uncertain. MT (and LXX) have qal imperative of רפה, understood as רפא, "heal/mend"; thus, "heal its breaks/fractures/fissures." Another option would be to take רפה as "sink down/relax/subside," reading with the idea of cracks in the earth (from an earthquake) which sink down into the earth. A. R. Johnson (*CPIP*, 166, n. 4) prefers to read from רפף ("to tremble"): "It is trembling, yea tottering, with its blows," understanding כ as emphatic. Dahood prefers רפה in the sense of "weak": "Weak from its fractures, much did it totter."

4.c. Or, "it is tottering/shaking"—even "collapsing," as in NJV.

5.a. NEB adopts the suggestion that ראה, "see/experience," should be read here as equal to רוה, "drink deeply" (D. W. Thomas, *TRP*, 23; see also Dahood, II, 78). But this is unnecessary (see A. R. Johnson, *CPIP*, 166, n. 5).

5.b. Lit. "wine (that is) staggering/reeling." Cf. Isa 51:17, 22. The metaphor is that of the cup of God's wrath which leaves the drinker dazed and staggering. Perhaps the image is derived from the drinking of water in an ordeal (see Num 5:11–31; cf. Ps 75:9; Jer 25:15; contrast the "cup of salvation," Ps 116:13; Kraus, II, 972).

6.a. This is a very difficult verse. נס means "standard/sign/signal/banner." The change to מנוס, "refuge," is frequently proposed (so Gunkel, Schmidt, Oesterley), and it is possible that נס itself can mean "refuge" (Thomas, ibid.). The verb could be read as a precative perfect and begin a petition, "Give [*or*, set] a rallying banner for those who fear you"(so Dahood, Buttenwieser); or the verb could be emended to תנה (impv. from נתן, "give/set/put"). However, MT in the usual sense is maintained above. A. R. Johnson (166, n. 6) cites Exod 17:15 (E); Isa 5:26; 11:10, 12; 13:2; 18:3; 49:22; 62:10; Jer 4:21; 51:12, 27) and translates, "Thou didst rally those that fear thee to Thy standard."

6.b. The hithpolel infinitive להתנוסס means "to take flight/flee" if derived from נוס, "flee/escape." If taken as a denominative from נס, the verb means "to rally (around a standard or banner)" or "to be displayed (of the banner)." Thus RSV, "to rally to it [the banner] from the bow"; JB, "to rally those who fear you"; NIV, "you have raised a banner to be unfurled against the bow."

6.c. LXX and other versions support the reading of קשט as an Aramaism for קֶשֶׁת, "bow." However, קשט means something like "truth" in Prov 22:21 (and in Aramaic in Dan 2:47; 4:37) and that meaning is preferred here by some interpreters; e.g., NEB, "to make their escape before the sentence falls [with a note, 'before truth']"; Johnson (CPIP, 166–67), "Only to let them flee before the truth," i.e., the reality of suffering a severe setback by the enemy's defeat of Israel's forces. Possibly a pun was intended between קֶשֶׁת ("bow") and קשט ("truth"); to flee from the bow is fleeing from the reality ("truth") which God has allowed to happen. See Comment.

7.a. The rather awkward construction is an attempt to get the force of the למען and the unusual position of the final clause (note 122:8, 9). The למען as a conjunction indicates result in response to prior action; 7a refers back to the action of God in the preceding verses (Johnson, CPIP, 166, n. 8, who translates, "That in return those dear to Thee may be delivered . . .").

7.b. Read "us" with kethiv rather than "me" with qere and 108:7. The singular in 108:7 is influenced by the context. Dahood reads "Grant us triumph," arguing that ענה can mean "to conquer, triumph" in some contexts (see I, 116; with support from R. T. O'Callaghan, W. L. Moram, and Buttenwieser, 252). Certainly, ענה frequently means more than a verbal answer. In this type of usage, its basic meaning is "to react/respond/to bring about a change of circumstances." The desire for a theophanic word may be indicated, but it would be a word announcing help and giving victory.

8.a. Lit. "God has spoken [or, spoke] in his holiness." Most commentators assume that the meaning is "in his holy place" or "sanctuary." However, "in his holiness" may be correct (cf. Pss 89:35; 105:42; Jer 23:9; Amos 4:2). Johnson (CPIP, 168, n. 4) prefers "God hath given His own sacred word." Dahood argues for the heavenly sanctuary and translates "from" rather than "in."

8.b. The verb עלז is not used elsewhere of Yahweh. NEB, "I will go up now," accepts the reading עלה זה (cf. Num 13:17; see C. R. North, VT 17 [1967] 242–43). See also Ps 108:8: Allen, n. 108:8.b., retains "I will exult"; LXX translates 'υψωθήσομαι, "I will be lifted up, exalted" = "I will be triumphant." JB has "I the victor will . . ."; Dahood prefers a hendiadys: "Exultant, I will make Shechem my portion" (cf. NAB, NIV), which is probably correct.

9.a. Lit. "the stronghold [or, protection] of my head," but a leather or bronze helmet is probably intended.

10.a. The metaphor is one of humiliation and servitude. Washpots were often dirty, used for bathing, and even for toilet purposes. The haplography supposed by Gunkel and Kraus to yield מי מואב, "waters of Moab," or ים מואב, "sea of Moab" (referring to the Dead Sea), is unnecessary. LXX, "Moab the bowl of any hope," appears to be the result of understanding רחץ in its Aramaic sense of "to trust" (so J. Barr, Comparative Philology and the Text of the Old Testament [Oxford: Clarendon Press, 1968], 55).

10.b. The translation depends on the meaning of this expression. The casting of the sandal or shoe may indicate the symbolic action of taking possession of Edom (cf. Deut 11:24; Ruth 4:7 is often cited, but is not really relevant). On the other hand, the metaphor may be one of domination; either in the sense of "the slave to whom the warrior flings his sandals to carry or to clean" (Kirkpatrick; in which case, it might be better to translate "at Edom"), or in the sense of a conqueror who puts his foot on a vanquished foe as a sign of victory (see Dahood, though his reading of the verb as "plant" is unacceptable). Buttenwieser's interesting comments (75–76) need supplementing by C. M. Carmichael, "Ceremonial Crux," JBL 96 (1977) 321–36. The Arabic custom cited of referring to a wedding day as "the day of putting on the shoe" goes back to a euphemism for sexual intercourse. However, an allusion to sexual activity does not seem probable here.

10.c. The text in Ps 108:10 is much easier, עָלֵי־פְלֶשֶׁת אֶתְרוֹעָע, "over Philistia I will shout (in victory)." LXX, "the Philistines have been subjected to me," apparently reads hithpael of רעע, II (cf. Isa 24:19; Prov 18:24). The verb is usually derived from רוע, "to raise a shout." In its other usage in Pss 108:10 and 65:14, the hithpael indicates "shout of joy, triumph." However, in its hiphil form the shout may be that of alarm or distress, which may be the meaning of the hithpael here. Dahood adopts the reading of התרע as hithpael infinitive construct with 1st person singular suffix, with עלי as in 108:10: "over Philistia will be my cry of conquest" (note Delitzsch, 226). Kirkpatrick, 342: "Mighty Philistia must raise the shout of homage to its conqueror." NJV: "acclaim me, O Philistia!"

11.a. Since the verb can sometimes mean "bring offering/tribute," it is sometimes read in that sense here (so Dahood, "who will bring me the Rock City?"). The מִי expresses a wish = "O for one to bring me [or, bring to me]. . . ." The "siege-proof city"—"entrenched city" (as in 31:22); 108:11 has "fortified city" (עִיר מִבְצָר)—probably ancient Petra, or Edom as whole, is thought of a fortress city in both psalms.

11.b. Haplography is usually assumed for יַנְחֵנִי = נָחֵנִי imperfect from נחה. However, Dahood may be correct in arguing that this is a case of two like consonants being written as one when the final letter of the preceding word (מִי, in this case) is the same as the first of the following (see Dahood, II, 81 for references).

12.a. See Johnson, *CPIP*, 166, n. 2; 170, n. 4; GKC, 155f. The הֲלֹא seems to have a force like that of הִנֵּה ("behold"); see Dahood, II, 24, on 54:2; BDB, 520; JB: "God, can you really have rejected us? You no longer march with our armies."

13.a. More commonly מִצָּר is read as "from the foe/adversary," but LXX reads θλίψεως, "trouble"; so, KJV, JB. Perhaps there is a deliberate wordplay between צָר, "foe," in v 14 and צָר, "trouble/distress," in v 13; (Johnson, 173).

14.a. Commonly translated, "we shall do valiantly," but the context indicates that the meaning should be "prove successful/prevail," or "get victory." Cf. Ps 118:15, 16; 1 Sam 14:48. NIV has "With God we will gain the victory." The *Translation* assumes that the imperfect forms of the verbs are modal in force. It could also be: "With God we can prevail; he can tread down our foes!" Cf. D. Michel, *Tempora und Satzstellung in den Psalmen* (Bonn: H. Bouvien, 1960), 148, no. 23, 63.

Form/Structure/Setting

This psalm is plagued with difficulties, and all interpretation is tentative. It appears to be a modified prayer of communal lament. Some of the familiar elements of the lament are present: the vocative address to God, the use of the word זנח (v 3), which occurs elsewhere in laments (see Pss 44:10, 24; 74:1; 88:15; Lam 3:15), the descriptions of conditions which form a complaint, petitions for divine aid in a time of great trouble, and perhaps a confession of trust (in modified form) in vv 8–10, 14. The psalm seems to express the prayer of the people (and their leader) during a time of national defeat and humiliation.

The psalm can be divided into three sections: vv 3–7, 8–10, and 11–14. The speaker in vv 3–7 and 12–14 uses the plural "us" for self-identification and addresses God as "you." The subject addressed in v 14 could be either God or the group included in the "we" of that verse. God is quoted in first person in the middle section (vv 8–10). The use of *Elohim* in each section is a rhetorical feature which seems to mark off the sections (vv 3, 8, 12). The use of זנח ("spurn" or "be angry") in v 12 links it back to v 3 and the first section. Ogden (*JSOT* 31 [1985] 84) notes also that the dual interrogatives in v 11 match the twin use of *Elohim* in v 12. The first question asks, "Who can take me to the siege-proof city?" The response in question form is, "Is it not you, O God?" The second question is "Who can lead me . . . ?" The parallel is another question, "Will you not go forth, O God . . . ?"

The *selah* division of the psalm is a twofold one. The division at v 6 seems premature in terms of the analysis above. Perhaps there are three possibilities for explaining the position of the *selah*. First, a pause after the description of the conditions of complaint may have been deemed appropriate, for one reason or another. Second, the severely unbalanced line in the MT may have attracted the *selah*. Third, the reading of v 6 may have been a positive one for the scribal interpreters (see Cohen, 190; NIV), or a prayer (using precative perfect) for God to set up a banner to rally the demoralized forces of Israel. If the last is the case, there may be a sequence of three calls for divine help in vv 3b, 4b, and 6 (so Ogden, *JSOT* 31 [1985] 86; see *Notes*). Kellermann (60) argues that the rally-sign is the Yahwistic holy place on Zion, citing Jer 4:6 as a close parallel. I have attempted to interpret this verse in another way and use a different analysis (see *Notes* and *Comment*).

The psalm is among those which seem to offer recognizable linkage with Israelite history. The wording is not precise enough, however, to preclude different theories—and not general enough to exclude others! Older critical commentators, in accord with a general approach, tended to think of the Maccabean period (Kraus cites Hitzig, Olshausen, Duhm, Buhl, Staerk). Joram's campaign against the Edomites has been suggested on the basis of 2 Kgs 8:20–22, 2 Chr 21:8–10, but seems most unlikely since the distress in the psalm does not appear in the prose accounts. The MT title associates the psalm with a campaign of David against the Edomites, and this setting is defended by some modern scholars (see Kirkpatrick, Buttenwieser, Kidner, and tentatively by Dahood). Those who defend a setting in the time of David postulate an invasion by the Edomites while David was busy in the North with the Syrians (e.g., Kirkpatrick). This is pure speculation and provides no firm basis for the psalm (1 Kgs 11:14–16 seems to indicate that Edom would have had more reason to lament than Israel).

The most probable setting reflected in the psalm is that of the time after the fall of Jerusalem in 587 B.C.E. (e.g., Kraus, Kellermann). The conditions described in the complaint would fit the exilic period, and the reference to Edom accords well with the Israelite animosity toward the Edomites exhibited in a number of passages (see Jer 49:7–22; Isa 63:1–6; Ezek 25:12–14; Obad; Ps 137; Lam 4:21–22). Lamentation ceremonies and fast days seem to have been a part of Israelite worship before the fall of Judah (see Jer 36:9) and afterwards (Zech 7:2–7; 8:19; see Kellermann; E. Janssen, *Juda in der Exilszeit* [Göttingen: Vandenhoeck & Ruprecht, 1956], 94–104), and the psalm would have been at home in such ceremonies. Ogden ("Psalm 60") argues that it stems from a lament ceremony (most probably post-exilic) in which it was linked with Isa 63:1–6 as a prophetic response. He thinks it probable that Ps 60, Isa 63, Ps 137, Obad, and Jer 49:7–22 all belong to the same "fundamental historical and liturgical context" (93), and this is probably correct. However, the caution and reservation of Kraus (*Psalms 1–59*, 3) regarding the hypothetical nature of all attempts to provide specific contexts for this psalm in the history of Israel is well taken.

Comment

The superscription (60:1–2). The historical note in the superscription is the result of the efforts of scribal interpreters to link psalms to accounts of the career of David. As noted above, the psalm is assigned to the context of David's conquest of Edom according to 2 Sam 8:13–14 // 1 Chr 18:12–13. Aram-Naharaim is a name for Mesopotamia and may allude to 2 Sam 8:3, which seems to refer to David marching to the Euphrates to establish his power and possibly to the hiring of Mesopotamian chariots and horsemen by the Ammonites to fight against him in 1 Chr 19:6. Aram-Zobah refers to a major Aramean state during the time of David, located on the eastern slopes of the Anti-Lebanon mountain range in the

Biqaʿ Valley. The scribal interpreter who provided the historical data for the title of Ps 60 may have had a text of 2 Sam 8:13 that read "and when he [David] returned, the son of Zeruiah defeated the Edomites" (see P. K. McCarter, Jr., *2 Samuel*, AB 9 246). Since Joab was the best known son of Zeruiah (rather than Abishai, his brother, who is credited with killing the Edomites in 1 Chr 18:12), the scribe identified him as the victor over the Edomites (Joab's attacks on Edom are also related in 1 Kgs 11:15–16). The precise location of the Valley of Salt is unknown, but it most probably refers to one valley or another in the region of the Dead Sea, probably in Edomite territory, rather than to the Wadi el-Milh, east of Beersheba. The number 12,000 differs from the 18,000 in 2 Sam 8:13 // 1 Chr 18:12. The variation is due either to a difference in traditions or to textual error.

The title most probably reflects the long animosity between Edom and the Israelites, which was exacerbated by the cooperation of the Edomites with the Babylonians in the destruction of Jerusalem in 587 B.C.E. Ps 137:7 indicates that the Edomites exploited the misfortunes of Jerusalem (see also Obadiah; Allen on Ps 137:7, n.b. 236). Thus two exilic and post-exilic interests converged: that of David and his exploits and the condemnation of Edom. It is quite probable that Ps 60 was composed as an *ad hoc* prayer which arose out of meditation on David during the terrible times after the fall of Jerusalem and out of the deep resentment of what was perceived to be a betrayal by the Edomites, who "should not have rejoiced over the people of Judah in the day of their ruin" (Obad 12), and who also participated in the looting of Jerusalem according to Obad 13 and in cutting off the escape of fugitives according to Obad 14.

Complaint and prayer for help (60:3–7). The condition of the people is perceived as being the result of divine anger and rejection. Their line of defenses had been broken through by an invader (v 3). The verb זנח is found in other laments (e.g., Pss 44:10, 24; 74:1; 78:15; Lam 3:17; compare v 3 with 44:10–12) and refers to rejection or anger—or both. The אנפת of v 3b is a denominative verb from אף, "nose/ anger," and carries the connotation of snorting in anger. A. A. Anderson notes that the verb is used on the Moabite Stone (line 5) for the anger of the Moabite god Chemosh against his people. The uncertain תשובב לנו, read here as "restore us," is an expression early in the prayer of the necessity of divine help. The distress of the present situation is beyond human remedy (v 11).

The invasion of an enemy has shaken the land like an earthquake (v 4); its terror has been like that produced when earthquakes break open the ground with fissures. According to the interpretation adopted here (see *Notes*), the situation is too bad to delay any longer a prayer for deliverance: "Heal its fissures!" Again, the need lies beyond the power of human hands. The people have experienced hard times (or "things," v 5a), in which the confusion and shock have left them staggering and reeling as if overcome by too much wine (cf. Isa 51:17, 22; Jer 25:15–16). The fearful violence of events has left the people dazed and traumatized, and it is God (v 3) who is responsible for it all.

As v 6 is interpreted here, it refers to a signal banner which had been raised (most probably thought of as on the walls of Jerusalem) to warn the inhabitants of the outlying areas to flee to the relative safety of the walls of a fortified town.

The situation in mind is like that envisioned in Jer 4:6:

> Raise a standard toward Zion,
>   flee for safety, stay not,
> for I bring evil from the north, and great destruction. (RSV)

See also Isa 13:2; 18:3; 30:17; Jer 50:2. The signal banner was not to rally troops
for a campaign or for a journey (as in some references, e.g., Jer 51:12, 27; Isa
49:22; 62:10) but to warn the farmers and tradesmen in the surrounding villages
to drop their work and to make for the walls of the town, with their wives and
children, hoping that they could get there before the gates were closed. Of course,
the safety of the walled town might prove to be deceptive. The invader might lay
siege, bringing about great suffering from shortages of water and food and
from disease, with the prospect of a terrible eventual violent overthrow of the town.

Kraus (II, 587) suggests that the situation depicted in vv 6 and 11 could be
that of the assembling of a group to flee as refugees to the safety of Edom (Obad
14; Jer 40:11), but he thinks it more probable that the content of vv 8–10 has to
do with the future subjugation of Edom. However, Kraus himself notes the
difficulty with v 14. It is possible that v 11 is ironic, reflecting bitter disappointment
that Edom proved to be a false refuge—perhaps the Edomites blocked the
escape of Israelites to Judah and turned refugees over to the Assyrians as in Obad
v 14. However, this approach is too speculative to engender much confidence,
and it seems better to think of Jerusalem as the failed place of refuge in v 6; thus
the verse continues the complaint in v 5. God is charged with failing to protect
his people who fled to the city from an impending attack. Yahweh (God) has
devastated the land and left the people with great suffering.

V 7 is a prayer for divine deliverance. A response to the great distress of the
people is urgently needed. God is reminded that these are "those dear to you"
("beloved ones") and "those who fear you" (v 6). The powerful action of the
divine right hand is needed for deliverance (see Pss 17:7; 18:36; 44:5 [4]; 74:11;
138:7; etc.). God is implored to respond: "Answer us!"

A holy promise recalled (60:8–10). The divine oracle in vv 8–10 (vv 8–11 are also
found in 108:8–11) is frequently interpreted as the response of a cult prophet or
priest to the complaint and prayer of the preceding verses (see the summary and
references of Johnson, 169–70). In this sense, the oracle would be a message of
assurance that Yahweh is the divine warrior who has conquered Israel's land and
controls the surrounding countries of Moab, Edom, and Philistia as well. Those
forced to take refuge in Jerusalem can take heart. However, it is more likely that
the divine message is a freely composed utterance from the past which is appealed
to as a basis for the prayer and hope which follows (so Johnson, *CPIP*, 170–71). The
rhetorical form of vv 8–10 is not intended so much as a divine oracle as a form of
prayer to God to remind him of his commitment to Israel (Ogden, *JSOT* 31 [1985]
87). These are the kinds of promises of divine sovereignty that Yahweh exultantly
declared to his people, but which lack fulfillment.

The message itself is in the form of a victory song by the Divine Warrior
(Gunkel), probably an *ad hoc* composition drawn from old traditions. The naming
of Shechem and Succoth may recall the Jacob tradition of Gen 33:17–18 and

49:10; Edom and Moab allude to the Balaam oracle in Num 24:17–19. The Mosaic tradition of Deut 31:1–10 may also be involved (so Weiser). The territories mentioned probably represent the major areas of the Davidic kingdom (so Weiser, Kellermann). Shechem, Succoth (in central Transjordan, perhaps, Deir ʿAlla in the Jordan Valley), Gilead, Manasseh, and Ephraim represent the areas of the Northern Kingdom, while Judah, Moab, Edom, and Philistia represent the South. The equipment of a warrior-king is applied piece by piece to the lands he intends to conquer: helmet, scepter or commander's rod, washpot, and shoe. The verbs in v 8 depict the division of conquered territory to those who will become its new residents, like the division of the land to the Israelites (e.g., Num 26:53, 55, 56; Josh 14:5; 18:2, 10; 19:51; Mic 2:4; Gen 49:7, 27; Exod 15:9; Judg 5:30, for חלק; for מדד, see especially 2 Sam 8:2, of David; Hab 3:6; Num 35:5). In the history of Israel, Yahweh had promised to carry out these intentions to be the Divine Warrior-King who would possess and measure out the land as indicated. From the standpoint of the speaker in the psalm, however, the divine program has been a failure. Yahweh has not kept his promises. What has happened to the exultant promises of the Divine Warrior?

A dismal present in contrast to past promise (60:11–12). The present reality in vv 11–12 is set against the exalted idealism of vv 8–10. The territory of the Northern Kingdom, now overrun by foreigners, still belongs to Yahweh, as do the vassal states of Moab, Edom, and Philistia (Kraus). The meaning of v 11 is an enigma. The verse leaves the reader with varied possibilities—and perhaps this is what it is intended to do. The informed reader brings a considerable repertoire to the verse. Is the speaker an Israelite king who is contemplating an invasion of Edom and needs divine assurance of the success of the campaign? The suggestion was made above that the verse is possibly the ironic statement of an Israelite refugee who has seen what happened to others who tried to flee to the safety of Edomite towns and fortresses entrenched in terrain almost impregnable to military invasion. Or is it the question of a person who actually longs for safety in Edom? Is there the hope that a flight of refugees to Edom would result in a new exodus and conquest of the promised land? Is the verse an old one framed in terms of Edom as the source of Yahweh's theophanic going forth to work mighty salvation for his people as in Hab 3? Perhaps the best interpretation is that of a continued appeal to the past commitments of Yahweh, as in vv 8–10, but with a transition into prayer in v 12. Yahweh is implored to return to his mighty divine warriorhood of the past, to revive Israel again and lead the Israelite forces in conquest of the mountain ramparts of the Edomites. The unidentified nature of the speaker is possibly an invitation to think of a new David, a king who would have the cooperation of Yahweh in new endeavors to fulfill old promises.

Prayer for relief (60:13–14). The achievement of חיל ("victory/wealth/strength/ success") and relief from distress can come only from God. Human help is vain; only divine intervention will suffice. V 14 expresses confidence that divine aid would bring success. God is able to save his own: "He could tread down our foes." Ogden (92) notes that the verb בוס ("tread down") appears in Isa 63:6 (an Edom passage) and in only five other passages in MT (Ps 44:6; Prov 27:7; Isa 14:19, 25; Jer 12:10). The usage in Ps 44:6 (5) is parallel with the pushing down and goring of an opponent by a wild ox: "through your name we push down our assailants."

Explanation

The psalm pictures a desperate situation for the people of God. The conditions lie beyond the power of any saving help from human sources (v 13b). This fundamental idea is touched upon briefly in v 3b, "return to us," and in v 4b, "heal its fissures." The prayer is equally urgent in vv 7 and 13. The psalm struggles to affirm faith in the sovereignty of Yahweh over history in a time when that faith is being tested. The speaker represents those who wait in distress for new action on the part of God. At the present time, Yahweh seems to have spurned his people (v 12) and left them at the mercy of their foes. His people, however, will not let him forget his commitments from the past. Perhaps the psalm belongs to a context like that set forth in Lam 2:18 of those who cry out to Yahweh day and night, without rest or respite, because of what he has done to Zion. Isa 62:6–7 may be even more pertinent for Ps 60. The prophet appoints "sentinels" ("keepers") upon the walls of Jerusalem with the charge:

> You who remind the LORD,
>   take no rest,
> and give him no rest
>   until he establishes Jerusalem
>   and makes it renowned
>   throughout the earth. (NRSV)

If I have read Ps 60 correctly, it belongs to a considerable tradition of prayer in the OT which confronts the divine presence with relentless complaint and petition, divine responsibility for promises made and judgments which threaten those promises (cf., e.g., Moses, Num 14:13–19). I hardly need to say that these are bold prayers which arise from strong faith. They are not for the weak and half-committed, but they belong to the meek who will inherit the earth, those who are of little stature by worldly standards but who have the power of prayer.

As noted above, this psalm has sometimes been dated to the Maccabean period and thus contemporary with the Book of Daniel. This is almost certainly incorrect, but it is interesting to note that the psalm expresses a theological position similar to that of Daniel. In Daniel, there is an emphasis on deliverance by means other than human hands. The great image in Nebuchadnezzar's dream is destroyed by a stone "cut out by no human hand" (Dan 2:34), a stone which becomes a great mountain and fills the whole earth (Dan 2:35). In Dan 8:23–25, the bold, arrogant, and destructive king, who is the "little horn" (Antiochus Epiphanes) of the preceding vision, will be dealt with by divine intervention: "By no [human] hand, he shall be broken." So it must be; for all saving-help of human beings finally is judged to be empty and worthless. The psalm is a stark reminder that the limits of human power are easily reached and that salvation is God's work. The Israelites are warned in Deut 8:17 of the temptation after settling in the lands to say: "My power and the might of my hand have gotten me this wealth" (עשׂה לי את החיל; cf. נעשׂה חיל in Ps 60:14). The antidote for such saying follows in Deut 8:18:

You shall remember the Lord your God,
for it is he who gives you power to get wealth [כח לעשות חיל].

The ancient promises still provide a basis for future hope. Surely God will not spurn and forget his people forever.

Though for a while the people reel under the assaults of the enemy, they will yet scale the crags of Edom. Superbly strong in the divine energy, they will at last *tread down* Satan under their feet. (J. H. Eaton, *Psalms*, 156)

We too wait with our ancient brothers and sisters for the Divine Warrior to arise and fulfill his promise to overcome the powers of this world. Even so, come, O Lord!

A Prayer from the End of the Earth (61:1–9)

Bibliography

Johnson, A. R. *CPIP*. 352–59. **Mayer, W. R.** "'Ich rufe dich von ferne, höre mich von nahe': zu einer babylonischen Gebetsformel." In *Werden und Wirken des Alten Testaments*. FS C. Westermann. Ed. R. Albertz et al. Göttingen: Vandenhoeck & Ruprecht, 1980. 302–17.

Translation

1	For the leader;[a] with instrumental music;[b] a Davidic (psalm).[c]	
2 (1)	*Hear my cry,*[a] *O God;*	(3+2)
	pay attention to my prayer.	
3 (2)	*From the end of the earth*[a] *I call to you,*	(4+2[4]4)
	when my heart is faint,[b]	
	lead me[c] *to a rock that is higher than I.*[d]	
4 (3)	*For you have been a refuge for me;*	(3+3)
	a tower of strength[a] *against the enemy.*[b]	
5 (4)	*O that I might sojourn in your tent forever,*[a]	(3+3)
	(and) take refuge under the shelter[b] *of your wing!* SELAH.	
6 (5)	*For you have heard my voice, O God;*	(4+4)
	You have given me the heritage[a] *of those who fear your name.*	
7 (6)	*Add*[a] *to the days of the king;*	(4+3)
	let his years span the generations.[b]	
8 (7)	*May he sit enthroned in God's presence forever;*	(4+4)
	assign[a] *Loyal-love and Truth*[b] *to safeguard him.*	
9 (8)	*Then*[a] *I will always sing the praise of your name,*	(4+3)
	fulfilling[b] *my vows day by day.*	

Notes

1.a. See n. 51:1.a.

1.b. See n. 54:1.b.

1.c. See n. 51:1.b.

2.a. Briggs translates as "my yell"; JB, "my cry for help."

3.a. Equal to "a distant place"(cf. 19:5; 46:10; 135:7; Deut 13:7; 28:49, 64; Isa 5:26; etc.). The meaning could be "from the edge of the land." Dahood thinks it is "from the brink of the netherworld."

3.b. For the meaning of "heart," see 27:3; 51:12. The "fainting heart" refers to ebbing vitality, failing courage, and fear of death. A. A. Anderson cites 1QH 8.29, "For (my life) has come near to the pit (i.e., Sheol) and my soul faints day and night." Cf. Pss 77:4; 107:5; 142:4; 143:4; Jonah 2:7; Isa 57:16.

3.c. Reading imperfect as jussive and equivalent to imperative. If the verse is read as a statement of confidence, the translation would read "You will lead me . . ." or, perhaps, past tense throughout: ". . . I called to you . . . you led me . . ." (as in LXX).

3.d. The translations of this line vary. E.g., NAB, "You will set me high upon a rock, you will give me rest"; NEB, "lift me up and set me upon a rock!" Both translations result from reading תְּרוֹמְמֵנִי for יָרוּם, with LXX and Syriac (cf. 27:5). Both translations assume תנחני to be hiphil imperfect from נוח, "cause to give rest to" or "put/place," rather than hiphil of נחה, "lead/guide" (also with deletion of מִמֶּנִּי). Dahood argues that יָרוּם is a jussive participle of ירם, which he argues is a by-form of רום (II, 85; I, 118), and translates, "the lofty mountain," a poetic name for God's heavenly abode. There seems to be no especially good reason to change MT.

4.a. Dahood argues for a compound noun, "a towered-fortress."

4.b. Lit. "from the presence of an enemy."

5.a. Or, "your eternal tent," assuming a construct chain with the pronominal suffix interposed. See Dahood and GKC, 131r.

5.b. Normally, צֵל, "shadow/shade" (17:8; 36:8; 47:2; 63:8; 91:1; Isa 49:2; 51:16; Lam 4:20; Hos 14:7), rather than סתר, "secret place/hiding place." LXX has σκέπη, "covering/protection."

6.a. The word ירשת is frequently considered to be a mistaken spelling for אֶרֶשׁ, "desire/request" (21:3), or as a by-form of אֶרֶשׁת (so Dahood, II, 86; I, 95; with interchange of *primae yod* and *primae aleph*; see also D. W. Thomas, *TRP,* 23). The change is not necessary, however, as the metaphorical use of "heritage," or "inheritance," is not especially difficult (note the נתן ירשה sequence in Deut 2:9; Josh 12:6; etc.). A. R. Johnson (355) thinks the meaning is clarified by the following line, which he reads in terms of positive statements: "You will be adding to the king's days. . . ."

7.a. Reading imperfect with imperative force, as in n. 3.c. (see Dahood, I, 29–30; Craigie, 84, n. 4.a.).

7.b. Literally, "his years as generation and generation"—a succession of generations with no defined end; forever. Note Pss 10:6; 45:18; Joel 2:2; 4:20 (3:20). The כְּמוֹ ("as/like") is sometimes changed to בְּמוֹ, "in/through," or to כִּימֵי, "as the days of" (perhaps LXX). If a change is made, כִּימֵי seems to be best.

8.a. Some ms evidence supports the omission of מן (see *BHS* and note the omission in Prov 20:28). Without the מן (piel imperative from מנה, "appoint/consign/assign," cf. the forms הַס, נַס, and צַו), the colon reads, "Loyal-love and Truth will guard him," or "let Loyal-love and Truth safeguard him." LXX apparently reads Aramaic מַן, "who?" "what?" However, the meaning of the Greek translation is not clear. Various emendations have been proposed.

8.b. A. R. Johnson (*CPIP,* 357) may be correct to conclude that חסד ואמת is a hendiadys, meaning "true devotion" or "true loyal-love."

9.a. כֵּן indicates "thus/so/then" = "in accordance with the foregoing."

9.b. Infinitive used as gerund (circumstantial infinitive; see GKC, 114o; Dahood, I, 167; II, 88).

Form/Structure/Setting

Ps 61 is classified as an individual lament in most form-critical analyses. If the translation above is accepted, such a classification fits vv 2–6. However, the prayer for the king in vv 7–8 is somewhat strange, but not without parallels (see below). The vow in v 9 is appropriate for a lament. Nevertheless, Weiser (443) finds a tone of thanksgiving in the psalm from v 4 onwards which "prevails . . . over the tone of lament and depression [and] the song is to be regarded as a thanksgiving." Like Pss 41, 56, and others, Weiser interprets Ps 61 as a recital by the author of the fulfillment of prayer for which thanksgiving can now be made (see also Kraus, II, 592). The thanksgiving character is enhanced if vv 7–8 are translated as positive statements rather than as petitions. See A. R. Johnson, *CPIP*, 354–59), who translates v 7 as

> Thou wilt be adding to the king's days,
> Making his years seem everlasting.

He treats v 8 as a conditional sentence:

> If he dwells ever in God's [Yahweh's] presence,
> true devotion . . . will be his safeguard.

The truth of the matter is that we probably have an individual prayer which was read differently in different contexts (see below).

The supplicant in the psalm is rather frequently identified as a king, perhaps David himself. Dahood puts the issue succinctly when he says,

> If with most modern scholars we classify this psalm as an individual lament composed by a member of the Old Testament community (cf. Kraus, *Psalmen*, I, p. 433), we shall find it difficult to account for the prayer for the king in vss 7–8. With Gunkel and Kraus we shall be forced to describe these two verses as the misplaced word of a later hand. If, however, we assume that the supplicant is a king, no such problem arises.

This may be the case, and a good number of interpreters have agreed. For example, S. Mowinckel (*PIW*, I, 226) argues that in both Pss 61 and 63 it is a king who prays. In Ps 63, according to Mowinckel, the king appears in the temple early in the morning to offer prayers and sacrifices for help against enemies. In contrast, Ps 61 is a prayer to accompany offerings before a battle, spoken by a king who is far away from the temple. The reference to the king in the third person in vv 7–8 is considered to be an example of court style (see Dahood, II, 84), with parallels in the OT (Jer 38:5) and in the Phoenician inscriptions of Yehawmilk, king of Babylon, from the fifth century B.C.E., in accord with the view that the speaker is a king.

Several interpreters assign the psalm to the period of the pre-exilic monarchy, and even to David when he was forced to flee from Absalom to the other side of the Jordan (e.g., Delitzsch, Perowne, Kirkpatrick, and Kissane). Others, however, think of the period of the exile after 597 B.C.E., when the prayer could have been for Zedekiah in Jerusalem (see Johnson, 353) and for Jehoiachin, who as an exile himself received favorable treatment by the Babylonian king, Evil-merodach (Barnes). Those who hold to the exilic setting do not think of the king as the speaker but of an Israelite who prays for the king.

The view that the psalm contains a prayer *for* the king is equally as probable as the conclusion that it is a prayer by a king. Kraus notes parallels of such abrupt prayers for monarchs in Mesopotamian prayers and notes Pss 28:8; 63:12; 72:15–17; 84:9–10. Johnson (*CPIP,* 359) thinks it conceivable, but not certain, that Ps 61 was composed for use on behalf of David in the years after his capture of Jerusalem when the emergence of eschatological hopes centered on his reign and his anticipated dynasty. Johnson thinks in terms of a cultic prophet speaking for the king and on his behalf.

It is common to interpret the supplicant in the psalm as one who was far away from Jerusalem and the festivals of the temple (cf. Pss 42–43) on the basis of v 3a: "From the end of the earth (or land) I call to you." Thus those who identify the speaker in the psalm with David think of some time when he was away from Jerusalem and might have expressed his longing to be back in the worship on Zion (note v 4), such as the occasion of his flight from Absalom's rebellion to Mahanaim beyond the Jordan. However, it is not necessary to assume a geographical reference in this statement. A number of interpreters (e.g., Mowinckel, Schmidt, Dahood, Eaton, Johnson) have understood the "end of the earth" as the edge of the netherworld; e.g., Dahood, "the brink of the nether world." Johnson (*CPIP,* 354) says that the speaker could have regarded himself "as slipping further and further down the gigantic cistern or well which leads to the waters of the underworld and there seeing the earth's surface receding further and further away." Dahood links this interpretation with an understanding of ארץ as the netherworld (which it almost certainly does have in some contexts; see Dahood, I, 106). However, it is not necessary to stress the netherworld aspect, though a condition involving the nearness of death may be suggested by the expression "as my heart grows faint." On the other hand, it may be read as a poetic metaphor expressing a sense of remoteness and existential distance from God, regardless of the cause. The language would certainly have been apropos for exiles, physically far from home, and physically and spiritually feeling themselves to be "at the end of the earth."

If we take a clue from the Greek text, and from the general characteristics of those psalms dealing with kingship, a conclusion that this psalm was read as an affirmation of messianic hope in the post-exilic period is highly probable. The psalm became an eschatological/messianic prayer for the fulfillment of the divine promise for an everlasting Davidic dynasty (2 Sam 7:16, 25–29)—a prayer which is more affirmation than it is petition (cf. Deissler, II, 71). In this case, the translation would be different from the one given above:

> Hear my cry, O God, pay attention to my prayer—
> from the end of the earth I called to you,
> when my heart was faint,
> You led me to a rock that was higher than I
> For you were a refuge for me,
> a tower of strength against the enemy.
> I will sojourn in your tent forever,
> [and] take refuge under the shelter of your wings!
> For you have heard my vows, O God;

You have given me the heritage of those who fear your name.
You will add to the days of the king;
his years will span the generations.
He will sit enthroned in God's presence forever;
Loyal-love and Truth will safeguard him.
There I will always sing the praises of your name,
fulfilling my vows day by day.

In this case the traditional language of lament in v 2 recalls the prayer which has now been answered. Either reading of the psalm is legitimate. The first would be more appropriate in the period from David to the end of the monarchy. The second fits the piety of the post-exilic period. The *Comment* is based primarily on the first translation.

Comment

Superscription (61:1). The expression עַל־נְגִינַת is usually translated as "on a stringed instrument" or "with string/instrumental music." The form of נגינת is that of a singular noun in the construct state. However, the form may be actually the feminine singular absolute (so Dahood, who cited Ugaritic support; much earlier was Delitzsch, who cited Phoenician parallels; GKC, 80f), though there is some textual and versional support for the plural absolute נ֫וֹת (see *BHS*). The על with נגינת appears only here in the psalm titles; elsewhere ב is used. Schmidt argues that על binds the word נגינת to "the leader" and thus, "for the leader who is in charge of string music." If the MT accents are followed, and the singular construct is accepted, the translation could be "for the leader in charge of stringed music relating to David." The LXX reads "among the hymns of David." The translation above assumes that the על is conditional and equivalent to ב in other instances of this expression.

A prayer for help (61:2–5). The address to God is direct and strong. A. A. Anderson notes that the Hebrew laments do not normally begin with a list of honorific divine names, as in Babylonian prayers. The "end of the earth" is used as a geographic term referring to faraway places, remote areas far from known surroundings (Pss 19:5; 46:10; 135:7; Deut 28:49; 30:4; Isa 5:26; etc.). The reference here could be to the "edge/frontiers of the land" (Buttenwieser), but it can refer equally as well to remote areas beyond the land to which the speaker has gone (or been taken) for some reason.

If the speaker is a king, he could be praying to God while on a distant campaign. Gunkel and J. H. Eaton (*Kingship*, 48) note the use of a similar phrase by Pharaoh Rameses II in a prayer at the Battle of Kadesh. However, some interpreters think of "the end of the earth" in existential terms: the sense of separateness and/or the awareness of being at the brink of death—an approach which is strengthened if ארץ is taken here as "netherworld" (as in Dahood; see note 3.a.; also see Johnson's view above). Some support for the existential interpretation is found in the use of the verb עטף ("fainting") in v 3b, which is used in contexts where life is under great stress and death seems near (e.g., Pss 102:1; 107:5; 143:4; Lam 2:11, 19; Jonah 2:8).

The two approaches are not mutually exclusive, however. Geographical separation that forces one to live his or her life in alien surroundings, far from home, friends, and familiar social groups, is usually lived in great anxiety and spiritual stress. The life of an exile is typically a "fainting one," lived at the "edge of the earth."

The speaker prays to be led to a rock that is inaccessible but secure. Whether we translate as "the rock that is higher than I" or as "the rock that is too high for me" (e.g., JB), the meaning is that of a request for a refuge which lies beyond the supplicant's strength and which can only be reached with God's help. The rock suggests a place where God abides and, especially in the context of the OT, the rock on which the temple was built on Mount Zion in Jerusalem. Dahood insists on reading "the Lofty Mountain" here, as a poetic name for the cosmic mountain of God's heavenly abode (citing Pss 121:1 and 123:1 in support; on 121:1, see the comments of Allen, 151 n. 1.b.). However, such a simple equating of the rock-mountain with the divine heavenly abode should be avoided. In the religious thought of the ancient world (and still present in some cultural areas of the modern), the cosmic mountain of the deity's abode functioned as the meeting place of heaven and earth, the axis of the world (see M. Eliade, *Patterns in Comparative Religions*, tr. R. Sheed [New York: Sheed & Ward, 1958], 375; for general discussion see R. J. Clifford, *The Cosmic Mountain in Canaan and the Old Testament* [Cambridge: Harvard UP, 1972]; J. D. Levenson, *Sinai and Zion: An Entry into the Jewish Bible* [New York: Harper & Row, 1985], 89–184). Levenson (122) describes it as follows:

> The cosmic mountain is a kind of fulcrum for the universe; it is on the line to which all the regions of the universe are referred, and it is somehow available to each of them. The base of the mountain lies in the chaotic underworld, and its head reaches into the heavens. On it, messages can be passed from heaven to earth and *vice versa*. It is the prime place of communication between transcendent and mundane reality.

All this is not conveyed directly by the prayer for refuge on a high rock, but it lies in the conceptual field surrounding the idea.

Three other metaphors for refuge are found in vv 4–5. The "strong tower" recalls the towers, sometimes massive in structure (such as the great tower at Jericho), which provided the anchors for city walls and served as surveillance points as well as places of refuge, and sometimes as places for the presentation of sacrificial offerings (2 Kgs 3:27; Jer 19:23; Zeph 1:5). To dwell in the "tent" of God is a metaphor for divine hospitality and the protective presence of the divine host (Cohen). The tent signified the dwelling of a deity and is sometimes applied to a temple (Pss 15:1; 27:5; Isa 33:20; cf. 2 Sam 6:17). The shelter of the divine wings (v 4b) alludes to the glyptic representation of the presence of God by the cherubim and their wings in the temple (1 Kgs 6:23–28; 8:67; Ps 91:1, 4), as well as to the protective care of a bird for its young (see *Comment* on Ps 57:2; also 17:8; 36:8; 91:4). V 4 is a statement of experience and provides the basis for the prayers in vv 2, 3, and 5.

A prayer for the king (61:6–8). V 6 is a continuation of the thought in v 4 (note כי־חיית in v 4 and כי־אתה in v 6), but it also provides a transition into the second section of the psalm and links with v 9 to form an inclusion for vv 6–9. A further basis for the petitions is laid by the statements that in the past God has heard the voice of the suppliant. The speaker recognizes that his/her heritage is that of those who fear the name of Yahweh. Thus the suppliant belongs to those who are reverent and faithful toward God (cf., e.g., Pss 24:32; 25:12; 34:8–10; 112:1).

The "vows" (see v 9; also Pss 50:14; 56:13; 65:2; 66:13–15) are not defined in this context, but they most probably involved promises regarding certain acts of behavior and of worship (see *Comment* on Ps 56:13). Vows added force to prayers by a commitment to give something to God if he would grant a request made in the prayer; though at times the vows may have been simple promises without being based on a favor from God (e.g., the vow of David in Ps 132:2–5; cf. the vow of Paul in Acts 18:10). On the theological significance of the name, see Craigie's comments on Pss 8:2; 9:2-3; also *Comment* on 54:3.

The prayer for the king (cf. Ps 72:15) concentrates on the extension of his life (v 7) and the permanency of his reign (v 8a). A wish or prayer for the long life of the king seems to have been a part of royal protocol; see 1 Kgs 1:31; Neh 2:3; 1 Sam 10:24; 1 Kgs 1:15, 34, 39; 2 Kgs 11:12//2 Chr 23:11. The prayer reminds us of the the prayer of Hezekiah for an extension of his own life (2 Kgs 20:1-7//Isa 38:1-6). The welfare of the people as a whole, and of each individual, was considered to be bound up with the life and reign of the king. Bigger-than-life language relating to kings and their reigns was common in the ancient Near East and in Israel (see comments on such kingship psalms as 2; 21; 72; 89; 110; 132; and for the whole matter of the nature of kingship, see O. Keel, *The Symbolism of the Biblical World*, 243–306; and for a prayer for the eternal life of a king, see Jacquet, II, 277). Nevertheless, the unusual expression כמו־דר ודר suggests that the years of the king's life be "as generations and generations," perhaps meaning "may the years he yet lives equal in number the many generations which will follow in his dynasty" (Cohen). Even in the form of the main translation above, there is a latent messianic hope in these verses, especially for post-exilic readers. Gunkel (261) argues that the prayer for the king was added by a later hand and declares that such prayers (as also in Pss 28:8–9; 63:12a; 84:10) are for the reigning king and not for the Messiah. Undoubtedly, the language is drawn from prayers by and for contemporary kings, language which could be extremely exalted. Nevertheless, we must ask why such prayers were added to psalms, or kept in psalms, during the post-exilic period when there were no kings. Surely they were retained to express the hope for a future king, whose reign would manifest the qualities of true monarchy, qualities longed for through so many disappointments (Deissler, Kidner, Maillot-Lelièvre). The words of the text convey a latent hope which transcends their finite limits. (The Targum in this psalm interprets the king as the King Messiah and indicates that the vows in v 9 will be paid on the day when he is anointed to reign.) In keeping with the mission of the king, the supplicant prays that God will appoint personified Loyal-love (חסד) and Truth (אמת) like guardian angels to keep and sustain the king (for these words, see *Comment* on Pss 51:3, 8; 57:4; also 40:12; 85:11–14; 89:15, 25; also Prov 20:28).

The Vow (61:9). The final verse of the psalm expresses the praise of the name of God which the supplicant will sing when God responds to the prayer in the preceding verses, and a basis is provided for a period of praise and vow-paying of indefinite duration. "Singing praise and making melody, he will make his whole life a continuous paying of vows" (Delitzsch, 232).

Explanation

The main value of this psalm probably lies in its metaphorical richness. The metaphors of the high rock, the strong tower, the perpetual dwelling in the tent of God, and the shelter under the divine wings enhance the prayer and contribute significantly to our repertoire of spiritual imagination. A well-stocked and fertile imagination is essential for spiritual strength, a strength that influences the whole being of the person and/or group that possesses it. The metaphors assist us to incorporate our own experience into the experience of prayer. Prayer should engage imagination both toward the one praying and toward God. The metaphors of the psalm pass into our own experience and expand our horizons. Walter Brueggemann has written of the Psalms:

> The Psalms do not insist that we follow word for word and line by line, but they intend us to have great freedom to engage our imagination toward the Holy God. . . . We will take liberties as the Psalm passes by and moves out into the richness of our experience and then back into the awesome presence of God. That is the way of metaphor (*Praying the Psalms* [Winona, MN: Saint Mary's Press, 1982], 35).

Without a good stock of metaphors and an active imagination, our prayers are crippled and reduced to flattened, formulaic expressions without much power.

Perhaps the dominant metaphor in the psalm is that of distance from God in v 3. A sense of far-awayness from the divine presence, an at-the-end-of the earth experience, seems to be endemic to the spiritual life from time to time (see, e.g., Pss 2:1; 10:1; 22:2, 12, 20; 35:22; 38:22 [21]; 71:12). Indeed, it is almost a continuous need: "The psalmist is here describing the human condition in existentialist terms: man constantly stands at the edge of the abyss, and only divine assistance can prevent his falling into it" (Dahood, II, 84). Werner R. Mayer discusses a provocative Babylonian prayer formula which says, "I call to you from distantness; hear me from nearness" ("'Ich rufe dich von ferne, höre mich von nahe,'" 302–17). The formula seems to mean that prayer suspends the distantness between the supplicant and the deity. Breaking down a perceived distance and the creation of sense of nearness and presence is a major function of prayer. The Psalms are of great importance in the recognition of distantness, which results from various kinds of stress and distress, and in the closing of that gap, which threatens spiritual health and even life itself. The very recitation of psalms like 61 serves to diminish distance and enhance nearness and presence.

Calm Faith under Attack:
A Psalm of Trust   (62:1–13)

Bibliography

Delekat, L. *Asylie und Schutzorakel am Zionheiligtum.* 186–89. **Honeyman, A. M.** *"ʾId, Du* and Psalm LXII 12," *VT* 11 (1961) 348–50; **Westermann, C.** *The Living Psalms.* 150–56.

Translation

1   For the leader;[a] ʿ *al-jeduthun;*[b] a Davidic psalm.[c]

2 (1)   *Yes,*[a] *my soul waits calmly*[b] *for God,*   (4[2+2]+2)
       from him is my salvation.

3 (2)   *Yes,*[a] *he is my rock where I am secure;*   (3+3)
       my stronghold where I am safe from ruin.[b]

4 (3)   *How long will you assault*[a] *a person;*   (3+2+4)
       all of you attacking[b]
       as you would a leaning wall or a battered parapet.[c]

5 (4)   *Yes, despite being a person of high status,*[a]
       they plan to push (him) down;[b]   (3+2+2+2)
       they delight in lies;
       they bless with their mouths,[c]
       but inwardly they curse. SELAH.

6 (5)   *Yes, calmly wait for God, O my soul,*   (3+2)
       for my hope is from him.

7 (6)   *Yes, he is my rock where I am secure;*[a]   (3+2)
       my stronghold where I am unshaken.

8 (7)   *My welfare and my power (depend)*[a] *on God;*   (3+3)
       I am rock-strong and secure in God.[b]

9 (8)   *Trust in him at all times, O people;*[a]   (3+3+3)
       pour out your hearts before him.
       God is our refuge! SELAH.

10 (9) *Yes, ordinary people*[a] *are only a breath;*   (3+2+2+2)
       an illusion[b] *are people of rank*[a]—
       rising[c] *on the balance!*
       Altogether they weigh less than a breath.

11 (10) *Trust not in extortion,*   (3+3+3+3)
       and in plunder take no empty pride;
       when wealth[a] *bears fruit,*
       do not set your heart on it.

12 (11) *God has spoken once—*   (3+3+3)
       twice I heard this—[a]
       that strength belongs to God.

13 (12)   *Yours is indeed* [a] *a loyal-love, O Lord,*   (3+4)
           for you reward each person
           according to what he [or she] has done.

Notes

1.a. See n. 51:1.a.

1.b. See *Comment.*

1.c. See n. 51:1.b.

2.a. This is an attempt to translate the Hebrew אַךְ, which occurs six times in this psalm (vv 2, 3, 5, 6, 7, 10). The force of the particle shifts back and forth between an affirmative meaning, "truly/surely/yes," and a restrictive meaning, "only/alone." Basically it seems to involve comparison, either overt or implied: "Yes, but on the contrary/nevertheless." N. H. Snaith ("The Meaning of the Hebrew אַךְ" *VT* 14 [1964] 221–25) compares it to the Yorkshire "nobbut" and to the Greek ἀλλά (though πλήν, "only/nevertheless/however/in any case," is used in Ps 62) and stresses the element of contrariness/exception/restriction, and even contradiction (225) in its usage.

2.b. Literally "silence/calm/stillness (is) my soul."

3.a. "My rock and my salvation" form a hendiadys (Dahood): "my rock of deliverance" or "my saving rock."

3.b. Traditionally, "I shall not be greatly moved"; רַבָּה is read adverbially; sometimes it is omitted (e.g., Kraus). The translation could be, "I am not severely shaken." Note the לֹא אָמוֹט in v 7b.

4.a. The verb תְּהוֹתְתוּ may be from הות, "shout/threaten/attack" (BDB; Briggs), or from התת, "speak incessantly," extended to mean "overwhelm with reproofs." Dahood associates it with the Ugaritic *hwt*, "word" (as in Job 6:30, *hawot*, "words"), and translates, "How long will you bluster." RSV has "set upon a man"; NRSV, "assail a person."

4.b. MT has pual imperfect 2nd plural, "all of you are slain" (or "will be slain"), as in KJV, "ye shall be slain all of you." However, the piel should be read here with the Ben Naphtali tradition and versional support (see GKC, 52g; Briggs). The verb רצח normally refers to illegal killing (Num 35:30 is an exception), murder, or manslaughter; though "shatter" (RSV) or "attack" in a more general sense is possible. NRSV, "batter your victim."

4.c. Reading as a military metaphor, with the wall and parapet referring to the persecuted person, which seems best. It is possible to read, however, with the bulging wall as a reference to the enemies; so KJV, "as a bowing wall shall ye be, and as a tottering fence." Dahood has, "All of you are like a leaning wall, a sagging fence." NEB has caught the most probable meaning: "How long will you assist a man . . . all battering on a leaning wall?"

5.a. The MT מִשְּׂאֵתוֹ is uncertain. Gunkel and others read מַשָּׁאוֹת from נשא ("to deceive") as meaning "deceptions" or "treachery": "They plan deception, they delight." However, MT may be retained with the sense of "dignity/status/high position," suggesting a person of eminent position in society, such as a king. LXX has "my honor/dignity/authority/office" (τιμήν), which may be correct.

5.b. The verb נדח carries the idea of "thrust out/away." If מִשָּׁאות is read as "deception" or "deceit," the verb can be read as "mislead/lead astray" (as in contexts like Deut 13:14; Prov 7:21). Dahood notes the odd use of the infinitive לְהַדִּיחַ without an accusative object and reads "to ruin they indulge in lies." Perhaps better would be:

> How they counsel deceit!
> They love to mislead with a lie;
> blessing with their mouths,
> but inwardly cursing.

5.c. MT, "with his mouth," but see *BHS.*

7.a. See n. 3.a.

8.a. Literally "my salvation/deliverance and my glory." Probably another case of hendiadys: "my glorious deliverance."

8.b. Literally, "the rock of my strength of my refuge," an extended construct chain, equal to, "my mighty rock-refuge." Note the chiasm in the verse "On God—my salvation and my glory—my mighty rock-refuge—in God" (ABBA).

9.a. LXX has "all the congregation of . . ." which may reflect Hebrew כָּל־עֲדַת and may be a better reading: "Trust in him, O whole congregation of the people."

10.a. The *Translation* assumes that the common assumption regarding the meaning of בְּנֵי אָדָם and בְּנֵי אִישׁ is correct when paired as here. See Pss 4:3; 49:3; Lam 3:33 (see A. A. Anderson, I, 374; Kraus, I, 169; Jacquet, II, 284). The distinction is made in some Babylonian and Egyptian sources. However, Kidner (223) correctly notes that the distinctions applied to these terms as expressions of "low estate" and "high estate" are only inferences. Both Hebrew expressions may mean "man" or "mankind." NEB has "all men."

10.b. Literally, "a lie," as in v 5.

10.c. Circumstantial infinitive; GKC, 114o. Cf. Perowne, 485.

11.a. The word חַיִל can mean "wealth/power/force, etc."

12.a. The expression "once . . . twice" may be a form of numerical saying, as in Prov 6:16–18; 30:15–31; etc. The message was repeatedly received. It is possible, but less likely, to read "two things have I learned" for the second expression (see NEB; NAB; NJV). It is possible that the ם at the end of שְׁתַּיִם is enclitic: שְׁתִּי־ם זוּ שָׁמַעְתִּי: "Two times of this I have heard" = "I have heard it twice."

13.a. The conjunction is emphatic.

Form/Structure/Setting

The outstanding characteristic of this psalm is the lack of any address or prayer to God until the last verse. Testimony and exhortation dominate the psalm. The sixfold repetition of the Hebrew אַך ("truly/surely/nevertheless/only") is a striking literary feature in the psalm (see note 2.a.). However, despite the presence of this feature, the psalm does not seem to have a very intricate design. The text moves forward with a fairly simple progression. Stuhlmueller (I, 284) notes that the refrain in vv 3 and 7 does not end major strophes, as would be expected, and that the conclusion seems "almost anticlimactic, like a later addition"—which it may very well be. As with many psalms, the somewhat vague structure allows for different outlines. Nevertheless, the *selah* placement (for whatever reason) seems to provide an adequate division of the psalm into three parts: vv 2–5, 6–9, 10–13. The first section is composed of two parts: vv 2–3, an opening affirmation; vv 4–5, a charge against enemies. V 4 is a relatively rare charge by a speaker directly to enemies (cf. Pss 6:9; 52:3; 55:14; 94:8), while v 5 is an indirect charge, addressed to whoever will hear. The second section is composed of three verses of personal affirmation (vv 6–8) and an exhortation to the people (v 7).

The third section begins with a reflection on the basic nature of humanity (v 16) and moves to exhortation of the people in v 11 (note that the exhortation in v 9 is positive but that in v 11 is negative). Vv 12–13 provide a conclusion in which God is directly addressed with affirmation of his loyal-love and fair dealing. The Hebrew אַך occurs three times in the first section, twice in the second section, and once in the third section. The occurrence of אַך in v 6 relates this verse back to v 2, as does the use of דּוּמִיָּה and דּוֹמִי, in vv 2 and 6 respectively. As noted above, vv 3 and 7 are the same, except for the word רַבָּה in v 3.

This psalm is clearly one of trust and affirmation, similar to Pss 4; 16; 23; 27:1–6; 91; 121; and 131. As such it shares features with the confidence sections of laments (e.g., Ps 22:23–32) and with the thanksgiving psalms (Pss 31:24–5; 32:6, 9–11; 34:10–23; 66:16–20), though strictly speaking the psalm lacks the major elements of a thanksgiving psalm. The psalm has a tone and some language common to the wisdom literature, and several scholars have put it in the wisdom tradition (e.g., Gunkel, Kraus, Deissler, Stuhlmueller). However, it seems to be "near wisdom" and does not clearly belong to the rather amorphous context known as wisdom poetry.

The condition of the speaker is clearly that of an endangered person, under attack by those who are seeking his (or her) ruin. In the face of assault (verbal or otherwise) by assailants, the speaker declares absolute confidence in God's protection. It is quite possible to think of a speaker who has taken refuge in a sanctuary (vv 3, 7, 8, 12), where assurance of divine help and safekeeping might be powerfully realized, possibly through receiving a *Heilsorakel* from God (v 12; S. Mowinckel, *PIW*, I, 219; Kraus, A. A. Anderson, Sabourin, 275). However, Schmidt, Leslie, and, tentatively, K. Seybold (*Das Gebet des Kranken*, 74–75) maintain that the speaker reflects an experience of severe illness, in which a weakened physical condition is likened to a bulging and falling wall, a condition made worse by enemies who batter the suffering person with vicious talk and curses. Community ceremonies for a person under attack by enemies, whether from outside the community or from inside, such as those postulated by Erhard Gerstenberger (*Der bittende Mensch*, esp. 126, 144) would be appropriate for Ps 62. In this case, the psalm would seem to be one spoken by a person being rehabilitated back into family and community life, who speaks in such a way as to challenge enemies and to profess a firm adherence to God.

Any attempt to assign a specific date for this psalm is hardly worth the effort to discuss. The scribes who provided the superscription either found the psalm in the Davidic tradition or put it there, no doubt thinking it suitable for the speaker to be David. However, this conclusion is not a substantial basis for dating the psalm (see Craigie, 31–35), and it may very well be post-exilic (cf. Westermann, 153).

Comment

The term *jeduthun* is found in Ps 39:1 with ל; with על, as here; it occurs also in Ps 77:1. Jeduthun is listed as one of David's chief musicians in 1 Chr 16:41, along with Asaph and Heman (1 Chr 9:16; 16:38; etc.). Mowinckel (*PIW*, II, 213) argues that the term should be understood as a noun, not as a personal name, and should be given the meaning "confession," drawing the word from ידה (which Craigie, 308, correctly notes could just as well indicate "thanksgiving" or "praise"). However, it may be more probable that the word is a personal name, like Asaph and Heman, which appear in titles of psalms. In that case, it could be a reference to a family of singers with this name and the title might be translated as "For the leader in charge of [the family singing group] Jeduthun, . . ." On the other hand, the name may have become a way of referring to a tune or musical setting, according to which the psalm was to be sung (the על would mean "according to" in this case).

Basic affirmation of trust (62:2–3). These verses express the assurance to which the speaker has come, and they suggest a previous struggle, a struggle that "had taken place in his soul, before he found in turning to God that stillness from which he is able to draw the inner strength he needed to overcome his affliction" (Weiser). Perhaps, we should think of the passage through a crisis, like that in Ps 73 and implied in Ps 131, to a turning point. The two parallel usages of אך in vv 2 and 3 indicate that the statements which they introduce do not come naturally and easily. Despite outward appearances, God is the speaker's salvation, rock, and strength (on the concept of rock see Ps 61:3). The speaker is confident of being "safe from ruin," of not being "*greatly* moved"—shaken and troubled, perhaps, but safe from ruin. Assurance is postulated on a calm, still waiting for God. The stillness, or calm resting, also suggests a previous time of restless spiritual agitation.

Charge against the enemies (62:4–5). The enemies are portrayed as false friends who persecute the speaker. They are pictured as brutally aggressive, deceptive, and delighting in lies. They have no respect for the status or dignity of the person they attack (v 5a). The purpose of their actions is destructive. Their attack is like that of a besieging army assaulting and battering the weakening walls of a city (v 4; cf. Pss 3:7; 56:2; 59:5). The speaker describes a condition (in third person) which is like a wall pushed in and ready to collapse at any moment.

The situation is made worse by the hypocritical behavior of the enemies, who verbally bless the speaker, but who pronounce curses in their hearts. The text may veil magical or semi-magical use of curses and abusive, occult terms against the speaker (S. Mowinckel, *PIW*, II, 3; Kraus, I, 112–17; II, 597). The question "How long?" (v 4) is found in charges and challenges addressed to opponents or persecutors (e.g., Exod 16:28; Josh 18:3; Job 8:2; 18:2; 19:2; cf. Pss 52:3; 58:2)— though it is also used in complaints addressed to God (e.g., Ps 13:2, 3). The expression is especially suitable for disputations in which opponents address each other directly.

Affirmation and exhortation (62:6–9). The statements of calm waiting, hope, and security in vv 6–7 parallel those in vv 2–3. There are some changes in nuances between vv 2–3 and vv 6–7, however. Kidner (I, 222) notes three: first, the speaker shifts from declaration in vv 2–3 to self-exhortation in vv 6–7; second, "hope" appears in v 6 rather than "salvation" in v 2; third, the somewhat open "where I am safe from ruin" ("not greatly moved") of v 3 becomes unqualified assurance in v 7. A fourth difference between the sections is the addition of v 8, which uses a chiastic structure to emphasize by repetition the concentration of the speaker on God (see note 8.b.). Everything which makes a person important and strong depends upon God's favor and help. The speaker turns attention to the people (probably to be understood as fellow worshipers) who are exhorted in v 9 to trust in God at all times and to "pour out" their hearts before him in prayer. (On "pouring out" prayer before God see Hannah's statement in 1 Sam 1:15: "I have been pouring out my soul before Yahweh"; also Pss 42:5; 102:1 [title]; 142:3; similarly, Hezekiah "spread out" the letter from the Assyrians before Yahweh, 2 Kgs 19:14 // Isa 37:14). The expression conveys openness and freedom in prayer to express to God all one's sufferings and distress. The third colon in v 9 ("God is our refuge") is a key statement in which the speaker extends personal faith to the community. The people are encouraged to follow the speaker in trusting God.

The weakness of mankind and the strength of God (62:10–13). The last major section of the psalm continues the instruction of v 9. The fundamental nature of humankind is set forth in v 10, and a warning against trusting in the products of oppression follows in v 11, which forms a concluding parallel with v 9 (note the repetition of "trust" and "heart"). V 10 forms a central affirmation around which the positive v 9 and the negative v 11 are placed. It is appropriate that v 10 have

the last אַךְ of the psalm, because the outward appearance of so many human
beings and their actions is deceptively positive (see Ps 73). Trust in the wealth
produced by human efforts, which so frequently involves some form of oppression and robbery, is most unwise (v 11). When wealth (חַיִל, "strength/wealth/
power") bears fruit and increases, it is not a thing on which to set one's heart,
because the essential nature of human beings is incredibly ephemeral (v 10)—
less in weight than a breath on scales!

The basis for all the affirmations in the preceding verses is found in v 12. A
message from God has been received, though there is no specific indication of
how it came, perhaps through some oracle of salvation or from the recital of
Yahweh's mighty acts (cf. Ps 136). The message which has been confirmed in a
twofold way is that strength belongs to God. Possibly the twofold hearing relates
to the first two parts of the psalm (vv 2–5 and vv 6–8). V 13 is added as a closing
statement and supplements the revelation of v 12. God's strength is linked with
his loyal-love and his faithfulness to reward people according to their works
(Exod 20:5–6; Deut 5:9–10; Prov 24:12; cf. Pss 28:4; 31:24–25; Prov 11:21, 31;
Rom 2:6; 1 Cor 3:8; 2 Tim 4:14; Rev 22:12)

Explanation

This psalm is mostly *about* God and faith in him; only v 13 is addressed *to* God.
The psalm is a strong affirmation of trust in God despite so much in life which
seems to countermand such confidence. For the speaker in the psalm, God is a
bastion of security and strength, even in the face of powerful foes who threaten
destruction. The truth is that power belongs to God, though the apparent
circumstances seem to favor extortion, plunder, robbery, and increasing wealth.
The speaker has found the strength of a calm stillness of soul before God, a
position which gives power for both self-encouragement (vv 6–8) and encouragement for others (vv 9–11). Stillness before God has exorcised the frequently
dominant elements of life—fearful anxiety, disappointment, pain of abuse—and
has become the source of assurance of the adequacy of divine power and divine
willingness to help those who are faithful. When we remain calm in trust before
God, we grow in strength and discipline.

The psalm is characterized by the sixfold use of אַךְ—the "nevertheless" quality
that marks the nature of a genuine faith commitment. However, the psalm does
not express a naive idealism which ignores the reality of evil in the world.

> The poet is aware of the contradictory character of human nature; he is
> aware of that ultimate lie which deprives man of any trustworthiness. And
> when he extends his grave indictment to all men, there is no reason to
> assume that in passing this pessimistic judgment on man he has in view
> only the behavior of his adversaries but wants to exempt himself from it.
> The profundity of the religious truth expressed in this psalm consists in the
> very fact that the psalmist knows that to see through the eyes of God means
> to get to the root of all things, of men and, last but not least, of one's own
> self, and to see life without any camouflage or self-deception as it actually is
> in its unadorned truth (Weiser, 451).

Weiser's treatment of the psalm is surely the most profound theological analysis of the psalm by any modern commentator.

The affirmation of faith in this psalm relates well to other biblical passages such as Ps 73; Hab 3:17–19; Dan 3:16–18; Matt 6:25–30; 25:31–46; Phil 4:10–13.

That Which Is Better Than Life Itself (63:1–12)

Bibliography

Auffret, P. *La Sagesse à Bati sa Maison.* 265–83. **Beyerlin, W.** *Die Rettung der Bedrängten.* 135–38. **Cerosko, A.** "A Note on Psalm 63: A Psalm of Vigil." *ZAW* 92 (1980) 435–36. **Johnson, A. R.** *CPIP.* 276–84. **McKay, J. W.** "Psalms of Vigil." *ZAW* 91 (1979), 229–47. **Michel, D.** *Tempora und Satzstellung in der Psalmen.* Bonn: H. Bouvier, 1960. 227–28.

Translation

1   A Davidic psalm;[a] when he was in the wilderness of Judah.[b]

2 (1)   *O God,*   (1+3+3+3+3)
    You are my God whom I seek;[a]
    my soul[b] *thirsts for you;*
    my body[c] *longs for you;*
    like[d] *a land parched and weary from lack of water.*

3 (2)   *So longing,*[a] *I have seen you in the sanctuary,*   (3+3)
    beholding[b] *your strength and glory.*

4 (3)   *For your loyal-love is better than life (itself);*[a]   (3+3)
    my lips have praised you.

5 (4)   *So I will bless you as long as I live*   (3+3)
    (and) in your name lift up my hands.

6 (5)   *As with the food of a feast*[a] *my soul is satisfied,*   (4+3)
    and with my joyful lips my mouth praises (you).

7 (6)   *As*[a] *I remember you upon my bed;*   (3+3)
    in the night-watches I meditate on you.

8 (7)   *For you have been my help,*[a]   (3+3)
    and in the shadow of your wings I have shouted for joy.

9 (8)   *My soul clings fast to you;*   (3+3)
    your right hand upholds me.

10 (9)   *Those who seek (to take) my life*[a] *will be destroyed;*[b]   (4+3)
    they will go down into the depths of the earth.

11 (10)   *Those who would hand over*[a] *the king*[b] *to the sword*   (3+3)
    will be left as food for jackals,

12 (11)   *but he*[a] *will rejoice in God.*   (3+3+3)
    Everyone who swears by him[b] *will rejoice,*
    for the mouths of lie-speakers will be shut up.[c]

Notes

1.a. See n. 51:1.b.

1.b. See *Comment.*

2.a. Relative clause, expressed by simple coordination. A. R. Johnson, *CPIP*, 280, n. 3; GKC, 155e.

2.b. The translation "my soul" (for נפשׁי) is for poetic purposes; "my life," "myself," or "I" is technically more accurate in this verse as well as in vv 6, 9, 10.

2.c. Lit. "my flesh."

2.d. Reading as *beth essentiae* (GKC, 119i).

3.a. This is NEB's way of expressing the force of the כֵּן, which has troubled commentators; see Perowne, 491; D. Michel, *Tempora,* 228.

3.b. A circumstantial infinitive; Dahood, II, 97; GKC, 114o.

4.a. Johnson (*CPIP*, 277, n.5) argues for the meaning "rich with life," on the basis that the מִן is used here to indicate the *source* of life rather than as a comparative (as usually taken). He appeals to the context of the psalm, which presents Yahweh as the author of all life. However, his argument seems forced.

6.a. Lit. "as marrow [חֵלֶב] and fat [דֶּשֶׁן]." Both words mean "fat" or "oil," and it is clear that the reference is to rich food (see Job 36:16; Ps 36:9). The two terms probably form a hendiadys meaning "very rich food."

7.a. אִם used in the sense of "as often"; as in Ps 78:34.

8.a. Cf. Pss 3:4; 60:13; 108:13; Job 31:21 ("because I saw my help in the gate").

10.a. Reading as relative clause without a relative particle; Johnson, 280, n. 3; GKC, 155m.

10.b. Lit. "for destruction," which may refer to either the speaker (i.e., "and they who seek my life for destruction") or to the enemies (as above). LXX's εἰς μάτην, "in vain" or "without a reason," may indicate לְשָׁוְא (note *BHS*), "for that which is vain" or "for that which is nothing." Dahood translates שׁוֹאָה in 35:8 as "pit" (cf. Isa 10:3). If he is correct that the word has this meaning, there may be an allusion in 63:10a to an idea parallel to the depths of the earth in 10b (equal to the depths of Sheol/Netherworld/Pit; 88:7; 86:13; Lam 3:55)—"They who seek my life are (destined) for the Pit; they are going down to the depths of the Netherworld."

The reading of the verbs in vv 10b and 11ab with jussive force is quite possible: "May they be destroyed who seek my life/may they go down to the depths of the earth/may they who would hand over him to the sword/be food for jackals" (or "may they be handed over to the sword . . . "; see n. 11.a.).

11.a. Reading as a relative clause, as in 10.a. The hiphil form of the verb נגר may carry the idea of extension or "handing over to" (note 77:3). The RSV, "they shall be given over to the power of the sword," follows a common emendation to a passive, with some versional support (see *BHS*). However, this is not necessary, nor is it necessary to explain the singular suffix as having collective or distributive force (i.e., "every one of them shall be given over").

11.b. The *Translation* assumes that the "him" of MT refers to "the king" in 12a.

12.a. MT has "the king."

12.b. The reference is to God/Yahweh; Johnson, *CPIP*, 281, n. 2.

12.c. The verb סכר is equivalent to סגר, "close/shut," and is used in Gen 8:2 for closing the fountains of the deep and the windows of heaven.

Form/Structure/Setting

The varied elements and flow of thought in this psalm have led to considerable chopping and shifting of verses by commentators. Gunkel prefers the verses in the following order: 2, 3, 7, 8, 9, 5, 6, 4, 10, 11, 12c, 12a, 12b. Schmidt proposes a similar arrangement: 2, 3, 7, 8, 9, 5, 6, 4, 10, 11, 12. Gunkel was concerned about the כֵּן at the beginning of v 3, which he believed had no proper reference; he was also concerned with what he judged to be a poor sequence of thought (e.g., vv 5–6, 4 should follow vv 7, 8, 9). Leslie links vv 6–8 to v 3 because of the reference to the sanctuary, on the assumption that vv 6, 7 reflect a worshiper meditating at night in the temple while lying close to the Holy of Holies, near the

Ark and the wings of the cherubim. Such rearrangements may do little harm to the psalm and may be satisfying to the interpreters, but they are unnecessary and highly unlikely to be original. How did the psalm get into its present condition if an earlier structure was so different?

While there is no consensus among commentators on the strophic structure of the psalm, the best division seems to be into three parts: vv 2–5; 6–9, and 10–12. Vv 3–5 are marked off by an introductory כֵּן at the beginning of 3 and 5, with 4 beginning with a כִּי (which correlates with the beginning of v 8). The כֵּן in v 3 establishes a link with v 2 (see *Translation*). A new section begins with v 6, which incorporates the use of נפשׁ ("my soul/life/desire"), as in vv 2, 9, 10. Each section of the psalm begins with a different nuance of נפשׁ (Ceresko, *ZAW* 92 [1980] 435). The "soul-body" merismus of v 2 (equals "my total being") shifts to "my desire/longing" in v 6 and to "my life" in v 10. The second strophe ends with v 9, which corresponds to v 6 (note use of נפשׁי)—and also to v 2. Ceresko (435) notes a chiasmus which centers on v 7: "my soul/desire" (v 6)—"joyful lips" (v 6)—"shout for joy" (v 8)—"my soul" (v 9). The subject matter shifts with v 10 to deal with the fate of the enemies and contrasts that fate with the joyful state of those who are faithful to God (note the reappearance of אלהים in v 12, parallel to v 2). Ceresko (436) also notes the presence of paronomasia between the verb שׁחר ("seek eagerly") in v 2 and the verb סכר ("shut up") and the noun שׁקר ("lie") in v 12 and suggests that the wordplay functions as an inclusion for the whole psalm.

The psalm begins with language which could point to a lament, but the affirmative, testimony-like statements in vv 4–5, 6–8, 9 indicate clearly that this is a psalm of confidence. The form is that of prayer to God, which expresses assurance and commitment (Schmidt classifies it as a thanksgiving psalm; also Weiser, 70, 443, 454; Beyerlin, 138). This analysis of the psalm is supported somewhat by its relationship to Pss 61, 62, and 64. Ps 61 is an individual lament, Pss 62 and 63 are psalms of confidence, and Ps 64 is an individual lament. Thus there is a ABBA arrangement of these four psalms, and they form a subgroup in the larger Davidic collection which extends from Ps 51 to Pss 70–71 (G. H. Wilson, *The Editing of the Hebrew Psalter,* 163). It is also worth noting that Pss 62 and 63 are joined consecutively in a Qumran psalm manuscript fragment (4QPs[a]; Wilson, 116).

The question of the identity and circumstances of the speaker in Ps 63 has provoked considerable discussion and varied conclusions. The scribal interpreters who added the historical note to the superscription obviously thought of David as the speaker. A goodly number of modern commentators have followed in this tradition, in a way, by taking the reference to the king in v 12 as an indication that the speaker is a monarch alluding to himself in third person (see discussion of Ps 61; so, e.g., Mowinckel, Kirkpatrick, Eaton, Dahood). Gunkel judges v 12 to be an addition and assumes that the psalm was the prayer of a severely distressed worshiper who longed for the intervention and nearness of God, along with the punishment of enemies. Kraus thinks of a suppliant who has taken refuge in the temple, where he spends a night (v 7) and prays for God's judgment on his enemies (vv 10–11). He treats v 12 as a prayer by a worshiper for the king as lord of the temple and chosen representative of the lordship of God. Weiser says that the poet was "probably in the sanctuary, where he has been allowed to behold the revelation of the majesty of God and experience his gracious help, and now knows himself to be safe, being under the protection of God." He argues for a setting in the pre-exilic festival of the Yahweh cult celebrated before the Ark (v 8) in the royal temple.

A. R. Johnson reads the psalm as a royal psalm, contending that "the suppliant is . . . no ordinary individual who has been caught up in some kind of social or political struggle in pre-exilic, exilic, or even post-exilic days" (*CPIP*, 276). He regards the speaker as a cultic prophet, speaking for a reigning king, "whether David or one of his successors" (277), and he believes that the speaker offers thanks to Yahweh for the assurance of a coming deliverance of the king from his enemies. J. W. McKay (*ZAW* 91 [1979] 229–47), supported by Ceresko, argues that Ps 63 is one of a number of psalms (he focuses on 5, 17, 27, 57, 63, 143) which were used (if not designed) by worshipers keeping vigil during night for a coming deliverance of God at dawn. He supposes that there were times, during festivals and on other occasions as well, when individual worshipers, perhaps accompanied by family members or friends, would come to the sanctuary to seek a blessing from God. Various vigil rituals would have been appropriate for a wide variety of distressful conditions, physical, mental, or spiritual. In this approach, stress is placed on v 7, and McKay translates v 3 as "And so I have come to seek a vision of you in the sanctuary to look upon your power and glory" (cf. NEB, "So longing, to come before thee in the sanctuary"). Ceresko (*ZAW* 92 [1980] 436) thinks that there are three progressively shorter strophes, in which the prayer becomes progressively more urgent, matching the three watches of the night.

As is true of many psalms, there seems to be no firm foundation for a decisive choice among the opinions about the setting and place. All of the proposals could be true for the setting of the psalm, and all of them could be wrong, because the psalm may be a purely literary work, using traditional ideas and expressions blended together into a unique composition (note that Gunkel calls this psalm "one of the pearls of the Psalter"—after he rearranges it!—and Weiser refers to it as containing "the finest testimonies to the piety of the Psalms"). In the present context of the Psalter, the psalm functions in a Davidic context, which has loosened it from any original cultic setting and made it available for individual worshipers, who could use it to enter into the inner spiritual life of David and make it their own. We would be wise to follow their trail and read the psalm with whatever contextual imagination proves meaningful, being careful to accept the discipline of good exegesis and literary analysis. The longing for the presence of God in this Davidic psalm is similar to longing in the Korahite Pss 42–43 and 84.

Comment

Superscription (63:1). The familiar מזמור לדוד ("Davidic psalm") is followed by a brief historical note, which relates the psalm to the wilderness time of David's career. However, the specific incidents or even the specific context in David's adventures in the wilderness are not indicated. See 1 Sam 23:14–15; 24:1 for David in the wilderness in flight from Saul. If the wilderness experience during the rebellion of Absalom is intended, and this seems more probable (Delitzsch), see 2 Sam 15:23, 28; 16:2. The historical note may have been stimulated by the בארץ־ציה ("in a land of drought") of v 2 (Gunkel, 267) and the use of the עָיֵף ("weary") in v 2 and היעף במדבר ("the wearied ones in the wilderness") in 2 Sam 16:2. In any case, the title is an exercise in scribal exegetical imagination which relates the psalm to the spiritual life of David.

Longing for the presence of God (63:2–5). The אלהים ("God") of v 2 was originally "Yahweh," which was changed to "Elohim" for some reason, as in numerous cases in Pss 42–83 (see Craigie, 29–30). The verb for "seek" is not the familiar cultic בקש but שחר, which may be a denominative of שָׁחַר, "dawn," and is often translated "to seek early," "early will I seek thee" (KJV). The verb's contextual meaning at least is clearly to seek eagerly, or to attentively anticipate. Its most frequent usage is in the wisdom literature (Prov 1:28; 7:15; 8:17; 13:24; Job 7:21; 8:5; 24:5; also note Ps 78:34; Hos 5:15; Isa 26:9). The suppliant expresses a powerful, longing desire for the near presence of God with the strong metaphorical language of thirst in a land of dryness (of Ps 42:2–3) and the fatigue brought about by a lack of water. Perhaps the effects of dehydration are indicated as may be suggested by the verb כמה, ("longs/yearns"), but which may connote the idea of its Arabic cognate "to be pale" or the Syriac verb "to be blind" (see KB, 441). In any case, "the poet is as thirsty for God as an exhausted wanderer is for water in a parched desert" (A. A. Anderson, I, 456). The geographical features of this verse are primarily metaphorical, and the physical location of the worshiper is secondary to the overpowering longing for the divine presence (see Leslie, 270, with reference to Mowinckel, who thinks of a sick person burning with fever, who comes to the temple to seek purification and healing—though prayers for healing should not be tied exclusively to the temple; they would have been more appropriate in family and community contexts).

The longing of v 2 becomes a testimony of assurance in the verses which follow. The speaker recalls past experiences of the strength and glory of God in the sanctuary in v 3. The visionary experience of the verb חזה ("to see/have a vision") is not described in detail, and doubtless differed in form and degree among worshipers. The experience may have involved some sort of rite using fire, smoke, and the blowing of a horn (cf. Exod 19), or it may have been more verbal and mental, combined with the rich symbolism of the temple, producing an internalized apprehension of the divine presence. The "strength [*or*, power] and glory" may suggest the presence of the Ark of the Covenant (cf. 1 Sam 4:21; Pss 24:7; 70:61; 132:8; see G. H. Davies, "The Ark in the Psalms," in *Promise and Fulfillment,* FS S. H. Hook, ed. F. F. Bruce [Edinburgh: T & T Clark, 1963], 51–61), which is also indicated by the "shadow of your wings" in v 8. Perhaps we should think of a worship experience which seems to lie behind the vision of Isaiah (Isa 6; see also 27:4; Hab 2:1).

Worship has made the speaker aware of the surpassing value of Yahweh's loyal-love (v 4), which is better than life itself. A vow of life-long praise follows in v 5. The lifted up hands refer to a posture of prayer, probably denoting that the empty hands wait in trust to be filled with the blessings of God (lit. "palms"—the open hand; the open hand may also show the nature of the one who is praying; cf. Pss 7:3; 24:4; 26:6; 73:13; Isa 1:15; 59:3, 6). For prayer in the name of Yahweh, see *Comment* on Ps 54:3.

The satisfaction of God's help (63:6–9). The vitalizing power of the divine presence is compared to the satisfaction and nourishment of rich food (v 6).
"Fatness" (חלב) represents the best and richest foods (Gen 45:18; Job 36:16),
which according to Lev 7:23 should not be eaten: "all fat is Yahweh's" (Lev 3:16).
Thus sacrificial god-like food is suggested by the words in v 6—the abundance
and pleasure of a feast before Yahweh (Ps 36:9). The divinely given satisfaction
results in praise (6b) and a satiation which is meditated upon during the watches
of the night (v 7). The good things of God's presence are recalled and meditated
upon in the personal and private nocturnal times in bed. For "the shadow of
your wings" in v 8, see *Comment* on Ps 57:2.

V 9 is a firm statement of commitment and trust. The speaker "clings fast" to
God—an expression which carries the meaning of "follow hard after" (as in Jer
42:16), with the verb "cleave/cling" used in the sense of Ruth 1:14; 2:8, 21, 23
and Ps 119:31. In Deuteronomy, דבק ("cling/cleave") is used for devotion to
Yahweh and to his commandments (4:4; 10:20; 11:22; 13:5; 30:20). It reflects a
commitment which will not fail. V 9b moves from the opposite direction and
affirms that Yahweh's right hand upholds the speaker, an expression of strong
support especially meant for kings and warriors (see Isa 42:6, 45:1; Ps 18:36; cf.
17:7; 41:13; 80:18; 89:22; 110:5; see J. H. Eaton, *Kingship,* 157–58). Yahweh's right
hand upholds servant-Israel—indeed all his servant people—in Isa 41:10.

The fate of the enemies (63:10–12). The enemies will be destroyed and go down
to the netherworld prematurely (v 10). V 11 contains language which is not
clear. If the *Translation* is correct, the enemies of the speaker would hand the
king over to the power of the sword; some sort of rebellion seems indicated. The
foes will go down to the depths of the earth, to the realm of the dead in Sheol.
The language shifts in v 11b to describe the unburied bodies of the foes, left as
carrion for jackals—unattended and unburied (cf. 2 Sam 21:10–14; 2 Kgs 1:9–10;
Jer 22:18–19). For a body to be left unburied was a dreaded misfortune. The
attack against the king will fail, and the king and all who "swear by him [God]"
will rejoice, while the lying mouths of the foes will be stopped. Swearing by God
is probably equal to swearing by the name of God (Deut 6:13; Jer 12:16; 1 Kgs
8:31; note NEB; JB). It is possible that oaths taken in the name of the king are
meant —or perhaps the king and Yahweh (see 1 Sam 17:55; 25:26; 2 Sam 11:11;
15:21; for non-Israelite parallels see comment on the verse by A. A. Anderson
and Kraus). The last part of v 12 sets forth the basic division in human society
between those who faithfully invoke Yahweh's name and the lie-speakers who
"make for chaos and confusion in the world of men" (Johnson, *CPIP,* 283). The
king's vindication and rejoicing are examples of the triumph that all those who
receive the loyal-love of Yahweh can expect to receive.

Explanation

This psalm may have been originally intended for the speaker as a king (or for
a speaker *for* the king); however such an identification of the speaker should not
be forced on the present psalm. As suggested in *Form/Structure/Setting* above, the
scribal attempt to link the psalm with the career of David was a way of making
both the psalm and the Davidic accounts available for all worshipers. All those

who are "in the wilderness," as David was, find that this is a psalm for them. The message of the psalm is that the loyal-love of God is of surpassing worth, worth more than life itself. The longing thirst for God is satisfied by the recall and realization of Yahweh's upholding power. Gerhard von Rad (*Old Testament Theology*, tr. D. M. G. Stalker [New York: Harper, 1962], I, 403) says that "extreme spiritualization" is attained in v 4—"a retreat into the realm of the most sublime communion with God which has made these men [*sic!*] practically unassailable from the outside." This sense of spiritual reality, which transcends the "lie-speakers" (v 12) and troubles of ordinary life, is also expressed in Ps 73:25:

> "My flesh and my heart may fail,
> but God is the strength of my heart
> and my portion forever (NIV).

Also in Ps 36:10: "For with you is the fountain of life; in your light we see light." And 16:5–6:

> Yahweh is my portion and my cup;
> You are the one who upholds my allotment.
> The lines have fallen for me in pleasant places;
> Yes, my heritage pleases me.

The upholding power of Yahweh makes one's "heritage" in life a pleasant one.

The lie-speakers and those who seek the speaker's life and the king's power (vv 10–12) make an arid spiritual climate: "a land parched and weary from lack of water" (v 2). A great soul-thirst for the living presence of God results—a thirst which does not go unsatisfied. The recall of the experience of the power and glory of Yahweh in the sanctuary and of his loyal-love breaks the sense of deprivation and thirst. There is a soul satisfaction which is like the satisfaction of the food at a feast (v 6)—a remembering at night (v 7) which produces meditation on the help which Yahweh had given. Even in the vigils of the night-watches, there is the certainty that

> My soul clings fast to you;
> your right hand upholds me.

In v 12, there is a broadening of confidence to encompass everyone who depends on Yahweh and who will rejoice while the lie-speakers will be reduced to silence in the depths of the netherworld. Stuhlmueller (I, 287) remarks that in this psalm the contradictions which are expressed by the speaker "melt away, for to such a person God's presence is most real in one's passionate desire, where love leaps beyond feeling and understanding."

This psalm may be profitably related to some NT passages. See especially Phil 1:21–23; 3:12–20; Gal 2:20; Eph 3:14–21; Rom 3:19; Rev 3:21. The psalm was used as a morning prayer by the early Greek churches and in the eucharistic liturgy of the Armenian church (see Jacquet and Stuhlmueller).

Poisoned Arrows and Wounds
without Warning   (64:1–11)

Bibliography

Beyerlin, W. *Die Rettung der Bedrängten.* 29–30. **Emerton, J. A.** "The Translation of Psalm LXIV.4." *JTS* 27 (1976) 391–92. **Jeremiah, J.** *Kultprophetie.* 119–20.

Translation

1	For the leader;[a] a Davidic psalm.[b]	
2 (1)	*Hear me,[a] O God, in my complaint;*	(4+4)
	protect my life from the dreadful threats[b] of enemies.	
3 (2)	*Hide me from a wicked mob,[a]*	(3+3)
	from a klavern[b] of evildoers,	
4 (3)	*who whet their tongues like swords,*	(4+4)
	who string (their bows)[a] for arrows of poison words,[b]	
5 (4)	*to shoot from hiding at the blameless,*	(3+4)
	who shoot without warning[a] and fear not,	
6 (5)	*who encourage themselves[a] in an evil matter.[b]*	(4+3+4)
	As they talk of laying snares secretly,	
	they say, "Who will notice them?[c]	
7 (6)	*Who will investigate the crimes?[a]*	(2+3+4)
	We have perfected a shrewd scheme![a] "	
	(The inward nature and the human heart—how deep they are!)[b]	
8 (7)	*Surely[a]—God will shoot an arrow without warning,[b]*	(4+2[3])
	(and) suddenly[b] they will have wounds!	
9 (8)	*Surely[a] they will ruin themselves with their tongues[b]*	(3+3)
	(and) everyone who sees them will be shocked.[c]	
10 (9)	*And then[a] all mankind will fear,*	(2+3+2)
	and[a] declare the works of God,	
	and his doings which they (then) will comprehend.[b]	
11 (10)	*The righteous will rejoice[a] in Yahweh;*	(4+3)
	(in Yahweh) they will take refuge,	
	and all the upright in heart will celebrate.	

Notes

1.a. See n. 51:1.a.
1.b. See n. 51:1.b.
2.a. Literally "my voice," here equal to "me."
2.b. Literally "from dread of an enemy." The פַחַד in some contexts seems to convey more than "dread" or "terror." See 91:5; Cant 3:8; Isa 2:4:17–18; Jer 48:43–44; Lam 3:47; Job 21:9; 31:25. Dahood translates as "pack"; a "hostile pack" in this case (II, 104; I, 81–82 on Ps 14:5). Dahood's Ugaritic

evidence seems weak (see Craigie on 14:5), and the biblical contexts do not indicate much evidence for "cabal" or "pack." The nuance of "threat" or "threatening action" seems convincing.

3.a. On סוֹד, see 55:15. Literally, "a council of wicked ones."

3.b. For רִגְשָׁה as "gathering" (in parallel with סוֹד, "council" in 55:15; and verb form in 2:1-2) see Dahood, I, 7. "Klavern" seems to get the meaning here. Perhaps "junto" would also do. JB has "mob of evil men."

4.a. Literally "they tread their arrow." For the use of דרך with bow and arrow, see BDB, 202; e.g., 58:8. For the translation above see J. A. Emerton (*JTS* 27 [1976] 391–92), who argues that דרך refers to using the foot to string a bow and that there is an ellipse of קַשְׁתָּם, "their bows," after the verb, followed by an asyndetonic nominal clause (or a circumstantial clause).

4.b. See Dahood (II, 104) for the argument for מר ("bitter/poison"). He translates the expression דבר מר as "poisonous substance." JB has "shooting bitter words like arrows."

5.a. Literally "suddenly/surprisingly." The relative clause continues the series from v 4.

6.a. More literally, "they hold fast to themselves." The idea is either that of strengthening themselves for their endeavor or holding fast to their plans.

6.b. The דבר רע, "destructive (or evil) word/thing," is an obvious match with דבר מר in v 4. The pair of expressions forms an inclusion which may be intended to stop the series of relative clauses. 6b and 6c refer back to the "council of wicked ones/wicked mob" of 3a.

6.c. לָנוּ, "to us" or "at us," is indicated by Syriac and Jerome: "Who will look at us?" Dahood argues that the change is unnecessary because the לָמוֹ ("for them") can also mean "for us/upon us" (he cites this as an "inescapable conclusion" for Pss 24:11; 64:6; 80:7; Isa 26:16; 44:7; 53:8; Job 22:17). LXX agrees with MT.

7.a. The text of v 7 is extremely difficult and no translation should be treated with confidence, including the one above. MT has literally "they search out/devise/think out evil acts; we have perfected a thought-out-device, and the inner part of a man and a heart is deep." Various proposals have been made: for example, to read in 7b תַּמּוּ (3 m.pl.) for תַּמְנוּ (1 c.pl.), or assume that תַּמּוּ = תַּמְנוּ (with נ standing instead of dagesh in the doubled מ), and translate "they have perfected . . ." (see Perowne, 495); or to read with some mss טָמְנוּ from טמן ("conceal/hide") and translate "Thou concealed"; or to retain תַּמְנוּ (see GKC, 67dd) and translate "They have devised injustice (saying), 'We have accomplished the device we had devised,'" or, "We are ready [assuming תמם is intransitive] with the device. . . ." Gunkel, followed by Schmidt and Kraus, reads 7a with 6c and reads as תַּעֲלֻמוֹתֵינוּ וְיִחְפֹּשׂ: "They say: who will notice us? Can our secrets be seen through? The scheme has turned out well. . . ."

7.b. Reading the last colon as an exclamatory observation by the narrator before the next section.

8.a. Gunkel notes the highly unusual occurrence of four *waw*-consecutive conjunctions in vv 8–10, noting that "certainty of hearing" sections elsewhere never begin in this manner, and proposes to read the simple conjunction instead. The normal usage of the *waw*-consecutive with imperfect produces past tense. However, this seems unlikely in this context. One option is to treat the verbs as equivalent to the so-called prophetic perfects or perfects of certainty, which have future reference (so Kirkpatrick). Buttenwieser (762) treats the imperfects here as functional precative perfects: "Let God shoot . . . let them be stricken instantly"—which certainly fits well in the context, because a petition is expected (not a "certainty of hearing"). The *Translation* takes the verbs as future (see GKC, 111; Delitzsch, II, 253) with a modal force appropriate for the supplicatory context of the psalm. The "surely" is used in the idiomatic sense in English of "Surely she won't do that!" or "Surely he will help me today!"—assurance, but assurance which falls short of certainty.

8.b. It is quite common and no great problem, to disregard the MT's *'athnah* accent and read פִּתְאֹם, "suddenly/unexpectedly," with the second colon; thus giving balance to the units. However, it may be that this is an example of unbalanced line-units for poetic effect. The idea of "suddenness" is carried by both units; the פִּתְאֹם does double duty. The extreme brevity of the second unit heightens the vividness of the sudden wounds produced by arrows which reach their target without warning.

9.a. See 8.a. above.

9.b. Eaton, *Kingship*, 163, proposes to read, "and by their tongue they bring him [i.e., God] down upon themselves." But it seems better to read the suffix הוּ on the verb as anticipatory (see GKC, 131m, o) and take "tongue" as the antecedent: literally, "they will cause it to stumble on themselves, i.e., their tongue." The argument that the suffix should be feminine (e.g., Delitzsch, Perowne, Kirkpatrick) is based on the false assumption that "tongue" has to be feminine. The anticipatory construction emphasizes the noun—in this case "their tongues." The meaning of "tongue" is, of course, "language" or "speech."

9.c. The verb יתנודדו can be from נדד, "to flee/retreat/leave," in a sense of fear, horror, or disgust (so KJV). The *Translation* assumes that the verb is from נוד, "to move the head back and forth" in shock, disgust, or scorn (cf. Jer 18:16; 31:18). NIV, "shall recoil in horror"; NEB, "all who see their fate take fright at it." For Dahood's arguments for נדד as "bow down" (and hence, "brought low") see Craigie, 324, n. 5.a.

10.a. *Waw* consecutive with imperfect returns to one of its normal usages—except that it is still in future tense.

10.b. The heavy "comprehend" is an attempt to get the meaning of the verb שׂכל, "be prudent/circumspect" (and in hiphil, "look at/give attention/have insight/ponder/teach"). JB, "they will understand why he has done it"; NEB, "they learn their lesson from what he has done," NJV, "and His deed which they perceived."

11.b. This verse can be translated as an exhortation: "Let the righteous rejoice . . ." (so RSV), or as a characteristic description, "The just man is glad in the Lord and takes refuge in him . . ."(NAB; also NEB, " The righteous rejoice . . .").

Form/Structure/Setting

The text is very troublesome in vv 7 and 8, but the literary structure seems simple enough. An opening call for help is found in v 2–3 with the familiar vocative address to God. There is no extensive description of the complaint of the suppliant, but the imperative supplications indicate a situation of great danger and terror. A description of the enemies is contained in vv 4–7. The expected judgment of God follows in vv 8–10. V 11 is a happy conclusion about the joy and security of the righteous. The two major internal parts of the psalm are marked by the use of פתאום ("suddenly," "unexpectedly," "without warning") used of those who shout from ambush (vv 4–5) and the sudden shooting of an arrow of judgment by God (v 8). The deceptive nature of the activity of the enemies is enhanced by their secret laying of snares in v 6 and their assumptions about their hidden crimes in v 7. Note also the use of the word סתר ("hide," "hidden") in vv 3 and 5.

The pivotal expression in the psalm seems to be v 7c—"The inward nature and the human heart—how deep they are!"—unfortunately, in a context that is uncertain in meaning (see *Notes*). The psalm portrays the work of evildoers as secret and mysterious. The anticipated judgment of God in vv 8–10 has some of the same mystery. V 11 is a closing affirmation regarding the righteous and the upright, which correlates with the "blameless" (תם) of v 5 (note the use of לב, "heart," in v 11 and in v 7c). The "all the upright in heart" is the counterpart of the deep mischief of the heart of evildoers.

This psalm is usually classified as an individual lament, and it has a complaint to God, a description of enemies, and an expression of confidence (v 11), characteristic of psalms of this type. The petitions are in the form of the extremely odd imperfects with *waw* consecutives in vv 8–9 (see *Notes*). The content of the psalm seems to reflect the danger of attacks by enemies which have not yet taken place. The speaker seems to anticipate the full result of the activity of the evildoers, rather than describe a situation which has resulted from their deeds. This quality of the psalm led Mowinckel (*PIW,* I, 219–20) to classify it with a group of psalms called protective psalms, which contain prayers to Yahweh against an imminent danger and are positioned *before* the full fury of distress comes. Among the psalms assigned to this class by Mowinckel are: 3; 5; 7; 11; 26; 28; 36; 52; 54; 57; 61; 62; 63; 71; 77; 86; 139; 140. The tone of these psalms is supposed to be brighter than the laments proper, containing prominent elements of assurance and confidence. In fact, Mowinckel declares that the psalms of confidence are a subgroup of the protective psalms. In any case, if we read the psalm in this way, we need to read vv 8–11 with future tense (as in the *Translation*) rather than with past tense, referring to actions which have taken place.

The psalm offers little in the way of clear evidence for the identity intended for the speaker or the setting, and of course the date is equally uncertain. There is little evidence for the view that the speaker is a person persecuted by enemies and who has taken asylum in a sanctuary (Kraus, Deissler). Surer ground is provided by taking a cue from the "blameless" in v 5 and the "righteous" and "upright" in v 11 and to think of faithful members of a Yahwistic community without attempting to relate the psalm directly to a specific situation-in-worship (cf. Leslie, Oesterley, Weiser, and the judgment of W. Beyerlin, *Die Rettung der Bedrängten*, 30). The speaker could be thought of as a leader of a community, who prays about evildoers who threaten his position and life. The use of the psalm in family and/or community rites for a distressed individual is quite possible. J. Jeremias (*Kultprophetie*, 119–20) argues that a cult prophetic lament-liturgy is reflected in the psalm, in the same category with Pss 12, 14, 52, and others. He finds a mixing of prophetic and wisdom language in these psalms. If this is the case, the speaker could be a prophet or prophet-like person in the community. In any case, the psalm is a literary entity, apparently without any strong ties to a specific ancient context. The text generates its own context in interaction with the reader.

Comment

Prayer and complaint (64:2–3). The prayer opens with a plea to God to hear an urgent complaint and to preserve the life of the speaker from threatening foes. The foes are not identified, but the use of "dread" regarding their threats provides an ominous beginning note which is continued in vv 4–7. The "hide me" of v 3 correlates with the "hidden places" from which the evildoers shoot their arrows in v 5 (תסתירני and במסתרים). The reference to the סוד of the wicked in 3a could refer to their meeting together to deliberate and make plans, action which, of course, was carried out in secret. The parallel expression "klavern" or "gathering" reflects the secret conspiracy-like nature of their threat. The reader is prepared for the deadly and secret actions of vv 4–6a.

The nature of the evildoers (64:4–7). The use of destructive language is the leading characteristic of the evildoers. They sharpen their tongues like swords and string their bows to shoot arrows of poison words. Undoubtedly, we are to think of bitter words of slander and false charges as well as calumnious innuendo and defamation. The attacks of the evildoers are made by plans devised in wicked councils and klaverns, and the attacks come without warning. The enemies shoot from ambush without any fear (v 5; cf. Ps 55:20; Deut 25:18), and they encourage one another in their evil purposes, confident that their snares laid secretly will not be discovered nor their crimes investigated (vv 6–7a). They are proud of their shrewd schemes (v 7b, though the translation of this verse is doubtful; see *Notes*). The sinister nature of the activity of the evildoers in these verses suggests to the reader that superhuman forces, or even agents, are at work. An interpretation of the "evildoers" as professional sorcerers is unlikely. However, it is another matter to think of a culture pervaded by awareness of the harmful powers of speech, combined with a sense of superhuman powers and demons. The sudden arrow, which comes silently and opens deadly wounds (v 8), and the sense of traps and snares contribute to a feeling of anxiety and apprehension of the uncanny. O. Keel-Leu (*The Symbolism of the Biblical World,* 89) remarks that nets and snares were important in magic (Ezek 13:17–21) and says, "Wherever they are evident, they spread uncertainty, anxiety, and sudden, inescapable disaster." The concealed nature of the devices of the foes adds to the general trepidation. Ps 64 reflects a cultural ambience full of destructive forces. I would not suggest that this psalm was used in exorcistic ceremonies, but such psalms as this would have served to strengthen the mind and heart of worshipers against the debilitating anxiety relating to evil powers in human society.

V 7c seems to be the pivotal statement of the psalm and is an exclamatory reflection on the depth of human nature which fosters such behavior as that described in vv 4–7b. The ability of the human mind to shrewdly connive and conspire in demonic ways against the blameless requires a depth of understanding which strains the human capacity of comprehension.

Anticipated retribution (64:8–10). The speaker seeks to move God to deal with the enemies by the use of the unusual statements in vv 8–10. The consequences would be appropriate for the actions of the foes. The retribution desired is of two types: (1) that God would shoot an arrow unexpectedly, with wounds suddenly appearing on those who are hit. The fate of the evildoers should correspond to their own methods (v 5). The action is not specifically defined, but we should probably think of failure, disease, and sudden calamity of any sort.

> They shoot, and shall be shot. A greater archer than they shall take sure aim at their heart. One of his arrows shall be enough, for he never misses his aim (C. H. Spurgeon, II, 84).

(2) That the retribution would result directly from the behavior of the evildoers (v 9). Their malicious speech should come down on them to their ruin. Again, the specific nature of the retribution is not spelled out; the emphasis is on the connectedness of the act and its consequence. Regardless of the exact nature of the retribution, it would be shocking to those who see it, so shocking in fact that, according to the hyperbole in v 10, all humankind would come to fear God and declare his word with new insight. The self-destructive work of these evildoers would eventually produce new human comprehension of the divine ways.

A closing statement (64:11). This verse seems to combine exhortation, confidence, and a wish for the future. The tense and mood of this verse should not be forced: "The righteous one rejoices/will rejoice/should rejoice . . ." On "upright hearts," see Pss 7:11; 11:2; 32:11.

Explanation

This psalm of complaint and judgment sets forth the demonic nature of much human behavior and the profound depths of human nature from which it stems. The speaker in the psalm has encountered treacherous and destructive actions by other people in society. These evildoers act with contempt for others and are bound together in klaverns of the wicked, where they encourage one another to persist in their evil designs. The evildoers work with no superficial wit but with the sagacity of practice and well-honed animosity. They are devious and often attack without warning. The blameless are often not "able to discover the quarter from which the weapon was shot, nor detect the hand which forged the arrowhead, or tinged it with the poison" (C. H. Spurgeon, II, 83).

As noted in the *Comment* above, there is an uncanny and sinister nature about the evildoers which involves an ambience of superhuman destructive forces and agents. The psalm communicates a sense of anxiety and perplexity about the nature of human society that is at home in every generation. The supposed sophistication of modern society is not immune to deep awareness of destructive forces which threaten to reduce our semi-ordered world to chaos. The power of viral disease, resistant to all known drugs, is an example from the area of medicine. Political and economic forces which seem to paralyze leaders and elude the grasp of government in the face of the threat of war or internal disorder are others. The demonic is a part of our way of life, and we are all subject to the danger of the poison arrow shot from hiding places.

The psalm is, however, finally an affirmation of faith in the judgment and saving power of Yahweh. The *Comments* above have made clear that there can be correspondence between sin and judgment. Those who shoot arrows (v 5) may be shot by God (v 8); those who whet their tongues like swords (v 4) may find them turned against themselves (v 9); the judgement upon those who encourage one another in evil matters in secret klaverns (vv 3, 6) can result in God-fearers who will declare the word of God. Glory and security may belong to the righteous (v 11). The psalm seems to express confidence in the judgment of God, but not certainty. It asks for faith.

As noted in the *Comment,* there is a combination of direct action by God in judgment (v 8) and of the built-in consequences of human actions (v 9). We should probably think of God's action as implementing the built-in consequence of v 9. The divine punishment is worked out through the nexus of intrahuman relationships between acts and consequences, but with a direct divine component. The appropriate rootedness of the judgment in the deeds of the evildoers is emphasized by the expression of direct divine action corresponding to human deeds. (On the matter of deed and judgment, see P. D. Miller, Jr., *Sin and Judgment in the Prophets* [Chico, CA: Scholars Press, 1982].)

The assurance of this psalm relates well to such NT texts as Matt 6:25–34; Phil 4:8–13; Rom 8:26–39.

Prayer for Rain and the Bounty of the Year (65:1–14)

Bibliography

Crüsemann, F. *Studien zur Formgeschichte.* 122–23, 192–93, 286. **Delekat, L.** *Asylie und Schutzorakel am Zionheiligtum.* 176–80.

Translation

1   For the leader;[a] a Davidic psalm;[b] a song.[c]

2   *Praise awaits you,[a]*   (3+2+3)
      O God on Zion;
      (O God on Zion),[b] vows[c] to you will be fulfilled.

3   *O Hearer[a] of Prayer,*   (2+3)
      unto you all flesh may come!

4   *When sinful deeds[a] overwhelm us,[b]*   (4+3)
      pardon[c] our rebellious acts.[d]

5   *How blest is the one whom you choose and bring near,[a]*   (3+2+3+2)
      the one who dwells in your courts.
      May we be sated with the goodness of your house, your holy temple!

6   *With awesome deeds which put things right,[a] answer us,[b]*   (3+2+3+2)
      O God of our salvation,
      the one who is trusted by all the ends of the earth[c]
      and the distant seas.

7   *Who by his[a] power sets the mountains in place;*   (3+2)
      who is girded with might;

8   *who stills the raging seas;*   (3+4)
      the raging of their waves, and the turmoil of the peoples.[a]

9   *So that[a] those who dwell at the ends (of the earth) will fear your signs* (4+4)
      (and) the outgoings of the morning and of the evening will sing for joy.

10   *You visit[a] the land and give it abundance,*
      greatly enriching it.[b]   (3+2+4+4)
      The divine channel[c] is full of water!
      You provide grain (for mankind)[d] by preparing [the land].

11   *Drench[a] its furrows;*   (2+2+2+2)
      soak down[b] its ridges![c]
      Let showers soften it;
      bless its growth.

12   *You crown[a] the year with your bounty;[b]*   (3+3)
      and your tracks drip fatness.

13   *(Even) the pastures of the wilderness drip (with fatness),[a]*   (3+3)
      and the hills gird themselves with rejoicing.

14   *The meadows[a] are clothed with the flocks,*   (3+3+3)
      and the valleys are dressed with grain;
      they shout and[b] sing for joy.

Notes

1.a. See n. 51:1.a.

1.b. See n. 51:1.b.

1.c. שִׁיר is a term used for both common (Amos 6:5) and secular songs (Amos 5:23). It is found in the heading of about 30 psalms in MT, appearing in various combinations. It probably had a more technical meaning than the general sense of "song" when used in psalm titles (Mowinckel, II, 207), but we do not know what it was. The form occurs together with *mizmor* ("psalm") thirteen times (Pss 30; 48; 65; 66; 67; 68; 75; 76; 83; 87; 88; 92; 108. A psalm could be a "song" (שִׁיר) and a *mizmor* (מִזְמוֹר)

at the same time. The technical cultic sense of שִׁיר is especially evident in the titles of Pss 30 and 92. The term is used consecutively with Pss 65–68, indicating that these psalms make up a small collection of the "song"-type (see *Form/Structure/Setting* of Ps 68).

2.a. An attempt to translate MT, borrowed from NIV. MT reads lit. "to you stillness is praise O God . . ."—perhaps with "stillness/silence" (דֻמִיָּה) in the sense of "silent-waiting is your praise, O God. . . ." KJV has, "Praise waiteth for thee, O God, in Zion." The versions have the idea of the fitness or appropriateness of the praise of God (LXX, πρέπει), which has led to the frequent reading of the consonants of דמיה as from a root "to be like/equal to" and in an extended sense "to be due/be fit" (reading qal participle דֹמִיָה or qal participle passive דְמִיָה). Thus, RSV, "Praise is due to thee"; JB, "Praise is rightfully yours."

2.b. The words "God in/on Zion" serve the second colon as well as the first; a pivot expression between the colons. "In Zion" probably is a short way of saying "in his temple on Zion."

2.c. Reading the singular as collective. Some Greek mss add "in Jerusalem."

3.a. LXX reads as an imperative with a first singular suffix on "prayer": "Hear my prayer . . ." However, the vocative address of the participle seems to fit the context.

4.a. Lit. "words/things/business of iniquities." Kirkpatrick refers to 105:27 and 145:5 for the use of "words" in the same sense; but see Allen's notes on both these verses. The *Translation* assumes that דברי is equal to "deeds of." Another option would be to consider the "words" as meaning the "story of sin" (perhaps, the "confession of sin"—NEB, "all men lay their guilt on thee"; D. W. Thomas, *TRP*, 25, "and confess their sin," lit. "with tales of iniquity;" also Gunkel; cf. Hos 14:3) or the "reality of sin." Some translations relate 3b to 4a, as in RSV, "To thee all flesh come on account of sin" or by changing "come" to a causative form (יָבִיאוּ for יָבֹאוּ) get the idea of "bringing words (confession) of iniquities"; thus, NEB, "All men shall lay their guilt before thee;" Dahood, "To you must all flesh bring its sinful deeds" (however, Dahood argues that qal of בוא can mean "bring" and does not make the change to hiphil; see I, 262). The first colon seems to function as a protasis of a conditional sentence (see Delitzsch, Kirkpatrick, et al.). It is possible that 4b should be read as a question without the interrogative particle: "When sinful deeds overwhelm us, will you pardon our transgressions?"

4.b. See n. 51:3.b.

4.c. Reading imperfect with imperative force, with LXX.

4.d. Traditionally, "transgressions"; see Ps 51:3b.

5.a. Reading a relative clause without a relative particle (GKC, 155f; cf. Ps 60:3; Kraus, 609).

6.a. Interpretation of the Heb. "in righteousness."

6.b. Following LXX ("Hear us . . .") and reading the imperfect with imperative force.

6.c. Lit. "trust/confidence of all the ends of the earth." For the construct form of מבטח see GKC, 92g. NEB has "in whom men trust from the ends of the earth and far-off seas." Syriac reflects וְעַמִּים, "and peoples," for יָם, "and sea."

7.a. For some evidence for a 2nd singular suffix, "by your strength," see *BHS*.

8.a. LXX has "the nations shall be troubled [*or*, in confusion], and they that inhabit the ends (of the earth) shall be afraid of your signs," connecting with 9a.

9.a. The *waw* consecutive refers back to the "answer us" in v 6a. The usual translation relates the conjunction to the immediately preceding descriptions of God with present continuing action: e.g., RSV, "so that those . . . are afraid . . ."; NEB, "The dwellers at the ends of the earth hold thy signs in awe." Another approach to the *waw* consecutive is to treat it as emphatic: "Thou who dwell . . . will fear indeed . . ." (see Dahood on Ps 119:90, and note such possible examples as Pss 3:5; 18:2; 38:13; 64:8–10).

10.a. Reading the perfect and following imperfects as characteristic. The verbal tense in this section is very uncertain. If vv 10–14 are thought of as thanksgiving language for blessings received, past tense would be best, as for example in NRSV and REB. Buttenwieser and Dahood translate the verbs as precative, expressing a wish or supplication, citing the imperatives in v 11 and reading the imperfects as passives.

10.b. The polel imperfect of שׁוּק, II, appears only here. The meaning of the verb is derived from the hiphil (Joel 2:24; 4:13) and the context. Dahood proposes a denominative verb from שׁוֹק, "leg/thigh," and supposes it to mean "make skip with mirth" (cf. Ps 114:6–8).

10.c. Lit. "channel of God"; possibly, "the mighty channel."

10.d. Lit. "their grain." The דְּגָנָם may involve an enclitic *mem*: דְגָנ־ם.

11.a. Reading the verb as piel imperative, rather than piel infinitive absolute or infinitive construct. If the infinitive is read, it could be taken as a substitute for the imperative (GKC, 117y, gg).

11.b. Either piel infinitive absolute or piel imperative. If רוה is read as imperative (as above), the infinitive also may follow: "Drench its furrows, soaking down its ridges . . ." The overtranslation "soak down" (for a verb which means "make descend") follows Dahood and seems to fit the context.

11.c. KB, 169, has גְּדוּד as "clods," which may be correct. "Ridges" here refers to those left between plowed furrows.

12.a. Reading as characteristic perfect, though the petitionary force of v 11 may be continued (see n. 10.a.).

12.b. Lit., "the years of your goodness"; years blessed by God with good conditions for agriculture and the economy.

13.a. Gunkel et al. propose to amend יִרְעֲפוּ ("drip") to יָרִיעוּ , "the pastures will shout for joy," supposing dittography from יִרְעֲפוּ in v 12. BHS suggests יַעֲרְפוּ, niphal imperfect from ערף, "drip/ trickle": perhaps, "the pastures of the wilderness are wet with fatness (rain)." But these changes are unnecessary, because the noun "fatness" in v 12 does double duty and is carried over as the object of the first verb in 13 (so Dahood). For "the pastures of the wilderness," see Comment.

14.a. LXX has "the rams of the flock"; see BHS.

14.b. The conjunctive particle אַף is here equivalent to the conjunctive "and" = "also/yea/how much more!"

Form/Structure/Setting

The literary structure of this psalm is enhanced by a number of key expressions and stylistic changes. The most important seem to be: (1) The expressions "O God on Zion" and "O Hearer of Prayer" are pivotal in vv 2 and 3. (2) The personal pronoun אַתָּה ("you") in v 4 is climactic: lit. "*you* must pardon them [our rebellious acts]." (3) The "how blest" (אַשְׁרֵי) of v 5 and the extended length of the verse with relative clauses probably marks the end of a section (cf. Ps 84:5); the concluding short expression "your holy temple" correlates with "on Zion" in v 2. (4) The "answer us" of v 6a correlates with "pardon our rebellious acts" in v 4. (5) The inverted statement at the beginning of v 6 calls attention to the beginning of a new section. (6) Vv 6bc–8 are marked by descriptive expressions for God, mostly in participial forms. (7) The *waw* consecutive on the first verb of v 9 indicates a conclusion which goes back to the prayer in v 6. The "sing for joy" (תרנין) closes this section and correlates with the "shout and sing for joy" at the close of v 14. (8) Vv 10–14 are set off by the use of perfect forms of verbs (except for vv 11 and 13) and by their context.

A form-critical judgment of the psalm depends on how it is read. The most common reading is that of a thanksgiving song, designed for use after God had answered the prayers for rain. Thus Mowinckel (*PIW*, I, 119–20) calls it a thanksgiving psalm of the harvest feast. Schmidt argues for a thank-offering liturgy. Leslie (108–10) describes it as a community utterance of thanksgiving for "the good earth of Palestine" and relates it to the celebration of New Year in the autumn. F. Crüsemann (*Studien zur Formgeschichte,* 201) argues for a hymn of praise in declarative style, and Kraus does not question its hymnic nature. The use of participles in vv 7–8 is definitely a hymnic feature, and the language of praise and thanksgiving is dominant throughout the psalm. However, the supplications in vv 4, 5, 6, and 11 make the psalm a prayer which is nearer to the laments.

The reading of the psalm as supplication based on praise is more compatible with the analyses of Delekat and Dahood. Delekat suggests that the psalm is a prayer written for workers on strike at harvest time who had gone to the temple as a place of asylum to seek protection from God. He makes much of v 5 and the ה cohortative on the verb, "let us be satisfied/sated." Delekat's theory has been severely criticized (see J. H. Eaton, *Kingship,* 7–8; Crüsemann, 201, n. 3), and it seems fair to say that his arguments for temple-asylum are too overextended to be given much weight. However, he seems to be correct in contending that the psalm is a petitionary prayer (178–79). Dahood follows Buttenwieser in reading precative perfects in vv 10–13 and also gives the imperfects jussive-cohortative force in vv 2–9, 13–14. He concludes that the psalm is a prayer for rain. I have been unwilling to read the verbs in vv 10 and 12–14 as precative (i.e., as supplications), but I see no good reason not to retain the imperatives in v 11. The poetic structure of this verse is different from vv 10 and 12–14, and it seems to be a key verse. The psalm is marked by an attitude of anticipation, in which the speaker awaits a new demonstration of the deeds of God, described in characteristic fashion in vv 10, 12–14. V 11 correlates with vv 5–6. Thus the psalm is a prayer for rain and the "bounty" which crowns a good year; it waits to become thanksgiving.

The distinctive nature of vv 10–14 has led some commentators to assume that Ps 65 is composed of two originally separate poetic pieces, now juxtaposed together. For example, Buttenwieser (346) argues that 65A (vv 2–9) should be identified with the deliverance from the Babylonian exile and is under the "sway of the broad universalism of Deutero-Isaiah." On the other hand, he argues that 65B (vv 10–14) is a prayer for rain dating from early in Israelite history: "There is nothing so primitive as this anywhere in the Psalter" (50; a short statement hardly likely to be proved either true or untrue since the determination of the qualities of "primitive" is so subjective). Some of the arguments for two psalms in one have force. Vv 2–9 are not specifically a prayer of thanksgiving for rain; rain is not mentioned (as in vv 10–12). Also, the portrayal of Zion as the rallying point for all mankind ("all flesh"; note Isa 40:5; 46:26; 66:23; Jer 32:26; Ezek 20:48; Zech 2:13; etc.) and the availability of the temple to all those whom Yahweh chooses to bring near relates well to passages like Isa 2:2–4; 56:7; 1 Kgs 8:41–43— all exilic or post-exilic passages (so Cohen, though he thinks the psalm reflects the Assyrian crisis of Hezekiah). The material in vv 10–14 is timeless in terms of Israelite worship and could come from any period, but the collocation of the nations coming to Jerusalem for the feast of booths with the giving of rain is interesting and may point to a post-exilic date.

A composition from formerly separate parts would be nothing foreign to the Psalter (cf. Pss 19 and 108), and the literary unity of the present form of Ps 65 may be the result of skilled scribal redaction. In any case, the speaker in the psalm cannot be identified except in terms of being any faithful Israelite, especially a priest, prophet, or king. The present psalm engages the reader in ways which allows freedom of interpretation and interaction.

Comment

Prayer for the forgiveness of sin (65:1–5). Vv 2–3 form a twofold introduction. V 2 has לְךָ ("for you") at the beginning of each major colon, which is complemented by the עָדֶיךָ ("unto you") in the second colon of v 3. It is possible that v 2 serves as an introduction both to Ps 65 and to the collection of Pss 65–68 (see *Comment* on 68:36c), with v 3 as the more specific introduction to Ps 65.

The word "praise" (*tehillah*) has a rather general reference to praise addressed to God. It is especially associated with the imperative hymns which summon various groups to praise Yahweh, with emphasis on the verbal root הלל, which is in "hallelujah" (e.g., Pss 113; 117; 96; 98; 100; 136; 159; Kraus, I, 20–21, 45). *T*ᵉ*hillah* appears in the superscription of Ps 145 and occurs rather frequently in the context of psalms (e.g., 22:26; 33:1; 34:2; 40:4; 71:8; 100:4). "Song" (שִׁיר) is related to תהלה ("praise") in Neh 12:46. The exact situation presupposed by v 2 is elusive, but it seems to be that of worshipers who have come for a festival celebration on Mount Zion. They wait, with ready praise and prepared to fulfill vows for the beginning of the festival—and perhaps especially for some indication of the presence of Yahweh. For vows, see 61:9. A. A. Anderson (I, 464) comments that "the vows may presuppose a time of trouble (drought?) or they may allude to promises made by the Israelite farmers at the time of sowing." Rain and a good harvest would be signs of blessing and forgiveness so that the vows could be joyfully fulfilled.

God (Yahweh) is addressed as being on Zion (v 2). The etymology of "Zion" (ציון) is uncertain, but it may mean "ridge" or "hillcrest." It refers to the hill in ancient Jerusalem on which the Israelite temple was built, located between what were the Tyropoean and Kidron Valleys, and which is known today as the Temple Mount, on which is located the beautiful Moslem shrine known as the Dome of the Rock (Haram esh-Sharif). The site was conquered for the Israelites by David (2 Sam 5:7). Before, it was the site of an ancient Jebusite/Canaanite town and worship place. The place is called "the stronghold of Zion" and the "City of David" in 2 Sam 5:7 (also 1 Kgs 8:1), which apparently refer to the hill Ophel south of the present Dome of the Rock area, overlooking the Kidron Valley and the Spring Gihon (which was Jerusalem's major source of water). In time the town was extended north beyond Ophel (original Zion) to include the Temple Mount; then it was extended west to include the hill which in modern times is erroneously called Mount Zion. Thus the name Zion came to be used more broadly and is found as a name for Jerusalem (Isa 10:24), the city of Yahweh (Isa 60:14), and even as a synonym for Israel (Ps 149:2; Isa 46:73) and for Judah (Jer 14:19). Zion is called הר-ציון, "Mount Zion," in a number of places (see Pss 48:3, 12; 74:2; 78:68; 125:1; and the "mountains of Zion" in Ps 133:3). It is also known as the הר-יהוה, "Mount of Yahweh" (Pss 24:3; 132:13). Yahweh is said to have his dwelling place or to be enthroned on Zion (Pss 9:12; 68:6; 76:3; 99:1–2). Zion is Yahweh's holy hill/mountain (Pss 2:6; 3:5; 15:1; 43:3; 48:2; 87:1; 99:9), the place of his holiness (Ps 24:3). The temple/house of Yahweh which was built on the holy hill was the place par excellence of the divine presence (Pss 5:8; 15:1; 24:2; 28:2; 138:2; etc.). For further treatment of Zion, see *Comment* on Pss 48; 50:2–3; 60:8; 76; 84. Zion is the place where Yahweh's teaching/word is dispensed (Isa 2:2; Mic 4:2; Pss 60:8; 108:8), and from there his help and support for the distressed and oppressed go forth (Ps 20:2–3). The idea of a rock of security and protection is also closely related to Zion (see *Comment* on Ps 61:3).

God is addressed as the Hearer of Prayer (v 3) and the one to whom "all flesh" may come (or, perhaps, "must come"). The Hebrew *t*ᵉ*phillah*, "prayer," is a general word for words to God, sung or spoken, in supplication, intercession, or praise. The word occurs seventy-seven times in the OT, with thirty-two usages in the Psalter (P. I. Heinen, "Das Nomen *t*ᵉ*filla* als Gattungsbezeichnung," *BZ*, n.f. 17 [1973] 103). It is found in six psalm titles, including Hab 3:1; Pss 17:1; 86:1; 90:1; 102:1; 142:1. All of the psalm titles are attached to laments (of the individual type in 17; 86; 102; 142 and of the community/people type in 90). Also, most of the uses of *t*ᵉ*phillah* in other places are in contexts of prayer out of distress of some kind (e.g., Pss 39:13; 61:2; 55:2; 1 Kgs 8:45, 49; Job 16:17; Isa 38:5; Lam 3:8), but the use of the word in Neh 11:17 and the notation in Ps 72:20; Hab 3:1 indicate that it can apply to thanksgiving/praise and should not be confined strictly to prayers of the complaint/supplication/lament type (contra Heinen). The poem in Hab 3 has been described as a lament, but it is actually hymnic in nature.

The expression "all flesh" can apply to all Israelites, but there can be little doubt that in the context of the Psalter it refers to all mankind. The coming of "all flesh" to God may be read with an eschatological thrust, but it is doubtful that we should go so far as Dahood and think of the final judgment. The idea of all flesh coming to Yahweh fits well with such passages as Pss 22:28; 86:9; Isa 2:2–4; Joel 3:1–4 (EVV 2:28–32) Isa 40:5; 66:23; Jer 32:27; Ezek 20:48; Zech 2:10–13. Zion will become the rallying point of all mankind. The juxtaposition of v 4 with v 3 suggests that one of the reasons for "all flesh" to come to Yahweh is the burden of guilt produced by human sins. Yahweh is the God who forgives sin. For פֶּשַׁע, "transgression," see Ps 51:3.

The verb כפר is usually translated "make atonement for" or "forgive" and is common in the Priestly material in the Pentateuch, especially in Leviticus (e.g., 4:20; 5:6, 10; 16:6, 11, 16, 34), but appears only three times in Psalms (65:4; 78:38; 79:9). Its origin and etymology are matters of dispute; the two most common explanations being that of "to cover" and "to wash away/wipe off." However, the general meaning in the OT is clearly that of the removal of the effects of sinful offenses against God, and such "wiping off/covering over" is necessary for a healthy divine-human relationship. The ritual acts of human beings are often related to the removal of guilt in the form of sacrifices (Exod 29:36; Lev 4:20; Deut 21:1–9), giving of atonement money (Exod 30:16), laying of guilt on a goat that it might be carried away into the wilderness (Lev 16:10), or prayers (as in the famous case of Moses praying for the sinful Israelites in Exod 32:30–32). However, in a few cases God makes atonement on his own for his own sake without such accompanying sacrifices. Such is the case in all three references to the verb כפר in the Psalter (see 78:38; 79:9). Of the three references in Psalms, L. Köhler (*Old Testament Theology*, tr. A. S. Todd [Philadelphia: Westminster Press, 1957], 213) remarks that "they have nothing to do with sacrifice or other expiatory rite. It is a question of propitiation or atonement by sheer grace." However, we should not press the element of grace to the point of excluding all human action. It is probable that various ceremonial exercises are presupposed for the process of confession of sin and forgiveness. The divine grace of God works through rituals as well as apart from them. However, human beings do not earn or buy forgiveness from Yahweh through any cultic process, as important as these may be (Isa 1:12–20; 43:25; 51; Ps 51:18; etc.).

The beatitude-like statement in v 5 expresses the blessed state of those who are chosen to draw near to Yahweh and dwell in the courts of his temple. For the meaning of אַשְׁרֵי ("how blest/how rewarding is the life of/to be envied is the person who . . .") see, e.g., Pss 1:1; 32:1, 2; 40:5; 84:5; 106:3). The reference is to that which is desirable to emulate (cf. W. Janzen, "'ASRE in the Old Testament," *HTR* 58 (1965) 215–16; E. Lipinski, "Macarismes et psaumes de congratulation," *RB* 75 (1968) 321–67; L. G. Perdue, *Wisdom and Cult* [Missoula, MT: Scholars Press, 1977], 328, n. 23). Does this wish for nearness to God and dwelling in the temple courts apply to priestly personnel only (G. von Rad, *Old Testatament Theology*, tr.

D. M. G. Stalker [New York: Harper, 1962], I, 405, n. 49), or does it include all who come to the temple area to worship? Cohen notes the use of the verbs "choose" and "bring near" in passages dealing with the ordination of priests (cf. Num 16:5), but then comments that the meaning is that "every Israelite is a member of a consecrated nation, 'a kingdom of priests.'" The request in v 5 seems to support the interpretation that the worshiping community is intended here; all those who are acceptable in the worship of Yahweh, and potentially every Israelite—and if v 3b has a universal expectation, every human being who comes to Yahweh. The satisfying "goodness" of the house of God is not defined, but we should think of the "spiritual refreshment" (Cohen) of festival worship, especially in the forgiveness of sins and the fellowship of sacrificial meals, along with the celebration of the divine blessings on the year in terms of rain, abundant agricultural production, and economic well-being (see Weiser's comments).

Prayer for God to put things right by awesome deeds (65:6–9). The "awesome deeds" (נוראות) is a word used for divine acts which both produce fear and terror in God's enemies (cf. Pss 47:3; 76:8; 89:8) and bring forth reverential awe and praise on the part of the faithful (68:36; 96:4; 99:2–3). The singular and the plural can be used of God's actions in saving his people (Exod 34:10; Pss 66:4; 106:21; 145:6). The "righteousness" in which God does his great works carries the idea of his saving-power demonstrated in victory, howbeit in deeds of justice which are appropriate for the "God of our salvation/deliverance" (on "righteousness" see *Comment* on Ps 51:16). The awe-inspiring, saving works of God (Yahweh) are such that they merit the confidence of all who live at the ends of the earth and on the shores of far-off seas ("sea of distant ones," v 6).

The participial descriptions of divine activity in vv 7–8 require little comment beyond translation. God is the one who is girded with strength like a warrior ready for battle (cf. Ps 93:1–2; Isa 51:9–11), the one who has set the mountains in place and stills the roaring of the seas and the turmoil of peoples. The mountains may represent the whole earth, or at least the piers which give it stability. Mountains represent the most fixed and stable parts of the world (cf. Pss 30:8; 46:4; 90:2; 96:10; 97:5; 104:5–6). The stilling of the raging sea (v 8) recalls ideas of divine struggle to overcome chaos, ideas widely associated with creation (cf. Pss 89:10–11; 93:3–4; 104:5–9; Jer. 6:22; 31:35). For further discussion of the struggle with chaos, see *Comment* on 74:13–14 and 89:9–14. The roaring turmoil among the nations is controlled by God (Yahweh) along with the raging powers of the natural world (cf. Isa 17:12–14; 25:5; Ps 74:23; Jer 6:23; 50:42; 51:55). The prayer in vv 6–9 is that the wondrous works of Yahweh will produce "fear/worship" and rejoicing among those who dwell over all the earth (v 9). The "outgoings of the morning and the evening" is a spatial reference to the whole world. The expression "those who dwell at the ends of the earth" (lit. "dwellers of the ends/boundaries") occurs in this form only here in MT. It seems to mean those "who dwell at earth's furthest bounds" (rsv) and is taken as equal to all who live on earth, near and far (cf. Ps 67:8). It is possible that the "ends" carries the connotation of ominous, demonic forces which lurk in mysterious faraway places and which may come forth from time to time to threaten the orderly course of life. Thus Mowinckel (*PIW*, I, 162) argues that "dwellers of the ends" refers to demonic powers of the *tehom* ("the deep/the primordial sea") around the earth, equal to the "helpers of Rahab" (Job 9:3; cf. Pss 74:4; 89:11; Isa 51:9), whom

Yahweh conquered in creation. The threat of Gog and his allies, coming from the remote north, against the people of Israel dwelling in secure well-being is similar (Ezek 38:6, 11; also cf. Jer 6:22–23; 25:32; 50:41–42).

A prayer for rain to crown the bounty of the year (65:10–14). The hymnic nature of vv 6–9 is continued in this section, though in different form. The land is dependent on God's actions for good crops and prosperity. God "visits" the land, not for punishment (as in some cases of the use of this verb; e.g., Ps 89:33; Isa 13:11; Jer 6:15; Amos 3:2) but in the sense of caring for it (e.g., Gen 21:1; Exod 13:19; Ruth 1:6; Ps 8:5). The divine channel of waters provides moisture for the land. The language is poetic and metaphorical, of course, for describing a heavenly source of rain. It reflects the idea of a conduit for rain water from reservoirs above the heavens down to the earth (cf. Job 38:25; Deut 11:11)—a divine irrigation system operated by God the master farmer! (Cf. "the windows of the heavens" in Gen 7:11; 8:9; Mal 3:10.) Allusion may also be present to the river that "makes glad the city of God" (Ps 46:5; cf. Isa 33:21; Ezek 47:1–12; Joel 3:18; Zech 14:8). The grain harvest results because the land is supplied with water and prepared to produce (v 10bc). Prayer for rain is made directly in v 11.

The crowning of the year with the bounty of God (v 12; cf. Ps 103:4) suggests an autumn harvest festival. The "tracks" of God may reflect the concept of God's passing through the land as he visits it, or the tracks of his chariot as he rides through the storm clouds which bring rain (see Pss 18:11; 68:5, 34). (These ideas seem more likely than the assumption that the tracks refer to those of the cart on which the Ark was carried [2 Sam 6:3–5] while being pulled over the fields in some sort of cultic fertility ceremony.) The verbal pictures in vv 13–14 portray stunningly luxurious growth on the hills and valleys. Even the pasture areas in the dry wilderness (מדבר), which normally have only a scanty growth of vegetation, are fertile and productive (they "drip fatness"; cf. Job 38:26–27). The grazing places seem clothed with flocks and the valleys dressed with grain (v 14). The whole land seems to rejoice and sing. The verb for "girded" (חגר in v 13) is rather frequently used for putting on mourning sackcloth (see Lam 2:10; Ezek 7:18; 27:31; 2 Sam 3:31; Joel 1:8), which suggests that the formerly dead hills and valleys have sprung into life—mourning has been turned into rejoicing!

Explanation

This psalm seems to move on two tracks through its three sections. One track is that of *hymnic praise* which sets forth the power of God. Those who are near him are blessed (v 5). He is the God of salvation, whose power controls the ragings of nature and human affairs (vv 6–8). He gives the land fertility and brings about the joy of great productivity (vv 10–14). His awe-inspiring "signs" bring about the reverential fear of all who dwell both near and far (v 9). He is trusted by all the ends of the earth (v 6). Yahweh is present on Zion, but his works extend out to immense horizons of creation and history. His work has universal scope; he is the Hearer of Prayer unto whom "all flesh" may come (v 3). He visits the land and moves through it like a conqueror, but unlike human conquerors he does not leave it desolate. His trail through the land leaves fertility and well-being behind. C. H. Spurgeon (IIa, 106) remarks that,

When the kings of old made progress through their dominions, they caused a famine wherever they tarried; for the greedy courtiers who swarmed in their camp devoured all things like locusts, and were as greedily ravenous as palmer-worms and caterpillars.

Unlike those kings, fatness drips from the tracks of the great Hearer of Prayer.

The second track in the psalm is that of the *petitions* which seek the activation of the powers of the Hearer of Prayer. There is need for forgiveness (v 4), for the satisfying goodness of festivals at the temple when Yahweh responds to his people (v 5), for the deeds which put things right (v 6), and for the rain which is essential for life (v 11). The strongest impact of the psalm is surely in the joy over the gift of rain and the flourishing growth which results. In dry areas like Palestine, rain produces an amazing coming forth of grass, flowers, and crops. The joy and wonder of such results can hardly be overemphasized in agricultural communities, where rain means the difference between life and death.

Praise for the One Who Keeps Those Who Fear Him among the Living   (66:1–20)

Bibliography

Becker, J. *Israel deutet seine Psalmen.* 57–58. **Crüsemann, F.** *Studien zur Formgeschicht.* 175–84, 228–31. **Haglund, E.** *Historical Motifs in the Psalms.* ConB OT Series 23. Lund: CWK Gleerup, 1984. 46–49. **Westermann, C.** *The Living Psalms.* 186–88, 216–21.

Translation

1	For the leader;[a] a song;[b] a psalm.	
	Raise a joyful shout to God,[c] all the earth!	(3+2+3)
2	*Sing of the glory of his name;*	
	set forth gloriously[a] his praise.	
3	*Say to God, "How awesome are your deeds!*	(4+4)
	So great is your strength that your foes cower[a] before you.	
4	*All the earth should bow[a] before you*	(3+2[3]+2[3])
	and sing your praise—	
	praise your name in song!" SELAH.	
5	*Come and consider[a] the works of God;*	(4+4)
	(his) awesome dealings[b] with mankind.[c]	
6	*He turned[a] the sea into dry land—*	(3+3+3)
	they[b] crossed the river on foot—	
	so[c] let us rejoice in him.	

7	*While he rules forever in his might,*	(3+3+3)
	his eyes watch the nations;	
	let not the rebellious rise in defiance![a] SELAH.	
8	*Bless our God, O peoples,*	(3+3)
	and let the voicing of his praise be heard!	
9	*He is the one who keeps us among the living,*	(3+3)
	who has not let our feet slip.	
10	*Indeed,*[a] *you have tested us, O God;*	(3+3)
	refined us as silver is refined.	
11	*You brought us into a snare,*[a]	(2+3)
	and put affliction[b] *on our backs.*	
12	*But you caused a man to ride at our head;*[a]	(3+3+2)
	we went through fire and water,	
	but you brought us out to abundance.[b]	
13	*I come to your house with burnt-offerings;*	(3+3)
	I will fulfill my vows to you;	
14	*those my lips promised;*	(3+3)
	(those) spoken when I was in trouble.	
15	*Burnt-offerings of fatlings, I will offer to you,*	(3+3+3)
	with the aroma[a] *of (burning) rams.*	
	I will offer bulls and goats.[b] SELAH.	
16	*Come, listen, all you who fear God,*	(3+2+3)
	and I will tell you what he has done for me.	
17	*I cried out to him with my mouth—*	(3+3)
	but praise was on the tip of my tongue![a]	
18	*Had I been guilty in my heart,*[a]	(3+3)
	my Lord would not have heard me.	
19	*But God did hear me.*	
	He listened to my voice in prayer.	
20	*Blessed be God,*	(2+3+2[3])
	who has not turned away my prayer,	
	or his loyal-love from me.[a]	

Notes

1.a. See n. 51:1.a.

1.b. See n. 65:1.c.

1.c. *Elohim* (אלהים) is used for *Yahweh*; common in Pss 42–83; see Craigie, 29.

2.a. The literal "set glory his praise" has been translated in different ways: KJV, "make his praise glorious"; RSV, "give to him glorious praise"; NIV, "offer him glory and praise"; JB, "glorify him with your praise"; NEB, "make glorious his praise." It is fairly common to add לֹ, ("to him"; cf. Josh 7:19; Isa 42:12) and take כבוד, "glory," as construct כְּבוֹד ("glory of"): "Give to him the glory of his praise ['his glorious praise']." The *Translation* assumes that כבוד is adverbial as in Dan 11:39, and possibly Ps 73:24, equivalent to בכבוד in Pss 112:9; 149:5 (cf. Crüsemann, *Studien zur Formgeschichte,* 175, n. 3).

3.a. The meaning of כחש is somewhat uncertain. The verb is used with the meaning of "to deceive/act deceptively" (e.g., Gen 18:15; Josh 7:11; Hos 4:2), but here it seems to denote unwilling homage or obedience/cringing/submission. Cf. Pss 18:45; 81:16; Crüsemann, 175, n. 5.

4.a. Modal use of imperfect, setting forth what ought to be.

5.a. Lit. "and see."

5.b. See *BHS.* The singular may be collective.

5.c. The עַל־בְּנֵי אָדָם generates different translations: KJV, "toward the children of men"; RSV, "deeds among men"; NJV, "who is held in awe by men for his acts." The *Translation* is close to NEB, "tremendous in his dealings with mankind." Cohen gives עַל the sense of "over" and suggests that it denotes the superior might of God.

6.a. LXX indicates a participle, "who turns . . ."; possibly a relative clause.

6.b. Indefinite personal subject (the Israelites); GKC, 144b.

6.c. The שָׁם ("there") has been considered difficult and dealt with in different ways. A fairly frequently suggested emendation is to read as an infinitive absolute שָׂמוֹחַ : שָׂמַח ("rejoice"), and thus, "rejoicing let us rejoice in him!" It is possible to retain the normal meaning of שָׁם, ("there") and translate the imperfect cohortative verb as past tense: "There we rejoiced in him indeed!"—at the river where the passage recalled in 6b occurred. Cohortative with past tense is rare but does occur in a few cases; e.g., Ps 73:17; 2 Sam 22:38 (cf. Ps 18:38); see GKC, 108g, h, for other possible examples, and Delitzsch. However, it is much more likely that שָׁם; is used here in the sense of "then/that being so/behold." Older commentators sometimes suggested that שָׁם is used here in the sense of אָז, ("then") in its sense of expressing logical sequence; see BDB, 23; cf. Delitzsch. More recent commentators cite Arabic usage (see R. Gordis, *The Book of Job* [New York: Jewish Theological Seminary of America, 1978], on Job 23:7 and 35:12) and El Amarna *summa*, "Behold!"; so Dahood (I, 81, II, 121), who translates "Come." See also Pss 14:5/53:6; 36:13; Prov 8:27; Judg 5:11; 1 Sam 4:4; 7:6; Hos 6:7. See further *Comment* on vv 1–7.

7.a. The *kethiv* has hiphil jussive of רום (יָרִימוּ); *qere* has qal imperfect, יָרוּמוּ. The meaning is essentially the same, but qal fits the לָמוֹ well: "Let not the rebellious exalt themselves [*or*, rise up in rebellion]." If the hiphil is used, an object may be assumed, such as "head," "hand," or "horn" (cf. Delitzsch). It is possible that לָמוֹ is here equal to לֹו : "Let not the rebellious rise up against him (God)"; cf. GKC, 103f; NIV.

10.a. Reading the כִּי as emphatic.

11.a. מְצוּדָה is commonly translated as "net" (of a hunter) or "snare" (Ezek 12:13; 17:20), but the word can also mean "stronghold" or "fortress," equal to "dungeon/prison" (see Delitzsch, Briggs, Cohen). Dahood translates "wilderness/steppe" from a root צוד, "to "range/wander," citing Lam 4:18 especially (cf. D. R. Hillers, *Lamentations* [Garden City, NY: Doubleday, 1972] 85, who thinks Dahood's reading of Lam 4:18 forces the Hebrew unidiomatically). See 91:2.

11.b. The word מוּעָקָה is unknown elsewhere (KB, 504, leaves it as "unexplained"), but it seems to be derived from the idea of "to press" (עקה, cf. Ps 55:4; LXX, θλίψεις) and thus "distress/oppression/affliction"; cf. modern metaphorical use of "pressure" in the sense of stress and strain (Kidner). NJV's note has "put a trammel on our loins"; NEB, "bound our bodies fast"; JB, "laid heavy burdens on our backs"; NIV, "laid burdens on our backs."

12.a. This expression is usually understood as "ride over our heads" (note *BHS* for plural). If the "over our heads" reading is accepted, the reference is probably to defeated troops lying on a battlefield and trampled by onrushing horsemen or run over by chariot wheels. See Jacquet for two examples from Iranian history of horsemen passing over the conquered. For לְ as "on" or "over," see BDB, 511; Pss 9:15; 21:4; 22:16; 132:11, 12; Job 36:7; Isa 3:26. The *Translation* follows Haglund (*Historical Motifs in the Psalms*, 48) and assumes that the reference is to Moses "riding at the head (of the host)" in the exodus from Egypt.

12.b. Lit. "to saturation/satiety" (Ps 23:5), equal to "abundance." A change of לִרְוָיָה to לִרְוָחָה, "to respite/relief" or "to a wide, spacious place," is often made; cf. LXX. Thus, NAB, "out to refreshment"; NEB, "out into liberty"; Kraus, "to freedom"; JB, more freely, "once more to draw breath."

15.a. קְטֹרֶת refers to incense in some contexts, but to the smoke and the aroma which goes up from sacrifices in others (cf. Isa 1:13; 1 Sam 2:28; see Allen's note 2.b. on Ps 141:2).

15.b. LXX adds "to you" = לָךְ.

17.a. Lit. "and he was exalted/extolled under my tongue." The verb is polel perfect 3rd masc. sing. from רום. LXX reads "I exalted (him) with my tongue," probably indicating רוֹמַמְתִּי, and it is possible that the final ת was omitted in MT because of initial ת in the next word (Briggs). It is probably best to read רוֹמַם as "extolling/praise." "Under my tongue" is an idiom equivalent to "on the tip of my tongue" (so NAB's translation); cf. 10:7. The idea is that of praise ready to be spoken, though the idiom may also carry the idea of a good taste in the mouth (see Kirkpatrick, 53).

18.a. More lit. "guilt . . . if I had seen (it) in my heart . . ."; the change of רָאִיתִי to אָמַרְתִּי, "if I had said in my heart . . ." (Gunkel et al.), is not necessary.

20.a. The MT accentuation binds "my prayer" and "his loyal-love" together: "who has not turned away my prayer nor his loyal-love from me." But it is better to assume the double use of the verb for two successive clauses (Dahood).

Form/Structure/Setting

This psalm contains a mixture of hymnic and thanksgiving elements. Vv 1–12 are predominantly hymnic in nature, with plural imperative calls to praise in vv 1, 2, 3, 5, and 8 and a modal imperfect in v 4. The participial constructions in vv 7 and 9 are also hymnic. The context is descriptive of God and his deeds (vv 3, 5, 6, 7, 9) and has in vv 10–12 the character of a "report addressed to Yahweh of his deeds," as defined by Crüsemann (*Studien zur Formgeschichte*, 191–99). These verses divide into three divisions: vv 1b–4, 5–7, and 8–12—note the placement of *selah* at the ends of vv 4 and 7. Each part begins with a plural imperative call to praise God, and all three sections are descriptive of divine works.

On the other hand, vv 13–20 are predominantly thanksgiving in nature, as is indicated by the twofold address of the speaker, who speaks to God regarding the fulfillment of vows in vv 13–15 and speaks to "all those who fear God" with a testimony of God's help in vv 16–20 (see Crüsemann, 228–35). The *toda*-formula (using the verb ידה, "praise/thank," as in Isa 12:1; Ps 118:1, 2; 138:1; etc.) is missing, but Crüsemann argues that the direct statements about sacrificial thank-offerings in vv 13, 15 take its place and point to a specific ceremony of presenting sacrifices in praise and thanksgiving to Yahweh, probably involving the laying of hands on the animal (cf. Lev 1:4; 3:2; 4:4; etc.) or other such actions. Vv 13–20 seem to reflect the presentation of sacrifices prior to the slaughter of the animals and the thanksgiving meal which follows. The speaker is ready to make sacrifices and fulfill vows.

Because of the difference in nature between vv 1–12 and 13–20, some interpreters have treated the psalm as composite and read the two sections separately (e.g., Briggs, Oesterley, Crüsemann, 229, n. 1; Westermann). The assumption that the psalm reflects a liturgy for the fulfillment of vows (e.g., Schmidt, Leslie, Weiser) is probable. The communal, hymnic material in vv 1–12 provides a suitable context for the individual thanksgiving in vv 13–20—"The voice of the individual worshiper thus joins the great chorus of the cult community assembled for the celebration [of a festival]" (Weiser, 469). Leslie declares that vv 1–12 are preliminary to what follows, but necessary for it. He envisions the payment of a vow by an individual worshiper, made previously when he was in distress:

> So following directly upon the choir hymn of congregational praise and thanksgiving comes the song of personal thanksgiving from the lips of the host of the feast himself. There in the inner court of the Temple, with throngs of worshipers around him, stands this individual worshiper, most likely a wealthy man and one of the leaders of the congregation. He has come bringing with him sacrificial animals as a whole burnt offering to the Lord, and as a peace offering for the sacrificial feast in which probably the whole congregation will share. The choir is now silent as all eyes are concentrated on him. He speaks and addresses himself to the Lord (298).

Such interpretations are more probable than that of Kraus, who thinks that the שׁם ("there") of v 6 refers to the cultic celebration of the crossing of the Sea of Reeds and the Jordan, originally celebrated at Gilgal near the Jordan (also see his *Worship in Israel*, 152–65; J. A. Soggin, *Joshua* [Philadelphia: Westminster Press,

1972], 51–54; for a critique of Kraus, see Crüsemann, 179–90, who points out that the Jordan is never "the river" in MT). Dahood argues on the basis of Ugaritic parallels that "sea" and "river" are "poetic alternates" and refer to the same event (namely, the Exodus). The recall of Yahweh's saving deeds would have been appropriate for ceremonies of praise and thanksgiving.

Literary explanations of the psalm provide alternatives to cultic ones, even if the psalm reflects worship situations (as it probably does). Weiser (also Dahood) argues that the two parts of the psalm should not be separated from each other, because the first would be left without a proper conclusion and the second without an introduction. Dahood suggests that the use of a natural word-pair in the "you brought us out" (תוציאנו) in v 12 and "I will come" (אבוא) in v 13 is not a "mere fortuity." Buttenwieser (357) notes the "come, see" (לכו וראו) of v 5 and the "come, listen" (לכו שמעו) of v 16. Note should be taken also of the use of the verb "to bless" (ברך) in vv 8 and 20. Tricolon verse constructions are found in vv 4, 7, 12, 15, and 20 (also in v 6).

Crüsemann (*Studien zur Formgeschichte*, 228–51) analyzes the succession of *Du-Teil* ("your-element") and *Er-Teil* ("he-element") statements in the speech of a number of praise-thanksgiving compositions, including Ps 66:13–20 (his list includes Isa 12; Sir 51:1–12; Pss 30; 32; 118; Isa 38:10–20). This exchange of address seems to be acceptable in the poetic compositions of the praise type and does not indicate separate compositions and mere mingling of elements. H. H. Guthrie, Jr. (*Theology on Thanksgiving* [New York: Seabury Press, 1981], 14–30) proposes a theological explanation for the mixing of hymnic and thanksgiving elements in psalms (see *Explanation* of this psalm), which adds further force to the literary unity of psalms with material such as that in Ps 66. Thus it seems best to treat the psalm as a composite literary unity, which reflects cultic thanksgiving liturgies. The borrowing of traditional elements (word pairs, ideas, expressions, whole or partial compositions) was undoubtedly a major feature of ancient poetic composition. However, the juxtaposition of such elements was usually intentional and designed. Literary and cultic approaches complement one another.

It is scarcely possible to date either the psalm as a whole or its parts, though Buttenwieser (355–57) gives very interesting arguments for the exilic time of Deutero-Isaiah or the early post-exilic period (also Deissler, II, 87). Becker (Israel *deutet seine Psalmen*, 57) says that the present form of the psalm looks back to freedom from exile and that the redactional joining of two separate parts together results in giving vv 13–20 a collective interpretation of the freed people.

Comment

Summons to praise God and his awe-inspiring works (66:1b–7). This larger section is divided into two parts: vv 1b–4 and vv 5–7. The first part is marked by the repeated use of plural imperatives (and the equivalent modal form of the imperfect in v 4). "All the earth" is addressed in v 1b and serves as a poetic inclusion with the same expressions in v 4. The opening verb means "raise a shout/make a joyful sound/sing and shout joyfully" and occurs also in Pss 47:2; 98:4; 100:1; cf. 95:1; 47:6. For the idea of glory, see 57:6; for name of Yahweh see 54:3–4. There are no כי ("because/for") sections in these verses, as commonly found in imperative hymns (cf. Pss 117; 125), but the references to the awesome works of God and to the greatness of his power—so great that his enemies cower before him (v 3)—function in the same way. These are the reasons that God (Yahweh) should be gloriously praised by all who live on the earth.

The second part begins with another plural imperative in v 5, an invitation to all who will (all the earth?) to come and become acquainted with the fearsome works of Yahweh in his dealings with mankind. The "come and see" word pair is used in connection with processionals to Zion/Jerusalem (Crüsemann, 181; cf. Pss 122:1b; 46:9; 84:8; 95:1; Isa 2:5). The passage reflects the pilgrimage of worshipers at festival time, when they moved toward the temple area.

V 6 recalls Yahweh's work of providing a passage for the Israelites on dry ground through the Sea of Reeds (Red Sea) in Exod 14–15; Ps 114:3. Commentators commonly assume that this passage refers to the crossing of the Jordan (Josh 3:14–17), citing 114:1–5 as a parallel passage. The two events are taken as representative of all the saving works of Yahweh. However, as noted above, the term "the river" is never applied to the Jordan elsewhere, while it is used in relation to the sea in Jonah 2:4; Ps 93:3–4 (see further in *Comment* on 74:13–15). It is probable that only one event is intended: the exodus crossing of the sea.

If the meaning of שם as "there" is retained in v 6, it is probably not a direct historical reference but refers to the cultic identification of the worshipers with the saving-history of the past: "There we really rejoice in him!" If this is the case, the worshipers were not physically "there" at the crossing, but they were there in the sense of the confessional statements of Deut 26:5–9:

> A wondering Aramean was my father, and *he* went down into Egypt and sojourned *there*. . . . And the Egyptians treated *us* harshly, and afflicted *us*. . . . Then *we* cried to the LORD . . . and [he] heard *our* voice . . . and brought *us* out of Egypt . . . and brought *us* into this place. (RSV, italics added)

Or as in Deut 6:20–22: "*We* were Pharaoh's slaves . . . and the LORD brought *us* out of Egypt" (italics added). Also, Deut 5:2–3. Thus Weiser says, "all historical differences of space and time disappear . . . so that participants in the cult, in facing God, faced the same situation in which the people of God had found themselves at the time of the Exodus" (470). The "there" becomes a present reality through the means of an actualizing identification with Israel's salvation-history. This may be the attractive interpretation we should give to v 6b. However, I have given evidence in the *Notes* above for a reading which seems to fit the context of the call to perceive the mighty works of God, i.e., reading the שם as "behold/so then/therefore": "So let us rejoice in him!"—because of his marvelous doings.

V 7 uses a hymnic participle (משל, "One who rules") to express the ongoing might and power of God as he watches over the affairs of the nations (cf. Pss 11:4; 14:2; 33:13–14; 113:5–6; Prov 15:3). Rebellious people, who obstinately reject God (cf. Ps 68:7; Jer 5:23; 6:28: Hos 4:16; 9:15), are warned not to try rising up in defiance of the divine will.

A call to bless God, who has kept his people among the living (66:8–12). A new section of the psalm is marked by the plural imperative call to "bless" God in v 8—addressed to the peoples of the earth (cf. "all the earth" in vv 1b and 4).

"Bless" (ברך) is equal to "praise" or "extol" (see further in *Comment* on 63:5). Note the "praise" in v 8 (see *Comment* on 65:2).

V 9 may be the key verse in the psalm: "He is the one who keeps us among the living, who has not let our feet slip." The slipping of the feet refers to misfortune in general (Pss 20:6; 55:23; 121:3), but in this context it seems to denote the slipping of the feet into the death of the netherworld. The force of the verse is to affirm the life-giving work of Yahweh, who has not allowed his people to be knocked off their feet into overwhelming misfortune, especially into premature death.

Vv 10–12 set forth the work of testing and refining on the part of God. The metallurgical figures in v 10 merge into historical ones in v 11. The verb for "test" in v 10 (בחן) has reference to the refining and testing of metal, but in usage with God as the subject it comes to mean try or test through action (cf. Jer 9:7; 12:3; 11:20; 17:10; 20:12; Zech 13:9; Pss 26:2; 139:23). The objective of God's testing is to reveal and to develop the character he wants (Ps 11:4–5, 7b). The verb בחן ("test") is closely related to צרף ("refine," in 10b) used of refining silver. The people have passed through testing and purifying experiences.

The "fire and water" in v 12b is a merism (cf. Isa 43:2) which means "from one extreme case to another"—comprehensive trials have been experienced. O. Keel (*The Symbolism of the Biblical World,* 184) notes that fire and water were the most important means of cultic purification (Num 31:23; cf. Ps 26:6). Assessment and refinement are both involved in the ordeals of the people. The language in this passage is too generalized for specific dating (though the parallels with Isa 43:2; 51:23 are striking), but v 12a indicates that the exodus and the wilderness wanderings constitute the event, or series of events, being recalled. Moses was the man who led the Israelites through "fire and water" into "abundance"—or to relief and freedom (with the versions; see note 12.b.).

The fulfillment of vows and personal testimony of God's saving work (66:13–20). V 13 begins an individual thanksgiving section, with a solo voice. The speaker is not identified, nor identifiable. A king or other representative leader of the people would be appropriate, of course. Vows to God made in a time of trouble are now ready to be fulfilled by the speaker (cf. Pss 22:26; 61:9; 116:18; Jonah 2:10). The vows involved sacrifices, in this case burnt-offerings (or holocausts), sacrifices in which the whole animal was burned and nothing (except the skin) was given back to the person who brought it (cf. Lev 1). Usually, sacrifices for thanksgiving and/or the fulfillment of vows were of the זבחים type, communion-peace offering type, in which only the fat and certain parts of the animal were burned, with the rest of the meat given back to the worshiper for human consumption in a *toda*-meal (i.e., a praise/thanksgiving meal; see Lev 3; 7:12–15; 22:29–30; Crüsemann, 229; R. de Vaux, *Ancient Israel: Its Life and Institutions,* tr. J. McHugh [New York: McGraw-Hill, 1961], 417; for the *toda*-meal, see H. Gese, *Essays on Biblical Theology,* 128–33). However, Lev 22:18, 21 and Num 15:3 link burnt-offerings with vows and free-will offerings. The reference to burnt-offerings rather than to communion offerings in Ps 66 in connection with vows indicates a very serious situation, "a mood of chastened rather than exuberant gratitude, as if to reflect the gravity of the threat that has now been lifted, and the depth of the offerer's debt" (Kidner; also R. Rendtorff, *Studien zur Geschichte des Opfers im Alten Israel* [Neukirchen-Vluyn: Neukirchener Verlag, 1967], 85, 117). The multiple nature of the sacrifices, involving different types of animals, also enhances the element of total dedication and profound thankfulness.

The second part of this section begins with the double plural imperatives of v 16, "Come, listen" (לכו־שמעו; cf. לכו־וראו in v 5). All those who "fear God" are addressed. Buttenwieser (357) argues that these are non-Israelites who are God-fearing proselytes. While the expression "all who fear God" does have some of the sweep of the "all the earth" expressions in vv 1 and 4 and of the "nations" in v 7, it probably refers to normal God-fearing Israelites. The speaker in vv 16–19 gives testimony of personal experience with God, who has heard his prayer and responded to his need. V 18 recalls the condition of nonguilt from which prayer had been made to God and recalls the declarations of innocence in the psalm of lament (e.g., Pss 7:4–6; 17:3–5; 18:21–25; 26:1–8; also Job 31). Even while the speaker cried out to God for help (v 17), "He was confident of deliverance and ready with praise, but with it under his tongue until the deliverance made it appropriate" (Durham, 303). God responded to sincere prayer and validated it as genuine (v 19).

V 20 is a closing verse for the entire psalm. The "blessed be God" reflects the "bless our God" in v 8. God has heard the speaker's prayer and responded with loyal-love (חסד, see 51:3, note 3.a.).

Explanation

The structure of the psalm in two distinct parts (vv 1–12 and 13–20) suggests at least two matters of importance. First, worship is set forth as both communal and individual. The individual experience of worship properly belongs in the context of the corporate. These two forms of worship are complementary, not mutually exclusive. Personal piety is nourished in fellowship with others who share faith. T. Butler declares that piety in the psalms has two major foci: the great moments of public religion and the crises of everyday life ("Piety in the Psalms," *RevExp* 71 [1984] 291). A division between these two is not encouraged by the Psalms: "The Psalter shows that biblical religion does not advocate such a cleft. . . . Biblical piety seeks to provide access to God for both the nation or larger community at worship and for the private individual" (ibid.). The individual becomes one with the group and the group becomes one with the individual in lament, praise, confession, and thanksgiving. The development of individual piety and the formation of a healthy spiritual life are functions of the worshiping community (see H. Ringgren, *The Faith of the Psalmists* [Philadelphia: Fortress Press, 1963], 20–26).

Second, the structure of the psalm reminds us that thanksgiving should be set in a theological context larger than that of purely personal concerns. Claus Westermann, in a well known section of his *Praise and Lament in the Psalm* (25–30), discusses praise and thanksgiving. In the process he points out that "thanks" can become a self-centered and even commercialized expression with little of the spontaneity of real praise. Praise requires concentration on the thing, person, or deity being praised. Thanks tend to be focused on what the *speaker has received*, and thus may become rather narrow and perfunctory. In the expression of thanksgiving the self may become the primary subject, but this is much less likely to happen in praise. Westermann's main point is that in OT texts thanksgiving to

God is a form of praise. He notes that the Hebrew texts have no verb that means only "to thank." The verb ידה, commonly translated "to thank," is not used to express thanks among human beings (*Praise and Lament in the Psalms*, 26–27), and the Hebrew *hodah* is a way of praising God. Westermann probably pushes the form-critical application of this idea too far (denying the validity of a thanksgiving genre, but dividing praise into two kinds: descriptive—hymnic in older terminology—and declarative, which sets forth how God has acted), but he is surely correct to stress the grounding of thanksgiving in praise of God. The juxtaposition of communal praise in vv 1–12 and individual thanksgiving in vv 13–20 holds the two types of praise together.

On the other hand, praise without thanksgiving moves toward a sterile religious experience in which the praise becomes purely ritualistic. Why should anyone sing the praise of God when there is nothing for which to be thankful? Descriptive praise of God tends to distance his presence from human affairs, which may be desirable, of course, when done in appropriate measure. However, praise continued indefinitely makes God into a fully celestial being and transfers the realm of real meaning and action to the heavenly sphere, or else renders divine action essentially moral. Praise alone would bring static quality to the religious experience. H. H. Guthrie, Jr. (*Theology in Thanksgiving* [New York: Seabury Press, 1981]) has stressed the theological aspects of the mixing of hymnic and thanksgiving materials in the OT. Yahweh, the cosmic sovereign worthy of all praise, made himself known to Israel as the one who used his cosmic power to save the Israelites (v 6) and to lead them through terrible ordeals of fire and water into abundance and freedom (v 12). He is the one who sustains his people among the living and gives them stability in a world of many dangers and pitfalls (v 9). Guthrie notes that the *toda* (thanksgiving) was an appropriate way of giving praise to Yahweh:

> Israelites might begin to sing *todah* to Yahweh, but as the singing proceeded quite unconsciously lapse into modes of expression rooted in the hymn. On the other hand, Israelites might set out to hail Yahweh as the ruler of the cosmos using the hymn form appropriate to doing that, but given the character and *modus operandi* of Yahweh, quite unconsciously lapse into words and phrases and forms associated with thanksgivings (23).

As Guthrie argues, this was the mix out of which Israel developed her theology (25). The personal, saving God of real-life experience is also the cosmic, order-bringing God, and all the earth may be summoned to praise him gloriously. Praise and thanksgiving have a symbiotic relationship in Yahwistic theology; one cannot live without the other.

W. O. E. Oesterley (316) says that Ps 66 teaches us the duty of the rendering to God of suitable responses to his many acts of love and deliverance. He suggests that some words from the Book of Common Prayer are appropriate:

> And here we offer and present unto thee, O Lord, ourselves, our souls and bodies, to be a reasonable, holy, and lively sacrifice unto thee (cf. Rom 12:1–2).

In Christian tradition, the title in both the LXX and the Vulgate relates this psalm to the Resurrection, probably because of the exodus motif in v 6, the setting of the soul in life in v 9, and the stimulus of v 12 to recall the work of Jesus for Christian readers. The references to "all the earth" in vv 1 and 4 led to the association of the psalm with the Feast of Epiphany, in which it is recalled that foreigners came to worship the newborn king (Matt 2:1–12).

A Prayer for Blessing and Summons to Praise *(67:1–8)*

Bibliography

Crüsemann, F. *Studien zur Formgeschichte.* 184–86, 199–201. **Jefferson, H. D.** "The Date of Psalm LXVII." *VT* 12 (1962) 201–5. **Michel, D.** *Tempora und Satzstellung in den Psalmen.* Bonn: H. Bouvier, 1960. 115–16. **Westermann, C.** *Blessing in the Bible and the Life of the Church.* Tr. K. Crim. Philadelphia: Fortress Press, 1978.

Translation

1   For the leader;ᵃ with instrumental music;ᵇ a psalm; a song.ᶜ

2 (1) *May God* ᵃ *be gracious to us and bless us;*   (3+3)
        may he make his face to shine among ᵇ *us.* SELAH.

3 (2) *Knowing* ᵃ *your way(s)* ᵇ *on the earth,*   (3+3)
        your saving-work among all the nations,

4 (3)   *let the peoples* ᵃ *praise you,* ᵇ *O God;*   (3+3)
        let all the peoples praise you.

5 (4) *Let the peoples rejoice and sing* ᵃ *for joy,*   (3+3+3)
        for you judge people with equity, ᵇ
        and guide people on the earth. SELAH.

6 (5)   *Let the peoples praise you, O God;*   (3+3)
        let all the peoples praise you.

7 (6) *The earth yields* ᵃ *its harvest!* ᵇ   (3+3)
        Continue to bless us, ᶜ *O God,* ᵈ *our God.*

8 (7) *May God bless us—*   (2+2+2)
        And all the ends of the earth
        will fear him!

Notes

1.a. See n. 51:1.a.
1.b. See n. 54:1.b.
1.c. See n. 65:1.c. LXX has "psalm to/for David"; omitting שׁיר, "song."
2.a. "Yahweh" is intended; written as "Elohim" rather frequently in Pss 42–83.

2.b. Num 6:25 has פָּנָיו אֵלֶיךָ, "his face toward/upon you," rather than אִתָּנוּ, "with you."

3.a. Reading the infinitive construct לָדַעַת as circumstantial (GKC, 114o); "then" is understood: "then knowing your ways . . ."; Dahood correctly links v 3 with v 4, translating "if your dominion (way) is known . . . The peoples will praise you, O God." I do not follow Dahood in reading future tense in vv 4–6, because the form of this section seems to be hymnic in nature rather than that of statements of confidence.

3.b. It should be noted that the singular "way" is read as plural in a few mss and may be collective. Two mss read "your way" as "his way" (see *BHS*) and the Syriac has "his ways," with 3rd singular suffix on "saving-work." A change to 3rd person is almost necessary if v 3 is read with v 2 (as in KJV, RSV, and several translations). However, the change appears to be an easing of an originally more difficult text. It is probable that this is one of the places where דֶּרֶךְ ("way") means "power/dominion." (cf. Amos 8:14; Prov. 31:3).

4.a. The plural should be retained in the five uses of עַמִּים and the two of לְאֻמִּים. Kidner comments that KJV's "the people" in v 5 seems like little more than "an appeal for hearty singing" (237). Basically the two words seem to have the same meaning (see BDB, 522, 766, 468, 710); both words are closely related to גּוֹיִם (v 3b), "nations." For Israel, "people" (עַם) is preferred to "nation" (גּוֹי), though the two words are sometimes used interchangeably (e.g., עַם in Isa 1:4; Ezek 36:15; cf. Exod 19:5–6). Gen 25:23 uses לְאֹם as the poetic counterpart of גּוֹי. The sense of distinction is clearly set forth in Num 23:9: "Lo, a people [עַם] dwelling apart, not reckoning itself among the nations [גּוֹיִם]." The distinction between עַם and גּוֹי has much in common with the differentiation in modern English between "people," which emphasizes common cultural and social characteristics, and "nation," which is a more political designation associated with social entities having organized governments. Israel undoubtedly existed as a state under the monarchy, but the predominant terminology was "the people" or the "people of Yahweh" (Judg 5:11, 13; 1 Sam 2:24), and frequently with personal pronouns ("his people," "your people," and "my people") with Yahweh as the subject. Some uses of "people" in the OT designate only a group within Israel, rather than Israel as a whole. For example, in Josh 3:4–6 "the people" (laity) are assigned places and roles different from that of the priests, and the Israelite troops are referred to as "the people" in Josh 8:5, 9–10, 20. Thus it is possible that "peoples" in Ps 67:4–6 refers to a subgroup of Israelites. However, "peoples" can be used of non-Israelites also (note Exod 15:14–15). This fact along with the reference to גּוֹיִם in v 3b makes it clear that the reference is to non-Israelite peoples (on the terminology of "people" and "nation," see E. A. Speiser, "'People' and 'nation' of Israel," *JBL* 79 [1960] 157–63; N. K. Gottwald, *The Tribes of Yahweh* [Maryknoll, NY: Orbis Books, 1979], 241–42, 509–12).

4.b. יָדָה, in hiphil imperfect, can be used to express thanksgiving or praise. C. Westermann, *Praise and Lament*, 25–35, argues that there is no word in Hebrew for "to thank"; יָדָה means "praise." But see Crüsemann, 279–82. Perhaps the meaning should be something like "thankfully praise."

5.a. Reading the imperfects as jussive rather than future; cf. LXX, KJV, Buttenwieser, Dahood.

5.b. מִישׁוֹר connotes straightness and evenness; thus "equity/fairness/rightly"; used here as an adverbial accusative (Buttenwieser). For a variant LXX reading, see *BHS* (followed by Gunkel and Kraus). V 5 does not require two sets of balanced colons because its tricolon structure is intended to call attention to its difference from the other verses and to emphasize it as the pivotal verse of the psalm.

7.a. Reading the perfect of the verb "to give" as characteristic or perfect of experience (actions which are usually repeated and expected).

7.b. Or, "increase/produce." See *Form/Structure/Setting* and *Comment*.

7.c. Reading the imperfect as jussive with progressive frequentative force.

7.d. "Yahweh, our God" is intended.

Form/Structure/Setting

This psalm presents major problems in determining the mood and tense of the verbs. A number of interpreters prefer to read the imperfects in vv 2, 7b, and 8 (and in some cases in vv 4, 5, and 6) as present indicatives expressing general or characteristic action (so, e.g., Eerdmans: "Elohim [God] is merciful and blesseth us . . . the clans confess thee . . . the peoples are glad . . ."; however, changing to present perfect in v 7: "The earth has yielded her increase, Elohim our God blesseth us . . .") or as present perfect (e.g., Leslie, 112):

God has been gracious to us and blessed us,
  and has caused his face to shine upon us, . . .
Let the peoples give thee thanks, O God; . . .
The earth has yielded its produce; . . .
God blesses us,
And all the ends of the earth shall fear him.

(cf. RSV for vv 7–8). Gunkel goes to past tense by changing the imperfect of חָנַן ("be gracious") in v 2 to perfect and the following imperfect to an imperfect with *waw* consecutive: "Yahweh [God] was gracious to us and blessed us." Crüsemann (199–201) follows Michel (*Tempora und Satzstellung,* 115–16) and reads the imperfect as general/characteristic: "God is gracious to us and blesses us"(vv 7b, 8); "God, our God blesses us, God blesses us." However, vv 4–6 are requests for praise in hymnic form: "Let the peoples praise you, O God . . . for you judge the peoples with equity . . . Let the peoples praise you" (Leslie, 112, calls v 5 a "little hymn complete in itself").

The decision is a difficult one, but I have decided that the psalm is most likely to be a prayer rather than a thanksgiving psalm and that vv 2, 7, and 8 should be expressed in this mode. The reasons are as follows: (1) LXX indicates jussive verbs, except in 7a; (2) the probability that the verbs in v 2 are jussive is good, and, if so, it is likely that the verbs in 7b–8 are also, because these colons match v 2 in the structure of the poem (Crüsemann, 200); (3) the perfect in 7a may be read as precative or optative (so Dahood, 126; *CBQ* 32 [1970] 632–33), but I have chosen to read it as characteristic: "the earth yields its produce," perhaps recalling Lev 26:4 (cf. Ezek 34:27), with the following prayer language asking for a continuation of that process. The statement in 7a forms the basis for the supplication in vv 2, 7b, and 8. Since the earth regularly yields harvests, it is reasonable to ask God to continue his blessing in that form.

The centerpiece of the psalm is v 5, which is surrounded on either side by a refrain in vv 4 and 6. V 5 is a tricolon with "peoples" (using two different words) repeated in each colon—in fact, "peoples" is found in each of the seven colons of vv 4–6. The major theme of the psalm is the importance of Yahweh's blessing Israel for the peoples of the world (Crüsemann, 201). V 3 is a statement of purpose for God's blessing on Israel and should be read with vv 4–6. The prayer for mercy and blessing in v 2 is matched by the prayer for blessing in vv 7b–8a. V 8a sets forth the same agenda as v 2a.

The psalm has frequently been read as a thanksgiving psalm for the harvest festival (S. Mowinckel, *PIW,* I, 120, 185; II, 30; with interesting detail, Leslie, 111). However, I prefer to read the psalm as a prayer for blessing, a plural self-benediction reflecting the Aaronic Benediction of Num 6:23–6. The speaker is not identified, but it is plausible to think of a priest leading a congregation in a prayer for blessing which will bring forth praise and reverence for Yahweh from the peoples of the world. An appropriate context would be that of a harvest/New Year festival, of course, or perhaps a congregational benediction at the end of a worship occasion (see C. Westermann, *Blessing in the Bible and the Life of the Church,* 42–45). A time before festival-goers left to go back to their home-places and routine lives would have been an effective context for the recitation of the psalm. The Jewish practice of reciting this psalm at the termination of the Sabbath is worth noting and should remind us that the psalm was not necessarily confined to any given context of worship.

The psalm provides little hard evidence for dating, being devoid of even a Davidic reference in the superscription. Several historical-critical scholars (e.g., Buttenwieser, Oesterley, Leslie, Taylor) date the psalm to the post-exilic era because of its seeming dependence on the Aaronic Benediction in Num 6:23–6 in the Priestly material of the Pentateuch and because its Deutero-Isaiah-like universalism. On the other hand, W. F. Albright ("The Psalm of Habakkuk," in *Studies in Old Testament Prophecy*, ed. H. H. Rowley [New York: Scribner, 1950], 6) declared that Ps 67, at least in its nucleus, goes back to the Tabernacle cultus in pre-monarchical Israel, a judgment made on the basis of his conclusion regarding Canaanite diction and imagery in the psalms. H. Jefferson (*VT* 12 [1962] 201–5) refined Albright's vocabulary comparison with Ugaritic (Canaanite) roots and found a 71 percent correlation. She concluded that her analysis supports a pre-exilic origin for the psalm. However, the vocabulary parallels of a short psalm with Ugaritic roots, made up of words with rather common usage in the OT, are not very persuasive for dating. The assumption that the psalm must be post-exilic because it is later than the Aaronic Benediction is equally unpersuasive because it is widely recognized that sections in the Priestly material of the Pentateuch (like Num 6:23–6) may be read as much older than their contexts. The psalm may be pre-exilic, but the emphasis on the peoples of the world and their relation to Yahweh points toward the post-exilic Israelite communities, when these communities must frequently have felt overwhelmed by the non-Israelite peoples around them, seemingly controlling the world. It is possible that the psalm is a composite creation from the post-exilic period made up of parts from exilic psalms. Vv 2, 7, and 8 could be from a thanksgiving-harvest song (reading "God has been merciful and he has blessed us . . . the earth has produced a harvest . . . Yahweh, our God has blessed us . . ."), and a hymnic section focused on the saving ways and judgments of Yahweh may be found in vv 4–6. If this should be correct, the redaction of originally separate parts has resulted in a new compositional genre.

Comment

Initial supplication (67:2). V 2 is an adaptation of the Aaronic Benediction found in Num 6:22–27:

> The LORD said to Moses, "Say to Aaron and his sons, Thus you shall bless the people of Israel: you shall say to them, . . .
>
> > The LORD bless you and keep you: . . .
> > The LORD make his face to shine upon you, and be gracious to you: . . .
> > The LORD lift up his countenance upon you, and give you peace. . . .
>
> So shall they put my name upon the people of Israel, and I will bless them."
>
> (RSV)

For the term "be gracious" (or "have mercy") see *Comment* on Ps 51:3. The major difference between the Num 6 passage and v 2 is that the speaker in the latter is identified with the recipients of blessing—he/she prays not that Yahweh will bless "*you*," but that he will bless "*us.*" The blessing of God manifests itself in different ways, but it is especially the intensification of life in such ways as to empower growth, fertility, and prosperity (Deut 7:13; 28:3–6). The blessing of God consists in his ongoing presence in life, his sustaining of the well-being of the world, and his providing family (Ps 128), food (Ps 132:15), dew (Ps 133:3), rain (Hos 6:3), etc. A. A. Anderson (478, on 66:20) remarks, "In a sense God's blessing was not an independent force, but rather the active help of God himself, so that one could not have the blessing without the giver." The presence of God comes with his blessing.

The shining forth of the face of God among his people is a metaphor for his goodwill and blessing (cf. Pss 4:7; 31:17; 44:4; 80:4, 8, 20; 89:16; 119:135). A shining, bright face reveals a person of good disposition and is a sign of inward pleasure. "In the light of a king's face there is life, / and his favor is like the clouds that bring the spring rain" (Prov 16:15, RSV). The opposite of God's shining face is his hidden face. When God hides his face, the life of his people is endangered (cf. Pss 10:1; 13:2; 30:8; 44:25; 104:29; Deut 31:18).

The hymnic core of the psalm (67:3–6). V 3 provides the basis for the calls to thankful praise in v 4. When the peoples of the earth know about God's (Yahweh's) ways (or, "power") and saving-work in Israel, they should respond with gratitude and praise. "Knowing" is not restricted to mental cognition; it includes experiential knowing and action. The "way of God" is a multifaceted concept (see M. H. Pope, *IDB*, IV, 817–18; K. Koch et al., *TDOT*, III, 270–93). The basic physical sense of the word is that of a stretch of road or of a journey. The metaphysical senses involve behavior and related matters such as "power." The meaning in v 3a seems closely linked with "saving-work" in 3b: The ongoing manifestations of the saving-work of Yahweh make known his will, especially in his choice of the Israelites and their "way" through history. There is merit in understanding "way" here in the sense of "dominion" or "power" (as does Dahood, II, 123), which matches well with "saving-work" or "victorious deliverance" in 3b. Yahweh's work in and through Israel is worthy of the praise of the nations.

A second call to rejoice and praise is found in v 5 with reasons attached. Yahweh "judges"—sets right things which are out of order—with equity, and he guides the peoples through their time on earth, though they may not know him (Isa 45:1–4). He guides the peoples of the earth as a shepherd does the sheep (note the use of the verb נחה in Pss 23:3; 78:52–3; also, see Exod 13:17; 15:13; Deut 32:12; Pss 77:21; 78:14; cf. Job 12:23). The God who exercises saving judgment and guidance for Israel does the same among the peoples of the world (for Yahweh as judge of the world, see Pss 58:12; 82:8; 94:2; 96:13; 98:9).

Concluding supplication (67:7–8). The prayer for God's blessing returns in 7b and 8a. A new basis is given for the blessing in v 7. The earth normally yields a harvest, understanding that it is made that way by Yahweh and empowered by his blessing. The "harvest" of v 7 is an attempt to get the meaning of יְבוּלָהּ, which could be "its increase" or "its production." The word is used primarily of agricultural productivity (Lev 26:4, 20; Deut 11:17; 32:22; Pss 78:46; 85:13; Ezek 34:27; Zech 8:12; Job 20:28). It may refer to the possessions or wealth of a household. The word probably carries a very old concept of the earth bearing fruit because of the blessing of a deity (cf. Gen 1:11–12, 28–30). Every harvest was a fulfillment of Yahweh's promise (Lev 26:4) and a demonstration of his blessing. The prayer which follows in 7b–8a is for a continuation of the blessing process. The blessing of earthly production is a visible token of the whole range of Yahweh's blessings, which merits the reverence of the inhabitants of the whole earth ("ends of the earth," see Ps 59:14).

Explanation

This psalm seems to involve two major subjects: blessing and the spread of life-giving knowledge of Yahweh to the people of the earth. As noted above, blessing is a multifaceted concept when used both of one human being to another and from God to human beings. Perhaps it is true to say that at its most fundamental level "blessing really means the power of fertility. God's blessing causes a developing and growing, a ripening and fruit-bearing, silent advance of the power of life in all realms" (C. Westermann, "Creation and History in the Old Testament," *The Gospel and Human Destiny*, ed. V. Vajta, 30–31, quoted by P. D. Miller, Jr., "The Blessing of God: An Interpretation of Numbers 6:22-27," *Int* 29 [1975] 24–27). The blessing of God takes diverse forms: posterity (Gen 26:23; 28:3), prosperity and wealth (Gen 24:35; Deut. 7:12–13), land (Gen 35:12; 48:3), the removal of the curse from the ground (Gen 8:21–2), fertility, health, and victory (Deut 7:14–16). The summary of blessings in Deut 28:1–6 conveys something of the comprehensive range of Yahweh's blessings.

> If you obey the voice of the LORD your God . . . all these
> blessings shall come upon you and overtake you . . .
> Blessed shall you be in the city, and
> blessed shall you be in the field.
> Blessed shall be the fruit of your body,
> and the fruit of your ground, and the fruit of your beasts, the
> increase of your cattle, and the young of your flock.
> Blessed shall be your basket and your kneading-trough.
> Blessed shall you be when you come in, and
> blessed shall you be when you go out. (RSV)

Perhaps what we miss here is overt mention of the spiritual dimensions of blessing. However, this is provided for in the Aaronic Benediction and in v 2 of our psalm by the face of God shining among his people in favor and fellowship. Further, the comprehensive nature of blessing encompasses both the physical side of life and its inner nature. Stuhlmueller comments: "God's blessings reach us first externally and physically, and then as we reflect upon our lives and the world, they seep ever more deeply into our thought and judgments." (300)

The blessing of God is closely linked with contexts of worship in the OT. The most appropriate place for blessing (however, not the only one; cf. Ps 118:26) is at the end of a worship service or festival (cf. 2 Sam 6:18; Lev 9:22; Westermann, *Blessing*, 43, 103–8). Mowinckel notes and emphasizes the worship-relatedness of blessing:

All worship reached its culmination in the priestly words of blessing. It was in order to receive blessing and make it secure in all its forms, that Israel, as a community and also as individuals, went to the sanctuary and took part in the worship offered there . . . through worship and all its rites, blessing was achieved, made secure and increased for individuals and for the community. (*Religion und Kultus*, 64, translated and quoted in Westermann, *Blessing*, 20)

Thus blessing is a bridge that joins worship with the ongoing life of the community outside the place of worship: "What has happened there is imparted to those who now leave one another to return to their daily lives" (Westermann, *Blessing*, 106). The benediction at the end of a worship service is a prayer that the blessing received at the sanctuary will go with the worshipers and link the going out of the worshipers with the ongoing blessing of God in all the fundamental aspects of their lives.

Westermann has argued for a distinction between God's saving action in the sense of acts of attention or intervention and the continuous action of God's blessing (see his *Elements of Old Testament Theology*, tr. D. W. Stott [Atlanta: John Knox Press, 1982], 102–4). Blessing is not a series of events as much as "the quiet, continuous, flowing, and unnoticed worship of God which cannot be captured in moments or dates" (103). Blessing runs through the growing, maturing, and fading of life, the providence of God in history and nature. As such, blessing is present outside the particular history of Israel (as in Job, the man from Uz) and has a scope wide enough to be common to all humankind. "Because the blessing (e.g., Gen 1:27–30) is given to all living things, it has universal character" (Westermann, 116). Thus the "spreading circle" (Kidner) of Ps 67, based on the concept of blessing, quite naturally reaches out to encompass the action of God to the ends of the earth. Cohen quotes a remarkable summary of Ps 67 from I. Abrahams, *Annotations to the Hebrew Prayer Book, Pharisaism and the Gospels:*

This psalm is a prayer for salvation in the widest sense, and not for Israel only, but for the whole world. Israel's blessing is to be a blessing for all men. Here, in particular, the Psalmist does more than adopt the Priestly formula (Num 6:22–27); he claims for Israel the sacerdotal dignity. Israel is the world's high priest . . . if Israel has the light of God's face, the world cannot remain in darkness.

Thus the psalm invites a messianic perspective which looks forward to an age when the relationship between Yahweh's saving-work in Israel and his blessing-work in all creation will no longer be obscure but will lead the peoples of the world to rejoice and sing of his judgments and guidance (v 5).

Blessed Be God   *(68:1–36)*

Bibliography

Aistleitner, J. "Zu Ps. 68." *BZ* 19 (1931) 29–41. **Albright, W. F.** "A Catalogue of Early Hebrew Lyric Poems (Psalm LXVIII)." *HUCA* 23 (1950) 1–39. **Caquot, A.** "Le Psaume LXVIII." *RHR* 177 (1970) 147–82. **Goodwin, E. W.** "A Rare Spelling, or a Rare Root in

Ps. LXVIII 10?"–*VT* 14 (1964) 490–91. **Gray, J.** "A Cantata of the Autumn Festival: Psalm LXVIII." *JSS* 22 (1977) 2–26. **Isserlin, B. S. J.** "Psalm 68, verse 14: An Archaeological Gloss." *PEQ* 103 (1971) 5–8. **Iwry, A.** "Notes on Psalm 68." *JBL* 71 (1942) 161–65. **Johnson, A. R.** *Sacral Kingship in Ancient Israel.* Cardiff: University of Wales Press, 1955. 68–77. **Keel-Leu, O.** and **Winter, U.** *Vögel als Boten,* Orbis Biblicus et Orientalis 14. Freiburg: Universitätsverlag, 1977. **LePeau, J. P.** *Psalm 68: An Exegetical and Theological Study.* Ph.D. Diss. University of Iowa, 1981. **Lipinski, E.** "Judges 5, 4–5 et Psaume 68, 8–11." *Bib* 48 (1967) 185–206. ———. "La colombe du Psaume LXVIII, 14." *VT* 23 (1973) 365–68. **Miller, P. D.** "Two Critical Notes on Ps 68 and Dtn 33." *HTR* 57 (1964) 240–43. ———. *The Divine Warrior in Early Israel.* Cambridge: Harvard UP, 1973. 102–12. **Mowinckel, S.** *Der achtundsechzigste Psalm.* Olso: Dybwad, 1953. **Podechard, E.** "Psaume LXVII." *RB* 54 (1947) 520. **Vogt, E.** "Regen in Fülle (Ps 68, 10–11)." *Bib* 46 (1965) 359–61. ———. "Die Wagen Gottes, zehntausendfach, Tasende *šin'an* (Ps. 68, 18)." *Bib* 46 (1965) 460–63.

Translation

1	For the leader;[a] a Davidic psalm;[b] a song.[c]	
2 (1)	*O that God would arise*[a] *and his enemies be scattered,*	(4+3)
	and those who hate him flee before him!	
3 (2)	*As smoke is blown away,*[a] *so may you blow them away,*[b]	(3+3+4)
	as wax melts before fire,	
	so[c] *may the wicked perish before God!*	
4 (3)	*But*[a] *the righteous, may they rejoice;*	(2+3+3)
	may they exult[b] *before God,*	
	and jubilate with joy!	
5 (4)	*Sing to God, praise his name*[a] *in song;*	(4+3+4)
	lift up (praise)[b] *to the Rider of the Clouds!*[c]	
	Yah is his name—celebrate[d] *before him!*	
6 (5)	*The Father of the Fatherless and Defender of Widows,*	(4+3)
	God, from[a] *his holy dwelling!*	
7 (6)	*God, who settles the homeless*[a] *in a household,*[b]	(1+3+3+3)
	who brings out prisoners with music,[c]	
	while[d] *the rebellious dwell in arid waste!*[e]	
8 (7)	*O God, when you go forth*[a] *before your people,*	(1+3+2)
	when you stride[b] *through Yeshimon*[c]*—Selah—*	
9 (8)	*the earth shakes and the heavens pour (rain)*[a]	(4+4+4)
	before God, the One of Sinai[b]	
	before God, the God of Israel.	
10 (9)	*You spread abroad*[a] *a good rain,*[b] *O God;*	(4+4)
	when your domain[c] *is weary*[d] *you sustain it.*	
11 (10)	*Your community*[a] *dwells in (your domain)*[b]	(3+4)
	which[c] *you prepare in your goodness for the poor, O God.*	
12 (11)	*When*[a] *the Lord*[b] *gives the word,*[c]	(3+3)
	a great host of messengers[d] *give the (good) news:*	
13 (12)	*Kings*[a] *of hosts flee; they flee!*	(4+4)
	And the "beauty of the house"[b] *will share the spoil!*	
14 (13)	*Although*[a] *you "rest between the saddlebags";*[b]	(4+4)
	the wings of the doves[c] *are covered with silver,*	
	and their pinions with green gold![d]	

15 (14) *When Shaddai* [a] *scattered* [b] *kings on it,* [c] (4+2)
  it snowed on Zalmon! [d]

16 (15) *O mountain of God,* [a] *Mount Bashan;* [b] (4+4)
  O mountain of peaks, [c] *Mount Bashan;*

17 (16) *O mountains with peaks,* [a] *why watch so enviously* [b] (4+4+4)
  the mountain God has desired for his dwelling?
  Yahweh will dwell there forever!

18 (17) *The chariots of God are twice ten-thousand,* (3+2+4)
  (with) thousands of warriors. [a]
  The Lord is among them, [b] *Sinai* [c] *is among the holy ones!* [d]

19 (18) *You ascended to the heights with captives,* (4+3+4)
  you received gifts from [a] *mankind;*
  even (from) those who rebel at the settling down [b]
  of the God Yah.

20 (19) *Blessed be the Lord,* (2+4+2)
  who day by day bears burdens for us, [a]
  the God (who is) our Savior! SELAH.

21 (20) *the God (who is) our God of Deliverance!* [a] (4+4)
  Through [b] *Yahweh, the Lord, (there is) escape* [c] *from death.*

22 (21) *(He is) indeed* [a] *the God who breaks the heads* (4+4)
  of his enemies;
  the hairy skulls of those who walk in their guilt.

23 (22) *(He is) the Lord who says,* (4+4)
  "I will bring back from Bashan, [a]
  I will bring back from the depths of the sea,

24 (23) *so that you may shake the blood off your feet,* [a] (4+4)
  (and) the tongues of your dogs may have a portion [b]
  from the enemy!"

25 (24) *Your processions are in view,* [a] *O God,* (3+4)
  the processions of my God,
  my King among the holy ones! [b]

26 (25) *Singers are in front; minstrels behind,* (4+3)
  in the midst of [a] *girls beating tambourines!*

27 (26) *"Bless God in the assemblies,* [a] (3+3)
  (bless) the Lord, (you who are) from the source [b] *of Israel!"*

28 (27) *Look,* [a] *Benjamin, the youngest,* [b] *is ecstatic!* [c] (3+4+3)
  The chiefs of Judah—their noisy leaders! [d]
  The chiefs of Zebulun—(and) the chiefs of Naphtali!

29 (28) *"Your God has ordained your strength."* [a] (3+4)
  Show your strength, O God, which you have exercised for us, [b]

30 (29) *from your temple above Jerusalem.* [a] (3+4)
  Let kings bring [b] *gifts to you!*

31 (30) *Rebuke the beast of the reed-thicket,* (3+4+3+4)
  a herd of bulls with calf-peoples, [a]
  (till) they submit themselves [b] *with pieces of silver* [c] *(as tribute).*
  Let peoples who delight in war be scattered! [d]

32 (31) *Let noble envoys* [a] *come* [b] *from Egypt,* (4+4)
  (and) Cush—let him hasten to stretch out his hands
  (with tribute) for God. [c]

33 (32)	*O kingdoms* [a] *of the earth, sing to God,*	(4+2)
	sing praise to the Lord! SELAH.	
34 (33)	*To the One who rides through the skies of the*	(4+4)
	primeval heavens! [a]	
	Lo, he thunders forth with his powerful voice! [b]	
35 (34)	*Yield power* [a] *to God;*	(2+2+2)
	his majesty is over Israel,	
	and his power is in the heavens.	
36 (35)	*How awesome you are, O God, from your sanctuary!* [a]	(3+3+3+2)
	He is the God of Israel,	
	who gives power and strength to the people. [b]	
	Blessed be God! [c]	

Notes

1.a. See n. 51:1.a.

1.b. See n. 51:1.b.

1.c. See n. 65:1.c.

2.a. The versions read יקום as jussive with a conjunction on the following verb (as in KJV, RSV, etc.). This interpretation is adopted in the *Translation*, which assumes that vv 2–4 express a series of supplicatory wishes. Albright (17) repoints as jussive. The verbs can be read as future, of course, or as generalized statements ("God will arise . . . ," as in NJV; or, "God arises . . . ," as in NEB). LePeau (Psalm 68) has a temporal clause and apodosis without the conjunction:

When God arises, his enemies are scattered,
and those who hate him flee before him.

(See also Briggs; A. R. Johnson, *Sacral Kingship*, 68; Dahood).

3.a. The word כְּהִנְדֹף is a mixed form combining the consonants of the niphal infinitive (כְּהִנָּדֵף) with the vowels of the qal infinitive (כִּנְדֹף), both forms having the preposition כְּ, from the root נדף (GKC, 51k). Most critics read niphal, as above: "is blown away/dispersed/drifted."

3.b. The verb is qal imperfect 2nd masc. sing. or 3rd fem. sing. with *nun* unassimilated (cf. 1:4; Job 12:13). A change to niphal imperfect 3rd masc. pl. or 3rd masc. sing. is fairly frequent (e.g., Dahood), sometimes with רוּחַ ("wind") as the subject: "When the wind drives it away" (D. W. Thomas, *TRP*, 25). For other conjectures, see LePeau, *Psalm 68*, 71–72. The emendations are unnecessary, since God is the subject and the enemies of v 2 are the object.

3.c. See *BHS;* LXX indicates כֵּן, "so/thus," written or understood.

4.a. Reading initial *waw* as disjunctive and adversative ("but") which shows contrast between the righteous of v 4 and the wicked of v 3.

4.b. The versions read with *waw* conjunction. Gray (*JSS* 22 [1977] 21) reads adverbially as "imperfect of attendant circumstances" ("But the true devotees rejoice exulting"). The conjunction should be understood. For the verb, see n. 5.d.

5.a. LePeau *(Psalm 68)* follows Dahood's reading of לאלהים as vocative and reads: "Sing, O gods; make melody, his heavens." The "his heavens" results from repointing שְׁמוֹ ("his name") to שָׁמָו ("his heavens") and parsing the statement as vocative, assuming double-duty לְ. V 33 is cited as support, but it is not very persuasive. The advantage of the reading is that the gods and the heavenly court are urged to prepare a way for God as he rides through the heavens (cf. Isa 40:3; 57:14; 62:10). However, the exegetical procedure is too contrived to be convincing, even if the verb סלל in v 5b is translated as "build a highway."

5.b. The verb סלל in the qal (as here) has limited usage in the OT (12 times), but is used of the action of building up a roadbed (Isa 57:14; 62:10; Jer 18:15; 50:26; Prov 15:19; Job 19:12; 30:12; cf. Isa 40:3, where the noun מסלה is used). However, it is used figuratively in Job 19:12; 30:12; Prov 15:19. Pilpael is used in sense of "exalt" in Prov 4:8, as is hithpael in Exod 9:7; this (along with the lack of an object) points to figurative use. However, Gunkel's objection that the verb cannot mean "build a road" because human beings cannot build a road for God (an argument utilized by Dahood for gods and not people in this verse) forces the logic of poetry too far. The synergistic nature of praise in the psalms, as well as in contexts like Isa 40, should be recognized (see Ps 148).

5.c. The word עֲרָבָה is used in MT to refer to three geographical areas (see LePeau, *Psalm 68*, 80): (1) the rift valley along either side of the Jordan River from the Sea of Galilee to the Dead Sea and south to the Gulf of Aqaba (e.g., Num 22:1; Deut 3:17; 4:49; Josh 4:13; 5:10); (2) the area along the southwest shore of the Dead Sea (1 Sam 23:24; Isa 51:3); (3) the area of the wilderness wanderings (Deut 2:8; Jer 2:6). In general, it refers to a sparsely vegetated, arid area (e.g., Isa 33:9; Jer 5:6; 17:6; 50:12; 51:43), usually translated as "desert" (though not a true desert), or "wilderness." The "Rider of the Clouds" terminology is derived from Ugar. usage of *rkb rpt* to designate Baal (e.g., Aqht 1:1:43–44; Baal 2:3:10, 17). The Hebrew "b/v" (בּ) is accepted as a mutation of the Ugar. "p"; thus:' *rpt.* See *Comment* for further discussion.

5.d. The verb עָלַז (24x) is probably the more normal spelling and the עָלַץ (9x) in v 4 is a variant. It is usually translated as "exult/be glad," but in a few contexts it conveys the idea of "celebrate a victory" (note 2 Sam 1:20; Ps 25:2), which seems appropriate here.

6.a. The בּ may have the meaning of "from" in this context; so Dahood, who cites Pss 18:10; 31:22, and 1QS 3.19 in Ugar. LePeau (*Psalm 68*) argues for "from," on the basis that in this context, as in Ps 18:10, God comes forth to help his people.

7.a. The most common meaning for יָחִיד in MT is that of "only child" (e.g., Gen 22:2, 12, 16; Judg 11:23; Amos 8:10; Jer 6:26). However, the word seems to mean "one living alone" in an isolated or friendless condition in Pss 25:16; 35:17. The plural, used only in 68:7, probably indicates a class of people: those who are lonely and friendless (such as sojourners and exiles), cut off from family contexts. Albright (*HUCA* 23 [1950] 19) suggested an unmarried man with no means to purchase a bride. LXX has μονοτρόπους, "those who live alone."

7.b. בַּיִת here means "family" or "household." See LePeau, *Psalm 68*, 90, n. 82; A. R. Johnson, "Psalm 23 and the Household of Faith," in *Proclamation and Presence*, ed. J. I. Durham and J. R. Porter (Richmond: John Knox Press, 1970) 264–71.

7.c. בְּכוֹשָׁרוֹת is a *hapax legomenon* of uncertain meaning. If related to כֹּשֶׁר, it would mean "prosperity" (cf. GKC, 124e, abstract plural of intensity; "complete prosperity"; see KJV, RSV, NAB). Ugaritic usage, in the form of *ktrt*, indicates the idea of "skilled," in contexts of weddings and birth, apparently referring to singing and midwifery. The meaning in 68:7 would be that of singing songs of celebration or more generally, "music" (so Dahood; LePeau, *Psalm 68*, 92; Johnson, *Sacral Kingship*, 70, n.`2., who, however, translates "skillfully").

8.a. Reading as characteristic action. See *Comment.*

8.b. צַעַד means "step," "pace," "marching."

8.c. "Yeshimon" without the article (as here) is used with reference to desert/wilderness wasteland (Deut 32:10; Pss 78:40; 106:14; 107:4; Isa 43:19, 20). With the article, it refers to a region or a place in Moab (Num 21:20; 23:28) and in Judah, southeast of Hebron (1 Sam 23:19, 24; 26:1, 3). As in v 6, the בּ may mean "from" (favored by Dahood; Miller, *Divine Warrior*, 106, 233, n.126). LePeau (*Psalm 68*, 98) cites theophanic accounts in Deut 33:23; Judg 5:4–5; Hab 3:3. The traditional "through" (KJV, RSV) conveys the idea of Yahweh coming through the desert to assist his people—or else the going forth before his people in the wilderness.

9.a. נָטַף, qal perfect pl., is given the meaning of "drop" or "drip" (e.g., Judg 5:4; Joel 4:18; Cant 4:11; 5:5, 13; Prov 5:3; Job 29:22). However, "dripping" or "drizzling" seems too weak. "When Yahweh appears the heavens ought to do more than just 'drip'" (LePeau, *Psalm 68*, 99; cf. Dahood, who thinks "sprinkled" is appropriate). Albright (*HUCA* 23 [1950] 20) derives from a root טָפַף, "to toss," compared with Arabic *taffa, taftafa,* "to flop the wings," and Aramaic *tptp,* "to flicker"; thus, "the heavens also tossed." Gray (*JSS* 22 [1977] 2–26), more probably, derives from the root טוּף, cognate with Arabic *tafa,* "overflow"; thus, "the heavens overflowed in a deluge"; pointing the verb as נַטֹּפוּ. Vogt (*Bib* 46 [1965] 207–9), proposes נָטָיוּ from נטה, "to totter/stagger." The verb can be retained and given a meaning more in keeping with "drop" (cf. Job 29:22, and hiphil references to "dropping" a message in Amos 7:16; Ezek 21:2/20:46; 21:7/2; Mic 2:6, 11; and cf. the noun in Job 36:27) than "drip"; thus, "pour" or "rained" or the like (so Buttenwieser, 29; Johnson, *Sacral Kingship*, 71, RSV, JB).

9.b. Literally, "this (is) Sinai" or "this Sinai," often translated as "yon [*or,* yonder] Sinai quaked at the presence of . . ." (cf. RSV, KJV, Delitzsch, etc.; supplying a verb from the first line, Kirkpatrick). More recent commentators (see Johnson, *Sacral Kingship*, 71, n.1; LePeau, *Psalm 68*, 101; Anderson; Dahood) assume that the Hebrew זֶה is similar here to the Arabic pronoun *du* and Ugaritic particle *d;* thus, "the One of Sinai," "He of Sinai," or paraphrased as "the lord of Sinai" (NEB). Johnson (71, n.1) takes "Sinai" with the force of a divine name: "Him of Sinai," equal to "the God of Sinai." Mowinckel (*Der achtundsechzigste Psalm,* 32) and Kraus are both critical of the appeal to the Arabic and Ugaritic parallels and omit the expression as a gloss, interrupting the metrical sequence (Kraus). However, this is not very persuasive; note the *Translation,* which shows balanced colons of 4+4+4.

10.a. An attempt to get the force of נוף, which connotes a back-and-forth movement; thus rain which is dispersed back and forth over an area. Albright (*HUCA* 23 [1950] 20) treats תניף as denominative of תנופה, commonly translated as "give-offering," but which he defines as "an extra offering of good will" and argues that the original meaning of נוף was "to surpass/exceed"; thus: "an abundance of rain wilt thou give freely."

10.b. Or "a generous rain." The colloquial English "good rain" seems to catch the idea of enough rain over a long enough period for the ground to be soaked.

10.c. So Dahood, who argues that נחלה, "inheritance," can have this meaning, or that of "patrimony." Goodwin (*VT* 14 [1964] 490–91) proposes to divide the consonantal text נחלתך into נחל, "wadi/stream," and the תך, which he interprets as an intransitive participle of a rare occurrence of a Hebrew root t-k-k, which must mean "stop/cease/be low/subside." He translates: "An abundance of rain wilt thou give freely, O God, a stream, subsided and exhausted, thou will restore it."

10.d. The *waw* can be understood as temporal determinative (as above) or as forming a hendiadys: "your exhausted heritage" (see LePeau, *Psalm 68*, 104).

11.a. חיה is normally "living creature" or "wild animal," and a few interpreters have tried to read the word here in terms of animals (e.g., Briggs, Kissane; cf. Perowne). LXX has "your creature." The appeal to 2 Sam 23:13, where the word has the sense of "troops," as a basis for "community," "family," or "flock" is weak. However, the appeal to Egyptian, Ugaritic, and Arabic parallels (see Albright, *HUCA* 23 [1950] 21; Gray, *JSS* 22 [1977] 22, n. 4; and Dahood) is strong enough to sustain the meaning of "tribe," "family," "household," or "community."

11.b. Literally "in it"; the antecedent is "your inheritance" of v 10.

11.c. Relative clause without a relative pronoun: GKC, 155f.; LePeau, *Psalm 68,* 107.

12.a. Reading as temporal clause without the conjunction (as in vv 2 and 15).

12.b. Reading with nominal afformative rather than pronominal ("my Lord"), giving the term a *status emphaticus*, probably meaning "the Lord of all." See O. Eissfeldt, "אדון *' adhon*," *TDOT*, I, 62–72; LePeau, *Psalm 68*, 110.

12.c. אמר refers to speech or spoken words. The exact force here is difficult to determine: "command"? "message"? "decision"? "news"? See Keel-Leu and Winter, *Vögel als Boten*, 23–27; cf. Ps 77:9, Job 22:28; Isa 33:3. "Word" leaves open varied shades of meaning.

12.d. Piel participle fem. pl. from בשר, "give news/tidings," traditionally translated as "bear good tidings." However, the news is not always good; it may be bad (see 1 Sam 4:17). The majority of usages in MT refer to the results of battles, but the word is also used of the birth of a son (Jer 20:15) and of the deeds of Yahweh (Isa 40:9; 52:7; Ps 96:2). The traditional interpretation has been to treat מבשרות as in apposition to צבא רב, "a great host," and to understand the fem. pl. participle as referring to female speakers (cf. 2 Sam 1:20): "women bear the glad tidings, a great army" (NJV); "the women who bring the news are a great host" (Cohen, 211); or, if the word is taken as a collective (plural, or as singular with -*ot* ending; so Dahood) the feminine element may be omitted: "The bearers of the word are a great host" (Miller, *Divine Warrior*, 108; similarly, Mowinckel, *Der achtundsechzigste Psalm*, 36). The unusual form of the word has led to varied interpretations and emendations. Albright (*HUCA* 23 [1950] 21, 370) reads: "Let Yahweh give an oracle / Rejoicing a mighty host." See also Dahood. Albright's reading involves assuming that the article should be attached to the preceding word (on the basis of the rare use of articles in poetry) making it אמרה (feminine), a division which Albright says is "obviously correct, besides making better sense"! Albright's translation has several weaknesses: (1) the article is not prolific in Hebrew poetry but appears often enough to caution against disregarding it; (2) בשר does not inherently mean good news; (3) it is doubtful that אמר should be used of an oracle (Mowinckel, 36). Among the emendations, Gray (*JSS* 22 [1977] 2–26) and LePeau (*Psalm 68*) accept the change by metathesis of מבשרות to משברת, from שבר, "break/shatter": "The Lord utters a word which shatters a great host." The *Translation* reflects the following decisions: (1) the "great host" is in apposition to the participle; (2) the news in this context is good, and consists of the material in vv 13–15; (3) we need not think of the messengers as women (though they should not be excluded absolutely, as LePeau does [112, 114]) because מבשרות is collective. In the *Comment*, I accept the interpretation of Eerdmans and Keel that the messengers are the doves of v 14, which has the merit of the agreement of gender (fem.) between "messengers" and "dove."

13.a. LXX has singular, "the king of . . ."; however, the rest of the text which follows differs in content from MT.

13.b. נות is an obscure word which has spawned varied interpretations. If derived from נוה, the meaning relates to the abode of animals, human beings, and God, and can refer to pastureland (e.g.,

2 Sam 7:8; Isa 65:10; Ps 23:2; see Dahood). If it is from נאה, regarded as defective, it is analogous to the construct of נְוֵה, which usually appears as נְאוֹת, referring to beauty and befitting characteristics (the adjective form is נָאוֶה/נָאוָה, see Ps 33:1). Kraus is among the commentators who take the first option: "On the floor of the houses they divide spoil," reading ובנות and תחלק as יחלק, pual 3rd masc. sing. Mowinckel (*Der achtundsechzigste Psalm,* 36) is more probable with no emendations: "On (each) floor booty will be divided," taking fem. 3rd pl. תחלק as impersonal or as 2nd masc., ("you will divide . . ."). Some, including Gunkel and Gray read the נות־בית as the spoil which is to be divided, which requires reading 3rd masc. or 3rd fem. passive; thus, Gray (*JSS* 22 [1977] 22): "And the fairest of the women of the palace are divided as spoil." LePeau (*Psalm 68,* 119) opts for נאה and the idea of "the beauty of the house." However, he interprets this not as the women at home but as the whole nation. It seems more probable to me that "the beautiful one" is idiomatic for "woman/women" (cf. Jer 6:2) and that the statement should be understood in terms of Judg 5:29–30. However, BDB (627), "she that is abiding at home" (Anderson, "the one dwelling at home"), is quite possible.

14.a. Reading as a concessive clause with Keel-Leu and Winter (30), Kissane (290, 294–95), and Deissler; joined to 14bc as the principal clause. Other readings are certainly possible: e.g., reading the אם as a question, "Why do you rest . . . ? The wings of the dove are . . . ," with a structure like Pss 8:4; 27:13 (for אם as a question, see BDB, 50). Another possibility is to read 14a as a suppressed apodosis (GKC, 159dd) followed by exclamatory statements: "If you rest among the saddlebags—The wings of the dove are covered with silver! . . ." (cf. LePeau, *Psalm 68,* 122) in the sense that anyone who remains with the baggage will miss out on the spoils.

14.b. The שׁפתים appears in similar forms in Ezek 40:43; Gen 49:14; Judg 5:16. Its meaning has been the subject of debate. Albright (*HUCA* 23 [1950] 22), utilizing the denominative verb שׁפת, argues for "hearths/hearth stones," where a pot is set (cf. kjv, "pots"), and for a reference to those who stay at home. It is more common to take the word to refer to the walls which converge into a corral for sheep: thus, "sheepfold" or "stall" (Briggs, Gray, *JSS* 22 [1977] 22, n. 10; rsv; et al.). Johnson (*Sacral Kingship,* 71, n. 6) follows KB (580) and reads as "saddlebags" or the "panniers" carried on either side of a donkey and suggests that the expression "to lie down (or squat) between the panniers," which donkeys are prone to do under heavy loads, was idiomatic for "lazy as a stubborn donkey." This proposal seems tolerably possible and is adopted above. See *Comment.*

14.c. Reading the singular as collective. So Keel-Leu and Winter, *Vögel als Boten,* 30, n. 3. Cf. Hos 7:11; 11:11; Isa 38:14; 59:11; Nah 2:8; Jer 48:28; Ps 55:7; and Isa 60:8.

14.d. The "green gold" may refer to gold plate over bronze (LePeau, *Psalm 68*). Albright (*HUCA* 23 [1950] 23) and Dahood translate "yellow gold," citing Ugaritic *yrg hrs,* which Albright says was "doubtless an ancient cliche by 1400 b.c.e." See also Anderson.

15.a. This is a verse with very uncertain meaning. *Shaddai* is frequently translated as "the Almighty" (kjv, rsv, neb, niv). Albright's explanation of the meaning of שׁדי as "the mountain one" (*JBL* 54 [1935] 180–93) has become widely accepted in one form or another (LePeau, *Psalm 68,* 130, n. 198; F. M. Cross, *Canaanite Myth and Hebrew Epic,* 52–60).

15.b. LePeau (*Psalm 68,* 126–27) prefers "spread out" rather than "scattered," but "scattered" seems to me to fit falling snow better.

15.c. The בה has been the subject of numerous explanations, most of them grammatically feasible (see the summary in LePeau, *Psalm 68,* 127–28). rsv and nasv, for example, adopt the locative "there" ("on Zalmon" or "in the land"). neb, jb, njv, niv adopt some form of the comparative, "it is like"; njv, "it seems like." Dahood adopts "then/thereupon," citing Ugar. Anat 3:29–30. LePeau follows GKC, 119p, and reads, "for her sake" with "dove" as the antecedent; "God acts on behalf of his people" (128). Others emend. Johnson (*Sacral Kingship,* 73, n. 2) takes the ב of בָּהּ as correlative with that of בְּפָרֵשׂ and indicates that the two ideas are complementary. "It is like the falling of snow on Zalmon" (cf. neb, jb, njv, niv cited above). For my translation see Buttenwieser, 29; Robinson in Oesterley, 322; Kraus, 625; reading as locative and referring to the location of the scattering of the kings, i.e., on Zalmon (so LXX). Keel-Leu and Winter (*Vögel al Boten,* 17, n. 1) reject this reading on the basis that mountains in Hebrew are masculine. This is generally true (GKC, 392e); however, in the case of several names of mountains in MT, including Zalmon, there is a lack of demonstrable evidence, and Pisgah in Num 21:20 is used with a feminine verb in MT. Also, the primary function of בה is not to refer to Zalmon, but to the preceding verbal idea correlative with the ב on בפרש (cf. GKC, 135p). Keel-Leu appeals to the same grammatical point, but takes Gen 24:14 as the controlling example and translates as *dadurch,* "thereby, by this means, in that way," disregarding the MT accentuation and reading בה with the second line, which has the merit of resulting in 3+3 lines rather than 4+2—if that is important.

15.d. Is a specific mountain intended? A Zalmon near Shechem is referred to in Judg 9:48, and Djebel Hauran (Jebel Druze) located in Transjordan on the borders of Bashan has peaks more than 6000 feet high on which snow falls in winter. The dark volcanic basalt rock and/or vegetation may have given it its name, "Dark Mountain/Black Mountain." In the present context, it is probable that the usage is more literary than geographic with the intention of heightening the contrast between the whiteness of the snow and the darkness of "Black Mountain."

16.a. Primarily a superlative term; "a godlike mountain," or "mighty mountain." However, D. W. Thomas, "A Consideration of Some Unusual Ways of Expressing the Superlative in Hebrew," *VT* 3 (1933) 215, and LePeau (*Psalm 68*, 134–35) caution that such terminology is not without religious reference and probably indicated a place linked with worship providing a contact between the heavens and the earth (see the discussion on Ps 61:2–5).

16.b. Bashan is located in Transjordan, extending from the Yarmuth northward to Mount Herman eastward to the Hauran rise (Jebel ed Druze). However, the usage here is probably more literary than geographic. See *Comment*.

16.c. Or, "summits," or, "humpbacked"; cf. גִּבֵּן in Lev 21:20.

17.a. The plural formation may contain an enclitic *mem* on "mountain" in a construct chain; so, "mountain of peaks"/"many peaked mountain" (Dahood).

17.b. The verb רצד appears only here in MT, but its meaning seems well established. See A. A. Anderson, I, 490–91. The *Translation* follows LePeau, *Psalm 68*, 133, 136, n. 210.

18.a. שנאן appears only here in MT; traditionally understood to mean "repetition" from שנה, "to repent/do again," thus: "twice ten thousand, thousands upon thousands" (RSV). If רבתים "twice ten thousand" is taken in a multiplicative sense (see GKC, 97h), the reading would be: "ten thousand times of thousands of repetitions." The meaning would be that of myriads, "thousands upon thousands"; large, indefinite numbers. The awkwardness of the Hebrew expression has led to numerous proposals for changes in the text (see LePeau, *Psalm 68*, 145–47 for a survey). The *Translation* follows Albright's solution (*HUCA* 23 [1950] 25; "Notes on Psalms 68 and 134," in *Interpretationes ad Vetus Testamentum pertinentes Sigmundo Mowinckel*, ed. A. S. Kapelrud [Oslo: Forlaget Land og kirke, 1955], 2–5; also Miller, *Divine Warrior*, 108–9; Dahood, Gray, *JSS* 22 [1977] 23). Albright omits the *aleph* on the basis of dittography (the original unpointed text would have been שנאאדני, in sequence) leaving שנן, which he equates with Ugaritic *tnn*, which designates a class of archers/warriors who accompanied the chariots. LePeau follows Caquot (*RHR* 177 [1970] 164–65) and reads from שנא, "to shine," with ן as plural suffix: "the Bright Ones," referring to the angelic members of the divine army. Cf. Kraus, who corrects to שאנן, translating *in Erhabenheit*, "in grandeur/nobility/stateliness"; cf. LXX, εὐθηνούντων, "those who thrive/prosper."

18.b. The change to בא מסיני, "The Lord came/comes from Sinai . . ." (*BHS;* RSV), is not necessary.

18.c. Perhaps we should read as in v 9, "the One of Sinai" or "the god of Sinai"; in any case, it is a divine epithet.

18.d. בקדש can be "among the Holy Ones," the members of the entourage of the Divine King; preferred by LePeau (*Psalm 68*, 147); others prefer "in holiness" (Mowinckel, *Der achtundsechzigste Psalm*, 41, "in holy power"). Most commonly, "into the holy place" (the sanctuary or temple which belongs to God). Gray (*JSS* 22 [1977] 2–26) prefers to read ב as "from" and קדש as the place name "Qadesh." See v 25.

19.a. Reading ב as "from." If *beth essentia*, the meaning would be that people are the gift; thus, NAB: "received men as gifts."

19.b. לשכן is difficult and has given rise to different readings (see LePeau, *Psalm 68*, 152–53). Anderson suggests that the verb be read in the sense of Ugaritic *škn*, "to establish" or "to accept" (and Syriac, "to submit"); thus: "Even the rebellious (did homage) in establishing (i.e., accepting) Yah as God." Perhaps better, accepting the ל in the sense of "with": "Even the rebellious are willing to dwell (or, may dwell) with Yah-God!" The entire statement is difficult enough to lead Albright (*HUCA* 23 [1950] 24) to write, "I do not know what to do with this three-beat colon."

20.a. Reading the relative clause, with omission of relative particle (GKC, 155f). The verb עמס can mean either "lift/carry" (Neh 4:11; Zech 12:3; Isa 46:3) or "load" and place a burden on another (Gen 44:13; Isa 46:1; 1 Kgs 12:11 //2 Chr 10:11; Nah 13:15; KJV, "who daily loadeth us with benefits"). Grammatically, the colon may be translated: "day by day God lays on us (or, carries for us) our salvation," cf. LXX, "the God of our salvation will prosper us [κατευοδώσει]" but this does not seem very meaningful (LePeau, *Psalm 68*, 156). "The God of our salvation" appears to be a divine epithet and should be retained.

21.a. מושעות is found only here, but it has a meaning similar to ישועה, "deliverance, salvation," found in v 20.

21.b. Translating לְ in the sense of BDB, 514g. The verse is difficult, but it seems to say that God (הָאֵל, perhaps "God himself," so Dahood here and in v 20) has control over death.

21.c. Literally "to (or of) death (there are) out-goings." LePeau (*Psalm 68,* 161) capitalizes "Death," with the idea of God's victory in battle and control of the realm of Death in the underworld.

22.a. For the force of the אַךְ, see n. 62:2.a.

23.a. MT lacks an object after the verbs in both colons, and this has given rise to many interpretations. Among the emendations, Gunkel and others change מִבָּשָׁן to מִכִּבְשָׁן: "From the furnace of fire I will bring them back . . . ," balancing "fire" and the "sea," and citing Isa 43:2; Ps 66:12 in support. Weiser repoints אָשִׁיב to אָשֻׁב, "I return"; of Yahweh's "homecoming" after the pursuit of his enemies. If אָשִׁיב is read as אֶשְׁבֹּם from a root שׁבם, "stifle/muzzle" (so Miller, *Divine Warrior,* 110; *HTR* 57 [1964] 240), the following results: אֶשְׁבֹּם בָּשָׁן אֶשְׁבֹּם מְצֻלוֹת יָם: "I muzzle the Serpent, I muzzle the Deep sea"; reading בָּשָׁן, "serpent," with Albright (see also Dahood). Albright (*HUCA* 23 [1950] 27–28) assumes the loss of מִמְּחַץ, "from smiting," before מִבָּשָׁן and changes מְצֻלוֹת to מִצְמַת (from צמת "end, exterminate"; thus, "From smiting the Serpent I return, I return from destroying Sea!" This is obviously too much emendation, but Albright's reading of "Bashan" as "serpent" (also in Deut 33:22) is more plausible and has been accepted by others (Miller, *Divine Warrior,* 110, and *HTR* 57 [1964] 240; Dahood; Gray, *JSS* 22 [1977] 9–10). However, without emendation the lack of an object is still a problem. As an implied object, we could think of God bringing his enemies back from whatever extreme places they may have fled to (see LePeau, *Psalm 68,* 167). This fits the context of a victory celebration of God's triumph over his enemies (vv 12–19) and the idea of returning the enemies so that people may participate in the victory (v 24; Durham). "Bashan" may be "Serpent" (perhaps with a play on the word for viper and the geographic region of Bashan) parallel with "Sea." However, the contrast between the mighty mountain of Bashan (v 16) and the depths of the sea is strong enough.

24.a. מחץ, "break to pieces," perhaps from Arabic "churn/beat/agitate" of milk, etc. (Dahood); e.g., Pss 18:39; 110:5; Job 5:18; 26:12; Num 24:8; Judg 4:26; Deut 33:11, with the meaning of "dip/plunge/wade" here. The verb is often emended to רחץ, "wash/bathe" in keeping with Ps 58:11b. Gray (*JSS* 22 [1977] 15) reads "dye your foot red . . . ," reading חמץ, II, "be red" (see BDB, 330). The reading above is tentative, but it assumes that מחץ here means "agitate, plunge" in the sense of shaking or stamping one's feet, and the דם is read as "from blood" (see n. 58:11.b. and Dahood on 58:11), i.e., to "shake your foot from blood." Even if "wash" is read, the idea may be that of washing blood from the feet.

24.b. Translation of a troublesome word (מִנֵּהוּ), usually taken as equal to מְנָת from מנה, and noun מְנָת, "part/portion" (BDB; Ps 58:4; Neh 12:44, 47; 13:10; Pss 11:6; 16:5; 63:11). Or, the form may be explained as the noun מֵן, "portion" (a *hapax*), from מנן, plus 3rd masc. sing. suffix (GKC, 103m; BDB, 585). In either case the suffix refers to the "tongue of your dogs," which will get its portion. Proposals for emendations are not unexpected, but none of them seem very persuasive (LePeau, *Psalm 68,* 175).

25.a. The verb is qal perfect 3rd masc. pl., literally "they saw." Proposals to repoint as qal imperative are sometimes made (e.g., Gunkel, Gray, Robinson, Oesterley, and Dahood). However, it can be translated with an indefinite subject, "they"; so NAB: "They view your progress, O God." The *Translation* follows Briggs, Johnson (*Sacral Kingship,* 74), GKC (144f), LePeau (*Psalm 68,* 177) in treating the Hebrew indefinite subject as corresponding to a passive construction in English.

25.b. Reading the singular as collective. LePeau (*Psalm 68,* 179) remarks that "into the sanctuary" (and "in the sanctuary"), "in holiness," and "among the holy ones" are all equally acceptable so far as the meaning of the expression goes. The context in v 18 is perhaps clearer and adds some support for the reading "holy ones" here. However, most commentators and translations have used "sanctuary" or "holy place." See *Comment* on this verse and v 18.

26.a. Some interpreters repoint בְּתוֹךְ to the absolute בַּתָּוֶךְ, "in the midst the maidens beat tambourines" (Briggs, Gunkel, et al.) . This is unnecessary because the singers and other members of the processional pass between the maidens playing tambourines (LePeau, *Psalm 68,* 181).

27.a. The word מַקְהֵלוֹת is a *hapax* with uncertain meaning. It is derived from the noun and verb קהל, "assembly/congregation" and "assemble." The noun קְהִלָּה, "assembly/congregation," appears only twice (Neh 5:7; Deut 33:4). The word refers to some sort of assemblies or groups. The assemblies could be made up of singers, ministers, or various groupings of the people. Though I have translated above in the plural, Dahood is probably correct to treat the form as "feminine singular of the Phoenician type" (148).

27.b. The word מקור ("source/fountain") can be taken in the sense of the source or fountain of Israel (Cohen, RSV, etc.); perhaps referring to the patriarch Jacob (Deut 33:28), or to the temple (cf. Zech 13:1), or to Yahweh. In any case, it is taken above in the sense of "you who are from Israel's source," i.e., all true Israelites. A reference to the Gihon spring at Jerusalem has been suggested (Eaton, 173; LePeau, *Psalm 68*, 185–86), but this seems unlikely. Kraus is among those who emend מִקּוֹר to read מִמְּקֹרָא, "from the convocation," and Dahood (cf. LePeau, 187) derives the word from a root רוק, "to call/convoke" (cf. Ugaritic *qr*, "a sound"), and translates, "in the convocation of Israel."

28.a. Reading שָׁם as in Ps 66:6, with Dahood; cf. LePeau, *Psalm 68*, 189. Gray (*JSS* 22 [1977] 17) notes that שָׁם rarely if ever is used in deictic sense and cites the evidence used by Dahood. However, he prefers to translate as "there" introducing the next stage of the narrative. He cites Ugar. *tm* (CTA 22:4, 6, 8, 9).

28.b. צָעִיר can mean "little," "insignificant," or "young." LXX has "the younger (one)," reading צָעִיר as with the article (which usually appears with it in this sense in narratives). Cf. Mic 5:1; 1 Sam 9:21.

28.c. The very uncertain word רֹדֵם is traditionally parsed as qal participle with 3rd masc. pl. suffix from רדם (see Briggs, etc.). Since the verb רדם means to fall into a heavy sleep or trance and the noun תַּרְדֵּמָה means a deep sleep or trance, it is assumed frequently that the root must be רדה, "to have dominion/rule"; thus, "their ruler" or the like. However, it is questionable whether or not this fits the context and the translation of "leads them" or "in the lead" used by RSV, NEB, NAB, JB, NIV, does not conform to the meaning of רדה (LePeau, *Psalm 68*, 189, n. 375), which usually means "to lord over" or "to dominate" when used of one Israelite in relation to another (note Lev 25:43, 46, 53; 1 Kgs 5:30; 9:23; 2 Chr 8:10; Jer 5:31; Ezek 34:4). Therefore, I have followed LXX's "in ecstasy," probably reading as participle of רדם in the sense of an ecstatic trance. Syriac has "in silence" (*BHS*).

28.d. The word רִגְמָתָם should probably be left untranslated because we do not know what it means. The traditional derivation is from רגם, "to stone," and thus a noun meaning רגמה to refer to a "heap of stones"; and in a colloquial way to "their heap (of people)," which Briggs (111) observes is an expression common in the southern part of the United States. However, רגם is used in the sense of stoning as a punishment, a legal procedure, and hardly refers to a heaping up of stones. A number of readings have been proposed (for a survey, see LePeau, *Psalm 68*, 192–97). Gunkel's change to read רֹב מְתִים "numerous in men," or "a crowd of men," which has led to the interpretation of רגמתם as the shouting crowd of people (KB, 873) gathered around the procession (or better, the shouting princes of Judah as they participate in the procession) is probably the most widely followed, though it has no real basis in the text except that it provides a good parallel to his emendation of צָעִיר רֹדֵם to צָעִיר אָדָם, "few in men." It is more likely that רגמתם is related to a root רגם, "to speak/shout," corresponding to the Ugaritic *rgm*, "to speak," and Akkadian *ragamu*, "to shout." See Johnson, *Sacral Kingship*, 75, 40, n. 3, who prefers, however, to translate as "honest spoken" on the basis of Gen 38:26; 44:18–34. LXX uses ἡγεμόνες αὐτῶν, "their leaders," which possibly suggests רוְנֵיהֶם (so *BHS*), but may only represent an attempt to interpret the רגמתם as the princes of Judah heading the processional and leading the shouting. It is interesting to note that the Greek ἡγεμών can be equal to πυρρίχιος, "of or belonging to the pyrrhic dance," and that πυρρίχη is used of a war song. Thus it is possible that the LXX translators were reading רגמתם in the sense of "their leaders in shouting and dancing"; i.e., the ecstasy of the first colon.

29.a. The perfect of צוה is frequently changed to imperative (so *BHS*) to give consistency in the verse as in LXX. However, this requires the emendation of אלהיך to אלהים or אלהי: "Command, O God [or, O my God], your strength." It is also possible to read צוה as precative perfect with optative force and not change the pointing or the following words: "Let your God command your strength." The reading above makes 29a a positive statement before the prayer which provides the basis for the requests which follow. The tentative translation above treats the line as a quotation, a possible *incipit*, a beginning line of a poem used as a kind of text for the prayer (on *incipits* in this psalm, see Albright, *HUCA* 23 [1950] 31, who however does not so treat v 28a; reading as imperative).

29.b. Reading the relative זו as equivalent of אֲשֶׁר, "who/which," with אלהים as the antecedent (LePeau, *Psalm 68*, 201). However, עזו (from which עֻזֶּה is derived) seems to mean "be strong/prevail," and as an intransitive verb, it could be read as: "Strengthen, O God, what you have done for us."

30.a. Perhaps a reference to the fact that the temple was on a small hill above the old town of Jerusalem; but more likely to the heavenly temple above Jerusalem. See *Comment*. The line is an example of enjambment in which v 30a completes the thought of v 29.

30.b. Reading jussive, as in Ps 76:12.

31.a. LePeau (*Psalm 68*, 208) points out that "calves of peoples" is grammatically epexegetical genitive or genitive of apposition (GKC, 128k–q; Johnson, *Sacral Kingship*, 76, n.1): "calves consisting of peoples," or "calves, the peoples"; thus, "calf-people." Emendation to בעלי, "lords of," is used by Gunkel et al. See *Comment*.

31.b. This line is very uncertain; only the word כֶּסֶף, "silver, money," is clear in meaning. The word מתרפס, a hithpael participle from רפש/רפס, means "to pollute a source of water" in qal, niphal, and noun forms in Ezek 32:2; 34:18; 34:19; Prov 25:26. Some translations read the hithpael in v 31 as "trample"; thus RSV, "Trample under those who lust after tribute," continuing the imperative "rebuke" at the beginning of the verse (Anderson). Johnson (176) links the מתרפס with the preceding "bulls of peoples," translating:

> Trampling on the bull-like peoples,
> On those whose pleasure was in silver.

However, רפס is found in hithpael imperative in Prov 6:3, and there carries the meaning "to allow oneself to be trampled on/to prostrate oneself/humble oneself" (see W. McKane, *Proverbs: A New Approach*, OTL [Philadelphia: Westminster Press, 1970] 322, who follows BDB and translates, "Swallow your pride"). The *Translation* follows this lead and links the participle with the herd of bulls and the calf-people. The "till" is supplied by the context. Another option is to emend the initial מ of מתרפס to ה and read as precative perfect (so LePeau, *Psalm 68*, 212–16, who translates: "That he [the beast] prostrate himself . . ."). A few Hebrew mss read מִתְרַפִּם, masc. pl. hithpael participle from רפה, "sink down/relax," thus "those who make themselves slack" = "humble themselves." LXX reads "so that those refined like silver may not be shut out." Perhaps this can be explained by reading a מן as negative of consequence and assuming that the following verb was niphal or hithpael infinitive with ה or התד (see Briggs). However, the verb assumed by LXX is uncertain: perhaps סגר, "shut/close," unless רפס was interpreted in the sense of excluding. The change in MT to התרפס (imperative) is sometimes made: "Trample underfoot . . ." (RSV, Kraus et al.)

31.c. BDB (954) defines רץ as "piece/bar" from רצץ, "to crush/crush in pieces"—in plural construct here. However, BDB adds "very obscure and dubious." Emendations are rife (see LePeau, *Psalm 68*, 212). LXX (see n. 31.b.) indicates צרף from צרף, "smelt/refine." LePeau reads בצרי by metathesis, a plural construct of בֶּצֶר, "ingot/bar," and then reads accusative of means (GKC, 118m): "That he [the beast] prostrate himself with bars of silver," i.e., with gifts of tribute for God. "Lust for silver," preferred by some (e.g., RSV), is derived by reading בִּרְצֵי (for בְּרֻצֵּי) from רצה, "be pleased with/delighted with."

31.d. בַּזַּר can be repointed to imperative (with versions) or read as precative perfect (as above).

32.a. חַשְׁמַנִּים is a *hapax*, but appears to be related to Egyptian *hsmn*, "bronze" (KB, 342, Anderson, Albright, *HUCA* 23 [1950] 30–34, et al.). Albright in his 1950 article (*HUCA* 23 [1950] 33–34) argued that Egyptian *hsmn* refers to natron (the more common meaning in Egyptian usage), rather than a kind of copper or bronze. He translated: "They are bringing natron out of Egypt." Natron is a compound of sodium which was used as a detergent and in the production of red dye. However, in 1955 (*Interpretationes Sigmundo Mowinckel*, ed. A. S. Kapelrud [Oslo: Forlaget Land og kirke, 1955] 5), Albright surveyed new evidence for Ugaritic *hušmanu* and concluded that the Hebrew refers to "red cloth": "They are bringing red cloth out of Egypt." Dahood, following *CAD* 6:142, prefers "blue cloth" (the Akkadian root refers to a stone or cloth of blue-green color). I have preferred to follow LXX (πρέσβεις) and Syriac and translate as "ambassadors/nobles/magnates/envoys." Possibly, this idea is related to the brightly colored (blue and red) clothing worn by nobles, diplomatic agents, and others of wealth and high social status.

32.b. Reading the verb as qal imperfect 3rd masc. pl., jussive from אתה ("come"). See LePeau, *Psalm 68*, 214–15, for other options; also Johnson, *Sacral Kingship*, 76.

32.c. Literally "let Cush run out his hands to God," reading תָּרִיץ as jussive, though the lack of gender agreement between verb and subject may be anomalous (see LePeau, *Psalm 68*, 217; however, see GKC, 146g; cf., e.g., Job 39:3, 16). Some interpreters (e.g., Johnson, *Sacral Kingship*, 76; Albright, *HUCA* 23 [1950] 34; Kraus) derive the verb from the Akkadian phrase *qata tarasu*, "stretch out the hand," postulating a root תרץ, "stretch out," for תריץ and reading as qal perfect 3rd.masc. sing.: "Cush has stretched out his hands. . . ." The connotation of "hand" can include that of "the work of one's hands" (cf. Ezek 28:15); in this case the context indicates the hands give handiwork as tribute to God.

33.a. Albright (*HUCA* 23 [1950] 34) objects that "kingdoms cannot sing while kings can" and understands ממלכות on the basis of Phoenician usage as "kings" (so also, Gray, *JSS* 22 [1977] 25; Dahood). However, LePeau (*Psalm 68*, 221, n. 476) argues that ממלכות does not have the meaning of "kings" when used in the expression ממלכות הארץ. In any case, ממלכות הארץ occurs with the idea of the people (who can praise Yahweh) as well as the land (LePeau cites Isa 23:17; 2 Kgs 19:15, 19 // Isa 37:16, 29; Ezra 1:2 // 2 Chr 36:23; cf. 1 Kgs 5:1 [4:21]; 11:11). Note Mowinckel (*Der achtundsechzigste Psalm,*

66), who points to long lists of inanimate things called upon to sing and praise—Pss 96:11–12; 98:2–8; 148:11.

34.a. See notes on v 5. בשמי שמי־קדם is literally "in the heavens of the heavens of antiquity/ancient times." LePeau (*Psalm 68*, 223, n. 480) argues for the double construct as a superlative, "the highest heavens" (citing GKC, 133i). He translates, "on the heights of ancient heavens" (cf. Gray, *JSS* 22 [1977] 25). Perhaps better: "through the primeval heaven of heavens," which should not be reduced to a mere "highest skies."

34.b. Literally "he gives with his voice a powerful, mighty voice/sound." To "give with his voice," using ב, denotes an emphasized construction; i.e., "he gives his voice mightily" (LePeau, *Psalm 68*, 224–25). קול is sometimes associated with thunder, roaring, or similar sounds (note the use of נתן קול in Jer 25:20; Joel 2:11; 4:16; Amos 1:2; 2 Sam 22:14; Ps 18:14).

35.a. Literally, "give," but give in what sense? Empower God? Ascribe (the most common word used in English translations) to God the source of power? I have chosen to understand the verb נתן as "yield" or "give over to." Equally good is "give out/give forth" (as the Lord "gives forth" the word in v 12), as in NAB, "Confess the power of God!"; NIV, "Proclaim the power of God." The use of נתן with עז or anything else in terms of giving to God is not common; God's giving to mankind is much more frequent. Cf. Ps 115:1; Jer 13:16.

36.a. The plural noun should probably be read as singular, "sanctuary" (for some versional support, see *BHS*). See Ps 73:17; the plural may be that of amplification (Anderson; GKC, 124e). Albright (*HUCA* 23 [1950] 35) reads "shrines," because he thinks the reference is to other sanctuaries before the building of the temple.

36.b. "The people" refers to the people of Israel. There is versional support for "his people," possibly reading לעמו with a 3rd singular suffix (adopted by Kraus, Weiser; cf. KJV, RSV, NAB, AB, NIV).

36.c. LePeau (*Psalm 68*, 231–32) reads לְעָם בָּרוּךְ אֱלֹהִים as "to the people blessed of God," on the grounds of metrical considerations, and so does not allow "blessed be God" to serve as a closing colon (in a similar way, Johnson, *Sacral Kingship*, 76). This is almost certainly incorrect. First, both Johnson and LePeau find it necessary to repoint בָּרוּךְ as construct בְּרוּךְ, as in Gen 24:31 and 26:29 (cf. Judg 17:2; Ruth 2:20; 3:10; 1 Sam 15:13; Ps 115:15). However, the usage in which blessing is directed *to* God is much more common. Second, the metrical argument is not very strong, since unbalanced colons are frequent. In this case, the first three colons are not necessarily unbalanced. The *Translation* reads as 3+3+3+2. Third, the blessing directed to God relates well to the statements about blessing God in vv 20 and 27.

Form/Structure/Setting

The difficulties of interpreting Ps 68 are almost legendary. H.-J. Kraus' (628) comment is repeated in essence by almost all commentators: "There is in the Psalter scarcely a song that, in its textual corruption and disconnectedness, presents the interpreter so great a task as Psalm 68." The amount of textual corruption is, however, in some dispute because of the high number of *hapax legomena* and low-frequency words in the psalm. How can we be sure that a word is corrupt when it does not appear elsewhere in MT? More than fifteen words and expressions in this psalm do not appear elsewhere in biblical literature. As many as two dozen words are used which are found less than twenty times in MT; half of them less than ten times (LePeau, *Psalm 68*, 2). J. A. Sanders ("Text and Canon: Concepts and Method," *JBL* 98 [1979] 5–29) says that the *lamedh* in the *massora parva* of MT, which marks a word appearing for the only time in that form in the MT, "stands like a soldier to remind the next scribe that the word in question must be copied precisely as written or corrected in the *Vorlage*" (17). Some thirty-two of these "soldiers" form a cordon around Ps 68. As in other psalms, the meaning conveyed by a colon or a verse may be very elusive, even if the meaning of each word is clear. In this regard, of course, Ps 68 is not unique, just more uncertain than most. In 1950, W. F. Albright (*HUCA* 23 [1950] 7) wrote that "Psalm 68 has always been considered with justice as the most difficult of all the Psalms." He noted the work of E. Reuss in 1851 in which he brought together some four hundred different commentaries on the Psalm, "with results which can easily be imagined." Such a summary today would be far more extensive but equally confusing.

These things make up the bad news about Ps 68. There is good news as well. The good news about Ps 68 is that its unusual nature has attracted the attention of a goodly number of competent scholars, who have been motivated to probe into the intricate nature of its text, content, and interpretation. The *Bibliography* is selected but still provides some idea of the attention the psalm has received. Commentaries are not listed, but some of them have extensive treatments. For example, Kraus uses thirteen very large pages in German for this psalm of thirty-six verses. Among the recent literature, the dissertation of J. P. LePeau (1981) is especially valuable for its reviews of research as well as for the author's own interpretation. In the following treatment of Ps 68, I am greatly indebted to LePeau's work. W. F. Albright's long study, the rebuttal of Albright by S. Mowinckel in his monograph, and the long article by J. Gray have been of great help also (see the *Bibliography* for references to these works).

Kraus refers to the "disconnectedness" (*Zusammenhanglosigkeit*) of the psalm, which has been a matter of major concern. T. H. Robinson (in Oesterley, 320) wrote in the introduction to the psalm that those interpreters seeking "a single (or even double) thread running through it" have to resort to textual emendation so extensive "as to necessitate a practical rewriting of the whole," without very satisfactory results. His own judgment was that the psalm is "a collection of sentences and phrases taken from a number of different poems, and strung together haphazard." The psalm is likened to a page from the index of a hymnal! With great linguistic skill and resources, W. F. Albright (*HUCA* 23 [1950] 1–39) argued for the psalm as a "catalogue of early Hebrew lyric poems," in reality the *incipits*, or the beginnings, of independent poems. He appealed to Sumerian and Akkadian catalogues of literary works or lyric poems. Assuming that Ps 68 is such a catalogue, Albright divided the psalm into thirty *incipits*: vv 1–3; 4; 5–6; 7; 8–9; 10; 11; 12; 13; 14; 15; 16–17; 18; 19; 20–21; 22; 23; 24; 25; 26; 27; 28; 29; 30; 31; 32; 33; 34; 35; 36. He used Exod 15:21 as a prime example from the MT. Miriam's song—"Sing to the LORD, for he has triumphed gloriously; / the horse and his rider he has thrown into the sea"—is the slightly changed first line of the poem which begins in Exod 15:1. Also, he cited Ps 68:2, which he claimed is repeated as an *incipit* in Num 10:35, the Song of the Well in Num 21:17–18, the beginning of a song honoring Saul and David in 1 Sam 18:7, and the Song of the Forgotten Harlot in Isa 23:16. These are all examples, according to Albright, of the practice of identifying Hebrew poetic compositions by their first lines or strophes. A longer type of *incipit* was needed when lyric poems were so numerous that more quotation was necessary for identification.

Albright's radical "disconnection" of the psalm has not met with general acceptance, though most commentators note the psalm's "kaleidoscope imagery" (Eaton, 169) and the free style of its formation. S. Mowinckel (1953) wrote explicitly to refute Albright's interpretation, concluding that "in the Old Testament itself no support for Albright's hypothesis is to be found" (9). He argues seriatim with Albright's examples and concludes that none of them is necessarily an *incipit*. J. Gray describes Albright's solution of the problem of the nature of Ps

68 as a "counsel of despair" (which Albright certainly did not intend) and argues that it "errs chiefly in showing no awareness of the relevance of each of the thirty passages he distinguished to a *Sitz im Leben* common to all" (*JSS* 22 [1977] 3). LePeau adopts a thesis similar to that of Mowinckel (*Der achtundsechzigste Psalm*, 9), who argues that one should begin with the assumption that Ps 68 is a cohesive psalm as it appears in MT. He notes that the separation of individual psalms from one another in the MT is usually correct. Further, the partition of a psalm into fragments, though certainly possible in the context of ancient literary composition, should not be done without good evidence. It is extremely unlikely that any psalm has been put together in its present form in the manner postulated by T. H. Robinson for Ps 68 (in Oesterley). Even a hymnbook is not a haphazard production! We must allow for skilled redaction of older materials into new compositions which then become greater than the sum of their parts (cf. Pss 19; 24; 40; 61; 99).

If we assume an essential unity for Ps 68, what is its basis? Schmidt (127) argues that the disparate elements of Ps 68 are bound together by the occasion (*Gelegenheit*) of the psalm's usage rather than by its subject matter (*Gegenstand*). Others take a similar approach (e.g., Mowinckel, Gray). Gray proposes that the psalm is a cantata for the Israelite autumn festival, during which there was a celebration of the enthronement of a victorious Yahweh as divine king, closely associated with the emphasis in the festival on the giving of rain (cf. Zech 14:16–17). Vv 26–28 do reflect a cultic setting, and it is reasonable to assume that the psalm was drawn from liturgies of the temple in Jerusalem (Mowinckel, *Der achtundsechzigste Psalm*, 72). Gray goes beyond this and argues that it was derived originally from the liturgy of an autumn festival held on Mount Tabor, considered to be a boundary sanctuary between Zebulun, Issachar, and Naphtali (Deut 30:18–19; Josh 19:34). He builds his argument on the peculiar and limited selection of tribal names in v 28 and on the assumption that the mountain of Bashan in vv 16–17 is equal to Mount Hermon, which is associated with Tabor in Ps 89:2–19 (especially in v 13), a psalm which is claimed to be similar in nature to 68 (Gray, *JSS* 22 [1977] 5). Appeal is also made to the victorious action of Zebulun and Naphtali under the leadership of Deborah and Barak in Judg 5:1–18 (note also the gathering of the troops of Naphtali and Zebulun on Mount Tabor in Judg 4:6).

Mowinckel (*Der achtundsechzigste Psalm*, 12; *PIW*, II, 75) cautions against separating too quickly between the connectedness of a cultic occasion and the subject matter of a psalm (as in Schmidt, see above). The subject matter of a liturgy should correspond to the inner connectedness of the cultic acts involved; a liturgy should reflect a closely related series of worship acts. Moving along this line, Mowinckel divides Ps 68 into nine self-contained strophes:

vv 2–4	vv 8–11	vv 16–19	vv 25–28
vv 5–7	vv 12–15	vv 20–24	vv 29–32
	vv 33–36		

However, Gray divides the psalm into twelve sections: vv 2–4; 5–7; 8–11; 12–15; 16–17; 18–19; 20–22; 23–24; 25–28; 29–30a, 31a, b, d; 30b, 32a, 31c, 32b; 33–36. Kraus also has twelve sections: vv 2–4; 5–7; 8–11; 12–15; 16–17; 18–19; 20–21; 22–24; 25–28; 29–30; 31–32; 33–36. LePeau uses the same nine divisions as Mowinckel and attempts to give a detailed poetic analysis of each strophe in the mode of biblical stylistics and rhetorical criticism. He is, however, somewhat inconsistent in seeking to allow the text of the psalm to generate understanding on its own terms (*Psalm 68*, 159), while insisting on understanding the "psalmist's thought" (60). The only access we have to "what the composer . . . intended to say" is the text of Ps 68 itself. We are on sounder ground if we do not try to speculate too much about the writer's mind. Whatever the writer meant, he or she can only mean for us what is written in the text. The writer left no commentary.

The unity of Ps 68 is defended by LePeau (*Psalm 68*, 234–73) on the basis of both internal consistency of metrical and strophic structure and thematic development. He attempts to demonstrate a fairly regular pattern of short, medium, and long verses in three movements (245–46):

vv 2–11, which stress the ideal kingship of God in an alternating pattern of medium and long verses;

vv 12–24, which focus on God as the cosmic king, using short verses;

vv 25–36, which emphasize the universal kingship of God in verses which are mostly of medium length.

J. P. Fokkelman divides the psalm into the same three large sections indicated above from LePeau (2–11, 12–24, 25–36), with each section organized thematically around three different mountains: Sinai, Bashan, and God's new abode, Zion (from an unpublished study cited by R. Alter in *The Literary Guide to the Bible*, ed. R. Alter and F. Kermode [Cambridge: Belknap Press of Harvard UP, 1987] 256). I find LePeau's overall arguments persuasive, and I have adopted the general outline of his analysis of the psalm. However, there are some weaknesses in his approach. He uses syllable counting to determine the length of verses, but he allows a rather wide range in his categories: 7–14 counts in short verses, 15–22 counts in medium verses, and 26–33 counts in long verses. Also, he fails to compare the variations in Ps 68 with other long psalms. I have not made any major comparisons with other long psalms, but the variations in syllable count in Ps 68 seem relatively high. The poetic structure in Ps 68 has an irregular quality at best and efforts to give it a uniform style should be resisted.

Form critics have had a rather difficult time in deciding upon a literary type for Ps 68 (LePeau, *Psalm 68*, 38–44). The choices include an eschatological hymn (Gunkel), a victory song (e.g., Briggs, Eaton, Miller, C. Westermann, *Praise and Lament in the Psalms*, 92), a processional hymn (e.g., A. A. Anderson, Stuhlmueller), and liturgy (e.g., Schmidt, Mowinckel, *Der achtundsechzigste Psalm*, 10; A. A. Anderson, Weiser). Hymnic elements are clearly evident (see vv 5–7, 20–24, 33–36). Vv 2–4, 8–11, 12–15, 16–19, 25–28 are descriptive of the actions of God and belong to the general category of praise in the reporting style as discussed by Frank Crüsemann (*Studien zur Formgeschichte von Hymnus und Danklied in Israel*, 192–99). However, supplicatory prayer is found in vv 29b–32, material which seems to fit Crüsemann's (184–91) hymnic praise-wish (*Lobwunsch*) addressed to God. Vv 2–4 are read as expressing a wish for supplication in the *Translation* and point to the overall category of the psalm as a supplicatory, hymnic prayer exalting the victories of Yahweh, but designed to petition him for further triumphs. The psalm seems to be the culmination of a short collection of such hymnic prayers, the beginning of which is marked by 65:2 and the end indicated by the "Blessed be God" in 68:36. The use of the term שִׁיר, "song," in each title indicates that the collection as a whole is of this genre.

Ps 68 seems to offer encouragement for dating by its references to specific tribal groups and geographic locations. The affinity of the psalm's language with Ugaritic words and expressions encouraged Albright to argue for its identification as an adaptation of original Canaanite *incipits*, and he dated the adaptation to the Solomonic period or a little later (the original material being from the thirteenth to tenth centuries B.C.E.). Albright's dating was influenced especially by the numerous cases of defective spelling in Ps 68 (sixteen or more) which are characteristic of Phoenician spelling and, assumedly, of the spelling in early Israel before being replaced by a more standard spelling c. 900 B.C.E. He also cited patterns of climactic parallelism like that in Ugaritic verse (105; Albright found this in vv 8–9, 16, 23, 24, 25, 28, 31). Mowinckel and Gray are among those who have questioned Albright's methodology in dating the psalm. Mowinckel (*Der achtundsechzigste Psalm*, 70–71) appeals to the psalm in Hab 3, which Albright demonstrated to be in accord with Ugaritic poetry (in *Studies in Old Testament Prophecy*, ed. H. H. Rowley [New York: Scribner, 1950] 1–18), but which Albright himself dated to the late pre-exilic era. Gray (*JSS* 22 [1977] 18–19) cites the scarcity of pre-ninth-century Hebrew epigraphic evidence and the relative lack of *scriptio defectiva* in what there is. He also notes the tendency to *scriptio defectiva* in Ecclesiastes, which is generally considered to be a later writing, and appeals even to the MT, which has less *scriptio plena* than the Qumran biblical texts. However, Gray does allow the cumulative evidence of syntax, spelling, vocabulary, phraseology, and motifs to indicate an early date. The similarity between 68:12–19 and the Song of Deborah is considered to be further support for an early date.

Attempts have been made to date Ps 68 by the historical allusions in its content. Thus Mowinckel (*Der achtundsechzigste Psalm*, 72) dates it to the time of Saul on the shaky ground of Benjaminite hegemony supposedly reflected in v 28. The notes in JB attempt to trace allusions in the psalm to events in Israelite history from the exodus to the exile. The similarities between Ps 68 and Deutero-Isaiah have received considerable attention (see LePeau, *Psalm 68*, 21–37), with both Gunkel and Buttenwieser arguing for the dependence of the psalm on Isa 40–55. However, all the allusions lack the specificity for any precision in dating. The psalm is probably post-exilic in its present form, but certainly contains traditional material from earlier periods. A history of development is probably lodged in the psalm, but it is impossible to reconstruct it with any certainty. The psalm may stream back to early poetry from a sanctuary on Mount Tabor and possibly other sanctuaries in the Northern Kingdom. At some later time it was taken into the Jerusalem tradition (vv 28, 30). The communities of the post-exilic period used it as a hymnic supplication for God to deal with Israel and the world powers in terms of his strength and character.

Like the date, the setting of Ps 68 defies precision. The cultic processional briefly described in vv 26–28 suggests a relatedness of some kind to a festival occasion and has been a major component in attempts to define the psalm as a liturgical composition. Other parts of the psalm may reflect other worship contexts. However, at no place is the content specific enough to be definitive.

Which festival? Where? As LePeau (*Psalm 68,* 44) notes (following Gunkel), if interpreters want to explain a text as a liturgy, they must be able to show how it relates to a worship context in some detail. It is not really possible to go beyond generalizations in the case of Ps 68 without becoming highly speculative. A context such as the autumn festival postulated by Gray is a generalized one. Few would doubt the use of such a psalm as 68 at one time or another in the autumn festivals of pre-exilic Israel (assuming that the psalm existed in some form during that time), but this does not necessitate the conclusion that the psalm is a liturgy. The argumentation in the cultic interpretation of psalms suffers from a circular nature in which worship acts and contexts are reconstructed from the texts of the psalms themselves and then used to explain the texts from which they are derived. However, the process can be useful in understanding texts, because worship situations are frequently reflected in their content. Imaginative reconstructions of the cultic contexts (using all external evidence available) frequently enhances exegesis. The literary structure of the psalm may reflect the liturgies of worship, even if they are not fully understood. The basic interpretive approach, however, should be a literary one in which the psalm is understood in terms of its own literary structure and content rather than in terms of a reconstructed cultic context.

Comment

A wish for Yahweh to arise in judgment (68:2–4). The psalm begins with a supplication in the form of a wish that Yahweh (Elohim, in the text) would rise up in a theophanic manifestation of judgment upon his enemies. The passage is probably an adaptation of the ancient so-called Song of the Ark in Num 10:35–36, in which Yahweh is exhorted to arise and let his enemies be scattered. The saying in Num 10 is associated with the movement of the Ark (cf. Ps 132:8), and those who read Ps 68 as a liturgy think in terms of some movement or presence of the Ark in a ritual act at a holy place celebrating the theophanic presence of God. The Ark may have been carried at the head of a procession to the holy place (A. R. Johnson, *Sacral Kingship,* 69; Kraus; A. A. Anderson). Dahood (II, 134) argues that there is no real basis for a direct confrontation of some kind with the Ark and that the theophany is celestial. It is better to say that it is poetic, a literary presentation of a theophany, though it may reflect ritual action in Israelite worship.

The verb קוּם is used rather frequently of God's rising up in judgment (Pss 3:8; 7:7; 9:20; 10:12; 17:13; 44:27; Isa 14:22; 33:10; Jer 2:27; Zeph 3:8; etc.). There are two contrasting results of God's "arising": on the one hand, his enemies are dispersed and flee before him, like smoke blown away by the wind or wax melting before fire; on the other hand, the righteous (see *Comment,* Ps 52:8) will rejoice with jubilation before God (v 4). The image of defeated soldiers, fleeing in a panic-stricken rout, with their strength leaving them like drifting smoke or melting wax, is contrasted with the joyful and stable state of the righteous who exult before the presence of the victorious Divine Warrior.

The enemies are primarily Yahweh's, but, of course, his people and their security are involved. The רְשָׁעִים, "wicked ones," are those who are opposed to the will of God; here they are identified with the enemies of God and those who hate him (for discussion of רְשָׁעִים, see Ps 55:4).

A summons to praise the Rider of the Clouds (64:5–7). The language of this section is in the form of a hymnic summons to praise the name of Yahweh (here in the short form, "Yah"), who as the great Rider of the Clouds is the father of the fatherless and deliverer of the homeless and the prisoners. As discussed in note 5.c. above, MT can be read as "the One who rides through the Wilderness." When read in this way, the figure is that of God who goes forth before his people and leads them through a wilderness experience (as in v 8), or as one who goes forth from his wilderness habitation to the aid of his needy people or to help his king (cf. Deut 33:2–5; Hab 3:2–15). The more likely interpretation (though it is quite possible that the expression deliberately has a double reference) is that of the use of a title of the Canaanite god Baal for Yahweh (note v 34). The psalm affirms that it is not Baal who makes the rain clouds his chariot and rides across the heavens to aid the defenseless, but Yah (Yahweh) (cf. Pss 18:10; 104:3; Deut 33:26; Isa 19:1). The two concepts of Cloud Rider and Wilderness Rider seem likely to be merged here.

Yah (Yahweh) is the one who rides the clouds and protects and defends those who are especially vulnerable (vv 6–7). Orphans, widows, and those without family were subject to oppression in the societies of the ancient world (as they still are). Repeated statements in the OT show Yahweh's special interest in these groups (e.g., Pss 10:13, 17; 145:13–20; 146:9; Isa 1:23; 10:2; Jer 49:11; Hos 14:3; Mal 3:5; Prov 15:25). He is the "father" of those who lack protection and a household (v 7, see note 7.a.; cf. Ps 25:16; on the love of God for his child, see Hos 11:1–4, Ps 103:13; Prov 3:12). He brings prisoners out of their confinement with rejoicing (cf. Ps 107:10–16). The nature of the prisoners is not given. The word אסיר is used of those imprisoned because they are charged with some crime (Gen 39:20, 22) and of prisoners of war or exiles (Pss 69:34; 79:11; Isa 14:13; Zech 9:11–12). The latter meaning seems more appropriate in this context.

The holy dwelling of God (מעון) is the divine heavenly abode (cf. Deut 26:25; Jer 25:30; Zech 2:17; 2 Chr 30:27). However, we need to keep in mind the synergistic relation between earthly and celestial dwelling places of God, especially the temples, which were considered to be places where heaven and earth met (Mowinckel, *Der achtundsechzigste Psalm*, 28–29; LePeau, *Psalm 68*, 87–88; cf. the discussion of Ps 61:2–5). As indicated in note 6.a., it seems more logical to read the בּ in v 6b as "from" rather than "in"; i.e., God rides the clouds through the wilderness, out from his holy abode to help the needy. However, the metaphysical role of the father of the household is also present in vv 6–7. The stubborn, rebellious ones are contrasted in v 7d with those who receive God's aid. The rebellious are left to live in arid wastelands, where life, if it continues at all, must be lived under greatly diminished conditions. Note the paralleling of literary structure in the first two sections of the psalm: descriptive language of the action of God (v 2 and v 5) followed by contrasting results (vv 3–4 and vv 6–7).

The rain-giving God of Israel (68:8–11). V 8 is generalized in language (see *Translation*), but it doubtless alludes to Yahweh going forth to lead his people out of Egypt and through the wilderness. Vv 8–9 are very similar to Judg 5:4–5. Different theories have been advanced to explain the relationship (see LePeau, *Psalm 68*, 96–97). The two accounts may be separate versions of a common tradition. In any case, the differences between the two should be considered intentional. Judg 5:4–5 is much more historical than Ps 68:8, which is more generalized and related to the giving of rain, rather than to victory over enemies as in Judg 5. The "going forth" of God (verb, יצא) before his people is military imagery for the idea of the Divine Warrior leading his army (cf. Judg 4:14; 2 Sam 5:24 // 1 Chr 14:5; Zech 14:3; Pss 44:10; 60:12 = 108:12), there is no reference to a specific battle.

The location of the *selah* at the end of v 8 may represent a usage in accord with the theory of M. D. Goulder (*The Psalms of the Sons of Korah* [Sheffield: JSOT Press, 1982] 102–4), who cites the verb סלל in v 5 as evidence for the meaning "lift up the voice" for *selah*, but with the technical meaning of "cantillation" or "recitative," during which some relevant section of the story alluded to would be recited. In the case of Ps 68:8, some account of the exodus from Egypt, the crossing of the sea, and the leading of Yahweh through the wilderness and on to Sinai (in other words, Exod 1–19) may have been recalled, or told, by those hearing or reciting the psalm. If the ancient Israelites did not, it is appropriate for us to do so.

The phenomenon in v 9 is described in language common to several theophanic accounts in the MT (Exod 19:16–18; 20:18; 1 Kgs 19:11–13; Hab 3:3–12; Mic 1:3–4; Nah 1:3–5; Pss 18:8–16 // 2 Sam 22:9–17; 77:19; 97:1–5; also, Judg 5:4). Storm and earthquake language, with lighting and fire, are used to describe the cosmic impact of the appearance and actions of Yahweh. LePeau (*Psalm 68*, 99) notes that the dripping or pouring of rain from the heavens is very unusual in theophanic accounts. God goes out in this section of the psalm not as in vv 5–7 to be the great Father of the orphans and solitary ones of the world, but to bring abundant rain for his people and his domain (v 10). The Rider of the Clouds and Father of the Fatherless gives victory both celestial and terrestrial over the forces which challenge his purposes and gives refreshing life-bringing rain to his weary land and peoples. In so doing, he sustains his "inheritance" ("domain," see note 10.c.). The result is that his "community" ("flock, family," see note 11.a.) will be settled in his domain, which is prepared for them in his "goodness" (v 11). The טובה, "goodness," surely includes the good rain which Yahweh gives, but it is too restrictive to translate it as "rain," as Dahood does. LePeau (107) points out that טוב can be used with food (Pss 34:11; 104:28; 107:9; Deut 26:11) as well as rain (Deut 28:12; Jer 5:25; Pss 65:12; 85:13; in some of these cases the reference may be wider than rain). The goodness of God is an expression of his comprehensive care for his people and the earth. The "poor" (עני) are sustained by the goodness of Yahweh. The "poor" (humble, dispossessed, without sufficient property for living, those with diminished powers, strength, and worth) refers in 68:11 to the people of Israel (cf. Ps 149:4; Isa 49:13; Ps 72:2), who do not really own the land which has been given to them. Yahweh owns the land, and the Israelites are but sojourners on it (Lev 25:23); Israel has the land by fief (see G. von Rad, *Old Testament Theology*, tr. D. M. G. Stalker [New York: Harper, 1962] I, 25–26; *The Problem of the Hexateuch and Other Essays*, tr. E. W. T. Dicken [Edinburgh: Oliver & Boyd, 1966] 85). "Technically, then they are the landless poor, completely dependent on God" (LePeau, 108). The word עני has the basic meaning of "afflicted" and is used of one who suffers as a victim. The עני is a person in a coerced situation, not in a condition of choice. However, the word should not be restricted to the meaning of "afflicted/ hurt." A range of meanings is attached to the word. S. J. L. Croft (*The Identity of the Individual in the Psalms*. JSOT SS 44 [Sheffield: JSOT Press, 1987], 55) provides a useful chart of the meaning of עני along a horizontal axis:

Afflicted, Destitute, in need = Righteous one, empty metaphor.

By "empty metaphor" he means that the expression has become conventional, without reference to any real need. The עני = righteous person is one who may or may not have severe physical needs but who has accepted the risk of dependence on Yahweh and commitment to his will. In this regard especially, the עני is closely related to the ענוים, "the needy," or "humble folk" (see Ps 69:33). Unlike עני, ענוים tends to refer to those who have chosen their situation, or accepted it as reflecting the divine will. The עני, the "poor one," tends to be alone with a strong sense of separation, but the ענוים are connected with congregations in acts of worship. Of course, the "humble folk" too participate in affliction and hurt. They are in this sense among the ענים ("humble folk"). Obviously, when עני moves to the "righteous" side of the scale of meaning, ענוים and עניים represent the same people.

The Lord's word of victory (68:12–15). This section is plagued with translation difficulties and uncertain meanings. A message from the Lord is cited abruptly in v 12, a message which seems to run through v 15. Its general nature is clear: Yahweh is the victor over kings and their armies. The news to be spread is that the Divine Warrior triumphs. Hostile kings are defeated, and a great number of messengers spread the news. The great Warrior has decreed the defeat of mighty foes, and the exciting and joyful news goes out to all the land. The identity of the messengers is not specified (see note 12.d., and below). The report of the rout of kings and their armies means that the women at home can prepare to celebrate the spoils of battle (v 13). The kings flee like frightened birds fluttering away (cf. use of the verb נדד in Isa 16:2; Jer 4:25; 9:9—or for the tossing about of an insomniac in Job 7:4; Esth 6:1; Gen 31:40).

An alternative interpretation is to understand "the beauty of the house" in v 13 as a figure of speech for Israel, on the basis that the division of spoil was the privilege and work of victorious warriors (Judg 5:30) rather than that of the women back home (so LePeau, *Psalm 68,* 119). Certainly, the term "house" (בית) can be used of the people of God (cf. v 7 above; Jer 12:7; Hos 8:1; 9:15) and נות ("beautiful") is used of the "daughter of Zion," a designation for Israel or Jerusalem (Jer 4:31; Mic 4:8; Lam 1:6; Ps 9:15). However, the reference in Judg 5:30 should not be pushed too far; surely the women anticipate that part of the spoil will be brought home (though not necessarily "a maiden or two for every man"!). Note David's distribution of the spoil from his campaign to his friends and to the elders of Judah in 1 Sam 30:26, and note the reference to women being clothed in scarlet and ornaments of gold from the spoils of Saul's victories in 2 Sam 1:24. The verb חלק should be translated with the meaning of "to share in" (see Keel-Leu and Winter, *Vögel als Boten,* 26–27; BDB, 323, though BDB assigns this meaning to qal, not to piel, as here).

V 14 seems to mean that though the people have behaved like a lazy donkey, "resting between the saddlebags" (cf. the behavior of Reuben in Judg 5:16), the victory has been won by Yahweh. Messenger doves spread the news abroad of

Yahweh-Shaddai's triumph without any real help from his people (cf. 2 Sam 5:24). However, the meaning of the doves in v 14 is uncertain and has been given widely varied interpretations. One of the prominent explanations is that the silver-covered wings of the dove refer to a fine piece of booty left behind by the fleeing kings, perhaps a winged helmet (Gray, *JSS* 22 [1977] 14, A. A. Anderson, Gunkel, Schmidt), or to some sort of bird-like object used in worship, either foreign or Israelite (Kraus, Gray, 14, Isserlin, *PEQ* 103 [1971] 8); possibly a standard of the goddess Astarte, whose symbol was the dove, or simply some *objet d'art* (Durham), or the winged symbol of Yahweh's theophanic cloud over the battlefield (Weiser). Kidner (I, 241) suggests that the reference is to women who preen themselves in new finery as they wait to share the spoil of battle—"peacocking around, as we might have put it." LePeau (*Psalm 68*, 124–25) follows Mowinckel (*Der achtundsechzigste Psalm*, 38–40) and understands the dove as a symbol of Israel, appealing to such references as Hos 7:11 and 11:11 as well as to the turtledove (תּוֹר) used as a symbol of God's people in Ps 74:19, relating this interpretation to the explanation of the "beauty of the house" in v 13 as Israel (see above), who leaves the battlefield with her wings adorned with victory and the wealth of her enemies. Another interpretation is to understand 14bc as a way of describing the luxuriance available to those who will participate in Yahweh's victory. A time of prosperity is at hand when "everything will gleam and glitter with silver and gold" (Delitzsch).

I have followed Eerdmans and Keel-Leu in understanding the doves to be messenger or signal doves released at the end of a victorious battle. The covering of the wings and feathers with silver and gold may be poetic language referring to the natural markings of the birds, whose wings are spangled with beautiful colors which look like silver and gold—though it is not impossible that birds with brightly ornamented wings were released (hardly plated with metal, however). The basis for this interpretation is the use of birds as messengers or signal givers. Eerdmans cites the Egyptian custom of releasing four geese to report the coronation of a king to the four winds of the heavens. His reference to Egyptian usage is worked out and greatly extended by Keel-Leu (*Vögel als Boten*, 109–41). Isserlin and Keel-Leu and Winter (in *Vögel als Boten*, 38–78) have researched extensive evidence of doves and other birds in ancient Near Eastern texts and in iconographic and statuary art in association with messenger functions (cf. Gen 8:6–12; Eccl 10:20). However, we should not think of the doves as carrier pigeons in the modern sense (Keel-Leu and Winter, 91, n. 1; 142). The message was conveyed by the release of the doves itself; those who saw them in flight would know what they meant.

V 15 is another obscure verse (see *Notes*). It is sometimes assumed to have a historical referent to a battle, otherwise unknown, in which the enemy forces were routed by a snowstorm on Mount Zalmon, similar to the hail on the the enemy force at Beth-horon according to Josh 10:11. If v 15b is translated in a comparative sense ("it is like"), the interpretation is usually that of kings and their armies put to flight like snow driven by the wind and spread across the slopes of the mountain, or that the kings and their troops drop their weapons and gear like falling snow as they run. As indicated in note 15.c., Keel-Leu (*Vögel als Boten*, 178) translates the בה with an instrumental sense: "thereby snow fell on

Zalmon." He argues for the snow as a means and manifestation of the divine judgment, relying heavily on Job 38:22–23: "Have you entered the storehouses of the snow, / or have you seen the storehouses of the hail, / which I have reserved for the time of trouble, / for the day of battle and war?" (RSV) (cf. Eccl 39:29; 2 Sam 23:20; Isa 30:30; Ezek 13:13). Snow is one of the natural phenomena used as a weapon by God. I have translated the expression in v 15 in the locative sense rather than in the instrumental, but the meaning is the same. The snow on Zalmon represents the divine intervention of God to destroy kings and their forces when they challenge the divine will and purpose. The verse is metaphorical rather than historical. The similarities between vv 13–14 and Judg 5:16, 30 have stimulated conjectures that Ps 68 reflects the war with the Canaanite kings of Judg 4–5. However, vv 13–15 differ significantly from the Judges account, and the descriptions are general enough to reflect many battle situations (LePeau, *Psalm 68*, 125). Zalmon in v 15 could refer to a hill near Shechem (Judg 9:48) and to a battle fought there in which enemy troops were defeated with the help of a snowstorm. But such a battle is otherwise unknown. Albright (*HUCA* 23 [1950] 23) argues that Zalmon does not refer to the hill near Shechem, because that hill is not over 3000 feet high and almost never has any snow. He (followed by others) prefers as the referent the crags of Jebel Druze (Hauran), in the area of Bashan, some of which are more than 6000 feet high and on which snow usually falls in winter and then rapidly melts on the dark lava slopes. The black basalt crags of the "Dark One/Black Mountain" (which the name "Zalmon" connotes) contrast with the lighter-colored limestone of Lebanon ("White One") as well as with the whiteness of the snow. The remoteness of these mountains from Israel (contrast Judg 4–5) and the lack of specific data encourage the conclusion that we are dealing primarily with poetic imagery rather than historical references (LePeau, *Psalm 68*, 132). Taking his case from Albright's location of Zalmon in Bashan, Keel-Leu argues that v 15 should be linked with vv 16–19 rather than with vv 12–15. However, I prefer to relate the kings of v 15 to the kings of v 13 and treat v 15 as the closing statement of the message which begins with v 13. Admittedly, v 15 is rather loosely related to the context in either case, but, as the ending of the preceding strophe, the verse prepares the reader for the otherwise very abrupt reference to the mountains of Bashan in v 16. V 15 says that Yahweh has already been there and demonstrated his power on the dark slopes of Zalmon. Why should the crags of Bashan think they can challenge his choice of a mountain?

The mountain where God dwells forever (68:16–19). This section is as obscure in details as the preceding. In general, the strophe sets forth the selection of a mountain for Yahweh's abode, which is contrasted with the mighty mountain of God in Bashan. Yahweh has ascended to his mountain habitation with a great entourage as the victorious Divine Warrior. As in the case of Zalmon in v 15, the reference to the mountain of Bashan is probably more literary imagery than geographic referent. However, Mount Hermon may lie behind the imagery, with its 9000 foot height. Bashan was the area where fat cows and strong bulls grew (Deut 32:14; Ezek 39:18; Amos 4:1; Ps 22:13) and was the home of fierce lions (Deut 33:22). It was a symbol of that which was lofty, rich, and powerful (cf. Isa 2:13; Jer 22:20). The mountain is personified and described as jealous with envy of the mountain chosen by God for his abode (v 17). The independent colon in v 17c is surely a key statement in the strophe and the psalm as a whole: "Yahweh will dwell there forever." The enduring dwelling of Yahweh on the mountain of his choice and up which he has ascended in mighty triumph (v 18) is of pivotal importance. The mountain of God is not identified, but in earlier contexts it may have been Mount Tabor (so Mowinckel, *Der achtundsechzigste Psalm*, 42–3, and Kraus) or some similar mountain. In the present psalm, the mountain is Zion in Jerusalem. Cf. Ps 132:13–14:

> For Yahweh has chosen Zion,
> He has desired [אוה] it for his dwelling place [מושב].
> "This is my resting-place [מנוחתי] forever [עדי־עד];
> Here will I dwell [אשב], for I have desired it [אותיה]."

(See notes by Allen, 203, on these verses.) NT readers will be aware of the rather radical reinterpretation of v 19 in Eph 4:8, where it is Christ who ascends on high with captives and *gives* gifts to mankind (see commentaries on Ephesians).

The movement of the great victor to the chosen mountain is described in vv 18–19 as being accompanied by a great host of chariots and warriors, the holy ones of the heavenly host (see *Notes*). The great conqueror leads captives as he goes to the heights (v 17) and receives gifts from all humankind, even from those who rebel at Yahweh's choice of a place on which to settle and reign (with due caution regarding the reading of v 19, see *Notes*). "Sinai" in v 18 is probably a divine epithet (see v 9 above) for God. Its use in this psalm serves to convey the meaning that Yahweh, long associated with Sinai, is not confined to that mountain and has now changed the place of his abode to another mountain, to Zion. Sinai and Zion are merged, or better, perhaps, Sinai has been moved to Zion. "The traditions of Yahweh's theophany, his earth-shattering apparition to man— even to some extent—his revelation of law, have been transferred from Sinai to Zion. In short, Sinai has not been forgotten so much as absorbed" (J. Levenson, *Sinai and Zion* [Minneapolis: Winston Press, 1985] 91). Sinai is wherever the God of Sinai is.

Blessed be Yahweh the great Victor (68:20–24). This strophe begins with blessing of the Lord Yahweh as the God who bears burdens for those worshipers for whom the speaker speaks (v 20). Yahweh as burden-bearer is contrasted sharply with such gods as those of Babylon, which had to be carried on weary beasts and human shoulders (see Isa 46:17; cf. Isa 63:9). Yahweh is also the God of deliverance, even from death (v 21), which means that he provides a way of escape from the threat of death. Perhaps we should capitalize "Death" (so LePeau, *Psalm 68*, 161) to show that it carries the connotation of the Canaanite lord of the underworld, Mot, the chief foe of Baal and his consort Anath in Ugaritic accounts. Mot is the god of "all that lacks life and vitality" (T. H. Gaster, *Thespis*, 125), who leaves the land desolate when he is away from it and spreads death. His habitation is either the deadly areas of sun-scorched desert or the dark, wet, and slimy regions of the netherworld. Of course, the point in Ps 68 is that Yahweh, not Baal, can deal with Mot.

Yahweh is the God who breaks the heads and the hairy skulls of those who are his enemies (v 22). It is possible, but not at all certain, that the hair has been allowed to grow long for sacred war or the keeping of a vow, as in the case of the Nazirites (Num 6:1–21; cf. Judg 5:2) or as a sign of power and vitality, as in the strength of Samson (Judg 13–16). There may be a hint of a demonic being behind the שֵׂעָר if the reader/hearer heard שָׂעִר, "goat/goat demon," or "demon" (Eaton, Albright, *HUCA* 23 [1950] 27, Mowinckel, *Der achtundsechzigste Psalm*, 49). The enemies move about "in their guilt [אשם]" used here (as in Gen 26:10 and Jer 51:5; cf. Prov 14:9) in the general sense of "guilt" or "sins"; this meaning is strengthened by the plural form of the word (only here; GKC, 1240; LePeau, *Psalm 68*, 165).

In v 23, the word "Bashan" is retained in the translation (see note 23.a.), and a contrast is drawn between the mighty, God-like height and strength of the mountains of Bashan and the depths of the sea. The language suggests a cosmic dimension to Yahweh's power. The object in v 23 is not expressed. It could be the Israelites who are dispersed in an area far from home (e.g., Mowinckel, 49–50; Buttenwieser, 257–61; Robinson in Oesterley, 325). However, taking the object as the enemies of Yahweh (v 22), who cannot escape from Yahweh regardless of the remote places to which they may flee, seems to fit the context better. Note the similar ideas in Amos 9:2–4; Ps 139:7–9. The poetic language conveys a sense of the power of God to overcome any foe, cosmic or historical.

V 24a may have the brutal portrayal usually assigned to it of a bloody celebration of vengeance by victors who wash (or "dye red," see note 24.a.) their feet in the blood of the vanquished. The *Translation* shifts the emphasis from such celebration to figurative language for freedom from war and oppression; in this case the imagery is that of stamping the blood of a battlefield off one's feet. V 24b expresses in idiomatic language a judgment on enemies like that imposed on Ahab and Jezebel, whose blood was licked up by dogs after each had been killed (1 Kgs 22:38; 2 Kgs 9:35–37).

Praising God in processions (68:25–28). A brief description of a festal procession into the area of a sanctuary is the subject of these verses. The procession comes into view from the perspective of a narrator, who describes a column of joyful groups. The reference by the narrator to "my king among the holy ones" is most probably a reference to the heavenly king, who comes with his people to worship (for "my king," cf. Ps 5:3; 44:5; 47:7; 74:12; 84:4). The "holy ones" is, of course, a collective reading of a singular word which may mean "holy place" or "in holiness" (see note 25.b.), which is also true for 18d. On the other hand, the "holy ones" may refer to a heavenly entourage of angelic beings and divine warriors (as in v 18), or, more probably, I think, there may be a merger of the heavenly and the earthly. The great king and his heavenly entourage mingle with his people in a triumphant procession.

Some of the major features are described by the narrator in vv 26 and 28. Singers and minstrels move along between girls beating tambourines. Four tribal groups are named (Benjamin, Judah, Zebulun, and Naphtali), led by their chieftains. Why these four tribal groups? Probably, because they embrace all Israel, North and South, with Benjamin being first because of Judg 5:14 and the location of Jerusalem in its borders. However, some interpreters (see *Form/Structure/Setting*) think the psalm reflects a time of Benjaminite hegemony, when there was a central cult place on Mount Tabor, located on the border between

Zebulun and Naphtali (Josh 19:34; cf. Judg 4:6, 10, 12, 14). According to this theory, the addition of Judah resulted from a reworking of the psalm for use in worship in Jerusalem (Mowinckel, *Der achtundsechzigste Psalm*, 54; Kraus, 470). It seems strange, however, for Benjamin to remain as the leader after such a reworking. The emphasis on the "youngest" (note 28.b.) is a more likely explanation, though Benjamin as the source of the first king of Israel (Saul) should not be ignored—paired with Judah the source of David. It is possible that the selection of tribes is representative of the practice of assigning particular tribal groups for special duties in the festivals (Weiser).

V 27 is probably a quotation of what the narrator hears from the singers and leaders of the procession. All who will, but especially the festal participants, are urged to bless God. All Israelites are called upon to celebrate the victorious power of Yahweh God. The picture seems to be that of groups in a solemn procession which appears before a festival congregation assembled in the courts of a temple and who call upon the waiting congregation to join in joyful, even ecstatic, praise of God. The passage reflects festival celebrations of Yahweh's triumphs over foes and hostile powers which threaten his people. The Victor moves in triumphant procession with his rejoicing people.

Prayer for God to demonstrate his strength (68:29–32). The understanding of this strophe is hampered by exegetical problems. However, the prayer language of supplication is clear in vv 29b–31. The prayer is directed to God who has "ordained your strength" (29a). This statement is treated in the *Translation* as a traditional expression (though a rather strange one) on which the following prayer is based. This, of course, may not be correct; the verb can be read as imperative with the versions and a few Hebrew mss (see note 29.a.). In any case, God is implored to manifest his strength from his temple above Jerusalem (v 30). As indicated in note 30.a., the temple can be thought of as the building on the small hill of Zion to the north and above the old city of Jerusalem. On the other hand, the temple may be the heavenly abode of Yahweh, as in v 6. A synergistic merger of thought in which there is no absolute differentiation between the two is probable.

In any case, God is asked to rebuke "the beast of the reed-thicket" and a "herd of bulls" along with the "calf-peoples." Understandably, the referent of these animal metaphors is the subject of diverse opinions. In terms of the primary physical referent, a lion, a crocodile, a hippopotamus, and a water buffalo have been suggested (LePeau, 206–7). In terms of historical and geographic referents, Egypt, Babylon, and Hazor (Gray, *JSS* 22 [1977] 19–20) are among the proposals advanced. Mowinckel (59–61) and Eaton (174) argue that the primary referent is to chaotic powers and demonic gods and their cults, while Kissane and Rogerson and McKay are among those who think the referent is a general one to any foe of warlike strength and a booty-loving character. In terms of historical and geographic reference, Egypt appears to be the most appropriate choice. Egypt is associated with reeds in 2 Kgs 18:21; Isa 19:6; 36:3; Ezek 29:6, and described in terms of a large dragon-like beast, Rahab, in Isa 30:7; Ps 87:4; cf. Isa 51:9. Even if Egypt is the primary referent, the powers of chaos embodied in land and sea monsters lie in the background. The animals embody the forces opposed to Yahweh and the ordered life of his people (cf. Pss 74:12–14; 89:10–11; Amos 9:3; Isa 27:1; Job 40:15–41:34; etc.). The "beast of the reed-thicket" probably should not be given an identity different from that of the "herd of bulls" and the calves, as, for example, by identifying the bulls as Assyria and Babylon (or Persia), with the beast of the reeds as Egypt and the calves as allied states of the great powers (e.g., Briggs, Buttenwieser, 270; Gray thinks that the calves are allies of Hazor, citing Josh 11:10). It is likely that we have the use of animal analogies for human beings, with the bulls representing the leaders and the calves referring to soldiers and the people. The prayer continues with the wish that those who delight in war would be scattered (v 31d) and that envoys would come from Egypt and Cush to pay homage to Yahweh (v 32). Cush is frequently translated as "Ethiopia," but seems to be a rather general term for the territory south of Egypt. LePeau (*Psalm 68*, 218) thinks that Cush is intended here as a figure for "the ends of the earth" and cites Zeph 3:9–10 as another example of such usage. He notes (217) that nowhere else in Psalms does a foreign people give homage and bring tribute to Yahweh. Outside the Psalter, however, this is not the case (see Isa 18:7; 19:18–25; Zech 14:16–19). The lack of other references in the Psalter is probably fortuitous.

A summons to praise the primeval Sky Rider (68:33–36). The kingdoms of the earth are urged to sing God's praise, who is described as having majesty over Israel (35b) and "power in the heavens" (35c). He is the Sky Rider who rides out from his heavenly sanctuary in awesome greatness. His powerful voice thunders forth (34; cf. Ps 29). He is the God of Israel (36b), who also is master of the primeval heavens, the dominator of "the sky that is spread over every land and people" (LePeau, 223). He merits the praise of all peoples and kingdoms of the earth.

The final colon of v 36 serves as a summary statement both for the psalm and for the collection of Pss 65–68 (see *Explanation*).

Explanation

Ps 68 is a psalm which has a steady focus on God and his great acts of powerful deliverance. Durham says that the most important feature of this psalm is

> its emphasis upon the coming and effectiveness of the Presence of God. With a comprehensive array of cross-references and imagery, some of it reminiscent of the Canaanite poetry to which Israel's poets were both stylistic and substantive debtors, the fact of God's movement toward and among men is extolled with great vigor and enthusiasm.

The focus of the psalm on the praise of God is strengthened by at least seven different words for God in its content: יהוה, Yahweh; יה, Yah; אלהים, God; אל God; אדני, Lord; שׁדי, Shaddai; זה סיני, the One of Sinai, which is more than in any other psalm (LePeau, *Psalm 68*, 61). In addition to the names of God, there are several descriptive epithets of God in the psalm: Rider of the Clouds (v 5), Sky Rider (v 34); Father of the Fatherless and Defender of Widows (v 6); God of Our Salvation (v 20); God of Deliverance (v 21); the God of Israel (v 36). The double name, יה אלהים, Yah-God, is used in v 19.

The "disconnectedness" of the psalm (see *Form/Structure/Setting*) is transformed into a "connectedness" by its concentration on God and his praise. Each strophe has as its subject some aspect of the presence and work of God, as LePeau has demonstrated by giving titles to each strophe of the psalm which include God in every case, plus some concept related to God. I have attempted to follow a similar process:

> Let God arise in judgment, vv 2–4
> Praise the Rider of the Clouds, vv 5–7
> The rain-giving God of Israel, vv 8–11
> The Lord's word of victory, vv 12–15
> The mountain where God dwells forever, vv 16–19
> The great Victor, vv 20–24
> Praising God in processions, vv 25–28
> Show your strength, O God! vv 29–32
> Praise the primeval Sky Rider, vv 33–36

All sections focus on God and divine action.

As noted in the *Comment* the "Blessed be God" at the end of v 36 both closes the psalm and the collection of שׁיר-psalms in 65–68. It also is a good summary statement of the thrust of all these psalms, especially 68. G. H. Wilson (*The Editing of the Hebrew Psalter*, SBL Diss Series 76 [Chico, CA: Scholars Press, 1985], 160–63) has argued for a grouping of Pss 62–68, noting that all of them, except 66 and 67, have "Davidic" in their titles; all except 63 have "for the leader," and all have "psalm." Wilson argues that there is a binding of Pss 65–68 by the use of the term "song" (שׁיר), which reflects a thematic unit (164, "a closely related unit of praise") and also incorporates the non-Davidic 66 and 67 into the unit. This binding operation is also strengthened by the concentration of Pss 66 and 67 on God and the effective use of the verb ברך ("bless") in 66, 67, and 68 (especially strong in 67). The "Blessed be God" at the end of 68 further binds the unit together (cf. Wilson, 190–91). In my opinion, Wilson should have included Ps 61 with 62–68. The psalm title of 61 shares "Davidic" and "psalm" (מזמור) with Pss 62–68. Since Ps 60 belongs to the *miktam* collection of Pss 56–60 (see *Comment* on 56:1), 61 is left isolated if 62–68 are defined as a unit. If Ps 61 is linked to Pss 62–68, the unit can be divided into two subunits. The first consists of 61–64, which fall into an ABBA arrangement of lament (61)—trust/confidence (62)—trust/confidence (63)—lament (64). The second subunit consists of the praise-wish psalms of 65–68. This unit is followed by the laments in 69 and 70–71, which close a Davidic collection that begins with Ps 51 (Wilson, 163).

LePeau (*Psalm 68,* 244–48) has called attention to a movement in the psalm relating to its focus on God. In the first half of the psalm (vv 2–17), there is an emphasis on God's "arising" and his mobility as he goes forth to scatter enemies and to set right what is out of order in human society. Throughout this section, God is appealed to as active and victorious in cosmic and historical endeavors. There is a transition in vv 16–19 as the emphasis falls upon God's choice of a dwelling place and his abiding there always. "The first half of the psalm thus concludes with a shift in thought from mobility to stability" (LePeau, 247). The pivotal expression is found in v 17c: "Yahweh will dwell there forever." This first use of *Yahweh,* which occurs only twice in the psalm (also in v 21; *Yah* is in v 5), serves to emphasize the transition and clearly to identify the God in both halves of the psalm as the same. LePeau (247–48) points out that all movement in the second half of the psalm is around, out of, or toward the divine residence. Yahweh victoriously ascends to the heights of his chosen mountain and receives gifts from mankind (vv 18–19). He brings back his foes from wherever they may flee (v 23) and in triumphal procession marches to the divine abode to celebrate in the midst of praise and prayer (vv 25–32). The God of Sinai, rejecting the mountains of Bashan, has made Mount Zion his dwelling place, and the kingdoms of the earth are exhorted to praise him with tribute and homage.

In the second half of the psalm, attention is consistently directed toward God's actions in relationship to his dwelling place. Theologically, the first part of the psalm expresses the divine presence in the form of the "coming God" (see W. Brueggemann, "Presence of God, Cultic," *IDBSup*, 680), who arises and comes forth as the theophanic victor. The "coming God" is "the one who comes, unexpectedly and irresistibly, and when he comes, the situation is decisively changed" (ibid.). The "coming God" is also the God who leads his people as he strides out into time and history (v 8). The second major manifestation of God's presence is that of the "abiding God" (ibid., 681), who dwells among his people and/or in his temple on his chosen mountain. He acts from his holy place, and human action is directed toward the holy place and the divine presence: "Bless God in the assemblies. . . . Show your strength . . . from your temple, O God" (v 27, 29, 30). These two aspects of the divine presence are emphasized in the central verses of the psalm by the use of the name Yahweh in v 17, associated with his abiding, and in v 21, associated with "deliverance," especially from death. The Coming God and the Abiding God are one, both are united in Yahweh, who is twice identified as the God of Israel (in v 9 as אלהי ישראל and in v 36 as אל ישראל)—which provides another connecting link in the psalm, bringing together the God of Sinai in vv 2–18 and the God of Zion/Jerusalem in vv 19–36. Blessed be God, who both comes and abides!

Hide Not Your Face from Your Servant   *(69:1–37)*

Bibliography

Allen, L. C. "The Value of Rhetorical Criticism in Psalm 69." *JBL* 105 (1986) 577–98. **Barre, M. L.** "The Formulaic Pair חסד (ו) טוב in the Psalter." *ZAW* 98 (1986) 100–5. **Becker, J.** *Israel deutet seine Psalmen.* 45–48. **Johnson, A. R.** *The Cultic Prophet and Israel's Psalmody (CPIP).* 386–96. **Lindars, B.** *New Testament Apologetic.* London: SCM Press, 1961. 98–108. **Michel, D.** *Tempora und Satzstellung in den Psalmen.* 19–21. **Mowinckel, S.** "The Verb *sîaḥ* and the Nouns *šîʰh, siha.*" *ST* 15 (1961) 1–10. **Seybold, K.** *Das Gebet.* 133–37. **Vogt, E.** "'Ihr Tisch werde zur Falle' (Ps. 69.23.)." *Bib* 43 (1962) 79–82.

Translation

1	For the leader;[a] according to *shoshanim;*[b] Davidic.[c]	
2 (1)	*Save me, O, God!*	(2+3)
	The water is already up to my neck.[a]	
3 (2)	*I am sinking in a deep swamp—*	(3+2+3+2)
	and there is no foothold.	
	I have reached the watery depths,	
	and a flood engulfs me.	

4 (3) *I am weary from calling out;*   (2+2+2+2)
    my throat is dry,
    *my eyes are failing*ᵃ —
    *from waiting*ᵇ *for God.*

5 (4)   *Those who hate me are more numerous than the hairs of my head;* (4+4+4)
    *my mendacious foes, who would destroy*ᵃ *me, are so many*
    *that*ᵇ *I am forced to restore what I did not steal.*ᶜ

6 (5) *O God, you know my folly;*   (4+3)
    my guilty deeds are not hidden from you.

7 (6) *Let none of those who wait for you be put to shame through me,*   (3+3+3+2)
    *O Lord,*ᵃ *Yahweh of Hosts;*ᵇ
    let none of those who seek you be humiliated through me,
    O God of Israel!

8 (7) *On your account*ᵃ *I endure reproach;*   (3+3)
    humiliation covers my face.

9 (8) *I have become a stranger to my brothers,*   (3+3)
    *and an alien to my mother's children.*ᵃ

10 (9) *On account of zeal for your house I am consumed,*   (3+4)
    and the reproach of those who reproach you has fallen on me.

11 (10) *Even when I wept in fasting,*ᵃ   (3+3)
    there was reproach for me.

12 (11) *And when I put on sackcloth as my clothing,*   (3+3)
    I became a byword for them.

13 (12) *Those who sit in the gate talk about me,*ᵃ   (3+3)
    *and the drunkards' songs are about me.*ᵇ

14 (13) *But I*ᵃ—*my prayer is to you,*   (2+2+2+3)
    *O, Yahweh, for a time of favor;*ᵇ
    O, God, in your great loyal-love,
    answer me with your sure salvation.

15 (14) *Rescue me from the mire; do not let me sink—*   (3+3)
    *let me be delivered from those who hate me,*ᵃ
    *even*ᵇ *from watery depths.*

16 (15) *Let not the flood of waters engulf me;*   (3+2+3)
    let not the depths swallow me up;
    let not the pit close its mouth over me.

17 (16) *Answer me, O Yahweh, because your loyal-love is good;*ᵃ   (4+4)
    according to your great mercy, turn to me.

18 (17) *Hide not your face from your servant;*   (3+3)
    *because of my distress,*ᵃ *answer me quickly!*ᵇ

19 (18) *Come near to my soul—redeem it!*   (3+3)
    On account of my enemies, ransom me.

20 (19) *You know my reproach—*   (3+2+2)
    *(you know) my shame and my humiliation;*ᵃ
    *all my foes are before you.*ᵇ

21 (20) *Reproach—*   (1+3+3+3+2)
    *it has broken my heart and I am sick (with misery).*ᵃ
    I expected compassion, but there was none,
    and comforters, but I found none.

22 (21)   *Instead,*[a] *they put poison in my food,*   (3+3)
            and for my thirst, they gave me vinegar to drink.

23 (22)   *May their table (set) before them become a trap;*   (3+2)
            a snare for their good friends.[a]

24 (23)   *May their eyes be darkened so they cannot see,*   (3+3)
            and make their loins tremble continually.

25 (24)   *Pour out your wrath on them,*   (3+3)
            and let your fierce anger overtake them.

26 (25)   *Let their encampments*[a] *become desolate,*   (3+3)
            and let no one dwell in their tents.

27 (26)   *As for you*[a]—*they hound whomever you strike;*   (3+3)
            and talk about[b] *the pain of those you wound.*[c]

28 (27)   *Add guilt to their guilt,*[a]   (3+3)
            and do not let them come into your righteousness.[b]

29 (28)   *May they be blotted out of the scroll of the living,*   (3+3)
            and not be recorded with the righteous.

30 (29)   *But I*[a]—*lowly and in pain*—   (3+3)
            defend me[b] *with your saving works, O God.*

31 (30)   *I will praise God's name*[a] *in song,*   (3+3)
            and magnify it with thanksgiving;

32 (31)   *that will please Yahweh more than an ox,*   (3+2)
            (more than) a bull with horns and hoofs.[a]

33 (32)   *Look!*[a] *The humble folk will rejoice;*   (3+2+2)
            those who seek God[b]—
            so let your hearts revive![c]

34 (33)   *For Yahweh hears*[a] *the needy,*   (3+3)
            and he does not despise prisoners who belong to him.[b]

35 (34)   *Let the heavens and the earth praise him;*   (3+3)
            the seas and all that move in them.

36 (35)   *For God will save Zion,*   (3+3+3)
            and build the towns of Judah;
            (his servants)[a] *will live there and possess it,*

37 (36)   *and the offspring of his servants will inherit it,*   (3+3)
            and those who love his name will dwell in it.

Notes

1.a. See n. 51:1.a.
1.b. The word is usually translated as "Lilies." It appears to be a musical term of uncertain meaning, probably the name of a tune or musical arrangement. See Pss 45:1; 60:1; 80:1.
1.c. See n. 51:1.b.
2.a. MT lacks the suffix, which is found in LXX.
4.a. From weeping; cf. Lam 2:11; Ps 119:28, 123.
4.b. MT has piel participle (cf. 31:25). LXX and Targum indicate a preposition plus infinitive, מיחל, "from hoping/expecting for my God," which is easier.
5.a. Lit. "they are mighty, my silencers/exterminators, my enemies, a lie." The translation above assumes a construct chain with interposed pronominal suffixes (cf. Dahood, I, 110; II, 157; GKC, 128d; 131r), rejecting the long-standing emendations to מִצַּמָּתִי, "than my locks of hair," or to מֵעַצְמוֹתָי, "than my bones" (with Syriac), though the parallelism is made smoother by these changes.

5.b. Reading the relative as indicating result in this case, a usage of אֲשֶׁר which does occur, but not commonly. The אָז, which is usually "then," here either has the force of "now" or is used emphatically. Dahood gives it the force of a demonstrative pronoun: "This."

5.c. Lit. "that which I stole not I must give back." Cf. Pss 40:8; 119:6, 92, for אָז in logical sequence (Briggs, BDB, 23). However, the statement may be a proverbial one, and a translation as a question may be in order; e.g., rsv, "What I did not steal must I now restore?" (see also, nab, njv). If this is the case, the speaker would be saying, "Is it right for this proverb to apply to me?" LXX reads as a temporal sequence, "Then I restored that which I took not away," followed by kjv. J. H. Eaton (*Psalms,* 175) reads the verb גָּזַל, "steal," as meaning "plunder," or "taken by plunder," in keeping with the interpretation of the speaker as a king. LXX has ἁρπάζω, "snatch away/seize/plunder" rather than κλέπτω, "steal/filch/purloin." For גָּזַל in the sense of "seize/plunder," see Gen 21:25; Judg 21:23; Mic 2:2.

7.a. Lord" (אֲדֹנָי) is lacking in some LXX mss, which brings the expression into harmony with "God of Israel."

7.b. On "Yahweh of Hosts, see Pss 59:6; 84:2, 4, 9, 13.

8.a. Cf. Ps 44:23, and note the Ugar. usage cited by Dahood.

9.a. Lit. "sons." The expression may mean a closer family relationship than that carried by "my brothers" (see Ps 50:20), since "brothers" may indicate kinship in a wider communal/tribal/people sense (cf. Gen 31:43; 47:1; Exod 2:11; 4:18; etc.). If this is the case, "children of my mother" means uterine siblings (see H. Ringgren, *TDOT,* I, 188–93). Dahood (I, 309–10) suggests, however, that the expression may be only a "poetic cliche."

11.a. MT, lit. reads, "and I weep/wept/will weep in/with the fasting." For the use of the verb בכה "weep," cf. Pss 78:64 (Job 27:15); 126:6; 137:1. The LXX has καὶ συνέκαμψα "and I bowed down," which could indicate וָאֶדְכֶה, from דכה, "crush/broken," or וָאֶכְפֶּה (וָאֶכֹּף) from כפה, "subdue/put down" (cf. Isa 58:5; Mic 6:6), or וָאֶעֱנֶה, from ענה, "humble/mutilate," or וָאֶכֶּה or וָאַךְ from נכה "smite/beat" (*HOTTP,* 299–300; 4QPsᵃ). Dahood proposes to repoint MT to וָאֶבְּכָה from נבך, which is supposed to be a dialectal variant of נפך, "pour/gush forth," and translates as "so I poured out my soul while fasting." If MT is retained, it is possible that "my soul" forms a second subject of the verb (Delitzsch, Briggs, Perowne). "I wept in fasting, my soul (wept)," probably equal to "and my very soul wept in fasting." Another option would be to take "my soul" as the object of the verb: "I wept for my soul (for myself)" (so L. Allen, *JBL* 105 [1986] 594, n. 77, following A. R. Johnson, *CPIP,* 388, n. 2, with Ezek 8:14, and repointing to piel [which is not really necessary since qal appears with objects; e.g., Gen 37:35; Judg 11:37, 38]). The "even when" is an attempt to reflect the *waw*-consecutives of the verbs.

13.a. The verb שִׂיחַ has the force of "complain" in several contexts (77:7; 105:2 = 1 Chr 16:9; Prov 6:22; and nouns in 1 Sam 1:16; Job 7:13; 9:27; 23:2; Ps 55:3). S. Mowinckel (*ST* 15 [1961] 1–10; cf. Allen, *Psalms 101–150,* 9, n.1.b.) has argued that the word does not mean "talk about" or "complain" in any of its contexts, but always means "to meditate on/to muse on," denoting inward, mental concentration on a matter or on a person. Mowinckel is correct to emphasize the element of mental concentration, but he goes too far when he denies all aspects of speaking or talking to for שִׂיחַ. It is true that the word does not apply to mere conversation; it denotes talk which results from intense mental and/or emotional concern. In a few contexts this may be properly expressed by the English "complain." The meaning in 69:13 is pejorative (cf. 2 Kgs 9:11) and "complain" or "talk about" is surely better than "meditate on." Mowinckel meets the problem in this verse by emending וּנְגִינוֹת ("and songs") to וַנֵגְנוּ בִי, "and they (the drunkards) sing about me," which gives the second colon of the verse a verb and frees it from dependence on יָשִׂיחוּ. An argument is usually pushed too far when such emendations are necessary to support it.

13.b. The verb in the first colon serves for the second also: "the songs of the drunkards talk about me."

14.a. For this construction see n. 27.a; also n. 30.a.

14.b. kjv and rsv adopt the interpretation of a prayer "in" or "at" a time of favor for the syntactically difficult עֵת רָצוֹן. But it seems more probable in the context that the meaning is a request "for" a time of favor/acceptance, when the prayer will be heard and God will respond to the suppliant's needs (cf. Isa 49:8; 58:5; 61:2; Pss 19:15[14]; 51:20[18]).

15.a. Some commentators consider "those who hate/reject me" to be unsuitable. However, the reference to foes may be deliberate in order to emphasize the nature of the metaphors used. Allen (*JBL* 105 [1986] 583) argues that MT is supported by the correspondent שֹׂנְאָי ("my haters/those who hate me") in v 5, and he also cites the frequent use of the hiphil הִצִּיל (נצל) in the sense of separation from enemies or trouble. Note the אנצלה ("I want to be delivered/let me be delivered") in the second colon, which sets up an action-request (factitive-passive) sequence, found fairly frequently in Heb. and Ugar. poetry (see M. Held, "The Action-Result (Factitive-Passive Sequence)," *JBL* 84 [1965] 272–82). This sequence also supports the equation of the "mire" with "those who hate me."

15.b. Reading the *waw* as an explanatory conjunctive (GKC, 154a), which emphasizes the "deep waters," corresponding to the "watery depths" in v 3.

17.a. Retaining MT. Some interpreters change כי־טוב to כטוב ("according to the goodness of your loyal-love") to make a smoother parallel with כרב רחמיך ("according to your abundant mercies"). The כי־טוב is possibly due to a failure to recognize טוב and חסד functioning as a formulaic word-pair and as a hendiadys without a conjunction (see Barre, *ZAW* 98 [1986] 103–5). If this is this case, the translation could be "according to your good loyal-love." However, Allen (*JBL* 105 [1986] 583) retains MT on the basis of 109:21 and the chiasmus in vv 17–18: "Answer me . . . —because your love is good/because of my distress—answer me." Vv 17b and 18a form corresponding elements.

18.a. The כי־צר־לי is as in 31:10. Usually צר is followed by ב (cf. Pss 18:7; 59:17; 66:14; 102:3; 106:44; 107:6, 13, 19, 28). Lit. "for distress is mine."

18.b. מהר functions as an adverb, even though it precedes the verb. See Allen, *JBL* 105 [1986] 589, n. 52.

20.a. Lit. "my scorn/reproach and my shame." The transfer of these two nouns to follow v 21a is rather frequently suggested, e.g. Kraus, NEB) so that it reads: "Scorn has broken my heart, / I am sick (because) of my shame and humiliation." This would leave v 20 as "You know my reproach, / before you (stand) all my foes." This transposition is defended by Allen (583) on the basis of structural parallelism with v 6, and also because v 6 would indicate only one noun in v 20. He argues that internal coherence is achieved for v 20 and a logical development results for vv 20–22, with v 20 as a heading which broaches the topic of humiliation (or reproach) in 20a and adversaries in 20b. The first is developed in v 21 and the second in v 22. However, the logical development of vv 20–22 is not negated by the retention of "my shame and my humiliation" in v 20, and the parallelism with v 6 need not be so exact. The translation above assumes that the verb in the first colon serves also for the second—a not uncommon occurrence. Transposition is unnecessary.

20.b. Some scholars follow the Syriac texts and read נגדך without the suffix (see *BHS*): "and my shame and humiliation are before [נגד] all my foes." The main point in the verse, however, is that Yahweh knows the suppliant's condition—not what the foes know. Some commentators (e.g., A. A. Anderson, I, 505) propose to read "all my foes" after the verb ואנושה in v 21, leaving v 20 as "You know my reproach, / and my shame and humiliation are before you." V 21 becomes: "Reproach has broken my heart; / I am in despair/sick (because of) all my foes." However, this disturbs the logical development of vv 20–22 (see n. 20.a.).

21.a. The verb is a qal cohortative form of נוש and appears only here. BDB, 633, gives the meaning as "be sick." LXX ταλαιπωρίαν ("hardship/misery") may indicate a qal fem. participle from אנש, "be weak/sick" (cf. Jer 15:18; Mic 1:9; see Briggs), and unpointed MT could be read as such. Dahood argues for a noun form from אנש, which he translates as "disease," but this necessitates too many changes in the colon. The חרפה ("reproach") at the beginning of this verse is an anacrusis.

22.a. Reflecting the *waw*-consecutive on the verb.

23.a. The plural of שלום appears elsewhere only in Jer 13:19, and with suffix in Ps 55:21 (see n. 55.21.a.), and as such the meaning would be "those at peace/secure." The plural in these references has been considered uncertain (BDB, Briggs, Gunkel, et al.). The Greek texts point toward ולשלומים > שלום, masc. noun, "recompense/vengeance/bribe/retribution" (cf. Mic 7:3; Hos 9:7; Isa 34:8). Syriac probably indicates ושלומם, "and their recompense/bribe/rewards." The Targum points to ושלמיהם > שלם, "fellowship sacrifice/peace offering." Dahood (I, 42–43; II, 162) repoints to qal passive participle pl. לשלומים > שלם, "to make a covenant/be in a covenant" = "those in covenant/covenanted ones/allies," which he interprets as the table companions in this context (cf. 41:10); Craigie (318–19) translates גם־איש שלומי in 41:10 as "even my good friend" (lit. "man of my peace"), who is a dining companion. Dahood treats the ל as emphatic: "even their [table] companions a snare." RSV follows the lead of the Targum and translates "their sacrificial feasts." KJV follows Calvin in assuming the omission of the relative and understanding שלומים in the sense of "welfare, prosperity": "And that which should have been for their welfare, let it become a trap."

26.a. For this meaning, see Num 31:10; Ezek 25:4; 1 Chr 6:39. The word (טירה) apparently designated a row of stones used to mark off encampments. However, in its developed usage its pl. form probably means "settlements" (so NEB; NIV has "their place").

27.a. The sing., emphatic כי־אתה ("you") is difficult: "For you, whom you have smitten." Frequently the versions are followed and the אתה is read as את, the sign of the accusative (see *BHS*): "For they hound/pursue whomever you strike." Dahood proposes אֹתוֹה, the sign of the accusative plus a 3rd pers. masc. sing. suffix, written as וה־: "they persecuted the one you smote." The translation above treats the emphatic אתה as an anacoluthon (cf. v 30).

27.b. The change of יספרו, "they talk about" to יוסיפו or יספו > יסף ("add to"), or יספיו > ספה ("add to/increase"), is supported by LXX and Syriac (see *BHS*). Allen (*JBL* 105 [1986] 583) defends the emendation on the grounds of a "blatant failure" of MT's יספרו to align with מספר in v 29, assuming a chiastic arrangement in vv 27–30. However, I fail to see why the chiastic parallelism of these verses requires such exact parallelism or how the emendation improves it. In fact, there seems to be a play on the words ספר, "talk/recount," and מספר, "scroll / book." Also, cf. v 13.

27.c. Syriac has "the wounded one" and a Heb. ms has "your wounded one" (see *BHS*), but MT may be retained unless we assume that the speaker is the only reference. Becker (*Israel deutet seine Psalmen*, 47), followed by Seybold (*Das Gebet*, 133, n. 4) argues that an original sing. was changed to pl. to agree with v 34 when vv 34–37 were added to an earlier form of the psalm found in vv 2–33.

28.a. Lit., "give iniquity onto their iniquity" = "reckon to them yet more guilt than they now have" (Gunkel). "Instead of taking away their iniquities by forgiveness, let one iniquity accumulate upon another" (Kirkpatrick).

28.b. "Your righteousness" refers to the saving work of God. See *Comment* on 52:8. JB has "strike them off the roll of the virtuous!" NEB has "exclude them from thy righteous mercy," which is better than RSV, "may they have no acquittal from thee."

30.a. The emphatic "I" is retained; cf. v 27.

30.b. Rendering the verse as expressing a prayer (see Allen, *JBL* 105 [1986] 582, reading the verb as jussive, KJV, RSV, NIV, NAB, NEB). The emphatic "I," with the conjunction, at the beginning of the verse could mark a shift of mood to confidence, which is found in the following verses; so LXX, and, e.g., Delitzsch, Perowne, Kirkpatrick, Kissane, NJV. However, vv 27–30 seem to form a unit in the psalm, and the תשׁגבני ("defend one") in v 30 may form an inclusion with the אל־תשׁטפני ("let not engulf me") in v 16 (see Allen, 582). Johnson (*CPIP*, 392, n. 7; 177, 190; see Pss 20:2; 91:14) has demonstrated that the verb שׂגב ("set on high/exalt") can mean "to defend/come to the defense of/protect."

31.a. LXX[L] and Targum indicate "the name of my God."

32.a. MT has the verse as only one statement without parallelism: "and better for Yahweh than an ox-bullock, horned, hoofed." Some mss and versions (see *BHS*) have the conjunction, "horned and hoofed" (see KJV, Buttenwieser, Cohen). Most modern translators assume two parallel colons, with the "more than" carried over to the second. The hiphil participle of פרס is used elsewhere of "dividing the hoof" (e.g., Deut 14:6–8; Lev 11:3, 7, 26), but is usually read here as the denominative of פרסה, noun fem., "hoof" (BDB, 828; Briggs): "hoofed." However, there appears to be no reason to avoid reading "with divided/cloven hoofs," cf. Lev 11:3. The point is that the animal is ritually clean and acceptable for sacrifice. The horns indicate that the animal is grown, probably three years old (cf. Gen 15:9; 1 Sam 1:24; Isa 15:5; Jer 48:34), a more valuable animal than a young one and suitable for sacrifice. Cf. P. K. McCarter, Jr., *1 Samuel*, AB 8, 63.

33.a. MT v 33 reads lit.: " They have seen/see/will see, poor/humble ones will rejoice; seekers after God, and let your heart rejoice." The *Translation* follows the fairly frequently suggested change of the perfect רָאוּ to imperative רְאוּ, read in the sense of "Behold/Look" proposed by Dahood (on Ps 68:35) and Johnson (*CPIP*, 394). Another treatment of ראו as imperative is reflected in NEB (also, Gunkel, Kraus): "See and rejoice, you humble folk." The perfect may be retained if it is read as precative/optative, "Let the poor see." However, the problem of an object of the verb remains. What do the poor see? God's work of deliverance must be assumed. A few mss and LXX have imperfect, jussive, יִרְאוּ, "let the poor see (and) rejoice" (cf. *BHS*, RSV).

33.b. LXX indicates an imperative, דִּרְשׁוּ, "seek God, and you shall live." Cf. Amos 5:4.

33.c. The expression "let your heart live" is equivalent to " Take heart," or "do not lose heart"; cf. Ps 22:27. The *waw* on the verb may be for emphasis in this case. Johnson (*CPIP*, 394) translates the verse as follows:

> Look, ye that are humble;
> Let those who are seeking God be glad.
> Yea, let none of you lose heart!

34.a. LXX and Jerome (followed by some commentators) may indicate a perfect, שָׁמֵעַ, for the participle, שֹׁמֵעַ. The change is not necessary (cf. Delitzsch, Gunkel).

34.b. Lit., "his prisoners." Cf. Pss 68:7(6); 79:11; 107:10–16; 102:21; 146:7; Zech 9:11–12; 22:25. BHS follows some commentators (e.g., Oesterley; cf. Gunkel) and suggests חֲסִידָיו, ("his godly/loyal ones") for אֲסִירָיו, ("his prisoners").

36.a. Lit., "they will dwell there." The subject is "his servants" in v 37. NEB reverses the order of the clauses in 36c and 37a in order to put the subject "his servant's children" (lit., "seed of his servants") with the verb in 36c.

Form/Structure/Setting

This psalm is easily recognized as having elements characteristic of individual laments, in which a speaker sets forth to God complaints about adverse situations and sufferings, along with strong petitions for divine action to relieve the distress. The speaker prays about a situation in which he/she is desperately in need of help before sinking into the oblivion of the deep waters of the netherworld. As in other individual laments, the speaker has been falsely attacked by foes. Family (v 9) and community (v 13) have turned against the suppliant, who claims to be a faithful servant of God (vv 8, 18), and whose piety (vv 11–12) and zeal for the temple (v 10) have been rejected and made matters of reproach and scorn (vv 11, 13). The status of the speaker is so Job-like (cf. Job 19) that it has become the talk of those in the gate and the subject of drunkards' songs.

The prayer of the suffering servant in this psalm involves fierce petitions regarding enemies in vv 23–29, petitions which end with the request that those who have so badly mistreated the speaker will be blotted out of the scroll of the living and not be recorded with the righteous (v 29). This is followed, however, by a section with a changed mood. The speaker expresses confidence in God and encourages other oppressed and depressed people to do the same. V 34 seems to be a key verse: "For Yahweh hears the needy / and he does not despise prisoners who belong to him." The last two verses of the psalm expresses confidence that God will save Zion, rebuild the cities of Judah, and reestablish the community of the offspring of his servants who dwell there.

The determination of the exact context intended for the suppliant in the psalm is very elusive: ". . . it is not concrete enough for us to grasp clearly the worshipper's historical situation and personal circumstances" (Weiser, 493). Vv 36–37 seem to presuppose an exilic situation after the destruction of Jerusalem in 587 B.C.E. However, v 10 may be understood as an indication that the temple of the pre-exilic period is still in existence. On the other hand, v 10 may be read as referring to one who was zealous to rebuild the temple (cf. Haggai and Zechariah) after 539 B.C.E., or else the expression "your house" here does not refer to the temple but to the "Household of Faith" or is used in some such wider sense (see Anderson; Johnson, CPIP, 389). The conflict which the speaker's zeal and piety seem to have provoked could refer to some reform effort in pre-exilic Israel, or to the period of rebuilding the temple in the early years of the return from exile in Babylonia (cf. Schmidt, Kraus), or later during the period of Ezra and Nehemiah (e.g., Briggs, Gunkel), or even in the period of party strife in Judaism reaching down to the Maccabean revolt in the second century B.C.E. (e.g., Oesterley). If the main part of the psalm is pre-exilic, vv 36–37 may be a post-exilic addition to adapt the psalm to conditions of that time (cf. Ps 51:20–21[18–19]). This conclusion may gain some support by the independent nature of vv 36–37, though they have been integrated with vv 31–35 by some stylistic features (see below). Vv 31–35 form a unit without the necessity of having vv 36–37.

L. Allen (*JBL* 105 [1986] 577–98) has addressed at some length the matter of the literary structure of this psalm. He recognizes that the mood and language of vv 31–37 sets these verses apart from vv 2–30, arguing that v 30 belongs with vv 27–29 to form a unit (see note 30.b.). He finds a balance between vv 2–14ab and vv 14c–30 in the first part of the psalm. Finding the division of v 14 into metrical colons to be difficult (accepting two bicolons of 3+2), he concludes that v 14 is the transition verse between v 2 and v 30 and divides it between the sections. The part of v 14 which begins with "O God" (אלהים) begins the second section of the psalm (note the use of Elohim in vv 2 and 6). The division of vv 2–30 at v 14 results in two sections of almost the same length. Further, there is a doubling arrangement of parallel elements in vv 2–14ab and vv 14cd–30. Allen (579) notes the following (modified):

vv 2–14ab		*vv 14cd–30*	
v 2	Save me	v 14d	your salvation
	waters	v 15	do not let me sink
v 3	I am sinking . . .		deliver . . . from waters depths
	watery depths	v 16	let not engulf me
	sinking in deep mire		flood
	flood		waters
	engulfs me		depths
v 5	those who hate me	v 15	those who hate me
	my foes	v 19	my foes
v 6	you know	v 20	you know
v 7	be put to shame		
	be humiliated		my reproach
v 8	reproach		my shame
	humiliation		my humiliation
v 10	reproach of those		
	who reproach you	v 21	reproach
v 11	reproach		
v 12	and I put on	v 22	they put
v 14a	but I	v 30	but I

These parallels (which are more evident in Hebrew) are sufficient to show the presence of roughly parallel and complementary sections in vv 2–30.

Allen (586) further divides the two main sections in vv 2–30 into two smaller units in each case:

vv 2–14ab		*vv 14cd–30*	
vv	2–5	vv	14cd–19
vv	6–14ab	vv	20–30

The section found in vv 31–37 divides into vv 31–34 and vv 35–37. A parallelistic arrangement of sections in vv 3–14b and vv 20–29 is possible as follows:

vv	3–5	A	vv	20–22	B'
vv	6–9	B	vv	23–26	A'
vv	10–14b	C	vv	27–29	C'

V 2 corresponds to v 30 to form an inclusion. Of course, vv 14cd–19 are left out of this scheme, interrupting the "reproach" material in vv 10–13, which is resumed in vv 20–22. Vv 14cd–19 form a subunit in the A X B literary insertion pattern (for this pattern see Allen, *JBL* 105 [1986] 533, n. 25; D. T. Tsumura, "Literary Insertion [A X B Pattern] in Biblical Hebrew," *VT* 33 [1983] 468–82; G. Braulik, "Aufbrechen von gepragten Wortbindungen und Zusammenfassen von stereotypen Ausdrucken in der alttestamentlichen Kunstprosa," *Sem* 1 (1970) 7–11, who works with verses in Deut 4:9, 15, 20–23, 30, 37).

Allen's division of the psalm represents a perceptive and skilled analysis. I have followed it in part in the *Comment* section below. Allen (585) argues that rhetorical analysis of this psalm establishes "a pervading structure" which "points to the integrity of the psalm." He concludes that while the literary integrity of the psalm cannot be proved, "the stylistic factors support it and suggest that evidence adduced to disprove it must be of a compelling nature to succeed." He offers further support for the validity of his literary analysis by observing the strong stylistic similarities between it and Ps 102 (591–95). The two psalms have a similar threefold structure and a good number of stylistic and terminological parallels, suggesting a close kinship between them. Note similarities between 69:18 and 102:3; 69:33 and 102:18; 69:36 and 102:17; 69:37 and 102:29; 69:34 and 102:21. Ps 22 has the same literary structure as Pss 69 and 102, much of the same basic context, and is about the same length. It is possible that these three psalms all emerged from the same context, whatever that may have been (note that Becker, *Israel deutet seine Psalmen*, 43–53, treats the three psalms in close sequence). A caveat should be entered relative to literary forms in the present structure of psalms relating to their possible composite nature and history of development. The composite artistry of a psalm does not exclude the use of earlier sections, which may have been parts of other psalms or have existed independently, or are additions to an original psalm core. A skilled composer/author is quite capable of blending formerly disparate parts into a well-constructed new composition—it happens frequently in choral compositions and sometimes in drama.

The personal situation of the speaker in the psalm is elusive. Commentators (e.g., Schmidt) have noted that the distress of the suppliant seems to have a double basis. On the one hand, enemies plague the speaker, apparently accusing the suppliant of robbery and forcing the repayment of what was not stolen (v 5). Foes taunt the suppliant and produce shame, humiliation, and agony of heart (v 19, 20–21). On the other hand, parts of the psalm can be read as indicating a severe sickness, as in v 21 ("I am sick"), v 30 ("lowly and in pain"), and v 27 (smitten by God). The descriptions in vv 3–4 and 15–18 could be understood as descriptive of the anxiety and suffering of a sick person who feels the nearness of death (see Seybold, *Das Gebet*, 133–37). However, the language in the psalm does not necessarily indicate a specific condition. As is generally true in individual laments, the metaphors are rather standard and designed to express a whole range of pain, suffering, and the machinations of enemies without being concretely specific about any situation. Perhaps the psalm does give "expression to the sorrows and hopes of some historical situation" (Eaton, 175), but, as Eaton adds, it is a situation which cannot now be identified.

We do not appear to be any better equipped, if as well, to determine where and how the psalm functioned in contexts of worship. Varied alternatives have been proposed, largely depending upon the theoretical reconstruction of Israelite worship adopted by particular commentators. For example, A. R. Johnson (*CPIP*, 386–94) thinks in terms of a cultic prophet in the context of the temple in Jerusalem who speaks possibly for his own case, but more likely for a king, who has suffered a defeat in battle, despite his dependence on Yahweh and zeal for the temple. The association of the speaker in the psalm with a king is assumed by S. Mowinckel and J. H. Eaton (*Kingship*, 51–53). As noted above, Kraus thinks of the psalm as emerging from a group of those who were zealous for the rebuilding of the temple in the very early post-exilic period. Seybold (*Das Gebet*, 133–37) proposes a tradition-history of the psalm in three stages. First, vv 2–30 formed the prayer for a sick person, under attack by enemies, and most probably intended for recital away from the areas of cultic worship in the temple. The second stage, vv 2–33, formed a prayer of praise for a healed person who would go to the sanctuary for appropriate ceremonies, including a public report of the illness and the healing. The third stage (which could involve the same worship situation as the second), vv 2–37, utilizes the earlier psalm as a testimony to the willingness of Yahweh to hear and deliver related to the wider concern for Zion/Jerusalem. An interpretive history, involving usage in differing contexts, may well be reflected in the psalm (cf. Becker, *Israel deutet seine Psalmen*, 45–48). However, its present form is best treated as a prayer expressing great distress by a pious and faithful person in the post-exilic period. The original forms of Pss 22, 69, and 102 probably were designed as prayers for the use of kings. The post-exilic versions of the psalms were probably deeply influenced by the servant concepts in Isa 40–55, and they may have been modeled also after the prophet Jeremiah and, perhaps, even emerged from disciples of that prophet (e.g., Stuhlmueller, who notes a number of rather striking parallels between Ps 69 and Jeremiah; also Deissler. See *Comments* below). As noted above, some parallels with Ps 22 are also evident, and the two psalms possibly stem from the same circles. Craigie (197–98) argues that Ps 22 was the basis of a liturgy, in which the worshipers moved from lament to prayer and on to praise and thanksgiving. If he is correct, the same understanding works remarkably well for Ps 69. Note, for example his summary of Ps 22:

> The words of the lament imply the worshipper's deep state of distress prior to the liturgy; although in their original compositions, the words presumably indicated the particular experience of a particular person. In the normal use of the liturgy they are simply words spoken by individuals whose personal circumstances may have differed.

Craigie suggests that Ps 22 was used for severely sick persons who were threatened by death and who participated in the liturgy as part of a congregation of worshipers hoping for favorable results. Ps 69 could have been used in like manner, as is also the case with Ps 102 (see Allen's excellent discussion of this psalm in *Psalms 101–150*, 11–16). However, too much emphasis should not be placed on sickness in 69. The powerful metaphors of the text are general enough to cover any great physical and spiritual distress. The superscription of Ps 102 indicates that regardless of a possible royal design in the original psalm, it was used in the post-exilic period as a prayer for "one afflicted, when he is faint and pours out his complaint before the LORD" (RSV)—for anyone in sickness or other severe distress.

There can be little doubt that psalms like 22 and 69 had similar usage. The use of these psalms during services of fasting and penitence in exilic and post-exilic Israelite communities is highly probable. In such cases the speaker would have been a priest or prophet who spoke as a representative of the community. However, the use of such psalms as these in family ceremonies, assisted by a ritual specialist (priest or prophet), during life-threatening crises (especially illness) in the lives of individuals (as projected in E. S. Gerstenberger, *Der bittende Mensch*) is highly probable. The probability of the usage of psalms in multiple contexts is high.

Comment

A plea and complaint (69:2–5). The psalm opens with a prayer to God for deliverance from a situation which is rapidly becoming desperate for the speaker, who is described as sinking into a bottomless muddy swamp and about to be drowned by floods of water. The speaker is sinking down into the watery depths, as in the great cosmic sea, down to the netherworld of the dead. The apparently terminal situation has produced great grief for the suppliant, expressed in the weariness of crying and the dry throat of one terrified, plus the dimmed vision of the exhausted and sick (v 4). The condition of the speaker is exacerbated by enemies who attack with false accusations and with demands for the repayment of goods not taken by robbery or plunder (v 5). The enemies are both numerous and vicious, apparently pretending to be concerned for justice while making unjust exactions from the speaker. The reader is not informed as to the details of the situation and a gap is left open to be filled by imagination. However, Jer 38:6, 22; 18:23; 23:9 may come to mind.

The reason for the humiliation of the suppliant (69:6–14b). This section begins with a confession in v 6. The folly and guilt of the speaker is not hidden from God. However, v 6 should not be over emphasized as a confession of sin since it is really a brief form of the speaker's protestation of innocence, delivered to provide efficacy for prayer: cf. Pss 7:4–5; 17:3–5; 38:6; 139:1–24. Both the suppliant and the enemies are before God and known by him.

Petitions directed to God (vv 7, 14ab) frame descriptions of the speaker's complaint in vv 8–13, though this section seems to divide into two subunits: v 8–9 and 10–13 (note the use of כִּי at the beginning of vv 8 and 10). The suppliant suffers as a loyal servant of God, who bears scorn, humiliation, and family alienation (v 9; cf. Jer 12:6) because of zeal for the "house" of God. The scorn directed toward the suppliant is really intended for God (v 10b). The nature of the suppliant's zeal for the "house" of God is not specified. We can think of a king who has devoted much effort to the upkeep and protection of the temple. However, a Jeremiah-like person who has advocated the proper correlation between behavior outside the temple area and worship at the temple is equally possible (cf. Jer 7:26; 23:10–12). The meaning of "your house" can extend beyond the temple to involve the idea of the "household" of Yahweh (see Jer 12:7–9)—the people of Yahweh. The nature of the speaker's zealous action is unfocused, but the context suggests deep concern about the behavior of some in the community whose actions are contrary to those appropriate for the "house" of God. The suppliant has participated in fasting and weeping because of the situation (vv 11–12)—perhaps we should think of a context like that reflected in

Isa 58:11–12 (cf. Pss 35:13; 109:24–25; Joel 1:8; 2:12–14; Zech 7:3–14). The reference to the town gate in v 13 recalls the rejection of prophetic reproof in the gate depicted in Amos 5:10–12. The wearing of a sackcloth garment was a visible sign of penitence, associated with grief and fasting (2 Sam 3:31; 1 Kgs 21:27; Isa 3:24; 58:5).

Regardless of the precise nature of the speaker's actions, the reader's attention is focused on the resulting treatment of the suppliant in the community. The suppliant is "consumed" (v 10a; cf. Pss 44:16; 83:17)—brought to a point of near extinction—and bears the scornful reproach of those who reproach God (v 10b). Members of the community mock and humiliate the speaker (vv 11–13), who becomes even the subject of drunkards' songs (13b) and of the scurrilous talk of those who sit in the town gate. If the understanding of the "house" of God suggested above is accepted, the speaker is portrayed as suffering both for God and for his or her own people, the estranged brothers and sisters of the family and community (v 9) for whom the speaker has done zealous service (cf. Jer 11:15; 12:7; 23:11; Ps 119:139; Isa 26:11; Ezek 36:5; Zeph 1:18; 3:8). In defiance of rejection, scorn, and humiliation, the suppliant prays to Yahweh for a time of favorable hearing and relief (v 14ab; cf. Ps 32:6; Isa 49:8; 55:6).

Petition and complaint (69:14c–18). This second large section of the psalm, corresponding to vv 2–14b, divides into two subsections. The initial statements in v 14cd constitute a plea for saving action on the part of God out of his great loyal-love, i.e., Yahweh's demonstrated willingness to deliver and protect when human resources are exhausted. Vv 15–16 pick up the muddy bog-like situation of v 3 and the waters which are about to overwhelm the suppliant. Yahweh must respond ("answer," 14c) and save. Otherwise the suppliant will slip down into the watery depths of death, and the "pit" (another term for *sheol* and the netherworld) will close its mouth over him/her. The peril of death is very near.

Vv 17–18 pick up the urgent plea for an "answer" in v 14d and constitute a small unit of urgent supplication to God on the part of the speaker. The "answer me" at the beginning of 17 is matched by the "answer me quickly" at the end of 18. The appeal to Yahweh's loyal-love in 17a corresponds to the loyal-love in 14b, and the "great" (כרב) loyal-love in 14c corresponds to the "great mercy" in 17b. A new, and a key element, is introduced in v 18a: "Hide not your face from your servant." The word "face," (פנים) sets up a wordplay with "turn" (פנה) in 17b. The speaker identifies himself/herself as a "servant" of Yahweh (v 18). The "servant" could be a king (used of David, 2 Sam 7:5; of Solomon 1 Kgs 3:7) or a prophet (1 Kgs 14:18; 2 Kgs 9:36; 14:25; 17:13, 23) or the righteous members of the Yahwistic community (see Ps 119:122, 125; Isa 54:17; 63:17). The description of a servant of Yahweh who undergoes such great distress because of faithful service easily recalls the striking passages in Isa 50:4–9 and 52:13; 53:12.

The concept of the hidden face of God is a major one in the literature of the Psalms (see Pss 13:2; 30:7–8; 27:9; 44:25; 88:15; 89:47; 102:3; 104:29; also, Gen 4:14; Deut 31:18; 32:20; Mic 3:4; Job 13:24). The hidden face of God is equal to his wrath and is the negative counterpart of the saving acts of God when his face is turned toward the distress of those in trouble (Pss 22:25; 25:26; 119:132).

> But I—I said in my security:
> "I will never be moved!"

> O Lord, in your favor you caused me to stand
>   with the strength of a mountain,
> Then you hid your face and I was dismayed.(Ps 30:7–8)

The hiding of God's face brings devastating results.

The consequence of the hidden face of God is separation, or at least perceived separation, from his presence. When God's face is hidden, he refuses "to see" with attention and care in times of distress and suffering (Pss 10:11; 13:4; Isa 54:7–8). The prayer in 69:18 wants the result expressed in 22:25: "he has not hidden his face from him but has heard when he cried to him." In 51:11, however, the hiding of God's face from the suppliant's sin has a positive meaning: "in effect the hiding of the face in this case suggests a divine response which the worshipper understands as an expression of grace and forgiveness" (S. E. Balentine, *The Hidden God* [New York: Oxford UP, 1983], 58). Possibly this was the original idea of God's hiding his face: hiding his face from sin and guilt. However, in most cases in the present MT the expression indicates a separation from God's presence and a divine refusal "to see" and respond to the need of a suppliant. Unless God is willing to forsake the hiding of his face and turn to the suppliant, oppression, suffering, and death loom ahead. A speedy response on the part of God is essential (69:18b).

A complaint (69:19–22). V 19 seems to me to correspond in terms of literary structure to v 2. Both are opening petitions for sections of complaint of almost equal length (vv 3–5 and vv 20–23). The "my enemies" (אֹיְבַי) of v 19 corresponds to "those who hate me" (lit., "my haters," שֹׂנְאַי) in v 15 (Allen, *JBL* 105 [1986] 588, notes) and also corresponds to "my foes" (צוֹרְרָי) in v 20 (also Allen, 578–79, 588). God is implored in v 19 to draw near in order to redeem the suppliant, who prays that God will "ransom" him (or her) from the enemies. For God as "redeemer" see Ps 78:35. The verb פדה ("ransom" or, better, "redeem") means "to take a thing or a man out of the possession and ownership of another into one's own possession and ownership by giving an equivalent for it" (L. Köhler, *Old Testament Theology,* tr. A. S. Todd [Philadelphia: Westminster Press, 1957] 233). See Exod 13:13; Job 6:22–23; Lev 27:27; etc. However, the paying of a price is only one method of "ransoming," and the verb may be used in the sense of "rescue" or "deliver" (see 1 Sam 14:45). The traditional translation as "ransom" is retained here (to distinguish the verb from גאל, "redeem"), but the reader should not make the mistake of assuming that it necessarily involves any kind of "equivalent price" or "release price." This is especially true when God is the subject. Köhler notes that in the thirty-three passages in the OT where God "ransoms," no equivalent is involved. "God ransoms always in grace, and since He is the supreme lord of the world, He gives no equivalent when he ransoms" (see Deut 7:8; 9:26; 13:6; 15:15; 21:8; 24:18; Mic 6:4; Ps 78:42; Neh 1:10; etc.). The only "price" which Yahweh pays when he "ransoms" is that of his punishment on those who oppress his people. He makes no deals!

The humiliation of the speaker is set forth in vv 20–23 in ways not unlike those in vv 8–10, especially with the repeated use of the word "reproach" (or "scorn," חֶרְפָּה) in vv 8, 10, 20, and 21, and "humiliation" (verb, כלם; noun, כְּלִמָּה) in vv 7, 8, and 20. There is an emphasis in v 20 on "you know"—the whole situation is known by Yahweh, before whom are all the speaker's foes (v 20b). The suppliant is without comforters, though broken-hearted and sick with misery (v 21; cf. "none to comfort" in Lam 1:2, 9, 17, 21, and "none to help her" in Lam

1:7; cf. Lam 1:3; 5:5; 5:8). Like Job, the suppliant expected compassion and comfort from friends but found none.

The language of v 22 should be understood as metaphorical, reflecting a poisoning at a meal normally supplied by sympathetic friends, probably a funeral meal provided for mourners, though the reference could include meals at other times of stress and need as well (Kraus, 645; cf. 2 Sam 3:35; 12:17). The poison and vinegar which the suppliant receives represents a radical form of betrayal by those who should have been comforters.

Petitions for punishment (69:23–26). The speaker has prayed repeatedly for personal deliverance in vv 2–22, but now prays for the punishment of the enemies who have treated him or her so badly. The language of these verses is harsh and need not be repeated here. The *Translation* and *Notes* above are sufficient without extended comment. The severity of the judgments requested is similar to that of petitions in Pss 58, 59, and 109. The punishments reverse the normal order of the good things of life (as it has been reversed for the suppliant). The requests are that the foes be deprived of:

- food and fellowship at their own tables v 23
- physical faculties and strength v 24
- divine mercy—unlike the goodness and loyal-love which pursue those who are members of Yahweh's household (23:6), let divine anger be poured on them and wrath overtake them.
- homes and families v 26.

(Rogerson and McKay, II, 99)

The judgment asked for on the tables of the enemies in v 23 reflects, of course, the poisoned food given the suppliant in v 22. Allen (*JBL* 105 [1986] 580) notes that the imprecation in 24b "brutally intensifies the sentiment of v 4 (note the reference to "failing eyes" in both verses) and that 24b reflects the inability to stand in v 3. The divine wrath in v 25 also corresponds to the "zeal" of the suppliant for the house of God in v 10 (though different words are used), and the homelessness prayed for in v 26 corresponds to the suppliant's family alienation in v 9.

Final complaint and petition for punishment (69:27–30). Allen (*JBL* 105 [1986] 578) has noted a chiasmic scheme in these verses: 27a = A, 27b = B, 28a = C, 28b = D, 29a = D', 29b = C', 30a = B', 30b = A'. The speaker directs attention to those who are hounded (or persecuted) because they have been chastened by God (v 27). The foes of the speaker have "usurped the role of God, and, not satisfied to let the divine punishment stand (or allow it to be a testimony of God's presence), have added to it by harassing one whom God has struck; by talking on and on about his suffering they have further added to it" (Durham, 312). The suffering of the speaker has moved the foes to talk and make false charges rather than to have compassion (cf. Job 19:21, 22). The plural "wounded" indicates that there were others who received the same treatment as the speaker.

In response to those who persecute such wounded people as the speaker, the suppliant prays that the guilt of the oppressors be added to until they are beyond any saving work on the part of God (v 28). Let them be "blotted out of the scroll of the living," i.e., removed from those who are preserved alive by God (for the scroll of the living, cf. Ps 109:13–14; Exod 32:32; Isa 4:3; Mal 3:16; Dan 12:1;

1 Enoch 47.3, 108.3; Rev 3:5). The speaker does not want them listed with the righteous, those who have received Yahweh's saving work and who are loyal members of the community of the servants of Yahweh. The reference is primarily to ordinary earthly human existence, but an eschatological dimension in the sense of eternal life should not be excluded entirely. On the other hand, an assumption that the text is fully eschatological and refers to immortality (see Dahood) should be eschewed. The language is general and should not be limited in either regard. Nor should exclusion from the scroll of the living be limited to the loss of membership in Israel (Cohen).

V 30 returns to the miserable condition of the sufferer and reiterates the "pain" recounted in v 27. The second part of the verse is a prayer asking to be defended from persecution by the saving work of God.

Praise and confidence (69:31–37). The mood of the speaker in this part of the psalm changes from complaint and petition to hope and assurance. The speaker is confident that God's saving work will not fail (v 30) and that he/she will be able to praise God with songs and thanksgiving (v 31). The word for "thanksgiving" in v 31 (תודה) can mean either a thank-offering or a song of thanksgiving (cf. Lev 7:12, 13, 15; Isa 51:3; 2 Chr 29:31; Neh 12:27; Pss 42:5; 50:14, 23; 56:13; 92:2; 107:22; 116:17; 147:7). The idea of song is dominant here, as v 32 indicates by referring to the "song" and "thanksgiving" as more pleasing to Yahweh than an ox (שור, note the wordplay with שיר, "song") offered as a sacrifice (see Pss 40:7–9; 50:13–14, especially, Craigie's comments on 50:7–15). The speaker addresses in v 33 the "humble folk" (ענוים), those who lack the material wealth and power to exercise much authority in ordinary human affairs but who are faithful to Yahweh and see his presence. Their deliverance and prosperity depend upon divine action. They are encouraged to let their "hearts revive" (v 33c), i.e., let their inner vitality and volition be quickened into new life by confidence in the work of Yahweh. The basis for this confidence is spelled out in v 34: Yahweh listens to the needy ones who are his own and does not reject them, even if they are "prisoners" (cf. Ps 22:25–27). Johnson (*CPIP*, 395–96) wisely warns against taking the "prisoners" (or "bonds") in v 34 too literally, in the sense of those imprisoned by legal procedures or as a result of war. He appeals to Ps 116:15–17 and understands the reference to be to those in the bondage of the "constant struggle with the forces of Death." This approach relates well to the desperate struggle with deathly conditions graphically described in vv 2–4, 15–16. However, the primary reference is more likely to be to the exile, to those who cannot return home unless Yahweh hears and delivers. NIV has "his captive people," which fits well with the interpretation of vv 31–37 as an exilic or post-exilic addition to the basic psalm in vv 2–30. The exile is a struggle with "Death," a metaphorical experience of sinking deep into the watery wastes of the netherworld (cf. Ezek 37:1–14.)

NEB and Dahood take another approach and think in terms of those bound to God by special religious ties. Thus, NEB reads, "those bound to his service." In any case, in the present context they are equivalent to the "humble folk" and the "needy" in vv 33a and 34a, defined in 33b as "those who seek God." Different groups of people in varied situations could, and can, identify with the "humble-needy-prisoners" of God.

Vv 35–37 form a second part of the section composed of vv 31–37. The praise of an individual in 31–34 gives way to cosmic praise in 35–37. The heavens, the earth (land), and the seas, along with all the creatures which belong to them, are summoned to praise God in v 35. The cosmic praise is focused on God's saving of Zion and rebuilding the towns of Judah (v 36). When this happens, the servants of Yahweh-God will live in restored Judah and take possession of it again as their divinely given inheritance, as the Israelites did long ago (described in Deuteronomy and Joshua). The restored servant community will dwell permanently in a restored land. The servant community is described as "those who love his [Yahweh's] name"; i.e., those who honor the divine presence and power in the "name" and trust in it (see Ps 5:12; 119:32; cf. 40:17; 70:5; 119:165; see Craigie, 88).

Explanation

The speaker in this psalm claims the status of a servant of God, whose zealous commitment to the "house" of God has stirred up malignant opposition which has put the supplicant in danger of sinking into the infernal depths of the netherworld. The speaker appeals to God for saving help, in part because loyalty to God has brought about overwhelming reproach and humiliation (v 8). The supplicant appeals for a favorable response from God out of his "abundant loyal-love" (v 14, רב־חסדך) and his reliable and sure saving-work, as well as to his "great mercy" (v 17), terminology which recalls the "mighty [or great] waters" (מים־רבים, in Ezek 1:24), of which variant descriptions appear in vv 2–3 and 15–16 (cf. Prov 18:4; Isa 43:16; Job 37:10; 38:34; Neh 9:11). Various adjectives are used with the "waters": deep, strong, broad, flood, etc. These watery depths represent the imminent nearness and power of Death.

The actions of the supplicant's enemies are described with graphic detail, and the petitions for punishment of the enemies in vv 23–29 are equally strong. The enemies are the kind of people who would put poison in the food of a meal intended for comfort, or offer sour and bitter vinegar to a person weakened by thirst (v 22). Indifferent to the actions of God which leave some smitten and wounded for his own purposes (v 27; cf. Isa 53), they tell cruel stories about the problems of God's "wounded ones." They are cruel where they should be merciful. When a stroke comes to any in the providence of God, the friends of the afflicted normally gather around them and comfort them, but these wretches hunt the wounded and vex the sick. "They lay bare the wounds with their rough tongues. They lampoon the mourner, satirize his sorrows, and deride his woes" (C. H. Spurgeon, II, 183). It is not surprising to find petitions for harsh punishment of the enemies—they deserve what is asked (for the theological problems raised by such petitions see Ps 58, *Explanation*).

Vv 17–18 clearly form the heart of the psalm. The supplicant is totally dependent on an "answer" from God, a response from his great and powerful love and compassion. If Yahweh hides his face and refuses to act quickly, there is no hope for the supplicant. The critical situation is known by Yahweh (v 20), who will surely not leave a devoted servant without compassion and without comforters. The supplicant urgently needs for God to "come near" to his/her life and redeem it (v 19) from a state of dereliction which seems to be removed from God's care.

The mood of the last part (vv 31–37) of the psalm is one of confidence and praise. The "humble folk" who seek after God (v 33) will not be disappointed (for meaning of ענוים, see C. Schultz, '*ANI and 'ANAW in the Psalms*, Ph.D. diss.,

Brandeis University, 1973. Also, S. J. L. Croft, *The Identity of the Individual in the Psalms* [Sheffield: JSOT Press, 1987], 49–72) Their vitality will be revived, because Yahweh hears and heeds such people as they (v 34). The community reflected in Ps 69 seems very much like the exilic groups responsible for the Book of Isaiah (note Isa 29:19; 32:7; 61:1; the Isaianic community is reflected in reference to those who are "humble [עני] and of a contrite spirit, and who tremble at my word" (66:2).

Vv 35–37 set the prayer of the suppliant in the larger context of Yahweh's saving-work. Indeed, the saving-work of Yahweh is always related to contexts which transcend the individual. "Here it is remarkable to see how this evidence of Yahweh's concern for but one among His devoted followers is held to be of cosmic significance and to warrant His being praised by the whole of creation" (A. R. Johnson, *CPIP*, 397).

Perhaps it would be more accurate to say that the psalm expresses the confidence that God's cosmic and historical work includes attention to the needs of faithful servants like the suppliant in Ps 69.

The NT refers and alludes to Ps 69 in several contexts. The emphasis on the suffering of a devoted servant for God's sake made the psalm especially adaptable to Christ's ministry and passion (John 2:17; 15:25; 19:29–30; Matt 27:34, 48; Mark 15:36; Luke 23:36; Rom 15:3). The references range over most of the psalm but seem to be concentrated on vv 21–29, verses which deal with enemies of the sufferer. Also, see Acts 1:20 (the judgment on Judas) and Rom 11:9–10, which refer to those in Israel whose "eyes were darkened," who were "hardened," and who "failed to obtain what was sought" (cf. Ps 69:22–24; cf. Rev 16:1). Stuhlmueller (I, 311) notes that the usage of the psalm in NT contexts provides some examples of how OT passages were utilized to enhance insights into the mystery of the work of Christ. For example, John 2:17 applies Ps 69:10 to Jesus' cleansing of the temple but adds a few verses later that Jesus "spoke of the temple of his body" (John 2:21–22), a saying which his disciples remembered and understood, after his resurrection, as a proper interpretation of the Scripture—a remembrance which strengthened their faith both in the Scriptures and in the words spoken by Jesus (cf. Mark 14:58).

A Prayer for God to Hurry to the Aid of a Needy Servant *(70:1–6)*

Bibliography

Johnson, A. R. *CPIP*. 404–12. Braulik, G. *Psalm 40 und der Gottesknecht.* Würzburg: Echter, 1975. 207–13, 265–67.

Translation

1   For the leader;[a] Davidic;[b] *lᵉhazkir.*[c]
2 (1) *Hasten,*[a] *O God, to rescue me;*   (2[3]+3)
       O Yahweh, for my help, hurry!

³ (2) *May those who seek my life* ª   (2+2+3+2)
             be brought to shame and disgrace; ª
           may those who are pleased by my misfortune
             be turned back and humiliated;

⁴ (3)   *may they turn back (in retreat)* ª *because of their shame,* ᵇ   (3+3)
             those who say, "Aha! Aha!"

⁵ (4) *May all who seek you be glad and rejoice in you,*   (3+2+4+2)
           and may those who love your saving help say continually, ª
           "God is great!" ᵇ

⁶ (5) *I am poor and needy* ª—   (3+2+3+2)
           O God, hasten ᵇ *to me!*
         You are my help and my deliverer, ᶜ
         O Yahweh, do not delay!

Notes

1.a. See n. 51:1.a.

1.b. See n. 51:1.b.

1.c. The expression is usually translated as "for the memorial offering" (RSV), or "to bring to remembrance" (KJV), or "for remembrance" (NAB), and is also found in the heading of Ps 38. The expression (אזכרה) may refer to the *azkarah* sacrifice (Lev 2:2, 9, 16, 5:12; 6:8 [15]; 24:7; Num 5:26), perhaps, a "memorial portion" (the part of the offering which was burned) (1) to remind God of the person who offered it and/or (2) as a pledge or token of the worshiper and commitment to the whole offering as owed to God, though most of it would be consumed by the priests or others. Thus, the use of *l'hazkir* in the titles of Pss 38 and 70 may refer (1) to the psalms as appropriate for chanting while the sacrificial act of *azkarah* took place (Cohen), or (2) to remind Yahweh of the distress of the worshiper (so Mowinckel, *PIW*, II, 212). The two ideas may be complementary, though the idea of "bring to remembrance" (note LXX, "for a remembrance that the Lord may save me") seems more appropriate for Ps 70 (see Craigie, 303).

2.a. The qal imperative רצה, "be pleased," appears in 40:14 but not here. The translation above is based on the assumption that the verb in 2b applies to both colons of the verse.

3.a. "Together" (יחד) is found after the verb (חפר, "disgraced") in 40:15. "To sweep away" or "to snatch away" (לספותה) is added after "my soul/my life" in 40:15. The addition of these words gives the verse a different poetic balance, but they should not be added to the text in Ps 70.

4.a. The verb appears as ישמו in 40:16: "may they be made desolate/stunned/appalled." The verb, ישובו means here "to turn back" in defeat, used as a military metaphor (cf. 6:11; 9:4; 56:10). It is possible that the difference arose from confusion between the Hebrew letters "M" and "B."

4.b. Apparently, the על-עקב means "according to the consequences of their shame," i.e., in consequence of the disgrace falling upon them (BDB, 784). LXX has "quickly received shame for their reward" in 40:16 and "be turned back and put to shame immediately" in 70:4. "Their shame" apparently refers to the humiliation of having plans fail, perhaps involving also an element of shame because their evil designs were exposed.

5.a. תמיד ("continually") disrupts the balance of the colons and is frequently deleted. However, it is probably a deliberate addition to join the psalm to a group of psalms which use תמיד. See *Form/Structure/Setting*.

5.b. There are some differences between this verse and 40:17, as follows: (1) אלהים for יהוה; (2) a conjunction before "they say" in 70:5; (3) ישועה for תשועה—both words mean "help/deliverance/salvation."

6.a. "Poor and needy" is probably a hendiadys = "Needy-poor" or "truly poor" (A. R. Johnson, *CPIP*, 227, n. 4). The words are a formulaic word-pair (e.g., see Pss 35:10; 109:16, 22). Note the pun on אני ("I") and עני ("afflicted/poor"); also in 69:30.

6.b. The colon is different in 40:18, which has אדני יחשב-לי, "the Lord will take account of me." The verb חשב means to "think/take account/reckon" and may be read as indicative: "the Lord takes thought (or will take thought) for me" (see KJV, RSV, NAB), or it may be read as jussive: "may the Lord take thought for me" (see NEB, NIV, NJB). The use of the imperative חושה ("hasten") in 70:6b makes a

better balance with אל־תאחר ("do not delay") than the יחשב in 40:18. The חושה in v 6b forms an inclusion with the חושה in v 2, and the "delay not" constitutes a nicely crafted negative parallel.

6.c. It is probable that these two words also form a hendiadys: "my delivering helper."

Form/Structure/Setting

The characteristics of an individual lament mark this psalm. (For the features
of individual laments, see *Form/Structure/Setting* of Ps 54.) Stuhlmueller describes
it as "a lapidary piece, carefully cut and polished from start to finish." It is a short
poem which catches up much of the force of the lament genre. Since it is found
in 40:14–18 (with variations), several commentators conclude that a section of
the liturgy (which Ps 40 is assumed to form) was detached and later given an
independent existence as a separate psalm (conveniently see Eaton, 114, 178).
Craigie (314) judges the relationship between Pss 40 and 70 to be uncertain, but
he accepts the hypothesis that Ps 40 is the "original, and hence oldest, composition," while 70 is "an adaptation and abbreviation, possibly undertaken to permit
'popular usage' of a part of the psalm, but more likely dating from a period when
royal psalms and liturgies were no longer in use." Since he accepts the thesis that
40 is a psalm for the king during the monarchical period, he suggests that 70 is
a "salvaged psalm" for use in a time after the monarchy, during the exile or later.
This may be correct, but it seems to me that the differences between 40 and 70
can be explained better as adaptation of material from 70 to 40 (so Braulik,
Psalm 40, 197–201), or they are two versions of common poetic material. Ps 70
forms a complete unit, which appears to have been adapted to the context of Ps
40. The petitionary pattern is held throughout 70, with חושה, "hasten," forming an
inclusion in vv 2 and 6. On the contrary, in 40:18 the inclusion with v 14 is
broken by the use of חשב, "think about/account to," in v 18. 40:18 is then transformed into an affirmative statement of confidence in God. The context of vv
14–18 in Ps 40 tends to give these verses a positive rather than a petitionary tone.
Craigie (316) notes that 40:14–18 "hovers between lament and a statement of
confidence," and he translates the statements in vv 15–18 (with the exception of
18d) as positive expressions rather than as petitions. Rather extensive similarities
of wording and content between Pss 22, 35, 38, 40, 60, 70, 71, and 102 point to a
common context for these psalms. For the parallels see G. H. Wilson, *The Editing
of the Hebrew Psalter* (132) and G. Baulik, *Psalm 40* (207–13 for parallels between
40:14–18 and Ps 35; see 208–11 for parallels between Pss 35 and 71). Some of the
major similarities of language and expressions are as follows:

38:23	חושה לעזרתי	hasten for my help
70:2	לעזרתי חושה	for my help, hasten
70:6	חושה לי	hasten to me
38:13	מבקשי נפשי	seekers of my life
	דרשי רעתי	seekers of my hurt
70:3	מבקשי נפשי	seekers of my life
	חפצי רעתי	desirers of my hurt
71:13	מבקשי רעתי	seekers of my hurt
71:24	מבקשי רעתי	seekers of my hurt
40:15	מבקשי רעתי	seekers of my hurt

40:17	כל־מבקשיך, all who seek you
70:5	כל־מבקשיך, all who seek you
69:7	מבקשיך, those who seek you

40:15	מבקשי נפשי, seekers of my life
70:3	מבקשי נפשי, seekers of my life
38:13	מבקשי נפשי, seekers of my life

The verb נצל, "deliver," is found in 40:14; 69:15 (2x); 70:2; 71:2, 11.

40:18	ואני עני ואביון, I am poor and needy
69:30	ואני עני ואביון, I am poor and needy
70:6	ואני עני ואביון, I am poor and needy

70:3	יבשו ויחפרו מבקשי נפשי, may those who seek my life be brought to shame and disgrace
71:24	כי־בשו כי־חפרו מבקשי רעתי, those who seek my hurt will be ashamed and disgraced
40:15	יסגו אחור ויכלמו, they shall be turned back and humiliated
69:7	אל־יכלמו . . . מבקשיך, don't let those who seek you be humiliated
69:20	בשתי וכלמתי, my shame and my humiliation
70:3	יסגו אחור ויכלמו, be turned back and humiliated
71:13	יעטו חרפה וכלמה, covered with reproach and humiliation

| 69:19 | נפשי גאלה, my life, redeem it |
| 71:23 | נפשי אשר פדית, my life, which you have ransomed |

Note use of תמיד, "continually," in 38:18; 40:12; 69:24; 70:5; 71:3, 6, 14.

Braulik (Psalm 40, 126–28; 208–11) provides lists of links between Pss 40 and 69, as well as between 40:14–18 and Ps 35 and between Pss 35 and 71. See the *Form/Structure/Setting* section of Ps 69 for similarities between that psalm and Pss 102 and 22 (Ps 71 also shows affinities with 22). This analysis is too limited to be definitive, but it is sufficient to show the probability that Pss 22, 35, 38, 40, 69, 70, 71, and 102 reflect much common language. In their present forms, these psalms may have emerged from post-exilic Israelite communities and groups who considered themselves to be the true, devoted servants of Yahweh, seekers after his presence (note the references to servant/servants in 35:27; 102:15, 29). They are characterized by deep devotion mingled with spiritual (and physical) agony. The communities behind them were probably closely related to those responsible for the Book of Isaiah. The members of these communities had eyes turned toward the future and a new salvation to come from Yahweh, for which they waited with both calm faith and eager anticipation.

The placement of Ps 70 between Pss 69 and 71 was a part of the redactional development of the second book of the Psalter. Ps 71 has no title in the MT, and it seems almost certain that 70 and 71 were intended to be read together (which is supported by some manuscript evidence; see *BHK*[3], *BHS*, Wilson, *The Editing of the Hebrew Psalter*, 177). The LXX supplies a Davidic title for 71 (the Targum does not), in keeping with the tendency to "davidize" the psalms in later traditions. In

Pss 3–89, only 10, 33, 43, and 71 lack titles in the MT. Wilson (131) notes that in each case there is manuscript evidence for combining each of the psalms in question with the psalm which precedes it. The LXX combines 9 and 10 but supplies titles for the others. Wilson (97) also notes that in the Qumran 4QPs[a] fragment g, 71:1 follows immediately at the end of Ps 38, with no indication of separation—the psalms were read together. The emphasis on "righteousness" in Ps 71 (see *Explanation* of that psalm) correlates well with the emphasis on "righteousness" associated with the king in Ps 72.

The speaker in Ps 70 is not identified. In the case of Ps 40, Craigie follows J. H. Eaton (*Kingship*, 42–44) and A. R. Johnson (*CPIP*, 399–412) in the conclusion that the psalm reflects a royal liturgy in which a king is the speaker. Johnson argues that the psalm "unfolds the relationship between the one and the many in Israelite thought" (317). The "One" is the king, who is the principal suppliant in the liturgy, and the "many" are the people of the kingdom, who make up the "great congregation" in 40:10, 11—and who pray for the king in psalms like 72. The king, of course, spoke on behalf of the people and shared their experience. It seems to me that the probability is high that psalms like 22, 35, 40, 69, 70, 71, and 102 were designed originally for recitation by kings in pre-exilic liturgies. However, in their present form and placement in the Psalter they are post-monarchical, democratized, and belong to post-exilic Israelite communities. They were available as the prayers of any faithful servant of Yahweh on any appropriate occasion, but were probably especially appropriate for days of prayer and fasting in the communities of those who waited for a new manifestation of the saving power of Yahweh. A servant king could no longer bear the burden of Israel. That burden now had to be borne by the needy-poor of Yahweh, his true servants, his "seekers," who lived in continual dependence on the help of God. They waited for Yahweh to hasten to their aid: "O Yahweh, do not delay!" They were the *Maranatha* people of post-exilic Israel (see 1 Cor 16:22).

Comment

"Hasten, O God, to rescue me" (Ps 70:2–6). The prayer begins with an urgent plea to God for help, help which is needed quickly. This short psalm is dominated at its beginning and at its end by emphasis on God's hastening to deliver: "hasten . . . hurry . . . hasten . . . do not delay." The prayer implies a period of painful and uncertain waiting for God to act on the part of a person who has been under attack from those who do not share his or her commitments. They gloat over the discomfort of the suppliant with their "Aha! Aha!" (v 4; see Ps 35:21, 25; Ezek 25:3; 26:2; 36:2). Weiser (340) is probably correct in surmising that the enemies were representatives of a specific group, but is probably not correct that the "whole cult community had disassociated itself" from the group. It is more likely that the groups were *within the cult community* and that the psalm reflects the kinds of group/party tension and conflict which pulse through the Book of Isaiah, especially, chaps. 56–66. Unfortunately, we cannot be very specific in exact historical terms about the definition and function of various groups in the post-exilic communities. On the other hand, the texts permit us to enter the emotionally charged atmosphere of the communities as reader participants.

The speaker in the psalm identified with those in the community who are described as the "needy-poor," the humble folk, who "love" God's saving help/salvation (for discussion of the "poor," see *Comment* on 68:11). The love for God's saving-work would involve longing for and anticipation of its delights. These are the folk who, despite their difficult circumstances, are encouraged to keep on saying, "God is great."

Explanation

See the *Explanation* for Ps 71.

A Prayer for Righteous Deliverance   (71:1–24)

Bibliography

Cogan, M. "A Technical Term for Exposure." *JNES* 27 (1968) 133–35. **Delekat, L.** *Asylie und Schutzorakel am Zionheiligtum.* 93–98, 207–15. **Tournay, R. J.** "Notules sur les Psaumes (Psaume, XIX, 2–5; LXXI, 15–16)." In *Alttestamentliche Studien F. Nötscher zum 60. Geburtstage.* Ed. H. Junker and J. Botterweck. Bonn: Peter Hanstein, 1950. 271–80.

Translation

1	With you, O Yahweh, I have taken refuge;	(3+3)
	may I never be put to shame.	
2	In your righteousness [a] rescue me and set me free;	(3+3)
	turn your ear toward me and deliver me.	
3	Be for me a rock of refuge [a]—	(3+3+3)
	for going to continually [b]—decreed [c] for my deliverance.	
	Yes,[d] you are my rock and my stronghold!	
4	O my God, set me free from the hand of the wicked,	(4+3)
	from the grasp of the unjust and ruthless.	
5	Yes, you are my hope,	(2+2+2)
	O Lord Yahweh,[a]	
	my trust from my youth.	
6	I have relied on you since I was born;[a]	(3+3+3)
	from my mother's womb, you have been my sustainer [b]—	
	continually the subject of my praise.[c]	
7	I have been a mystery [a] for many,	(3+2)
	though you (have been) my strong refuge.[b]	
8	(And) my mouth has been filled with your praise,	(3+2)
	with your renown all day long.	
9	Cast me not off [a] in the time of my old age;[b]	(3+3)
	as my strength fails, forsake me not.	
10	For my foes talk about me,[a]	(3+4)
	and my "soul watchers" have formed a conspiracy,	

11	saying: [a]	(1+2+2+2)
	God has forsaken him;	
	after him! Catch him!	
	For no one will rescue him.	
12	O God, be not far from me;	(3+3)
	O God, hasten to my help!	
13	Let my adversaries [a] end up in complete shame; [b]	(4+3+2)
	let them be wrapped in reproach and humiliation,	
	those who seek my hurt.	
14	And I, I will have hope continually,	(3+4)
	(ready) to add to all [a] your praise.	
15	My mouth would tell of your righteousness,	(3+3+3)
	of your salvation all day long.	
	Though I do not know the scribal art, [a]	
16	I would come [with an account of] (your) mighty deeds, [a]	(2+2+3)
	O Lord Yahweh;	
	I would commemorate [b] your righteousness, [c] yours alone!	
17	O God, you have taught me from my youth,	(3+3)
	and unto now I have told about your wondrous deeds.	
18	So even to gray-haired old age, [a]	(3+3+3+2)
	O God, forsake me not,	
	till I can tell about your [strong] arm;	
	[and tell about] your mighty deeds,	
	to all the generation [b] to come. [c]	
19	Your righteousness, O God, is heaven-high,	(3+3+3)
	the great things you have done—	
	O God, who is like you?	
20	Though [a] you have made us [b] see troubles—	(3+2+2)
	many hurtful (troubles) [c]—	
	will you let us [b] live again? [d]	
	And from the depths of the earth bring us [b] up again?	
21	Restore me to a good status, [a]	(2+2)
	and comfort me again. [b]	
22	Then [a] would I praise you with a lute;	(3+2[3]+3+2)
	(then would I praise) your faithfulness, O my God; [b]	
	I would sing to you with a harp,	
	O Holy One of Israel!	
23	My lips would give a shout of joy;	(2+2+3)
	I would sing to you indeed! [a]	
	(With) my very soul [b] which you will have ransomed.	
24	Then [a] my tongue would tell of your righteousness all day long;	(4+4)
	How [b] put to shame, how [b] disgraced will be those who seek my hurt!	

Notes

2.a. For "righteousness," see *Comment* on 52:8. "Righteousness" in this context refers to God's actions which "put things right"—his saving actions. I have retained the traditional "righteousness" in the translation in order to show the emphasis on the word in this psalm.

3.a. Reading מָעוֹז, "place of protection/refuge" for מָעוֹן, "dwelling/habitation." The change follows 31:3, the versions, and a few Heb. mss (see *BHS*). However, it may be that MT should be retained and read as "be for me a rock for dwelling"—a safe place; cf. 27:5. The reading in 31:3 could be a deliberate change (Kidner).

3.b. The לבוֹא תמיד ("to go continually") is frequently changed to לבית מצודות, "a house of defense/protection"="a stronghold" (see RSV, JB, NAB). However, as noted in the treatment of Ps 70, the תמיד ("continually") seems to be a deliberate feature of a group of psalms and should not be lost.

3.c. The literal expression, "to come continually you have commanded (or decreed) for my deliverance," is difficult and sometimes considered to be meaningless (so Kraus). The emendation in 3b above would smooth out the colon, but it does not commend itself. The *Translation* treats the "you have decreed for my deliverance" as a relative clause without a connecting particle (cf. GKC 155m). Dahood (II, 172, and comment on 42:9; I, 259) has demonstrated that צוה can mean "send/promise/confer" rather than "command" in some contexts (cf. 91:11). However, the meaning of "command" or "decree" seems to fit the context better in v 3, and so it has been retained.

3.d. An attempt to get the force of the כי in this context, treating it as an inducement for an action (see KB, 432, #17; cf. Gen 40:15; Isa 29:16; 36:5; Mal 3:14). It is possible that the כי introduces a rhetorical question (cf. KB, 432, #12): "Are you not my rock and my stronghold?"

5.a. Following MT. Translations frequently break up the divine name into parallel colons (disregarding the accentuation). So Dahood: "For you, O Lord, are my hope, / my trust, O Yahweh, from my youth." Dahood and some translators do the same in v 16. The division of the divine name in this way gives a 3+3 balance in the line, if that is desired.

6.a. It is possible that this expression means "from before I was born" (מבטן)—"from within the womb." But the context seems to indicate "from birth."

6.b. BDB (159) derives the uncertain גוזי from גזה, which they propose means "cut off/sever," hence, "to be severed from a mother's womb." A similar verse in Ps 22:10 has גחי from גיח or גוח, "burst forth/ draw forth," as from the womb (cf. Job 38:8). LXX has σκεπαστής, "protector" (22:10 has ἐκσπάσας, "the one who drew me out"—of the womb). Delitzsch (335), followed by Briggs, argues that the σκεπαστής in 71:6 is erroneous for ἐκσπάστης, which would result in the translation: "Out of the bowels of my mother you are the one who drew me forth." Kraus follows Gunkel and changes to עוזי, "my refuge" or "my strength" (as also 4QPsᵃ and Targum). Dahood reads "my sustainer," and argues that the Qumran text represents "an easy way out of the difficulty." Perhaps the best clue is the use of the verb גוז in Num 11:31 for being carried by the wind (also see Ps 90:10). The גוזי in 71:6 can be read as a participle with a suffix (so Eerdmans), "my bearer/sustainer." This is close to the LXX idea of protection or shelter and fits the context.

6.c. Reading בך ("in you") in the sense of "on account of you" (see BDB, 90a, 5); thus more literally, "on account of you my praise is continual."

7.a. See *Comment*. The prep. is probably a *kaph veritatis* (see GKC, 118x), with the meaning of "fully equivalent to a mystery" rather than "like a mystery."

7.b. A construct chain with interposed suffix (see Dahood, II, 86; cf. GKC, 131r).

9.a. Cogan (*JNES* 27 [1968] 133–35) has demonstrated that the hiphil verb השליך can mean "leave/ abandon/expose" in some contexts. See Ezek 16:5; Gen 21:5; Jer 38:6; Exod 1:22. "Abandon" is the meaning in v 9 (note the parallel verb "forsake"), though I have retained the traditional wording.

9.b. Dahood (II, 174) notes that the literal "to a time of old age" borrows the suffix from "my strength"="to a time of my old age." The verse is composed in a balanced chiasm.

10.a. Some commentators (e.g., Gunkel and Jacquet) prefer to emend אמרו, "they say," to ארבו, "they lie in wait/ambush," which matches well with שמר as "to spy on/lie in wait for" in the next colon. Dahood argues for a meaning of אמר as "to see" (from Ugar.' *mr*), here in the sense of "eye me," with hostility (cf. 3:2). However, the idea of "saying about one" is appropriate for the context, in which the enemies are depicted as still making their plans. The ל in לי is that of reference or relation (cf. Ps 41:6).

11.a. A prose-like addition to the text.

13.a. The expression could be read as "my accusers"; cf. Ps 109:4, 20—lit. "adversaries/accusers of my soul/life." Dahood (II, 174; I, 237, on Ps 38:21) argues for "slanderers."

13.b. Reading יבשו יכלו ("they will be put to shame; they will be at an end/consumed/fail") as a hendiadys without a conjunction (so Dahood). יכלו is frequently emended to יכלמו, "they will be humiliated." If the hendiadys is accepted, the emendation is unnecessary and the meaning is that of "May they be put to shame, finished" or "finished in shame." Dahood translates "be utterly humiliated."

14.a. The כֹּל ("all") seems redundant and may be the result of dittography from the preceding על-.

15.a. The ספרות appears only here in MT, and its meaning is uncertain. Some LXX manuscripts (see BHS) read it as γραμματείας, "writings," while others read πραγματείας, "business/occupation/affairs." RSV's "for their number is past my knowledge" follows Symmachus' ἐξαριθμῆσαι, ("number-ing/recounting"), which is a possible reading (Anderson, Kraus). NJV seems to assume that the כ in the statement is concessive (BDB, 473b) and that ספרות means something like "reckoning/account of/treatment of a subject," translating "though I know not how to tell it." The Translation assumes that the כי is concessive (cf. Hos 13:15; Ps 21:12; Prov 6:35; Eccl 4:14) and that the ספרות has to do with writ-ing and the scribal art (see L. Delekat, Asylie und Schutzorakel, 95).

16.a. More likely than KJV's "I will go in the strength of the Lord," which is, however, the reading of LXX—and the "mighty deeds" can hardly refer to deeds of the speaker. The suffix on "your righteousness" in the second colon applies to "mighty deeds" of the first, it is quite possible that אבוא; ("I will come/enter") here means "to enter upon/begin with" (so D. W. Thomas, TRP, 29; following G. R. Driver, "Hebrew Notes," VT 1 [1951] 249). NEB reads, "I will begin with a tale of great deeds, O Lord God." This translation has the advantage of a good parallelism with the second colon.

16.b. The hiphil of זכר has a wide range of meanings. In a cultic sense the hiphil acts as a denominative of zeker (זֵכֶר), which refers to an act of utterance, especially of the divine name in prayer and praise (see B. S. Childs, Memory and Tradition in Israel [Naperville, IL: Allenson, 1962] 11–16, 70–73). Childs (71) notes that the speaker in Ps 6:6 asserts that "in death there is no remem-brance (zikhrekha) of you, in Sheol who can give you praise," and he comments that the speaker "suffers not because of the inability to remember Yahweh in death . . . rather . . . the problem arises from the failure of the dead to share in the praise of Yahweh which characterizes Israel's worship" (see Craigie, 93; Allen, notes on Pss 111:4; 135:13; 145:7). The commemoration in v 16 is of the "righteousness" of God rather than of the divine name.

16.c. For "righteousness," see 52:8, and n. 71:2.a.

18.a. The words for "old age and gray hair" form a hendiadys (see Dahood).

18.b. Dahood argues that this is one of the places where דור ("generation") means "assembly" (see 14:5; also Craigie, 145, 5.b.). However, it is difficult to see how old age in the first colon has to do with an assembly or congregation, unless we understand the speaker as fearing a loss of enough strength to give a testimony. LXX supports "generation" ("the generation that is to come"), as do the similar verses in Ps 22:31–32.

18.c. The meaning is "to all of the coming generation." As BHS and GKC, 155f, note, the לכל- = לכל־דור, and the clause is formed without a relative pronoun (cf. n. 71:3.c.). JB, freely: "let me live to tell the rising generation about your strength and power."

20.a. Reading אשר as concessive (cf. BDB, 83g); it should not be deleted.

20.b. Reading plural suffix in all three verbs with kethiv; the marginal qere has singular "me." See Comment.

20.c. Lit. "many and evil/harmful/hurtful." The translation assumes a hendiadys and an under-stood repetition of "troubles" in the second colon.

20.d. See GKC, 120d, g. Lit. "You have/will turn/return; you have/will preserved/preserve our life/let us live/revived/revive us" = " You will let us live again." The translation assumes an implied question without an interrogative particle (GKC, 150a, b), though reading as a petition (jussive, as in v 21) changes the meaning very little. See Comment.

21.a. Lit. "Increase my greatness," equal to "dignity/honor/esteem/status." The meaning is very similar to that of כבוד, "weight/glory/reputation/distinction."

21.b. The verb תסב (from סבב) is equivalent to תשוב; see the two examples in v 20. It is not neces-sary to change to ותשוב, as, e.g., Buttenwieser, 601.

22.a. cf. Ps 52:7.

22.b. The balance of the colons results from assuming that "then I would praise you" is under-stood before "your faithfulness, O God" in the second colon.

23.a. If the כ is read as emphatic (see Dahood, I, 301; cf. 49:16), there is no need for the deletion of this clause on the grounds that it is a duplication from v 22 (e.g., BHS; Kraus). The suffix "to you" in the second colon has a double function and serves the first colon also: "a shout of joy (to you)."

23.b. נפשי, "myself/my soul," has the stronger meaning here of "my total being/self." For נפש, see 54:5.

24.a. See n. 22.a.

24.b. The כי is emphatic in both cases. See n. 23.a.

Form/Structure/Setting

The literary structure of this psalm is not clearly defined, but it seems best to allow the direct address to God in some verses to mark off its main section, which is in vv 1–19. However, vv 19–20 seem to form a short section outside the main outline of the psalm, with v 19 doing double duty. (Note the twofold "O God" in this verse.) These verses may be an addition to an earlier form of the psalm. In line with this analysis, the outline of the psalm is as follows:

vv 1–4	opening petitions
vv 5–12	the main complaint
vv 13–18	petitions, vows, complaint
vv 19–20	praise and prayer
vv 21–24	petition and vow of praise

The psalm seems to contain a high degree of traditional elements, and it has been called "a filigree of other laments or songs of thanksgiving" (Stuhlmueller, I, 317). Compare the following:

vv 1–3 and Ps 31:1–3a
vv 5–6, 17 and Ps 22:10–11
v 12a and Ps 22:1, 11, 19
v 12b and Pss 38:12; 40:13
v 13 and Ps 35:4, 26
v 18 and Ps 22:30–31
v 19 and Ps 36:6

For other references, see *Comment* below. As noted in the *Form/Structure/Setting* section of Ps 70, Ps 71 may be read together with that psalm. Several parallel statements bind the two psalms together. Note the pleas for haste to help on the part of God in 70:2, 5 and 71:12, the prayer for deliverance or rescue in 70:2, 5 and 71:2 (note v 11 also), the prayer for help in 70:2, 5 and 71:12, and the prayers regarding putting enemies to shame in 70:3 and 71:13, 24.

The psalm has more characteristics of an individual lament than of any other type—note the petitions, complaints, and vows to praise when relief comes. However, elements of confidence, thanksgiving, and praise are smoothly modulated into the content. It is a kind of confident, even jubilant, psalm of lament. The reason for this may be that the speaker in the psalm addresses God from the viewpoint of one who has attained mature adulthood and who is approaching old age (vv 17–18). The suppliant manifests a serenity often denied to the young, the product of "a long memory of God's faithfulness and a growing hope in His life-renewing power" (Kidner, I, 250). The speaker is not identified, of course, but readers/hearers of the psalm may well have thought of David, or of Jeremiah, or of others, who spoke from mature experience. However, the psalm is available to anyone who finds it helpful, regardless of age.

Attempts to relate the psalms to specific liturgical acts in worship contexts do not inspire much confidence. For example, Eaton (*Kingship*, 54) who represents the "kingship" approach, classifies Ps 71 among the "Psalms with clearly royal content" and assumes that the speaker was intended to be the king as he participated in royal rites associated with the autumn festival in pre-exilic Israel. Mowinckel (*PIW*, I, 220) puts 71 in a special group of individual laments called "protective psalms" (3; 5; 7; 11; 26; 27; 36; 52; 54; 57; 62; 64; 77; 86; 139; 140), because they contain prayers for Yahweh's protection against danger, especially danger from enemies. He notes that the tone of these psalms is "brighter than that of the psalms of lamentations." They contain more assurance of help and move closer to a group of psalms which can be called "psalms of confidence." The "protective psalms" belong to Mowinckel's larger category of "National Psalms of Lamentation," psalms designed for *ad hoc* cultic festivals with days of humiliation and prayer, usually observed in times of crises. The "protective psalms," according to Mowinckel, were not intended for days of lamentation *after* a disaster or time of distress, but for "days of antecedent prayer and fasting" *before* an impending crisis, prayers for the favor and protection of Yahweh. Delekat (*Asylie und Schutzorakel,* 207–15, 93–98) puts 71 among a group of psalms which refer to seekers of asylum at the temple in a literal sense. Hounded by personal enemies, a refugee had fled to the temple area for protection: "With you, O Yahweh, I have taken refuge" (or, "I have fled to you for refuge"). Delekat takes such statements as reflecting a literal sense of fleeing to the sanctuary and, in the case of 71:1–3, of standing on a rock in the court of the sanctuary and addressing a prayer for protection to the Rock (God)—translating לצור in v 3 as "O Rock," a term for God (treating the preposition as emphatic, 210, v 5). The prayer would probably have been accompanied by a sacrifice. Seybold (*Das Gebet,* 76) includes Ps 71 among a group of psalms that were "probably" (but not certainly) intended as prayers of the sick.

In my opinion, Mowinckel is probably the nearest to the target for a psalm like 71. The historical setting for the present form of such psalms was, however, not that of pre-exilic Israel, but rather the communities of faithful Israelites in the earlier post-exilic period (see *Form/Structure/Setting* of Ps 70). The primary community was undoubtedly Jerusalem and the rebuilt temple. But these psalms do not have the temple-centered hope of Ezek 40–48 and Haggai. As noted in connection with Ps 70, the communities are likely to have been the same or similar to those responsible for the Book of Isaiah (which begins in chap. 1 with a severe critique of temple worship and ends in chap. 66 with the same). One can speculate that prayers like those in Pss 70 and 71 were particularly at home with those Israelites who did not want to join in the noisy celebration at the rebuilding of the temple after the exile (see Ezra 3:10–13; Hag 2:3; 1 Esdr 5:59–65). Some Israelites waited for a new glory from Yahweh which would transcend the temple on Mount Zion, whose rebuilding was for them "a day of small things" (Zech 4:10). There were certainly worship services, e.g., fast days (cf. Zech 7:5; Isa 58), when such psalms could have been recited appropriately.

Mowinckel (221–24) notes that a "regularly repeated psalm of lamentation borders on the ordinary psalm of prayer," and that we should not assume that there was *always* an *ad hoc* crisis immediately behind the complaints of such laments. The language of disaster was suitable for ongoing distress as well as for periods of intense danger and trouble. The conditions of the post-exilic communities generally justified the use of the language of crisis, especially for individuals who felt themselves trapped in unconstructive and oppressive life-situations.

We must also allow for the conventionalization of metaphors, in which the language comes to be "stock metaphors," words and expressions which form a code lacking the direct references of earlier usages.

The speakers in this group of psalms link their own salvation with that of the nation (see Pss 69:36–37; 102; 13–23) and to the creative-saving works of Yahweh (see Pss 22:28–32; 35:23–28; 102:24–29). The situations of individual persons were related to the conditions in the communities in which they lived. In this connection, the use of the plural in the written text of 71:20 (see note 20.b.) rather than the singular of the marginal reading is relevant. Mowinckel (I, 221) comments:

> In the eyes both of the prophets of re-establishment and of pious people, gentile supremacy over God's people would often appear to be the cause of all misery and sin to be found among the people. Thus the prayer for deliverance from foreign supremacy would involve prayer for the salvation and re-establishment of Israel in general, a "turning of the destiny."

The terrible disturbance of the exile and the continuing domination of the people of Yahweh by foreign powers was viewed as having cosmic dimensions, upsetting the underlying world order and requiring an intervention and "putting right" by Yahweh, the creator, sustainer, and world judge.

Comment

Petition for freedom and protection (71:1–4). The psalm begins with a formulaic expression in v 1a, which is rooted in the ancient custom of seeking asylum and protection in a sanctuary (cf. 1 Kgs 1:49–53; 8:31–32; Exod 21:13). The expression "I have taken refuge with you, O Yahweh" is rather common in individual laments (with variations in form; see Pss 7:2; 11:1; 16:1; 25:20; 31:2; 57:2; 41:8; 144:2; and also 5:12; 16:31; 31:20; 34:9; 23; 37:40; 64:11; 118:8–9). The expression usually stands at the beginning or near the end of a psalm. "It does not introduce the theme to be developed, but asserts the mental stance or attitude of the worshiper" (J. Gamberoni, *TDOT*, V, 67). The expression in 1a forms an inclusion with v 3d ("you are my rock and my stronghold") to provide a context for the petitions between.

The supplications which follow in vv 1b–3b make use of traditional language, but the force of the combination of terms is considerable. The supplicant prays never to be "put to shame," but to be "rescued," to be "set free," etc. God is implored to turn his ear toward the speaker (v 2b) so that the petitions can be heard (these verses are very similiar to 31:2–3a). The appeal to divine "righteousness" in v 2a is a plea for the activation of Yahweh's will for justice, for the vindication of the innocent who are oppressed; in general, for the setting right of affairs in human life and for the saving of those devoted to Yahweh (see Ps 52:8). The divine righteousness will be manifest when the supplicant is freed from the grasp of unjust and ruthless persons (v 4). V 4 forms an inclusion with v 1; note the direct address to Yahweh/God in both verses.

The main complaint (71:5–12). These verses set forth, in rather traditional language, the conditions of the supplicant which merit complaint to God. The complaint begins with a succinct statement of confidence in God, which is followed by an affirmation of life-long trust and praise in v 6. The meaning of v 7 is not entirely clear. The word for "mystery" (or "like a mystery," see note 7.a.) denotes a "wonder" or a "portent," something extraordinary, which is so out of the routine course of things that it baffles. The reference here can be understood (1) as an unusual case of God's care (so Weiser: "He is the sign or portent which in a visible way makes manifest 'to many' God's providential rule, his power and his help"), or (2) as an outstanding public example of divine punishment (cf. Deut 28:46)—perhaps, the evidence for life lived under a divine curse. The term מוֹפֵת is rather frequently used to convey a display of divine power as a sign or warning to make the enemies of God afraid (Exod 7:3; 11:9; Deut 6:22; 1 Kgs 13:3, 5; Isa 20:3)—so NEB in 71:7, "To many I seem a solemn warning." The word appears in a word-pair with אוֹת ("sign"); see, e.g., Exod 7:3; Deut 4:34; 6:22; 7:19; 13:2, 3; 26:8; 28:46; 29:2; 34:11; Isa 8:18. *Mopheth* is used especially to describe the events of the exodus from Egypt. In these contexts, the "signs and wonders" are demonstrations of divine power and explicit or implicit warnings to all who might dare to oppose the divine will. If the meaning of a "solemn warning" is understood in 7a, then 7b indicates that the speaker ignores the wrong (and for the enemies, gratifying) conclusions about his or her sufferings, while persisting in trust in God—"looking to God to see through to a conclusion the work He began so long ago" (Kidner, I, 251). Perhaps, however, we should not draw the lines of meaning too sharply. The verse may mean that the suppliant continues with unshaken trust in God regardless of how the "many" (v 7a; the people in the community) choose to interpret the situation. Some members of the community would have seen the suppliant as a "sign" of God's providential care; others would have understood his or her condition as a divine judgement. A "sign" is subject to the interpretation of the viewer.

The condition of the suppliant is the subject of talk and conspiracy on the part of enemies who are described as "soul-watchers" (v 10), those who wait for any opportunity to harm the life of the speaker. The foes assume that the suppliant has been forsaken by God and left at their mercy (v 11). The situation is made worse by the failing strength of advanced age (v 9); it is imperative that the suppliant not be abandoned by God while foes are strong and personal strength declines. V 12 forms the closing petition of this section (note the direct address to God which corresponds to the direct address to Yahweh in v 5). God is asked not to be far away (cf. Ps 22) and to hasten to help one who needs divine presence.

Petitions and promises (71:13–18). I have linked v 12 with the previous section, but it actually seems to be the pivot verse in the psalm which focus toward both vv 1–11 and vv 13–24. In any case, v 13 contains a petition to God for the punishment of enemies. The request in 13a ("let my adversaries end up in complete shame") echoes the petition in 1b ("may I never be put to shame"; cf. Ps 35:4, 26). The suppliant prays that the adversaries will end up "wrapped" in ignominy and humiliation (13b). The prayer for the punishment of enemies in v 13 is matched by a petition for personal care in v 18—"even to gray-haired old age."

The petitions in vv 13 and 18 frame 14–17, which are composed of statements of confidence and promises of praise if Yahweh responds to the pleas for help. The suppliant has continual hope and is ready to praise Yahweh more and more (v 14), even though there is a lack of scribal skill in expressing such praise (if this is what 15c means). Vv 15–16 seem to reflect the practice of bringing written prayer before Yahweh for his attention and response (perhaps, letter-prayers; see the discussion of *miktam* in note 56:4.a.) We need not accept the thesis of Delekat that prayers such as this were written on sanctuary walls by those seeking asylum or by prisoners, though his proposal is certainly possible. Writing and reading in ancient Israel was not restricted to a small group of professional scribes (for a convenient survey of this subject, see A. R. Millard, " The Question of Israelite Literacy," *Bible Review* 3 [1987] 22–31), and individual worshipers very probably offered written prayers along with oral prayers and sacrifices on some occasions. See 2 Kgs 19:14 // Isa 37:14 for Hezekiah's spreading out the letter from the Assyrian messengers in the temple before Yahweh, accompanied by a prayer of petition and complaint (cf. Job 31:35–37). The speaker in 71:15b–16 seems to be saying that he or she would come before Yahweh with a written account of Yahweh's mighty deeds of righteous power. This interpretation may be strengthened by the verb זכר in 16b; a verb which is used in the hiphil participial form in some references to designate a scribal recorder (e.g., 2 Sam 8:16; 20:24; 1 Kgs 4:3; 2 Kgs 18:18, 37; 1 Chr 18:15; Isa 36:3), though the role of the official involved is the subject of disagreement by commentators and may refer to a "remembrancer" or a herald, whose duty was to make reports to the king and communicate royal decrees (which would most probably have been written; for convenient surveys of the matter, see G. H. Jones, *1 and 2 Kings* [Grand Rapids, MI: Eerdmans, 1984] I, 135–36; P. K. McCarter, Jr., *2 Samuel,* AB 9, 255). In a few references, other forms of the verb זכר may refer to the production and or use of written material (e.g., 1 Chr 16:4; Isa 43:26—where is it used with the verb ספר— Exod 20:24; 2 Sam 18:18). The term להזכיר is the title of Ps 70 (a title which also covers Ps 71), and Ps 38 should also be noted (see 70:1, note c.)—the term may refer to the psalms which follow as suitable written prayers designed to cause Yahweh to remember those bringing them.

The verb "to hope" (יחל) in v 14 means "to wait for with expectation" or "to put hope in," and it is used in contexts which express positive anticipation, not anticipation of adverse judgment or punishment. The translation is often "wait/ wait for" (see Pss 31:25; 33:18; 38:15; 42:6; 43:5; 69:4; 130:5; 147:11)—sometimes used with קוה, "to wait for/look eagerly for," as in Ps 130:5–7; Isa 40:31; etc. NEB reads 16a as "I will begin with a tale of great deeds, O Lord God," which reflects the opinions of G. R. Driver (*VT* 1 [1951] 249 and D. W. Thomas [*TRP*, 29]) that the verb בוא can have the meaning of "enter upon/begin with/commence" (cf. Prov 18:6). This seems too forced for the context, as does KJV's "I will go in the strength of the Lord God," since the verb normally means "come," rather than a generalized "going." The best approach is to understand the verse as reflecting the speaker's willingness to go to the sanctuary for a thanksgiving service in which Yahweh's deeds of deliverance and blessing would be commemorated in a written account, accompanied by sacrifice, fellowship, and testimony of thanksgiving and praise (for the thanksgiving ceremony, see *Form/Structure/Setting* and *Comment* of Pss 30 and 66; also 40:6.

In v 17 the speaker recalls the teaching of God which has extended from youth to mature age (cf. vv 5–9). The subject matter of the teaching is not specified, but the wondrous deeds of Yahweh's righteous saving-work must be intended. On the basis of the statements in v 17, the suppliant prays that God will not forsake him or her in old age (18; cf. 22:31–32 [30–31]. The speaker looks ahead to old age and prays that God will not abandon him or her when the vital forces of life begin to be depleted—at least not until the next generation has been told about the might and saving-power of God (v 18). The speaker wants the strength to make the coming generation know that no god can compare with Yahweh (19c; cf. 35:10; 86:8; 89:7, 9 [6, 8]; Mic 7:18), the incomparable God (see Isa 40:10–31).

Praise and prayer (71:19–20) . These two verses seem to be an intrusion into the psalm, even if the singular of the marginal reading is accepted (see note 20.b. above). Vv 19–20 in their plural form serve to adapt the individual prayer of the original psalm to community application. On the other hand, the plural forms in v 20 do not nullify the validity of the prayer for an individual. The speakers in the group of psalms to which 71 seems to belong identify their personal welfare with that of the nation (Pss 22:23–25c; 102:22–23). If the singular reading of these verses is adopted, they should be understood as statements of confidence, expressing praise for past deliverance and assurance about the future (cf. LXX; KJV; RSV). In the plural, however, v 19 is a hymn-like expression of praise, and v 20 is an acknowledgment of the troubles which Yahweh has allowed his people to see (the exile?), followed by supplications for renewal of life and deliverance from the depths of the netherworld ("depths of the earth" refers to the netherworld). The literal meaning of the language should not be pressed, but when read as the prayer of a speaker in advanced age it points to a resurrection-like restoration of life (with regard to the nation and the exile, cf. Ezek 37:1–14; Isa 26:19–21). It is clear from other contexts that the language of the netherworld and the revival of life can be used in relation to the calamitous troubles of the living. For example,

> O Lord, you brought up my soul from Sheol;
> from those going down to the pit, you made me live. (Craigie, Ps 30:4)

Craigie (253) says of the speaker in 30:4 that: " The meaning is not that the psalmist had died and been restored to life; rather he had been so close to death that it was as if he were already dead, and from that grave situation [no pun intended!] he had been rescued by God's act of healing." See also his *Comment* (93, 95) on Sheol in 6:16 (also Ps 88:6–8). Any diminution of vital power could be considered as a Sheol-condition, an invasion of life by death. In Sheol, life continued at minimal levels of vitality, devoid of praise and joy. The suppliant in Ps 71 speaks as one already in the depths of Sheol—though expecting to live to old age! The plural reading evidently points to the nation's similar condition because of the oppression of the exile.

Petition for restoration and vow of praise (71:21–24). The suppliant prays for restoration to a satisfactory status in life and for comfort in v 21 (cf. Job). If vv 19–20 are understood as a prayer for the restoration of the nation, v 21 is a prayer for the individual suppliant to share in its new well-being and to have a significant place in its society (on the תרב גדלתי, lit. "increase my greatness," of v 21, see note 21.a; "greatness" is normally used of God or of princes and people in high positions; Ps 143:3, 6; Esth 1:4; 6:3; 10:2). The LXX and Vulgate avoid the prayer for greatness by an individual by changing to "your [God's] righteousness" (or "your greatness" in some manuscripts): "You multiplied your righteousness."

A vow to praise God when deliverance comes follows in vv 22–24. The speaker promises to give praise and thanksgiving to the "Holy One of Israel" (v 22), a title for God which is seldom found outside the book of Isaiah (see Pss 78:41; 80:19). Whatever its origin, the title "Holy One of Israel" indicates Yahweh's possession of Israel and his claim on the people for their obedience (see W. H. Schmidt, *The Faith of the Old Testament: A History*, tr. J. Sturdy [Philadelphia: Westminster, 1983] 152–56). God demonstrates his holiness both in acts of judgment and in the punishment of his own people (Isa 5:16) and in acts of deliverance (Isa 41:14, 16; 43:14–15, etc.). The Holy One of Israel is exalted both in judgment and in salvation, and he holds both Israel and the nations accountable. The suppliant's praise will emphasize the righteousness of Yahweh—his acts which bring right order into the world, his "putting things right." V 24b is a statement of confidence about the fate of foes who have sought to injure the suppliant (cf. vv 3, 13).

Explanation

As explained in the *Form/Structure/Setting* of Ps 70, Ps 71 should be read together with 70. The speaker in 70 is presented as one of the "poor and needy," who prays that God will hasten to aid and deliver without delay. The suppliant is distressed because unnamed persons seek her life (מבקשׁי נפשׁי, "seekers of my soul/ life") and long for her hurt (חפצי רעתי, "those who desire my hurt," 70:3). The prayer of the speaker contains a threefold petition: (1) let God turn to help, (2) let the enemies be ashamed, frustrated, and humiliated, and (3) let those who seek God (מבקשׁיך, "seekers of you") be glad and rejoice.

The speaker in Ps 71 is also identified as one who has enemies "who seek my hurt" (מבקשׁי רעתי, v 24), enemies who are further identified as "adversaries of my soul" (שׂטני נפשׁי) in v 13 and as "watchers of my soul" (שׁמרי נפשׁי) in v 10. The opponents are also characterized as "unjust and ruthless" (v 4). The speaker is characterized as one of mature age, perhaps approaching old age (vv 9, 18), who looks back on a lifetime of reliance on God (v 6), and who has been instructed in recounting the praiseworthy acts of God from youth to mature age (v 17), one who is at home among those who praise and worship. The speaker is one who shares the terrible troubles of exilic life and the yet-to-be restored Israel (v 20, see *Comment*) and waits to "live again" in a proper status among Yahweh's restored people (21). As in Ps 70, the suppliant wants God to hurry (חושׁה) to help (v 12) and to nullify the words of those who propose to chase and seize him because they have concluded that God has forsaken him (vv 11–12). There are petitions that adversaries be put to shame and wrapped in ignominy and humiliation (see v 13; cf. 70:3). The suppliant is ready to come to the sanctuary for a praise and thanksgiving service (v 16).

Readers may discover numerous angles of approach to meaning in these two psalms. I will mention only two in these brief remarks. First, commentators have observed that 71 is one of the few psalms in which the speaker is identified as a person of mature age, a mature adult at or near the boundary of old age, already feeling the diminishing of strength which age brings. Ruthless enemies assume that the speaker has been abandoned by God, and they are ready to seize him. The speaker might have expected mature age to bring exemption from such attacks, but such is not the case. Family or friends are not mentioned; the speaker is alone—except for God.

However, the psalm seems to indicate that advanced age has at least one major advantage: a long memory of God's presence and of being taught to understand the ways of God (vv 6, 17). Hope in God (v 5) may become a more vital element of life for those who are both devout and old. These are the people who can tell a new generation about the mighty deeds of God (vv 16–18), if they will listen. They are people of wisdom whose knowledge and skill are essential. They are also the people who know that enduring wisdom is a gift from God.

> [You say] with the aged is wisdom,
>   in length of days is understanding.
> [But I say] with God is wisdom and strength,
>   his are counsel and understanding. (Job 12:12–13)

Those who can look back on a long trail of trust in God know better than those who are younger that both statements are true.

A second major aspect of these psalms is the theme of divine righteousness in 71. The expression "your righteousness"—addressed to God—occurs five times: vv 2, 15, 16, 19, 24. The "heaven-high" righteousness of Yahweh (71:19) is clearly a main point of emphasis. Yahweh's righteousness is often referred to in the OT (e.g., Pss 7:9; 35:24; 97:6; 119:7, 62, 75, 103:17; 111:3; 116:5; Jer 9:24; Dan 9:14; Zeph 3:5). The contexts frequently deal with some function of judgment, especially in upholding the cause of the oppressed (e.g., Ps 9:4–5, 9–11—see *Comment* of Craigie, 118—50:6; 96:13; 99:4; Isa 5:16; 58:2; Jer 11:20). Thus appeal is made to Yahweh for deliverance from various kinds of trouble (also Pss 31:1; 143:11), from enemies (Pss 5:8; 143:1–3), from the wicked (Pss 36; 71:2, 4), and for the vindication ("putting right") of those falsely charged or deprived of justice (e.g., Pss 14:5; cf. 53:6; 35:24; 69:28; 94:21–23; 103:6; 116:5–6; 140:13–14; 146:7–9; Isa 62:1–5). The righteous acts of Yahweh are also his saving acts (36:6), and righteousness often appears in contexts which indicate that the meaning is that of deliverance and salvation (e.g., Pss 22:32; 40:10–11; 51:14–16; 65:6; Isa 46:12; 51:1, 5–6, 8). Yahweh is a "righteous God and a Savior" (Isa 45:21).

> There are two sides to his righteousness: salvation and condemnation; deliverance and punishment. However—and this is an important point— Yahweh's righteousness is never solely an act of condemnation or punishment. . . . Because his righteousness is his restoration of the right to him from whom it has been taken, it at the same time includes punishment of the evildoer; but the punishment is an integral part of the restoration. Only because Yahweh saves does he condemn. His righteousness is first and foremost saving. (E. R. Achtemeier, *IDB*, IV, 83)

The righteousness of God is not a strict apportionment of justice according to some divinely fixed norm, used to measure all actions involved. The righteousness of God is his will for order and fairness in all the realms of the world (W. Zimmerli, *Old Testament Theology in Outline*, tr. David E. Green [Atlanta: John Knox Press, 1978] 142–43). Ps 71 (with Ps 70 included) is a prayer for deliverance in terms of divine righteousness. See further, *Comment* on 52:8.

A Prayer for the King   (72:1–20)

Bibliography

Eaton, J. H. *Kingship.* 141–42, 159–60, 160–65. **Johnson, A. R.** *Sacral Kingship in Ancient Israel.* Cardiff: University of Wales Press, 1955. 6–14. **Kselman, J. S.** "Psalm 72: Some Observations on Structure." *BASOR* 220 (1975) 77–81. **Paul, S. M.** "Psalm 72:5—A Traditional Blessing for the Long Life of the King." *JNES* 31 (1972) 351–54. **Saebø, M.** "Von Grossreich zum Weltreich: Erwägungen zu Pss. lxxii8, lxxxix26; Sach ix 10b." *VT* 28 (1978) 83–91. **Skehan, P. W.** "Strophic Structure in Psalm 72 (71)." *Bib* 40 (1959) 302–8. **Veugelers, P.** "Le Psaume LXXII Poeme messianique?" *ETL* 41 (1965) 317–43. **Wilson, G. H.** " The Use of Royal Psalms at the 'Seams' of the Hebrew Psalter." *JSOT* 35 (1986) 85–94.

Translation

1   A Solomonic psalm [a]   (4+2)
    O God, your justice [b] give to the king
        and your righteousness to the son of the king.[c]
2   *May he judge your people with righteousness*   (3+2)
        and your poor with justice.
3   *May the mountains bring well-being [a] for the people*   (4+2)
        and the hills righteousness.[b]
4   *May he vindicate [a] the poor of the people,*   (2+2+2)
        deliver the children of the needy,
        and crush any oppressor.
5   *May he live [a] while the sun endures*   (2+4)
        and as long as the moon [b] through all generations.
6   *May he be [a] like rain upon fertile land,[b]*   (3+3)
        as showers that irrigate the earth.
7   *May righteousness [a] sprout in his days*   (3+4)
        and well-being abound until the moon is no more.
8   *May he rule from sea to sea*   (3+3)
        and from the River [a] unto the ends of the earth.
9   *Before him may his foe [a] bow*   (3+3)
        and his enemies lick the dust.
10   *May the kings of Tarshish [a] and the islands [b] render tribute*   (4+4)
        and the kings of Sheba [c] and Saba [d] bring a gift.
11   *May all kings fall down before him*   (3+2)
        all nations serve him.
12   *For [a] he will rescue the needy who cry for deliverance,*   (3+3)
        the poor, and the one with no helper.
13   *He will look with compassion upon the weak and needy*   (3+3)
        and their lives he will deliver.
14   *From oppression and violence he will redeem [a] their lives*   (4+3)
        and their blood will be precious in his eyes.

15   *May he live!*   (1+3+3+2)
        Let gold of Sheba be given [a] *to him;*
        let (the people) pray [b] *for him continually;*
        let them bless [c] *him through the day.* [d]
16   *May there be abundance* [a] *of grain in the land—*   (3+2+3+4)
        even on the mountaintops!
        May his crops (of grain) thrive [b] *as (the trees) of Lebanon,*
        and (people) blossom forth from the town, [c] *like the grass of*
        the land.
17   *May his name endure forever*   (3+3+2+2)
        and increase as long as the sun. [a]
        May people bless themselves by him,
        and all nations call him happy.
18   *Blessed be Yahweh God,* [a]   (3+2+3)
        the God of Israel,
        who alone does wondrous things.
19   *Blessed be his glorious name forever*   (4+3+2)
        and may all the earth be filled with his glory!
        Amen and Amen.
20   *The prayers of David son of Jesse are ended.*

Notes

1.a. לשלמה—lit. "to Solomon/of Solomon," or "belonging to Solomon/concerning Solomon." This is one of two psalms that mention Solomon in the title. The other, Ps 127, is one of the "Processional Songs" (see the discussion of Allen on Ps 120).

1.b. משפטיך "your judgments/ordinances," but both the LXX and the Syriac translate the word in the singular: "your justice." Since the term is parallel with "your righteousness," the reading given here has both textual and poetic support.

1.c. לבן־מלך—lit. "to a son of a king." This phrase parallels "the king" earlier in the line and is often a different way of referring to the same individual. This terminology emphasizes the place of the new king in the royal dynasty.

3.a. שלום—usually translated "peace" but in this context "well-being" seems more appropriate. The reader should be aware of the connotation of "completeness, wholeness." This same note applies to this word in v 7.

3.b. בצדקה—lit. "in" or "by righteousness." The prep. ב is missing from some of the versions (see BHS).

4.a. ישפט—a form of the root שפט from which משפט, "justice" (which appears two times in these four verses), is derived.

5.a. ייראוך—lit. "May they fear you." The pl. verb has no clear antecedent and changes the focus of the psalm from the relationships of the king to his subjects and to other kings to the relationship between (probably) the people and God. Dahood takes the verb as sing. and translates "May he fear you," which is more appropriate but is a difficult reading. However, the LXX reads καὶ συμπαραμενεῖ, a translation of ויאריך ("May he prolong" or "continue long"), which fits easily into the context of the psalm and is followed in the translation above.

5.b. עם־שמש ולפני ירח—lit. "with sun and before/in the presence of the moon." Ps 89:37–38 describes the line and throne of David as enduring "as the sun before me, as the moon it will be established forever." S. M. Paul interprets this verse as a traditional blessing for the king's longevity: the sun/moon image is found in Sumerian, Akkadian, and Assyrian court blessings as well.

6.a. ירד—lit. "May he come down, descend."

6.b. גז is literally "mown grass, shearing," but rain on mown grass is not desirable. BDB gives "land to be mown" as the meaning of גז in this verse. Dahood (II, p. 181) interprets this phrase as "may the influence of the king be felt in all the cultivated regions of the world."

7.a. צדיק—literally "righteous one," which Dahood sees as the counterpart of עשׁק ("oppressor") at the end of v 4 (II, 181). Some Heb. manuscripts as well as the LXX and the Syriac read צדק ("righteousness"), which matches the parallel שׁלום ("welfare").

8.a. נהר often refers to the Euphrates (Gen 15:18; 31:21; 2 Sam 10:16), but not invariably. This may be a reference to the great stream that issues from the temple in Israel's visions of Zion (cf. Ps 46:5; Ezek 47). In this case the poet would be seeing the power of the king extending from Jerusalem over the world.

9.a. ציים—literally "wild beast" or "desert-dweller." This is frequently emended to צרים ("foes") or צריו ("his foes"); the second alternative is supported by the parallel איביו ("his enemies").

10.a. תרשׁישׁ is usually identified as Phoenician Tartessus in southern Spain, although some locate it in Sardinia (Dahood, I).

10.b. איים probably refers to the Mediterranean coasts and islands.

10.c. שׁבא is the Hebrew spelling of the South Arabic Saba, an area known for its wealth (Isa 60:6; Jer 6:20; Ezek 27:22–25).

10.d. סבא is either an Arabian kingdom, perhaps located in modern Yemen, or a Sabean colony in North Africa. See Gen 10:7; Isa 43:3; 45:15; Joel 3:8; 1 Chr 1:9.

12.a. The כי at the beginning of this sentence may mean "for" or "because" and sometimes "if," among other meanings. Dahood (II) translates it as "if," making the conditional protasis extend through v 14 and beginning the apodosis with ויחי ("*then* may he live") of v 15. Thus the promise of life for the king is dependent on his establishing justice towards the poorest of the people. Grammatically this translation is defensible. There is no strict form which a Heb. conditional sentence must follow, and כי is among the particles which may begin one. Ps 89:30–32 asserts that the Davidic king will be punished if he violates the commandments of the Lord (although the line will endure). Theologically Dahood's translation is not incompatible with the one given here. Both show a connection between the king's work for justice and the prayer for his life.

14.a. The verb גאל means "to redeem, to act as kinsman" (BDB). It is used in connection with levirate marriage, when the kinsmen of a dead man marries his widow and has children by her in her first husband's name (cf. 1 Cor 3:13). It also means "to avenge the blood" of murder (cf. Num 35:19–27 passim). The word implies that there is a personal relationship between the redeemer and the one on whose behalf he is acting. They are connected in some way, which is why the redeemer is willing to pay the price.

15.a. ויחי ויתן־לו—lit. "and so he will give to him," but both the LXX and the Syriac translate this passively. The jussive force continues from the first verb.

15.b. ויתפלל בעדו—lit. "and may one pray for him," apparently referring to those who have received the king's justice in vv 12–14. The passive construction is simpler in English.

15.c. יברכנהו—lit. "may one bless him." See n. 15.b.

15.d. כל־היום—lit. "all the day." This is a difficult verse, largely because there are no stated subjects or objects. Instead, there are four 3rd pers. masc. sing. verbs and three 3rd pers. masc. sing. pronominal suffixes. Some read the verse as a continuation of v 14 with the needy as the subject: "that he may live, and gold of Sheba be given to him, and that he may pray for him" (the king) "continually and may bless him at all times" (Weiser, 501). H. Schmidt offers a similar translation (136–37), as does B. Duhm. The main problem with this is that the weak and needy are represented by pl. suffixes in v 14 while in v 15 the verbs and suffixes are sing.

16.a. פסה is found only here in MT, but it apparently means "plenty/abundance." KJV has "an handful."

16.b. ירעשׁ, usually translated "shake" or "wave." Briggs (II, 139) reads as ירעשׁה, "may sheep pasture," in order to avoid an unlikely translation of the root רעשׁ, which usually refers to earthquakes or storms. However, the "shaking" motion is not always severe; in Job 39:20 it is used of the jumping of a horse. One option is to understand the verb as referring to the rustling of the wind in the grain, which sounds like the wind moving through the cedars of Lebanon—hyperbolic language, of course. The *Translation* assumes that רעשׁ can mean "thrive/flourish" (see KB, 903). For discussion of emendations, see Gunkel, 310.

16.c. The emendation of מעיר ("from a town") is rather common. *BHS* suggests יציץ ועמירו for מעיר ועמיר (as in Gunkel): "may it flourish and its sheaf." However, "city/town" may be retained (with LXX), with the meaning of (1) the people flourishing out of the towns (where they were born and reared)—coming forth like the grass of the fields, or (2) that prosperity would come forth from the towns. The first option seems preferable.

17.a. לפני־שׁמשׁ—lit. "before/in presence of the sun."

18.a. While the Elohim (אלהים) is missing from several ancient manuscripts as well as LXX and the Syriac, and its presence could be the result of confusion with the following word, caution is in order about its deletion. The "heaping up" of divine names in an introit is found elsewhere (see Kraus, I, 487, 491).

Form/Setting/Structure

Ps 72 is universally considered to be a royal psalm. Hermann Gunkel, who pioneered form criticism in the psalms and discerned five basic types among them (the others are hymn, communal lament, individual lament, and individual song of praise), identified ten psalms as royal: 2, 18, 20, 21, 45, 72, 101, 110, 132, and 144:1–11. The royal pslams bear no specific stylistic characteristics. Some are hymns of praise, and some are laments, but all deal with the person or the office of the king. Since Israel saw her kings as standing in a relationship of special endowment by and responsibility to God, her worship included concerns about them. Others have expanded the royal classification to cover more psalms, but 72 continues to be included among them. More specifically, Ps 72 is probably also an accession or coronation psalm, a prayer for the king at the beginning of his reign. It may have formed part of the coronation ceremony as well as of less spectacular occasions when praying for the king's welfare was required. This psalm focuses not on the relationship between the king and God, such as we find in Ps 2, but on the relationship between the king and the people with glimpses of the response of the nations and of the land itself to the reign of this royal son.

The dating of the royal psalms has been the subject of scholarly debate. Older source critics such as J. Wellhausen and his followers put them in the post-exilic period and conjectured that the community of Israel itself, a foreign monarch, or a Maccabean prince was the subject of these psalms. Later scholarship has found these suggestions untenable and assigns the royal psalms to the period of the monarchy in Israel. It is clear that the king in Ps 72 is highly idealized, and some have suggested that he is a messianic figure (Briggs). However, he is not the king of the messianic kingdom since there are still oppressors tormenting the poor, and nowhere else do we find the people interceding on behalf of the messianic king. The idealization apparent in the psalm is the result of the hope attendant at every new beginning. However, in its present canonical context, the psalm is a prayer for the future realization of the idealized hopes of monarchy, especially reflecting the hope of Israelites in exilic and post-exilic communities for the restoration of the Davidic dynasty and the fulfillment of the promises attendant to the Davidic kingship.

Ps 72 bears the title "A Solomonic Psalm," which may mean it is to, for, or concerning Solomon as well as by him. Since this psalm also has a postscript saying that this ends the prayers of David, the title probably does not indicate Solomonic authorship, certainly not in the opinion of whoever wrote the postscript—which may be earlier than the title. Apparently Ps 72 concludes an early collection of Davidic psalms which was later incorporated into the larger psalter that we now have. There are psalms after this that are identified as Davidic. Aside from the title and postscript there is very little material within the psalm itself that indicates a specific date. In its present canonical placement, the note at the end (v 20) suggests that the psalm was read in later times as a prayer of David for his son and successor, Solomon. The psalm is a prayer that the Davidic hopes and expectations be fulfilled in his descendants (see G. H. Wilson, *JSOT* 35 [1986] 85–94).

This psalm has irregular meter but apparently does consist of five stanzas of approximately equal length. Throughout it shows a concern for the well-being of the dispossessed and the intricate relationship among God, the king, and the people. The first stanza (vv 1–4) focuses on the prayer that God's justice will be manifest in the king for the people. The second stanza (vv 5–8) begins with a prayer for the king's life and shows life flowing from him to the land. The third stanza (vv 9–11) is a tightly constructed excursus in which it is asked that the influence of the king might be worldwide. In the fourth stanza (vv 12–15) the themes of the first two are echoed. The king's establishment of justice is life-giving, and so the people are urged to pray continually for him. In the final stanza (vv 16–17) this completed reciprocal relationship between king and people makes itself felt in the fertility of the land as well as in the minds of the nations. Each of these stanzas ends with the king fulfilling his function, and, except for the first, each ends with a reference to the effect the harmony of his reign has on the nations of the earth. Ps 72 ends the second book of psalms (Ps 42–72), so vv 18–19 act as a benediction to the preceding section and v 20 (as discussed above) marks the end of the collection.

Comment

May God give justice through the king (72:1–4). In the first stanza the prayer is for the king to be endowed with the justice and righteousness of God. The king's function as the agent of Yahweh (1 Sam 10:1–2) is evident in the emphasis in v 2 on his extending God's righteousness and justice to God's people, especially the poor; both the attributes and the people belong to God, and the king is the instrument that brings them together. V 3 shows that the completed well-being of the people flows out of the natural order of things; when the righteous king is blessed with God's justice, the earth itself participates in the positive relationship existing among God, king, and people. Harmony and righteousness become part of all of creation. In v 4 the son of the king delivers the sons of the needy; the one blessed by God in turn blesses the poor. The complex literary structure of vv 1–4 enhances the forcefulness of the language. The word-pair "justice" ("judgments")-"righteousness" of v 1 is matched by the word-pair "well-being"–"righteousness" in v 3, and the verses have the same 4+2 metrical construction. V 2 is paired with v 4ab in a chiastic ABBA pattern:

May he judge your people in righteousness	A
and your poor with justice.	B
May he vindicate the poor . . . ,	B'
deliver the . . . needy	A'

V 4c stands outside these patterns and pairs with 1a to form another 4+2 statement:

O God, your justice give to the king (v 1a)
    and crush any oppressor. (v 4c)

(cf. J. S. Kselman, *BASOR* 220 [1975] 77–81).

May God give life through the king (72:5–8). The second stanza contains a prayer for the long life of the king. Again, as in the first stanza, the king is related to people and land. He will be "like rain upon fertile ground" that enables it to bear (v 6), and the land will indeed bear righteousness and well-being, as it did in the first section. God makes the land bear, but through the reign of the king. This psalm compares the effect of the king on the nation to the effect of rain on fertile soil; he does indeed give life, but (as we shall see in stanza four) the life he gives enhances but does not create the physical existence that the people already possess. Because the king fulfills his God-given function, the land is blessed as well, though the blessing is always ultimately from God. The link between the king and fertility is found more directly elsewhere in the ancient Near East where the king's special relationship with his deities (sometimes incarnational and sometimes representational) gives him the ability to confer life upon the land. The linking of this trait with social justice in stanza four gives this characteristic of kingship a Yahwistic flavor. This section concludes with the prayer that the king's power might extend over the entire earth.

Let foes and foreigners yield to the king (72:9–11). This section develops the closing thought of the previous one. God is petitioned to make hostile, distant, and powerful monarchs submit in service to the just and life-giving king of Israel. His power has the effect of drawing together the rest of the world to serve him (v 11). Since he serves God, by implication he brings the nations to Yahweh's service as well. The theme of the people of the world coming to worship God in Jerusalem is found in Zechariah (8:20–23; 14:16–17). The mention of Sheba recalls the rich gifts the queen of that country presented to Solomon (1 Kgs 10:1–10), although here not a queen but kings are mentioned (v 10).

The basis for the king's dominion (72:12–15). In stanza four the reason for the prayer is made explicit; the king's life-giving activity does more than enhance the fertility of the earth. Its major characteristic is his intervention on behalf of the poor among God's people (vv 13–14). He is the compassionate one who helps those who have no one else to stand up for them. He redeems their lives as a kinsman would (see textual note on this word). Oppression and violence, which are unnatural, can no longer rule the existence of the people. V 15 gives the conclusion which follows from vv 12–14—verses which serve as a protasis for the apodosis in v 15 (cf. Dahood). The speaker prays for long life for the king and for the precious gold of Sheba (see note 10.c.) that it be given to him. In addition, the speaker calls for continual prayer for the king that he may be constantly sustained by the divine blessing. The ויחי ("and may he live!")at the beginning of v 15 extends the thought of v 5, and the gifts called for in v 10 are enhanced by the gold of Sheba in v 15b.

Closing prayer for the prosperity of the king's reign (72:16–17). The final stanza prays for an abundance of life springing forth in profusion. The fruit of the land, the grain that supplies physical life to the inhabitants of the land, multiplies, and then the redeemed people themselves do the same (v 16). The reading of v 16d is uncertain. If the translation above is correct, the meaning is that the towns (where the people lived) would become fertile like the fields and blossom forth with a profusion of new people for the king's reign. It is clear from the psalm, however, that the life which the king gives is more than physical. The fertility of the land is part of God's blessing on Israel, but it is not because of a good harvest that the people increase and grow strong. It is because the king is truly God's agent, giving hope and fullness to their lives, that the people flourish. The land is part of God's promise to Israel, part of the relationship between them, and so it participates as well in the welfare of the nation. As people and land respond to the life-giving activities of the king, his fame increases. Eventually he becomes a model for all the nations as they desire to be similarly blessed (v 17).

A benediction and concluding statement (72:18–20). These verses serve as a benediction not only to Ps 72 but to the second book of psalms (42–72) as well (see *Form/Structure/Setting*). In the context of Ps 72 they serve as a reminder that God alone is the giver of life, justice, and power. The glory goes to him rather than to any earthly agents, no matter how great they might be. V 20 is a concluding note to the second book of the Psalter (Ps 42–72) in its present context. As noted above, it also probably indicates that Ps 72 was understood in later tradition as a prayer by David for Solomon.

Explanation

Psalm 72 offers a glimpse of the ideal relationship among ruler, God, and people. The people pray for the empowerment of the king, who uses the gifts God gives, not for his own benefit or even for the benefit of the powerful, but for the least of all among the people. The constant prayers of the people enable him to continue in his kingly function.

In the *Comment* the themes of justice, life, and power were traced through the psalm. It is worth noting that the first prayer is for the king to bring justice and deliverance to the poor. The essential nature of social justice in the service of God is found throughout the OT (cf. Isa 1:12–17; Amos 5:14–15, 24). Second to that is the plea that the king may live and give life to the land, and third is the hope that his power may go to the ends of the earth. As the psalm progresses we see that these are not three separate goals, but one. The familiar ancient belief in the king as giver of fertile life is here echoed and amplified; establishing justice is also a life-giving activity, and to the psalmist a much more important one. When the king gives the life of God's justice to the people, then the blessings of fertile land and far-reaching power follow. All of these themes add up to the biblical concept of *shalom* ("peace/well-being"). Though the word *shalom* appears only twice in this psalm (vv 3 and 7), it brings together into a wholeness the political, economic, social, and spiritual dimensions of life—which is what *shalom* is all about. The integration encompassed in *shalom* extends into an integral unity between heaven and earth (Stuhlmueller, I, 320). The blessing of *shalom*, in which there is life and harmony for all creation, is a central concept of the Bible (see Lev 26:4–6; Ezek 34:25–29; Eph 2:14). *Shalom* is the salvation which embraces all creation.

The people have responsibility in this relationship as well. They need to respond to the king. They are to invoke God's blessing on him all his days. Although in the context of the psalm it appears that these prayers come only as a result of his work for the people, the probability that this is a coronation psalm indicates that the people begin to pray for the king even before he takes on his tasks in order that he might be empowered by God to fulfill them. While the king stands in special relationship to God as the anointed son of David, the people are privileged to be able to intercede for him because they are in relationship to God as well. They pray for the life of the king in order that the king may give them life which enables them, in turn, to pray. It is a complex relationship, but when it is established the world itself is changed through it. An exhortation from the NT is in order: "First of all, then, I urge that supplications, prayers, intercessions, and thanksgivings be made for all men, for kings and all who are in high positions, that we may lead a quiet and peacable life, godly and respectful in every way" (1 Tim 2:1–2, RSV).

As stated under *Form/Structure/Setting*, this psalm is not in the strict sense messianic. It deals with an earthly king. It was at least in part the frustration of these hopes that led to the development of the messianic idea in Israel. No king in Israel's history ever matched the ideal, but the hope for one never died. As Christians we affirm the life-giving power of Jesus (John 10:10), who is concerned for the poor and oppressed (Matt 25) and before whom every knee should bow (Phil 2:9–11). Like the citizens of the Davidic monarchy, we pray that the relationship between our King and ourselves may be dynamic enough to change the world.

From Theodicy to Credo   (73:1–28)

Bibliography

Allen, L. "Psalm 73: An Analysis." *TynB* 33 (1981) 93-118. **Brueggemann, W.** *The Message of the Psalms: A Theological Commentary.* Minneapolis: Augsburg, 1984. 115–21. **Buber, M.** *Right and Wrong: An Interpretation of Some Psalms.* London: SCM, 1952. 34–51; also in *Theodicy in the Old Testament.* Ed. J. L. Crenshaw. Philadelphia: Fortress Press, 1983. 109–18. **Buss, M. J.** " The Psalms of Asaph and Korah." *JBL* 82 (1963) 382–92. **Caquot, A.** "Le psaume LXXIII." *Sem* 20 (1971) 29–55. **Crenshaw, J. L.** *A Whirlpool of Torment: Israelite Traditions of God as an Oppressor.* Philadelphia: Fortress Press, 1984. 93–169. **Kraus, H.-J.** *Theology of the Psalms.* 168–75. **Luyten, J.** "Psalm 73 and Wisdom." In *La Sagesse de l'Ancien Testament.* Ed. Maurice Gilbert. Leuven: Leuven UP, 1979. 59–81. **Mannal, M.** "Sur le quadruple *avec toi* de Ps. LXXIII 21–26." *VT* 21 (1971) 59–67. ———. "Les adorateurs de mot dans le Psaume LXXIII." *VT* 22 (1972) 425–29. **McCann, J. C.** *Psalm 73: An Interpretation Emphasizing Rhetorical and Canonical Criticism.* Ph.D. Diss. Duke University, 1985. **Nasuti, H. P.** *Tradition History.* **Perdue, L. G.** *Wisdom and Cult.* SBLDS 30. Missoula, MT: Scholars Press, 1977. 286–91. **Rice, G.** "An Exposition of Psalm 73." *JRT* 41 (1984) 76–86. **Ross, J. F.** "Psalm 73." In *Israelite Wisdom.* Ed. J. G. Gammie et al. Missoula, MT: Scholars Press, 1978. 161–75. **Westermann, C.** *Praise and Lament.* ———. *The Psalms: Structure, Content and Message.* Tr. R. D. Gehrke. Minneapolis: Augsburg, 1980. **Würthwein, E.** "Erwägung zu Psalm 73." In *Wort und Existenz.* Göttingen: Vandenhoeck & Ruprecht, 1970. 161–78.

Translation

1   An Asaphite Psalm.[a]
    Truly,[b] God is good to Israel,[c]   (3+3)
    to those who are pure in heart!

2 But for me, my feet had almost stumbled;   (4+3)
       my step had nearly slipped,

3   because I envied the arrogant,   (3+3)
       and coveted [a] the prosperity of the wicked.

4 For they have no pains at their deaths;   (3+3)
       and fat are their bodies. [a]

5 They are not troubled like mortals,   (3+3)
       nor plagued like humans.

6 Consequently, pride is their necklace,   (3+3)
       and violence drapes them like a robe.

7 Their eyes bulge from fatness; [a]   (3+3)
       the conceit of their hearts is unlimited.

8 They scoff and speak with malice;   (3+3)
       in their arrogance they threaten oppression.

9 They set their mouths in the heavens,   (3+3)
       while their tongues strut on the earth. [a]

10 So his people turn to them, [a]   (4+4)
       and they swill the waters of abundance. [b]

11 And they say, "What does God know?"   (3+3)
       and, "Does the Most High know anything?"

12 Behold, these are the wicked;   (3+3)
       always carefree, their prosperity increases.

13 It surely seemed as nothing that I kept my heart clean,   (3+3)
       and washed my hands in innocence—

14 I was plagued all during the day,   (3+2)
       and my punishment [a] (began) each morning.

15 If I had said, "I will speak thus"—   (3+4)
       Behold! I would have betrayed your children.

16 When I tried to understand this,   (3+3)
       it was torment in my eyes; [a]

17 until I entered the sanctuary [a] of God,   (3+2)
       then I comprehended their destiny. [b]

18 Truly, you will put them on slippery places;   (4+2)
       making them fall into deceptive places of ruin. [a]

19 How suddenly they can be destroyed!   (4+3)
       completely swept away by terrors. [a]

20 Like a dream when one awakens   (2+4)
       (so) when you rouse yourself, O Lord,
       you will despise them as mere images. [a]

21 When my heart was as sour as vinegar,   (3+2)
       and my insides were torn-up, [a]

22 I [a] was senseless and ignorant;   (3+3)
       I was a brute beast before you.

23 Yet, I [a] am always with you;   (3+3)
       you hold my right hand!

24 With your counsel, you guide me,   (2+3)
       and afterward, with glory, you will receive me. [a]

25	*[With you] what can I lack in heaven,*[a] *And with you I desire nothing else on earth.*	(2[3]+3)
26	*My flesh and heart were spent,*[a] *but my strength*[b] *and portion*[c] *is God, forever!*[d]	(3+4)
27	*Behold! Those far from you will perish;* *you destroy all who are faithless to you.*	(3+3)
28	*But for me, the nearness of God is my good;* *I have made the Lord, Yahweh,*[a] *my refuge—* *telling*[b] *of all your works!*	(4+4+3)

Notes

1.a. This is the first of eleven consecutive psalms bearing the superscription לאסף. The same precautions regarding the similar superscription לדוד to authorship apply here as well (Craigie, 31–35 and n. Ps. 51:1.a.). The collection of Asaphite Psalms (Pss 50, 73–83) is one of six basic collections which form most of the Psalter (Craigie, 27ff.). The Chronicler's tradition seems to link the Levites of the Ephraimite tradition and the Asaphite singers (Anderson, *Psalms*, I, 45; Buss, *JBL* 82 [1963] 382–92; Mowinckel, *PIW*, II, 79–82; Nasuti, *Tradition History*, 117).

1.b. This Hebrew particle "truly" (אך) strikes a note of certainty (Cohen, 231). It appears at key points in the psalm; see vv 13 and 18. See further in *Comment*.

1.c. The inclinations of most twentieth-century commentators in rejecting "to Israel" for "to the upright" (לְיָשָׁר אל for לְיִשְׂרָאֵל) is reflected in the textual notes of *BHS* (Gunkel, 316; Jacquet, 431; Kraus, III, 502). The RSV and NEB translations follow the emendation. There is much to say for it, since it retains the consonantal text, improves the meter, and offers a good parallelism between "upright" and "pure in heart." However, it is not without problems, not the least of which is that there is absolutely no textual evidence for the suggested reading. MT should be retained. See *Comment*.

3.a. Lit. "watched," but the parallelism with "envied" seems to suggest the "watching" is more than just seeing, rather watching with desire; hence "covet."

4.a. This literally reads "There are no bands in their death, and fat are their bodies." The overwhelming majority of modern commentators agree with the revision of למו תם למ ("in their death" as suggested by the textual notes of *BHS* (Dahood, II, 189; Gunkel, 316; Kraus, II, 664; Schmidt, 138; Weiser, 505). The arrangement divides למותם into למו (concluding the first phrase) and תם (beginning the second phrase). The reading which results is like that in RSV: "For they have no pangs: their bodies are sound and sleek." This preserves the consonantal text, gives a good meter, and offers a parallelism as good, or better, than the MT. Nonetheless, the literal is not unintelligible. As Spurgeon reads: "They have a quiet death; gliding into eternity without a struggle" (Spurgeon, I, 247). "Fat bodies" as a positive attribute may offend our modern health-consciousness, but it is an ancient picture of healthy prosperity. The "wicked" not only have enough to eat; they enjoy an overabundance!

7.a. LXX and Syriac indicate עֲוֹנָמוֹ ("their iniquity") for עֵינָמוֹ ("their eye[s]"). The text in this verse has inspired a number of proposed readings. However, Schmidt's assessment that it is "incomprehensible" (138) is too extreme, though understandable. There is also some dispute over יצא ("bulge" or "protrude"). Gunkel translated "Their eyes are milky white" by repointing the text, assuming that this also was a picture of healthy prosperity (Gunkel, 317). Similarly, Dahood has suggested "their eyes glisten more than milk" (Dahood, II, 189), which involves an argument that יצא can mean glisten (I, 93–94) and the emendation of מֵחֵלֶב ("from fat") to מֵחָלָב ("from milk"). Obviously, we are dealing with an archaic metaphor here, and fair equivalence is all that is necessary. The NEB, while free, is good: "Their eyes gleam through folds of fat, while vain fancies pass through their minds."

9.a. A caricature of the arrogant talk of the wicked, who are pictured as some sort of extraordinary giants whose mouths reach from heaven to earth. Kraus (II, 668), crediting Helmer Ringgren, recalls a Canaanite text (CTA 23:61–62) which reads "a lip to earth and a lip to the heavens, tongue to the stars" (see also, Dahood, II, 190; Crenshaw, *A Whirlpool of Torment*, 102).

10.a. This is perhaps the most difficult verse in the psalm. Briggs (144) omits it as a bad gloss. He assumes that it was a marginal note of consolation, emphasizing the divine promise to restore Israel which eventually crept into the text. The translation is not particularly difficult, but the critical issue is whether this verse is a promise to restore Israel or an indictment of the people for joining the wicked. There is no question that it is "his people" who have turned, even though some translations unjustifiably emend the text to "their people" (see for example NIV). If the verse is a promise that God will return his people, it is unintelligible in this context. Thus, we have Briggs' omission of the entire verse, or Gunkel's creative translation: " They sit around with the fools, and greedily drink all their words." The problem verb "return" has a *qere* in the MT which assumes a confusion of " י " for " ו " in the text (יָשִׁב for יָשׁוּב). If the *qere* ישׁוב is used, it means "turn back" in the sense of apostacize, as found in Judg 2:19; 8:33; Jer 8:4; et al. With this reading, the Israelites are seen to be so impressed with the prosperity of the wicked and their impunity that they "turn to" them "turning from" God (see v 27).

10.b. The "waters of abundance" is read as a metaphor for prosperity, akin to the more familiar "my cup runneth over" (Ps 23:5; McCann, *Psalm 73*, 35). Some have interpreted this as "drinking up their words" (Cohen, 232; Gunkel, 317; Kraus, II, 664). The verse is too uncertain in meaning to claim very much for it, but it seems to indicate that the ordinary people turn to the rich and drink down their language with unthinking desire for their affluent lifestyle. Regardless of how vile they may be, the ways of the rich are very attractive to many people. Even their foolish language (v 11) is treated as wise.

14.a. The proposal in *BHS* to read "and I am reproved/admonished/reproached" (from יכח) eases the reading but is not necessary.

16.a. Lit., "it was a wearisome thing in my eyes." Translations vary: KJV has "it was too painful for me," which follows LXX, and has been assumed to be the meaning in other translations (e.g., NEB, REB, "too hard for me"). RSV, "it seemed to me a wearisome task," is closer to MT. I have adopted the translation of Kraus (*Psalms 60–150*, 83). "My eyes" is equal to "for me."

17.a. " The sanctuary of God" for (מקדשׁי אל) is lit. "the holy places/things of God." The use of the pl. to refer to the sanctuary of God is unusual (but see Ps 68:36). It may be to intensify the holiness of the place (Briggs, 146; Cohen, 234), or may simply refer to the temple and all its precincts (see Jer 51:51; Ezek 21:7; Lev 21:23; and others). Dahood has noted that it was a common Canaanite practice to designate dwellings with pl. forms (Dahood, II, 192). Obviously, whether the reference is to the Solomonic temple, the ruined temple site after 587 B.C., the post-exilic temple, or simply a family "holy place" cannot be discerned.

17.b. The noun and pronoun suffix אחריתם is traditionally translated as "their end," but it seems to be more abstract in nature and means "that which comes after," though it can mean "end" or "result" in derived senses. In this context, it surely includes "future" (for usage in future sense, see Prov 13:17–18; 24:14; Isa 46:9–10; Jer 29:11). However, the future perceived in 73:17 includes the result of the actions of the wicked (cf. Num 23:10; Jer 17:11; Deut 32:20; Amos 8:10; Dan 12:8). Thus the translation as "destiny" or "fate" (Crenshaw, 104) seems better. J. Ross ("Psalm 73," 162, 171) translates, "the outcome of their deeds." For full discussion of אחרית, see H. Seebass, *TDOT*, I, 207–12. The verb אבינה (from בין) is a simple imperfect cohortative and carries the ideas of "discernment/understanding/consideration of a matter/perception" (Note Deut 32:4, 29; Prov 7:7; Neh 13:7; Ezra 8:15; Pss 28:5; 50:22; Dan 9:2).

18.a. The word משׁואות is used only here and in Ps 74:3. Its meaning is obscure. If derived from שׁוא ("emptiness/vanity," BDB, 996), its meaning is "ruins" (which fits well in 74:3). If from נשׁא, II ("deceive"; BDB, 674), it means "deception." The *Translation* represents an attempt to combine these two ideas.

19.a. The pl. "terrors" (בלהות) is an expression of death; perhaps, we should read Death. The "King of Terrors" in Job 18:14 seems to be an epithet of Mot, Death who rules the netherworld (see M. H. Pope, *Job*, AB 15, 126; Dahood, II, 193). See also Isa 17:14. JB has "terrified to death."

20.a. The ancient versions read בעיר as "in the city" and צלמם as "their image"; so LXX, "As the dream of one awakening, O Lord, in your city you will despise their image." Modern translators frequently assume that בעיר is a contracted form of בהעיר from עור, "raise oneself/awake" (Crenshaw, *A Whirlpool of Torment*, 106). The exact reading is uncertain. RSV ignores the "Lord" and reads: " They are like a dream when one awakes, / on awaking you despise their phantoms." The meaning of this reading is, as expressed by Durham (320), that the wicked are "in fact like the contemptible images of a bad dream, gone when one awakens, except for a brief shudder of recollection." Gunkel and Kraus ignore the accent and emend אדני ("O Lord") to אינמו or אינם ("it is not" or "they are not") and read "Like a dream, when one wakens, they are gone" (Kraus), or, "Like a dream which disappears when one awakens" (Gunkel). See other translations for further conjectures. The *Translation* assumes that "image" is used in the sense which appears in Ps 39:7, and I have adopted Craigie's translation—"mere images," in the sense of transitory, phantom-like existence. Dahood argues that בזה, (normally, "despise") can be used in the sense of "undervalue/treat lightly" (see Gen 25:34). And he may be correct. However, I have retained the "despise," assuming that the idea is probably that of a bad dream. "The sinners who occasioned such consternation are actually no more than fleeting images in a divine nightmare" (Crenshaw, *A Whirlpool of Torment*, 106). In any case, the general sense of the verse is that the wicked who seem so prosperous and stable can disappear as quickly as a dream and have no more real substance than the "mere images" of a troublesome dream.

21.a. Literally "and as to my kidneys, I was pierced." This is a metaphor for deep, internal anguish.

22.a. Here, and again in v 23, an emphatic personal pronoun אֲנִי ("I") is used.

23.a. See n. 22.a.

24.a. There are three problems with the latter half of this verse. First, what is the meaning of "and afterward," וְאַחַר? Second, what is the meaning of "glory," כָּבוֹד? Third, what is the meaning of "take or receive," לָקַח? The question with "afterward" has to do with whether it refers to this life, or the life after death (Anderson, II, 535). Is the psalmist expressing a faith that all the things now troubling him will pass, or the hope that in the afterlife God's justice will be manifest? See *Comment*. In Christian circles "glory" is synonymous with "heaven," but is that the meaning here? Gunkel reads: "you give the soul courage/strength on the way" (Gunkel, 312; Schmidt's treatment is similar, 138). Cohen accepts the word "glory" but says that it is not referring to the Hereafter, "since glory never has such significance in the [Hebrew] Bible" (Cohen, 235). However, Briggs finds it to be an unambiguous eschatological statement: "The Psalmist finds the solution of the inconsistencies of this life in the final reward to the righteous after death" (Briggs, 147).

Three meanings have been given to "take" (לקח) in this verse. The first is "take up" in the sense of "receive." The second is "take" meaning to "lead," as in Gen 48:1 or Exod 14:6 (Cohen, 235; Dahood, II, 195). The third alternative is that "take up" is a technical word for "assumption" like Enoch's or Elijah's in Gen 5:24 and 2 Kgs 2 (Briggs, 142; Kraus, II, 672; Weiser, 195). Of course, the meaning here depends upon the understanding of "after" and "glory." Dahood argues for אחר as a preposition "with" (I, 302; II, 195), both here and in Ps. 49:18. LXX in both cases translates with the meaning of "with" (μετὰ δόξης in 73:24). In this case, 73:24 would mean "and with glory you will take me." However, the correlation of אחר ("afterwards") with אחרית ("afterwards/future/destiny") in v 17 and the context point toward retaining the adverbial force.

25.a. Dahood (II, 195) points out that this verse is an example of "swivel" or "enjambment" in which the phrase "with you," וְעִמָּךְ, serves both clauses of the verse:

> What shall I lack in heaven
>   with you
> I desire nothing on earth

He argues that מִי־לִי has the force of מִי־אַתְּ בִתִּי, "What ails you, my daughter?" in Ruth 3:16 and Ugar. Krt:38–39, *mn krt kybky*, "What ails Kirta that he would cry?" For מִי in the sense of "What?" see Judg 13:17 and Mic 1:5; cf. Job 21:15. The meaning of the verse seems to be that the rediscovered presence of God is sufficient for the most comprehensive realms of life: heaven and earth.

26.a. Usually the verb is read as characteristic ("fails") or future ("will fail"), but I have read v 26 as forming a frame with vv 21–22, describing the human condition before the sanctuary experience of v 17 and enclosing the vital information about the relationship with God in vv 23–24.

26.b. Gunkel notes the peculiarity of the expression צוּר־לְבָבִי "strength of my heart" (Gunkel, 320). Some (e.g., Kraus, II, 503; Schmidt, 138) read צוּרִי ("my rock") for צוּר. If "rock" is read, it seems clear that it is a metaphor for "enduring strength." Dahood offers a unique (if unconvincing) translation: "My flesh and heart may waste away, O Mountain, but my heart and my body, God, will be eternal." Dahood claims that צור is a divine appellation to be rendered "O Mountain" (Dahood, II, 195).

26.c. "Portion" (חלק) originally referred to the land allotted to the individual families, the heritage into which all members of the family enter. God as a "portion" may recall the inheritance of the Levites—Yahweh himself (Deut 10:9).

26.d. The textual notes of *BHS* suggests the deletion of לְעוֹלָם ("forever") but offers no textual evidence (Kraus, 503; Schmidt, 138). Dahood's peculiar translation (see n. 26.a.) assumes that there is a reference to "the new heart and body that God will give the Psalmist after death."

28.a. The appearance of two divine names אֲדֹנָי יְהוָה ("my Lord, Yahweh") is unusual. The textual notes of *BHS* are undecided as to which should be deleted. Gunkel (320) and Schmidt (138) claim that יהוה ("Yahweh") is a later addition. Briggs (142) omits the entire verse (along with v 27) as a Maccabean gloss. Omitting either divine name does not particularly change anything, although the redundancy may serve to emphasize the object of the speaker's hope.

28.b. Circumstantial infinitive; see 63:3.

Form/Structure/Setting

Form critics have not arrived at a consensus regarding this psalm. Allen (*TyndB* 33 [1981] 93–118) finds four primary suggestions for its genre. First, it has been called a "wisdom psalm" or *Lehregedicht* by such notables as Gunkel (312) and Jacquet (432). However, Gunkel seems undecided, since he refers to it as an individual "psalm of lament" as well. Kraus, likewise, calls it a wisdom psalm, noting that the form is not clear-cut (Kraus, *Theology*, 169). Westermann (*Praise and Lament*, 53, 114) identifies it as an individual psalm of lament (53) but then uses it as an example of a wisdom psalm! Though Ps 73 may be popularly identified as a wisdom psalm, the ambivalence about this designation should be noted. Brueggemann argues that classifying in terms of wisdom is a problem for it is "an intensely religious statement" (115–16), a probe into faith which is not usually associated with the wisdom teachers. This is not a very convincing argument, however. B. W. Anderson (*Out of the Depths: The Psalms Speak for Us Today* [Philadelphia: Westminster, 1974] 218) has emphasized that only one of eight criteria for the wisdom form is found in Ps 73. Nonetheless, he calls it "the greatest of the wisdom psalms" (Anderson, *Depths*, 225).

The second suggested form is that of an individual song of thanksgiving. Mowinckel and others have championed this form (Mowinckel, *PIW*, II, 114; Schmidt, viii, 139; Weiser, 89). The thanksgiving may be for divine insight, or for recovery from illness.

These two forms are the most widely mentioned. The two remaining are less so. The third form, an individual psalm of lament, was mentioned previously in the discussion of wisdom. Gunkel's and Westermann's affinities with this designation were noted. The fourth form is a "psalm of confidence," as mentioned by Westermann in *Praise and Lament*, 80, who lists it among psalms which show the transition from psalms of individual lament to those in which lament has been turned to praise.

Obviously, Ps 73 represents an impasse in form criticism. In my opinion, the psalm belongs to the large genre of testimony, which encompasses both the thanksgiving type of psalm and the reflection. The latter is more indigenous to the wisdom literature. Ps 73 seems more nearly to be a reflection than a thanksgiving, though these two types are similar. R. E. Murphy (*Wisdom Literature: Job, Proverbs, Ruth, Canticles, Ecclesiastes, and Esther*, FOTL 13 [Grand Rapids: Eerdmans, 1981] 130) has set forth succinctly the characteristics of the reflective mode in terms of Ecclesiastes:

> *Use of phrases* —
> "I said in my heart"; "I gave my heart to know"; "I saw again"; "I know." Phrases from other sources could be added: "I have been young and now am old, yet I have not seen . . . (Ps 37:25); "I have seen the wicked . . . " (Ps 37:35); "I sought him, but he could not be found" (Ps 37:36); "But as for me" (Ps 73:2); etc.
> *Use of rhetorical questions* (See Eccl. 2:2, 12, 15, 19, 25)—
> A rhetorical question is used in Ps 73:15; also note the questions of the wicked in v 11.

Various subgenres are incorporated into reflections. A saying/proverb (for this genre, see Murphy, 4–6) and command/instruction material may be included (for the former, see 37:1–11; in fact the whole of Ps 37 is an instructional poem; see Craigie, 196). The example story may be used (as in Eccl 9:13–16; note Ps 37:35–38). Ps 73 does not seem to have an example story, unless the entire psalm constitutes one. Thus Ps 73 is a reflective testimony, not directly instructional but certainly intended to function in that mode. The reflective testimony differs from the thanksgiving in that the latter celebrates a direct deliverance by God in more exhortative language and directly addressed to those who hear the testimony (note Pss 22:23–27; 66:16; 32:11; 33:1; 40:10–11). Ps 73 does have the element of direct address to God (note vv 18–25) which is characteristic of the thanksgivings but does not give the reader the same sense of congregational awareness—though the framing formed by vv 1 and 28 certainly suggests that the speaker is addressing a group.

No less than thirty-seven literary patterns have been proposed for Ps 73 (see Allen, *TyndB* 33 [1981] 93–118, and McCann, *Psalm 73*, 49–51, for reviews, especially of those not readily in English). Rhetorical criticism, making use of stylistic analysis, has been particularly useful in the analysis of this psalm. The psalm is set off by an inclusion ("good," טוב, in vv 1 and 28) and by the repetition of a proverbial form in the first and last verse as well. "Heart" (לבב) occurs five times within the psalm, leading Buber to call it a "meditation of the heart" (Buber, *Right and Wrong*, 37f.). The exclamatory "truly" (אך) occurs in verses 1, 13, 18, and "behold" (הנה) occurs twice (vv 12 and 27), both times in reference to "the wicked." These are not simply mechanical repetitions, but as Allen has noted "the poet seems to be deliberately ranging over earlier vocabulary and reversing its contexts." Everyone agrees that v 17, the sanctuary experience, is the turning point of the psalm.

Based on these features, the following eight-part structure is offered for Ps 73. (1) "Surely God is good to Israel"—a proverbial statement which is both the beginning proposition of the psalm and the conclusion arrived at by the psalmist after a struggle of faith (v 1); (2) "I was on slippery ground"—the plight of the psalmist (vv 2–3); (3) "Behold! These are the wicked"—the prosperity and arrogance of the wicked, which troubled the speaker (vv 4–12); (4) "It surely seemed as nothing"—the psalmist fears his faith has been futile based on his observation of the wicked (vv 13–16); (5) "Until I entered the sanctuary"—the place of worship becomes a turning point in the faith of the psalmist (v 17); (6) "Truly, you have put them on slippery ground"—in contrast to the fears of the psalmist (see #2), it is the wicked who are really "on thin ice" (vv 18–20); (7) "Behold! Those far from you will perish"—in contrast to the apparent prosperity and impunity of the wicked (see #3), their doom is sealed (vv 21–27); (8) "The nearness of God is good"—in contrast to the apparent futility of the psalmist's faith (see #4), his pure heart has been blessed by the continuing presence of Yahweh; also, the proverb of v 1 is affirmed, but the understanding of "how God is good" has changed—divine goodness is not prosperity but presence. Vv 1–3 and 27–28 provide framing sections for the content of the psalm (Crenshaw, *A Whirlpool of Torment*, 99–100).

With the form critics in some disarray, it should be no surprise that the *Sitz im Leben* is equally confused. Those who emphasize the wisdom form of the psalm conclude that it had a noncultic setting and was used as a teaching tool. Those who find a cultic setting are divided as to whether it has an individual or corporate focus. Thus, the psalm may be a song of thanksgiving for recovery from sickness and highly individual. Schmidt even suggests that the psalmist may have seen a wicked man have a heart attack and die in the temple courts—and literally saw the "end" of the wicked as described in v 17 (Schmidt, 139). Cohen, though not working within form critical categories, sees the psalm as cultic, but highly personal: "the outspoken confession of a man whose faith has been sorely tested" (Cohen, 231; Weiser, 507, sounds similar). Perdue (*Wisdom and Cult,* 291) argues that the psalm is a theological reflection concerning "the good fortune of the wicked and the validity of the lament-thanksgiving response to the problem of suffering." He notes the absence of some of the characteristics of the thanksgiving psalms: introduction with announced intention of praising god; address and admonition directed toward a congregation. However, Perdue also argues that the sage who speaks in the psalm had found that an intellectual understanding of evil was beyond his grasp and that the only way to deal with the incongruities between a theology of retribution and personal experience was through a cultic experience which transcended the problem. He thinks it most probable that v 17 refers to some sort of theophanic experience in a sanctuary. Beaucamps, Ringgren, and Würthwein find a corporate, cultic setting (Beaucamps, II, 5; H. Ringgren, *The Faith of the Psalmists* [Philadelphia: Fortress, 1963] 59, 72–73; Würthwein, "Psalm 73," 177). However, the suggestion that the speaker is the king performing a cultic function, or that the psalm is part of the autumn feast of the covenant, seems unjustifiably speculative. Kraus has pointed out that seeking a specific speaker is pointless, for it is "characteristic of didactic poems in the wisdom tradition that they are marked by autobiographical stylization" (Kraus, *Theology,* 173).

It seems safe to conclude that the psalm, in its canonical form, was read, or recited, before the religious assemblies of Israel (v 1). The further identification of a specific speaker or occasion is not only impossible but also unnecessary. The psalm seems to be a good example of what Miller has called "openness to new contexts" (Miller, *Interpreting the Psalms,* 18–28). That is, the psalms are not locked into any one particular setting in history, but their openness in language and universality of concerns invite the sincere participation of twentieth-century Americans with fifth-century B.C.E. Israelites.

An attempt to grasp the literary structure of the psalm is provided by the diagram on the following page. The pattern seems to be: A–v 1a; B–vv 2–3; C–vv 4–12; D–vv 18–20; E–v 17; D'–vv 18–20; B'–vv 21–26; C'–vv 27–28; A'–v 16 (ABCDED'B'C'A')

Comment

Since the meaning and major exegetical problems have been dealt with for the most part in the *Translation, Notes,* and *Form/Structure/Setting* sections, the comments in this section are limited to the following remarks.

1. *Retention of "to Israel" in v 1.* The change to "God is good to the upright" would make the psalm more definitively a composition concerned with individuals and the retributive and rewarding ways of God. Brueggemann (*The Message of the Psalms,* 116) comments that there is "more at stake than grammar. The change

Structural Diagram of Psalm 73

1 An Asaphite psalm,
Truly, God is good to Israel,
to those who are pure in heart!

2 But for me, my feet had almost stumbled;
my foot steps had nearly slipped.
3 Because I envied the arrogant,
and coveted the prosperity of the wicked.

4 For they have no pains at their deaths;
and fat are their bodies.
5 They are not troubled like mortals,
nor plagued like humans.
6 Consequently, pride is their necklace,
and violence drapes them like a robe.
7 Their eyes bulge from fatness;
the conceit of their hearts is unlimited.
8 They scoff and speak with malice;
in their arrogance they threaten oppression.
9 They set their mouths in the heavens,
while their tongues seize the earth.
10 So his people turn to them,
and they swill the waters of abundance.
11 And they say, "What does God know?"
and, "Does the Most High know anything?"
12 Behold, these are the wicked;
always carefree, their prosperity increases.
13 It surely seemed as nothing that I kept my heart clean,
and washed my hands in innocence.
14 I was plagued all during the day,
and my punishment (began) every morning.
15 If I had said, "I will speak thus"—
Behold! I would have betrayed your children.
16 When I tried to understand this,
it overwhelmed my eyes;
17 until I entered the sanctuary of God,
then I comprehended their destiny.

18 Truly, you will put them on slippery places;
making them into deceptive places of ruin.
19 How suddenly they can be destroyed!
Completely swept away by terrors.
20 Like a dream, when one awakens—
(so) when you rouse yourself, O Lord,
you will despise them as mere images.
21 When my heart was as sour as vinegar,
and my insides were torn-up,
22 I was senseless and ignorant;
I was a brute beast before you.
23 Yet, I am always with you;
you hold my right hand!
24 With your counsel, you guide me,
and afterward, with glory, you will receive me.
25 [With you] what can I lack in heaven?
And with you I desire nothing else on earth.
26 My flesh and heart were spent,
but my strength and my portion is God,
forever!
27 Behold! Those far from you will perish;
you destroy all who are faithless to you.
28 But for me, the nearest of God is my good;
I have made the Lord, Yahweh, my refuge—
telling of all your works!

from Israel to 'upright' changes the religious world in which we do our interpretation." The term "upright" would indicate that the psalm which follows is that of
a wise person, grounded in human experience with the ways of God. This would not
be false, of course, for the testimony which follows is that of such a person indeed.

If "Israel" is retained, the speaker is an Israelite whose message is intended for
other Israelites. Further, the Israelite speaker embodies in personal experience
the experience of Israel itself. Martin Buber (*Right and Wrong*, 35–36) has understood this point and expressed it in excellent language:

> Certainly only one who had plumbed the depths of personal suffering
> could speak in this way. But the speaker is a man [*sic*] of Israel in Israel's
> bitter hour of need, and in his personal suffering the suffering of Israel has
> been concentrated, so that what he now has to suffer he suffers as Israel. In
> the destiny of an authentic person the destiny of his people is gathered up,
> and only now becomes truly manifest.

Thus the struggle for faith in the psalm is more than an individual and personal
trial. The testimony is that of "those who are pure in heart" in Israel, i.e., those who
are willing to be faithful until they know that Yahweh is good to Israel despite evidence
which seems to contradict that assumption. The psalm works in the context of
Israel's faith in Yahweh and should not be reduced to personal experience alone.

2. *The adverb "truly"* (אך). As stated in note 1.b., the Hebrew particle אך appears at three crucial places in the psalm: vv 1, 13, 18 (see Ps 62, note 2.a. for
discussion of this word). Its force is that of "yes, even though the evidence seems
to give it little support"—a condition which is contrary of what is expected. The
threefold אך gives this psalm its character of " The Great Nevertheless." In v 1,
the force of the "truly" is "in spite of everything to the contrary, God is good to
Israel." In v 13, the force is: "in spite of all the indications of well-being of the
wicked, I kept my heart clean and washed my hands in innocence"—which
means that the speaker refused to run after the prosperous wicked and adopt
their ways. He/she remained among those Israelites who were "pure in heart,"
those who could "wash their hands in innocence." The language in v 13 alludes
to rituals in which the washing of hands declared one's innocence and indicated
that the person was "clean" (or "pure") for worship. See Ps 26:6; Deut 21:6; Matt
27:24. Priests were to wash their hands before entering the tent of meeting
(Exod 30:19–21), a symbol of moral purity (Ps 23:4). A terrible portrayal of
hands unwashed and unfit for worship is found in Isa 1:15–16:

> When you spread forth your hands,
>   I will hide my eyes from you;
> even though you make many prayers,
>   I will not listen;
>   your hands are full of blood.
> Wash yourselves, make yourselves clean;
>   remove the evil of your doings
>   from before my eyes;
> cease to do evil. (RSV)

The third אַךְ ("truly/nevertheless") is found at the beginning of v 18. Despite the outward appearances of stability on the part of the wicked (vv 4–12), the speaker has become confident that God will put them on slippery places until they fall into unexpected ruin.

3. *The "afterward, with glory, you receive me" of v 24.* The problems in this enigmatic verse have received some attention in note 24.a. above. A long line of interpretation, especially Christian interpretation, has understood "glory" (כבוד) as equal to "heavenly glory" and the verb form "take me" as equal to "take me up" (see Buber, *Right and Wrong*, 47–48). However, neither of these two assumptions is necessarily the case. The word "glory" does not appear to be used of "heaven" elsewhere in the MT. The "glory" of Yahweh may be above the earth (Ps 108:6) or above the heavens (Ps 113:4), and the heavens recount his glory (Ps 19:2), but most references are to the divine glory *on* earth (e.g., Exod 14:4, 17–18; 16:7, 10; 24:16–18; 34:29–35; 40:34–35; Isa 35:2; 40:5; 59:19; see the comments of Craigie on Ps 21:5, pp. 190–91). Buber (48) points to Isa 14:18–19 where "glory" and death are linked:

> All the kings of the nations lie in glory [בכבוד],
>> each in his own tomb;
> but you are cast out, away from your sepulchre; (RSV)

The reference in these verses is to the king of Babylon who aspired to a heavenly destiny but is denied the "glory" of an honorable burial—a "glory" granted to most kings. "Glory" is the honored end given to those worthy to receive it. It does not, however, specifically refer to a postmortem existence in a heavenly realm. Thus the meaning in v 24 is most probably that of a life guided by the counsel of God and coming to its end with a "glory" which testifies of its worth and fulfillment.

However, generation after generation of readings have understood more than the cryptic words actually say in this verse. A perception of ultimacy in the context warns against any final closure, and the declarations in the context seem to support this conclusion. The speaker affirms, "Yet, I am always with you" (v 23)—with the god who holds the right hand of the faithful (23), as of a king, Isa 45:1; 42:1. God gives those who are pure in heart their "strength" ("rock") and "portion," which will endure forever, though "flesh and heart (mind)" will be terminated. These features tell the reader that the "glory" in v 24 has a dynamic quality which has the power to transcend death and displace it with life, guided and endowed by God.

H.-J. Kraus (*Theology of the Psalms*, 173) observes that Luther's famous translation of v 23 (*"Dennoch bleibe ich stets bei dir,"* "Nevertheless I remain constantly with thee") does not represent the Hebrew syntax of the verse very well. V 23a is a verbless clause which expresses an ongoing state: "Yet I am continually with you." Kraus argues that "Verse 23 gives expression not to a 'nevertheless' of faith nor of a defiant piety, but to a quite surprising assurance that nothing can destroy the covenant or disrupt the believer's communion with God." Crenshaw (*A Whirlpool of Torment*, 108) also perceives the openness of the context:

Mind and body will eventually decay, but is that the end? If so the moment will mark the close of a relationship in which God has been a rock and a portion from the occasion of the psalmist's visit to the divine sanctuary. But if death does not signal the end . . .

Likewise, Martin Buber (*Right and Wrong*, 48–49) summarizes the text of v 24 as "When I have lived my life, says our Psalmist to God, I shall die in *kabod* (glory), in the fulfilment of existence." Then Buber adds immediately two other sentences: "In my death the coils of Sheol will not embrace me (says the Psalmist), but thy hand will grasp me. 'For,' as it is said in another Psalm related in kind to this one, the sixteenth, 'Thou will not leave my soul to Sheol.' Buber might have recalled another verse in Ps 16 as well—v 11, " Thou dost show me the path of life; / in thy presence there is fullness of joy, / in thy right hand are pleasures for ever-more (KJV). A. Weiser (178) comments on this verse as follows:

> In view of the context in which this saying stands, the phrase "path of life" can hardly be understood in any other sense than as a life lived in com-munion with God which will be carried on even after death; in other words, as the consummation of salvation, the future form of which is at present still hidden from the poet.

The speaker in Ps 16 waits for God to reveal the mystery, living in a faith which encompasses both life and earth. Can there be any doubt that the testimony in Ps 73 emerges from a like faith? Nothing can finally separate those who are pure in heart from the presence of God (cf. Rom 8:35–39).

Explanation

Ps 73 is surely one of the greatest of the psalms in terms of reader response. Readers over and over again find that the words of the psalm "fit their condition" and give them new strength. The psalm is an ancient composition, but it always seems contemporary. Readers identify easily with the speaker in the psalm; they know about the struggle for faith in a world which usually holds the active presence of God in contempt (v 11)—though more often in deeds than in words. These readers know how hard it is to stay on the course of purity and faithfulness when the tongues of the wicked strut through human society with lies, malice, and scoffing. We know them well. Of course, when we meet them we often recognize that they are us and their names are ours. We envy them to the brink of disaster and drink down their words as those who are thirsty drink water. The power of the wicked is in large measure their ability to evoke jealous coveting in the hearts of the righteous (vv 2–3). When we watch the wicked with envy as they live out their opulent ways, an agony of spirit begins.

I have borrowed a title for this psalm from the stimulating remarks of S. Terrien on it in his *The Elusive Presence* (San Francisco: Harper & Row, 1978). Terrien's full statement is that "the poet of Psalm 73 began a song on the issue of theodicy and ended it as a credo on the eternal presence" (316). He notes that in the psalm "an inquisitive essay becomes a prayer." The crucial point of the psalm is found in v 17, which recounts in a very brief statement that the speaker attained a Godward orientation during a time in the sanctuary, which constituted a revelation of things seen but not seen, of things known but not known. We are not told how the new insight happened. Perhaps the speaker was a participant in the worship at the temple in Jerusalem on one of the high days of festival time, where, like Isaiah of Jerusalem, a vision appeared of Yahweh high and lifted up upon his great heavenly throne, while priests and people chanted: "Holy, holy, holy is the LORD of hosts; / the whole earth is full of his glory" (Isa 6:3, RSV). Or perhaps on a similar occasion the speaker heard an unnamed prophet declare that

> "The grass withers, the flower fades,
>> when the breath of the LORD blows upon it;
>> surely the people is grass.
> The grass withers, the flower fades;
>> but the word of our God will stand for ever.
> And the glory of the LORD shall be revealed,
>> and all flesh shall see it together,
>> for the mouth of the LORD has spoken." (Isa 40:7–8, 5, RSV)

Or did the new understanding come in a moment of meditation and quiet reflection on the ways of God and humankind—a moment of disclosure which opens the eyes of a mind blinded by envy and the "glory" of the wicked? Who can say? In any case, v 16 seems to indicate that the sanctuary experience came after strenuous intellectual effort. Worship is no substitute for rigorous mental pondering. The efforts to understand are supplemented by the disclosures of worship. The sanctuary is no place for a pious fool who thinks that piety can take the place of reflection and the quest for knowledge.

W. Brueggemann has utilized in helpful ways a pattern of orientation, disorientation, and new orientation in the interpretation of psalms (conveniently set forth in his *The Message of the Psalms;* earlier in "Psalms and the Life of Faith: A Suggested Typology of Function," *JSOT* 17 [1980] 3–32). The seasons of well-being in human life are times of orientation; the seasons of hurt, alienation, suffering, and death are times of disorientation, seasons of new orientation are those when "we are overwhelmed with the new gifts of God, when joy breaks through the despair" (Brueggemann, *The Message of the Psalms,* 19). Ps. 73 is a masterpiece of reorientation, though Brueggemann somewhat inexplicably places the psalm under the rubric of disorientation, commenting that it "seems to be the last word on disorientation, even as it utters the first word of new orientation" (115).

The latter part of Ps 73 (vv 17–28) contains three new orientations or reorientations. First, there is *reorientation toward the wicked.* The sanctuary experience stimulated a new awareness of the outcome of the actions of the wicked. When viewed from the perspective of envy they seemed invincible and the struggle for purity and faithfulness seemed foolish—a cruel daily torture of the soul (v 14). A renewed sense of time opened the eyes of the speaker to the fragility of the strength and power of the wicked. They are real enough, but their security is an illusion. Prosperity can be gone so suddenly (cf. Ps 30:7–8), leaving no more behind than a nightmare (vv 18–20).

The second reorientation is a *new understanding of the self* (vv 21–22). The speaker experiences a "flashback" in these verses and recalls that the trauma experienced in vv 2–16 was largely "a matter of the heart." As M. Buber put it in his great essay on this psalm ("The Heart Determines," in *Right and Wrong*, 34–52):

> The state of the heart determines whether a man [or a woman] lives in the truth, in which God's goodness is experienced, or in the semblance of truth, where the fact that it "goes ill" with him [or her] is confused with the illusion that God is not good to him [or her].

Buber points out that "heart" (the volitional center of being) is a key word in this psalm, appearing six times: vv 1, 7, 13, 21, 26 (2 times). A soured heart had left the speaker reacting to the well-being of the wicked at the level of a brute beast. As noted previously, the greatest strength of the wicked is their power to stir up envy and discontent in the hearts of those faithful to God. The sanctuary experience has revealed that the "state of the heart . . . [was] at stake" (Crenshaw, *A Whirlpool of Torment*, 97). This aspect of the psalm should not be taken as either indifference or resignation to the evil works and ways of those described in vv 4–12. There are times and ways to resist them; no society should allow them to go carefree and unjudged in their increasing wealth (v 12). Nevertheless, the condition of the heart is always critical.

The third reorientation is that *toward the presence of God*. The sanctuary experience had broken through all "ideology of self-sufficing, affluence, and self-sufficiency" (Brueggemann, *The Message of the Psalms*, 121) and allowed a resurgence of a sense of God's presence. Now the speaker knows that "I am always with you" (v 23); flesh and heart may fail, but "the rock" of God endures forever (v 27). Those who are far from God will perish (v 27), but an unforeclosed future lies before those who make Yahweh their refuge (v 28). The counsel of God (עצה, "purpose/guidance"), not jealous envy of the wicked, now controls the speaker's life, as he/she moves toward the "afterwards" and the experience of a glorious reception by God (v 24; Terrien, *The Elusive Presence*, 319). "Blessed are the pure in heart, for they shall see God" (Matt 5:8).

God's Scorned Name and Drawn-Back Hand *(74:1–23)*

Bibliography

Ackroyd, P. R. "נצח– εἰς τέλος." *ExpTim* 80 (1969) 126. **Auffret, P.** "Essai sur la structure littéraire du Psaume LXXIV." *VT* 33 (1983) 130–48. **Dahood, M.** "Vocative Lamedh in Psalm 74, 14." *Bib* 59 (1978) 262–63. **Day, J.** *God's Conflict with the Dragon and the Sea.*

21–25. **Emerton, J. A.** "Notes on Three Passages in Psalms Book III." *JTS* 14 (1963) 374–81. ———. "Spring and Torrent in Ps. 74:15." VTSup 15 (1966) 122–33. ———. "Translation of Psalm 74:4." *JTS* 27 (1976) 391–92. **Gelston, A.** "A Note on Psalm LXXIV 8." *VT* 34 (1984) 82–87. **Johnson, A. R.** *CPIP.* 131–36. **Lelièvre, A.** "YHWH et la Mer dans les Psaumes." *RHPR* 56 (1976) 253–75. **Ploeg, J. P. M. van der** "Psalm 74 and Its Structure." In *Travels in the World of the Old Testament,* ed. M. S. H. G. Heerma van Voss et al. Assen, The Netherlands: Van Gorcum, 1974. 204–10. **Roberts, J. J. M.** "Of Signs, Prophets and Time Limits: A Note on Psalm 74:9." *CBQ* 39 (1967) 181. **Robinson, A.** "A Possible Solution to the Problems of Psalm 74:5." *ZAW* 89 (1977) 120–21. **Sharrock, G. F.** "Psalm 74: A Literary-Structural Analysis." *AUSS* 21 (1983) 211–23. **Smick, E. B.** "Mythopoetic Language in the Psalms." *WTJ* 44 (1982) 88–98. **Willesen, F.** "The Cultic Situation of Psalm LXXIV." *VT* 2 (1952) 289–306. **Young, W. A.** *Psalm 74: A Methodological and Exegetical Study.* Ph.D. diss. University of Iowa, 1974. Ann Arbor: UMI, 1979.

Translation

1   An Asaphite[a] *maskil.*[b]

Why, O God, are you unrelenting[c] *in anger?*[d]   (4+4)
     Why does your anger[e] *smoulder against the flock of your pasture?*

2   *Remember your congregation, acquired of old;*   (4+3+4)
       the tribe of your patrimony,[a] *which you redeemed;*
       Mount Zion, where[b] *you have dwelt!*

3   *Stride forth*[a] *to a total*[b] *ruin,*   (4+3)
       (to) all the damage in the sanctuary[c] *done by an enemy.*

4   *Your foes have roared in the midst of your meeting-place;*   (4+3)
       they set up their own signs as signs.[a]

5   *It seemed like men bringing up (or swinging) axes*   (3+3)
       into (or in) a thicket of trees[a]*—*

6   *So then*[a] *they hacked away*[b]   (3+3)
       all its carved work[c] *with axes and pikes.*[d]

7   *They set your sanctuary on fire,*   (3+3)
       they defiled to the ground[a] *the dwelling-place of your name.*

8   *They said in their hearts,*   (2+2+3)
       "let us destroy them altogether!"[a]
       (So) they burned[b] *every meeting-place of God in the land.*

9   *We see no signs for us,*[a]   (3+2+3)
       there is no longer a prophet (with us),
       nor one with us who knows for how long.

10   *How long, O god,* |*will the foe taunt?*   (4+4)
       Will the enemy scorn your name forever?

11   *Why do you draw back your hand, even your right hand?*   (4+3)
       (Draw it) from the midst of your bosom; end it![a]

12   *O God, my King*[a] *from long ago;*   (3+4)
       Salvation-Worker in the midst of the earth!

13   *You put down*[a] *the Sea*[b] *with your strength;*   (4+4)
       you broke the heads of Sea-Monsters in the waters.

14   *You smashed the heads of Leviathan,*   (4+4)
       giving him as food for the creatures of the desert.[a]

15	*You cleft open both spring and stream;*	(4+4)
	you dried up flowing rivers.	
16	*The day belongs to you, the night also;*	(4+4)
	you put the moon [a] *and the sun in place.*	
17	*You set* [a] *all the boundaries of the earth;*	(4+4)
	summer and winter, you formed [b] *them.*	
18	*Remember this:* [a]	(2+3+3)
	An enemy has taunted (you), O, Yahweh;	
	a fool-people [b] *have scorned your name!*	
19	*Give not the life of your dove* [a] *to a wild beast;* [b]	(4+4)
	forget not completely [c] *the life of your poor ones.* [d]	
20	*Consider the covenant* [a]—	(2+3+2[3])
	for the hiding-places [b] *of the land are full;*	
	(they) are domains [c] *of violence.*	
21	*Let not the oppressed sit* [a] *humiliated;* [b]	(3+4)
	let the poor and needy praise your name.	
22	*Arise, O, God, defend your cause;*	(4+4)
	remember that you are taunted all day long by fools. [a]	
23	*Do not forget the clamor* [a] *of your foes,*	(3+4)
	the din of those who rebel against you, which goes up continually.	

Notes

1.a. See Ps 73:1.

1.b. See Ps 52:1.

1.c. The terms לנצח and נצח (vv 1, 3, 10, 19) are frequently given a temporal meaning of duration in time: "forever/prepetuity." The four usages in this psalm relate to the anger of God (in vv 1, 19) and to the nature of the actions of enemies (vv 3, 10). The durative force seems appropriate in passages like Pss 77:9; 103:9; Isa 13:20; 57:16; and probably in v 10 of this psalm and in עד־מתי ("How long?") passages; e.g., Ps 79:5; 89:47. However, in many passages, such as in Ps 44:24 (cf. Young, *Psalm 74,* 62), either the nontemporal meaning of "totally/completely" is appropriate, or the meaning is ambiguous and seems to move back and forth from "forever" to "totally." Even in the עד־מתי passages, the meaning does not seem to me to be unambiguous. "Unrelenting" is Young's choice of a word to reflect the ambiguity of the Hebrew. The LXX εἰς τέλος has much of the same ambiguity (see Ackroyd, *ExpTim* 80 [1969] 126).

1.d. The verb זנח is traditionally translated as "reject/spurn/cast off" (cf. Ps 60:3, 12), but in this verse, with the object "us" assumed, it has an intransitive meaning, "to be angry." This is now recognized as its meaning in several contexts (cf. Pss 44:10, 24; 77:8; 89:39; Lam 3:31.). See R. Yaron, "The Meaning of זנח," *VT* 13 (1963) 237–39; Sharrock, AUSS 21 (1983) 213, n. 5.

1.e. Lit. "your nose," an idiomatic expression for anger.

2.a. The combination of (שבט) "tribe," and נחלתך is found elsewhere only in Jer 10:16 = 51:19 and Isa 63:17 (pl.). The meaning seems to be that of a people and their territory which forms a special "tribe" of Yahweh, his "inheritance." Young (*Psalm 74,* 67–68) follows Dahood (I, 13) in using "patrimony" as an attempt to get the scope of the expression נחלה. For discussion of "tribe," see N. K. Gottwald, *The Tribes of Yahweh* (Maryknoll, NY: Orbis Books, 1979) 245–56; G. A. Mendenhall, "Tribe," *IDB* 13–15, 919–20; idem, *The Tenth Generation* (Baltimore: Johns Hopkins UP, 1973) chap. 7.

2.b. The demonstrative pronoun, זה, "this," serves here as a relative pronoun (Dahood).

3.a. A strange expression (lit. "lift up your steps"), which has provoked emendations and different ideas of its meaning. LXX's τὰς χεῖρας implies Heb. כפיך, "your palms/hands," while Syriac indicates פעליך "your deeds/works"; cf. NEB, "now at last restore what was ruined beyond repair." The meaning may be one frequently given: "hasten your steps" (more idiomatically, "pick up your feet") = "Come quickly to a total ruin." I have adopted essentially this idea in the *Translation.* Another approach would be to follow JB, "Pick your steps over these endless ruins," and NIV, "Pick your way through these everlasting ruins." That is, God is asked to walk carefully as he makes his way through the debris at the site of the sanctuary.

3.b. Reading נצח as in v 1 above, which seems to make better sense than "everlasting." JB's "endless" may be acceptable hyperbole.

3.c. Young (*Psalm 74*, 17) connects 3b with 4 as the beginning of the description of the situation in the temple: "Your enemy wreaked havoc in the sanctuary." However, this necessitates taking כל as an adverbial accusative. It seems better to keep 3b related to 3a as the completion of the petition begun in 2a. Sharrock (*AUSS* 21 [1983] 215) comments that 3b links the first and second paragraphs of the psalm thematically, introducing the subject in vv 4–9.

4.a. Kraus notes P. R. Ackroyd (*JTS* 17 [1966] 392–93), who proposes to read שאגו צרריך בקרבו במועדך שמו אותם, omitting the אתות: "Your adversaries roar in the midst (of it); in your assembly place they have their signs." Kraus translates: "Your adversaries roared in your festival-place; they set up their signs in its midst"—assuming בתוכו for אתות. Young (*Psalm 74*, 74) argues against emendation and contends that the awkward construction of the verse puts emphasis on the repeated "signs." Johnson (*CPIP*, 132) translates 4b as "Who left these signs of themselves as signs." Since the meaning is not certain (see *Comment*), I have retained MT and translated as in RSV.

5.a. NEB has a note on this verse which declares the Heb. "unintelligible," but the translators have provided a very free rendering: "They brought it crashing down, like woodmen plying their axes in the forest." Apparently, the translators have read the first verb (יִוָּדַע) as יְדָעוּ (as proposed in BHS) from גדע, "hew/cut down," or else יְדָעוּ or יִדְעוּ from a supposed root דעה, "raze/burn" (Emerton, *JTS* 14 [1963] 376; cf. RSV). The NEB has retained כמביא ("like someone who brings") and translated freely as "like woodmen plying (their axes)," but transposing it from the first colon to the second. This convoluted mixture of emendation, transposition, and free translation clearly indicates the difficulty of this verse. LXX presupposes a negative before the first verb (καὶ οὐκ ἔγνωσαν = ולא ידעו, "and they did not know") and כמביא ("as one who causes to come/bring") as כְּמָבוֹא ("as an entrance") and attaches 5a to 4b with the idea that the adversaries have set up their standards ignorantly in the entrance of the temple—apparently the Greek translators were as perplexed as their modern counterparts! Among the emendations, that of A. Robinson (*ZAW* 89 [1977] 120–21) involves minimal changes of the consonantal text and gives an interesting meaning: יודע כמבוא למעלה כסבך־עץ קיר דומות, "The way to the ascent seemed like a tangled mass of timber, a city of desolation"—treating מבוב as the entryway leading to the processional steps in front of the temple.

I have chosen to try to translate the text as it stands, though with no great confidence. The lack of an object after the first verb is a problem, but יודע can be taken to mean "it seemed" (lit. "it is known"; see BDB, 394; Robinson, 120; A. R. Johnson, *CPIP*, 143, "it called to mind"). Young (*Psalm 74*, 76–77) reads יודע as jussive, "let it be known," or more freely, "Look!" The indirect object is the speaker, "it seemed to me." The mental image is that of ax wielders going up into a thicket of trees to bring them down in tangled masses of limbs and underbrush. There seem to be two lines of interpretation: (1) "It seemed as if someone swung axes upward"; (2) "It seemed as if someone brought axes up . . ." (see *HOTTP* 3, 322). RSV: "At the upper entrance they hacked the wooden trellis with axes." The RSV translators have read גדע ("hew down") for the first verb (see above) and read מבוא ("entrance") for ("bringing up"), with סבך־עץ as "wooden trellis" assuming סבך from שבכה, "latticework/network" (see 1 Kgs 7:18, 41).

6.a. Reading עתה ("and then") with *qere*, reflecting a temporal sequence, "so now" or "so then." The *kethiv* would apparently be ועת ("and a time"), yielding the meaning: "Its carved work at one time (or "all at once")"—reading יחד with a temporal sense.

6.b. Lit. "to smite/hammer/strike down." LXX indicates גדעו or כתתו, "cut down / beat down," for the עתה ("and then") at the beginning of this verse.

6.c. LXX indicates פתחיה, "its entrances" (Syriac indicates, פתחים), which is accepted by some commentators (e.g., Dahood). However, the meaning of פתוח as "carving" or "engraving" seems to be no problem (for carvings on the interior wall of the temple, see 1 Kgs 6:29; for inscriptions, Zech 3:9; Ezek 28:11; cf. Ezek 8:10; 23:14). In the *Translation* the יחד is read as quantative ("all together"), but it may be temporal ("at the same time/at once"; see J. C. DeMoor, "Lexical Remarks Concerning Yahad and Yahdaw," *VT* 7 [1957] 355). Johnson (*CPIP*, 132, n. 5) divides the consonants to read פתוחי־היחד, "the carved work, everywhere." The fem. suffix on פתוח is odd, referring to the "meeting-place" in v 4 (which is masc.).

6.d. See KB, 433–34.

7.a. Or, "utterly desecrated," or, "brought low (to the ground) in dishonor."

8.a. The word נִינָם should be read as a simple imperfect (plus 3rd pers. masc. pl. suffix) from ינה, "to oppress/mistreat/suppress." The change of vowels to נִינָם (or to hiphil, נוֹנֵם) is not really necessary (see Delitzsch, II, 380, who cites גִּירֵם, "we hurled them down," in Num 21:30; cf. Exod 34:19; also, Sharrock, *AUSS* 21 [1983] 215, n. 10; cf. GKC 76f). For ינה, "oppress," see Pss 17:12; 123:4 (*qere*). However, a long tradition of interpretation takes the word as a noun with a plural suffix meaning "offspring" or "progeny" (LXX; see Johnson, *CPIP*, 132, n. 6; also, Dahood). However, the idea of "kindred" or "progeny" seems to fit the context poorly. It is worth noting that both Johnson and Dahood have to make rather drastic changes in the following colon in order to sustain the reading of a substantive. Johnson repoints מוֹעֲדֵי־אֵל ("meeting-place of God") to מוּעֲדֵי־אֵל, "those appointed of God" = "who hold office from God"—influenced by concern for proposals to date the psalm in the later post-exilic period. Dahood (II, 202) reads the verb שָׂרְפוּ as a simple passive (שׂוֹרְפוּ) used as a precative perfect: "Let all their progeny be burned" (followed by Young, *Psalm 74*, 81, 83)—a procedure which balances the colons (into 3+3), but is not very convincing.

8.b. LXX and Peshitta indicate a reading of נִשְׁבִּיתָה or נִשְׁבַּת, "let us cause to cease" for MT שָׂרְפוּ, "they burned," which seems to involve too much change to be likely (see Gelston, *VT* 34 [1984] 83, 86, n. 4).

9.a. Reading the suffix as objective rather than as genitive (with Dahood, II, 202; Young, *Psalm 74*, 85; cf. GKC 135n).

11.a. The meaning of this verse is uncertain. The *kethiv* reads חוקך (or חקך), "your decree/statute," and the *qere* reads חיקך, "your bosom" (Emerton, *JTS* 14 [1963] 378). LXX reads, "Why do you turn away your hand, / and your right hand from the midst of your bosom forever [or completely]?" The LXX εἰς τέλος for the כלה at the end of the verse indicates that the translators understood כלה in the sense of "to complete" (perhaps assuming an infinitive absolute, "completely"), equivalent to לנצח ("forever") in v 10 (see n. 1.c.). The *kethiv* ("your decree") has little support among versions or commentators. Emerton (380) translates as "Why drawest thou back thy hand, / Even thy right hand from the midst of thine assembly." He achieves this by an elaborate process of appeal to the Syriac text of the Peshitta, which seems to indicate קהלכה "your assembly/congregation," for MT's חיקך כלה, "your bosom; end it." Emerton thinks the question in 11a extends into 11b and considers the subject to be God's holding back his hand from helping Israel.

The *Translation* is obviously a conjecture but attempts to stay with MT. It assumes that the וימינך ("and your right hand") does double duty as the subject of both colons. The *Translation* assumes that the כלה is piel imperative and that the question in 11a does *not* continue in 11b. A more lit. meaning of 11a would be, "Why do you let your hand return," which is equivalent to "draw back." There is a problem with the lack of an object for כלה , but this construction has a parallel in Ps 59:14. The object is the destruction and taunting of the foe in the temple (כלה can be understood as equivalent to כלהו—"destroy him/it"; Johnson, *CPIP*, 135, n. 3). If the continuation of the question in 11a into 11b is desired, it can be obtained by the widely adopted change of כלה to some form of the verb כלא ("restrain/withhold/keep back") and read: "Why do you draw back your hand, / and hold back your right hand in the midst of your bosom?" (as, e.g., in Kraus, II, 676, 677). But this seems to be a very forced use of the preposition in מקרב as well as the adoption of an emendation, unless, of course, מקרב is emended to בקרב (as in Young, *Psalm 74*, 91). Another possibility is to retain the *kethiv* (חוק) and recognize that it has a range of meaning which encompasses "action prescribed" or "obligation" (see Exod 5:14; 30:21), along with assuming that the כַּלֵּה is a piel infinitive absolute (which occurs 6 times in this form) and is used for both colons, resulting in a translation such as "Why would you hold back your hand (forever), / even your right hand forever from the midst of your obligation (to us)?" In this case, מקרב is awkward, but may be used for balance in the colons and correlates with בקרב in v 12.

12.a. LXX has 1st pers. pl. suffix, "our king"; Syriac has no article: "king from of old" = "the ancient king." For "my king," see Pss 44:5[4]; 68:25; 84:4.

13.a. Reading פֵּרֵ, "shatter/break/destroy/frustrate/make ineffectual" (BDB, 830). פרר, II ("rend asunder/break apart") is weakly attested, only in Isa 24:19, Job 16:12, and possibly here. It is possible that the idea of "shaking back and forth" is present and thus "rouse the sea." But this does not go well with 13b. The idea of "split" is strongly influenced by the assumption that the object is the Reed Sea (see *Comment*).

13.b. Heb. ים ("sea") is the Yamm of Ugar. sources.

14.a. Lit. "for a people, for desert ones," an obscure construction which is equivalent perhaps to "for a people of desert ones" (unless ציים means "hyenas"; Johnson, *CPIP*, 135, n. 7). The meaning of

ציים is uncertain. If it is a denominative of ציה, "dryness," it may refer to animals like the hyena who live in desert places. The word צי, however, can mean "ship" (Isa 33:21; Num 24:24; Ezek 20:9), which could mean that לציים means "for the people belonging to ships" = "sea-farers, sailors," or the like. However, the pl. of צי, "ship," in Num 24:24 is צים, though it is possible to disregard the pointing and read לצי ים (see Young, *Psalm 74*, 101): "for the people of the ship of the sea" = "sea-farers." LXX has "Ethiopians," which probably means "desert dwellers." the emendation to "for the sharks of the sea" (see *BHS*) has been widely adopted (NEB; NAB, "for the dolphins"), but it involves too much change and has been strongly refuted by J. Barr (*Comparative Philology and the Text of the Old Testament* [Oxford: Clarendon Press, 1968] 236–37). Johnson (135) is probably correct when he reads עם, "people," as "an army," in the sense used of a "people/army" of locusts in Joel 2:2 (cf. Prov 30:25–26). Thus, "an army of desert creatures" may be what is intended. NJV has "for the denizens of the desert."

16.a. It is possible that the singular מאור ("luminary") is collective ("luminaries"); "the luminaries, even the sun," or "the luminaries (moon and stars) and the sun."

17.a. The verb נצב, with God as the subject, is used for fixing or protection of boundaries (Deut 32:8; Prov 15:25), of giving a king his dominion (1 Chr 18:3). The verb seems to carry the idea in hiphil of "to stand up/to erect," as to set up a pillar (Gen 35:14, 20) or "stood" as the waters of the Reed Sea (Ps 78:13). Thus, to fix, set, or establish boundaries.

17.b. "Formed" (יצר) is used in the sense of "made" (cf. Pss 94:9; 95:5; 104:26; Amos 4:13; Isa 44:2).

18.a. The referent of זאת, "this," is not entirely clear. Young (*Psalm 74*, 110) calls it a "forensic admonition that God take the speaker's argument seriously." It seems to refer to the statements which follow and is a form of the use of the fem. to refer to something already said (see GKC 135p).

18.b. This expression appears elsewhere only in Deut 32:6; there of the Israelites who act as if Yahweh is not their father. For נבל, "fool," see *Comment* or Pss 14:1 and 53:1.

19.a. LXX and Syriac indicate תודך is a hiphil 2nd pers. sing. fem. from ידך, "praise/thank," for MT's תורך ("your turtle dove"), yielding the translation: "Deliver not to the wild beasts a soul that gives praise to you." This reading fits the context well and has been adopted by some commentators (e.g., Gunkel and Kraus). However, the metaphor of a dove given to a wild beast is stronger. The traditional ET of תור is "turtledove," to distinguish it from יונה ("dove").

19.b. The versions had some difficulty with this word (see *BHS*). Some modern interpreters emend (without textual support) to למות ("to death"): "Give not your dove to death" (e.g., Kraus). However the unusual fem. ending (which may have led LXX to read pl., "to the wild beasts") is not a problematic construct ending (so Kraus), but a fem. absolute ending (see GKC 80f, g; Dahood; Young, *Psalm 74*, 112), which may be collective (and may indicate that LXX was reading MT). The לחית ("to a wild beast") forms a pun with חית ("life") in v 19b. As Young (113) notes, there is an ironic identification of the life of the poor ones with the "wild beasts" who oppress them.

19.c. See n. 1.c.

19.d. See *Comment* on 68:11. The term, "your poor ones," appears in MT three times: here, 72:2, and Deut 15:11.

20.a. LXX reads with 2nd pers. sing. suffix, "your covenant," which is probably what MT means without emendation (see לעם, "to the people," in Ps 68:36). The covenant is the one Yahweh made with Israel. Changes such as לבריתיך, "for your creatures" (from בריאה) which is represented in NEB, are not persuasive.

20.b. Dahood and Young (*Psalm 74*, 115–16) change מחשכי, "dark places of/hiding places of," to מחשכי, "from/with darkness," and assume that the verb "filled" does double-duty for the first and second colons, thus giving a fairly well-balanced tricolon: "Consider your covenant! / The earth is filled with darkness; pastures [see n. 20.d.] are overrun with violence."

20.c. נאות is properly "pastures/meadow/countryside" (cf. Ps 23:2), but here it means "habitations" or "domains" (NAB, "plains") in a metaphorical sense. The emendations to אנחה (*BHS*), "groaning," or נאוה, "pride/haughtiness," are not necessary. LXX has "houses/abodes/habitations of lawlessness."

21.a. Reading ישֵׁב (with Syriac) from ישב, "sit/remain/dwell" (see Dahood, Young, *Psalm 74*, 118), for MT ישֹׁב from שוב, "turn, return/turn away." The idea is that of those who sit amid ashes or on the ground in despair and humiliation (cf. Jer 2:12–13; Lam 2:10; Neh 1:4; Isa 29:1; Pss 44:26; 137:1).

21.b. LXX^B has conjunction before נכלם: "Let not the oppressed *and* humiliated one be turned away (rejected)," which appears to be reading the verb ישב as hiphil imperfect (from שוב) rather than MT's simple imperfect.

22.a. Lit. "remember your taunting from a fool."

23.a. Lit. "the voice of your foes." The word קוֹל ("voice") is used here of the roar and din of violent foes (for the idea of roaring, cf. Ezek 1:24; 43:2; Pss 29; 93:3, 4).

Form/Structure/Setting

A number of linguistic and poetic features mark this psalm and bind it together. G. F. Sharrock (*AUSS* 21 [9183] 211–23) has chosen to begin an analysis with the pattern of the main verbs in the psalm:

2–3 imperatives
4–9 perfects
10–11 imperfects and imperative (?) in v 11
12–17 perfects
18–23 imperatives and jussives

Sharrock concludes that the psalm has an inverted symmetrical structure in the following order:

A imperatives
  B perfects
    C imperfects
  B' perfects
A' imperatives

He treats v 1 as an introduction to the whole psalm, which it is, but the rhetorical questions in this verse are equivalent to the supplicatory imperatives in 2–3. There are certainly other ways to analyze this psalm, but Sharrock's makes sense and seems to have a "good fit" with the psalm. I have adopted his outline in the *Comment*. P. Auffret (*VT* 33 [1983] 130–48) offers a considerably more complex analysis of the psalm, but one which has much in common with Sharrock. Auffret finds the following succession of sections: vv 1–2; vv 3–11 and 1–11; vv 12–17; vv 1–17; vv 18–23; and the complete psalm in vv 1–23. In the formation of vv 1–11, he finds that vv 1–3a (ending with נצח, "forever/completely," as does 1a, לנצח) deal with *the people*, while vv 3b–11 concentrate on *the enemies*.

Various other literary aspects are easily identifiable in the psalm. The initial זכר, "remember," in v 2 is matched by זכר, "remember," in v 18 (the A and A' sections are thus related; a secondary זכר appears in v 22). The "roaring" of the foes in v 4 (שאג) is matched by the "din" (שאון) of the rebels in v 23. A thematic element in the psalm is found in the use of נצח ("forever/completely") in vv 1, 3, 10, 19. Thus the sequence of זכר—נצח—שאג in vv 2–4 is matched by the slightly varied sequence of זכר—זכר—שאון in vv 18–23. Also, note the use of צוֹרְרֶיךָ ("your foes") in v 4 and in v 23.

Young (*Psalm 74*, 144–45) calls attention to the so-called stair-like parallelism in vv 1–11, which has a crescendo effect, that reaches a climax with the imperative "end it" of v 11 (if the *Translation* is correct). A similar intensifying effect occurs in vv 18–23, ending with the din of the rebels against God rising up continually (תמיד). The use of אֶרֶץ ("land/earth") in v 12 and in v 17 marks in an appropriate way the beginning and end of a major section. The sevenfold אתה ("thou/you") in the form of a separate personal pronoun also characterizes these verses, with their powerful direct address to God. The key words of v 18 (זכר, חרף, and נבל,

"remember," "taunting," and "fool") form an inclusion, or frame, for vv 18–23. (Note their reccurrence in v 22.) The prayer for God to "arise" in v 22 (קוּמָה) is matched ironically by "those who rebel ("rise up," קוּם) against you," in v 23. A similar frame is noted by Auffret (134) for vv 1—10—11 (לָנֶצַח—אֱלֹהִים—לָמָה) "Why . . . O God . . . forever" in v 1 and לָמָה—אֱלֹהִים—לָנֶצַח in vv 10–11—though the order in vv 10–11 is actually לָמָה—לָנֶצַח—אֱלֹהִים, giving an ABCB'C'A' pattern with v 1). There seems to be a chiastic aspect to the placement of these verses: v 10 relates primarily to vv 12–23, while v 11 relates best to vv 1–9. Thus the two larger sections of the psalm, vv 1–9 and vv 13–23 are joined together by the inverted placement of vv 10 and 11:

v 10   vv 1–9
v 11   vv 12–23

The language of vv 1–11 and vv 18–23 is clearly that of communal lament, a prayer voiced for the people because of the great distress they have experienced (cf. Pss 44; 79; 89; Jer 14:1–15:4; Isa 63:7–74:11; see Young, 159–74). Both sections expose the roaring enemies who have wreaked great damage to the divine dwelling place and to the people. The great distress which has resulted and the behavior of the enemies are described for God's attention, and he is implored to intervene with power to rectify the situation. The fourth section (vv 12–17) is different, however; it is hymnic in nature, describing in a glorifying way the cosmic actions of God. These are, of course, put in the form of address to God (for a congregation, as in the thanksgiving mode; see F. Crüsemann, *Studien zur Formgeschichte*, 191–99, 289–94; Kraus). This section serves two major purposes in the psalm: (1) it looks back to the great acts of God and lays a foundation for the present appeal; (2) it contrasts in a striking way the cosmic strength and power of Yahweh with the seeming weakness which he has displayed toward his own major concerns: covenant, temple, and the poor and needy people of his "pasture." He is a powerful cosmic king who is failing as a Divine Warrior in the view of the speaker in Ps 74—failing because of his unrelenting anger against his own people—while he tolerates outrageous behavior on the part of those who slander his name and destroy his temple (cf. Young, 155–57). This section serves as a major motivation in the prayer (motivations are rather common in laments; see Gunkel-Begrich, *Einleitung*, 125, 129–32; S. Mowinckel, *PIW*, I, 204–6).

The setting and date of Ps 74 have been the subjects of much variation in opinion. Quite expectedly, critical scholars during the past 100 years, primarily concerned with a historical approach, have sought with great diligence to relate the psalm to an actual historical event. For example, Kirkpatrick relates the psalm closely to Ps 79 and argues for a date contemporary with Lamentations, some fifteen or twenty years after the destruction of Jerusalem in 587 B.C.E., though he surveys at some length the arguments for dating during the time of Antiochus Epiphanes (170–165 B.C.E.) and the Maccabees. Further he leaves open the possibility that the psalm might have been retouched to adapt it to the circumstances of the later period. The period after 587 B.C.E. commends itself toward dating the psalm because of the destruction of the temple and the city of Jerusalem (2 Kgs 25), the hostility of neighboring peoples (Ps 137; Ezek 24), the similarity to Lam 2:5–17 (including the "her prophets obtain no vision from the LORD" in v 2; cf. Ps 74:9), and various other parallels with Jeremiah, Lamentations, and Ezekiel (Kirkpatrick, 441).

Also, there is the widespread acceptance of the difficulty of dating any canonical psalm as late as 165 B.C.E. because of the discovery of texts of some of the Psalms at Qumran, dating from the first century B.C.E. (Dahood). On the other hand, the absence of prophets in Ps 74:9 relates well to references to such absence from Maccabean times (see Macc 4:46; 9:27; 14:41). Further, the reference to the destruction of the "meeting-places of God" in 74:8 has been thought to refer to synagogues, and it has been assumed that these would have been present during the religious persecution of Antiochus Epiphanes. The "signs" in the temple in vv 4, 9 have been applied to the profanation of the temple and the introduction of non-Jewish emblems during the time of Antiochus. However, the psalm lacks the definite descriptions and references to make either of these dates absolutely decisive, though on largely general grounds the exilic, sixth-century date has been more popular among recent writers (e.g., Anderson, Dahood, Kidner, Kraus). At various times, other dates have been advocated: an Edomite destruction of Jerusalem in 485 B.C.E. (by J. Morgenstern, "Jerusalem— 485 B.C.," *HUCA* 27 [1956] 101–79) and a Persian attack on Jerusalem c. 344 B.C.E. (see Leslie, 234; Buttenwieser, 555–66). 1 Kgs 14:25–26; 15:18; 2 Kgs 14:14; 16:3; 24:13 indicate that plunderings of the temple were not limited to the destructions by the Babylonians and by Antiochus.

Scholars with greater form critical and cultic interests, beginning with Gunkel, have argued against trying to date Ps 74 in relation to any specific historical event. Few scholars, however, have gone so far as F. Willesen (*VT* 2 [1952] 289– 306) in attempts to detach the psalm entirely from historical contexts and relate it to a cultic drama involving the ritual profanation and purification of the temple. For Willesen, Ps 74 was originally a ritual lament from the celebration of an Israelite New Year Festival. Such extreme "myth and ritual" interpretation has been rejected by most scholars (see the critique of Willeser in Dahood, II, 205, and Sabourin, 303–4). Most interpreters continue to think in terms of some sort of a historical relatedness. For example, Kraus thinks of the period between 586 B.C.E. and 520 B.C.E., probably nearer to 520 than to 587, and the psalm as belonging to lament ceremonies from this period (cf. Jer 41:8; Zech 7:1–7; 8:18–19), though he wants to remain open to other possibilities (so similarly Johnson, *CPIP*, 131). After a long and wandering investigation of the setting of Ps 74, Young comes to the tentative conclusion that the date and cultic context were exilic, "around the time of Second Isaiah—though with a much different outlook" (*Psalm 74*, 227). Undoubtedly the psalm had a date of composition and a cultic history, but the specific contexts now seem beyond our power to recover, though a date and setting among the people left behind in Palestine after 587 B.C.E. are highly probable. The psalm exists for us not primarily as a historical or as a cultic document but as a literary entity which generates its own intratextual context. Its use in public worship as well as in private study and devotion need not be doubted.

Comment

Question and petition (74:1–3). The question which is put to God (Yahweh) in prayer is "Why are you so angry with us? Is it total anger—never to be assuaged?" God's anger is described as "smoldering/smoking" (v 1), like mountains as a result of a nature-convulsing theophany of God (cf. Exod 19:18; Pss 104:32; 144:5).

His anger is not directed at the enemies of his people but against "the flock" of his own "pastures" (v 1)—those for whom he has assumed a shepherd-like responsibility, the people he acquired for himself long ago, his own patrimony (v 2). The "long ago" (קֶדֶם) can mean "ancient times," times when God created the world and defeated his cosmic foes (as in vv 13–17; Isa 51:9; Pss 55:20; 68:34; Deut 33:25). It can also refer to indefinite times when God determined his purpose in history (Lam 2:17; 2 Kgs 19:25 = Isa 37:26; Ps 119:152), or to the early times in Israel's history when God demonstrated his care for his people in ways which became paradigmatic (Ps 44:2; Lam 1:7; 5:21; Mic 7:20; Jer 30:20). All of these are blended together in Ps 74. Perhaps the most striking element is the anger of God which has allowed Mount Zion, his own dwelling place and his sanctuary/meeting-place/temple (vv 2, 3, 4), to be brutally attacked and possessed by enemies. Why does God turn against his own dwelling-place and allow it to become a total ruin? For the significance of Mount Zion, see Ps 62:2.

The ravaged sanctuary (74:4–9). These verses constitute a complaint which sets forth to God (Yahweh) what his foes have done to his meeting-place/sanctuary. The purpose of the prayer is not, of course, to inform Yahweh of what has happened (surely he knows!), but to move him to the action asked for in vv 2–3—to lay out the situation before him. The use of מוֹעֲדֶךָ ("your meeting-place/ assembly") in v 4 in this way is rare in MT (see Lam 2:6; Isa 33:20). The usual meaning of the word is that of "appointed time" or "festival." Young (*Psalm 74*, 74, citing R. J. Clifford, *The Cosmic Mountain in Canaan and the Old Testament*, 44–48) notes that in some Ugaritic usage the word means "assembly of El" (the Canaanite high god), while Baal's temple is referred to as *gdš*, "holy place/sanctuary." Both terms are used in Ps 74 for the temple of Yahweh.

The actions of the enemies are described with strong language. They have roared in the sanctuary like lions (v 4), and the damage they have done has left it in total ruins. They have hacked away and beaten up the fine carved panels of the temple (v 6). In fact, the attack on the temple was like woodcutters or lumberjacks going up to swing their axes in a thicket of trees growing on a hillside (v 5). They have set the sanctuary on fire and "defiled it to the ground" (v 7), which means that the whole sanctuary was brought down to the ground by those who profaned the holy place of worship. The expression conveys both the total religious profanation and physical destruction. The praise and prayer of the temple have been replaced by the crude bellowing of pagan soldiers bent on a destructive orgy, intending no stopping of their pillage until they have done away with all the people related to the temple (v 8, probably religious leaders and worshipers and their families in the temple area; Johnson, *CPIP*, 172, n. 6). The enemy invaders have erected their own standards and emblems in the temple (v 4). The symbols and rites of Israelite worship have been replaced by pagan equivalents (Anderson; cf. 1 Macc 1:45–49).

Two matters in this section merit some special attention. First, there is the matter of the signs in v 4 (also in v 9). In the context of v 4, the signs seem to be either military signs and emblems of the invaders (cf. Num 2:2; etc.), or their religious emblems (cf. Deut 6:8; Ezek 4:3), or both. The invaders would probably raise the standards and emblems of their victorious gods in the main cultic place of a conquered people. The situation is different in v 9, for the Israelites are said to see no signs: "We see no signs for us" (which could be, of course, "we see none of our signs," see n. 9.a). These are probably to be understood as signs of Yahweh's saving actions—signs of divine intervention to change the situation (on "signs," see *Comment* on 65:7). Even if there were signs, there was no prophet to explain them—no one to tell them how long the present distress would continue (v 9). We should probably not make too much of the verse as an indication of the physical absence of prophets and prophecy, especially in terms of dating the psalm. The main point is that there is no person who can answer the dilemma presented by the invaders—"the whole situation was unintelligible, inexplicable in view of the relation of Israel to God" (Briggs, II, 154; cf. Lam 2:9). Weiser (519) comments, "There was no sign of the divine presence (we might think of the cultic tradition or of symbols or of the evidence of sacrifices), no comforting word spoken by a prophet, no counsel of a wise man which could have saved the people from their gloomy despair."

The second matter is that of the "every meeting-place of God in the land" (v 8). What is the "meeting-place of God"? The idea of מועדי־אל as "the appointed times of God" seems to be ruled out by their being the object of "burning" (A. Gelston, *VT* 34 [1984] 83)—though it seems possible, but remote, that the reference could be to "festivals" at the temple, all of which the enemies want to prohibit by its destruction. Also, it seems unlikely that the "meeting-places" (or "assemblies") in v 8 are to be identified with the "meeting-place/assembly" in v 4. Gelston cites the parallel in Lam 2:6 between שׂכו ("his booth") and מועד as evidence that the מועד can have reference to buildings used for worship, though the meaning of this verse is not clear (the verse may be defining the temple as a place of festal assembly, or, possibly, the reference is to festival structures used by worshipers). Gelston (83–86) suggests four possibilities for dealing with the plural "meeting-place of God": (1) Take as a reference to non-Yahwistic sanctuaries (perhaps with ארץ being taken as "world/earth")—but why such lament over non-Yahwistic worship-places? (2) Take as a reference to local sanctuaries or "high places"—but if the psalm is later than Josiah's reform (621 B.C.E.), the "high places" should be gone as places of Yahwistic worship (see 2 Kgs 22–23); unless they were restored, but even so such lament for such places seems unlikely. (3) Take as a reference to the several buildings in the temple area. Possible support for this interpretation may come from Lam 2:6 and the fact that some Hebrew manuscripts have the plural "meeting-places" in v 4 and "sanctuaries" in v 7 (note *BHS*), which could possibly refer to the courts and buildings of the temple used as places of festal assembly (note that NJV translates as "God's tabernacles"). This is a possible interpretation, but it seems strained with the כָּל־ ("every") and "in the land" language of v 8. (4) Take as a reference to other places of Yahwistic worship besides the temple area—"non-sacrificial Yahwistic cult centers in Judah, and, as such, precursors of the synagogue" (85). A possible reference to such a place is found in 1 Macc 3:46, where there is reference to a former "place of prayer" at Mizpah—probably the place where Gedaliah set up a short-term administration after the fall of Jerusalem in 587 B.C.E. (2 Kgs 25:23; Jer 40:10). Was Mizpah the only community with a place of prayer? Hardly. There were probably other places as well. Some of the former "high places" may have been adapted to non-sacrificial worship places after the reform of Josiah—possibly the "meeting-places of God" in Ps 74:8.

The fourth interpretation seems the most likely. The Greek versions of Aquila and Symmachus understood the expression in v 8 to mean "synagogues," which is, of course, very probably anachronistic; the "meeting-places" were more probably the prototypes of the synagogues. It is possible, of course, that this whole discussion has been too much ado about nothing and that 8b should be read as a hyperbole about the invaders: "They have burnt every meeting-place of God on the whole earth!"—which receives some support from LXX, which has the invader boast (see n. 9.b.): "Come, let us abolish the feasts of the LORD from the earth." Gunkel's change of the verb שׂרף from third person plural ("They have burned") to first person plural ("We will burn") is not really necessary for this interpretation (the perfect in 8b could read as precative-optative: "Let's burn"— an interpretation that would have the advantage of continuing the arrogant, almost insane boasting of the attackers in 8a, b). However, on the whole, I prefer the fourth alternative presented by Gelston.

God's scorned name and drawn-back hand (74:10–11). As noted already, these verses are the hinge section of the psalm. The crux of the psalm is found in the backward look to the terrible damage done to the worship place and the seemingly endless scorn of Yahweh's name. Why does he hold his hand in his bosom? Why does he not pull out his right hand and with one mighty blow end the arrogant invasion of his domain? Will he tolerate forever the brutal treatment of his own patrimony, the "flock" of his pasture, the people of his covenant—giving them over like a dove about to be devoured by a wild beast, leaving them poor and needy to sit humiliated, while the enemy taunts and clamors unceasingly?

The background of this psalm reflects the type-scene of an attack on a cosmic king and his mountain/temple home, which appears in Canaanite form in the Baal cycles found in the Ugaritic literature (Young, *Psalm 74*, 179–80, 193–95, 219–23). In terms of these stories, the rivals who attack the mountain temple and challenge the power of the divine king are supposed to fail, as reflected in Isa 14:10b–15, where the assault on El/Elyon results in the attackers being cast down to the realm of the dead in Sheol. (The pattern of the impregnable nature of the divine temple/home is reflected in the inviolability of Zion: Pss 46; 48; 76; Isa 36–39 = 2 Kgs 18:13–20:19.) Will the Divine Warrior of Israel, whose victories have been both historical and cosmic (vv 12–17) prove to be inferior to Baal and allow his temple to be wrecked and his people to be brutalized? Surely not. The prayer of Yahweh's people is "End it?"—and do it now; strike forth in power (v 2) and put things right!

An address to the Salvation-Worker in the midst of the earth (74:12–17). The "my King" in v 12a lets the reader know that the speaker in this psalm is an individual voicing a prayer for the commuinty—not simply a detached narrator of events or some purely professional mediator. With one expression, the speaker identifies the deity addressed as "my King from long ago," or "my ancient King" (cf. Pss 55:20; 93:2; Hab 1:2; Mic 5:10; Dan 7:13). The speaker expresses "ownership" of the long history of Yahweh and Israel, who is described as the "Salvation-Worker" (or "salvation," see Ps 51:14). The word for "salvation" here is ישׁועות, "deliverances" or "victories" (cf. Pss 44:5; 68:20). The image is that of a king whose leadership and power win victories for his people over hostile foes (cf. Pss 20:6; 21:2; 67:3; 118:14, 15, 21; et al.).

Of course, the tone and mode of address in vv 12–18 are quite different from those in vv 1–11. In vv 4–9, a kind of report is made—as if a messenger from battle brought a message of the course of events. In vv 12–18, the address is direct (seven times, God is addressed with the emphatic "You"), and the language is affirmative, hymn-like in setting forth the mighty deeds of the Salvation-Worker. There are no imperatives in these verses; the cosmic power of Yahweh is contrasted with the roaring foes, swinging their destructive axes, in vv 4–9. The common interpretation of the "sea" in 13a is that the referent is the dividing of the waters of the Red (Reed) Sea at the time of the Israelite exodus from Egypt, with the Sea-Monsters in 13b taken as symbolic representation of Egypt (e.g., Cohen). However, as observed in n. 13.a., the verb (פוררת) carries ideas of shattering or breaking rather than of splitting or dividing. This combined with the creation language and the lack of explicit reference to the exodus makes it reasonable to conclude that the primary referents are the cosmic forces commonly treated as gods in ancient Near Eastern thought. For example, in the Ugaritic literature there is a struggle for cosmic kingship between the god Baal (thunderstorms and fertility) and Yam or Yamm (sea) and with the sea-monsters associated with Yamm (see Young, *Psalm 74*, 179–227 for a full review of the texts and their counterparts in the OT; also A. Lelièvre, *RHPR* 56 [1976] 253–75). The Tannim (תנינים), "Sea-Monsters" or "Sea-Serpents" (cf. Ezek 29:3; Job 7:12; Ps 148:7), are described as creatures with seven heads (cf. Rev 12:3; 13:1; 17:3), which has led M. Dahood (II, 205) to suggest that this accounts for the sevenfold "you" (אתה) in vv 13–17 (rejected, however, by J. Day, *God's Conflict with the Dragon and the Sea*, 24, though his reasons are not too strong). Leviathan seems to be another name for the Sea-Monster, who is described as a coiled serpent with seven heads (see *ANET*, 138; cf. Isa 27:1; Job 41:1; Ps 104:26). O. Keel-Leu (*The Symbolism of the Biblical World*, 50–51) notes that the sea-monster/dragon is variously named in ancient literature and variously depicted in ancient Near Eastern pictorial representations (see the iconographic reproductions in Keel-Leu, 50–55). The concept was a fluid one which flowed into different conceptualizations. The multi-headed feature of the monster was quite widespread and may have arisen from the extreme agility of a snake's head, which may give the impression of multiple heads (Keel-Leu, 52).

In Ugaritic sources the battle between Baal and Yamm and associated beings is primarily related to a struggle for cosmic power and divine kingship rather than to creation, which is the case also in Ps 74:12–14. God/Yahweh is the great victor-king of the cosmos, who crushes the heads of sea-monsters and gives their bodies as food for the creatures of the desert (v 14; Ezek 32:2–8). However, in vv 15–17 the text reflects the creative work of God in the world. The Victor-King is also the Creator. In this regard, the text reflects the cosmic struggle to gain a created order (the *Chaoskampf*) which is so well known from the Babylonian creation account, *Enuma Elish*, in which Marduk (the divine king, roughly equivalent to Baal) overcomes Tiamat, who represents the primeval waters, equal to the sea and associated monsters. However, the Baal myths may have associated creation with the conflict with Yamm, the sea-monster, even though the emphasis is on the affirmation of the divine kingship (see Day, 17; note that Baal is credited with the establishment of the seasons; see *Comment* on v 17 below). It is also possible, as Young (*Psalm 74*, 175–224) argues, that the Hebrew texts reflect the blending of traditions associated with El with those of Baal. El in the Ugaritic texts is the father god, head of the divine assembly, and the eternal and wise king, the "ancient one," and "creator of all creatures." The attributes of El and Baal are merged in the Yahweh of the OT.

Emerton (VTSup 15 [1966] 122–33) has argued persuasively that v 15a does not refer to the breaking open of rocks and the earth in order to produce flowing water for people and animals (as commonly interpreted; cf. Ps 18:15–16; Exod 17:6. Num 20:28)—especially relating to the provision of water for the Israelites in the wilderness. Emerton argues that the verb בקע ("cleave, split") does not go well with the idea of opening up a flowing spring (cf. Dahood's, "released springs and brooks"; cf. Ps 104:10–12; Prov 3:20), but reflects a creation idea of the draining away of covering waters so that dry land appeared (cf. Gen 1:9–10), and that this is also the explanation of v 15b, which reverses the process described in the flood narrative in Gen 7:11. The purpose of the springs and rivers was to drain the waters into a cosmic abyss and allow the dry land to appear.

The creative work of God is also demonstrated by his control of day and night, the establishment of the sun and moon, and the division of the climate of the world into seasons (vv 16, 17b). The fixing of the boundaries of the earth (v 17a) is not entirely clear. We should probably think of divisions/boundaries in a general sense, including: divisions between land and sea (cf. Ps 104:9; Job 38:8–11; Jer 5:22), the divisions of the land among the peoples of the earth (Deut 32:8; Acts 17:26; cf. Ps 82), and the divisions of the seasons (cf. Gen 1:14). Dahood translates גבולות as "zones" and associates it with the temperature zones of the earth. In the Baal texts, the establishment of the seasons is ascribed to Baal by the goddess Asherah in a speech to the high god El: "Behold now, Baal has appointed his rains; / He has appointed the wet and snowy seasons, / He has thundered in the storm clouds, / He has blazed his lightning bolts to the earth." (Young, *Psalm 74*, 190; the text is CTA 4.5. 68–71, and the translation is from F. M. Cross, *Canaanite Myth and Hebrew Epic*, 148–49).

Prayer for God's help (74:18–23). The last major division of the psalm is composed of intense appeals to God for his intervention. Imperative and jussive verbs dominate these verses. According to the interpretation which I have given to v 18 (see notes), it contains a summary of the distress described in the lament in vv 10–11. A "fool-people" have taunted Yahweh, the cosmic sovereign, and reviled his name. Young (111) notes the pun on the verb חֵרֵף, "taunt," and the noun חֹרֶף, "winter," in v 17. God has used his power to form winter (חֹרֶף), but he remains silent while foolish foes taunt (חֵרֵף) and scorn (נאץ, also in v 10; a verb which may also be translated as "despised") his name. The use of Yahweh as the name of God heightens the sense of a close relationship among God, his people, and the speaker (note the second person of "your name" after the third person of the prior line, and compare the sevenfold "you" in vv 12–17).

The reference to the covenant in v 20 is an unusual expression ("to the covenant," cf. Jer 14:21). It assumes that God is being charged with ignoring the obligations of his covenant. The reference is most probably to Yahweh's covenant with Israel (Exod 19:4–6; 24:8) rather than to the Davidic covenant (Pss 89:3, 39; 143:11–12) or to the covenants with Noah (Gen 9:8–17) or to that with Abraham (Gen 17:2–14). Cf. Ps 78:10; Isa 64:8. The idea of "covenant" is that

God has taken on himself commitments to his people which he should not forget (for ברית, "covenant," see Ps 55:21). Israel is God's helpless dove, in danger of being devoured by a wild beast; they are the "poor ones" of God who must be remembered by God if they are to live (v 19). V 20 indicates a situation in which law and order have broken down and the "hiding-places" have all become the haunts of robbers and others who treat the people with violence. Wherever one turns, the land is full of danger.

Explanation

Ps 74 is a communal lament, designed for use in public prayer and lamentation ceremonies, which begins with a cry of distress, "Why, O God?" and ends with an extended entreaty to God for his intervention: "Arise, O God, defend your cause!" (v 22). The distress is caused by a ferocious attack by enemies against the central place of worship. The sanctuary has been burned and left in total ruins (vv 3–7). However, the distress voiced by the speaker in the psalm is a distress which extends beyond physical damage. The major problem is the seeming indifference and inactivity of God. The temple could be rebuilt, but what of the faith in God which it represented? Claus Westermann (*Praise and Lament*, 177) says of the question "Why?" in the laments that it is "like the feeble groping of one who has lost the way in the dark." It has the sense of a desperate seeking on the part of those who are trying to find a way through God's seeming alienation; an absence which goes beyond momentary experience to become an ongoing travail.

The sense of the absence and inactivity of God, despite great provocation by his enemies, is heightened by the hymn-like section in vv 12–17, which recalls the cosmic power of God. He is the basher of sea-monsters' heads and the one whose power overwhelms every challenge to divine kingship. Why then does he tolerate the "monsters" who are loose in his own patrimony? Why does he hold back his right hand rather than immediately end this gross challenge to divine authority? Why are the poor ones of his people (v 21) sitting in humiliation when they would gladly rise and sing the praise of his name if he would prove to be the real Salvation-Worker on the earth (v 12)? Why does the mighty Lord of the Covenant draw back his powerful right hand from the accomplishment of his purpose for his own people (v 11), while brutal perpetrators of violence lurk in all the dark places of the land (v 20)?

Ps 74 is a good illustration of Westermann's emphasis on accusatory questions and complaints directed at God (*Praise and Lament*, 177). The questions and complaints "tread that thin line between reproach and judgment" (ibid.). However, personal address dominates these laments; they do not turn away from God but *toward him in an act of faith*. He must reverse a situation which has developed beyond human resources. Westermann goes a bit too far in his analysis of the communal laments by the way in which he forces the elements of trust and praise into these psalms (see 52–57). In fact, praise in the communal laments is usually latent and not overtly expressed, and the laments usually end with the problems laid out before God but unresolved. The hymnic section in vv 12–17 is more descriptive than declarative and is not really praise but rather prayer intended to emphasize God's painful inactivity. The language of praise is put to use in the service of lament. Nevertheless, Weiser (520) is correct to write that this psalm (especially in the supplication of vv 18–23), "expresses the unshakable belief that God, who has shown himself in the creation of the universe to be Lord over the chaos, has now also the power to suppress the revolt of the chaotic powers and that in view of his covenant promise he will not allow his downtrodden people to become the defenseless prey . . . of the cruel lust for power of these enemies." The confidence lies close at hand that God will pay attention to this covenant and remember his needy congregation (v 2), and that he will not forget the snarling, tumultuous taunting of the fools who have wreaked havoc on Mount Zion.

Some further consideration of vv 12–17 is appropriate here. As noted above in the *Comment,* the mythical referents in these verses seem to have been Ugaritic-Canaanite in an ultimate sense. In a more immediate sense, Ps 74 was probably dependent on Israelite traditions such as those reflected in Pss 104:1–9; 89:10–15; 65:7–8; 93; 24; Gen 1. In the Israelite traditions, Yahweh's kingship is closely related to the creation of the world. The Ugaritic accounts of the struggle between Baal and Yam (Sea) do not express overtly a relationship to creation. The emphasis in the Baal texts, as in the Babylonian Marduk texts, is upon the establishment of the power of divine kingship and the building of a temple for the victorious god. Lelièvre (*RHPR* 56 [1976] 266–68) and Day (24) suggest that this may be reflected in Ps 74:12–17, which is motivated by a description of the destruction of Yahweh's temple in vv 1–11. It would be inappropriate for a divine King to allow his house, a house which was rightfully his because of his victories over the Sea and the sea-monsters, to be so ill-treated.

Vv 12–17 should not be read as a treatment of the exodus from Egypt in metaphorical-mythical language, as is sometimes done (see Smick, *WTJ* 44 [1982] 90), equating the monster with Egypt and the Red Sea and thus separating the area of myth from history. The point is not (as Kidner, 268, argues) that Yahweh had done in history what Baal claimed to do in the realm of myth. In the first place, the emphasis is not on the exodus at all, though it should not be excluded entirely. The stress is on God's creative and saving power, especially demonstrated in his works of creation by the one who is the Salvation-Worker in the midst of the earth (v 12). In the second place, the function of mythical language should be kept in mind. The definition of myth is a very complex subject which cannot be expounded here (see J. W. Rogerson, *Myth in Old Testament Interpretation,* BZAW 134 [Berlin: de Gruyter, 1974]; B. Otzen, H. Gottlieb, and K. Jeppesen, *Myths in the Old Testament,* tr. F. Cryer [London: SCM Press 1980]; F. R. McCurley, *Ancient Myths and Biblical Faith* [Philadelphia: Fortress Press, 1983]). In some cases in biblical literature, there is a historicization of myth, or conversely, a mythicization of history, in which mythological images are used to describe historical acts of Yahweh in the experience of Israel, or a myth is applied to an event in history (cf. Isa 21:1–9), or a historical event is given cosmic or universal dimensions by the use of mythic language (cf. the accounts of the deliverance from Egypt in Exod 1–15; see McCurley, 3–4). Ps 74 seems to represent a mythicization of history, if we assume that some historical actuality lies behind vv 1–11. The history, however, has been put in a mythic context which serves to express realities of life in the language of human imagination in the form of mythical images. The value of this language of imagination lies in its capacity to comprehend and express those realities which so often lie beyond the power of the logical constructs of the "reasons of the mind." In the mythical language of the Bible there is no escape from the experiences of the senses or from the actuality of historical happenings. The use of mythical language occurs when the inability to deal with the great questions of humanity with a 1+1=2 model is recognized, either explicitly or implicitly. The "reasons of the heart" and the modes of imagination must be utilized in the inward and outward journeys which the reality of human life in God's creation requires.

"There Is a Cup in Yahweh's Hand" *(75:1–11)*

Bibliography

Dahood, M. "The Four Cardinal Points in Psalm 75, 7 and Joel 2, 20." *Bib* 52 (1971) 397. **Eaton, J. H.** *Kingship.* 55–56. **Jeremias, J.** *Kultprophetie.* 117–20. **Johnson, A.** *CPIP.* 317–22.

Translation

1   For the leader;[a] *al-tashsheth;*[b] an Asaphite psalm;[c] a song.[d]

2 (1) *We give thanks to you, O God;*   (4+4)
    we give you thanks, and your Name[a] *is near,*[b]
    your wondrous deeds declare it![c]

3 (2) *When I choose a set time,*[a]   (3+3)
    I will indeed[b] *judge with equity.*

4 (3) *When the earth and all her inhabitants are shaking,*[a]   (3+3)
    I am the one[b] *who makes her pillars*[c] *firm. SELAH.*[d]

5 (4) *I say to the boastful, "Do not boast,"*   (3+3)
    and to the wicked, "Do not lift up your horns;[a]

6 (5) *do not lift your horns up high,*   (3+3)
    or speak with an insolent neck."[a]

7 (6) *For neither from the east, nor from the west,*   (3+3)
    nor from the wilderness,[a] *is there such [power] for lifting up.*[b]

8 (7) *For God is the one who judges;*   (2+4)
    he puts one down, and he raises up another.

9 (8) *Indeed, there is a cup in Yahweh's hand,*   (3+2+2+2+3+2)
    and the wine foams, fully mixed[a]*—*
    when he pours it[b] *out,*
    all the wicked of the earth will surely drink it—
    drink it down, dregs and all!

10 (9) *But I, I will declare forever (his wondrous deeds);*[a]   (3+3)
    I will sing praise to the God of Jacob.

11 (10) *And all the horns of the wicked? I will cut (them) off,*[a]   (3+3)
    but the horns of the righteous will be lifted up.[b]

Notes

1.a. For למנצח, see n. 51:1.a.

1.b. אל־תשחת, "Do Not Destroy," generally understood to be the opening lines of a song to whose music this psalm was to be sung. The phrase appears in Deut 9:26 and, with suffixes, in 1 Sam 26:9 and Isa 65:8; it is likely that the song referred to appears in one of these passages. See n. 57:1.b.; the term also appears in the titles of Pss 58 and 59.

1.c. For לאסף, "to/for/of Asaph," see n. 73:1.a.

1.d. The word שיר may mean a cultic song, as here, or a secular one (cf. Amos 6:5). See n. 65:1.c.

2.a. Yahweh's name is of great signficance (cf. Exod 3:13–15). In the biblical world names meant more than designations of people; names conveyed their essential being (cf. Gen 32:27, Mark 5:9). Consequently Yahweh's name reveals his character (Exod 34:14; Jer 33:2; Amos 5:8; 9:6) and is the focus of love (Ps 69:37), fear (Ps 61:6), and praise (Isa 26:10; Ps 18:50; 1 Chr 16:10). Yahweh's name is his presence in the place of worship (Exod 20:24; Deut 12:5, 11). According to G. von Rad, Yahweh's name "takes the place which in other cults was occupied by the cultic image" (*Old Testament Theology*, tr. D. M. G. Stalker [New York: Harper, 1962] I, 183). See *Comment*, 54:3.

2.b. וְקָרוֹב שְׁמֶךָ סִפְּרוּ—literally "and your name is near; they will recount." The LXX and the Syriac apparently read as וְיִקְרָא בִשְׁמֶךָ סַפֵּר ("and calling on your name one will recount"). rsv has "we call on thy name and recount" in order to match the context of 2a (also Briggs, II, 160). *BHS* proposes וְקֹרְאֵי בִשְׁמֶךָ סִפְּרוּ ("and those calling on your name recount"), which utilizes the 3rd pers. masc. pl. סִפְּרוּ of MT. This proposal is a fairly minor emendation, moving the last letter of MT's וְקָרוֹב to the beginning of שְׁמֵךְ and using the form of סִפֵּר in the text. It is followed by Kraus (683), Jeremias (*Kultprophetie*, 117), Schmidt (143), and Gunkel (326). However, the translation above is based on the conclusion that קָרוֹב should be retained as an adjective ("near") and that the nearness of the divine name is equivalent to the nearness of God; so, njv, "we praise You; Your presence is near." A slightly different option is found in niv, "we give thanks, for your Name is near." The *Translation* assumes that the Name/Presence comes near when thankful praise is given to God.

2.c. Reading "your wondrous deeds" as the subject of the verb. The deeds of Yahweh manifest the nature of his "Name." Cf. neb, "thy name is brought only near to us in the story of thy wonderful deeds"; "Thy wondrous deeds tell of thy nearness through Thy Name" (Johnson, *CPIP*, 319). Others assume an indefinite "they/men/people" as the subject: "men tell of your wonderful deeds" (niv).

3.a. מועד is literally "appointed time/place/meeting." Dahood (II, 211) prefers to translate as "assembly," interpreting this as the final judgment at which all people will come before Yahweh's court (cf. Ps 65:3–4, Joel 3:12, Hab 2:3). The translation "designated time" still indicates an appropriate and planned occasion but does not limit the reference to the end of the world (so Jacquet, Schmidt, and Anderson).

3.b. The use of the first common sing. pronoun plus the qal imperfect first common sing. verb emphasizes the subject. The verb itself would still mean "I will judge"; the pronoun stresses Yahweh as the one who acts. The כי at the beginning of the verse may also be emphatic (see Johnson, *CPIP*, 319).

4.a. Traditionally the verb מוג is understood as "melt/dissolve," a metaphor for helplessness, terror, and the resulting disorganization (e.g., Exod 15:15; Josh 2:9, 24; 1 Sam 14:16; Amos 9:5). However, in more recent study it has been recognized that the verb can mean "wave" or "move to and fro/swerve" (see KB, 501; Dahood, II, 211; also see Ps 82:5).

4.b. As in 3b, the use of the pronoun plus the imperfect verb stresses Yahweh as the performer of the action.

4.c. The pillars of the earth are its foundations (1 Sam 2:8; Ps 104:5; Job 9:6; 38:4, 6). In this context they may be seen as the moral bases of human life (Johnson, *CPIP*, 320).

4.d. For סלה, see n. 52:5.a.

5.a. Lit., "a horn," but the possessive suffix is added to it in v 6. The horn is a symbol of strength (Job 16:15; 1 Sam 2:1), power (1 Sam 2:10; Lam 2:17), dignity, and glory (Pss 89:18, 25; 92:10; 132:17). In Ps 132:17 and Dan 7:7, 8, 24, horns represent kings. Yahweh lifts the horn of the Davidic king (Ps 89:18, 25), of the faithful worshiper (Ps 92:11), and of (or on behalf of) his people (Ps 148:14). Exalting one's own horn is synonymous with haughtiness and arrogance. Cutting off the horn (Jer 48:25; Lam 2:3) is a humiliating judgment: power and arrogance are overwhelmed and brought to nothing.

6.a. In the case of בצואר עתק, some commentators follow the LXX and read the first word as בְּצוּר, "to the Rock," taking it to be a divine title (cf. 1 Sam 2:2). The translation would then be "do not speak arrogantly to the Rock" (Jacquet). The MT is acceptable, however; "speak with an arrogant neck" parallels "exalt your horn on high." A synonym for צֹואר, ערף, is used in the phrase קְשֵׁה־עֹרֶף ("stiff-necked") to describe obstinate behavior (Exod 32:9; 33:3, 5; 34:9; Deut 9:6, 13; 31:27). In Job 15:26 צֹואר is used to describe insolence and defiance.

7.a. מִמִּדְבַּר הָרִים ("from the wilderness of the mountains"). Some commentators prefer to emend MT to מִמְּדַבֵּר, which gives the meaning "Is it not from he who speaks that there is lifting up?"—assuming a hiphil infinitive construct from רום for הרים (Jacquet; Schmidt; Johnson, *CPIP*, 319). This translation goes well with the next verse. "Wilderness," however, can also be meaningful here. It was in the wilderness that Israel received Yahweh's revelation (Exod 19:1, where it is pointed as it is in this psalm), and there Elijah heard the voice of Yahweh (1 Kgs 19), and yet the wilderness itself is not the source of powerful exaltation any more than east and west are.

7.b. הרים may be the hiphil infinitive construct from רום, lit. "to lift up," or the word "mountains." The forms are identical. The LXX and other ancient versions support the first translation. Those who read "from the wilderness to the mountains" see this verse as spanning the four cardinal points; "mountains" is needed to complete the pattern (Dahood, Jacquet, Jeremias, and Schmidt). The textual evidence leans toward "to lift up," and since forms of רום are found throughout this psalm (vv 5, 6, 8, 11) it is a reasonable reading.

9.a. מלא מסך ("fully mixed") appears only here in the MT. The "mixed" comes from מסך. Probably it refers to mixing wine with spices. Cf. "wine of staggering" in Ps 60:5.

9.b. מזה, sometimes "from it" (the cup), but זה as the masculine demonstrative adjective must refer to the masculine יין ("wine"), not to the feminine כוס ("cup").

10.a. אֲגִיד לְעֹלָם—lit. "I will declare forever." The LXX apparently translates אֲגִיל ("I will rejoice"). *BHS* suggests אֲגַדֵּל ("I will magnify"). Accepting this emendation and taking לְעֹלָם as a divine title following Gen 21:33, Dahood reads "I shall extol the Eternal One" (II, 215, following Driver, *JTS* [1943] 14). This translation parallels the next line perfectly but requires a reading for which there is no textual evidence. The object is the "wondrous deeds" of v 2.

11.a. אֲגַדַּע—"I will cut off." *BHS* suggests an alternate reading of יגדע ("he will cut off") and is followed by RSV, Anderson, Jacquet, Kraus, and Schmidt. There is no evidence to back up this reading; the LXX and Syriac support MT. Heb. has no quotation marks, so this verse can represent Yahweh's speech as vv 3–6 do. The biblical concern that the people take responsibility for justice is strong (Isa 1:16–17; Amos 5:15; Mic 6:8), so it is possible that a worship leader is speaking here. Eaton (*Kingship*, 55–56) suggests that it is the king identifying himself with Yahweh's cause. However, the best option is to treat God as the speaker.

11.b. The polal imperfect תרוממנה is from רום ("lift up/exalt"). It is Yahweh who exalts the righteous.

Form/Setting/Structure

This psalm does not fit easily into any of the traditional psalm types (hymn, lament, royal psalm, etc.). It has been classified as a communal thanksgiving, but this interpretation ignores some aspects of the psalm. It contains a traditional hymnic introduction, an oracle and pronouncement of judgment, and a response of praise. Most attempts to categorize Ps 75, therefore, assign it to a hybrid form. Jacquet sees the psalm as embodying an original literary form combining characteristics of the hymn, blended with prophetic and wisdom genres with a didactic intention. Mowinckel (*PIW*, II, 64) believes it is an oracle fitted into a thanksgiving psalm. Eaton (*Kingship*, 55) suggests that the psalm has royal elements and that the primary speaker is the king. But most commentators emphasize its prophetic nature. Gunkel classifies it as a prophetic liturgy. Like Jacquet, Sabourin considers it a didactic psalm, which he views as a loose category embracing wisdom psalms, historical psalms, liturgies, and prophetic exhortations. The didactic psalms hold in common a teaching purpose, although they express that purpose in different forms. Sabourin (394–95, 401–2) classifies it as prophetic exhortation, a form that characteristically includes an oracle and prophetic

speech with promises and threats. Ps 75 fits this description well. V 2 clearly gives
the psalm a place in public worship; probably Johnson is correct in assigning it to
the cultic prophets (*CPIP*, 317–22). The reference to Asaph in v 1 may give
credence to the prophetic character of the psalm (see note 1.c.).

Ps 75 is generally given a setting in the pre-exilic cult. Mowinckel links it with
the pre-exilic Enthronement Festival of Yahweh (I, 142). Various commentators
have suggested that it celebrates a historical event such as the defeat of
Sennacherib during Hezekiah's reign, mentioned in 2 Kgs 19:35 (Kirkpatrick)
or an episode of the Maccabean revolt (Duhm). Such settings naturally provide
their own date. There is nothing in the psalm itself to tie it to either of these
events, however, and without a specific event as a setting there is little evidence as
to the psalm's date. A post-exilic dating is sometimes defended on the grounds of
the psalm's similarity to the Song of Hannah in 1 Sam 2:1–10 (e.g., Deissler). It is
more probably an earlier psalm reworked after the exile (Anderson). It provided
the people at worship with a chance to praise Yahweh and to hear his promise to
judge the wicked and exalt the righteous in the context of the community. Either
the king (Eaton, *Kingship*, 55–56) or more likely a prophet (Johnson, *CPIP*, 317–
22) spoke on behalf of the worshiping community to God and then on behalf of
God to the community, elaborating on the oracle in vv 3–6. (J. Jeremias,
[*Kultprophetische*, 119] concludes that the psalm is an abbreviated cult-prophetic
lament liturgy.)

The psalm itself falls naturally into an introductory statement of congregational praise (v 2), an oracle of assurance and judgment (vv 3–6), a prophetic
exhortation (vv 7–9), a vow of praise (v 10), and another short oracle in v 11. The
oracles promise God's upright judgment and steadying presence in the trembling
world (vv 3–4) and give specific words of condemnation to the boastful and
wicked. The exhortation replicates and supplements this, saying that judgment is
nowhere in the world but with God and that he will indeed exercise it (vv 7–8),
moving then to describe specifically the judgment of the wicked (v 9). V 10 is a
vow of praise to God for his wondrous deeds. The verse forms a frame with v 2
and we can assume that the speaker is the same—king, prophet, priest, or other
worship leader. The psalm ends with a final word from God which announces
the divine intention to cut off the power of the wicked and give victory to the
righteous.

Comment

Introduction (75:2). This verse sets the context of the psalm in the worshiping
community and shows by example part of the nature of worship. Yahweh has
established his name in the place of worship (Deut 12:5, 11), and it is foundational
to his relationship with his people (Exod 3:13–15). The presence of Yahweh is
invoked by praise and by recounting Yahweh's wonderful deeds in the life of the
community as a whole and of the individuals in it. His actions have formed and
sustained the community in specific ways, and the memory of this activity in the
past gives a solid basis for hoping for similar salvific intervention in the future.
Praise actualizes the divine presence in the divine name.

Oracle (75:3–6). Here Yahweh speaks to the people through a worship leader,
probably a prophet. V 3 contains a promise that judgment is Yahweh's and will

come at the time that suits his purposes. Justice and vindication for the righteous, although not apparent in the present, will come (cf. Hab 2:1–4). In v 4 this assurance is linked to the steadiness of the earth itself: Yahweh who created and sustains the world and all that is in it can be depended upon to establish justice upon it in good time. Yahweh is the basis both of the world's stability and of the moral order. If either is challenged, chaos may erupt, but Yahweh's steadying hand will be there to restore order. Vv 5 and 6 are Yahweh's word of warning to the boastful and wicked, those who deny his lordship or try to take it into their own hands. Those who exalt themselves instead of trusting in him are denying the fundamental nature of reality: Yahweh is in charge, and judgment will come. To the congregation this is a word of hope. This may be interpreted as an eschatological judgment (cf. Dahood), but need not be.

Exhortation (75:7–9). In these verses the worship leader continues in the same vein as in the oracle. Nowhere can true exaltation be found but with Yahweh, so it is senseless to look for it in oneself or in the rest of the world. He is the one who judges, setting some up and putting some down. Although the judgment is not apparent yet, it is prepared and in Yahweh's hand now. At the designated time Yahweh's lordship will become apparent, and those who have denied or ignored it will have to consume the full amount of his wrath. The cup as the instrument of Yahweh's judgment on the nations is found elsewhere (Isa 51:17; Jer 25:15–17, 28f; 49:12; 51:7). It may be reminiscent of the ordeal of bitter water described in Num 5:11–31, where a woman accused of adultery must drink a specially prepared potion. If she is innocent, she will be unaffected by the experience, but if she is guilty the poison will enter her system and cause her agony. "The cup of salvation" appears in Ps 116:13.

Vow to praise God (75:10). In this verse the speaker vows to declare and sing the praise of Yahweh's great deeds—Yahweh is here designated as the "God of Jacob" (see Pss 20:2; 46:8, 12; 76:7; et al.). The verse presupposes an audience for the speaker, as in v 2.

A closing oracle (75:11). I have read this verse as a short oracle, which corresponds to vv 3–6, and affirms again that the wicked will lose their power while that of the righteous is exalted. Another approach is to postulate an explanation like that of Gunkel and assume that the speaker is cooperating with God in the divine judgment. A modification of this explanation is to treat the speaker as a king who has the responsibility for cutting off the power of the wicked, as in Ps 101:8:

> Morning by morning I will destroy
> > All the wicked of the land,
> cutting off [להכרית] all the evildoers
> > from the city of the LORD. (RSV)

(See J. H. Eaton, *Kingship*, 55.)

Explanation

Perhaps, this psalm is worthy of being remembered mostly because of three striking metaphors in its content. The first of these is the portrayal of a shaking world, about to fall into ruins as in a great earthquake, whose pillars (עמודיה) are made firm by the mighty intervention of God (v 4). "The times are, like our own," says Leslie (208), "unsteady, shaken, and insecure." "Enormous disorder is in the earth," he continues, "and unrest is felt in the whole populated world."

If the foundations are destroyed, what can the righteous do? (Ps 11:3) In the context of Ps 11, this is a taunt of the wicked. The answer in Ps 75 is to trust in Yahweh, who is able to stabilize the great pillars which are conceptualized as supporting the earth. The power to put the pillars of the earth in place and make them firm in creation power (1 Sam 2:8; Job 38:4)—here applied to the terrible shaking endured by human society (cf. Isa 24:17–20; Deissler, II, 123);

> For the pillars [מצק] of the earth are the Lord's,
> and on them he has set the world. (rsv, 1 Sam 2:8)

The second metaphor is that of the foaming cup of the wine of judgment in the hand of Yahweh (v 9). At first it may seem to be a cup for a festival crowd, ready to celebrate and enjoy blessings received. But it is not. It is the cup of the wrath of God (Ps 11:6; Isa 51:17, 22; Jer 25:15; 49:12; Hab 2:15–16; Jer 51:7; Ezek 23:31–33; Zech 12:2; Rev 14:10; 16:19; 17:4; 18:6)—the worshipers would have expected a "cup of salvation" (Ps 116:13), or a "cup of consolation" (Jer 16:2), or a "cup of blessing" (1 Cor 10:16). Yahweh holding a great cup in his hand is ready to pour out its foaming wine of judgment "into the throats of all the world's boastful till the last dregs are downed" (E. M. Poteat, "Exposition of Psalms 42–89," IB, IV, 402). The wine of humiliation and confusion is substituted for the wine of blessing and salvation.

The third metaphor is that of the "horns"—a word which appears in singular or plural four times in the psalm (vv 5, 6, and twice in 11). The "horn" (קרן) can be a symbol of power, majesty, and dignity (of animals, Num 23:22; Deut 33:17; of human beings, 1 Kgs 22:11; Dan 7:8). (To raise the horn of a person is to give power or dignity as in Ps 89:18. Horns can be raised in pride and defiance, however, and they can symbolize the threats of the arrogant, as in 75:5–6.) The horns of the wicked will be cut off, but those of the righteous will be lifted up in victory. This is an affirmation of faith, for which no proof yet appears. But it is the basis for which the righteous give thankful praise to God. The righteous see the cup in Yahweh's hand for what it is.

The Mighty God of Judgment   (76:1–13)

Bibliography

Day, J. "Shear-Jashub (Isaiah VII 3) and the Remnant of Wrath (Psalm LXXVI 11)." VT 31 (1981) 76–78. Eissfeldt, O. "Psalm 76." ThLZ (1957) 801–8. Emerton, J. A. "A Neglected Solution of a Problem in Psalm LXXVI 11." VT 24 (1974) 136–46.

Translation

1   For the leader;[a] *with instrumental music;*[b] *an Asaphite psalm;*[c] *a song.*[d]
2   *The Renowned One in Judah is God;*[a]   (3+3)
     in Israel his name is great.

3	*His lair*[a] *came to be in Salem*[b]	(3+2)
	and his den[a] *on Zion.*	
4	*There he shattered the fiery arrow,*[a]	(3+3)
	the shield, the sword, and the battle weapons.[b] SELAH.	
5	*You are the Resplendent One;*[a]	(2+2)
	the Majestic One from the mountains of prey![b]	
6	*The stouthearted (lay) plundered,*[a]	(3+2+3)
	slumbering in their last sleep;[b]	
	no man of war could lift a hand![c]	
7	*At your rebuke, O God of Jacob,*	(3+3)
	horses and chariot-riders lay stilled.[a]	
8	*O You!*[a] *You are the Awesome One!*	(3+4)
	Who can stand before you when you are angry?[b]	
9	*From the heavens you caused judgment to be heard;*	(3+3)
	the earth feared and was quiet	
10	*when God rose for justice,*	(3+3)
	to give deliverance to all the oppressed[a] *of the land.* SELAH.	
11	*For the rage of humankind will praise you;*	(3+3)
	[*when*] *you gird on the residue of* [*their*] *raging.*[a]	
12	*Make vows to Yahweh your God and fulfill them;*	(4+4)
	let all round about him give tribute to the Fearsome One,[a]	
13	*he who mortifies*[a] *the spirit of princes,*	(2+2)
	who is the Awesome One to the kings of the earth.	

Notes

1.a. See 51.a.

1.b. See 54:1.b.

1.c. See 73:1.a.

1.d. See Ps 65:1; LXX adds "concerning the Assyrian."

2.a. Elohim (אלהים, "God") has been substituted in MT for Yahweh.

3.a. The words for "lair/covert" (סך) and "den" (מענה) are frequently treated figuratively as "abode/tabernacle/dwelling" and "dwelling place" (note KJV and RSV). However, in this psalm the imagery seems to be more that of a lair or covert for lions or other wild beasts (note Jer 25:38; Amos 3:4; Job 38:40; Pss 10:9; 104:21–22). The imagery of God in v 2 is that of a leonine warrior who takes a powerful position in Jerusalem on Mount Zion and defeats all attackers.

3.b. "Salem" is an ancient poetic name for Jerusalem (cf. Gen 14:18).

4.a. רשפי־קשת—lit., "flames of a bow," a poetic reference either to the swiftness of the arrows or to incendiary arrows—probably the latter; see Ps 7:14.

4.b. ומלחמה—lit., "and battle," but in this context the weapons of war are clearly meant (see Dahood, II, 218).

5.a. The niphal particle of אור is found only here—lit., the expression נאור אתה is "you are lighted up/enveloped in light." NEB (also Kraus) reflects the assumption of an interchange of consonants to נורא (from ירא, "fear"); "thou art fearful" or, "the fearful one." LXX reflects תאיר, "you shine forth. . . ." (see *BHS*). NRSV has, "Glorious are you. . . ."

5.b. Reading with MT, מהררי־טרף ("from mountains of prey/booty"), but LXX and the Syriac read "everlasting mountains," leading to the reading מהררי עד, with עד in the sense of "eternity" (Kraus, *Psalms 60–150,* 108). It is possible that a copyist, understanding עד to mean "prey" (as it does in Gen 49:27; Isa 9:5; 33:23; and Zeph 3:8), substituted טרף. עד means "ancient" or "everlasting" in over forty occurrences, according to BDB (cf. Job 20:4; Hab 3:6; Amos 1:11; Pss 83:18, 92:8). This translation is rather popular, e.g., in RSV and NRSV. However, it is likely that the lion imagery of v 3 is continued; the imagery is that of a lion returning from the mountains where animals and bandits, who lurk there, spare no prey. It is possible, of course, to translate the "majestic" with a comparative: e.g., RSV, "more majestic than the everlasting mountains"; or, retaining MT in the last word, "more majestic than mountains rich with game" (NIV). The LXX uses ἀπό, "from/away from," which is probably correct.

6.a. The expression אשתוללו (from שלל, "spoil/plunder") appears only here in MT. The hithpael impf. 3rd pers. masc. pl. would have been ישתוללו. The א in MT is either a scribal error or the form is Aramaic (Briggs).

6.b. נמו שנתם—lit., "they slept their sleep," but in the context of vv 6 and 7 the sleep of death is indicated.

6.c. Lit., "and all the men of strength could not find their hands"; in death their strong limbs were useless to them.

7.a. Again, the sleep of death is probably intended. Weiser, Dahood, Kraus, RSV, and NRSV have "lay stunned," indicating the unnatural nature of the sleep but allowing for the possibility of a brief period of unconsciousness. The "chariot(s)" assumes "chariot-riders." Cf. LXX.

8.a. The word אתה, "you," is not found in LXX, and Kraus (*Psalms 60–150*, 108) says it "should surely be eliminated," so that v 8 begins like v 5. But its presence in the text emphasizes that God, not the strong soldiers or their weaponry, is to be feared; its omission would leave a very short colon in 8a.

8.b. מאז אפך is lit., "from the time of your anger." *BHS* and others suggest a possible reading of מאז, "from the strength of your anger."

10.a. See *Comment* on Ps 69:33.

11.a. This verse is difficult and has been translated, emended, and interpreted in a number of ways. Literally, MT reads "Surely [or, "for"] the wrath of humanity will praise you, a remnant of wraths you will gird on [yourself]." The noun חמה appears in two forms in this verse (construct sing. and absolute pl.). Are two kinds of wrath meant? Those who follow MT suggest that the first clause means that the wrath of God's enemies will turn into praise after their defeat (Briggs), or that the rebellion of wrathful humanity enables God's power and glory to be displayed, eliciting praise from his people (Maillot and Lelièvre). LXX reads the first colon as, "For the thought [or, "things much thought about," ἐνθύμιον] of mankind will give you thanksgiving"; possibly reflecting a word from חמד ("desire/ take pleasure in"), though Emerton (*VT* 24 [1974] 139) suspects "no more than free translation."

The meaning of the second clause is even less clear. Weiser translates: "He who has been spared death must extol thee." LXX reads the verb as ἑορτάσει, which is a translation of תחגך rather than תחגר, and is translated: " The remnant of wraths will keep a pilgrim-festival to you." Frequently אדם in the first clause and חמת in the second are emended to אֱדֹם, and חֲמָת, rendering the verse as "Surely wrathful Edom [Aram] shall praise you / the remnant of Hamath will keep a pilgrim-festival to you" (Schmidt, Jacquet, Kraus). It is possible that Hamath and Edom are symbolic for north and south (Schmidt). Eissfeldt (*ThLZ* [1957] 801–8) believes this verse refers to the time of David, when these states were of political importance, but this requires ignoring LXX's superscription referring to Assyria.

J. A. Emerton (*VT* 24 [1974] 136–46) argues that a solution to these problems is possible without emending the consonantal text. He suggests that תודך be read as תָּדֹך (from דכך) or תָּדוּך (from דוך) and translated as "you crush." He cites Houbigant (*Notae criticae in universos Veteris Testamenti libros*, II, 1777) and Kahan (in Kittel, *Die Psalmen*, 1922) as having suggested this reading earlier, although he did not discover this until he had advanced the solution himself. He also advocates translating תחגר as "restrain" rather than "gird," a solution involving nuances of the word in MT rather than a different reading, arguing that the translation fits well into the context of the psalm: in the previous verse God has delivered the helpless poor and in v 13 he inspires awe in the powerful kings of the earth. He translates: "Surely thou dost crush the wrath of man / Thou dost restrain the remnant of wrath." Readers are referred to his article for a further discussion of the issues involved. J. Day (*VT* 31 [1981] 76–78) agrees with Emerton.

I have chosen to stay close to MT in the translation above. No interpretation of this verse inspires much confidence (see *Comment* below). The lit. plural of "angers/wraths/rages" in the second colon is treated as a plural of intensification.

12.a. The expression למורא is lit., "to the fear," but the meaning is clear (cf. Isa 8:12, 13; Ps 9:21). LXX's τῷ φοβερῷ ("to the Terrible One/Fearsome One") is consistent with v 8 where the same Greek word is used for "awesome/terrible/fearsome." However, the poetic variation should not be smoothed away completely.

13.a. The verb בצר has two lines of meaning: (1) "to cut off" (as of grape clusters, e.g., Lev 25:5, 11; Deut 24:1), thus KJV, RSV, and NRSV have "cuts off the spirit"; (2) "to make inaccessible/enclosed/ unattainable," mostly in simple passive participle (e.g., Num 13:28; Deut 1:28; 3:5; Josh 14:12; Hos

8:14; Jer 33:3). Thus the translations vary: cf. NAB's "checks the pride," NEB's "breaks the spirit," NJV's "curbs the spirit," and JB's "snuffs out the lives." The translation, "mortifies," is an attempt (perhaps ill-advised) to combine the two lines.

Form/Structure/Setting

Psalm 76 is traditionally considered to be one to the Songs of Zion (e.g., Gunkel, Dahood, Sabourin). Other psalms in this category are 46, 48, 84, 87, and 122. They are characterized by devotion to Zion as the center of Yahweh's presence with his people. Like hymns in general, the Songs of Zion consist of an introduction proclaiming the praiseworthiness of Yahweh, a main section in which the reason for praise is given (Yahweh's deeds and/or his attributes), and a conclusion urging response to the majesty of God. Although it is an Asaph psalm, it is similar in content to Ps 46; indeed, to all the Korah psalms of 46–48.

Yahweh's deliverance of Israel from her military foes is the reason for praise. This has understandably led scholars to look for a specific historical setting for the psalm. The title in the LXX ("concerning the Assyrian") refers to the mysterious defeat of Sennacherib before the gates of Jerusalem in 701 B.C.E. as found in 2 Kgs 19 and Isa 37. There is nothing in the text of the psalm that invalidates this possibility, and vv 6 and 7 could be interpreted as indicating an unusual sort of victory over Israel's foes. On the other hand, nothing in the text *requires* this interpretation. Weiser suggests that the subject of the song is David's defeat of the Philistines in 2 Sam 17–25. If the Masoretic text is emended to read Edom (or Aram) and Hamath in v 10, then a Davidic setting is indicated (Eissfeldt [*ThLZ* (1957) 801–8]). It is also possible to read the psalm as focusing on a future eschatological deliverance of Israel by Yahweh rather than on a past historical one. Dahood (II, 218) states that the psalm functions on both levels as it describes "the destruction through divine intervention of historical foes who sought to plunder Jerusalem, and at the same time announces the eschatological defeat of the nations at the last judgment."

The psalm may have emerged in some original form from an actual historical event; several commentators have preferred the time of David and Solomon rather than that of Hezekiah (late 700s B.C.E.), but the psalm has the generalized imagery of cultic celebration and all efforts to relate it closely to a specific historical context should be avoided. The psalm reflects a context of festival worship at Jerusalem on Mount Zion. The theological context is that of the Zion theology (see H.-J. Kraus, *Theology of the Psalms*, 78–84; also see the treatments of Pss 46, 47, and 48 by Craigie). S. Mowinckel's theory that Ps 76 belonged to the context of the celebration of the kingship of Yahweh in the festivals at Zion (see *Psalmenstudien*, II, 58–59; *PIW*, I, 149–51; followed by Kraus, I, 689) is probable. The psalm

. . . hardly refers to any single real historical event, as earlier interpreters of the psalm used to think, nor is it meant to be a description of what is going to take place in the "latter days," in eschatological times. It is described as something just experienced, something the congregation "itself has seen" (Ps 48:9). But at the same time it is something it "has heard of" before. . . . The explanation is that there is a reference to the realities of faith being re-experienced as repeated reality in the cult (S. Mowinckel, *PIW*, I, 151).

The eschatological force of the psalm, which was not dominant for pre-exilic festivals, according to Mowinckel, is likely to have been much stronger in post-exilic usage. In its present canonical context, Ps 76 invites the reader to look backward and forward, but especially to the latter, to the time when the resplendent majesty of Yahweh will be demonstrated in great acts of rebuke and judgment. The shape of the future lies in the past.

Modern commentators commonly divide Ps 76 into four sections: 2–4, 5–7, 8–10, and 11–13. This arrangement fits the contours of the text and provides four stanzas of nearly equal lengths. Each of the sections begins with distinctive statements: vv. 2, 5, 8, and 11. Vv 2 and 12–13 seem to form a frame or inclusion for the psalm; they can be read together as a summary of the content of the psalm. The tightly worded v 5 is rather obviously a key statement.

The four-part literary analysis is adequate, but a division following the placement of *Selah* in the psalm seems equally valid. *Selah* occurs at the end of vv 4 and 10, yielding a three-part arrangement: vv 2–4, 5–10, and 11–13. In this case, vv 1–4 and 11–13 provide a frame for the main section in 5–10. The frame sections are of almost equal length, and each is approximately half as long as the main section. Vv 2–4 could be read with vv 11–13 to form a complete psalm and vv 5–10 could be read independently, so that the psalm is composed of two psalms, with one interposed into the other in a kind of "sandwich" construction. However, this feature of the psalm should not be pressed, because the traditional nature of the content in many psalms means that they can be read in this way.

I have chosen to use the three-part arrangement in the *Comment* which follows. One of the striking literary features of the psalm is the repeated use of participial expressions for God: נודע (v 2), נאור (v 5), נורא (v 8), מורא (a closely related noun form in v 12), and נורא (v 13): Renowned—Resplendent—Awesome—Fearsome—Awesome. The concentration on God is intensified by the double use of אתה ("you") in v 8 (also note the אתה in v 5).

Comment

The renowned lion of Judah (76:2–4). As observed in notes 3.a. and 5.b. above, the imagery of "lair" and "den" in these verses is that of a lion who has come forth to establish his domain on Mount Zion. The leonine imagery of Yahweh is well known from OT texts (e.g., Amos 1:2; 3:8; Hos 5:14; 11:10; Isa 31:4; 38:13; Jer 4:7; 5:6; 25:30, 31, 38; 49:19; 50:44). The language of Isa 31:4 reflects the same motif of Yahweh coming like a lion to Mount Zion to manifest his power: "As the lion roars, even the young lion, . . . so Yahweh of Hosts will come down to fight on (על) Mount Zion" (RSV). In the Isaiah passage the meaning is obscure, but the motif of Yahweh coming as a lion to Mount Zion to fight against his enemies is probably reversed and he comes to attack Jerusalem, not defend it (על used in the sense of "against"). In Jer 25:30–38, Yahweh roars his judgment from heaven to destroy the nations (note Ps 76:9–10); his going forth is described with leonine imagery: "Like a lion he has left his covert or 'lair'" (סכו, as in Ps 76:3) (Jer 25:38). Yahweh is the Lion-Warrior who establishes his shelter on Mount Zion and wreaks destruction on those who attack.

V 4 is a poetically effective description of the breaking of battle equipment (cf. Ps 46:9–10). The leonine and divine warrior motifs are merged in this context.

R. Bach ("Der Bogen Zerbricht, Spiesse Zerschlägt und Wagen mit Feuer verbrennt," in *Probleme biblischer Theologie*, FS Gerhard von Rad, ed. H. W. Wolff [Munich: Chr. Kaiser, 1971] 13–26) has analyzed the tradition-history of the motif of Yahweh's breaking of weapons and his destruction of the materials of war, which appears here and in Ps 46:10. The two psalms are Zion-songs, but the motif also appears in several prophetic texts: Hos 1:4; 2:18 (20); Jer 49:35; Mic 5:9–13; Zech 9:10. Bach contends that the basic message in all these passages (with the exception of the LXX of Zech 9:10) is: "Yahweh breaks the weapons of war"—bows, swords, chariots, spears, shields, etc. Bach (18–19) argues that the motif was older than the Zion traditions and has been utilized as an existing motif in Pss 46 and 76. He thinks the motif belonged to the older and wider traditions of Yahweh-war—related to Yahweh's victories in delivering Israel, but transformed in the prophetic traditions to express Yahweh's wondrous power and ability to deliver his people without their use of weapons (22)—so that Yahweh breaks not only the weapons of enemies, *but also the weapons of Israel*, which are to be purged from Israel by Yahweh along with idols and soothsayers according to Mic 5:10–13:

> In that day, says the LORD,
>   I will cut off your horses from among you
>   and will destroy your chariots;
> and I will cut off the cities of your land
>   and throw down all your strongholds;
> and I will cut off sorceries from your hand,
>   and you shall have no more soothsayers;
> and I will cut off your images
>   and your pillars from among you,
> and you shall bow down no more
>   to the work of your hands. (NRSV)

Bach (23–26) points out that this motif is very important in prophetic eschatological hope: "I will make for you a covenant on that day with the wild animals, the birds of the air, and with the creeping things of the ground; and I will abolish the bow, the sword, and war from the land; and I will make you lie down in safety" (Hos 2:18 [20]; NRSV). See also Mic 4:3–4; Isa 2:4; 9:5; Ezek 39:9–10; and Zech 9:10. In Ps 76:4 ownership of the weapons of war is not entirely clear. The verses which follow describe a great victory over foreign foes, but v 4 is related primarily to vv 2–3 and may allude, at least, to the tradition of Yahweh as Israel's sole warrior, the Mighty One whose people need no weapons. His "rebuke" is sufficient to still horses and chariots and leave men-of-war slumbering in their last sleep (vv 6–7).

The victory of the leonine warrior (76:5–10). The central section of the psalm describes the great victory of Yahweh, who is the shining Resplendent One, majestic in mien and action, who has come from "the mountains of prey." The attackers have been stunned into a sleep of death by the mighty rebuke of the God of Jacob (vv 6–7). For "rebuke," גערה, see Pss 18:16; 80:17; 104:7; Isa 50:2; 51:20; 66:15; note the verb in Ps 9:6; Isa 17:13; Ps 119:21; Mal 3:11; Ps 106:9; Nah 1:4; Isa 54:9. The thrust of גערה (and related words) is "almost always . . . a threatening manifestation of the anger of God" (A. Caquot, *TDOT*, II, 51). The rebuke of God is that of the divine warrior/judge who drives away his enemies and the counterforces which produce revolts in history and eruptions of chaos in nature.

> For behold the LORD will come in fire,
>   and his chariots like the stormwind
> to render his anger in fury,
>   and his rebuke (גערתו) with flames of fire.
> For by fire will the LORD execute judgment,
>   and by his sword, upon all flesh,
>   and those slain by the LORD will be many.
>   (Isa 66:15–16, RSV)

In Ps 76, the awesome Warrior/Judge has spoken his mighty judgment from heaven and the earth is stilled in fear and awe (v 9). He is the awesome, terrible one, before whose anger all men-of-war are helpless (vv 8, 6d). V 10 provides the basic purpose for the great display of divine energy: Yahweh has risen, as he is wont to do, to bring liberation and justice to the poor and oppressed of the "land"—though, in its larger canonical context, we should probably read ארץ as "earth"; in the immediate sense, Israel, but in the larger sense all the oppressed of the earth.

A call for homage to Yahweh (76:11–13). Yahweh is presented as a great king who overcomes the raging of humankind (v 11) and waits for the fulfillment of vows made to him by homage-paying vassals. The neighboring people, along with the Israelites, are exhorted to bring tribute to the God who awes kings and mortifies the rebellious wills of princes (vv 12–13; cf. Isa 52:13–15). The vows may reflect the idea of vows made in times of peril (cf. Judg 11:39; 2 Sam 15:7, 8; Jer 44:25; Jonah 1:16).

Explanation

This psalm emphasizes Yahweh's power and his willingness to use it on behalf of his people. Vv 2 and 3 portray him as the one who dwells on Zion, a common theme (cf. Pss 48, 87, 132), where he has come to establish his lair as the mighty Lion-Warrior of Israel. The rest of the psalm, however, shows him moving out from Zion. The psalm celebrates the powerful theophanic victories of Yahweh over his foes and the forces of disorder. The Great Lion has his "den" on Mount Zion, but his rebuke and judgment go out to still the raging of humankind. By the end of the psalm the world is under his leonine power (cf. Amos 1:2). He has used his liberating strength to counter the destructive strength of humanity.

Ps 76 does not specifically refer to Yahweh as ending war or to the age when "nation will not again go to war against nation, neither will they learn war any more" (Isa 2:4). Still, it is clearly the intent of the psalm to show that warlike powers are helpless before Yahweh, who delivers the poor and whom all kings will fear. The OT seems to say more about war than about peace, but it always sees peace as Yahweh's goal. Its visions of the age when Yahweh's will is brought about on earth include a peaceful world worshiping him (Zech 14:16; Isa 11:6–9), and one of the generally accepted titles of the messiah is "Prince of Peace" (Isa 9:6).

In the Book of Revelation the rider of the White Horse defeats the evil nations and destroys their armies (19:11–21) and the redeemed of all the peoples enter into the New Jerusalem where there is no death, grief, or pain (21:1–4). The celebration of Yahweh's victory over warlike humanity in Ps 76 is part of this tradition. Its language is appropriate for a theophany of deliverance and judgment (e.g., see Ps 18), language and imagery which form a major component in both prophetic and apocalyptic literature (e.g., Isa 2:12–22; 10:33–34; Ezek 1; Hab 3; Dan 7; Rev, passim). Yahweh rises in power and glory to save and to break the strength of opposing persons and forces.

The violent nature of the imagery is offensive to many people. However, at least three things should be kept in mind. First, the imagery is a poetic depiction of the terrible evil which pervades life in this world. Ours is not a utopian world, devoid of the power of chaos, free of the demonic, and basically loving. On the contrary, it is a context where brothers and sisters deny the "keeping" of their brothers and sisters, where thieves "break through" and steal, where friends either do not comfort or else betray other friends, where the entrenched social, religious, and economic structures of society systematically exploit, oppress, and suppress the poor of the earth. The world groans in its suffering and cries out for judgment. Like those dying from thirst in a desert place, the "little people" of the world long for the Lion of Judah to come forth from his lair and roar out his mighty rebuke until shields, swords, horses, and chariot riders all lay in stunned stillness. For those who know how to listen (who "have ears to hear"), that roar will mean that God's

> children shall come trembling from the west.
> They shall come trembling like birds from Egypt,
>   and like doves from the land of Assyria;
> and I will return them to their homes, says the LORD.
>   (Hos 11:11, NRSV)

Second, the language seeks to engender a catharsis, a purification and empowerment of the soul so that a healthy life can be lived. The language is rooted in cultic worship, with all the accompanying liturgies, designed to intensify the worshipers' perceptions of reality and purge away alien loyalties and despair. A. Y. Collins (*Crisis and Catharsis: The Power of the Apocalypse* [Philadelphia: Westminister, 1984] 154) writes of the Book of Revelation as a whole:

> Feelings of fear and resentment are released by the book's repeated presentations of the destruction of the hearers' enemies. The element of persecution represents the present, conflict-ridden, and threatened situation in which the author invites the hearers to see themselves. The second two elements in the repeated plot, judgment and salvation, represent the resolution of that situation: the persecutors are destroyed by divine wrath and the persecuted are exalted to a new, glorious mode of existence.

Catharsis occurs when feelings are so intensified that purging becomes transformed into praise. Psalms like 76 may serve this purpose.

Third, the psalm seeks to provocate and evocate a commitment to a counter world-view. The reality of divine judgment seems remote in a world so apparently dominated by natural and human powers. The psalm invites the reader to join the company of those who affirm, in the teeth of seemingly overwhelming evidence, that there is a judgment which sets right the horrible endemic evil in human existence. The one whose name is great in Israel will arise to judge the earth and possess all the nations (Ps 82:8). That, however, is an affirmation of faith, a judgment out of "the assurance of things hoped for" and "the conviction of things not seen" (Heb 11:1–3); certainly it is not for those who have no eyes to see or ears to hear. But those who hear and those who see will say "Amen."

Will God Spurn His People Forever? *(77:1–21)*

Bibliography

Brueggemann, W. *Israel's Praise.* 136–40. **Driver, G. R.** "Reflections on Recent Articles." *JBL* 73 (1954) 125–36. **Haddix, J. L.** *Lamentation as Personal Experience in Selected Psalms.* Ann Arbor, MI: UMI, 1986. 91–112. **Jefferson, H.** "Psalm LXXVII." *VT* 13 (1963) 87–91. **Jeremias, J.** *Theophanie: Die Geschichte einer alttestamentlichen Gattung.* WMANT 10. Neukirchen-Vluyn: Neukirchener Verlag, 1977. 26–28, 90–97, 156–57. **Kselman, J. S.** "Psalm 77 and the Book of Exodus." *JANESCU* 15 (1983) 51–58.

Translation

1 For the leader;[a] according to Jeduthun;[b] an Asaphite psalm.[c]

2 *With my voice I cry out to God,* (3+4)
crying with my voice to God that he would give ear to me.[a]

3 *In the day of my distress I have sought the Lord,* (3+3+3)
at night my hands[a] *have been extended*[b] *(toward him)
without respite;*
(but) my soul[c] *has not been comforted.*

4 *I remember God, and then I groan;* (3+3)
I ponder (on it)—and my spirit grows weak. SELAH.

5 *You hold open*[a] *my eyelids;* (3+3)
I am so distraught that I cannot speak.[b]

6 *I reflect on the days of the past,* (3+2 [3])
of years long ago.[a]

7 *At night I remember my songs;*[a] (3+3+2)
I ponder in my heart,
and my spirit seeks (an answer).[b]

8 *Will the Lord spurn*[a] *(us) forever,* (3+3)
and never be favorable (to us) again?

9 *Has his loyal-love completely come to an end?* (3+3)
Will his promises fail for generation after generation?

10 *Has God forgotten to be gracious?* (3+3)
Has he locked up his compassion in anger? SELAH.

11 *And so I say, "My sorrow is this:*[a] (3+3)
the changing[b] *of the right hand of the Most High!"*

12	*(Then) I remember*[a] *the deeds of Yah*[b]—	(2+3)
	for I do remember your wonders of old—	
13	*I reflect on all your work*[a]	(2+3)
	and ponder on all your acts.	
14	*O God, your way is in holiness*[a]—	(3+3)
	Who is a great God like Yahweh?[b]	
15	*You are the God who works wonders;*[a]	(4+3)
	you made known your strength among the peoples.	
16	*By your arm*[a] *you redeemed your people:*	(3+2)
	the sons of Jacob and Joseph. SELAH.[b]	
17	*The waters saw you, O God;*	(3+3+3)
	the waters saw you and writhed;	
	even the deeps roiled!	
18	*The clouds poured out*[a] *water;*	(3+3+3)
	the heavens rumbled with the voice of thunder;	
	your arrows[b] *darted everywhere!*	
19	*The voice of your thunder was in the storm;*[a]	(3+3+3)
	lightning flashes[b] *lit up the world,*	
	(while) the earth trembled and shook.	
20	*Your way went through the sea;*[a]	(2+3+3)
	your paths[b] *went through the great waters,*	
	though your tracks[c] *were unknown.*	
21	*You led*[a] *your people like a flock*	(3+2)
	by the hand of Moses and Aaron.	

Notes

1.a. See n. 51:1.a.

1.b. See n. 62:1.b. *Kethiv* has ידיתון; *qere* has ידותון. The name also appears in the title of Ps 39 with the same *kethiv-qere* spellings.

1.c. See n. 73:1.a.; also see Craigie, Ps 50:1, n. a.

2.a. For the form of the verb, see GKC 63o.

3.a. Reading plural with LXX.

3.b. An unusual meaning for the verb נגר (niphal perf. 3rd pers. sing.), which normally means "pour out," like water. Commentators frequently note that the verb would be suitable with tears and assume that the original reading was "mine *eye* poured out in the night and slacked not" (e.g., Kirkpatrick; Lam 2:18, 19; 3:49). The peculiar reading of KJV ("my sore ran in the night, and ceased not") derives from the KJV translators taking יד, "hand," to mean "blow/wound/sore" (with Rashi). LXX has "before him" (נגדה). Job 23:2, "his hand [God's] is heavy in spite of my groaning" (reading with LXX ידו, "his hand" for MT's ידי, "my hand") tends to support the "his hand" in Syriac (see *BHS*), i.e., "God's hand," with the text changed to avoid referring to God so directly in such harsh terms. Dahood (II, 226; I, 241–42; II, 100) argues for the verb נגר as meaning "attack/smite" and takes both "hand" and "soul" as referring to God: "His hand attacks at night . . . his mind refuses to relent." J. L. Haddix (*Lamentation*, 91, 97) takes "my hand" as "my strength" (which is common enough), which eases the use with נגר ("pour out"): "At night my strength was poured out. . . ."

3.c. For נפשׁי ("soul/self"), see Ps 54:5.

5.a. The reference is to God, who will not allow the suppliant to sleep. The versions suggest that שׁמרות ("guards/watches") refers to the "nightwatches," with the meaning "I do lay hold of the night watches with mine eyes" (see Briggs, II, 173; Perowne, 53). The verb אחז normally means "grasp/take hold of/seize," but the context seems to indicate the idea of "holding open the guards of my eyes" (Kraus, II, 695).

5.b. This expression can be translated as "but I will not speak." Gunkel (336) protests that it is strange that such a person could *not* speak in his distress and argues that the reader expects "and cannot rest/sleep"; proposing a change to אֶרְגִּיעַ, "and I cannot rest." Kraus rejects Gunkel's emendation and reads "yet I will not speak" (as in Ps. 39:2–3) in the sense that the suppliant will not quarrel with God.

6.a. Several commentators (e.g., Kraus, Dahood) and translations (e.g., RSV) follow LXX, Symm, and Syr and connect the first word of v 7 ("I remember") to this colon. This eases the balance in v 7, but is not really necessary in v 6 since the verb in the first colon ("I think about") serves the second also.

7.a. Lit., "My music," but the meaning is probably that of a song sung with the accompaniment of an instrument. See Job 30:9; Lam 3:14. LXX suggests וְהָגִיתִי "and I meditate" or "and I meditated." If זכר is transferred to v 6b (cf. n. 6.a.), it is usual to assume that נְגִינָתִי, "my music/songs," should be changed to וְהָגִיתִי, "and I meditate."

7.b. This phrase appears only here. The piel impf. 3rd pers. masc. sing. form of the verb (חפש) with a *waw* consecutive is unexpected in a poetic context and the versions read 1st pers. sing. וָאֲחַפֵּשׂ "and I diligently searched my spirit." The meaning is not significantly different.

8.a. The verb זנח is usually translated as "spurn/reject," but it can mean "to be angry" and that may be the meaning here: "Will the Lord be angry forever?" (supported by Kselman, *JANESCU* 15 [1983] 55, n. 15; see Pss 60:3; 89:39; Dahood, II, 77).

11.a. The best choice for חַלּוֹתִי is to take it as a piel inf. with the sing. suffix from חלה , "become sick/be weak"; lit., "to sicken me is this" = "my grief is this" (cf. Kraus, *Psalms 60–150*, 113: "Then I said: I am indeed sorry about this . . ."). See GKC 67r; BDB, 317, takes the form as qal inf. with the suffix, repointing to חֲלוֹתִי (which is supported, perhaps, by Aquila, see *BHS*), which would yield the same meaning: "my sickness is this" = "my grief/sorrow is this." Also, Kselman (*JANESCU* 15 [1983] 52): "And I said, 'This is my sorrow, that the right hand of Elyon is changed'" (following W. A. Goy, "Dieu a-t-il changè? Psalm 77," in FS Wilhelm Vischer, ed. J. Cadier [Montpellier: Causse Graille Castelnau, 1960] 56–62). Briggs (II, 177) takes the form as piel inf. from חלל, "to pierce/wound" = "my piercing wound," with some support from some versions. LXX seems to suppose a verb, הַהֲלוֹתִי, from חלל, "begin": "And I said, 'Now I have begun,'" which makes little sense. Gunkel (336) follows a long line of commentators (also Jacquet, II, 506) who read v 11 as questions, "Yet, I say: 'Can it become weak? Is the right hand of the Most High changed?'" But this necessitates reading חַלּוֹתִי as חֲלֹתָה and שְׁנוֹת in 11b as שְׁנֹתָה.

11.b. Reading qal inf. of שׁנה, "change" (see Pss 34:1; 89:35), which seems more probable than understanding as "years" as in v 6 (שְׁנוֹת)—"the years of the right hand of the Most High," years when the Most High acted favorably (preferred by Briggs).

12.a. Following *qere, kethiv* has אַזְכִּיר "I will cause to remember/mention/commemorate/celebrate" (cf. 71:16; Isa 63:7). The *kethiv* fits well with the cohortative of the verb in the second colon, and the translation may be: "I will commemorate [or, proclaim] the deeds of Yah; / yes, I will remember your wonders." This translation avoids the repetition of "remember" in the verse, which is sometimes considered as tautalogical. However, I read the text as continuing the complaint made in the previous verses. How can God fail to continue his mighty deeds of the past? Does he intend to reject his people forever?

12.b. "Yah" is a short form of Yahweh.

13.a. Perhaps we should read as pl., with some versional support (see *BHS*).

14.a. The meaning is "your way is holy," or "your ways are holy" (NIV); though קֹדֶשׁ is sometimes read as "holy place/sanctuary" (LXX, KJV, cf. 73:17): "Your way is in the sanctuary"—but this seems unlikely in the context.

14.b. MT has substituted (rather frequently in Pss 42–83) "Elohim" for Yahweh, who is clearly the subject in the present context. LXX has "like our God."

15.a. The singular in MT is collective. Note the occurrence of פֶּלֶא ("wonder") in v 12, and see *Comment* below.

16.a. Lit., "with an arm," but the versions are correct in understanding a 2nd pers. sing. suffix, "your arm."

18.a. The verb is a polel perf form of זרם, "pour forth in floods/flood away." The polel is found only here. Cf. *qal* in 90:3, apparently a denominative of זֶרֶם, "rain-storm/heavy rain" (e.g., Isa 4:6; 32:2; 25:4; Hab 3:10).

18.b. "Your arrows," חִצֶּיךָ, is a metaphor for lightning flashes, though in other references חָצָץ means "gravel" (Prov 20:17; Lam 3:16). The usual explanation is that חָצָץ is here a fuller form of חֵץ, "arrow" (see Briggs; BDB, 346; GKC, 93bb).

19.a. The word גַּלְגַּל denotes "what goes round" and is usually used of a wheel (Jer 47:3, of wheels of a war chariot; Ps 83:14) but it is also used of a whirlwind (Isa 5:28). The word is sometimes read as "wheels [of chariots]" in this context (reading כגלגל instead of בגלגל), as in NJV, "your thunder rumbled like wheels." However, this seems unlikely in the context. Cf. Ps 97:4.

19.b. LXX, Syr, and Jerome add a 2nd pers. sing. masc. suffix: "your lightning flashes"—which matches "your thunder."

20.a. Some translators add "Yahweh" or "God" to the colon for better balance (e.g., Gunkel and Kraus).

20.b. *Kethiv* has "your paths"; *qere* has "your path."

20.c. Lit., "your heels," but used in the sense of "footprints/steps/tracks."

21.a. Dahood translates the verb as a preccative perf., giving it the petitionary sense of "lead your people like sheep," forming an inclusion with the perfect in v 16, "redeem . . . the sons of Jacob and Joseph." He comments, "It is much more likely that a lament would end with a prayer than by stating an historic fact" (II, 233). However, the statements in vv 17–21 are an indirect form of prayer, an appeal to the great acts of God in the past.

Form/Structure/Setting

This is not an easy psalm to read because of the uncertainty about the tenses and modes of the verbs. The translation above assumes that the psalm belongs to the broad genre of lament, which is within a well-established interpretative tradition. However, it is possible to read the psalm in terms of thanksgiving, with the verbs in vv 2–4 read in past tense and recalling a time of lament (as in the thanksgiving psalms; e.g., Ps 30), with vv 15–16 expressing a deliverance by God. In this reading, vv 17–21 would be hymnic praise of the God who has saved his people. Thus, J. Gray ("The Kingship of God in the Prophets and Psalms," *VT* 11[1961] 9) designates the psalm as "a public thanksgiving after relief from distress." The translations in LXX, KJV, and NIV are compatible with this interpretation. Nevertheless, the language of the psalm seems to indicate a situation of present distress existing for the speaker, a prayer which waits for an answer.

Ps 77 is sometimes read as a composition of two originally independent psalms, or parts of psalms. The psalm is usually divided into vv 2–10 and 11–21 or 2–11 and 12–21. Thus Gunkel (333–34) calls vv 2–10 a lament by form and content and describes vv 11–21 as hymnic. A. A. Anderson (II, 55), though defending the literary unity of the psalm, says that vv 2–11 can be taken as having the form of an individual lament, while vv 12–21 resemble a hymn. Kraus (*Psalms 60–150,* 114) finds a prayer song of an individual person (speaking for the community) in vv 2–10, with vv 11–21 as a retrospection on the great deeds of Yahweh in the form of hymnic address, and with vv 17–20 being an independent description of a theophany. Cohen (246–48) follows the *selah* division of the psalm, which divides it into vv 2–4, 5–10, 11–21 (reading v 11 with vv 11–16 and as meaning: "The cause of all my mental and spiritual distress is that I dare to imagine that God is capable of such a change of purpose with respect to Israel").

The formation of the psalm could be the result of an intended liturgical usage or fashioned after the form of a liturgy. For example, Stuhlmueller (II, 22) suggests that the individual lament in vv 2–10 (following the *selah*) expresses loneliness and separation from God, while vv 11–16 is a confession of faith that "God's ways do not change," with a meditation by the worshiper on God's redemptive acts set forth in the liturgies and confessions of faith, and vv 17–21 form a hymn which points toward a new creation/exodus for Israel and continued leadership. A. Weiser (532) argues that the hymn in vv 12–21 "presupposes a cultic situation, and it may be assumed that the whole psalm was recited in such a context." Weiser argues that the change in the speaker's attitude "is not to be accounted for only by the newly gained knowledge that he walked in the wrong way as he doubted God" (532, Weiser assumes that v 12 reflects an inward change in the speaker's attitude; "I will tell of all thy work. . . ."), but the knowledge itself goes back to a living encounter with God in worship, which constrains the speaker to bear witness to the congregation of God's wonderful deeds. Weiser thinks his case is strengthened by the nature of vv 17–20 as a description of theophany (assuming that theophanic experiences were a major element in worship). J. Jeremias (*Theophanie*, 26–27) agrees that vv 17–20 form a description of a theophany. On the whole, however, attempts to explain this psalm on the basis of liturgy do not seem to be very successful.

    J. Kselman (*JANESCU* 52 [1983] 51–58) has drawn together an impressive array of evidence pointing toward the rhetorical unity of the psalm and to the probability that it is "the literary creation of a single poet" (57). The major features in his analysis are as follows:

A. Structural features:
1. The word קוֹלִי ("my voice") in v 2 forms an inclusion with קוֹל in v 18 and 19—the voice of lament in v 2 is answered by the "voice" of God's thunder in vv 18–19 and the theophany of vv 17–20.
2. Another inclusion is formed by the extended hand of the speaker in v 3 and the hands of Moses and Aaron in v 21. Also, the lament in vv 2–11 is marked off by the use of יד ("hand") in v 3 and ימין ("right hand") in v 11.
3. The fourfold use of the root זכר ("remember") binds the psalm together: once in v 4, once in v 7, and twice in v 12 at the beginning of the hymn section. Between the "remember" in vv 4 and 7 and the "remember" (2 x) in v 12, the antonym השכח ("forget") is found in v 10.
4. Kselman (57) refers to אשׂיחה ("I ponder/think about") in vv 4, 7, and 13 as a "fusing device": vv 4 and 7 use it in lament; v 13 uses it in praise
5. The psalm is marked by the use of concentric, chiasmic structure that cuts across the division of the lament and hymn:
    A vv 9–10   Questioning of creedal tradition
      B v 11   End of lament: God's right has changed
        C vv 12–14   Beginning of the hymn: the incomparability of God
      B¹ vv 15–16   The answer to B: God still redeems
    A¹ vv 17–21   The answer to A: God is still the God who redeemed Israel.

B. Content:
1. Kselman argues that the questions in vv 9–10, which with v 11 culminate the lament, are answered by "the hymnic representation of God's mastery over the sea" (53) in vv 17–20.
2. As part of his case, he contends that the questions in vv 9–10 are framed in terms of the creedal statement found in Exod 34:6:

Yahweh, Yahweh
El Compassionate and gracious,
slow to anger,
and abundant in kindness and fidelity

3. In effect, Kselman thinks that vv 9–10 are a commentary on Exod
34:6, questioning each point of the formula:

Has his loyal-love ceased forever?
Will his promise fail?
Has El (God) forgotten to be gracious?
Has he locked up his compassion in anger?

(For Exod 34:6 in the Psalter, see Pss 86:15; 103:9–13; 145:8). The
argument is that the speaker answers the questions posed in vv 9–10
by calling to mind the great acts of wonder and power in Yahweh's
victory over Egypt and his mastery of the sea in the defeat of the
chariots and soldiers of Pharaoh (see Exod 15): "The God who delivered Israel from Egypt can deliver the psalmist from the present
distress as well" (Kselman, 53). Thus the questions in vv 9–10 are
answered by recalling the demonstration of the truth of the creedal
statement in Exod 34:6, in his gracious act of salvation, and in the
display of his faithful love.

Kselman's analysis seems to offer the best reading of Ps 77, and I would
modify his approach only in minor ways. I agree that the questions in vv 8–10 (v 8
should be included) form the heart of the psalm and raise the questions of the
basic character of Yahweh and the continuation of his love. These are the questions
which the speaker ponders day and night (vv 6–7). Can Yahweh still be declared
to be compassionate, merciful, slow to anger, and abundant in loyal-love? The initial
response of the speaker is in v 11: "I am wounded by the changing of the right
hand of Yahweh." The mighty right hand of Yahweh, famed for its punishing
power against such foes as the Egyptians, is no longer active—or is it?
Kselman seems to think that the psalm affirms the incomparability of Yahweh
and provides a positive answer to the troubling questions: "Yes, I can still affirm
the old credo!" The psalm certainly moves in this direction, but it seems to me
that the psalm has no change of mood; the questions are left open. Will the
God who did such marvelous things in the past do them again? Will his loyal-
love continue? Will he never be favorable to us again? Has he locked up his
compassion in unending anger? Must the groaning and the sleepless pondering
(vv 4–5) go on forever? These questions hang unanswered in the psalm. The
reader must answer—though there is little doubt that the psalm is intended to
prompt the reader to respond with "No" to the questions in vv 8–10.
Commentators are wont to argue that Ps 77 is old, or at least some sections are
old (e.g., Dahood, Jacquet). The reasons given are primarily linguistic in nature.
H. Jefferson (*VT* 13 [1963] 87–91) argues that tricolons in vv 17–20, which is like
the ABC/ABD pattern characteristic of Ugaritic literature, combined with the
nature of their vocabulary, points to a very archaic origin; finding thirteen words
in these verses used less than fifty times in the OT. A high percentage of the
uncommon words are found in Ps 18:8–16, which is judged to be early (ninth or

eighth centuries or even tenth century B.C.E.): 52 percent of the vocabulary in
77:17–20 is found in Ps 18:8–18 (45 percent of the vocabulary of 77:17–20 is used
in Hab 3:10–12) and 57 percent of the vocabulary of 77:17–20 has Ugaritic
parallels. Jefferson also argues for a close literary relationship between 77:12–15
and Exod 15:11–13 (note the use of "working wonders," עשה פלא, in both passages). This kind of argumentation must be allowed some weight and it points to
the high probability that Ps 77 is composed of older material, much of it traditional. However, the common vocabulary may be due in large measure to a
common literary genre. Ps 18:6–18 is a description of a theophany as is 77:17–20
and it is not surprising that they share common language, because they are part
of a common tradition. It is possible that the reference to "the sons of Jacob and
Joseph" (v 16) may point to an origin in the Northern Israelite Kingdom before
722 B.C.E. However, the present psalm seems more at home in the time of the
exile (after 587 B.C.E.) and especially in the post-exilic period. The speaker is
likely to speak for the perplexed and fearful Israelite communities in the great
catastrophe of the exile and its aftermath.

Comment

The first complaint (77:2–5). The speaker is not identified, but the psalm could
be the personal prayer of any individual Israelite who felt the burden of the
people among whom he/she lived. The distress of the people oppresses the
individual who shares it with them. Crying out to God, seeking him in the day of
distress, and praying through the night with lifted hands are familiar themes in
laments (Pss 6:7; 22:2–3; 86:2–7; 88:2–7; 88:2–3, 10; 102:2–3; 120:1; 141:2; 142:2).
The imperfect verb אצעקה ("I am crying out") as well as the repeated expression
"with my voice to God" in v 2 indicates the perpetual nature of the speaker's
praying. It is not a passing sorrow or even a sudden tragedy that has caused this
distress; the speaker's life has become defined by the doubt and anguish of the
circum-stances. Although the speaker hopes that God may hear and respond,
this does not seem to happen, and there is no comfort for the soul (v 3). God's
lack of re-sponse worsens the already miserable situation. Now the very thought
of God, who is the hope of deliverance, has become a source of pain and
spiritual distress (v 4).

V 5 accuses God of "holding open" the psalmist's eyelids, a continuation of
the thought in vv 3–4 when the remembrance of God brings on groaning and
pondering of the spirit. Now the speaker is unable to sleep and attributes that fact
to God as well. The disturbance is so great that the sufferer cannot even speak of it,
but broods instead. The verbs זכר ("remember"), שיח ("ponder"), חשב and הגה
("reflect"), and דרש ("seek") appear a total of ten times between vv 4 and 13, indicating the energy that the speaker is turning inward (זכר "remember," appears four
times). V 5 is a transition verse which relates to the night in v 3 and the night in v 7.

The second complaint (77:6–11). The painful depression of the speaker has been
described in vv 2–5; a troubled distress which comes from unanswered prayer and
pondering about God. The process of remembering and pondering (זכר and שיח) continues in vv 6–11 with more description and with the troubling questions in vv 8–10.

The apparent absence of God in the present leads to meditation about the
past, when divine love and protection were evident. This makes the present look

even worse as the speaker remembers the favor, lovingkindness, graciousness, and compassion of the former days. Even God's eternal promises seem to have come to an end. In sorrow and abandonment the speaker ponders on the disturbing questions in vv 8–10. The confident songs of praise, sung in the past, evoke dire questions about the present. This complaint reaches a climax in v 11 when the speaker laments the wounding which has resulted from the "changing of the right hand of the Most High." In v 11 the speaker attributes a weakened/grieving condition to the failure of God to use his right hand for the defense and deliverance of his people. Cf. v 16, which recalls how God (Yahweh) redeemed his people with his arm. The "songs" in v 7a probably refers to the songs of thanksgiving and praise which had been sung in happier times.

A meditation on the deeds of God (77:12–16). Several commentators read these verses as expressing a change of mood in the speaker from lament to confidence (see the references above to Stuhlmueller and Weiser; also Kraus, II, 695–96). A sudden change of mood is found in some laments and it is possible here. It seems to me, however, that Dahood makes better sense. Dahood reads v 12 as a positive affirmation of intention ("I will recite your magnificent deeds . . ."), but he argues that the purpose of the song about God's primordial deeds is "to persuade God to repeat such feats on Israel's behalf" (II, 78).

I prefer to read these verses as continuing the painful reflection of vv 4–11 on God's failure to duplicate his great works in the present. The recall of God's wonderful works of the past—culminating in the deliverance of Israel in v 16—is the counterpoint to the divine passivity in the present. Note the use of the verb שׂיח ("muse/reflect/ponder") in vv 7 and 13. The pondering of inscrutable questions continues—even in reflection (indeed, more so) on God's holiness and greatness (v 14). How can Yahweh maintain his holy way with Israel while refusing to use his great arm and powerful right hand for her deliverance?

A description of a theophany (77:17–21). The distressful meditation of vv 12–16 is intensified by the description of the demonstration of God's power in theophanic intervention (cf. Ps 18:8–18). The language of v 17 reflects the ancient motif of a divine struggle with chaotic forces in bringing forth creation. The turbulent waters of the great primeval seas writhed before the presence of God and the deeps roiled, so great was his power. The language draws from the widely spread myth of the primeval conquest of the waters of chaos (see the discussion of 74:12–17; 104:2–7; J. Day, *God's Conflict with the Dragon and the Sea,* 96–97). However, in this context the chaos struggle has been adapted to divine intervention for deliverance (as in Pss 18:8–18; 93) and the historization of the myth in the description of divine action in the Exodus (see Isa 51:9–11; Exod 15:5–10; Ps 114:3–5; Isa 63:12–14). The descriptive elements in these verses reflect various religious traditions from the ancient Near East (see Kraus, *Psalms 60–150,* 116–17; Day, 96–101, for details and references). The shepherd motif in v 21 is a common one in the Bible (see, e.g., Pss 78:52–53; 95:7–11; 100; cf. Pss 23; 80:2; Ezek 34).

Explanation

The speaker in this psalm voices great personal distress caused by the unrelieved condition of Israel. The psalm is a prayer of unanswered lament. Nevertheless there is a feeling of expectancy about it. The reader knows what the speaker in the psalm can only seek in perplexity and reflection: God has surely not rejected his people forever; his promises will be kept. At the close of the psalm the reader senses that a theophanic intervention of the wonder-working God of creation and exodus is imminent, though the worshiper waits for it to come.

The complaints in vv 2–11 focus on the hurt of a person whose anguish stems from unanswered prayer and doubt about God. The pain is too great for speaking (v 5), and the night has become a time not for sleeping but a time of constant pondering and seeking for the answers to disturbing questions. The possibility of God's desertion from his people and the end of his loyal-love is confronted in the dark hours of sleepless night. The reader can hardly miss the references to night in vv 3 and 7. The speaker knows of spiritual terror at night (cf. Ps 91:5). The recall of God's power and greatness in vv 12–21 does not bring an immediate end to doubt and waiting. The psalm seems to suggest that God moves on his own schedule and often the faithful must endure the anguish of waiting. Perhaps we should read the psalm with a passage like Isa 40:31:

> They who wait for the LORD
> > shall renew their strength,
> > > they shall mount up with wings like eagles,
> They shall run and not be weary,
> > they shall walk and not faint. (RSV)

Those who wait pray, "Come Lord!"

As noted above, most commentators read this psalm with a major shift of mood in v 12. In this case, a different explanation is required for the text. For a vigorous exposition of the psalm along these lines, see W. Brueggemann (*Israel's Praise*, 137–40). Brueggemann reads the psalm in the context of "Pain as the Matrix of Praise" (136) and argues that a connection between "canonical memory of credo and concrete pain" is articulated in its content (137). In this approach, God becomes the center of attention as the speaker shifts away from "I" to "thou" (vv 13–21). The speaker's remembering of the past "takes the mind off the hopelessness of the self" and "conceptualizes present hurt, as yet unresolved" (138). The remembering of the speaker is aided by identification with "your people" (vv 16, 21); the remembering and the identification allow present trouble to be "recontextualized and thereby transformed" (138)—"The trouble has been set in the context of remembered praise." There is much in this exposition with which to agree. However, it seems to me that the recontextualization and transformation in this psalm is incomplete; the speaker is at the threshold of a new understanding but has not entered, and the reader is left to ponder his or her own willingness to enter. The speaker and the reader wait for a new revealing of the unperceived steps of God through the great waters (v 20), which will become a new mystery, a reality not discoverable by ordinary observation. The psalm invites us as readers to ponder the mystery of the "unknown tracks" of God in the midst of our distress. Has his loyal-love (v 9) failed? Can we still trust his promises? Vv 12–21 give us the basis for an affirmative answer, but the decision is ours.

The Riddle of God and Israel
from Zoan to Zion   *(78:1–72)*

Bibliography

Campbell, A. F. "Psalm 78: A Contribution to the Theology of Tenth Century Israel." *CBQ* 41 (1979) 51–79. **Carroll, R. P.** "Psalm LXXVIII: Vestiges of a Tribal Polemic." *VT* 21 (1971) 133–150. **Clifford, R. J.** "In Zion and David a New Beginning: An Interpretation of Psalm 78." In *Traditions in Transformation*, ed. F. M. Cross. Winona Lake: Eisenbrauns, 1981. 121–41. **Coats, G. W.** *Rebellion in the Wilderness.* Nashville: Abingdon, 1968. 109–24. **Eissfeldt, O.** "Das Lied Moses Deuteronomium 32:1–43 und das Lehrgedicht Asaphs Psalm 78 samt einer Analyse der Umgebung der Moses-Liedes." *Berichte über die Verhandlungen der Sachsischen Akademie der Wissenschaften zu Leipzig* (Phil.-hist. Klasse 104, 5). Berlin: Akademia, 1958. Esp. 34–37. **Haglund, E.** *Historical Motifs in the Psalms.* Lund: CWK Gleerup, 1984. 88–101. **Johnson, A. R.** *CPIP.* 45–66. **Junker, H.** "Die Entstehungszeit des Ps. 78 und des Deuteronomiums." *Bib* 34 (1953) 487–500. **Nasuti, H. P.** *Tradition History.* **Westermann, C.** *Praise and Lament.* 228–49.

Translation

1	An Asaphite *maskil*. [a]	
	Give ear, O my people, to my teaching;	(3+3)
	bend your ear to the words of my mouth.	
2	*I will open my mouth in a story,*[a]	(3+3)
	speaking about riddles [b] *of things past,*	
3	*things that we have heard and known about,*	(3+3)
	that our fathers told us.	
4	*We will not keep them from our children;*[a]	(3+3+3+3)
	telling them to the next generation:	
	the praiseworthy acts of Yahweh, his power,	
	and the wonders he has done.	
5	*He instituted a set of requirements* [a] *in Jacob,*	(3+3+3+2)
	and established a body of teaching [b] *in Israel,*	
	which he commanded our fathers	
	to make known to their children,	
6	*that the next generation might know;*	(4+2+3)
	children yet to be born,	
	who in turn [a] *would tell their children,*	
7	*that they (in turn) would put their confidence in God,*	(3+3+2)
	and forget not the deeds of God,	
	but keep his commandments;	
8	*not becoming like their forefathers,*	(3+3+3+3)
	a rebellious and defiant generation,	
	a generation that did not keep its heart steady,[a]	
	and whose spirit was not faithful to God.	

9	*The sons of Ephraim, well-equipped bowmen,*[a]	(3+3)
	turned back[b] *on the day of battle.*	
10	*They did not keep the covenant of God,*	(3+3)
	and refused to obey his instruction.	
11	*They forgot his deeds*	(2+3)
	and his wonders[a] *that he had shown them.*	
12	*In front of their fathers he did a wonder,*	(4+3)
	in the land of Egypt, in the region of Zoan.[a]	
13	*He split the sea and brought them through it,*	(3+3)
	and caused the water to stand up like a wall.[a]	
14	*And then he led them with a cloud by day*	(3+3)
	and all night by a fiery light.	
15	*He split*[a] *rocks in the wilderness*	(3+3)
	and let (them) drink[b] *as from a great deep.*	
16	*Then he caused streams to flow from a crag*[a]—	(3+3)
	water ran down like rivers!	
17	*But they continued to sin against him,*	(3+3)
	defying the Most High (even) in the arid land.	
18	*They willfully put God to the test,*[a]	(3+3)
	asking about the food they craved.[b]	
19	*And they spoke against God, saying,*[a]	(3+2+3)
	"Is God able?—	
	to prepare a table[b] *in the wilderness?*	
20	*True, he struck a rock,*	(3+4+3+3)
	and water gushed out and streams flowed—	
	But can he also provide bread?	
	Can he supply meat for his people?"	
21	*When*[a] *Yahweh heard about it, he was furious,*	(4+3+3)
	and fire broke out against Jacob,	
	and (his) wrath flared up against Israel,	
22	*because they did not trust in God,*	(3+3)
	and did not rely on his saving work.	
23	*And so he commanded the skies above,*	(3+3)
	opened the doors of heaven,	
24	*and rained down on them manna to eat;*[a]	(4+3)
	he gave them the grain of heaven!	
25	*Each person ate the bread of angels;*[a]	(4+3)
	he sent them plenty of bread!	
26	*Then he set the east wind blowing in*[a] *the heavens,*	(3+3)
	and by his might he guided the south wind,	
27	*and so he rained meat down on them like dust;*	(4+4)
	flying birds like the sand of the seashore,	
28	*making them fall inside his camp,*[a]	(3+2)
	round about his[a] *dwelling-place.*[a]	
29	*And so they ate more than enough;*	(3+3)
	he brought them what they wanted.	
30	*(But) before they ate all they wanted,*[a]	(2+3)
	with their food still in their mouths,	

31   the wrath of God flared up against them,   (3+2+3)
         and he killed their best men;
         he brought down (to death) the youths of Israel.

32   Despite all this, they kept on sinning,   (3+3)
         and did not trust in his wonders.

33   And so he ended their days in a breath,[a]   (2+2)
         and their years in sudden calamity.[b]

34   True, when he was killing them they searched for him;   (2+2)
         they repented and looked diligently for God.

35   They remembered that God was their Rock,[a]   (3+3)
         and that God Most High was their Redeemer.

36   But they deceived him with their words,   (2+2)
         and with their tongues they lied to him.

37   Their heart was not steadfast with him,   (3+3)
         and they were not faithful to his covenant.

38   But he is compassionate;   (2+3+3+2)
         he forgave their waywardness and did not destroy (them);
         frequently turning back his anger,
         he did not fully rouse his wrath.

39   He remembered that they were flesh,   (3+3)
         spirit[a] which passes and does not return.

40   How often were they rebellious in the wilderness   (3+2)
         and caused him pain in the desert!

41   Repeatedly[a] they tested God   (3+3)
         and vexed[b] the Holy One of Israel.

42   They did not remember his hand,   (2+3)
         on the day when he ransomed them from the foe:

43   how[a] he set his signs in Egypt   (3+2)
         and his wonders in the region of Zoan;[b]

44   how he turned[a] their rivers into blood,   (3+3)
         so that they could not drink (from) their streams.

45   He sent against them a swarm[a] and it devoured them,   (4+2)
         and frogs that ruined them.

46   And he gave to the grasshopper[a] their crops,   (3+2)
         and their produce to the locust swarm.

47   He killed their vines with the hail,   (3+2)
         and their sycamore trees with the frost.[a]

48   He delivered their livestock to the hail,[a]   (3+2)
         and their flocks to the lightning bolts.

49   He sent his burning anger against them: (3+3+3)
         fury and indignation and distress;
         a band of angels[a] of calamity,

50   who prepared a path for his anger.   (3+3+3)
         He did not spare them from death
         and their lives he delivered to the plague.

51   He struck down all of the firstborn of Egypt,   (3+3)
         the firstfruits of virility[a] in the tents of Ham.[b]

52	And then he set his people moving,^a	(3+3)
	and guided them as a flock in the wilderness.	
53	He led them safely and they were not afraid,	(3+3)
	but their enemies (were left) covered by the sea.	
54	And then he brought them to his holy territory,	(3+3)
	to the mountain which his right hand got.	
55	He drove out nations before them	(3+3+4)
	and apportioned them by lot as a possession,	
	and so he settled the tribes of Israel in their tents.	
56	But they tested and rebelled against God Most High,	(4+3)
	and his requirements they did not keep.	
57	They turned aside and acted faithlessly like their father	(3+3)
	and they failed like a treacherous bow.	
58	They provoked him with their high places,	(2+2)
	and with their idols they made him jealous.	
59	When God heard about it, he was furious,	(3+3)
	and he vehemently repudiated Israel.	
60	He forsook the tabernacle at Shiloh,	(3+3)
	the tent where he dwelt among humanity,	
61	and he gave up to captivity his power,^a	(3+2)
	and his glory^a to the hand of the foe.	
62	He allowed his people to be given to the sword,	(3+2)
	and he was furious with his heritage.	
63	Fire devoured their young men,	(2+3)
	and their maidens were not praised.^a	
64	Their priests fell by the sword,	(3+3)
	and their widows did not bewail them.	
65	And then the Lord awoke as from sleep,	(3+3)
	like a strong man shouting from wine.	
66	He hit his foes in the rump^a;	(2+4)
	he gave them to eternal reproach.	
67	And he repudiated the tent of Joseph,	(3+3)
	and he no longer chose the tribe of Ephraim.	
68	But he chose the tribe of Judah,	(3+4)
	Mount Zion, which he loved.	
69	He built his sanctuary like the heights,^a	(3+3)
	like the earth that he established forever.	
70	And he chose David his servant,	(3+3)
	and took him from the sheepfolds,	
71	from tending ewes he brought him	(3+3+2)
	to shepherd Jacob his people,	
	and Israel his inheritance.	
72	And so he^a shepherded them with his upright^b heart;	(3+3)
	with his skillful hands he led them.	

Notes

1.a. For Asaph (found in the titles of Pss 50, 73–83), see n. 73:1.a. For maskil, see n. 52:1–2.c.

2.a. The word מָשָׁל is usually translated as "proverb," though "parable" is frequently used in translation of Ps 78:2. The word is associated with the wisdom literature (e.g., Prov 1:1, 6; 10:1; 25:1; 26:7, 9; note also Ezek 12:22–23; 18:2–3) and refers to a carefully constructed, short statement, usually of one or two colons, which expresses some truth about life that has been verified by long human experience. These short statements occur in several forms and contain highly varied content. However, מָשָׁל is also used for various types of figurative sayings which have the character of allegory (see Ezek 17:2; 20:49), discourse (Num 23:7, 18; 24:3, 15, 21, 23; Job 13:12; 27:1; 29:1), and a taunt or "taunt song" (Deut 28:37; Jer 24:9; Isa 14:4; Mic 2:4; Hab 2:6). מָשָׁל and חִידָה "riddle," are found together in Ps 49:5; Ezek 17:2; Hab 2:6; also in Wisd 8:8; Ecclus 39:3. "Parable" is acceptable for Ps 78:2, but the more general word "story" seems better. The psalm is presented as a teaching psalm in the form of a story, told in poetry.

2.b. The word for "riddle" (חִידָה) is also associated with wisdom literature. In a strict sense, "riddle" occurs in the OT only in Judg 14:10–18, though a number of passages refer to "riddle speech" (see Num 12:8, 1 Kgs 10:1–5; 2 Chr 9:1–4; Prov 1:6; Ezek 17:2). Riddles use words that belong to common knowledge but which conceal special meanings known only to those who know how to solve the riddle. The riddle connotes ambiguity and mystery, often revealing a "paradox of reality." Thus, Ps 78 deals with the paradox of Israel's inability to trust God's great acts of deliverance, despite the long-continued and repeated nature of those acts. The story of Yahweh's relationship with Israel is truly full of "riddles."

4.a. Lit., "sons." The reference is to posterity and is not exclusively male, thus "children" is appropriate.

5.a. The word עֵדוּת is usually translated as "testimony" or "decree." A. R. Johnson (*CPIP*, 6, n. 5; 59, n. 4; *Sacral Kingship in Ancient Israel* [Cardiff: University of Wales Press, 1955] 58, n. 4) has argued that עֵדוּת is a corresponding term to עֵדָה (which appears in the plural in v 57), traditionally rendered as "testimony," and is used in a specialized sense (1) of Yahweh's promises to his followers (as in Ps 93:5), or (2) of the undertakings which he requires of his people, i.e., his "laws" (Johnson cites Pss 25:10; 132:12). The second meaning is rather clearly the correct one for 78:5. See also Pss 119:2; 60:1.b.

5.b. Lit., *torah* (תּוֹרָה), the teaching or instruction which Yahweh gave to Israel.

6.a. Lit., "they will rise up and tell. . . ." The versions supply a conjunction: "And they will rise up. . . ." (*BHS*). The translation above reads the colon as a relative clause without a relative pronoun; relative by parataxis.

8.a. "Heart" (לֵב) is equal to "purpose" or "will." REB has: "a generation with no firm purpose."

9.a. Following Johnson (*CPIP*, 49, n. 3) who argues that superlative force results from the use of a construct form (נֹשְׁקֵי, "equipped/armed") with a partitive genitive (רוֹמֵי־קָשֶׁת, "bow-shooters/bowmen"); literally: "the equipped ones of the bow-shooters" = "the able bow-shooters." Johnson translates as "the best equipped of bowmen." Gunkel proposes an extensive reconstruction of this verse, reading בָּנִים פֹּרְעִים ("unrestrained/undisciplined children") for MT's בְּנֵי־אֶפְרָיִם ("sons of Ephraim"), מְשַׁקְּרִים ("deceptive/treacherous ones") for נֹשְׁקֵי רוֹמֵי ("those equipped with the shooting of")—assuming an unvocalized נֹשְׁקְרִים behind MT—and כְּקֶשֶׁת הַפּוֹכָ(ה) ("as a bow which turned/bent"). His translation is: "Unrestrained sons, treacherous / as the bow which fails on the day of battle." Such a massive reconstruction is hardly convincing (cf. Kraus).

9.b. Or, "gave way" (Johnson, cf. v 57); Dahood has "who turned tail."

11.a. The words נִפְלָאוֹת (niphal participle, fem. pl.) and פֶּלֶא refer to wonderful or marvelous deeds; actions done in an astonishing manner (e.g., Exod 3:20; 34:10, Josh 3:5; Pss 9:2; 26:7; 40:6; 71:17; 77:12; 88:13; 89:6; 119:129). When used of God, they are acts which lie beyond the powers of human performance, certainly in any normal sense.

12.a. Usually translated as "the field(s) of Zoan." However, שָׂדֶה frequently means "region" or "adjacent territory," and sometimes means "a plain" or "level land." Zoan (LXX, Tanis) was a city in northeastern Egypt, known also as Avaris, and possibly the same as Raamses/Rameses in Exod 1:11, though this identification is now questioned (see *Harper's Bible Dictionary*, 848, 1166, also 81). See also T. O. Lambdin, *IDB*, IV, 961; J. van Seters, *IDBSup*, 424–25. Zoan is not mentioned in the exodus accounts in the Pentateuch.

13.a. MT has נֵד, "wall/dam/barrier." LXX has ἀσκόν ("leather bag/wine skin") = נֹאד (or נֹד) with the same meaning. The verb נָצַב is more appropriate for the idea of a wall.

15.a. Note the use of the same verb (בָּקַע) for splitting the sea in v 13.

15.b. MT is without an object. The implicit object is supplied by the versions. Note the omission of object suffixes with verbs in vv 6, 21, and 38.

16.a. See Num 20:7–11.

18.a. Lit., "they tested God in their heart."

18.b. Lit., "for their *nephesh* (לנפשם)," which can mean "for themselves." However, נפש may also refer to desire, emotions, and appetite (cf. Deut 21:14; 23:25; Jer 34:16; Pss 35:25; 105:22). Vv 29–30 indicate that the food referred to in v 18 was not so much to sustain life as to satisfy undisciplined appetites.

19.a. Sometimes unnecessarily deleted on metrical grounds (see *BHS*). The proselike "saying" is unexpected, but it is not out of place in the epic nature of this psalm.

19.b. Frequently translated as "spread a table" (cf. Ps 23:5). The word for "table" (שלחן) probably originally referred to a leather hide spread on the ground for the serving of food. However, other references indicate that it can be used with the idea of a "table" in our sense of the word (e.g., Ps 69:23; Exod 25:23, 27, 28, 30; 30:27; 37:10; 1 Kgs 7:48; Ezek 40:41, 42).

21.a. The לכן is usually "therefore/as a result" (occasionally "surely"), which is the force of the "when" in the translation above. The word is possibly a scribal supplement for emphasis (cf. Kraus)— its omission allows for more balanced colons, though balanced colons are not especially characteristic of this psalm.

24.a. As in the case of the לכן in v 21, the infinitive לאכל ("to eat") unbalances the colon and may be a clarifying comment (cf. Kraus).

25.a. MT's אבירים means "strong/valiant ones" (note 1 Sam 21:8; Job 24:22; 34:20; Lam 1:15; cf. Judg 5:22; Isa 10:13). LXX has "angels" (cf. Ps 103:20) and this is widely adopted. The meaning is that of strong ones of the heavenly host of God; even possibly "the mighty gods," see Johnson, *CPIP*, 52, n. 1.

26.a. LXX has "out of heaven."

28.a. MT has "his camp," but most translations follow the versions and read "their camp" and "their habitations/dwelling places." The "his" may, of course, be collective and refer to Israel or to Jacob. On the other hand, Johnson (*CPIP*, 52, n. 2) argues extensively for the meaning of "his" as a reference to Yahweh (with a convenient survey of commentators pro and con). The camp is Yahweh's, in the midst of which he has his earthly dwelling place in the tabernacle. The plural form of משכן (tent of meeting/tabernacle in the P material of the Pentateuch) can be an intensive plural (GKC 124g–i) to emphasize the dwelling place of God (cf. Pss 43:3; 84:2; 132:5, 7; see L. Allen, 201, n. 5.b.), or the plural form משכנות actually may be singular with an old feminine וה-ending. Thus, the משכנות refers to the divine "dwelling-place." or "tent-shrine" of Yahweh.

30.a. Lit., "they were not estranged from their desire/lust."

33.a. The בהבל could be understood in the sense of "nothingness/futility." The word הבל is primarily a reference to "vapor/wind/breath"—that which lacks substance and is without any real gain (e.g., Deut 32:21; Isa 57:13; Jer 8:19; 10:8; 51:18; Prov 13:11; 21:6; Eccl passim). The word also can carry the notions of the enigmatic and anomalous. The meaning in Ps 78:33 is probably that of the swift and unexpected end of life, which can happen as quickly as a breath. But the idea of futility may also be present (note NIV, NJV; NAB, "he quickly ended their days").

33.b. The word בהלה seems to refer to any unexpected and frightening calamity, though its usage is very limited in MT (Lev 26:16; Jer 15:8; Isa 65:23). Note the word play with בהבל ("in the nothingness") in the first colon. Lev 26:16 suggests that בהלה denotes an attack of acute illness.

35.a. The divine epithets "Rock" (צור or סלע) and "Stone" (אבן) appear rather frequently (33x) and seem to be quite old (see Gen 49:24; Deut 32:4, 15, 18, 30, 31; Pss 18:3, 32, 47; 19:15; 28:1; 42:10; 62:3, 8; 78:35; 86:27; 92:16; Isa 44:8; Hab 1:12). Possibly the terms were linked to Mount Sinai and the "most holy place" built on a rock foundation (see Craigie and Ps 28:1–4; also Kraus on Ps 28:1). However, it seems more probable that the epithets are borrowed from ancient Near Eastern traditions, and they may also allude to the rock in the wilderness which became a source of water for the thirsty Israelites (Exod 17:1–7; Num 20:2–13). The rock epithet expresses the idea of the reliability, the protection, the stability and the permanence of Yahweh. D. N. Freedman ("Divine Names and Titles," in *Pottery, Poetry, and Prophecy* [Winona Lake: Indiana: Eisenbrauns, 1980] 114–5) argues that צור has the basic meaning of "mountain" (also Dahood in Ps 78:35 and passim; however, not in 95:1), apparently a cognate for שדי. The meaning "mountain" may be appropriate for some contexts, but it should not be insisted on in all cases. See also G. W. Ahlstrom, *Psalm 89* [Lund: Haaken Ohlssons, 1959]115; A. S. van der Woude, *THAT*, II, 542–43.

39.a. רוח here is usually translated as "wind": "like the wind which passes and does not return," relating, of course, to the transient nature of human life. Johnson (*CPIP*, 55, n. 3) observes that רוח is normally fem. and does not relate well to the masc. participle which follows. He suggests "the spirit of that which departeth and returneth not," noting the correspondence of language with רוח in v 8. Perhaps a better translation would be "(that they were) like [a spirit] which goes but does not return"—life is a one-way street.

41.a. Or, "But they turned back and tested God" (cf. kjv). However, שׁוב here more likely denotes repetition.

41.b. The verb תוה means "mark off/set bounds to"; thus to grieve or pain God in this context by doubting and testing the limits of divine power.

43.a. The translation assumes that the relative participle אשׁר has the sense of the English "how" in the sense of "manner" or "way of doing something." Cf. the usage in Deut 6:15 and 2 Kgs 8:5.

43.b. See n. 12.a.

44.a. Note the use of the verb הפך, "turn/turn over/overthrow," in vv 9 and 57.

45.a. The word ערב is frequently understood as meaning "swarms of flies" (cf. Exod 8:20–32; Ps 105:31). However, the identification of the insects involved is not certain, and the "mixture" (the basic idea of the word) probably refers to swarms of different kinds of insects. LXX uses a word which means "dogfly," an insect known for its vicious and painful attacks.

46.a. This verse uses חסיל and ארבה in parallel. Both are generally translated "locust" (BDB), although the latter is more common. Weiser suggests "rodent" for the former and Dahood has "grasshopper." Jacquet proposes "cricket," and rsv uses "caterpillar." The verb חסל means "to finish/consume," and so חסיל in parallel with ארבה may refer to any rapacious insects.

47.a. The word חנמל is a hapax which is translated as "frost" in LXX. KB, 316, has "devastating flood," which is followed by neb and reb, "torrents of rain"; niv has "sleet."

48.a. Several MSS and Symm read לדבר, "to the pestilence/plague." In this case, v 48 would correlate with the livestock plague in Exod 9:1–7. If "hail" is retained, the correlation is with Exod 9:9, 25. If the change to "pestilence" is accepted, the word for "lightning bolts" (רשׁפּים) in 48b should be read as "plagues" or "disease." רשׁף seems to have been derived from Canaanite/Phoenician רשׁקדּחץ ("fiery arrow") and can apply to lightning (cf. Ps 76:4; Hab 3:5). In Ugar. usage, רשׁף is equal to the Egyptian god Seth and to the Mesopotamian god Nergal, who was a god of pestilence (cf. Deut 32:24; Hab 3:5; Job 5:7). Thus רשׁף can denote either lightning flashes or the "arrows" of pestilential disease (see D. Conrad, "Der Gott Reschef," *ZAW* 83 [1971] 157–83, who argues that Resheph was more than a minor god of plague and the underworld, being an important god of sky, weather, fertility, and war).

49.a. Lit., "a sending of messengers/angels" (construct of משׁלחת), a word that refers to "sending out/discharge" (Eccl 8:8); thus it means "detachment/deputation/band." Cf. Exod 12:23.

51.a. Or, "manhood" (niv). The word (אוֹן) refers to generative power, sexual virility in this context. The plural is either intensive, or should be read as אנם "their virility."

51.b. Ham is a name for Egypt; see Gen 10:6; Pss 105:23, 27; 106:12.

52.a. Note the use of the verb נסע ("move/set out on a journey/march") in v 26.

61.a. LXX has a 3rd pers. pl. suffix in both cases: "their power" and "their glory." If "his power—his glory" is retained, the reference is to the ark, which is called "the ark of your power" (ארון עזך) in 132:8. See G. H. Davies, "The Ark in the Psalms," in *Promise and Fulfillment,* ed. F. F. Bruce (Edinburgh: T. & T. Clark, 1963) 51–61; cf. 1 Sam 4:3–8; Ps 24:8. The word for "glory" is תפאָרה, more properly, "beauty" or "renown."

63.a. The meaning is most probably "not praised (in marriage songs)" (cf., e.g., Cant 7:1–9; Jer 7:34; 16:9). However, the verb has sometimes been treated as a hophal form from ילל, "howl/wail/lament," which is reflected in LXX., but it is unlikely.

66.a. In agreement with translations and commentators who take אחור as "the rear part"; thus, jb: "to strike his enemies on the rump"; kjv: "and he smote his enemies in the hinder parts." Dahood (II, 247) argues for a double entendre in the sense of the posterior and of the rear guard of an army. The double entendre is probable, and the smiting (נכה) of the Philistines with boils or hemorrhoids in 1 Sam 5:5, 9 (cf. 6:4, 11, 17) may be in mind—though the exact nature of the "tumors" referred to in these verses is uncertain.

69.a. The translation is literal. The "heights" (רמים) may refer to the earthly temple or the divine sanctuary in the heavens. If the earthly temple is intended, the meaning may be that the temple is as stable and enduring as the mountains (Cohen; niv). Johnson (*CPIP,* 61, n. 3) does not follow the emendation to כמרמים (*BHS*), but reads, "He built His sanctuary like the heavenly heights" on the basis that רמים is an adjective used with the force of a substantive (so also Dahood). Cf. Ps 148:1. jb has "he built his sanctuary, a copy of high heaven" (similar to Briggs). The idea of the "heights of heaven" is most probable, which corresponds well with 69b; the temple relates to heaven and to earth and has the glory and enduring qualities of both.

72.a. The subject is David.

72.b. The word תם refers to integrity and wholeness; sometimes translated as "blameless" or "sincere" (cf. 101:2; Job 1:1, 8; 2:3). The concept is that of personal integrity and good moral character rather than sinless perfection (cf. Josh 24:14; Judg 9:16, 19).

Form/Setting/Structure

Most commentators agree on the general nature of Ps 78, although they use different terms to identify its form. Westermann sees it as a descriptive hymn of praise with a wisdom introduction (*Praise and Lament*, 141), while to Jacquet it is a historical psalm (a genre devoted to the recital of Israel's history). Maillot and Lelièvre, Schmidt, and Sabourin view it as at least partly a historical psalm with affinities to the wisdom genre because of its narrative nature and a stated purpose of educating the next generation. Dahood, Mowinckel, Briggs, Carroll, and Weiser are among those who consider the psalm to be didactic. Although its subject matter is similar to those psalms that enumerate Yahweh's activity in Israel's history (cf. Pss 105, 114, 135, 136), Ps 78 does not seem interested in presenting a mere list of the events of Israel's past. Schmidt (150) describes it as offering "a philosophy of history," and Jacquet adds that it differs from those hymns that use Israel's history as an occasion for praising Yahweh in that it presents history not as a recital but as a subject for meditation. Von Rad calls the psalm a meditation on history which becomes "a somber confession of Israel's failures" (*Old Testament Theology*, tr. D. M. G. Stalker [New York: Harper, 1962] I, 357), although it also celebrates the salvation-history in such a way as to draw from it lessons for living as God's people and does not lose its character in praise. Von Rad notes that the verb הודה (hiphil of ידה), which is generally translated as "to praise" (or, "give thanks"), more properly means "to confess" or "to accept" and usually refers to some sort of divine datum which precedes. God's acts of judgment as well as his acts of deliverance may be the subject of praise (cf. Josh 7:19; Ezra 10:7–11; Dan 3:31–4:34 [4:1–37]; Isa 12:1–6)—the so-called doxology of judgment.

Date and historical setting. All the psalms are notoriously difficult to date. R. P. Carroll (*VT* 21 [1971] 133–50) makes the point that, since all of the psalms have undergone post-exilic editing, they could conceivably all be dated to that period. Arguments about dating, he says, concern possible original forms rather than the work as it now exists (144). However, this does not prevent him from offering opinions as to the original period of this or any other psalm, but it does serve as a reminder of how complex the transmission of these poems was and makes it difficult to offer any final conclusions on the subject.

Ps 78, despite its strong historical allusions, has generated a wide range of proposed dates. To some scholars the psalm's triumphant ending with the reign of David indicates a date of composition during that period. The earliest possible date would be in the mid-tenth century, with the argument that because the temple is not mentioned the psalm was probably composed before it was built. Campbell (*CBQ* 41 [1979] 51–79) agrees that the origin of the psalm must be close to David's era; the loss of the ark and the subsequent destruction of Shiloh would have been a pressing concern in the tenth century. He argues that Ps 78 provides a theological interpretation of the period between the loss of Shiloh and the establishment of the Davidic monarchy in Jerusalem. Dahood, remarking on the antiquity of the language (specifically the consistent use of the imperfect to refer to the past), is also willing to date the psalm to the tenth century. He reads the condemnation of Ephraim and the rejection of Israel by Yahweh as a reflection of the Judean reaction to the revolt of the Northern tribes against the Jerusalemite hegemony. However, since the psalm makes no mention of the end of the Northern Kingdom, which would have fit well into its theological system, Dahood puts the *terminus ad quem* at 922. Jacquet agrees. Johnson (*CPIP,* 64–65) suggests that the psalm's celebration of Yahweh's choice of Judah rather than Ephraim, of Zion rather than Shiloh, may point to a time before the disruption of the monarchy, perhaps during the reign of Solomon. Much of the approach to an early date for this psalm is found in the succinct statement of B. D. Eerdmans (379): "With the reign of David the psalmist has reached the end of his historical reflections. Apparently his criticism had to stop here. The natural reason seems to be that he had arrived at his own period."

Other scholars, still holding to a pre-exilic date for the psalm but unwilling to set it so early, place it after the fall of the Northern Kingdom but before the exile of Judah. Sabourin states that the psalm ends with David for theological reasons and not because the author had reached a contemporary period. With the election of David as Israel's shepherd in the city loved by Yahweh, Israel's relationship with her God was secure. Haglund (*Historical Motifs,* 95, 100) suggests that the psalm comes from shortly after the Northern Kingdom fell, since its use of the desert traditions indicates that they had not yet coalesced into their present form. He believes the psalm's purpose was to explain why the Northern Kingdom came to an end. Sabourin, Briggs, Weiser, and Maillot and Lelièvre (who would be willing to set the psalm later in the pre-exilic period) agree that the fall of the Northern Kingdom is presupposed by the psalmist: Yahweh utterly rejects Israel. Since the Judean monarchy is presented as the culmination of Yahweh's relationship with his people, it is argued that the psalm must antedate its fall.

However, not all scholars are willing to limit the discussion of a date to the pre-exilic era. Gunkel (342) is among those who set the psalm in the early post-exilic period, arguing that its picture of the Northern tribes as completely faithless may indicate the anti-Samaritanism of early Judaism, making much of his reconstruction of v 9. Judah consistently condemned Israel's worship practices, but the utter rejection of the Northern tradition as far back as the desert seems more like the separatism of Ezra and Nehemiah. Thus Kraus (II, 704) thinks it conceivable that the psalm belongs close to Deuteronomistic circles and the Chronicler's history, with a renewed emphasis on the election of Zion and David over against Northern Israelite claims.

Arguments from silence are weak at best; the fact that the building of the temple, the revolt under Jeroboam I, the destruction of Israel, and the captivity of Judah are not mentioned does not necessarily mean that they had not taken place at the time of the psalm's composition. The psalm was, after all, considered valuable enough to be included in Judaism's sacred literature by people living long after all of those events had occurred even though it mentioned none of them. The reference to "Mount Zion, which he loved" (v 68) and the establishment of the Davidic monarchy in the city of Yahweh's sanctuary is certainly compatible with the temple tradition. There does not seem to be any reason to suppose the psalmist to have antedated it. Again, while the division of the United Monarchy is not explicitly referred to, the separation of North and South in Yahweh's eyes (and, therefore, in the eyes of his people) is certainly indicated. The statements that Yahweh "completely rejected Israel" (v 59) and "the tribe of Ephraim he did not choose, but he chose the tribe of Judah" (vv 67b–68a) seem more vehement than any reference to the mere political separation of the two nations could be. Seen in this light, the actual fall of the Northern Kingdom is irrelevant. Once Yahweh had rejected it, it ceased to exist in any meaningful sense anyway. Its omission cannot be used as a reliable indication of the psalm's date.

Campbell's argument that the psalm belongs to the tenth century because that is the period that needed to assimilate the developments in the time from Shiloh to Jerusalem may be valid and deserves some attention; certainly parts of the psalm may be that old. The body of the psalm dealing with the disobedience and testing in the wilderness could have come from the Northern tradition, although its setting as an explanation of the disinheritance of Ephraim must have been added by a Southern editor. Vv 40–51 may be part of an older work describing the events leading up to the exodus (Briggs). However, one of the requirements for Campbell's argument is that "it is crucial that Ephraim/Jacob/Joseph is not to be identified with the northern Kingdom, nor Judah with the southern kingdom" (*CBQ* 41 [1979] 61), and this is difficult to countenance. He interprets Ephraim as "the old order" of Shiloh, while Judah is "the new order" of Jerusalem. This may be correct, but many of the phrases of this psalm would be offensive to the northern part of the newly United Kingdom that Campbell believes the poem to have been written to legitimate. No Northerner would likely have accepted religious literature which claimed that Yahweh "rejected the tent of Joseph and the tribe of Ephraim he did not choose. But he chose the tribe of Judah. . . ." (vv 67–68a); after all, Joseph was the honored progenitor of the Northern tribes of Ephraim and Manasseh, and Ephraim was the largest tribe in the region. Tribal loyalties were strong in that period; it is worth remembering that the United Kingdom itself survived less than eighty years. No one trying to provide a theological basis for the new nation would word it in a way calculated to offend half the country.

Carroll, arguing also that the psalm served to pave the way from Shiloh to Jerusalem, explains that its most pressing need was to legitimate Judah's claim to be the heir of greater Israel's salvation history. The Northern tribes preserved the exodus and desert traditions. Joshua, who mediated the covenant to the tribes in the land of Canaan, was from Ephraim. So was the great judge Samuel, whose tradition presents him as anti-monarchical (cf. 1 Sam 8). The Southern David/Zion tradition needed to be related to the complex of exodus and settlement traditions that were largely Northern property, and the only way to demonstrate Judah's inheritance of these traditions was to prove that Ephraim was no longer chosen. Consequently the anti-Ephraim language is very specifically anti-Northern. Moses is never mentioned. The only individual named in the psalm is David of Judah. While Carroll is reluctant to set an ironclad date for any psalm (see above), he sees Ps 78 as being at least extensively reworked if not originally written after the fall of Samaria.

Setting in worship. The setting of the psalm in worship is almost as controversial as its date. The speaker addresses a group in vv 1–5, and there is good reason to assume that the psalm was intended for use in public worship. Note the communal setting of the historical Pss 105 and 106 in 1 Chr 16 (cf. Deut 31:30; 32:44–54). Who was the speaker? Kraus (II, 703) suggests a Levitical priest, and Nasuti (*Tradition History*, 323–26) pursues this possibility further, pointing to its close parallels with Deut. 32 and 1 Chr 16, both associated with "Levitical performers." The psalm in 1 Chr 16 is specifically associated with "Asaph and his brethren," and the Levitical preacher who responds to the lament of King Jehoshaphat is identified as an Asaphite. Contexts like the ceremony of national lamentation in 2 Chr 20 would have been appropriate for the recitation of Ps 78 (Nasuti, 259–62, argues for the Asaphite psalms as belonging to such ceremonies, which in some cases may have been restoration ceremonies for the rededication of a defiled temple, with a high probability for a prophetic role in their recitation). Johnson (*CPIP*, 47) too argues that the speaker belonged to "the circle of cultic prophets who had so important a part to play in connection with the musical aspects of Israel's worship," although he dates the psalm to the time of Solomon.

Any one of the different functionaries in Israelite worship—kings, priests, prophets, teachers, and laypersons—could be the speaker in Ps 78, but we will probably be nearer its original design if we think of a prophet. The setting of the psalm need not be restricted to lamentation and restoration ceremonies. Its recitation would have been appropriate from the time of David on—perhaps, especially appropriate for the reform of Hezekiah (late 700s B.C.E.) when there was an attempt to unite the worship of the North and the South in Jerusalem (according to 2 Chr 30; cf. also Josiah's efforts in 2 Kgs 22:15–20). The suitability of the psalm for the Hezekian reform is argued at some length by Clifford (138–41, citing common language between the psalm and 2 Kgs 17:7–23). The use of the psalm in post-exilic contexts would have served to continue the emphasis on the choice of Zion and David—with an increasing futuristic emphasis, the Zion and David yet to be (as in Jer 31:1–6).

Literary structure. R. J. Clifford ("An Interpretation of Psalm 78"), noting the lack of consensus among commentators on the outline of the psalm's literary structure, has given the psalm a rhetorical analysis with good results. His outline in summary form is as follows:

Introduction: vv 1–11

First Recital:	Second Recital:
Wilderness events vv 12–32	From Egypt to Canaan vv 40–64
gracious act (vv 12–16)	gracious act (vv 40–55)
rebellion (vv 17–20)	rebellion (vv 56–58)
divine anger and	divine anger and
punishment (vv 21–32)	punishment (vv 59–64)
Sequel vv 33–39	Sequel vv 65–72

In vv 1–11, the speaker addresses all Israel with the intention of laying out a teaching about the true condition of the nation, recalling the infidelity and failures of her history with Yahweh. The first recital in vv 12–32 is a presentation of Israel's history in the wilderness, which is followed by a reflective sequel in vv 33–39 on the results of the wilderness experiences. The second recital, in vv 40–64, also focuses on the wilderness and Israel's inadequate response to the signs and wonders that Yahweh did in Egypt. The second sequel, found in vv 65–72, describes the intervention of Yahweh in action for Israel, his repudiation of Joseph / Ephraim and his choice of Judah, Zion, and David. I have adopted Clifford's analysis of the psalm in the *Comment,* with minor modifications. For a more complex analysis, see A. F. Campbell (*CBQ* 41 [1979] 51–79), who confines the introduction to vv 1–8 and divides vv 9–72 into two major recitals:

A. Recital of rejection   vv 9–64
  1. Rejection of Yahweh by Israel   vv 9–58
    a. Event and interpretation   vv 9–11
    b. First recitation   vv 12–39
    c. Second recitation   vv 40–58
  2. Rejection of Israel by Yahweh   vv 59–64
B. Recital of election   vv 65–66

This analysis has a good bit in common with that of Clifford, but it seems more unwieldy and less responsive to the text of the psalm.

The same is true of Coats (*Rebellion in the Wilderness,* 199–224), who argues for an introduction of two parts in vv 1–8 (vv 1–4 and vv 5–8), and four units of material in the verses which follow. Two units (vv 9–16 and vv 42–66), according to Coats, have their roots in the positive traditions of Yahweh's aid to Israel in the wilderness, matched by Israel's idolatry in the land. Two units (vv 17–41 and 67–72) have their roots in the murmuring tradition as it is known in the Pentateuch, with vv 67–72 being "untouched by the Deuteronomist"—arguing that the polemic of this unit "most likely . . . reflects the stimulus which gave rise to the murmuring tradition itself" (224). Nevertheless, the combination of these units into the present psalm belongs to a post-deuteronomistic date (after the fall of the Northern Kingdom), and probably much later, since the psalm as a whole reflects the connected account of wilderness traditions in the Pentateuch.

Comment

Introduction (78:1–11). The first verses of this lengthy psalm establish the intention of the author. Through it Israel is to learn "about riddles of things past" (v 2) that will teach future generations (v 6) to place their confidence in God.

1–4 The speaker urges the audience to pay heed to the "teaching" about to be offered. The word used, תורה, is found also in v 5, where it refers to the "instruction" (or, as above, "body of teaching") God appointed in Israel (a reference to the giving of the law at Sinai); the speaker seeks to pass on the "story" of God and Israel, which includes the commands that are part of תורה.

The knowledge to be conveyed is ancient, "riddles" handed down from previous generations that apparently must be understood if Israel is to continue as the people of God. The "riddle," of course, is not immediately accessible. It is not even explicitly stated, but apparently its solution lies in telling the "story" to those yet to come, a "story" of Yahweh's wonderful deeds and Israel's failures.

2–8 Israel has been able to know Yahweh in two ways. One way is through his words, the law that he has established for her. Even before the law, however, was the divine action: exodus preceded covenant. Both are necessary for an understanding of Yahweh and the way to live in relationship with him. In Deut 6, immediately after the giving of the Ten Commandments, Moses tells Israel: "And this is the commandment, the statutes and the ordinances which the Lord your God commanded me to teach you" (v 1); the people are told to "teach [these words] carefully to your children and speak of them when you sit in your house and when you walk along the way and in your lying down and in your rising up" (v 7). God's instruction is to be the subject of discourse among God's people. Deut 6:20–21 link the תורה with the tradition of the signs and wonders God has performed: "If your son asks you in the future, saying 'What are the testimonies and the statutes and the ordinances which the Lord our God commanded you?' you will say to your son, 'We were servants to Pharaoh in Egypt, and the Lord brought us out from Egypt with a mighty hand. . . .'" The commandments and practices need the tradition of God's active love to give them life and to set them in context. *Torah* is a combination of story and commandments; the commandments are understood in the context of the story and the story is incomplete without the commandments. Only by understanding the old traditions can the present generation avoid repeating the sins of the previous ones. Maillot and Lelièvre (171) point out that "the man without memory is not able to be a faithful man."

9–11 V 9 contains a reference to an occasion on which Ephraim failed God. The tribe of Ephraim, descended from the younger of Joseph's two sons who nonetheless received the greater blessing from his grandfather Jacob (Gen 48:13–20), was the strongest and most numerous of the Northern tribes. Its warriors had a reputation for fierceness in battle, and a specific instance where they showed cowardice before the enemy is not found in the Bible. Because the tribe was the largest in the North, it is reasonable to suppose that the reference is to the Northern people in general and not this specific tribe alone. Referring to a nation or a group by the name of a component part or of a famous ancestor is a common practice in Semitic poetry. It is found elsewhere in Ps 78 in vv 5, 21, 51, 67, and 71.

The incident referred to in v 9 has occasioned speculation. One's solution is, of course, dependent on the date held as the time of origin for the psalm, which is the subject of debate (see *Form/Structure/Setting*). One suggestion, coming from Campbell, is that this is a reference to the loss of the Ark to the Philistines described in 1 Sam 4. 1 Sam. 4:10 says that "each man fled" on that day, and Campbell sees this as constituting the rejection of Israel by God, who did not renew his association with his people until David's time, when he "awoke as from sleep" (v 65; for more on Campbell's argument see *Form/Structure/Setting*).

Weiser believes that v 9 refers to the lost battle of Gilboa at which Saul of Benjamin and his sons were killed (1 Sam 31:1–13). This constituted Saul's ultimate rejection by God and made the way clear for David of Judah to assume the kingship, an occurrence that obviously was of great importance to the author of Ps 78. While this battle was not lost through the cowardice of Ephraim or any other tribe, it did mark the end of the old order in Israel and the beginning of the Davidic era.

Haglund, on the other hand, argues for an evocation of the fall of Samaria, when the Northern Kingdom was destroyed forever (*Historical Motifs*, 89). Certainly the judgment of v 10 is typical of the Southern opinion of the North: 2 Kgs 17:7–18 states that Israel fell because the people sinned against Yahweh by following other gods and forsaking his commandments. This may well be the best solution, but there are not enough details given to make a definite decision easy. Perhaps at this point the psalmist felt no need to be too explicit. One of the psalm's themes is that God's people have constantly forgotten his goodness and failed to learn from their own history; thus v 10 could be a description of Israel's endemic behavior, not a reference to a specific event. If so, perhaps the verbs in v 10 should be understood as characteristic. Cohen (250) cites an explanation of v 9 by Jewish commentators, from a tradition based on 1 Chr 7:21, that the Ephraimites left Egypt on their own, without waiting for God's redemptive acts, and subsequently suffered a heavy defeat in a battle with the men of Gath— though Cohen himself understands the verse as directed at the tribe of Ephraim, whose lack of steadfastness is likened to well-armed warriors who run away at the time of battle. The value of the Jewish tradition is that it reminds us that the psalm may draw on traditions not recorded elsewhere in MT.

The recital of wilderness events (78:12–39). This section begins with a recall of a great "wonder" done by God in Egypt and witnessed by the Israelite ancestors (v 12). For "the region of Zoan," see note 12.a. There is no reference to Zoan in the exodus accounts in the Pentateuch. The text seems to merge the wonder in the region of Zoan with the crossing of the sea and the provision of water in the wilderness. There are two matched pictures, both using the verb בקע ("split") in vv 13 and 15: God "split" the sea and he "split" the rocks in the wilderness—note also the "sea" in v 13 and the "great deep(s)" in v 15, and the "streams" and "rivers" in v 16. There is no indication in vv 12–16 of the murmuring of the people recorded in Exod 17:1–7 and Num 20:2–13; the miracles in Ps 78 are of God's initiative and of pure grace (Clifford, "An Interpretation of Psalm 78," 132).

17–20 The recital of God's gracious and marvelous acts in vv 12–16 is followed by an account of the rebellion of the Israelites in vv 17–20. The people "continued to sin" against God defying him even in the arid wasteland of the wilderness (v 17). The statement in 17a, "they continued to sin against him," seems to relate back to vv 8–11 (so Clifford, 133). As the fathers "forgot" the wondrous deeds of God which they had seen, so the wilderness generation continued to sin by putting God to the test with questions about his power and ability to supply the needs of his people (vv 18–20).

Campbell (*CBQ* 41 [1979] 54–5) notes the harsh but balanced juxtaposition of the material in vv 12–20. Ten colons in vv 12–16 set forth the wonders of God's action passage of the sea, guidance by day and night, and provision for water (four colons for the first, two for the second, and four for the third)—followed by ten statements in vv 17–20 setting forth the rebellious spirit of the Israelites. The multiple nature of vv 18–20 stresses the willful and mocking nature of the testing of God—they did not ask God sincerely for food nor wait to see whether or not he would provide it.

As noted above, v 9 is difficult to fix historically, and it is also a problem for the logical development of the poem, interrupting the sequence of thought between vv 8 and 10. Campbell (54) notes that the plural subject of the verb, "they continued to sin," in v 17 cannot be the Ephraimites since they were chronologically later than the wilderness generation—at least in a logical sequence. The best solution seems to be to recognize that the poem does not move on the plane of historical chronology. Thus the chronologically later sin of the Ephraimites is put at the head of a series of transgressions because of (1) its paradigmatic nature and (2) because of the significance of Ephraim later in the psalm. The position of the behavior of the Ephraimites among the sins of the fathers is *historically* anomalous but *theologically* in order—the Ephraimites embodied the rebellious and forgetful behavior of the ancestors.

21–32 Yahweh is described as furious at the Israelites because of their failure to trust in him and rely on his power to save (vv 21–22). The verb for "trust" אמן is frequently translated by "believe"—"they believed not in the God"—in this context and in others. "Believe" is usually not a good translation in modern English. The basic ideas usually associated with the verb אמן are "constancy/stability/relying on/giving credence to/trust." Of course, they may involve the modern "believe," but the fundamental idea is "to trust/have confidence in/depend on"; i.e., to have faith in someone or something. Yahweh's wrath flared up because the Israelites did not trust him enough to depend on his saving work. "Old Testament faith is not (at least primarily) an intellectual consent to certain ideas about God. Rather it is an attitude toward him which takes seriously his commands and promises" (A. A. Anderson, II, 567; cf. Deut 9:23; Ps 119:66; Gen 15:6; Exod 4:31; 14:31; Jonah 3:4–5, 10). Faith in the NT is not essentially different. Trusting-dependence is at the heart of all discipleship.

There is an element of irony in the actions of Yahweh in vv 23–31. On the one hand, he demonstrates his power to provide for his people by "raining down" on them manna and meat. Note the use of the verb מטר, "to rain" in vv 24 and 27: Yahweh, like Baal, can produce a "rain" of fertility and abundance. Yahweh, who commands the winds and the skies, "rained" meat in the form of flying birds that fell in the camp of the people round about the dwelling place of Yahweh in the middle of the Israelite encampment (vv 27–28). No Israelite could have missed Yahweh's power to provide—manna and birds were falling all over the place! However, this abundance is not the result of pure grace; "unlike the Pentateuchal traditions of the graceful gift of manna, manna is here given under the sign of divine wrath, like the quail in Num 11:31–35" (Clifford, 133). Yahweh's response to Israel's testing (note the verb נסה, "test/try," in vv 18, 41, and 56) is to give them what they want and to strike them at the very moment when they are filling themselves on the food they craved (vv 29–31; note v 18). Weiser (541) comments that these verses make "evident how closely God's grace and his judgment are related to each other." The sad result is found in v 32: the Israelites kept on sinning and refused to trust in the wonders of God.

33–39 A sort of reflection on the divine actions and their results follows as a sequel in vv 33–39. The narrator recalls that the response of the Israelites was not totally negative. Under severe punishment, they repented and searched for God, remembering that he was their redeemer and source of security (vv 33–35), their Rock. But the turning to God was not genuine (v 36); it was done out of necessity and not out of steadfast loyalty and consistency of commitment to Yahweh (v 37).

In contrast to the history of the behavior of his people, Yahweh was (and is) compassionate, turning back from his anger to forgive and to remember their human condition (vv 38–39). The narrator reflects on Yahweh's compassion in juxtaposition with his wrath; the reader knows, of course, that the fury of Yahweh did not run its full course: "he did not fully rouse his wrath." His anger can rage terribly, but that is not his most essential nature (cf. Exod 34:6–7).

A second recital: a history of rebellion from Egypt to Canaan (78:40–64). Vv 40–41 introduce this section by placing the "whole wilderness time under the dark shadow of the wrath of God and the incessant testing (*Versuchung*) of the Holy One of Israel" (Kraus, II, 710). Israel's behavior in the wilderness was characterized by a massive forgetfulness: "they did not remember" (לא־זכרו; cf. זכר also in vv 35 and 39). The failure to remember the power and works of God is equal to forgetting: "They forgot his deeds" (v 11).

A series of divine acts of power and deliverance follow in vv 42–55. All the acts are gathered around "the day he ransomed them from the foe." The reference is to the deliverance at the exodus and related events. The "day " (יום) here means "time" or "times" and ties the diverse traditions into a single account. The plagues are the central feature of the "signs" and "wonders" of God, which were "not remembered" by the Israelites. The plague account is presented in a form independent of that found elsewhere, even from the account in Ps 105:27–36. The following table will help to bring the plague accounts into focus (the account in Exod 7–12 is composed of three traditions according to source analysis; for tables see Campbell, *CBQ* 41 [1979] 69; Haglund, *Historical Motifs*, 95):

Ps 78	Exod 7–12	Exod 7–12(J)	Exod 7–12(E)	Exod 7–12(P)	Ps 105
rivers to blood	Nile to blood	Nile to blood	Nile to blood	waters to blood	darkness
swarm (flies)	frogs	frogs	hail and lightning	frogs	water to blood
frogs	gnats	swarm	darkness	boils	frogs
grasshoppers (mosquitos; caterpillars)	swarm	livestock plague	firstborn	firstborn	swarm
locusts	livestock plague	hail and lightning		hail and lightning	gnats
hail and lightning	boils	locusts		locusts	hail and lightning
firstborn of Egyptians	hail and lightning	firstborn		firstborn	locusts
	firstborn				firstborn
	locusts				
	darkness				
	firstborn				

It is sometimes argued (see Haglund, *Historical Motifs*, 95) that Ps 78 represents the oldest version of the tradition and Ps 105 and Exod 7–12 are variants. Of course, if source analysis of Exod 7–12 is accepted, the J, E, and P accounts would be as old or older on this basis. However, this kind of argumentation inspires little confidence. It is much more probable that the plague traditions were relatively fluid and malleable enough to be fashioned in different ways for different contexts. The exact details of the plagues were not a matter of great concern. What mattered most was the impact of the account. The recital shows part of what the Israelites "did not remember."

The death of the Egyptian firstborn in v 51 is the climax of the dramatic description of the sending of a band of angels to prepare the way for the anger of God (vv 45–50). This passage has similarities to the account of the Destroyer (המשחית) who is not allowed to enter houses with blood on the lintel and door-posts in Exod 12:23 (cf. Exod 12:13; 2 Sam 24:16; 2 Kgs 19:35; Ezek 9:1–7; Heb 11:28).

The climactic act of God among those acts which the Israelites "did not remember" is set forth in vv 52–55: the safe leading out of his people from Egypt, guiding them through the wilderness, to be settled in his holy territory. His people were delivered, but God left their enemies covered by the sea (Exod 14:24–31). The "they were not afraid" (perhaps better, "they were not in dread," from פחד) of v 53 contrasts with the great fear of the Israelites before the Egyptians in Exod 14:10–14—though the Israelites learned to fear and trust Yahweh when they were delivered and they saw the Egyptians dead on the seashore (Exod 14:30–31).

Vv 52–53 summarize the guidance and care of the Israelites in their wander-ings. He "set his people moving" and kept them safe until he brought them to places to live in his holy land in v 55 (cf. Isa 63:14; 49:10; Ps 80:9; 1 Chr 17:21). However, the saving work of God was matched by the incessant rebellion of the Israelites (vv 56–58). They "tested" God (נסה, note the verb in vv 18, 41, and in Ps 106:14) and "rebelled" against him (note "rebellious" in v 8, and the verb in vv 17, 40; cf. Pss 106:7, 33, 43; 107:11). They were guilty of apostasy and faithless (or, treacherous) behavior (v 57), which provoked God to furious anger (vv 58–59). The result was the destruction of the sanctuary at Shiloh and the severe punishment of the people (vv 60–64; cf. 1 Sam 4; Jer 7:12, 14; 26:6, 9).

Clifford ("An Interpretation of Psalm 78," 135) correctly argues, I think, that the mountain of v 54 was not Mount Zion. His argument is based on (1) the correspondence between vv 44–51 and Exod 15:1–18: the divine attack in vv 44–51 corresponds to Exod 15:1–12, and the procession in vv 52–55 to Exod 15:13–18. He follows F. M. Cross (*Canaanite Myth and Hebrew Epic,* 112–44) in his argu-ment that Exod 15:1–18 is an Israelite adaptation in the pre-monarchical period of an ancient myth of a storm god's victory over the sea and his triumphant return to his throne. Also, the mountain of Yahweh's sanctuary in Ex. 15:17 was not originally Mount Zion, though it is understood as such in the present context of Exod 15:1–18. Thus there is no necessity of forcing a leap to the Zion tradition in v 54 (as in Kraus). (2) The shrine in v 60 is explicitly identified as Shiloh, and Zion-Jerusalem is clear in vv 68–69. Thus it is most likely that the poem considers Shiloh and Zion as "successive central shrines for all Israel" (135). Note the language of vv 54 and 68: "which his right hand got" and "which he loved"—"The destruction of one shrine does not mean that God will not choose another" (Clifford, 135).

Shiloh (v 60) was an early shrine of Yahwism in Canaan, the site where Joshua established the tent of meeting containing the ark of the covenant after Israel occupied the land (Josh 18:1) and where Samuel served under Eli (1 Sam 1:9; 3:1). It was destroyed by the Philistines c. 1050 B.C.E., at which time the ark was captured (1 Sam 4, Jer 7:12; 26:6). The "power" and the "glory" of v 61 are references to the ark (cf. Ps 132:8). As v 64 says, the priests of Shiloh (Phinehas and Hophni, Eli's sons) were killed on that day. Phinehas' widow was so shocked and horrified at the capture of the ark that she immediately went into childbirth and died, unable to mourn her husband (1 Sam 4:17–22). The loss of Shiloh was a theological problem for Israel, since the ark was the sign of God's presence with his people. The speaker makes clear in this passage that the destruction did not represent God's defeat at the hands of the Philistines but rather God's judgment on his own faithless people.

The Great Awakening (78:65–72). In the final section of Ps 78, God returns to his people and delivers them from their enemies He continues to reject the North, which has been the more rebellious part of the nation, but he establishes an even more glorious relationship with the South by giving them David his chosen king. These verses correspond to the sequel of the first recital of history in vv 33–39 (Clifford, 136).

65–67 In v 65 the Lord awakes "as from sleep." There are other places in the Hebrew Scriptures where reference is made to God's sleeping. In Pss 7:7, 35:23, 44:24 and 59:5–6 he is implored to waken and save his people, and in Zech 2:13 the return from the Babylonian Exile is described as God's rousing himself from his dwelling place. This should not be interpreted to mean that the speaker believed that Yahweh was really asleep; both Ps 121:4 and Isa 40:28 state the opposite. Instead, God's wakening is a vivid metaphor for what the speaker understands as the end of a period of divine inactivity in Israel's life. After the destruction of Shiloh, God had no dwelling among the people. The ark, which survived the battle, was returned by the Philistines and housed at Kiriath-jearim (1 Sam 6:1–7:2), but there was no shrine there to take the place of the one at Shiloh. The people suffered at the hands of the Philistines to such an extent that they chose a king to fight their battles (1 Sam 10:1). But under Saul there was still constant war with the Philistines (1 Sam 13–31 passim); it was not until his death and the coming of David that these enemies were defeated and Israel knew peace (2 Sam 8:1). To the composer of Ps 78, David represents Yahweh's powerful reintervention in Israel's affairs after the chaotic period of Samuel and Saul.

V 65 portrays Yahweh as a strong man "shouting from wine." This is generally understood as an even more daring image of God as having slept like a drunkard (Weiser, Dahood), but some commentators (e.g., A. A. Anderson, II, 576) suggest that the image is not of wine-induced sleep but of wine as a stimulant: God is roused with the sudden unstoppable vigor of the intoxicated. However, the imagery here is almost certainly that of the Divine Warrior who wakes from sleep to do battle once more for Israel (note Isa 51:9–11, where Yahweh is asked to awake and come forth as a warrior; also Isa 42:13–16). The background of the idea of the deity sleeping in the Baal traditions should not be overlooked (see 1 Kgs 18:27).

67–72 At this point God rejects the Northern sanctuary and the tribe of Ephraim as the locus of his worship. This is different from the rejection of v 59. When God "vehemently repudiated Israel" at the fall of Shiloh, he judged the whole people and removed himself from all of them for a period. Now he denies only the tent of Joseph and the tribe of Ephraim and chooses instead Zion and the tribe of Judah, upon whom he bestows the Davidic monarchy. The emphasis in this passage is not upon the rejection of the Northern tribes—indeed, Clifford (137) is probably correct to argue that the Northern tribes are not rejected at all. The issue is the location of Yahweh's chosen sanctuary and his establishment of the Davidic kingship. (Note the chiastic arrangement in vv 67 and 68: repudiated—tent of Jacob—tribe of Ephraim—no longer chose—chose—tribe of Judah—Mount Zion—he loved: ABBAABBA.)

The sign of God's choice of Judah is the fact that his dwelling is established in Zion and is as secure and eternal as the earth (Ps 132:13–18). It is the capital of David, his chosen king (2 Sam 6:21; 1 Kgs 8:16), who moved from being a shepherd of sheep (2 Sam 7:8) to being a shepherd of God's people. One of David's first acts upon making Jerusalem his capital was to bring in the ark of the covenant (2 Sam 6:1–19). Installing the ancient vehicle of Yahweh's presence with Israel in the new capital served to link David's regime with the religion of the period of the judges, but the most precious emblem of God's presence with Israel was David himself, the king chosen by God.

Explanation

This long psalm moves to a climax in the choice of Zion as the place for Yahweh's sanctuary and of David as his servant who will be the shepherd of Israel, which is Yahweh's "inheritance" or patrimony in the world (vv 68–72). The true continuation of the ancient pre-monarchical history of Israel continues in Zion and David, because God has rejected the worship in Ephraim. "The introduction of David is the climax of the argument [in the psalm], which has been carefully built up from the first with this conclusion in view. . . . By acting as the counterpart of the Divine Shepherd . . . he was to be instrumental in leading Yahweh's people along right paths and thus ensuring that the hopes which Yahweh continued to have for them might yet be realized" (A. R. Johnson, *CPIP*, 62). The recitals of the history of Israel in the psalm are not intended, of course, as mere exercises in historical epic. The history is the essential story, the root story, from which Israel understands her life in every generation. Parents are to pass on to their children the accounts of the great acts of Yahweh and his teaching, each generation passing on the teaching in a continual network (vv 4–8). The object is for each generation of Israelites to "put their confidence in God and forget not the deeds of God, but keep his commandments" (v 7). The psalm is "meant to search the conscience: it is history that must not repeat itself" (Kidner, II, 280).

The psalm also sets itself forth as a "parable," which speaks of "riddles" from the past (v 2). The "riddle" is the mystery of God's saving work in Israel's history and of Israel's behavior. It is the "story" which sets forth "the mysterious conflict between the power of God and the power of sin" (Weiser, 541). The psalm deals with terrible stories of Yahweh's own people's lack of faith, disobedience, and the consequences which followed, but it also is "meant to warm the heart, for it tells of great miracles, of a grace that persists through all the judgments" (Kidner, II, 280). There is an "irrational quality about the things that have come to pass" in Israel's history (Weiser, 538). The gracious acts of God are "irrational" (or perhaps better, "supra-rational") and the behavior of God's people defies all logical analysis. This is the "riddle" at the heart of the "parable" out of which the Israelites lived and out of which we live. Ours is a God who does not

> . . . perpetually rebuke
>   nor does he retain his anger forever,
> He has not treated us in proportion to our sins
>   nor has he dealt with us as our iniquities deserved.
>   (Ps 103:9–10; tr. L. Allen, *Psalms 101–150*)

Rather, his loyal-love toward us continues to be demonstrated through all our sin histories. The psalm establishes the point that "no matter how heinous the infidelity, God stands ready to begin again" (Clifford, "An Interpretation of Psalm 78," 138).

Ps 78 is referred to in the NT in several places. Matt 13:35 cites v 2 as a prophecy of Jesus' speaking in parables (apparently referring to Asaph in the title as a prophet). V 3 is alluded to in 1 John 1:1–4, as is v 18 in 1 Cor 10:8. V 24 is cited from the LXX text in John 6:31, Peter quotes from v 37 in Acts 8:21, and v 44 is evoked by Rev 16:4.

A Communal Complaint and Prayer for Deliverance   (79:1–13)

Bibliography

Brueggemann, W. *The Message of the Psalms: A Theological Commentary.* Minneapolis: Augsburg, 1984. 71–74. **Janssen, E.** *Juda in der Exilszeit: Ein Beitrag zur Frage der Entstehung des Literatur Judentum.* FRLANT 69. Göttingen: Vandenhoeck & Ruprecht, 1956. 19–20. **Nasuti, H. P.** *Tradition History.* 193–200.

Translation

1   An Asaphite psalm.[a]
 O God, the nations [b] have come into your inheritance;   (4+3+3)
  they have defiled your holy temple;
  they have reduced Jerusalem to ruins.
2   *They left the corpses of your servants*   (3+3+3)
  as food for the birds of the heavens,
  the flesh of your devoted ones [a] for the beasts [b] of the land.
3   *They poured out their blood like water—*   (3+2+2)
  all around Jerusalem,
  and there was no one to bury (the dead).
4   *We have become subjects of contempt to our neighbors,*   (3+3)
  of scorn and derision to those around us.

5	*How long, O Yahweh?*	(2+2+3)
	Will you be angry forever?	
	Will your jealousy burn like fire (forever)?	
6	*Pour out your wrath on* [a] *the nations,*	(3+2+2+3)
	those who do not know you; [b]	
	(Pour out your wrath) on kingdoms	
	who have not called on your name.	
7	*For they devoured* [a] *Jacob,*	(3+2)
	and devastated his living place.	
8	*Remember not (our) wayward acts* [a] *of the past;* [b]	(3+3+2)
	let your compassion come quickly to meet us,	
	for we are down and out. [c]	
9	*Help us, O God of our salvation!*	(3+2+3+2)
	For the glory of your name, [a]	
	deliver us and pardon our sins	
	for your name's sake.	
10	*Why* [a] *should the nations* [b] *say,*	(3+2+3+3)
	"Where is their God?"	
	Before our own eyes let (your name) be known among the nations	
	by the vindication [c] *of the outpoured blood of your servants.*	
11	*Let the groans of the prisoners reach you—*	(4+2+3)
	How great [a] *is your arm!—*	
	Reprieve [b] *those condemned to death.* [c]	
12	*Pay back sevenfold into the bosoms of our neighbors*	(4+4)
	the contempt in which they have held you, [a] *O Lord.*	
13	*Then we, your people,*	(2+2+3+3)
	the flock of your pasture,	
	will give you thanks forever;	
	to every generation we will declare your praise.	

Notes

1.a. See n. 51:1.a. and n. 73:1.a.

1.b. "Nations" is used here in the sense of non-Israelites; the peoples who do not honor Yahweh (cf. v 6).

2.a. On, "loyal ones," see n. 52:11.a.

2.b. Note the לחיתו ("beasts of"), cited as having an "old case ending (poetic)" by BDB, 312; also in Pss 50:10; 104:11, 20; Isa 56:9; Zeph 2:14. Dahood (II, 250) calls it an archaic nominative ending, in an anomalous position after a preposition (which would normally have a genitive), and suggests that it is a fossilized expression used by "a deliberate archaizer who no longer appreciated the fine points of case endings and their function."

6.a. אל is used in the sense of על, "on/upon." See *BHS*. Note Jer 10:25.

6.b. Or, "who have not known you." "Know" (ידע) is used in the sense of "acknowledge/respect/be well acquainted with."

7.a. MT has the singular, "he devoured." Some ms evidence and Jer 10:25 support the plural (see *BHS*).

8.a. More commonly, "iniquities." See n. 51:4.b.

8.b. עונת ראשנים is a phrase frequently translated as "the iniquities of our forefathers" (e.g., RSV, Kraus, Dahood, Gunkel), taking ראשנים as a substantive noun meaning "ancestors" (cf. Deut 19:21; Lev 26:45). However, the word is actually an adjective usually meaning "former" (cf. Gen 25:25; Deut 10:1–4; 24:10; Hos 2:9; Hag 2:3, 9); if read in this way, the phrase is "former iniquities" (BDB, Jacquet, Sabourin). Neither word has a possessive suffix ("our iniquities" or "our former/forefathers"), so in either case it must be added for smoother reading. Translating the phrase as "former iniquities" or "wayward acts of the past" fits well with the following verse, where the sins are not "our forefathers'" but "ours."

8.c. This is Dahood's colloquial translation of "for we are brought very low." NIV has "for we are in desperate need."

9.a. Lit., "concerning the word of the glory of your name." For רבד in the sense of "for the sake of," see Ps 45:5; Gen 20:11; Exod 8:8[12]; BDB, 184.

10.a. Dahood argues for המל with the nuance of "lest": "Lest the heathen should say"—which may be correct. Cf. Eccl 5:5; 7:16, 17.

10.b. There is some evidence for reading "Why should they say among the nations. . . ." (See BHS and LXX.)

10.c. Better than "avenging" or "vengeance"; see n. 58:11.a.

11.a. Reading the כ on ליגד as a kaph veritatis (see GKC, 118x), which gives emphasis.

11.b. The Syriac text indicates רתד for MT's רתוה (hiphil impv from רתי, "remain over/preserve"). Cf. Ps 105:20. MT would be hiphil impv or inf abs from רתנ, "let go free." The change is not significant, and MT may be retained.

11.c. Lit., "sons of death."

12.a. More lit., "their reproaches/taunts [with] which they have reproached/taunted you."

Form/Structure/Setting

Ps 79 is a communal lament. It implores God to take action against Israel's enemies in the face of national disaster, acknowledging that Israel has sinned and asking for forgiveness. The situation is desperate and portrayed in emotion-laden terms. There is no disinterested observation here; the speaker is deeply involved in the plight of God's people. This psalm is similar to Pss 44 and 74, both of which seek to move God to salvific action in the face of Israel's shame before her mocking neighbors.

Although the psalm appears to deal with a specific set of circumstances, scholars have not been able to agree on which event in Israel's history inspired it, which is also the case with Ps 74. Most consider both psalms to deal with the destruction of Jerusalem and the temple in 587 B.C.E. (e.g., Delitzsch, Briggs, Kissane, Jacquet, Dahood, Anderson). Kidner holds that the psalm comes from eyewitnesses of the final fall of the kingdom, most likely ones who remained in the land after the deportation.

However, there are some specific problems with Ps 79 that have led commentators to consider other solutions (see Gunkel and Schmidt, who think of some unknown event after the fall of Jerusalem and probably after the time of Ezra). The psalm makes no mention of any detail that matches only the destruction of Jerusalem by Nebuchadnezzar's soldiers and no other situation. It does not refer specifically to the burning of the temple, mentioned in 2 Kgs 25:9 and Jer 52:13, or to the uprooting of the whole people. According to Isa 35:8, 52:1, and Lam 1:10, the mere presence of the heathen in the sacred precincts of the temple would be sufficient to defile it; its destruction is not required. In addition, the references to "our neighbors" in vv 4 and 12 lead some to believe that Jerusalem had been invaded not by one nation, as was the case in 586, but by the troops of several (E. Podechard, cited in Jacquet). These verses are also sometimes interpreted as specific references to Moab, Edom, and Ammon; nations bordering on Israel and frequently engaged in wars with her, several of which have been offered as settings for this psalm. They plundered Jerusalem before its fall to Babylon (2 Kgs 24:2) as well as afterwards (Ezek 35:10; 36:5). The notes in The New Oxford Annotated Bible (RSV) suggest that both Pss 74 and 79 reflect "some otherwise unknown event of the post-exilic period (cf. Isa 64:11)." Finally, the fact that vv 2c–3a are quoted in 1 Macc 7:17 has led some scholars (e.g., Oesterley) to argue for the atrocities of Antiochus Epiphanes in the fourth century as the occasion for Ps 79.

In spite of all of these problems and theories, the time after the fall of Jerusalem in 587 seems to be best for the original setting of the psalm. The fact that it does not mention the burning of the temple is not so important; Ezek 25:3, which recapitulates the end of Jerusalem, refers only to the profanation of the sanctuary, and nowhere in the Book of Lamentations is the fire of God's judgment (1:12; 2:3; 4:11) specifically linked with the destruction of the temple. Further, it is not absolutely necessary to find a setting in which Israel's neighbors were involved in war against her, although in this case the antagonism that the speaker feels for the neighbors could be an oblique reflection of the Edomites' plundering of southern Judah during and after the destruction of Jerusalem by the Babylonians. As to the citation of this psalm in 1 Macc 7:17, Dahood points out that it is quoted there as scripture, indicating that it must have originated quite a bit earlier in order to have had time to attain that status. The fact that the psalm gives no concrete details tying its origin to the events of the fall of the Southern Kingdom does not mean that it does not reflect those events. The psalm seems to presuppose the same situation as that in Isa 63:7–64:11 [63:7–64:12], which H. G. M. Williamson ("Isaiah 63:7–64:11: Exilic Lament or Post-Exilic Protest?" *ZAW* 102 [1990] 48–58) has argued is an exilic penitential liturgy probably recited at the ruined site of the temple in Jerusalem before 515 B.C.E. Williamson relates the Isaiah passage more closely with Ps 106 and Neh 9, both of which he argues belong to the exilic period. He does not make much of Ps 79 except to note that it lacks any historical retrospect (56). There are no significant lexical parallels between Ps 79 and the Isaiah passage, but the situational relationship is strong enough to support their belonging to the same context.

Thus it seems most probable that Ps 79 belongs to a sizeable corpus of OT literature (including Ps 74) which emerged from the community which remained in Palestine during the exile and was used in penitential liturgies during that period. The relevance of the psalm need not be restricted to that period, however. Penitential liturgies were used throughout the post-exilic era, and Ps 79 continues to be used with the Jewish observance of the Ninth of Ab, which commemorates the destruction of the temple at Jerusalem. The fall of Jerusalem in 587 B.C.E. became a paradigm for all other invasions and oppressions.

Literary structure. The uneven literary structure of Ps 79 may be due, in part at least, to its anthological style. Stuhlmueller (II, 32) remarks that the psalm "belongs as much to the entire psalter as it does to Asaph." A considerable amount of the content of the psalm appears in other contexts. For example:

v 1c	see Jer 26:18; Mic 3:12
v 4	see Ps 44:15
v 5	see Pss 6:4; 13:2; 89:47
vv 6–7	see Jer 10:25
v 8c	see Pss 142:7; 116:6
v 9d	see Pss 23:3; 25:11; 31:4; 54:3; 106:8; 109:21; 143:11
v 10ab	see Pss 115:2; 42:4; Joel 2:17
v 11a	see Ps 102:21

v 11c   see 1 Sam 26:16
v 12   see Pss 89:51–52; 44:14; Gen 4:15, 24; Lev 26:18, 21, 24

These examples are enough to demonstrate that much of the language of Ps 79 is borrowed from the traditional expressions and words of Israelite laments.

The psalm can be outlined in various ways: e.g., Gunkel, Kraus, and A. A. Anderson divide into vv 1–4, 5–12, 13; Stuhlmueller has vv 1–4, 5–7, 8–9, 10–12, 13. Jacquet divides the psalm into two major parts: vv 1–7 and 8–13. A division into two parts seems sufficient to me, but the division seems better after v 5, which concludes the complaint in vv 1b–4. Thus vv 1–5 are made up of complaints and vv 6–13 are made up of petitions and supplications, except for the vow of praise in v 13.

Comment

The Complaint (79:1–5). The first section of the psalm describes the horror that Jerusalem has become. It presents her as totally vulnerable to human violence and mockery as well as Yahweh's continued anger.

1 The historical referent is not given, but the psalm most likely reflects Nebuchadnezzar's destruction of Jerusalem and the temple in 587 B.C.E. (see *Form/Structure/Setting*). "The nations" are, according to v 6, those who do not know Israel's God, and so they are heathen coming into the holy places of Israel. Generally Yahweh's "inheritance" is his people (1 Sam 10:1; 1 Kgs 8:35), but the reference here is inclusive and includes the land and Jerusalem. Although only the defiling of the temple is mentioned, its parallelism with the destruction of the city indicates that it, too, has been ruined. Jerusalem would hardly be described as "stone heaps" or "ruins" with the temple left intact.

2–3 These verses refer to the many people slaughtered in the taking of the city, but the actual massacre is too terrible for the speaker to relate. Instead, we see its aftermath: Jerusalem has become a city of the dead where the corpses outnumber those who could bury them. Certainly those who killed them would not perform such a service; throughout the ancient Near East, the bodies of the conquered dead were dishonored by being left as carrion (cf. Deut 21:23; Isa 14:18–19). Bones and corpses made a sanctuary ceremonially unclean and unfit for worship (2 Kgs 23:16). The pathos is greater in that the dead were those who were faithful to Yahweh, his devoted servants. Innocent as well as guilty perished in the sack of Judah's capital, and their steadfastness in relationship to God did not protect his saints.

4 Although the fighting is over, Israel's suffering continues. The people must bear the contempt of their neighbors with the misery of their physical conditions.

5 The destruction of city, temple, family, and friends was not the full extent of Israel's loss. The taunts of her neighbors she can bear; her greatest loss was the care of her God. The speaker knows that it is because of his divine anger that they have suffered so; because of God's anger, they are still in pain. Yahweh's wrath continues to burn although the fires that consumed the city have long since cooled, and the speaker laments the duration of the anger. Surely the carnage and destruction already experienced is enough. "How long?" is Israel's cry under judgment. See Pss 13:2, 44:24, 80:5, and 89:47 as well.

Supplications (79:6–13) **6–7** The people plead with Yahweh to pour out his wrath on the nations that have defeated his people. The enemies are described as nations and kingdoms who "do not know you"; i.e., they acknowledge no relationship with him, have no claim on him, and it is these godless people who have razed the temple and murdered Yahweh's holy ones.

8 Although the nations know no relationship with Yahweh, the people are quick to point out that they themselves have not always lived up to their commitments. There are indeed former "wayward acts" that can be remembered against them. Their sin has led to this judgment and they do not argue against it. Instead, they plead for Yahweh's judgment to be matched by his compassion, for they have no other hope.

9–12 In these verses the people beg for Yahweh's power to be joined with his forgiving compassion for the deliverance of his doomed people. Some of the faithful are in the prisons of their human captors (and others, perhaps, in the prisons of frustrated faith); only Yahweh can save them from their fate.

Frequently in laments Yahweh is reminded of the power he showed in creation (74:12–17) as well as in Israel's times of need (44:1–8). A petition is addressed to the God of Israel's salvation (cf. Pss 22:5–6; 44:2–5) for pardon and deliverance. The motivation for the petition is an appeal to the glory and honor of Yahweh's name. For the significance of appeal to the name of God, see *Comment* on 54:3. The appeal to God's name is an appeal to his reputation, which is what he really is. God's name is inextricably intertwined with Israel—ultimately it is God's glory which is at stake. Such is the boldness of Israelite prayer.

It is on this basis that the nations have taunted Israel. Their mockery is less of Israel's people than of Israel's God. The fact that the nation has been defeated and her people deported leads others to think that Israel's God has been defeated as well, that her much-vaunted special relationship with him has ended. To the nations, Israel is a people without king, nation, home, or deity. Certainly Yahweh's own people must have wondered about this as well. The loss of temple, king, and nation was nearly a deathblow to Israel's understanding of her relationship with Yahweh. To hear her deepest doubts and fears echoed sarcastically by her enemies was painful. It is apparently this insult to Yahweh that angers the people most. In desperate faith they pray that when they are delivered, when the innocent victims of vv 2–3 are vindicated, then those who have laughed at Yahweh's power will see it in action and know that they were wrong. Yahweh's strength is greater than that of the nations; he is able to deliver those that the scoffers have marked for death.

13 The last verse in the psalm foresees an end to this nightmare period of death, confusion, and isolation. In confidence the people assert that Israel is Yahweh's people, his flock, and that when his redemption comes they will recount his praise for generations. It is worth noting that the last word in the psalm is "praise"—hardly expected at the beginning of the psalm.

Explanation

This psalm deals with one of the basic issues in religious thought: how do the people of God cope with disaster in the face of God's seeming absence? The answer is: by hanging on to hope in him. The fall of Jerusalem in 587 B.C.E. was a horrible, bloody episode that changed the lives of all Israelites forever. The ones who survived had lost family and friends, some to death and some to captivity. They had lost their nation and their homes, all that had made for stability in their lives. But the disruption went much deeper than that. They had believed that, as God's chosen people, such a disaster could never befall them (Amos 9:10). They had thought that the nation would endure forever and that its Davidic dynasty would never fail and always enjoy God's love and watchful care (2 Sam 7:8–17; Ps 89:19–37).

The destruction of the nation, therefore, was a theological crisis as well as a political, economic, and social one. The problem was even greater than that, however. The temple had survived the Babylonian assault of 598 B.C.E. when King Jehoiachin, the legitimate ruler, had been taken away and his uncle was placed on the throne (2 Kgs 24:1–17). In the battle of 587 the temple itself—situated on God's chosen and beloved Mount Zion (Ps 78:68) and serving as his eternal abode (Pss 48:1–14; 76:1–3; 1 Kgs 8:12–13)—was burned to the ground (2 Kgs 25:9) and his faithful followers killed by heathen (Ps 79:2–3, 6). The destruction of God's own dwelling, his home on earth, was more than the loss of the national worship center; it seemed to indicate that God had either abandoned his temple and his people or had been defeated himself. This is apparently how Judah's neighbors interpreted the events of that year (v 10). Ps 79, therefore, is more than a response to the extremity of the situation in which Jerusalem's survivors found themselves. It is a heartfelt effort to integrate God into their understanding of the events that have wrecked their lives.

Ps 79 is not, however, an ordered theological assessment of the experiences of 587 B.C.E. and its aftermath. It is instead a desperate and honest plea for God to show himself to be the God that the people had always known, the God of their salvation. They had become a people with nothing. Conventional faith had been shattered along with everything else. In spite of this, they do not take the easy way made available to them by their neighbors of denying their God's existence and they are unable to believe that he is no longer concerned with them. In the midst of the chaos caused by the destruction of everything that had ever given them security, the people still hold onto faith in God.

This psalm is not particularly easy to read. It is full of anguish at the unspeakable things the people have seen and anger at those who are responsible for them. It is not pretty. It is not full of noble religious sentiments. It is too real for that. The people are too tired and confused to pretend. Instead, they tell God exactly what is in their hearts. They do not hide the pathos of their situation or their horror at the unmerited deaths of God's holy ones. They hope for a vengeance as bloodthirsty as the siege they themselves have lived through. Their faith and their need are great enough that they trust God with their honesty. They trust him with themselves, and what they are feeling is neither beautiful nor humane. W. Brueggemann (*The Message of the Psalms* [Minneapolis: Augsburg, 1984] 71–72) comments that "the psalmist only wants Yahweh to feel what we feel. It is like a patriot watching the flag burned, a lover watching his beloved raped, a scholar watching the library burn—a helpless revulsion that can scarcely find words." In this way the psalm points to an important theological affirmation: God loves us as we are. Christians recall that Christ died not for perfected human beings but for sinners (Rom 5:6–8). That does not justify sin and ungodliness, but it does assure us that God knows all about us. Our weakness cannot horrify him. As this psalm shows, we can trust him even with our weakness and unloveliness.

It must be noted that even in the people's cry for vindication—if not revenge—it is God's action they seek. They are asking for his deliverance, not trying to wreak their own vengeance. Although they have been unable to see his help in their immediate past, they have not forgotten his delivering power and have not lost hope that they will see it again. The psalm ends in v 13 with a vow of thanksgiving and praise forever, which Kraus (*Psalms 60–150,* 136) thinks expresses an assurance of being heard. It is, however, predicated on the response of God to the petitions in vv 8–11. Without divine help, there can be no praise.

This psalm continues to be recited at the Western Wall (Wailing Wall) of the temple in Jerusalem on Friday afternoons and, as noted above, is used in the liturgy of the Ninth of Ab, a fast day which commemorates the destruction of the temple. Part of v 3 is quoted in Rev 16:6, and v 6 is quoted in 1 Thess 4:5.

A Prayer for the Restoration of the Ravaged Vineyard of the Shepherd of Israel (80:1–20)

Bibliography

Beyerlin, W. "Schichten im 80. Psalm." In *Das Wort und die Wörter,* FS Gerhard Friedrich, ed. H. Balz and S. Schulz. Stuttgart: Kohlhammer, 1973. 9–24. **Eissfeldt, O.** "Psalm 80." In *Kleine Schriften,* III, ed. R. Sellheim and F. Maass. Tübingen: Mohr, 1966. 221–32 (originally in *Geschichte und Altes Testament,* FS Albrecht Alt. BHT 16. Tübingen: Mohr, 1953). **Gelston, A.** "A Sidelight on the 'Son of Man.'" *SJT* 22 (1969) 189–96. **Heinemann, H.** "The Date of Psalm 80." *JQR* 40 (1949/50) 297–302. **Hill, D.** "'Son of Man' in Psalm 80 v. 17." *NovT* 15 (1973) 261–69. **Johnson, A. R.** *CPIP.* 136–150. **Mettinger, T. N. D.** *The Dethronement of Sabaoth.* Tr. F. H. Cryer. ConB, OT 18. Lund: CWK Gleerup, 1981. ———. *In Search of God: The Meaning and Message of the Everlasting Names.* Tr. F. A. Cryer. Philadelphia: Fortress, 1988. ———. "YHWH Sabaoth—The Heavenly King on the Cherubim Throne." In *Studies in the Period of David and Solomon and Other Essays,* ed. T. Ishida. Winona Lake, IN: Eisenbrauns, 1982. 109–38. **Schreiner, J.** "'Hirte Israels, stelle uns wieder her!' Aulegung von Psalm 80." *BibLeb* 10 (1969) 95–111. **Thomas, D. W.** "The Meaning of רֹן in Psalm LXXX.14." *ExpTim* 76 (1965) 385. **Victor, P.** "Note on Psalm LXXX.13." *ExpTim* 76 (1965) 294–95.

Translation

1   For the leader; [a] according to *shoshannim;* [b] an *Eduth;* [c]
    an Asaphite psalm. [d]

2 (1) *O Shepherd* [a] *of Israel: Give ear;*   (3+3+4)
      the one who guides Joseph like a flock.
      O Cherubim-enthroned-One, shine forth, [b]

3 (2)   *before Ephraim, and Benjamin and Manasseh.*   (4+2+3)
            Rouse your mighty power
            and come for our salvation!
4 (3)   *O God, restore us;*   (2+4)
            make your face shine [a] *that we may be saved.*
5 (4)   *O Yahweh God Sabaoth,* [a]   (2+2+2)
            how long will you fume [b]
            at your people's prayers?
6 (5)   *You have fed them tears for food,*   (3+3)
            even made them drink tears by the keg. [a]
7 (6)   *You have made us an object of strife for our neighbors,* [a]   (3+3)
            and our enemies mock (at us) among themselves. [b]
8 (7)   *O God Sabaoth, restore us;*   (3+4)
            make your face shine that we may be saved.
9 (8)   *You transplanted* [a] *a vine from Egypt;*   (3+3)
            you drove out nations and replanted it.
10 (9)   *You cleared (the ground)*   (2+2+2)
            so that it took root
            and filled the land.
11 (10)   *The mountains were covered by its shade,*   (3+3)
            and mighty cedars [a] *by its vines.*
12 (11)   *Its branches stretched to the Sea,*   (3+3)
            and its tendrils to the River.
13 (12) *Why have you broken its wall,*   (3+3)
            so that vagrants [a] *may pluck its fruit?*
14 (13)   *Wild boars* [a] *root it up,*   (3+3)
            and field animals [b] *feed on it.*
15 (14) *O God Sabaoth: please turn* [a] *again,*   (3+3)
            look down from heaven and see!
            Inspect [b] *this vine—*   (3+3+3)
16 (15)   *the stock* [a] *planted by your right hand,*
            the "son" [b] *you made strong for yourself—*
17 (16)   *(now) burned with fire and cut down,*   (3+3)
        May they perish at the rebuke of your face! [a]
18 (17)   *Let your hand be upon the man of your right hand,*   (3+3)
            upon the son of humanity [a] *you made strong for yourself.*
19 (18)   *Then we will never turn from you.* [a]   (3+3)
            Give us life, and we will invoke [b] *your Name!*
20 (19) *O Yahweh God Sabaoth, restore us;*   (4+4)
            make your face shine that we may be saved!

Notes

1.a. See n. 51:1.a.

1.b. *Shoshannim* (שׁשׁנים) literally means "lilies," which may be either the name of a melody, or an unknown stringed instrument (Anderson, I, 50); *eduth* (עדות) means "witness" or "testimony." Regarding the "Asaph" ascription, see Ps 73:1. The LXX adds "concerning the Assyrians."

1.c. For עדות, "testimony," see n. 60:1–2.b. and n. 78:5.a.

1.d. See n. Ps 73:1.a.

2.a. Three participles with nominative force are used in this verse as divine epithets. Appeal is made to God as "one shepherding" (רֹעֵה), "one guiding" (נֹהֵג), and "one enthroned-on-the-cherubim" (יֹשֵׁב הַכְּרוּבִים). Dahood (II, 254) chooses to translate נֹהֵג as a participle with imperative force: "lead Joseph like a flock."

2.b. The hiphil verb form הוֹפִיעָה (יפע) is also found in Ps 94:1; for other forms see Deut 33:2; Job 10:3; 37:15; Ps 50:2; Job 3:4; 10:22. Ugar. texts (*CTA* 3.D.34 // 3.D.49) indicate that the term is related to battles between the gods and implies "shining" forth victoriously in battle. In Ps 80 the battle between deities is transposed into a battle between Yahweh and the enemies he shares with Israel (B. C. Ollenburger, *Zion: The City of the Great King,* JSOT SS 41 [Sheffield: JSOT Press, 1987] 72; P. D. Miller, Jr., *The Divine Warrior in Early Israel,* [Cambridge, MA: Harvard UP, 1973] 75–78). The petition seeks success from God for the tribes named.

4.a. This refrain (vv 4, 8, 20) contains two pleas to God expressed as hiphil imperatives: הֲשִׁיבֵנוּ "restore us" and וְהָאֵר "let shine." The call for God to "let his face shine" is a plea for a theophanic shining forth as in Ps 50:2 (also Asaphite) and Ps 94:1. It is also reminiscent of the Aaronic blessing of Num 6:24–26 (Anderson, II).

5.a. The divine epithet יהוה אלהים צבאות, which is found in vv 5, 20; Pss 59:6 and 84:9, is grammatically difficult. The MT scribes probably read it as equivalent to אלהים צבאות ("God Sabaoth") in vv 8 and 15, with אלהים substituted for יהוה (which would not have been pronounced in this Elohistic psalm; cf. Kraus, II, 719). Beyond this, it is probable that the *mem* was originally enclitic with the construct form אלהי; thus יהוה אלהי צבאות: "Yahweh, the God of Sabaoth" (see B. K. Waltke and M. O'Connor, *An Introduction to Biblical Hebrew Syntax,* 158–60). In later transmission of the texts, the enclitic *mem* became confounded with other common morphemes (in this case with the masculine plural ending ים־). The enclitic *mem* in this instance probably had a mild emphatic force ("God indeed of Sabaoth"), though it is possible that it was only stylistic with little or no strengthening force.

The two occurrences of אלהים צבאות (vv 8 and 15; not found elsewhere) are almost certainly cases of the substitution of אלהים for יהוה, and so the expressions were properly "Yahweh Sabaoth" in both cases. Perhaps the presence of the יהוה אלהים צבאות in vv 5 and 20 encouraged the use of אלהים צבאות, without יהוה, in vv 8 and 15. The retention of יהוה in vv 5 and 20 ensured that אלהים צבאות would be understood as יהוה צבאות, "Yahweh Sabaoth."

The epithet יהוה צבאות is frequently used in the OT, but the distribution of occurrences is uneven (see the chart in T. N. D. Mettinger, *The Dethronement of Sabaoth,* 12; idem, *In Search of God,* 152). For example, the designation does not appear in the Pentateuch, but is found 56 times in Isa 1–39 (only 6 times in Isa 40–55, and not at all in chaps. 56–66). It occurs 82 times in the MT of Jeremiah (but only 10 times in LXX). Its usage is limited in the Deuteronomistic history (11 times in Samuel and 4 times in Kings), and it does not appear in Ezekiel at all. On the other hand, it is found 14 times in Haggai, 53 times in Zechariah, and 24 times in Malachi, indicating a resurgence of usage in post-exilic literature. The designation יהוה צבאות is found 8 times in Psalms (Pss 24:10; 46:8, 12; 48:9; 69:7; 84:2, 4, 13), יהוה אלהי צבאות occurs in Ps 89:9, יהוה אלהים צבאות is found 4 times (Pss 59:6; 80:5, 12; 84:9), and אלהים צבאות appears 2 times (Ps 80:8, 15), for a total of 15 times for the epithet in the Psalter. Limited usage of the designation occurs in Hosea, Amos, Micah, Nahum, Habakkuk, Zephaniah, and Chronicles. The designation אדני יהוה צבאות ("Lord/my Lord Yahweh Sabaoth") appears a few times (e.g., Isa 3:15; 10:23, 24; 19:4; 22:5, 12, 15; 28:22) as does הָאָדוֹן יהוה צבאות ("the Lord, Yahweh Sabaoth"); Isa 1:24; 10:16, 33). The form of the designation as יהוה אלהי צבאות ("Yahweh God of Sabaoth") occurs fairly frequently outside the Psalter (e.g., 2 Sam 5:10; 1 Kgs 19:10; Amos 3:13; 4:13; 6:8, 14; Jer 5:14; 15:16).

The word צבאות (sing. צבא) means "armies" or "military forces" with reference to human affairs (e.g., Gen 21:22; 26:26; Num 1:3; Judg 4:2, 7; 1 Sam 12:9; 2 Sam 3:23; 1 Chr 7:4; Ps 60:12). It can also mean "compulsory service" of one kind or another (as in Isa 40:2; Job 7:1; 10:17; 14:14), and "service of worship" (as in Num 4:3, 23, 30, 35, 39, 43; 8:24, 25; Exod 38:8; 1 Sam 2:22). It is also used for the stars and heavenly bodies (e.g., Deut 4:19; 17:3; 2 Kgs 17:16; 21:3; 23:5; Isa 34:4; Jer 33:22; 2 Chr 33:3, 5; Neh 9:6).

T. N. D. Mettinger ("YHWH Sabaoth," 123–28) has isolated and analyzed a number of texts which provide insight into the meaning of צבא/צבאות with reference to the divine realm:

1 Kgs 22:19–23 / 2 Chr 18:18–22	"All the host of heaven" (כל צבא השמים) is beside Yahweh's throne on his right hand and the left.
Ps 103:19–22	"All his host" (צבאו, *kethiv; qere* has "all his hosts," צבאיו) is among the heavenly throng of his "messengers" (מלאכיו), "mighty ones" (גבר כח) and his "ministers" (משרתיו), who are exhorted to bless Yahweh.

Ps 148:1–5	The divine entourage includes "his messengers" and "all his host(s)" (כל־צבאיו or כל־צבאו) with the "sun and moon" and "all your shining stars."
Dan 8:10–13	The "little horn" grows great even up to "the host of heaven" and the "Prince of the host" (שׂר הצבא).
Ps 89:6–19	Yahweh Sabaoth (v 9) is supreme in the council of the mighty holy ones of the heavenly realm.

See also, Dan 8:10, 11, 12, 13; Josh 5:13–15 (where the commander of the army of Yahweh—שׂר־צבא־יהוה—meets Joshua); Isa 13:4; 40:26; and 45:12. Mettinger concludes that צבא refers to the heavenly council that gathers about Yahweh as the divine king: "the צבאות . . . alludes to the heavenly council, the צבא around the heavenly king" (126). This seems to be correct: צבאות refers to the agents (such as angels), powers, and heavenly bodies in the service of and under the command of the heavenly monarch, who is Yahweh.

The syntactical relation of Yahweh and Sabaoth has been the subject of considerable discussion. The traditional translation has been "Yahweh of hosts," viz. as a construct chain, which is usually considered to be a violation of Hebrew grammar. F. M. Cross (*Canaanite Myth and Hebrew Epic*, 65, 70) makes this grammatical feature an important element in his argument that "Yahweh" was originally derived from a causative form of the verb "to be" and was a sentence name for the high god El: "El—who creates—the Heavenly Armies." However, Mettinger (127–28) argues that the construct relation is "the least problematic option" (he prefers that the question of the construct relationship remain open, citing the "YHWH of Samaria" and "YHWH of Teman" designations from the Kuntillet Ajrud inscriptions; *In Search of God*, 133–35).

Regardless of its original meaning, we should probably take our cue from the יהוה אלהי צבאות forms ("Yahweh, God Sabaoth"). These forms may be secondary (argued strongly by Cross, 69–70), but they indicate how "Yahweh Sabaoth" was understood in the Israelite traditions. It is possible that the original designation was אל צבאות (note Mettinger, "YHWH Sabaoth," 134), which is preserved in the אלהי צבאות form. In any case, the epithet יהוה צבאות in conventional usage was probably used without reference to heavenly armies or hosts, but simply as an epithet consisting of an abstract plural with the meaning of "Powers" or "Powerful One" (thus, O. Eissfeldt, "Yahwe Zebaoth," *Kleine Schriften* 3, ed. R. Sellheim and F. Maass [Tübingen: Mohr, 1966] 103–23). In this sense, the word is an adjectival, descriptive genitive. Thus, the translation "Almighty" in NIV is probably not out of line: "Yahweh God Almighty." However, Kraus (*Theology of the Psalms*, 19–20) is wise to counsel that the more abstract qualities of the epithet be subordinated to its active connotations: "What it means is that the divine reality designated by יהוה (*Yahweh*) could include and connote the צבאות (*Sebaoth*) in the sense that in Yahweh's actions and in his exclusivity those features which were found in the צבאות (*Sebaoth*) are expressed in one being. Yahweh himself was and did that which was represented by the צבאות (*Sebaoth*)."

The uneven, and even odd, distribution of the epithet in the OT suggests that it involves a complex history of religion. Space excludes a discussion of the matter here. Mettinger (in *The Dethronement of Sabaoth*) has reviewed the work of other scholars before him and has gone beyond them especially in the Deuteronomistic materials (which substituted name-theology for Sabaoth-theology) and in Ezekiel (*kabod* ["glory"]-theology is substituted). Also, see *Comment* on vv 2–4 below for limited discussion.

5.b. Lit., "you smoke" (עשׁנת). Usually it is in conjunction with "anger" (Anderson, II, 583; Briggs, II, 207). The idea may be that God is "fuming" during his people's prayers (בתפלים) and therefore not answering them. But עשׁן is used with -ב in the sense of "against" (Ps 74:1). There may be a wordplay involved with the verb, since the noun עָשָׁן is used of smoke enveloping God in theophanic appearances (2 Sam 22:9; Ps 18:9; Isa 4:5; 6:4; 14:31), which is suggestive in the theophanic context of Ps 80—the "smoke" of Yahweh's anger replaces the "smoke" of his benevolent appearances.

6.a. The Hebrew שׁלישׁ indicates a measure which is one-third of a larger quantity (Anderson, II, 583). Gunkel and most others have assumed it means a "great stein" of drink (Gunkel, 354; Kraus, II, 554). In that spirit, "keg" is offered here.

7.a. Lit., "you have made us a contention/strife (מדון) to our neighbors." The RSV reads מנוד for מדון, meaning the neighbors "wag" or "shake" their heads in mockery (Gunkel, 354; Anderson, II, 584; etc.). The change to מנוד, "head-shaking/amazement" (cf. Ps 44:15), eases the reading: "You have made us a head-shaking for our neighbors" = "object of head-shaking." However, there seems to be no textual evidence for this change and LXX indicates מדון, "strife/controversy." If מדון is retained, the construction with לשכנינו could be considered as a so-called ethical dative, or more probably, a dative of interest, which expresses either advantage or disadvantage (R. J. Williams, *Hebrew Syntax*, #271; GKC 119s; 135i; B. K. Waltke and M. O'Connor, *An Introduction to Biblical Hebrew Syntax*, 206–9, refer to a "*lamed* of interest or advantage"); i.e., the enemies use the strife for themselves, for their own interest (not likely, "have strife among themselves").

7.b. Again, as in 7.a., an example of the so-called ethical dative, or dative of interest: our enemies mock among themselves; for their joy (*HOTTP*, 337).

9.a. The verb נסע means "to pull up" or "to move." "You plucked up a vine" could be used, as in NJV, and "brought" appears in more than one translation (e.g., NIV, REB, NRSV). The context rather clearly indicates that the vine was moved from Egypt to new ground prepared for it; thus, "transplanted."

11.a. Lit., "cedars of god" (אל), and some commentators translate this way (Gunkel, 354; Kraus, II, 554; Weiser, 547; Briggs, II, 202). Dahood cites similar usages in Ugar. to indicate the superlative, and translates "towering cedars" (Dahood, II, 259; also Cohen, 265).

13.a. Lit., "passersby" (עברי). However, the tone of this section of the psalm is not particularly neutral, as "passersby" would suggest. Therefore, "vagrants," with more negative overtones, may not be out of place.

14.a. Lit. "boar from the forest" (חזיר מיער). Not only is this an unclean animal, it is undomesticated. Briggs prefers the emendation "boar of the Nile" as the "most probable reading" (Briggs, II, 206; cf. Gunkel, 355). He supposes the suspended *ayin* in MT is a clue to shift the reference from an assumed original with reference to Egypt in order to indicate a reference to Rome. But the suspension is more likely due to the fact that this was assumed to be the middle consonant of the entire Psalter—a fact worth noting in itself, if it is true (see Delitzsch's note on this matter). The ע in יער ("forest") is elevated above the line in Heb. mss because it was assumed to be the middle letter of the entire Psalter (Ps 78:36 is the middle verse of the Psalter). The ע suggests the "eye"—in the scribal tradition it would connote the "eye" of God watching over Israel.

14.b. The exact meaning of the word זיז ("animals"?) is unknown. Victor ("Note on Psalm LXXX.14") believes it refers to the "leader boar," while Thomas ("The Meaning of זיז") believes it is some sort of insect. "Field animals" is a good guess.

15.a. The verb is שוב meaning to "turn" or "return." Many translate it with the meaning of "come back," but the sense of the psalm seems to be that God has turned his back on Israel. Thus the plea is to "turn around" and "look" toward us.

15.b. Lit., "visit." The verb פקד implies to visit for *action*, either for a gracious purpose or for a punitive reason (Anderson, II, 585). Dahood uses "take care of" and Cohen translates "be mindful" (Dahood, II, 255; Cohen, 265). It is in this sense that "inspect" is used: "Come and see, and do something about it."

16.a. The word וכנה appears only here in the OT and its meaning is unknown. The LXX assumed it was an imperative verb "restore" from כון (Anderson, II, 585; Briggs, II, 208). Gunkel and Kraus both use "garden" (וגנה; Gunkel, 355; Kraus, II, 554). Others have opted for "shoot," "sapling," "root," etc. Dahood and JB keep it ambiguous: "Take care of what your (own) right hand has planted" (Dahood, II, 255). In the context, it seems that the reference is to what God planted in v 10—the nursery stock for his vineyard.

16.b. Some commentators and translations omit this colon as an editorial repetition of the same statement in 18b, which has almost the same wording. Transposition in these verses is also suggested by some: e.g., Jacquet (II, 566) rearranges to read: vv 14ab, 15ab, 17ab, 15c, 16a, 18a, 16b (18b), 19ba. Such transposition inspires no confidence, but it is probable, however, that 16b is an editorial revision in order to re-interpret the kingship language in v 18 as applying to the vine, which is Israel.

17.a. This verse is not particularly difficult to translate, but it presents several problems. Is it a description of the situation, a curse upon the enemies, or some of both? Briggs omits the entire verse as the addition of a later editor (Briggs, II, 207). He believes the first part of the verse is a description of the situation: "She is burned with fire; she is cut off." But the second part is an imprecation against the enemy: "At the rebuke of thy countenance let them perish." Anderson essentially agrees with Briggs, but translates the first part: "They have burned it with fire" (Anderson, II, 586). Dahood's translation is similar: "Those who burned it with a full blazing fire—at your angry rebuke may they perish" (Dahood, II; similarly RSV, REB, NRSV, NAB). However, Cohen, Weiser, and KJV all translate: "It is burned with fire, it is cut down / they perish at the rebuke of thy countenance" (Cohen, 266; Weiser, 546; cf. NJV). Grammatically, the antecedent for the qal passive fem. sing. participles "one burned" (שרפה) and "one cut down" (כסוחה) is "vine" (v 15) which has been the topic since v 9.

Thus, the first part of the verse is a description of the destruction of the vineyard. However, the "they" of the second part of the verse is ambiguous, and could refer to either Israel or the enemies. If "they" refers to Israel, the devastation of the vineyard is the result of God's wrathful visitation (perhaps mediated by Israel's enemies). But if "they" refers to the enemies (so, e.g., Briggs, II, 207), it is a plea that God will turn his wrathful face upon Israel's enemies. It seems better to regard the enemies as the subject and to treat v 17b as a petition directed to God.

18.a. Lit., "son of mankind/humanity" (בן־אדם) = "human being."

19.a. Dahood is in the minority in translating this "we have never turned away from you" (Dahood, II, 255). It is a promise not to be disloyal *again* (Cohen, 266).

19.b. The verb קרא in this context (with ב) means to "call with the name" or "invoke the name" (cf. Gen 4:26; 12:8; 2 Kgs. 5:11; Jer 10:25 (= Ps 79:6); etc.). The meaning is to invoke the name of Yahweh in prayer, praise, curse, and blessing.

Form/Structure/Setting

There is almost universal agreement that Ps 80 is a good example of a communal lament. Westermann actually uses this psalm as an example of the form, illustrating its various parts: address and introductory cry for help, reference to God's earlier saving deeds, lament, confession of trust, petition, motifs, double wish, and vows of praise (Westermann, *Praise and Lament*, 53).

It is true that the communal lament form provides the general structure for the psalm, but there are additional features. One immediately recognizes a refrain: "O God, restore us, and let your face shine that we might be saved." This refrain occurs in vv 4, 8, and 20, consequently dividing the psalm into three parts (using the verb ישׁע, "save/restore" in each case). However, the refrain is not consistent. The address changes: "O God" (v 4), "O God Sabaoth" (v 8), "O Yahweh God Sabaoth" (v 20). Some commentators have assumed that the refrain recorded in v 20 is the correct one, and that vv 4 and 8 are corruptions of it. Thus they emend their translations accordingly (Anderson, II, 583; Briggs, II, 202; Gunkel, 351; Jacquet, II, 565–66; Kraus, II, 554). Most also assume that "Yahweh" is original and that Elohim was substituted (see n. 5.a.).

Some have not been satisfied with the natural division of the psalm into three unequal segments by the refrain and have suggested two other locations for it, resulting in a psalm of five strophes and refrains. Briggs, for example, inserts an additional refrain between vv 11 and 12, and sees in v 15 the remnants of a refrain ("O God Sabaoth: Please turn again"). Thus, v 15a is emended to the standardized refrain, and the fifth strophe begins, "Look down from heaven and see" (Briggs, II, 202; see also Gunkel, 351). Jacquet reads with a uniformly worded refrain in vv 4, 8, between 12 and 13 and between 17 and 18, and in v 20. Nonetheless, the imposition of a preconceived notion of poetic structure (strophes of equal length interrupted by a standardized refrain) has not been followed by everyone and has little to commend it (Cohen, 263–64; Dahood, II, 254–55; Kraus, II, 554; Schmidt, 152; Weiser, 545–46). The suggested insertion between vv 11 and 12 and the emendation of v 15a to be a refrain are especially problematic because they disrupt the poetic "Parable of the Vine."

Maintaining the integrity of the text, the following overall structure is offered:

Invocation and petition (vv 2–4)
Lamentation (vv 5–8)
Parable of the vine
    1. Recitation of God's saving acts (vv 9–12)
    2. Description of the vine's present condition (vv 13–17a)
    3. Petitions and vow (vv 17b–20)

The communal nature of the lament and the recurring refrain immediately suggest a cultic setting for Ps 80. We may think of it as a prayer offered in time of national disaster, perhaps as a litany with the people repeating the refrain after the priest offered each portion of the prayer. Can a more specific setting be described?

Setting and date. The LXX's addition of "concerning the Assyrian(s)" to the title represents a scribal attempt at contextualization of the psalm, probably with the assumption that it reflects the period of Assyrian conquests after 745 B.C.E., especially the time between 732 and 722 when the Northern Kingdom was destroyed. The use of the designations "Israel" and "Joseph" in v 2 with the mention of the tribes of Ephraim, Benjamin, and Manasseh may indicate that the psalm is concerned with the destruction of the Northern Kingdom by the Assyrians. It is an open question, of course, as to who is doing the praying and when. Is the psalm a prayer of the Northern tribes from their captivity in Assyria for their restoration? Or, is it a prayer from the Southern Kingdom (Judah) for the restoration of the whole nation after the fall of the Northern Kingdom in 722 B.C.E.? Or is it a post-exilic prayer for the restoration of the nation?

Modern scholars have adopted approaches similar to that of LXX. Gunkel (353) judged that the reference to the Joseph tribes and Benjamin indicates that the content originated in the North, with a *terminus a quo* of 722 B.C.E. The present psalm is later, according to Gunkel, but it derived its content from the former Northern tribes (Gunkel and Begrich, *Einleitung in die Psalmen*, 139). Gunkel's judgment of the Northern derivation of the content (or at least part of it) has received rather widespread support (e.g., T. H. Robinson in Oesterley, 366 [conditions of Northern Israel after 721 B.C.E.]; Weiser, 547; Dahood, II, 255; Anderson, II, 581, is uncertain).

The Northern origin of the psalm received strong support from Eissfeldt in 1953 when he argued for dating it during the time of Hoshea ben Elah (2 Kgs 15:29–30), who murdered his predecessor Pekah ben Remaliah about 732 B.C.E. and reigned until he was taken captive by the Assyrians in 722 ("Psalm 80," 227–32; "Psalm 80 und Psalm 89" [1964] 132–36). Kraus (*Psalms 60–150,* 141) rejects Eissfeldt's effort, saying, "This dating is altogether too bold an attempt at an explanation." Kraus himself (140) is more comfortable with the arguments of those like Schmidt (153) who locate the psalm in Judah and Jerusalem, probably during the time of Josiah when there was a strong idea of the restoration of the old union of twelve tribes and when Josiah may actually have extended his control into the old territories of Ephraim, Benjamin, and Manasseh (following M. Noth, *The History of Israel,* tr. S. Godman [New York: Harper & Brothers, 1958] 273–74). The refrain in vv 4, 8, and 20 with its prayer for restoration correlates well with this context.

Other scholars have turned away from a purely historical and geographical approach to tradition-historical interpretations. Among these are W. Beyerlin ("Schichten im 80. Psalm"), who begins with the conclusion that vv 2–3 are the oldest stratum of the psalm; probably stemming from the pre-monarchical period of Israel's history (11). The communal lament in vv 5–7, 17b–19 was integrated with the early prayers in vv 2–3 by the use of the refrain in vv 4, 8, and 20. This was probably done during the time of Josiah, according to Beyerlin (17, 19), when there would have been concern for the distress of the occupied Northern territories. The vine passage in vv 9–17a is an allegorical interpolation added to the basic psalm in vv 2–7, 17b–20 and was brought into the psalm after 587 B.C.E. (119). Thus the opinion of some commentators that Ps 80 as a whole originated from the post-587 period is not groundless, according to Beyerlin (15).

Nasuti (*Tradition History*) is more interested in relating the psalm to a tradition than to a precise determination of the historical development of the tradition. He examines Ps 80 in the context of his thesis that the Asaphite psalms belong to the Ephraimite tradition; the psalms are part of the *traditum* (traditional content itself) of the Ephraimite *traditio* (the process of passing on the *traditum*). The Ephraimite tradition originated in the pre-monarchical period of Israel's history and was at home in the Northern Kingdom, but actually had a Southern locus (frequently peripheral, except during the reigns of Hezekiah and Josiah) for most of its history (205).

Nasuti concentrates on linguistic links and features in the Asaphite psalms and the Ephraimite tradition. In the case of Ps 80, he notes the following distinctive words and expressions:

צאן, "sheep/flock," for the people	v 2 and Pss 74:11; 77:21; 78:52; 79:13; 95:7; 100:3
יוסף, Joseph	v 2 and Pss 77:16; 78:67; 105:17
עשן, "be angry/fume"	in v 5, Ps 74:1; Deut 29:19
נסע, "pull out/lead out" (hiphil)	v 9 and Ps 78:52
זיז שדי, "field animals	in v 14 and Ps 50:11.
Also, הופיעה, "shine forth"	in v 2 and Ps 50:2
and נהג, "one who guides"	in v 2 and Ps 78:2

Further, the tradition elements in the psalm's central metaphor of the vine in vv 9–17 are compatible with Northern traditions; see Hos 10:1; cf. 14:6–7; Jer 2:21 (used with נטע, "planted," as in Ps 80:9), cf. Exod 17:17; 2 Sam 7:10; Amos 9:15; Jer 11:17; Ps 44:2. The use of the vine image in Ezekiel (chap. 17; 19:11) is a later allegorical elaboration of the earlier metaphor (204).

Nasuti does suggest that the imagery of the walled vineyard in v 13 (פרצת גדריה, "you have broken down her wall/fence") reflects a stream of Southern tradition like that in Isa 5:3 (פרץ גדרו, "breaking its wall"). In fact, Nasuti says that though the listing of tribes in v 2 and the image of the vine both reflect a dominant Northern locus, they betray some links to the South upon close analysis. The grouping of Ephraim, Benjamin, and Manasseh would be "most at home in such times of Ephraimite ascendency as the reign of either Hezekiah or Josiah" (205), because in both periods some efforts were made out of Jerusalem to reclaim parts of the Northern Kingdom. The possible link with Isaiah supports this historical conclusion, and also represents at least a minor opening to another stream of tradition associated with Judah. Such openness is not really surprising because the Ephraimite tradition established itself in Jerusalem, especially after 722 B.C.E.

Nasuti (206–9) notes two or three parallels between Ps 80 and Jeremiah: obviously the use of the verb "plant" (נטע), used of the vine in vv 9 and 16, with Jer 1:10; 2:21; 11:17; 12:2; 18:8; 24:6; 31:28; 32:41; 42:10; 45:4 (its other usages are found in Exod 15:17; Ps 44:3 [note the close parallel to 80:9]; Ezek 36:36; Num 24:6; 2 Sam 7:10 [= 1 Chron. 17:9]; Amos 9:15—the last three references are arguably from the Ephraimite stream of tradition). Also note the use of אכל (hiphil, "fed") and שקה (hiphil, "give to drink") in v 6 with Jer 9:14 and 23:15 (cf. Ps 42:4; Jer 2:14; 19:9; 25:15, 17). Nasuti does not note the major use of "shepherd" (Ps 80:2) in Jeremiah (see Jer 2:8; 3:15; 10:21; 12:10; 17:16; 22:22; 23:1–4; 25:34, 35, 36; 31:10; 33:12; 43:12; 49:19; 50:6, 44; 51:23). Also the designation "Sabaoth" (80:8, 15, 20) occurs some 82 times in the Book of Jeremiah (56 times in Isa 1–39, but it does not appear at all in Ezekiel; Mettinger, *In Search of God,* 152). Other scholars have suggested that Ps 80 relates well to the preaching of Jeremiah in Jer 30–31. The compatibility of the psalm with Jeremiah strengthens its relatedness to the Ephraimite tradition since Jeremiah seems to have belonged to this stream in its Jerusalem locus (R. R. Wilson, *Prophecy and Society in Ancient Israel* [Philadelphia: Fortress, 1980] 231–51). This relatedness also strengthens the case for a date for the psalm during the time of Josiah (c. 640–609 B.C.E.).

The descriptive title "the Cherubim-enthroned One" in v 2 seems to be well established in the Ephraimite tradition, probably originating from the worship center at Shiloh in the pre-monarchical period, but which was transferred to Jerusalem and was at home there (1 Sam 4:4; 2 Sam 6:2 [= 1 Chr 13:6]; 2 Kgs 19:15 [= Isa 37:16]; cf. 1 Kgs 6:23, passim; 7:29, 36; 8:6, 7; Nasuti, 208–9; Kraus, *Psalms 60–150,* 141; see note Ps 88:1.c.). The same is true for "Yahweh Sabaoth" (Ps 80:4, 8, 5, and 20; see note 5.a.; Mettinger, "YHWH Sabaoth," 128–38).

This discussion is sufficient to demonstrate that firm conclusions about the dating of Ps 80 are hard to come by. Vv 1–3 may go back to ancient sanctuaries at Gilgal and Shiloh when the three tribes mentioned in v 3 were dominant. On the other hand, the cumulative indications for the historical context of the whole psalm in the time of Josiah is rather strong. Heinemann (*JQR* 40 [1949/50] 297–302) argues for the identification of the "man of your right hand" (איש ימינך) in v 18 as Saul, whose father is said to be איש מבן־ימין ("a man from Benjamin") in 1 Sam 9:1 איש ימיני, "a Benjamite man" is found later in this verse and also in 2 Sam 20:1; Esth 2:5 [Mordecai]). Heinemann (301) contends that "The psalm must have been composed in the time of Saul. Thus it becomes obvious why the author should think that the salvation of Israel depends on Benjamin, or rather on the איש ימיני." But if the איש ימינך in v 18 is a king (which is not at all certain), it probably refers to the Davidic king, who is told by Yahweh to "sit at my right hand" (ישב לימיני); see Beyerlin ("Schichten," 13). In this case, the psalm can hardly date to the time of Saul. Nasuti's arguments for relating Ps 80 to the Ephraimite tradition are persuasive, but this conclusion may not help us very much since the Ephraimite stream of theology was so wide and was at home geographically both in the North and in the South and historically both in pre-exilic and post-exilic Israel. Beyerlin may be correct in his judgment of the vine metaphor as the latest stratum of the psalm.

It seems plausible to argue that the present psalm originated in the period of Josiah and Jeremiah (and Ezekiel; note the shepherd metaphor in Ezek 34; 37:24; Zimmerli, *Ezekiel* 2, Hermenia, tr. J. D. Martin [Philadelphia: Fortress, 1983] 214, who says that Jer 23:1–4 is "unmistakably the model for Ezekiel 34"); i.e., c. 640–587 B.C.E. On the other hand, when the nature of psalm formation is considered, with the extensive use of traditional language, stock metaphors, and whole poetic sections, there is no reason to exclude the possibility that a skilled Asaphite scribe composed the psalm in the post-exilic era, or, more probably, reworked an older psalm into the present psalm. V 18 is not an insuperable difficulty for this view. The איש ימינך ("man of your right hand") may be a reference to the vine in v 16 (ימינך נטעה, "planted by your right hand") and/or to Benjamin (בנימין, "son of the right [hand]," v 3). The "son of humanity" (or, "human son") in 17b may be a reference to the "sonship" of Israel in relation to Yahweh (see Exod 4:22–23; Hos 11:1; Ephraim is called Yahweh's firstborn in Jer 31:9). The scribal writer may have intentionally applied kingship language to the vine (Israel) in order to reinterpret such language for Israelites when the Davidic monarchy no longer existed.

Another option is the possibility that v 18 refers to the messianic expectations which gathered around Zerubbabel in the late sixth century B.C.E. (see HAG 1:1; 2:2, 20–23; Zech 4:6b–10a; Ezra 3:2, 8; 4:2, 3), who is referred to as "the Branch" (איש צמח) in Zech 3:8 and 6:12 (cf. Jer 23:5; 33:15), or possibly some other potential messianic king in the post-exilic time. It may be worthy of note that the vine (גפן) in Ezek 17 is allegorized in terms of kingship. It seems rather certain that messianic expectations in the post-exilic period could be conceptualized in terms of growing plants (cf. D. L. Petersen, *Haggai and Zechariah 1–8*, OTL [Philadelphia: Westminster, 1984] 210; KB, 867, n. j.; cf. Isa 4:2 in addition to the references above). The Targum's indication that v 18 was read as a prayer for a messiah, a new "man of your right hand" and "son of man," may represent an old interpretation of this verse. Further, the "son of humanity" in 18b may reflect tradition like those associated with the "one like a son of humanity" in Dan 7:13–14 (cf. Kraus, *Psalms 60–150*, 143). However, I think this option is less likely than that of the re-interpretation of kingship in terms of the nation.

The naming of the three tribes, Ephraim, Benjamin, and Manasseh, in v 3 can of course go back to a pre-monarchical source (as noted above), or reflect the movements of Josiah in his efforts to reclaim the territory of the old Northern Kingdom. However, it is possible that the selection of tribes resulted from scribal exegesis of older writings in the post-exilic period. The three tribes are in the order of march immediately behind the Ark in Num 2:17–24. Perowne (84) remarks: "This explains their mention in the Psalm. The prayer of the Psalmist is, that God would again lead His people, again go forth at the head of their armies as He did of old." He continues to say that the psalm is a prayer for national restoration, "for the same divine succour which had been so signally vouchsafed to their fathers in the wilderness" (I should add that Perowne is arguing for the psalm as having originated fairly early in the history of the Northern Kingdom, but his observations are valid for a post-exilic scribal interpretation which I suggest as possible). The reference to Joseph, as a name for Israel, in v 2 would naturally lead to the Rachel triad of tribes in v 3, regardless of the historical ambiguities of the political relationship of Benjamin to Ephraim and Manasseh (Ephraim, Manasseh, and Benjamin appear together in this order in the tribal lists in Num 1:5–15; 1:20–43; 2:3–31; 7:12–83; 10:14–28; Gen 46:8–27; the listing varies in Num. 26:5–51; 34:16–29; cf. Gen. 49:3–27; only Num. 13:4–15 has Ephraim, Benjamin, and Manasseh in that order, but Zebulun intervenes between Benjamin and Manasseh). The absence of Judah is striking, but the Rachel tribes, sons of Jacob-Israel, may have been understood as representative of all Israel in a post-exilic context (note Jer 31:15–26). Possibly there was the idea of going back to pre-monarchical traditions as the basis for a new future. Thus the date and provenance of this psalm remain open questions, but I suspect that the present psalm stems from post-exilic scribal interpretation and that it was used as a prayer of lamentation during this period.

Comment

Invocation and petition (vv 2–4). The psalm begins with one of the great titles for Yahweh: Shepherd—though it appears directly in the Psalter only in Ps 23:1 and here. The designation "Shepherd of Israel" appears only here in the OT, but the idea is a common one. In Gen 48:15, Jacob, having blessed Ephraim and Manasseh (with crossed arms so that his right hand was on Ephraim's head, who was the younger), turns to bless Joseph and in his blessing refers to "the God who has been my shepherd all my life to this day" (הָאֱלֹהִים הָרֹעֶה אֹתִי מֵעוֹדִי עַד־הַיּוֹם הַזֶּה). The concept is in the song at the sea in Exod 15:13, although neither the noun or the verb is used:

> In your unfailing love [בְחַסְדְּךָ]
> you will lead [נָחִיתָ] the people
> you have redeemed.
> In your strength you will guide [נֵהַלְתָּ] them
> to your holy dwelling. (NIV)

See Johnson, *CPIP*, 139; also 2 Sam 24:17; Ezek 34:11–16, 31c ("And you are my sheep, the sheep of my pasture, and I am your God, says the LORD God," RSV); Ps 100:3. "Shepherd" is a widely used metaphor for kingship, and appears both in ancient Near Eastern literature and in the OT (in the OT, see Ps 78:71; 2 Sam 5:2; Jer 10:21; 23:1–4; Ezek 34:1–10; for nonbiblical references, see Zimmerli, *Ezekiel* 2, 213). Christian readers will recognize the powerful use of the shepherd metaphor in Luke 15:1–7 and John 10:1–21.

For the epithet "Cherubim-enthroned One," see *Form/Structure/Setting*. In combination with Yahweh Sabaoth, it probably originated in Israelite traditions from the worship at the sanctuary at Shiloh (1 Sam 4:4; 2 Sam 6:2), though both designations came to be at home in Jerusalem (2 Kgs 19:14–16; Pss 18:11; 97:2; 99:1). The imagery of "enthroned on the cherubim" seems to carry at least three ideas: (1) the mobility of Yahweh, who comes to his people in times of need and manifests his power in deeds of deliverance; (2) the divine warrior who rides his throne chariot across the heavens and through the storm to save (Ps 18:8–18); (3) the one whose great wings provide relief and protection for those who are under them (Ps 91:4; cf. Deut 33:11–12).

The Shepherd of Israel is implored to "give ear" to the speaker's petition, to guide (נֹהֵג) Jacob like a flock, and to "shine forth" (הוֹפִיעָה, see Pss 50:2; 94:1) in a dazzling display of his theophanic glory. He is urged to rouse his mighty power and come forth for the saving of his people (v 3).

The petitions in vv 2–3 use four imperatives: *Give ear* (הַאֲזִינָה), *shine forth* (הוֹפִיעָה), *rouse* (עוֹרְרָה), and *come* (לְכָה). The parallel with the deliverance from Egypt is striking. In the call of Moses, Yahweh says, "I have seen, I have heard, I am concerned, so I have come to lead" (Exod 3:7–8). The speaker illustrates a strong faith based on the firm foundation of tradition (Weiser, 547). He longs for Yahweh to appear in theophanic glory and "shine forth" as he did at the beginning of Israel (Exod 25:10; Deut 33:2; Pss 50:2; 94:1). By implication, the cause of the present calamity is the *absence* of Yahweh, with resultant darkness and devastation (Dahood, II, 555–56). The metaphor is bold: God must be sleeping! Therefore, he must "rouse himself" and "come."

The refrain both concludes and summarizes the plea, which is reiterated at v 8 and v 20. "Restore us" is a hiphil imperative (הֲשִׁיבֵנוּ) from the root שׁוב ("turn"), and could be translated "O God cause us to turn," or "O God turn us." A broken relationship exists, and only a new covenant, or at the very least the renewal of the previous covenant, can restore Israel (Anderson, II, 582). It is possible that the speaker is also begging God to "help the exiled tribes to repent, as the essential preliminary to their restoration" (Cohen, 263). "Restoration" is not just a readjustment of the material situation in Israel; the content of the psalm makes it clear that physical well-being is of major concern. "Restore" applies simultaneously to external welfare and what takes place in the human soul (*metabasis* and *metanoia;* Weiser, 548). This is a cry for "re-creation" in a comprehensive sense. Causing the face to shine (v 4b) is a sign of favor and good will (cf. Num 6:25).

Complaint (vv 5–8). After the invocation and petition the psalm moves to the complaint. Laments have a threefold dimension: interior ("us"), exterior ("them" or "enemies"), and divine being ("Thou") (Westermann, *Praise and Lament*, 53). Each dimension is found in Ps 80. The "us" is a picture of bitterness and absolute powerlessness. The "enemies" have joy among themselves as they mock the Israelites, which is more probable than a reference to the enemies as fighting among themselves for the spoils of the nation they have overcome (see note 7.a.). The divine "Thou" has turned a deaf ear, fuming in anger even at the prayers of the people (v 5). Cohen (264) refers the reader to Lam 3:44: "Thou hast covered Thyself with a cloud [of smoking wrath], so that no prayer can pass through."

The "How Long?" in v 5 (עַד־מָתַי) is a fairly common feature in laments. It suggests that the endurance of the people is nearly exhausted. The imagery of "tears" as "food" appears in Isa 30:20 and Hos 9:4. God's neglect is being deliberately contrasted with his care in the wilderness where the people dined on manna and quail and had fresh water provided from rocks. The "How long?" is not a rejection of punishment itself. Rather, it implies that the punishment is deserved: "Why?" is not asked. The thing at issue is the claim that the punishment has gone on "long enough!" (Anderson, II, 583).

The affliction is fundamentally a trial of faith (Weiser, 548). Yet the people hope enough to offer this lament. That is the paradox of faith: "God has chastised; therefore he will also heal" (Weiser, 549). God has led Israel out of bondage and created a nation before; he can do it again. The appearance of the refrain in v 8 at the close of this section sounds with a note of urgency. "God Sabaoth: this has gone on long enough!" For "Sabaoth," see note 5.a.

The great vine, now ravaged (vv 9–17a). These verses form an extended section of poetry which could be called a "Parable of the Vine." The vine and vineyard are well-known symbols of the people of God (Anderson, II, 584). In his blessing of Joseph, Jacob promises he will be a "flourishing vine" (Gen 49:22). The prophets especially use the imagery, perhaps its most beautiful expression being that of Isaiah in his "Song of the Vineyard" (Isa 5:1–7; also see 27:2–6; Jer 2:21; 12:10; Ezek 15:1–8; 19:10–14; Hos 10:1; cf. John 15:1–6).

The exodus is recast as God's "plucking up" a vine out of Egypt to plant in his vineyard. Israel is repeatedly described as having been "planted" in Canaan, even when trees and vines are nowhere in the context (Briggs, II, 205). Yahweh is an active vinedresser, who cleared a place for the vine he "plucked" out of Egypt (v 9). The verbs of vv 9–10 emphasize God's causative action in the establishment of the vineyard (Dahood, II, 258). God took the vine out of Egypt and cleared the ground so that it took root and filled the land. Obviously, it is an allegory of the total conquest of the promised land. The vine has incredible size, as it covers mountains, mighty cedars, and reaches out its branches and tendrils from the sea to the river. Vv 11 and 12 are not just poetic pictures of a land dominated by a vine; they parallel the dimensions of the land promised in Deut 11:22–25. Cohen (265) finds the four points of the compass in "mountains," "cedars," "sea," and "river," but this goes too far. The land was filled from the Sinai mountain range in the south, to the cedars of Lebanon in the north; from the shores of the Mediterranean in the west, to the bank of the Euphrates in the east. The thought in historical terms can hardly be of anything else but of the great empire of David, whose territory extended from the Mediterranean to the Euphrates (Kraus, *Psalms 60–150*, 142).

The picture of the flourishing vineyard changes dramatically in v 13. A dark catastrophe overshadows the great success of vv 9–12. Just as God caused the vine to "take root" and "fill the land," he has now broken the "fence" or "hedge" which protected it. God's continuing protection of his people is often depicted as a "fence" around them. Satan, for example, complains to God that he has "hedged Job about" as a protection from evil (Job 1:9–11). Vv 13–17a suggest some sort of severe military defeat and conquest by enemies, but the historical context eludes us (see *Form/Structure/Setting*). In any case, the psalmist depicts Yahweh as the immediate cause of the clearing, planting, and dressing of the vine, and likewise as the immediate cause of the present devastation of the vineyard. In contrast to the beautiful, private vineyard which once existed, the "broken fence" allows strangers to enjoy the fruit, wild hogs to "root up" the plants so carefully transplanted, and field animals (or insects, see note 14.b.) to chew up the foliage, and the vines to be cut down and burned with fire. The sight is so heartbreaking that the speaker can only cry: "O God Sabaoth! Please turn again! Look down from heaven and see!" The speaker wants God to intervene against the enemies, who really do not have the power to do what they are doing without his permission.

Petition and vow (vv 17b–20). V 17b is a petition that the enemies be rebuked by the face of Yahweh, doubtless shining forth in power and anger at what he would find if he looked at his vineyard. Cf. the refrain in vv 4, 8, and 20. V 18 is a request that God's protective and strengthening hand be available to the "man of your right hand" and the "son of humanity" whom God has made strong. The language is that of intercession for a king, but in the present psalm the primary reference is probably to the "son" in v 16b which is the vine (Israel). As discussed in note 16.b. and *Form/Structure/Setting*, it is probable that v 16b is a redactional addition used to bring the kingship language of v 18 into alignment with the metaphor of the vine in vv 8–17a. The use of the language for the vine (Israel) may have been eased by the associations of Ephraim (v 3) with the right hand of Jacob in the blessing in Gen 48:14, 17, 18—Ephraim is the "son of the right hand," of Yahweh, of course. Likewise, Benjamin is literally "son of the right hand." The association was further eased by the confluence of kingship and the nation in ancient Near Eastern thought; the king embodies the nation and his fortunes are those of his people, and vice versa.

The "son of humanity" (בֶּן־אָדָם) in the present context simply becomes a poetic variant of "son" in 16b and "man" (אִישׁ) in 18a. The expression may have had
more exalted connotations in the usage of an earlier form of the psalm without
the vine metaphor (vv 2–8, 18–20). Later Jewish tradition interpreted vv 16–20 in
a messianic sense, but that is probably not the case with the present psalm,
although it is possible to read v 18 in a future sense: "Let your right hand be on a
man of your right hand / on a son of humanity whom you will make strong for
yourself." Without the redactional addition in v 16b, this would be a very acceptable reading. The situation in the psalm is confusing, but I take it that the MT
edition represents a "de-monarchializing" and "de-messianizing" of the psalm.
The future hope should be focused on the restoration of the vine, without
monarchy.

The vow in v 19 is noteworthy because of its use of the verb סוג, "move away/
backslide"; freely translated: "We will never be backsliders again!" (cf. Ps 53:4;
Prov 14:14; Ps 44:19; Isa 50:5; Ps 78:57; Zeph 1:6). The people promise to be loyal
to Yahweh if he will restore them again and let his face shine with favor toward
them. Without the restoring work of God there is no basis for promises of
commitment; for, indeed, there is no future. If God will give them life (v 19b),
the people will invoke his name in prayer and praise (see note 19.b.).

Explanation

I have little to offer beyond what has already been said in the sections above.
The contrast in the mood and situation of the speaker in this psalm with that of
the speaker in Ps 23 is striking. The protection and restored life longed for in Ps
80 is a reality in Ps 23: there the Shepherd "leads" (נהל), "restores" (ישׁובב) life, and
"guides" (נחה) the speaker in safe paths. The verbs "lead" and "guide" differ from
those in Ps 80, but the meaning is the same. The speaker in Ps 23 has received
what the speaker and the congregation in Ps 80 want.

Ps 80 is among the communal laments that boldly put to God the situation
which has developed among his people (cf. Pss 44; 74; 79; 89). There is no
confession of sins in this psalm, apart from the implied backsliding in the vow in
v 19, and perhaps there is no need of such; the situation speaks for itself. The
psalm speaks for a people who have been fed on tears, which they have drunk by
the keg (v 6)! The face of their Shepherd no longer shines forth toward them in
victory and favor. Instead, he "fumes" in anger at their very prayers (v 5).

The most vivid part of the psalm is the extended metaphor of Yahweh's great
vine which he took from Egypt and planted in his land. In the vineyard that was
Israel, the vine once spread its branches and tendrils until it transformed a large
territory into a vineyard and covered mountains and mighty cedars with its
shade. But now the great vine is ravaged, uprooted by wild hogs and trampled by
vagrants who pluck its fruit as they will. Yahweh is implored to come and "inspect"
("visit") the devastated vineyard to see the condition of the vine for himself (vv
15c–17a). V 17b seems to assume that if Yahweh came and saw what had happened,
the anger and rebuke in his face would cause the ravagers to perish. The
fundamental need is expressed in v 19b: "Give us life, and we will invoke your
Name!"

"Open Wide Your Mouth and I Will Fill It" (81:1–17)

Bibliography

Boer, P. A. H. de. "Psalm 81:6a: Observations on Translation and Meaning of One Hebrew Line." In *The Shelter of Elyon.* FS G. W. Ahlstrom. Ed. W. B. Barrick and J. R. Spencer. JSOT SS 31. Sheffield: JSOT Press, 1984. 67–80. **Booij, T.** "The Background of the Oracle in Psalm 81." *Bib* 65 (1984) 465–75. **Haglund, E.** *Historical Motifs in the Psalms.* ConB, OT 23. Lund: CWK Gleerup, 1984. 15–18. **Goulder, M. D.** *The Psalms of the Sons of Korah.* JSOT SS 20. Sheffield: University of Sheffield, 1982. 109–11. **Jeremias, J.** *Kultprophetie.* 125–33. **Johnson, A. R.** *CPIP.* 3–18. **Layton, S. C.** "Jehoseph in Ps 81, 6." *Bib* 69 (1988) 406–11. **Mowinckel, S.** *PIW.* II, 156–60. **Nasuti, H. P.** *Tradition History.* 210–23.

Translation

1	For the leader;[a] on the *gittith;*[b] Asaphite.[c]	
2 (1)	*Sing out in exultation to God, our strength;*	(3+3)
	shout for joy to the God of Jacob.	
3 (2)	*Take up a song; sound a timbrel;*[a]	(3+3)
	(play) the melodious lyre with the harp.	
4 (3)	*Blow a horn at the new moon;*[a]	(3+3)
	at the full moon for the day of our festival.[b]	
5 (4)	*For this is a decree for Israel*[a]—	(3+3)
	a mandate of the God of Jacob[a]	
6 (5)	*that he appointed as a testimony in Joseph—*	(3+3+3)
	when he (the God of Jacob) went out against the land of Egypt.[a]	
	I hear speech I have not understood[b]—	
7 (6)	*I relieved*[a] *his shoulder of the burden;*	(3+3)
	his hands were freed from the basket.	
8 (7)	*In distress you called and I delivered you;*	(3+3+3)
	hidden in thunder, I answered you.	
	I tested you at the waters of Meribah. SELAH.	
9 (8)	*Hear (me), my people, and let me admonish you;*	(3+3)
	O Israel, if you would only hear me!	
10 (9)	*There should not be among you a strange god,*[a]	(3+3)
	and you should not bow down to a foreign god.[a]—	
11 (10)	*I am Yahweh your God,*[a]	(3+3+3)
	who brought you out of the land of Egypt.	
	Open wide your mouth and I will fill it![b]	
12 (11)	*But my people did not heed my voice;*	(3+3)
	Israel would not yield to me,	
13 (12)	*And so I let them*[a] *go after the stubbornness*	(3+3)
	of their hearts,[b]	
	that they might do what they wanted to do.	

14 (13)   *O that my people would listen to me,*   (3+3)
          that Israel would walk in my ways!
15 (14)   *Straightway, I would subdue their enemies,*   (3+3)
          and turn my hand against their foes.
16 (15)   *Those who hate Yahweh would submit* [a] *to him,* [b]   (3+3)
          and their time [c] *would be (over) forever.*
17 (16)   *Also, he would feed him (Israel)* [a] *from the*   (3+3)
          best of the wheat [b]—
          and with honey from the rock, [a] *I would satisfy you!*

Notes

1.a. See n. 51:1.a.

1.b. The term הַגִּתִּית appears also in the headings of Pss 8 and 84. Craigie (105, n. 1.a.) summarizes the three major explanations given for the meaning of גִּתִּית: (1) a type of musical instrument, such as a "Gittite lyre," viz. an instrument named after a place (Gath), analogous to the "Spanish guitar"; (2) a musical tune or setting—again, perhaps, named after a place: "according to the Gittitic tune," or possibly, "Song of the Winepress" (note that LXX translates as "winepresses"; probably understanding גִּתּוֹת, as in Neh 13:15, rather than the adjective גִּתִּית, which might suggest that the title intended the psalm to be used when wine was being pressed from grapes; cf. L. Delekat, "Probleme der Psalmenüberschriften," *ZAW* 76 [1964] 293–94); (3) a festival or ceremony of some kind, as in Mowinckel, *PIW*, II, 215. Mowinckel also suggests a family connection for the term with the "Githite," Obed-edom in 2 Sam 6:10–11, in whose house the ark of Yahweh stayed until it was moved to Jerusalem. Later tradition ascribed a Levitical genealogy to Obed-edom and described him as a musician (1 Chr 15:21; 16:5, cf. v 38) and gatekeeper (1 Chr 15:18–24; see also 1 Chr 26:4–8, 15). The exact meaning of the expression in the titles remains uncertain.

1.c. See n. 73:1.b. A few mss and LXX add מִזְמוֹר, "psalm."

3.a. The "timbrel" (תֹּף) was an instrument used by women, especially for dancing (see Exod 15:20; Judg 11:34; 1 Sam 18:6; Pss 149:3; 150:4). E. Werner (*IDB*, III, 474) argues that timbrels were not allowed in the temple, perhaps due to their strong association with females. The "timbrel" was carried and beaten by hand, originally perhaps shaken with pieces of bronze between two membranes. If timbrels were not used in the temple, the celebration took place outside, perhaps in the temple courts or outside the gates (A. A. Anderson, II, 587).

4.a. Lit., "on the new" (בַּחֹדֶשׁ), i.e., the moon/month, which began with a full moon according to v 4b. According to Num 29:1, 6, the new moon began the lunar months, but this hardly seems likely here. The text in Ps 81 seems to indicate a calendar in which the months began on the full moon. See A. R. Johnson, *CPIP*, n. 4.

The "horn" is the שׁוֹפָר, not the silver trumpets blown at each new moon according to Num 10:10. The *shophar* was made from the horn of an animal, usually a ram (Josh 6:4–13). The first reference to the *shophar* is in Exod 19:16, and there are many others after that verse. The classification of the *shophar* as a musical instrument is questionable, though it does appear among such instruments in Pss 98:5–6; 150:3–5. Mostly it was an instrument to give signals, or to herald some important announcement (Judg 3:27; 6:34; 7:8–22; 1 Sam 13:3; etc.). The first day of the seventh month is described in Num 29:1 as the "day of the blowing of the *shophar.*"

4.b. The festival intended is most probably the autumn festival, which is known in the OT as Tabernacles, or the Festival of Booths/Shelters (חַג הַסֻּכּוֹת); Heb. *Sukkoth.* This festival seems to have been the major festival in pre-exilic Israel: note, "the feast of Yahweh" in Judg 21:19; Lev 23:39; Hos 9:5; "the feast" in 1 Kgs 8:2, 65; 2 Chr 7:8; Neh 8:14; Isa 30:29; Ezek 45:23, 25. The Festival of Tabernacles began on the fifteenth day of the seventh month, which was a time when the moon was full. The first day of the seventh month was a day when the *shophar* was blown (see n. 4.a. above); cf. Num 10:10.

5.a. The לְיִשְׂרָאֵל perhaps should be read as vocative, "O Israel" (as in Dahood). The לֵאלֹהֵי, "of the God of . . ." or "from the God of . . ." is an example of the use of לְ as possessive (cf. R. J. Williams, *Hebrew Syntax*, 270) or the ablative sense of "from" (Dahood, II, 264, with reference to O. Loretz, *BZ* 2 [1958] 288). See GKC 129. T. Robinson in Oesterley (372) suggests that "Israel" may be a contracted form of "the God of Israel," parallel with "the God of Jacob" (for the "God of Jacob," see Pss 20:2; 75:10; 76:7; 84:9; 94:7; 2 Sam 23:1; Isa 2:3; Mic 4:2). The God of Jacob seems to be synonymous with the God of Israel. The expression recalls the Jacob traditions (see Gen 35:1–3), and possibly was preferred terminology in the worship at Bethel (note Hos 12:2–6). Also note Gen 33:19–20.

6.a. The LXX reads "when he came forth from the land of Egypt," making the subject Joseph rather than God. This is followed by some translations: NEB, NAB, JB, NJV; cf. KJV and RSV. Kraus judges the LXX to be an easing of a difficult text and retains MT. A. A. Anderson (II, 488) follows G. R. Driver and W. Thomas (*TRP*, 34), who argue that על has the meaning "from" in Phoenician, and that it may be the case here (also Dahood, II, 264). A. R. Johnson (*CPIP*, 6, n. 6) argues that the preposition ב in this context has a causal force rather than the temporal one usually given it, and that על means "against." The reading which results is: "who imposed it on Joseph as a testimony, because of His sallying forth against the land of Egypt." (For the causal meaning of ב, see Gen 18:28; 19:16; 29:20; Exod 16:7, 8; 2 Chr 28:36.) In Johnson's translation, the God of Jacob in v 5 is the subject of the verb; it is he who went forth against Egypt.

On the other hand, de Boer ("Psalm 81.6a") argues that Joseph is the subject in v 6b. He then understands the expression בצאתו על־ארץ מצרים as "in his rising (to power) over the land of Egypt." This is based on Gen 41:45: ויצא יוסף על־ארץ מצרים, "and Joseph went forth (with authority over the land of Egypt)"; cf. Gen 19:23; Zech 5:3; Esth 1:7; 2 Kgs 24:12 for other occurrences of יצא על־. De Boer suggests that this psalm expresses (originally in any case) a hope of restoration, with the house of Joseph as its center, rather than Judah. He thinks that in some exilic and post-exilic circles there were non-Judean or even anti-Judean hopes (76). The Joseph story originally belonged to these circles: "Most of the Hebrew texts collected and revised, enlarged and rewritten, in order to encourage the remnants of the people in Palestine and elsewhere, have a Judean tendency, but there are scattered fragments wherein non-Judean, sometimes even anti-Judean, ideas are preserved" (76). De Boer may be correct about the psalm's relatedness to a Joseph-hope in the late pre-exilic, exilic, and post-exilic periods. But the present psalm is Judean, in any case, and the editors intended to read the "God of Jacob" (who is Yahweh) as the subject of the verb in v 6b rather than Joseph. Therefore, I have retained that reading.

De Boer (75–77) suggests that the unique spelling of Joseph in v 6a (יהוסף) rather than יוסף) was "intentionally manufactured to suggest an alternative reading, namely Jehudah [יהודה] instead of Joseph [יוסף]." The unique spelling would indicate opposition to the hope of restoration centered in the house of Joseph and the Joseph traditions. The scribal interpreters (probably post-exilic) could not change the text radically, but they could change it enough to indicate to any alert reader that יהוסף really refers to יהודה as Israel. For Yahweh's going out against Egypt before the exodus, see Exod 11:4. Layton (*Bib* 69 [1988] 406–11) notes that the expanded form of the name is a hapax legomenon in MT but occurs fairly frequently in postbiblical inscriptions from the period 200 B.C.E.– 200 C.E. He concludes (411) that the name Jehoseph was a "popular, colloquial form of the name of Second Temple vintage." The expanded spelling (with a theophoric יהו that violates modern philological principles) was intended to stress the Yahwistic faithfulness of Joseph and probably belongs to a later redaction of Ps 81. The spelling of the name is in keeping with a post-exilic date for the present psalm.

6.b. The statement in v 6c has been given several interpretations. (1) Earlier interpreters understood the expression "lip (language/speech) I did not know" as the speaker identifying with the Israelites who had to endure the oppression of Egyptians who spoke a foreign language (e.g., Calvin). (2) Others have understood the "unknown language" to be the voice of God: "The Psalmist speaks in the person of Israel at the time of the Exodus . . . Israel then *began to hear* Jehovah . . . whom it had not yet learned to know as the self-revealing God of redemption. . . ." (Kirkpatrick, 491). (3) More recently, most commentators have assumed that the voice is that of Yahweh whom the prophet-speaker hears speaking the words which follow in vv 7–17. The speaker's "ear has been opened to hear an unearthly *voice,* divine words which he will now give forth again in what follows" (Eaton, 202). Goulder (*The Psalms of the Sons of Korah,* 111) has a modified interpretation along these lines. He objects to the strong emphasis on the speaker in Ps 81 as a cultic prophet, arguing for a priest-poet who leads the people in a new commitment to obeying the voice of Yahweh. The meaning is: "I am now ready to hear and obey the voice that I did not lay to heart before" (note the use of the verb שמע, "hear," in vv 6c, 9a, 12, and 14). This is a plausible reading, even though I have not adopted it. (4) A few commentators have treated the statement as a marginal note, which should be disregarded, as in NEB, and by W. Thomas (*TRP*, 34 ["a lectionary rubric"]). (5) Dahood (II, 264–65) argues that the לא־ידעתי ("I did not know") is a relative clause without a relative pronoun used as a substantive (cf. Job 18:21;

Isa 41:24; 43:19; Jer 2:8; also Ps 35:15; Job 29:12, 16; Prov 9:13; 23:35; Ps 85:9). In this case, the relative clause would serve as a genitive of the construct שְׂפַת (note GKC 130d, 144f, n). Dahood translates: "I (God) heard the speech of one unknown to me"—i.e., Israel, crying out under Egyptian oppression and heard by God before he "knew" Israel (note Exod 2:23–24; Amos 3:1–2). His translation would be stronger if שְׂפַת were understood as "lament" (note that שָׂפָה, "lip," is sometimes used in contexts of lament: 1 Sam 1:13; Job 13:6; Pss 16:4; 17:1; 21:3; Jer 17:16; Hab 3:16). This is an attractive interpretation, but it seems to me that v 6c should be linked with 11c, which seems to be a reference to prophetic inspiration.

7.a. LXX has a 3rd pers. masc. sing. verb ("he relieved"). However, modern commentators and translations have preferred to go the other way and read "your shoulder" in 7a and "your hands" in v 7b (e.g., RSV, JB, Gunkel, Schmidt, Oesterley, and Jacquet). This change is arbitrary and need not be adopted. The change of person in Hebrew poetry is not uncommon (e.g., see Pss 44, 84, 85).

10.a. The term for "a strange god" (אֵל זָר) does not appear often (see Ps 44:21; cf. Deut 32:16); "a foreign god" (אֵל נֵכָר) is somewhat more common in varied forms (see Deut 32:12 and Mal 2:11; cf. Dan 11:39), but also see the plural "strange gods" (אֱלֹהֵי נֵכָר) in Josh 24:20, 23; Jer 5:19; Gen 35:2; 1 Sam 7:3; Deut 31:16.

11.a. An alternative translation is: "I, Yahweh, am your God, the one who brought you up from the land of Egypt." This translation is syntactically acceptable and appears in some English versions; e.g., JB, NAB, NJV; also, see Jacquet, Maillot and Lelièvre, and Johnson (CPIP, 9, n. 70), who caution against exaggerating the similarity between 81:10–11b and the statement in Exod 20:2 and Deut 5:6, where the "I am Yahweh your God" translation expresses the self-revelatory emphasis. Johnson argues that in Ps 81 the words which correspond to the self-representation formula at the beginning of the Decalogue no longer function as a self-disclosure in a theophany, "but simply with a view to reinforcing this fundamental prohibition [in v 10] against the worship of any other god." W. Zimmerli, whose long study, "Ich bin Yahweh" (see in English, I Am Yahweh, tr. D. W. Stott [Atlanta: John Knox Press, 1982] 1–28) has been very influential in establishing the basic nature of אֲנִי יהוה אֱלֹהֵיכֶם ('ny yhwh 'lhykm) as a generic self-representation formula, allows for a "ruptured" (Sprengung) form of the formula as "I, Yahweh, am your God" in cases where it is required (e.g., Exod 20:5), although the determination of acceptable instances is not certain (Zimmerli, 26). Despite Johnson's caution, the close correspondence to Exod 20:2 and Deut 5:6 tilts the decision toward the more basic form of the saying as a self-representation of God. The context in both Exod and Deut is basically that of theophany. One of the elements of theophany is the self-introduction of the deity with an emphatic "I am" (note Gen 17:1; 26:23–25; Exod 6:2, 6, 8; Ps 50:7). The deity's identity is revealed in part by a name: "I am Yahweh." Beyond the name, the identity involves relatedness to antecedent events: "I am the God of Abraham your father"; "I am Yahweh your God who brought you out of the land of Egypt." In addition to Zimmerli, I Am Yahweh, cited above, see J. K. Kuntz, The Self-Revelation of God (Philadelphia: Westminster Press, 1967) 47–71.

11.b. The colon in v 11c is often moved in translation. Gunkel, Kraus, Jacquet, and Johnson (CPIP, 8, n. 2) transfer it to a place after 6c, translating 6c in the sense of "I became aware of a strange voice" (Kraus), or as Johnson: "I can hear the speech of one whom I know not, / 'Open thy mouth wide that I may fill it.'" NEB and S. Mowinckel (PIW, I, 157) place the colon after 8c: "I tested you at the spring of Meribah; / 'Open your mouth, I will fill it'—" although NEB reads the imperative form of the verb "open" as perfect: "Where I opened your mouths and filled them." For a negative criticism of such transposition, see Goulder, (The Psalms of the Sons of Korah, 109–11). Dahood suggests reading the hiphil impv. הַרְחֵב ("widen/open") as hiphil inf. const., הַרְחֵב (or, הַרְחִיב), in a construct chain with "your mouth," which is the direct object of the postpositive verb. He treats the conjunction on the verb as an emphatic waw, and the following translation results: "What is more, I filled your wide-open mouth." Such a reading has the advantage of requiring a very small change in MT, but the treatment seems rather forced and the interpretation wrong.

13.a. See BHS; there is some manuscript evidence for הֵם, "them" rather than MT's הֹדּוֹ, "him," though the "him" is collective.

13.b. The word שְׁרִירוּת, always used with heart/will, occurs only here and in Deut 29:18 outside of Jeremiah, where it is rather frequent (3:17; 7:24; 9:13; 11:8; 13:10; 16:12; 18:12; 23:17). See A. B. Spencer JBL 100/2 (1981) 247–48, who argues that שְׁרִירוּת is primarily "self-reliance," with three metaphorical dimensions associated with its usage: self-reliance, doing one's own will, and idolatry.

16.a. The verb כָּחַשׁ has usually been taken in the sense of "to feign submission/fawn/adulate/cringe." However, J. H. Eaton (JTS, 19 n.s. [1968] 603–4) has argued for a basic idea of "grow lean/wither/become small/shrink," suggesting, "they become small in view of me" (for the preposition לְ

in this sense, see BDB, 514b) or "they shrink at my presence." See Ps 18:45–46. The English "submit" seems adequate—if somewhat bland. The expression "knuckle under to him" is another possibility.

16.b. The pronoun "him" is somewhat ambiguous: Yahweh? Israel? *BHS* suggests reading "those who hate them/him" for "those who hate Yahweh." In this case the object would be Israel; so NEB, "Let those who hate them come cringing to them. . . ." (note Deut 32:29; Ps 18:45). However, this is not necessary and the meaning seems to be more likely that of enemies cowering before Yahweh, as in Ps 66:3. The use of third person in direct addresses by God is found in other contexts; e.g., see Amos 2:4; Ps 50:21–22.

16.c. The "their time" (עתם) seems to be a pregnant way of saying that their time of rebellion would be over or that "their time of submission will be forever." J. H. Eaton (*JTS* 19 [1968] 607–8) argues that עת ("time") is derived from ענה, "be bowed down/afflicted/lowly" (note BDB, 773a and KB, 719). The sense would be "their submission/subjugation will be forever." Of course, 16b could be understood in the sense of "a good time for Israel will be forever." But the plural suffix ("their") points easily to the "haters of Yahweh" in 16a, and the reference to adversaries seems highly probable.

17.a. The consecutive impf. form of the verb would normally point to past tense: "And so he fed him . . ." However the context seems to call for a conditional idea, though a return to a retrospective view is possible. The frequently suggested emendation of ויאכילהו to ואאכילהו, "and I would feed him" (e.g., Delitzsch, Gunkel, Kraus) would ease the construction. But the consecutive impf. is used a few times with a future and contingent sense (see *Notes* on Ps 64). The "him" refers to Israel.

17.b. Lit., "from fatness of wheat." The idea is that of "fine wheat flour."

17.c. The parallelism suggests that this refers to the "best honey," and Dahood (II, 267) proposes "essence of honey," assuming that צור ("rock") is actually derived from a root צרר and צררת meaning "heart/inwards" (see Dahood, I, 38, 63, 189). But the traditional explanation of rich food coming forth from barren and unfruitful rocks seems more probable (see Job 29:6; Deut 32:13). See Gunkel, 360. It is possible that the "rock" also carries an allusion to Yahweh (so N. C. Habel, *The Book of Job* [Philadelphia: Westminster, 1985] 409, on Job 29:6, where the rock pours out streams of oil).

Form/Structure/Setting

Ps 81 is generally considered to be closely related to Pss 50 and 95, and this judgment is probably correct (see J. Jeremias, *Kultprophetie,* 125–27). All three psalms have a sermonic style, with preaching and admonition. The psalms are often described as having a liturgical quality. E. Gerstenberger (210) declares of Ps 50: "This psalm is a sermon given before a small audience," and classifies it as a liturgical sermon. The liturgical features are more pronounced in Ps 81, but its overall structure is that of preaching, with instruction in the past history of Yahweh's dealings with Israel and strong admonition. The character of vv 6c–17 as an oracle of God strengthens this judgment.

The speaker in Ps 81 is frequently identified as a prophet, usually with the designation "cult prophet" (e.g., Johnson, Kraus, and, conveniently, Sabourin, 403). However, the style of the preaching is that associated with Levitical preaching in Deut and Chr (e.g., Jeremias, Gerstenberger, and Kraus; note Deut 33:8 and Pss 81:8; 95:8). As stated in n. 6.b., Goulder objects to the "oracle hypothesis" in relation to the speaker as a cult prophet. He argues for a priest-poet who leads an assembly of worshipers, who announces his faith in Yahweh and admonishes the people. He makes much of the מנצח ("leader") in the title, "the priest who leads the music" (*The Psalms of the Sons of Korah,* 111). He asks how a prophetic speaker could repeat the message of inspiration (in vv 6c and 11c) each time the psalm was recited; or if taken over by the priestly choir, the words of inspiration would have been meaningless—or so he claims. Goulder seems to have confused the literary design of the psalm with its cultic usage. The design is that of a prophetic call to praise followed by admonition. The reader/reciter of the psalm is quite another matter. The appeal to inspiration in the psalm authenticates its authority but relates to the reader or worship leader (priest, prophet, or layperson—the מנצח) only so far as he or she "owns" the psalm as his or her experience. The psalm invites the reader/hearer to enter into the speaker's experience of inspiration and to hear the voice of God. It is important to think of psalms in terms of readers/hearers as well as the speaking voices of their content.

There is wide agreement among commentators that Pss 50, 81, and 95 are psalms which reflect festival settings and were most probably recited on such occasions, probably being composed for use in them. (For an imaginative reconstruction of the worship situation reflected in Ps 81, see T. Robinson in Oesterley, 372.) Jeremias (125) calls them "the great festal psalms." As already indicated in n. 4.a. above, the primary festival reflected by the texts is almost certainly that of the autumn Festival of Booths/Tabernacles. In addition to the content of v 4, the giving of *torah* in vv 6, 10–11, along with the promise of a good harvest and fine food in v 17 are features which would enhance the probability of a Tabernacles context. Major features of worship during the Festival of Tabernacles are undoubtedly represented in Pss 50, 81, and 95. However, attempts to reconstruct *specific ceremonies and liturgies* from the content of these psalms has generated more disputation than consensus and there seems to be little basis for much improvement. In general, looking back through psalms to see the details of Israelite worship is "seeing in a mirror dimly"—the major features are clear; the details are blurred.

Scholars have long suggested that Ps 81, and indeed most of the Asaph psalms, originated in worship circles of the Northern Israelite tribes. The references to Jacob and Joseph are suggestive of this, though they are not conclusive, as is the reference to Meribah (also in 95:8) which may represent a variant tradition from those in Exod 17:1–7; Num 20:1–13. If the psalm originated in Northern circles of worship, it probably dates from the period prior to 722 B.C.E. Even if a pre-exilic date for the origin of the psalm is correct, however, its present form and position in the Asaph collection (Pss 50, 73–83) point toward exilic and post-exilic contexts (cf. Deissler, II, 148; Gerstenberger on Ps 50, 210; note Nasuti, *Tradition History*, 223, 385–95). In these contexts Pss 50, 81, and 95 represent the preaching of Levitical priests, who carried on the prophetic tradition. It is also possible that the psalm was a Joseph-hope psalm re-read as applying to Judah-Israel (see n. 11.a.).

The psalm divides into two major sections: a hymnic festal summons in vv 2–6b and an oracle in vv 6c–17. Older critical commentators were prone to treat these sections as two unrelated parts, sometimes referring to Ps 81A (vv 2–6b) and Ps 81B (vv 6c–17), as, for example, in Buttenwieser who argues that the combination of the two parts into one psalm was "one of the vagaries of text transmission" (54). The nature of psalm composition, however, makes it abundantly clear that such a hypothesis is not necessary. The psalms in the Psalter are full of bits and pieces of traditional material which have been combined into literary unities. Indeed, the composite nature of psalmody is almost a norm.

The oracle section in vv 6c–17 may be subdivided into vv 6c–11 and vv 12–17, though another option is to follow an analysis like that found in Stuhlmueller (II, 38–39) who divides the oracle section into two prophetic speeches: v 7 plus 12–17, addressed to Israel in the third person (except for 17b) and vv 8–11 in the I-Thou form of personal dialogue. My own approach, however, is that an oracle is properly formed by vv 6c and 11c, which has been separated into two parts to frame the material in vv 7–11b. The result is a "sandwich" type of construction of the A x B type (see *Form/Structure/Setting* of Ps 69, and the works of D. T. Tsumura, G. Braulik, and L. C. Allen cited there). The oracle has been split for the insertion of the content in vv 7–11b, which then contains an "oracle within an oracle" in vv 9–11b. V 11c also serves as a linking statement to bring vv 12–17 into the oracle. V 9 does double duty as a summons for the oracle material in vv 10–11b and for the material in vv 12–17; note the reference to "my people" (עמי) in vv 9 and 12, and again in v 14, which relates back to vv 9 and 12 also with the use of the verb שמע, "hear."

Comment

A summons to praise (81:2–6b). The reader is invited to think of a crowd gathered for a festival (probably Tabernacles, see note 4.b.) and of a speaker (priest, or prophet, or lay leader) who urges that the celebration begin with singing and joyful shouting, accompanied by musical instruments (cf. Pss 47:2; 95:1–2; 98:4–6; 148:2–3; 150:3–4). V 4 refers to the blowing of signal horns to mark the beginning of the feast. The basis for the summons is set forth in vv 5–6b as a divine decree. The festival is mandated for Israel by God, appointed when he (Yahweh) "went out against the land of Egypt" (cf. Lev 23:41–43). The festival is a celebration rooted in the events of the exodus from Egypt and the wilderness (vv 7–8). The reference to Joseph (the only usage of the enlarged spelling יהוסף, "Jehoseph") may be evidence of an origin of the psalm among the Northern tribes (note 81:2; 78:67; so, e.g., Schmidt, Weiser, Dahood), though it falls short of proof, since Joseph may be used in one or two places in the sense of Israel—especially "Israel in Egypt" (see Kraus, II, 730, and 722 on 80:2; cf. 77:16; 105:17; Obad 18; Amos 5:6, 15; 6:6; also A. A. Anderson, II, 588, 560, 582).

An admonitory oracle (81:6c–17). As noted above the oracle has a sermonic quality; it is preaching. The oracle begins with a report by the speaker in v 6c of hearing a message previously unknown, probably in the sense of not understanding its full meaning (cf. Job 42:3, 5). The reference to the message received from Yahweh vouches for the authenticity of the oracle which follows. The speaker is the mouthpiece of God whose mouth is filled with the divine message (note 11c; cf. Jer 1:9; 2 Sam 23:1–2).

The oracle itself begins with a soliloquy by God in v 7, as he recalls how he freed the Israelites from their oppression in Egypt. The oracle flows without interruption into the direct address of v 8, which recalls the thunderous delivering action of God. The "hidden in thunder" is often taken as an allusion to the theophany on Mount Sinai (Exod 19; 20:18). However, the context is that of the deliverance from Egypt (cf. Exod 14:19, 24) and a reference to the Sinai experience should not be pressed. The reference seems more compatible with theophanic accounts in which God comes forth with power to save and deliver; as in Pss 18:12, 14; 77:19; 104:4; cf. Hab 3:2–19. The expression recalls the awesome intervention of the Divine Warrior, who went out victoriously against the land of Egypt (6c) and made himself known in the wilderness.

The testing of Israel at the waters of Meribah recalls the traditions which appear in Exod 17:7; Num 20:13; Deut 6:16; Pss 78:20; 95:8–9; 106:32; cf. Deut 32:51; Ezek 47:19; 48:28. However, in these references the Israelites *test* God, whereas in 81:8b God is said to have *tested* Israel. Possibly the text intends to suggest that those who test God are actually testing themselves (A. A. Anderson, II, 590), but it is more probable that a variant tradition has been used (along the lines of Exod 15:25; Deut 33:8; cf. Exod 16:4; Deut 8:2, 16; Judg 2:22; 3:1, 4) in which Yahweh tests Israel. There may have been a covenant tradition associated with Meribath-kadesh (note the relation of Meribah-kadesh in Deut 32:5; Ezek 47:19; 48:28) parallel to the Sinai tradition in which Yawweh gave the people his commandments and tested their loyalty (Weiser, 554, who cites Deut 33:8–9; 32:51; Exod 15:25–27; 16:4; Num 20:13; 27:14). The people passed the test by assuming the obligations of a covenant with Yahweh. Note that the idea of "testing" is associated with the covenant-making at Sinai. (Cf. Exod 20:20, where the verb is נסה rather than בחן as in 81:8a.) In the variant tradition it is probable that the theophanic response from a storm was linked with the giving of the commandment against the worship of other gods than Yahweh (vv 10–11).

B. S. Childs (*The Book of Exodus*, OTL [Philadelphia: Westminster Press, 1974] 372) has stressed that "theophany and the giving of law belong together" in the present sequence of the narrative in Exod 19–20. In the context of Ps 81 the theophanic language in 8b is loosely attached to the deliverance from Egypt, though the reader also thinks of Sinai. In their present context, vv 10–11 are doubtless intended to recall the statements in the Decalogue found in Exod 20:3; Deut 5:7, and similar expressions of the prohibition against the worshiping of foreign gods in Exod 22:20; 23:13; 34:14; Deut 13:2–40—a fundamental tenet on which all else in the relationship with Yahweh is dependent.

V 9 also belongs to the oracle in vv 12–17, and matches v 14 to express the longing of God for a responsive people. There is a tone of lament in these verses, a reflection of the grief of God because of a wayward people. The sad story of their rejection of the will of God is told in vv 12–13. The Israelites would not heed the divine voice, would not yield to the divine will (v 12)—"would have none of me," as the RSV has it (note the repeated use of the verb שמע, "hear/heed" in vv 9, 12, and 14). The result was a divine letting go of the people to follow their own stubborn ways and to do whatever they wanted to do (v 13; cf. Hos 2:5–7; Rom 1:24, 26, 28). The disastrous results of the faithlessness of the people are not spelled out in this psalm, but clearly the reader is expected to bring to the text a repertoire in which the results are "familiar territory."

Vv 9–11b seem to form an oracle within an oracle, which represents the oracle by which God tested the Israelites at Meribah (8c). In v 11ab, Yahweh's self-introduction is recalled. As noted above (see note 11.a.), the expression in 11ab is very close to that in Exod 20:2 and Deut 5:6 and is properly understood as a theophanic self-representation of deity. At Meribah, the Israelites were not left to deal with an unnamed deity. Yahweh had made himself known as "your God, who brought you out of the land of Egypt." He had made his personal name recognizable to his people. The self-introduction is expanded to include the statement of his saving action: "who brought you out of the land of Egypt." Yahweh's identity includes *both* his name and his acts of deliverance and salvation. He is not simply: "Yahweh, who, incidentally, brought you out of Egypt." The divine self-identity is inclusive of his saving action: "I am Yahweh who brought you out of Egypt." Yahweh is not identified apart from his action; thus his identity is also revealed in vv 7–8, though his name is not given there—the passage moves to a climactic statement in vv 11ab; the reader is held in suspense about the identity of the speaker in vv 7–10, even with some question about the identity of the God of Jacob in vv 2–6b, until v 11 is reached, at which point "Yahweh with his majestic I appears on the scene" (Kraus, *Psalms 60–159*, 152). V 11 is clearly the central statement of Ps 81.

The exhortation in v 11c, "Open wide your mouth and I will fill it," immediately suggests one whose mouth is to be filled with good food and drink, and that idea may not be missing entirely since v 17c could follow naturally after 11c: "Open wide your mouth and I will fill it [v 11c], / and with honey from the rock, I will satisfy you [v 17c]." However, the varied forms of the expressions for "putting" or "filling" the mouth in the OT are used mostly of putting words of speech in the mouth: e.g., Exod 4:15; Num 22:38; 23:5, 12, 16; Deut 18:18; 31:19; 2 Sam 14:3, 19; Isa 30:27; 59:21; Jer 1:9; 5:14; Pss 10:4; 71:8; 126:2; Job 8:21, 23:4, Prov 20:18. The verb רחב, "enlarge/widen," is not used often with mouth: 1 Sam 2:1; Ps 34:21; Isa 57:4—in all three of these cases the meaning is something like "deride/taunt"; e.g., Hannah "opens wide" her mouth in 1 Sam 2:1 to gloat over her enemies. Cf. P. K. McCarter, Jr. (*I Samuel*, AB 8 [Garden City, NY: Doubleday, 1980] 72) who argues that the meaning is not opening the mouth to "mock" or "gloat" but stretching the mouth open to swallow something. He compares Isa 5:14 where the נפש ("throat/appetite/maw") of Sheol gapes wide (הרחיבה) and its mouth is opened (פערה) to swallow up a multitude of the living. This meaning hardly seems appropriate for Hannah in 1 Sam 2:1 or for Ps 35:21 (despite v 25), or for Isa 57:4. It is possible, however, that in Ps 81:11c the meaning is: "Open wide your mouth and I will fill it with something to swallow"—hardly the figurative swallowing of the enemies, as McCarter (72) seems to suggest, but possibly the honey from the rock in v 17c. But the predominance of filling the mouth and opening the mouth to receive and express speech tilts the meaning strongly in that direction.

The question remains, however: What words are to fill the speaker's mouth? They could be words of praise like those in vv 2–6b, especially after Yahweh deals with the enemies, as put forth in vv 15–17. In view of the usage of רחב and "mouth" with gloating or exulting over the failure of foes, I think it is possible that the meaning here is: "Open wide your mouth and I will fill it with words of exultation over the failure of your foes and of praise for Yahweh's saving works."

The oracle ends with "a forward, not a backward, look" (Johnson, *CPIP*, 10) in vv 15–17. The future could hold good things for the people, dependent on their willingness to listen and obey God: "walk in my ways" (see Johnson, 13–14; the references to "his way" and "his ways" are too numerous to list). The reference to enemies in v 15 may be indicative of a context in which the Israelites are surrounded and threatened by foes (Kraus). However, such language is rather stereotypical and should not be pressed into a specific historical context. Indeed, Israel (North, South, and together) always lived ringed about with enemies, especially in the post-exilic period when the state existed only in a diminished puppet status. The "haters of Yahweh" may be either foreign or domestic; in both cases they are those who try to do what they want to do in terms of their stubborn wills (if the reading, "those who hate them" [i.e., the Israelites] is adopted [see note 16.b.] the meaning is not essentially different; in OT contexts the enemies of Israel are usually the enemies of Yahweh and vice versa, although there are some notable exceptions, e.g., Isa 10:5-6; Jer 25:8–9; 27:1–11). The reference to the "best of the wheat" ("fat of the wheat") and "honey from a rock" are very similar to expressions in Deut 32:13–14, and indeed are probably free adaptations of commonly known sayings (cf. Num 18:12; Ps 147:14), though "honey from a rock" with צור appears only here (Deut 32:13 has מסלע, "from a crag"). Honey may be found at times in the clefts of rocky cliffs, but the primary meaning is probably that of rich and valuable food produced from any naturally barren sources. A. Caquot (*TDOT*, III, 129) declares that it would be "absurd" to assume that the honey in Deut 32:13 and Ps 81:17 refers to wild honey collected from the honeycombs of bees in the clefts of rocks: "'Honey out of the rock' was not something to be collected any more than the 'oil out of the flinty rock' which is connected with it [in Deut 32:13]." Perhaps, but bees find shelter for their combs among rocks, and olive trees grow well in rocky soil. Olive presses were also built out of large rocks. In any case, v 17 indicates that Yahweh would supply his people with rich and desirable food.

Beyond the use of honey as food, it is worth noting that two or three references relate honey and sweetness to words which God puts in the mouth: "How sweet are thy words to my taste, / sweeter than honey to my mouth" (Ps 119:103, RSV). The scroll, given to him by the hand of God and with writing on front and back, which Ezekiel eats, is said to have been sweet as honey in his mouth (Ezek 3:3; also, see Ps 19:11; Jer 15:16; cf. Prov 16:24; 24:13–14; Rev 10:8–11). The usage of the metaphor of words "sweet as honey" points to the free allusion, at least, of v 17c with v 11c (see above).

Explanation

Ps 81 is an example of liturgical preaching, similar to Pss 50 and 95. As Kraus notes, the two distinct parts of the psalm can be perplexing. The psalm begins with a joyful summons to festival celebration and praise; a celebration which is established for Israel by the mandate of God (v 5). The oracle which begins in 6c starts with a review of the merciful acts of God in relieving the Israelites of hard oppression, but moves to recall the failure of the people to obey the command of God and his "letting them go" to follow their own ways (vv 12–13). At first this arrangement may seem strange.

T. Booij (*Bib* 65 [1984] 466–69) offers some help from the form critical sector of analogies. He points out that the oracle resembles that of other texts in which Yahweh speaks in first person. These texts seem to have a "pattern of remembrances" composed of stock elements. The major features are:

1. Yahweh recalls the deliverance from Egypt (Judg 2:1; 6:8–9; Jer 7:22; 11:7; Ezek 20:10; Ps 81:7–8).
2. The giving of commandments—or the "ways" of life—in or about the exodus period is cited, sometimes with the powerfully affirmative theophanic self-presentation of "I am Yahweh your God" (Judg 2:2; 6:10; Jer 7:23; 11:7; Ezek 20:17, 11–12, 18–19; Ps 81:10–11; Lev 18:4–6, 21, 30; 19:3, 4, 10, 12 [see W. Zimmerli, *I Am Yahweh*, tr. D. W. Stott (Atlanta: John Knox Press, 1982) who says of

this statement, "It is a statement laden with final significance . . . in this self-introduction we hear the ultimate statement Yahweh can make about himself," 19]).

3. The divine complaint that Israel would not listen to and obey the will of God (Judg 2:2; 6:10; 7:24–25; 11:8; Ezek 20:8, 13; 21; Ps 81:12).

Booij notes that the "pattern of remembrances" is worked out in varied ways in different contexts, but the pattern is consistent enough to suggest that this was a standard pattern of preaching in festival contexts. The purpose of such preaching was (1) to recall the great acts and commandments of Yahweh which warrant praise, and (2) to admonish the worshipers not to repeat the failures of the early Israelites (note Ps 95:7–8). The doxological nature of the festival is by divine mandate (vv 5–6), but there is an even greater and fundamental admonition of God (note v 9) in the commandment given at the waters of Meribah (vv 8b, 10–11b; Booij, *Bib* 65 [1984] 468). The intention of such preaching was not to stifle doxology and joyful celebration but rather to heighten the meaning of Israel's experience of her saving-history by recalling her sin-history along with it. A. Weiser (555) comments that "The fact that the history of salvation manifested itself as the history of God's judgments is, however, by no means to be considered as a sign that God has abandoned his people; on the contrary, behind this history is the same will to save that is behind his promises; the judgment of God is the hand which he stretches out to restore the sinner to himself and lead him in his ways." Thus the preaching in Ps 81 lays before the congregation an open future of blessing (vv 14–17). The central statement of the psalm seems to be in v 11:

> I am Yahweh your God,
> who brought you out of the land of Egypt.
> Open wide your mouth and I will fill it (with words of praise).

Yahweh, with his divine "I" of self-introduction, is at the center of things. The congregation is urged to sing and shout for joy at the festival (vv 2–6b). Yahweh has a record of relieving the distress of his people, though his admonitions are often disregarded because of their stubborn hearts (vv 7–14). The divine pathos of Yahweh is expressed in v 14:

> O that my people would listen to me,
> that Israel would walk in my ways!

Yahweh is not a God of abstract absoluteness, who holds himself aloof from the world. He is moved and affected by what his people do or do not do. He has a dynamic relationship with his people, his family, and their welfare (cf. A. Heschel, *The Prophets*, vol. 4 [New York: Harper & Row, 1962] 1–11). Yahweh "has a stake in the human situation" (Heschel, 6), and he becomes frustrated with the intractable behavior of his own people. Yet he stands ready to fill the mouth of a messenger with words of victory and praise—and "honey from the rock" to swallow with all its delightful taste of sweetness.

"Arise, O God, Judge the Earth!"   *(82:1–8)*

Bibliography

Ackerman, J. S. *An Exegetical Study of Psalm 82.* Ph.D. diss. Harvard University, 1966. **Anderson, F. I.** "A Short Note on Psalm 82,5." *Bib* 50 (1969) 393–94. **Budde, K.** "Ps. 82, 6f." *JBL* 40 (1921) 39–42. **Buss, M. J.** "The Psalms of Asaph and Korah." *JBL* 82 (1963) 382–92. **Cooke, G.** "The Sons of (the) God(s)." *ZAW* 76 (1974) 22–47. **Emerton, J. A.** "The Interpretation of Psalm lxxxii in John x." *JTS* 11 n.s. (1960) 329–34. ———. "Melchizedek and the Gods: Fresh Evidence for the Jewish Background of John X.34– 36." *JTS* 17 n.s. (1966) 399–401. **Fleming, D. M.** *The Divine Council as Type-Scene in the Hebrew Bible.* Ph.D. diss. Southern Baptist Theological Seminary, 1989. **Gonzalez, A.** "Le Psaume LXXXII." *VT* 8 (1963) 293–309. **Hanson, A.** "John's Citation of Psalm LXXXII Reconsidered." *NTS* 13 (1966/67) 363–67. **Hoffken, P.** "Werden und Vergehen der Götter: Ein Beitrag zur Auslegung von Psalm 82." *TZ* 39 (1983) 129–37. **Jeremias, J.** *Kultprophetie.* 120–25. **Jüngling, H.-W.** *Der Tod der Götter eine Untersuchung zu Psalm 82.* Stuttgart: Katholisches Bibelwerk, 1969. **Kingsbury, E. G.** "The Prophets and the Council of Yahweh." *JBL* 83 (1964) 279–86. **Miller, P. D., Jr.** "When the Gods Meet: Psalm 82 and the Issue of Justice." *Journal for Preachers* 9 (1986) 2–5; and in *Interpreting the Psalms.* Philadelphia: Fortress, 1986. 120–24. **Morgenstern, J.** "The Mythological Background of Psalm 82." *HUCA* 14 (1939) 29–126. **Mullen, E. T., Jr.** *The Assembly of the Gods: The Divine Council in Canaanite and Early Hebrew Literature.* HSM 24. Chico, CA: Scholars Press, 1980. 226–44. **Neyrey, J. H.** "'I Said: You Are Gods': Psalm 82:6 and John 10." *JBL* 108 (1989) 647–63. **Niehr, H.** "Götter oder Menschen—eine falsche Alternative, Bemerkungen zu Ps 82." *ZAW* 99 (1987) 94–98. **O'Callaghan, R. T.** "A Note on the Canaanite Background of Psalm 82." *CBQ* 15 (1953) 311–314. **Robinson, H. W.** "The Council of Yahweh." *JTS* 45 (1944) 151–57. **Smick, E. B.** "Mythopoetic Language in the Psalms." *WTJ* 44 (1982) 88–98. **Tidwell, N. L. A.** "WAᵓOMAR (Zech. 3:5) and the Genre of Zechariah's Fourth Vision." *JBL* 94 (1975) 343–55. **Tsevat, M.** "God and the Gods in Assembly." *HUCA* 40 (1969) 123–37.

Translation

1 An Asaphite psalm.[a]	
God[b] is standing[c] in the divine assembly,[d]	(3+3)
in the midst of the gods he pronounces judgment:	
2 (1) *"How long[a] will you judge unjustly,*	(3+3)
and favor[b] the wicked?—SELAH.	
3 (2) *Judge the powerless[a] and the orphan;*	(3+3)
maintain the rights[b] of the poverty-stricken.[c]	
4 (3) *Make the powerless poor[a] secure;[b]*	(3+3)
save[c] them from the hand of the wicked."	
5 (4) *They neither know nor understand;*	(4[2+2]+2+3)
they wander about in darkness,	
(while) the very[a] foundations of the earth shake![b]	
6 (5) *Indeed I said:[a]*	(4[2+2]+3)
"You are gods,	
and sons of Elyon are you all!"	

7 (6)   *"But, no!*[a] *You will die like humankind.*[b]   (3+3)
        and fall like any chieftain!"[c]

8 (7)   *Arise, O God, judge the earth!*   (4+4)
     For you have patrimony in every nation.[a]

Notes

1.a. See n. 73:1.a.

1.b. In the Elohistic section of the Psalter, אלהים stands for "Yahweh" (יהוה); note that אלהים in 1c refers to the "gods" or "divine beings," other than יהוה. The two words do not mean the same in both cases.

1.c. For the use of the verb form נצב (niphal participle), see Gen 24:13, 43; Exod 5:20; Num 22:23, 31, 34; Isa 3:13. The participle could express past tense ("he took his stand / place"), or present perfect ("he has taken his place," NRSV), but the poetic character of this psalm seems to indicate present tense. See *Comment.*

1.d. The עדת־אל is lit., "assembly of El (God)." It is probably, however, a fixed formula for "divine assembly" or "divine council." (Objection is occasionally made to the use of the word "council" [e.g., Kidner, II, 297–98], insisting on the word "assembly"; the difference, however, appears to be a matter of semantics and of little importance.) However, עדה does not appear in construct with Yahweh elsewhere in the OT to indicate the divine council, referring instead to the congregation of Israel (Num 27:17; 31:16; Josh 22:16–17; Ps 74:2). The "council of Yahweh" is elsewhere formed with סוד (Amos 3:7; Jer 23:18, 22; Job 15:8; Ps 25:14), and עדה does not appear in any other place in construct with El (Ackerman, *An Exegetical Study,* 283). LXX reads ἐν συναγωγῇ θεῶν, "in the assembly of the gods," which may represent אלם or אלים, parallel with אלהים in 1a and בני־עליון ("sons of Elyon") in 6b (Briggs, II, 217). Aq has ἐν συναγωγῇ ἰσχυρων, in "the assembly of the mighty," but Symm has ἐν συνόδῳ, "in the assembly of God." It is probable that the Greek versions represent a variant Heb. textual tradition of בעדת אלים, "in the assembly of the gods." It is unlikely that the LXX translators would have gone to the plural θεῶν, "gods," without finding it in the Heb. texts (Ackerman, 278–79, 284)—unless it was possibly the result of an error in the Greek transmission of the texts (see Ackerman, 284, n. 532), or the Greek translators took an enclitic *mem* as a plural: אל־ם as אלם or אלים (Mullen, *Assembly,* 230, n. 197). Symm and Jerome (*in coetu Dei,* "in the assembly of God") represent the tradition of "assembly of El (God)" which became the standard Heb. text c. 100–200 B.C.E. The Ugar. evidence is somewhat mixed, but Ackerman (281) concludes that it more likely indicates בעדת אלים. The expression in MT is probably what has been called a "frozen formula" for "divine council" or "divine assembly" borrowed from Canaanite sources (Mullen, 230). If this is the case, it is not likely that (1) אל is used as an epithet for Yahweh—the עדת־אל is not equal to the עדת־יהוה; (2) אל is not here the god El used over against Yahweh, with Yahweh pictured as a participant in the high god El's assembly, bringing charges against his fellow gods for their failure to provide justice (as advocated by Eissfeldt, "El and Yahweh," in *Kleine Schriften,* ed. R. Sellheim and F. Maass, vol. 3 [Tübingen: Mohr, 1966] 386–97; discussed at considerable length by Ackerman, 309–33, who finds it unconvincing, 331; Mullen, 230).

2.a. "How long?" (עד־מתי) is an expression found in some laments (see n. Ps. 90:13.b. and *Comment*). Here, however, the question has the character of a charge against the gods (cf. Ps 94:3–5; Exod 10:7; 1 Sam 1:14; Jer 4:14, 21; Ps 74:10; Prov 1:22).

2.b. Lit., "You lift up the faces of the wicked," i.e., you show respect, favor, and partiality.

3.a. The word דל refers to the "weak/lowly/helpless" people (e.g., Lev 19:15; Judg 6:15; Job 31:16; Ps 113:7; Isa 10:2; Jer 5:4).

3.b. The hiphil imperative form הצדיקו (from צדק) literally means "to cause to be righteous," but the meaning in contexts like this is "do justice/justify/vindicate" or "to pronounce a person guiltless" (KB, 794). The idea is that of helping persons get their rights, e.g., Deut 25:1; 2 Sam 15:4; Isa 5:23; 53:11.

3.c. Treating the עני ורש as a word pair which forms a hendiadys: lit., "afflicted/oppressed (one) and the one in want." For רש, see Ps 34:1; 1 Sam 18:23; 2 Sam 12:3; Prov 10:4; 13:8, 23.

4.a. Again, as in 3.b., treating the expression as a hendiadys: דל ואביון; lit., "the lowly and poor." The combination of words appears also in Ps 72:13.

4.b. Traditionally the פלטו (piel imperative) is translated as "rescue," but the verb can mean "to bring into security," or "keep safe" (BDB, 812): Mic 6:14; Pss 22:5, 9; 31:2; 37:40; 71:2; 91:14. The meaning in v 4 seems to be: "See that the lowly and the poor are free from oppression."

4.c. The verb הצילו > נצל (in hiphil imperative) is normally rendered "deliver," but the English "save . . . from" seems better here.

5.a. Reading the כל־ here as emphatic. Lit., "all of the foundations of the earth," or, "everything about the foundations of the earth." The translation above is almost the same as that of Tsevat, *HUCA* 40 91969) 125.

5.b. The verb מוט means to "totter/move/shake." Anderson (*Bib* 50 [1969] 393–94) argues that the meaning here has nothing to do with the shaking of the foundations of the earth. He notes the use of מוט for the tottering walk of a stunned or drunk person (Lev 25:35), and the activity of the legs (Pss 17:5; 38:17; 66:9; 94:18; 121:3). Further, he contends that מוסדי ארץ ("foundations of the earth") refers to the abode of the dead in the netherworld; the "foundations" are to be understood as the lower part of the physical structure of the world. He translates: "Those who do not care and do not understand will/walk around in darkness;/All of them will totter in the lower structures of the earth." This requires understanding כל־ as כלם, "all of them," with the preposition ב on בחשכה doing double duty with מוסדי ארץ, and the assumption of chiasm in the colon. Such forced treatment of the text generates no confidence.

6.a. Since the study of Budde in 1921 (*JBL* 40 [1921] 39–42) it has been rather common to translate the אני אמרתי at the beginning of v 6 as "I thought" (more literally, "I said to myself"). Budde argued that this is the meaning when the sequence אמרתי followed by אכן (v 7) occurs: Isa 49:4; Jer 3:19–20; Zeph 3:7; Ps 31:23; Job 32:7–8; cf. Exod 2:14; 1 Sam 15:32; Isa 40:7; 45:15; 53:4; Jer 3:20; 4:20; 8:8. Tsevat (*HUCA* 40 [1969] 125) has "Once I had thought you to be gods"; Kraus, "I thought: gods are you"; NJV, "I had taken you for divine beings." A. R. Johnson (*Sacral Kingship in Ancient Israel* [Cardiff: University of Wales Press, 1955] 90) reads as a positive statement in present tense: "I admit that ye are gods. . . . Nevertheless ye shall die like men" (citing GKC 106g). Johnson's solution avoids the difficulty of having Yahweh say, "I thought . . . but I was wrong"—a mistaken judgment about the gods, who presumably had fooled him about their true nature.

It is unlikely that we should read "I thought" in v 6. The examples of the אמרתי אכן sequence are impressive, but the number is limited and it is debatable whether the meaning is "said" or "thought" in some cases (e.g., Isa 49:4 is found in a dialogue: v 3—"And he [Yahweh] said [ויאמר] to me"; v 4—"Then I said [ואני אמרתי]" "But surely/nevertheless [ואכן] my judgment is with Yahweh"; v 5—"And now Yahweh says [אמר]," etc.). Does אני אמרתי in v 5 mean, really, "I thought"? In Jer 3:19–20, it is doubtful that Yahweh only *thinks* the content of v 19 (note the context of command which goes back to 3:12), though it is quite possible that אמרתי . . . ואמר here means "I intended." In Jer 8:8, איכה תאמרו, "How can you say . . . " is an accusation in lawsuit language (followed by אכן), similar to the question in Ps 82:2, and it is unlikely that the charge against the defendants would be: "How can you think, 'We are wise and the *torah* of Yahweh is with us.'" It seems doubtful to me that in 1 Sam. 15:32 we should conclude that Agag, having been brought before Samuel, "thought" the words which follow: "Surely (אכן) this is the bitterness of death" (NRSV). Thus it is better in 82:6 to retain the idea of Yahweh's recall of a definitive statement on his part in the past about the gods, although Johnson's translation is quite possible. Perhaps we should remember that silent reading, or talking to oneself (as Hannah in 1 Sam 1:12–13), was considered abnormal, or at least odd, in ancient culture.

7.a. The adverb אכן is usually taken with the force of "surely/truly/nevertheless," expressing a change from what is expected. In BDB (38) it is said to be stronger than אך (see n. Ps 62:2.a.). It functions in contrastive modes in most cases, rather than as asseverative. "The word ordinarily opens a speech that indicates a sudden recognition in contrast to what was theretofore assumed" (W. L. Holladay, *Jeremiah*, Hermeneia [Philadelphia: Fortress, 1986] 124, who notes that F. J. Goldbaun, "Two Hebrew Quasi-Adverbs לכן and אכן," *JNES* 23 [1964] 135, says that אכן means "Ah!"—a "grunt substitute," an interjection). The translation into English is usually better as "No!" or "Ah!" or "Oh, no!" I have chosen "But, no!" for Ps 82:6, which conveys the strong adversative force in the contrast between the statements in v 6 and those in v 7.

7.b. Mullen (*Assembly*, 243) argues that the אדם in this colon refers to the biblical "Adam" in Gen 2–3, who rebelled against God by eating the fruit of the "tree of knowledge of good and evil," which carried the penalty of death. For his transgression Adam was driven from the garden (Gen 3:24). This may be correct and would be an interesting reference to Gen 2–3, which is generally ignored in the rest of the OT. The meaning would differ little, if any, from the usual assumption that אדם refers to "humanity."

7.c. Traditionally, "and like one of the princes" (וכאחד השרים). A שׂר may be a representative of a king, or an official (Gen 12:15; Jer 25:19; Num 22:13, 35), or a chieftain or ruler (Num 22:8; Judg 7:25), or simply a leader or commander (Gen 21:22; 37:36). The plural שׂרים may refer to notable people, leaders, and officials (KB, 929). I take it that there is some irony, even sarcasm in v 7, and I have chosen "chieftain" because it is within the range of the meaning of שׂר and has a pejorative connotation in contemporary English.

It is unlikely that וּכְאַחַד should be re-pointed to וּכְאֶחָד and read adverbially with the meaning "all at the same time" or "together" (as, e.g., Kissane, II, 58, who translates "suddenly, ye princes, shall ye fall"). The parallelism with 7a ("like humankind") should be maintained in 7b ("like any שׂר"). See Tsevat, *HUCA* 40 [1969] 130, n. 29. Mullen (*Assembly*, 239–40) understands שׂר as a name, meaning "Shining One" (noting Akkadian *šorāru* "to be brilliant/shine," and the parallel with הילל, "the Shining One" in Isa 14:12 ("Lucifer" in Vg), who is cast into the netherworld (Isa 14:15). He also cites *CTA* 23.57 with a reference to *šarī puḫri*, "the Shining Ones of the Council." Mullen translates Ps 82:7b as "And like one of the 'Shining Ones' you shall fall." Ackerman (*Exegetical Study*, 402–23) pursues this matter at exhaustive length, but concludes that the interpretation of the שׂרים as gods cast out of heaven is not provable. He suggests that it is more probable that the imagery is that of the execution of שׂרים ("princes/nobles/leaders") after being captured in battle. His argument depends on his interpretation of the sentence in 7a as a death sentence of immediate execution, rejecting the idea that it is a divestiture of immortality (399). This seems to me to force the logic of the poetic account too hard and to fail to take into adequate account the כ on both אדם and אחד שׂרים. Does a sentence to die "like humanity" mean immediate death? Becoming subject to the mortality of humankind is sufficient.

8.a. The exact meaning of the colon in v 8b is not clear. RSV has "for to you belong all the nations," and NRSV and REB are very similar. This translation is probably accurate, but seems understated. LXX has ὅτι σὺ κατακληρονομήσεις ἐν πᾶσιν τοῖς ἔθνεσιν, which probably is equal to "for you will inherit all the nations," and has the advantage of recognizing the use of the verb נחל (qal), which means "get/take as a possession/inherit" (a denominative from נחלה, "possession/inheritance/property"). KJV argues with LXX, reading: "for you will inherit all the nations." NIV has, "for all the nations are your inheritance."

Part of the difficulty arises from the use of the verb נחל in *qal* followed by the preposition ב. There are some other examples of this, e.g., Judg 11:2: "and they said to him [Jephthah] you will not inherit in the house of our father" (לא תנחל בבית אבינו). See also, Num 18:20; Deut 19:14; Josh 14:1; cf. piel in Josh 13:22. Ackerman (430–34) argues that the qal of the verb נחל has three major usages: (1) "to receive, or be allotted, an inheritance" (Num 18:20, 23–24; 26:55; 35:19; Deut 19:14; Josh 14:1; etc.); (2) "to take possession of" (Exod 23:30; 32:13; Isa 57:13; Ps 69:37; Zeph 2:9); (3) "to allot, divide the land"—with only three clear references: Num 34:17–18; Josh 19:49; Ezek 47:14; cf. Ezek 34:9; Zech 2:15–16). The first two meanings are not suitable for the context in Ps 82 because Yahweh cannot receive or take possession of an inheritance which he already has. The territories assigned to the gods are in his realm and they are condemned for misrule in his נחלות ("inheritances"). Ackerman considers the possibility that the verb should be piel תְּנַחֵל or תְּנַחֵל, with the meaning of "to allot/divide inheritance" (437), but piel imperfect of נחל is not attested in MT. The hiphil (תַּנְחִיל or תַּנְחֵל), which is found in Deut 32:8–9, would mean to "grant inheritance" or "to allot." However, the hiphil in Deut 32:8–9 does not appear with the ב, and is unlikely to be correct in Ps 82:8, though Ackerman believes that the two passages refer to the same concept (438).

I find the flow of thought to be difficult if 8b is read to mean that Yahweh will allot territories *among* the nations since it is assumed that such apportionment has already happened. Ackerman (433–34), however, proposes that 8b be read in *past tense*, which is grammatically quite possible: "For you divided [inheritances] (תנחל) among the nations." V 8b is then a justification of the plea for Yahweh to take rule vacated by the deposed gods: It is his duty, because he assigned the gods their territories in the first place.

A weakness in this reading seems to occur in Ackerman's rejection of the present tense translation, "for you are in possession over all the nations" (*An Exegetical Study*, 432, n. 820), on the grounds that in attested usages the imperfect of נחל occurs in future tense with a direct object. There is, of course, no direct object in 8b. It is arguable that the imperfect form of נחל in Prov 3:35; 11:29; 28:10 expresses persistent present action, and the verb is found without an object in Num 18:20; 32:19. Therefore it seems possible to translate in present tense despite the more frequent future tense of the imperfect of נחל. The reading above assumes that Yahweh has the right of נחלה in all nations, rather than being a reference to his allocation of נחלות in the past. נחלה can mean "proprietory right(s)" or "patrimony" (Dahood argues for "patrimony" in a number of cases: Pss 2:8; 68:10b; 74:2; I, 13; II, 139, 200; he translates as "kingdom" in Ps 47:5 [I, 285]). In this approach, justification is given for the plea in 8a on the basis that Yahweh has patrimonial rights in every nation; he is, and has been, the "manor lord" (Schmidt's translation: *Erbherr*) over all the nations.

The verb could be read as jussive, parallel with the imperatives קוּמָה and שָׁפְטָה in 8a; so Dahood (II, 271), who wants to avoid three successive imperatives in the same verse and judges the change to imperfect to be a stylistic variant. In this case, the translation could be: "Exercise your patrimonial rights in every nation." Dahood, however, contends that נחל can mean to "rule over": "rule over all the nations yourself"—giving the expression with כִּי precative force. However, the understanding of 8b as a basis for the petition in 8a seems more likely to be the better reading.

NEB's "for thou dost pass all nations through thy sieve" follows G. R. Driver (*HTR* 29 [1936] 187), who argues that the verb נחל is to be associated with Assyrian *naḥālu*, "to sift." JB paraphrases (correctly, I think): "since no nation is excluded from your ownership."

Form/Structure/Setting

A glance at the bibliography above (which is not exhaustive) will reveal at once that this short psalm has generated an enormous amount of scholarly attention. And well it may, because it is *sui generis* in the Psalter; there is no other psalm like it. It has been described as "poetry with narrative context" (Fleming, *Divine Council*, 132), but it has not been easily definable in terms of genre or of function.

Since the work of Gunkel, especially, Ps 82 has been defined as having prophetic character, a prophetic psalm in the collection attributed to the Asaphites. Mowinckel (*PIW*, II, 64) finds it to be a "peculiar mixing of psalm and oracle, where the oracle is the chief thing but is organically fitted into a short prayer." Similar descriptions using the term "prophetic" are rather widespread: prophetic hymn, prophetic liturgy, prophetic tribunal, prophetic social critique, and prophetic lawsuit (see Fleming, *Divine Council*, 134–35). Jeremias (*Kultprophetie*, 120–25) deems Ps 82 to be a prayer which belongs very close to the cultic-prophetic liturgies of lament, though it differs in important respects, and belongs in the context of the judgment speeches of the cult prophets against the evildoers in Israel (also, Deissler, II, 151; Kraus, 154).

Over the past fifty years, several studies have grounded Ps 82 firmly in the tradition of accounts of the meetings of the divine council or assembly of the gods, notably the works of J. Morgenstern, H.-W. Jüngling, J. S. Ackerman, M. Tsevat, E. T. Mullen, and D. M. Fleming. The best source for clues as to the literary nature of the psalm is in the reports of such assemblies, especially in 1 Kgs 22:19–23; Job 1:6–12; 2:1–6; Zech 1:7–17; 3:1–5; Isa 6:1–13; 40:1–8.

Two or three characteristics of these reports are important for understanding Ps 82. First, the reports have a visionary character, in which a narrator reports what was "seen": "I saw Yahweh sitting on his throne" (1 Kgs 22:19); "In the year that King Uzziah died I saw the Lord seated on a throne" (Isa 6:1); "I saw at night; and behold!" (Zech 1:8); "And he showed me Joshua the High Priest standing before the angel of Yahweh" (Zech 3:1). Second, there is a direct and immediate style in the narration of the descriptions of the council or court scenes: the narrator speaks as a direct observer, which is particularly evident in Isa 40:1–8; Zech 1:8; and Ps 82. The style in Ps 82 is like that in the report of what Athaliah sees when she enters the temple in 2 Kgs 11:13–16: "And Athaliah heard the sound of the guards . . . and she came to the people in the house of Yahweh, and she looked, and behold, the king was standing [עֹמֵד] by the pillar." The action of an ongoing narrative is stopped as it were for a vignette, without much context, of the scene. Thus Ps 82 begins without the benefit of any introduction: "God is standing [נצב] in the divine assembly." Third, the narrator may be identified, as in the case of Micaiah in 1 Kgs 22 and the prophet Isaiah in Isa 6 (in both cases simply saying, "I saw"), but in other cases the voices seem almost at random: as when God speaks to his divine court in 1 Kgs 22 and responses are described as "and one said one thing, and another said another." In this regard, Ps 82 seems to share much with the unidentified voices in Isa 40:1–8 (a text which has recently received careful attention from C. R. Seitz, "The Divine Council: Temporal Transition and New Prophecy in the Book of Isaiah," *JBL* 109 [1990] 229–47). Seitz (245) argues that the voices in Isa 40:1–8 belong to anonymous members of the heavenly council responding to Yahweh. The narrator as it were overhears what is said in the council and puts it in the written form of a narrative, in such a way that "God speaks directly from the divine council without the need of prophetic agency" (Seitz, 246). This type of account represents a shift in prophetic literature from accounts of prophets as those who address an audience directly to accounts in which the prophet is addressed and conversation between God and his divine agents is reported. This is scribal prophecy and the accounts are literary productions rather than reports of the oral speeches of the prophets themselves.

Ps 82 seems to have the major features of such "scribal prophecy" and probably emerged from a similar matrix. The date of the origin of the psalm is probably impossible to fix precisely. It has been dated from the time of David, or earlier, to the time of the Maccabees. Mowinckel (*PIW*, I, 150–51; II, 132) related it to a new year festival which celebrated Yahweh's enthronement as the divine king, contending that the idea of a council or assembly of gods was a feature of this festival, though Ps 82 probably comes from a comparatively late time because of the connection between the idea of judgment and Yahweh's universal kingship. He also relates Ps 82 to Pss 12, 14, 58, 90, and others which he classifies as psalms of national lamentation (*PIW*, I, 221), derived possibly from the period of the late monarchy.

On the other hand, there are interpreters who want to to date the psalm to the early monarchy or to the pre-monarchical period. Ackerman exemplifies this position, arguing that the psalm originated in liturgies of the tribal league and was used later in the liturgies of the monarchy and in new year celebrations of the post-exilic period (see his summary, *An Exegetical Study*, 483–97). This position is based on the archaic nature of the psalm's language (Dahood, II, 269, cites this in agreeing with Ackerman's dating), its probable Canaanite prototype, and its place in the history of Israelite religion with the development of Yahweh as the supreme God.

Generally, however, a later date seems more probable and is supported by most commentators. Jungling (*Tod*, 78–79) summarizes a series of reasons for giving the psalm a *Sitz im Leben* in the time of the exilic prophets, especially Deutero-Isaiah, or somewhat later. Gonzalez (*VT* 8 [1963] 293–309) rejects the Ugaritic parallels as determinative of date and also relates it to the time of Deutero-Isaiah. Jeremias (*Kultprophetie*, 120–25) argues for the context of the psalm in the late monarchy and says that it is a "prototype (*Urbild*) of cultic-prophetic proclamations of justice" (see also, Kraus, 154–55). It seems to me, however, that it is more likely to be a literary composition which has dependence on the preaching of the prophets (such as Micaiah in 1 Kgs 22) rather than being a "prototype," and is probably from a later date. Years ago, Morgenstern (*HUCA* 14 [1939] 119–26) concluded that the psalm belongs to a date of c. 500–475 B.C.E., which is still a good guess.

I have suggested above that the speakers in Ps 82 are members of the heavenly assembly. There is no good reason to doubt that God is the speaker in vv 2–4 and v 7. There is some question about v 6, though I think the speaker is God (see *Comment*), and quite a bit about v 5. Vv 1 and 8 are framing verses for the speech in between, and are probably to be understood as from an anonymous member (or, members) of the divine council, rather than from a prophet who is directly describing a vision. The account of the scene in the divine council is narrated from the perspective of a participant(s).

The psalm seems to be developed with a familiar chiastic type literary structure of ABCDCBA.

> v 1 God is judging in the divine assembly
>> v 2 Charge against the gods
>>> vv 3–4 Charge violated by the gods
>>>> v 5 Result of the failure of the gods
>>> v 6 Proclamation of the gods' former status
>> v 7 Sentence of judgment on the gods
> v 8 prayer for God to rise and judge the earth.

Vv 3 and 4 recall the commission of the gods, which is completed by v 6. V 7 is the pronouncement of judgment which responds to v 2. God has risen to stand in the assembly of the gods in v 1, but he is implored to rise to judge the earth and exercise his patrimonial rights in v 8. The language of v 8 is that of petition in the laments (see *Comment*), but I take it to be more of a prayer of exclamation than of lament. Yahweh is encouraged to exercise his patrimonial rights in all the nations. The imperative קומה is used in the sense found, for example, in Isa 21:5: "Rise up, commanders, / oil the shield!" (NRSV). Or as Isa 51:17: "Arouse yourself; rise up, Jerusalem . . ." (REB). Or as Isa 60:1: "Arise, shine, for your light has come" (NRSV). Or Mic 4:13: "Arise and thresh, / O daughter Zion / for I will make your horns iron / and your hoofs bronze" (NRSV). The kingship and power of Yahweh is firmly established and the divine assembly acclaims its support of his action and encourages him to assume judgment of the earth for himself. "It sounds like man's Amen in response to the divine promise when the appeal is now made to God to appear and take direct charge himself also of the office of Judge of the earth and by virtue of his own authority to enter upon his exclusive Lordship over the nations, which like the possession of an inheritance by the heir is his by right" (Weiser, 560).

Comment

Ps 82 opens abruptly, without an introduction, with an immediate focus on God (Yahweh) having taken his stand in the midst of a council, or assembly, of divine beings while he pronounces judgment (v 1). He is clearly in charge, presiding over the meeting. "God" is not further identified, but he is surely Yahweh, the "Great God" who is designated as the "Great King over all the gods"

(מֶלֶךְ גָּדוֹל עַל־כָּל־אֱלֹהִים) in Ps 95:3; cf. 96:4 (Kraus, *Psalms 60–150,* 155). The "gods" (אֱלֹהִים) are the divine beings who function as his counselors and agents. Cf. v 6; Pss 8:6; 29:1 ("sons of gods," בְּנֵי אֵלִים); 89:6–7; Exod 15:11; Job 1:6; 2:1; Gen 6:2. The scene is pictured as that of a divine assembly in which the great king pronounces sentence on some of the gods who have failed in their duties. Tsevat (*HUCA* 40 [1969] 127) notes that the psalm's opening suggests that what "might normally be a routine assembly, where the gods report or participate in deliberations, has unexpectedly turned into a tribunal; God has stood up to judge the assembled." See also, Mowinckel, *PIW*, I, 151. In this regard the meeting is similar to that in Job 1:6–12, which seems routine until Yahweh and Satan come into conflict over Job.

The portrayal of God as standing is somewhat surprising, because one might assume that a king or judge would be seated (as represented in drawings from ancient Near Eastern sources in O. Keel-Leu, *The Symbolism of the Biblical World,* tr. T. J. Hallett [New York: Crossroad, 1978] 207–8). However, the OT seems to have two sets of concepts regarding this matter. Moses sits while judging, while the people stand (Exod 18:13); Deborah sat under a palm tree while judging Israel (according to Judg 4:5—though the יֹשֶׁב here may mean "lived"); David had a seat by the wall (1 Sam 20:5); see also 1 Kgs 7:7; Isa 16:5; 28:6; Ps 122:5; Prov 20:8. However, God is commonly spoken of as standing (see Tsevat, 127, citing Isa 3:13 with Ps 82:1; cf. Acts 7:54–55; Rev 5:6; 14:1; 19:17) although in the account of a divine council setting in Dan 7:9–14, which functions as a tribunal, the Ancient of Days is seated (יְתִב) and surrounded by a myriad host (cf. also Zech 3:1–10, where the Angel of Yahweh seems to be seated).

Ackerman (*An Exegetical Study,* 310–11) comments on the use of the verb נצב in Joseph's dream account in Gen 37:5–8 in which Joseph's sheaf rose (קָמָה) and remained standing (וְנִצָּבָה) while the sheaves of his brothers bowed down (תִּשְׁתַּחֲוֶיןָ) before it. The language is that of a royal court with subjects bowing down before their lord (Ackerman, 311–14, also notes that Yahweh stands [נִצָּב] over or on [עַל] the altar in Amos 9:1–4, and follows de Vaux, *Ancient Israel,* tr. J. McHugh [New York: McGraw-Hill, 1961] 156, in considering God's standing [קוּם] to give judgment in Ps 76:9–10). De Vaux argues that during the arguments in a case the judge remained seated, but stood up to pronounce the sentence, while the contending parties remained standing (cf. Isa 50:8). Ackerman (314–15) is inclined to agree, and concludes that נצב is used (1) to refer to the stance taken by a sovereign to receive acknowledgment of his lordship in his court, and (2) to address the accused in order to state charges and to pronounce sentence. On occasions, kings are noted as standing: Absalom, giving judgment while standing in the gate area in 2 Sam 15:1–6; Joash (Jehoash) in 2 Kgs 11:14; Josiah in 2 Kgs 23:3, who "stood by the pillar and made a covenant." The standing of Yahweh indicates that a very important matter is being decided.

The expression of the indictment in the form of a question, as in v 2, seems to have been a feature of Israelite judicial procedure (Ackerman, 336–37). See 1 Sam 22:13; 2 Sam 1:14; 1 Kgs 2:42–43. The use of the question form was probably to give the person (or persons) charged an opportunity to explain the offending actions. Ackerman (337) argues that the עַד מָתַי ("how long?") question in v 2 does not seek an answer, however, but introduces a complaint and a demand that the offending activities be halted, having the force of imperative "stop/

cease!" (citing Exod 10:3; Num 14:27; 1 Sam 1:14; 16:1; 1 Kgs 18:21; Jer 23:26). Thus he contends that v 2 is both an indictment and a command that the gods cease judging unjustly. This may be correct, but it seems to push the meaning of a formulaic saying too far. Of course, the speakers who use עד מתי in questions want the action at the point of concern stopped, but I fail to see that the question itself is a command (note that in some cases the question is followed by a command, as in Ps 82:3–4; Exod 10:3; 1 Sam 1:14; 16:1; 1 Kgs 18:21; Jer 23:26, 28; and with the command first, Jer 4:14).

Vv 3–4 are composed of a set of commands to the gods, following the question in v 2. They must recall the commission of the gods, since it would make little sense to command them to do what they will no longer have the opportunity to do because of their sentence in v 7. Their commission has been to provide judgment for those who lack the wealth and power to defend themselves in human society. The repetition of words for poor and needy people in vv 3–4 is an effective poetic device (Tsevat, 128): דל—רש—עני—יתום—דל: "weak"—"orphan"—"humble" (or, "oppressed")—"needy"—"weak." The imperative verb "judge" in 3a doubtless means "judge justly," but it seems to me that it may indicate the need for elders, judges, kings, and other leaders to actively intervene in the interest of powerless people who cannot defend their rights. V 2 expresses the positive action of the gods in giving advantage to the wicked, and v 3 sets forth their failure to act on behalf of the needy.

Yahweh expects judges and leaders to protect the marginalized people in society: the poor, the oppressed, and those without family support. Thus Job in his days of power and wealth testified that he went into the gate (where legal cases were tried) and "delivered the poor [עני] who cried, / and the orphan who had no helper. / The blessing of the poor [אבד] came upon me, / and I caused the widow's heart to sing for joy" (Job 29:12–13, NRSV). Further he declared: "I was eyes to the blind, / and feet to the lame. / I was a father to the needy, / and championed [ריב] the cause of the stranger. / I broke the fangs of the unrighteous [עול] / and made them drop their prey from their teeth" (Job 29:15–17, NRSV). Also, note the reference in Amos 5:10–12 regarding the hatred of wealthy oppressors for "the one who reproves [מוכיח] in the gate" and the "one who speaks the truth" about those who "trample on the poor [דל]" in order to build their fine houses and maintain their affluent lifestyle. The contrast with the performance of the gods is evident; they have failed to do their duty.

The identity of the speaker in v 5 is ambiguous. God may continue his charge against the gods, or else further describe the condition of the oppressed people in vv 3–4, as in Johnson (Sacral Kingship, 90), who translates: "Rescue the weak and the poor / who have neither knowledge nor understanding, / But live persistently in darkness, / So that all the foundations of the earth are shaken." Also, Kidner (II, 298), who takes the verse as describing "the plight of the misgoverned and misled."

However, it seems more likely that v 5 describes the condition of the gods; it is part of their indictment. The speaker could be God addressing other members of the assembly who are not under judgment, turning aside for a moment from direct address to the condemned gods and perhaps presupposing a pause after v 4 when the gods could have responded but did not (Gunkel, 362; Ackerman, 380–83). Tsevat (HUCA 40 [1969] 129) suggests that the speaker is God and that the verse is "not an address or a proclamation but the deliberation of the judge in camera in preparation for the verdict." It is, of course, possible that it is the voice of the psalmist who interrupts the flow of the account with a reflection or commentary on the nature of the gods—or possibly on the condition of the lowly and poor in vv 3–4. It seems more probable to me, however, in view of the form critical nature of the psalm (see *Form/Structure/Setting*) that the speaker in v 5 is an anonymous voice of one of the members of the heavenly assembly, the narrator in vv 1 and 8.

V. 5 makes it clear that the failure of the gods is not accidental or incidental, although Tsevat (128) may go too far when he evaluates the verse as saying of them that it is "Not that they are unwilling to do what they are bidden—if that were the case, there would be hope that they would change their minds—but they are incapable of grasping the issue, of walking in the light. As long as they are in office there is no hope for the world; the whole present order is corrupt, and the corruption affects the foundation of the earth." Should we say, however, that as inherently faulty as the performance of the gods is they are simply captives of their benighted nature? If so, how is the judgment of Yahweh justified? In that case, the gods could do no other than what they have done! Ps 82 certainly partakes of the general polemic in the OT against the basic lack of power on the part of other gods vis-à-vis Yahweh, but that does not mean that they are totally impotent. The psalm assumes that the gods are responsible for their grievous malpractice, and v 5 is better taken as descriptive of resulting conditions. The verse is a general statement of what happens to all those who disregard the commands of God relating to justice and the care of the marginalized people in human society. The "darkness" in which the gods wander about (walk back and forth) may be either (1) the darkness they have brought to the lands because of their malfeasance in judgment—and in this respect the interpretation of Johnson and Kidner referred to above may be partially correct—or (2) the darkness may be what they use to cloak their deeds from the scrutiny of their sovereign (Ackerman, *An Exegetical Study,* 373), or (3) it may reflect their be-nighted nature which has resulted from their refusal to "know" and understand the ways of God—or all three!

The shaking of the foundations of the earth in v 5c refers to the subversion of the order which sustains creation. "In the Old Testament just judgment is the real substructure of the universe—the foundations of the whole creation. . . . The demonic power-plays of the gods call the existence of the world into question" (Kraus, 157). H. H. Schmid (*Gerechtigkeit als Weltordnung,* BHT 40 [Tübingen: Mohr, 1968] 81–82) comments that when judgment is not rendered properly, the "foundations of the earth shake . . . the cosmic order is destroyed." The world-view behind v 5 is a holistic one, with interconnections between all spheres of life.

Some commentators think v 6 is a continuation of the speaker's evaluation of the gods in v 5; e.g., Dahood (II, 270) says that "the psalmist had been under the impression that the pagan deities were of some importance, but now realizes that they are nothing" (see Perowne, 105–7, who thinks it likely that vv 2–7 are a "rebuke addressed, in the true prophetic strain, by the poet himself," though he notes that most interpreters do not agree; also Kissane, II, 57–59). Another approach is to take v 6 as the recall on the part of God of a particular moment in time when he had spoken a decree which established the duties of the gods (e.g.,

Schmidt, 156), translating the אֲנִי אָמַרְתִּי as "I said" or "I once said." In this case, Yahweh would now be revoking his former decree. This is the interpretation which I prefer, despite the strong support for reading אֲנִי אָמַרְתִּי followed by אָכֵן as "I thought . . . but, no . . ." (see note 6.a.; Ackerman, *An Exegetical Study*, 385, adopts the "I thought" reading and says, "Yahweh is . . . stating a misconception which he had wrongly held . . . the condemned were at no time truly 'gods' and 'sons of Elyon'"). Is it likely that Yahweh would have been fooled in his judgment about the true nature of the gods? Again the question arises, as in v 5, if the gods are and have been hopeless miscreants, what is the basis for the judgment in vv 2–4? How can they be held liable for what they were never empowered to do? V 6 must recall God's appointment of the gods to their duties; the pronouncement by which they were "invested with divine authority to execute judgment in His name" (Kirkpatrick, 497). The statement could be treated as sarcastic, of course: "I accepted you as really gods, even sons of Elyon, all of you!" But this seems unlikely.

For Elyon (אֶלְיוֹן) as a divine name, see note Ps 92:2.b.

The judgment on the gods in v 7 strips them of their divine status and condemns them to "the human fate of death" (Kraus, 157). They will no longer have an exalted status, free from the ravages of disease and death. It is too much to say, however, that the sentence is that of capital punishment with immediate execution (cf. Cohen, 271; Ackerman, 398). The sentence is that of becoming mortal and subject to the sudden "falls" of human leaders. Ackerman (400) observes that the verb נפל is often used for sudden and disastrous death: assassination, death in battle, or execution (e.g., Exod 19:21; 33:28; Josh 8:25; Judg 8:10; 12:6; 20:44, 46; 1 Sam 4:10; 31:8; 2 Sam 1:19, 25, 27; 3:38; 11:7; 21:9; 1 Kgs 22:20; Isa 14:12; Jer 20:4). The gods will become vulnerable to the destructive "falls" of tyrants, chieftains, princes, generals, and other kinds of leaders and officials. They are to be deposed from their divine prerogatives.

The judgment on the gods has some similarity to the rather widespread mythical imagery of the revolt and punishment of a god. A god could be killed if he became rebellious and failed to carry out his functions; as, for example, Kingu in *Enūma eliš* (4.119–28); *dWe-ila* in *Atra-hasis* (1.4.123–24); however, the claim that one god renders a whole group of gods to be mortal seems to be without parallel elsewhere (Miller, *Interpreting*, 123). In the OT, the fall of a great king is described in Isa 14:4–21, who had been of such high status as to think of himself as seated in the assembly of the gods, but who is now fallen down to Sheol where he has fellowship with maggots and worms along with his fellow tyrants who have become as weak as he. For extensive treatment of the motif of the revolt of a god and the fall from heaven, see Morgenstern, *HUCA* 14 (1939) 76–114; Ackerman, *An Exegetical Study*, 402–23.

In the case of Ps 82, however, there is no indication of a challenge to divine authority, as seems to have been the case in the mythical framework of the account in Isa 14. Cf. the case of the prince of Tyre in Ezek 28:1–10, who has this charge lodged against him by Yahweh (v 2, NRSV): "Because your heart is proud / and you have said, 'I am a god [אֵל אָנִי]; / I sit in the seat of the gods [אֱלֹהִים] / in the heart of the seas, / yet you are but a mortal [אָדָם] and no god [אֵל], / though you compare your mind with the mind of a god [אֱלֹהִים].'" Cf. also, the "little horn" (Antiochus Epiphanes) in Dan 8:9–11; 11:21–45. The sentence of mortality and deposition from high rank in Ps 82 results from the simple failure of the gods to do their job of maintaining the welfare of the lowly and poor among human beings (Mullen, *Assembly*, 243).

In fact, in the conceptual field of ancient thought, the loss of immortality by the gods means that they are no longer capable of keeping their position (Tsevat, *HUCA* 40 [1969] 129–30). The matter is put forcefully by some lines from the Old Babylonian version of the Gilgamesh epic: "When the gods created mankind, / they set apart death for mankind, / but retained life in their own hands" (X.3:3–5). In the Ugaritic Aqhat epic, Prince Aqhat, after refusing an offer of immortality from the goddess Anat, declares: "I shall die the death of all (men), / I, too, shall certainly die" (see 2 Aqht.6.26–38). Gods are no longer gods when they must eventually fall and die like human beings.

In v 8, God is implored to arise and judge the earth. The "arise" (קוּמָה) is rather common in the petitions found in laments (e.g., Pss 3:8; 7:7; 9:20; 10:12; 44:26; 74:22; cf. Num 10:35; Jer 2:27). As discussed in *Form/Structure/Setting*, however, it seems to be more acclamation than supplication in this context. The implication of the petition seems clear that Yahweh is being encouraged to do what the gods have not done. They have failed in their responsibilities and Yahweh is the one to correct their error by judging the world properly. Ackerman (433) may be correct to conclude that v 8b provides further justification for Yahweh to act in the absence of the deposed gods because it is assumed that he assigned the gods their duties in the various נחלות ("patrimonies/inheritances") of the earth. This conclusion could be correct without following Ackerman's translation of תנחל as "allot" or "divide" the land among (ב) the nations. Perhaps it matters little whether we take 8b as referring to Yahweh's past allotment of נחלות among the nations or to his right of patrimony in every nation. In either case, he is the supreme ruler and judge who alone can bring justice to the oppressed peoples of the world.

V 8 calls for a "realignment of world order" (Fleming, *Divine Council*, 146), with Yahweh himself assuming the duties of the neutralized gods. Their failure and sentence is similar in some respects to that passed on the semi-divine Keret (or, Kirta) by his son in the Ugaritic texts:

> You do not judge the case of the widow,
> Nor do you judge the case of the wretched.
> You do not drive out the oppressor of the poor!
> You do not feed the orphan before you,
> Nor the widow behind you!
> You have become a companion of the sick-bed,
> You have become a friend of the bed of sickness!
> Descend from the kingship that I might reign,
> From our dominion that I might sit enthroned over it!
> (*CTA* 16.6.45–54)

Keret's son, Yassib, is trying to oust him from his throne on the grounds that he cannot fulfill the essential duties of kingship. Keret does not take kindly to his son's pronouncement and in turn pronounces a curse on him, asking that the god Horon and the goddess Astarte smash his skull: "May you fall at the prime of your life" (tr. M. D. Coogan, *Stories from Ancient Canaan* [Philadelphia: Westminster,

1978] 74). There is no debate with Yahweh in Ps 82, of course; his pronouncement is nondebatable and there is no call for any other gods to judge the world.

The meaning of v 8b is treated at some length in note 8.a. above. Three major
translations seem to be possible: (1) "for you granted inheritances among all the
nations," taking the verb תנחל as past tense in the sense of allot or grant territory;
(2) "for you will possess (as inheritance) all the nations," or, taking the imperfect
verb with כי־אתה as jussive or precative: "take possession of all the nations as your
inheritance"; (3) "for you have possession of all the nations," or "you have
patrimony in every nation."

I prefer the third option; the basis for the petition in 8a is the patrimonial
rights which Yahweh has in every nation. He may judge the earth if he chooses,
because his "inheritance" extends into every country.

In any case, the conceptual horizon of v 8, and of the entire psalm, is that of
the assignment of the gods to each nation as patron deities, who would be
responsible for the welfare of each nation. This idea finds expression in the
corrected text of Deut 32:8–9:

> When the Most High (עליון) apportioned (בהנחל) the nations,
> When He set up the divisions of mankind (אדם),
> He fixed the boundaries of the peoples
> According to the number of the sons of "God" (or, "El"),
> But Yahweh's own allotment in His people,
> Jacob His apportioned property.

(The translation is that of Tsevat, 132; for textual details, see his notes and
BHS). See also, Deut 4:19–20; Jer 10:14 = 51:17–19; 16:19–20; Dan 10:13, 20–21;
12:1; Ecclus 17:17; *1 Enoch* 20.5; *Jub.* 5.31–32; 35.17. Yahweh apportioned the nations among the gods, selecting Israel for himself and retaining ultimate hegemony
over all the nations; "When God established the existing order, He turned over
to others part of what was His. It never ceased to be His; may He, then, today
reenter into His own" (Tsevat, 133). The gods serve only so long as their service
is in accord with his purposes. Their time of service has come to an end. The
Sovereign of the heavens and the earth himself will now rise in judgment to the
acclaim of the heavenly assembly.

Explanation

I will give attention, and only briefly, to two major aspects of Ps 82. First, who
are the "gods" referred to and judged in this psalm? A very old stream of
interpretation interprets the "gods" as human judges or officials. This is based
primarily on references in Exod 21:6; 22:6–7, 8, 27; 1 Sam 2:25 (cf. also, Exod
2:27; Judg 5:8), in which the parties in legal procedures are directed to come
before "God" (אלהים). In Exod 21:6, Hebrew slaves who wished to remain in
service to their masters after six years of service are to be brought to God at the
doorpost and have an ear pierced with an awl. The *Targum Onqelos* translates אלהים
as דיניא, "judges," and forms the basis for the conclusion that אלהים = "judges" (also
in Exod 22:6–7, 8; see C. H. Gordon, "אלהים in Its Reputed Meaning of *Rulers,
Judges*," *JBL* 54 [1935] 139–44; Jüngling, *Tod,* 24–37). Much is made of Exod 22:27

[28]: "you shall not revile God (אלהים), and you shall not curse a ruler (נשׂיא) among your people." It is assumed that אלהים and נשׂיא are synonymous.

The interpretation is not well grounded in the exegesis of the texts. The exact meaning of being brought before אלהים (as in Exod 21:6) is not known, but it most probably involved some sort of ceremony, not necessarily, or even probably, conducted by judges in a legal sense. Further, regardless of the meaning of אלהים in these texts, it does not follow that אלהים in Ps 82 refers to judges or other leaders. In fact, if the unity of the psalm is maintained, and there is no real reason not to do so, the simile, "like humankind" and "like the princes/chieftains" in v 7 makes it impossible to assume that the "gods" (who are also called "sons of Elyon" in v 6) could be human beings.

Despite its exegetical weakness, however, the old tradition of relating Ps 82 to human actions has a strong element of truth in it. Niehr (*ZAW* 99 [1987] 94–98) argues that to conclude that Ps 82 must be understood as either relating to gods or to human beings is a false alternative. Both are involved because God's judgment of the gods has its parallel in God's judgment of unjust human officials (Niehr attempts to ground God's judgment in the psalm in the social critique of rulers in the eighth century B.C.E., which need not detain us here). In the content of the Bible, there is a persistent nexus between the heavenly realm and the realm of the world. Judgmental activity on earth interacts with that administered by heavenly authorities (cf. Kraus, I, 576). The gods as patrons of the various nations were responsible for the type of kings, judges, and officials they appointed and empowered; however, the gods, not even Yahweh, do not act directly. Their will is administered by human agents, who are extensions of the divine presence in earthly affairs. Thus the judgment of the gods is at the same time a judgment of their human agents.

The second aspect of Ps 82 which merits attention is the matter of the meaning of this psalm for modern readers. Christian readers will be aware of its importance in the interpretation of John 10 in the NT (see the article by Neyrey, *JBL* 108 [1989] 647–63, for treatment of this matter and full references to other works). Apart from this, however, the psalm has its own message. The powerful divine concern for justice in human society is certainly a major feature of that message regardless of what other components it may contain. The issue of the governance of human affairs is a matter of life and death to God Almighty. He does not take lightly the mistreatment of the lowly and powerless in the world. Injustice shakes the very substructure of the cosmic order and the "world threatens to fall apart into chaos once more" (Miller, *Interpreting*, 124). The artistically constructed psalm—a fine piece of imaginative poetry composed of 59 Hebrew words—depicts judgment in the divine realm, but we know as human beings that God does not intend to be any less rigorous with us. The responsibilities of the gods are ours. Thus despite the heavenly setting in the psalm it points us toward firmly grounding our religion in the earthly needs of people (Stuhlmueller, II, 43). An abstract theology which seeks to separate itself from human affairs leads to a sentence of death. At the same time the psalm encourages us to keep our attention on heavenly matters as we conduct the business of the world. The gods are under a sentence of mortality; they have become no-gods. But the world is prone to believe that this is not true; it thinks the gods of indifference and injustice are still in control. Ps 82 says that there is ultimate accountability. God is standing, even now, in the divine assembly and charges his agents, divine and human:

Judge the powerless and the orphan;
maintain the rights of the poverty-stricken.
Make the powerless poor secure;
save them from the hand of the wicked.

A Prayer for the Punishment of Enemies   (83:1–19)

Bibliography

Buss, M. J. "Psalms of Asaph and Korah." *JBL* 82 (1963) 382–92. **Costacurta, B.** "L'aggressione contro Dio: Studio del Salmo 83." *Bib* 64 (1983) 518–41. **Lahau, M.** "Who Is the 'Ashurite' (2 Sam. 2:9) and 'Asher' (Ps. 83:9)?" *BMik* 28 (1982–83) 111–12 (Heb.). **MacLaurin, E. C. B.** "Joseph and Asaph." *VT* 25 (1975) 27–45. **Ogden, G. S.** "Joel 4 and Prophetic Responses to National Laments." *JSOT* 26 (1983) 97–106. **Wifall, W.** "The Foreign Nations: Israel's 'Nine Bows.'" *Bulletin of Egyptological Seminar* 3 (1981) 113–24.

Translation

1   A song;[a] an Asaphite psalm.[b]

2 (1) *O God,[a] do not rest;[b]*   (3+3)
       do not be silent or still, O God.[c]

3 (2) *For lo, your enemies are roaring[a]*   (3+3)
       and those who hate you have raised[b] their heads.[c]

4 (3) *Against your people they make plans,*   (3+3)
       and they conspire together against your treasured ones.[a]

5 (4)   *They say:[a]*   (1+3+3)
       "Come and let us exterminate them as a nation,
       and the name of Israel will be remembered no more."

6 (5) *For they have consulted together[a] with one mind;*   (3+3)
       (even) against you they are making a covenant.[b]

7 (6) *The tents of Edom and the Ishmaelites,[a]*   (3+2)
       Moab[b] and the Hagrites.[c]

8 (7)   *Gebal[a] and Ammon and Amalek,[b]*   (3+3)
       Philistia with the inhabitants of Tyre.

9 (8)   *Also, Assyria is joined with them,*   (3+3)
       they have become the arm for the sons of Lot.[a] SELAH.

10 (9) *Do to them as with Midian[a]—*   (3+2+2)
       as with Sisera and Jabin[b]
       at the river Kishon,

11 (10)   *who were destroyed at En-dor,[a]*   (2+2)
       who became dung for the ground—

12 (11)	*Deal with their nobles* [a] *as with Oreb and Zeeb,*	(4+3)
	and with all their princes as with Zebah and Zalmunna,	
13 (12)	*who said,*	(2+2+3)
	"Let us take possession for ourselves	
	of the pasturelands [a] *of God."*	
14 (13)	*O my God, treat them as whirling dust,*	(3+2)
	as chaff before the wind,	
15 (14)	*as a fire which burns a forest,*	(3+3)
	as flames which set mountains ablaze!	
16 (15)	*So pursue them with your tempest;*	(3+2)
	terrify them with your storm;	
17 (16)	*fill their faces with humiliation,*	(3+3)
	so that they will seek your name, [a] *O Yahweh.*	
18 (17)	*Let them be put to shame and terrified, continually;*	(3+2)
	let them be abashed and perish, [a]	
19 (18)	*that they may know that you,*	(2+3+3)
	whose name is Yahweh, you only, [a]	
	are the Most High over all the earth.	

Notes

1.a. See n. 65:1.c.

1.b. See n. 73:1.a.

2.a. Cf. אלהים here and in v 13 with יהוה in 17b, 19. Briggs sees the occurrences of יהוה as glosses within the "Elohistic Psalter" (Pss 42–83). Kraus treats יהוה as the original form which was emended to אלהים in the first two instances by the Elohistic redactor and proposes that we read יהוה in vv 2a and 13. The occurrence of both divine names in the psalm may indicate that it was used as a part of more than one collection.

2.b. LXX, Vg, and Syr indicate מי ידמה, "Who will be like you?" But MT is satisfactory, and LXX probably represents either dittography or haplography (see Briggs, II, 223). Cf. Ps 89:7; Isa 62:6.

2.c. The divine name אל is used here in place of אלהים. Dahood suggests that this is a vocative form, "O El," and that it forms an inclusion with a vocative אלהי (which he assumes as correct), as in v 14, at the beginning of the verse. Similar usage of vocative אל can be found in Pss 10:12, 16:1, 17:6, and 139:23.

3.a. The verb המה pictures a crowd-like murmuring or mob-induced confusion or tumult.

3.b. The phrase ומשנאיך נשאו, "and those who hate you have raised," has a wordplay on the verbs שנא and נשא.

3.c. Lit., "have raised a head." The collective idea conveys the idea of raising their heads in haughty arrogance or in victory. REB has "carry their heads high"; NJV is rather flat: "assert themselves." Cf. Judg 8:28, where the defeated Midianites are said to "lift up their heads no more." Heads are lifted up at the news of victory in Ps 24:7, 9. Cf. also Job 10:15; Zech 2:4 [1:21].

4.a. צפוניך, "your treasured one," (qal pass participle of צפן, "to treasure/hide"). Some ancient sources read צְפוּנֶךָ, a singular noun meaning "your jewel" or "your treasure" (Gunkel; Schmidt), possibly indicating a sanctuary or temple. Dahood (II, 274) prefers the alternate reading and leans toward the meaning as a complement to עמך ("your people") at the beginning of the verse. Kraus (*Psalms 60–150*, 160) retains MT, but understands the צפוניך as "your charges" or "your protégés"— "those entrusted to your care." NRSV has "those you protect."

5.a. The translation above treats the אמרו ("they say") as an anacrusis outside the colons which follow. The colons in 5b and 5c are reasonably balanced without the deletion of עוד or שם (as proposed by Briggs, II, 223). Note the similar construction in v 13.

6.a. The expression לב יחדו is difficult to translate literally and is the recipient of suggested emendations: Gunkel (366) emends לב יחדו to read לב אחד, "one heart." For the verb without ("heart/mind"), see Ps 71:10; Isa 45:21; Neh 6:7. Briggs (II, 223) suggests a conflation of two readings: נועצו יחדו and נועצו לב אחד, which may be correct.

6.b. The phraseology, . . . עַל . . . בְּרִית . . . כָּרַת, "make a covenant *against* " is not used else-where in the OT. Covenants are usually made "with," not "against," another entity. Therefore, Dahood suggests reading עָלֶיךָ as a pl. participle from עלה ("your assailants make a covenant," with עלה in the sense of "rise up against to attack." But Dahood fails to give any convincing example of the verb with this meaning, although he could have cited Isa 7:6; Jer 4:13; Joel 4:9 [3:9]; etc.

7.a. The Ishmaelites are generally associated with tribes south of Judah. Paralleled here with the Edomites (descendants of Esau, Gen 36:1–17) we have a pair of references to the tradition of sons whose brothers were chosen over them (Isaac and Jacob) as patriarchs.

7.b. Moab refers to a tribal people located to the east of the Jordan, active in the time of Saul (as attested by 1 Chr 5:10).

7.c. The identity of the Hagrites (הַגְרִים) is uncertain. They are associated with territory in North-ern Arabia in 1 Chr 5:10, 19–20. Their mention with the Ishmaelites makes it natural to assume some connection with Hagar and Abraham (cf. Gen 16:1, 15). Hagrites are also mentioned in 1 Chr 11:38; 27:30.

8.a. Gebal (גְּבָל) is identified by some (e.g., Dahood) as the Philistine city of Byblos. Mentioned elsewhere only in Ezek 27:9 (with *pathah*). More likely it refers to a location south of the Dead Sea near Petra in Edom since it is listed with Ammon. Syr has "borders of Ammon," which is adopted by Kissane, II, 62–63 (reading גְּבָל). Briggs (II, 223) also eliminates the possibility of a placename by translating "lords of Ammon," emending MT to גְּבוּלֵי ("borders/territory of"), which he suggests may be a garbled form of בַּעֲלֵי, "lords/masters of."

8.b. Amalek was primarily a southern tribe from the area of the Negeb with very ancient roots (see e.g., Exod 17:8; Num 24:20).

9.a. The expression לִבְנֵי לוֹט, "for the sons of Lot," is a traditional reference to peoples surround-ing Judah; here most likely Ammon (Deut 2:19) and Moab (Deut 2:9).

10.a. The shift of "as Midian" (כְּמִדְיָן) to the beginning of v 11 is fairly common in commentaries (e.g., Gunkel, Schmidt, Oesterley, Kraus; see *BHS*), which gives the colons better balance. However, I have taken the formation of vv 10–12 as an envelope structure, with the insertion of the material in vv 10b, 10c, 11a, and 11c within the larger reference to the Midianites in vv 10a and 12–13 (the pattern is A X B [for references, see *Form/Structure/Setting*, Ps 69]). The short colons in 10b, c, and 11a, b are then well balanced.

10.b. Sisera and Jabin are defeated enemies mentioned in Judg 4–7.

11.a. The place name עֵין־דֹּאר is spelled variously: עֵין־דֹּר (Josh 17:11), עֵין־דּוֹר (1 Sam 28:7). Some commentators prefer to read עֵין־חֲרֹד as in Judg 7:1, a location associated with the Midianite raids on the Israelites. E.g., Gunkel (366) suggests that חֲרֹד was corrupted to דֹר and then identified with En-dor (עֵין־דֹּאר) in 1 Sam 28:3–25 and Josh 17:11–12. See *Comment*.

12.a. The construction שִׁיתֵמוֹ נְדִיבֵמוֹ, "make them, their nobles," seems redundant. Perhaps the verb should be reduced to the nonsuffixed imperative, as in *BHS* (following LXX): שִׁית(ה) or שִׁית. If MT is retained, the construction is probably emphatic. Delitzsch (II, 470) says that "the heaped-up suffixes . . . give to the imprecation the rhythm and sound of pealing thunder."

13.a. The word נְאוֹת is the plural of נָוֶה, "place where one pastures/pasture ground," or more generally, "place/abode"; of Yahweh, see Exod 15:13; 2 Sam 15:25; Jer 25:30. Perhaps, we should read the singular (cf. *BHS*). LXX has θυσιαστήριον or ἁγιαστήριον: "the altar" or "the sanctuary" of God.

17.a. The second colon is problematic because of its seeming incoherence within the context of the psalm. As such, several have suggested emendations: Gunkel (and Schmidt) suggest reading שְׁלֹמְךָ for שִׁמְךָ and thus reading "that they may seek peace with you [your peace]." Dahood emends by placing the final *waw* of בַּקֵּשׁוּ on שִׁמְךָ(וּ) and reading בַּקֵּשׁ as "avenge" or "exact a penalty" (see Gen 31:39; 43:9; 1 Sam 20:16; 2 Sam 4:11; Ezek 3:18, 20; 33:8; Josh 22:23): "Let your name, Yahweh, avenge itself." It hardly needs to be said that his reading is highly questionable, especially since the verb with this meaning is normally followed by an explicit direct object. The difficulty of the statement is sometimes overstated; e.g., Dahood (II, 277) claims that it is "hardly amendable to coherent exegesis." Kraus (*Psalms 60–150*, 164) rejects Gunkel's idea of the nations "looking for peace" with Yahweh and correctly points to the expectation that the nations are to recognize the universal lordship of Yahweh.

18.a. Reading the imperfects as jussives. Gunkel (367) adds יֹחַד to the end of the second stich to complete the meter, thus rendering "and let them perish together," but this is unnecessary.

19.a. Frequently commentaries and translations follow LXX and take לְבַדְּךָ ("alone") with the second half of the verse, sometimes with the omission of שִׁמְךָ ("your name") as in Kraus (*Psalms 60–150*,

160): "That they may realize that you, O Yahweh / alone are the Most High over all the earth." Oesterley (376) deletes both שמך and יהוה to read: "And let them know that thou alone / art Most High over all the earth." NJV seems to read וידעו ("and they will know/and let them know") as an anacrusis (cf. v 5): "May they know / that your name, Yours alone, is the LORD, / supreme over all the earth." I have chosen to read the verse with an A X B pattern (cf. the envelope pattern in vv 10–12), with שמך יהוה לבדך as the middle element, which is an explanatory statement emphasizing that the Most High (עליון) over all the earth is indeed Yahweh.

Form/Structure/Setting

Ps 83 is generally accepted as a national lament, manifesting several character-istics of this form. It implores Yahweh to come to the aid of his people who are being surrounded by a host of enemies. The speaker perceives the problem as being rooted in the evil of the heathen nations around Israel and not due to sinfulness within Israel. In this regard it is like other national laments with the absence of a call to repentance (e.g., Pss 44, 74, 80, 137). The psalm focuses on a petition urging Yahweh not to remain passive toward present threats; reminding him of his interventions in the past in destroying earlier enemies of Israel (vv 10–13).

The careful enumeration of Israel's enemies might lead the reader to believe that the psalm's historical setting could be easily determined. But the number of nations listed and their combination confuses the issue since there was never a period in Israel's history when all of these enemies threatened concurrently.

Kraus (*Psalms 60–150,* 161) comments on the "amazing" confidence of some commentators in their ability to fix the historical situation in this psalm: from the Assyrian period of pre-exilic Israel to the period of the Maccabees (one of the more popular contexts argued for is that reflected in 2 Chr 20, but the nations in Ps 83 are not mentioned in that passage). Kraus himself thinks that the list of nations is freely composed, as a more or less standard portrayal of an "assault of nations" against Israel. The fact that there are ten nations named supports the conclusion that we are dealing with a stereotypical list (cf. Dan 7:7, 20, 24). Such a large coalition of nations in alliance against Israel is both unknown and improbable (Deissler, II, 156).

The dating of the psalm tends to follow the historical situation presupposed. If "Assyria" in v 9 is taken as a direct historical reference, contemporary with the composition of the psalm, it would point to a date between the ninth and seventh centuries B.C.E. (cf. Schmidt, 158). It is more likely, however, that Assyria is mentioned as an *example* of one of the great world powers allied with the small states around Israel. It is rather strange that Egypt and Babylon are not mentioned, but Ezra 6:22 provides some evidence of Assyria as a stereotyped reference to a foreign power (the "king of Assyria" there seems actually to refer to Persia; cf. Hos 9:6; Zech 10:10–11; Lam 5:6; Isa 11:11; 19:23–25; 27:13; Jdt 2:1; 1 QM 1.2; 18.2; 19.10.

If the lexical criteria for dating Hebrew poetry set forth in *Form/Structure/Set-ting* of Ps 93 have any validity, Ps 83 is a late composition, with prose-like constructions (e.g., the את in v 13; also the relative pronoun אשר in 13.a). The psalm probably originated from a post-exilic context (Deissler, II, 156, cites v 2 as dependent on Isa 62:1), though a late pre-exilic date is possible. The "Judean perspective" and the "cultic traditions of Jerusalem" (Kraus, 162) are not out of harmony with a post-exilic date. In any case, Gunkel's proposal to refer אשור to the North Arabian Asshurim, who are listed as descendants of Abraham through his wife Keturah in Gen 25:3-4 (cf. Num 24:2-4) is unlikely. Kraus (163) notes that such an insignificant group would not have been able to be an "arm for the sons of Lot" (the Moabites and Ammonites; Deut 2:9, 19; cf. Gen 19:37-38). To be an "arm" for someone is to provide strong and effective help (cf. Exod 6:6; 15:16; 2 Kgs 17:36; Job 22:8 ["a man of arm" possesses the land]; Isa 33:2; Jer 21:5; Dan 11:6).

The literary structure of the psalm is not complicated. V 2 is an opening plea to God, followed by complaint in vv 3-9; vv 10-19 is an extended run of petitions about the enemies. B. Costacurta notes a chiastic sequence in vv 3-6, framed by the use of כי at the beginning of vv 3 and 6:

> v 3: enemies of God (כי . . . אויביך . . . משנאיך)
> v 4: enemies of Israel (על-עמך . . . על-צפוניך)
> v 5: enemies of Israel (נכחידם מגוי . . . ולא-יזכר שם)
> v 6: enemies of God (כי נועצו . . . עליך)

A schema in vv 10-13 focuses on the names of ancient foes and their fate in a way which highlights the present situation (Costacurta, *Bib* 64 [1983] 520):

> v 10: names of ancient foes
> v 11: the fate of ancient foes
> v 12: names of ancient foes
> v 13: the threat of present foes

Also, see note 10.a. above.

The speaker is not identified, but we can think of a pious Israelite leader voicing a prayer for the people. A suitable setting would have been lamentation ceremonies in exilic or post-exilic Israelite communities.

Comment

A plea to God (83:2). God, who is Yahweh, is implored not to be at rest or quiet, i.e., inactive and silent when help is needed. The meaning is expressed well by NJV's translation of the second colon (where the verb is חרש): "do not hold aloof." The speaker seeks God's active help.

A complaint about enemies (83:3-9). These verses set forth to God an urgent complaint about an imminent military attack against the people of the speaker, who are referred to as "your people" (v 4). God is reminded, indirectly, of his obligation to defend Israel. The enemies are described with rather typical language: they are in a roaring rage (v 3; המה; cf. Pss 46:7, 4; 59:7, 15; Jer 6:23), arrogantly lifting up their heads, perhaps already sure of victory, and united in mind and purpose as they make their shrewd plans to attack and exterminate. Their overweening confidence is expressed in the short speech attributed to them in v 5. The complaint makes it clear that these are not only Israel's enemies but are also Yahweh's enemies: they are those "who hate you" (v 3) and they are about to try to exterminate "your people," "your treasured ones." The political alliance (ברית, "covenant") they have made (v 6) is "against you." Yahweh cannot afford to ignore this threat.

The enemies named in vv 7–8 are known from other references in the OT, though this combination is unique. For Edom, note Ps 137:7; Isa 34:5–6; 63:1; Ezek 35:1–15; for the Ishmaelites, see Gen 17:20; 25:18; 37:25–28; for Moab, see Judg 3:12–30; 1 Sam 14:47; 2 Sam 8:12; 2 Kgs 3:4–24; Isa 15–16; Jer 48; Zeph 2:8–11; for the Hagrites, a tribe with territory east of the Jordan with whom the Transjordan tribes of Reuben, Gad, and Manasseh fought, see 1 Chr 5:10, 19–20; cf. 1 Chr 27:30; 11:38; for Ammon and Amalek, see Judg 3:13; 2 Kgs 24:2; Jer 41:15; 49:1; Exod 17; Num 24:20; 1 Sam 15. Gebal may be a reference to a Canaanite and Phoenician port some twenty miles north of modern Beirut and known in Greek traditions as Byblos (modern Jebeil), listed in Josh 13:5 as among the lands not yet possessed by the Israelites (the expression in Josh 13:5 is הָאָרֶץ הַגִּבְלִי, "the Giblite land"; this term is also found in 1 Kgs 5:32 [18] and Ezek 27:9 in the expression זִקְנֵי גְבַל, "elders of Gebal").

Commentators have usually preferred to identify Gebal as some tribal area south of the Dead Sea in relation to Edom and Moab. Perhaps insufficient attention has been paid to the possibility that the peoples listed form a rough circle around Israel, beginning in the south, up the Transjordan region, over to Tyre (and Gebal), and back down the coast to Philistia. This approach would be strengthened if there were some kind of neat pattern in the way the ten names are listed, but at the moment I do not see one (except in v 8 there could be a kind of chiastic pattern: Gebal—Ammon and Amalek—Philistia—Tyre.

```
A  Gebal ─────────────────── Philistia  B
B  Ammon and Amalek ──────── Tyre  A
```

If the Phoenician Gebal (Byblos) is intended, archaeological excavations have shown it to have had a long history from the Neolithic period (c. 8,000 B.C.E.) down to its conquest by the Muslims in 636 C.E. It was a major trade center, but lost some importance and power to Tyre after c. 850 B.C.E. It remained, however, as a significant city throughout the entire period of Israelite history. Philistia and Tyre are well known and hardly need references (e.g., Judg 3:3, 31; 1 Sam 4–6 for the Philistines and Amos 1:9–10; Isa 23:1–18; Jer 25:22; Ezek 26–28 for Tyre).

Assyria is the great power which joined with and supported hostile nations ringing Israel. As already discussed above, "Assyria" is probably a stereotyped name for the great nations of the ancient Near East. Typically in several periods of history, the small states in Palestine-Syria were either in coalition against Mesopotamian powers (as against the Assyrians in 853 B.C.E.) or in some sort of league with Mesopotamian states, or with Egypt.

The "sons of Lot" is most probably a direct reference to the Moabites and Ammonites who were traditionally considered to be descendants of Lot through incestuous intercourse with his daughters (see note 9.a.). The references are lacking to demonstrate it, but I suggest that the expression had also become stereotypical by the time this psalm was composed, in the manner that Edom became the prototypical enemy of Israel after the exile (as, e.g., in Obadiah; note Ps 60:1 [title], 10–11).

Petitions for divine judgment of the enemies (83:9–19). This is a rather extensive and vivid section of petitions asking for varied forms of judgment on the enemies. The requests for judgment are rooted in the traditions of the salvation-history of

Israel, which had accounts of how Yahweh dealt severely with those who attacked his people in the past (vv 10–13). The defeat of the Midianites and the execution of their leaders Oreb, Zeeb, Zebah, and Zalmuna by Gideon (Judg 6–8) is recalled—a victory which was really Yahweh's, of course. Included in this account is also a retrospect in vv 10b–11 to the defeat of Sisera and Jabin and their forces (Judg 4–5). These were "close-in" enemies (like those in vv 7–8) who threatened the whole enterprise of Yahweh and his people.

V 13 matches v 5 in recalling the arrogant speech of foes in the past, who sought to take possession for themselves of the very "pasturelands" of God (reading the speaking in v 13 as that of the ancient enemies in vv 10–12 rather than to current enemies in vv 2–9, as in most interpretations on the grounds that there is no reference to such a statement by the Midianites in Judg 6–8 [e.g., Oesterley, 377], but such expectation of exact quotation is not required; note Durham, 343). The present enemies are trying to play the role of ancient enemies and they should suffer the same fate; at least that is the prayer of the speaker. That fate is, of course, a terrible one: a "hideous picture of corpses that were scattered like so much dung on the field" (Kraus, 163, on v 11b; cf. Jer 8:2; 9:22).

In the middle of the petitions, the speaker makes a personal appeal to God in v 14a: "O my God." The petitions are personalized in this way; the speaker's personal welfare merges with that of the country. The individual and the corporate are inseparately meshed. The speaker could be a king, especially if the psalm is from the pre-exilic period, but it matters little. Any congregational leader could integrate personal concern with community distress. The kings were not the only ones who were concerned with the nation's welfare.

Vivid figures of speech are used to describe the desired defeat of the enemies in vv 14–19. The "whirling dust" of v 14a (גלגל) is derived from גלל, "to roll," and the word גלגל can mean a "wheel." It could be simply a "rolling thing," but it is frequently identified as the wheel-shaped dry calix of the wild artichoke (*Gundelia Tournefortii*) which rolls over the fields before the wind like thistledown or tumbleweeds. I assume that the reference is to rolling thistles, dry leaves, mixed with dust and driven by the wind. The simile of chaff or stubble whirling in the wind is found in other contexts: see, e.g., Isa 40:24; Jer 13:24; with מץ ("chaff"), see Ps 1:4; 35:5; Hos 13:3; Job 21:18. The graphic depiction of a fire burning in a dry forest and roaring up the sides of mountains, as it were, to set the mountains themselves ablaze (v 15), may be compared with Deut 4:11; 5:20 [23]; 9:15; Isa 9:18–19; Ezek 21:3 [20:47]. For the rout of enemies by a storm (v 16), compare Josh 10:11; Isa 28:2, 17; 29:6; Hos 8:7; Amos 1:14; Nah 1:3; Job 21:18; 27:20–23; Prov 1:27; 10:25. For v 17, compare Mic 7:10; Ezek 7:18; Obad 10; Jer 46:12. This psalm is a good example of traditional language being put together in a composition with good poetic artistry. The language is basically conventional, but the composition is unique and effective.

The ultimate result of the treatment of the enemies prayed for in the petitions is expressed in v 19: that they may know that Yahweh rules as the Most High (עליון, see Ps 92:2b) over all the earth. God is asked to act in such ways as to bring the prototypical enemies to recognize his universal lordship. To "know" Yahweh is to recognize his name and submit to his will. The concept emerges out of a long tradition in the OT: e.g., Exod 5:2; 7:5; 14:4, 18; 1 Kgs 2:13, 28; Ezek 7:2–4; 25:3–5; 28:25–26. Of course, "knowing" Yahweh applies to Israelites as well as to foreigners; both are brought together in the Deuteronomistic text in the prayer of Solomon in 1 Kgs 8:43 (also, 2 Chr 6:33): "in order that all the peoples of the earth may know thy name and fear thee, as do thy people Israel, and that they may know that this house which I have built is called by thy name" (RSV). Cf. Ps 46:11. The tradition of "knowing" God is extensively treated by W. Zimmerli in his *"Erkenntnis Gottes Nach dem Buch Ezekiel"* (originally published in 1954 [ATANT 27], now in English in *I Am Yahweh,* tr. D. W. Stott [Atlanta: John Knox, 1982] 29–98). Weiser (564) summarizes the end of Ps 83 with the contention that the power and the grace of God have the final say: "The ultimate goal of God's terrible judgments . . . is that his enemies, too, will be made ashamed and will seek him, that they will turn to him in penitence and will come to realize that power and glory upon the whole earth belong alone to God who has revealed his name Yahweh."

Explanation

One is tempted not to bother with the message of this little-read psalm. It could be said that its main claim for attention is that canonical tradition has placed it between two better-known psalms: 82 and 84. The language and the content of the psalm are conventional and seem to offer nothing really different from that found in a number of individual and communal laments. On the other hand, the canonical tradition, however it was transmitted, is worthy of our respect. In church tradition, the psalm has been excessively spiritualized and the speaker, ringed by enemies, has been taken as a prototype of Christ on the cross. As such, the psalm has been included in liturgies for Good Friday (see Deissler, II, 158; Jacquet, II, 615–16). Although we will do well to respect the piety of this tradition, we will do better to read the psalm more directly in its context.

Ps 83 merits our consideration from at least two perspectives. First, it is a good example of relatively late Hebrew poetry. Its style is not marked by great subtlety; it is rather straightforward and simple. The fine distinctions and intricate patterns of some psalms are missing. However, it is effective and expresses prayer with both economy of words and well-crafted figures of speech.

Second, the psalm serves as a paradigmatic prayer of lament and complaint for a people surrounded by hostile nations and threatened with overwhelming force. The psalm reminds us that the greatest resource of the people of Yahweh is prayer, which appeals both directly to him and is based on his powerful acts of intervention and deliverance in the past. The foes that ring the land would ravage the very "pasturelands of God" (v 13) for themselves; appearing "as a sinister counterfeit of God's kingdom, a kind of anti-church. . . . But Israel relies on a passionate intercession in which two features stand out: the remembrance of ancient salvation, and the controlling motive of serving God's glory" (Eaton, 208). The most severe judgments of God are reserved for those, whether individuals or nations, who set themselves to take over the "pasturelands of God," seeking to exterminate his people and his enterprise in human history. Let all kings and tyrants, all oppressors whatever their role and status, take notice. Let the people of God whenever they are ringed about with threatening foes lift up their hearts. The king of all nations and the judge of all the earth hears prayer and will in his own time and ways sweep his foes away as a fire roars through a forest and sweeps over the mountains in blazing fury. "Vengeance is mine, I will repay, says the LORD."

A Psalm of Pilgrimage for Those Who Trust God   (84:1–13)

Bibliography

Booij, T. "Royal Words in Psalm LXXXIV 11." *VT* 36 (1986) 117–20. **Buchanan, G. W.** "The Courts of the Lord." *VT* 16 (1966) 231–32. **Goulder, M. D.** *The Psalms of the Sons of Korah.* 37–50. **Grollenberg, L.** "Post-Biblical חֲרוּרִים in Ps. lxxxiv 11?" *VT* 9 (1959) 311–12. **Johnson, A. R.** *Sacral Kingship in Ancient Israel.* Cardiff: University of Wales Press, 1955. 93–97. **Mulder, M. J.** "Huibert Duifhuis (1531–1581) et L'Exégèse du Psaume LXXXIV 4." *Oudtestamentische Studiën,* ed. P. A. H. DeBoer. Leiden: E. J. Brill, 1969. 227–50. **Smothers, E. R.** "The Coverdale Translation of Psalm LXXXIV." *HTR* 38 (1945) 245–69.

Translation

1   For the leader;[a] upon (according to) the Gittith;[b] a Korahite psalm.[c]

2 (1) *How beautiful is your dwelling place,*   (3+2)
    O Yahweh Sabaoth!

3 (2) *My soul[a] yearns—even wastes away[b]—*   (3+2+2+3)
    for the courts of Yahweh;
    my heart and my flesh cry out
    to the living God.[c]

4 (3) *Even a bird finds a home,*   (3+3+3+3+2)
    and a swallow a nest for herself,
    where she can put her young
    near[a] your altars, O Yahweh Sabaoth—
    my King and my God[b]—

5 (4) *How blest are those who dwell in your house,*   (3+2)
    who can continually praise you! SELAH.

6 (5) *How blest are those whose strength[a] is in you,*   (3+2)
    with pilgrim-ways[b] in their hearts!

7 (6) *Those passing through the Valley of Baca[a]*   (3+2+3)
    will make it an oasis;[b]
    moreover the early rain will clothe it with blessings.[c]

8 (7) *They will go from strength to strength[a]*   (3+3)
    till each appears before God in Zion.[b]

9 (8) *O Yahweh Sabaoth!*   (3+2+3)
    Hear my prayer;
    give ear, O God of Jacob. SELAH.

10 (9) *Behold our shield (with favor),[a] O God,*   (3+3)
    and look at the face of your anointed.

11 (10) *How much better is a day in your courts than a thousand (others)![a]*   (4+4+3)
    I choose waiting at the threshold[b] of the house of God
    more than dwelling in the tents of wickedness.[c]

12 (11)   *For Sun and Shield is Yahweh-God;*   (4+4+4)
           grace and glory, Yahweh bestows;
           he withholds no good thing from those who walk in integrity.[a]
13 (12)   *O Yahweh Sabaoth!*   (2+2+2)
           How blest is the one
           who trusts in you.

Notes

1.a. See n. 51:1.a.

1.b. The הגתית also appears in the superscriptions of Pss 8 and 81. Its meaning is unclear, and varied suggestions about it have been made: (a) a musical tune or setting; (b) a kind of musical instrument, possibly a "Gittite lyre" (viz. an instrument named after a place, i.e., Gath) and LXX has "for the winepresses" (it is possible that something like "Song of the Winepress" is intended [גת is used for winepress in Hebrew: Neh 13:15; Lam 1:15; Isa 63:2; Judg 6:11; for more on the "winepress" theory, see L. Delekat, "Probleme der Psalmen—Überschriften," *ZAW* 76 (1964) 293–94]); or (c) some sort of ceremony or festival. Mowinckel (*PIW,* II, 215) thinks the expression may have something to do with Obed-edom, "the Gittite," in 2 Sam 6:10–12, in whose house the Ark of Yahweh stayed until David brought it to Jerusalem. Mowinckel says that the account in 2 Sam 6 is probably not about a one-time event but reflects a fixed festal rite: the house outside the precincts of the temple from which the Ark was brought to the temple in a festal procession each new year. However, Mowinckel is not sure about the exact relationship of הגתית to this rite: The place from which the procession started? The ritual act of lifting up the Ark? Or a special "Gittite lyre" to be played during the procession?

1.c. Lit., "for (or, belonging to) the sons of Korah, a psalm," a title which appears with Pss 47, 48 (in reverse order), 49, 85, 87, and 88 (in the same order as Ps 48: שיר מזמור לבני קרח). The "sons of Korah," also appear in the titles of 42–43 and 44 (with למנצח in each case), and in 45 (with משכיל and "a love song," שיר ידידת).

According to Exod 6:21–24, the Korahites are descendants of Levi through Kohath and Izhar. In 1 Chr 6:7 [6:22], Korah is also a Levite and a descendant of Kohath, but with a different lineage. The Korahites were a guild of temple singers according to 2 Chr 20:19; they also appear as temple gatekeepers in 1 Chr 9:19; 26:1, 19, and as bakers in 1 Chr 9:31. Num 16 contains an account of a revolt by Korah and 250 leaders of the people against Moses and Aaron, an account now conflated with a revolt of lay people led by the Reubenites, Dathan, and Abiram (cf. Deut 11:6; Ps 106:17). Korah himself and his allies died when the earth swallowed up Dathan and Abiram according to Num 16:31–35, but the "sons of Korah" survived (Num 26:9–11). The account in Num 16 is a complex one, which shows signs of an extensive tradition history. The Korah material is probably from the later stages of the tradition and may reflect Levitical conflict with the priestly hierarchy supported by exiles returning from Babylon after 515 B.C.E., led by such leaders as Ezra and Nehemiah. It is possible that the Korahites were members of a Levitical group who were active in Palestine during the exile (note the survival of the sons of Korah in Num 26:11; P. J. Budd, *Numbers,* WBC 5 [Waco, TX: Word, 1984] 189–90). The present material in the OT points not to a subordination of the Korahite status as priests but to a continuation of their function as Levites under the supervision of the Aaronite-Zadokite priests (note Num 4:17–20).

This brief discussion is sufficient to indicate that the OT references indicate a complex history of the Levites, the priesthood in general, and the role of the Korahites in all of it. Goulder (*Psalms of the Sons of Korah,* 51–84) attempts to strengthen his case for the origin of the Korah psalms from the sanctuary at Dan by arguing that the priesthood there was partially Korahite. He begins with the establishment of a priesthood at Dan (Laish) by the migrating Danites according to Judg 17–18, a movement accompanied by a Levitical priest of Judah ("of the family of Judah"), although the Danite priesthood is said to have been composed of the descendants of Gershom, a grandson of Moses, in Judg 18:29. Num 26:58 is a key text for Goulder. This text divides the Levites into five families: Libnites, Hebronites, Mahlites, Mushites, and Korahites. Disposing of the Mahlites with LXX, Goulder argues that the Libnites and Hebronites are associated with places in the south and that it is probable that it was the Mushites and Korahites who migrated north. He then assumes that the main priesthood at Dan was Mushite (Moses), associated with Gershom, and that the Korahites formed an assistant

Levitical priesthood there. Goulder also argues that Exod 32 is based on an original legend which legitimated the priesthood of Moses, assisted by Levites, who in the story answered his call of loyalty to Yahweh against their fellow Israelites (Exod 32:26–29), which he thinks reflects the situation at Dan of a Mosaic (Mushite) main priesthood with a wider circle of Levites (the Korahites) assisting.

After the Assyrian conquests c. 730, Goulder assumes that some of the Korahites went south and ultimately established themselves as part of the Levitical priesthood in Jerusalem. They remained there and became more influential in the post-exilic period, but they never became the priests of the altar. Though they did not preside over the sacrificial rituals, they and their fellow Levites "kept the Temple, they led worship, and they were the guardians of the sacred tradition. . . . The real threads of national religious life were in their hands" (Goulder, 83).

Goulder's case obviously depends on considerable conjecture about texts that are far from clear. Korah is linked with Hebron in 1 Chr 2:43 and may refer to a town in the south of Judah. A reference to the "sons of Korah" on an inscribed bowl found at the site of the temple of Arad points to the probability of a southern locale, and it is probable that all five names refer to southern sites where Levites originally lived (Budd, *Numbers*, 297; Y. Aharon, "Arad: Its Inscriptions and Temple," *BA* 31 (1968) 11; N. M. Sarna, "The Psalm Superscriptions and the Guilds," in *Studies in Jewish Religions and Intellectual History: Presented to Alexander Altmann*, ed. S. Stein and R. Loewe [London: Institute of Jewish Studies; University of Alabama Press, 1979] 285, 297, n. 28; Aharoni dates the bowl to stratum VII, c. 715–687 B.C.E., the time of Hezekiah). This does not rule out the possibility that a group of Korahites migrated with a group of Mushites to the north, but it does nothing to strengthen the case. The Korahites may very well have remained in the south.

G. Wanke, *Die Zionstheologie der Korachiten* (Berlin: Töpelmann, 1966) is at the other end of the critical spectrum in regard to the Korahites, arguing that the Korahite psalms first originated in post-exilic times, becoming prominent about the fourth century B.C.E. The highly developed Zion theology in the Korahite psalms is taken as reflecting the post-exilic religious situation. The Zion theology is composed of a variety of themes and motifs, according to Wanke, put together by Korahite temple singers in the post-exilic period. Zion motifs, such as the mountain of God, paradise, and the combat with chaos, were applied to Jerusalem as the city became the focus of Israelite hopes in the post-exilic communities. Wanke considers all these motifs to be late, finding their major parallels in other parts of the OT that are considered late. He also considers the divine epithets Yahweh Sabaoth, Elyon, and the God of Jacob (typical in Korahite Zion psalms) as late pre-exilic or post-exilic. Wanke's extreme position on dating suffers from major weaknesses in methodology and has received little support; e.g., Ps 45 is rather clearly pre-exilic in origin (which he does not deny; *Zionstheologie*, 5, 109), and Wanke finds it necessary to assume that it was taken into the Korahite songbook from an earlier time. It is also hard to believe that the emphasis on inviolability of Zion would be a purely post-exilic product, or that the Jerusalem cult tradition as a definable entity has no pre-exilic history.

The best conclusions relating to the Korahites seem to be the following: (1) The Levitical Korahites probably belonged to Judah and to sanctuaries in the south. (2) The Korahites were active in both pre-exilic and post-exilic times; they may have been a Levitical priesthood which functioned in Palestine during the exile (Budd, *Numbers*, 190) and opposed the efforts by the priestly hierarchy, supported by the returning settlers from Babylon, to take control. The chances are good that they held their own, despite being forced to accept a subordinate role to the Zadokite priests in the temple. "The Korahites had a head-start on the other priesthoods, having been in Jerusalem since the eighth century. They . . . lost the battle for equality at the altar, but they . . . won most of the other battles" (Goulder, 79). (3) The Korahites probably drew on multiple traditions for poetic motifs and content, possibly including some material from Northern sanctuaries and festivals. The present Korahite psalms, however, emerged primarily from the Jerusalem cult tradition. (4) The Zion psalms continued to be important for post-exilic Jewish communities because of the continuing focus on Jerusalem and Zion as the center of Israel's life and as the center of the world, and the eschatological orientation given to the psalms in these communities. The songs of Zion praise Zion as it was and as anticipation of its role in an idealized future.

3.a. The word נֶפֶשׁ refers to the innermost being. It can, of course, be reduced to the simple pronoun "I," but too much is lost in some contexts if it is reduced in this fashion. For "soul," see n. Ps 54:5.b.

3.b. Dahood insists on his reading of גַם in 4a as "aloud," which he argues establishes a parallelism between 3a and 3c (with גַם added to 3c): "My soul longs and pines aloud; / My . . . heart and flesh cry out." It seems improbable that anyone would "pine" (כלה, "waste away") aloud. The parallelism is somewhat improved ("pines aloud" // "cry out"), but the supplementary aspect of parallelism needs to be remembered (B often goes beyond A with new elements).

3.c. Briggs (II, 226) argues for "El, the God of my life," reading אֵל חָיַי (from חיים) for אֵל חַי, a change which he proposes for Ps 42:3 also. Dahood (II, 280) argues for the vocative case, "O Living God" (a change he also would make in Ps 42:3), but his argument depends on reading אֵל, "to," as אֵל, "God." Having made the change, he reads "O God, O Living God" as the first colon of v 4 (ending v 3 with "cry out"), and forming an inclusion with "O Yahweh Sabaoth, my King and my God" at the end of v 4; the inclusion frames the three cola in 4a, b, and c. The proposal is attractive and may be correct, but it should be noted that "Yahweh Sabaoth" in v 2b can be taken as forming an inclusion with "Yahweh Sabaoth" in 4d. The result is a chiastic framing of the content in vv 2–5:

A	How beautiful is your dwelling place (v 2a)
B	O Yahweh Sabaoth (v 2b)
B'	O Yahweh Sabaoth (v 4d)
A'	How blest are those dwelling in your house (v 5a)

In addition, "Yahweh Sabaoth" appears again in vv 9 and 13 and provides framing for the entire psalm.

4.a. MT is difficult unless the אֵת is read as a preposition meaning "near" or "at the side of." See Gunkel, 370, Dahood, II, 280. However, a long line of commentators disagree: e.g., Delitzsch, Oesterley, Schmidt, who stop the reference to the "birds" after "her young." See the extensive review in Mulder, "Huibert Duifhuis."

4.b. This colon may be an addition as *BHS* suggests, but it need not be deleted.

6.a. The word עֹז may mean "refuge" rather than "strength," as Dahood (II, 280) and Kraus (II, 746) argue; derived from the root עוז, which means "take refuge" in Isa 30:2. In this case, the reading would be: "How blest is the one whose refuge is in you"; or reading עוז as infinitive: "How blest is the one taking refuge in you." However, the idea of "strength" or "power" for the pilgrims in v 9 (though the words are different, of course) may point to retention of the rare *scriptio plena* עֹז here.

6.b. The meaning of מְסִלּוֹת בִּלְבָבָם is the subject of some debate, but the meaning "pilgrimage" seems to be strongly supported by LXX and the context. LXX's ἀναβάσεις, "a going up," could be equal to תַּעֲלוֹת, "ascent," but this is equal to "pilgrimage" (so Kirkpatrick, 507), and it is probable that the LXX translators were reading חֲסִלּוֹת, "roads/highways." In the context the "roads" are the pilgrimage roads of ascent to the temple (one always goes "up" to a temple). RSV and NRSV have, "in whose heart are the highways (to Zion)." NEB has, "whose hearts are set on pilgrim ways"; Weiser (565): "when he meditates in his heart on pilgrimages"; NJV: "whose mind is on the [pilgrim] highways." Dahood (II, 281) opts for the metaphorical sense of סלל, "think highly of/exalt" (cf. Prov 4:8) and reads as "extolments": "from whose heart are your extolments." It is true that this parallels nicely with v 5b: "How blest . . . / who continually praise you // How blest . . . / from whose heart are your extolments." But it seems better to read v 6 with vv 7–8 (dwelling in the temple in v 5 does not correlate too well with "extolments in the heart" in v 6). V 6 may very well have a double entendre (in a good sense) on the "ways": the "ways" of pilgrimage and the "ways" of God in a metaphysical sense. They are both in the heart of the pilgrim.

7.a. A frequent, traditional understanding of the phrase is "valley of tears" (assuming בֶּכֶה or בֹּכֶה for בָּכָא). Thus Briggs reads "vale of weeping," supposing that it reflects "the experience of sorrow in which the pilgrims approach the sacred places." But "sorrow" seems unlikely to be the primary meaning in a context of pilgrimage joy. On the other hand, a hot, arid valley without water can be cause enough for tears on the part of travelers struggling through it.

It is more likely, however, that בכא refers to a place, though the place is unknown. Cohen derives "baca" from "balsam tree" (see 2 Sam 5:23–24) and assumes the reference is to a valley where these trees, known to grow in arid places, are found en route to Jerusalem. NEB follows this lead with its more interpretational translation "thirsty valley" (REB has "waterless valley"). This reading makes a good contrast with the following line which speaks of "springs" and "showers." This interpretation is not without its detractors. Anderson (II, 604) disputes the existence of such a valley on the pilgrim route, and even the growth of balsam trees in Palestine. P. K. McCarter, Jr. (*II Samuel*, AB 9 [Garden City, NY: Doubleday, 1984] 155–56) examines the evidence for the plural בכאים (sometimes identified as balsam trees) as well as the עמק הבכא in Ps 84:7 and comes to the conclusion that the meaning may be something like "The Parched Place," some arid place on the way to Jerusalem; in the case of 2 Sam 5:23, somewhere north or northwest of Jerusalem. The references in 2 Sam 5:23 and Ps 84:7 do not necessarily refer to the same place, but it is possible that they do (cf. Judg 2:1, 5: הבכים, "the Weepers Place"). There is probably a play on the sound of the word with the verb "to weep," hence the Valley of Baca (Dry Place) is also the Valley of Baca (Weeping). It is possible that the name is related to a tree which exudes ("weeps") sap or some substance (see KB, 126; Kidner, II, 305, n. 1; cf. Hagar in Gen 21:17 and her weeping when the water was all gone).

7.b. Lit., "they make it a spring." REB has, "the LORD fills it with springs," a free translation of what is assumed to be the meaning. NJV provides another approach: "regarding it as a place of springs, as if the early rain had covered it with blessing."

7.c. The *Translation* agrees with Goulder (*Psalms of the Sons of Korah*, 257, n. 41) that the difficult Hebrew is best read as it is in MT; מורה is used for "early rain" in Joel 2:23 (the "early rain" is the autumn rain in October-November). The hiphil of עטה means "to wrap" or "envelop." "Blessings" (ברכות) is left as it is; it is unlikely that the meaning would be: "The valleys are wrapped/enclosed in pools" (which would assume a change to בְּרֵכוֹת; בְּרֵכָה > בְּרָכָה; Gunkel, 371). The גם, "also/even/moreover," is rhetorical: "Yes, the early rain clothes it with blessings" or, "Even the early rain wraps it in blessings!"

8.a. "From strength to strenth" is a frequently used translation of מחיל אל־חיל. Some commentators prefer to read מחל אל־חל, "from rampart to rampart" (e.g., Briggs, II, 230), which Dahood (II, 282) takes by metonymy to mean "from village (or, town) to village." Cf. NJV. The translators of NEB and REB assume that the reference is to the ramparts of Jerusalem: "So they pass from outer wall to inner"—of pilgrims making their way into the city and the temple area. It seems appropriate to understand the expression as referring to the endurance and renewal of strength on the part of pilgrims as they make their journey to the sanctuary. The word חיל may mean "wealth" or "military force," but here it means "power/strength." The word can refer to the strength to act effectively (cf. Prov 31:10). Cf. "from glory to glory," 2 Cor 3:18.

8.b. MT is apparently a short form of the technical expression for appearing at the sanctuary in the presence of God, as found in יראה כל־זכורך אל־פני האדן יהוה, "every male is to appear before the Lord Yahweh" (with variations, also in Exod 34:23; Deut 16:16; cf. Exod 23:15; 34:20). The expression is similar to that in Ps 42:3, ואראה פני אלהים, "and I shall appear before God," or "I shall be seen by the face of God." There is some Hebrew ms evidence that these passages represent scribal corrections to avoid a direct reference to "seeing God"; thus Ps 42:3 would be read with qal (וְאֶרְאֶה) rather than niphal: "and I will see the face of God." In 84:8b, the reading would be: "each one will see (unless יראו is read, in that case, "they will see") the God of Gods in Zion" (assuming that the preposition אֶל should be אֵל, "God," in the expression אל־אלהים. LXX takes the אל־אלהים as "God of Gods" and makes it the subject of the verb: "the God of Gods will be seen (or, appear) in Zion." This approach is reflected in such translations as REB, "and the God of gods shows himself in Zion"; NRSV: "the God of gods will be seen in Zion." I have retained MT as in NIV, as not being overly awkward. The reading "till they see (יראו) the God of Gods in Zion" involves minor changes and is plausible.

10.a. Lit., "see our shield, O God." An optional reading is: "O God, our Shield," treating מגננו as vocative and coordinate with "God." This has the support of LXX and is followed in KJV. The parallelism with v 10b, however, supports the interpretation of "shield" as a reference to the king, or possibly the high priest. A. R. Johnson (*Sacral Kingship*, 96, n. 1) points out the chiastic nature of the verse: "our shield—look—O God—look—face of your anointed." Dahood (II, 278, 282) pursues his elaborate argument for reading "shield" as "suzerain" (see Dahood, I, 16–18; for a critique, see Craigie, 71, n. 4.a.) and assumes that the reference is to God: "O God, our Suzerain, behold." The word מגן may at times refer to the protective action of God as a "suzerain," but it is unlikely in this context.

11.a. The problems of reading this verse are multiple and are subject to no easy solutions. V 11a is lit.: "For better is a day in your courts than a thousand." Goulder (47, 257, n. 45) wants to read טוב ("good/better") as a noun (as in v 12) rather than as an adjective: "a day of good" = "a good day" (which he argues refers to a feast day). But this makes it necessary to read בחרתי ("I choose") in 11b with מאלף, "more than/rather than a thousand," and to take this with the following infinitive הסתופף: "For a feast-day in your courts / I choose more than a thousand (shekels) / To keep the threshold in the house of my God / than to dwell in the tents of wickedness." This is possible, but it seems forced. L. Grollenberg (*VT* 9 [1959] 311–12) argues for בְּחֵרָת, derived from חרות, which had the sense of "freedom/liberty" in postbiblical Hebrew, denoting the status and domain of a חר, "free person/noble" (of Neh 6:17; 13:17), and thus: "For a day in your courts is better than a thousand in my own domain/estate." This is, of course, a variant form of the commonly adopted emendation of בחרתי to בְּחֲדְרִי, "in my chamber" = "at home" (e.g., Kraus, *Psalms 60–150,* 166). G. W. Buchanan (*VT* 16 [1966] 231–32) seeks to improve on Grollenberg by the drastic emendation of the text to מאלף בכמת און: "For a day in your courts is better than a thousand high places of iniquity"—hardly an improvement! Dahood (II, 282–83) offers a quixotic reading of בחרת as "Cemetery" (חרת from Akkadian-Ugaritic, "grave/cemetery," plus the preposition ב and the *yodh* as an archaic genitive ending. "Cemetery" is taken as a poetic name for the netherworld. Dahood may be commended for his linguistic ingenuity, but it is hardly likely that the speaker would bother to say that a day in the courts of God is better than a thousand in the cemetery!

In the translation above, I have chosen to follow what seems to be the pattern of MT, and of LXX, which reads: ὅτι κρείσσων ἡμέρα μία ἐν ταῖς αὐλαῖς σου ὑπὲρ χιλιάδας / ἐξελεξάμην παραρριπτεῖσθαι ἐν τῷ οἴκῳ τοῦ θεοῦ / μᾶλλον ἢ οἰκεῖν ἐν σκηνώμασιν ἁμαρτωλῶν ("Because better is one day in your court than a thousand; I have chosen to cast my lot in the house of God rather than dwell in the tents of sinners") I assume that Dahood (II, 282) is correct to insist that כי טוב has the force of "how much better." The reference of "more than a thousand" is unexpressed. Goulder (*Psalms of the Sons of Korah*, 47) thinks it is "more than a thousand shekels," but it is more probably "more than a thousand (days) at home," or (as above), simply "more than a thousand other days anywhere." The verb בחר is retained and read with the second colon. Another option would be to accept the reading of בחרתי as "in my chamber" = "at home," and assume that the כי טוב "how much better," does double duty with 11b: "How much better is a day in your courts than a thousand at home; (how much better) waiting at the threshold of your house than dwelling in the tents of wickedness!"

11.b. The hithpoel infinitive form of the verb (הסתופף from ספף) is apparently a denominative of סף, "threshold," but its meaning is uncertain. It is traditionally understood as "to be a doorkeeper" with the assumption that this was a menial task. However, the position of doorkeeper seems to have been a major office with dignity and authority: note Eli in his seat by the doorpost of the temple at Shiloh in 1 Sam 1:9; see also 2 Kgs 12:9; 22:4; 25:18; Jer 35:4; 52:24; Esth 2:21; 6:2; 1 Chr 9:19, 22; 2 Chr 23:4. Thus it has been common to assume that the meaning of the verb here is to stand, or to lie prostate, at the threshold of the temple as a pilgrim supplicant seeking admission (e.g., Kraus, 170). Whatever the exact meaning is, the context seems to suggest that a lowly status in the temple is better than a well-established status elsewhere (note the use of the verb דור, which suggests permanent, well-established living; the verb can mean "to heap up" or "to stack in circles": as in Ezek 24:5, and is related to the word "generation/family circle"). Although it is possible that the contrast is between the assembly of festival participants at the entrance to the temple and the assembly of the wicked in their tents (on the possibility that the verb דור is a denominative of דור in the sense of "people" or "congregation"; note Pss 14:5; 49:20; 73:15; cf. Craigie, 145, n. 5.b.).

11.c. The suggested change of רשע, "wickedness/wrong doing," to עשר, "wealth," is unsupported and unnecessary; as is Gunkel's proposal (372) to read באהלי, "in my own tent," with רשע, "wickedness," added as a misunderstanding.

12.a. The colons in this verse seem somewhat overloaded and out of balance, at least on first reading. Thus it is not surprising that some commentators try to improve the structure of the verse. For example, Kraus (166) deletes אלהים in 11a and "Yahweh" from 12b and restructures to begin a new verse with יתן, "he gives," with the following translation resulting: "For sun and shield is Yahweh, / grace and honor. / He grants, he does not withhold good things / from those who walk blamelessly." I see no particular harm done by this procedure, but on the other hand, is it really necessary? The colons are not severely out of balance. LXX has a different content for 12a ("For the Lord loves mercy and truth") and has God as the subject of 12b ("God gives grace and glory"), and takes the second occurrence of Yahweh as the subject of 12c ("the Lord will not withhold good things from them that walk in innocence"). For an attempt to reconstruct the text of vv 11 and 12 in the light of LXX and MT, see Briggs (II, 230). The result is not encouraging. An option to the translations above could be to delete אלהים and read as: "For Sun and Shield is Yahweh: / grace and glory, he bestows; / Yahweh withholds no good thing / from those who walk in integrity." The word unit count would be 3+3+3+2 (as in Schmidt, 159).

Form/Structure/Setting

Ps 84 is a psalm which contains mixed elements, although it is usually described as a hymn which expresses devotion to the temple in Jerusalem (Gunkel, 368). Mowinckel (*PIW*, I, 88) includes it with the hymns of praise, but he says that in it Yahweh is "praised more indirectly, by exalting all that belongs to him: his Temple, his holy city, and the blessings which flow from that place where the fountain of life is and where strength is to be found." Zion appears only once in the psalm (v 8b), but it reflects a longing for festival worship in Jerusalem (as in Pss 42–43) and the pilgrimage of worshipers to the autumn festival (Tabernacles). Assuming that the psalm belongs to this setting-in-worship, T. H. Robinson (in Oesterley, 378) has written a beautiful description of it:

> The great autumn festival is at hand. The long year's toil in field and vineyard is over, the produce of the land is gathered in, and the cycle is about to begin once more with solemn ritual and stately ceremony. The ground is parched, and all the wadis are dry, but the summer is nearly at an end, and almost before the feast is over the autumn rains may be expected, to soften the earth and make it once more fit for husbandry. From every village in the country comes a train of pilgrims, and as they draw near to their journey's end they sing a song like this.

The speaker in the psalm is unidentified, though usually considered to be a faithful Israelite on pilgrimage to Zion.

Goulder (*Psalms of the Sons of Korah*), in keeping with his general thesis, argues that Ps 84 was originally a pilgrimage psalm for the sanctuary at Dan in the Northern Kingdom. He thinks it comes from the tenth-ninth centuries B.C.E., earlier than the Korahite Pss 42–43, and reflecting a shift toward the more general term Elohim in reference to Yahweh (which agrees broadly with the scheme proposed by Freedman for the dating of poetry in terms of the usage of divine names and titles; for references and summary, see *Form/Structure/Setting*, Ps 93). Goulder (44–46) assumes that "in Zion" in v 8b is an addition to adapt the psalm to Zion usage after the fall of the Northern Kingdom (the difficult אֶל־אֱלֹהִים, "towards/to God," in MT is a substitution for an original אֵל־דָּן, "the God of Dan," followed perhaps by "on Herman"—the mountain near the sanctuary at Dan).

It is possible that Ps 84 did originate from circles of priests at the sanctuary at Dan, but the present psalm is clearly a Zion-psalm, more probably from Jerusalem, and must be dealt with on that basis. Also, regardless of the original date and context of the psalm, the present psalm is "a timeless expression of the ultimate satisfaction of pilgrimage, and the privilege of worship" (Rogerson and McKay, II, 170). Indeed, a pre-exilic date for the psalm is by no means certain, and the present psalm may represent post-exilic piety. Kissane (II, 66) proposes to read the psalm in the context of the Babylonian exile, treating the "supposed description of a toilsome journey to Jerusalem" in vv 7–8 as a figurative description of the present distress of the exiles and anticipation of a change of the arid desert-like conditions of life into future glory (similar to Isa 35; 51:3; 58:11). I do not care to spiritualize vv 7–8 to this extent, and Kissane's translation of אֶת־מִזְבְּחוֹתֶיךָ as "in your altars" (= in the ruins of the altars in the destroyed temple) seems improbable (see 4.a. above), but his reading does caution us against trying to read the psalm in a tightly restricted context. We simply do not know its date or precise originating context. Thus major attention should be given to the literary context derived from the content of the psalm itself.

Ps 84 begins a second series of Korahite psalms in the psalter: 84–85, 87–88). The first series is found in Pss 42–43, 44–49. The Asaphite run of psalms in 73–83 ends and a Korahite run begins. G. H. Wilson (*The Editing of the Hebrew Psalter*, 164) notes the appearance of the מִזְמוֹר ("psalm") in the titles of Pss 82–85 and 87–88, while it is absent in Ps 81 and Ps 89. In this small way the editors of the Psalter may have bound the Asaphite run of psalms with the Korahite run (for the place of Ps 86 in the Korahite run, see *Form/Structure/Setting* of that psalm). The longing for participation in worship at the sanctuary of Yahweh marks the beginning of both the Korahite series in Pss 42–49 and the series in Pss 84–88.

How the two series of Korahite psalms are related is an open question. Goulder (18–19; 86–87; 172; 199–200; 217–19; 228–29) argues that all of the Korah psalms, plus Ps 89A, originally belonged to the liturgy of the sanctuary at Dan, with Pss 84 and 85 having been displaced from their place in the festival sequence (a sequence represented in the present Psalter by Pss 42–49) by Pss 42–43 and 44. In addition, Ps 87 was displaced by Ps 48. Goulder gives as a reason for this displacement the serious political situation in the Northern Kingdom after the death of Jeroboam II, when the situation required a "more chastened, more political, more anxious" (18) set of psalms. Pss 84, 85, and 87 were retained and eventually placed in a "supplement" in Book III of the Psalter (according to Goulder, Pss 88 and 89A were taken out of their original liturgical sequence at Dan later in Jerusalem when Book III was prepared for post-exilic celebration of the Feast of Tabernacles).

Goulder's thesis is interesting and some of the Korah psalms, or parts of the psalms, may have originated out of the worship of Northern Israelite sanctuaries. On the other hand, his thesis involves too much conjecture about adaptations and too many forced readings to be persuasive without further evidence. It is important to note that even Goulder (199) makes it clear that all of the Korahite psalms in the present Psalter represent usage in Jerusalem. If this is true, the fact that later scribes and worshipers could use Northern psalms from Dan with such relatively little adaptation warns us against pushing the poetic language too hard in terms of actual physical descriptions (as in the case of 84:7–8, see below).

The literary structure of Ps 84 seems fairly simple: after the title in v 1, there is a longing for the dwelling place of Yahweh in vv 2–5, followed by a brief section setting forth the well-being of the pilgrim in vv 6–8. A short intercessory prayer for the anointed of Yahweh follows in vv 9–10, and the last part of the psalm in vv 11–13 is a meditation on the joy of participation in the worship of Yahweh. The threefold use of אַשְׁרֵי, "How blest," in vv 5, 6, and 13 binds the psalm together and sets its tone (Kidner, II, 303). This is the only psalm in which אַשְׁרֵי appears three times. Another distinctive feature of the psalm's literary structure is the fourfold use of יהוה צבאות, "Yahweh Sabaoth" (traditionally, "Lord of Hosts"), in vv 2, 4, 9 (with אלהים), and 13. This usage provides inclusion for the content of the psalm; see note 3.c. above and observe the inclusion formed by Yahweh Sabaoth in vv 2 and 13:

מה־ידידות משכנותיך	How beautiful are your . . .
יהוה צבאות	Yahweh Sabaoth
יהוה צבאות	Yahweh Sabaoth
אשרי אדם בטח בך	How blest is . . .

The formation is chiastic: ABBA.

Comment

Longing for the dwelling place of Yahweh (84:2–5). The language of these verses expresses a passion for the temple and the presence of Yahweh which rivals that of Ps 42. Kraus (*Psalms 60–150,* 167) says that the מה which begins v 1 is an "exclamation of amazed glorification," and he calls attention to the literal wording of 1a: "How well-loved [יְדִיד] are your dwelling places!" The plural may refer to the multiple buildings of the temple area (cf. Pss 43:3; 46:5; 132:5, 7), or it may be an emphatic plural expression to enhance the term (cf. Ezek 37:27), or both. Perhaps the longing is expressed more intensely in Ps 42–43, but there is no lack of artistry in Ps 84, especially with the vignette of the birds who nest in the temple area near the altars of Yahweh Sabaoth (v 4). The reference must be to the nests of birds located in crevices in the walls of the buildings or in trees in the temple courts (for olive trees in the temple area, see Ps 52:10 and *Comment* there). The birds are symbols of the life, freedom, and joy of those who dwell close to God.

The plural "altars" in v 4 probably refers to at least two altars in the temple: a larger altar for the burnt offerings located in front of the temple (Exod 27:1–8; 38:1–7; 1 Kgs 8:64; 2 Kgs 16:14) and a smaller altar for incense situated before the Holy of Holies (Exod 30:1–10; 37:25–28; 1 Kgs 6:20–22; 7:48). A third altar may have been installed when King Ahaz had the priest, Uriah, build one according to the pattern of one he had seen in Damascus (2 Kgs 16:10–16). It is possible that there were more than two altars in the temple (for altars in Israelite worship, see M. Haran, *Temples and Temple Service in Ancient Israel* [Winona Lake, IN: Eisenbrauns, 1985] 15–18; R. deVaux, *Ancient Israel*, tr. J. McHugh [New York: McGraw-Hill, 1961] 406–14).

The speaker yearns for a privilege like that of the birds. Driven by inner motivations to build safe nests in which to hatch their young, they seem to be at home in the confines of the temple: "The holy place is the epitome of the undisturbed, fulfilled life" (Kraus, *Psalms 60–150,* 168). The birds are truly blessed, for they have found a safe residence in the house of the living God. The privileged status of birds recurs in Scripture and perhaps there is a similar longing in Jesus' lament: "Foxes have holes and birds of the air have nests, but the Son of Man has no place to lay his head" (Luke 9:58, NIV). Likewise, in his admonition not to worry about tomorrow, Jesus points to the birds: "They do not sow, or reap, or store away in barns, and yet your heavenly Father feeds them" (Matt 6:26, NIV).

From their privileged position in the nooks and crannies of the temple precincts, the birds fill the air with joyous song. The birds are like the temple singers, whose *hallels* to Yahweh Sabaoth—King and God—are never ending (for "Yahweh Sabaoth," see note Ps 80:5.a.). The temple courts, the site of festival celebrations and spiritual experiences of the presence of Yahweh, are idealized.

The temple, of course, is conceptualized as the home of God, and those who worship there are his guests (cf. Ps 23:5–6). V 5 contemplates the happy status of those who have the privilege of continually dwelling in the temple. The pilgrim who finds such joy in the temple courts at festival time thinks longingly of priests and ministers who live in the temple area all the time (cf. 1 Chr 23:30–32; 2 Chr 29:27–28; Eccl 47:8). The view is utopian of course; the priests and Levites who stayed at the temple and did all the work involved there (including, no doubt, caring for pilgrims at festival times!) may not always have considered it so ideal. Nevertheless, the zest and vision of the poetic enthusiasm is refreshing. Holy places are indeed sources of joy and praise for priests and pilgrims alike.

The blest state of pilgrims (84:6–8). The dual אַשְׁרֵי ("blest/happy") in vv 5 and 6 correlate the joy of the permanent temple dweller (v 5) with that of the pilgrims (v 6). Blessing and happiness are not confined to the priests and Levites. Those who have set their minds on pilgrimage have found strength in Yahweh (v 6), which moves them on from strength to strength (מֵחַיִל אֶל־חָיִל) even as they pass through such a fearsome place as the Valley of Baca (v 7). Vv 7–8 present a vignette of pilgrims making their way through difficult terrain on their way to the temple. As they trudge through this arid "valley of weeping," the early rain comes (or is anticipated) and turns it into a valley of springs, clothed with the blessings of revived growing plants. Such blessings move them from "strength to strength," which they know streams out from the God in Zion to whom they look throughout their journey. They are strengthened by anticipation of appearing before the presence of God in the temple. They will "see" him there and his face will be turned toward them in favor. The prospect of a beatific vision gives them energy to keep going on their arduous trek. The joy of festival time will make up for all their hardships on the journey.

Goulder (*Psalms of the Sons of Korah*, 39–40) argues that v 7 refers to a place called Baca, mentioned by Josephus as a small town in Galilee, supposedly situated at the head of a dry valley leading from the sea at Acco up toward the waters of Merom. He assumes that the most likely pilgrimage route from the region around Samaria to Dan (postulated as the sanctuary originally intended in Ps 84) would have followed the Kishon Valley to the sea, up the coast to Acco, up the Baca Valley to Merom, and then north via Gischala (el-Jish) and Kedesh to Dan. Water would be a problem on the climb from Acco to Merom.

He argues further that the early rain referred to in v 7 would be unlikely to occur on a pilgrimage to Jerusalem for the festival of Tabernacles, since the festival in Jerusalem was held in the seventh month (mid-September to mid-October) and rainfall during this period is rare all over Palestine. On the other hand, the festival in the Northern Kingdom was held in the eighth month (1 Kgs 12:32–33) which falls in the period of mid-October to mid-November when the rains usually fall. Thus, he argues, it would be unlikely for pilgrims going to Jerusalem to expect rain to cover their way with blessings; whereas Northern pilgrims could always have a reasonable expectation of rain on their journeys.

This is an interesting argument, but not totally persuasive. First, there are, of course, dry and difficult routes for pilgrims on the way to Jerusalem. For example, Cross (*Canaanite Myth and Hebrew Epic*, 109–10, n. 57) argues that the Valley of Achor in Josh 7:24–26 and Hos 2:15 was the site of an ancient road from the Dead Sea area at the fords of the Jordan, up the Wadi Dabr, through the Buqêʿah, and along the Kidron to Jerusalem (an alternate route from the Jordan to Jerusalem to that via the Wadi Qelt). Cross even suggests that Hosea may have had reference to the transformation of the Achor Valley into a garden by elaborate irrigation works built by King Uzziah (cf. 2 Chr 26:10). Of course, irrigation fits poorly with "early rain" as the source of blessings for a dry valley—unless we should follow Dahood (II, 281) and read מורה as "the raingiver," with reference to Uzziah! (Dahood, however, considers it to be a divine appellative for Yahweh.) LXX has "lawgiver," or "teacher," followed by Vulgate: "the lawgiver will give blessings." Regardless, the point is that there was no shortage of dry valleys in October-November leading to all the pilgrimage places in ancient Palestine.

Second, despite the fact that rain at the time of Tabernacles in October is rare, the association of rain with this festival seems to have been persistent (note Zech 14:16–19). We should also allow for a metaphorical dimension to v 7. The poetry should not be forced into a physically exact description. The psalm is about the pilgrimage itself which turns parched valleys into oases and clothes barren slopes with flowers whether it rains or not. Blessings are transmitted wherever the pilgrims go, because they are looking to God whose presence is at home in Zion (cf. T. H. Robinson, in Oesterley, 89).

Even in the eighth month there would be no assurance of actual rainfall on a pilgrimage. Doubtless there were occasions when rare October showers fell at the time of Tabernacles, and the fall rains were never far away (hopefully, at least). Kissane (II, 70) gives this verse the meaning of a figure of future hope, the future glory of Zion (cf. Isa 35; 51:3; 58:11). However, the idea of future hope should not be pressed. It is also possible that this verse reflects an earlier calendar when the autumn festival was in the eighth month and that the establishment of the festival in that month by Jeroboam, according to 1 Kgs 12:32–33, was not a novelty but a continuation of accepted tradition. In this case, the use of the seventh month in Jerusalem was actually the innovation (for the argument and references, see Goulder, 62–63).

A prayer for the anointed one (84:9–10). The references to "our shield" and "your anointed" are usually understood as applying to the king. If this is the case, it is an indication that this psalm dates from some time in the monarchy. For "shield" with reference to kings and rulers, see Ps 47:10; Hos 4:18; but much more frequently of God: Pss 3:4; 7:11; 18:3, 31, 36; 28:7, 33; 115:9–11; 119:114, 144; Prov 30:5. For "anointed" with reference to kings, see Pss 2:2; 18:51; 20:7; 28:8; 89:39, 52; 132:10, 17; 1 Sam 16:6; 24:7[6]; 26:9, 11, 16, 23; 2 Sam 1:14; Isa 45:1; Lam 4:20. The ancestors of Israel are referred to as "my anointed ones" in Ps 105:15. In post-exilic times when there was no monarchy, v 10 was probably understood with reference to the high priest in Jerusalem (for משׁיח with reference to priests, see Lev 4:3, 5; 6:15[22]; for the verb משׁח, "anoint," with priests, see Exod 28:41; 29:7, 36; 30:30; Lev 16:32; Num 3:3; 35:25; Zech 4:14; 1 Chr 20:22; Dan 9:25, cf. Isa 61:1; 2 Macc 1:10; see de Vaux, *Ancient Israel,* 105, 347, 399–401). The most natural explanation of v 10 is that the king is intended as the object of the prayer, but the high priest could have been intended in post-exilic times. There is little tension between the king as "our shield" in v 10 and Yahweh as "shield" in v 12, because the king embodied and exercised the divine protective power (as Kraus, 170, notes, with reference to Ps 72:12–14). The king was considered to be an "extended arm" of Yahweh, who intervenes and establishes justice (e.g., Mowinckel, *PIW,* I, 53–55). The prayer in 84:10 is for Yahweh to look with favor on the king/priest so that his reign can be established and prosper. The king would have been much involved, of course, with major festivals in pre-exilic Israel, and the same can be postulated for the high priest in post-exilic Israel.

Meditation on the goodness of festival time with Yahweh (84:11–13). One day in the courts of Yahweh is declared to be better than a thousand anywhere else. Far better for a person to wait as a pilgrim at the gates of the temple courts than to be separated from the joyful celebration of Yahweh's blessings. The "tents of wickedness" represent an area of life which are antithetical to the "house of God." Weiser (569) thinks that the meaning in v 11c is that it is better to stand like a beggar at the threshold of God's house than to dwell in the tents with godless Gentiles, assuming that the speaker in the psalm lives abroad in a pagan country. This is a widespread interpretation (see note 11.c.) and may be true, but nothing in the psalm really requires a setting outside of Israel, and we need assume no more than a contrast between festival joy of the courts of the house of God and the "tents of wickedness."

The central focus of pilgrimage and Ps 84 is Yahweh-God, who bestows grace and glory and good things on those who live lives of integrity (v 12). "Walking" is another positive double entendre: those who walk in pilgrimage and those who "walk" with obedience and faith in the way of Yahweh. The word for "grace" (חֵן) appears elsewhere in the Psalter in Ps 45:3 (though the related חַנּוּן, "gracious," is found in Pss 86:15; 103:8; 111:4; 112:4; 116:5; 145:8, and in Joel 2:13; cf. Exod 22:26[27]; 34:6). The word means "favor/acceptance/mercy," which is freely given. In v 12b it is linked with "glory" (כָּבוֹד; for this word, see *Comment*, Ps 96:1–6), which means "honor" or "favorable situation" in this context.

Yahweh is described as sun and shield in v 12a. "Sun" (שֶׁמֶשׁ) is not used elsewhere as a metaphor for Yahweh, and has sometimes been read as meaning "buckler" or "battlement" on the basis of Isa 54:12 (שִׁמְשֹׁתַיִךְ, supposedly "your shields" or "your battlement/rocky crag"; cf. Gunkel, 372; KB 995; the reading in Isa 54:12 is based on the assumption that the shields or pinnacles catch the rays of the sun, as part of the glittering description of restored Zion). But this should be resisted; Kraus (170) terms it "unwarranted" and notes that "sun" is a rather common royal epithet in ancient Near Eastern texts (e.g., Pharaoh is called "my Sun-god" in Tell El-Amarna text 288 and "Sun" or "Sun-god' was a favorite title of Hittite kings [D. R. Hillers, *Covenant* (Baltimore: Johns Hopkins UP, 1969) 29, n. 2]). Cf. the "Sun of righteousness" (שֶׁמֶשׁ צְדָקָה), which will arise for those who fear the name of Yahweh in Mal 3:20[4:2], and Ps 19:5–7.

This psalm is noteworthy for its concentration of divine epithets, which serves to emphasize that the precincts of the temple and the celebration of festivals have meaning because of the gracious presence of Yahweh. Festivals are exciting times of feasting and joyful celebration, but they are finally nothing without fellowship with God.

> "For with thee is the fountain of life; in thy light do we see light" (Ps. 36:9). This is the key sentence for our understanding of Israel's cultic life. Fulfilled life is not the result of some magic power, but the result of the power of the *Deus praesens,* the gift of his steadfast love; it is blessing and *shalom* received from him (Kraus, *Theology of the Psalms,* 78).

The *Deus praesens* makes just one day in the temple courts, or even a day of only waiting at the entrance, more meaningful than a thousand others elsewhere. Ps 84 closes with a burst of enthusiasm in v 13, using Yahweh Sabaoth (also in vv 2 and 9) and אַשְׁרֵי ("How blest") as in vv 5 and 6. These are the ones who go "from strength to strength" as they look toward God and turn valleys of tears into ways of blessings.

Explanation

Ps 84 expresses the longing of a pilgrim for the joy of participation in the worship of temple courts of Yahweh. It is a psalm for pilgrimage, which may profitably be read with other psalms which express yearning for the temple of God:

> One thing I ask of the Lord,
> it is the one thing I seek:
> that I may dwell in the house of the Lord

all the days of my life,
to gaze on the beauty of the Lord
and to seek him in his temple.

(Ps 27:4, REB)

As a hind longs for the running streams,
so I long for you, my God.
I thirst for God, the living God;
when shall I come to appear in his presence?

(Ps 42:1–2, REB)

I rejoiced when they said to me,
"We are going to the house of the Lord."
Our feet stood inside your gates, O Jerusalem,
Jerusalem built up, a city knit together,
to which tribes make pilgrimage,
the tribes of the Lord,
—as was enjoined upon Israel—
to praise the name of the Lord.

(Ps 124:1–4, NJV)

If I forget you, O Jerusalem,
may my right hand forget its skill.
May my tongue cling to the roof of my mouth
If I do not remember you,
If I do not consider Jerusalem my highest joy.

(Ps 137:5–6, NIV)

Pilgrimages and festivals are almost universal features of religious life. They are concerned with the physical aspects of religion: journey, temple courts, feasting, liturgies, fellowship with fellow pilgrims, and the like. These physical aspects, however, have meaning because they bear spiritual realities with them. The experiences of pilgrimages and festivals stay with the worshipers when they return to everyday life. They have seen what they would never have seen had they stayed at home.

Ps 84 bears witness to a strong and living faith which longs for the "living God" (v 3) and the context of holiness, life, and love in the temple courts and beyond. We may read this psalm, as it often has been read, with sensitive awareness of its spiritual dimensions. For example, the transformation of the Valley of Baca into an oasis (v 7) is indeed "a classic statement of the faith which dares to dig blessing out of hardships" (Kidner, II, 305). J. Levenson (*Sinai and Zion: An Entry into the Jewish Bible* [Minneapolis: Winston, 1985] 177–78) writes of this same verse: "it implies a kind of natural/spiritual transformation: *Natural* in that a valley becomes a mountain, Zion, and *spiritual* in that the ascent somehow enables the worshippers to make the water of tears into springs. . . . In other words, the road up to the Temple is the objective correlative of an inner spiritual development which is crowned by a vision of God in his place on Mount Zion. The physical ascent is also a spiritual ascent." This is a way of saying that pilgrimage and festival are sacraments: visible actions become the means of grace and revelation of the presence of God. Pilgrimage and festival have surplus meanings which engage the participants in spiritual encounter.

Beyond actual participation in pilgrimage and festival, the poetic descriptions of the joy of the celebrants are themselves sacramental. The poems become signs of the presence of God for those who read them. They serve as a kind of *vade mecum:* psalms which the readers can take with them for regular use and the renewal of memory and the spirit of pilgrimage (a suggestion made for Pss 120–34 by K. Seybold, *Die Wallfahrtspsalmen: Studien zur Entstehungsgeschichte von Psalm 120–134* [Neukirchen-Vluyn: Neukirchener, 1978] 73). The pilgrimage psalms probably functioned for ancient Israelites in this way. When they were far away from Jerusalem, some doubtless found the psalms to be an encouragement for the difficult journeys at festival times; journeys they might have avoided otherwise. Others who could not go found that the psalms revived their memories and kindled their imaginations, either from their own experiences or from the stories of those who had been to Zion. The pilgrimage psalms helped them to visualize the beauty of the temple and its courts, the birds nesting near the altars, the dry valleys on the journey which were transformed by rain, and the crowd in the temple courts, shouting with joy and thanksgiving (Ps 42:5).

For many there could be no physical journey to Zion, but the psalms allowed them to be pilgrims and festival celebrants in memory and imagination. We too can have spiritual kinship with the ancient pilgrims and feel the anticipation of festival times well up in our hearts. The ancient pilgrims left Jerusalem behind when the festivals were over to return to their worldly occupations, but the memories and the faith engendered were not lost:

> If I forget you, O Jerusalem,
> let my right hand wither!
> Let my tongue cleave to the roof of my mouth,
> if I do not remember you.
>
> (Ps 137:5–6, RSV)

We remember also, and we know forever, that even one day in the courts of God is worth more than a thousand anywhere else. Through the psalms we may become pilgrims too. Those who have ears to hear and eyes to see, let them hear

Revive Us Again   (85:1–14)

Bibliography

Becker, J. *Israel deutet seine Psalmen.* 58–59. **Broyles, C. C.** *Conflict of Faith.* 165–68. **Cragham, J. F.** *The Psalms: Prayers for the Ups, Downs, and In-Betweens of Life.* Wilmington, DE: Michael Glazier, 1985. 148–51. **Johnson, A. R.** *CPIP.* 199–209. **Kselman, J. S.** "A Note on Psalm 85:9–10." *CBQ* 46 (1984) 23–27.

Translation

1   For the leader:[a] a Korahite psalm.[b]

2 (1)   *O Yahweh, you favored* [a] *your land;*   (3+3)
        you "turned" the fortunes [b] *of Jacob.*

3 (2)	You lifted off the guilt of your people;	(3+3)
	you covered all their sin,[a] SELAH.	
4 (3)	You pulled back[a] all your wrath;	(3+3)
	you turned away[b] from your hot anger.	
5 (4)	Turn us,[a] O God of our salvation!	(3+3)
	Put an end[b] to your displeasure with us.	
6 (5)	Will you be angry with us forever?	(3+3)
	Must your anger be prolonged for generation after generation?	
7 (6)	Will you not turn[a] (and) give us life,	(3+3)
	that your people may rejoice in you?	
8 (7)	O Yahweh, show us your loyal-love,	(3+3)
	and grant us your salvation!	
9 (8)	I will hear what God has to say:[a]	(3+3+3+3)
	Yahweh indeed[b] will command[c] well-being	
	for the loyal members of his people[d]—	
	But don't turn back to folly![e]	
10 (9)	Surely[a] his salvation is near to those who fear him,	(4+3)
	so that Glory[b] may dwell in our land.	
11 (10)	Loyal-Love and Faithfulness[a] have met together;	(3+3)
	Righteousness and Well-Being have embraced.[b]	
12 (11)	Faithfulness will spring up from the earth,	(3+3)
	and Righteousness will look down from heaven.	
13 (12)	Yahweh will indeed bestow what is good,	(3+3)
	and our land will yield its harvest.	
14 (13)	Righteousness[a] will go before him,	(3+3)
	and prepare a way for his footsteps.[b]	

Notes

1.a. See n. 51:1.a.

1.b. See n. 84:1.c.

2.a. For the tense of the verbs in vv 2–4, see *Form/Structure/Setting* below. I have left the translation "turned" literal and in quotation marks in order to emphasize the play on the verb שוב and its varied uses in the psalm.

2.b. The *kethiv* is שבות, but שבית, "captivity," is the marginal reading. שוב means "returning" or "restoration." The words are derived from two different Heb. roots: שוב, "turn/return," and שבה, "take captive." The technical expression שוב שבות occurs in a number of contexts, e.g., Pss 14:7 (53:7); 126:4; Deut 30:3; Jer 29:14; 30:3, 18; 31:23; 33:26; 48:47; 49:39; Hos 6:11; Amos 9:14; Zeph 2:7; 3:20; Ezek 16:53; 29:14; Joel 4:1; Lam 2:14; Job 42:10. In some cases, the meaning may be that of "bring back/restore captives," as the scribal tradition on the margin of Ps 85:2 indicates: "brought back the captivity of Jacob," probably thinking of the return of exiles from Babylonia. However, the more comprehensive meaning "restore the fortunes/well-being" is to be preferred in most contexts, even where שבית occurs. See H. W. Wolff, *Joel and Amos*, tr. W. Janzen et al. (Philadelphia: Fortress, 1977) 76, n. 19; Goulder, *Psalms of the Sons of Korah*, 99, 266, n. 19, for summaries and references; also W. L. Holladay, *The Root SUBH in the Old Testament with Particular Reference to Its Usages in Covenantal Texts* (Leiden: Brill) 110–15; A. R. Johnson, *CPIP*, 67, n. 4; cf. Johnson, *CPIP*, 200, n. 2). Note the parallel in Hos 6:11 of שוב שבות with רפא in Hos 7:1, leading Kraus (II, 756) to translate "the restoration of the wounded body politic" (following Wolff, *Hosea*, tr. G. Stansell, ed. P. D. Hanson [Philadelphia: Fortress, 1974] 123).

3.a. The versions indicate plural, "sins" (*BHS*). See, however, 2 Chr 6:25–26; Dahood, II, 286.

4.a. The verb אסף means "gather/remove"; "gather and take away," BDB, 62, no. 4. For, אסף as "draw back/withdraw," see 1 Sam 14:19.

4.b. Some commentators find difficulty with "you turned (away) from the heat of your anger." Kraus (II, 753) proposes to read הִשְׁבַּתָּ מֵחֲרוֹן, "you have stilled/calmed your anger from hotness" (lit.); "you have stilled the heat of your anger" (see also Gunkel, 375), reading the verb as שׁבת "cease/desist." The problem arises because of MT's hiphil form of שׁוב, which is normally transitive, "cause to return/restore XXX," rather than qal, which would be intransitive. If emendation is rejected, one solution is to assume that the hiphil is used here as qal (for qal with מִן, see Exod 32:12; Jonah 3:9; for somewhat similar construction, see Ezek 14:6; 18:30; 21:35; Delitzsch, III, 10; Perowne, 127), with the object "yourself" understood, as in KJV. An easier solution is to assume that the text originally used an enclitic *mem:* הֲשִׁיבוֹתָ־ם חֲרוֹן אַפֶּךָ: "You turned back the heat of your anger." The parallel with 4a is improved and the intransitive problem with the hiphil is solved (H. D. Hummel, "Enclitic *MEM* in Early Northwest Semitic, Especially Hebrew," *JBL* 76 (1957) 102; Dahood, II, 287, who, however, thinks that the hiphil may have an intransitive sense here, relying on the internal hiphil הֲשִׁיבֵנוּ, "return to us/restore us," in Ps 80:4, 8, 20).

5.a. The meaning of this verbal expression is a major problem in this psalm. One option is to read the qal שׁוּבֵנוּ ("turn us") as equal to the hiphil in Ps 80:4, "O God, restore (הֲשִׁיבֵנוּ) us" (as in Gunkel, 375; Kraus, II, 253; RSV; NAB; NIV; REB; and probably intended by LXX ἐπίστρεψον ἡμᾶς "turn us." Another proposal (as, e.g., Oesterley, 383) is to read the שׁוּבֵנוּ of MT as שׁוּב־נָה, "Turn now, O God . . . and bring an end to your displeasure." Another approach is to assume that the verb has dative force, rather than accusative: "turn/return to us"; see Dahood, II, 287, and now embraced by Johnson, *CPIP*, 200, n. 2; also Buttenwieser (the suffix is "an accusative of direction," 281), Kissane, NEB. Kidner (II, 308) comments correctly that "the grammatical evidence is indecisive"; the meaning depends on the interpretation of the psalm and may have varied as it was used in different contexts. See *Form/Structure/Setting* below.

5.b. See Johnson, *CPIP*, 200, n. 3. The verb is lit., "break off" (פָּרַר), as in Ps 89:34. However, Dahood (II, 287) argues for פָּרַר as "flee," on the basis of the Ugaritic text, 1 Aqht 120 (*pr wdu*, "flee and fly"), also citing Ps 89:34; Job 15:4; Eccl 11:10. However, the Ugaritic root *pwr* = *prr* can mean "break/violate/annul" (G. R. Driver, *Canaanite Myths and Legends* [Edinburgh: Clark, 1956] 163; C. H. Gordon, *Ugaritic Manual*, 314, no. 1594. B. Margalit (*The Ugaritic Poem of AQHT* [Berlin: de Gruyter, 1989] 408, n. 11) argues that the root in the AQHT text is properly *tpr*, "sew/sew up," rather than *prr*, "flutter/fly," as generally assumed. Therefore "brush off/invalidate" should be retained as the meaning of the Heb. verb.

7.a. Kraus (II, 253; also, Briggs, II, 234; Gunkel, 375; Oesterley, 383) omits אַתָּה (the personal pronoun "you") because of supposed overloading of the colon; possibly bring a misreading of הֲלֹא תָשׁוּב as הֲלֹא אַתָּה תָשׁוּב. However, the colon is not seriously overloaded and the emphatic "you" adds intensity to the plea. LXX has ὁ θεός, "O God," indicating Heb. הָאֵל or אֱלֹהַ (*BHS*), perhaps influenced by 9a. NJV translates "Surely you will revive us again," assuming that the הֲלֹא indicates a strong affirmative statement (see GKC 150e), unless it is taken as ironic, i.e., "Surely you wouldn't fail to . . ."—which is unlikely.

9.a. The combination of הָאֵל יהוה, "the God, Yahweh," is strange, and some commentators prefer to omit the הָאֵל (e.g., Kraus, II, 753; Schmidt, 160, propose הֲלֹא for הָאֵל: "I am listening [for] what he says! Is it not that Yahweh speaks of salvation?"). However, the MT punctuation indicates that "the God" (or El; Dahood has "El himself") and "Yahweh" should be read with different colons, though, of course, they are in apposition.

9.b. Reading the כִּי as emphatic (cf. Ps 77:12, etc.).

9.c. Reading the piel יְדַבֵּר ("he will speak") in the sense of "command," as in Gen 12:4; Exod 1:17; 23:22, or possibly "promise," as in Gen 18:19; 21:1–2; Deut 1:14; 6:3. See W. H. Schmidt, *TDOT*, III, 97 (cf. in proclamation, *TDOT*, III, 100–101, and God's intention "to speak peace" or "to speak good"; Num 10:29).

9.d. Treating "to his people and to his loyal ones" (אֶל־עַמּוֹ וְאֶל־חֲסִידָיו) as a hendiadys, with Dahood (II, 289). However, it is possible that the construction is appositional: "to his people, that is to those who are his loyal-ones."

9.e. The last colon of v 9 is considered perplexing by some commentators. Gunkel (375) thinks that it does not fit in the context, and Kraus (II, 753) calls it *sinnwidrig* ("nonsensical/absurd"), which is surely incorrect, though Dahood (II, 289) claims that it "defies analysis." Gunkel proposes to change to וְאֵלַי שָׁבִי־לוֹ כִסְלָה, which reads: "and to those who turn their hope/confidence to him" (followed by Oesterley, 383), understanding כִסְלָה as "hope/confidence" as in Job 4:6, where it is parallel to תִקְוָה, "hope" (see also Ps 78:7; Prov 3:26). Schmidt (160–61) reads וְאֵל יָשִׁיבוּ אֵלָיו לִבָּם, "and to those who turn their heart to him"; reflecting LXX's καὶ ἐπὶ τοὺς ἐπιστρέφοντας πρὸς αὐτὸν καρδίαν, see also, John-

: אל ישבו בלי כסלה to אל־ישובו לכסלה son, *CPIP*, 206. Kraus (II, 754) follows F. Notscher and changes
"Let them not dwell without hope!" (suggested also in *BHS*). NEB, "and to all who turn and trust in
him," probably reflects ואל שבי לכסלה, lit., "and to those coming back to hope." The revisers of NEB in
REB have wisely returned to MT: "Let them not go back to foolish ways." A. R. Johnson (*CPIP*, 205)
translates: "But let there be no reverting to folly!" MT does not require enendation, though LXX
offers an acceptable optional reading. J. S. Kselman (*CBQ* 46 [1984] 23–27) reconstructs vv 9–10 to
read: "Let me declare [hiphil for qal] what El decrees, / What Yahweh says—for he promises
peace, / to the devoted ones of his people, / to the one who dwells in security. / Surely, near is his
salvation to those who fear him; / Near is his glory to him who dwells in our land." Kselman emends
the imperfect ישובו to the qal participle of ישב, "one who dwells," and understands כסלה as meaning
"confidence/assurance." See n. 10.b. for his reconstruction of v 10b.

10.a. For the meaning of the particle אך, see n. 62:2.a.

10.b. The suggestion that כבודו, "his glory," be read for MT's "glory" is fairly frequently made
(*BHS*). Dahood (II, 289) argues that the suffix on ישע, "his salvation," does double duty for כבוד (=
"his glory") and that the text does not need changing. Kselman argues that the lack of real synonymous parallelism in v 10 (cf. Dahood) points to the need for an alternate reading (following
Dahood). He argues that אך קרוב and לשכן are syntactically parallel, as are also ישע and כבוד, "his
salvation" and "[his] glory," but that ליראיו ("to those who fear him") and לשכן ("to dwell") are not
really parallel although they are both prepositional phrases. He proposes to emend the infinitive
לשכן to a participle (לשׁכן) and read "(Near is) his glory to the one who dwells in our land," citing
כבודו and כשעותו ("his salvation" and "his glory" in Ps 96:2–3; also, Isa 62:1–2; Ps 62:8). He contends
that "his salvation" and "(his) glory" function as a hendiadys: "The poet asserts that God's glorious
salvation is near to those who fear him and who consequently dwell in the land" (24).

The resulting reading is attractive and well balanced, although the word order is unusual (as
Kselman notes, *CBQ* 46 [1984] 25). But Kselman begins with a dubious assumption: that the parallelism in v 10 has to be fully synonymous. Most parallelism is *not*, and the now well-established thesis
that parallelism is basically supplementation rather than repetition of content applies here. V 10b
goes beyond 10a to explicate what the nearness of Yahweh's salvation means. Thus, I have treated
"Glory" in v 10b as a personification, as with Loyal-Love, Faithfulness, Righteousness, and Well-Being
(Peace) in vv 11–12. Goulder (112) suggests that there is here a tetrad of supernatural powers,
similar to a tetrad in Ps 96:6 and another in 89:15. If Glory is included, there is a pentad rather than a
tetrad. Of course, it is *his* (Yahweh's) glory which dwells in the land, as well as *his* mercy, etc.

11.a. Or, "Truth."

11.b. The niphal נשקו, "have kissed each other" would ease the reading (MT has נשקו, qal). Op-
tionally, the emendation to נשקו, niphal from שקק, "rush together/embrace" (cf. Joel 2:9; Nah 2:5) is
frequently adopted (e.g. Kraus, II, 754; REB, "have embraced").

14.a. Syr indicates וצדיק, "and the righteous one," for MT's צדק, "righteousness," but MT should
be retained.

14.b. The meaning of this colon is not clear. To what or to whom does the suffix on "his steps"
refer? Will "Righteousness" set a way for the steps of Yahweh? Or does the suffix refer to "Righteousness" itself ("and he will put its steps to/on a way")? Or should something like the sense of שים לב
(e.g., Job 4:20) with the idea of "set the heart to" = "pay attention/regards/heed" be understood (as
in Delitzsch, III, 12; cf. Gunkel, 375) with the meaning: "Righteousness shall go before . . . and
attend unto the way of his (Yahweh's) steps." Delitzsch argues, though he does not prefer it, that the
לדרך פעמי can be understood as a construct relationship: "(Righteousness) will set (his footsteps) to
the footsteps of him (Yahweh)," understanding the "his steps" as doing double duty, meaning that
Righteousness both goes before Yahweh like a herald in 10a and follows closely in his footsteps in
10b.

Emendation is common of course. Kraus (II, 754) suggests instead of וישם either וישר, "straightness/
rightness," or ושלום, "peace/well-being": Righteousness goes before him / and well-being follows in
his tracks" (see also Jacquet, II, 632, 637, and others). Dahood (II, 290) prefers to read the *lamedh*
on "way" as emphatic, vocalize the דרך ("way") as a qal participle, and derive the ישם from the Ugaritic
root *ysm* (Aramaic *wsm*), "pleasant/beautiful," yielding "beauty," and thus: "beauty will indeed tread
in his steps."

I prefer to read "Righteousness" as the subject of ישם, with the verb used either in the sense of (1)
determine/fix a way or (2) make/prepare a way, with דרך as construct with פעמיו ("his steps"): "the
(way) of his steps" = "the way for his steps." The construction may mean that Righteousness, like the
herald of a king, will *prepare* the way for the king or else will determine or set the way the king will go.

Gunkel (374, 375), who prefers to read וְשָׁלוֹם or וִישַׁר, thinks the figure is that of a king who has heralds going before and footmen who trail behind: Righteousness is the forerunner and Peace/Rightness follows behind. The emendations are unnecessary, but the idea of a herald going before a king is probably correct.

Form/Structure/Setting

In terms of general genre, Ps 85 is a prayer for the favor and saving work of Yahweh. Complaint is not expressed directly in the psalm, but conditions of distress are presupposed behind the statements and petitions in vv 2–8. It is clear that the speaker and those who are represented by him/her have understood their distress as the result of the wrath and displeasure of Yahweh. They want to be revived, given a restoration of "life" by Yahweh (v 7). The second part of the psalm (vv 9–14) contains affirmative statements about the saving work of Yahweh which is near at hand for those who are faithful to him. The psalm closes with a fine section of poetic depiction of the great qualities of Yahweh's presence and power: Glory, Loyal-Love, Faithfulness, Righteousness, and Well-Being (Peace); all are ready to go forth to participate with Yahweh as he bestows his goodness on the land and its people.

What kind of context in life and worship is reflected in the psalm? Mowinckel (*PIW*, I, 223) argues that Pss 85 and 126 are prayers for peace and a happy new year which belonged to harvest and new year celebrations, having the idea of a "turning of destiny" (the "turning" refers to every new year, especially in Ps 126). Weiser (571–72) also argues that the scene in Ps 85 is "probably that of a service of supplication of the cult community, held within the framework of the festival cult," and eschews a historical context for "the tradition of the festival cult celebrated at the autumn feast . . . when the cult community continually witnessed at first hand . . . the *Heilsgeschichte* as the representation of the gracious acts of God's guidance (deliverance from Egypt, bestowal of the promised land)." Weiser is willing to assign a pre-exilic date to the composition of the psalm.

Many interpreters, however, have assumed that the psalm belongs to the period after the exile (including Mowinckel, *PIW*, I, 223; not evident, however, in *Psalmenstudien*, III, 54–59). Kissane's well-expressed summary of Ps 85 puts forth the general approach of many commentators: "This psalm is a message of hope to the returned exiles who during the early years after the return from exile were discouraged because their condition fell far short of the glorious and happy state which had been foretold by the prophets. The exile is at an end, and the sins of Israel which caused it are now pardoned. But the sad condition of the people implies that the anger of God is not yet fully appeased" (II, 72). In this approach, the perfect forms of the verbs in vv 2–4 are usually translated as English present perfects: "you have been gracious . . . you have forgiven," etc.

Two or three problems plague this view. First, the content of vv 2–4 remains in serious tension with that in vv 5–8. If Yahweh has favored the land, turned the fortunes of Judah, lifted away and covered sin and guilt, and drawn back his wrath, why is it necessary to continue to pray for these things? "This is a direct contradiction in Hebrew as in English," Goulder (*Psalms of the Sons of Korah*, 100) comments. "If God has taken away all his wrath and turned from the fierceness of his anger, then he has already caused his indignation to cease, and is not *drawing* his anger out to perpetuity." Second, the "turning of the fortunes," in v 2 is a comprehensive expression, found as early as Hos 6:11, and is not necessarily tied to the return of Israelite exiles and the restoration of Jerusalem. Third, it is argued that there is a lack of direct evidence from the OT that contemporary Israelites regarded the return of some exiles and the rebuilding of Jerusalem as a sign of a mighty act of forgiveness and restoration on the part of Yahweh (Goulder, 100, who has reference to Haggai ["You expected much, but it came to little," 1:9] and Zechariah ["O LORD of hosts, how long will you be without mercy for Jerusalem and the cities of Judah that have felt your anger these seventy years," 1:12]).

The main weakness of these objections, however, lies in the assumption that the speaker in Ps 85 is reflecting the context of the *early* return and restoration. If we assume a later period, for example that of Ezra and Nehemiah, the "turning of the fortunes of Jacob" in the return of exiles becomes plausible. It is frequently assumed that MT's *qere* reading of שְׁבִית for שְׁבוּת indicates a reference to the return of exiles from captivity in Babylonia, which is reflected in LXX. This is probably true, though the early meaning of שְׁבוּת and שְׁבִית may not have been significantly different in the formulaic saying of "turn the turning/captivity," both meaning to restore (see v 2b above). It seems highly probable that Ps 126:1 reflects the return from exile, which is described as one of Yahweh's great works (see the comments of Allen, 169–75). From the perspective of a later context (postexilic), the "turning of the fortunes" by Yahweh in the return and restoration becomes one of the examples of such action. The question which Ps 85 seeks to answer is: Will Yahweh "turn our fortunes" again and demonstrate his loyal-love in further saving works? To this, the answer of the psalm is "Yes" (vv 9–14).

Thus, it does not seem necessary to treat the perfects in vv 2–4 as prophetic with a future, eschatological force (see Gunkel, 373; Oesterley, 302; NJV), or as precative perfects with imperative force (as, Buttenwieser, 272; Dahood, II, 286: "Favor your land . . . restore . . . withdraw, etc."; note A. R. Johnson's change of mind on the precative perfect, in *CPIP*, 202, n. 1), or as characteristic perfects, as in JB: "Yahweh you favour your own country, you bring back the captives of Jacob." It seems to me that it is better to understand the perfects in vv 2–4 as expressing simple past tense, without fixing the historical context too tightly. The original composition and use of the psalm may have been much earlier, with the primary reference of the language of vv 2–4 to the events of the exodus from Egypt and the wilderness wanderings (note Johnson, *CPIP*, 208), but its present role in the Psalter reflects post-exilic experience (on the reinterpretation of the psalm, see Becker, *Israel deutet*, 58–59; cf. Aejmelaeus, *The Traditional Prayer in the Psalms*, 13). The exile and the return of some exiles were experiences of a piece with Yahweh's saving acts in earlier history (cf. Allen, 174, on Ps 126). Ps 85, of course, is concerned with the extension of those saving works into the future.

Goulder (98–111) seeks a different explanation for the language in Ps 85. He begins, of course, with the assumption that all the Korahite psalms originally belonged to the festival celebrations at the sanctuary at Dan in the Northern Kingdom, and thus must date prior to 722 B.C.E. (see *Form/Structure/Setting* of Ps 84). His main case is that the *selah* indicates a pause in which the story of apostasy, judgment, and forgiveness in Exod 32–34 would be set forward in a cantillation or recitative. He argues that the emphasis on forgiveness of sins and withdrawal of wrath in vv 2–4 does not fit well with the events of the exodus and conquest, but are very appropriate for Exod 32–34. He finds five phrases in common between Ps 85 and the Exodus passages: (1) "Turn from the heat of your anger" (שׁוּב מחרון אפך) in Exod 32:12 with Ps 85:4b; (2) "Yet now if you will forgive their sin" (תשׂא הםאתם) in Exod 32:32 (also see 34:7) with 85:3; (3) "Yahweh, Yahweh, God" (יהוה יהוה אל) in Exod 34:6 with the use of אל ("God") in 85:9; (4) "loyal-love and faithfulness (truth)" (חסד ואמת) in Exod 34:6 and in Ps 85:11; (5) "Behold, my angel shall go before you" (ילך לפניך) with Righteousness going before in Ps 85:14 and in Exod 32:34 (לפניו יהלך). Goulder's is an interesting hypothesis, but only that: a hypothesis. The expressions in Exod 32–34 and Ps 85 are not distinctive enough to these contexts to constitute very persuasive evidence. A minor flaw in Goulder's case is that MT has the *selah* after v 3 rather than after v 4 where it would be expected. The value of Goulder's study is to strengthen the case against the exclusive application of the language in the psalm to the return from exile. For a similar treatment of a psalm, though not tied to a *selah,* see Freedman's interpretation of Ps 23 in *Pottery, Poetry, and Prophecy,* 275–302.

Modern commentators have argued for more than one speaker in Ps 85, giving it a liturgical character (Gunkel, 373). In particular, the view that it is a prophetic or other cultic official who gives an oracle as God's answer to the prayer of the congregation in vv 2–7 has been popular (e.g., Leslie, 122; Weiser, 571, 573; Anderson, II, 611; Johnson, *CPIP,* 199–209; Kraus, II, 757; and the summary in Goulder, 108–9). This may be true, but I see little reason to require a change of a speaker in Ps 85. The speaker may be understood as a prophet or priest, who hears the message of Yahweh in v 9, but the postulate of a change of speaker is built on general theories rather than on the content of the psalm. In this, I agree with Goulder (111), though on different grounds. Goulder argues that the priest-poet (whom he identifies with the מנצח, "leader," in the title) requires no hearing of "the mysterious voice of God speaking" (Weiser, 571) because the message has been heard by all the assembly in the recall of the story in Exod 32–34. In my opinion, the message would have been clear to any priest or prophet or faithful Israelite from the traditions recalled in vv 2–4 without necessary recourse either to an oracle from the "mysterious voice of God" or to the recitation of Exod 32–34. The formulation of the message in vv 8–14 is done from traditional elements in the proclamation of Israel's faith which would have been known to any informed speaker.

Comment

A recall of Yahweh's favor in the past (85:2–4). These verses have received considerable attention in the *Notes* and *Form/Structure/Setting* sections above and the material there need not be repeated here. The "land" (ארץ) is Israel's dwelling place, but it is really Yahweh's land (Lev 25:23; Kraus, II, 756), even though it is called "our land" in v 13. It is "our land" because Yahweh favored it and gave his people prosperity in it ("turned the fortunes of Jacob"). The "favor" shown to the land was especially manifest in Yahweh's forgiveness of sins, by the removal of sin-guilt (Isa 40:2), and his pulling back his wrath from destroying his people.

These verses provide the basis for the petitions which follow in vv 5–8. "The members of the congregation, whose eyes are firmly focused on God, know who it is to whom they pray and what they can hope for from him in their present affliction" (Weiser, 572). The supplications are rooted in a firmly established tradition of faith. They are addressed to God who "turns fortunes" and turns away from wrath. (Kraus notes the frequent use of "Jacob" as a name for Israel in Isa 40–55; e.g., 40:27; 41:8; 42:24; 43:1, 22, 28; 44:1, 2, 5, 21, 23; 45:4, 19).

Supplication for Yahweh's saving work (85:5–8). The difficulty with the verb in 5a has been discussed in the *Notes* (5.a.) and in the *Form/Structure/Setting* section. I take it that the best sense is that of "turn us" = "restore us" (as in Pss 80:4, 8, 20; 126:4), with "again" or "further" understood. It is possible that we should understand the expression שׁוּבֵנוּ as a contracted form of שׁוּב שְׁבוּתֵנוּ, "turn our fortunes (as you did in the past)"—the full form would have made the colon too long; assuming that the poet thought it important to use אֱלֹהֵי יִשְׁעֵנוּ, "god of our salvation" (note the threefold use of נוּ-, "us," in the verse). The prayer seeks an end to Yahweh's anger, which is a prerequisite to restoration. The rhetorical question in v 6, designed to be persuasive, conveys a sense of the experience of long-endured wrath, which threatens the very life of the people (v 7). The suppliants have experienced adverse conditions so long that they feel dead and in need of a renewal of life, a revitalization by the one who gives life (cf. Pss 71:20; 80:18; 138:7; 143:11; Hos 6:2; 14:87; Ezek 18:27). For an extensive study of life in the OT, see H. Ringgren in *TDOT*, IV, 324–44. The verb שׁוּב ("turn") is used again in v 7. Yahweh is implored to "show" (v 8), that is, "demonstrate/manifest" his loyal-love (חֶסֶד) in action. For חֶסֶד, see note Ps 51:3.a.

A message of assurance (85:9–14). The speaker in v 9 declares intention to hear what God, Yahweh, has to say. As noted above, a goodly number of commentators think of some kind of oracular experience in which a prophet/priest receives a message from Yahweh for the worshiping community. Weiser (573) argues that the recipient of the oracle receives only one word: שׁלוֹם, "peace/well-being," translating: "The Lord, yea, he speaks: 'salvation' to his people . . ." The material which follows could be considered as the filling out of the oracular message of *Shalom* by the prophet/priest. This seems somewhat forced to me, and the text lends itself to understanding it as an indirect report of the message of Yahweh: "In the present case the psalmist does not go on to speak *qua* Yahweh in the first person but seems, rather, to be giving the gist of the divine response" (Johnson, *CPIP*, 205). Johnson says further that the situation is like that in Ps. 20:7, where the speaker says, "Now I know that Yahweh saves . . ." If this is the case, it suggests a message which results from reflection and observation rather than from some oracular voice. The message is the speaker's interpretation of what Yahweh has to say (cf. Kraus, II, 757; Kissane, II, 74, argues that there is no new revelation, but the message is derived from prophecies such as those in Isa 40–66).

The message is one of encouragement and assurance, designed to build confidence and hope. As I have read it, v 9d is a warning by the speaker to the people not to turn back to old ways of folly, which would nullify the saving work of Yahweh. The apostasy of the past should be avoided (Goulder, *Psalms of the Sons Korah*, 111, cites Exod 34:12–17 and Jer 10:8 as relevant; the latter passage uses the root of "folly" in connection with idolatry). The positive statements in vv 10–14 are made up of traditional material, but they are artistically constructed into a brilliant and unique passage, which reminds the reader of Deutero-Isaiah. Buttenwieser, 273–80, even argues that Ps 85 is from the same author as Isa 40–55, though earlier. He notes the striking similarity of Ps 85 to Isa 40–55 but says there is no "labored imitation"; the psalm shows the "poetic spontaneity" which marks the works of genius.

The poetry of vv 10–14 is marked by the personification of the primary qualities of Yahweh and his action. His "salvation" is near (cf. Isa 51:5; 56:1; Matt 3:2; Mark 1:15), and his "Glory" will again dwell in the land (for "glory," cf. Pss 19:1; 26:8; 57:6, 12; 63:3; Isa 6:3; 40:5; 60:2; 62:2), Kraus (II, 758) remarks that the message corresponds to that in Isa 46:13 (RSV):

> I bring near (קרבתי) my deliverance (צדקתי),
>   it is not far off,
> and my salvation (תשועתי) will not tarry;
> I will put salvation (תשועה) in Zion,
> for Israel my glory (תפארתי).

Cf. the desertion of the temple and Jerusalem by the glory of Yahweh in Ezek 11:22–25 and its return in Ezek 43:1–4.

Glory, Loyal-Love (חסד), Faithfulness (Truth), Righteousness, and Well-Being (Peace/*Shalom*) are presented as living agents of Yahweh's work of bestowing goodness and productivity on the land. The four great "agents" in v 11 have met together, like kings or generals preparing for some action, and they are in harmony. All the "agents" are partners in concord; there is no meeting of opposites in a picture of atonement as some older interpretations would suggest (see Kidner, II, 310; Perowne, 126). The qualities of divine action and life are set forth in these verses; contrast the absence of faithfulness (אמת) and loyal-love (חסד), and knowledge (דעת) from the residents of the land in Hos 4:2 (cf. Isa 59:14–15). The land will receive the action of the "agents" in coordinated endeavor from below and above, according to v 12. Faithfulness springs up from the earth (cf. Isa 58:8–9) while Righteousness looks down from heaven, prepared to go as a herald before Yahweh in a theophanic advent (v 14). For the verb שקף, "look/gaze," see Pss 53:3; 102:20; Deut 26:15. For v 12, cf. Isa 45:8 (RSV):

> Shower, O heavens, from above,
>   and let the skies rain down righteousness;
> let the earth open, that salvation may sprout forth,
> and let it cause righteousness to spring up also;
> I the LORD have created it.

Cf. the return to chaotic conditions in the flood narrative in Gen 7:11. See also Hos 2:21–22; Isa 32:15–18. All of this action will bring goodness and productivity to the land (v 13).

I have retained the traditional translation "harvest" in v 13, but too much emphasis should not be put on "harvest" as such. There is no need to deny the appropriateness of Ps 85 for the celebration of harvests, and יבול can refer to agricultural produce of the ground (note Deut 11:17; Lev 26:4, 20; Hab 3:17; Hag 1:10–11; Ps 78:46); there is no reason to deny this as the basic meaning. A few references, however, seem to point toward a more general meaning of "production" or "productivity" (cf. Deut 32:22; Judg 6:4; Job 20:28). Gunkel (374) calls attention to the rich harvests and fertility which is associated with the new era that Yahweh will bring to his people in Hos 2:21–23; Amos 9:13–15; Isa 4:2; 30:23–25; Jer 31:12; to which may be added Zech 8:11–12; cf. Ps 65:10–14.

The "agents" do the work of Yahweh, of course, as is made clear in v 13. It is Yahweh who gives goodness and fertility to the land, however they may be mediated. V 14 reflects the idea of a theophanic coming of Yahweh (cf. *Comment* on Ps 65:10–14). Righteousness will go before Yahweh as a herald before a king and prepare a way for his journey through the land (cf. Isa 58:5; 62:11; 40:3–5, 10; Gunkel, 374; Kraus, II, 758). For discussion of "faithfulness" (truth), see *Comment* on 51:8; for "righteousness," see the *Explanation* of Ps 71. "Righteousness" in this context refers to Yahweh's judging and saving acts which bring deliverance to his people. The concept differs little from "salvation" (as in Deutero-Isaiah; e.g., see Isa 42:21; 46:12–13; 51:1, 5–6, 8; 62:1), but the judging aspect of the "righteousness" of God should not be lost (Kraus, *Theology*, 42–43). Though his judgments are ultimately saving judgments (Ps 36:7), Yahweh is the one who "puts things right." "The righteousness of Yahweh is the perfection of the manner in which he sees through everything, evaluates, judges, and saves. It is the perfection of the one who, true to his responsibilities to the community, helps all who are oppressed, falsely accused, persecuted, or suffering, and reveals himself as their deliverer" (Kraus, *Theology*, 43; cf. Pss 31:2; 71:2).

The expression which encompasses all that Yahweh will do is שלום, "Well-Being/Peace," used in vv 9 and 11. The "agents" will produce the *shalom* which Yahweh commands for his people in v 11 (see note 9.c). *Shalom* is the comprehensive concept of well-being, peace, and welfare which includes love, faithfulness, righteousness, prosperity, and glory. W. Brueggemann (*Living Toward a Vision: Biblical Reflections on Shalom* [Philadelphia: United Church Press, 1982] 16) has summarized *Shalom* in vigorous descriptive language with reference to Lev 26:4–6 and Ezek 34:25–29a: "It is well-being that exists in the very midst of threats—from sword and drought, and from wild animals. It is well-being of a material, physical, historical kind, not idyllic pie in the sky, but salvation in the midst of trees and crops and enemies—in the very places where people always have to cope with anxiety, struggle for survival, and deal with temptation. It is well-being of a very personal kind . . . but it is also deliberately corporate. If there is to be well-being, it will not be just for isolated, insulated individuals; it is rather security and prosperity granted to a whole community—young and old, rich and poor, powerful and dependent. Always we are all in it together." This is the word of Yahweh for his people. For further discussion of *shalom*, see Kraus, *Theology of the Psalms*, 82), who says that *shalom* in the Psalms is used with four meanings: (1) the fruitfulness and undisturbed growth, prosperity, and life of the land and the whole earth: Pss 72:3, 7; 85:11; 147:14; (2) well-being of the whole nation: Pss 29:11; 85:8–9; 125:5; (3) the basic function of the king: Ps 72:3–7; and (4) the distinctive force available to the city of Jerusalem: Ps 122:6–9.)

Explanation

I will not repeat the explanations already given in the sections above. Perhaps it is sufficient here to call attention to v 7, which seems to be the key verse in the psalm: "Will you not turn (and) give us life / that your people may rejoice in you?" Ps 85 is a prayer for renewal of "life" among the people of Yahweh. The supplication in v 7 looks back to Yahweh's life-giving actions in the past and it looks forward to the great message of the future *shalom* in vv 9–14. "Life" is, of course, more than physical existence, and to "revive" or "renew" life is more comprehensive than a new surge of physical vitality. H. Ringgren (*TDOT*, IV, 333) points out that the piel form of the verb היה can be used for the restoration of the walls and ruins of a city, which can be "revived" (Neh 3:34 [4:2]; 1 Chr 11:8). "Living water" is fresh running water or water from a spring, not from cisterns (Lev 14:5–6, 50–52; 15:13; Num 19:17; cf. Jer 2:13; 17:13; Zech 14:8). Life, like *shalom*, is the capacity for healthy action and well-being. "The word *chayah* thus means not merely 'be or stay alive,' but also to enjoy a full, rich, and happy life" (Ringgren, 334). The verb can refer to healing (see Num 21:8–9; Josh 5:8) and the restoring of strength (as in the case of Samson in Judg 15:19; cf. Gen 45:27; also 2 Kgs 1:2; 8:8–10, 14; 20:1, 7 = Isa 38:1, 9, 21). In Psalms, see 71:20; 30:4; 80:19; cf. 56:14.

Life in the OT is especially characteristic of Yahweh. He "lives" (Ps 18:46) and never dies (Ps 121:4). He is the God of life (Pss 36:9; 42:8), the "Living God" (Josh 3:10; Pss 42:3; 84:3; Hos 2:1 [1:10]; 2 Kgs 19:4, 16 = Isa 37:4, 17; Deut 5:23 [26]; 1 Sam 17:26, 36; Jer 10:10; 23:36), and the power of life flows from him (Ps 145:16; 36:8–10; 80:18; 1 Sam 2:6; Deut 32:39; cf. Jer 2:13; 17:13). Those who are far from him will perish (Ps 73:27). He provides the "Way (or Path) of Life" (דרך חיים): Ps 16:11; Prov 5:6; 6:23; 15:24; Jer 21:8; cf. Prov 2:19; 10:17. Thus all of life is a gift and a trust from Yahweh, just as the land is (Ps 16:5–6; 17:14; Kraus [*Theology of the Psalms*, 163] notes the idea of a "portion in life" for humans in Ps 17:14; note also the use of חלק, "portion," in 142:6; Isa 17:14; Lam 3:24; Eccl 9:5–6, 9). In 1 Sam 25:29, Abigail says to David that he is "bound up in the bundle of life with Yahweh" (cf. A. R. Johnson, *The Vitality of the Individual in the Thought of Ancient Israel* [Cardiff: University of Wales Press, 1949] 105–6; the reading in 1 Sam 25:29 may refer to being "tied up in a document," cf. Job 14:17; Isa 8:16; P. K. McCarter, Jr., *I Samuel*, AB 8 [Garden City, NY: Doubleday 1980] 399, translates in 1 Sam 25:29 as "tied up in the Document of the Living" = to the "Book of the Living" in Ps 69:29).

Thus "life" and the "revival of life" refers to the well-being of an individual or a people, not to mere duration of living (Johnson, *Vitality,* 102). Kraus (*Theology,* 163) remarks: "The life that he [Yahweh] imparts is not primarily . . . the natural fullness of vitality and vegetation, from which the power of being emanates. It is rather, transcending all seasonal rhythms, the power of blessing that is active in the history of the chosen people and in the created world that shall never be moved (Ps 93:1)." It is worth noting that "life" is sometimes combined with *shalom*, and in the case of Prov 3:16–18 (RSV), with wisdom:

> Long life is in her [wisdom's] right hand;
> in her left hand are riches and honor.
> Her ways are ways of pleasantness,
> and all her paths are peace [שלום].
> She is a tree of life [עץ חיים] to those who lay hold of her;
> those who hold her fast are called happy.

See also Mal 2:5; for association with "blessing," see Deut 30:16, 19 (Ringgren, 333). When Yahweh traverses his land and visits his people, as v 14 implies, he will bestow on land and people goodness, fertility, life, and *shalom.*

"Bend Your Ear, O Yahweh . . .
Teach Me Your Way . . . The Godless Have
Risen Against Me"   (86:1–17)

Bibliography

Auffret, P. "Essau sur la structure littéraire du Psaume 86" *VT* 29 (1979) 385–402.
Beyerlin, W. *Die Rettung der Bedrängten.* 30–31. **Brueggemann, W.** *The Message of the Psalms: A Theological Commentary.* Augsburg OT Series. Minneapolis: Augsburg, 1984. 60–63.
Delekat, L. *Asylie und Schutzorakel.* 98–101. **Johnson, A.R.** *CPIP.* 226–36.

Translation

1   A Davidic prayer.[a]
    Bend your ear, O Yahweh, give me an answer!   (4+3)
      For I am poor and needy.[b]

2   Protect[a] my life for I am loyal (to you);[b]   (4+4+2)
    save your servant, O You, my God,[c]
    (save)[d] this one who trusts in you,

3   Have mercy on me, O my Lord,   (2+3)
    for[a] I call to you all day long.

4   Bring joy to the soul[a] of your servant,   (3+4)
    for[b] I lift up my soul[a] to you, O my Lord.[c]

5   For You, O my Lord, are good and forgiving,[a]   (4+3)
    abounding in loyal-love for all who call to you.

6   Listen, O Yahweh, to my prayer,   (3+3)
    and give attention to my pleas for mercy.[a]

7   In my time of distress I call to you,   (3+2)
    for you can answer (my prayers).[a]

8   None is like you among the gods, O my Lord,[a]   (3+2)
    and there are no works to compare with yours.

9   All the nations that you have made[a]   (3+4+2)
    will come and bow down before you, O my Lord,
    and they will glorify your name.

10   For great[a] you are, a Worker of Wonders!   (4+3)
    You, O God, are without a peer.[b]

11   Teach me, O Yahweh, your way   (3+2+4)
    that I may walk in your faithfulness;[a]
    unite my heart[b] to fear your name.

12   I promise to thank you,[a] O my Lord, my God,   (3+2+3)
    with all my heart,
    and glorify your name forever,

13   because of your great loyal-love for me,   (3+4)
    in that you will deliver my soul from Sheol's lowest part.[a]

14   *O God, the godless* [a] *have risen against me;*   (3+4+3)
        a ruthless gang [b] *has sought my life;* [c]
        they have no regard for you. [d]

15   *But you, O my Lord, a compassionate and merciful God,*   (4+4)
        slow to anger and abounding in loyal-love and faithfulness, [a]

16   *turn to me and have mercy on me;* [a]   (3+3+3)
        give your strength [b] *to your servant*
        and save the son of your handmaid. [c]

17   *Work* [a] *a sign that all will be well for me,* [b]   (3+3+4)
        that those who hate me may see and be dismayed [c]
        that you, O Yahweh, have helped and comforted me. [d]

Notes

1.a. See n. 51:1.b. Ps 86:1 has לדוד תפלה rather than לדוד מזמור, "Davidic psalm," but the formation is the same.

1.b. For the word pair עני ואביון see n. 70:6.a; also *Comment,* 68:11; also, Pss 9:19; 12:6; 35:10; 37:14; 40:18; 49:3; 69:34; 72:4, 12, 13; 74:21; 82:4; 109:16, 22; etc; also, G. J. Botterwick, *TDOT,* I, 27–41. Johnson (*CPIP,* 227) translates as "I am the one who is humble with need," treating the word pair as a hendiadys.

2.a. For the *metheg* on the imperative, שמרה, see Delitzsch, III, 14; GKC 48i; 9v; 61f; cf. Ps 119:167.

2.b. Or, "loyal-one/devoted one." For חסיד, see n. 52:11.a.

2.c. The אתה אלהי, "You are my God," is frequently transferred to the beginning of v 3, resulting in a better balance in the colons: "Save your servant, the one who trusts you. / You are my God, have mercy on me, O Lord, / for to you I call . . . " See, e.g., Kraus, BHS, JB, NAB, REB.

2.d. This translation assumes that the verb in 2b serves also for 2c, which puts the colons into an acceptable balance. The חנני, "Have mercy on me," in v 3 appears elsewhere in short colons: see Pss 9:14; 25:16; 26:11; 27:7; 30:11; 57:2.

3.a. Dahood (II, 293) takes the preposition כ as emphatic: "it is to you I cry. . . ."

4.a. Retaining the traditional "soul" for נפש here, though I used "my life" in v 2a. On נפש, see Ps 54:5. Johnson (*CPIP,* 228, and *The Vitality of the Individual in the Thought of Ancient Israel* [Cardiff: University of Wales Press, 1949] 17–18) argues for the meaning "desire/yearning" in this usage: "Because it is to you that I look with yearning." Cf. נפש with the verb נשא ("lift up") in Ps 24:4; Hos 4:8; Ezek 24:25. The idiom means to have an attitude of desire and expectancy toward some person or object.

4.b. Perhaps, again with Dahood, the כ should be emphatic: "it is to you that I lift up my soul. . . ."

4.c. Some Greek texts and Jerome omit the "my Lord" (see, e.g., *BHS,* Kraus, Oesterley), but the repeated use of אדני (or יהוה) in this psalm is a caution against its omission in order to balance the colon. Note the occurrence of אדני in vv 3, 4, 5, 8, 9, 12, and 15 = seven times. Yahweh appears in vv 1, 6, 11, and 17.

5.a. The adj. סלח is a hapax legomenon but probably means "ready to forgive" (see Briggs, II, 238).

6.a. Some mss have לקול for בקול, a change of no significance. The plural noun (occurs only in pl.) תחנונות means "cries for favor" or "supplications"; in prayer to God, see Pss 28:2, 6; 31:25; 116:1; 130:2; 140:7. Other translations are equally as good: "my pleadings," "my imploring cry," or "pay heed to me as I plead for Thy grace" (Johnson, 228).

7.a. This verse is often taken as a statement of confidence, expressing the usual behavior of Yahweh as a basis for the prayer which is made to him in times of trouble ("for you will answer me" or "for you answer me"). However, it seems probable that in some usages such as this, the preposition כ and the following imperfect verb explicate the basis of the plea not on the basis of the confidence of the speaker but on the ability of Yahweh to respond (note that vv 8–10 follow, which praise the might and power of Yahweh; cf. this grammatical construction in contexts like Pss 3:8; 17:6; 49:16; 118:10, 11, 12; 128:2; cf. 59:10, 18). Dahood (II, 294; III, 404) appeals to his theory of an emphatic precative כ, reading: "O that you would answer me!" He cites some of the references I have given above (esp. Ps 17:6) plus others in which perfect forms of verbs are used, and 2 Chr 6:26. His reading is attractive and may be correct, though the whole grammatical validity of the precative perfect remains moot. The translation above is based on Michel, *Tempora und Satzstellung in den Psalmen,* 82.

8.a. Some mss have "Yahweh"; Syr indicates "Yahweh my God" (*BHS*).

9.a. The transfer of עשׂית אשׁר ("which you have made") to the end of v 8 (as, e.g., Kraus) is unnecessary. Dahood's reading of אשׁר as conditional (II, 294, citing, BDB, 83b), "When you act all the pagans will come," is possible, but it seems unlikely. See *Comment*.

10.a. Dahood (II, 294) treats the כי־גדול as emphatic (giving a full beat to the כי, resulting in a scan of 3+2+3: "How great you are, / O Worker of Miracles / you, O God, alone." The conjunction on "worker" can be treated as emphatic, explicative, or vocative (as Dahood).

10.b. I have translated rather freely. Johnson (*CPIP*, 230, n. 4) notes that the meaning in this context is not likely to be that of a statement of monotheism. The לבדך here carries the meaning of "matchless" or "unique"; cf. Ps 71:16; Isa 26:13; Ps 83:19; Deut 4:35 (מלבד; cf. Gen 26:1; Num 17:14 [16:49]). Note JB: "Since you alone are great, you perform marvels / you God, you alone." Similarly, Dahood (see n. 10.a.; LXX adds ὁ μέγας ["the great one"]): "You are God alone, the great one," which may equal: "You, God, (you) alone are the great one." Cf. Briggs, II, 237; Oesterley, 388.

11.a. Traditionally, "truth," for אמת, see *Comment*, Ps 51:8. The meaning is "walk in fidelity to you" (Dahood, II, 295); the suffix is an objective genitive (cf. Ps 26:3); Williams, *Hebrew Syntax*, 11, no. 38.

11.b. Some Greek texts have "let my heart rejoice," indicating that the piel imperative יחד in MT (from יחד) is read as יחד from חדה, "rejoice" (cf. GKC 75r). The piel יחד is a hapax legomenon, but the reading is acceptable and may be retained (see Kraus, II, 760). Cf. Briggs, II, 238. My "unite my heart" is literal, but awkward. NRSV has, "give me an undivided heart."

12.a. Note the cohortative form of the piel verb אכבדה in 12b. From a form-critical perspective, vv 12–13 form a vow of praise (see Kraus, II, 763); the speaker promises to proclaim God's praise if there is divine intervention and deliverance from distress.

13.a. This verse is difficult to translate because of uncertainty of its syntax in this context. In the context of the hymnic-thanksgiving content of vv 8–12, v 13 should read rather easily as: "For your loyal-love for me is great, / and you have delivered my soul from Sheol's depth." In this way it would ground the praise and vow of thanksgiving in divine action already experienced. However, in the context of Ps 86, I take it that there is a contingency factor in these verses; *the divine action of deliverance has not yet occurred.* Dahood (II, 296) comments that "to translate the verb as past, 'You have rescued me' (*The Jerusalem Bible*), is to render the following imperative and precatives meaningless," which is, perhaps, an overstatement because it is possible that the supplications in vv 16–17 are based on Yahweh's previous merciful actions, but Dahood is sensitive to the context. Note the transfer of vv 8–13 after vv 1–17 are rearranged in Jacquet, 645–46 (with vv 14–17 after v 7).

V 13 seems to be integrally related to v 12 which anticipates future praise based on the action in v 13b (see Kidner, II, 213; Delitzsch, II, 13; Michel, *Tempora und Satzstellung*, 96). I take the conjunction and the perfect (והצלת) in 13b as explicative of the causal clause in 13a, with the perfect expressing future tense (cf. Michel, 96, Oesterley, 389). Buttenwieser (831) opts for a precative perfect in 13b (with the conjunction omitted): "Oh, save my soul from She'ol below." (See *Form/Structure/Setting* below.)

14.a. The word זד (here pl. זדים) carries the meaning of "insolent/presumptuous/arrogant." "Conceited" seems too weak. In a few contexts, it seems to denote those who rebel against God, the "godless" who scorn the divine will and purposes (note Jer 43:2; Isa 13:11; Mal 3:19 [4:1]; Allen translates "godless" in Ps 119:21, 51, 69, 78, 85, 122; cf. Ps 19:14). Note v 14c. The זדים are those who defy God and try to disregard his will.

14.b. The עדה is traditionally "assembly/congregation," but here seems more appropriately that of "company/band/gang," or even "pack" (עדה is used of animals in Ps 68:31; cf. Judg 14:8).

14.c. נפשׁ, as in vv 2, 4, and 13.

14.d. Lit., "And they do not set you before themselves"; apparently an idiomatic statement which means that those involved have no regard for the will of God. See Ps 54:5.c. Cf. Pss 16:8 ("I have set Yahweh before me always"); 119:30.

15.a. This verse is without an expressed verb, and I take it as describing the subject addressed by the imperative verbs in v 16. The word pair חסד ואמת ("loyal-love and faithfulness") is probably a hendiadys (see A. R. Johnson, *CPIP*, 56, n. 2; 66) meaning "true/faithful loyal-love."

16.a. Gunkel (377), Kraus (II, 760–61), and others, transfer 16a to the beginning of v 17 on the basis of sense and parallelism. Others (e.g., L. Delakat, *Asylie und Schutzorakel*, 98) read 16a with 15a, b. The transfer seems unnecessary, though neither is objectionable. I suspect that there is a wordplay between פנה and תנה ("turn" and "give") which indicates that the colons in v 16 should be read together. The subject of the verbs in 16a, 16b, 16c, and 17a is the Lord in v 15.

16.b. Gunkel (378), followed by others (e.g., NEB and REB), understands עֹז as "refuge/protection" (cf. also Pss 21:2; 84:6). The assumption is that in such cases as these (cf. also Ps 59:18; 62:8; Exod 15:2; Isa 12:2; 49:5; and others) the noun is derived from עוז, "to take refuge," rather than from עוֹז, "to be strong" (see KB, 693): "Give your servant protection."

16.c. Dahood (II, 296; III, 150) changes the reading here and in Ps 116:16 to לבן־אֲמָתֶךָ (MT, אֲמָתֶךָ) and translates as lit., "the son of your fidelity" (from אמה), thus, "your faithful son." Johnson (*CPIP*, 233, 372–73) follows Dahood's lead, but prefers the ־בן as "the 'son' to whom Yahweh has said 'Amen' (אמן)" and equal to "Thine adopted son," arguing that "son" and "Amen" are used in the sense of a covenant. Cf. F. C. Fensham ("The Son of a Handmaid in Northwest-Semitic," *VT* 19 (1969) 312–21), who defends reading "son of your handmaid."

17.a. Dahood (II, 296) notes the parallel of the verb (עשׂה) with the title "Worker (עשׂה) of Wonders" in v 10. For the verb, cf. Pss 83:10; 109:21; 119:124; thus I have used the rather awkward "work a sign."

17.b. Lit., "with me a sign for goodness," which means "a sign for my welfare/benefit." Johnson (*CPIP*, 234) paraphrases: "a sign that all will be well." JB, "Give me one proof of your goodness"; similarly, NEB and NAB.

17.c. Traditionally, "ashamed"; בושׁ means to be disgraced or humiliated for something that has happened which made a former position look foolish or weak or both. See H. Seebass, *TDOT*, II, 50–60.

17.d. The translation of v 17 follows the pattern in Johnson (*CPIP*, 234) and Cohen (282), also Delitzsch (II, 13), and Michel (*Tempora und Satzstellung*, 70, 179–82). Cf. Aejmelaeus, *The Traditional Prayer in the Psalm*, 65. Cf. Ps 109:26–27.

Form/Structure/Setting

Dahood (II, 292) begins his brief summary of Ps 86 by saying that "Modern scholars approach unanimity in classifying this psalm as the lament of an individual." Indeed, this is the case; the psalm is a prayer in which an individual speaker expresses supplication and complaint to God. The speaker, the pray-er, is in great distress, and apparently in danger also (note vv 2, 14). The supplications for mercy and relief are pressed toward God with urgency. The psalm is dominated by the imperative mode of prayer.

The psalm is frequently divided into two major parts: 1–13 and 14–17 (e.g., Kraus, II, 761; Deissler, II, 166–68). However, it has a somewhat more complex structure than that of two divisions. The language of lament in vv 1–7 changes into hymnic praise language in vv 8–10, followed by a request to be taught by Yahweh in v 11 and a vow of praise-thanksgiving in vv 12–13. H. Schmidt (162) and Jacquet (also, Leslie, 383–84) put vv 8–13 at the end of the psalm (after v 17), treating them as a thanksgiving for a gracious response on the part of God. Such a rearrangement of the psalm is too arbitrary to be convincing, especially when insuperable problems in MT are not involved. See also Weiser (576), who argues that the present order of the psalm is correct for its cultic ceremony.

In the present design of the psalm, the lament and complaint are carried in the supplications in vv 1–7 and in vv 14–17. These verses form a frame around vv 8–13, which contain hymnic praise and a vow of thanksgiving, with a request to be taught by Yahweh and to be given single-heartedness in fearing his name (v 11). This section is enclosed by vv 7 and 14, which carry the complaint elements (time of distress in v 7 and the opposition of the godless in v 14), though v 7 is a general statement while v 14 contains a specific complaint. Thus vv 8–13 constitute a positive core (or "hinge," Deissler, II, 168) in this lament and set up a kind of dialectical tension between praise and supplication. G. Giavini

("La Struttura Letteraria del Salmo 86 (85)," *Riv. Bib. It.* 14 [1966], 455–58, given in P. Auffret, *VT* 29 [1979] 385) finds a concentric outline in Ps 86:

A 1–4 (עבדך, "your servant," in 2 and 4)
   B 5–6 (רב־חסד, "abounding loyal-love")
      C 7 (ביום צרתי, "in the day of my distress")
         D 8–10 (יכבדו לשמך, "they will glorify your name")
            E 11 (שמך, "your name")
         D' 12–13 (אכבדה שמך, "I will glorify your name")
      C' 14 (אלהים זדים קמו־עלי, "O God, the godless have risen against me")
   B' 15 (רב־חסד, "abounding loyal-love")
A' 16–17 (עבדך, "your servant")

In this approach, v 11 is a key verse: "Teach me, O Yahweh, your way . . . make me single-hearted in fearing your name." W. Brueggemann (*The Message of the Psalms,* 62) notes the sixfold direct use of the pronoun אתה ("you") in the psalm and suggests the possibility of a chiastic order with v 10 as the pivot: v 2(A), v 5(B), v 10a(C), v 10b(C'), v 15(B'), v 17(A'). Brueggemann's analysis also points to the significance of vv 10–11, which form a sort of "core within a core" (of vv 8–13). The psalm exists in an artistic format however it got the way it is.

A major characteristic of this psalm is the use of language found in other psalms (most of these usages will be noted in the *Comment*). It has been called a "mosaic of fragments from other Psalms and scriptures," with no claim to "poetic originality" (Kirkpatrick, 514; though Kirkpatrick later claims that the psalm "possesses a pathetic earnestness and tender grace of its own"). Johnson (*CPIP,* 226) notes the practice among older critical commentators of con-cluding that the psalm was built from bits and pieces borrowed from the work of other authors with little sign of logical development. Johnson, however, notes the growing recognition among contemporary interpreters of the psalm's artistic poetic structure. Buttenwieser (832) calls it "only a second-class poem," but defends its coherence, sequence, and "literary worth in general." In this regard, the comments of Weiser (576) on Ps 86 merit quotation at some length:

> The peculiar character of the individual laments does not lie in the origi-nality of each example, but in the fact that their form and thoughts are both typical and generally valid. . . . Moreover, we are not justified in regarding the affinity of the psalm with other songs as the result of borrow-ing from other literature in order to mask the author's own incompetence. On the contrary, we are here dealing with a liturgical style which is deliber-ately used to incorporate the personal concern of the worshipper in the larger context of the worship of the cult community and of the speech-forms and thought-forms proper to it.

Weiser's judgment has been supported by studies of the use of traditional lan-guage in the psalms, such as those of Culley, *Oral Formulaic Language in the Biblical Psalms,* Aejmelaeus, *The Traditional Prayer in the Psalms,* with L. Schmidt, *Literarische Studien zur Josephsgeschichte* (Berlin: de Gruyter, 1986). See also Alter's treatment of "artful use" of "conventional" or "stock" imagery in the Psalms (*The Art of Biblical Poetry,* 189–92). Alter argues that "stock imagery" is "the staple of biblical poetry" (190), but it is often supplemented by poetic intensification and the innovative use of "intensive imagery." The process of intensification of a stock expression may occur because of the context in which it is used; e.g., the use of the verb, שׂבע, "be satisfied/sated," in Job 19:22 (Alter, 192).

The use of language found in other psalms and OT writings has sometimes been given as a reason for dating the psalm to a later date (after the exile); e.g., Briggs, II, 235, who calls it "a prayer composed for public worship in the synagogue." If the psalm depends on finished and defined works of scripture, a later date would be indicated. However, actual direct borrowing from written works may not be the case. Buttenwieser (831; note Gunkel, 376, also) contends that the number of lines copied from other psalms (if that is the case) is not so numerous as frequently thought and that the psalm incorporates popular expressions which "might be common to any two writers." See also the comments of Oesterley (387), Anderson, II, 613, and Durham (347). Thus the use of traditional content, stock expressions, and conventional imagery does not point necessarily to an especially late date. On the other hand, it is compat-ible with a later date and the artistic use of traditional prayer language. There is wisdom on the part of commentators who refuse to date the psalm (Oesterley, 387: "It is hopeless to attempt even an approximate dating"; Rogerson and McKay, II, 178: "It is impossible to date the psalm, or to identify the psalmist and his troubles"), but I prefer to agree with the judgment of those who find it probable that the psalm belongs to the post-exilic era (e.g., Stuhlmueller, II, 51).

As is typical of the psalms, the speaker (or pray-er) in Ps 86 is not identified nor is the context and situation of his/her prayer clear in precise detail. The prayer obviously arises and/or is designed for situations of distress and trouble. The descriptions, however, are quite generalized and lack specificity. Some effort has been made to identify the speaker as a king. Dahood (II, 292) seeks to strengthen this case by observing that terms in v 16 are familiar from royal correspondence from El Amarna and Ugarit. The vassel addresses the suzerain as "my lord" and refers to himself as "your servant." Dahood also argues that the large-scale effects in v 9 would be inappropriate for a private citizen (a curious point, since the private citizen in v 9 does not produce the results, but only affirms what will be true of Yahweh) and that the dangers referred to in v 14 "are not those that beset a simple citizen" (see also Eaton, *Kingship,* 79–80). Thus Dahood describes the psalm as "a royal letter addressed to God." L. Delekat (*Asylie und Schutzorakel,* 98) suggests that the two parts of Ps 86 (86A = vv 1–13; 86B = vv 14–17) are prayer inscriptions for use in a sanctuary for those of faith who need protection, probably a farmer who is threatened because of some mismanagement of his affairs. Kraus (II, 762) is content to think of a pray-er, in great distress and under pressure from enemies, who seeks a hearing by Yahweh and divine help.

The suggestion that the psalm reflects the language of royal correspondence is interesting and may be correct. However, there is no reason to deny the use of the language of kingship by pious Israelites in the post-exilic era. The use of the terms חסיד ("loyal-one/devotee") in v 2 (cf. Ps 52:11a) and עבד ("servant") in vv 2, 4, and 16 (cf. Isa 65 and 66) point in the direction of loyal Israelites of piety and devotion in the post-exilic communities, faithful believers who have appropriated for themselves the language of kingship for their prayers. The psalm could have been at home in formal worship contexts (note the careful suggestions of Beyerlin, *Die Rettung der Bedrängten*, 30–31; also, Weiser, 576, who postulates a thanksgiving service conducted after the prayer in vv 1–7 was answered, though Weiser has difficulty with vv 14–17), but it probably originated and was used primarily in the learned scribal circles of the pious in the postmonarchical Israelite communities (Diessler, II, 168). In my opinion, it is best to read the psalm as a literary composition, written for the use of any who found its content helpful. See Aejmelaeus, *The Traditional Prayer in the Psalms*, 104–6, on Pss 86 and 143: "The skilfulness of the composition seems to imply the written form in the original." She refers to these psalms as examples of "the developed form of the traditional prayer."

The composition of Ps 86 in terms of the skilled use of traditional material means that the title, "Davidic prayer," must be assumed to be a scribal construct to give the psalm Davidic authority. It belongs to the tendency of LXX, Syr, and QPss mss to extend Davidic authority by the use of more Davidic super-scriptions (cf. Wilson, *The Editing of the Hebrew Psalter*, 156). A Davidic tradition of prayers seems to have existed, regardless of its date(s) and provenance (see Pss 17:1; 72:20; 142:1; 143:1), though not much of it remains. Ps 86 interrupts the run of Korahite psalms in 84–85 and 87–88–89 (89 is bound to 88 by a similar type of title). The reason for the placement of 86 between 85 and 87 is not apparent, other than the understanding of 87 as an amplification of the reference to the Gentile nations in 86:9 (Cohen, 283). It is possible that a Davidic prayer in the Korah sequence adds authority to these psalms. Possibly, also Ps 86 was simply considered to be a desirable individual prayer after the communal prayer in Ps 85.

Comment

A prayer for God's merciful response (86:1–7). The language of these verses is that of supplicatory prayer, in which the speaker seeks mercy and pro-tection from the Lord of heaven, Yahweh. These verses constitute the "voice (or, expression) of my supplications for mercy" in v 6b. The style is that of a "servant" (vv 2 and 4: "your servant") who addresses an overlord or great king ("my Lord," vv 3, 4, 5), who is clearly Yahweh (vv 1 and 6). A loyal servant, who is "poor and needy" (1b, see note 1.b.) places a claim on Yahweh, who is the protector of those who trust in him (cf. Pss 9:19; 40:18; 25:2, 20; 57:1–2).

The speaker's life is in danger from unspecified causes (v 2). V 7 alludes to times of distress and v 4 indicates a lack of joy in the present situation, all in the rather generalized and formulaic language of prayers and laments. Each reader or hearer can use these verses for his or her own situation; they are a kind of model prayer. The content is respectful but direct; the "servant" does not waste words getting to the point: "Bend your ear, O Yahweh . . . protect my life, save your servant . . . have mercy on me . . . listen, O Yahweh, to my prayer." The pray-er longs for the joy of deliverance (v 4; cf. Pss 46:5; 51:14; 90:14; 92:5), a joy which only the Lord can give.

The speaker does not doubt the ability of Yahweh to deal with the distress expressed in the supplications: "The problem is making it Yahweh's concern, in order to mobilize God's mercy and God's power" (Brueggemann, 62). Yahweh is described as "good and forgiving" (or, "ready to forgive") with abundant love and loyalty for those who are loyal to him (v 5). The adjective סלּח ("forgiving") does not appear elsewhere in MT, but the verb סלח is fairly common, with God (or the action of God) always as the subject (Anderson, II, 615; cf. Pss 25:11; 103:3; Jer 31:34; 50:20; 2 Chr 7:14). The expression "abounding in loyal-love" (רב־חסד) also occurs in v 15 in the form רב־חסד ואמת. V 7 corresponds to v 5 in expressing confidence in Yahweh's capacity to deal with times of distress; vv 7 and 5 bracket the intense appeal to Yahweh in v 6 (for v 6, cf. Pss 5:2; 28:2; 130:2; for v 7a, cf., e.g., Pss 20:2; 77:3; for 7b, see 17:6; perhaps אל ["O God"] is missing from 86:7b or is understood, but cf. Dahood, II, 294). I have read the ביום צרתי in a general collective sense: "in my times of trouble," but it may be that the more literal "in the day of my distress" should be understood, as, e.g., Kraus (II, 763) who thinks of a situation at a sanctuary in which the speaker appears with his enemies before God and expects an oracle of vindication and deliverance from God (cf. Pss 20:2; 50:15), or at least with the expectation of some sign or favorable omen (cf. Schmidt, 162–63; Leslie, 383–84). The present psalm, however, has probably lost the immediacy of direct cultic relatedness and is more generalized.

Affirmation of the incomparable sovereignty of Yahweh (86:8–13). These verses, which form the core of the psalm, are really in two parts. The first, vv 8–10, sets forth the incomparable nature of the lordship of Yahweh, using language found in other contexts as well (e.g., on v 8, see Exod 15:11; Deut 3:24; Ps 35:10; for v 9, see Isa 2:3–4; 66:18–19; Zech 14:9, 16; 2 Kgs 19:15, 19; Neh 9:6; Jer 16:19, Tob 13:11; 14:6; Pss 66:4; 22:28–29; for v 10, see Pss 72:18; 77:14–15; 83:19. Yahweh is declared to be a "Worker of Wonders," one who does acts of deliverance and salvation which lie beyond human powers (cf. Ps 9:2). Brueggemann (*The Message of the Psalms,* 63; "'Impossibility' and Epistemology in the Faith Tradition of Abraham and Sarah [Gen 18:1–15]," *ZAW* 94 [1982] 615–34) proposes to translate נפלאות ("wonders") as "impossibilities," arguing for a faith tradition involving the word פלא especially manifest in Gen 18:1–15, Judg 13:1–20, and Jer 32:16–35, and reflected in numerous references in the Psalms (e.g., 72:18; 78:4, 11, 12, 32; 96:3; 98:1; 111:4; 139:14; 145:5; also 105:2, 5; 106:7, 22; 107:8, 15, 21, 24, 31; 136:4). He contends that the varied usages of פלא point to acts of God, or potential acts, which "challenge accepted definitions of reality" (*ZAW* 94 [1982] 620). The "impossibility" may be of two kinds (as in Jer 32:17, 27): that which causes endings to what is valued and that which brings unexpected and unanticipated newness. In general, the usage of פלא-language refers to "the inversions and discontinuities by which something emerges in historical experience for which there was no ground of expectation" (*ZAW* 94 [1982] 623). Brueggemann does not doubt that in more "standardized liturgic uses" some of the concreteness, intensity, and sharpness of usage in narratives like Gen 18:1–15 are lost. But it is important that "Israel's classic tradition of liturgy and hymnody continued to speak about the radical freedom of God and the disjunctive character of Yahweh's way over-against and distinct from every presumed world" (622). Indeed, Yahweh is without a peer among the gods, and he cannot be confined within the parameters of normal life. He is the "Worker of Wondrous Impossibilities," the one who gives hope to the hopeless, and the one who destroys the pretensions of those who think themselves secure from judgment.

The second part of this section is a petition by the speaker to be taught the "way" of Yahweh (v 11) and a vow of thanksgiving (vv 12–13). Again, the language of these verses is similar to that found in other contexts (for v 11, see Pss 27:11; 25:4–5, 8, 11; 26:3; for v 13, see Ps 9:2; for v 13, see Deut 32:22; Pss 56:14; 57:10, 11). The petition to be taught the "way" of Yahweh is appropriate after vv 8–10 (note Ps 25:4–5). The God without a peer is the one who provides an incomparable way of life for those who know and glorify his name. It is a "way" in which the speaker wants to "walk." "Way," of course, refers to the behavior and actions of God; his "way" of doing things in the world (cf. Exod 33:12–14). At the same time, the divine "way" involves a commitment from those who walk in it to behavior patterns that are in conformity with the will of Yahweh (in Gen 18:19, Abraham is told to charge his descendants to keep the "way" of Yahweh, doing "righteousness" [צדקה] and "justice" [משפט]). The "way" of Yahweh is not an abstract ideal, because it is not divorced from the acts of Yahweh and his people (cf. Ps 119:33).

V 11c is a "penetrating climax" (Kidner, II, 312), a key statement in the psalm. A reverent and obedient response to God involves a "united heart" (i.e., "mind" or "will") toward God (cf. Jer 32:39–41; Ezek 11:19–20). The uncentered and divided will toward Yahweh is destructive (cf. Ps 12:3; 1QH 4.14; James 1:8; 4:8). There is a unity in Yahweh himself (a "oneness") which is complemented by a "oneness" in his people's response to him (cf. Deut. 6:4–5; 10:12; Eph 4:1–6).

A vow of thanksgiving follows in vv 12–13. The vow is made with the assumption that Yahweh will respond to the speaker's supplications. The "united heart" in 11c will respond to God's action with a "whole heart" ("all my heart") in v 12, and the name that speaker is made single-hearted to fear (v 11) will be glorified unceasingly (v 12c). The speaker would be able to enter into the future glorifying (or, honoring) the name of Yahweh with the nations in v 9; the "fetters of the distress" (Kraus, II, 763) would be broken by Yahweh's glorious manifestation of his name and glory. V 13 further grounds the vow of praise in the action of Yahweh's loyal-love (חסד) expressed in deliverance from "Sheol's lowest part," which could mean deliverance "away from" death, especially premature death, but the usage here may be metaphorical with reference to severe distress, probably involving the danger of death (e.g., Deissler, II, 169; Kidner, II, 313). Sheol is the realm of God-forsakenness, a dark "land of forgetfulness" (see *Comment*, Ps 88:11–13; Pss 30:4; 71:20; Craigie, 93, 95–96).

Complaint, affirmation, and petition (86:14–17). The lament in vv 1–7 returns in this section. A direct complaint is registered in v 14 (cf. Pss 28; 54:5). The language is concrete and seems to be descriptive of an actual situation. However, as is usually the case in the psalms there is nothing to identify what is going on with any degree of specificity. Johnson (*CPIP*, 232) argues that the likelihood is that the supplicant is not a pious individual citizen but a reigning king who seeks Yahweh's aid. However, the experience of being threatened by godless and ruthless people is not confined to kings. Individuals from various socioeconomic levels may be attacked by those who have no regard for God. The reason for the attack of the godless is not given, though the use of the verb קום ("rise up") suggests a legal or semi-legal situation in which the speaker has been charged with some offense (cf., e.g., Pss 27:12; 82:8; Job 30:28; 31:14; Deut 19:15–16; Isa 54:17; Mic 6:1; Zeph 3:8, etc.). On the other hand, קום can be used in the sense of "rise up to attack" (e.g., Josh 8:1, 19; Deut 19:11; 22:26; Judg 8:21; Ps 27:3; Amos 7:9). The context of Ps 86 does not offer decisive evidence for one meaning over another. Perhaps, the language in v 2 and the general tone of the content of v 14 tilts toward the physical danger of one whose life is in peril, though a combination of physical peril and false charges in a legal hearing is also possible.

V 15 is a form of the basic description of the nature of Yahweh found in Exod 34:6. Other forms of the affirmation are found in Num 14:18; Pss 103:8; 145:8; Neh 9:17; Jonah 4:2; Joel 2:13. The expressions in the differing contexts represent liturgical usage of a confession of faith. The formulaic expression was not rigidly fixed and appears with variations in the different contexts (Jonah 4:2 and Joel 2:13 are the same). Yahweh is declared to be merciful and loyal in his love, restraining his anger (he has an "extended nose," takes a "long breath"!). The ancient formulation provides the basis for the petitions which follow in vv 16–17. A God who is merciful (v 15, חנון) is asked to show mercy (v 16, חנני) and to empower and use saving action for one of his faithful servants who is now in great trouble. If "son of your handmaid" is retained (see note 16.c.), the expression denotes a person who belongs to the household by birth, not an outsider or slave purchased by the master of the household (cf. Ps 116:16; Exod 2 1:4; 23:12; Cohen, 282; Allen, 113:16.b). de Vaux (*Ancient Israel,* tr. J. McHugh [New York: McGraw-Hill, 1961] 82) notes that slaves bought for money were distinguished from those born in the household (citing Gen 17:12, 23, 27; Lev 22:11; cf. Jer 2:14), but in the final analysis there was probably little difference between a household-born slave and one brought in from outside. All of them were members of the household and were due acceptable treatment. The rights of the slave as a human being were recognized (cf. Exod 20:21; 21:26–27; Deut 23:16–17; Exod 20:8–11 // Deut 5:12–15; Job 31:13–15).

The "sign" (אות) requested in v 17 refers to some sort of favorable demonstrations of divine action. Mowinckel (*PIW,* II, 66) contends that the meaning here is that of a "token for good" or "favorable token," such as could result from casting lots. If the token or omen was positive, a priest or temple prophet would interpret the "sign" in the words of a cultic oracle. This is not the only interpretation possible, however (cf. F. J. Helfmeyer, *TDOT,* I, 175). The meaning of "sign" (אות) is wide-ranging in the OT. Helfmeyer (170) agrees with Gunkel's basic definition of אות as "an object, an occurrence, an event through which a person is to recognize, learn, remember, or perceive the credibility of something." In the case of a "sign" done by God, it is something which affirms and makes recognizable divine action. The functional nature of a "sign" is basic—not the "sign" itself or its content. "The substances of signs are as protean as the world in which they occur" (Helfmeyer, 170), and they may occur in different contexts: history, creation, and worship. In the case of Ps 86:17, the context does not permit a precise definition of the nature of the "sign." Its function, however, is clear: to confirm the faith of the speaker, giving evidence of divine comfort, while serving as a token to the speaker's enemies which will leave them abashed. For אות elsewhere in the Psalter, see Pss 69:9; 74:4, 9; 78:43; 105:27; 135:90.

Explanation

Though skillfully composed, this psalm would have little to distinguish it stylistically except for its relatively high cluster of imperative petitions (twelve in vv 1–7 and 14–17; 2 in vv 8–13, for a total of fourteen). Only a few prayer psalms have clusters of similar length; Aejmelaeus (*The Traditional Prayer in the Psalms,* 51) notes 69:17–19 and 119:33–40 along with 86:1–6 (clusters of four prayer imperatives are much more common: e.g., Pss 6:2–3; 22:20–22; 26:1–2; 51:3–5; 55:2–3).

The core of the psalm is found in vv 10–11, which form a transition in the prayers in vv 8–13. The incomparable God, the Worker of Wonders, is implored to teach the supplicant his, Yahweh's, "way," so that the supplicant may walk in it with single-hearted obedience. This is followed by the prayer: "Unite my heart to fear your name." Then, the supplicant will join in the worldwide praise of Yahweh's deliverance (vv 8–9; 12–13), whose name will be glorified forever. What is the significance of this "prayer within a prayer"?

I have no great wisdom on this subject. But I suggest that prayers for deliverance and restoration of well-being (vv 1–7; 14–17) need to be expressed with an adequate understanding of God. It is important that the supplicant have the three qualities expressed in v 11:

(1) Understanding of the divine "way" in the world. Complaint and lament need to be informed by insight into the nature of life in God's creation and the manner of divine action. A catharsis of faith (as in Job) is necessary for power in petitions, and this must come about through divine instruction. Times of trouble and fear are times when wise supplicants especially seek to learn the ways of God. The openness to being informed by the spirit of God opens channels of grace and power. The deepest need of the supplicant is for understanding.

(2) Petitions in prayer, regardless of how many times repeated, mean little unless the supplicant is committed to a life-style which reflects the "truth" (better, "faithfulness") of God (v 11b). A life of trust and faithfulness empowers petitions.

(3) The "single-heart," devoted to God and united in purpose, makes the petitions authentic. The "double-minded" person is unstable and motivated by falsehood (see Ps 12:3; cf. 1 Chr 12:33). According to the Letter of James, "the double-minded man, unstable in all his ways" will not receive anything from prayer. Such people must purify their hearts and cleanse their hands if they are to draw near to God (James 4:8). The pure heart is one which is united in purpose and concentrated on the divine will. "Heart" (לבב/לב) refers to the mind, the inner volitional self, which shapes the will and the forms of behavior (cf. 1 Tim 1:5; 2 Tim 2:22); "Blessed are the pure in heart, for they shall see God" (Matt. 5:8, RSV). S. Kierkegaard's treatise on *Purity of Heart Is to Will One Thing* (tr. D. Steere [New York: Harper and Brothers, 1961]) comes to mind. His prayer at the end of his "edifying address" on this subject closes as follows: "Oh, Thou that givest both the beginning and the completion, give Thou victory in the day of need so that what neither a man's burning wish nor his determined resolution may attain to, may be granted unto him in the sorrowing of repentance: to will only one thing." Indeed, single-heartedness to fear the name of God is finally the gift of the Worker of Wonders, the "One-who-does-Impossibilities" (v 10).

Zion: The Birthplace of All Nations (87:1–7)

Bibliography

Beaucamp, E. "Le problème du Psaume 87." *Liber Annuus* 13 (1962–63) 53–75. **Booij, T.** "Some Observations on Psalm LXXXVII." *VT* 37 (1987) 16–25. **Chopineau, J.** "Midrache des Sources (Sur le psaume 87)." *Foi et Vie* 76 (1977) 7–11. **Schmuttermayr, G.** "Um Psalm 87 (86), 5." BZ 7 (1963) 104–10. **Smith, M.** "The Structure of Psalm LXXXVII." *VT* 38 (1988) 357–58. **Wanke, G.** *Die Zionstheologie der Korachiten.* BZAW 97. Berlin: Töpelmann, 1966. 21–22, 31–40.

Translation

1   A Korahite psalm;[a] a song.[b]
    His foundation[c] is upon holy mountains—
2   *Yahweh loves*[a] *the gates of Zion*   (4+3)
    more than all the dwellings of Jacob.
3   *Glorious things are spoken of you,*[a]   (3+2)
    O City of God! SELAH.
4   *I will declare*[a] *that Rahab and Babylon are among*   (4+4+2)
    those who know me;[b]
    even (of) Philistia, Tyre, and Cush too,[c]
    (I will declare):[d] *"This one*[e] *was born there!"*   (2+3+3)
5   *Of Zion indeed*[a] *it will be said,*[b]
    "Every one[c] *was born in her!*
    The Most High himself[d] *has established her."*
6   *Yahweh recorded in the register*[a] *of the peoples,*   (4+3)
    "This one was born there." SELAH
7   *And singers sing as they dance,*[a]   (2+2)
    "All my springs are in you!"

Notes

1.a. See n. 85:1.b.

1.b. See n. 65:1.c.

1.c. Dahood (II, 299) proposes to read יסודתו (noun, fem. sing. with suffix) as a qal fem. passive participle with a 3rd pers. masc. suffix: "O city founded by him," with the pronominal suffix acting as the agent of the verbal form. He argues that a vocative expression makes an inclusion with "O city of God" at the end of v 3. This makes it unnecessary to posit a hapax legomenon nominal form. Pronominal suffixes may express the agent in the action of a verbal form (e.g., Pss 37:22; 83:12; Prov 7:26; Job 29:3). On the other hand, the nominal form with suffix has good analogies in Hebrew (Booij, *VT* 37 [1987] 18; Perowne, 138). Delitzsch (II, 17) also prefers a participle (with the normal reading of the suffix: "his founded [city]") but notes that there is little, if any, difference in meaning. The suffix refers to Yahweh (cf. Anderson, II, 620). LXX has "his foundations." Booij (18) notes that the pronominal suffix refers to a noun following later, as, e.g., Prov 14:14, 20, 32; 29:11. He also notes that in such references as Ps 114:2 and Lam 3:1 the pronominal suffix is used of God and he is not named at all. Thus it is not necessary to reverse the order of 1b and 2a, as is sometimes done (e.g., NEB—corrected in REB; Gunkel; Oesterley). Kraus (II, 765) is among those who prefer to read the suffix as referring to Zion and thus corrects the text to יסודתה "her foundation."

2.a. The first two words of v 2a ("Yahweh loves") are sometimes read with v 1b: "His foundation upon holy mountains / Yahweh loves"; as, e.g., in NAB; Briggs, II, 239; Booij, *VT* 37 (1987) 18. Delitzsch (II, 18) says that "ver. 2 is decapitated" by this procedure, which is not true, I think, but I have preferred to retain the single colon in v 1 as either (1) a title for the psalm (cf. translation of Beaucamp in Sabourin, 212), or (2) a *casus Pendens* construction (e.g., Nah 1:3; Pss 18:31; 104:17; 125:2; Eccl 2:14; 2 Sam 23:6; GKC 143).

3.a. The expression could mean "in you," but the context indicates that the meaning is that of "concerning you [Zion]," as in LXX, περὶ σοῦ. The pl. subject with a sing. verbal form is a bit odd, but it is found in other cases (see Delitzsch, II, 18): "the glorious things are conceived of as the sum-total of such," a unity in plural form. The בְ is used as, e.g., in Pss 50:20; 119:46; 1 Sam 19:3; Cant 8:8. Some commentators (e.g., Briggs, II, 239; Dahood, II, 300) change the pual sing. participle מְדֻבָּר to piel מְדַבֵּר, with an unmentioned subject: "He (Yahweh) speaks glorious things of you," or, in the case of Dahood: "(Yahweh) speaks in you, O City of God." It is better to retain the pual (see Booij, *VT* 37 [1987] 18–19). Kraus (II, 768) notes that דבר ("say/speak") can also mean "sing," citing Judg 5:12; Ps 18:1.

4.a. The hiphil form of זכר could mean "I cause to remember," but it is usually read in the sense of "I will mention" or "I tell of." Dahood (II, 300, 251–52) mounts an argument for the hiphil as "record/inscribe" in some cases (cf. Delitzsch, II, 19), and thus here: "I shall inscribe Rahab and Babylon. . . ." This interpretation relates well to v 6 and may be correct. However, I take the verb to be used in the sense of "set forth the case" (as in Isa 43:26; see B. S. Childs, *Memory and Tradition in Israel* [Naperville, IL: Allenson, 1962] 14) or as "proclaim" (see Jer 4:16; Isa 12:4, where זכר (hiphil) is parallel with ידע (hiphil), "make known"; cf. also Ps 45:18. I take it that v 4 has at least a semi-forensic sense, being a proclamation by the divine king.

4.b. The preposition לְ may be read as dative, "to those who know me" (as in Jer 4:16, "to the nations"), as in LXX. This may be the correct meaning: "I declare of . . . to those who know me." However, the preposition may mean "with respect to," to express "for what purpose," or "as what" (Delitzsch, II, 19, who cites 2 Sam 5:3; Isa 4:3); note also the idea of "product," when an action produces a state or a condition in Williams, *Hebrew Syntax*, 50, n. 278; cf. Exod 7:15; 1 Sam 15:1; Exod 21:2). Also, Gunkel, 380; cf. GKC 119t, u. Thus Rahab and Babylon are declared to be among those who know Yahweh.

4.c. LXX has the "Philistines" (lit., "foreigners") for Philistia and "the people of the Ethiopians" for Cush, while retaining the singular for "Tyre," using ethnic terminology for Philistia and Cush. The Hebrew text means "the people of" each of the nations named, rather than the nations as political and geographic entities (as in Isa 19:24–25). The Heb. "Cush" can refer to either land or people, or both: Isa 20:3, 5; 43:3; 45:14; 2 Kgs 19:9 = Isa 37:9; Nah 3:9; Ezek 30:4, 5, 9 (BDB, 469).

4.d. The *Translation* assumes that the verb אזכיר in 4a does double duty in 4b, c.

4.e. LXX has "these were born there," which eases the text, but probably does not change the meaning. MT's זה ("this one") refers to the nations named in 4b, one by one, not to individuals (contra NEB) nor to the sum total of the nations (Delitzsch, II, 19). Each of the peoples named is given a Zion-birth status. The demonstrative זה ("this") rather than הוא ("that") may indicate a new subject rather than one already known, which would be more probably הוא (GKC 136a).

5.a. Treating the conjunction as "more or less emphatic, functioning as a transition to a statement which underlines and varies the preceding one" (Booij, *VT* 37 [1987] 20). Or the conjunction may be merely stylistic (see. n. 5.d.).

5.b. LXX has Μήτηρ Σιων, ἐρεῖ ἄνθρωπος, "a man will say, 'Zion is mother,'" which may indicate a reading of the Heb. text as לציון אם [י]אמר (Gunkel, 380; Kraus, II, 765). Kraus (also Gunkel) reads "I call/name Zion, Mother," assuming אמר ל־ as in Isa 5:20; 8:12; Eccl 2:2. This reading balances the colons (3+3+3) and is acceptable as a case of haplography, though I suspect that LXX's reading is simply interpretative, and I have retained MT. For variation in the Greek texts, see Perowne, 137; G. Schmuttemayr, *BZ* 7 (1963) 104–10; Kissane, II, 82.

5.c. Lit., "a man (person) and a man (person) is born in her." "Man and a man" probably means "every person" or "each and every one"; see GKC 123c; Kraus, II, 765; Booij, *VT* 37 (1987) 20–21; note Esth 1:8; Lev 17:10, 13.

5.d. Treating the conjunction again (as in 5a) as emphatic—or else merely stylistic (cf. Williams, *Hebrew Syntax*, 71).

6.a. The simple inf. const. in MT, "in (or, as) writing of peoples," should be corrected with LXX to בִּכְתָב in the writing/register/enrollment" (see Briggs, II, 242; *BHS*). The verb ספר has the meaning here of "record/write down" as in Ps 56:9 (Gunkel, 380); cf. Job 31:4.

7.a. The reading of this verse is problematic at best (Gunkel, 380, calls it "completely meaning-less"). Lit., "And singers like dancers/pipe-players / all my springs/fountains are in you." LXX has ὡς εὐφραινομένων πάντων ἡ κατοικία ἐν σοί, perhaps: "As all those who rejoice is the settlement (dwelling, foundation) in you." The only thing that seems clearly related to MT is "dwelling/settlement" (Heb. מעון) for MT's מעיני, "my springs." LXX also seems to put "singers" (שרים) in 7a after the זה in v 6: זה עמים ושרים מילד בה, "these peoples and princes that were born in her" (reading the plural of שר, "prince/leader," and reading the זה as distributive singular). This would, of course, leave the way open to use the verb εὐφραίνω, "cheer/delight/make merry" for חללים, "dancers/pipe players" (εὐφραίνω is used elsewhere for חלל only in the piel in Deut 20:6), but the verb is used for גיל, "rejoice/give enthusiastic cries"—possibly related to dancing—in Zeph 3:17 and Isa 41:16, and for רנן, "shout for joy," in Isa 12:6; 42:11, 44:23; 52:8. Booij (*VT* 37 [1987] 21) argues that MT is intelligible, though terse: (1) the participles are used in a durative sense with indefinite subjects (e.g., Gen 39:22; Exod 5:16; Jer 33:5; 30:23; Neh 6:10; 2 Chr 9:28) and (2) the preposition כ is understood as temporal (cf. Gen 38:29; 40:10; Williams, *Hebrew Syntax*, 47). Booij translates: "And they sing while dancing: / All my springs are in you.'" He assumes that חללים is an irregular polel participle without the prefix מ (cf. GKC 525) from חול, "whirl about/dance" (cf. Judg 21:23; 1 Kgs 1:40, LXX). My translation is similar and based on the same approach, with מעיני, "springs," retained. For the rather widely adopted reading, "And singers like dancers / all of them respond to (sing praise) to you," see Kraus, II, 765; Oesterley, 390.

Form/Structure/Setting

Generally, Ps 87 is a poem which praises Zion as the city of God and the center of life, eventually at least, for all peoples. This short psalm is, however, full of difficulties, and its exact reading and meaning are uncertain. In addition to its linguistic difficulties and abrupt style (Kidner, II, 314, refers to "its enigmatic, staccato phrases"), there is a major problem in deciding what vv 4–6 really mean. One approach, exemplified by Kraus, is to assume that these verses deal with Jews living in the various nations of the Dispersion, possibly also including proselytes. For all of these, Zion is their "mother," just as for those living in Jerusalem (see also Jacquet, II, 657–68). The more common approach is to assume that the psalm envisions Zion to be the world center of Yahweh worship, which will be for all peoples, symbolized by the Gentile nations mentioned in the psalm. Weiser (580) assumes that the setting of the psalm is that of a great pilgrimage festival at the temple in Jerusalem: "The festal throng moves along in solemn procession, in step with the rhythm of the hymns. People from all over the world pass by before the eyes of the singer. It is as if the whole world had arranged to meet in this place." Yahweh counts the peoples of the nations "Not as so many Egyptians or Babylonians, Philistines, Tyrians, or Ethiopians, but as sons and daughters of Zion" (Leslie, 35, though Leslie thinks of the foreigners as scattered Israelites among the nations).

Wanke (*Zionstheologie*, 22) says that Ps 87 is probably the "purest Zion-song" in the Psalter and in the OT. However, Goulder (*The Psalms of the Sons of Korah*, 170–80) argues that the psalm was originally a song from Dan which was taken south with all the Korahite psalms (plus Ps 89) and adapted to become a Zion-song. The modification involved the addition of three phrases: "the gates of Zion," "Yea, of Zion" (ולציון in v 5), and "with Ethiopia (Cush)" (Cush/Ethiopia being used to turn "the geographical balance southwards"). In addition there was, according to Goulder, some repointing (two verbs) and the deletion of a repeated verb in v 7 (179). He relates Ps 87 closely with 48; two hymns originally praising Dan as the city of God which were altered in Jerusalem to become Zion-hymns.

Goulder (176–79) argues that he offers a new solution to the problem of
the meaning of vv 4–6. The "this one was born there" in v 4 is taken as a
reference to the birth of a prince who will continue a royal dynasty, a birth by a
pregnant queen who had come to Dan at a time when the birth of her baby
and the celebration of the autumn festival coincided. The surrounding nations
are declared to be "among them that know me" (see note 4.b. above), anticipating their acknowledgment of Yahweh and their paying tribute to his anointed
king. Thus Goulder understands the psalm as a kind of Dan version of the
expression of the extended power of the son-king of Yahweh in Jerusalem
found in Ps 2.

Goulder's argument is tied to his thesis that all the Korah psalms (plus part of
Ps 89) originated from Dan (see *Form/Structure/Setting*, Ps 85). In my opinion, his
contention that "the gates of Zion" is an addition to the original psalm is his
strongest point. His interpretation of the "this one" in v 4 as referring to the birth
of a prince seems to founder on v 5–6, where he finds it necessary to repoint the
verb יֹאמַר and rather lamely reads 5b as "Each man shall say, 'He was born in
her,'" with "Yea, Zion" (for וּלְצִיּוֹן) added in Jerusalem. Goulder (*Psalms of the Sons
of Korah*, 179) admits that the present text of Ps 87, reflecting its Jerusalem
adaptation, means by "this one" one of the peoples mentioned and that 5b is
intended to be read, "Each man was born in her," prefaced by "Yea, of Zion" to
clarify the "in her."

I prefer to take the approach to the Psalm expressed by Booij (*VT* 37 [1987]
17): "The interpretation of Ps. lxxxvii must start from the current Masoretic
text." We cannot escape uncertainties about the exact meanings of statements in
the content of the psalm, but we are surely on firmer ground to stay with MT and
its substantial support by the versions than to build on an extensively reconstructed text. The NEB illustrates the latter approach with the note at the beginning of the psalm that "the text of this psalm is disordered, and several verses
have been re-arranged," followed by four notes indicating "probable reading,"
involving alteration of consonants in five cases. The scholars responsible for REB
are to be commended for a return to the order of MT, with only modest
emendation.

There is little evidence for dating the psalm. If Goulder should be correct, the
original psalm would belong to a time before 722 B.C.E., being transferred to
Jerusalem sometime after the fall of the Northern Kingdom of Israel. Probably,
the importance of Dan yielded to Bethel in the later stages of the Northern
Kingdom, and thus the psalm would have originated back in the period of
perhaps 922–750 B.C.E. (cf. Goulder, 18–19). This is very tenuous, however, and
the psalm may have been a Zion hymn (or part of one) from its beginning,
originating sometime during the monarchy in Jerusalem. The failure to mention
Assyria among the nations (cf. Isa 19:25) is striking and possibly points to a time
after c. 610 B.C.E. when Assyria was no longer a major power. On the other hand,
the similarity of the content of the psalm with a series of passages which envision
a universal aspect for Zion (see *Comment*) may point to a kind of utopian strand
of theology and expectation in the early post-exilic period (note the comments
by D. L. Petersen, *Haggai and Zechariah 1–8*. [Philadelphia: Westminster, 1984]
181–83, on Zech 2:15 [11]).

Comment

Smith (*VT* 38 [1988] 357) calls attention to what he calls a "concentric pentacolon" in Ps 87 which unifies its structure:

A בְּךָ, "in you" (v 3)
 B שָׁם, "there" (v 4)
  C בָהּ, "in her" (v 5)
 B' שָׁם, "there" (v 6)
A' בְּךָ, "in you" (v 7)

The ABCB'A' pattern ties vv 3–7 into a unit and probably indicates that vv 1–2 form a thematic introduction to what follows. The placement of בה ("in her") at the center of these verses, followed by a statement of the Most High's establishment of Zion (5c), is striking and makes rearrangement of the verses dubious. Beyond the analysis of Smith, it seems possible that the colon in 5c correlates and completes the single colon in 1b (note Wanke, 38): "His foundation (is) upon (the) holy mountains [1b]; / the Most High himself has established it [5c]." If this is the case, the material in vv 2–5b is inserted in an "envelope" construction, which concentrates on 4c and 5b; v 2 is an introduction to vv 3–7.

Whatever the previous history of the content of Ps 87 may have been (possibly the psalm is only a section from a longer psalm or a liturgy), the present psalm seems to set forth the role of Zion as the universal spiritual center of the world. It is unlikely that the references in vv 4–6 refer to Jews living in such nations as those named. The exiles from Israel and Judah would hardly have been referred to as "Rahab," or as Babylonians, or Philistines, or Tyrians, or Cushites. The ethnic identity of Israelites is consistently maintained in the OT, regardless of their geographical, political, and cultural contexts.

Thus there is no need to question that Ps 87 deals with Gentiles. The present location of the psalm in the Psalter is most probably due to its reading as an amplification of Ps 86:9 (Cohen, 283). The psalm expresses the expectation that Zion will become the "mother city" in a universal worship of Yahweh. It belongs with a number of passages which anticipate and envision a time when the gentile peoples will worship Yahweh: "It shall come to pass in the latter days / that the mountains of the house of the LORD / shall be established (נכון) as the highest of the mountains, / and shall be raised above the hills; / and all the nations shall flow to it" (Isa 2:2 // Mic 4:1 with minor differences; RSV). Isa 19:23–25 foresees a time when Israel's role as a blessing in the world will be shared with Egypt and Assyria, all to be blessed by Yahweh, saying: "Blessed be Egypt my people, and / Assyria the work of my hands, and Israel my heritage" (v 25; RSV). Zion is called upon to rejoice in Zech 2:10 because Yahweh is coming to dwell in the midst of her: "And many nations shall join themselves to the LORD in that day, and shall be my people" (Zech 2:11, 14 [15], RSV). See further Isa 45:22–23; 56:6–7; Zech 8:22–23; 14:16–19; Mal 1:11; Ps 86:9; Esth 9:27. The concept of being "born" in Zion as a means of expressing spiritual kinship does not seem to appear elsewhere (however, see Isa 49:20–21 for a closely related concept), but the maternal role of Zion is found in Isa 49:19–26; 54:1; 62:4–5; 66:7–8; cf. Isa 60:4–5. Zion's status

as "mother city" is clearly apart from dependence on the LXX's reading of v 5b
(see note 5.b. above).

Because of a lack of similar references and contexts, the exact meaning of the
declaration of birth in Zion ("This one was born there") is elusive. It could be
that of being "recorded for life [לחיים כתוב] in Jerusalem" (Isa 4:3). In any case,
the words in 4c and 5b are performative utterances which legitimate those
referred to in the statements (cf. T. N. D. Mettinger, *King and Messiah* [Lund: CWK
Gleerup, 1976] 266–67). Anderson (II, 621–22) comments that the "native"
status of foreigners "does not depend upon the fact that one happened to be
born in Zion, but rather upon one's obedience to Yahweh," which is probably
true, but that goes somewhat beyond the text of Ps 87, where there is no mention
of obedience. The Zion-status of the Gentiles is the result of the performative
declaration of Yahweh. The psalm suggests, at any rate by the absence of any
requirements of the Gentiles, a massive act of divine grace.

The recording in the "register of peoples" in v 6 recalls Ezek 13:9: "My hand
will be against the prophets. . . . They shall not be in the council of my people,
and not be enrolled in the register of the house of Israel." Closely related, or the
same, is the "scroll of the living" (Ps 69:29; cf. 109:13–14; Exod 33:32; Mal 3:16;
Dan 12:1; *1 Enoch* 47.3; 108.3; Rev 3:5). The actual place of birth does not matter
if Yahweh records that a person was "born" in Zion: " The most glorious thing
that He can say of each of them, the crown of all their history, shall be this, not
the record of their separate national existence or polity or dominion, but the
fact that they have become members by adoption of the city of God" (Perowne,
138). However, since reference to birthplace and entry of names in a register do
not seem to be associated with the formal process of adoption, it is better to
speak of the *legitimization* of people from the nations as Zionites. The key to the
political procedure reflected in these verses is possibly found in the Assyrian
practice of justifying the deportation and movement of peoples involved in
empire building by the use of a common refrain, found in Neo-Assyrian inscriptions about conquered peoples: "I counted them among the Assyrians" (D. L.
Smith, *The Religion of the Landless* [Bloomington, IN: Meyer Stone, 1989] 29, citing a work of M. Liverani, "The Ideology of the Assyrian Empire," *Mesopotamia*
7:307; see *manu*, CAD, 224, no. 6j, e.g., of four thousand men of the land of Hatti:
"I look and considered [counted = ספר] as people of my own land"). The meaning of the Akkadian verb in this sense is "to consider a person, a region, or an
object as belonging to a specific class, region, or destination" (*CAD*). Thus the
process recalled in vv 5–6 is analogous to that of a conquering king who declares
foreign peoples to belong to his royal realm and registers them among the
people of the conquering country.

V 5b has a universal range which includes all humanity: "Everyone was born in
her!" The exuberance of the vision breaks the bounds of even the widespread
geography of v 4 and is inclusive of all human beings. Yahweh is the "empire
builder" par excellence! Such poetic vision should neither be diminished by
prosaic theological fears of universal salvation nor pressed into the confines of
dogma.

In v 1, "his foundation," refers to the city founded by God; cf. Isa 14:32,
"Yahweh has founded [יסד] Zion"; see also Isa 28:16. The plural "mountains"

may refer to the hills on which Jerusalem is built (note Ps 125:2), or it may be a plural used to intensify or amplify the basic concept (cf. GKC 124d–f), in which case it really means "on *the* holy mountain." Two other ideas about the plural are worthy of note: (1) the word הַר ("mountain") in both singular and plural can refer to separate mountains or to mountain ranges (Talmon, *TDOT*, III, 429, 433), thus possibly to the hill country of Canaan which was the territory of Yahweh's special heritage. (2) The connotation of a cosmic or world mountain may be present; see Kraus, (II, 767–68), who suggests that הַרְרֵי־קֹדֶשׁ alludes to the "primitive mountains" which projected up out of the depths of the primeval seas and became the places where deities lived and decided "cosmically important matters" (Talmon, 441). Kraus calls attention to such references as Pss 36:7; 24:2; 89:12; 102:26; 104:5, and especially 78:69 (also note Deut 32:22), arguing that when the parallel to 1b in 5c is considered there can hardly be any doubt that mythical elements are set forth in the psalm.

All of the nuances of meaning may be present in the text of 87:1b, allowing the reader a repertoire of meaning (Talmon, 430, comments in passing on "the inherent mythical qualities of mountains"). Yahweh's "foundation" on the mountains is a mighty "city of God" (v 3b), both a city belonging to God and a powerful, mighty, God-like city, which is built on earth with cosmic dimensions (note also Ps 48:2–8). The "foundation" of Yahweh, which he (the Most High) has established (v 5c) is probably envisioned as Mount Zion in the midst of concentric mountain ranges (Ps 125:1–2) reaching out to distant lands, even to the ends of the earth (Ezek 5:5; Ps 46:9–10; cf. Isa 42:10–13; Talmon, 436). If this reading is correct, the peoples of the world can be encompassed in Zion without difficulty (vv 4–5). The "foundation" of Yahweh is the glorious metropolis which is to become the home city of the peoples from every nation.

"Rahab" in v 4 is used as an epithet for Egypt (on Rahab, see *Comment* on Ps 89:6–15), as in Isa 30:7; cf. Isa 51:9–10. The designation of Egypt as a dragon-like chaos-monster (Rahab), one of the creatures which threaten the well-being of existence in ancient myths, is a clue to the nature of the peoples named as representative of the nations. Babylon represents the great powers from Mesopotamia (Kraus, II, 769). The great power centers of the ancient Near East were Egypt and Mesopotamia. Philistia and Tyre represent lesser powers lying near to Israel. Cush represents distant foreign peoples. Cush is usually taken to refer to the Nubian kingdom, located along the Nile River south of Egypt—though the term is not strictly defined and is used for the Kassites in Gen 2:13 and 10:8, who lived in what is modern Kurdistan, a mountain area east of Babylonia. It is probably a mistake to use Cush for modern Ethiopia; LXX has Αἰθιόπων in Ps 87:4, which is properly "burnt-faces," people with dark, sunburnt skin, and could refer to any southern land. See O. Wintermute, *IDBSup*, 200–201. All these peoples (and more) will be assigned the birthright of the people of Zion.

The "gates of Zion" (v 2) is the use of a part for the whole (synecdoche). The importance of gate areas in walled towns as centers of social and economic life is well known (cf. Pss 9:15; 24:7–9; 69:13; 122:2 where "your gates" is in apposition with Jerusalem). Yahweh "loves" the gates of Zion more than the "dwellings of Jacob." Kraus (II, 767) seems to limit "love" to Yahweh's choice, or election, of

Zion for his sanctuary (see Ps 78:67–68; cf. 132:13), but there is no need to exclude his care and protection of Zion (note v 5c and Yahweh's "love" for the righteous in Ps 146:8–9). The "dwellings of Jacob" may refer to other towns and cities in Israel: "Though Yahweh himself built and beautified these towns, he did not choose them as the site of his revelation; this perogative was Jacob's" (Dahood, II, 299). However, we should not exclude reference to other sanctuaries and temples in Israel; see Kraus (II, 767), who leans heavily on the "tent of Joseph" rejected by Yahweh in Ps 78:67–68, which refers to the sanctuary at Shiloh; note Ps 78:60. See also Anderson (II, 620), who notes that the "contrast seems to be between Zion as a religious centre, and other cities . . . of a similar significance," and who also notes the possibility of an allusion to the Samaritan temple on Mount Gerizim, depending upon the date of the psalm.

Kraus (II, 768) is probably correct to conclude that the language in vv 2–3 and 7 reflects the singing and dancing which marked entry processions of worshipers coming to the chosen city at festival time (cf. Ps 122; 2 Sam 6; see Excursus: "Songs of Ascents" in Allen, 219–21). The verb in v 2, דבר, "say/speak/declare," can be understood as "sing" (noted by Kraus, II, 768, citing Judg 5:12; Ps 18:1); thus the "glorious things" about Zion are sung, I suppose, by the singers and dancers in v 7, who include in the "glorious things" the affirmation: "All my springs are in you!" "Springs" or "fountains" is a metaphor for the source of life and blessing (see Ps 36:10; Isa 12:3; Joel 3:18, Heb 4:18; cf. Isa 41:18; Hos 13:15; note also the river of Zion in Ps 46:5). V 7 seems to call up the vision of joyful people singing and dancing in a procession into Zion, or perhaps around the walls of Jerusalem (cf. Ps 48:13; see Craigie's comments, 355).

Explanation

If I have read the psalm in an acceptable way, it is a declaration of God's intention to make Zion the spiritual metropolis of the world. A speaker sets forth the love of Yahweh for Zion, "his foundation upon holy mountains," in vv 1b–3, which is said to be the "City of God" (3b). Weiser (581) uses his imagination to depict the context of the psalm: "The poet stands on the top of Mount Zion absorbed in thought. What he sees and what he thinks takes shape in his mind under the impression of the festive mood that surges round about him everywhere, and becomes a song of praise glorifying Jerusalem, the Holy City of God." The praise of Zion stops in vv 3–5b and Yahweh speaks of his intention for the peoples of the world in regard to Zion. The speaker in vv 4–5b seems to be God (probably in the voice of a prophet), while another voice is heard in vv 6–7, unless these lines represent a return to the speaker in vv 1b–3. Yahweh is visualized as proclaiming that Gentile peoples will be among those who will "know" him and are to be given birthrights in Zion.

"Know" is used in the sense of those who have been brought into a special relationship with God (cf. "many nations will be joined to [לוה] Yahweh" in Zech 2:15 [11]). The verb "know" is used of Yahweh's special relationship with Israel in Amos 3:2: "You only have I known out of all families of the earth" (cf. Deut 10:15; Jer 1:5; Gen 18:19; Exod 33:12, 17; cf. also Pss 9:11; 36:11; 79:6; 79:6, 91:14). Those who "know" Yahweh, and who are "known" by him, belong to his legitimate people. It is Yahweh's intention to make peoples from nations far and wide to be citizens of Zion, joining with those native to the city: "It is a bold picture—Yahweh taking inventory of the peoples of the world, all of them . . . , and giving every one a birth certificate marked 'Zion'" (Durham, 350). The reader is invited to think that the testimony of the singers in v 7 includes the foreigners in vv 4–6. The song of the singers in v 7, "All my springs are in you," is a response to the "glorious things" of Zion in v 3, now expanded to include the "one great family of God" (cf. Weiser, 584).

The vision of Ps 87 lives on in Judaism and in Christianity. The latter developed, especially with Paul of Tarsus, the concept of the inclusion of the Gentiles as an integral component of its understanding of the work of Christ and the polity of the church. The Gentiles are "fellow heirs, members of the same body and partakers in the promise of Christ Jesus throughout the gospel . . . the plan of the mystery hidden for ages in God" (Eph 3:3–9, RSV). The speaker in Heb 12 declares that "You have come to Mount Zion and to the city of the living God, the heavenly Jerusalem, and to innumerable angels in festal gathering, and to the assembly of the first-born who are enrolled in heaven" (vv 22–23, RSV).

The mother-role of Zion is used by Paul in his letter to the Galatians: "The Jerusalem above . . . she is our mother" (Gal 4:26). The "redeemed from the earth" will stand with the triumphant Lamb on Mount Zion, with the name of the Lamb and his Father's name on their foreheads; they will number 144,000, but are only the firstfruits for God and the Lamb of a great harvest, of a "great multitude which no one could count, from every nation, from all tribes and peoples and tongues" (Rev 14:1–5; 7:9). Their song of victory and salvation confirms the vision of Ps 87.

A Bitter Prayer of Distress *(88:1–19)*

Bibliography

Brueggemann, W. *The Message of the Psalms: A Theological Commentary.* Minneapolis: Augsburg, 1984. 78–81. **Grelot, P.** *"HOFŠĪ* (Ps LXXXVIII:6)." *VT* 14 (1964) 256–63. **Haag, E.** "Psalm 88." In *Freude an der Weisung des Herrn: Beiträge zur Theologie der Psalmen.* Ed. E. Haag and F.-L. Hossfeld. Stuttgart: Katholisches Bibelwerk, 1986. 149–70. **Haddix, J. L.** *Lamentation as Personal Experience in Selected Psalms.* Ph.D. diss., Boston University, 1980. Ann Arbor: UMI, 1980. 113–30. **Tate, M. E.** "Psalm 88." *RevExp* 87 (1990) 91–95.

Translation

1   A song;[a] a Korahite psalm.[b] For the leader:[c]
according to *mahalath-leannoth.*[d]
A *maskil*[e] of Heman the Ezrahite.[f]

2(1)   *O Yahweh, the God of my salvation:*   (3+2+2)
daily I cry out for help,[a]
nightly (I am) before you.[b]

3(2)	Let my prayer come to your attention;[a] bend your ear to my cry (of distress)![b]	(3+3)
4(3)	For my soul is sated with troubles, and my life is brought near to Sheol.	(3+3)
5(4)	I am reckoned with those going to the Pit;[a] I have become like a strong man without strength;[b]	(3+3)
6(5)	"set free"[a] among the dead; like the slain,[b] who lie in a (common) grave,[c] whom you remember no longer, those[d] who are cut off from your hand.	(2+4+3+3)
7(6)	You have put me at the bottom of the Pit,[a] (down) in the utter darkness[b] of the depths.	(3+2)
8(7)	Your wrath has come down[a] on me; you have squashed (me)[b] with all your waves.	(3+3)
9(8)	You have caused my close friends[a] to stay away from me; you have made me repulsive[b] to them; (I am) closed in[c] and I cannot get out;	(3+3+3)
10(9)	my eye[a] has grown weak from suffering.[b] I have called to you, O Yahweh, every day; I have stretched out my palms to you.	(3+3+3)
11(10)	Do you do wonders[a] for the dead? Do even the Rephaim[b] rise up (and) praise you? SELAH.	(3+3)
12(11)	Is your loyal-love declared in the grave? Your faithfulness in Abaddon?	(3+2)
13(12)	Are your wonders known in the darkness? Your righteousness[a] in the Land of Forgetfulness?	(3+3)
14(13)	As for me, I have cried for help to you, O Yahweh, and in the morning my prayer has been before you.[a]	(4+3)
15(14)	Why, O Yahweh, do you spurn me? Why do you hide your face from me?	(4+3)
16(15)	I have been afflicted and nearly dead[a] since boyhood;[b] having borne your terrors, I despair of life.[c]	(4+3)
17(16)	Your wrath[a] has swept over me; your terrors have annihilated me.[b]	(3+2)
18(17)	They swirl around me all day like water; they close in on me from all sides.[a]	(3+3)
19(18)	You have caused lover and companion to stay away from me; (caused to stay away from me) my close friends— darkness![a]	(4+2)

Notes

1.a. See n. 65:1.c.
1.b. See n. 85:1.b.
1.c. See n. 51:1.a.
1.d. The meaning of *mahalath-leannoth* is uncertain, but it is often assumed to be a tune or chanting pattern to be used with the psalm. The word *mahalath* is used in Ps 53:1 (see n. 53:1.b.), but *mahalath-leannoth* appears only here. Mowinckel (*PIW*, II, 210) suggests that *mahalath* is equal to "song" or "playing instrument" (probably a "reed-pipe") and suggests the reference is to the flute or "flute playing," which he argues would indicate a psalm of lament (reed pipes/flutes were played at

lamentation ceremonies; see Jer 48:36; Matt 9:23). However, he argues that in 88:1 the עַל־מָחֲלַת means "in connection with (properly 'over') illness" and relates to purification from illness (cf. מַחֲלָה, masc "sickness," and מַחֲלָה, fem "sickness"). He takes *leannoth* (212) as "for penance" (properly "to humiliate/abase"; a piel inf. const. from עֲנה) and argues that it indicates that the psalm was used as a psalm of penitence and lamentation, probably in rituals associated with purification from illness. Goulder (*The Psalms of the Sons of Korah*, 202) suggests that *mahalath* was derived from חלל, "to pierce," and referred to holes in the ground or apertures to pits (cf. Isa 2:19). He relates this to his theory of the festal rites at Dan, which included the taking of a priest or prophet as representative of the people to a pit or cave outside the city to cry out to Yahweh in laments and pleas during the days of the festival (198). He notes, of course, the pit-language of Ps 88, with references to water, darkness, and the distress of being in such frightening places. He thinks it likely that *mahalath* was originally the pit-cave at Dan where one of the streams of water disappears underground for some distance outside the southwest corner of the ramparts of the city. In this case, the meaning of the expression *mahalath-leannoth* would have been something like the Pit of Lament. However, Goulder says that when Ps 88 was transferred to the Jerusalem community, *mahalath* was probably taken as "appeasement"; thus "about appeasement of affliction" (Leslie, 397, reads as "for self-abasement") and could, of course, have continued to give expression to rites of affliction and lamentation. Eerdmans (138, 412, 416) notes that in Assyrian incantation texts for healing, the name of the patient had to be mentioned when they were recited, and he supposes that such is the case in the use of Pss 53 and 88. The עַל־מָחֲלַת . . . לְעַנּוֹת would mean "on account of the sickness of . . . ," with the name of the sufferer added in each case. In the case of Ps 88, "On account of the sickness of . . . to humble oneself (or for contrition)." The confession of contrition would, supposedly, make the prayer more acceptable to God. The theories are interesting, but assured conclusions are nonexistent.

1.e. See 52:1–2.c. The term probably indicates a well-written poem which gives powerful expression to its subject matter.

1.f. A person named Heman is mentioned in 1 Chr 2:6 as being one of the sons of Zerah, along with Zimri, Ethan, Calcol, and Dara. Zerah is a descendent of Judah. In 1 Kgs 5:11 [4:31], Heman is mentioned with Ethan the Ezrahite (note Ps 89:1) as one of the famous wise men of Solomon's reign. Heman is referred to as the king's seer in 1 Chr 25:5 and is mentioned along with Ethan in 1 Chr 15:17, 19 as among the Korahite Levitical singers. He is also called a singer in 1 Chr 6:18–23 [6:33–38] and his ancestry is traced back to Korah. Thus linkage is made between Heman and the Korahites to which Ps 88 is assigned. It is not certain, of course, that all the references to Heman and Ethan are to the same persons. The references to Heman (Ps 88:1) and Ethan (Ps 89:1) as Ezrahites are mysteries, as no direct connection between the Ezrahites and the Korahites is known elsewhere. The suggestion has been made to consider אֶזְרָחִי ("Ezrahite") as a patronymic equivalent to זַרְחִי ("Zerahite") and to identify Heman as in 1 Chr 2:6, which would make him a member of one of the clans of Judah. But Heman, Asaph, and Ethan are listed as Levitical singers in 1 Chr 15:17, 19, and Ethan is said to be an Ezrahite in 1 Kgs 5:11 [4:31]. There seems to be no real answer to all this confusion. We are probably dealing with more than one Heman in the traditions.

Dahood (II, 302) represents another approach and follows W. L. Albright to argue that Ezrahite means "native-born," thus, "Heman the native-born" (also in 89:1), proposing that אֶזְרָחִי originally meant an "aborigine" and then "from a pre-Israelite family" (note the noun אֶזְרָח, "a native," as in Lev 23:42; Num 15:13; Exod 12:19, 48; Josh 8:33). See W. L. Albright, *Archaeology and the Religion of Israel* [Baltimore: Johns Hopkins UP, 1956] 127, 210).

The inscription is probably a double one, perhaps derived from two different sources, possibly indicating that a Heman psalm has been taken into a Korahite collection, regardless of the lineage of Heman. Goulder (203) may be correct to conclude that "Ezrahite" has been added to Heman in the title of Ps 88 from "Ethan the Ezrahite" in the title of Ps 89. Since Heman is reckoned as a colleague of Ethan, a link with the Korahite psalms was provided for Ps 89 by also designating Heman in 88:1 as an Ezrahite. Thus relationship between Ethan and Heman as Ezrahites draws together Pss 88 and 89, and both Heman and Ethan are identified as Korahites (note 1 Kgs 5:11 [4:31]; 1 Chr 6:33–38), though Ethan is from the line of Merari in 1 Chr 6:44 and is possibly the same as Jeduthun (see 1 Chr 25:1; 2 Chr 5:12; and cf. 1 Chr 15:17, 19).

2.a. The text is often changed to אֱלֹהִי שׁוַּעְתִּי יוֹמָם צָעַקְתִּי, "my God, I call for help by day / I cry out in the night before you" (note RSV; cf. v 14). Sometimes צָעַקְתִּי ("I cry/have cried") is changed to צַעֲקָתִי ("my cry"): "my cry in the night is constantly before you" (Gunkel, 382). It is possible to read the יוֹם as "on the day when" or "when" (e.g., in Pss 56:4; 78:42; cf. 102:3; 18:1 which has בְּיוֹם; see Delitzsch, III, 25): "when I cry before you in the night." Goulder (*The Psalms of the Sons of Korah*, 201, 204) adopts this approach and reads: "On the day that I have cried by night before thee, let my prayer enter . . . ," assuming that 2b is a clause whose main sentence follows in v 3. This fits his theory that the psalm is a prayer of a representative of the community who prays through the night in a penitential rite, perhaps intended to be a prayer at dawn. Kraus (II, 771–72) reads vv 1–2 as: "O Yahweh, God of my salvation, / at daytime I cry to you, / at night I stand before you. / May my prayer come before you! / Incline your ear to my lamentations!"—a self-description of the speaker, who wants to declare that the prayer is that of one who holds on unceasingly to trust in Yahweh: "The darkest of all Old Testament psalms stands under the certitude: You are the 'God of my salvation'" (774). This is a possible reading which avoids emendation, but it seems to me that v 2 should be read as complaint rather than as a statement of confidence. LXX reads: "I have cried by day and in the night before you," which seems in keeping with the idea of incessant prayer, as in v 14. I assume that יוֹם is equivalent to בְּיוֹמָם (cf. Pss 18:1; 102:3) or the adverb יוֹמָם ("daily"), and that the statement means: "I have cried out for help before you day and night."

2.b. Dahood (II, 302) argues that נֶגְדְּךָ ("before you") should be understood here as "to you" (adopted by Haddix, *Lamentation as Personal Experience*, 120).

3.a. It is possible to read this statement as an affirmation: "my prayer will come before you" (Kraus, Schmidt, Haag, "Psalm 88," 150). The לְפָנֶיךָ ("to your face/presence") has the force of "to your attention" (cf. Gen 6:13; Lam 1:22; Jonah 1:2).

3.b. LXX adds κύριε, "O Yahweh," which gives the colons better balance.

5.a. The participle may mean "those about to go to the pit"— expected imminent action.

5.b. The expression אֵין אֱיָל is a hapax, found only here in MT. אֱיָל is frequently taken as an Aramaic loan word, "help" (see BDB; Briggs, II, 248; Gunkel, 382) and is read as such in LXX and Syr, followed by NEB ("like a man beyond help"). However, the word probably means "strength" (see KB; Dahood, II, 303; KJV, RSV, etc.). NJV combines the two readings very nicely: "a helpless man." The גֶּבֶר indicates a strong, vigorous man.

6.a. The usual meaning of חָפְשִׁי is "free" (e.g., Exod 21:2, 5; Deut 15:12, 13, 18; Job 3:19; Isa 58:6. KJV translates literally as "free among the dead," but RSV goes to "forsaken." NEB has "abandoned," so also NJV with the note "lit. 'released.'" LXX supports "free" with ἐλεύθερος, and Symm has ἀφεὶς ἐλεύθερος ("one set free"). Nevertheless, proposals for textual changes have been prolific (for surveys, see Grelot, *VT* 14 [1964] 256–63; Haag, "Psalm 88," 151, n. 6; Jacquet, 675, n. 6a). One major alternative is to assume that חָפְשִׁי means "cot/couch/bed," utilizing the meaning of חֹפֶשׁ in Ezek 27:20 and understanding it as "bed/couch."

Attempts have been made to strengthen this understanding from the usage of בֵּית הַחָפְשִׁית ("in the separate house"), referring to a king's case of leprosy and separation from the normal community (cf. 2 Chr 26:21) in 2 Kgs 15:5. Dahood (II, 304) argues that this is equal to Ugaritic *ḥptt* in UT 51.8.7–8: *wrd bt ḥptt arṣ* which he reads as "and go down to the nether house of cots," citing also the motif of Sheol as a place of beds in such texts as Ps 139:8; Job 17:13; Prov 7:27. Dahood translates: "In Death is my cot"; Haag is similar.

However, this approach is beset with difficulties. The meaning of the Ugaritic *ḥptt* is uncertain and is variously rendered as "filthy" or "uncleanness" or as "netherworld" (Anderson, II, 625). The meaning of חֹפֶשׁ in Ezek 27:20 (בְּבִגְדֵי־חֹפֶשׁ) is usually taken as something like "saddle-cloths" and probably has nothing to do with "cot" or "bed." The expressions in 2 Kgs 15:5 // 2 Chr 26:21 may refer to the king's "house of freedom" rather than separation to some sort of unclean place. The king is free from the normal burdens (cf. 1 Sam 17:25) of royal functions. REB translates 2 Kgs 15:5 as "he was relieved of all duties and lived in his palace." Thus it seems better to retain the sense of "free" in Ps 88:6. I have, however, understood it in an ironic sense: "relieved of duties among the dead!"—equal to the strong man without strength in 5b and those who lie in the grave.

6.b. Some Greek texts have ἐρριμμένοι, indicating מֻשְׁלָכִים, "cast out ones," added to the text, but the extra word does not seem to help much: "Free among the dead / like the slain ones who are cast out / (like) those who lie in the grave." Cf. Jer 14:16.

6.c. The word קֶבֶר is the typical word for "grave," but in this context it seems to refer to the common grave(s) of those slain and buried without proper attention (cf. Isa 14:19; Ezek 32:20–32).

6.d. Lit., "and those . . ." The conjunction seems to be explicative, "even" or "specifically," and explanatory.

7.a. Lit., "the pit of the lowest (places)." Cf. Lam 3:55; Pss 63:10; 86:13; Ezek 26:20; 31:14, 16, 18; 32:18, 24; Isa 44:23. The translation above is that of NJV.

7.b. LXX has ἐν σκοτεινοῖς καὶ ἐν σκιᾷ θανάτου, "in dark places, even in the shadow of death," which assumes וּבְצַלְמָוֶת for בְּמְצֹלוֹת, "in deep places." The "deep places" (or "bottom") appears especially with reference to the sea (note Exod 15:5; Neh 9:11; cf. מְצוּלָה in Job 41:23; Pss 68:23; 69:3, 16; 107:24; Jonah 2:4; Mic 7:19; Zech 10:11). V 7b is lit., "in the dark (places) in the depths." The plural may indicate intensity ("utter darkness"), ב on במצלות may be the result of failure to recognize an enclitic *mem* on the preceding word: מצלות, במחשכי־ם, "in the darkness of the deep places." See n. 19.a. for מחשך as "darkness."

8.a. The verb סמך normally means "support/lean on," but here it appears to be as in Ezek 24:2, "to lean on aggressively/attack."

8.b. Assuming piel perf. from ענה, II, "bow down/afflict," with the suffix assumed from עלי ("on me") in the first colon. LXX has "you have brought upon me all your waves," probably assuming אניה לי from אנה, III, "meet/encounter," in piel, "cause to meet" or "allow to meet" (see *BHS*, Gunkel, Kraus). Delitzsch (III, 25–26) argues for כל־משבריך ("all your waves/billows") as an adverbial accusative with the verb ענה (in piel) used in the sense of "to bow down/press down," here used of turning or directing the waves down on the afflicted one like a cataract. In any case, the sense seems to be that the speaker has been crushed beneath the "waves" of God.

9.a. Or, "my companions," sometimes read as "my acquaintances," but the pual participle of ידע expresses more than the English "acquaintance."

9.b. Lit., "you have made (set) me an abomination to them."

9.c. The expression probably should be read as equivalent to כלא אני or נכלאתי, with the versions, "I have been imprisoned." However, an indefininte "one" from the suffix in the previous colon (שתני) may be assumed and no pronoun need appear: "Imprisoned, I cannot escape" (Dahood, II, 305; also Haddix, *Lamentation as Personal Experience*, 115).

10.a. The noun is singular, "my eye," probably influenced by the דאבה, "languish," taken as simple perf. 3rd pers. fem. sing. The plural or dual is often read (with LXX), but the singular may refer to the appearance of the suffering person (so Haddix, *Lamentation as Personal Experience*, 115, citing Lev 13:55). Indeed, it is probably synecdoche here for the body or the whole person.

10.b. The word עני refers to "affliction," "poverty," and the like; e.g., Gen 16:11; 29:32; Exod 3:7; Job 10:15; 36:8, 15, 21; Pss 9:14; 25:18; 31:8; 44:25; Lam 1:9.

11.a. The sing. "wonder" is collective.

11.b. Usually translated as "the shades" (RSV) or "the dead" (KJV). The exact meaning of the word רפאים is uncertain, except to say that it "clearly suggests the inhabitants of Sheol" (Anderson, II, 628). The word is frequently understood as "shadowy replicas" of persons who have died, the diminished selfhoods which survive death, and taken as derived from the Heb. root רפה, "sink/relax," so that the noun denotes "the powerless ones" (cf. Isa 14:9–10). On the other hand, the word may be from רפא, "heal," and denote "healers," as in Ugaritic (K. Spronk, *Beatific Afterlife in Ancient Israel and in the Ancient Near East* [Neukirchen-Vluyn: Neukirchener, 1986] 51–52). A major problem arises in both Phoenician and Hebrew sources in that two different usages of Rephaim appear. (1) They appear as a pre-Israelite people (e.g., Deut 2:10–11; 2:20; 3:11; Josh 12:4; 13:12; 17:15; 18:16; Deut 14:5; 15:20)—located in association with the Jordan or in the south of Jerusalem. (2) They appear as the dead (e.g., Isa 14:9; 26:14; 26:19; Prov 2:18; 21:16; cf. 9:18). How are the two related? The key to this matter probably lies in Ugaritic usage (see S. B. Parker, *IDBSup*, 739; Spronk, *Beatific Afterlife in Ancient Israel*, 161–96, 227–29), where *rp'um* is a name for the privileged dead, royal ancestors, who live as the dead, but sometimes in the roles of warriors and healers, who have superior power; functioning like lower deities of the underworld. The *rp'um* may come up from the netherworld on occasion, as in a new year festival, and the living ruler may be counted among the *rp'um* (Spronk, 196; KTU 1.15.3.2–4 and 1.108.23–24). In KTU 1.161, the ancient kings of Ugarit are invited to a banquet for the dead ancestors, in order to bless the reigning royal family. The kings are called *rp'um*, and indicates why Keret in KTU 1.15.3.2–4, 13–15 is given a status among the *rp'um*: "he is in fact being blessed with ancestral apotheosis" (J. F. Healey, "The Last of the Rephaim," in *Back to the Sources: Biblical and Near Eastern Studies*, ed. K. J. Cathecart and J. F. Healey [Dublin: Glendale Press, 1989] 38). Healey (39) concludes that the Ugaritic *rp'um* are the ancestral spirits of royal families and, perhaps, associated heroic figures.

Thus it is understandable that legendary peoples of the past may have been known as *rephaim*, "healers," after their posthumous status as the mighty among the dead. The meaning of the term as "healers" should not be pressed too hard, but it is rather clear that the word is related to רפא rather than to רפה ("be weak"). In time, the term tended to lose its reference to privileged status and become a general term for the dead, who are considered generally in the OT to be weak and powerless. For example, the kingly status of the dead is mocked in Isa 14:9–10, where deceased kings still sit on thrones in the netherworld, but declare to an incoming tyrant: "You have become weak (חלה) like us." The mighty רפאים are as weak (or "sick," the common meaning for חלה) as the ordinary dead, or even worse, as those whose dead bodies received no proper respect or burial (Isa 14:18–20). In the Isaiah passage, the mighty "healers" (of disease—a function of kings—and of a country; cf. 2 Chr 7:14) and the like are denied the status of the elite among the dead, since they have all become weak, living with maggots and worms. Thus I take the sense in Ps 88:11 to retain an element of the old idea of the *rephaim* as the elite, the heroic ones, among the dead, which the strong אם construction tends to support: "Do *even* the Rephaim rise (and) praise you?" Perhaps the strong "healers" among the dead should be able to do what the ordinary dead cannot, but they are as weak as all the dead.

13.a. "Righteousness" is equal to "righteous acts," equal to "acts of putting things right." See *Explanation* of Ps 71.

14.a. The translation is similar to that of NJV. The verb קדם means "to be in front" or "to meet," or "to confront" if in hostility. NAB paraphrases: "with my morning prayer I wait upon you."

16.a. MT's נוע has the meaning of "dying" or "near to death/about to die." LXX has καὶ ἐν κόποις, and וינע, "in trouble/suffering/weariness," possibly reflecting וְיָגֵעַ, "weary/weak/spent" (cf. Deut 25:18; 2 Sam 17:2; Eccl 1:8; Kraus, II, 773, who translates *todkrank*, "sick unto death/dangerously ill").

16.b. Dahood (II, 306) reads "groaning" for "from my youth" (assuming an enclitic *mem* and taking the root as נער, (cf. KB, 622) "to roar" or "to growl," like a lion.

16.c. The word אפונה occurs only here and appears to be from פון which seems to denote "perplexity/embarrassment/benumbness." LXX has ἐξηπορήθην, "be in great difficulty/doubt/despair." The suggestion is made frequently (e.g., BDB, 806) to read אפוגה from פוג, "grow numb/helpless" (see Gen 45:26; Pss 38:9; 77:3; Hab 1:4). Other proposals are rather numerous, but not very persuasive. I have followed the Greek text, which probably reflects MT, but no major change is involved in reading as from פוג. For discussion of the cohortative form of the verb, see GKC 108g. The translation above is rather free, but seems to fit the context.

17.a. Treating the plural (lit., "wraths/furies") as an intensive or plural of amplification (GKC 124e).

17.b. For the form of the verb, see BDB, 856.

18.a. Lit., "together" or "altogether."

19.a. The מחשך, "dark place or region" (it can mean a "hiding place," see Ps 74:20; "darkness" [?], Isa 29:15), poses a well-known problem. LXX has ἀπὸ ταλαιπωρίας ("away from [my] distress/suffering"), indicating that the translators took the *mem* as a preposition, perhaps reading חשך as "darkness" in a metaphorical sense for "distress," or understanding the adj. חָשֵׁךְ, "obscure/low." *BHS* indicates that a few Heb. mss read מחשך, perhaps מֶחֱשָׂךְ (from חשך) "withholding/keeping back": "keeping back (or, away) my close friends" (see Anderson, II, 630). Another option from חשך is to assume the חשכה perfect ("you have kept back"); less probable is שכחוני, "they (my close friends) have forgotten me" (adopted by Gunkel, 384). I have followed Kraus (II, 772, 773) and retained "darkness" as a closing word for the psalm, with the recognition, however, that the end of the text may have suffered damage and appears to be incomplete. An option would be to read "my close friends (are) darkness" (cf. Job 17:13–14), which would of course be eased by reading מידעי ("my close friend is darkness," and would be eased even more by reading ורק for ורע: "and only the darkness is my close friend"; cf. Gunkel, 384). Note the appearance of מחשך ("darkness/dark places") in v 7 in the plural, which I translated as an intensive plural.

Form/Structure/Setting

Ps 88 is easily recognizable as having the features of the individual laments. An individual speaker pleads before God for divine attention and response to a complaint about great distress. The complaint is set forth in vv 4–10, and is followed by a series of rhetorical questions, all of which expect a negative answer in vv 11–13. The latter verses intensify the complaint and add urgency to the speaker's prayer. The complaint is resumed and extended in vv 14–19, ending (in the present text, at least) with the emphatic word "darkness." Expressions of trust in Yahweh and vows of praise, found in some individual laments, are either missing or veiled in the psalm.

Goulder (*The Psalms of the Sons of Korah,* 203) protests against the bleakness ascribed to the psalm by many commentators and argues that v 14b should be read as the speaker's confidence that a night of lamentation is almost over and a morning of joy is at hand when the laments of the speaker will change into celebration (see *Notes* on v 14 and *Comment*). In Goulder's interpretation, the entire psalm becomes a kind of prelude to celebration and good things that follow on the last day of the fall festival. This depends on an elaborate scenario for the psalm, which is very interesting and may be true, but which is too speculative to inspire much confidence as a basis for interpretation.

The situation of the speaker is clearly one of great distress, though a specific definition of the distress has the typical elusive quality of descriptive language in the psalms. The impact of the poetic expressions is powerful, but the focus on a definite, particular context remains blurred at the edges. Most interpreters of the psalm have read it as reflecting a prayer for a very sick person, who is near death (e.g., Kraus, II, 773; Dahood, II, 302, describes it as the "lament of a desolate man in mortal illness"). Seybold (*Das Gebet*, 113–17) places Ps 88 among those psalms which can be understood with assurance as relating to illness and healing (Pss 38, 41, 88, and 11QPs^a 155 [Syr. 3 = 11QPs^a 155]). Interpreters who take this approach include loneliness and spiritual distress along with sickness. "To his physical suffering is added the excruciating mental pain that his friends are estranged from him and his acquaintances have forgotten him" (Leslie, 397).

Among those who read the psalm as a liturgical composition from some sort of communal atonement ritual, perhaps the most interesting is Goulder, who argues that the Korahite psalms originally related to festival contexts at the ancient sanctuary at Dan. He argues that Ps 88 belonged to an atonement rite for the sixth day of the festival in which a human scapegoat was banished from the community for a day and a night. In such rites, the king was probably originally the representative of the people in ritual humiliation and penitence (201; see Eaton, *Kingship* 177–81). However, it is unlikely that major kings like Solomon and Ahab would have submitted to the ordeals, and if there was such a ritual it is probable that a priest was assigned the role. As discussed in the *Notes* on v 1, Goulder thinks that the psalm reflects the experience of a representative priest who was placed in a pit-cave not far from the sanctuary. The sufferer was left alone in the pit to undergo an experience like one in the realm of the dead, down in the depths of the pit with darkness and water, while the frightening ghosts of the dead whispered as they milled about in the dark. The priest was there to pray and plead for himself and the people.

Goulder suggests that after the fall of the Northern Kingdom (722 B.C.E.), worshipers from the Northern sanctuaries at Dan and Bethel brought the Korahite psalms to Jerusalem, where some of them were associated with David and Zion theology (transferred from Mount Tabor and Dan theology; see *Form/Structure/Setting* of Ps 89). In the case of Ps 88, the ordeal it reflects probably seemed too strange and barbarous for the people and priests in Jerusalem, especially after the exile, and the psalm (with Ps 89) was assigned to a supplementary collection. Goulder theorizes that there was a "tribulations-of-David" sort of liturgy used in the autumn festival in Jerusalem which is reflected in Pss 51–72 (with these Psalms extending from the Bathsheba incident in Ps 51 to the triumph of Solomon's accession in Ps 72; based on 2 Sam 10–1 Kgs 2). The use of Pss 51–72 forced some of the Korahite psalms into an appendix to Book III of the Psalter (Pss 73–89), which is now Pss 84–89. Otherwise Book III is composed of Asaphite psalms—assuming that Ps 89 is a Korahite psalm.

Such an elaborate reconstruction is highly conjectural and can hardly be used as a firm basis for exegesis without further historical evidence. Goulder, *Psalms of the Sons of Korah*, 209, himself recognizes the theoretical nature of his proposals. Even if the liturgical history is correctly reconstructed, it does not follow necessarily that the psalms involved were written for actual use in liturgical rites. In fact it seems rather improbable to me that a priest assigned to a scapegoat role in a pit would be provided with a particular psalm of eighteen verses to recite (over and over?); though one would expect such a priest to recite many stock verses and even entire psalms, while extemporizing extensively in his prayers.

A sounder conclusion is that of assuming the possibility of such an ordeal for the *metaphorical* milieu of the psalm. P. K. McCarter ("The River Ordeal in Israelite Literature," *HTR* 66 [1973] 403–12; also Widengren, *The Accadian and Hebrew Psalms of Lamentation as Religious Documents*, 205–9) notes that there are several psalms in the Psalter which share the motif of a judgment by water (or the threat of death from water), citing Pss 18 (2 Sam 22); 66; 69; 88; 124; and 144, plus the psalm in Jonah 2. The following elements are present to one degree or another: (1) the speaker is beset by raging waters; (2) he/she is surrounded by accusers; (3) he/she protests his/her innocence and affirms reliance upon God, pleading to be delivered from the waters; in some cases (4) the speaker has been drawn from the waters and offers praise for being brought to safety. McCarter suggests that ancient customs of water judgment, especially in Mesopotamia, lie behind such language. The water judgments were intended to determine guilt or innocence by plunging the accused person into a river. Survival indicated innocence; drowning was proof of guilt. The survival or death of the accused was assumed to be the action of gods, of course. Widengren (207–9) discusses the possibility that the poems which allude to such legal procedures may actually have reference to judgment in the netherworld, or the earthly legal procedure may have symbolized one in the netherworld. The river ordeal does not appear in OT legal material, and the language in the psalms of the Psalter is unlikely to have direct reference to such procedures, but it may be drawn from a "general mythological backdrop" widely shared by the literature of the ancient Near East (K. Seybold and U. B. Mueller, *Sickness and Healing* [Nashville: Abingdon, 1981] 53).

The metaphorical language of sickness is sufficiently varied enough to encompass the statements in Ps 88 (see Seybold and Mueller, *Sickness and Healing*, 43–56; Seybold, *Das Gebet*, 35–36). Sickness involves an increased danger of death and heightens the awareness of the nearness of dying. Death language is "stereotypically associated with the image of sickness" (Seybold and Mueller, 53; note: Isa 38:10–19; Job 33:22, 28). "The sick person feels near to death, or believes himself to be caught in the flow of those who are descending to the Pit; indeed he already feels himself leaning toward the underworld, towards Sheol, the collecting center for all the living" (Seybold and Mueller, 53). On the other hand, there appears to be no language in Ps 88 which *necessitates* a direct reference to illness. The language of lamentation similar to that in Ps 88 is found in contexts with no direct reference to sickness: e.g., see the pit-water language in Pss 18:5–6; 28:1; 30:2–4; 40:3; 42:8; 69:2–3; 124:2–5; Lam 3:54; Jonah 2:4, 6, 7; Zech 9:11—though some of these contexts could involve illness. The lack of any reference to enemies or accusers in Ps 88 also mitigates against relating the psalm exclusively to sickness (note the presence of enemies in Pss 38:20–21; 41:3, 6, 8, 10; Seybold and Mueller, 46–47; Mowinckel, *PIW*, II, 6–8). However, the isolation of the speaker from friends and family (88:15, 19) aligns well with illness (note Ps 38:12; 41:10; Job 19:13–22).

Thus, Ps 88 may be classified generally as an individual lament, lacking some common elements (enemies, confession of guilt, direct petition for divine intervention, vow of praise or statement of confidence; Kraus, II, 773; Haag, "Psalm 88," 155). There is no difficulty in associating the psalm with serious and chronic (v 16) illness, but the metaphorical backdrop is wider than sickness and can encompass any severe distress or life-threatening situation (see *Form/Structure/Setting* of Ps 69). The variegated metaphorical tapestry in the psalm has threads from penitential rites (possibly including those proposed by Goulder), river ordeals, and sickness, including the partially family-based rituals for sickness postulated by Seybold (see *Form/Structure/Setting* of Ps 69) and the family community rites of lament and petition suggested by Gerstenberger (*Die bittende Mensch*).

The psalm offers little or no evidence for dating. If the theory of Goulder is correct, or other interpretations which would assign the psalm to humiliation rites for the king (advocated by G. Widengren, *Sakrales Königtum: Im Alten Testament und im Judentum* [Stuttgart: Kohlhammer, 1955] 75–76), the psalm would be pre-exilic—if from the sanctuary at Dan, before 722 B.C.E. W. F. Albright (*Archaeology and the Religion of Israel* [Baltimore: Johns Hopkins UP, 1956] 126–29) says that Pss 88 and 89 "swarm with Canaanitisms" and may indicate an original date as early as David. However, Albright (128) notes an abundance of Canaanite material in exilic and post-exilic books (Job, Proverbs, Deutero-Isaiah, Ezekiel, and Habakkuk) and adds that "we cannot . . . establish any definite correlation at present between the date of a Psalm and its Canaanite content." It seems to me that the linguistic criteria for dating a psalm spelled out in the *Form/Structure/Setting* of Ps 93 are inconclusive when applied to Ps 88, though they are not incompatible with a date in the monarchy of pre-exile Israel. If we must have a date, the period of the monarchy before 722 B.C.E. seems to be a good guess. However, it is worth remembering that there is a long tradition of interpretation (including Theodore of Mopsuestia, Theodoret, Tarqum, and Kimchi) which treats the psalm as an exilic or post-exilic prayer of the nation or of faithful Israelites. This approach is found in Briggs (II, 244) and recently in Haag, "Psalm 88"; see Jacquet, II, 670, 674 for references.

Comment

Introductory petition (88:2–3). These are words of petition which indirectly express a complaint. The speaker has prayed day and night but feels deserted; the prayers have not reached the ear of God. The speaker has cried out for help (צעק), an expression which suggests strong cries; "not a dignified prayer, but protracted wailing" (Goulder, 204; e.g., Deut 22:24; 2 Kgs 4:1, 40; 8:3; Num 11:2; 12:13; 20:16; Isa 33:7; 65:14; Ps 107:6, 28). The language is typical of lamentation (note Pss 17:1; 22:3; 61:2; 77:2; Exod 14:10, 15), but the distress of vv 2–3 is not ordinary. The expression "Yahweh, God of my salvation" conveys a continuing faith in Yahweh despite his failure to respond. "In the midst of his agonies he clings to his faith in God as the only source from which his salvation can come"

(Cohen, 285). The speaker's faith is troubled but unbroken (Kraus, II, 774), and Kidner declares that this is "the only positive note in the psalm" (II, 317).

The first complaint (88:4–10). The speaker's "soul" ("self," see Ps 54:3) is "sated," not with the good things of God's house (65:5), but with troubles and with a life that is lived on the brink of disaster and death (cf. Pss 123:3, 4; Isa 1:11; Lam 3:30). The heart of the complaint is the description of life near to death and to Sheol, of being reckoned with the stream of humanity going down to the Pit (another term for the netherworld and the abode of the dead; cf. Pss 28:1; 30:4; 40:3; 143:7; Prov 1:12; Isa 14:15, 19; 24:22; 38:18; Ezek 26:20; 31:14, 16; 32:18; also, Ps 107:18; Job 33:22, Prov 2:18; 5:5; 7:27). The speaker feels like a strong man who has lost his strength (5b).

The meaning of חפשי in v 6 is uncertain (see note 6.a.), but I have taken it in the ironic sense of "set free," released from the normal obligations of life—but "free" among the dead! Like King Uzziah in 2 Kgs 15:5, whose leprosy caused him to dwell in a "freedom-house" (see commentaries) and exempted from royal duties, the speaker has been cut loose from community responsibilities and given "freedom" among the dead and near-dead—a living hell. Durham's summary (351) is well put: "He is like a valiant man whose strength has failed, like a wounded man deserted among the dead in the field of battle; like one defiled, lying in a grave; like all of these, whom Yahweh no longer remembers, as they are gone from his 'hand.'" Like the dead in a common grave, the speaker is cut off from the power of Yahweh. The "slain ones" (חללים in v 6) is probably a shortened form of the "slain by the sword" (חללי־חרב; Ezek 31:17, 18; 32:20, 21) which according to Eissfeldt ("Schwerterschlagene bei Hesekiel," in *Studies in Old Testament Prophecy,* ed. H. H. Rowley [Edinburgh: Clark, 1957] 71–81) includes those who are murdered or executed as well as those who are killed in battle, those like miscarriages and the "uncircumcised" who do not receive an honorable burial (cf. Deut 21:1–9; Isa 34:1–3; Jer 41:9; Lam 4:9).

The speaker complains that he/she is in the darkness at the bottom of the Pit (v 7), with waves of divine wrath surging over (cf. Lam 3:53–55; cf. vv 4–6, 7–9). The subject changes in v 9 to the shunning of the speaker by friends (cf. Job 19:13–32; 30:9–15; Pss 31:12; 38:12), who has become "repulsive" (lit., "an abomination") even to close friends, closed in and isolated from normal community life. V 9c suggests some sort of confinement, such as a quarantine (Anderson, II, 627; cf. Lev 13:4–46) or imprisonment (cf. Jer. 32:2), but it may be only a metaphorical account of the confinement of the distress in which the speaker is shut in by loss of strength and power. The "eye" of the speaker has grown weak or dim (9d); probably more a reference to a loss of strength, an ebbing loss of life, rather than to the loss of sight (Anderson, II, 627). The "eye(s)" is a synecdoche for the whole person, an indicator of the vitality and health of a person (cf. 1 Sam 14:27, 29; Deut 34:7; Ps 19:9; Ezra 9:8) or of the lack of vitality and of depleted strength (Gen 27:1; Job 17:7; Ps 6:8; 38:11; Lam 5:17). Job's eye grew dim because of anguish (כעש) rather than from old age (Job 17:7). There is also a play on words between עיני ("my eye") and עני ("my suffering/anguish").

The last part of v 10 (10bc) relates back to vv 2–3 and reiterates the repeated praying of the speaker. The complaint in vv 2–10a is enclosed by an "envelope" formed by vv 2–3 and 10bc, with the center of the framing verses formed by the petitions in v 3. At the same time v 10bc provides a transition to the rhetorical questions in vv 10–13. It is also possible to read two strophes in vv 2–10 (cf. Haag, "Psalm 88," 153–54): vv 2–6 and vv 7–10, with an ABCDCBA pattern: vv 2–3; v 4; v 5; v 6; v 7; vv 8–10a; v 10b, c. The description of the dead in v 6b, c, d is the central focus of the first part of the psalm. V 6a is the key expression in the entire psalm: "'set free' among the dead!"

The Land of Forgetfulness (88:11–13). The rhetorical questions in these verses present the realm of existence in the netherworld as without the wonderful deeds of Yahweh and without praise for him. Even the mighty among the dead (the Rephaim; see note 11.b.) are incapable, or unwilling, to rise and praise Yahweh. Abaddon does not hear proclamation of Yahweh's wonders, loyal-love, faithfulness, and saving deeds of righteousness. It is a terrible Land of Forgetfulness, where no voice is raised to praise the wonder of Yahweh (cf. Eccl 9:5). The praiseless quality of death is found in a number of references (see Pss 6:6; 30:10; 115:17; Isa 38:18–19; Ecclus 17:27–28). Praise of God is from the living; "The living, the living, he thanks thee" (Isa 38:19); "From the dead, as from one who does not exist, thanksgiving has ceased; he who is alive and well sings the Lord's praise" (Ecclus 17:29, RSV; see also Pss 115:17; 118:17; 119:175). "Where death is, there is no praise. Where there is life, there is praise" (C. Westermann, *The Praise of God in the Psalms*, tr. K. R. Crim [Richmond: John Knox, 1961, 1965] 159). G. von Rad declares that "Praise is man[kind]'s most characteristic mode of existence: praising and not praising stand over against one another like life and death" (*Old Testament Theology*, tr. D. M. G. Stalker [New York: Harper & Row, 1962] I, 369–70). Westermann (159) adds that, while it is not expressly stated in the OT, the conclusion must be drawn that "There cannot be such a thing as true life without praise. . . . Praise of God, like petition, is a mode of existence."

Vv 11–13 intensify the complaint of the speaker in Ps 88. They imply the need of a swift and effective divine intervention for one who is already near to Sheol and reckoned among those on their way to the pit of death. Sheol is the realm of the dead, of the Rephaim, of the grave, Abaddon, darkness, and forgetfulness. "Abaddon" is another term for the netherworld to which the dead go; the "place of destruction and perishing" (see Prov 15:11; 27:20; Job 26:6; 28:22; 31:12). Both Sheol and Abaddon were probably originally names of gods of the netherworld, as was the Greek Hades (R. Gordis, *The Book of Job* [New York: Jewish Theological Seminary of America, 1978] 278). Note that in Rev 9:11, Abaddon is the name of "the angel of the bottomless pit" (Healey, "*Rephaim*," 38, cites *rpʾ u* as a divine title; KTU 1.108.1, 19, 22: *rpʾ u mlk ʿlm* has a part in a mythical banquet).

The second complaint (88:14–19). In these verses the speaker returns to direct complaints: unanswered prayer (v 14), spurning by God (who hides his face from the speaker), long-continued affliction (perhaps physical disability which has forced the person out of normal life and into inactivity), terrors which have brought despair of life (v 16), crushing by divine wrath, and annihilation by God's terrors (v 17)—which close in on the speaker from all sides (v 18)—and desertion by lovers and friends (v 19). The reader will recognize, of course, that the complaints are similar to those of Job.

The reference to unanswered prayer in the morning in v 14 has a bitter note because the morning was a time to expect God's help (cf. Pss 46:6; 90:14; 143:8; 2 Sam 23:3-4; Zeph 3:5; Kraus, II, 776). Two words for "terrors" are used in vv 16 and 17. The word אֵמָה (אֵימָה) used in v 16 ("your terror") is used in other contexts for the terror or dread which Yahweh produces in his enemies or sends against them (see Exod 15:16; 23:27; Deut 32:25; Job 9:24; 13:21; cf. Josh 2:9). The "terrorizing power" is sent out from Yahweh and intimidates his foes. A second word for "terrors" is in v 17 in the plural noun בעותים, occurring elsewhere only in Job 6:4, though the verb בעת, "startle/terrify," appears in a number of places (Job 3:5; 7:14; 9:34; 13:11, 21; Isa 21:4; 1 Sam 16:15; Job 18:11) and the word בעתה, "terror/dismay," is found in Jer 8:15 = 14:19. The references point to a degree of hypostatization at least, in which the "terrors" of Yahweh act as his agents of destruction (cf. plague and pestilence in Hab 3:5, and "the spirit" in 1 Kgs 22:21-22). They are the demon-like beings and powers which afflict the speaker—and they are God's "terrors" and do his bidding, as they swirl around and close in for the kill. In the midst of all this, the speaker experiences the loneliness of being deserted by lovers and friends (v 19). The final word of the psalm is "darkness" (מחשך), or "dark place," such as the dark region in which travelers lose their way and places where criminals hide, waiting for an opportunity to attack violently (cf. Isa 42:16; Pss 74:20; 143:3; Isa 29:15; Lam 3:6). The colon in v 19b seems defective (see note 19.a.), but in its present form it ends the psalm with the grim prospect of the dreadful darkness of the impending netherworld confronting the speaker (cf. Job 17:13–16; 18:18).

Explanation

Ps 88 is frequently described as a gloomy psalm: "the saddest Psalm in the whole Psalter" (Kirkpatrick, 523); "unrelieved by a single ray of comfort or hope" (Weiser, 586); "stark and lonely and pain-riddled" (Durham, 352). Such descriptions are justified, though they should not be applied out of context. Fortunately, the psalm does not have to be read alone. The reader knows that the very next psalm in the present Psalter, though a lament, opens with the words חסדי יהוה, "Yahweh's deeds of loyal-love" and the speaker declares a desire to sing on and on about the merciful deeds and faithfulness of Yahweh. Praise is not far away from Ps 88, and glimmers in the opening affirmation: "Yahweh, the God of my salvation."

But these qualifications must not be allowed to dim the starkness of the lonely pain and terror of the psalm. It offers no easy comfort, derived from "cheap grace." It opens with an encouraging word, and the reader expects a change to confidence and praise as the poem develops, but the end is "the final *darkness* thumping leadenly like some muffled drum in the poet's own funeral cortege" (Durham, 352). The nocturnal silence of the long night of death is at hand.

M. Marty in his book *A Cry of Absence: Reflections for the Winter of the Heart* ([San Francisco: Harper & Row, 1983] 68) writes of Ps 88 that it deals with a "wintry landscape" of the soul: "The psalm is a scandal to anyone who isolates it from the biblical canon, a pain to anyone who must hear it apart from more lively words. Whoever devises from the Scriptures a philosophy in which everything turns out right has to begin by tearing out this page of the volume." Ps 88 may be "an embarrassment to conventional faith" (W. Brueggemann, *The Message of the Psalms,* [Minneapolis: Augsburg, 1984] 78), but it is an "embarrassment" which we should keep. Whenever we pass through the "valley of the shadow of death" we may find that it prepares the way for divine comfort.

With other laments, Ps 88 stands as a witness to the intent of the Psalms to speak to all of life, to remind us that life does not always have happy endings. Long trails of suffering and loss traverse the landscape of human existence, even for the devoted people of God. There are cold, wintry nights of the soul, when bleakness fills every horizon, and darkness seems nearly complete.

The distress in Ps 88 has the added dimension of being perceived as caused by God. The lack of explicit references to enemies in this psalm has been noted (see *Form/Structure/Setting*), but their place is taken by God and his agents of destruction. The psalm gains poetic power and intensity by the repeated complaints of God's actions; note vv 7–9, 15–19:

> You have put me . . .
> Your wrath has come down on me
> You have squashed me
> You have caused close friends to stay away
> You have made me repulsive
> Your wrath has swept over me
> Your terrors have annihilated me.

The similarity to Job is obvious. The anguish of spiritual and physical dereliction is expressed in the psalm; the speaker speaks as one forsaken whose faithful prayers are unanswered. As in the case of Job (see Job 12:1–5; 13:1–8; 16:1–5; 19:13–22), the spiritual distress is made worse by the desertion of the speaker by companions and friends. The abandonment by God is embodied and intensified by the abandonment of friends (cf. Ps 31:11–19). The "recall of personal biography" (Marty, *Cry of Absence*, 146) is of no help: "I have been afflicted and nearly dead since boyhood." God seems hidden, impervious to all prayer. This is a landscape which some have never known and perhaps never will. For others, however, its bleak features are well known because of journeys there. Some will know of it only as passing tourists, but others are longtime sojourners in it and know it well—too well.

However, all is not perplexity and hopelessness in the psalm; it is not "a psalm of mute depression" (Brueggemann, *The Message of the Psalms*, 80). The prayer is addressed to God and the speaker assumes that God hears the complaints. The speaker has "no option but to deal with Yahweh"—which is basic for all the life of Israel—the speaker must deal with Yahweh even in the silence of divine absence. Prayer and speech form a lifeline human beings cannot do without. God is addressed throughout the psalm, though he cannot be praised. The reader knows, however, that the complaints could become praise. The speaker is on the brink of death, but prayer is the lifeline which keeps him/her from the Pit. Even the greatest of those in Sheol cannot rise to praise Yahweh, but the speaker keeps death away by conversation directed to God. "This author, like Job, does not give up. He completes his prayer, still in the dark and totally unrewarded" (Kidner, 319). Further, the silence of God will not last forever. Our memory stirs and we recall a line from another psalm: "Even the darkness is not dark to thee, / the night is bright as the day, / for darkness is as light with thee" (139:12, RSV). Or, perhaps, we leap ahead and remember that "The light shines in the darkness, and the darkness has not overcome it" (John 1:5, RSV).

Will God Keep His Promises? (89:1–53)

Bibliography

Ahlström, G. W. *Psalm 89: Eine Liturgie aus dem Ritual des leidenden Königs.* Lund: CWK Gleerup, 1959. **Brunner, H.** "Gerechtigkeit als Fundament des Thrones." *VT* 8 (1958) 426–28. **Clifford, R. J.** "Psalm 89: A Lament Over the Davidic Ruler's Continued Failure." *HTR* 73 (1980) 35–47. **Craghan, J. F.** *The Psalms: A Literary Experiential Approach.* Wilmington, DE: Glazier, 1985. 151–57. **Dumortier, J.-B.** "Un Ritual D'intronisation: Le Ps. LXXXIX 2–38." *VT* 22 (1972) 176–96. **Eissfeldt, O.** "Psalm 80 und Psalm 89." *Kleine Schriften* 4 (1968) 132–36. Tübingen: Mohr, 1968. ———. "The Promises of Grace to David in Isaiah 55:1–5." In *Israel's Prophetic Heritage,* ed. B. W. Anderson and W. Harrelson. New York: Harper & Row, 1962. 196–207. **Haglund, E.** *Historical Motifs in the Psalms.* ConB, OT 23. Uppsala: CWK Gleerup. 77–82. **Johnson, A. R.** *Sacral Kingship in Ancient Israel.* Cardiff: University of Wales Press, 1955. 97–104. **Lipiński, E.** *Le Poème Royal du Psaume LXXXIX 1–5, 20–38.* Paris: Bagalla, 1967. **Mettinger, T. N. D.** *King and Messiah: The Civil and Sacral Legitimation of the Israelite Kings.* Lund: CWK Gleerup, 1976. 173, 254–56, 262–64. **Milik, J. T.** "Fragment d'une Source du Psautier (4Q Ps 89)." *RB* 73 (1966). 94–106. **Mosca, P. G.** "Once Again the Heavenly Witness of Psalm 89:38." *JBL* 105 (1986) 27–37. **Mullen, E. T., Jr.** "The Divine Witness and the Davidic Royal Grant: Ps. 89:37–38." *JBL* 102 (1983) 207–18. **Neusner, J.** "The Eighty-Ninth Psalm: Paradigm of Israel's Faith." *Judaism* 8 (1959) 226–33. **Pardee, D.** "The Semantic Parallelism of Pslam 89." In *Shelter of Eyon: Essays on Ancient Palestinian Life and Literature,* FS G. W. Ahlström, ed. W. B. Barrick and J. R. Spencer. JSOT SS. Sheffield: JSOT Press, 1984. 121–37. **Sarna, N. M.** "Psalm 89: A Study in Inner Biblical Exegesis." In *Biblical and Other Studies,* ed. A. Altmann. Cambridge, MA: Harvard UP, 1963. 29–46. **Terrien, S.** *The Elusive Presence.* New York: Harper & Row, 1978. 298–304. **Tournay, R.** "Note sur le Psaume LXXXIX, 51–52." *RB* 83 (1976) 380–89. **Veijola, T.** "Davidverheissung und Staatsvertrag." *ZAW* 95 (1983). 9–31. ———. *Verheissung in der Krise: Studien zur Literatur und Theologie der Exilszeit anhand des 89. Psalm.* Annales Academiae Scientarum Fennicae, 220. Helsinki: Suomalainen Tiedeakatemia, 1982.———. "The Witness in the Clouds: Ps. 89:38." *JBL* 107 (1988) 413–17. **Ward, J. M.** "The Literary Form and Liturgical Background of Psalm LXXXIX." *VT* 11 (1961) 321–39.

Translation

1   An Ethan-the-Ezrahite [a]-*maskil*.[b]

2 (1)   *I want to sing forever*[a] *of Yahweh's deeds of loyal-love,*[b]   (4+2+3)
     (sing of them) to one generation after another,[c]
     (and) use my mouth to make known your faithfulness.

3 (2)   *For I have declared*[a] *that your loyal-love is built to last forever,*[b]   (4+4)
     (and) that you have fixed your faithfulness in the heavens.[c]

4 (3)   *"I have made a covenant-obligation*[a] *to my chosen one;*   (3+3)
     I have sworn (an oath) to my servant David:

5 (4)   *I will establish your offspring forever,*   (3+3)
     and sustain[a] *your throne for one generation after another."* SELAH.

6 (5)   *So the heavens have praised*[a] *your wondrous work, O Yahweh;*   (4+4)
     your faithfulness also in the assembly of the Holy Ones.

7 (6)   *For who in clouds above*[a] *is equal to Yahweh?*   (4+4)
     Who is like Yahweh among divine beings?

8 (7)   God, dreaded in the council of the holy ones,   (4+4)
            great^a and awesome above all around him!

9 (8)   O Yahweh God Sabaoth!   (3+3+3)
            Who is like you, O Mighty Yah?^a—
            with your faithfulness^b around you?

10 (9)   You are the ruler of the surging sea;   (4+4)
            when its waves rise up,^a you can still them.

11 (10)   You crushed Rahab; she was like a corpse;   (4+4)
            you scattered your enemies with your powerful arm.

12 (11)   The heavens are yours; so is the earth,   (4+4)
            the world and its fulness; you have founded them!

13 (12)   You have created the North and the South;^a   (4+4)
            Tabor and Hermon sing for joy in your name.^b

14 (13)   Your arm is enclosed with might;^a   (3+2+2)
            your hand is strong;
            your right hand is raised (to strike).

15 (14)   Righteousness and justice are the foundation of your throne;   (4+4)
            Loyal-Love and Faithfulness stand before you.

16 (15) How blest are the people who know the festal shout;   (4+4)
            O Yahweh, they will walk in the light of your face!

17 (16)   They will rejoice in your name all day long,   (3+2)
            and be jubilant^a in your righteousness,^b

18 (17)   for you are the glory of their strength.^a   (3+3)
            In your goodwill you raise^b our horns.^c

19 (18)   Truly,^a Yahweh is our shield,   (3+3)
            and the Holy One of Israel is our king!

20 (19) Once^a you spoke in a vision to your loyal people,^b (4+4+3)
            and you said: "I have set a boy over warriors;^c
            I have raised up a chosen one from the people.

21 (20)   I found David my servant;   (3+3)
            with my holy oil I anointed him,

22 (21)   whom my hand will firmly support,   (3+3)
            as also my arm will make him strong.

23 (22)   No enemy will get the better of him;^a   (3+3)
            no evil person will humiliate him.^b

24 (23)   I will beat to pieces his foes before him,   (3+2)
            and strike down those who hate him.

25 (24)   My faithfulness and my loyal-love will be with him;   (3+3)
            through my name his horn will be raised.

26 (25)   I will put his (left) hand^a on the sea,   (3+2)
            and his right hand on the rivers.

27 (26)   He will declare of me, 'You are my Father,   (4+3)
            my God and the Rock of my Salvation.'

28 (27)   Also, I will make him my firstborn;   (3+3)
            the most high of the kings of the earth.

29 (28)   Forever I will keep my loyal-love for him,   (3+3)
            my covenant obligation^a to him is steadfast.

30 (29)	*I have ordained that his offspring last forever;*	(3+3)
	his throne, as long as the heavens last.[a]	
31 (30)	*If his descendants forsake my teaching,*	(3+3)
	and do not follow my commandments;	
32 (31)	*if they profane my requirements,*	(3+3)
	and do not keep my commandments,	
33 (32)	*I will punish their rebellion with a rod,*	(3+2)
	and their waywardness[a] *with plagues.*	
34 (33)	*But I will not break off*[a] *my loyal-love from him;*	(3+3)
	I will not betray my fidelity (to him).	
35 (34)	*I will not profane my covenant,*	(2+3)
	or alter what I have promised.[a]	
36 (35)	*Once for all I have sworn by my holiness;*	(3+2)
	I do not lie to David:	
37 (36)	*His offspring will continue forever*	(3+3)
	and his throne as the sun before me;	
38 (37)	*as the moon it will be established forever.*[a]	(3+3)
	And a witness in the clouds will be faithful. "[a]	
39 (36)	*But (now) you have rejected, spurned,*[a]	(3+3)
	and become enraged with your anointed.	
40 (39)	*You have repudiated*[a] *the covenant with your servant;*	(3+3)
	you have defiled his crown in the dirt.[b]	
41 (40)	*You have broken through all his walls,*	(3+3)
	(and) reduced his fortifications to ruins.[a]	
42 (41)	*All who pass by have plundered him;*	(3+3)
	he has become the scorn of his neighbors.	
43 (42)	*You have raised the right hand of his foes;*	(3+3)
	you made all his enemies rejoice.	
44 (43)	*You have even turned back (on himself) the edge of his sword,*[a]	(3+3)
	and failed to support him in battle.	
45 (44)	*You have made his glorious rulership*[a] *cease,*	(2+3)
	and thrown his throne to the ground.	
46 (45)	*You have cut short the days of his youth;*	(3+3)
	you have robed him with shame. SELAH.	
47 (46)	*How long, O Yahweh?—Will you hide forever?*[a]	(4+3)
	Will your wrath burn like fire (forever)?	
48 (47)	*Remember how short my life is!*[a]	(2+4)
	Have you created human beings for naught?[b]	
49 (48)	*What human being can live and not see death?*[a]	
	Who can save themselves from the hand of Sheol?	
50 (49)	*Where are your former deeds of loyal-love,*[a] *O Lord?*[b]	(4+3)
	(Those deeds) you promised on oath to David?	
51 (50)	*Remember, O Lord, your scorned*[a] *servants,*[b]	(4+4)
	(scorn that) I have borne in my bosom from so many people;[c]	
52 (51)	*(it was) your enemies who scorned, O Yahweh,*	(4+4)
	who scorned your anointed at every step.[a]	
53 (52)	*Blessed be Yahweh forever;*	(3+2)
	amen and amen.	

Notes

1.a. Cf. n. 88:1.f. A man named Ethan is given as a Levitical musician in 1 Chr 15:17, 19, along with Heman, Asaph, and others, and as a traditional wise person in 1 Kgs 5:11 [4:31]. A Levitical singer named Ethan is also mentioned in 1 Chr 6:42. For full discussion, see Lipiński, *Le Poème Royal du Psaume LXXXIX*, 11–19.

1.b. See n. 52:1–2.c.

2.a. The עולם ("forever/always") in 2a and 3a can be explained as an accusative of time or adverbial accusative. There is support in the versions and in some mss for reading לעולם (see *BHS*), and this form appears in vv 29a, 37a, and 53a. The word appears without a preposition in vv 2a, 3a, and 38a, and as עד־עולם in v 5a. See Mullen (*JBL* 102 [1983] 213–14). I have read the verb as modal, expressing desire or wish: "I would like to sing (if I could)."

2.b. For the plural of חסד as "deeds/acts of loyal-love," see n. 50.a. Dahood (II, 311) argues that the suffixless חסדי יהוה is equivalent to "your love, Yahweh" (citing Pss 77:12; 84:2–3; 102:16; Prov 5:16 for similar constructions and parallels), which would solve the problem of the change of persons within v 2. LXX and Theod also indicate a 2d masc s suffix: "Your loyal-loves, O Yahweh." LXX, however, retains MT's interchange of persons in 77:12 and 84:2–3, but does not in 102:16 and Prov 5:16, which may indicate that uniform person references within verses is not required (cf. Ahlström, 42).

2.c. I have retained the traditional reading for לדר ודר with the meaning of "as long as I live," but דור may have the meaning "family" or "assembly," as in Ps 14:5 (see Dahood, I, 82; III, 127; Craigie, 145, n. 5.b). In this case, the expression means that the speaker sings the praise of Yahweh in assembly for worship or in family gatherings. In any case, the expression indicates indefinite duration.

3.a. This expression seems awkward and some commentators propose a change to אָמַרְתָּ, "you have said," with support from the LXX (cf. v 20), though some versions have an imperative (Ahlström, 44). The speaker seems to be the same as in v 2 and the change to Yahweh as the speaker of the statements that follow in v 3 is not necessary. RSV adopts אמרת ("Thou hast said") and transfers it to the beginning of v 4 (Anderson, II, 631), but NRSV retains MT in v 3 and adds "You said" at the beginning of v 4.

3.b. "Loyal-Love" (חסד) is suffixless in MT, which Gunkel (390), calls "impossible." I have adopted Dahood's argument that the suffix on "your faithfulness" in v 2c serves also for "loyal-love" in 3a. Kraus (II, 779, 780), having adopted the "you have said" reading, follows with "my loyal-love" (חסדי, on the basis of haplography) and "my faithfulness." Cf. Dahood (II, 312). The עולם functions adverbially, as noted in 2.a. above. An optional reading could be: "Your loyal-love built the heavens forever; / you have made your faithfulness firm in them."

3.c. This translation assumes that שמים ("heavens") belongs with the second colon. "Heavens" is emphasized in the sentence (for the sentence construction, see GKC 143) and is parallel to עולם. Kraus (II, 778, 779) is an example of those who read כשמים, "as the heavens," which requires בהם, "in them," to be ignored or read as כהם, "as them" (Gunkel, 390; Schmidt, 166). Dahood (II, 312) wants to read a comparative *beth*, "than these"; namely, the heavens—taking "heavens" with the first colon: "your love created the heavens / but you made your fidelity more steadfast than these."

4.a. Lit., "I have cut a covenant." See *Comment*.

5.a. Lit., "build" (בנה) as in v 3.

6.a. Or, "They praise your wonders in the heavens," if we assume that the preposition "in," attached to "the assembly of the Holy Ones," applies also to "heavens" (see Dahood, II, 312–13, who rejects Gunkel's addition of the preposition to "heavens" as "both unnecessary and disruptive"). The double-duty preposition could be assumed, but inanimate subjects can be subjects which praise Yahweh (see Pss 19:2; 148:3–4, 7–9), and I have read "heavens" as the subject. The meaning in 89:6 is probably that of heavenly beings ("the heavens") who praise Yahweh; assuming metonymy (i.e., the container for the thing contained). The tense of the verb resumes that of v 3.

7.a. The sing. שחק usually means "cloud" ("clouds" in plural), but here seems to be equal to "sky/heavens" (cf. Job 37:18). The reference is to the heavenly realm, conceptualized as the sky. Thus, the rather free translation above.

8.a. This translation reads the רבה with the second colon, with LXX, Syr, and Vg, rather than with the first as in MT, which probably indicates that the masc רב should be read rather than the fem רבה (see *BHS*). However, the use of רבה as an adverb in Pss 62:3 and 78:15 (or as an accusative of extent; see GKC 118d) may mean that MT should be retained and read: "God is greatly dreaded in the council of the holy ones, / awesome above all around him." (Ahlström, *Psalm 89*, 58; the reading of

Symm with רבה as an adjective modifying סוד, "the great council of . . . ," is less probable). Cf.
Dahood (II, 313). Some interpreters propose רב הוא (e.g., Johnson, *Sacral Kingship,* 99): "He is great
and awesome above all" (the הוא has slight support in the Heb. mss, see *BHS*).

9.a. The *Translation* retains חסין, "mighty," with the "Who is like you?" as in MT; LXX and Vg read:
"O Lord God of Hosts, who is like you? / You are mighty O Lord, and your truth is round about you."
The translation above assumes three colons. The word חסין, "mighty," is not found elsewhere in MT,
though the adjective חסן occurs in Amos 2:9 ("strong") and in Isa 1:31 ("the strong one"). I take יה חסין
as a divine epithet: "Mighty Yah," which balances with Yahweh Sabaoth at the beginning of the verse.
For emendations, see Gunkel (390) and Ahlström (64). The most common change proposed is to
read חסנך, "your power" (as in Kraus and *BHS*): "Your power and your faithfulness are around you"
(Kraus). Another option is to read: "Who is a strong one, like you, O Yah / you whom faithfulness
surrounds."

9.b. Dahood (II, 313) understands the abstract "faithfulness" as meaning "faithful ones," of the
celestial court, and he may be correct.

10.a. For the unusual form of the inf. const. שאו, see Briggs, II, 266; GKC 76b.

13.a. LXX has "the north and the sea" (see *BHS*), assuming וים or וימים, perhaps understanding the
"north" (צפון) as the "mountain of God in the north" (cf. Isa 14:13; Ps 48:3); thus the two great
objects of creation: mountains and seas (Ahlström, 75).

13.b. There is slight evidence for לשמך (*BHS*): "to/about your name." Dahood (II, 314) argues
that שם ("name") has here the nuance of "presence"; thus: "in your presence."

14.a. Lit., "there is for you an arm with might (or, of a valiant person/warrior)." Dahood (II, 314)
suggests that the abstract גבורה is equal to "warrior," which he identifies as an appelletive for Yahweh:
"Yours is a powerful arm, O Warrior" (cf. 76:16). Pardee ("Semantic Parallelism," 124) reads: "Yours
is the (mighty) arm along with power."

17.a. Usually ירומו would mean "they will be exalted/uplifted" (so LXX), but the meaning seems
here to be "extol" or "be jubilant" (Dahood, II, 315; I, 77, 134–35), making the proposed emendations
to ירננו ("they will sing aloud") or ירימו ("they will lift up their voice") unnecessary. Cf. the usage of
the polel of רום in Pss 30:2; 34:4; 99:5, 9; 107:32; 118:28; 145:1.

17.b. "Righteousness" is equal to "victory" or "salvation."

18.a. The poetic suffix on עזמו ("their strength") is equal to עֻזָּם (see Briggs, II, 267; GKC 91.b).
Clifford (*HTR* 73 [1980] 43) reads "our strength" (עֻזֵּנוּ) following Cross, *Canaanite Myth,* 161, n. 71,
who observes that in old Hebrew script *men* and *nun* are frequently confused, especially in the seventh and sixth centuries B.C.E. Cf. Dahood (II, 315), who also reads "our" rather than "their," and
argues that מוֹ may refer to first person plural.

18.b. Reading hiphil with *kethiv; qere* has simple 3rd pers. sing.: מוֹ-, "our horn is exalted."

18.c. Some Hebrew texts have קרנינו, "our horns" (cf. *BHS; Briggs*, II, 267). LXX and other texts
have sing. "our horn."

19.a. The כי is read as emphatic. The ל on יהוה and קדוש is also emphatic.

20.a. The אז is used adverbially (Buttenwieser, 251; as in Ps 2:5; Gen 4:26).

20.b. Or, "godly ones" (for הסיד see Ps 52:11.a). A number of Heb. mss have the singular, "your
loyal-one," probably with Nathan and 2 Sam 7 in mind. LXX has "your sons" (τοῖς υἱοῖς σου = בָּנֶיךָ).
The Qumran fragment 4QPs 89 has בחריך [לֹ], "[to] your chosen ones." Lipiński (*Le Poème Royal du
Psaume LXXXIX,* 34) calls attention to the correlation of 4QPs 89's בחריך, "your chosen ones," with
בחירי, "my chosen one" in v 4 and argues that the חסידים ("your godly ones") is derived from the later
post-exilic period when the חסידים ("godly/pious/loyal ones") played a major role in Jewish religious
communities. Lipiński follows Milik (*RB* 73 [1966] 99) in arguing that the LXX reading is evidence
for בחריך, which can mean "your young sons/people" (from בחור, "young man").

20.c. Or, "aid/help." The reading נזר, "crown" is often adopted for עזר, "strength" (as in RSV, and in
agreement with v 40 [cf. Ps 132:18; 2 Kgs 11:12]). Cf. Dahood, II, 316; see Anderson, II, 640. It is
more probable that the reading should be "lad/boy/stripling" in keeping with the Ugaritic *gzr,* with
David and Saul in mind, or David and Goliath: "I have set (or exalted) a boy over the warrior / I have
raised up a young man from the people." I have adopted this translation (see Clifford, *HTR* 73 (1980)
44, n. 22; Dahood, II, 316; Mettinger, *King and Messiah,* 263). Otherwise, MT would read "I have put
strength on a warrior/mighty man," or "I have empowered a warrior."

23.a. The meaning of ישא is obscure, but seems to be a hiphil imperfect from נשא, which is given
the meaning "act the creditor against/make exactions of" (BDB, I, following LXX, though Symm has
"deceive/beguile," followed by others; see Briggs, II, 268; BDB, II; Ahlström, *Psalm 89,* 105). The
meaning seems to be "to take advantage of," especially with unfair means. Thus, the general

expression "get the better of." rsv has "shall not outwit him." KB (951a) derives from שוע, "treat badly."

23.b. LXX reads προσθήσει τοῦ κακῶσαι αὐτόν = יוֹסִיף לְעַנּוֹתוֹ: "no evil person will add to his mistreatment" or "mistreat him again"; cf. 2 Sam 7:10.

26.a. Lit., "his hand," but it probably means his "left hand," paralleling "his right (hand)" in the next colon. In any case, the meaning is inclusive: his power encompasses the sea and the river (see *Comment*). Cf. Dahood (II, 317) for interesting comments.

29.a. Lit., "my covenant" (בריתי), but בריח (as in v 4) represents the obligations which God has undertaken to his king.

30.a. Lit., "like the days of heaven." Cf. Deut 11:21; Eccl 45:15; Bar 1:11.

33.a. For עון, see Ps 51:4.b.

34.a. The verb is hiphil imperfect from פרר, "break/frustrate/make ineffectual" (BDB, I, 830). A change to אסיר (from סור, "turn aside/remove/take away") is sometimes suggested (e.g., Briggs, II, 269; Kraus, II, 781) but does not seem necessary (Ahlström, *Psalm 89*, 127).

35.a. Lit., "that which has gone forth from my lips."

38.a. Clifford (*HTR* 73 [1980] 46, n. 28) proposes to read עד ("witness") as part of a break-up of the stereotyped phrase עולם וָעֶד ("forever and ever"), found, e.g., in Pss 10:16; 21:5; 45:7; 48:15; 52:10; 104:5. For the phenomenon of the break-up of stereotyped expressions, he cites E. Z. Melamed, "Break-up of Stereotyped Phrases as an Artistic Device in Biblical Poetry," in *Studies in the Bible*, ed. C. Rabin, ScrHieros 8 (Jerusalem: Magnes, 1961) 115–53. rsv: "while the skies endure," represents בעד השחק or לעד כשחק. Mullen (*JBL* 102 [1983] 213–14) notes that normally the expression עולם ועד ("forever and forever") occurs with the preposition as לעולם ועד (see Pss 9:6; 45:18; 119:44; 145:1, 2, 21; Dan 12:3; Mic 4:5; Exod 15:18).For occurrences without the preposition, see Pss 10:16; 21:5; 45:7; 48:15; 52:10; 104:5. Thus the reading of עולם ועד ("forever and ever") is possible, but the retention of לעולם in vv 29a, 37a, and 53a, plus the necessity of assuming corrections in vv 2 and 3 as well as in 38, points to the wisdom of concluding that MT should be kept. The witness possibly could be the moon, as often understood, but it seems more probable that it (or he) is another entity, and that the sun (37b) and the moon (38a) refer to the durative nature of the throne.

The translation, "an enduring witness in the clouds/sky/heavens" (as in njv; Mosca, *JBL* 105 [1986] 30), is unlikely to be correct, because normal Hebrew grammar requires an attributive adjective to follow the noun immediately, except in a genitive construction (Veijola, *JBL* 107 [1988] 414). G. W. Anderson (*Peake's Commentary on the Bible*, 432b) renders v 38 as, "As the moon which is established forever, a faithful witness in the sky," assuming that יכון עולם is an implicit relative clause qualifying כירח, which is unlikely, because כסאו, "his throne," in 37b is rather clearly the subject of the verb יכון, as in 2 Sam 7:16 (see Mosca, 31, n. 16).

39.a. Dahood (II, 318) may be correct to read the two verbs as a hendiadys: "you spurned in your anger," or, "you have thoroughly rejected (your anointed)." The verb זנח, "reject/spurn" (II, "stink"), is used absolutely without an object also in Pss 44:24; 74:1; 77:8. rsv, "But now thou dost cast off" represents ועתה ("but now") for MT's ואתה (cf. Gunkel, 395, who rejects the change as "an offense against Hebrew style"). See *Comment*.

40.a. The verb is a piel perf. from נאר, "abhor/spurn," a meaning parallel to חלל, "profane/defile" (Gunkel, 394). The verb occurs elsewhere only in Lam 2:13 (see Anderson, II, 644; Ahlström, *Psalm 89*, 132, translates as "break"). "Disdain" is another possibility.

40.b. Lit., "to the ground/earth"; perhaps referring to the Underworld, the realm of the dead (cf., e.g., Isa 26:19; Jonah 2:7; Ps 22:30; Job 17:16), a land of gloom and darkness. Metaphorically, of course, the meaning is "utterly/worst-case" (as Dahood, II, 318).

41.a. For מחתה, "terror/destruction/ruin," see Isa 54:14; Jer 17:17; 48:39; Prov 10:14–15, 29; 13:3; 14:28; 18:7; 21:15. Ahlström (*Psalm 89*, 133) argues that in Prov 13:3, מחתה is antithetical to life and can be a word for Sheol, the realm of the dead. Also, Prov 18:7.

44.a. Lit., "the stone of his sword," but here צור must mean "edge of." Emendations are suggested: e.g., change to צר, "flint knife" (Josh 5:2, 3), but the "flint of his sword" (a sword sharp as flint?) is little improvement. A change to מצר, "from a foe/enemy" or "from the distress/oppression," yields translations like: "You have let the sword turn back before the foe" (Gunkel)—i.e., become ineffective in battle or even be turned back against the one using the sword (cf. Kraus, II, 792). LXX reads τὴν βοήθειαν ("the help/support"). G. R. Driver (in *Studies in Old Testament Prophecy*, ed. H. H. Rowley [Edinburgh: Clark, 1950] 55) argues that צר is related to Akkadian *sarāru*, "to dart/flash," and thus "the flash of his sword" or "his flashing sword" (reading צר חרבו). It seems sufficient, however, to conclude that צור was originally a flint knife, or that flint formed the cutting edge of a knife made from other material, which in time came to be used as an idiom for the sharp edge of a knife or sword (see Eerdmans, 425; Anderson, II, 645–46).

45.a. The expression מטהרו is not found elsewhere in MT. The form appears to be a hiphil perf. 2nd pers. masc. sing. (of טהר, "to be clean, pure") plus the prep. מן. However, the mss and interpretative history vary, and the expression has often been treated as a noun (with a "euphonic" dagesh, as in מקדש, "sanctuary," in Exod 15:17 or מנזר, "consecrated one," in Nah 3:17). If the prep and verb are assumed, the reading is: "You have made (him) cease (or be removed) from his purity/splendor." If a noun is read, the reading is: "You have removed his purity/splendor." For the linguistic history, see Delitzsch, III, 43; Perowne, 156; Briggs, II, 270. It seems better to treat the word as a noun, derived from the common idea of טהר as "cleanness/purity" and thus "luster/splendor/brilliance." The idea of "splendor" is supported by the versions and finds a bit of additional strength from the Ugaritic *thr*, "jewel/pearl" (Ahlström, 137; Dahood, II, 319). The translation above is based on NEB, but follows a correction of the text proposed by Johnson (*Sacral Kingship*, 103, n. 1), reading מטה טהרו, "the rod/scepter of his purity/splendor," which assumes a case of simple haplography, a correction which is strengthened by the short colon in v 45a, which seems to lack a word. The translation "his glorious rule" in NEB (REB has, "You have put an end to his splendour") is based on the emendation מטה הדו ("the scepter of his majesty"), but its meaning is probably correct and fits the emendation I have adopted and, indeed, that of the unchanged text, since even if the meaning "purity" is adopted, it must refer to the brilliant quality of the royal rule. For other proposed changes, including the change of the verb (here hiphil perf. of שבת = הסיר, "remove," BDB, 991–92, or else "cause to cease to exist/destroy") to שברת, "you have broken," see *BHS*, Briggs, Gunkel (395), and others. Ahlström (*Psalm 89*, 137) mentions the possibility that the מטהר refers to some sort of insignia of the royal office: a crown, scepter, or jewel worn on a king's robe.

47.a. For the superlative force of לנצח, see n. 52:7.b.

48.a. MT probably has אנ- missing after the verb זכר ("O remember . . ."), which is more probable than the assumption that אדני ("O my Lord") is missing. The meaning appears to be: "O remember that I am not of long duration," or, "Think about me! How long is my life?" (cf. Alhström, *Psalm 89*, 153). The change of חלד "lifetime," to חדל (with the support of two mss), "close/come to an end," and the pointing of חדל as an adj. חָדֵל, "fleeting, passing") would ease the reading somewhat: "O remember! I—how transitory (am I)!" Or with אני מה-חדל yielding: "O remember, how transitory I am" (Anderson, II, 647). LXX reads: "Remember what my real nature (ἡ ὑπόστασις) is." Cf. Dahood (II, 326), who proposes another line of emendation to get: "Remember my sorrow (אוני), the few days of my life."

48.b. The second colon of this verse also has some difficulty. Lit., "Concerning what vanity (or futility) have you created all the sons of humankind?" *BHS* proposes to read עולם השוא for על-מה-שוא, taking the עולם with the first colon: "Remember, I am not everlasting / Did you create all humankind for nothing (vanity)?" This reading seems to follow Johnson (*Sacral Kingship*, 103, n. 2, who argues that מה corresponds to an Arabic negative, as in 1 Kgs 12:16; Cant 8:4, and that חלד corresponds to an Arabic word for "lasting"). LXX has: "For have you created all humankind in vain (or without reason)?"—expecting the answer "No."

49.a. Lit., "Who has become a human being (גבר), and he (or, who) will not see death?"

50.a. Lit., "your loyal-loves," but the plural refers to deeds of mercy, love, and kindness; e.g., Gen 32:11 [10]; Isa 63:7; Ps 25:6; cf. Isa 55:3; 2 Chr 6:42; Lam 3:22; Pss 17:7; 107:43–44. The same is true in v 2. See C. R. North, *The Second Isaiah* (Oxford: Clarendon Press, 1964) 257, who stresses the distinction between the singular חסד and the plural חסדים.

50.b. Many Heb. mss have יהוה for אדני here and in v 51.

51.a. Lit., "the reproach of your servants." The word חרפה can mean "reproach/scorn/taunting/humiliation" and probably "abuse." Cf. Pss 69:8, 10, 11, 20, 21; 71:13; 74:22; 78:66; 79:4, 12.

51.b. Twenty-four Heb. mss and Syr read the singular ("servant"), probably with the king in mind. LXX and Jerome agree with MT's plural. Dahood (II, 320) explains the plural עבדיך ("servants") as a plural of majesty referring to the king, parallel to the plural "loyal people" or "devoted ones," in v 20, which is also a plural of majesty referring to the king, according to Dahood. I think he is incorrect in both cases.

51.c. A difficult colon, which has usually been judged to be defective (e.g., Briggs, II, 270; Perowne, 157). The singular number of the speaker, after the plural in 51a, the strange כל-רבים ("all the many people"), and the use of "fear in my bosom" have been questioned. The use of "bosom" (חיק) with the verb נשא in Num 11:12 and Isa 40:11 suggests that the combination is an expression of care and love, like a parent for a child or of a good shepherd caring for sheep. If a negative connotation is assumed for v 51, the usage may be ironic: a strong expression of personal pain and hurt. The scorn (חרפה) from many peoples is borne in the speaker's bosom (an understanding of the colon which is supported by LXX) rather than "All the many peoples I bear (with love) in my bosom." I have assumed that "scorn" (חרפה) is the object of the verb; lit., "remember the scorn of your servants" = "scorn heaped on your servants." The expression כל־רבים עמים is taken to mean "all the many different peoples," semi-parallel, at least, to כל גוים רבים ("all the many nations") in Ezek 31:6, which probably means "all great nations of every kind" (so W. Zimmerli, *Ezekiel 2*, Hermeneia, tr. James D. Martin [Philadelphia: Fortress, 1969, 1983] 143). Ahlström (*Psalm 89*, 160) notes the unusual word order of רבים עמים, but observes that רבים or רבות is found before the word it modifies in Ps 32:10; Prov 7:26; 31:29; Neh 9:28. Zimmerli (*Ezekiel 2*, 143) thinks that גוים רבים, ("many nations,") is a "fixed comprehensive expression" which occurs in Ezek 26:3; 38:23; 39:27 (with the article); also עמים רבים ("many peoples") is found in Ezek 3:6; 27:33; 32:3, 9–10; 38:6, 8–9, 15. I assume that v 51b is an asyndetic relative clause (so Ahlström, 160). rsv's "the insults of the peoples" seems to have the correct meaning, but the emendation of כל־רבים to כלמת ("insult/reproach of"), as in Ezek 36:15, does not seem to be necessary (cf. Thomas, *TRP*, 37). *BHS* proposes, with some versions (also Gunkel, 396) כל־ריבי עמים, "all of the controversy (quarrels/wrangling) of the peoples," or כל־דבת עמים, "all the defamation of the peoples." See the discussion by Tournay (*RB* 83 [1976] 382–86).

52.a. Lit., "the heels of your anointed."

Form/Structure/Setting

Ps 89 opens with a declaration of praise in vv 2–3, with the speaker affirming a willingness to sing and speak the praise of Yahweh to generation after generation. This is followed in vv 4–5 with the quotation of an oracle from Yahweh in which he declares that he made a covenant with David. Vv 6–19 are hymnic in nature, setting forth reasons for the praise of Yahweh and closing with the affirmation in v 19 that Yahweh is Israel's shield and king. A long oracle-vision follows in vv 20–38, which recalls and quotes a long list of divine promises to David and his posterity. This section is followed by a complaint in vv 39–46, expounding the strong contrast between the promises in vv 20–38 and the present reality. The complaint is followed by expostulation and petitions in vv 47–51. V 53 is a closing benediction for the psalm and for Book III of the Psalter.

Generally speaking there are three main types of material in the psalm:

2–3, 6–19	Hymnic praise
4–5, 20–38	Recall of divine oracle about David
39–52	Lament relating to the divine failure to maintain the servant-king

How do all these parts function together? Obviously, it would be easy to conclude that the psalm is a collection of disparate parts, probably reflecting a history of composition, and this conclusion is not uncommon in critical commentaries. E.g., Briggs (II, 250) divides the psalm into 89A (vv 2–3, 6–15, plus 16–17) and 89B (vv 18–46, with vv 47–52 appended by the editor who combined the psalms; Buttenwieser (239) also divides the psalm into 89A (vv 2–3, 6–19) and 89B (vv 4–5, 20–52, plus the last words of v 2 and the first two words of v 3, partially emended, read at the beginning of v 4). Gunkel (386–94) argues for a hymn in vv 2, 3, 6–19, joined to a lament in vv 39–52 by the insertion of the material in vv 20–38 (for further references, see Clifford, *HTR* 73 [1980] 35). Lipiński (*Le Poème Royal du Psaume LXXXIX*, 20–38) argues on the basis of the

Qumran text 4QPs 89 for an original royal psalm of vv 2–5 and 20–38 to which the other parts were added at later times. In his opinion vv 6–19 form an early insertion and vv 39–52 are later. With some rearrangement of the psalm he concludes with a unified poem of a preamble (v 2) and seven strophes as follows: 2, 3–5, 20b–22, 26, 23–24, 25, 27–28, 31–33, 34–36a, 29b*, 30, 37–38.

The tradition-history approach is also found in Kraus (II, 781–85) who suggests that vv 2–3, 6–19 formed a hymn (or were hymnic elements) on the power of Yahweh, which were taken over by the singer of the oracle material in vv 4, 5, 20–38 and the lament in vv 39–52; all elements of a lament over the death of Josiah in 609 B.C.E. (citing Zech 12:10–14, which he understands as referring to a great lamentation over the death of Josiah at Megiddo; see also 2 Chr 35:25). Veijola (*Verheissung in der Krise*), influenced heavily by his analysis of the psalm's stichometric structure, argues that the oldest part of the psalm is a hymn in vv 2–3, 6–19, which was expanded into a long psalm of a different type by the material in vv 4–5, 20–46. The earlier long psalm was supplemented by the lament material in vv 47–52 (divided into two strophes of vv 47–49 and 50–52), which made it suitable for lamentation ceremonies in the later exilic period (210). He relates the psalm to Deuteronomistic material and argues for the location of such material at Mizpah and Bethel in the exilic period and positions Ps 89 at Bethel (in relation to later phases of the Deuteronomistic history). He suggests that the hymn is probably an adaptation of a Northern Israelite prototype (120, 210). Veijola (133–43) treats the psalm as a collective expression, a lament of the people (communal lament). Haglund (*Historical Motifs*, 82) agrees with Veijola's conclusion that Ps 89 shows strong Deuteronomistic influence (Veijola, 60–70, 76) but argues that the oracles and lament parts are older than 2 Sam 7 // 1 Chr 17 and should be traced back to monarchial times rather than be dated in the exile.

Goulder (*The Psalms of the Sons of Korah*, 213–19) argues that, despite the lack of explicit reference to Korah in the title, the psalm is a Korahite psalm, with an original hymn in vv 2–5, 6–19 (89A; minus any reference to David) composed for use in worship on Mount Tabor (note v 13), later accepted by the priests at Dan (which Goulder argues was the original context of all the Korahite psalms), and transferred to Jerusalem after the fall of the Northern Kingdom. In Jerusalem the psalm was greatly expanded with the oracle and lament material, probably as the result of a historical disaster; possibly the death of Josiah, but much more probably the situation with King Jehoiachin (also called Jeconiah and Coniah) after 597 B.C.E. Thus, he argues for a hymn from Tabor, adapted to the Danite autumn festival in the eighth century, and later expanded for use at Jerusalem in the early part of the sixth century.

An alternative explanation of the structure of the psalm, and not necessarily antithetical to a history of composition, is to explain it as some sort of liturgy. Johnson (*Sacral Kingship*, 22–23) argues for a lamentation-type ceremony after the royal forces, or at least the king, have been overtaken by some disaster and the king is deeply humiliated, attributing his trouble to the anger of Yahweh. However, later in the same book (103–4) and in *CPIP*, 80, he argues that the psalm reflects "not an historical event . . . but a ritual drama which served to remind both king and commoner that salvation for Israel and indeed for the world at large could only be brought about by self-denial on the part of the David king."

He suggests that the king is identified as the Servant of Yahweh in the psalm, and also as a "humble Messiah" who realizes that he can wield power only by "ultimate dependence upon the goodwill and power of Yahweh." Ahlström (*Psalm 89*, 26) attempts to understand the psalm in terms of the Davidic king in renewal-of-life rites. Eaton (*Kingship*, 121–22) favors the psalm as relating to royal humiliation in festal drama, and argues for a coherence in the psalm which represents the autumn festival's themes of the creator-kingship role of Yahweh and that of the Davidic covenant. J.-B. Dumortier (*VT* 22 [1972] 176–96) argues for vv 2–38 as originally a poem for a royal enthronement celebration, probably related to enthronement rites in the new year festival.

The theory of a ritual humiliation ceremony for the Israelite king (succinctly summarized by Eaton, *Kingship*, 109–11, 121–22) postulates that the king underwent a rite of humiliation analogous to that for the Babylonian king in the Babylonian new year festival (for discussion, see H. Frankfort, *Kingship and the Gods* [Chicago: University of Chicago Press, 1948] 318–20). According to the theory, after being humiliated by ritual suffering and attacks by foes, the king was delivered and restored to power with renewed vigor. The ceremony would have been a ritual lesson in dependence on Yahweh for life and power for king and people. Johnson's cumulative arguments for this theory involving numerous psalms, have a degree of persuasiveness, and it is possible that such rites were conducted.

On the other hand, the evidence is not very firm when put to the test. The theory has been vigorously rejected by Mowinckel (*PIW*, I, 244–46; II, 253–55; idem, *He That Cometh*, tr. G. W. Anderson [Oxford: Blackwell, 1956] 86–87; idem, review of Ahlström, *Psalm 89*, in *JSS* 5 [1960] 291–98) and others (see Ward, *VT* 11 [1961] 327–37). Ward (334) points to serious difficulties in assuming that Ps 89 belonged to such a ritual: (1) the psalm says nothing about a ritualistic humiliation of the king; the problem in Ps 89 is violation of the covenant by God (vv 39–40)—involving not the discipline of the king (vv 31–34) but a breaking of a solemn oath on the part of God; (2) no restoration after humiliation is described, nor is there any certainty of hearing expressed; (3) in Ps 89 the exaltation of the king *precedes* the humiliation; and (4) the evidence for ritual humiliation in other royal psalms is either nonexistent or conjectural. The evidence for the direct relationship of psalms to an actual rite of humiliation seems too uncertain to be a very firm foundation for any psalm, but it is especially weak for Ps 89.

Other scholars have defended the unity of Ps 89 with less conviction about a definite ritual context. Stuhlmueller (II, 62) writes, "The psalm's principal purpose is to serve as a liturgical lament over military defeat and is general enough to express the people's sorrow and dismay over any defeat." Ward (*VT* 11 [1961]) marshalls a number of arguments based on metrical considerations, logical coherence, and vocabulary (a table is given on p. 339 of twenty-five key words which occur in all the major divisions of the psalm; see also the tables in Sarna, "Psalm 89," 31, 32) for the unity of the psalm from its time of origin. Ward is very tentative about the context of the psalm, but seems to lean toward a private literary composition after 587 B.C.E. (338).

More recently Clifford (*HTR* 73 [1980]) has endeavored to support the unity of the psalm by explaining it as a "coherent poem of lament," without giving any specific context of worship. The case in his valuable article is weakened somewhat by a considerable amount of textual emendation and rereading. On the whole, however, the cumulative impact of the arguments for the unity of the psalm is considerable and the treatment of it as an integrated unit in its present form is a sound procedure. It is well to remember, however, that "an intelligible unity" (Ward, 323) may result from the skilled re-use and juxtapositioning of already existing literary material; we need not assume that only a "patchwork" results from the use of originally unrelated elements. A fine artistry may be produced by the interweaving and shaping of disparate components borrowed from older traditions and preexisting material. This is especially true when the purpose of the composition is directed toward the presence of ambiguity and contradiction.

The key to the interpretation of the psalm in its present form is found in the lament in vv 39–52. The hymn and the oracle must be read in relation to the distress reflected in these verses. The promises of Yahweh and his praise have been called into serious question by the trouble and pain of disasters and unfulfilled expectations which are expressed in the last part of the psalm. The situation projected in these verses is typically (for the Psalms) both specific and generalized. The Davidic king has been humiliated in defeat; the walls and fortifications of his city have been breached and reduced to ruins (v 41). His crown has been defiled in the dirt by foes who plunder and scorn him (vv 40, 42). His sword has failed in battle and turned back on himself (v 44), and the days of his youth have been cut short (v 46). His rulership has ended in shame, with his throne thrown to the ground (v 45). The speaker in vv 47–52 pleads the case with Yahweh on the basis of the brevity of human life and the inability of human beings to save themselves from death. Yahweh is implored to remember that those who scorn his loyal servants are his enemies (vv 51–52). Yahweh's former deeds of loyal-love are not now in evidence (v 50).

Do these verses indicate a specific historical situation? Many interpreters have answered the question in the affirmative, but there is no agreement as to the specific context. The time of King Rehoboam after the reign of Solomon has been suggested (Delitzsch, II, 33; Eerdmans, 428; a view which Kirkpatrick, 531, calls "wholly improbable"). Sarna ("Psalm 89," 44–45) argues strongly for the crisis during the reign of Ahaz of Judah in 735–34 B.C.E. The best arguments, at least for me, are those for the time of the youthful Jehoiachin and his aborted reign after the attack on Jerusalem by the Babylonians in 597 B.C.E. The shocking death of Josiah (609 B.C.E.) could still have been a major factor in the disappointment and distress over the promises of God for the Davidic dynasty (see Kraus, II, 784; Anderson, II, 631). Goulder (*The Psalms of the Sons of Korah*, 218) argues for a play on the name of Jehoiachin-Jaconiah-Coniah (כניהו—יכניה—יהויכין) and the verb כון ("establish/fix") in vv 3, 5, 23, and 38 in Ps 89. But none of these historical contexts is totally convincing and the elusive nature of a historical setting suggests that the fixation of a specific context may not be very important (note Clifford, *HTR* 73 [1980] 47).

My own approach is as follows. First, the psalm probably reflects different contexts and may have been used on various occasions. The hymnic-oracle material in vv 2–39 may have been derived from royal enthronement ceremonies in pre-exilic Israel (cf. Weiser, 591). The psalm probably had a history of supplementary additions related to its use on different occasions (Durham, 352; cf.

Lipiński's argument that the core of the original psalm was composed of vv 1–5 [*Le Poéme Royal du Psaume LXXXIX*, 20–38]). The lament in vv 39–52 was never an independent work and was intentionally designed to follow vv 20–38 (Mosca, *JBL* 105 [1986] 29, n. 9).

Second, the arguments against the post-exilic period for the present psalm are weighty (e.g., silence about the destruction of Jerusalem and the temple and the deportation of large numbers of people; see Sarna, "Psalm 89," 42–43), but I do not find them to be as persuasive as do some commentators. It is not clear that vv 41–45 *cannot* refer to the ruin of Jerusalem, more likely in 597, but not totally incompatible with 587 (see the extensive argumentation in Veijola, *Verheissung in der Krise*, 95–112). Beyond this, suppose we think about the period after 515 B.C.E. when the temple had been rebuilt and Jerusalem restored, though not yet in a splendid way. The Davidic monarchy had not been restored and the old hopes and expectations had languished, though still remembered and repeated. The collapse of high anticipation associated with Zerubbabel, as reflected in Haggai (1:1; 2:4–5, 20–23) and Zechariah (3:8; 4:6–10; 6:9–15), for whatever reasons, could have precipitated a crisis of faith like that found in Ps 89. The extensive similarity of vocabulary between Ps 89 and the Deuteronomistic literature set forth by Veijola (50–53) is no barrier to the later dating since Malachi, for example, shows considerable influence from Deuteronomic language. Veijola's comparison with other exilic literature (54–59; Lamentations, Pss 44; 60; 74; 77; 79; 80; 102; 108; Isa 63:6–64:11, Mic 7:8–20, Jer 33:19–26, and Deutero-Isaiah) shows an affinity with such writings but does not rule out the use of such language at a later date (Mettinger, *King and Messiah,* 256, argues that Ps 89 is a "re-working of the prophecy of Nathan in the spirit of the Dtr movement," but he resists dating the psalm in the exile). All in all, the fixing of a specific historical context is an uncertain business, but the present psalm is probably either exilic or post-exilic (i.e., after 597 B.C.E., but more probably after 500 B.C.E.).

Third, the speaker in vv 39–52 need not be the king or a member of the Davidic family. It is more probable that we should identify the speaker throughout the psalm as one of Yahweh's faithful "servants" (v 51), pious people who struggled to maintain faith in the bleak spiritual contexts of periods like that reflected by the Book of Malachi (perhaps, 500–450 B.C.E.). The "servants" of Yahweh seem to be a descriptive expression for loyal worshipers during exilic and post-exilic times (e.g., Isa 54:17; 56:6; 63:17; 65:8, 9, 13, 14, 15; 66:14; Dan 1:12, 13; Neh 1:6, 7, 10, 11; Job 42:7, 8).

Fourth, the relationship of Ps 89 and the Nathan oracle for David in 2 Sam 7 has received much attention, notably the argument of Sarna that Ps 89 is an "exegetical adaptation, not another recension" of the oracle ("Psalm 89," 45; supported by M. Fishbane, *Biblical Interpretation in Ancient Israel* [Oxford: Clarendon Press, 1985] 466–67). The dependence of Ps 89 on the tradition of the Nathan oracle need not, however, mean that Ps 89 is dependent on the *text* of 2 Sam 7. Both Sarna (37–39) and Fishbane (466–67) note the "strategic changes" and modifications of the content of 2 Sam 7 in Ps 89: (1) the key reference to the temple project in 2 Sam 7:10–13 is missing in Ps 89; (2) the promise in 2 Sam 7:10 (of respite for the people from their enemies) is applied to David alone in Ps 89:23–24; (3) the father-son relationship in 2 Sam 7:14 refers to David's son, but in Ps 89:27–28 it applies to David alone; (4) the threatened punishment of David's son for sin in 2 Sam 7:14 is referred to the entire Davidic dynasty in Ps 89:31–33; (5) there is no reference to a dream-vision (Ps 89:20) given to the devotees of Yahweh in 2 Sam 7 (though the reference to night in 2 Sam 7:4 might suggest one, and "loyal ones" could conceivably be Nathan and David); and (6) the strong emphasis on covenant in 89:4, 35–36, 50 is lacking in 2 Sam 7. Thus Ps 89 is likely to be a reinterpretation of an earlier text or a recension of the same tradition. In any case, the emphasis in Ps 89 is on the promises of lasting stability for the Davidic dynasty. The author of Ps 89 had as a sole concern "the Divine Pledge of perpetuity to the Davidic dynasty as such and . . . the glaring contrast between the promised ideal and the present reality" (Sarna, 39).

Finally, the placement of Ps 89 in the canonical form of the Psalter is worth consideration. Goulder (*The Psalms of the Sons of Korah*, 211) notes that there are verbal links between Pss 88 and 89: "loyal-love," "faithfulness," "righteousness" in 88:11–13 and the same words in 89:2, 3, 5, 9, and 17 and notes the use of the verb ידע ("known/make known") in 88:13 and 89:2. A planned placement of the royal psalms in the formation of the Psalter is suggested by Childs, who argues that the royal psalms are the backbone of the Psalter, strategically situated through the collections rather than gathered together in groups, as is the case with other major categories of psalms. These psalms arose originally out of kingship ideology in monarchial Israel, but "were treasured in the Psalter for a different reason, namely as a witness to the messianic hope which looked for the consummation of God's kingship through his Anointed One" (*Introduction to the Old Testament as Scripture* [Philadelphia: Fortress, 1979] 517).

A student of Childs, G. H. Wilson, has pursued this matter further (see his *The Editing of the Hebrew Psalter*, 212–15; idem, "The Use of Royal Psalms at the 'Seams' of the Hebrew Psalter," *JSOT* 35 [1986] 85–94; see also, D. M. Howard, Jr., "Editorial Activity in the Psalter: A State-of-the-Field Survey," *Word and World* 9 [1989] 279, 281) and argued that Ps 89 is primarily concerned to recall the covenant between Yahweh and David and represents a theological reevaluation of this relationship as it is reflected in Pss 2–72. The covenant with David in the content of Ps 89 is an event of the distant past, and most importantly, it is a *failed covenant* (Wilson, *JSOT* 35 [1986] 91; idem, *The Editing of the Hebrew Psalter*, 214). "It is this problem of the failure of YHWH to honor the Davidic covenant that stands at the heart of Ps. 89 and is the object of the plea with which the psalm and the first major segment of the Psalter end" (Wilson, *JSOT* 35 [1986] 91).

Wilson suggests that Pss 2–72 reflect a more positive and hopeful view of the Davidic kingship, "while the extension of 73–89 modifies these hopes in the light of the exilic experience" (91). Further, Wilson thinks that Pss 90–106 (Book IV) function as an editorial "center" of the present Psalter and provide "answers" to the problem of the failed covenant put forth by Ps 89 as follows: (1) Yahweh is king; (2) Yahweh was a "refuge" long before the monarchy (in the Mosaic period); (3) Yahweh will continue to be a refuge without the monarchy; (4) Yahweh will bless his faithful servants who trust in him (see Wilson, *The Editing of the Hebrew Psalter*, 215; Howard, *Word and World* 9 [1989] 281). This approach needs additional study and reflection (for example, how are Pss 88 and 89 related?), but it seems to make sense and suggests a plausible rationale for the placement of Ps 89 in the Psalter.

Comment

Hymnic introduction and recall of the covenant with David (89:2–5). In vv 2–3 an unidentified speaker declares his/her desire to sing the praise of Yahweh. Some key ideas in the psalm appear in these verses: "deeds of loyal-love" (חסדי), "your faithfulness" (אמונתך), "forever" (עולם), "generation after generation" (לדר־ודור), "heavens" (שמים), and the verbs "build" (בנה) and "fix/establish" (כון). Obviously, the emphasis is on the firmly fixed faithfulness of Yahweh and his deeds of loyal-love for his people. The "deeds of loyal-love" are those acts by Yahweh which have demonstrated his grace and saving actions in keeping with his faithfulness to his covenant obligation to Israel (cf. Pss 17:7; 25:16; 36:6; 107:43; Isa 63:7; Kraus, II, 585). Cf. the חסדי דוד, "the sure mercies of David" or "deeds of loyal-love for David" in Isa 55:3, which is a reference to the commitment and loyalty of Yahweh to David, transferred to the nation Israel—or better, to those servants of Yahweh who compose the true and faithful nation (cf. Isa 54:17; 56:6; 63:17; 65:8, 9, 13, 14, 15; 66:14; on Isa 55:3 and Ps 89, see Eissfeldt, "The Promises of Grace to David in Isaiah 55:1–5"; C. Westermann, *Isaiah 40–66* [Philadelphia: Westminster, 1969] 283–84). Whether or not there is actual literary dependence of Isa 55:3 on Ps 89 remains an open question, but both were drawn from the same traditions, and Westermann (284) is probably correct to argue that Isa 55:1–5 is a refutation of laments about the breach of the covenant with David, such as that found in Ps 89. Note the importance of the verb "build" (בנה) in the Nathan oracle (2 Sam 7:5, 7, 13, 27; 1 Chr 17:4, 10, 12; also of כון ("fix/establish") in 2 Sam 7:16, 24, 26; 1 Chr 17:11, 12, 14, 24, and the verb אמן (see Ps 89:29, 38; the root of אמונה, "faithfulness," in 89:2, 3, 6, 9, 25, 34, 50) in 2 Sam 7:16; 1 Chr 17:23, 24.

The brief oracle in vv 4–5 is a quotation of Yahweh's covenant commitment forever to David and to his offspring. The meaning of ברית ("covenant") has been a controversial subject in biblical study, but there are good grounds for assuming that its primary meaning is that of "obligation/commitment/responsibility." Many biblical scholars have assumed that the primary meaning of ברית is "relationship" rather than "obligation" or "binding responsibility." The most basic idea in the usage of ברית, however, seems to be that of "obligation" or "duty": to take an obligation upon oneself, or to impose an obligation or duty on another, or to mutually accept obligations, and the like. In reality, the difference between the obligation idea of covenant and the relationship idea is not so great. No relationship of any significance can exist without obligations, and the assumption or imposition of obligations creates relationship of some kind. Thus Yahweh assumed responsibility for the saving and care of Israel as an act of loyal-love on his part; at the same time he imposed obligations on Israel as a part of the covenant relationship. Ps 89 is concerned with the terrible problem of the apparent failure of Yahweh to keep the obligations which he assumed for the Davidic dynasty (for a survey of the complicated course of covenant study in the past hundred years, see E. W. Nicholson, *God and His People: Covenant and Theology in the Old Testament* [Oxford: Clarendon Press, 1986]; also, M. Weinfeld, *TDOT*, II, 253–79).

Vv 2–5 present the major thesis that the stability of the Davidic dynasty should be as lasting as the faithfulness of God in the heavenly realm, though the reader is not fully aware of the import of the first part of the psalm until the entire psalm is read. Vv 4–5 seem to be a deliberate interruption of the context in order to alert the reader to an unexpected message.

The close of the opening section of the psalm is marked off by the *selah* in the present text after v 5; a pause which serves to intensify the beginning of the hymn in v 6. The expression "forever" (עולם) and "generation after generation" (לדר ודר) in vv 2 and 5 serves as an inclusion, or framing feature, for this section, which is also bound together in a chiastic ABBA pattern of the verbs "build" (v 3)—"fix" (v 3)—"fix" ("establish") (v 5)—"build" (v 5): בנה—כון—כון—בנה (Stuhlmueller, II, 63–64). Within the frame of these four verbs there are two verbs which express Yahweh's commitment to David: "I have cut a covenant/assumed the obligations of a covenant" (כרתי ברית) and "I have taken an oath" (נשבעתי), both in v 4. A covenant is confirmed by the taking of an oath (see Weinfeld, *TDOT*, II, 256; note Gen 21:22–24; 26:26–28; Deut 29:9–13 [10–14]; Josh 9:15–20; 2 Kgs 11:4; Ezek 16:8, 59; 17:13–15, 18). Occasionally, "oath/curse" (אלה) is used for "covenant"; e.g., Deut 29:11 [12]; Neh 10:30 [29].

A hymn of praise to Yahweh as the cosmic ruler (89:6–15). These verses seem to form a segment of the larger section of vv 6–19. The praise of vv 2–3 is continued, with vv 4–5 functioning as the insertion in an "envelope" (or AXB) pattern between vv 2–3 and vv 6–8. The direct address to Yahweh in 2c–3 is resumed in v 6, and the third-person testimony-language of v 2a,b is resumed in vv 7–8 (an AB X BA pattern in vv 1–8).

The main subject of vv 6–15 is the cosmic rulership of Yahweh, who is incomparable among the holy ones, the divine beings, in the heavenly skies (vv 7–8). Yahweh's cosmic rulership is (1) marked by the praise of the heavenly beings (vv 6–8), and (2) characterized by his "faithfulness" (note the אמונתך ["your faithfulness"] in vv 6 and 9). The "assembly of the holy ones" (קהל קדשים) is equivalent to the "council of the holy ones" (סוד־קדשים) in v 8. Cf. Ps 82:1; Jer 23:18; 1 Kgs 22:19–21; Isa 6:1–3; Job 1–2. For the idea of סוד, see n. 55:15.a. For the "sons of God/divine beings" (בני אלים), see Ps 29:1; cf. Ps 82.

The metaphorical content of vv 6–9 is drawn from the concept of a heavenly assembly around a great kingly God, who rules as a respected, even dreaded, sovereign. The use of אמונתך ("your faithfulness") stresses the reliability of Yahweh. The word suggests a "conscientious way of acting" which reflects inner stability and consistency (A. Jepsen, *TDOT*, I, 317; cf. v 34; 2 Kgs 12:16 [15]; 2 Kgs 22:7 // 2 Chr 34:12; 1 Chr 9:22, 31; Lam 3:22–23; Pss 33:4; 36:6; 40:11; 88:12; 92:3; 96:13; 98:3; 100:5; 143:1). "Faithfulness" is contrasted with *sheqer* ("falsehood/lie," שקר); see Prov 12:17, 22; 14:5; Jer 5:1, 2; 9:2 [3]; Isa 59:4; Ps 119:29, 20. Jeremiah laments the terrible lack of אמונה in Jer 5:1, 3; 7:28; 9:2 [3]; cf. Isa 59:1–8; Prov 12:2 [1]; 20:6; Deut 32:4, 20. Yahweh's אמונה is important in Ps 89 because it forms a major basis for the lament and petitions later in the psalm. The prayer in the psalm reminds God of the inseparable linkage between his faithfulness and his promises. For him to ignore his promises would violate the reliability which is inherent in his personhood and in his relationship with Israel (cf. Hos. 2:22 [20]). Note that אמונה occurs in Ps 89 in vv 2, 3, 6, 9, 25, 34, 50—a sevenfold usage which can hardly be accidental. In other psalms the word appears more than once only in Ps 119 (vv 30, 75, 86, 90, 133).

In v 9 the language of praise shifts to second person, direct address to Yahweh, who is called Yahweh God Sabaoth. The divine epithet Sabaoth is traditionally translated as "Hosts"—"Yahweh of Hosts." But it is a complex term which may mean "Powers" as much as "Hosts" (see note Ps 80:5.a). Vv 10–14 are important verses in this section of the psalm, because they provide the basis on which Yahweh's cosmic rulership is founded. They are set off from other verses by the repetition of the emphatic אתה, "you", at the beginning of vv 10 and 11, and the equivalent לך, "to you" or "yours," at the beginning of v 12 followed by אתה in 12b, 13a, and לך in 14a. The victory of Yahweh over Rahab and other powerful enemies is described. Rahab is a name for the chaos monster in ancient stories; referred to several times in the Hebrew scriptures (Ps 87:4; Isa 30:7; 51:9–10; Job 9:13; 26:12). The name is used of Egypt in Isa 30:7 and Ps 87:4, but its primary referent is the story of the conquest of the raging sea and the forces it represents, as in the myth of Baal's establishment of his kingship by overcoming Yam (Sea). See *Comment* on Ps 74:12–17; also see the discussions of Pss 29:10, 93, and 95. Because of his victorious power over the great forces of disorder, Yahweh is established as the creator and ruler of the heavens and the earth (v 12).

The mention of Tabor and Hermon in v 13b may be due to their use as centers of worship in ancient Palestine. The evidence for Tabor may be somewhat stronger (see Hos 5:1; cf. Deut 30:19; Josh 19:34; Jer 46:18; and the discussion of *Form/Structure/Setting* of Ps 68), though the reference to Baal-Hermon in Judg 3:3 may indicate that it was once a major Canaanite sanctuary (cf. 1 Chr 5:23), and its history as a sacred site is probably reflected in the name הרמון from חרם ("to consecrate/devote/put under a ban") and thus חֵרֶם a "devoted thing (to God)." Thus Hermon may mean "a sacred mountain" or "consecrated place." Later traditions also indicate the cultic importance of Mount Hermon.

Some commentators think that Tabor and Hermon are mentioned because of their impressive size (e.g., Kirkpatrick, 535). However, in the case of Tabor this is difficult to justify (Goulder, *The Psalms of the Sons of Korah*, 213), since it is only 1,843 feet high (compared to Hermon at 9,100, Gerizim at 2,849 and Ebal at 3,077), though Tabor is a prominent landmark in the Jezreel Valley. A few interpreters (e.g., Dahood, II, 314; Kraus, II, 788) argue for four mountains on the basis that צפון וימין ("north and south") are actually the geographical designations for Zaphon and Amanus (reading אמן or אמנה for ימין), with Zaphon referring to Mount Casius (the mountain home of Baal at Ugarit) and Amanus (mentioned with Shenir in Cant 4:8) as either a spur of the Taurus mountains or the Anti-Lebanon range (see also, Cross, *Canaanite Myth and Hebrew Epic*, 161, and 37–39). In this case it is highly probable that all the mountains were associated with traditions of worship, either that of Yahweh or of other gods, and are now declared to be under the lordship of Yahweh (cf. Rogerson and McKay, II, 192). If the expression "north and the south" is retained, the reference is to the worldwide dimensions of Yahweh's creative work which is (1) praised by the splendor of the great mountains Tabor and Hermon, or (2) the praising of Yahweh's creative work at two ancient places of worship is recalled. It is possible that Goulder (214) is correct to suggest that the hymn part of Ps 89 originally came from the cult center on Mount Tabor before it was transferred to the sanctuary at Dan, which was at the foot of Mount Hermon.

In v 14, Yahweh's arm and hand are declared to be strong (cf. Isa 48:13; Exod 15:6–12; Pss 17:7; 18:35; 139:10; cf. 89:11). I have read v 14c (lit., "your right hand is raised") as meaning "raised and ready to strike" (as is apparently the meaning in Isa 26:11) rather than as "exalted/triumphant/victorious arm" (cf. Exod 14:8; Num 33:3). S. R. Driver (*The Book of Isaiah*, ICC, 442) comments on Isa 26:11 that "the uplifted hand is power in action as the dropped hand is absence of power, or power held in check" (cf. 2 Sam 4:1; 17:2; 24:16).

The idea of a throne supported by the qualities of righteousness (or "right order") and justice (v 15) occurs also in Ps 97:2, and with "righteousness" alone, in Prov 16:12 (and LXX has "righteousness" in Prov 20:28). Similar concepts are found in Egyptian literature (see Brunner, *VT* 8 [1958] 426–28). The metaphorical concept is that of the pedestal or platform on which the throne rests (cf. 1 Kgs 10:18–20 for the raised throne of Solomon). The Hebrew "righteousness" (צדק) is equivalent to the Egyptian *maat* ("fundamental order/truth/justice"); the throne of the king was thought of as resting on a pedestal of *maat*, a divinely established order which sustained the kingship and to which the king was responsible. Yahweh's throne (kingship) is founded upon and characterized by the fundamental, cosmic characteristics of right order and justice. Loyal-love and Faithfulness (חסד ואמת) are personified as royal attendants who do the bidding of the Cosmic King. They are expressions of the righteousness and justice which are fundamental in the rulership of Yahweh.

The joyful people of the divine king (89:16–19). These verses are descriptive of the praise and strength of the people who worship and trust the Cosmic King in vv 6–15. They are worshipers who have experienced the thrill of the "festal shout" during worship times (v 16). The "festal shout" (תרועה), *teruah*, is used in varied ways: of the blowing of horns (Lev 23:24; 25:9), at the acclamation of a king (Num 23:21), as a war cry or alarm signal (Num 10:7, 9; Josh 6:10, 16, 20; Judg 7:21; 1 Sam 17:52; Isa 42:13; 2 Chr 13:15), and as a victory shout over enemies (Jer 50:15; Ps 41:12). In religious worship, it is a cry or shout of acclamation and joy toward God (see Pss 47:2; 66:1; 81:2; 95:1, 2; 98:4; 100:1; and for a combination of praise and war cry, see 1 Sam 4:5–6). The prolonged battle yell becomes a roar of praise for God and his victories in worship contexts.

Those who know the experience of the festal *teruah* are happy and rejoicing people, who know the strength and victory which flow out of the goodwill of Yahweh (vv 17–18)—or at least they are supposed to be. They cry out in homage to their cosmic king who is their shield (v 19) and the one who lifts their horns in victory (v 18b; for the idea of horns lifted in victory, see note 92:11.b. and *Comment*). The "horn" is also a symbol of strength and power, of course (e.g., Pss 75:6; 112:9; 1 Sam 2:1), as well as of success. The raised horn is a sign of conspicuous good fortune; "a *visible* sign of success" (P. K. McCarter, Jr., *I Samuel*, AB, I, 73). Cf. Deut 33:16b–17. Those whose horns are raised know the elation of elevated circumstances and the joy of participation in the saving work of Yahweh. For the "Holy One of Israel," see Pss. 71:22; 78:41; 99:3, 5, 9; the expression is prominent in Isaiah, e.g., Isa 1:4, 5:24; 30:11, 12, 15; 43:3, 14, 15; 60:9, 14. See *Comment* on Ps 71:22.

The great oracle of the Holy One of Israel about David and his posterity (89:20–38). This section can be divided into two subsections: vv 20–28 and vv 29–38 (cf. Dumortier, *VT* 22 [1972] 186–192). The first part (vv 20–28) sets forth in divine speech the status of David as the chosen and anointed servant of Yahweh. The status of David as the divinely empowered warrior, chosen from among the people, is emphasized (v 20b). Yahweh "found" him and anointed him to be his servant-king (v 21). "Found" (מצא) is used in the sense of "elect/choose," as in Hos 9:10; Deut 32:10; cf. Ezek 16:4–7, 7–8. Dumortier has called attention to the parallels between the qualities attributed to David in vv 20–28 and those attributed to Yahweh in vv 6–19. For example:

1. David possesses power proportional to that of Yahweh; cf. vv 6–19 and 22–28. David is the highest of the kings of the earth (v 28) just as Yahweh is the most exalted cosmic ruler (vv 7–9).

2. The mighty arm and hand of Yahweh (v 14) used to establish and maintain his cosmic rulership is used to empower David so that no enemy can defeat him (vv 22–24).

3. Yahweh raises the horns of his faithful people in v 18 and raises the horn of David through the divine name in v 25 (note also the use of "name" in vv 13 and 17).

4. David will exercise power over the rivers and the sea (v 26), as Yahweh rules the surging sea and stills its roaring waves (vv 10–11).

5. Righteousness (צדק) and justice (משפט) support the throne of Yahweh while Loyal-Love (חסד) and Faithfulness (אמת) stand ready to do his bidding (v 15); David is sustained by Yahweh's faithfulness (אמונה) and loyal-love (חסד) in v 26.

6. David is given the status of the Most High (עליון) in relation to other kings of the earth. Mettinger (*King and Messiah,* 263) argues that though עליון is not used of Yahweh in Ps 89, the first part of the psalm describes him as the head of the heavenly assembly (vv 6–9) and עליון is used elsewhere for Yahweh as head of the divine council (cf. Ps 82:6). Thus the עליון-status of the king is the counterpart of that of Yahweh in the heavenly realm: "The king does on earth what God does in heaven." The cosmic ruling power of God is invested, in considerable measure at least, in the Davidic king.

The terms "sea" and "rivers" (v 26) should, perhaps, be considered as personified concepts (Sea and River) of the chaotic enemies of the order maintained by the divinely chosen and established servant-son-king of Yahweh. Historically the terms denote the boundaries of David's empire, at least in a rough sort of way: the Mediterranean on the west and the Euphrates and Tigris on the east (though some commentators have thought of the Euphrates and the Nile; Anderson, II, 641; Dahood, II, 317; Mowinckel, *PIW,* I, 55; Veijola, *ZAW* 95 [1983] 9–31, 22–24; cf. Ps 80:12). But a purely either/or choice between mythical and sociogeographic understandings of this language should be avoided. The powers overcome by Yahweh (Ps 89:10–13) have their counterpart in the Davidic ruler's domination of an earthly kingdom (vv 26). The cosmic taming power of Yahweh in vv 10–13 is demonstrated in the ruling power of the king.

At the same time, the king remains "manifestly a human being" (Mettinger, *King and Messiah,* 263). He has been "found" and "chosen" from among the people (vv 20–21), and he calls Yahweh, "My God" and the "Rock of my Salvation." Mettinger suggests that the designation בכור ("firstborn") in v 28 was chosen "to retain the human side of the king," who as a human being belongs to Yahweh, despite his special status. Veijola (*ZAW* 95 [1983] 23) argues that in OT accounts it is always Yahweh who overcomes the chaos powers and that this power is not given to the king. The king's mandate, according to Veijola, is expressed in purely earthly and geographic terms (cf. Ps 72:8). However, it is questionable whether or not such a clear distinction can be made between the sociogeographic and the cosmic powers of kingship, especially in Ps 89.

David rules for Yahweh as his anointed servant and as his firstborn son, and he addresses his heavenly sovereign as "my Father" (v 27); see Ps 2:7 and 2 Sam 7:14. The metaphorical background of the "my son—my father" relationship between Yahweh and the Davidic king was derived from the language of adoption (see M. Weinfeld, "The Covenant of Grant in the Old Testament and in the Ancient Near East," *JAOS* 90 [1970] 190–93; Dumortier, *VT* 22 [1972] 188–89, who cites the Code of Hammurabi, 170, 192, for the formulaic expressions "my son" and "my father" in legal adoptions; Mettinger, *King and Messiah*, 265–67). David was chosen by Yahweh from among the people (not from among the "sons of God" or divine beings), raised to power by divine will, and anointed as king (vv 20–21). He was "found" among his people; not divinely born (v 21). Mettinger (268) says that v 28 refers to a status "bestowed upon the king by a divine act of will, and not of a right held by descent": "I will make him my firstborn"—David is Yahweh's "firstborn"!

In Israelite society, the firstborn son received the paternal blessing (Gen 27) with succession to the authority of his father (Gen 27:1–4, 29, 35–37; 2 Kgs 2:9; cf. Gen 37:21–22; 43:33) and was entitled to inherit a double portion of the family estate (Deut 21:15–17; Isa 61:7). As the "firstborn" of Yahweh, David is given an exalted status of privilege and power (cf. Heb 1:6); a status higher than that of any other king (v 28b), comparable to Yahweh's own status among the divine beings of the heavenly realm (vv 7–9). Mettinger (173) suggests that the word "firstborn" (בכור) in Ps 89 takes the place of the term נגיד, "leader/one especially selected by God from the people of Israel" (in 2 Sam 6:8; equivalent to "son" in 2 Sam 6:14—though, according to Mettinger, נגיד is a more precise specification of sonship: the "son" chosen for leadership). The supreme expression of a king's position is that of a בכור ("firstborn")-status (Mettinger, 263).

Vv 29–38 form the second part of the large oracle in vv 20–38, and set forth the promises and conditions relating to the offspring of David in the Davidic dynasty. The word "seed/offspring" (זרע) in vv 30 and 37 is a key term in this section, along with "his sons/descendants" (בניו) in v 31. *Vv 20–28 deal with the great promises to David and vv 29–38 extend those promises to the Davidic dynasty.*

The commitment of Yahweh to David, a covenant-obligation, is repeated in v 29 and continued in vv 34–36 as the frame and basis for commitment to David's offspring in vv 30, 37–38. Vv 31–33 deal with the divine response to sinful and rebellious behavior on the part of David's kingly offspring. The violation of divine commandments will bring about severe punishment (v 33), but will not cause Yahweh's covenant-obligation to David to be broken off (v 34). Yahweh will not betray his fidelity to him or profane his holy covenant with him. He has made his promises to David on oath and he has not lied about it (v 36; see also Ps 132:11). The throne(ship) of David's dynasty is founded upon irrevocable commitments by Yahweh and should endure like the sun and the moon (vv 37–38).

The identity of the "witness" (עד) in v 38b is a matter of debate. In the translation above, I have chosen to separate the witness from the moon in 38a, rejecting a translation such as that in NJV: "as the moon, established forever, / an enduring witness in the sky." As pointed out in note 38.a, the reading "faithful witness" or "enduring witness" is grammatically suspect. Veijola (*JBL* 107 [1988] 413–17) appeals also to the colometrical and syntactical structure of vv 37–38, arguing that 37a, 37b, and 38a make up a tricolon followed by a separate colon in 38b (see also Veijola, *Verheissung in der Krise,* 33–34):

37a His offspring shall endure forever,
37b his throne as the sun before me,
38a as the moon it shall be established forever
38b And a witness in the clouds shall be faithful.

I think that this is correct (note that it is also the arrangement adopted by Mullen, *JBL* 102 [1983] 209). Veijola leaves v 38b as an independent colon with no parallel. Perhaps we should enlarge the unit to include v 36 and find the parallel of 38b in 36a:

36a Once I swore by my holiness—
36b I do not lie to David,
37a his offspring will continue forever
37b and his throne as the sun before me;
38a as the moon it will be established forever.
38b And a witness in the clouds will be faithful.

The counterpart of 38b is 36a; two colons which form a frame, or "envelope" around vv 36b–38a (or alternatively we have *two* tricolons: 36a, 36b, 38b and 37a, 37b, 38a, with 38b separated to enclose the second with 36a). The affirmation of a witness in the clouds is part of the oath which Yahweh takes in 36a.

The further question of the identity of the witness remains, however. Mosca (*JBL* 105 [1986] 27–37) has directed his attention to this matter with the unusual thesis that the witness is the throne in v 37b. Mosca's article is a valuable and interesting study, but his thesis seems to encounter insuperable difficulties. First, the grammatical improbability of reading "his throne . . . an enduring witness" has been noted above. Mosca himself (32) admits that throne is not elsewhere designated as a witness, though he argues that there is "nothing inherently improbable" about it being designated as such, since other inanimate objects often serve as witnesses in the OT. Third, Mosca has to argue at considerable length for the concept of the throne "in the sky" (heavens) as existing in the divine presence. His treatment of the mythical and cosmic dimensions of the throne concept (divine throne theology) is valuable, but the throne of David in Ps 89 can hardly be conceived of as a "witness in the clouds"—even though later Jewish legends did postulate David sitting on a throne directly opposite to that of God (Mosca, 35). Also, the reference to the fallen throne in the lament in v 45 can hardly offset the other liabilities of this thesis (which has to assume that the fall of the throne is from heaven to earth).

Veijola (*JBL* 107 [1988] 413–17) has followed some earlier commentators (notably, Kirkpatrick, 540) in defending the thesis that God himself is the witness, after rejecting the theses of Mosca and Mullen. He appeals to the dwelling place of Yahweh "in the clouds" in v 7 and to the role of Yahweh as witness in a number of OT texts (Gen 31:50; 1 Sam 12:5; 20:23, 42; Jer 29:23; 42:5; Mic 1:2; Mal 2:14; 3:5; Job 16:19). He (as does Kirkpatrick) emphasizes Jer 42:5 where Yahweh is invoked as witness to an oath. He also refers to Josh 24:22 where the people are asked to be witnesses against themselves, suggesting by analogy that Yahweh could have a double role as partner and as guarantor. He also appeals to Job 16:19 and the interpretation of the "witness in heaven" as part of a "dialectical conception of God"; God versus God. This thesis too seems highly improbable. None of the passages in which Yahweh acts a witness involve him as *a witness to his own oath;* he is a witness of covenant agreements and oaths taken by others. In Ps 89 Yahweh affirms that there is a witness to the commitments he has taken, and the witness can hardly be himself, unless he is playing word games.

Both Veijola and Mosca are concerned about the lack of reference to the "witness" in the lament which follows in vv 39–52; with Mosca citing the "throne" in v 45 as support for his theory and Veijola (417) arguing that the "supposed double role of Yahweh" fits well with these verses. The arguments do not seem very cogent to me. It would be extraordinary indeed for a speaker in *a prayer addressed to Yahweh,* as Ps 89 is, to appeal to a witness *against* Yahweh in that prayer. This does not happen in Job, who declares the existence of a "witness in heaven" in Job 16:19 but does not appeal to the "witness," even in v 20 (nor to the "redeemer" in Job 19:25–27, nor is such appeal involved in the "arbiter" wish in Job 9:33 or in the case of the "mediator" of Elihu in Job 33:23–28). In Ps 89, Yahweh has indicted himself with his own oath in vv 36–38.

In my opinion, the thesis of Mullen (*JBL* 102 [1983] 207–18) is essentially correct. He rejects the surprisingly widely adopted view that the "witness" is the rainbow of Gen 9:12–16 (advocated by Ahlström, *Psalm 89,* 130; also Eissfeldt, "Psalm 80 and Psalm 89," 132–36; see Mosca, 28, n. 3), which is a "sign" (אוֹת), not a "witness," although it is in a covenant context (it is not, however, ever associated with the Davidic covenant). Mullen argues that the language of vv 37–38 (which should be extended to v 36) is that of ancient royal-grant covenants, and the language includes vv 4–5 and 30 also. In these covenants a deity unilaterally establishes and empowers a king or other favored person. Gifts and privileges are bestowed on faithful servants by a divine suzerain (as with Abraham in Gen 15:17).

A very important facet of Mullen's case is the function of divine witnesses in covenant making of the royal-grant type and in ancient treaty texts (see Mullen, 210). Veijola (*JBL* 107 [1988] 414–15; *ZAW* 95 [1983] 19–20) adds significantly to the brief documentation of Mullen regarding witnesses, noting the function of "clouds" as witnesses in some texts, e.g., in the treaty between Mursilia II and Duppi-Teshub of Amurru, a list of gods are invoked as witnesses, and after the gods are named the list ends: "the mountains, the rivers, the springs, the great sea, heaven and earth, the winds (and) the clouds—let these be witnesses to this treaty and to the oath"; see *ANET,* 203–5). In treaty-covenant texts from the ancient Near East, witnesses were invoked as guarantors of the terms of the treaty. In polytheistic cultures, gods were designated as witnesses, along with the mighty aspects of nature such as heaven and earth as well (for the invocation of the forces of nature see Deut 4:26; 30:19; 31:28; cf. Deut 32:1–2; Isa 1:2–10; Jer 2:12; Mic 6:1–12; for the Israelites themselves as witnesses, see Josh 24:22, though note the stone as witness in 24:27: "for it has heard all the words of the LORD which he spoke to us").

In the case of Ps 89:38, the affirmation of a witness in the heavens is similar to that of Job 16:19 (RSV): "Even now, behold, my witness is in heaven, / and he that vouches for me is on high." The witness is defined in Job 16:20 as the interpreter of thoughts to God and the one to whom "my eye pours out tears (of complaint)." The function of the witness will be to plead Job's case before God and verify the truth of his complaints about God (Job 16:21; cf. Job 33:23–24). The force of the text in Ps 89 is that Yahweh's promises and commitments to David are known by a reliable heavenly witness. The witness is unidentified, possibly not a definite figure ("witness" lacks the definite article in the text; Mullen, *JBL* 102 [1983] 215, cf., Veijola, *JBL* 107 [1988] 416, who notes that the lack of the definite article may have been to avoid the word sequence וָעֶד עוֹלָם, "forever and ever," see note 38.a above). Mullen (218) vacillates on this position and finally concludes that the "witness in the heavens" is "possibly" the sun or the moon, "two of the older gods so often called upon as witnesses to treaties within the ANE and biblical materials" (cf. Mosca, *JBL* 105 [1986] 29, n. 7; 27, n. 3), though this seems to be an unnecessary complication of the matter. The point is that Yahweh cannot deny his oath to David without such perjury being revealed. M. Weinfeld (*Deuteronomy and the Deuteronomic School* [Oxford: Clarendon Press, 1972] 75) notes that the grant type of covenant served mainly to protect the rights of the servants who received the "grant" from a master rather than the rights of the master. David is the servant of Yahweh who has received a "royal-grant" and Yahweh is under obligation to keep the terms of his oath.

Complaint and petition (89:39–53). The mood of the psalm changes drastically at v 39. After the extensive sections of praise and recall of the great promises of Yahweh to David, the reader is hardly prepared for the abrupt shift to the charges made against Yahweh in vv 39–46. The intensity of the complaint is heightened by the long sections of praise and promise which go before it. In vv 39–46, Yahweh is charged with having broken his covenant-obligations to David by his rejection of the Davidic kingship and by giving victory to the foes of the king (cf. v 24). The irony of the raised right hand of the foes in v 43 can hardly be missed when the raised hand of Yahweh (v 14) and the affirmation of support of the Davidic king, by the divine hand (v 22) are recalled. Yahweh had declared that he would beat to pieces the foes of David (v 24), but it is the walls and fortifications of the Davidic king, not those of his enemies, which now lie in ruins (v 41). David was to have his right hand of power on the "rivers" (v 26), but his offspring has seen the victorious raised right hand of his enemies as they rejoiced over his defeat (v 43; cf. v 23). The "firstborn" of Yahweh (v 28) has experienced the turning back of the edge of his sword against himself (v 44) and "the highest of the kings of the earth" in the divine scheme of things (v 28) has not been sustained in battle and has had his throne thrown down to the dirt (v 45).

It is no wonder that the speaker in these verses, either king or ordinary Israelite, cries out "How long, O Yahweh?" Will Yahweh try to hide himself forever from the reality of the situation and his own commitments?—Will he burn with wrath forever? (v 47). Pleas to remember the finite nature of human beings are made in vv 48–49. These two verses seem rather strange in the context, since they introduce subject matter not mentioned before in the psalm and are placed in an "envelope" structure, or insertion pattern, between vv 47 and 50 (note this structure also with vv 2–8 and 28–38 above).

The rhetorical questions in v 50 follow naturally after v 47 but are very loosely related, if at all, to vv 48–49. The imperative "remember" at the beginning of 48 relates well to the "remember" at the beginning of v 51. One may suspect that vv 48–49 have been added to the psalm to bring it into line with individual laments, probably in the post-exilic period (the language of human finitude seems rather conventional; e.g., Pss 39:6–7; 90:5–6, 9–10; 102:12; Kraus, II, 792). The intensity of the complaint is increased by reminding Yahweh that he is dealing with the frailty and finitude of all humankind. Israel and Israelites cannot be isolated from humankind; Yahweh's actions in repudiating his commitments to the Davidic kingship call into question his purpose for all human beings; none of whom can save themselves from death.

The individual speaker in vv 48 and in v 51 personalizes the tragic loss of the monarchy. The absence of Yahweh from his people (v 47) is not a mere matter of national and corporate concern and of sociopolitical realities. "The pragmatic history of the king becomes in these verses the paradigmatic history of moral man[kind]. . . . The fate of the individual and the fate of the king have met. They are one and the same" (Neusner, *Judaism* 8 [1959] 232). The servants of Yahweh now bear the brunt of the divine judgment in their own bosoms (vv 51–52). The identity of the speaker in the psalm is revealed in these verses; one from among those servants of Yahweh who bear the scorn and shame of the enemies of Yahweh, the same enemies who were allowed to shame and humiliate the Davidic king (v 52).

The petition in v 50 is expressed in the form of questions, which are both complaints and petitions. The speaker wants Yahweh to remember his former deeds of loyal-love and activate them in the present. The rhetorical question (beginning with איה, "where?") expresses earnest longing (as in Jer 2:6, 8; Job 35:10; Isa 63:11, 15; Judg 6:13). If we take our cue from the use of the formulaic question in Job 35:10, the question reflects trust that Yahweh will respond; other references containing איה indicate weakened faith because of distress. The matter is left open, except that there can be little doubt that the scribal interpreters who added v 53 read with faith.

Explanation

The explanation of this psalm lies in its last major section, vv 39–52. It is a lament which deals with the "riddle of the inscrutability of God's way of acting in history" (Weiser, 593). The psalm reflects the perplexing experience of the contradiction between old promises and understandings of the ways of God and the actuality of the developments of history. The high hopes and expectations gathered around the Davidic monarchy seem crushed to the speaker. Is this to go on forever? Has Yahweh really broken his oath and repudiated his covenant-obligation? The psalm reflects on these questions. Vv 4–5 seems to be a "text" for the psalm, recalling the covenant, the oath, and the promises of Yahweh to David and to his dynasty:

> I have made a covenant-obligation to my chosen one;
> I have sworn (an oath) to my servant David:
> I will establish your offspring forever,
> and build your throne for one generation after another.

The sad counterpart of these verses is found in vv 39–46. God seems to have renounced his commitments to the Davidic monarchy and the "glorious rulership" has ceased, with the crown and the throne thrown to the ground, plundered, and treated with contempt by victorious enemies. Vv 31–33 allow, of course, for severe punishment of Davidic kings for disobedience of divine teachings and commandments, but this should not mean the total repudiation of the divine commitments (vv 34–38).

The perplexity and hurt are not resolved in this psalm; the matter is left open. The speaker cannot solve the problem: "He [*sic*] can only state that contradiction with a bleeding heart; he can only lift his hands to God in prayer and bring his affliction before him and lay before him the problems which his own thinking and reasoning are unable to master" (Weiser, 593). The speaker and fellow servants of Yahweh lodge their faith and hope in the repeated prayer that Yahweh will "remember" (vv 48, 51): remember the finitude of human beings and his divine purpose in creation (v 48) and the historical condition of the servants of Yahweh as they bear the scorn of many peoples.

The meaning of "remember" is, of course, in many contexts much more than mere mental recall. The mental recollection is for the purpose of appropriate action (e.g., randomly selected: Gen 8:1; Exod 2:24; 6:5; 20:5; Pss 25:6–7; 74:2, 18, 22; Jer 14:21; 15:15). Two things are worth mentioning in connection with "remember" in Ps 89. First, a major object of praise in Israelite worship was centered on Yahweh's faithfulness in remembering his covenant-obligations (B. S. Childs, *Memory and Tradition in Israel*, SBT 37 [Naperville, IL: Allenson, 1962] 41): see Pss 105:8, 42; 106:45; 111:5–9; 1 Chr 16:12–28; cf. Pss 98:3; 136:23). The situation described in Ps 89 threatens the praise which remembering Yahweh's past mercies should bring forth. Second, Childs has pointed out that to remember, especially in worship, was "to bridge the gap of time" and space so that later generations could form a solidarity with earlier ones and actualize the presence of God through recall and identity with his saving works in the past (see *Memory and Tradition*, 74–80, 83–89). The speaker in Ps 89 wants Yahweh's "former deeds of loyal-love" (v 50) and his commitments to David and his offspring actualized in the present. The gap between the traditions and reality yawns open like an abyss. A bridging by divine remembering is imperative.

The reader should consider Ps 89 with Ps 74 (and also with Ps 80), which sets forth the same theological dilemma, except that in the case of Ps 74 the emphasis is on Yahweh's forsaking of his covenant-commitment to Israel and the temple in Jerusalem rather than to the Davidic dynasty (see the discussion in the *Explanation* section of Ps 74). Interestingly, these two psalms form "bookends" which frame Book III of the Psalter (Pss 73–89). Ps 73 deals with the confession of an individual whose faith has been pushed to the brink of failure by the prosperity of the wicked, while 74 deals with the inexplicable inactivity of Yahweh in history. Ps 88 is a powerful individual lament which challenges God's treatment of its speaker, and Ps 89 is a lament about the incongruity of Yahweh's commitments and the actuality of history. Thus at both ends of Book III there is a psalm which deals with the theological distress of an individual followed by a psalm which expresses the distress in terms of the nation. In fact, Book III seems to deal over and over with the bafflement of believers who are struggling with the gap between promise and reality (the expression "How long?" in the form of עַד־מָה, occurs in the Psalter elsewhere in Pss 4:3, 74:9, and 79:5; it is also found in Num 24:22).

Both Ps 88 and 89 end without a resolution (v 53 is not properly a part of Ps 89, but if it is so treated, it only adds to the sense of incompletion in the psalm); these psalms (and others as well; e.g., 44 and 74) have no proper closure. The lack of closure is painful for the reader who seeks answers for difficult theological questions arising out of the enigmas of life. But we need to think carefully about this lack of closure, the failure to tie up loose ends so that a supposed satisfactory "answer" emerges. Closure has its liabilities. The subject matter tends to become purely historical and is no longer the living matter of ongoing life. Closure can be like the sealing of a tomb which signifies the acceptance of death and the giving up of life.

Elie Wiesel, a survivor of the concentration camps of the Holocaust and a powerful witness to the contemporary world, disturbs his readers by postponement of images of the end in his writings and by a reluctance to deal with closure. "His stories are part of a process that destroys the enchantment of reality and reveals the jagged edges of events which have not been domesticated by memory and reduced to consonance" (G. B. Walker, Jr., *Elie Wiesel: A Challenge to Theology* [Jefferson, NC: McFarland, 1988] 32). The same description applies rather well to psalms like 44, 74, 88, and 89. They do not end with domesticated consonance. In the long run, however, their dissonance may be a greater source of strength and comfort. Strength is not built on easy stories with happy endings. In Wiesel's short story called "The Wandering Jew," the young speaker says of one of the wandering teacher's dazzling expositions: "That was beautiful." He is rebuked by the teacher, who says: "When will you understand that a beautiful answer is nothing? Nothing more than illusion? Man defines himself by what disturbs him and not by what reassures him. When will you understand that you are living and searching in error, because God means movement and not explanation?" ("The Wandering Jew," *Legends of Our Time* [New York: Holt, Rinehart & Winston, 1968] 93). Pss 88 and 89 give no "beautiful answers"; rather lament, questions, and pleas. The psalms do, however, presuppose a listening God (as do the stories of Wiesel; see Walker, 66, 80), who hears both praise and bitter lament, and who always has the capacity to remember—a God who does not forget. The world may little note or refuse to listen at all, but Yahweh-God hears the stories of his people's pain and hurt. We who read these psalms join with Yahweh's servants of old as we wait to see how the ancient commitments and promises will be worked out in history.

Christians believe that the Davidic promises have been given a fulfillment in Jesus, who is the Messiah (Christ; Acts 2:30), the "firstborn of the dead" (Rev 1:5), "the ruler of the kings of the earth." He has borne the abuse and scorn directed toward the anointed king (Ps 89:52) and shared by the servants of God (89:51; Heb 13:13; cf. Heb 11:26; Matt 27:44; Luke 18:32). Yet there is no final closure. Christians still wait for a second coming, for a final denouement. We pray with our brothers and sisters out of the past:

> Where are your former deeds of loyal-love, O Lord?
> (Those deeds) you promised on oath to David?
> Remember, O Lord, your scorned servants.

We pray because we know that God listens, and we also know that Christ prays this prayer with us. We are not alone, though friend and neighbor may be far away and we are bereft of companions (Ps 88:19).

A Prayer: "Teach Us How to Number Our Days" (90:1–17)

Bibliography

Auffret, P. "Essai sur la structure littéraire du Psaume 90." *Bib* 61 (1980) 262–76. **Booij, T.** "Psalm 90, 5–6: Junction of Two Traditional Motifs." *Bib* 68 (1987) 393–96. **Brueggemann, W.** *The Message of the Psalms.* Minneapolis: Augsburg, 1984. 110–15. **Goitein, S. D.** "'Maon'—A Reminder of Sin." *JSS* 10 (1965) 52–53. **Levenson, J. D.** "A Technical Meaning for NᶜM in the Hebrew Bible." *VT* 35 (1985) 61–67. **Müller, H.-P.** "Der 90. Psalm: Ein Paradigma exegetischer Aufgabe." *ZTK* 81 (1984) 265–85. **Rad, G. von.** "Psalm 90." In *God at Work in Israel.* Tr. J. H. Marks. Nashville: Abingdon, 1980. 210–23. **Schreiner, S.** "Erwägungen zur Struktur des 90. Psalms." *Bib* 59 (1978) 80–90. **Thomas, D. W.** "A Note on זרמתם שנה יהיו in Psalm XC 5." *VT* 18 (1968) 267–68. **Tsevat, M.** "Psalm XC 5–6." *VT* 35 (1985) 115–17. **Vawter, B.** "Postexilic Prayer and Hope." *CBQ* 37 (1975) 460–70. **Westermann, C.** "Der 90. Psalm." In *Forschung am alten Testament. Theologische Bücherei Altes Testament* 24. Munich: Kaiser, 1964. 344–50. ———."Psalm 90: A Thousand Years Are But as Yesterday." In *The Living Psalms.* Tr. J. R. Porter. Grand Rapids, MI: Eerdmans, 1989. 156–65. **Whitley, C.** "The Text of Psalm 90, 5." *Bib* 63 (1982) 555–57.

Translation

1 A Moses-prayer;[a] the man of God.
   O Lord, you are our help,[b]   (3+3)
   (our help) in every generation.[c]

2 *Before the mountains were born,*   (3+3+3)
   and (before) you travailed[a] with earth and world—
   from everlasting to everlasting you are God!

3 *You turn human beings back to dust,[a]*   (3+3)
   saying,[b] "Turn back you mortals!"[c]

4 *For a thousand years in your eyes*   (3+3+2)
   are like a day that is past,[a]
   (like)[b] a night watch when it is over.[c]

5 *When you pour[a] sleep[b] on them,*   (2+4)
   they become like nonlasting[c] grass in the morning,[d]

6 *which springs up in the morning, but is nonlasting;[a]*   (3+3)
   toward the evening it withers and shrivels up.[b]

7 *So[a] we are consumed by your anger,*   (2+2)
   and overwhelmed[b] by your wrath.

8 *You set our waywardness[a] before you,*   (3+3)
   our hidden (sins)[b] in the light of your face.[c]

9 *So all[a] our days pass by[b] in your wrath;*   (4+3)
   we finish[c] our years like those who sigh.[d]

10 *The number of our years[a] may be seventy,[b]*   (4+4+3+3)
   or eighty, if we are strong;[c]
   yet their span[d] is toil and trouble,
   soon gone[e]—and we fly away!

11	*Who knows the power of your anger?*	(3+2[3])
	And your wrath according to the fear due you?[a]	
12	*Teach (us)*[a] *how to number*[b] *our days*	(3+3)
	that we may obtain[c] *a mind of wisdom.*	
13	*Turn back,*[a] *O Yahweh!—How long?*	(3+2)
	Change your mind[b] *about your servants!*	
14	*Satisfy us*[a] *each morning*[b] *with your loyal-love,*	(3+3)
	and we will sing out joyfully[c] *every day!*	
15	*Give us joy as many days*[a] *as you have afflicted us;*	(3+3)
	the years when we have seen distress.	
16	*Let your works*[a] *appear*[b] *to your servants,*	(3+2)
	and a majestic vision of you[c] *to their children.*	
17	*Let the approval*[a] *of the Lord our God*[b] *be upon us;*	(4+4+3)
	the work of our hands, establish[c] *it for us;*	
	the work of our hands, establish it![d]	

Notes

1.a. The form is the same as that of "a psalm to/for David," on which see n. 51:1–2.b.

1.b. The מעון, traditionally translated as "dwelling place" (KJV, RSV), is often changed to מעוז, "safe place/hiding place/habitation" (see such contexts as Ps 27:1; 28:8; 37:39; 52:9; Jer 16:19; Neh 8:10). מעון is used of the habitations or dens of animals (as in Nah 2:12; Jer 9:10; 10:22; 49:33; 51:37) and also for the habitation or dwelling-place of God: Deut 26:15; Jer 25:30; Ps 68:6; 2 Chr 36:15. LXX is often said to support מעוז, but καταφυγή simply means "refuge," which can be the extended meaning of מעון in such contexts as Deut. 33:27; 71:3, 91:9. The change to מעוז is unnecessary, though there seems to be little difference in meaning between the two words. Dahood (II, 322, 172) argues that מעון is derived from Arabic *ana* which denotes "aid/give succor" and translates as "our mainstay" in 90:1 and as "your mainstay" in 91:9. The argument for the meaning "help/aid" is presented more extensively by Müller, *ZTK* 81 (1984) 269, and I have adopted this meaning. The proposal of Goitein (*JSS* 10 [1965] 52–53) that מעון is derived from עון, "sin/iniquity/waywardness" (note עון in v 8), with the idea that God's dwelling place is a place for sin, is too forced and improbable—though a play on the words in vv 1 and 8 is possible.

1.c. Or, "in generation after generation," or "from generation to generation," or "in each generation."

2.a. MT has a consecutive polel imperfect from חול ("whirl/travail/give birth"). There is versional support for reading polal (see *BHS*): "be brought forth" (as in some translations: JB, "before the earth or the world came to birth"); cf. Prov 8:24, 25; Ps 51:7. Taking the verb as 3rd pers. fem. is unlikely: "or even the earth and the world were in travail," understanding the object as "the mountains" (Anderson, II, 650; Kraus, II, 798–8). KJV and RSV have "or ever thou hadst formed the earth and the world," which seems to represent more interpretation than translation, following LXX, and is correctly criticized as "too vaguely rendered" by Alexander, II, 296). The consecutive imperfect in 2b has the force of making the birth of the earth and the world coincide with the birth of the mountains (Delitzsch, III, 50): "Before the mountains were born and you were in labor with the earth and the world." The "before" (בטרם) in 2a serves 2b also. The conjunction at the beginning of 2c is explicative: "Even!"

3.a. Lit., "crushed/pulverized matter" (דכא), a word not found elsewhere in MT, but the adj. is found in Ps 34:19; Isa 57:15 as "contrite (crushed)/humble." LXX has ταπείνωσιν, "a low place," of the condition of persons: "brought down/humbled/of low rank." Possibly, the דכא refers to the dust of Sheol, the place of the dead (see Dahood, II, 323; Müller, *ZTK* 81 [1984] 271, n. 33)

3.b. The consecutive imperfect functions the same as in 2b and there is no need to change to a simple conjunction as frequently suggested (e.g., *BHS*, Kraus). Cf. Michel, *Tempora und Satzstellung in den Psalmen*, 276. I have taken the imperfect of שוב and אמר as iterative, rather than as past tense, as Müller (271): "You let mankind turn back to dust, and you say . . . ," taking the meaning as the fate determined for humanity by the decree of God. Dahood (II, 323) transposes אל ("God") from v 2 and vocalizes as the negative אַל: "Do not send man back . . ."; a reading which has support from LXX and Vg and agrees with the hiphil jussive form תֹּשֵׁב in 3a (earlier, Briggs, II, 276). However, the jussive form may be used here for the ordinary imperfect or else is an archaism (see GKC 109k; Müller, 271, citing W. V. Soden, *Tempus und Modus im Semitischen*, Akten des 24. internat. Orientalistenkongresses [Munich, 1959] 263–65).

3.c. The reading of the verb שׁוּב in 3b with the meaning "come back (to life)," as in Westermann, *The Living Psalms* (Edinburgh: Clark, 1989) 160–61, is improbable. Westermann postulates a chiastic parallelism between vv 3 and 5–6 as follows: v 3: dying—being born // v 5: being born—dying. He compares this "impressive picture of the rhythm of birth and death" to Eccl 3:2. Unfortunately, this interpretation depends (1) on taking the second שׁוּב in v 3 with a different meaning than the first, (2) emending the uncertain verb זרם in v 5 to זרע, "to sow (life)," (3) reading שֵׁנָה, ("sleep") in v 5 as "year after year," and (4) transposing v 4 to a position following v 2—though the transposition in not really necessary since vv 3 and 5–6 provide a frame around v 4 in an envelope (A X B) pattern.

4.a. יוֹם אֶתְמוֹל = "a day formerly" = "yesterday." See Isa 30:33. At least this is the meaning usually given. Actually, יוֹם ("day") appears with אֶתְמוֹל (adv. "formerly/recently") only here, though the meaning of אֶתְמוֹל alone seems to be "yesterday" in some cases, otherwise it is "formerly/recently/ before."

4.b. The preposition on "like a day" does double duty and there is no need to add another to אַשְׁמוּרָה ("night-watch"). See Dahood, II, 324.

4.c. Reading the verb יַעֲבֹר (which need not be changed to perfect) as (1) serving the third colon as well as the second and (2) in a temporal sense (see Gen 50:4; 1 Kgs 18:29; Amos 8:5; Cant 2:11).

5.a. The verb זרם is traditionally taken in the sense of "flood/overwhelm/sweep away as by a flood." The noun זֶרֶם means a heavy pouring out of water, rain or hail, as in a storm (see Isa 4:6; 25:4; 28:2; 30:30; 32:2; Job 24:8) The poel form of the verb is used in Ps 77:18 with reference to the clouds pouring forth water; it is not used elsewhere. The idea of washing human beings away so that they become as sleep, followed by images of passing away like grass (vv 5b, 6) is strange (Booij, *Bib* 68 [1987] 393)—Why should people who have been washed away to the sleep of death spring up like grass in the morning and fade away during the day? The problem of the relationship of 5a to 5b–6 does not seem to be solved by the paraphrase of the Targum: "and if they do not turn back, you bring death upon them, like sleeping ones they will be."

Some ancient versions reflect MT: Symm has "like a squall you have shaken them out, they will be sleeping"; Jerome has, "when you hit them violently, they will be asleep" (probably assuming the verb זרם, see Booij, 394). LXX and Syr, however, seem to reflect difficulty with the text. LXX has τὰ ἐξουδενώματα αὐτῶν ἔτη ἔσονται, "their contempts [*or*, contemptible things] will be years," which does not seem to make much sense unless a Hebrew text שָׁנָה יִהְיוּ is assumed, with זרמותם being understood as "phallus" or "ejection of semen" (note the use of זרמה in Ezek 23:2 and the LXX of that verse, with שׁנה understood as plural [as in v 10]). Even so, the translation hardly makes sense. Syr's "their issue (progeny, generation) will be a sleep" (apparently reading זרמתם as a noun with a plural suffix [see Whitley, *Bib* 63 (1982) 557; Booij, 398]) makes more sense: their reproductive powers will fail. If we assume that the probable text was an offensive one, which MT has obscured, the Syr probably provides the best result. The suggestion of Thomas (*VT* 18 [1968] 267–68) moves in the same direction. He notes N. H. Tur-Sinai's proposal (*VT* 16 [1951] 309) to transfer the final letter of זרמתם to שׁנה, resulting in מִשְׁנָה and understanding it as meaning "bladder," and reads as "an emission of the bladder are they." Thomas, however, proposes to transfer the final letter of זרמתם to the beginning of the word, thus מִזְרָם: "from emission of semen in sleep are they." Whitley (556–57) too reads זרמתם as a noun ("their offspring") and changes the following ("sleep") to שֹׁנֶה (participle from שׁנה, "change") and translates as "Their offspring changeth, as grass undergoing change" (omitting both יהיו and בבקר as intrusions).

For an interpretation of the verb זרם as "shorten/cut short" or "interrupt," see Müller, *ZTK* 81 (1984) 272; Vawter, *CBQ* 37 (1975) 460, based on Arabic *zarima* and *zarama*. If זרמתם is understood as "cut them off," it is possible to read it with v 4c: "like a watch in the night you cut them off (in) sleep" (cf. G. R. Driver, *ZAW* 80 [1968] 177–78). For the double accusative after the verb, see Schreiner, *Bib* 59 (1978) 83, n. 19, who observes that after verbs of covering, clothing, and the like such usage is normal (see GKC 117, 5ab). Kraus (II, 795) represents several commentators who emend זרם to זרע, "sow (seed)": "You sow them year by year" (assuming שֵׁנָה שָׁנָה). For a good list of other emendations, see Booij, *Bib* 68 (1987) 393, n. 1.

The translation above retains the verb, because the meaning "pour out/flood/ejaculate" is fairly well established (see Tsevat, *VT* 35 [1985] 115–17, and Booij). "Sleep" is also retained, with the meaning of either "sleep of death," or else a sleep which makes those who receive it dull and vulnerable to the action of God (note the discussion by Booij, 395, and see the usage of sleep in Ps 76:6–7, 10; Nah 3:18; *Enuma elis* I 60–65; Gilgamesh Epic XI 199–233). I have followed Booij in reading 5a and 5b as protasis and apodosis (cf. such texts as Job 7:20; 21:31; 23:10; 35:6; Prov 6:22; 18:22; 22:9; GKC 159h). The antecedent of the plural suffering is the "sons of humanity" in v 3. For שׁנה as equivalent to death see Job 14:12; Jer 51:39, 57. The translation above also assumes that יהיו should be read at the beginning of the second colon.

5.b. As already noted in n. 5.a, the meaning of שׁנה ("sleep") is debated. Dahood (II, 324) takes it as an accusative of time: "If you pluck them at night (in the period of sleep)" (reading the verb זרם as "pluck" and as conditional without an indicator). But this does not seem to fit the context very well. *BHS* proposes, with versional support, to read שׁנה שׁנה, "year after year," assuming that the text has suffered a haplography as well as a changed vocalization, and that the verb יהיו should be read with 5b, deleting בבקר as dittography from 6a (Kraus, II, 794–95; also Anderson, II, 651). I have retained the meaning "sleep," which is surely the simpler procedure.

5.c. The verb חלף seems very doubtful in the sense of "flourish/renew" in its qal forms, though it is taken in this sense rather frequently (e.g., KJV, RSV, NIV, NJV). The meaning in the qal form is "pass on/change/disappear" (e.g., 1 Sam 10:3; Isa 8:8; 21:1; Job 4:15; 9:26; 11:10; Isa 2:18). Usage in piel and hiphil seems to support the idea of "renew/sprout" (see Job 14:7; 29:20) and in some cases "substitute/exchange" (Isa 9:9 [10]; Isa 40:31; 41:1). The context in vv 5a and 6 seems to favor the idea of "fading/passing/withering." The translation above assumes a relative clause, used as a substitute for an adjective: lit., "like grass that fades away" (see Schreiner, *Bib* 59 [1978] 84; GKC 155, 2b, 1). Booij (*Bib* 68 [1987] 396) translates without בבקר ("in the morning"): "they become like grass which is not lasting."

5.d. The בבקר may be the result of dittography and omitted, as is done frequently. This shortens the second colon and reduces the lack of balance between 5a and 5b. However, the balance of colons may not need to be taken too seriously (note Booij's discussion of the 2+3, *Bib* 68 [1987] 395, n. 16— if "in the morning" is removed the colons are still out of balance). I have assumed that the literary feature of the "expanded colon" is used in vv 5 and 6, as in v 17 (cf. v 10). For "expanded colon," see n. Ps 92:8.b, 10.a.

6.a. Reading the conjunction as adversative and giving the same meaning to the verb חלף as in v 5b.

6.b. LXX adds ἀποπέσοι = יבול from נבל "shrink/droop," before the verbs for "withers" and "shrivels," and assumes that the verbs are jussive: "Let it flower and pass away, . . . let it droop, let it be withered."

7.a. The כי is frequently taken as emphatic ("indeed"), but some versions have a causal or resultative force (LXX has ὅτι, "because/for" or "so that"). The force of the כי is equivalent to כן, cf. Briggs.

7.b. The verb is assumed to be a niphal perfect common pl of בהל, "be disturbed/dismayed/terrified," and in a secondary sense "to hasten/act quickly." If the secondary meaning is taken, the idea is that of "being hurried (away to an untimely end)." The first meaning yields the idea of "terrified" or "overwhelmed (with dismay)." Dahood proposes to read the verb as from בלה, "wear out": "worn out by your rage," which makes a better parallel with כלה, "consumed" in 7a.

8.a. Traditionally, "our iniquities"; see n. 51:4.b.

8.b. A defectively written plural passive participle from עלם, "be concealed/hidden," thus, "our secret/hidden things"—with the assumption that the reference is to faults and sins. LXX understands as ὁ αἰών, "our age/generation," or possibly "our past (life)." The Targumic tradition understands the reference to be to "the sins of our youth"; cf. 89:46; Isa 54:5; Job 20:11; 33:25; Briggs, II, 277; Dahood, II, 325.

8.c. The combination of the noun מאור ("luminary/lamp/light") and the preposition ל appear only here in MT (more lit., "to the lamp of your face"). Dahood (II, 325) proposes to read למו אור פניך, "to the light of your face," noting a poetic balance with כמו in v 9. He may be correct, but note Briggs (II, 277) and Prov 15:30.

9.a. The כל loads the colon heavily and is frequently deleted (e.g., Kraus). On the other hand, the emphasis on "*all* our days" is appropriate (and a pattern of 4+3 in the verse may still be maintained), which leads Dahood (II, 325) to comment that its deletion "need not enlist our further attention." So be it!

9.b. LXX adds another verb, the equivalent of כלינו: "All our days are gone, and we are consumed in your wrath." The verb פנה, "turn/change," in used here in the sense of its use in Jer 6:4, "the day is waning," which suggests that the time of opportunity is swiftly passing. Perhaps we could say, "our days spin by."

9.c. The change of the piel perf. כלינו ("we finish/consume/end") to כָלוּ ("our years end/are consumed like") to balance with the פנה in 9a (e.g., Kraus, II, 796) is unnecessary.

9.d. Lit., "like a sigh." The word הגה is strange, but it apparently means a "moaning sound" or a "sigh," from הגה, "utter/speak/growl/muse" (sometimes, "to read in an undertone," KB, 224; cf. Ps 1:2). The use of הגה in the sense of "moaning" or "mourning" is found in Ezek 2:10 and in the sense of the "rumble of thunder" in Job 37:2. The meaning of "lamentation/mourning" is possible in 90:9: "like a moan of woe." Some commentators understand this obscure colon to mean that the whole of life is "one long sigh or moan" (Anderson, II, 652). I take it as a reference to the whimpering, sighing end of the swift course of toilsome and troubled life.

LXX translates הגה as "spider": "Our years are spun out (or, told) like a spider"—perhaps, understanding "spun out (told) like a spider's web" (cf. KJV: "We spend our years as a tale that is told"). The LXX's "spider" (also, Syr) seems to be without much explanation; possibly a scribal error produced Heb. גוגה (*gogah*), which was then identified as Syriac *gewagay*, "spider" (Jacquet, II, 724). See also Dahood's note (II, 325).

10.a. Lit., "the days of our years in them (are) seventy years," a type of *casus pendens* construction (Müller, *ZTK* 81 [1984] 274, n. 49). The "days of" apparently is equal to "the number of" in this case (Kraus, II, 796). The "in them" (בהם) is difficult and frequently omitted as a gloss, or emended to גְּבְרָם, "their highest limit" or שָׂבְעָה, "their fill" (see Gunkel, 401). However, the "days" and "years" relate v 10 to v 9 and the language in 10a need not be changed though it is awkward. The masc. suffix of "in them" refers to the "days of the years"; not to the fem. "years" alone.

10.b. Traditionally understood as a statement of the typical life expectancy of human beings, which seems unrealistic by normal patterns of life in the ancient world. Conditional clauses in 10a and 10b seem more plausible.

The subject of the verse is clearly the ephemerality of even a long human life, as 10c and 10d make clear. The occurrences of conditional statements without an indicator (e.g., אם) is fairly common (note Allen's translation of and note on Ps 104:20).

10.c. The form is apparently an intensive plural: "great strength/might/vigor" (cf. Pss 20:7; 71:16; 106:2; 145:4, 12, 150:2; Job 26:14—all used of God and usually understood as "mighty acts" or "power"; cf. Ezek 32:29). The meaning is that of "by strong performance/strong efforts" or "in good health" (JB, "eighty with good health").

10.d. Reading רחבם ("their breadth/width") with the versions for MT's רהבם which would mean "their pride," or perhaps "their frenetic activity," relating to the verb רהב, "storm against/importune" (note KB, 876, "eagerness/insistence"). LXX's πλεῖον may indicate רְבָּם (from רבב, "be/become many"), yielding the idea of "the greater part of them are toil and trouble" : NAB, "most of them are fruitless toil."

10.e. The verb גז is simple perfect 3rd pers. masc. sing. from גוז, "pass along/disappear" (cf. Num 11:31)—though the form could be a participle. The singular fits poorly with the subject "our days - our years" in vv 9–10 if 10d is taken as bringing vv 7–10 to a close, but poses no difficulty if נחבם/נהבם in 10c is the subject. The כי may be taken as causal or emphatic ("Indeed!"). Müller (*ZTK* 81 [1984] 273) takes it as emphatic and the combination of גז חיש as adverbial and proposes the translation: "Indeed, declining rapidly we fly away" (*"ja, eiling schwindend fliegen wir davon"*). In this case the consecutive imperfect ונעפה relates to the plural subject in vv 7–9. Gunkel and others suggest the option of גזו. I have left the translation somewhat ambiguous.

If the present verse division and MT accentuation are modified, a translation similar to that of Briggs (II, 271) fits vv 9–10 with a well-balanced 3+3 colon pattern: "So all our days pass away; / in your wrath we complete our years. / As a sigh are the days of our years; / in them there may be seventy years, / or even eighty with good health, / but their span is toil and trouble; / soon gone—and we fly away."

11.a. This is a translation which is very near that of the RV, but very uncertain. Lit., "and as your fear (is) your wrath." LXX's καὶ ἀπὸ τοῦ φόβου σου τὸν θυμόν σου suggests the Hebrew ומיראת עברך, "and from the fear of your wrath"; though some LXX texts have τοῦ φόβου σου τὸν θυμόν σου, which is apparently the literal of MT and suggests that the other texts represent interpretations, which in turn may suggest a Hebrew text of ומי ראה חך עברתך (or . . . ומי ירא) "and who fears the stroke (or, force) of your wrath?" (see Briggs, Gunkel, Kraus, Anderson, Jacquet). Dahood (II, 326) proposes to assume a defective כי in וכיראתך and reads "that those who fear you are (the object of your) fury"; cf. NEB, "Who feels thy wrath like those who fear thee?" But it seems best to assume that the force of "who knows" (or, "feels/experiences") in 11a carries over to 11b.

12.a. The verb lacks a suffix (הוֹרְעֵנוּ would be expected), but the suffix on "our days" (נו—) does double duty, probably avoiding a redundancy (Müller, *ZTK* 81 [1984] 276; Dahood, II, 326). For the force of the כן with the verb, see 1 Sam 23:17 (Gunkel, 401): "so make it known/that it may be known" = "teach (us) so."

12.b. LXX links למנות (simple infinitive construct of מנה, "count/number") with v 11: "Who knows the power of your wrath, to number (our days) because of the fear of your wrath." V 12 follows: "So make known your right hand" (ימינך) for MT's ימינו; i.e., "your right [hand]" for "our days"). This has the merit of balanced colons in both verses, but probably represents an effort to understand MT.

12.c. The hiphil of בוא ("come/go") means to "bring in/gather," and thus "get/obtain." Unnecessary changes are proposed by some commentators to alter the meaning to "bring wisdom into the heart/mind" or "to bring the heart/mind to wisdom" (e.g., Gunkel, 401–2; Oesterley, 405; Anderson, II, 654; BHS).

13.a. Reading the שובה as the simple imperative of שוב as in Exod 32:12; Job 6:29; Ps 6:5; 80:15; in imperfect: Josh 7:26; Job 7:7; Isa 12:1; Jer 23:20. The meaning is that of "turn (aside)/divert/stop/stay/relent." If Yahweh is thought of as having left his people and the prayer is for his return, then the traditional "Return!" is in order.

13.b. The niphal imperative of נחם is usually translated as "have pity/compassion," but when it is used with the preposition על it regularly means "to change one's mind about something planned" (Exod 32:12, 14: Jer 18:8, 10; Jonah 3:10; Job 42:6). Thus the meaning may be "relent/change a course of action" (see D. Patrick, "The Translation of Job 42:6," VT 26 (1976) 369–71).

14.a. LXX indicates perfect (שבענו) rather than MT's imperative: "We have been satisfied."

14.b. Lit., "in the morning." The expression is equal to "at dawn" and in the context means "each morning."

14.c. The colon is heavy and perhaps ונשמחה ("and we will rejoice") should be omitted (Gunkel). I have read the two words ונרנה ונשמחה as a hendiadys: "joyfully rejoice/sing out" (Pss 35:27; 67:5; Zech 2:14 [10]).

15.a. This form of "days" occurs elsewhere only in Deut 32:7; ימות rather than ימי. The plural שנות ("years") instead of שני appears for the first time in MT also in Deut 32:7. Both words are in construct with the verbal expressions which follow them. In both cases, the unusual forms may be due to assonance (see Dahood, II, 326).

16.a. MT's singular is probably collective as indicated by the plural ("your works/deeds") in the versions.

16.b. LXX indicates ראה, imperative: "And look upon your servants and upon your works."

16.c. The expression הדרך is usually taken as "your splendor/majesty," though the meaning "vision/revelation/apparition" is rather widely adopted. See Levenson, VT 35 (1985) 63–64; Cross, Canaanite Myth and Hebrew Epic, 152–53, n. 28; cf. Kloos, Yhwh's Combat with the Sea, 36–37. Much attention is focused on the parallelism of הדר with hlm, "dream/vision" in Ugaritic text CTA 14.3.155, and the meaning of the expression בהדרת קדש in Ps 29:2; 96:9; 1 Chr 16:29 (possibly 2 Chr 20:21), which is more likely to mean "appearance in holiness" than refer to the "holy garments" of worshipers, but is more likely still to mean "holy splendor" (see n. 96:9.a). The idea of "splendor/majesty" surely remains with the word in its theophanic sense; hence, "majestic vision." The meaning in 90:16 does not necessarily result in the same meaning in 96:9, though glory and theophany are common to both texts.

17.a. The word נעם is usually understood in the sense of "pleasure/delight/favor," as well as "beauty" (KJV; LXX has λαμπρότης, "brilliancy/radiance/splendid conduct"; cf. Ps 27:4; Prov 3:17; 15:26; 16:24; Zech 11:7, 10). Sometimes "sweetness" is used (JB, "May the sweetness of the Lord be on us!"; note Prov 16:24; KJV of Ps 141:6, following LXX). Levenson (VT 35 [1985] 61–67) has made a case for the meaning of נעם in Ps 27:4 and in 90:17 as a reference to an affirmative, visible sign from God, probably originally rooted in forms of divination, especially through fire as it consumed or failed to consume a sacrifice (noting Ps 4:6–7, the departure of the angel in the flame from the altar in Judg 13:20, and the description of Yahweh as a "devouring fire" in Exod 24:17; Deut 4:24; 9:3; Isa 30:27; cf. Isa 33:14). Thus in Pss 27 and 90 the longing is for "a theophanic fire employed as an affirmative omen" (63). Possibly the idea of the fire of a theophanic appearance is reflected in the LXX's reading of 90:17 (above). This technical sense does not, however, mean that there is not a more general meaning of "brightness/pleasantness," which is favorable and affirming (64). I have chosen "approval" in the translation of 90:17, which seems to fit the context, but it is rather bland. See also Levenson's treatment of Ps 16:5–6, 11 (VT 35 [1985] 64–66).

17.b. The colon is too long and perhaps "our God" should be omitted (BHS). Possibly both אדני and אלהינו are variant words for יהוה; the reader is either to pronounce one or the other. The two together are equivalent, of course, to "Yahweh our God."

17.c. The polel form כון may be factive and translated as "affirm/approve," or "say 'yes' to " (Levenson, *VT* 35 [1985] 64). The meaning "give attention to" is also possible; note the polal of כון in Job 8:8, though the meaning there could be also "affirm/approve"; cf. Isa 51:13.

17.d. The last colon should not be omitted on the basis of dittography (as in NEB). V 17 is a tricolon, using the expanded colon technique (see notes on Ps 92:8, 10), or else 17a should be read with v 16, forming a tricolon.

Form/Structure/Setting

Ps 90 is treated as having two major divisions (vv 1–12; 13–17) by most commentators, with a number arguing for two different poems put together as one (see Jacquet, II, 720). Gunkel (399) says that the first part deals with God and human beings, of matters which are of concern to all persons, while the second part is more characteristically Israelite relating to Yahweh and Israel. The meditation, or reflection, in vv 1–12 is the context and foundation for the petitions in vv 13–17. These divisions of the psalm are also woven together by a rather intricate literary structure. Vv 1b–2 form an introduction to the psalm, a frame which is completed by vv 16–17 as the conclusion. Vv 11–12 form a pivotal linkage between vv 3–10 and vv 13–15.

The literary structure of the psalm seems to be marked by the use of an envelope formation (A X B), either deliberate or incidental. V 4 follows v 2 more naturally than it does v 3 (and commentators sometime transpose the verses), so that vv 1b–2 and 4 form an envelope around v 3, which properly begins a unit composed of vv 3, 5–10, and interlocks the introduction of the psalm with the first main part. In turn, vv 3 and 5–6 form a frame around v 4. Vv 7 and 9 put v 8 in an envelope, and vv 9 and 11 frame v 10. As already noted, vv 11–12 link the two main parts of the psalm. V 12 relates best to "our days" in vv 9–10, while v 11, though closely related to vv 9–10, provides a transition to vv 13–15. Vv 13 and 16 frame vv 14–15 (cf. Auffret, *Bib* 61 [1980] 272–75); note the "servants" in both verses. The four-colon structure of vv 5–6 and v 10 encloses the two-colon verses in vv 7–9 and vv 14–15 have a total of four colons with unity of content between the two-colon verses 13 and 16 (Auffret, 275). The three-colon structure of v 2 matches the three-colon formation of v 17. The use of שוב in v 13 rather obviously relates to the use of the same verb in v 3 (see *Comment* on v 13). For further discussion, see the studies by Schreiner and Auffret.

The content of the psalm is also intricately formulated. Vv 1b–2 express confidence in God and gratitude for his help through the generations, affirming his everlasting nature. These verses are directly addressed to God in the language of prayer, which continues throughout the psalm. Vv 3–11 reflect on the human condition of mortality and life under divine wrath and ends with the petition in v 12. The reflective language constitutes a kind of complaint, but is not in the language common to the individual and communal laments (see the discussions by Westermann, "Der 90. Psalm"; idem, "Psalm 90," 158–65), though the complaint becomes rather specific in vv 7–10. The petitions of vv 13–17 are direct and contain language common to the laments. Thus the psalm is a communal prayer composed of grateful reflection, complaint, and petitions for gracious divine action.

The speaker in the psalm is not specifically identified (apart from the title), but vv 13 and 16 clearly indicate that the prayer represents the experience, reflection, and petitions of a community of people who identify themselves as the "servants" of Yahweh. The post-exilic use of the term "servants" for faithful members of the Israelite communities (see Isa 56:6; 65:8–9; 65:13–15; 66:14; cf. Mal 3:18; 3:22[4:4]; Ps 123:2; 134:1; 135:1) is evidence for the origin of this psalm in those communities. We may assume that the speaker is one of the "servants," whose prayer is designed to encouraged and instruct his/her distressed fellow "servants."

Though the context(s) of the psalm's composition and use cannot be absolutely fixed, the ascription of the psalm to Moses in the title is undoubtedly the result of later (probably post-exilic) scribal exegesis, even though the Mosaic origin of the psalm is still defended by a few scholars; among older commentators Delitzsch is notable. Dahood (II, 322) argues that archaic language in the psalm points to an early date of composition, possibly in the ninth century B.C.E., but not to Moses. We cannot follow exactly the midrashic tracks of the scribes who attributed this psalm to Moses, but their general course is reasonably clear. Earlier traditions had associated him with songs and poetry (Exod 15; Deut 31:30–32:47), and the similarities of language between Ps 90 and the song of Moses in Deut 31:30–32:47 was probably the starting point for either the composition of Ps 90 and/or its assignment to Moses, who is further designated as "the man of God" (cf. Deut 33:1; Josh 14:6; Ezra 3:2). Various linguistic parallels between the song of Moses and Ps 90 strengthen the relationship with Moses: e.g., the unusual ימות ("days") and שנות ("years") in v 15 are found together in Deut 32:7; the noun פעל ("work") in v 16 occurs in the Pentateuch only in Deut 32:4 and 33:11 (Delitzsch, III, 59). Freedman has observed that only Moses and Amos, apart from Ps 90, are able to intercede with God and get him to "repent" (נחם, "change one's mind/relent/ repent"): see Exod 32:12, 14; Amos 7:1–3, 6, though Yahweh does נחם in other contexts for other reasons (e.g., Jonah 3:10; cf. Jer 15:1, 6)—in fact only Moses *tells* God to נחם (Amos only says "Forgive" and "Stop it!"). Thus it is likely that the scribe(s) who put Moses in the title of Ps 90 was/were aware that only Moses could tell God to "turn" and "change his mind." Freedman suggests that Ps 90 was composed with the episode of Exod 32 in mind and "imagined in poetic form how Moses may have spoken in the circumstances of Exodus 32." See "Who Asks (or Tells) God to Repent?" *Bible Review* 1, 4 (1985) 56–59. In any case, such clues are all the scribes needed; the assignment to Moses required no extraordinary exegetical ingenuity (see E. Slomovic, "Formation of Historical Titles in the Books of Psalms," *ZAW* 91 [1979] 376).

The content of the psalm indicates long-lasting communal distress and need (vv 13–15), perhaps long and exhausting hardships from famine and disease (Johnson, *CPIP*, 191). The speaker and the community appear to have lived close to death for an extended time. The communal distress is not specifically defined, but the scribal interpretation of the psalm as Mosaic naturally took the time of affliction and distress in v 15 as a reference to the servitude of Israel in Egypt (Eerdmans, 430), which is reflected in the Targum for v 1: "A prayer of Moses the prophet, when the people of Israel sinned in the desert" (an interpretation which influenced older commentaries such as that of Barnes, *Notes on the Old Testament: Psalms*, III, 1–2). However, the experience of exile after 587 B.C.E. is much more probable. Vawter (*CBQ* 37 [1975] 460–70) argues for a close relationship between Ps 90 and the developed wisdom of the post-exilic period, and finds similarities between the psalm and the wisdom inspired prayer in the Wisd 9:1–18; 15:1–3. Mowinckel (*PIW*, II, 102) asserts that "Obviously the psalm derives from Jewish times, not from the earliest period." Von Rad ("Psalm 90," 221) is satisfied to assume that the psalm "derives from about the same intellectual and theological situation as Ecclesiastes," associating it with wisdom thought (also Müller, *ZTK* 81 [1984] 266–68) and judges it: "certainly post-exilic. We cannot fix the date of its writing any more precisely than that" (222).

The psalm has the general nature of a prayer of lament: complaint in vv 7–10 and petitions in vv 13–17. Features common in individual laments are found in the use of the imperative שׁובה ("turn/return") directed to Yahweh in v 13 (Ps 6:5; 7:8; 80:15; cf. 126:4), in the "How long!" of v 13 (cf. Ps 6:4; 74:10; 94:3), and the commitment to praise when the petitions are answered in v 14b (Müller, 268). Because of these features the reader might postulate a worship service of communal prayers of lament as the appropriate context of Ps 90—and, indeed, the psalm may have been used in such ceremonies (Kraus, II, 796–97). A model for such an occasion is provided by Joel 2:12–17 which depicts the community gathered in the temple to pray for divine mercy and deliverance (note the use of שׁוב and נחם in Joel 2:14 and Ps 90:13). See also Kraus, *Psalms 1–59*, 51; 1 Kgs 8:33–40; for evidence of regular services of repentances and fasting in Jerusalem after 587 B.C.E., see Jer 41:4–8; Zech 7:1–7; 8:18–19.

On the other hand, the sharply delineated conditions of immediate distress which seem to characterize the communal laments are missing in Ps 90 (Kraus, II, 797; Müller, *ZTK* 81 [1984] 266–67): complaint about the actions of enemies, cries of distress, drought or famine, and pleas for God to intervene to deliver the people from oppression (cf. Pss 44; 80; 84; 137; Lam 5). Thus it seems more probable that Ps 90 is a literary composition, belonging to the category of "learned psalmography," i.e., psalmography from circles of sages and scribes for the use of individuals and groups, but especially for personal piety and devotion. Von Rad ("Psalm 90," 222) summarizes this interpretation: "The genre of the national song of complaint, which gives the psalm, even in its present form, its unmistakable stamp, is accordingly to be understood only as an art form. It is no longer cultic, but a freely chosen literary figure which an unknown poet used for his poem." Von Rad suggests that the author would have been someone like Ben Sira, whose work is set forth in the Book of Ecclesiasticus. According to Mowinckel, the "learned psalmography" was characterized by the pastiche-like nature of compositions; intermixed materials which "do not keep to the rules" and make genre classification difficult, and by the reuse of old primary forms (see Mowinckel, *PIW*, II, 104–25; J. L. Kugel, "Topics in the History of the Spirituality of the Psalms," in *Jewish Spirituality: From the Bible through the Middle Ages*, vol. 13 of *World Spirituality*, ed. Arthur Green [New York: Crossroad, 1986] 129–34). Thus Ps 90 probably owes its existence and preservation to learned scribal composers, collectors, and interpreters of psalms and teachings in post-exilic Israelite communities who considered themselves servants of Yahweh, and prepared prayers and teaching for Israelites who sought to live as the devoted servants of Yahweh during hard times long endured.

Comment

Title and address to God (vv 1–2, 4). The designation of the psalm as a "prayer" (תפלה; Pss 17:1; 86:1; 102:1; 142:1; also 72:20) is appropriate for a psalm in the tradition of "learned psalmography" (Mowinckel, *PIW*, II, 108). The didactic material of such psalms is expressed in the forms of prayers addressed to God. The ascription of the prayer to Moses incorporates both the authority of Yahweh's servant par excellence and the ancient cultural feature (commonplace in Jewish literature) of grounding statements in antiquity. Overt newness was suspect; the more ancient the saying, prayer, or instruction, the more legitimate was its authority. Note the testimony of Wisdom in Prov 8:22–31 and the use of David, Solomon, Job, Daniel, Enoch, et al. in later literature. The appeal to "apostolic authority" is well known in Christian history.

The prayer begins with 1b, which is linked with v 2 in an artistic structure. Auffret (*Bib* 61 [1980] 263) notes the framing provided by "O Lord . . . you" and "you are God," and the pivotal expressions "were born" (ילדו)—of the mountains—and "travail with" (תחולל)—of the earth and the world; also the parallel between "in generation after generation" and "from everlasting to everlasting." The result is a powerful address to God which sets forth his enduring help from creation on; merging the historical and the transcendent realms of God (Vawter, *CBQ* 37 [1975] 463). God has been a source of help and a refuge (מעון may convey both ideas, see note 1.b. above) from the beginnings of the world— "from everlasting to everlasting" (or "from beginning to end," Müller, *ZTK* 81 [1984] 270).

Creation is conceptualized in the cosmogonic mode of being given birth, known from other creation stories in the ancient world (cf. Prov 8:25 for a similar statement). The statements in v 2 may assume the generative power of the earth, which produced the mountains (cf. Gen 1:20, 24; Job 38:8, where the primeval waters of the seas gush forth from an unspecified "womb"—the primordial waters below the earth[?]; cf. Job 28:14; Gen 7:11; 49:25; Deut 33:13; Isa 51:10; Ps 36:7). Kraus (II, 798), however, incorrectly argues that God was not a participant in the process. The passive verb "was born" in 2a has an indefinite subject, which could be understood as the earth. But the verb "travailed with" in 2b refers to God; it is God who has given birth to the earth and the world, along with the mountains (v 2a), as massive evidence of his creative power.

The synergistic nature of biblical creation accounts is often overlooked, especially when creation is defined in terms of the narrow scope of creation out of nothing. Creation is the result of divine initiative, but the process involves a working together of the divine with earthly and human powers. V 2 roots the confident testimony of v 1b, c in the wider horizon of God's works. The God who has been "our" help or refuge for generation after generation is the Creator who was God before the world began, and who still is. The eternal God who continually helps his people does not suffer from the transitory nature of humanity and of all earthly things which is set forth in the following verses (Westermann, "Psalm 90," 159).

In this section, v 4 relates most directly back to v 2; the eternal God is not vulnerable to the passage of time as are human beings, though we should not say that "time has no meaning with God" (Cohen, 298). The language is comparative, not absolute (cf. Isa 40:15–17 for a similar comparison). "It puts our world into its context . . . and our time-span into its huge setting of eternity" (Kidner, II, 329). On the "night watch," see Ps 63:7. A thousand years, of course, is an exceedingly long time for human history—a millennium—but to God only like a night watch, which may seem like an eternity for some, but for those who sleep it is as nothing.

The mortality of humankind (vv 3, 5–6). A complaint begins with v 3a which sets forth the divine responsibility for the death of humankind. The meaning of v 3b is the subject of different interpretations. One line of interpreters (e.g., Luther, Kissane, Delitzsch, Westermann) understand it to mean a return to life in the sense that "Human life will go on!" (Westermann, "Psalm 90," 161)—human beings die, but they do not die out (Delitzsch, III, 51). But it is more probable that 3b adds to the expressiveness and intensity of 3a and means that human death is as much the result of divine fiat as is creation. Humankind lives under a divine mandate of mortality, which no human being can escape.

Vv 5–6 further define the process and nature of human mortality. As von Rad ("Psalm 90," 214) says of v 3: "God himself is the cause of bleak transience." He pours out on humanity a "sleep" which pervades all of human existence (though no translation of v 5a inspires much confidence). The "sleep" is a bad sleep, which leaves those engulfed by it unable to respond adequately to life. In Ps 76:6–7, stout-hearted warriors are immobilized by sleeping a sleep which keeps them from raising a hand; at the rebuke of Yahweh, riders and horses are thrown into a deep sleep. The "shepherds" (leaders) of Assyria slumber under the deactivating wrath of Yahweh in Nah 3:18 (cf. 1:2). See also Jer 51:39, 57.

In Ps 90 all human beings are under a "sleep" which leads to death, but which anesthetizes them to the transitory nature of life and the reality of the wrath of God (vv 7–10). They do not know how to "number" their days (v 12), and are beguiled by short-lived flourishes of life, symbolized by the morning grass. The mortality of humankind is compared to the transience of grass in a dry climate, which flourishes in the coolness of the early morning dew only to wither and shrivel under the heat of the day. There seems to be a two-way comparison in vv 2–6: (1) humankind's "days" of life are very brief in comparison to the being of God, and (2) the transience of human existence is emphasized by the enduring nature of the mountains and the world.

Life under the wrath of God (vv 7–10, 12). The life of humankind is not only brief, it is also lived under wrath, wearisome with toil, and in trouble. The "somber reflections" (von Rad, "Psalm 90," 214) in this psalm continue in these verses; the "bleak transience" of vv 3–6 moves to an even more "somber horizon": "We are consumed by your anger, / and overwhelmed by your wrath." The relationship of humanity to God is complicated both by transience and by sin: the guilty waywardness of human beings is constantly before the face of God; sins kept secret from other human beings are not hidden from him (v 8). The light which streams out from the divine face illumines the dark places of human culpability; God knows human beings—all of us—as they actually are. These verses recall, of course, the accounts in Gen 2–3, and also the analysis of sin by Paul in the Book of Romans (Westermann, "Der 90. Psalm," 347): "Here, as there, what is in question is the fallibility of the whole human race and not just the sinfulness of the people of God" (Westermann, "Psalm 90," 161).

Vv 7 and 9 form a frame around v 8 and constitute a literary unit (Westermann, "Psalm 90," 161); note the use of ("for/so") at the beginning of vv 7 and 9, and the use of the verb כלה ("finish/complete/consume") in the same verses. V 9 expresses the meaning of v 7 in a complementary way. The human guilt which God keeps before his face (v 8) is like a radioactive core which poisons all of life; which is completed like a הגה, a "sigh," a short expression of resignation and weariness (cf. Ezek 2:10 and note 9.d. above), or, a "breath of the mouth" (Targum). The days pass by in the wrath of God, only to end with a sigh! Von Rad's description of these verses as presenting a "somber horizon" is well taken.

Vv 10 and 12 form an addendum to the material in vv 7–9 and develop further the description of human distress (cf. Müller, ZTK 81 [1984] 274–77; Westermann, "Psalm 90," 162). Even when human life is extended to its full length, the span of the years is full of toil and trouble, and as the years fly by they are soon gone (v 10). A somewhat similar reflection on the eternity of God and the brevity and evil of human life is found in Ecclus 18:1–14, where, however, human life is said to be possible for a hundred years (see also Isa 65:20). *Jub.* 23.8–15 contains a reflection on the decline in longevity in the accounts of the patriarchs in Genesis: after the flood, human beings began "to grow old quickly and to shorten the days of their lives due to much suffering and through the evil of their ways." With Ps 90:4, 10 in mind, an evil generation will say: "The days of the ancients were as many as one thousand years and good. But behold, (as for) the days of our lives, if a man should extend his life seventy years or if he is strong (for) eighty years, then these are evil. And there is not any peace in the days of this evil generation" (tr. O. S. Wintermute, in *The Old Testament Pseudepigrapha,* ed. James H. Charlesworth [Garden City, NY: Doubleday, 1985] 100). It is worth noting, however, that none of the pre-flood patriarchs in Gen 5 actually lived a thousand years; even the long life span of Methuselah (969 years) falls short of the millennial ideal (cf. *Jub.* 23.27).

V 12 is a petition which corresponds most closely to v 10. The need for human beings is for a mind wise enough to sort out the days, with their events, responsibilities, and opportunities, so that they can cope with the transience and evil of human life (v 10). This verse represents mainstream wisdom theology and acknowledges that the wisdom required lies beyond the power of humanity. It is the gift of God, a power of discernment which is not the result of human endeavor, but must be taught by God (cf. Prov 2:6–15). Cf. Eph 5:16, "making the most of the time, because the days are evil" (rsv), and Col 4:5, "conduct yourselves wisely . . . making the most of the time" (rsv).

V 12a is traditionally understood as "numbering days" (מנה) in the sense of realizing how few the days of human life are; i.e. a constant awareness and response to the temporality of life—the wisdom which emerges from contemplation of "the fleeting character and brevity of our lifetime" (Delitzsch, III, 57). This is doubtless true, but "numbering our days" is surely more than checking them off on the calendar and thinking about the reduced number left! After all, we hardly need to ask God to teach us how to count days. We can do that very well. The verb מנה does mean to "count/number off" in its simple forms: e.g., 2 Sam 24:1; 2 Kgs 12:11. But some contexts suggest that more than mere numbering is involved: e.g., 1 Kgs 20:25; Isa 53:12 (KB, 537, suggests "summed up with"); Ps 147:4; Ecclus 40:29. Thus the meaning probably includes the ideas of "evaluation/judgment" and the like. Perhaps the English "deal with our days" gets to the meaning rather well.

Appeals to Yahweh for a reversal of wrath (vv 11, 13–17). V 11 serves as an interlocking verse between vv 7–10, 12 and vv 13–17 (see *Form/Structure/Setting* above). The subject matter of the wrath of God relates back to vv 7–9: note the repetition of עברתך ("your wrath") in both vv 9 and 11 and the use of אפך ("your anger") in vv 7 and 11. Vv 9 and 11 form an envelope around v 10, which without v 11 would lead easily to v 12. At the same time the use of the verb ("know" in v 11 and "cause to know/teach" in v 12) binds these verses together.

Unfortunately the meaning of v 11 is less than certain. Kirkpatrick interprets the rhetorical questions in the verse with one of his own (552): "Who understands or lays to heart the intensity of God's wrath against sin so as to fear Him duly with that reverence which is man[kind]'s safeguard against offending Him?" The answer assumed is "No one." Though the consuming power of God's wrath has been experienced (vv 7–10), its full extent and potential lies beyond human ken. If the translation above is correct, v 11b means that the same ignorance of the power of God's wrath is manifest in the disproportionate human responses in worship ("the fear due you"). Both the power of God's wrath and the quality of reverence due him elude the "knowing" of human beings, which makes imperative the petitions in vv 12–17. Perhaps, also, the measure of the homage not given to God is the measure of judgment (Kidner, II, 330, n. 2).

The language in vv 13–17 is easily recognizable as that of petitions in psalms of lament (Westermann, "Psalm 90," 163; idem, "Der 90. Psalm," 348; Gunkel and Begrich, *Einleitung in die Psalmen*, 128–29). The "turn back" of 13a relates to v 3 with some irony. The "turn back" (שוב) in v 3 (twice) is used to describe God's sending humankind back to dust, but the "turn back" in v 13 petitions for a turning of God *from* wrath, i.e., "relent" (cf. Exod 32:12). Yahweh is implored to change his mind about his servants, who have endured long distress, and to make manifest to them his enduring love, which satisfies and evokes joyful responses of praise (v 14). For the expression עד־מתי, "How long?" see Pss 6:4; 49:5; 74:10; 82:2; 94:3; Exod 10:7; 1 Sam 1:14; Jer 4:14, 21; Prov 1:22; a "poignant exclamation rather than a question" (Cohen, 13), which expresses the weariness and perplexity of acute distress long endured. In this case, how long will Yahweh continue wrath without relief?—an interpretation that seems more probable than the idea that Yahweh has been absent and is asked to return to his people (cf. Ps 79:5).

The "morning" in v 14 is the use of a conventional idea of the time for the answer and help of God (Kraus, II, 800; see Pss 5:4; 30:6; 46:6; 143:8; also, 59:17; 88:14; 2 Sam 23:4; Zeph 3:5 (for discussion of "God's Help in the Morning," see C. Barth, *TDOT*, II, 226–28). The idea is rooted in worship experiences of prayer and the sense of the renewed presence of Yahweh, sometimes concretely symbolized in the temple by such means as fire and smoke, and with the coming of dawn which brought the worshipers from the darkness of night into the light of a new day. Historical traditions which associated Yahweh's saving intervention with the morning were doubtless a factor also (e.g., Exod 14:27; 2 Kgs 19:35; Isa 37:36; also Josh 10:9–11; Judg 6:28).

The "days-years" combination in v 15 is a *leit* motif which appears also in vv 4 and 9. "By repeating this parallelism, the author deliberately links the plea in distress from the communal lament with the motif of human transitionness"

(Westermann, "Psalm 90," 164). The years of distress ("evil") in v 15 is a specific example of the more universal statements about human life in vv 3–12. The time of great distress for Israel is presented against the background of the days of "toil and trouble" for all human life as described in vv 3–10.

The petition in v 15 is for days of joy equal to the years of distress. This will be possible when Yahweh is no longer hidden and his glorious works are again apparent to his servants (v 16). When Yahweh "changes his mind" (נחם, v 13) about the condition of his servants and bestows upon them his gracious approval (v 17, נעם, see note 17.a.), productive life will be possible; the work of human hands will be effective and enduring, despite the transience of life. The prayer is for stability and worthwhileness in normal human endeavors, so that the somber human conditions described in vv 3–10 do not overwhelm the spirit of the servants of Yahweh and so that they will know that their work is "not in vain" (cf. 1 Cor 15:58; Kidner, II, 331). The visible success and effectiveness of the "work of our hands" would be a sign of the appearance of Yahweh and of the "change of his mind" (v 13) which is expressed in his gracious approval (vv 16–17; Levenson, *VT* 35 [1985] 63). The "work(s)" (פעל) of Yahweh in v 16 is/are that of salvation and "providential intervention" (Anderson, II, 655; cf. Pss 92:6; 95:9; 111:3; 143:5; Hab 1:5; 3:2). The divine epithet "Lord" (אדני) used in v 1 is now identified as "our God," who is Yahweh (v 13).

Explanation

Ps 90 is well known for its treatment of the transitory nature of human life in the context of the eternal nature of God (vv 1–12). The mere brevity of human life is not, however, the major concern of the psalm. "The main point of Ps 90 is not the hymn, praising the eternity of Yahweh, nor the contemplation of the shortness of human life, but the prayer for the Eternal God not to overlook the short life of a man [*sic*] and let it pass away in misfortune, but to have mercy upon his congregation which consists of such short-lived people" (Mowinckel, *PIW*, II, 75). Mowinckel's fine summary points toward the tension in the structure of the psalm in which the reality of the limited and troubled course of the lives of human beings is framed by the confident confession of faith in God at its beginning and by petitions for divine intervention at the end (Westermann, "Der 90. Psalm," 349). The somber portrayal of the brevity of life and its waywardness under the wrath of God forms one pole while the joy and majestic vision of the saving work of Yahweh for his servants form another. The psalm reaches out for "the eternity of God in the midst of man[kind]'s passing life" and the faith in God's grace which frames the psalm shines "like a star from another world" (Weiser, 603).

Without the use of precise analysis, Ps 90 witnesses to a direct relationship between sin and death, probably with Gen 2–3 in the background. A connection between the wrath of God and the shortness of life seems to be assumed as necessary, though the same lack of direct statement regarding the relationship found in Gen 1–11 is also present. In Genesis the shortened life span is regarded as the judgment of God because of human sin (so most commentators from Luther on), or as the result of diminished vitality because of increasing distance from the original vitality of the starting point of creation (G. von Rad, *Genesis*, [Philadelphia: Westminster, 961] 67) and the deterioration resulting from the spread of sin (see

D. J. A. Clines, *The Theme of the Pentateuch,* JSOT SS 10 [Sheffield: JSOT Press, 1978] 64–77). "The author of Psalm 90 sees sin and death as interconnected, but an intellectual calculation of the relation . . . is not possible for him" (Westermann, "Psalm 90," 161–62). Westermann argues that this is the point of v 8: the "unverifiable and incalculable" relationship is "shifted to where it ought to be, into the light of God's countenance"—which displays gracious love as well as anger.

The world-view which lies behind and around Ps 90 (as of all the Bible) differs in some significant particulars from that we commonly know today. One of these particulars is that of what may be called a theological-ecological understanding of life. Modern analyses tend to separate the physical and spiritual realms of life and to demarcate the realm of nature from other aspects of life. Even in theological studies a separation of creation from history is common. The biblical approach, generally, is much more systemic and ecological; one in which the spiritual and the physical, the divine and the human, are in constant interaction. Human behavior and what we know as nature are dynamically interconnected; a relationship continually maintained by the creative-judging-saving presence of God. Therefore the miserable condition of life in post-exilic Israelite communities is integrated with the universal situation of humankind in vv 3–10 and with the broad horizons of Yahweh's saving work in vv 1b–2 and 13–17. The biblical propensity to move back and forth from the general to the particular is also evident. The specific distress of the servants of Yahweh in vv 13–17 is juxtaposed with the universal condition of humankind in vv 1–10; the specific is dealt with in the context of the general. The converse is also true. The Bible usually refuses to postulate generalized doctrines without moving swiftly to personalized particulars: "Who is my neighbor?" Jesus replied, "A certain man went down from Jerusalem to Jericho, . . ." (Luke 10:29–30). The accounts in Gen 1–3 shift from humankind in the context of the whole of creation until the focus is on Adam and Eve and God in the Garden in chap. 3, and on to the family in chap. 4. The general and the particulars must be held together in a continual dialectic.

The message of the psalm seems to cluster around two poles. First, v 12 points to the "heart (mind) of wisdom" which can be ours when we allow God to teach us how to "number our days"; that is, the wisdom to cope with the days and years of our mortal existence in ways which will be healthy and happy. Such wisdom makes it possible for God to establish "the work of our hands" (v 17). Second, the psalm's broad horizons, somber though they are, help us to persevere until the saving work of God is fully apparent in a majestic appearing of this glory to his faithful servants (v 16). See 2 Pet 3:8–10. Isaac Watts' (1719) paraphrase of Ps 90 still stirs us:

> O God, our help in ages past,
> Our hope for years to come,
> Our shelter from the stormy blast
> And our eternal home. . . .
>
> Be thou our guard while life shall last,
> And our eternal home.

Amen.

When God Is Your Refuge   (91:1–16)

Bibliography

Brueggemann, W. *The Message of the Psalms.* Minneapolis: Augsburg, 1984. 156–57. **Caquot, A.** "Le Psaume XCI." *Sem* (1958) 21–37. **Eissfeldt, O.** "Eine Qumran-Textform des 91. Psalms." In *Bibel und Qumran*, ed. H. Bardtke. Berlin: Evangelische Haupt-Bibelgesell-schaft, 1968. 82–85. ———. "Jahwes Verhältnis zu 'Eljon und Schaddaj nach Psalm 91." In *Kleine Schriften*, Bd. 3, ed. R. Sellheim and F. Maas. Tübingen: Mohr, 1966. 441–47. **Fraine, J. de** "Le demon du mid.' (Ps 91 [90], 6)." *Bib* 40 (1959) 372–83. **Hugger, P.** *Jahwe meine Zuflucht: Gestalt und Theologie des 91. Psalms.* Münsterschwarzacher Studien, 13. Münsterschwarzachen: Vier-Turma-Verlag, 1971. **Macintosh, A. A.** "Psalm XCI 4 and the Root סחר." *VT* 23 (1973) 56–62. **Ploeg, J. Van der.** "Le Psaume XCI dans une re-cension de Qumran." *RB* 72 (1965) 210–17.

Translation

1
Whoever dwells under the protection[a] of the Most High[b]   (3+3)
will abide[c] in the shade of the Almighty.[d]

2
I say:[a] O Yahweh,[b] (you are) my refuge[c] and my fortress,[d]   (4+2)
my God in whom I trust.

3
Truly,[a] he will save you from the fowler's[b] trap   (4+2)
(and) from the threat[c] of destruction.[d]

4
With his feathers[a] he will cover you,   (3+3+3)
and under his wings you will take refuge;[b]
his faithfulness[c] will be (your) shield of protection.[d]

5
Do not fear[a] the terror[b] of the night,   (3+3)
or the arrow that flies in daytime,

6
or the plague[a] that stalks in the dark,   (3+3)
or the scourge[b] that rushes forth[c] at noonday.

7
A thousand may fall beside you;   (3+2+3)
ten thousand on your right,
(but) it[a] will not come near you.

8
You will only look at it with your eyes,   (3+3)
and watch the punishment of the wicked.

9
Truly you, O Yahweh, are my refuge![a]   (3+3)
If you make the Most High your haven,

10
no harm will happen to you;   (3+3)
no disaster[a] will come near your tent.

11
For he will command his angels about you,   (3+3)
to guard you in all your ways.

12
They will hold you up with their hands,   (3+3)
lest you stub your foot on a stone.[a]

13
You will tread on the lion[a] and the cobra,   (3+3)
(and) trample the young lion and the serpent.[b]

14
"Truly,[a] I will keep safe[b] the one devoted to me;[c]   (3+3)
I will protect[d] the one who knows my name,

15   *who will call upon me, and I will answer,*   (2+2+2)
           with whom I will be in (time of) trouble,
           whom I will free from trouble and bring to honor.
16   *I will satisfy them with long life,*[a]   (3+2)
           and show them [b] *my saving-work.*"

Notes

1.a. Traditionally, "shelter/secret place." The noun סתר means a "hiding place" or "secrecy." In some usages, it means "under the cover of/protection," as here. See 1 Sam 20:20; Job 40:21; Pss 31:21; 61:5; cf. Ps 27:5.

1.b. For עליון, see n. 92:2.b.

1.c. The participle in 1a is continued by the finite verb in 1b (Johnson, *CPIP*, 186, citing GKC 116x). The verb לון means, basically, "to lodge" or "spend the night," but in more extended usage it means to "live in" or "abide" (see n. 55:8.a.). NIV has "rest"; JB, "make your home."

1.d. I have retained the traditional "shadow of," but בצל "in the shade of" is also metaphorical for "under the protection/security of." See Isa 30:2, 3; 49:2; 51:16; Lam 4:20; Eccl 7:12; cf. Cant 2:3; Ps 121:5. For "under the shadow of the wings of," see Pss 17:8; 36:8; 57:2; 63:8. In the sense of political protection, see Judg 9:15; Ezek 17:23; 31:6, 12–17; Hos 14:8[7]. For שדי, "Almighty," see n. Ps 68:15.a., a name for God which appears only twice in the Psalter.

2.a. LXX, supported by Syr and Vg, presents a well-known problem here, becasue its ἐρεῖ indicates either (1) אמר (simple [qal] participle) or (2) יאמר (3d sing. impf.): (1) "saying/the one saying" or (2) "he will say." The Qumran text 11 QPsAp[a] has האומר, evidently a participle with the article: "The speaking one/the one who says" (see J. van der Ploeg, *RB* 72 [1965] 212). The resulting translation could be: "Living under the protection of Elyon / abiding in the shade of Shaddai / is the one who speaks to Yahweh: my refuge and my fortress / my God in whom I trust" (see Eissfeldt, "Eine Qumran-Textform des 91. Psalms," 83).

The linkage of vv 1 and 2 as in the versions and in the Qumran text is certainly an acceptable option, regardless of the interpretation of the verse. Nevertheless, MT also seems acceptable and I have retained it (see *Form/Structure/Setting*). For examples of translations with the LXX-Qumran option, see JB and NEB. Dahood, Eerdmans, and NAB vocalize אמר in 2a as an imperative addressed to the person being encouraged: "Say to Yahweh (or O Yahweh), 'my refuge and my fortress.'" Johnson (186) vocalizes as אֹמֵר but treats it as a descriptive vocative (see 154, n. 1), equal to "Thou that sayest of Yahweh." He also reads the participle ישׁ in 1a as a descriptive vocative: "Thou that dwellest in . . . and lodgest in . . . ," assuming that the finite verb in 1b continues the force of the participle in 1a.

2.b. Reading the ליהוה as vocative (as in Dahood, II, 330; Hugger, *Jahwe meine Zuflucht*, 31; cf. C. Scheldl, "Die Hieligen' und die 'Herrlichen' in Psalm 16:1–4." *ZAW* 76 [1964], 172): "I say, O Yahweh. . . ." It may be, of course, "of/concerning" Yahweh. LXX has ἐρεῖ τῷ κυρίῳ, "he will say to the LORD," which is quite possible for ל אמר (e.g., Gen 3:13; 1 Kgs 14:2): "I say to Yahweh: (you are) my refuge. . . ."

2.c. Hugger, *Jahwe meine Zuflucht*, 58–116, has an extensive review of the verb חסה, "seek refuge," and of its noun forms. He argues that the expression אתה מחסי, "you are my refuge" (as in v 9), is an emphatic cultic formulaic statement of trust in Yahweh; more a formulaic declaration than the expression היית מחסי, "You have been my refuge" (as in Ps 61:4), which is a testimony of experience. The combination of מחסי and אתה occurs five times: Pss 71:4; 91:2; 91:9; 142:6; Jer 17:17.

2.d. Perhaps the MT accentuation should be disregarded and "my fortress" read with 2b in order to balance the colons: "I say, O Yahweh, (you are) my refuge / and my fortress, my God in whom I trust"; so Kugel (*The Idea of Biblical Poetry*, 115–16), who argues that this is an example of scribal "forgetting" of parallelism, resulting in the misplacement of the medial pause. V 3 has the same unbalanced formation (4+2), however, and the misplacement of the medial pause is not a solution in its case. It is better to recognize that the colons in both vv 2 and 3 are balanced in thought: אתה ליהוה is repeated, in the mind of the reader before 2b, and the same is the case with כי הוא יצילך ("truly he will deliver/save you from") before 3b. The expression in each case does double duty.

3.a. Reading the כי as emphatic (asseverative), with the meaning "verily," "truly," or "indeed," or the like. Johnson (*CPIP*, 186) has: "Be assured that He will deliver you." Gunkel (406) suggests that the כי is equivalent to אשרי ("how blest is") as in Pss 112:1, 6; 128:2; Prov 3:13–14; 8:34–35; Job 5:17–18.

3.b. The word for "fowler," יָקוּשׁ (Prov 6:5; Jer 5:26) appears as יָקוֹשׁ in Hos 9:8 (cf. Ps 124:7). The יָקוֹשׁ makes the colon long, and Dahood wants to read it with 3b, postulating a verb יָקֹשׁ, "to shield/ protect," sharing the accusative prefix with the preceding verb and reading (with 3a) as: "He alone will free you from the snare/shield you against the venomous substance."

3.c. Reading מִדֶּבֶר ("from the pestilence/plague of") as מִדָּבָר (from דָּבָר, "word/matter/thing/ way of"), and understanding with Johnson (*CPIP*, 186) as equal to the "threat of destruction," or as "destructive word" (cf. Pss 38:13; 52:4, 6; Kraus, II, 802–3), or as "destructive event." LXX has "troublesome/disordered matter." Duhm's emendation to מִבּוֹר ("from the pit of") is adopted by Weiser. The vocalization in v 3 may have been influenced by the appearance of דֶּבֶר in v 6. Either reading in v 3 is acceptable and differs little in meaning.

3.d. For חַוּוֹת, "destruction," see n. 52:4.a.; n. 57:2.d.

4.a. The versions read MT's sing. noun as plural (see *BHS*). MT may represent defective spelling. However, the Qumran text has the sing. and the word may be collective. Cf. Hugger, *Jahwe meine Zuflucht*, 30.

4.b. 11QPsApᵃ has תשכון "you will dwell" (cf. Dahood, II, 331), which may be the use of a more contemporary verb for one not so common (see Eissfeldt, "Eine Qumran-Textform," 83).

4.c. On אֱמֶת, "truth/faithfulness," see *Comment* on Ps 51:8. Johnson (*CPIP*, 186) translates as "his pledge," in the sense of a solemn promise (56, n. 2; 72, n. 3), as in Ps 132:11.

4.d. The hapax legomenon וְסֹחֵרָה is the subject of a study by Macintosh (*VT* 23 [1973] 56–62). The word is derived from the root concept of "circle/circumference," and was interpreted in the Targum as a "round shield" (עֲגִילָא), an interpretation followed by some versions and represented in KJV and RSV as "buckler." LXX, on the other hand, treats the word as a verbal form (probably simple fem. sing. participle סֹ(וֹ)חֵרָה): "his truth will encircle you with a shield"; followed by Briggs, II, 280, 282; also by the Jewish commentators Rashi and Ibn Ezra; Macintosh, 58. Macintosh appeals to Akkadian and Arabic cognates, and to the use of סָחַר in Isa 47:15 and Ps 38:11 (less helpful), to support the idea of "protection," especially with a background of enchantments and magical defenses against demons. He suggests that Buttenwieser's proposed emendation (819) is unnecessary to sustain an essentially correct translation: "His faithfulness will protect you like a shield." The translation above treats "shield and protection" as a hendiadys: "protective shield/shield of protection." NEB's "rampart" for סֹחֵרָה follows a Syriac root with the idea of "Walled enclosure/bulwark" (also in Gunkel, KB, Macintosh, 61).

5.a. A command form of prohibition (Johnson, *CPIP*, 187, n. 3; cf. Decalogue; GKC 107o); more emphatic than a jussive. Obedience is expected.

5.b. See n. Ps 74:2.b.; cf. Job 15:21; 21:9; 22:10; Cant 3:8; Jer 49:5; Lam 3:47.

6.a. Retaining MT's דֶּבֶר, "pestilence/plague/epidemic"; e.g., Exod 5:3; 9:3, 15; Lev 26:25; Num 14:12; Deut 28:21; Ezek 33:27; 38:22; Amos 4:10. The plagues afflict livestock as well as human beings (Exod 9:3–7; Ezek 14:19; Exod 9:15). They are always lethal (Exod 9:6; Jer 14:12; Ezek 5:12; 14:19). The word occurs in lists that include flood, famine, sword, hail, fire, and enemies. Note the tripartite sword, famine, and pestilence in such passages as Jer 14:12; 21:6, 7, 9; 24:10; 27:8, 13; 29:17, 18; Ezek 6:11, 12; 7:15; pestilence, flood, and sword in Ezek 28:23; sword, wild beasts, and pestilence in Ezek 33:27. Note that דֶּבֶר, "threat of destruction," appears in v 3.

6.b. The word קֶטֶב may carry the idea of "sting" or "thorn" (KB, 834; de Fraine, *Bib* 40 [1959] 397). BDB (881) suggests "destruction" from a root (assumed) "cut off" (also Briggs, Anderson).

6.c. MT's יָשׁוּד is usually taken as from שָׁדַד, "devastate/deal violently with." The form יָשֹׁד would be expected (but see GKC 67q), unless יָשׁוּד is from a verb שׁוּד. Cf. Dahood, II, 332. LXX has "demon/ evil spirit" for יָשׁוּד, reading וְשֵׁד (שֵׁד, "demon/evil spirit," see Deut 32:17; Ps 106:37; cf. Gen 14:3, 8, 10). The Qumran text 11QPsApᵃ has ישוד, which may represent the normal spelling of the qal imperf. from שָׁדַד. Hugger (*Jahwe meine Zuflucht*, 41) argues that the Qumran text (ישוד) should be read as וְשֹׁד (using the noun שֹׁד, "devastation," which appears some 25 times in MT), but he does not adopt this as the best reading, preferring to assume that ישוד in MT is a verb with the meaning "go forth/rush with force" (R. Gordis, *JTS* 41 [1940] 34–41; see also idem *The Book of Job* [New York: Jewish Theological Seminary, 1978] 59). The meaning of שׁוּד as "pour/rush in with force" is found in Syr and provides a superior meaning in Ps 91:6. The assumption that the verb is שׁוּד solves the spelling problem in the vocalization.

7.a. For the "it," see *Comment*.

9.a. V 9 presents major problems for translation and interpretation. To whom does the emphatic "you" (אַתָּה) apply? The 1st common sing. suffix on "refuge" usually generates emendation from מַחְסִי to מַחְסֶךָ, "for Yahweh is your refuge" (e.g., Gunkel, Kraus, Oesterley), understanding the "you" as the one (or those) who are encouraged to have faith in Yahweh. Dahood (II, 333) and Johnson (*CPIP*,

189) assume that מחסי is an archaic spelling which retains the final *-y* and that the suffix "your" is borrowed from "your haven" in 9b (so Dahood; Johnson: "Because thou hast made of Yahweh a refuge"). Another approach is to conclude that a verb is either missing (e.g., Gunkel, Kissane) or understood (Dahood argues that the verb in 9b serves double duty in 9a). E.g., the verb אמרת has been assumed after the אתה or in place of it (see Gunkel, 107) on the participle אמר (Caquot, *Sem* [1958] 31): "for/ if you say that Yahweh is your refuge" (also, Kissane). If MT is retained, one could read the verse as in NIV: "If you make the Most High your dwelling—even the LORD, who is my refuge—" (see also, KJV; Kirkpatrick, 557, who notes that this type of translation involves "an intolerably harsh construction"). LXX retains the first suffix on "my refuge" (reading ἐλπις μου, "my hope / object of hope") but reads the verb (ἔθου) as in middle voice: "For you, O Lord, are my hope / you have made (for yourself) the Most High to be your refuge"—the "you" refers to the speaker in the first part of the verse.

The Qumran text is damaged and the reconstruction of the verse is uncertain. Eissfeldt ("Ein Qumran-Textform," 85) reconstructs as [יהוה קר]את מח[סי עליון שם] מחמדך, which would read: "Yahweh you have named as 'My Refuge' / made the Most High your desire (or, beloved one)." The reconstruction is made in support of Eissfeldt's thesis that the psalm is the testimony of a convert to Yahwism (see also, Hugger, *Jahwe meine Zuflucht*, 47, n. 24).

I have chosen to retain MT and read v 9a with v 2 as forming a frame around vv 3–8, in which case v 9b begins a new section of the psalm (cf. Hugger, 48). The כי ("truly") is taken as asserative, as in vv 3 and 14.

10.a. נגע is a "stroke/plague," such as a disease (Lev 13:2; 14:3, 32, 54) or a wound inflicted on a person or a blow (Deut 17:8; 21:5; Prov 6:33; Ps 89:33). "Disease," "calamity," "plague," "scourge," or "disaster" are all acceptable; the parallel with ("harm/evil") suggests a more general term. The QPsAp[a] text has a verb (יגע), "strike/smite" (Eissfeldt, "Eine Qumran-Textform," 85; Hugger, *Jahwe meine Zuflucht*, 49).

12.a. The translation could be: "lest your foot hit a stone" (taking תגף as imp. 3rd pers. fem. sing. from נגף).

13.a. LXX and Syr seem to read שחל ("lion") as having the meaning "serpent." LXX has ἀσπίδα καὶ βασιλίσκον, "asp and basilik." It is possible that זחל (for MT's שחל) was being read; a word used of crawling things or reptiles in Deut 32:24 and Mic 7:17—though LXX does not indicate זחל in those references. However, the emendation of MT, or the postulation of a different text, may not be necessary. Mowinckel's study of שחל (*Hebrew and Semitic Studies*, FS G. R. Driver, ed. D. W. Thomas and W. D. McHardy [Oxford: Clarendon Press, 1963] 95–103) has set forth a case for the word as blending leonine and serpentine features, citing Semitic cognates and Job 28:8 (and possibly Job 10:16 and Prov 26:13). Mowinckel originally translated שחל in Job 28:8 as "lizard"; in his study he adopts the idea for Ps 91:13 of the sea dragon or mythical *Lindwurm* ("serpent" is adopted in Job 28:8 by M. H. Pope, *Job*, AB 15, 180). The LXX translators may have understood שחל in Ps 91:13 as "serpent," helped, of course, by the feeling that "lion" is out of place with "serpent" in the same poetic colon. The Qumran text QPsAp[a] has פתן ("cobra") in the first place followed by a lacuna in the text, which van der Ploeg (214) argues probably had אפעה ("viper"), which LXX renders as βασιλίσκος in Isa 59:5 (and used for פתן in Deut 32:33). Eissfeldt ("Eine Qumran-Textform," 84), however, reconstructs the lacuna with שחל, which he treats as meaning a mythical sea serpent, following Mowinckel.

Some interpreters argue for a reptilian sense for both שחל and כפיר in Ps 91:13. Johnson's (190) proposal to carry over the force of the "lest" from 12b to v 13a ("Lest you . . . step upon . . . a viper, tread upon . . . a snake") works very well, but it demands the reading of שחל and כפיר ("lion"—"young lion") in reptilian senses. Thomas (*TRP*, 38–39) cites Mowinckel and translates שחל as "asp" and כפיר ("young lion") in 13b as "viper," citing the use of *kurpha* in Syriac with the meaning "asp/viper" (also, Johnson, *CPIP*, 190, n. 3), and noting the LXX use of δράκοντων ("dragons/large serpents") for כפירים ("young lions") in Job 4:10, where the "arrogance (or exultation) of the dragons/serpents will be quelled." Hugger (*Jahwe meine Zuflucht*, 50–52), after discussion of the versional variations (and noting Luke 10:19), adopts van der Ploeg's reconstruction of אפעה in the Qumran text and translates *"Kobra und Otter"* ("cobra and viper") in 13a, retaining "lion," however, in 13b.

The case for reading שחל as referring to a serpent or reptilian creature has merit. The verbs דרך and רמס, while metaphorical for "subdue," convey the imagery of "stepping on" (דרך with על is elsewhere only in Deut 33:19; Amos 4:13; Mic 1:3; Job 9:9; hiphil in Hab 3:19) or "trampling," meanings which it could be argued do not fit too well with lions. However, note the use of רמס in Dan 8:7 of a ram, and of דרך with human beings in Judg 20:43; cf. the important parallel to 91:13 in Isa 63:3 (using the verbs דרך and רמס; cf. Hugger, 249–50; whose argument that 13b is figurative language in contrast to treading on serpents in 13a is not very convincing).

Despite the evidence for the reptilian sense of שַׁחַל, I have retained the meaning "lion" in v 13a, though with doubt. There seem to be enough contexts in which to establish the basic meaning of שַׁחַל as "lion," at least in biblical Hebrew (Job 4:10; 10:10; 28:8; Hos 5:14; 13:7; Prov 26:13). There is really no question about כְּפִיר as "lion" in 13b. The parallelistic sequence is: lion/snake // lion snake (ABAB). The incomplete Qumran text may have had: snake/lion // lion/snake (ABBA)—a sharper parallelism; though it is possible, of course, that this text had: snake/snake // snake/snake. The verbs seem somewhat strained with "lion" (as noted above); however, they are not necessarily unsuitable.

13.b. תַּנִּין is a sea serpent or sea dragon in some contexts (see *Comment* on 74:12–17), but in Exod 7:9, 12; Deut 32:33 it is a snake (parallel to נָחָשׁ in Exod 4:3; 7:15). LXX uses δράκων, "dragon/large snake" in Exod 7:9, 10, 12 and Deut 32:33.

14.a. Reading the כִּי as asseverative, as in vv 3, 9. Otherwise it is causal ("or/because") or conditional ("if," Dahood, II, 333).

14.b. In both piel (as here) and hiphil, פלט can mean to "bring into security" (KB, 762). The masc. sing. suffix is read as collective.

14.c. The verb (חשׁק) means to "cling to/desire/be attached to/love" (see Gen 34:8; Deut 7:7; 10:15; 21:11; 1 Kgs 9:19; Isa 38:17).

14.d. The verb שׂגב means to make inaccessibly high (see Pss 20:2; 69:30)—out of the way of harm.

16.a. Lit., "with extended (number of) days I will satisfy him."

16.b. *BHS* suggests a change of וְאַרְאֵהוּ ("and I will show him") to וְאַרְוֵחוּ, "and I will cause him to drink deeply/be satisfied" (from רוה; so, e.g., Gunkel, *"schlürfen mein Heil"* ("swig my salvation"); Thomas, *TRP*, 23, 38, with reference to *VT* 12 (1962) 499–500; Anderson, II, 659; rejected, however, by Kraus, II, 803. Johnson (*CPIP,* 190) has: "the continual enjoyment of my salvation," explaining רָאָה בְ- as idiomatic for looking with special pleasure and/or having an enjoyable experience (Pss 54:9; 106:5; 118:7; Eccl 2:1; Isa 52:8; Jer 29:32; Obad 12–13; Mic 7:9; cf. Ps 50:23).

Form/Structure/Setting

It is generally agreed that Ps 91 has two main parts: vv 1–13 and vv 14–16. The latter verses have the form of a divine oracle with God assumed as the speaker. After the opening declarations of trust and commitment in vv 1–2, vv 3–13 form a sermonette of encouragement (Stuhlmueller, II, 73), which is given added authority and intensity by the oracle in vv 14–16. The oracle matches the one in Ps 95:7d–11 (though the context is quite different), being the only two oracles in Pss 90–100. This feature is combined with the preaching character of Ps 95 to suggest that Pss 91 and 95 form an inclusion around Pss 92–94 (see *Form/Structure/Setting* of Pss 93, 94, and 95). The psalm is intended for instruction and exhortation and is designed to challenge and strengthen the faith of those who trust in Yahweh.

The main part of the psalm, vv 3–13, is marked by direct address, linguistically to a singular person, who is told of Yahweh's sure protection from different forms of peril and threats to life. Vv 14–16 should also be understood as direct address to the one spoken to in vv 3–13, even if they are not technically an example of the descriptive vocative (as with Johnson, 185–86, see note 2.a.). See *Comment* below.

The alternation of first and second persons in the psalm has given rise to a long-continued antiphonal interpretation, in which it is assumed that two human voices speak: first voice, vv 1–2; second voice, vv 3–4; first voice, vv 5–8; first and second voices, v 9 (first voice 9a; second voice, 9b); second voice, vv 10–13; God speaks, vv 14–16 (see Cohen, 301–3; Delitzsch, III, 60–61, whose division of the voices is slightly different; Perowne, 176). The psalm can be read antiphonally, but it is not necessary to assume that two or more speakers (in a few cases, choirs have been assumed) are involved. One speaker sets forth the claims of faith in a prayer (note vv 2 and 9a) which is designed for teaching. In this respect, the psalm is like Ps 90, which is also a prayer with didactic/sermonic intention.

How shall we identify the speaker? The reader of psalm commentaries will not be surprised at a potpourri of answers. The MT has no title for Ps 91, but LXX has αἶνος ᾠδῆς τῷ Δαυιδ ("Praise by a song of David") which may represent שׁיר מזמר לדוד (*BHS*): "a Davidic song-psalm." The attribution of the psalm to David probably developed because of the momentum of the Davidization of psalms in later scribal interpretation and the large number of words in Ps 91 which are common in psalms in the older Davidic collections (see Briggs, II, 279). In any case, the reference to David is also found in the Targum which explains the psalm as a dialogue between David and Solomon (Cohen, 301; Kirkpatrick, 554)—David begins to speak at v 2 and Solomon answers in v 9, but God speaks in v 10.

Modern commentators do not take seriously the idea of David and Solomon as the speakers, but a goodly number have supposed that the psalm should be understood as addressed to a king. Eaton (*Kingship*, 17) says, "The individual on whom such promises are lavished could hardly be any but the king" (also, Caquot, *Sem* [1958] 21–37; Dahood, II, 329; Johnson, *CPIP*, 188). In this approach, the psalm may be considered as "forming the climax" of a liturgical worship service intended to encourage a king to meet the threat of an enemy and "set out for the scene of battle with the confident assurance that under Yahweh's protection he will emerge both unscathed and victorious" (Johnson, 188). The speaker would be a priest or a prophet addressing the king.

The ancient rabbinical interpretation of the psalm as "A song for evil encounters" (Bab. Talmud, *Sheboth* 15b; Hugger, *Jahwe meine Zuflucht*, 331–33), i.e., one to be used to avert the attacks of demons (who were thought to be responsible for illnesses and various kinds of pestilences), has found its modern counterpart in the interpretation of several scholars (e.g., Briggs, II, 278–79; Oesterley, 407–11; in terms of testimony of a pious person healed for sickness: Kraus, II, 804; K. Seybold, *Das Gebet*, 164, both with qualification). Mowinckel (*Psalmenstudien*, III, 102–5) combines the idea of defense against demonic powers and refuge under the protection of Yahweh. According to Mowinckel, the psalm has the form of a liturgy, spoken by a priest in response to a worshiper who has come to a worship place to pray to Yahweh for deliverance from life-threatening conditions (see also, idem, *PIW*, II, 50–51). Schmidt (171–73) takes the psalm as a form of "entrance liturgy" (as in Pss 15 and 24A), similar to Ps 121, addressed to pilgrims coming to the temple. Delekat (*Asylie und Schutzorakel*, 235–39) argues for the psalm as a priestly speech to someone who seeks protection for himself and for his family in the sanctuary from the onslaught of a pestilence.

Eissfeldt responded to the concentration of divine names in vv 1–2 (four names) by arguing that Ps 91 is a "psalm of conversion" of a pious person, formerly devoted to Elyon-Shaddai, who has converted to Yahweh (see Eissfeldt, "Jahwes Verhältnis zu ʿEljon und Schaddaj nach Psalm 91"; idem, "Eine Qumran-Textform des 91. Psalms"; idem, *The Old Testament: An Introduction*, tr. P. R. Ackroyd [New York: Harper & Row, 1965] 126). In this approach, the speaker in the psalm is a priest, who confirms that the convert now has Yahweh's protection. In this case the tense in v 4 should be past: "He has covered you with his feathers / and under his wings you have taken refuge" Delekat (237), however, notes that the expression of taking refuge under God's wings occurs elsewhere only in Ruth 2:12, with reference to a foreign woman. The concept appears in similar expressions in Pss 17:8; 36:8; 57:2; 61:5; 63:8. However, there is no reason to assume that the reference has to be to a foreign convert. Eissfeldt seeks to strengthen his thesis by reconstructing the incomplete v 9a in the Qumran text to read "Yahweh have you named (called), 'My refuge'" (יהוה קר[את מח]סי). He also argues for an early date for the psalm, perhaps reflecting the conquest of Jerusalem by David (c. 1000 B.C.E.) and a subsequent subordination of El Elyon theology to that of Yahweh (which he argues may be inferred from Gen 14:18–24 and Ps 110:4). He even offers as a conjecture that Zadok (assumed to be a priest of El Elyon) was the speaker of Ps 91:1–2 and that Abiathar (a priest of Yahweh) was the speaker of 91:3–13 ("Jahwes Verhältnis zu ʿEljon und Schaddaj," 447).

My own conjecture is as follows. First, it seems to me that Mowinckel's argument (*Psalmenstudien*, III, 102–3) that the psalm was originally part of a larger liturgy has some probability. Mowinckel calls attention to the isolated nature of v 1 (which is not the subject of the "I say" in v 2), and which may have been the continuation of a description of the secure status of the righteous; possibly involving the use of אשרי ("how blest is . . .") at the beginning of v 1 (as in Gunkel)—with אמר (participle; see note 2.a.) read in v 2: "How blest is the one who dwells . . . who says to Yahweh, (you are) my refuge." In the present text, however, v 1 is a general statement of the subject matter of the psalm and is separate from v 2.

Second, the nature of the liturgy from which the psalm was borrowed is too elusive to recover with any assurance. Mowinckel assumed a lamentation ceremony, with the complaints and petitions of a distressed person missing, leaving a blessing (vv 1–13) and an oracle of assurance (vv 14–16) in the psalm, probably spoken by one (or two) priests. He may be correct, but the use of the psalm content originally in a prebattle liturgy of worship for the king (as in Johnson) also has some probability.

On the other hand, the liturgy may have been designed for any pious believer, though Eissfeldt's argument for the use of the psalm in the confirmation of a convert, or for a transfer of allegiance from El Elyon and El Shaddai to Yahweh, does not seem likely. I would expect a stronger emphasis on loyalty to Yahweh and some warning against defection in the psalm if that were the case; especially since the psalm seems to resemble Deut 32 in several references. A relatively early date for most of the content may be correct (it checks out fairly well with the poetic criteria for early dating discussed in *Form/Structure/Setting* of Ps 93; note the tri-colons in vv 4, 7, and 15), possibly modified in the post-exilic period by the addition of the guardian angels in v 11 and an eschatological thrust in v 16 (Loretz, II, 31).

Third, the present psalm has been attached to Ps 90 (which supplies a form of the complaint/lament that Mowinckel found lacking for 91) by scribal interpreters who may have thought of Pss 90–106 (Book IV), especially Pss 90–100, as a "Moses-collection," designed to call post-exilic Israelite communities and individuals to a wise and confident faith in the kingship of Yahweh, and to set forth that "Yahweh is the Great God / and the Great King over all gods" (95:3). The similarity of Ps 91 to wisdom poetry (as in Gunkel, 403, and others; noting a close likeness to Job 5:17–26) is not decisive for the date of its content (wisdom content may be prexilic), but it does fit well with the theological milieu of the post-exilic period, and it is not out of harmony with the "learned psalmography" represented by Ps 90; perhaps, we can speak of "learned redaction and anthologizing" in the case of Ps 91. These conjectures should not be taken as certain, of course. Kraus's (II, 404) negative remarks about the efforts of commentators to put the psalm in the context of specific situations is a caution well taken though not necessarily to be completely heeded. Ps 91 has its own validity as a literary entity without regard to a historical setting-in-life.

Comment

A thematic statement (91:1). V 1 is a statement of the general subject matter of the psalm; Eerdmans calls it a "motto." It is a kind of "text" for the prayer-exhortation in vv 2–13. The content is deeply rooted in the traditions of faith in Yahweh's power and willingness to protect those who trust in him (e.g., see Pss 17:8; 27:5; 31:21; 32:7; 36:8; 57:2; 61:5; 63:8; 121:5).

The protective function of the "shade of the king" is a widespread metaphor in the ideology of ancient Near Eastern kingship. For the protective "shade" of the Davidic monarch, see Lam 4:20; cf. Judg 9:15 (see F. Crüsemann, *Der Widerstand gegen das Königtum,* WMANT 49 [Neukirchen-Vluyn: Neukirchener, 1978] 21–22). See also Isa 49:2; 51:16; Hos 14:8–9 [7–8]. The royal features of Ps 91 make it appropriate for Pss 90–100, which are dominated by kingship-of-Yahweh ideas. The "shade" or "shadow" is that of the divine king, the Almighty One.

The divine names Elyon and Shaddai are also well known in the Yahwistic traditions (see Gen 17:1; 28:3; 35:11; 49:25; Exod 6:3; Deut 32:8; Ruth 1:20, 21; Job passim; Ps 18:14; Joel 1:15). Their usage represents significant developments in the history of Israelite religion, and they were used in cults other than that of Yahweh, but in the present context there is no doubt that they are names for Yahweh. The use of both terms intensifies the parallelism in the verse and prepares for the use of "Yahweh" in v 2. Gunkel's (406) claim that the verse in its present form is "a clear tautology" ignores the factor of poetic intensification (see Alter, *The Art of Biblical Poetry,* 62–84).

A testimony of faith and exhortation (91:2–9a). As noted above (see note 9.a.), I take vv 2 and 9a as forming a frame, or inclusion, around vv 3–8. The problem with the אמר is discussed in note 2.a. I have retained the "I say" in the sense of a testimony, addressed to God, but intended to be heard (or read) by other people. In vv 2 and 9a the speaker addresses his/her own expression of faith to God before encouraging others to share that faith. V 2 is the speaker's own response to v 1 (cf. Ps 18:4). The idea of "refuge" (מחסה) in the psalm seems to be that of a secure, protective area guaranteed by Yahweh himself with his presence (see Kraus, II, 805; cf. Pss 14:6; 46:2; 61:4; 62:8, 9; 71:7; 73:28; 94:22; 142:6). For "my fortress," see Pss 18:3; 31:4; 71:8.

The content of vv 3–9a seems to fall into two sections: vv 3–4 and vv 5–9a. It may be incidental, but interesting, to note that there are five colons in vv 3–4 and ten colons in vv 5–9a—and ten colons in vv 9–13, if 9a is counted; that is, if 9a is a transition statement which does double duty for vv 5–8 and vv 9–13. The case for a division after v 4 is strengthened by the presence of a סלה (*selah;* see Ps 62:1) at the end of the verse in the Qumran (11PsApa) text. V 9a is a pivotal statement in vv 2–13; there are sixteen colons in vv 2–8 and sixteen colons in vv 9b–16.

Vv 3–4 encourage whoever is addressed to trust Yahweh, as a savior and protector. The notes on vv 3 and 4 have dealt with most of the exegetical problems. These verses provide a detailed metaphorical language which undergirds the statement of trust in v 2 and instructs the addressee in the nature of the saving power of Yahweh (cf. Kraus, II, 805). The "fowler's trap" and the "threat of destruction" (v 3) are not specifically defined; the language is metaphorical for all kinds of traps and threats from enemies and from natural causes. The "threat (or word) of destruction" probably refers primarily to slander and the vocal threats of enemies, though דבר can mean "anything/everything/something." The expression may mean simply "anything that destroys." Both traps and the threat of destruction imply the danger of violent death (for "fowler's trap," cf. Ps 124:7; Hos 9:8; also Pss 119:160; 140:6; 141:9; 142:4; Jer 18:22).

The metaphor of Yahweh as a mighty bird is found in v 4 (hardly an actual description). Whoever trusts in him for refuge is protected under his wings (cf. Exod 19:4; Deut 32:11; Pss 5:12–13; 17:8; 63:8). The wings may also allude to the wings of the cherubim in the temple of Jerusalem (see *Comment* on Ps 57:2). Those who seek to destroy those who stay under the wings of the Almighty will find them surrounded by Yahweh's faithfulness like a protective shield (v 4c). In American parlance, these are the "teflon" people, whose shield is nothing less than the faithfulness of God.

V 5 begins a new subsection with its rather startling use of the command form: "Do not fear." The dangers listed in vv 5–6 are fourfold and alternate between action in periods of darkness and light: (1) terror-night, (2) arrow-daytime, (3) plague-dark, (4) scourge-noonday. This has the appearance of a merism, i.e., dangers which may occur at anytime, day or night; a comprehensive statement of the perils of life.

The "terror" (or "dreadful thing") in the night is any sudden onslaught, especially a physical attack (cf. Cant 3:8) which would threaten life; as is the "arrow" by day. It is often suggested that the "arrow" by daytime refers to sunstroke (cf. Ps 121:6), but the language is metaphorical and conveys the sense of any sudden and lethal attack. One may be hit by an "arrow" shot from concealment even at high noon. Sunstroke may hit suddenly, but lightning also strikes suddenly, and "arrows" can be a synonym for "flashes of lightning" (Pss 18:15; 77:18; 144:6; Zech 9:14; T. H. Gaster, *Myth, Legend, and Custom in the Old Testament* [New York: Harper & Row, 1969] 674). "Arrow" is used, for example, of the "arrow of Yahweh" (see Deut 32:42; 2 Sam 22:15; Ps 64:8; Zech 9:14; Pss 38:3; 77:18; Job 6:4; Ezek 5:16) and in a metaphorical sense of human actions (Isa 49:2; Jer 9:8; Pss 57:5; 64:4; Prov 25:18; Hugger, *Jahwe meine Zuflucht*, 186–89).

Hugger (182) argues that the expression "terror of the night" differs from the more precise time designations for "in the daytime" (יומם is an adverb) "in the dark" (באפל), and "at noonday" (צהרים) and refers to the fear of the night itself which anyone under the protection of God should not worry about. The poetic construction need not be pushed so hard, however. The "terror (dread) of the night" can mean "a night-terror," i.e., a terror which operates in the night (cf. Cant 3:8, פחד בלילות, "terror in the nights"; see M. H. Pope, *Song of Songs*, AB 15 [Garden City, NY: Doubleday, 1977] 435–41). For unexpected attacks at night, see Exod 4:24–26; 11:4–5 (the going forth of Yahweh at midnight so that the firstborn of the Egyptians would die); 12:29–30; Judg 7:19; 16:2–3; 20:5; 2 Kgs 6:14;

Obad 5; Neh 6:10; and for texts with similar features to 91:5, see Gen 32:23–33; Prov 3:24–25; Job 4:14; 22:10–11. Midnight and noonday seem to have been times of special anxiety (for midnight, see Exod 11:4–5; 12:29–30; Ruth 8:9; for noonday [less evident]: Deut 28:29; 1 Kgs 18:26–29; 2 Kgs 4:20; Job 5:14; Jer 6:4; Isa 59:10; Amos 8:9; Zeph 2:40. Jer 15:8 is of special significance, because of its reference to the "destroyer at noonday," שדד בצהרים).

The "plague" and the "scourge" in v 6 are metaphors which suggest attacks of illness, whereas the "terror" and the "arrow" in v 5 suggest the attacks of human enemies, though the words are inclusive and the context resists specific interpretation. Some interpreters have argued that all four perils of vv 5–6 represent demons and/or malignant spirits (conveniently presented by T. H. Gaster, *IDB*, I, 820), which are often associated with illness. For example, the "night-terror" has a parallel in the description of Zaqar, a god of dreams, in a Mesopotamian magical incantation known as *paluḫtum ša litâti*, "the terror of the night" (Gaster, *Myth, Legend, and Custom in the Old Testament*, 813), and the Babylonian pest demon, Namtar, has been suggested for the "plague" (דבר) in 6a (Anderson, II, 657), Gaster (*IDB*, 820) notes the association of דבר with Resheph (a Canaanite god of plague and pestilence) in Hab 3:5. Dahood (II, 331) notes the possibility that "arrow" should be identified with Resheph, citing Ugaritic references, though he also says that if v 5 is read looking back to vv 1–3, rather than forward to the "plague" (דבר) in v 6a, the primary reference is probably to the hunter's arrow. Hugger (*Jahwe meine Zuflucht*, 186) notes that the Targum on this verse refers to "the arrow of the death angel" (see also de Fraine, *Bib* 40 [1959] 375–76).

Despite all this, the exact nature of the concepts in vv 5–6 remains elusive (Kraus, II, 806); probably intentionally elusive. The language is metaphorical and designed to encompass a whole range of potentially lethal happenings. Nevertheless, there is no reason to doubt that the content of the psalm reflects a thought world in which the presence of demons, demonical possession, and malignant spirits and powers was considered commonplace. The text of the psalm reflects a sense of synergistic inner connection between ordinary life and the sinister powers of the occult. The demons and powers were especially manifest during epidemics and unexpected physical attacks, along with other varied catastrophies which threaten human existence.

The interpretation of v 7 as a reference to the actual fall of opponents in battle seems to me to be improbable (but note Ps 3:7). For example, Johnson (*CPIP*, 188–89) takes the whole section of vv 5–8 as referring to the perils of war: surprise attacks at night, shots from bows by day, the death and disease which follow in the unsanitary conditions of camp life and the aftermath of battles, and the seeing of enemies mown down right and left while the one addressed (a king) remains unscathed because of the shielding power of Yahweh. His presentation is an impressive exercise in poetical imagination, but the highly metaphorical language of the psalm makes it improbable that the references have been so specifically understood. V 7 certainly suggests a battle scene, but its juxtaposition with vv 5–6 suggests, but does not say, that the thousands who fall do so as a result of the plagues in these verses. The "it" in v 7c may refer to the "plague" or to the "scourge" in v 6 (so Dahood, II, 332: "the plague that frequently broke out during military campaigns"), but it is more likely an indefinite subject which refers to whatever causes the thousands to fall in 7a,b.

V 7c should not be omitted from the text as a gloss (as, e.g., Hugger, *Jahwe meine Zuflucht*, 42–45; Kraus, II, 802, 806). The verse is a tricolon; perhaps a bit of very old poetry (see *Form/Structure/Setting* of Ps 93), which should not be read as a simple statement of the result of the scourge in v 6 (as Hugger, 207–9; Kraus, II, 806). The retention of 7c makes it probable that 7a, b should be read in a conditional sense and as a description of a new terror from which Yahweh provides protection, though the juxtaposition with the preceding verses should not be ignored. The point is not that a thousand or ten thousand have fallen, but if they do, the cause of their destruction "will not come near you" (the addressee). If such dreadful events do transpire, the one who is under the protection of Yahweh will simply look on as punishment comes to the "wicked" (v 8). The "wicked" are those who are the bipolar opposites of the "righteous," those whose behavior threatens the peace and well-being of the community. They are those who live outside of trust in the protective care of Yahweh; those who are not willing to say of Yahweh "You are my refuge" (v 9a).

Under the protective care of the angels of Yahweh (91:9b–13). This section forms a parallel to vv 5–9a. As noted above in *Form/Structure/Setting* there is an almost even colon count in both sections. The message of assurance is the same: Yahweh provides a sure refuge against the onslaught of destructive forces. The word נגע ("disaster") in v 10 has the basic meaning of a "blow/stroke/plague" and its range of meaning seems about the same as דבר and קטב in v 6 (as a wound inflicted by a human being, Deut 17:8; 21:5; Prov 6:33; punishment by God, Gen 12:17; Exod 11:1; 2 Sam 7:14; Ps 39:11; disease, Lev 13 and 14, passim; Deut 24:8; Ps 38:12). Note also the appearance of דבר in MT of v 3 (see note 3.c.). The word translated "harm" (10a, traditionally, "evil," רעה) is a widely used word for moral and physical "evil": intentions of the heart (Ps 28:3), consequence of sin (Prov 13:21), unfaithfulness to God (Deut 13:5, 11[12], blemish on a sacrificial animal (Deut 17:1), and misfortune or disaster (Jer 1:14; 2:3; Amos 3:6; etc.).

Johnson (*CPIP*, 189) argues that the reference to the tent (v 10) which belongs to the person under the protection of Yahweh "gains in significance if it is taken quite literally as referring to the temporary dwelling used by the king while on a campaign . . . even in camp he [the king] will enjoy complete security" (also, Dahood, II, 333). Such an interpretation may have been true of v 10 in another context, more specifically directed toward the king, but it seems improbable in a psalm which makes such extensive use of metaphorical language. The "tent" is the "home/habitation/dwelling place" of the faithful person—wherever he/she may be (see Kraus, II, 807; Hugger, *Jahwe meine Zuflucht*, 226–29, who surveys the references to אהל in the Psalms: 15:1; 19:5; 27:5, 6; 52:4; 61:5; 78:51, 55, 67; 83:7; 84:11; 91:10; 102:26; 118:15; 120:5; 132:3. For Ps 91:10, cf.: Prov 14:11; Pss 52:7; 118:15; Job 18:14–15; 19:3–10; 20:26).

A further expression of the protection of Yahweh for those who trust him is given in vv 11–12. The angels of Yahweh will be given charge over the faithful ones to protect them in all their "ways," i.e., in their activities and conduct of life, though some commentators argue that the reference here is to actual travel, "ways" in the sense of journeys (so Hugger, 243; Johnson, *CPIP*, 189, "where'er thou goest"; cf. Brueggemann, *The Message of the Psalms*, 156, who, however, uses the idea of a "safe journey" in the psalm in a metaphorical sense). "Ways" is more probably used here in the sense found in such references as Pss 1:1, 6; 10:5; 26:4; 39:2; 51:15; Prov 3:6.

The "ways" are the "ways of life." The idea of a journey fits better with v 12, but again there is no need to leave the realm of metaphorical language. The traveler may dash a foot against a stone while on the road, but an ordinary person may also stump a foot on a stone any day while walking about a village or in the fields. Perhaps it is correct to say, however, that the use of "tent" (אהל) in v 10 and דרך in v 11 indicates that divine protection is effective both at home and away from home.

The idea of angels bearing up persons so that no foot is injured in hitting a stone (12) is a metaphor of special care; like parents who support a child to keep him / her from painful and dangerous falls and bruises (cf. Exod 19:4; Isa 63:9; Prov 3:23). Stumbling is a fairly frequent metaphor for trouble and misfortune: e.g., Pss 37:31; 38:17; 56:14; 73:2; 94:18, 116:8; Prov 3:23, 26; note the "stone of stumbling" in Isa 8:14—a "stone to strike against." For angels who protect people from harm, see Ps 34:8; cf. Ps 103:20–21; Gen 24:7; 48:16; Exod 15:19; Isa 63:9; Tob 5–10; Matt 4:6; Heb 1:14; cf. Johnson, *CPIP*, 126.

The angels are considered to be divine beings whose superior power can protect human beings from harm (Weiser, 611). Cohen (303) refers to the Talmudic teaching that two ministering angels accompany a person through life and testify about that person's conduct to the heavenly tribunal after death. The expression "his angels" is probably equivalent to "the angel(s) of Yahweh" (e.g., Gen 16:7, 9, 10, 11; 22:11, 15; Exod 3:2; Num 22:22; Judg 5:23; Ps 34:8; 35:5, 6; Zech 3:1), a form of the manifestation of Yahweh himself "appearing to human beings in human form" (von Rad, *Old Testament Theology*, I, tr. D. M. G. Stalker [New York: Harper & Row, 1962] 287; for the whole matter, see 285–89). The "angel of Yahweh" (מלאך יהוה) ordinarily acts to protect and serve Israel (2 Sam 24:16 is an exception), but in Ps 91 the angel will guard individuals who trust Yahweh and abide under his power.

The protective metaphors in vv 3–12 give way in v 13 to one of positive subjugation. The person who is under the protection of Yahweh and under the protective charge of his angels (v 11) will have the power to tread down and trample deadly snakes and lions (v 13). Lions and poisonous snakes are dangerous animals who attack with little warning from hidden places (for lions, see Jer 25:28; Judg 14:5), but they will be put down and mastered by the person of faith—the language is metaphorical, of course, for all persons and powers which threaten human beings with lethal attacks (cf. Ps 58:4–6; Deut 32:33). For the verb רמס, "trample," in v 13, cf. Isa 63:3; more generally, cf. Isa 11:6–9.

An oracle of assurance (91:14–16). These verses constitute an oracle from Yahweh, spoken by a priest, prophet, or more probably a teacher respected for wisdom, which responds to the prayer-testimony in vv 3–13 and gives authority to its exhortation. The oracle is also an explication of the thematic statement in v 1 (Caquot, *Sem* [1958] 35). The assurance is addressed to the person who is "devoted to" Yahweh (v 14, "cleaves to/clings to"), a term used of the love of person for person (Gen 34:8; Deut 21:11) and of Yahweh's devotion to Israel (Deut 7:7; 10:15), but not elsewhere of a person's devotion to God. The one who is devoted to Yahweh knows his name (v 14b). Note Ps 20:2, where "name" and the verb שגב ("make high/make inaccessible") are also used (cf. also Ps 148:13). To "know" the name of God is, of course, to have a close relationship with him (cf. Ps 9:2, 11); the "name" of Yahweh involves his whole being and is the foundation of trust (see Craigie, 118–19; *Comment* on Ps 54:3). V 14 specifies the kind of person who will be the recipient of the promises in vv 15–16. "To honor," or "glorify" (v 15c), means to bring to dignity and success; to achieve as one blessed by God (cf. 1 Sam 2:29–30; Prov 4:8 (Hugger, *Jahwe meine Zuflucht*, 275–76, notes that God's honoring a human being is unusual). For long life (lit., "extension of days") as a sign of divine favor, see Exod 20:12; 23:27; Deut 30:20; Ps 21:5; Prov 3:2. Seeing Yahweh's "saving work" (v 16b) is possibly a reference to the future, eschatological, salvation of Yahweh. For example, Stuhlmueller (II, 74) says, "We are intrigued by a hint of messianic salvation at the end of a long life" (similarly, Kissane, II, 109; Dahood, II, 334; Luke 2:29–30). A "hint," an openness, there is perhaps, but the meaning is basically that of the perception of the divine saving work along the course of life, ever knowing that the full expression of that work lies in a future yet to be (cf. Kirkpatrick, 558; Pss 50:15, 23; 98:1–3; Isa 49:6; 51:1, 6, 8; 56:1; 62:1).

The presence of an oracle of Yahweh at the close of this psalm parallels that at the close of Ps 95, except, of course, the context is quite different. These are the only two oracles in Pss 90–100, which seem to form an anthological subunit, introduced by the Moses-psalm in Ps 90 and recalling the early days of Israel's history under the leadership of Yahweh's great servant (note the wilderness content in 95:8–11). In the larger context of Pss 90–99 the great acclamations of Yahweh's kingship are given under the rubric of Moses, who proclaimed the kingly reign of Yahweh in the context of the deliverance at the sea (Exod 15:18). In their present form, these are psalms of the exilic and post-exilic period. The Davidic monarchy is gone, but "the Great God, Yahweh, the Great King over all the gods" who has saved Israel and made them his people (95:7) reigns with might and power. The temple may not be available for worship, but on every Sabbath day "it is good to give thanks to Yahweh" and to praise his name (92:2). The faith expressed is like that of Isaiah: "In the year that King Uzziah died I saw the Lord [Yahweh] sitting upon a throne, high and lifted up" (Isa 6:1, RSV).

Explanation

Ps 91 is a prayer-oracle of encouragement to trust God for protection and security. The speaker is an individual person of faith who bears testimony of his/ her commitment while delivering a sermonette-like exhortation on the basis of a "text" (thematic statements) in v 1: "Whoever dwells under the protection of the Most High / will abide in the shade of the Almighty." The direct address to God in v 2 is the speaker's testimony to personal appropriation of the statement in v 1. This basic thesis is then explicated in a series of striking metaphors in vv 3–13, interrupted by another affirmation to God in v 9a. The whole is given divine authenticity in the form of the oracle in vv 14–16, where God declares that he does indeed do what the speaker has said. The last words in the psalm are not spoken *to* God but are spoken *by* God to us (Brueggemann, *The Message of the Psalms*, 157).

The metaphors convey assurance in different ways. First, protection is available from the deadly dangers of life. The metaphors have a concreteness about them which keeps them centered on real threats to physical well-being, but at the same time there is a sinister quality about them which suggests that powers of a "fifth dimension" are involved. The realm of the occult, the realm of the superhuman and supramundane, lies close at hand. Lethal forces lurk along the ways of life and the abiding protection of the Almighty is essential for safety. Traps are ready to snap shut, arrows may fly suddenly, plagues stalk through dark nights and even rush forth to ravage at noonday. Ps 90 deals with the somber reality of the finitude and temporality of life under the judgment of God while Ps 91 expounds the divine protection which is available against the sinister powers which threaten human welfare. The prayer of Ps 90 is answered by the confident instruction of Ps 91.

Second, the metaphors also set forth the declaration that Yahweh's protective care is not limited to certain times and places. He gives security by day and by night—constantly (vv 5–6), in the dark as well as in the brightness of noontime. The psalm says nothing about the restriction of Yahweh's gift of security to the temple or other sanctuary, though it is possible that the language of the psalm's content was drawn, in part at least, from rituals associated with someone who had sought asylum (and assurance) from some threat (perhaps an epidemic; cf. Delekat, *Asylie und Schutzorakel*). The protecting wings and shadow (shade) of Yahweh reach out to wherever the one who trusts in him is, whether at home or on a journey (Brueggemann, 156, says that the psalm interweaves two kinds of images: a *safe place* and a *safe journey,* which is true, but the idea of a journey is not as explicit as he assumes). The person of faith is given assurance of security wherever and whenever he/she may be—in the midst of physical threats or social chaos: "A thousand may fall beside you / ten thousand on your right / but it will not come near you" (v 7).

The final emphasis in the metaphors is the guardianship and empowerment of angels (vv 11–13), who will make secure all the "ways" of the trusting one; holding him/her up with their hands and giving power to subdue lions and serpents (v 13). Weiser (611–12) argues that v 13 does not point to "dangerous and terrifying journeys through the jungle in the course of which a lion suddenly jumps up from the reeds or the wanderer treads on a serpent," but rather involves old mythical ideas of a god killing a dragon and putting his foot on its neck as a sign of victory. This is more than the text actually says, and we should be cautious about too much emphasis on it, but it is the kind of ideation that lies in the background. Commentators sometimes suggest that the lion is a symbol of open, devouring attack and the serpent is a symbol of cunning, underhand dealings (e.g., Jacquet, 747). However, lions and snakes have in common the reputation of attacking from hidden places (for lions, see Pss 10:9; 17:12; 1 Kgs 13:24; cf. Job 28:8, and note Mowinckel's argument for a blending of lion and serpent qualities referred to in note 13.a.), and perhaps we should think of them both as representative of attacks from ambush—again both physical and social.

Thus Ps 91 is an enduring encouragement of faith, which asks us to respond to its affirmations. The case for faith is not put in the language of argument; it declares the reality. We are challenged to ground our endeavors in trust in Yahweh, a trust which will not fail and which leads us along a way where we will see more and more of the saving work of God until finally our knowledge will be complete. Weiser's profound piety and exegetical skill merge in his fine summary of this psalm (613): "The hymn is a sturdy comrade; its boldness and unbroken courageous testimony to God has already enabled many a man [*sic*] to overcome all sorts of temptations. By virtue of the soaring energy of its trust in God it leaves behind every earthly fear, every human doubt and all inhibiting considerations, and lifts man [*sic*] up above the depressing realities of life to the hopeful certitude of a faith which is able to endure and to master it." Amen.

A Psalm for the Sabbath   (92:1–16)

Bibliography

Booij, T. "The Hebrew Text of Psalm XCII 11." *VT* 38 (1988) 210–13. **Loewenstamm, S. E.** "*Balloti* bᵉšāmān raᶜanān." *UF* 10 (1978) 211–13. **Sarna, N. M.** "The Psalm for the Sabbath Day (Ps. 92)." *JBL* 81 (1962) 155–68. **Thomas, D. W.** "Some Observations on the Hebrew Word רַעֲנָן." In *Hebraische Wortforschung*, FS Walter Baumgartner. VTSup 16. Leiden: Brill, 1967. 387–97.

Translation

1	A psalm[a]: a song for the Sabbath Day.	
2	*It is good to give thanks to Yahweh;*[a]	(3+3)
	to praise your name, O Most High,[b]	
3	*to declare your loyal-love*[a] *at dawn,*[b]	(3+2)
	and your faithfulness at night,[c]	
4	*with zither*[a] *and lute,*[b]	(3+3)
	with a song[c] *on the harp.*	
5	*For you have made me glad by your work, O Yahweh;*[a]	(4+3)
	because of your handiwork I sing out!	
6	*How great are your works, O Yahweh,*	(3+3)
	how[a] *profound*[b] *are your designs!*[c]	
7	*(Only) a dunderhead*[a] *would not know (this),*[b]	(3+3)
	and (only) a fool would not understand it.	
8	*When the wicked thrive, they are like grass*[a]—	(3+3+2)
	and when all the evildoers blossom out,[b]	
	it is to be forever destroyed.	
9	*But you are the One-who-is-on-High,*[a]	(2+2)
	forever, O Yahweh.[b]	
10	*For lo, your enemies, O Yahweh,*[a]	(3+3+3)
	for lo, your enemies will perish,[b]	
	all the evildoers will scatter.[b]	
11	*As if I were a wild ox, you have raised my horn;*	(3+3)
	which I have rubbed[a] *with fresh oil.*[b]	
12	*My eyes have gazed (in triumph)*[a] *at my attackers;*[b]	(3+3+2)
	when evil foes rose against me,	
	my ears heard (them scatter).[c]	
13	*The righteous will thrive like a date-palm;*	(3+3)
	grow like a cedar in Lebanon.	
14	*Planted*[a] *in the house of Yahweh,*	(3+3)
	they will flourish[b] *in the courts*[c] *of our God.*	
15	*They will still bear fruit*[a] *in old age;*	(3+3)
	they will (still) be green and full of sap,[b]	
16	*declaring*[a] *that Yahweh is upright*[b]—	(3+3)
	my Rock, in whom there is no wrong-doing.[c]	

Notes

1.a. See n. 51:1.a.

2.a. Dahood seeks to avoid having Yahweh addressed in the 3rd pers. in the first colon and directly in the second by parsing the ל as vocative and rendering "O Yahweh." However, a shift from 3rd pers. to direct address occasionally occurs in Hebrew poetry (e.g., see 66:8–10; 93:1–2, 4–5; 94:12–14).

2.b. The divine name עליון suggests the idea of "ascend," and connotes "the Highest" (cf. the adjective in 2 Kgs 15:35; Isa 7:3; 36:2). The name indicates the exalted status and power of God (e.g., Pss 47:2, 6–7; 83:19; 82:6; 91:1, 9; 97:9). It is an epithet of kingship (H.-J. Kraus, *Theology of the Psalms*, 28; T. N. D. Mettinger, *In Search of God: The Meaning and Message of the Everlasting Names*, tr. F. H. Cryer [Philadelphia: Fortress Press, 1988] 122).

3.a. See n. 51:3.a.

3.b. Lit., "in the morning."

3.c. Lit., "in the nights." Briggs (II, 286) takes the plural as intensive and understands as "in dark night," citing 134:1; Cant 3:1, 8. See L. C. Allen on Ps 134:1, n. 1.c. The simple plural "nights" or "night hours" (Dahood has "watches of the night") may be sufficient (see 16:7; though cf. Briggs, I, 121; Craigie, 154–55).

4.a. Lit., "on ten," apparently referring to a multiple stringed musical instrument; perhaps, something like the zither (JB).

4.b. The word נבל refers to a stringed musical instrument, usually appearing with כנור ("harp") and translated as "psaltery" or "viol" in KJV. See n. 57:9.b. LXX allows only one instrument in 3a: "on a psaltery of ten strings," a judgment followed in some translations (NEB, NJV, NIV; note 33:2; 144:9).

4.c. The verbal root הגה refers to "uttering/speaking/musing." In the sense of "murmur/medi-tate," see Pss 1:2; 63:7; 77:13; 143:5. For the noun הגיון, which appears here, see Ps 19:15 and, in a negative sense, Lam 3:62. It is thought to refer to the sound of music produced by a harp in 92:4; cf. 9:17 (see Craigie, 116, n. 17b). It may, however, refer to soft or meditative singing or chanting to the accompaniment of a stringed instrument. Possibly, "strumming."

5.a. The extension of the psalm's dominant metrical pattern of 3+3 to 4+3 by the word "Yahweh" has led to suggestions for its omission (e.g., Briggs, Gunkel, Kraus). However, v 9 would also be too long on the basis of this judgment. See n. 9.b. below.

6.a. The interjection in 6a does double duty.

6.b. Lit. "exceedingly deep." On the usage of עמק, see A. A. Wieder, *JBL* 84 (1965) 162–63. In some contexts, עמק may carry the Ugaritic idea of ʿmq, "strength/violence." The parallel with גדל ("great") may indicate that the meaning here is "strong/powerful."

6.c. Or, "thoughts," as traditionally translated. If creation is the subject in the verse, "designs" seems better.

7.a. Or, "brutish person"; see n. 94:8.a.

7.b. The pronoun in 7b does double duty.

8.a. See Job 27:14 for a similar construction (R. Gordis, *The Book of Job* [New York: Jewish Theo-logical Seminary, 1978] 294). The last two words (כמו עשב) constitute an apodosis. Note the *passeq* after בפרח רשעים.

8.b. The infinitive with a preposition followed by a consecutive imperfect usually denotes past tense (with ב , see Lev 16:1; 1 Kgs 18:18; Isa 38:9; Ezek 16:36; Ps 105:12–13; Job 38:7–8; with other prepositions, see Gen 24:30; 39:18; Josh 8:24; Jer 9:12–13). N. H. Sarna (*JBL* 81 [1962] 159–60) ar-gues that past tense should be read in v 8 ("a particular event that has taken place in the past"). However, in the case of v 8 the tense is determined by the infinitives in 8a and 8c; i.e., it is an indefinite "whenever." The colon in 8b is parenthetical and adds to the description in 8a. For similar use of the consecutive imperfect, see Ps 29:5, 9; 50:16; 90:3 (note D. Michel, *Tempora und Satzstellung in den Psalmen* [Bonn: Bouvier, 1960] 41). Perhaps v 8 should be considered a variant type of the expanded colon, which is found in the tricolon in v 10. S. E. Loewenstamm ("The Expanded Colon in Ugaritic and Biblical Verse," *JSS* 14 [1969] 176–96; idem, "The Expanded Colon, Reconsidered," *UF* 7 (1975) 261–64) notes the variations and free development of ancient patterns in expanded colons (verses in which the sentence is interrupted and then expanded and completed in a second and/or third colon) in biblical verses. See also, Y. Avishur, "Addenda to the Expanded Colon in Ugaritic and Biblical Verse," *UF* 4 (1972) 170. Neither Loewenstamm or Avishur include 92:8, but it seems probable that it belongs to this category. The sentence in 8a is interrupted by 8c. For a similar verse structurally, see Ps 29:9, where the consecutive imperfect also appears. For the consecutive imperfect after an infinitive, see Ps 50:16. An alternative translation would be: "When the wicked flourish like grass, / then all the evildoers blossom forth / to be forever destroyed."

9.a. Reading מרום as a divine epithet, as in 56:3. Otherwise, the translation is "you are (on) high," as traditionally. LXX has ὕψιστος, "highest one"; cf. Isa 24:4, 21. See Dahood, II, 337. JB has "whereas you are supreme forever." Note the use of מרום in 93:4.

9.b. As in n. 5.a., "Yahweh" is sometimes omitted. However, its retention in both places forms a frame for vv 5–9 and it should not be omitted.

10.a. V 10 is a tricolon with the pattern A+B+C/A+B+D/E+F+G (Dahood, II, 337), which has Ugaritic parallels, as in "Behold, thine enemies, O Baal, / Behold, thine enemies shalt thou crush, / Behold, thou shalt crush thy foes!" (though the pattern here is A+B+C/A+B+D/A+D+E). See, e.g., Kidner, II, 336, n. 1.; see also I, 2, n. 1. Cf. Exod 15:6, 11, 16 and several verses in Judg 5:2–31. See D. N. Freedman, *Pottery, Poetry, and Prophecy: Studies in Early Hebrew Poetry* (Winona Lake: Eisenbrauns, 1980) 188–89. As noted in 8.b. above, v 10 is an example of the use of the expanded colon in biblical verse, and any effort to reduce the verse to a bicolon (as in LXX[B]) should be eschewed (Loewenstamm, *JSS* 14 [1969] 193). The subsequent colons after the interruption of the sentence are expressive as well as informative. For examples of the use of expanded colons, see Pss 29:1–2, 5, 8; 67:4, 6; 77:17; 93:3; Judg 5:12; Hab 3:8; Cant 4:8.

10.b. The verbs אבד ("perish") and פרד ("divide/separate") are used in parallel in Job 4:11, on which see E. Dhorne, *A Commentary on the Book of Job*, tr. H. Knight (London: Thomas Nelson and Sons, 1926, 1967), 48.

11.a. The word בלתי is frequently taken as a simple perfect 1 c.s. from בלל, "mingle/mix," and given the meaning, "I am anointed" (BDB, 117), a meaning not found elsewhere in the usage of the verb, which occurs mostly in the simple passive participial form. The word could be a piel inf. const. (with 1 c.s. suffix) from בלה, "become old/worn out/used up," thus, "my being used to the full/ completely." This appears to be the basis for LXX's "But my horn shall be exalted . . . and my old age with rich mercy" (perhaps assuming simple inf. const., בלתי)—with the verb in 11a doing double duty. "You have exalted (raised up) . . . (exalted) my old age (my worn-outness) with fresh/luxuriant oil." Since a passive meaning of the perfect בלל is not found, translators frequently follow Syriac and Targum and read בלתני, "and you have anointed me"—assuming that בלל can mean "anoint." RSV has "thou has poured over me fresh oil"; the meaning "poured" may receive some support from the use of בלל in Exod 29:2. T. Booij (*VT* 38 [1988] 210–13) argues that there is no convincing interpretation of בלתי and proposes to assume the verb בלג, which means to "gleam/smile/look cheerful" (BDB, 114), appearing only in hiphil. Booij suggests that the verb in v 11 (an assumed בלגתי) can be taken in simple perfect with the meaning "shine/be bright"; thus: "And my horn is exalted [reading single imperfect for MT's hiphil, with LXX and Jerome] like that of the wild ox, I shine with fresh oil." S. E. Loewenstamm (*UF* 10 [1978] 211–13) has proposed that בשמן רענן be read as "like a fresh oil-tree," arguing that שמן is equivalent to שמן עץ("oil-tree"), noting that זית ("olive") is used for "olive-tree(s)," and occasionally more explicitly with עץ (Hag 2:19), and rather frequently with שמן ("oil"; e.g., Deut 8:8; Isa 41:19 and Ps 52:10: ואני כזית רענן בבית אלהים, "I am like a fresh (green) olive (tree) in the house of God." He follows Symmachus in reading כשמן for בשמן and the infinitive reading of בלתי (from בלה) to get: "My old age is like a fresh olive tree." Buttenwieser (842, n. 11) takes בלתי as "my old body" and reads רענן as the predicate ("fresh") with בלתי: "my old body will be freshened as if [כשמן] anointed with oil." The translation above assumes that the object of the verbal action in 11b is the "my horn" in 11a, as in the proposal of D. G. Pardee (*UF* 8 [1976], 252; idem, *UF* 7 [1975], 358): "You have raised my horn like that of a wild bull; I have smeared it (or myself) with fresh oil." The anointing of a horn is mentioned in an interesting way in a Ugaritic passage (UM 76.22, 23; IV AB 2.22, 23; CTA 10.2.21–23):

qrn dbàtk btlt ʿnt	Your powerful horn, girl Anat,
qrn dbàtk bʿl ymšḫ	your powerful horns will Baal anoint,
bʿl ymšḫ hm bʿp	Baal will anoint them in flight.

(See D. Pardee, "The Preposition in Ugaritic," *UF* 8 [1976] 252; G. R. Driver, *Canaanite Myths and Legends*, OT Studies 3 [Edinburgh: Clark, 1956] 116; E. Kutsch, *Salbung als Rechtsakt*, BZAW 87 [1963] 8; S. E. Loewenstamm, *UF* 10 [1978] 111, for translations.) The word *dbàt* is translated as "prowess" by Driver and as "strength" by C. H. Gordon (*Ugaritic Literature* [Rome: Pontificium Institutum Biblicum, 1949] 50; also Kutsch, 8). In the Baal text, Anat is to be prepared for a fight by anointing her horns. The Ugaritic verb is *mšḫ*, which seems to correspond to the Heb. משח, commonly understood as "anoint." However, Kutsch (7–9) argues that משח is basically "to make fat/make greasy/rub oil into," and thus only in an extended sense "to anoint." The references to rubbing shields with oil in 2 Sam 1:21 (reading with *qere*) and Isa 21:5 are especially interesting. Leather shields had to be rubbed with oil to make them ready for use. In the case of Saul's shield in 2 Sam 1:21, it lay soiled on the slopes of Mount Gilboa, unrubbed with oil, and not ready for action (see the discussion of P. K. McCarter, Jr., *II Samuel*, AB 9 [1984] 75, 76). The parallel usage of בלל with משח in such texts as Exod 29:2; Lev 2:4; 7:12; and Num 6:15 indicates that it can have the meaning of "make fat (with oil)/mix (oil) with," and then "to smear/rub on/anoint" (Kutsch, 10–11). With a small emendation of בלתי to בלה, the colon in 11b would run in smooth parallelism with 11a: "You have rubbed/anointed it (my horn) with fresh oil." However, I have retained MT despite the strange meaning. See *Comment*.

11.b. For שמן רענן as "fresh, oil," see D. W. Thomas, "Some Observations on the Hebrew Word רַעֲנָן" in *Hebraische Wortforschung*, FS Walter Baumgartner, VTSup 16 (1967) 387–97; Booij, 213, n. 1. Most contexts use the word with reference to trees (e.g., Deut 12:2; 1 Kgs 14:23; Job 15:32; Jer 11:16; Pss 37:35; 52:10) and the meaning is that of "thick with leaves, luxuriant, dense, spreading" (Thomas, 396); figuratively, "flourishing/thriving." The meaning "green" is a secondary meaning derived from the thick foliage of a thriving tree. The association of רענן with (olive) oil indicates that it is a fresh, high-quality oil (greenish-white in color); possibly "thick" or "rich" oil. Thomas, 396, notes Briggs, II, 285, who explains the language of 11b as "anointed so richly with oil by Yahweh that he will be saturated with it as are cakes when prepared for sacrifice," and who translates as "thou dost enrich me with fresh oil."

12.a. The verb ותבט (hiphil of נבט, "look/gaze at") is used in the sense of "gaze at/over enemies in triumph" or "look in fulfilment of desire" or "gloating over." It is used several times with ראה ("see") in parallel, and the usage in v 12 corresponds to the usage of ראה in Pss 22:18; 37:34; 54:9b; 59:11; 112:8; cf. 52:8.

12.b. MT בשורי is a noun (masc. pl.) with a 1 c. s. suffix, plus a preposition, apparently from שׁור, II, "behold/regard"; thus, "my watchers." The emendation to בשוררי (see *BHS*) is widely adopted (e.g., Kraus, II, 810). שורר is perhaps a polel participle from שׁור (with *mem* omitted; see BDB, 1004; note GKC 52s, cf. KB, 958). For usage of שורר, see 5:9; 27:11; 54:17; 56:3; 59:11 (see n. 56:3.a.). The translation in some cases may be "slanderers" rather than "watchers" (Dahood has "defamers," see II, 25). The context in Ps 92 suggests, however, that the meaning is "those who watch insidiously/those who lie in ambush"; cf. מארב in 59:4 (note 59:11); 10:8, 9; Lam 3:10; Judg 9:25; etc.—though the language of "rising up against" could easily refer to verbal or legal attacks. "My attackers" in v 12 corresponds to "your enemies" (איביך) in v 10.

12.c. The subject of the hearing is not specified and various suggestions to fill the gap have been made: the plots of the evil foes, their fall/downfall, cries of terror. The context suggests a military expression such as "rout" (as in NIV), which would convey the noisy retreat of foes in disorder and defeat. A Qumran text has שמעה, simple perfect, for MT's plural imperfect (see *BHS*), which strengthens the case for reading the imperfect in 12b as past tense (LXX reads as future).

14.a. The verb (שׁתל) carries the meaning of "transplanted"; see Ps 1:3; Ezek 17:22, 23; 19:10, 12–13 (Dahood, I, 3–4).

14.b. Perhaps the verb should be read as simple imperfect, with 4QPs^b (*BHS*), rather than MT's hiphil. Dahood (II, 338), however, suggests an elative hiphil with the denotation of "richly flourish" (on the elative function of hiphil, see E. A. Speiser, *Genesis*, AB 1, 273). The reader of Ps 92 will note that the verb פרח ("sprout/bud/send out shoots") in vv 8 and 13 is translated as "thrive." Perhaps, "flourish" is elative enough for the hiphil in v 14.

14.c. "House" (temple) is understood. The addition of בית (see *BHS*) is unnecessary and makes the colon too long.

15.a. Usually taken as simple imperfect from נוב, "bear fruit." Also in 62:11; Prov 10:31. Dahood (II, 336) translates v 15a as "still full of sap in old age," assuming that נוב has the basic sense of "flowing" (see his note on 62:11).

15.b. Lit., "fat ones (דשנים) and thriving fresh ones (רעננים) they will be." For רענן, see v 11.c. above.

16.a. Reading להגיד as a circumstantial infinitive construct (see n. 61:9.b.; GKC 114o).

16.b. For this epithet of Yahweh see Deut 32:4, 18, 30, 31; 1 Sam 2:2; 2 Sam 22:3, 32, 47 (Pss 18:3, 32, 47); 2 Sam 23:3; Pss 19:15; 28:1; 31:3; 62:3; 78:35; 144:1; Isa 30:29; 44:8; Hab 1:12; cf. Deut 32:37; Pss 62:3; 73:26; 89:27; 95:1.

16.c. The *kethiv* עלתה is defective for the fuller form עולתה in *qere*. The meaning of עולתה is usually given as "unrighteousness/evil/injustice/wrongdoing." The word suggests the idea of deviation (a contrast to ישׁר—"to go straight/level"), of coming up short/lacking, or failure. See 2 Chr 19:7; Zeph 3:5. The negative construction points to the positive dependability of God.

Form/Structure/Setting

In terms of a general category, Ps 92 belongs to the genre of the thanksgiving psalms, especially in some verses. Vv 1–4 are more of a testimony and an encouragement for others to praise God, which is typical of the thanksgiving psalms, than a hymnic summons to praise. The recall of gracious action on the part of God toward the speaker in vv 5, 11–12 is an expected element in individual thanksgivings. On the other hand, vv 6, 9–10 are composed of descriptive praise of God, more in keeping with a hymn. Vv 7–8, 13–16 have the characteristics of wisdom poetry, setting forth the contrast between the fool (v 7) and the wicked (v 8) with the righteous (vv 13–16). H.-J. Kraus (*Psalms 1–59*, 51) remarks on "the confluence of several elements of form . . . clearly observable in Psalm 92" (also *Psalmen,* II, 810). He notes that individual songs of thanksgiving may take on didactic characteristics and be "shaped by wisdom poetry in both form and content (cf., e.g., Psalm 34)" (*Psalms 1–59*, 59). Thus Ps 92 is an individual psalm of thanksgiving (note the תודה-formula in v 2, "to give thankful praise to Yahweh"); Kraus, *Psalms 1–59*, 51.

The literary structure of the psalm is marked by the use of short double colons (or else a single colon) in v 9 to express the exaltation of Yahweh. Vv 1–4 provide an introductory section of praise for the goodness of the loyal-love (חסד) of Yahweh. The position of v 9 in the center of the psalm suggests a balanced structure and a chiastic arrangement is possible as follows:

> A vv 1–4
>   B vv 5–7
>   C v 8
>   D v 9
>   C' v 10
>   B' vv 11–12
> A' vv 13–16

(suggested by R. M. Davidson, "The Sabbatic Chiastic Structure of Psalm 92," paper delivered at SBL meeting, Chicago, IL, Nov. 18, 1988). The rejoicing in the work of Yahweh in vv 5–7 is continued in vv 11–12. The tricolon in v 10 matches the tricolon in v 8. The confident testimony regarding the future of the righteous in vv 13–16 complements the testimony of praise in vv 1–4. Also, some linguistic features assist in holding the psalm together. Note the use of Yahweh seven times in the psalm (vv 2, 5, 6, 9, 10, 14, and 16)—perhaps a happy coincidence for a sabbath psalm? (See N. H. Sarna, *JBL* 81 [1962] 167–68.) The use of Yahweh in a four-part colon in 5a relates it to the four-part unit which constitutes v 9 and provides a literary frame for vv 5–9, which is enhanced by the use of Yahweh in v 6 (in the dominant 3 + 3 structure). The contrast between the depth of Yahweh's "designs/thoughts" in v 6 with this high status in v 9 adds further complementation, and, indeed, produces a merismic effect: how great is Yahweh from the depths to the heights; i.e., everywhere. The double colon in v 9 seems to find its parallel in 16b, possibly forming a verse which has been split for the insertion of the material in vv 10–16a. (The pattern is possibly that of an A X B insertion; see L. C. Allen, "Rhetorical Criticism in Psalm 69," *JBL* 105 [1986] 583, and *Form/Structure/Setting* of Ps 69). Also, v 16a could rather easily form a tricolon with v 15.

The title of Ps 92 in MT designates it for use on the sabbath day, the only psalm with this rubric in the Hebrew texts. In the Greek texts, however, seven psalms are associated with the sabbath week: 24; 48; 82; 94; 81; 93; 92—in this order for each of the days. The liturgical selection was designed to have a psalm to accompany the libations of wine after the daily *tamid* offering (see Sarna, 155; Mishnah, *Tamid* 7:4; S. Mowinckel, *PIW*, I, 2-3). The Greek psalter has sabbatic superscriptions for five of the seven psalms: 24; 48; 94; 93; 92; possibly also originally for 81; 82 (Sarna, 155, n. 3). The fact that only Ps 92 is specified for the sabbath in MT probably indicates that its selection for this liturgical use was earlier than that of the other six, being used with the *tamid* offering on sabbaths, or other sabbath worship, in the post-exilic temple in Jerusalem (Sarna, 156). Of course, the psalm probably had an earlier history unrelated to sabbath worship; most likely in thanksgiving services during festival times to commemorate the mighty works of Yahweh (J. H. Eaton, 225).

An analysis in terms of the literary characteristics applicable to the dating of Hebrew poetry, as spelled out in *Form/Structure/Setting* of Ps 93, indicates that Ps 92 qualifies for a moderately early dating; e.g., frequency of Yahweh as a name for God (with Elyon, but no Elohim), no prose particles, and the use of tricolons. The psalm is rather liberally supplied with conjunctions, however, which indicates that it is not of a very early date. In general, it probably originated during the monarchical period of pre-exilic Israelite history.

The speaker in the psalm is not identified beyond the generalized descriptions of one who has been delivered from the peril of evil foes by the gracious intervention of Yahweh. The assumption that the speaker should be given a primary identification as a royal figure lies close at hand, especially for commentators with a propensity for relating psalms to kingship. Thus, Dahood (II, 336) says that Ps 92 is "a royal song of thanksgiving to be classified with Ps. XVIII." J. H. Eaton (*Kingship*, 58–59) places Ps 92 among the "Psalms with clearly royal content" and argues that the psalmist is a king because of the way his victory (vv 11–12) is joined to Yahweh in triumph (vv 9–10): "God's foes and the king's are one." Further, "the figure of the horn is obviously appropriate of royal triumph" (citing 75:11; 89:25; 132:17; 1 Sam 2:10). He takes the term "righteous one" (v 13) as a reference to a king (see 151; 2 Sam 23:3; Zech 9:9; Ps 18:21; cf. Ps 101:2–4; G. von Rad, *Old Testament Theology*, tr. D. M. G. Stalker [New York: Harper, 1962] I, 322), who is compared to strong and flourishing trees (see Judg 9:8–16; Ezek 17:22–24). The plural reference in v 14 ("our God") denotes the "participation of the community in the triumph of God and the king" (59); the royal vitality was a major communal interest. "Our God" in v 14 is matched by "my rock" in 16a, which Eaton argues refers to the royal covenant (cf. 28:1; 18:3, 47; 62:2, 7; 144:1).

The appropriateness of the language of Ps 92 for a king should not be doubted. It may very well have been composed with a king in mind; indeed, even for the victory celebration of some king. On the other hand, the shift of royal language to common worshipers in later usage of the psalms is beyond dispute. Any attempt to confine a psalm like this to royal situations should be rejected. Perhaps the speaker is a king, but any reader may fuse his or her identity with that of the speaker.

Comment

An affirmation of thanksgiving to Yahweh (92:2–4). The speaker in these verses sets forth the desirability of praising Yahweh for his loyal-love and faithfulness. Instrumental music (v 4) enhances the aesthetic satisfaction and pleasure of the praise (Kraus, II, 811). For the meaning of "loyal-love" (חסד), see note 51:3.b., and for "faithfulness" (אמונה), see 88:12. V 3 is sometimes interpreted as a reference to singing (or chanting) at the times of the daily burnt offering at the temple (the *tamid*), i.e., in the early morning and late afternoons (see N. M. Sarna, "The Psalm Superscriptions and the Guilds," in *Studies in Jewish Religious and Intellectual History*, ed. S. Stein and R. Loewe [London: Institute of Jewish Studies, University of Alabama Press, 1979] 291; cf. 2 Chr. 29:20, 27; 1 Chr 16:40–42; 23:30–31; Sir 50:11–19). The absence of ערב ("evening") is, however, unexpected (note ערב in 1 Chr 16:40; 23:20; 2 Chr 2:3; 13:11; 31:3; Ps 141:2). The night is associated with such activities as watching for intruders or other dangers (Neh. 4:3 [9], 16 [22]; cf. Ps 90:4), visions (Job 35:10; Ps 77:7; cf. Ps 149:5–6), remembering the name of Yahweh (Ps 119:62), and the servants of Yahweh standing in the temple (Ps 134:1). Therefore it is unlikely that the primary reference in v 3 is to the *tamid*, and it is probable that "morning/dawn" and "night" form a merism which means to declare Yahweh's loyal-love continually, day and night. It may be, however, that in later usage, the verse was understood with reference to the *tamid*.

The great works of Yahweh (92:5–7). The speaker has been made glad by the experience of Yahweh's works. The singular "work" in v 5a could refer to specific help received by the speaker, but the parallels in 5b ("works of your hands") and 6a indicate that the statement is a general one. It is unlikely that two different divine activities are intended (as in Barnes, II, 448). The "works" of the hands of God may apply to creation (see Pss 19:2; 102:26) and to other actions as well (Ps 28:3, Isa 5:12). If read with the sabbath in mind, the expressions should most probably be understood in relation to creation. ("Your designs" seems better for מחשבתיך in 6b, rather than "your thoughts." The meaning of the expression encompasses "plans" and can be equivalent to "ways" (cf. Isa 55:8, 9; 59:7; 65:2; 66:18; Jer 6:19; 18:12; Ps 56:6; Prov 19:21; Job 21:17). The "dunderhead" (traditionally, "brutish man"; RSV, "dull man") and the fool are not persons of "low I.Q., but . . . people who deliberately reject true wisdom, the beginning of which is the fear of Yahweh" (A. A. Anderson, II, 662). See Pss 77:12–13; 104:24; 106:2; 111:2. The knowledge of God's works is "unmindfully ignored" (Weiser) only by those who live like animals.

The wicked are like grass (92:8). The wicked are described as being like grass or green herbage (עשב) which springs up after rain, but which withers and dies in the heat and dryness that follow (see the comparison with grass in 90:5–6; 37:2; 103:15; Isa 40:6, 7, 8; also 76:16; 102:5, 12; Isa 37:27). The wicked blossom out like the flowers that accompany the growth of herbage but are soon destroyed; they bloom and are gone like wildflowers. The force of the simile is greater, of course, in climates where grass shoots up in luxuriant growth after a rain and then dies back quickly. The wicked are not identified, but they are generally all those whose behavior is disruptive of community life; behavior which is frequently violent (note Pss 94:3–6; 37:4; 119:110; 140:5; Jer 5:26–28; Hab 1:2–4).

The exalted status of Yahweh (92:9). This is the pivotal verse of the psalm. The word מרום refers to the realm where Yahweh lives and works and from whence he sends forth his power and help for those in need, or against those whom he punishes (e.g., Ps 18:17 // 2 Sam 22:17; 93:4; 102:20; 144:7; Isa 32:15; 33:5; 57:15; 58:4). The basic meaning of מרום is "height" and it serves as a synonym for the heavens where God dwells and is enthroned (93:2–4; Jer. 17:12). The conceptual field of מרום is undoubtedly inclusive of the idea of the cosmic mountain which is the dwelling place of deity. See *Comment* on 61:2–5. Yahweh is beyond any successful attack by human beings (cf., e.g., 9:8; 10:16; 11:4–6; 14:2; 68:34; 102:13; see Kraus, II, 812). He rules over the world as the "One-who-is-on-High."

The fate of the enemies of Yahweh (92:10). The expanded colons of 10b, c present the total failure which awaits the enemies of Yahweh, who are undoubtedly the wicked of v 8. V 10 is a verse from an old victory hymn, celebrating a triumph over foes. The reflexive form of the verb (פרד) suggests the ideas of "disintegration/bursting/dispersion," though this element should not be over stressed. Note how the verbs of v 10 (אבד, "perish," and פרד, "scatter") are used together of the dispersal of lions in Job 4:11.

The raised horn (92:11–12). The difficulty with the second colon of this verse has been set forth in note 11.b. The first colon refers to an empowering of the speaker, whose "horn" (strength and power) has been raised like that of a wild ox ready for combat. Rubbed with oil, the speaker's "horns" gleam with virility and health, as his head is lifted to look over his fleeing attackers, and his ears hear them running away in panic. V 11 probably does not refer to some sort of anointing ceremony (such as that of a king) or to the anointing of an honored guest on a festive occasion (Pss 23:5; 45:8; 133:2; cf. Isa 61:1–3), but the uncertain nature of 11b makes it unwise to exclude the possibility completely.

The thriving of the righteous (92:13–16). The future of the righteous in v 13 contrasts to that of the wicked in v 8. The wicked are like grass, springing up in profusion, but only to perish quickly. The righteous, on the other hand, will thrive like the fruitful date-palm and like the towering cedars of Lebanon. The contrast between the "wicked" (רשעים) and the "righteous" (צדקים) is familiar in the wisdom literature (e.g., Prov 10:3, 6, 7, 11, 16, 20, 24, 25, 28, 30, 31, 32) and Ps 1. The righteous are like trees that grow in the courts of the temple (v 14). For trees in the temple courts see *Comment* on 52:10; Kraus, II, 813. The date-palm (תמר) is a tall, slender tree with a plume-like foliage at the top. Its deep tap roots seek out water in the ground, and it is associated with water sources and oases (Elim, Num 33:9; Jericho, Deut 34:3; Judg 1:16; 3:13). The fruit of the date-palm can be consumed as food, and a drink can be made from its sap. The leaves were used for roofs and woven into mats and baskets. Palm branches were used on festive occasions (Tabernacles, Lev 23:40; victorious entry into Jerusalem, 1 Macc 13:51; John 12:13; purification of the temple, 2 Macc 10:7). The palm tree is used as a metaphor for a beautiful woman in Cant 7:8[7], 9[8] and for Wisdom in Ecclus 24:13–14 (used along with the cedars of Lebanon). The "cedar" (ארז) of Lebanon is renowned in biblical references for size and quality (e.g., Judg 9:5; 1 Kgs 4:33 [5:13]; 2 Kgs 14:9; Ezra 3:7; Isa 2:13; 14:8; Ps 104:16). The deep-rooted coniferous tree lives to a great age and grows very high and large. The wood, durable and resistant to insects, is a prime choice for fine products, such as musical instruments, chests, panels, and coffins. For the majestic and cosmic nature of a cedar of Lebanon, see Ezek 31:1–9, where the magnificent world-tree, drawing upon the rich waters of the primeval deep in the Garden of God, is a metaphor for the royal power of Egypt. Neither of these trees would likely have grown in the temple courts (v 14), though smaller cedars may have been there. The palm tree was at home around Jericho and in places of similar climate—most palm fronds are brought to Jerusalem from the Jordan Valley. We should not try to insist on the literal accuracy of the poetic and metaphorical language. Vv 14–15 probably allude to the idea of the courts of the temple as a paradise, a garden of God with ample water and highly productive trees (Gen 2:46–3:24; Ezek 28:13–14; cf. Ps 36:7–10; see J. Levenson, *Sinai and Zion* [Minneapolis: Winston Press, 1985] 128–37). Those who are "planted in the house of Yahweh" have enduring vitality, even when old they will be like trees full of sap and with green foliage (v 15). The primal fertility of creation will mark their lives.

I have retained the traditional "upright" in 16a, but the word (ישׁר) should be understood in the sense of Pss 19:9; 25:8; 33:4. Yahweh's "uprightness" is good (25:8) and involves a cluster of words and expressions descriptive of his character and works: "rejoices the heart" (19:9), perfect, trustworthy, pure, clean, true, and faithful. There appears to be some literary artistry in the relationship of v 16 to vv 2 and 9. V 16b provides a satisfactory parallel colon for v 9 (perhaps with "Yahweh" as a pivot word between the colons: a 3+1+3 pattern), and creates a frame for vv 9–16. In general, v 16 corresponds to vv 2–4 (note the use of the infinitive of נגד, "declare," in vv 3 and 16). The alternation of descriptive language in 2a with direct address in 2b is matched by the direct address in v 9 and the descriptive language in 16b (ABB'A' pattern). Also, the descriptive language of 2a and the direct address of 2b is matched by the same pattern in 16a, b (ABA'B'). Thus the psalm is framed in a rather intricate manner.

The rocklike quality of God is expressed in terms of his lack of failure; i.e., in terms of his reliability and consistency (16b, traditional, "injustice/unrighteousness/wrongdoing"). The flourishing of the righteous (vv 13–15) is living testimony to this characteristic of God. The sense of this is expressed in Zeph 3:5:

> The LORD within her is righteous,
>   he does no wrong [עולה],
> every morning he shows forth justice,
>   each dawn he does not fail [עדר];
> but the unjust [עול] knows no shame. (RSV)

Explanation

The title of Ps 92 designates it as a psalm for the sabbath day. Most modern commentators consider the title to be a rubric, which reflects the practice of using the psalm for sabbath worship, but which has little or no connection with its content (Sarna, *JBL* 81 (1962) 158–59). Thus the psalm originally had nothing directly to do with the sabbath, being a *todah* (thanksgiving) psalm suitable for various occasions; perhaps, originally a victory song (vv 10–12). This conclusion is supported by the lack of anything *specifically* sabbatical in the psalm.

Nevertheless, one may assume that whoever introduced it into the sabbath liturgy "must have discovered something in it that intimately corresponded to the dominant themes of the day for which it was selected" (Sarna, *JBL* 81 (1962) 159). This assumption is strengthened by the fact that Ps 92 is the only psalm in MT with the sabbatical rubric; indicative of a deliberate choice (unless it was merely fortuitous, of course). Sarna (158–68) sets forth what he considers to be sabbath themes in the psalm. The first is that of creation. The association of sabbath with creation is well known in biblical texts (see Gen 2:1–3; Exod 20:11; 31:17). According to Exod 31:17, Yahweh ceased from his work of making the heavens and the earth on the seventh day and he was "refreshed" (וינפש). Thus the presence of creation concepts in Ps 92 would be expected, but are they there? Vv 5–6 can be read as such, though the language is not very specific. The "work" (פעל) of Yahweh in v 5 can encompass creation work, though it appears in 90:16 in terms of divine providence (see also 95:9; Isa 52:10; Job 36:24; Pss 44:2; 64:10; 77:13). For the sense of "work of creation," see Isa 45:9, where פעל appears with the "hands" of God. Note the "works (מעשי) of his hands" in Ps 19:2 applied to the firmament ("work of your hands" in Ps 143:5, however, is probably that of deliverance and divine care). The context in 92:8–12 seems to suggest an action of deliverance from wicked foes rather than a work of creation. However, Sarna argues that vv 8 and 10 reflect the combat-victory motif (*Chaoskampf*) of creation; the overcoming of chaos is depicted in terms of the overcoming of rebellious forces. The events in v 8 (which Sarna takes as referring to past happenings) are those described in v 10 (162, 164), and v 10 is a "historicized, if fragmentary, version of the popular Israelite combat epic" (cf. Isa 17:12–14; 27:1; 51:9–10; Hab 3:8–15; Ps 74:13–15; Job 26:10; 38:8–21; Prov 8:27, 29). The exalted status of God in v 9 intensifies the combat motif, according to Sarna (cf. Isa 33:3, 10). The argument seems somewhat forced, but it is certainly possible for vv 5–6 to be read with reference to creation regardless of vv 8 and 10.

M. Weinfeld ("Sabbath, Temple and the Enthronement of the Lord," in *Melanges biblique et orientaux*, FS M. H. Czalles, ed. A. Caquot and M. Delcor, AOAT 212 [Neukirchen-Vluyn: Neukirchener, 1981] 501–12) suggests another linkage of Ps 92 to sabbath in terms of the three-way relationship of creation-victory over enemies and temple. The temple was typically the house and resting place of the deity after combat and the work of creation (cf. Gen 2:1–3). The deity defeats enemies and is enthroned in his "dwelling place" (note Exod 15:17), which is a temple, as in the Babylonian accounts in which Marduk's victory over his enemies (the forces of chaos) brings about his enthronement and a temple for him. In the Ugaritic Baal epic, the building of Baal's sanctuary and his enthronement is associated with victory over the sea, which probably includes creation in its conceptual context, though the matter of the combat with the sea and creation in the Baal text has been the subject of debate: for an extensive survey, see C. Kloos, *Yahweh's Combat with the Sea: A Canaanite Tradition in the Religion of Israel* (Amsterdam: G. A. van Oorschat, 1986) 70–93, whose conclusion is negative; J. Day, *God's Conflict with the Dragon and the Sea: Echoes of a Canaanite Myth in the Old Testament* (Cambridge: Cambridge UP, 1985) 1–18, whose conclusion is positive. Much depends on what is meant by "creation" (see L. R. Fisher, "Creation at Ugarit and in the Old Testament," *VT* 15 [1965] 313–24).

If "Creation" is understood as primarily *creatio ex nihilo* ("creation out of nothing"), then such concepts as "subduing," "separating," "fixing," and "ordering" are likely to be excluded. Regardless of the conclusion relative to the Baal texts, the association of the *Chaoskampf* motif with creation in the OT seems to be undeniable (see Pss 29:10; 74:12–17; 89:10–15; 93:1–5; 104:1–9; Job 9:5–14; 26:5–14; 38:7–11). The temple in which the deity finds rest follows victory over enemies and the establishment of order. The entry of Yahweh into his sanctuary is an entry into rest: "This is my resting place forever; / here will I dwell, for I have desired it" (Ps 132:14). Also, "Arise, O Lord, to your resting place / you and the ark of your might" (Ps 132:8). Thus, the interrelated ideas of creation and temple function to make Ps 92 appropriate for sabbath usage, regardless of its original compositional context.

Weinfeld (502–6) notes also the association of tabernacle/temple with sabbath in OT texts. The sabbath commandment in Exod 31:12–17 follows instructions for building the tabernacle; instructions which are framed by six commands with the formula "And Yahweh said to Moses" (Exod 25:1; 30:11, 17, 22, 34; 31:1). The seventh command is the sabbath command in Exod 31:12 (using אמר, as in 30:34, rather than דבר as in the others). The typological parallels between the completion of the tabernacle sanctuary in Exod 39:1–40:33 and Gen 1:1–2:3 are striking (Weinfeld, 503); also note the parallelism between the cloud-glory of Yahweh on Mount Sinai for seven days in Exod 24:15–16 and the cloud-glory of Yahweh covering and filling the tabernacle in Exod 40:34–Lev 1:1. Another form of the sabbath stipulation follows the interlude of the golden calf and begins the account of the building of the tabernacle in Exod 35:1–3. Note also Lev 19:30 ("You shall keep my sabbaths and reverence my sanctuary," RSV) and Lev 26:2 (N. M. Sarna, *Exploring Exodus* [New York: Schocken Books, 1986] 214).

The idea of the temple courts as a paradise (see *Comment* on vv 13–16 above) is worth noting again because sabbath has something of the same quality. The account of the seventh day in Gen 2:1–3, which presupposes the sabbath, is marked by a lack of morning and evening. Thus the seventh day (sabbath) has no darkness; darkness in which malevolent works of injury and death are done by evil persons and malign powers (cf. Gen 32:27; Exod 4:24; 12:12, 22; Job 3:3–9; 24:13–17; 34:20–25; 36:20; see J. Levenson, *Creation and the Persistence of Evil* [San Francisco: Harper & Row, 1988] 123). Without darkness the seventh day is a day of light and the powers of darkness are banished. The idea of the paradisiacal quality of sabbath is reflected in Isa 58:14 and in Jewish tradition. The Mishnah (*Tamid* 7:4) declares that Ps 92 is "a song for the time that is to come, for the day that shall be all sabbath and rest in the life everlasting." The Sabbath is a proleptic glimpse of the eternal life of the coming age: "Those who observe the Sabbath experience an earnest of the coming redemption" (J. Levenson, *Sinai and Zion*, 183–84). So it is with the righteous in Ps 92:13–16; they both anticipate and experience the paradisiacal life.

The reader will readily recognize that the arguments for Ps 92 as a psalm for sabbath are rather subtle and indirect, and he or she may well ask: If this psalm was intended for use on the sabbath, why was it not written with more specific reference? As already indicated, the lack of direct relatedness to sabbath probably indicates that the psalm was composed for some other context and later adopted for the sabbath (S. Mowinckel, *PIW*, II, 205–6). The original context was perhaps that of thanksgiving after victory (of a king?) or a festival occasion (perhaps at the close of such a celebration; Weiser, 614; J. H. Eaton, 225–26). Nevertheless, the title and liturgical tradition ask the reader to read it with a sabbath repertoire (a referential context of norms and allusions; the "familiar territory" of a text). We are not bound by this referential context and may prefer to shift the psalm to another. I doubt, however, that there will be much improvement over the ancient liturgical wisdom which asks us to read it with the Sabbath in mind.

An Acclamation of the King Who Reigns on High (93:1–5)

Bibliography

Becker, J. *Israel deutet seine Psalmen.* 73–74. **Day, J.** *God's Conflict with the Dragon and the Sea.* 35–37. **Eaton, J. H.** "Some Questions of Philology and Exegesis in the Psalms." *JTS* 19 (1968) 608–9. **Howard, D. M., Jr.** *The Structure of Psalms 93–100.* Ann Arbor: University Microfilms International, 1986; Ph.D. diss., University of Michigan, 1986. 38–57, 145–59, 200–201. **Jefferson, H. G.** "Psalm 93." *JBL* 71 (1952) 155–60. **Jeremias, J.** *Das Königtum Gottes in den Psalmen.* Göttingen: Vandenhoeck & Ruprecht, 1987. 15–29. **Michel, D.** "Die sogenannten Thronbesteigungspsalmen." In *Tempora und Satzstellung in den Psalmen.* Bonn: Bouvier, 1960. 215–21. **Shenkel, J. D.** "An Interpretation of Psalm 93:5." *Bib* 56 (1965) 401–16. **Watts, J. D. W.** "*Yahweh Malak* Psalms." *TZ* 21 (1965), 341–48.

Translation

1[a] *Yahweh reigns![b] He has robed himself with majesty.*   (4+4+3)
Yahweh has robed himself; belted himself with strength!
The world is firmly established;[c] immovable.

2 *Your throne was established long ago;*   (3+2[3])
You are from eternity, (O Yahweh).[a]

3 *The floods[a] roared,[b] O Yahweh;*   (3+3+3)
the floods roared with their thunderous voice;
the floods roared[c] with their pounding.[d]

4 *(But) greater than the roar of many waters,*   (3+3+3)
mighty (waters), breakers of the sea,
was the Mighty One on high, O Yahweh![a]

5 *Your testimonies[a] are sure indeed;[b]*   (3+3+3)
holiness[c] befits[d] your house,
O Yahweh, for endless days.

Notes

1.a. LXX has the title: Εἰς τὴν ἡμέραν τοῦ προσαββάτου ὅτε κατῴκισται ἡ γῆ· αἶνος ᾠδᾶς τῷ Δαυιδ. "For the day before the sabbath, when the land was inhabited: a praise song for David." The filling of the land may refer to creation, and thus to the Sabbath, or to the return from the exile (Delitzsch, III, 74; Kirkpatrick, 563).

1.b. The expression יהוה מלך has received much attention, especially since S. Mowinckel's proposal in 1921 to translate it as a cultic affirmation in the celebration of Yahweh's kingship, with the meaning "Yahweh has become king" (*Psalmenstudien*, II, 6–8). The expression occurs elsewhere in 96:10; 1 Chr 16:31; Pss 97:1; 99:1. The most significant critique of Mowinckel's proposal was made by D. Michel, "Studien zu den sogenannten Thronbesteigungspsalmen," *VT* 6 (1956) 40–68; also his *Tempora und Satzstellung*, 215–21; also see H.-J. Kraus, *Psalms 1–59*, 86–89; and brief treatments with references to the literature in K. A. Kitchen, *Ancient Orient and Old Testament* (London: Tyndale Press, 1966), 102–6; D. M. Howard, *Structure*, 39–40. Since the work of Michel, most scholars have translated the expression as "Yahweh reigns" (Michel: "Yahweh, is the one who exercises kingship") or "Yahweh is king." Howard (40) notes that no major English Bible version has adopted Mowinckel's "Yahweh has become king!" The major argument against the formulaic expression "*x* has become king" is based on 2 Sam 15:10 and 2 Kgs 9:13, where the exclamation "*x* has become king" is clearly indicated, but where the word order is "*x* מלך" (see also Isa 52:7). The argument is supposed to be strengthened by 1 Kgs 1:18, where the word order is מלך XXX, but which is commonly read as "*x* is king" or "*x* reigns as king" (note the "*x* מלך" in 1 Kgs 1:11, 13).

The argument from 1 Kgs 1:11, 18 does not seem very strong to me. The context is that of Adonijah's attempt to seize the kingship in view of the impending death of David. The durative aspects of Adonijah's kingship could hardly be the major subject of Nathan (v 11) and Bathsheba (v 18). They are concerned with the fact that Adonijah has seized power and *become* king. The context of Ps 47:9[8] may favor the translation "God has become king" rather than "God is king."

The placement of subject and verb does not provide very persuasive evidence against the idea of beginning a reign. "The placing of the subject first simply gives added emphasis to it" (J. Day, *God's Conflict with the Dragon and the Sea*, 36). In his later work, Mowinckel still defended the meaning of "Yahweh has become king" (*PIW*, II, 222), but he recognized that the argument for a shout of homage does not depend on the translation: "It is of secondary importance whether we *translate* 'reigns as king,' for in every case the attention is turned toward the 'ingressive' element." He asks why the MT did not vocalize as מֶלֶךְ if the idea of a durative state of being king was intended. Mowinckel (*PIW*, II, 223) is surely justified in arguing that the treatment of יהוה מלך as a cry of homage in the sense that "Yahweh has become king," or "Yahweh reigns (anew)" does not destroy the idea that Yahweh always *is* king. Cultic terminology should not be pushed into such rationalistic modes of thinking. The dramatic nature of worship does not require an exact metaphysical delineation of words in liturgies. Note Rev 11:17, cf. v 15; 19:6 which follow the LXX texts. I have adopted "Yahweh reigns" for the *Translation*, but in an acclamatory sense which celebrates the repeatedly new enthronement of Yahweh.

1.c. Some versional evidence points to תִּכֵּן, "he has established," cf. Ps 75:4 (reading as piel perf. of תכן, "measure/regulate/mete out"; see Job 28:25; Isa. 40:12 for the niphal imperfect from כון which is in MT). See *BHS* on Ps 96:10. The אף ("surely/also/indeed") intensifies the action of the verb; thus, "firmly established," see the comment of Dahood, II, 340.

2.a. This colon is frequently considered to be incomplete and אל ("God") or אלהים ("God") is added; e.g., Kraus. Howard argues for "From long ago was your (throne)!" on the basis that both the subject ("your throne") and the verb ("established") in 2a do double duty and serve in 2b. The subject is reinforced in 2b by "the echoing . . . of its suffix through the use of the independent personal pronoun" (אתה). It seems likely that "Yahweh" is understood but need not be added to the text. The fivefold use of Yahweh in this psalm is probably intentional.

3.a. Lit., "rivers" (see Pss 24:2; 46:5; 74:15; 98:8; Ezek 31:15; Hab 3:8; Jonah 2:4).

3.b. Lit., "lifted up"—"The rivers raised. . . ." The object is "their voice" (קולם) in 3b.

3.c. The imp. is frequently changed to perf. (see *BHS*), but this need not be done. The imp. may continue the past tense of the perfs. in 3a, b in a qtl–qtl–qtl sequence, a phenomen present in both Ugar. and Heb. poetry (see Dahood, II, 341; Howard, *Structure*, 43–44, for discussion and reference). Howard points out that the sense would differ very little if the verb is read as habitual past ("used to lift up") and also that it is possible to read as future: the waters would continue to rebel, as in the past, but Yahweh would be their master. LXX^A has "the floods will lift up their waves"; a colon which is missing in some Greek texts (see Briggs, II, 311).

3.d. The word דכים appears only here, and it is usually taken from דכה, "crush," as the noun form דכי, the "crushing/pounding/raging" of waves in the sea (BDB, 194). For its possible relationship to *dkym* in the Ugar. UT 49.5.1–3, see Kraus, II, 819; Dahood, II, 341; Day, *God's Conflict with the Dragon and the Sea*, 37.

4.a. This verse would be expressed more smoothly in English with some change in the order of words. Howard (44) suggests: "More majestic in the heights is Yahweh / than the thunders of many waters, / majestic waters, breakers of the sea." But he follows Freedman, and translates more literally as a broken construct chain: "More than the thunders of many waters, / Majestic (waters), breakers of the sea, / (More) majestic in the heights is Yahweh." This supposes that the מים ("waters") is assumed to be repeated (in sense) before אדירים ("majestic/mighty ones"), synonymous with "breakers of the sea" (lit., "More than the voices of many waters, mighty ones, breakers of the sea. . . ."). This avoids the textual emendation of אדירים to אדיר ממשברי, "mightier than the waves.", as, e.g., in RSV. For the broken construct chain, see GKC 130; Dahood, III, 381–83; D. N. Freedman, *Pottery, Poetry, and Prophecy* (Winona Lake: Eisenbrauns, 1980) 339–41. J. H. Eaton (*JTS* 19 [1968] 608) suggests that 4b be understood as a title, analogous to various Ugar. usages (*bl ym*, "Prince Sea"; *zbh yrh*, "Prince Moon," etc.): "(Over) their Majesties the Breakers of the Sea." He also suggests that "many waters" in 4a has titular force: "their Lordships the Waters" (likewise מים אדירים in Exod 15:10). It is also possible that the *mem* at the end of אדירים is an enclitic in an extended construct chain: "majestic ones of the breakers of the sea" = "mighty breakers of the sea." In this case, the מקלות ("more than the sounds of") does double duty: "Greater than the roar of many waters // (than the roar) of mighty breakers of the sea // is the Mighty One on high, O Yahweh." The *Translation* assumes that Yahweh is addressed in the vocative, and אדיר in 4c is treated as a divine epithet (as in Isa 10:34; Ps 76:5). The vocative "O Yahweh" forms a frame with the "O Yahweh" in 3a and 5c.

5.a. So MT, reading as a noun (fem. pl.) of עדה (BDB, 730), closely related to עדות (and עדה). These terms appear numerous times in Ps 119 and often elsewhere (e.g., Pss 25:10; 78:56; 99:7; 132:12; Deut 4:45; 6:17, 20). The meaning of the term is "testimonies" or "affirmations." The usage of עדות in close relation to "commands," "decrees," and "covenant" (as, e.g., in Deut 6:17, 20; Ps 25:10, and extensively in Ps 119) shows that the meaning is that of "stipulations" or "commandments." Weiser (620) suggests that "testimony" involves the tradition of salvation-history, which was recited in worship ceremonies and fits well with Deut 6:20 and 4:45. A. A. Anderson (II, 669) suggests that it may refer to "the Covenant as a whole (cf. 119:2) which includes not only the mighty deeds of Yahweh, but also his promises and commands (cf. 25:10; 132:12)." J. D. Shenkel (*Bib* 56 [1965]) and Dahood (II, 342) argue that the meaning "testimonies/decrees/affirmations" is unlikely in this verse. Shenkel argues that the meaning of עדה should be derived from the Ugar. word *'dt* meaning "throne," and translates in 93:5 as "Your throne." Dahood, like A. Bentzen (cited by Shenkel, 404), derives עדה from the verb יעד, "appoint" (cf. עדה, n.f. "congregation/assembly"). Bentzen understood עדה as "sacred assemblies," but Dahood argues for a derivative meaning "appoint to a seat/throne," vocalizing as inf. const. עדתך, and thus "your enthronement." Bentzen's proposal of "your sacred assemblies" relates well to "your houses" in 5b. MT, however, almost certainly intended the meaning "testimonies/affirmations," as in Ps 19:8 and Ps 119 (see J. Becker, *Israel deutet seine Psalmen*, 73–74).

5.b. The traditional translation of מאד is "very sure" (KJV; RSV). NAB has "Your decrees are worthy of trust indeed"; NJV, "Your decrees are indeed enduring." Howard (*Structure,* 47) argues for "affirmed," thinking of a liturgy or a ceremony affirming the surety of the divine decrees and assuming that לביתך should be read as "in your house." Dahood has "was confirmed."

5.c. Shenkel (*Bib* 56 [1965] 412) argues for קדש as a collective noun meaning "the saints/holy ones," i.e., divine beings in the heavenly court of Yahweh; citing Ps 68:18; Deut 33:2; Exod 15:11, and probably Ps 77:14. See Ps 68:18d. Shenkel's translation of 93:5 is, "Your throne has been firmly established; / in your temple the holy ones glorify you, / Yahweh, for length of days."

5.d. The word נאוה is usually understood as piel perfect (or pilel/palel) from נאה, "be comely/befitting" (see BDB, 610; GKC 75x, KB, 585). The form is a hapax in MT (cf. נאוו for נאוו, "they are beautiful" in Isa. 52:7; Cant 1:10, and the adjective form נאוה, [fem. נאוה] is found in Cant 1:5; 2:14; 4:3; 6:4; Pss 33:1; 147:1; Prov 17:7; 19:10; 26:1) which is usually taken to mean "befitting." Perhaps we should understand the meaning as "adorn"; note the LXX's πρέπει, which has the basic meaning of "clearly seen/meets the eye/conspicuous" and thus "fitting/suits."

Shenkel (*Bib* 56 [1965] 401–16) argues for a verb meaning "to praise" on the basis of an apparent mispointing of MT in Pss 33:1 and 147:1, where נאוה ("comely/befitting") is found, but where verbal forms are expected. In Ps 33:1–3 there are five imperative verbs, and reading נאוה as imperative of the intensive stem (with תהלה, "praise" as object) does not seem unreasonable. Dahood (I, 200) reads as piel inf. const. with fem. ending from נאו (a by-form of נוה), which is understood in Exod 15:2 by LXX as δοξάζω, "glorify/praise." In Ps 147:1, the pointing of נאוה as infinitive is easier in the context and is adopted by some commentators (see Kraus, II, 1135, following J. Blau, *VT* 4 [1954] 410–11; also L. C. Allen, 304–5, who translates v 1b as "it is indeed pleasing to engage in fitting praise"). Thus Shenkel and Dahood assume an original verb "to praise/glorify/laud" in Ps 93:5.

Howard (*Structure*, 48) follows the reading נוה in Qumran 4QPsᵇ and assumes that it is נוה in the sense of an abode for shepherds and flocks (see נָוֶה in BDB, 627). He suggests that נוה קדשך ("your holy habitation") in Exod 15:13 is relevant, and translates Ps 93:5 as "Your decrees are affirmed, O Mighty One, / In your house, (your) holy habitation, / O Yahweh, for length of days." This assumes that the ל on לביתך ("to your house") should be read as "in" (or "at," see Ps 51:12) and that the מאד ("exceedingly") be read with Dahood as מְאֹד and understood as an epithet of Yahweh ("O Mighty One"), though Dahood in Ps 93:5 reads as "of old," matching the מעולם ("from old") in v 2 (see also Freedman, *Pottery, Poetry, and Prophecy*, 347; e.g., in Pss 46:2; 78:59; 109:30; 142:7; see "Grand One" in Dahood's index, III, 473).

Form/Structure/Setting

Ps 93 is a hymn or praise psalm that celebrates Yahweh's kingship and victory over primordial forces. It does not have the summons to praise or call to worship found in some hymns (e.g., Pss 33:1; 47:2; 95:1–2; 96:1–3; 98:1; 100:1–4; 105:1–3; 149:1–3, and vastly extended in 148). Hymns primarily express praise of Yahweh for his deeds and qualities, which has a proclamatory character shared by praise in the thanksgivings (E. S. Gerstenberger, *Psalms*, I, 15, 17). Ps 93 is a combination of proclamation (v 1) and direct address to Yahweh (vv 2, 5, and probably vv 3–4).

V 1 is set off as the opening acclamation, with a longer metrical pattern than the other verses. Howard (*Structure*, 55–56) treats 1c in relation to 2a, b as a unit, noting a 3+3+3 pattern in the remainder of the poem. I prefer, however, to read vv 1–2 as a unit. The affirmation of Yahweh's eternal enthronement in v 2 matches the acclamation of his kingship in 1a, b. V 1c is the central affirmation of the stability of the world which stands between the two. Vv 3–4 deal with the cosmic forces whose overcoming marked the establishment of the reign of Yahweh as the one who has "belted himself" as victor. V 5 attaches the stability of the "testimonies" (or commandments) of Yahweh to the power of his kingship.

Ps 93 is usually treated with Pss 47, 96–99 as a subgroup of hymns that declare the kingship of Yahweh. J. D. W. Watts (*ThLZ* 21 [1965] 343) has isolated five characteristics of the kingship of Yahweh psalms:

1. Concern with all the earth, all peoples, or all nations.
2. References to other gods.
3. Signs of exaltation and kingship.
4. Characteristic acts of Yahweh: making, establishing, sitting, judging, etc.
5. Expressions of the attitude of praise before the heavenly king.

Watts finds that Pss 96 and 97 (also 89) have all five characteristics. Pss 98 and 99 have 1, 3, 4, and 5 (also Ps 47); Ps 95 has 2, 3, 4, and 5. Ps 93 has 3 and 4. This rough survey is sufficient to show that Pss 47, 93, 95–99 share a good number of characteristics, but they also differ from one another.

The thesis that these psalms (and other closely related material, such as Pss 24:7–10; 89:6–15) emerged from a festival of Yahweh's enthronement has been widely accepted since the work of S. Mowinckel, who argued that in the autumn festival, which marked the beginning of the new year, Yahweh was acclaimed as newly enthroned and praised as the Creator King. The thesis has been extensively criticized and modified (see A. R. Johnson, "The Psalms," in *The Old Testament and Modern Study*, ed. H. H. Rowley [Oxford: Clarendon Press, 1951] 152–81; for a review and summary of earlier reactions, see H.-J. Kraus, *Psalms 1–59*, 86–89 [with a negative judgment]; see E. Gerstenberger, "Psalms," in *Old Testament Form Criticism*, ed. J. H. Hayes [San Antonio: Trinity UP, 1974] 214–16, for a positive approach; also Gerstenberger, *Psalm*, p 1, FOTL 14, 197–98; and W. Brueggemann, *Israel's Praise: Doxology against Idolatry and Ideology* [Philadelphia: Fortress, 1988] 4–6). The thesis of the praise of Yahweh's kingship in festival contexts seems to be well established in general terms at least, and Brueggemann (6) argues that "Even scholars who are not in sympathy with the proposal appeal either to the hypothesis [of Mowinckel] itself or to some derivative form of the hypothesis." The acclamation and praise of Yahweh as king was surely a major element of Israelite worship. However, the exact nature of the worship, precise dating, and cultic contexts are matters which are too elusive to determine with any certainty. Gerstenberger ("Psalms," 215) wisely comments that "We leave the dating open and just state that the Yahweh kingship psalms are sufficient evidence for an Israelite festival which praised Yahweh's taking power over the nations and which probably was tied to the seasonal cycle of cultic activities."

In a similar manner, B. C. Ollenburger (*Zion the City of the Great King*, JSOT SS 41 [Sheffield: JSOT, 1987] 25–33) surveys the scholarly discussion in the period since Mowinckel and concludes that the available evidence points to the celebration of Yahweh's kingship, established by primordial victory over chaos and exercised from Zion in the autumn festival in Israelite worship. He adds, however, that "there is insufficient evidence, it seems to me, to recounstruct this festival in detail, to ascribe a dominant role within it to the earthly king [as in A. R. Johnson, *Sacral Kingship, passion*] or to assign a whole range of Psalms to specific movements within the festival" (33). I take this as a sound conclusion.

D. M. Howard (*Structure*, 93–100) has done an extensive analysis of Pss 93–100, in terms of linguistic comparisons, structural comparisons, and context, and concludes that the psalms form "a logical coherent unit within Book IV of the Psalter" (216). He argues that Ps 93 introduces the section composed of Pss 93–100, while 95 and 100 bracket the heart of the section in 96–99. Ps 94 is usually considered to be disjunctive in this section, according to Howard shows significant ties with its present context (See *Form/Structure/Setting*, Ps 94; Howard, 201–6).

Ps 93 in context. In its present context in Book IV of the Psalter, Ps 93 is a short psalm, that praises the kingship of Yahweh, positioned between the thanksgiving-sabbath Ps 92 and Ps 94. The latter is a form of communal instruction with some similarity to a thanksgiving psalm. As noted above, Ps 93 is frequently considered to be anomalously placed, separated from Pss 95–99 (and more especially 96–99) which share with it the praise of Yahweh's kingship. There are, however, some reasons for considering Pss 92–94 as a unit, with Ps 93 as the pivot psalm between the two longer Pss 92 and 94.

First, the lines of continuity between Pss 92–93 merit some attention. We can begin with the presence of a title in MT for Ps 92. In the MT of Pss 90–99 there are only three titles: 90:1; 92:1; 98:1 (LXX has titles for all of Pss 90–99). G. Wilson (*The Editing of the Hebrew Psalter*, SBLDS 76 [Chico, CA: Scholars Press, 1985] 131–32,

135–36, 173–81; idem, "The Use of 'Untitled' Psalms in the Hebrew Psalter," *ZAW* 97 [1985] 404–13; idem,"Evidence of Editorial Divisions in the Hebrew Psalter," *VT* 34 [1984] 337–52) has argued that in Books I–III of the Psalter there are good reasons to conclude that the juxtaposition of an untitled psalm with a preceding titled one is the result of editing in order to indicate a tradition of combining the psalms in usage, and he reviews the five good cases for such combinations in the first three books of the Psalter: Pss 1–2; 9–10; 32–33; 42–43, and 70–71 (*Editing,* 173). In the cases of Pss 9–10 and 42–43, the second psalm was probably originally a unified part of the prior psalm (which is supported by mss evidence and by content). The relationship of untitled psalms to preceding titled psalms has also received attention from W. Zimmerli, who argues for "twin-psalms" in some cases, notably: Pss 111–112 and 105–106 (see "Zwillings-psalmen," in *Wort, Lied, und Gottespruch,* FS J. Ziegler, ed. J. Schreiner [Würzburg: Echter, 1972] 105–130; also reviewed and discussed by D. M. Howard, Jr., "Psalms 93–94 and the Editing of the Hebrew Psalter," unpublished paper dated June 1989, and kindly provided to me by the author). The situation in Books IV–V of the Psalter is not so clear because of large runs of untitled psalms in these books. Nevertheless, it is suggestive for the relationship of Pss 92 and 93; at least it is not surprising to find that the untitled Ps 93 is closely related, editorially, to titled Ps 92 (which stands out in the midst of one of the longer runs of untitled Psalms in the Psalter). Wilson (*Editing,* 178) concludes that an *original* unity of Pss 92 and 93 "seems out of the question." In this regard, he is probably correct, but this does not exclude an *editorial* unity of tradition and usage.

There are some links between Pss 92 and 93 which support concluding that the two psalms should be read together. Of course, the unequal length of the two psalms limits the comparison of lexical and content factors of relationship, nevertheless there are some features worth noting. The use of מרום ("high") in the pivotal v 9 of 92 and in the final statement of 93:4 is striking (מרום appears elsewhere in Book IV only in 102:20, and does not appear in any other consecutive psalms). The root רום ("to be exalted/high") also appears in 92:11. Also note the use of מאד ("exceedingly/very/indeed") in 92:6 ("Your thoughts are very deep") and 93:5 ("Your testimonies are sure indeed"), and the use of the "house/temple" of Yahweh in 92:14 and 93:5 (in Pss 90–99, בית, "house," of Yahweh appears only in 92:14; 93:5; 98:3). The use of tricolons in 92:8, 10, 12 and in 93 is an obvious similarity, a feature that is also found in 94:23. The parallel nature of 92:9 and 93:2 should be noted also. V 5 in Ps 93 in its present form, seems to be an addition to the content of vv 1–4, serving to relate 93:1–4 to 92:16 in content and to act as a transition verse into Ps 94.

The links between 92 and 94 may indicate also that 93 is to be read with 92. Note the use of בער ("brutish/dull/dunderhead") in 92:7 and 94:8, in the context of language at home in the wisdom literature in both psalms. Also note the צור ("rock") in 92:16 and 94:22; the speakers in both psalms claim Yahweh as their "Rock" (צור also occurs in Ps 95:1 and only elsewhere in Book IV in 105:41). The "evildoers" (פעלי און) appear in 92:8, 10 and in 94:4, 16; and only elsewhere in Book IV in 101:8, though noun forms of פעל occur in 90:16; 92:5; 95:9; 104:23. The significant wisdom features of Pss 92 and 94 also provide linkage between these two psalms. Howard ("Psalms 90–94," 32) notes that the wisdom section in 94:8–15 reflects 92:6.

Further evidence for reading Ps 93 with 92 comes from usage of the psalms in the Jewish liturgies for sabbath observance. According to the Mishnah (*Tamid* 7:4), Ps 93 was recited by the Levites in the temple on Friday (note the Greek title) and Ps 92 was sung on the sabbath (Saturday). A reason for this reversal is ascribed to Rabbi Aqiva (b. *Rosh Hash.* 31a): God's work of creation was completed in six days ("The world is firmly established," 93:1); presumably so that he could sit enthroned on high (see J. Levenson, *Creation and the Persistence of Evil: The Jewish Drama of Divine Omnipotence* [San Francisco: Harper & Row, 1988] 108; following M. Weinfeld, "sabbath, Temple, and the Enthronement of the Lord— The Problem of the Sitz im Leben of Genesis 1:1–2:3," in *Mélanges biblique et orientaux*, FS M. H. Czaelles, ed. A. Caquot and M. Delcor, AOAT 212 [Neukirchen-Vluyn: Neukirchener] 1981, 501–12). Weinfeld argues for the association of divine enthronement with sabbath in rabbinic tradition and perhaps earlier.

The basis for the linkage of sabbath and enthronement derives from the idea of divine *otiositas,* found in creation myths from many places (N.-E. A. Andreasen, *The Old Testament Sabbath: A Tradition-Historical Investigation*, SBLDS 4 [Missoula, MT: Scholars Press, 1972] 174), including ancient Near Eastern creation stories. *Oiositas* is used to refer to the inactivity/rest/relief of a god following a struggle or great expenditure of energy in transforming chaos into cosmic order, or else following a struggle with some disruptive crisis. In the calmness and stability of the established order, the deity sits in peace on a throne in his palace (Andreason, 174–82; Levenson, 100–11). The idea of Yahweh's "rest" is present several times in the OT: see Ps 132:14; Gen 2:1–3; Exod 31:16–17; Ps 95:11 (see *Comment* on the verse); note 2 Sam 7:1: "when the king [David] sat enthroned in his palace and the Lord had granted him rest from all his enemies around him" (trans. Levenson, 107). Thus the association of Sabbath and enthronement was easy, and the use of kingship/enthronement psalms in sabbath observance is understandable. Sabbath is rooted in the "repose of the enthroned creator" (Levenson, 109), whose work has been completed ("declared very good," Gen 1:31) and which has produced a time of order and well-being.

A further bit of evidence for linking Pss 93 with 92 is found in the Qumran text, 4QPs[b], which probably originally contained Pss 91–103 and 112–18 (so P. W. Skehan, "A Psalm Manuscript from Qumran [4QPs[b]]," *CBQ* 26 [1964] 313–22; G. H. Wilson, "The Qumran Psalms Manuscripts and the Consecutive Arrangement of Psalms in the Hebrew Psalter," *CBQ*, 45 [1983] 381). Only a part of 93:5 is found in the 4QPs[b] material (*[l]bytk nwh qdš/[y]hwh l'r[k]*), but the following line is left blank and a *waw* of large size is found in the lower margin, probably as a marker between Pss 93 and 94. Wilson (381, n.7) concludes that 93 "originally bridged the gap between 91–92 and Psalm 94." All in all, it seems to me that Ps 92 is appropriately complemented by the exaltation of Yahweh's kingship in Ps 93.

On the other side of Ps 93, D. Howard ("Psalms 93–94," and "Psalms 90–94 and the Editing of the Psalter," a paper read at the national meetings of the Evangelical Theological Society, San Diego, CA, November 16, 1989; both papers used by permission) has argued for strong links between Pss 93 and 94. His arguments have been summarized in some detail in *Form/Structure/Setting* of Ps 94 and need not be repeated here. He concludes that there is a significant cohesiveness between them, at least "in the minds of the Psalter's editors" ("Psalms 93–94," 13) and that the ordering of the psalms in the sequence of Pss 90–94 is purposeful: "Psalm 93 affirms YHWH'n sovereignty over rebellious nature, while Psalm 94 affirms his sovereignty over rebellious humanity." Thus it seems to be arguable, at least, to read Pss 92–93–94 as an editorial triology of psalms. Howard

("Psalms 90–94," 33) argues that there are significant links between all the psalms in 90–94 and that they form a coherent unit of five psalms. His conclusion makes sense to me. I would suggest that this larger unit of psalms is marked by affinitives with the wisdom traditions (probably adopting Ps 93 from other sources), and that we should think of the speakers in all of them as theologically informed leaders and teachers involved in communal and liturgical instruction in post-exilic Israelite communities (though the dating of psalms is a very elusive business).

In regard to date, it is possible that the origin of the content in Ps 93 was quite early in Israelite history. At least, this is the conclusion of some commentators influenced by similarities between the psalm and Ugaritic poetry. For example, H. G. Jefferson ("Psalm 93") concludes that the evidence of vocabulary, style, and thought content points to an early pre-exilic, possibly Canaanitish origin. Dahood concludes that its closest counterpart is Ps 29, which he judges to be from the tenth century B.C.E. (also advocated by E. Lipiński, see J. D. Shenkel, *Bib* 56 [1965] 402; Kraus, II, 816). Mowinckel and Weiser are content to think of the broad context of the pre-exilic period. Of course, there is no lack of defenders of the post-exilic period: e.g., Kirkpatrick argues for the return from Babylon and the early days of the restoration; Buttenwieser (317–43), who is an ardent defender of Pss 93, 96, 97, and 98 as post-exilic psalms dependent on Isa 40–55, argues that perhaps Deutero-Isaiah himself is the author (Ps 99 is not included by Buttenwieser in this group, because he contends that Ps 99 is "spiritually akin not to Deutero-Isaiah but rather to Ezekiel and his later follower, Joel," 362).

After careful analysis, Howard (*Structure*, 48–55) concludes that the data point to an origin in the "earliest stages of Hebrew poetic writing," probably the tenth century, but possibly as early as the twelfth century. The major factors in Howard's analysis are as follows:

1. Absence of the definite article, of אשר and את (relative pronoun and sign of direct object) from the psalm, i.e., no prose particles. The assumption of this criterion is that there was a tendency to insert prose particles in later poetry.

2. Absence of conjunctions; later Hebrew poetry has conjunctions.

3. Use of tricolons rather than bicolons. The tricolon is common in Ugar.; less common in most MT poetry.

4. The alternation of prefixed (imperfects) and suffixed (perfects) verb forms without apparent change of tense seems to be more characteristic of early Heb. poetry, and this apparently occurs in 93:3; see n. 3.d.

5. Absence of אלהים for God and the occurrence of Yahweh; cf. Exod 14; Judg 5, early poems which use Yahweh in most cases. Also, the Balaam oracles, Gen 49, and Deut 33. D. N. Freedman, "Divine Names and Titles in Early Hebrew Poetry" (in *Pottery, Poetry, and Prophecy* [Winona Lake: Eisenbrauns, 1980] 77–129) finds three stages in the use of divine names and titles:

   I.   Militant Yahwism (twelfth century)—Exod 15; Ps 29; Judg 5.

   II. Patriarchal revival (eleventh century)—Gen 49; Num 23–24; Deut 33.

   III. Monarchic syncretism (tenth century and later)—1 Sam 2; 2 Sam 1; 2 Sam 23; 1 Sam 22 = Ps 18; Deut 32; Pss 78, 68, 72.

The name Yahweh is used exclusively or predominantly in Phase I; El, Shadday, Elyon, and El Olam appear with Yahweh in Phase II; Yahweh continues to be used in Phase III, but Elohim appears for the first time in the sense of "God," along with Adonay, and other names and titles.

A sixth criterion is, of course, that of content (non-linguistic reasons). The similarities in language and content between Ps 93 (and the same is true of 96–99) and Isa 40–55 have been interpreted to indicate that these psalms should be dated during the exile or afterwards. However, the dependence of the psalms on Deutero-Isaiah should not be assumed; it is equally as probable that both draw from common pre-exilic Jerusalem traditions. Thus the evidence for the date of the content of Ps 93 tilts toward the conclusion of an early pre-exilic date for its content. The present psalm, however, may be only a section from a larger psalm, selected for its present position in Book IV and interpreted in the exilic or post-exilic context of Pss 90–99 (note the suggested reinterpretation of 93:5 in Becker, *Israel deutet seine Psalmen*, 72–73).

Comment

An acclamation of divine kingship (93:1–2). The language in these verses belongs to the realm of kingship. Yahweh, like great earthly kings, is presented as having clothed, or robed, himself in majestic garments. The King himself is no newcomer; his going forth is from eternity, and his throne was established long ago. The King is also the warrior who has "belted himself with strength" and who is acclaimed as victorious over his foes (cf. 24:8). The language suggests a victory celebration for the Warrior-King, who has conquered the forces which threaten the earth and now sits in power on his throne on high. For the "belted with strength," cf. Ps 18:40 = 2 Sam 22:40; also Ps 65:7; Isa 8:9; 45:5; Job 38:3; 40:7. Yahweh declares that he has "belted/girded" Cyrus in Isa 55:5, but the worshipers who acclaim the kingship of Yahweh in Ps 93 declare that "he has belted himself" (note the reflexive form of the verb). Yahweh's victory, of course, is the stable establishment of the earth (1c)—the divine Champion has made the earth as secure as his throne (for the idea of the exalted throne of Yahweh, see 9:5–8; 11:4; 45:7; 47:9; 97:2; 103:19.

Yahweh's cosmogonic victory (93:3–4). The awful roaring of the chaotic floods— the "mighty waters" and "breakers of the sea" (4b)—is recalled in these verses. The expressions used were doubtless conventional in Israelite worship and perhaps should be treated as personifications of the primeval forces which threaten creation: thus, Floods (or Rivers), Many Waters, Mighty Waters, "Breakers of the Sea" (or "Yamm's Waves"; Howard, *Structure*, 45). For the significance of the floods/ sea in divine kingship, see *Comment* on Ps 74:12–17. Also, see *Comment* for Pss 29 (also *Form/Structure/Setting*); 68:23; 89:10–15; 104:1–9; also Job 9:5–14; 26:5–14; 38:8–11. The imagery was doubtless used in hymns for festivals in Israel, especially the autumn festival with its new year characteristics.

If the "floods" are translated into historical reference, they could refer to the "roaring" of hostile nations against Yahweh and Israel (see Isa 17:12; 51:9–15; Jer 6:23; 50:52; cf. Ps 2): "The sea with its mighty breakers thundering against the shore as though it would engulf the solid land is an emblem of the heathen world menacing the kingdom of God" (Kirkpatrick, 565). The "floods" may have a double meaning, with reference to foes, foreign and domestic, as well as to cosmic forces which threaten the order and stability of creation (A. A. Anderson, II, 668). However, the historicizing of such passages as this should not be pursued to the extent of stripping them of their mystic reality and power. They seek to express dimensions of reality which transcend ordinary historical events, though these events embody that reality. The roaring, pounding turbulence of the seas represents a cosmogonic challenge to God and the world regardless of its implementation.

The appearance of an imperfect form of the verb נשׂא in its third usage in v 3 (see note 3.d.) is a matter of controversy in interpretation. The case for the continuation of the past tense in such verb sequences seems to be well established for both Ugaritic and Hebrew poetry and has been adopted in the translation of v 3. This is consistent with Yahweh's sovereignty as "having been established from ages past" and the affirmation that the rebellious waters are no longer a threat. "YHWH's established throne prevents them from any longer lifting up their voices in opposition to him" (Howard, *Structure*, 44). The past tense in v 3c also agrees with the literary description of the throne and presence of Yahweh: the throne was established "long ago (from of old)" and Yahweh is "from eternity." In a literary sense, vv 3–4 recall the victory over the surging floods which was followed by the establishment of Yahweh's throne on high.

Nevertheless, the cosmogonic victory of Yahweh should not be treated as a purely past event. The context of acclamation indicates a continuing threat: Why the acclamation of Yahweh as the Victor King if the "floods" have long ceased to be a problem? The pounding, surging, and roaring of the "floods" are never far away. The seas of chaos are tamed, but their mighty roar hangs in the air like an echo, which is suggested by the use of the vocative ("O Yahweh") in vv 3 and 4. Such images are never "cut flowers" in a vase (P. Ricoeur, *The Symbolism of Evil*, tr. E. Buchanan [Boston: Beacon Press, 1967] 203). Ricoeur argues that in the case of the biblical images of creation there is "fundamentally . . . no longer a drama of creation . . . the images of the old system no longer survive except as cut flowers"; the images continue to be used but their "significations" have changed. For a critique of Ricoeur, see J. Levenson, *Creation and the Persistence of Evil*, 50 and passim. The "significations" do change, but *not fundamentally*. The drama is still real and it is actualized every time Yahweh is acclaimed King and the stories of his victories are told. In a sense the "floods" belong to the distant past, but their primordial roaring is also contemporary.

The trustworthy testimonies of Yahweh (93:5). The juxtaposition of this verse with vv 1–4 implies that Yahweh's guidance for human conduct has proved true and reliable—as stable as the throne of God and the earth. The juxtaposition is similar to that in Ps 19 (vv 8–12), though 19:2–7 is quite different from 93:1–4. The meaning of v 5b is rather elusive (and may indicate that it is not properly understood; see notes 4.c. and 5.d.). The primary idea is probably that of the holy presence of Yahweh which fills the temple (possibly land, if "house" is extended in meaning). The temple is holy because Yahweh, or some form of his presence, makes it his abode (Pss 11:4; 15:1–5; 24:3–5; 47:9; also 2:6; 5:8; 11:4; 79:1; 138:2; Isa 6:3). The "holiness" makes the house/temple a source of blessing for the people (cf. 36:9; 65:5; S. Mowinckel, *PIW*, I, 164). The holiness of the people who worship at the temple would follow as a corollary.

Through strong moral compliance with the Lord's will, Israel adorns the house of the Lord with holiness. The way by which the Lord lives effectively in the daily lives of his people determines the holiness of liturgy and temple (C. Stuhlmueller, II, 80).

The relation of the "for endless days" in 5c to the first two parts of the verse is ambiguous: Is it the sure testimonies is 5a? Or the befitting holiness of 5c? Perhaps we should understand the verse as follows:

> Your testimonies are sure indeed;
> the holiness (which) befits your house,
> O Yahweh, (let) it be for endless days.

Explanation

The psalm is a song which praises Yahweh's kingship and his mighty deeds of (1) giving stability to the world (v 1) and of (2) giving sureness to those who depend upon his "testimonies" (v 5). The psalm is brief but powerful; it "rushes along like the roaring water of which it speaks" (Weiser, 618). It expresses the fervent emotion of festival celebrations of Yahweh's power and enthronement as the mighty king, who reigns from his throne on high. His is a kingship established in the remote past, as was the world, but which continues to be actualized in the acclamations of the present. Yahweh comes from eternity, not the present. The worship reality presupposed by the psalm (and by others of its type) has been gathered up in some sentences by Weiser (618):

> He is the God who was, who is and who is to come, and before whose reality the barriers of time disappear so that what happened long ago and what will come to pass in the future both simultaneously call for a decision at the present moment. The eye of faith, focused on the reality of God, is opened to a living under-standing of reality by means of which pre-history and the end of time, creation and eschatology, acquire an actuality that is charged with energy and is concentrated on the present by the very fact that God shows himself at work in it.

The psalm is designed to energize those who recite it, and is charged with the majestic beauty and holiness of the sovereignty of Yahweh.

> Hallelujah!
> For the Lord our God the Almighty reigns. (Rev 19:6, RSV)

The Creator-King has fixed the earth so that it will not be moved (v 1)—his work of creation will not fail. In like manner his commandments have proven to be sure and trustworthy. Mankind can live with assurance in both realms. The holy presence and power of God overcome the threat of the surging floods, both in the physical world and in the world of human society.

Christian readers will think immediately of the disciples with Jesus during the storm on the sea and of his words, "Peace, be still!"—more properly, "Be silent"; "be muzzled!" (Mark 4:39; cf. the use of the verb "muzzle" in Mark 1:26; Luke 4:35 of the demons). The "testimonies" of God are sure indeed; their power is greater than that of any roaring flood of calamity.

Reassurance for the Righteous   *(94:1–23)*

Bibliography

Auffret, P. "Essai sur la structure littéraire du Psaume 94." *BN* 24 (1984) 44–72. **Howard, D. M., Jr.** *The Structure of Psalms 93–100,* 58–73.

Translation

1[a]	O God of Vindication,[b] O Yahweh; O God of Vindication, shine forth![c]	(3+3)
2	Rise up, O Judge of the Earth, turn back[a] on the proud what they deserve![b]	(3+3)
3	How long will the wicked, O Yahweh, how long will the wicked celebrate—	(3+3)
4	spewing out[a] arrogance when they speak, (and) all the evildoers[b] vaunting themselves.	(3+3)
5	They crush your people, O Yahweh, and oppress your heritage.[a]	(3+2)
6	They kill widows and resident aliens, and murder orphans.[a]	(3+2)
7	And they say, "Yah[a] will not see! Jacob's god won't understand."	(3+3)
8	Understand (this)—you dunderheads[a] among the people! You fools, when will you get smart?[b]	(3+3)
9	Does the one who shapes the ear not hear? Or the one who forms the eye, does he not see?	(4+4)
10	Does the one who disciplines nations[a] not rebuke? The one who teaches humankind knowledge?[b]	(4+3)
11	Yahweh knows human intentions[a]— that they amount to nothing![b]	(4+2)
12	How blest is[a] the person whom[b] you discipline, O Yah, and whom you teach from your law,	(1+3+1+2)
13	giving[a] them assurance[b] because of evil days,[c] until a pit is dug for the wicked.	(4+4)
14	For Yahweh will not desert his people, and his heritage he will not forsake.	(4+3)
15	Justice will turn back on the righteous,[a] and likewise[b] to all the upright.	(3+3)
16	Who will rise up for me against wrongdoers? Who will take a stand for me against evildoers?	(3+3)
17	Unless Yahweh had been a help for me, I would soon have dwelt in the silence (of death).[a]	(4+4)

18	*Though I said, "My foot is slipping!"*	(3+3)
	Your loyal-love, O Yahweh, sustained me.	
19	*When my cares* ᵃ *were great within me,*	(3+3)
	your comforts brought joy to my soul.	
20	*Can a seat of destruction* ᵃ *be allied* ᵇ *with you?*	(3+3)
	—one who forms misery by decree? ᶜ	
21	*They band together* ᵃ *against the life of the righteous*	(3+3)
	and condemn innocent blood. ᵇ	
22	*But Yahweh has become* ᵃ *a fortress for me,*	(3+3)
	and my God is my rock of refuge.	
23	*He will turn back on them* ᵃ *their iniquity,*	(3+2+3)
	through their evil he will destroy them;	
	Yahweh our God will destroy them!	

Notes

1.a. LXX has a title: Ψαλμὸς τῷ Δαυιδ, τετράδι σαββάτων, "A psalm for David for the fourth day of the week."

1.b. "Vindication," "justice," "retribution," or "avenging" are better than "vengeance" for the fem. pl. נקמות (נקמה). For the word נקם, see n. 58:11.a.

1.c. Reading as הופיעה hiphil impv., which has good versional support (see *BHS*), though LXX indicates 3rd per. perf., which the MT has with הופיע (from, יפע, "shine out/beam"). The perfect occurs in Deut 33:2, but the imperative הופיעה in Ps 80:2 forms the best parallel to 94:1. The defective spelling in MT may be due to haplography, involving the ה of the first word in v 2 (cf. GKC 53m; 69v). The translation of the verb as a perfect would be as follows: "The God of vindication has shone forth" (cf. Dahood, II, 346, who retains the perfect in the same manner as in Ps 50:2, seeking an inclusion with vv 22–23).

2.a. Often translated as "render/give," but the force of the expression seems to express the principle of retribution. "Pay back" (NIV) or "put back on" seem better.

2.b. The word גמול means "dealing/recompense/benefit" (so BDB, 168a); that which is merited by behavior.

4.a. Reading as a circumstantial clause; see GKC 120g; Exod 15:9; Job 29:8.

4.b. For פעלי און see excursus: "The Nature of Enemies in the Psalms."

5.a. The word נחלה refers to the family property, land, and possession. It is translated in varied ways, usually by "inheritance." "Patrimony" is another possibility. Note the occurrence of the word, also with reference to Yahweh, in v 14.

6.a. Some Greek texts follow the order of "widow-orphan-alien," which is more nearly the pattern in the OT. But MT should not be changed (Kraus, II, 820–21).

7.a. A short form of "Yahweh."

8.a. Or, "brutish among the people" (KJV) or, "dullest . . ." (RSV). Dahood has "dolts," and JB has "you most stupid of men, you fools." "Dullards" is another good option. A. A. Anderson (II, 672) suggests the paraphrase: "You have behaved like animals among your own people." In 96:7, the בער-person is one who "does not know," a fool who does not understand (see Ps 73:22; Prov 12:1; 30:2). The "brutish" person is one characterized by animal instincts which lead to a stubborn and insensitive will.

8.b. The verb שכל, in hiphil, means "To act prudently" or "successfully," with understanding and due consideration of circumstances. The colloquial translation above seeks to get the force of the expression in the context.

10.a. KJV and RSV follow the versions and read הַיֹסֵר, "he who chastens" for MT's הֲיֹסֵר, "is he not the one who chastens," which is considered to be defective (the same is true for הֲנֹטַע, "is he not the one who plants/forms" in v 9a). LXX has ὁ παιδεύων, "The one who educates/trains/disciplines/punishes" (the same range of ideas as in the Heb. יסר). MT is probably defective. The meaning of יסר in 10a is not clear. Tentatively, I have chosen "discipline" rather than "instruct," despite the parallel "Teach" in vv 10b and 12b. The idea of "disciplining nations" is not common in the Old Testament, but see Ps 2:10; cf. Ps 59:6, of Israel; Hos 7:12, 15, of Jerusalem; Jer 6:8; Zeph 3:7; cf. further Isa 26:9, 10; Judg 8:16.

10.b. Frequently modified to אָדָם מִדַּעַת and read as "is the one who teaches mankind without knowledge?" E.g., see *BHS*, also Duhm, Gunkel, and Kraus (Dahood [II, 81, 348] argues for this reading on the basis that the final *mem* on אדם is a single writing of a consonant where morphology and syntax require two). Another option is to assume הלֹא ידע for דעת, "he that teacheth men, should he not have knowledge?" (Oesterley). The changes are acceptable but probably unnecessary. The rhetorical question in 10a carries over into 10b, and the הלֹא יוכיח is understood after the colon in 10b: "The one who teaches humankind—does he not rebuke?" This is probably an example where voice inflection indicated the meaning.

11.a. Or, "Thoughts/schemes/designs." Perhaps it would be better to translate: "Yahweh knows human designs."

11.b. The word הבל is well known from its usage in Eccl (see Eccl 1:2, 14; 2:1, 11, 15, 17, 19, 21, 23, 26, etc.; see also, Pss 39:6, 7, 12; 62:10; Jer 10:3; etc.). It connotes a vapor or a breath and conveys the nuances of temporal ephemerality, existential futility, and absurdity (see J. L. Crenshaw, *Ecclesiastes: A Commentary* [Philadelphia: Westminster Press, 1987] 57–58).

12.a. The word אשרי, "blest," or "how blest!" is a masc. pl. construct form used as an interjection. The noun from which it is derived is uncertain (see H. Cazelles, *TDOT*, I, 445). See further in *Comment.*

12.b. *BHS* refers to two mss which delete the relative pronoun אשר. It is not really needed because the relative clause does not require it. Howard (63–64) defends its retention, noting that it is included in the text of this verse in 4QPs^b, observing, however, that this is the only occurrence of the relative pronoun in the psalm and that its presence makes v 12a the psalm's longest colon. He defends the retention of אשר on the basis of its usage with אשרי ("blest/happy") at the beginning of the colon. In 23 of the 26 occurrences of אשרי in the Psalter, it is followed by a relative pronoun or by a participle. The phrase אשרי הגבר, "how blest is the man," in v 12 is found also in Pss 40:5 and 127:5, and the structure (but not the wording) is the same in Pss 1:1 and 33:2. Exceptions are found in 34:9; 65:5; 84:6, and Howard notes that "the pattern is not inviolable." He says, correctly, that the deletion of the אשר does not remove the "heaviness" in v 12a.

I have retained the relative pronoun, though it probably is a scribal addition which could be deleted (possibly added because of its presence in Ps 40:5 and perhaps 127:5). I have read the אשרי outside the following bicolon as anacrusis. There are other examples of overloaded colons with אשרי, and in some of them it should probably be read outside the colons; e.g., see Pss 1:1; 32:1, 2; 33:12; 65:5; 127:5; 137:9; 144:15b; 146:5; Job 5:17; Isa 32:20. In 144:15, both occurrences of אשרי are probably outside the colons:

> Blest are
> the people for whom this is so;
> blest are
> the people whose God is Yahweh.

In the translation above, I have agreed with Dahood that the Yah (יה) belongs between the colons in 94:12. The relative pronoun does double duty in 12a and 12b, which makes unnecessary the argument of Dahood (II, 348) that the conjunction of the first word of 12b serves as a relative pronoun; however, if the אשר is deleted, Dahood is probably correct. For discussion of pivot patterns, see W. G. E. Watson, "The Pivot Pattern in Hebrew, Ugaritic, and Akkadian Poetry," *ZAW* 88 (1976) 239–53.

13.a. Translating the infinitive as circumstantial, with Dahood (II, 348) and NEB (see Ps 63:3b).

13.b. The hiphil form of the verb שקט suggests "calmness/quiet confidence/inward quietness in the face of troubles" (see Isa 7:4; 30:15; 32:17).

13.c. Dahood (II, 348) translates "after the evil days," taking the preposition in the sense of Hos 6:2; Isa 24:22 (Dahood cites Ps 30:4 also), but the meaning of מן as "after" in this verse is doubtful as is interpreting it in the sense of "eternal repose after death." This does not fit well with 13b (Dahood rather lamely explains the "pit" in this colon as "a special pit . . . in the underworld for the oppressors of Israel") and the general, descriptive nature of the expression (Howard, 64). I have read the מן as causal; as, e.g., in Nah 1:5–6; Exod 2:23; Deut 7:7. It can, however, be temporal: "during evil days."

15.a. Reading צדיק with some mss and versional support (see *BHS*). However, the abstract noun צדק, "righteousness," in MT can be read with the same understanding by metonymy (Howard, 65). The more common reading is "for justice will return to righteousness," assuming some meaning such as "judgment shall again accord with justice" (NJV) or "judgment will again be founded on righteousness" (NIV); similarly NAB. JB has "for verdict will return to righteousness again," which hardly makes sense unless the meaning is that "verdict [vindication?] will return to the righteous (singular read as collective)"; see Maillot and Lelievre, II, 264. Another alternative is to understand the meaning as "judgment turns into righteousness (i.e., salvation)"; see Weiser, 622, n. 4; Barnes, II, 455.

15.b. Some commentators (e.g., Gunkel, Kissane, Kraus) read ואחריו, "and after him/it," as ואחרית לכל־, "and a reward shall come to all the upright of heart"—i.e., "a (good) final lot (or end)." Oesterley prefers to emend to ואחריתו כישרי־לב, "and his latter end (be) like the upright in heart." The translation above follows Dahood (I, 275, 302, II, 195) in reading אחריו as "with him," or "after him (in turn, or in like manner)."

17.a. See Ps 115:17, where דומה, "silence," is clearly the realm of the dead—"another name for Sheol" (Gunkel, 416).

19.a. שרעפי, "my cares/doubts/worries," is also in Ps 139:23 (cf. שעפים in Job 4:13 and שעפי in Job 20:2), where it is often translated as "Thoughts"; i.e., dividing and distracting thoughts and concerns. I have used "cares," but that may be too bland. Perhaps, "Troubled thoughts."

20.a. As Dahood (II, 350) remarks, this "phrase is metonymic for iniquitous rulers." Also, Kraus, II, 826. Cf. Ps 122:5; see L. C. Allen, 156; BDB, 442b. See *Comment.*

20.b. For the anomalous form of the verb see GKC 60b; 63m; BDB, 288a; KB, 273a.

20.c. This seems to be a more likely translation than "Can a seat of destruction form mischief against (your) statute?" as Syr indicates (see Anderson, II, 675; Oesterley, Kraus).

21.a. The imperfect is taken as persistent or durative in the present tense; the action is a continuing one. This is a debatable conclusion, of course. The verbs may be read as expressing past tense, and past tense may be held throughout vv 21–23 (as in Dahood, II, 346; D. Michel, *Tempora und Satzstellung in den Psalmen.* [Bonn: Bouvier, 1960] 28, 138). The *waw*-consecutive forms in vv 22 and 23 can be used to support this reading since in most cases such verb forms indicate past tense. However, v 20 seems to set the tense context into present time (note the participle in 20b), differentiating the temporal frame from that in vv 17–19 and going back to the tense of v 16. Vv 16 and 20 frame vv 17–19, which recall past experience, and take the action back to the same time as that in vv 1–7. The conditions described in vv 20–21 correspond to those in vv 1–7.

The "banded together" is read as from גדד, "gather together against" (BDB, 151; KB, 169a). Since the simple form of this verb does not appear elsewhere, some commentators (e.g., Gunkel, 416) prefer to read יגורו, from גור (II), "stir up strife/assail," as in Pss 56:7; 59:4 (cf. BDB, 158b). NEB reads as ינידו, hiphil impf. from נגד, "to make known/put before someone," and translates: "for they put the (righteous) on trial for his life" (REB, however, reverts to either גדד or גור: "they conspire to take the life of the righteous").

21.b. Gunkel proposes אדם ("man") for ודם ("and blood") = "and an innocent man." So, also Oesterley. The "blood" may be retained, however, as metonymy or synecdoche.

22.a. The *wayyqtl* form (ויהי) in v 22 represents a sequential explanation of a situation in the same time frame as that of the persistent imperfects in v 21 (so B. K. Waltke and M. O'Connor, *An Introduction to Biblical Hebrew Syntax* [Winona Lake: 1990], 33.3.3c, who translate: "so YHWH has become my fortress"). In poetry it seems probable that the use of *wayyqtl* forms indicates an emphatic construction: "Indeed/surely YHWH has become/is a fortress for me." I have not, however, treated it as emphatic in the translation. Cf. Ps 64:8–10.

23.a. The *wayyqtl* form וישב could continue the action in this verse in the same present tense frame as that in v 22, and this may be the case, at least in a strict sense: "and so he repeatedly turns back on them their iniquity." However, the sequence of thought is much easier with future tense: "Yahweh has become a fortress for me and he will turn back on them their iniquity"—probably with the sense: "He will certainly turn back on them." The use of *waw*-consecutive forms (*wayyqtl* forms) for future tense is sometimes disputed, but it seems clear in a number of cases. See L. McFall, *The Enigma of the Hebrew Verbal System* (Sheffield: Almond Press, 1982) 18; Waltke and O'Connor, 33.1.2d; 31:1.1e(3); 33.3.3c. For examples, see Isa. 9:5[6]; 51:3; Pss 16:9; 22:30; 41:13; 55:18; 64:8–10; 109:28; Mic 2:13; Job 14:17. Emendations are sometimes suggested because of the failure to recognize the future tense of *wayyqtl* forms in some constructions. For the על־הם, "on them," cf. Ps 79:12; for שוב in *qal* in relation to the "turning back onto" of the consequences of actions, see Pss 7:17; 54:7.

Form/Structure/Setting

H. Gunkel classifies Ps 94 as a poem of mixed styles: a communal lament in vv 1–7; a sermonic section directed toward those who despise God in vv 8–11; a speech of blessing and encouragement in vv 12–15 (contrasting sharply with the previous verses); and an individual lament in vv 16–23. The diversity of sections in the psalm raises the question of unity and led H. Schmidt (175) to postulate Ps 94a in vv 1–11 and Ps 94b in vv 12–23 (Schmidt is followed by E. Leslie, 253–55; 330–40, who divides the psalm, however, into vv 1–15 and 16–23).

The unity of the psalm is defended or assumed, however, by most commentators. For example, Kraus (II, 822) argues for a coherence of meaning in the context of the psalm and says that H. Schmidt should not have overlooked the relationship between vv 5 and 14 (v 14 responds with a promise of protection of "his heritage," נחלתו, to the threat against "your people," עמך, and "your heritage," נחלתך in v 5). Also, the verb יסר ("discipline/instruct") and the piel of למד ("Teach") link vv 10 and 12, joining the sections composed by vv 8–11 and vv 12–15. The verb שׁוב, "Turn/turn back," is found in vv 2, 15, and 23 and ties the psalm together with the act-consequence idea of retribution. The "righteous" form a common subject for vv 12–15 and 16–23 (see vv 15 and 21). The verb בין, "understand/comprehend" occurs in vv 7 and 8 and binds vv 3–7 and 8–11. The "evildoers" (פעלי־און) and the "wrongdoers" (מרעים) in v 16 link back to the "evildoers" (פעלי־און) in v 4 and the "wicked" (רשׁעים) in v 3.

The juxtaposition of disparate elements is a common feature of poetry from the ancient Near East, including the OT. For Ps 94, C. Stuhlmueller (*Psalm 2*, 81–82) follows E. Beauchamp (*Le Psautier*) and proposes a chiastic structure for the psalm:

Introduction vv 1–2

A vv 3–7		A' vv 20–23
B vv 8–11		B' vv 16–19
	C vv 12–15	

This is not entirely convincing, but it stresses the central role of vv 12–15 and suggests a structural unity for Ps 94. Howard (*Structure*, 71–73) argues that Ps 94 is a "non-alphabetic acrostic," contending that while the verses in the psalm do not follow an alphabetic pattern for the most part, v 1 begins both colons with *aleph;* v 12, which marks the beginning of the central section composed of vv 12–15, begins with the same letter (used twice); and v 13 begins with *lamed*, the middle letter of the alphabet. The acrostic is a typical wisdom feature and if the semi-acrostic nature of the psalm could be sustained it would strengthen other wisdom features in the psalm. It must be admitted, however, that the case for an acrostic is not very strong (but note the ה—ה—ה in v 2 and the עד—עד in v 3, the י—י in v 4, the ר—ר in v 7, the ה—ה—ה in v 10, the כי at the beginning of 14a and the כי at the beginning of 15, etc.). Even so, the psalm should be treated as a unity.

Dahood (II, 346) rejects the conventional lament label for Ps 94 and insists that it is properly a psalm of thanksgiving, with interposed individual and group lament, which "elicited a favorable response from God, who delivered the suppliants from corrupt oppressors." Although I do not read the verbs in vv 1–2, nor in vv 21–23, as expressing past tense, I think that Dahood is moving in the right direction. The thanksgiving psalm may recall the lament and complaint of a past situation (e.g., Ps 30:3, 9–11) from which the speaker has been delivered and now praises God with thanksgiving and testimony to others about what God has done. The testimony in the thanksgiving psalms has a didactic and exhortative character; it is intended to encourage and instruct others (in addition to Ps 30, note Pss 22:23–31; 40:2–11; 66:16–20; 118:1–19; 138:1–8). These psalms assume that people are listening to a speaker recite them, and even when they are addressed directly to God they are designed for the instruction of those who hear. The use of prayer directed to God for instruction and even preaching may seem strange to us, but it seems to be a characteristic of biblical prayer. Perhaps we should remember that silent prayer, and also silent reading, was rare in the ancient world. For example, in the famous story in 1 Sam 1, Hannah attracted the suspicion and concern of the priest Eli when he watched her mouth while she prayed: "Only her lips were moving; her voice could not be heard" (1 Sam 1:13). He assumed that she must be drunk and admonished her to put aside her wine drinking! Normally people nearby heard the prayers as they were prayed.

Ps 94 is not really a thanksgiving psalm, however. It is true that the speaker draws on past experience of deliverance in vv 17–19, but in the psalm as a whole the situation is a current one; the speaker shares the present distress with the community whose petitions and lament are expressed in vv 1–7. The speaker addresses the situation in vv 1–7 (and returned to again in vv 20–21), in vv 8–19, and in vv 20–23. This includes a relatively rare direct rebuke of opponents in vv 8–11 (cf. Pss 52:3–5; 58:2–3).

The psalm's basic nature is found in vv 8–15 and 22–23. These verses have the character of communal instruction intended to strengthen the faith and resolve of a community of believers and to rebuke a group who are advocating what has been termed practical or functional atheism (v 7; cf. the discussions of Pss 14 and 53) which is that of the "dunderheads" and fools who try to live as if they have no accountability to God. The psalm has a sermonic quality, but the speaker is unlikely to be a cultic prophet. The wisdom elements in the psalm (especially in vv 12–15) point to an origin in circles concerned with such teaching. The speaker fits the mold of "a well-informed, theologically versed leader" who "presents the psalm to a listening congregation" (E. S. Gerstenberger, *Psalms*, pt. 1, FOTL 14 [Grand Rapids, MI: Eerdmans, 1988] 21, on the wisdom psalms; cf. "Didactic Poetry" in Kraus, *Psalms 1–59*, 58–60, who notes that the macarism [אשרי, "how blest/happy"] is a characteristic element introducing wisdom teaching: Pss 1:1; 32:1; 33:12; 34:8; 40:4; 41:1). In general, Ps 94 has the same genre as Pss 91 and 112. These psalms were probably developed for use as liturgical instruction in the Jewish communities of the post-exilic period; i.e., in pre-synagogal or synagogal study and worship (Gerstenberger, 21), although their use in the temple at Jerusalem should not be ruled out.

This conclusion assumes a dating for the psalm which (typical of the psalms) is impossible to fix exactly. Howard (*Structure*, 66) says it is "especially elusive," and commentators differ (e.g., Briggs, Gunkel, Kraus argue for late dates; E. J. Kissane [II, 116] says that there is "little doubt that the psalm was written during the Exile"; S. Mowinckel, "Psalm Criticism between 1900 and 1935," *VT* 5 [1955] 29–30, prefers the later period of the monarchy, though he adds: "but possibly from the time of the Persians"; Dahood contends for a pre-exilic date on the basis of the frequency of the *yytl* verb forms used to express past time in vv 5, 6, 12, 16, 18, 19, 21, and 23, according to him). Howard (67) comes to the conclusion that a pre-exilic date is plausible; however, later than Ps 93. The application of the lexical indicators for date (see *Form/Structure/Setting*, Ps 93), however, does not point to a very early date (There are several prose particles, the prefixing verb forms are ambiguous, and the divine epithet "Yah" is not decisive).

It seems to me that the psalm probably makes use of traditional language and elements which may be much older than its composition. For example, G. E. Mendenhall (*The Tenth Generation* [Baltimore: Johns Hopkins UP, 73, 85) argues that the ABC:ABD pattern in v 1 is archaic and that the early date of this verse is supported by the use of the feminine plural form נקמות ("vindication/vengeance"), found also in Judg 11:36 and Ps 18:48 (see also 2 Sam 4:8; 22:48; Ezek 25:17). The psalm itself, however, is more likely to belong to exilic or post-exilic communities. There is no title in MT (LXX has one, indicating its use on the fourth day of the week; a usage supported by Talmudic sources also), which indicates the probability of later dating. The proud evildoers in vv 3–7 could be foreigners, which would fit well with the foreign oppression of Israelites after 587 B.C.E., and this can certainly be the reference of the "seat of destruction" in v 20. On the other hand, I doubt that the evildoers in vv 3–7 are foreigners, though it is quite possible that v 20 does refer to the oppressive rule of foreign overlords (see *Comment*). If the evildoers in vv 3–7 are domestic, the OT accounts provide ample evidence for the discord and strife in the Israelite communities of the post-exilic period (e.g., Isa 58:3–12; 59:1–15; 63:16–19; 65:5, 13–16; Ezek 44:10, 12–13, 15; Mal 3:5, 13–15; Ezra 9:1–15; Neh 5:1–6:14; 13:23–31; Mic 7:1–7). Thus I assume that the provenance of Ps 94 is post-587 B.C.E.

The position of Ps 94 in Book IV of the Psalter has often been considered to be anomalous, because the psalm separates Ps 93 from Pss 95–99; psalms which overtly refer to the divine kingship of Yahweh. At first glance, the psalm seems out of place or simply given its position at random. When the larger context of Pss 90–99 is considered, however, the function of the psalm in its present placement makes sense, whether the placement is by design or merely incidental. G. H. Wilson (*The Editing of the Hebrew Psalter*, SBLDS 76 [Chico, CA: Scholars Press, 1985] 216–17) notes that Ps 94 shares a common concern with Ps 92 with reference to those who are "dull" (see 92:7 and 94:8: בער, which I have translated as "dunderhead," though "dullard" is a good option). The wicked are flourishing in both cases, and the "dull people" fail to realize that the wicked are doomed to failure and judgment. The righteous suffer now, but they will prosper in the future. Both psalms seem to deal with a current situation among the people which is keeping them from recognizing the kingship of Yahweh, set forth in Pss 93, 95–99. Ps 94 summons those with weak faith and lax commitment to a renewed perception of the work of Yahweh which would permit them to join in the acclamation of his kingship. At the same time, both psalms (92 and 94), especially 94, serve as a rebuke and warning to the wicked (as does the oracle in 95:8–11). The Great King is coming to judge on earth with equity and faithfulness (96:1, 10, 13; 98:9). He did not overlook the sinfulness of the early generations of Israel (99:8c) and he will not ignore wickedness.

D. M. Howard, Jr. has pursued further the matter of the placement of Ps 94 (in "Psalms 90–94 and the Editing of the Psalter," a paper read at the national meetings of the Evangelical Theological Society in San Diego, California, November 16, 1989), especially with reference to the relationship of Ps 94 to Ps 93.

He isolates eight lexemes which these two psalms have in common:

גאות	"proud majesty" (93:1)	גאים	"proud ones" (94:2)
דכים	"pounding" (93:3)	דכא	"crush" (95:5)
נשא	"raise" (93:3)	נשא	"raise" (94:2)
מוט	"move/stagger" (93:1)	מוט	"move/slip" (94:18)
כסא	"Throne" (93:1)	כסא	"seat/throne" (94:20)
יום	"day" (93:5)	יום	"day" (94:13)
רב	"many" (93:4)	רב	"many" (94:19)
יהוה	"Yahweh" (93:1, 3, 4, 5)	יהוה	"Yahweh" (94:1, 3, 5, 11, 14, 17, 18, 22, 23).

Most of these are probably incidental, especially since Ps 93 is so much shorter than 94. Howard (26, 28–29) thinks, however, that the two paired roots גאים—גאות and דכא—דכים may have some significance. The proud majesty of Yahweh which reigns over the rebellious waters in 93:1, 3–4 finds a strong contrast in the proud arrogant people of Ps 94:2, who seem to continually celebrate their wicked ways, which they carry out in confidence that Yahweh is indifferent and impotent. They forget, of course, that he is the mighty ruler, whose powerful throne is secure from the onslaught of the floods and the sea of chaotic powers, who is coming to judge the earth. Likewise, the "crushing" of the pounding waves in 93:3 finds its counterpart in the "crushing" oppression of the wicked in 94:5 directed against the people of Yahweh. The confidence in Yahweh affirmed in Ps 93 provides a basis for the rebuke and exhortation in 94:8–15 (Howard, 27). In addition, the play on the "lifting up" of the floods in 93:3 and the petition for Yahweh to "rise" in 94:2 (נשא in both cases) is worth attention: "the roars of the waters arise in rebellion against YHWH in Psalm 93, and YHWH is called to arise in vengeance [נקמות] against his enemies in Psalm 94" (Howard, 27). Also, מוט in 93:1 in a negative construction refers to the stability of the world established by Yahweh, whereas in 94:18 it refers to the slippery, unstable condition of the footing of the speaker. Also the secure throne (כסא) of Yahweh in 93:2 contrasts with the "throne of destruction" in 94:20, which is destroyed by Yahweh.

Thus there is an editorial cohesiveness, at least, between Ps 94 and its context in Book IV (Howard, 32). Since I have proposed that there is a close relatedness between Pss 92 and 93 (see *Form/Structure/Setting* of Ps 93), it is at least arguable that Pss 92–94 form an editorial unit. Indeed, it is probable that Pss 90–94 form a five-psalm unit with some coherence of meaning and function (with Howard, 34). This unit is gathered around the significance of the sabbath (see Ps 92) and was designed to revive the languishing faith of troubled communities in the post-exilic era.

The meaningful function of Ps 94 in its context is strengthened further by the recognition that the opening petitions in vv 1–2 address Yahweh in language that denotes kingship and finds parallel language in Pss 96–99. The function of נקמות ("vindication/vengeance") is a royal one, a function of a king or king-like person, who "rises" to judge and to mete out the proper recompense for the proud ones of the earth (v 2). Mendenhall (*The Tenth Generation,* 76–77) summarizes the evidence for the usage of the root נקם and finds that it refers to executive rather than to judicial action; the exercise of an imperium, not the exercise of private self-help, though it transcends normal legal procedures.

Yahweh exercises the divine imperium of the heavenly King and Judge of the Earth (v 2). The concepts here comport well with the judging function of Yahweh in Pss 96–99, who will put things in right order and correct the injustice and inequity of human society.

Further, the petitions in Ps 94:1–2 are for a theophany, a "shining forth" (יפע) of the God of vindication and a "lifting up" or rising (נשׂא) of the Judge of the Earth. The "shining forth" of Yahweh appears in Deut 33:2 in connection with his coming from Sinai and "shining forth" from Mount Paran to become king in Jeshurun (v 5). God (Yahweh) also "shines forth" (יפע) from Sinai in the theophanic context of Ps 50:1–6 (the verb is in v 2). The shepherd of Israel, who is the "One Enthroned on the Cherubim" is implored to shine forth in Ps 80:2 (cf. Ps 99:1). Clearly, we are involved with the language of a theophany of the Divine Vindicator-Judge which correlates with the theophany of the Divine Warrior-Judge of Ps 97 (note the "judgment" of Yahweh in 97:8). Ps 94 is not directly a kingship-of-Yahweh psalm (it is not a hymn), but it is in good company with Pss 93, 95–99.

Comment

Address to Yahweh and Petitions (94:1–2). These verses are typical in form of the opening of laments. The meaning of נקמות has been discussed in note 1.a. and in *Form/Structure/Setting* above and need not be repeated here. The speaker wants Yahweh to act as Divine Judge and "turn back" (שׁוב) on those who vaunt themselves in arrogance and pride a recompense that their behavior deserves. The recompense (גמול) is not defined more precisely, but cf. Judg 9:16; Ps 28:4; Joel 4:4[3:4]; Lam 3:64. The speaker seeks a divine judgment which will have an appropriate correlation with the deeds of the "proud ones."

For the nature of divine judgment in the OT, see K. Koch, "Gibt es ein Vergeltung dogma im Alten Testament?" *ZTK* 52 (1955) 1–42 (EV in *Theodicy in the Old Testament,* Issues in Religion and Theology 4, ed. J. L. Crenshaw [Philadelphia: Fortress, 1983] 57–87), and P. D. Miller, Jr., *Sin and Judgment in the Prophets,* SBLMS 27 (Chico, California: Scholars Press, 1982), esp. chap. 4, 121–39. Koch's thesis is that (1) the consequences of an action have a "built-in and inherent connection" (*Theodicy,* 59) with the nature of the action itself (there is a sin-disaster connection on the one hand and a good-action-blessing connection on the other), and that (2) the correspondence between actions and consequences is the result of God's faithfulness at work in the process (73). The prayer in Ps 94:1–2 is for Yahweh to exercise his faithfulness in making the system of built-in consequences work (note the reference to Yahweh's חסד, "loyal-love," in v 18; cf. Ps 62:13). Yahweh's judgment is the completion in good order of the built-in consequence process: disaster and failure for the wicked; vindication and blessing for the righteous. The right correspondence between actions and judgment is dependent on the faithfulness of God to his purposes and commitments. Thus there is an interaction between human behavior and divine action. Miller (138) points out that the process is not trivialized by a reduction either to some sort of deistic system of automatic response or to capricious "acts of God," but that there is "a kind of synergism in which divine and human action are forged into a single whole or the divine intention is wrought out through human agency."

For Yahweh as the world judge or judge of the nations, see Pss 7:7–8; 9:8–9; 58:12; 76:9–10; 82:8; 96:10, 13; 98:9.

Lament about present distress (94:3–7). The prayer begun in vv 1–2 continues with language characteristic of laments. For the formulaic saying, "How long?" (עד־מתי), see Ps 90:13 note b. and *Comment* (cf. Pss 6:4; 80:5; 82:2). The wicked, whoever they are, celebrate the success of their crushing of the faithful people of Yahweh. They spew out insolent words and vaunt themselves as they carry out their vicious business. Their oppression is especially heavy upon the dependent classes of people, represented by widows, resident aliens, and orphans (v 6). These are groups of people who need special protection and care (cf., e.g., Exod 22:22; Deut 24:17; 26:12; 27:19; Isa 1:17; Jer 7:6; 22:3; Zech 7:10; Mal 3:5). Such groups are of special concern to Yahweh, and he is not supposed to deal lightly with those who mistreat them (cf. Pss 68:6; 82:3–4; 146:9; Mal 3:5).

The "killing" and "murdering" in v 6 is not described further. The meaning probably includes a range of results from oppression, all the way from the deprivation of things necessary for life to legalized murder (cf. A. A. Anderson, II, 672). Kraus (*Psalms 60–150*, 240) suggests venal judges (cf. v 20) who fail to protect the wards of Yahweh (and of the community) and allow them to suffer violent treatment, even death in some cases.

The question arises as to the identity of the proud evildoers referred to in vv 3–7. Since they are addressed directly by the speaker in vv 8–11 (at least that is the most natural conclusion regarding the "dunderheads" and "fools" in v 8), it follows that they are probably domestic foes, internal to the life of the community, rather than foreigners. The language in vv 5–6 is not inappropriate, however, for foreign oppressors, and it is possible that we should understand a strong indictment of the leaders of the community who act in the manner of foreign rulers. In any case, the ruthless evildoers act with disdain for Yahweh's willingness to intervene or even of his ability to do so (v 7). The implication is that Yahweh lacks the sense even to understand the situation, let alone do anything about it! Perhaps these are the insolent words which the evildoers spew out of their mouths as they vaunt themselves (v 4).

V 20 may also refer to the evildoers in vv 3–7 (so, e.g., Kraus, 242, who argues that the כסא הוות is the "judge's bench," citing Ps 122:5 for support). Some occupant of the "seat of destruction" forms, or shapes (יצר) "misery" or "misfortune" by decrees which do not uphold an order of justice and equity but lend support to those who band together to attack the righteous (v 21). To the righteous person who is speaking, of course, this is an intolerable situation which is not compatible with partnership with Yahweh. How can Yahweh tolerate such a thing?

The "seat of destruction" (כסא הוות) is probably a parody of the "seat of judgment" (cf. the כסאות למשפט, "seat/throne for judgment," in Ps 122:5). The tribunal intended for the establishment of justice has been perverted into a tribunal of destruction. The judge who sits there now makes decrees of misery and oppression. The term חק is used of ordinary enactments and decrees (such as the legal conditions of a deed of purchase in Jer 32:11), and the same is true of the closely related חקה. S. Mowinckel, however, has noted that in a number of cases חק and חקה are used about the laws of nature and the world order (e.g., seasons of the year, Jer 5:24; celestial bodies, Ps 148:6; the limits of the ocean, Jer 31:35–36 and Job 28:26; the laws of the heavens and constellations, Job 38:33; see also

Sir 43:7, 10; cf. 16:26. Job 38:33a refers to the "laws [נחקות] of the heavens" [cf. Job 38:10], which have a corresponding "order," משטר, on earth in Job 38:33b). Mowinckel argues that חק in Ps 94:20 refers to "established law" or "cosmic order" ("The Hebrew Equivalent of Taxo in Ass. Mos. ix," *Supplements to Vetus Testamentum,* I, ed. G. W. Anderson et al. [Leiden: Brill, 1953] 90–91; idem, "Psalm Criticism between 1900 and 1935," *VT* 5 [1955] 30; also see H. Ringgren, *TDOT,* V, 141–47). The laws and decrees which function in human society derive their authority from their correlation with the laws and decrees of the divinely created world order. Thus the situation in Ps 94:20 contradicts the fundamental nature of things. The tribunal which should produce judgment and justice, as from the ministers of God" (Rom 13:6), in harmony with the cosmic order is instead a "seat of destruction" which produces a counterorder of misery and oppression.

The occupant of the "seat of destruction" may be one of the proud evildoers of vv 3–7 (a venal Israelite judge or ruler). However, another scenario is possible. V 20 may refer to a foreign governor or ruler who now occupies the position represented by the "seat of judgment" and encourages, by actual decree and/or default, the oppression of the evildoers described in vv 3–7 and vv 21–23. Thus, Mowinckel ("Psalm Criticism," 30) thinks in terms of a foreign potentate and his "co-operators among the Israelites." He also notes that the oppression seems to be permanent (the product of "decree," חק) rather than the result of an acute attack. The "thrones (or seats) of judgment" in Ps 122:5a are defined in 122:5b as belonging to the Davidic dynasty (cf. "the throne of kingdoms" in Hag 2:22). The reference is to the judging function of the king (cf. 1 Kgs 7:7; 2 Sam 15:2, 6; 1 Kgs 3:28; Isa 11:3; 16:5; Jer 21:12; see Kraus, *Psalms 60–150,* 433–35). If we think of Ps 94 as reflecting the post-exilic period, the Davidic "seat of judgment" belonged to the past and it was now a "seat of destruction" occupied by a foreign governor allied with Israelite evildoers.

The verb חבר in v 20a ("allied with") may mean nothing more than "joined with" or "united with," but the use of the word with reference to Jerusalem in Ps 122:3, of Israel "allied" with Judah in Ezek 37:16–19, and of political alliances in Gen 14:3; Judg 20:11; 2 Chr 20:35, 37; Dan 11:6, may be a clue that the occupant of the "seat of judgment (destruction)" is a foreign official whose alliances with Yahweh would be as anomalous as Ephraim being "joined" or "allied" with idols in Hos 4:17. At least the terminology is not out of harmony with such an interpretation of the rhetorical question in v 20 (which demands the answer "No," of course). However, this is speculative, and it is our good fortune that the fundamental message of the psalm does not depend on the exact definition of such matters.

Rebuke of the fools (94:8–11). I assume that the "dunderheads" and "fools" addressed in the disputation speech of vv 8–11 are the proud evildoers of vv 2–7. It is possible, however, that we should think of members of the speaker's community who have failed to perceive the true nature of the evildoers' actions, perhaps because of envy of their short-term success or because of intimidation and the violent oppression of the people by the evildoers. Because of the strong language used ("dunderheads"—or "brutes"—and "fools") the first option seems more probable.

With the courage of a prophet, the speaker confronts the evildoers as a teacher and disputes their basic thesis expressed in the quotation from them in v 7. This "obdurate lot" (Kraus) is called to return to sense and sanity. The rhetorical questions put to the "fools" in vv 9–10 confront them with the reality of the God they have so arrogantly dismissed. In case the questions fail to make the point, the speaker affirms the ability of Yahweh to know in no uncertain terms in v 11. Yahweh knows the ways of human beings; even their intentions— and they amount to nothing unless they are in harmony with his ways. Kraus (*Psalms 60–150*, 241) thinks that a notion of the effect of preexistent wisdom, as in Prov 8, may be reflected in v 10, with reference to "the one who teaches mankind knowledge." In Prov 8, Woman Wisdom claims that she is a source of "knowledge" (דעת) and "instruction" (מוסר, from the verb יסר, "instruct/discipline" as in 94:10a), as well as one who gives "counsel," "truth," "good sense" (or, "prudence," ערמה), "wisdom," etc. "By me kings reign," she declares (v 15), "and princes decree [יחוקקו, from חקק, cf. חק, "decree," in 20b] righteousness." Only fools would assume that the great teacher and disciplinarian of humankind and nations would be deterred from knowledge of those who crush his people.

Reassurance for the righteous (94:12–15). These verses are intended as encouragement for those who are trying to be faithful to Yahweh. Vv 12–13 are addressed to Yahweh as a prayer in the form of thanksgiving-praise. Gunkel (414) refers to it as a speech of blessing, commonly found in the wisdom literature; e.g., Pss 1:1–3; 32:1–2; 34:9b; 112:1–10; 119:1–2; 127:5; 128:1, 2; cf. Prov 3:13–17; 8:32–36; 14:21–22; 16:20; 28:14; 29:18; Job 5:17; Isa 3:10; Jer 17:7–8. These speeches are marked by the use of אשרי ("blest/happy/fortunate") and sometimes ברוך ("blessed") or טוב ("good," as in Isa 3:10). The אשרי-person is one who enjoys good fortune, or even has an enviable status (W. Janzen, "'Ashrê in the Old Testament," *HTR* 58 [1965], 215). H. Cazelles (*TDOT*, I, 446) defines אשרי as "a liturgical cry [which] points to an act in which believers seek happiness." (Perhaps it is better to say "in which believers receive happiness.") Cazelles thinks that it was probably a foreign expression taken into the language of the OT during a late period (447). He finds no satisfactory parallels in cuneiform literature, though the Akkadian *ašru* from the Neo-Babylonian period extols humility and trust (*CAD*, I, 455; *ašru* B, *CAD*, I, 456, is used as an adjective in personal names in the sense of "taken care of") and possibly has some relevance for the context in Ps. 94:12–15. The Egyptian parallels stress deeds of faithfulness and steadfastness, and may have influenced the Israelite use of אשרי (447–48). The word is never used to describe God; being applied only to the condition of human beings who meet with the favor of God. The Greek texts use μακάριος for אשרי (except in Prov 31:28), which is well known from the Latin *beatus* and the English "beatitude" in Matt 5:3–12; Luke 6:20–23). The אשרי-person is: one who comes to Zion and participates in the celebrations of festival times in the temple courts (Pss 65:5; 84:5; Isa 30:18–19); one who takes refuge under the protection of Yahweh (Pss 2:12; 34:9) and who trusts him (Ps 84:13); one who "fears" God (Pss 112:1; 128:1) and whose behavior is "blameless" (Ps 119:1–2, תמימי דרך) because he/she obeys the *torah* of Yahweh with delight and turns away from the counsel and ways of the wicked (Ps 1:1–3). The "blest-person" considers the poor (Ps 41:2) and is committed to doing justice and "righteousness" at all times (Ps 106:3). The splendid former status and behavior of Job described in Job 29:2–25 (Job is referred to as "blest," using the verb אשר, in v 11) exemplifies the full-blown ideal of the "blest-person." See also Prov 3:13; 8:33–34; 14:21; 16:20; 20:7; 28:14; 29:18; Mal 3:12; Ps 72:17; Cant 6:9.

The "blest" or "happy" state in Ps 94:12 is that which results from the discipline and instruction of God. In this respect, it is similar to Eliphaz's statement in Job 5:17 that whoever is reproved and disciplined by God is "blest" (the verbs are יכח and יסר; Eliphaz's saying is probably a deliberate revision of Prov 3:13: "Blest is the person who finds wisdom"). Prov 3:12 says that "Yahweh disciplines (יוכיח) the one whom he loves, even as a father does the son who is dear to him." (God is asked not to correct in anger in Pss 6:2 and 38:2). Deut 8:5 declares that Yahweh disciplines (יסר) Israel as a man disciplines his son (cf. Deut 4:36). Thus the אשרי-person is one who has God-given happiness; bestowed through a positive and trusting response to the discipline and instruction of God.

The "comforting instruction" (Kraus, *Psalms 60–150*, 241) in vv 12–15 is intended for righteous and upright persons (v 15) who are trying to make their way through the troubled situation indicated in vv 3–7 and 16–23. These are the people who know the *torah* of Yahweh (12b) and his ways. At the moment they are passing through "evil days" (v 13, ימי רע), but they can gain reassurance from three factors. (1) Yahweh does not desert his people (v 14), or cast off and forsake his own heritage. He is not a deity who leaves his people forever to the ravages of lawless violence and oppression. He is, after all, the judge of the Earth (v 2). (2) An appropriate result will eventually "turn back" on the proud evildoers (vv 2b and 12b). Their hegemony will last only until the pit for the wicked is dug, and the implication is clear that they are now digging their own pit and will fall into it when it is finished (see Pss 7:16; 57:7, using בוא; for שחת, as in 94:13, see 7:16 also, and Prov 26:27: "Whoever digs a pit will fall into it / whoever rolls a stone will have it turn back [שוב] on himself"). The act-consequence process, maintained and empowered by Yahweh, will work. See v 23. The "pit" also suggests the Pit which is the Netherworld of the dead—there is an ominous nuance to the expression in v 13. The judgment of death delays, but only till the digging is done! (3) Justice will "turn back" on the righteous (v 15). The "turning back" of judgment on the wicked and justice on the righteous is not based on the merit of the righteous per se, but is rooted in the faithfulness of Yahweh to his people. His consistent reliability is the "best comfort for the one who is tempted" (Kraus, 241). Yahweh is the God of vindication, who establishes and maintains right order in the world (v 1). The righteous need not fear to wait for him to shine forth from his heavenly abode and rise up as the judge of the Earth.

It is worth noting that Ps 94:12–15 is found almost at the exact center of Pss 90–99. The message of these verses is central both for Ps 94 and for the entire section of Pss 90–99. These psalms were intended for the flagging faith of Israelites who were living under long-continued "evil days," days "passed in your [God's] wrath" (90:9), when the vision of the future had grown dim and hope had waned. Some had turned to cruel and violent ways, making common cause with foreign oppressors, and disdaining the power of Yahweh. Thus these psalms are designed to revitalize faith and create a new awareness of the kingship of Yahweh.

Reassurance based on personal experience (94:16–23). In these verses the speaker identifies with the experience of the righteous in vv 2–15. Up to this point, he/she has addressed the situation in terms of traditional wisdom theology, but now teaches out of reflection on actual confrontation with the wrongdoers and the misery made by decree from the "seat of destruction" (vv 16, 20–21). The speaker recalls the question asked in a time of distress because of the violent evildoers: who would rise and take a stand to defend against them (v 16)? The question is now rhetorical and everyone knows the answer, but it recalls a situation of risk when the answer was far from clear. Yahweh has given the "help" which has saved the speaker from the silence of death (v 17). But the danger had been acute; the "slipping foot" in v 18 is metaphor for a near-disastrous fall (as in Ps 38:17). V 19 suggests that the "slipping foot" was a near collapse of faith (as in Ps 73:2): the cares ("troubled thoughts") within were great—greater than the external threats? Perhaps faith was at the brink of failure.

However, Yahweh had not failed the speaker in the time of great trouble. He was a "help" (עזרתה, see Pss 22:20; 27:9; 35:2; 38:23; 40:14, 18; 44:27; 46:2; 60:13; 70:2; 71:12; 108:13). Once again, a speaker can declare of Yahweh: "thou art my help and my deliverer" (as KJV and RSV have it in Ps 40:18). The exact nature of Yahweh's help is not stated, just as the precise nature of the troubled situation is not provided. The language is personal without being specific. In the second place, the speaker has been sustained (סעד) by Yahweh's loyal-love (חסד, see note 51:3.a.). The confidence expressed in vv 12–15 is rooted in the experience of Yahweh's loyal-love, his enduring love which has remained faithful through centuries of trouble, sin, rebellion, and more trouble. Will it fail now? Surely not.

In the third place the speaker has received divine comfort (intense comfort; note the plural "comforts" in v 19). The comfort has brought joy to his/her "soul" (the inner being, נפשׁ, "my soul"). For תנחומים ("comforts/consolations") in the face of death, see Jer 16:7 (see also Isa 66:11 for the comforting breasts of a mother; for תנחומות, see Job 15:11, "the consolations of God," also Job 21:2). The word carries the ideas of relief of emotional stress and grief as well as the satisfaction of the mind. The righteous in vv 15 and 21 can expect to have the same joyful relief. Kraus (*Psalms 60–150*, 242) observes that the speaker's "own existence is a paradigm for the fate of the צדיק, for the hope which Yahweh affords him [*sic*] in all afflictions" (see also Weiser, 624).

Vv 20–21 again describe the situation of oppression and danger. The antecedent of the "they" is apparently the evildoers in v 16 (and the same as the evildoers in v 4). They "band together" (or possibly, "stir up strife") against the righteous in ways which threaten life (v 21; נפשׁ is used for "life," as, e.g., in Ps 33:19), no doubt supported by oppressive decrees from the "seat of destruction" (v 20, see *Comment* above). The speaker has confidence, however, that the protective and comforting action of Yahweh will continue (vv 22–23). Yahweh will be a fortress of refuge and safety, and he will "turn back" the sinfulness of the evildoers onto themselves so that they will be destroyed. He will sustain the act-consequence process (see *Comment* on vv 1–2) and the evildoers will get what they deserve. The final colon in v 23 allows the speaker again to identify with the people addressed: "Yahweh *our* God will destroy them" (note the double use of the verb יצמיתם, "destroy them"). The Judge of the Earth, who dispenses discipline to nations, will not long tolerate the vaunting pride of the evildoers and their "seat of destruction." Yahweh is a "turn-backer" of judgment onto the wicked and of justice onto the righteous (v 15).

Explanation

The explanation of Ps 94 has been set forth in the sections above in a fairly full way. It need not be repeated here. V 11 of this psalm is cited in 1 Cor 3:20 (with Job 5:13) and v 14 is in mind in Rom 11:1–2 (with 1 Sam 12:22).

Meribah and Massah in the Context of Jubilant Worship   (95:1–11)

Bibliography

Auffret, P. "Essai sur la structure littéraire du Psaume 95." *BN* 22 (1983) 47–69. **Davies, G. H.** "Psalm 95." *ZAW* 85 (1973) 183–98. **Jeremias, J.** *Das Königtum Gottes in den Psalmen.* Göttingen: Vandenhoeck & Ruprecht, 1987. 104–14. ———. *Kultprophetie.* 125–33. **Johnson, A. R.** *CPIP.* 18–22. **Howard, D. M., Jr.** *The Structure of Psalms 93–100.* 74–84, 168–70. **Riding, C. B.** "Psalm 95:1–7c as a Large Chiasm." *ZAW* 88 (1976) 418.

Translation

1	*Come, let us sing out to Yahweh;*	(3+3)
	let us raise a shout to the Rock of our salvation,[a]	
2	*Let us approach his presence*[a] *with thanksgiving;*[b]	(3+3)
	let us raise a shout to him with songs of praise!	
3	*For Yahweh is the Great God,*[a]	(3+3)
	the Great King[a] *over all gods.*	
4	*The depths*[a] *of the earth are in his hand,*	(3+3)
	and the mountain peaks[b] *are his.*	
5	*The sea is his;*[a] *he made it,*[b]	(4+3)
	and his hands formed the dry land.	
6	*Enter, let us prostrate ourselves and kneel;*[a]	(3+3)
	let us kneel[b] *before Yahweh our maker.*	
7	*For he is our God,*	(3+3+2[3]+3)
	and we are the people of his pasture,[a]	
	a flock under his care.[b]	
	Oh, that today you would hear his message![c]	
8	*Do not harden your hearts as you did at Meribah,*	(3+3)
	as on that day at Massah in the wilderness,	
9	*when your fathers tested me,*	(3+3)
	when they put me to the proof,	
	though they had seen my work.	
10	*For forty years I detested*[a] *that generation,*[b]	(4+4+3)
	and I said:	
	"They are a people who have wayward hearts,	
	and they do not (want to) know my ways."	
11	*So*[a] *I swore in my anger:*	(2+3)
	"They will never come[b] *to my resting place!"*[c]	

Notes

1.a. A. R. Johnson (*CPIP*, 19) has "the Rock that is our salvation." For "Rock" as an epithet for God, see n. 78:35.a. D. M. Howard (*The Structure of Psalms 93–100*, 75) notes that the wilderness experiences of water from a rock (Exod 17:1–7; Num 20:2–13) are recalled in vv 8–11, which makes "Rock" more appropriate in the context of this psalm.

2.a. Or, "meet him." For the use of the verb (קדם), see Deut 23:5; Neh 13:2; Pss 18:6; 21:4; 59:11; 68:26; 79:8; 88:14; 89:15; Mic 6:6; Amos 9:10. The meaning "greet"—"let us greet him with thanksgiving" (NAB)—is sometimes suggested, but it seems less probable. Johnson (*CPIP*, 19) has, "let us approach His Person with . . ."

2.b. For תודה, see n. 100:1.a.

3.a. Lit., "a great god and a great king." The usage of the expression "a great king" in Pss 47:3, 7, 8; 48:2–3 indicates clearly that the expressions are definite. Yahweh is not only *a* great god and *a* great king, he is *the* great one (A. A. Anderson, II, 677). Cf. Exod 15:11; Pss 96:4; 97:9; 136:2 (see Deut 10:17); 149:2.

4.a. The מחקרי does not appear elsewhere (cf. חקר in Job 38:16) and perhaps means "places to be explored" (so BDB, 350; deriving the noun from the verb חקר, "search/explore." LXX reads πέρατα, "opposite sides/quarters," and seems to presuppose מרחקי, "the distant places of." The idea of the remote parts of the earth makes sense, but it is probable that the parallel with "peaks/summits" in 4b points to a merismus; i.e., a combination of polar terms (e.g., day and night) so that together they express a concept of totality. In this case, the power of God extends from the lowest and most inaccessible parts of the earth to the mountain peaks: "the whole world is in his hand."

4.b. The word תועפות is uncertain, appearing also in Num 23:22, 24:8, and Job 22:25. BDB (419) links the word to "horns" and thus "towering eminence," assuming a root יעף, II, "ascend." KB (1022) suggests "the best, the hair of the head," which fits well in Job 22:25 (cf. Sir 45:7; R. Gordis, *The Book of Job* [New York: Jewish Theological Seminary, 1978] 242, translates as "real treasure"; see his work, 250, and S. R. Driver and G. B. Gray, *The Book of Job* [New York: Scribner's Sons, 1921] II, 157, for discussion of the word's etymology), but not well in the other references. KJV follows the Rabbinic interpretation of "strength" in the Num references and uses "strength" in Ps 95:4. NIV goes to "peaks." (KJV has "plenty" in Job 22:25; NIV has "choicest.") NEB's "folds of the hills" is not a very good way of expressing the undulations of hill country (REB goes to "peaks of the mountains").

5.a. The relative pronoun אשר is omitted from the beginning of this verse and from the beginning of v 4 by some commentators on metrical grounds (so Kraus). If the two occurrences are retained, the force is probably causal: "in that . . ." and used like כי—Yahweh is a great king in that the depths of the earth are in his hand, etc.

5.b. Probably a circumstantial clause, which may be translated "since/because he made it" (Briggs, II, 296).

6.a. LXX adds "and weep" (κλαύσωμεν = נבכה); followed by the Vg.

6.b. A kneeling position follows the act of prostration, an act of complete homage (Kraus, II, 661) and leaves worshipers respectfully attentive for new developments in the service of worship (Durham, 365).

7.a. *BHS* suggests the reading עמו וצאן מרעיתו, "his people and the flock of his pasture"; adopted by, e.g., Gunkel and Kraus. The ידו ("his hand") is read with the next colon in this case. Gunkel appeals to Jer 23:1; Ezek 34:31; Pss 74:1; 79:13; 100:3. The change is supported by one Heb. ms, the Syr, and Tg.

7.b. Gunkel, Kraus, and *BHS* suggest the addition of the plural imperative דעו at the beginning, with the reading: "Know today (of) his rule/works / power (lit., hand)." The change is based on an appeal to haplography. NEB ("you shall know his power today") seems to reflect תידעונה, which is unlikely. Howard (Structure, 77–78) retains MT (citing Dahood, Anderson, Delitzsch, and Leslie) and notes the syntactical parallels between 79:13 and 95:7:

	(1)	(2)	(3)
79:13	and we	your people	flocks of your pasture
95:7	and we	people of his pasture	flocks of his hand.

The first element is identical in each case; the second and third each have a noun or a compound noun with a suffix referring to Yahweh.

7.c. Lit., "his voice"; "his message" results from understanding קול in the sense of "command/entreaty," as in Gen 3:17; 4:23; Exod 3:18; 4:1, 9; Deut 1:45; 21:18; etc. NJV has "heed his charge this day." The אם is to be read in the optative sense (BDB, 50, b.3).

10.a. Or, "loathed" (קוט).

10.b. Lit., "with a generation"; LXX smooths out the text with τῇ γενεᾷ ἐκείνῃ = בדור ההוא "with that generation." Also, Syr and Jerome.

11.a. A rare use of אשׁר to indicate result (like כי); cf. 2 Kgs 9:37; Gen 13:16; 1 Kgs 3:12–13; see R. J. Williams, *Hebrew Syntax*, 465.

11.b. For the construction with אם, see R. J. Williams, *Hebrew Syntax*, 456; GKC 149abc; BDB, 50.

11.c. Johnson (*CPIP*, 21) translates מנוחתי as "my home" (in *Sacral Kingship*, 60, 19, n. 1, he has "my homeland"). He argues on the basis of Ruth 1:9 and Ps 132:8 that the thought behind the word is that of "taking up one's abode, or as we should say, 'finding a home' for oneself" (21, n. 1). L. C. Allen (200, 202, n. 8.a.) translates "your home of rest" in Ps 138:8; see his note for further discussion and references to secondary literature. G. von Rad ("There Remains Still a Rest for the People of God: An Investigation of a Biblical Conception," in *The Problem of the Hexateuch and Other Essays*, tr. E. W. T. Dicken [New York: McGraw-Hill, 1958, 1966] 94–102) argues that the concept of "rest" (נוחה) has no eschatological expectation in Deuteronomy, there the promised "rest" is that of the people of Israel dwelling in the "pleasant land" with rest from enemies round about. In 1–2 Chr, however, "rest" becomes relief from enemies, granted from time to time, or given as a gift of God (1 Chr 22:9; 2 Chr 15:15; 30:30), along with the idea that God finds his rest among his people (2 Chr 6:41–42)—not that the nation finds rest, but God finds rest (as in Ps 132:8). The two ideas are combined in 1 Chr 23:25–26, and Ps 95:11 has the idea of Israel entering into God's rest (or resting place). It is this form of the idea which appears in Heb 3:7–4:11, a warning against a lack of faith like that of the wilderness generation which would cause Christians to be denied entry into God's rest. God's rest on the seventh day of creation (Gen 2:2) is also quoted, but the passage in Heb is a Christian midrash on Ps 95. A. R. Johnson (*CPIP*, 21, n. 1) contends that Deut 12:9 is a key passage for the doctrinal play on the noun and verb forms in Deut and 1–2 Chr.

Form/Structure/Setting

Like Pss 50 and 81, Ps 95 is a psalm which is usually thought to reflect a festival context, with widespread agreement among interpreters that vv 1–7c form an extended call to worship. The call to worship is combined with an oracle of prophetic-like preaching in vv 7d–11. The compositional pattern is very similar to Ps 81. Of course, it is not surprising to find a number of critical commentators who regard the psalm as made up of two originally independent poems (e.g., Briggs), but the majority in this century have treated the psalm as one literary unit. The unity between the two major parts is frequently explained on a liturgical basis; the psalm is often described as a liturgy (e.g., Gunkel [a "prophetic liturgy"], Schmidt, Buttenwieser, Kraus). The liturgical explanation for the literary shape of the psalm makes sense, though the actual "cult functional" nature of it is more problematic ("cult functional" is an expression from S. Mowinckel, *PIW*, I, 32). We are on safer ground to work on the basis that liturgical occasions provided the compositional shape of the psalm rather than to assume that it is part of an actual liturgy and recited while the liturgical actions were happening.

The psalm has excited the imagination of more than one commentator into rather colorful descriptions of the worship event reflected in it (e.g., Oesterley, Leslie, and G. H. Davies, *ZAW* 85 [1973] 183–98). According to this interpretation, in v 1 worshipers approaching the place of worship for some festival occasion encourage each other, or are encouraged by a speaker such as a priest, to move on to the sanctuary with shouting and singing. A second call to move toward Yahweh is given in v 2, envisioning worshipers about to enter the inner areas of the sanctuary (perhaps into the inner court of the temple). A third exhortation is found in v 6, calling on the worshipers to enter farther into the inner place of worship and to bow down before Yahweh. A choir or chorus is assumed to have chanted vv 3–5 and 7ab, or else the worshipers would have done so themselves.

The flow of the psalm changes dramatically with v 7d. Leslie (215) describes it as follows: "Then suddenly comes a change in person. The hymn ceases, and a prophetic voice, either that of a cultic prophet or of a priest imbued with prophetic spirit, speaks in the Lord's name a prophetic oracle, a message of warning to the entire worshiping throng." The prophetic preaching continues to the end of the psalm. At best, of course, the psalm reflects only bits of a larger liturgy. Mowinckel reminds us that "the ritual of a festival service is in fact a very complex affair with many subdivisions . . . which involved a number of very different acts and ceremonies" (*PIW,* I, 32–33). Perhaps, we should think of an act of sacrifice or some comparable act of worship for which the psalm would have been a suitable prelude (G. H. Davies, *ZAW* 83 [1973] 193). The use of Ps 95 in evening worship in the synagogues was at the beginning of the sabbath and as an "Invitatory Psalm" (see Cohen, 312; Kirkpatrick, 572) at the commencement of worship services supports the conclusion that it could belong to an entrance or beginning-of-worship liturgy.

The question of the exact occasion or situation-in-worship has evoked different opinions, which is no surprise. As noted above, a long Jewish tradition links the psalm with the celebration of the sabbath (see Oesterley, 520). Modern scholars have tended to think of the autumn festival of Tabernacles/Booths (as in the cases of Pss 50 and 81 see note 81:4.a.). The nature of the autumn festival and its chief emphasis have been matters of dispute. Mowinckel has argued forcefully and effectively for Pss 47, 93, 95–99, 100 as belonging to the festival context of the celebration of the enthronement of Yahweh as Divine King, which was at the same time a new year festival (see *PIW,* I, 106–92). According to Mowinckel, the first part of Ps 95 is an enthronement psalm in which "Yahweh, creator of the world and of Israel, has come to take his seat on his throne and receive the homage of his people" (*PIW,* I, 156). The second part is a renewal of the covenant through the mouth of a cultic prophet, which imposes on the people "the supposed commandments of Mount Sinai and of Kadesh" (178). Thus the psalm (as also Ps 81) joins together two essential elements of the festival: epiphany (or theophany) and covenant renewal (156–57; II, 71–73, 76). Weiser, well known for his advocacy of the covenant renewal nature of the autumn festival, mentions the renewal of the covenant in his commentary on Ps 95, but he wisely does not press the point. The psalm offers little or no direct support to a theory of a covenant renewal ceremony, though it would have been appropriate for such if there had been one.

The festivals (especially the autumn festival of Tabernacles) were undoubtedly the contexts for the praise of the Great God who is the Great King (95:3). The preaching of the prophets, or Levitical priests, in festival contexts is highly probable, and Ps 95 (as in the case of Pss 50 and 81) sets forth an example of such preaching (see Jeremias, *Kultprophetie,* 126–27). The preaching role of the prophet-priests is illustrated in such passages as Deut 27:9–10; 31:9–13; 15:2–7; 2 Chr 17:7–9; 20:13–17. An exhortation directed to festival participants to remember the past and the obligations incumbent on the people of Yahweh, would not have required a formal covenant renewal ceremony nor a dramatic enactment of the enthronement of Yahweh, with the ark carried in a festive procession to symbolize the personal presence of Yahweh (as in Mowinckel).

While it seems most probable that Ps 95 reflects the rituals and liturgy of the central sanctuary in Jerusalem, the possibility of the use of such psalms as 50, 81, and 95 in family or small community groups should not be excluded (see E. S. Gerstenberger, *Psalms*, 6–7, 30–34; 207–11). Even if the psalm originally emerged early in the history of Israel, it was surely used, with all the psalms, in the post-exilic communities. Gerstenberger (28–29) has argued, I think correctly, that we should read the Psalter in the light of Jewish community organizations in Persian and Hellenistic times (after 539 B.C.E.) in terms of local assemblies and meetings, as well as in the temple community in Jerusalem. In some cases, Zion seems remote (Pss 42:7; 87:1–7; 137:5), but it should be remembered that sacrifice and temple worship remained important, though true worship did not depend upon either (Pss 40, 50, and 51; Isa 58). "In short, at this latest stage the Psalter is not exactly a hymnbook of the second temple but more precisely a hymnbook of the many synagogal communities that lived with their hearts turned toward the Holy City but ritually independent of her" (Gerstenberger, 28).

Thus a date for the composition of Ps 95 cannot be established with any certainty. The opinions of commentators vary, usually in terms of their theories about the development of Israelite worship and the usage and date of the kingship of Yahweh psalms as a group (Pss 47, 93, 95–99). A. R. Johnson (*CPIP*, 19) thinks that it is conceivable to trace Ps 95 (like Ps 81) back to the pre-monarchical years of the settlement of the tribes in Palestine. On the other hand, several interpreters have been impressed enough by similarities between the psalm and Deuteronomy, Isa 40–66, and the prose oracles in Jeremiah (the so-called C sections) to date it to the exilic or post-exilic period (after 587 B.C.E.)—e.g., Oesterley (421) thinks Ps 95 reflects spiritual conditions like those in Hag 2; Mal 2:2; Isa 57–59 and suggests a date of c. 450 B.C.E. or a little later. Similarly, Gunkel (420, who links it with the time of Isa 56–66), Stuhlmueller (in early post-exilic age), and Jeremias (127). Kraus (II, 830) tentatively puts it between the publication of Deuteronomy and 1–2 Chronicles.

If the psalm is considered to be a composition actually used in pre-exilic festival contexts, its date would be prior to 587 B.C.E. (e.g., Mowinckel, *PIW*, I, 121–22). Perhaps the lack of a title in the Hebrew text (LXX has: "a song of praise to David") is a slight clue indicating that Ps 95 is later than Pss 50 and 81, which are in the Asaphite collection. On the other hand, Mowinckel (*PIW*, II, 72) argues that the Meribah tradition in 95:8 is found in the Yahwistic material of the Pentateuch and is "certainly older than Amos and Isaiah." However, a post-exilic psalm could easily incorporate an old tradition. Thus one can do little more than guess about the date of the psalm. Mowinckel (*Psalmenstudien* II, 146; *PIW*, II, 71–72) argues strongly that Ps 50 is not understandable without the exile—separating 50 from 81 and 95 (81 may have been Northern in origin, but it has been "remodeled in Jerusalem"; see also Jeremias, 127). Perhaps, but I find such differentiation to be less than convincing. The most probable guess for Ps 95 is that of an origin in early post-exilic Israelite communities.

Comment

A multiple summons to worship (95:1–7c). This section is marked by three calls to worship, each beginning with a different verb (vv 1—הלך, 2—קדם, 6—בוא).

Possibly the change of verbs is due simply to poetic variation, but it seems more probable that the verbs suggest liturgical movement. The first call (v 1) reflects a procession moving toward a sanctuary. The second (v 2) is given as the procession nears the entry to the worship place or is already in the outer courts, while the third (v 6) is at the entry to the holy place of worship. The בוא ("come/enter") of v 6 may be the beginning of an actual formula of entry (see G. H. Davies, *ZAW* 85 [1973] 191) which encourages worshipers to prostrate themselves and then kneel so that they can see and hear the activities of worship. However, the multiple calls also serve to emphasize the coming-to-God aspect of worship. Only those who are prepared to enter the presence of the Great God are prepared to worship. It is possible that vv 1–2 should be treated as a refrain, a general summons which was sung (or could have been sung) by the congregation as the members encouraged themselves to come to the worship of a festival (Stuhlmueller, II, 84). The motivation sections in vv 3–5, 4abc could have been sung by a choir or schola.

Barnes (II, 457) correctly notes that our English "O come let us sing unto the LORD" is too tame for the text. "The Psalm opens with a crash of words: The Psalmist calls upon his hearers to 'shout' and 'sing aloud.'" Oesterley too (421) notes "this noisy mode of worship," but then qualifies it with the unfortunate remark that it is "thoroughly characteristic of emotional Orientals." What he should have said is that it is "thoroughly characteristic of the enthusiasm of Israelites for Yahweh"—the Great God and the Great King over all gods. The "thankful-praise" or "thanksgiving" of v 2 could refer to a sacrifice made with accompanying praise, but in the context of Pss 50 and 81, it more probably refers to a sacrifice *of* thankful praise (cf. 50:14).

For the "Rock" as an epithet of God, see note 1.b. For the movement of the worshipers to a position before the "face" of God ("into his presence," v 2), see Pss 17:13, 89:15. The "face" or "presence" of a deity referred to an image of the deity in the ancient religious context of Israel, but in the OT it is used in a metaphorical way for the presence of God (Kraus, II, 830).

The basis for hailing Yahweh with praise and thanksgiving is given in the two כי-sections in vv 3–5 and 7abc. In the first section, Yahweh is described as the creator of the world, the owner and manager of all creation. "The highest God, who is the king of the gods, is the creator of the world and lord of the world" (Kraus, II, 830). The sphere of his power extends throughout all creation, from the depths of the earth, where the powers of death reside, to the peaks of the mountains, where deities have their assemblies (see Craigie's *Comment* on Ps 48:2–3). Land and sea are his (cf. 24:1–2); his lordship extends to all creation. In the second section, Yahweh is described as the maker (עשה) of Israel (6b). The worshipers claim and confess him as their God (7abc). They affirm their relationship to him in the metaphor of "a flock under his care."

Kraus (II, 831) notes the relationship of the creator of the world in vv 3–5 with the creator of Israel in vv 6–7. The God of Israel is both creator and shepherd (the strongest parallels to this dual role for Yahweh are found in Second-Isaiah, e.g., 43:1, 15; also see Deut 32:6 and Ps 100:3). For v 7abc, note the similarity with Jer 31:33. For the shepherd concept, see Pss 23:1; 80:2; 100:3; Isa 40:11; John 10:11-14.

A message from God (95:7d–11). The transition from the first part of the psalm to the second part is provided by the admonitory introduction of a divine oracle in 7d. The worshipers kneeling before Yahweh are encouraged to hear his message for them. Kraus (831) notes the parallelism between ידו ("his hand/care") and קלו ("his voice/message"). The confession of Yahweh's lordship over the world and over his people provides a context for hearing his word of instruction. The "today" (היום) recalls the prominent use of this stylistic device in Deuteronomy (see, e.g., Deut 4:40; 5:3; 6:6; 7:11). The expression stresses the urgency of hearing the message and also links the past with the present, as in Deut 5:2–3: "The LORD our God made a covenant with us in Horeb. Not (only) with our fathers did the LORD make this covenant, but with us, who are all of us here alive this day (היום)" (RSV). The hardening of hearts and the testing of God, as at Meribah, cannot be relegated to the past and left there. The matter still lives and the congregation is at Meribah again. Massah ("testing") is now.

The divine message has the character of a sermonic admonition, which recalls and reactualizes the old tradition of testing God, of putting him to the proof. "At Meribah" refers to the events in Exod 17:7 and Num 20:13, where the people of Israel "contended" (רבו from ריב) with Yahweh (ריב is found in Exod 17:7, while מרה, "be rebellious/disobedient/stubborn," is used in Num 27:7). Meribah (מריבה) is literally "contention" or "controversy," while Massah connotes "testing" or "tempting" (from נסה). See also Deut 33:8; Ps 106:32. The testing of Yahweh at Meribah is not spelled out specifically, but the use of Meribah with Massah suggests a double meaning (see G. H. Davies, ZAW 85 [1973] 193–94). Meribah and Massah occur together in Deut 33:8 and in Exod 17:7. Massah only is mentioned in Deut 6:16 and 9:22. Meribah occurs without Massah in Num 20:1–13 and in Ps 81:7.

Perhaps, the key passage for Ps 95:8 is Exod 17:7: "And he called the name of the place Massah and Meribah, because of the faultfinding (ריב) of the children of Israel, and because they put the LORD to the proof (נסה) by saying, 'Is the LORD among us or not?'" (RSV). The testing of the Meribah-generation was the questioning of the reality of the presence of Yahweh. "The oracular warning is saying not only 'Do not be rebellious as your fathers were about the waters of Meribah,' but it is also saying 'Do not question the presence of God here today, as your fathers questioned it at Massah'" (Davies, 194). V 10 recalls the loathing of Yahweh for the wilderness generation, which would not trust his demonstrated works of deliverance (v 9) and whose wayward hearts would not let them commit themselves to his ways. The Meribah-generation is presented as an example of heart-hardening and erring ways of life. V 11 recalls the oath which Yahweh took with himself regarding the Meribah-generation. For discussion of "my resting-place," see note 11.c.

The unusual use of the relative אשר at the beginning of v 11 (where one might expect the more common לכן, "therefore," which is customary in prophetic preaching, especially to introduce the announcement of a divine judgment: as in Amos 4:12; Hos 2:8, 9[6, 9]; Isa 8:4; Mic 3:12; Jer 28:16; 38:30–31; etc.) may be an indication that the preaching in this psalm is both like and unlike that found in the prophetic literature—and the same can be said for the preaching in Pss 50 and 81. The dominant characteristic of the preaching in these psalms is that of admonition. V 11 recalls an announcement of judgment in fact, but the purpose of the recall is to encourage the congregation to hear the message of Yahweh and avoid the mistakes of the past. C. Westermann (*Basic Forms of Prophetic Speech*, tr. H. C. White [Philadelphia: Westminster Press, 1968] 163–68) has analyzed the prophetic speeches in the Books of Chronicles. He finds that these speeches, for the most part, contain "a good genuine prophetic tradition" but that they have lost the "sharpness" of the original forms of prophetic judgment-speech. The style of preaching in Pss 50, 81, and 95 has lost some of the immediacy of earlier prophetic oracles of judgment and is similar to the prophetic instruction of the speeches in Chronicles (see 1 Chr 17:15 // 2 Sam 7; 2 Chr 11:2–4; 15:2–7; 20:14–18; 25:7–8). Of course, this kind of preaching is prominent in Isa 40–55 (see 42:18–43:7; 43:25–28). Judgments of the past are recalled for instructive purposes. Gerstenberger (*Psalms*, 210) says that the elements of Ps 50 fit the genre of a liturgical sermon and adds that "The genre is widely used in later OT writings but has been far too little explored." It seems very probable that this type of prophetic preaching was most at home in circles of Levitical priests and became of major significance in the exilic and post-exilic periods of Israel's history.

Explanation

The hymn section of this psalm (vv 1–7c) is a fine expression of the joyful celebration of Yahweh's kingship and shepherdhood, which reflects a festival liturgy. The jubilation of festival worship fills these verses. The Great God, who is King over all the gods, is hailed as the creator of the earth and the sea. The members of the great shepherd's flock are exhorted to prostrate themselves before him and to kneel expectantly in his presence. In v 7a, Yahweh is confessed as the worshipers' own God: "He is our God." These verses urge the reader to join in the celebration and confess with others: "We are the people of his pasture, a flock under his care."

The second part of the psalm (vv 7d–11) is a sermonic challenge to hear the message of God derived from the Meribah experience of the wilderness generations. The message is a "direct and stern word" (Durham, 366), which recalls the putting of Yahweh to the proof by the wilderness generation with the resulting disastrous consequences. The worshipers are warned that hardening of hearts, like that at Meribah, could happen to them. The hardening of the heart (קשׁה) refers, of course, to the stubborn and rebellious will of those who followed their "wayward hearts" and refused to learn the ways of God for them. "Contention" and "testing" were more congenial to them than were obedience and faith (vv 1–11). Further, the psalm attempts to bring home the fact that worship is more than an act of formal praise and remembering the long ago. Yahweh addresses them "today" and confronts them with his demands (see Mowinckel, *PIW*, I, 186; Johnson, *CPIP*, 22). Jubilation is one pole of worship; obedience of the demands of God is the other. The "resting-place" of God is closed to those who only jubilate.

Vv 1–7c are often called the *Venite* in Christian worship; an invitatory hymn which calls people to worship. The Epistle to the Hebrews uses this psalm in exhortation to Christians who may be in danger of falling away from their commitment to God (see Heb 3:1–4:13). The treatment in Hebrews is a Christian *midrashic* treatment of the psalm, which focuses on the failure of the wilderness generation to reach the "rest" of God. The "rest" of God is a yet unrealized goal, though there is a sense in which those who have faith have already entered the "rest" (4:3, 10). The central message is set forth in Heb 4:11: "Let us therefore strive to enter that rest, / that no one fall by the same sort of disobedience" (RSV). The text in Heb 3:7 attributes the oracle in the psalm to the Holy Spirit, and it is the voice of God himself which urges his people to give heed "today" and to persevere in a faithful life. An "evil, unbelieving heart" (3:12) can result in their falling away from the living God. The old trek through the wilderness toward the promised land always passes by Meribah, where hearts may harden and the pilgrimage be lost: "So we see that they were unable to enter because of unbelief (lit., "un-faith" or "unfaithfulness")" (Heb 3:19; see also 4:2).

Yahweh Reigns as King   (96:1–99:9)

Bibliography

General: **Brueggemann, W.** *Israel's Praise.* **Gray, J.** "The Kingship of God in the Prophets and Psalms." *VT* 11 (1961) 1–29. **Gunkel, H.** *Einleitung in die Psalmen.* 94–116. **Howard, D. M., Jr.** *The Structure of Psalms 93–100.* **Johnson, A. R.** *Sacral Kingship in Ancient Israel.* Cardiff: University of Wales Press, 1955. **Kraus, H.-J** *Die Königsherrschaft Gottes im Alten Testament: Untersuchungen zu den Liedern von Jahwes Thronbesteigung.* Tübingen: Mohr, 1951. **McCollough, W. S.** "The 'Enthronement Psalms.'" In *A Stubborn Faith,* ed. E. C. Hobbs. Dallas: Southern Methodist UP, 1956. 53–61. **Michel, D.** *Tempora und Satzstellung in den Psalmen.* **Mowinckel, S.** *Psalmenstudien,* II: *Der Ursprung der israelitischen Eschatologie.* Amsterdam: Schippers, 1961 (1922). ———. *PIW.* II, 106–92. **Ollenburger, B. C.** *Zion the City of the Great King.* **Schmid, H.** "Jahwe und die Kulttraditionen von Jerusalem." *ZAW* 67 (1955) 168–97. **Watts, J. D. W.** "Yahweh Malak Psalms." *TZ* 21 (1965) 341–48.

Form/Structure/Setting

Pss 96–99 are treated here as a unit, though each psalm has its own particular set of characteristics. These psalms, usually linked with Pss 47, 93, and 95, belong to the form-critical category of hymns of descriptive praise of Yahweh (using the "descriptive praise" category of Westermann, as in his *Praise and Lament*). Since the work of Gunkel and Mowinckel, they have commonly been called the enthronement psalms (see Westermann, *Praise and Lament,* 145), celebrating the kingship of Yahweh and frequently associated with proposed enthronement ceremonies in the pre-exilic temple in Jerusalem. However, there is some unhappiness among scholars about the grouping of these psalms in a common category and about the rubric "enthronement psalms." Westermann (150) argues that there is no proper form-critical category which can be designated as "enthronement psalms"; they are mixed psalms of descriptive praise that have been expanded and modified by exclamations and descriptions of divine kingship.

Years ago Buttenwieser (320–21) contended that Pss 93, 96, 97, and 98 do not form an organic group with Pss 95, 99, and 100. According to him, Pss 93, 97, 98, and 96 (in that order, 334–43) form a single poem of four parts, with Ps 99 being a distinctly different psalm, "narrow and particularistic" and lacking the universal perspective of Isa 40–55 (32, 361–63). Kraus (II, 851) also argues that Ps 99 is differentiated from Pss 96–98, chiefly on the basis of a lack of establishable dependence on Isa 40–55 and the strong possibility, at least, of a pre-exilic date of origin in the time of the kings. He thinks Pss 93 and 99 are probably pre-exilic (possibly belonging to the background of the call and preaching of Isaiah), but that Pss 96–98 originated after Isa 40–55 in the post-exilic cultus. F. Crüsemann (*Studien zur Formgeschichte*, 70) wishes to differentiate Pss 96 and 98 (also Ps 47) from Pss 93, 97, and 99 on the basis that 96 and 98 belong to the category of "imperative hymns" (which he postulates), while 93, 97, and 99 do not.

Some scholars prefer to avoid the descriptive word "enthronement" because of its strong association with a theoretical liturgical celebration of Yahweh's kingship (linked especially to Mowinckel, *Psalmenstudien*, II). For example, Anderson (I, 33) uses the title "Psalms Celebrating the Kingship of Yahweh." Gerstenberger (*Psalms*, 19), though open to the use of Pss 47, 93, and 96–99 in enthronement rituals, uses the designation "Yahweh-kingship psalms" (see *Form/Structure/Setting*, of Ps 93). Not surprisingly, Kraus, who contends that there never was a real ritual of Yahweh's enthronement, uses the designation "hymns of Yahweh as king" (see *Psalms 1–59*, 45).

The reservations are worthy of note, but Pss 93, 96–99 (and Ps 47) share a substantial thematic unity, despite predictable variations in poetic style and form. Kraus (I, 45) says of Pss 47, 93, 96, 97, 98, and 99 that they "are clearly identified by the theme of Yahweh's kingship, by which the group is held together." Also Howard (*Structure*, 216) concludes that "Psalms 93–100 form a logically coherent unit within Book IV of the Psalter." It may be that Pss 93 and 99 (and possibly Ps 95) originated at dates much earlier than 96–98, though caution should be exercised in assuming that similarities to Isa 40–55 are positive proof of a later date. Regardless of the dates of individual psalms, it is most probable indeed that Book IV is post-exilic and that Pss 93, 96–99 in the present Psalter reflect post-exilic usage.

The designation "enthronement psalms" is well established in scholarly literature and is not likely to go away. It may be prudent, however, to use a more neutral descriptive category such as that of Kraus and others. I will designate Pss 93, 96–99 as "kingship-of-Yahweh psalms," without a necessary link to enthronement ceremonies as such. Of course, the term *enthronement psalms* does not necessarily carry a full commitment to enthronement rites like those proposed by Mowinckel. The psalms celebrate the conviction that Yahweh is *enthroned as king* and reigns as king (as in Ps 29:10) quite apart from any ritual enactment. One could argue also that these psalms celebrate the enthronement of Yahweh as king at creation and in the course of history apart from any repeated ritual enthronement in festival ceremonies (note Kraus' treatment of Ps 47).

The matter of the dating of Pss 96–99 is worth some further consideration. The evidence for Ps 93 tilts toward a pre-exilic date, perhaps quite early (see *Form/Structure/Setting* for Ps 93), while the situation for Ps 95 is uncertain but possibly pre-exilic (see *Form/Structure/Setting* for Ps 95). Possibly all of the kingship-of-Yahweh psalms are from the monarchical period of Israelite history (prior to 587 B.C.E.). Howard (*Structure*), whose work was used extensively in dealing with Ps 93, applies the criteria formulated there to Pss 96–99 with the following results:

Ps 96   Few clear indicators, but likely post-ninth century, pre-exilic.
Ps 97   Likely pre-exilic, but not too early.

Ps 98   Conceivably from the pre-monarchical period, or else from late
        pre-exilic or exilic periods.

Ps 99   Nothing militates against a date in the pre-exilic monarchical
        period, though the dating must be tentative as with the other psalms.

In each case, Howard has applied the criteria of prose particles, bicolons versus
tricolons, prefixed and suffixed verbs, and divine names, and his analyses seem
to be well done.

Nevertheless there is enough uncertainty to exclude a certain conclusion for a
pre-exilic date for all of Pss 96–99. The criteria are only approximate at best. The
parallels between the kingship-of-Yahweh psalms and Deutero-Isaiah are not as
determinative as some scholars have argued. The strongest advocate for dependence on Deutero-Isaiah has been arguably Kraus (in his *Die Königsherrschaft Gottes
im Alten Testament;* see also his *Theology of the Psalms,* 90–91, and his commentary
on Ps 96–99). Buttenwieser (326–32) goes beyond Kraus, however, and contends
that Deutero-Isaiah himself was the author of Pss 93, 96, 97, and 98! For a survey
of arguments and analysis, see A. R. Johnson, "The Psalms," in *The Old Testament
and Modern Study,* ed. H. H. Rowley (Oxford: Clarendon Press, 1951) 192–95;
recently, Ollenburger, *Zion,* 35, 176, n. 76).

Two or three additional factors are worthy of consideration. First, Ps 93 may
be only a psalm fragment, functioning as an independent psalm, but selected
and put in its present place at a time much later than its composition. Second,
the mixed form critical nature of these psalms points in a general way to a later
date (see Westermann, *Praise and Lament,* 142–51, who notes that the kingship-
of-Yahweh psalms manifest a mixture of the three formal categories of hymns
advocated by F. Crüsemann, *Studien zur Formgeschichte:* imperative, participle, and
direct address). Third, the form critical evidence is strengthened by the presence
of a high degree of traditional, formulaic language as determined by R. C. Culley
(*Oral Formulaic Language in the Biblical Psalms* [Toronto: University of Toronto Press,
1967] 102–11): 65 percent in Ps 96; 42 percent in Ps 97, and 50 percent in Ps 98.
It is true that Culley (108) appeals to this evidence in order to defend a date for
these psalms *prior* to Deutero-Isaiah, but this is based on the grounds that the
formulaic language relates to earlier contexts and not on the formation of such
language in the present psalms. A. Aejmelaeus (*The Traditional Prayer in the Psalms,*
13) remarks with some overstatement that the tendency of scholars to date
psalms on either side of the exile (and it may be added, with a fair degree of
dogmatism) is alleviated if "the psalms are not regarded as literary manifestations of a certain author at a certain time, but are understood as the result of a
process of growth throughout the centuries," and if one is open to the possibility
that one psalm may contain both ancient and late elements. (Also, see Culley,
esp. 112–19, who notes the remarks of Johnson on Pss 96 and 98 in *Sacral Kingship,* 90, n. 6).

Third, the lack of titles for Pss 93, 96–99 (and 95) in MT points to the
possibility of (if not probability of) a later compilation of these psalms. The
addition of titles referring to David in the Greek texts indicates that the scribal
tradition of interpretation in the post-exilic period felt the need of "Davidizing"
them. Generally speaking, the psalms found in the Psalter within runs of titles that
attribute them to David seem to be earlier. Thus it is not unreasonable to conclude

that Pss 93–99 were outside the earlier Davidic collections and also not in the sons-of-Korah tradition in which Ps 47 appears. The use of שׁירו ליהוה שׁיר חדשׁ ("sing to Yahweh a new song") in 96:1 and 98:1 indicates the use of a formulaic saying, found also in Isa 42:10–13 and Ps 149:1 (a psalm with six points of contact with Isa 61 alone; see Allen, 319), and forms another bit of evidence for the exilic or post-exilic dating of the psalms in question, especially if "new song" praises the coming new and unprecedented intervention of Yahweh in history. It should be noted that a similar formulaic statement is found in Ps 33:3, an untitled psalm of uncertain date, but which may be exilic or post-exilic.

The use of the content of Ps 96:1–13 in 1 Chr 16:8–34 does not prove that the date of origin for this material is late—indeed, it almost certainly indicates that the content is earlier than Chronicles—but it points again to a post-exilic provenance for Pss 96 and 105 (which also appears in 1 Chr 16; for the date and setting of Ps 105, see Allen, 49–44, who is uncertain about its date but reads it in terms of a post-exilic congregation, and Kraus, II, 892, who thinks its origin is no earlier than the exile).

Thus I think it best to work with the following hypothesis: (1) There was a long tradition of kingship-of-Yahweh poetry in Israel, reaching back to early pre-exilic periods, probably represented in Ps 93; (2) the dates of origin for Pss 95 and 96–99 as individual psalms are uncertain—possibly all pre-exilic, but more probably post-exilic in their present forms; and (3) the cultic situations of Pss 93–99 in the Psalter are mostly post-exilic, and these should be considered the primary contexts for their interpretation.

The setting in worship for the kingship-of-Yahweh psalms eludes any certain conclusion and probably varied at different times in different communities. Kraus (*Psalms 1–59*, 45, 71) thinks the references to "bowing down" in Pss 95:6; 96:9; 99:5, 9; 132:7, 138:2 indicates that kingship-of-Yahweh praise was chanted when festival congregations moved in solemn processions and prostrated themselves in adoration and obeisance before the perceived presence of Yahweh: "It was probably at this cultic act of homage that the hymns were sung. The praise of God breaks out. The glorification knows no bounds. Also the heavenly powers join in the praise of Yahweh (Pss 29:1; 103:20f.; 149:1ff.). All creatures, the whole creation, chime in (Psalms 96 and 98). At this act of homage sacrifices were probably presented" (Kraus, 71). The reference to Yahweh's status as "cherubim-enthroned" in Ps 99:1 (see also Ps 80:2 and *Comment* below) may also indicate an association with the movement of the ark, which was considered to be either the throne of God or the footstool of the enthroned king (note 99:5), at least in pre-exilic ceremonies. Ps 96:1b–13 is found as a part of the psalm in 1 Chr 16, along with Ps 105:1–15 (plus v 34 from Pss 106:1; 107:1; 118:1; 136:1; and vv 35–36 from Ps 106:47–48), and related to the cultic ark procession into the temple (cf. Ps 132 and the usual theories about Ps 24:7–10). Ps 47:6 may refer to the "going up" of the ark to the temple with the people shouting and blowing horns as they rejoiced (e.g., see the treatment of 132:7–8 by Kraus). The ark was not present in the post-exilic temple (see Jer 3:16–17), and the use of the kingship-of-Yahweh psalms would not have involved its physical presence. Cultic processions were, however, almost certainly a part of the worship of the second temple and the bowing of the people in adoration of Yahweh in the outer court of the temple would have been continued as a part of worship (cf. Ps 100:4; Joel 2:15–17; Kraus, *Theology of the Psalms*, 91; idem, *Psalmen*, II, 835).

A more precise fixing of the worship context of the kingship-of-Yahweh psalms is hard to come by with any assurance. The larger nature of the pre-exilic festival has been fiercely debated (see *Form/Structure/Setting*, Ps 93). The emphasis on some sort of ritual of enthronement (as with Mowinckel) has been popular, but new year, covenant renewal, and royal-Zion festivals have been advocated with great vigor. Regardless of its exact nature and the liturgical proceedings, the chief festival involved in pre-exilic Israel was almost certainly that of Tabernacles, the comprehensive autumnal festival in the Israelite cultic calendar. Presumably this would have been true also in the temple after 515 B.C.E., though there was probably a rise in the significance of the spring festivals of Passover and Pentecost (the relatively little attention given by OT scholars to worship in the second temple, in comparison with the enormous energy devoted to the pre-exilic temple, is a rather striking lacuna in the scholarly endeavors of this century). Beyond the worship of the festival, allowance should be made for the use of the kingship-of-Yahweh psalms in sabbath worship (as argued years ago by N. H. Snaith, *Studies in the Psalter* [London: Epworth, 1934] 47–87; see *Form/Structure/Setting*, Ps 93). And apart from the use of these psalms in the temple, we should remember their use in pious study and prayers by family groups and by individuals.

The segment of psalms in Pss 96–99 seems to divide into two major divisions of twin-psalms: 96–97 and 98–99. In both cases the psalms are of approximately the same length: 96 has 13 verses (29 colons) and 97 has 12 verses (29 colons) (actually the first colon of 96 serves as a title); 98 has 9 verses (24 colons) and 99 has 9 verses (25 colons). The content patterns of Pss 96–97 and 98–99 are similar; for example:

96	97	98	99
a new song	Yahweh reigns	a new song	Yahweh reigns
earth called to praise Yahweh	thanksgiving to Yahweh	sea and world called to praise Yahweh	exaltation of Yahweh
Yahweh's coming to judge the world	Zion	Yahweh's coming to judge the world	Zion
	holy name		holy hill

The tendency for a juxtaposition of an untitled psalm with a titled one (as in 42–43; 32–33; 70–71; see *Form/Structure/Setting*, Ps 93) points to the pairing of 96–97 and 98–99. Ps 98:1 has a one-word title (longer in LXX) and Ps 96:1a probably serves as a title for that psalm (cf. G. H. Wilson, *The Editing of the Hebrew Psalter*, 178; idem, "The Use of 'Untitled' Psalms in the Hebrew Psalter," *ZAW* 95 [1985] 410).

Howard (*Structure*) has examined the lexical relatedness of Pss 96–99 at some length. He (176–79) notes that Pss 96 and 97 have 22 words in common, a few of which are significant. For example, "heavens (שמים) is found in 96:5, 11 and 97:6 and "glory" (כבוד) is found in 96:3, 7, 8 and 97:6 and only in these verses in Pss 93–100. Also גיל, "rejoice" (96:11 and 97:1, 8) occurs nowhere else in Book IV, and חיל, "tremble" (96:9; 97:4), occurs elsewhere in Book IV only in 90:2. Only Pss 96 and 97 have all five of the themes characteristic of the Yahweh-*malak* psalms according to a study by Watts (*ThLZ* 21 [1965] 341–48; see *Form/Structure/ Setting*, Ps 93). Pss 98 and 99 have 13 words in common, plus some thematic links (Howard, 194–95). Howard notes that the words in common tend to come together at the end of Ps 98 and the beginning of Ps 99 in a "concatenation of ideas between the two psalms" (195): especially, earth (ארץ), peoples (עמים), judging (שפט), righteousness (צדק), and equity (ישרים).

Pss 96 and 98 have much in common with "more common vocabulary and closer structural affinities" (Howard, *Structure*, 179) than is the case even with Pss 96 and 97. The similar beginnings and endings of these two psalms are well known: 96:1–2 and 98:1–2; 96:13 and 98:9. Likewise, Ps 97 has several expressions and themes in common with Ps 99. Howard (190) notes that the total of 19 words and particles shared by Pss 97 and 99 is more than 97 has in common with 96, although many of these are incidental. The most striking usages are those of Zion in 97:8 and 99:2 and the word "cloud" (ענן) in 97:2 and 99:7; the only occurrences of these words in Pss 90–100. Howard (192) remarks that these usages "confirm the relatedness of the two psalms." (ענן is found again in Book IV only in Ps 105:39, and Zion only in 102:14, 17, 22). The lines of evidence seem to point to a parallelistic pattern of Pss 96–99 of ABAB.

Admittedly this type of evidence is weakened by the fact that so much of the language is traditional. It does, however, point to the coherence of Pss 96–99 as a unit and the cumulative evidence supports treating 96–97 and 98–99 as psalm-pairs. Incidentally, the combination of psalms in the Hebrew manuscripts collated by Kennicott and de Rossi indicates a higher combination of Pss 96 with 97 than of 94 with 95 or of 95 with 96 (according to Snaith [*Studies in the Psalter* (London: Epworth, 1934) 53]; Pss 94 and 95 are written together in 9 manuscripts; 95 and 96 in 4; 96 and 97 in 14; 98 and 99 in 8; see also Briggs, I, xlix; also table 4 in Wilson, *Editing*, where the data are different but the ratios are about the same). This evidence is, of course, late and influenced heavily by liturgical usage. It may, however, confirm other indications (see Wilson, *Editing*, 133, n. 11). In brief, Pss 96–99 can be treated as a literary unit, divided into two psalm-pairs.

Psalm 96

Bibliography

Brueggemann, W. *The Message of the Psalms: A Theological Commentary.* Minneapolis: Augsburg, 1984. 144–46. ———. *Israel's Praise.* 30–38. **Jeremias, J.** *Das Königtum Gottes in den Psalmen.* Göttingen: Vandenhoeck & Ruprecht, 1987. 121–31. **Martin-Achard, R.** "Israël, peuple sacerdotal." *Verbam caro* 18.3 (1964) 25–27. **Ringgren, H.** "Behold Your King Comes." *VT* 24 (1974) 207–11.

Translation

1a	*Sing to Yahweh a new song;*[b]	(4+3)
	sing to Yahweh, all the earth.	
2	*Sing to Yahweh; bless his name;*	(4+3)
	proclaim his salvation day after day.[a]	
3	*Declare his glory among the nations,*	(3+3)
	his wondrous deeds among all peoples.	
4	*For great is Yahweh, most worthy of praise;*[a]	(4+3)
	he is to be feared above all gods.	
5	*For all the gods of the peoples are mere idols,*[a]	(4+3)
	but Yahweh made the heavens!	
6	*Honor and Majesty are before him;*	(3+3)
	Might and Glory[a] *are in his sanctuary.*[b]	
7	*Ascribe to Yahweh, you families of peoples,*	(4+4)
	ascribe to Yahweh glory and might;	
8	*ascribe to Yahweh the glory of his name;*	(4+4)
	bring tribute[a] *and enter his courts;*	
9	*bow down before Yahweh in (his) holy splendor;*[a]	(4+3)
	writhe before his presence,[b] *all the earth!*	
10	*Say among the nations: Yahweh reigns!*[a]	(4+3+3)
	the world is firmly established,[b] *immovable;*	
	he will judge the peoples with equity.[c]	
11	*Let the heavens rejoice and the earth be jubilant;*	(4+3)
	let the sea and all within it resound;	
12	*let the fields and everything in them exult.*	(4+4)
	Then[a] *let all the trees of the forest raise a shout*	
13	*before*[a] *Yahweh, for he is coming,*[b]	(3+3+2+2)
	he is coming to judge the earth.	
	He will judge the world with righteousness,	
	and its peoples with his faithfulness.	

Notes

1.a. LXX has a title for this psalm: "When the house was built after the captivity; a song of David."

1.b. For a "new song," see Pss 33:3; 40:4; 98:1; 144:9; 149:1; Isa 42:10. See *Comment* below. Vv 1a and 2a are missing in 1 Chr 16:28.

2.a. 1 Chr 16:23 has מיום־אל־יום for ליום מיום. For the verb בשׂר, "proclaim," see *Comment*, 96:1–6.

4.a. Lit., "ones to be praised [pual ptcp] exceedingly."

5.a. The word אלילים denotes "weak/insufficient/worthless things"; cf. Job 13:4; Zech 11:7; Lev 19:4; 26:1; Isa 2:8, 18, 20; 10:10, 11; 19:1–3; 31:7; Ezek 30:13. The original meaning may have been "gods," used in MT as a term of contempt. LXX uses δαιμόνια, "demons," but the word can also means "gods."

6.a. I assume that honor, majesty, might, and glory form a tetrad of personified divine powers. The word translated "glory," תפארת, is often translated as "splendor" or "beauty." It applies to apparel of a high priest in Exod 28:2, 40; the greatness of a king in Esth 1:4; the house of David and inhabitants of Jerusalem, Zech 12:7, 7. Yahweh's תפארת is found in Ps 71:8; 1 Chr 29:11; of his name in Isa 63:14; 1 Chr 29:13; of his arm in Isa 63:12. Associated with כבוד, "glory," in Exod 28:2; Isa 4:2; Prov 4:8–9 (from כבד, "be heavy/honored"); 1 Chr 29:11–12; Esth 1:4.

6.b. 1 Chr 16:27 has עז וחדוה במקמו, "Might and joy in his place." "Place" is the more general term, probably meaning "holy place." Since the material in 1 Chr 16 is attributed to David, the redactors may have wanted to avoid referring to the "sanctuary" before the temple was built (cf. Gunkel, 425).

8.a. Or, "gift(s)."

9.a. The expression בהדרת־קדש has been given more than one interpretation. Traditionally הדרת is taken from הדרה, "ornament/adornment/splendor" (kjv: "beauty of holiness"). The expression elsewhere appears in Ps 29:2; 1 Chr 16:29; 2 Chr 20:21; note the plural בהדרי־קדש in Ps 110:3, "in holy adornments" (though see Allen, 80, n. 3.d, who prefers to emend to "on the holy mountains"). The reading "beauty of holiness" was interpreted by older English speaking commentators in a spiritual sense; the beauty of holy deeds and disposition on the part of the worshiper.

LXX ἐν αὐλῇ ἀγίᾳ αὐτοῦ equals בחצרת קדש, "in his holy court," a reading followed by Calvin and reflected in some older commentaries (e.g., D. Dickson, *A Commentary on the Psalms,* from the seventeenth century, who writes of Ps 29:2 that worship should take place "in the glorious sanctuary, the place of public meeting" because it was a place of grace and worship showing forth the glory of God [150], also for Ps 96:9 [178], "his church represented by the sanctuary"). LXX may have been influenced by 1 Chr 16:27 (see above, and P. R. Ackroyd, "Some Notes on Psalms," *JTS* 17 [1966], 396, n. 2). The interpretation as "holy attire" is also well established, appearing as a marginal reading in the Revised Version. Note Briggs, I, 255; Kirkpatrick; cf. Exod 28:2; 2 Chr 20:21 (?).

A more recent line of interpretation takes its starting point from the Ugaritic word *hdrt* (*Keret* text, *CTA* 14.3.155) translated as "vision/apparition/dream," with the assumption that some sort of theophanic appearance of a deity is involved, or at least the strong sense of the presence of a deity. For the data and arguments, see Ackroyd (*JTS* 17 [1966] 396), Dahood, I, 176; II, 358; F. M. Cross, *Canaanite Myth and Hebrew Epic,* 152–53, n. 28. Cross (155) translates in Ps 29:2, "Fall down before Yahweh who appears in holiness!"; Dahood: "Bow down to Yahweh when the Holy One appears." This interpretation appeals also to LXX which changes the subject from the worshipers to Yahweh (see Cross, 153). See Craigie (242, n. 2) for a critique of this interpretation, arguing that the Ugar. *hdrt* is a hapax legomenon in the Ugar. texts and possibly a scribal error for *d(h)rt,* "dream/vision" (C. H. Gordon, *Ugaritic Textbook,* 735) and thus may provide no parallel for the Hebrew הדרת. If בהדרת refers to Yahweh rather than to the worshipers, it is better to take it as "splendor/array," with a suffix on קדש, with LXX, or else consider it understood: "Worship Yahweh in (his) holy splendor/array." The idea is that of being clothed in brilliant garments (cf. such passages as Job 40:10; Ps 104:1; Prov 31:25) or simply the royal dignity of a king and his court (cf. Prov 14:28; cf. Howard, *Structure,* 88–89). The "his courts" at the end of 8b suggests that the corresponding element in 9a should refer to Yahweh rather than to the worshipers.

Another option is to assume that קדש, with or without the suffix, refers to "the holy place," parallel to "his courts" in 8b, and read simply: "Bring a gift and come to his courts // fall down before Yahweh in the splendor of the holy place (or, his holy place)," as in Loretz, II, 56–57. The concept of theophany is reflected in the psalm, but it should not be pushed too hard in specific words.

9.b. Kraus (II, 834) argues that the מפני, "from the face of/because of," supports the interpretation of "his holy appearing/revelation" in the parallel 9a. There may be a small variation in meaning between מלפני and לפני (see BDB, 817–18; KB, 889; Howard, *Structure,* 97). If so, מלפני indicates movement away from a person or thing and לפני indicates a position in front of or in the presence of. מפני, which occurs here, seems to be equal to מלפני, which occurs in this context in 1 Chr 16:30 and in the context of Ps 97:5.

10.a. For יהוה מלך, see n. 93:1.a. 1 Chr 16:31 has this colon after v 11a.

10.b. For discussion of אף־תכון, see n. 93:1.b.

10.c. A colon also found in Ps 9:9b.

12.a. A change of אז, "then," to אף, "also/the more so," is adopted by some commentators (e.g., Gunkel, 433; Kraus, II, 834): "also let the trees of the woodland shout for joy." This seems to smooth out the parallelism. However, the "then" is retained in LXX, and I suspect that the rejoicing of trees in a theophanic context is a traditional feature: see Ezek 17:22–24; 31:2–18; Isa 10:33–34; 2 Sam 5:22–24; cf. Isa 55:12. See also Dahood (II, 359), who argues that 1 Chr 16:33 helps to establish the stichometric division of the prayer.

13.a. 1 Chr 16:33 has מלפני rather than לפני in Ps 96:13. Perhaps, מלפני has more of the sense of "because of/on account of" (cf. BDB, 817–18, 5.b; KB, 767b), whereas לפני means "in the presence of/before." But there is probably little or no difference in meaning. If there is, perhaps the מפני (= מלפני) in v 9 indicates moving away from the presence of Yahweh and the לפני in v 13 points to the joyful shouting of the trees in the anticipated divine presence. See n. 9.b.

13.b. Reading the twofold בא as a participle (so Delitzsch, III, 93) and not as a perfect (so Briggs, II, 313). The personal pronoun expected as the subject is omitted, as frequently (cf. GKC 116s). The participles express imminent action. If the perfect is read, the verbs could be descriptive of character-istic action ("he comes") or refer to an advent that has already taken place (Briggs, II, 313), "for he is come/has come/came"). Gunkel (421) and Kraus (II, 833, 838) read the verbs as expressing an eschatological concept, which I take to be correct.

I have read the כי as causal, but it may be temporal: "when he comes."

Comment

A call to praise Yahweh, who is greater than all other gods (96:1–6). Imperative sum-mons mark the first division of this psalm in vv 1–3. Note the series of six impera-tives: sing—sing—sing—bless—proclaim—declare. The threefold use of שׁירו, "sing," is impressive, followed by the verbs בשׂר and ספר in vv 2 and 3. The verb בשׂר carries the idea of "bringing news/a message," which involves "good news" in the OT (one exception seems to be the use of the word מבשׂר, "messenger" in 1 Sam 4:17; see *TDOT*, III, 314). Its use in the proclamation of Yahweh's saving acts is appropri-ate in Ps 96 (cf. Isa 40:9; 41:27; 52:7; 60:6; 61:1; Nah 2:1 [1:15]). The usage of בשׂר in Deutero-Isaiah has the force of reporting a victory which Yahweh has won elsewhere. For example, in Isa 41:25–29, a messenger (מבשׂר) will bring the news to Jerusalem that Yahweh has caused to come forth "one from the north" (Cyrus) who will do the will of Yahweh for the salvation of Israel (Brueggemann, *Israel's Praise*, 32).

Something of this approach seems to be present in Ps 96, except that the proclamation is directed toward the people and nations of the world. The news of Yahweh's saving work should be spread abroad day after day, until all people and nations know about his glory. The message is intended to arouse joy and evoke faith in Yahweh as the nations come to understand that he reigns as king over the whole world. The verb ספר in piel means to "recount/declare," perhaps the collo-quial English "tell about it" is a good translation (for "wondrous deeds" and praise, see Pss 26:7; 44:2; 73:28; 78:3, 4; 79; with the preposition ב, see Exod 9:16; 10:2; Ezek 12:16). The verb ברך in piel with God as the object means "praise" or "extol."

The "glory" of Yahweh in v 3 refers to more than the majestic aura of the divine presence, though that is included. "כבוד is by and large that asset which makes people or individuals, and even objects, impressive, and usually this is understood as something that can be perceived or expressed" (von Rad, *Old Tes-tament Theology*, tr. D. M. G. Stalker [New York: Harper & Row, 1962] I, 239). The possessions of Jacob in Gen 31:1 are his "glory," that which gives him standing in society (cf. Job 19:9; 29:20). For the "glory" of a people and its leaders, see Isa 5:13 (cf. Isa 16:14; 17:3; 21:16; Jer 2:11). Yahweh's "glory" is the manifestation of his presence, as in Num 16:19, 42; Ps 102:16, Isa 8:7; 40:5; 60:1–2; cf. Exod 16:10; 24:16–17; 40:34). His "glory" is also seen in the "work of his hands" (as in Ps 19:2) and in his "marvelous deeds" (נפלאות) in Ps 96:3 (cf. Exod 3:20; 34:10; Josh 3:5; Job 5:8–15; 9:10; 37:14–16; Pss 9:2; 26:7; 40:6, etc.). The whole of the created world is filled with the "glory" of Yahweh (Isa 6:3), and his power over the processes of creation is acclaimed as "Glory!" in Ps 29:9. His "glory" also mani-fests itself in history (cf. Exod 14:4, 17–18; Ezek 28:22; von Rad, 239–40). Thus the "glory" of Yahweh is an active, not a static, concept. It is his presence, power, and action in the world. For the "glory" of Yahweh in theophanic contexts, see *Comment* on Ps 97:6. For discussion of "name," see *Comment*, Ps 54:3.

The meaning of the "new song" (see note 1.b. above), which is called for in v 1, is somewhat ambiguous; perhaps deliberately so. In terms of form critical history, the probability is that "new song" referred to the celebration of a military victory (T. Longman III, "Psalm 98," *JETS* 27 [1984] 269) argues that each of the seven usages of "new song" in the OT (Pss 33:3; 40:3; 96:1; 98:1; 144:9; 149:1; Isa 42:10) occurs in a holy war context (plus the two NT occurrences, Rev 5:9; 14:3; see Longman, "The Divine Warrior: The New Testament Use of an Old Testament Motif," *WTJ* 44 [1982] 290–307). However, the use of the expression in its present context has been demilitarized and applied broadly to the comprehensive saving work of Yahweh. Thus in cultic terms the reference may be to a "new song" for a new festival occasion. Every festival, or other occasion of worship, merited a new song to celebrate Yahweh's new and renewed works. If there were some sort of enthronement ritual, which celebrated Yahweh's victory over his foes and the renewal of his reign as divine king, there would have been even more reason for a new song. The new, or renewed, reign of a king was the occasion for new expressions of celebration.

It is possible that the "new song" is the psalm itself which follows the summons (so Dahood, II, 357), perhaps having been a "new song" for some festival occasion. If we take our orientation for a "new song" from Isa 42:10 (cf. the "new name" in Isa 62:2), the emphasis will move toward a song which anticipates the new acts of redemption and deliverance which Yahweh is about to perform. The context in Isaiah is focused on the new works that Yahweh will do:

> Remember not the former things,
>   Nor consider the things of old,
> Behold, I am doing a new thing;
>   Now it springs forth, do you not perceive it?
>   (Isa 43:18–19, rsv)

> You have heard; now see all this;
>   and will you not declare it?
> From this time forth I make you hear new things,
>   hidden things which you have not known.
> They are created now, not long ago;
>   before today you have never heard of them.
>   (Isa 48:6–7b, rsv)

See Kraus, II, 835–36, 847. Another approach to the "new song" is that of an "ever-new-song" (Anderson, II, 682), which celebrates the "ever-newness" of Yahweh and his works:

> The steadfast love of the LORD never ceases,
>   his mercies never come to an end;
> they are new every morning;
>   great is thy faithfulness.
>   (Lam 3:22–23, rsv)

All these elements of "new song" are probably valid in one context or another. In the context of Pss 96 and 98 it seems to me that the anticipation of new actions and victories on the part of Yahweh is dominant. Ps 96 is a call for universal praise of Yahweh who is coming to judge the earth. The "new song" is to express a new realization and acknowledgment that the future belongs to Yahweh. "A new song must be sung for a new orientation" (Brueggemann, *The Message of the Psalms*, 144). The new song is the song which breaks through the restraints of the present circumstances and voices expectation and confidence in the future works of God (see Kraus, II, 836).

The second part of the first section of Ps 96 in vv 4–6 sets forth the reasons for praising Yahweh, in typical hymnic fashion. The use of כי in vv 4 and 5 provides a double emphasis on the high status of Yahweh, who is greater than all other gods and more worthy of reverence (fear) than any other deity. The second כי-statement in v 5 extends and intensifies the declarations in v 4: all the gods of the peoples are "mere idols"—the common and devastating critique from Yahwistic theology of other gods: they are nothing but idols made by human hands. Yahweh "made the heavens" (cf. Ps 8:4); he is the creator from whom all life and newness flows. The "heavens" lie beyond any human power to make.

I have read v 6 as expressing the great qualities of Yahweh's kingship as personifications, who attend him in the temple (cf. Pss 85:14; 89:15). The entourage of Yahweh is not made up of a company of lesser gods, who are in reality no gods, but of those "agents" of his own which are manifest in his saving work and wondrous deeds. Yahweh's escorts in v 6 are in keeping with his glory in v 3. For the ancient religious background of these verses, see Kraus, II, 837.

A call to praise Yahweh, who is coming to judge the earth (96:7–13). The wide scope of those who are summoned to praise Yahweh in vv 1–6 is extended in vv 7–13. The "families of the people/nations" (v 7) are urged to praise Yahweh and his kingship is to be proclaimed among the nations (v 10). Beyond the realm of strictly human affairs, however, the great components of creation are encouraged to be glad and rejoice before Yahweh (vv 11–13). "The creator of the world and the judge of the world has to be praised by the entire range of his lordship and his possessions" (Kraus, *Psalms 60–150*, 252).

"Families" (משפחות) is a difficult word to define in precise sociological terms, but in general it refers to the subdivisions of human society, basically the extended family, tribe, clan, etc.; subdivisions based on kinship and common interests (cf. N. K. Gottwald, *The Tribes of Yahweh* [Maryknoll, NY: Orbis Books, 1979] 257–70). The concept of "family" is sometimes extended to include the nation, the whole people as one enormous family (cf. Num 26:5–62; 1 Chr 1–9; Ezek 20:32; Zech 14:17–18). All the "families" of the world are urged to ascribe to Yahweh glory and mighty power (which means, of course, that they would not attribute these qualities to their gods) and to come with gifts of tribute to join in a great "bowing down" before Yahweh, who reigns as king over all creation (vv 7–10). Prostration before Yahweh in homage and adoration (already referred to in *Form/Structure/Setting* above) was probably a regular part of Israelite worship. Kraus (*Theology of the Psalms*, 91) surmises that "During festival weeks, bowing in prayer must have taken place again and again. In terms of the history of religion, this was comparable to the great throngs at prayer in Islam. In the course of the festival the clans and families probably took advantage several times of the opportunity to enter the temple and pray to the God who was present in the דביר ('inner sanctuary')." In Ps 96, the congregation is vastly extended to encompass the "families of the peoples," who are encouraged to bow in homage before Yahweh. The contrast with Ps 29:1–2 is often drawn, because there the heavenly beings are summoned by a worshiping congregation to give glory to Yahweh and to join them in praise of Yahweh (Craigie, 246).

V 10 contains three great affirmations: (1) Yahweh exercises the power of divine kingship; (2) the created world is immoveably fixed, having been made that way by Yahweh; (3) Yahweh will "judge" the peoples of the world with equity (for Yahweh's judgment of the nations, see Gen 15:14; 1 Sam 2:10; Pss 7:9; 9:9; 76:9; 110:6; Job 36:31). Yahweh's judgments "set things right," punishing the wicked and granting help and protection for the righteous (cf. Deut 32:36; Ps 135:14; Job 35:14; Dan 7:22 with Isa 3:13–14; Ps 50:4). Sovereignty, stability, and equity are the key concepts. Howard (*Structure*, 91–93) argues for v 10 as an independent unit in Ps 96, serving as a bridge between vv 1–9 and vv 11–13. He notes the parallel between the almost identical formulas in v 3a, "declare among the nations" and that in 10a, "say among the nations." Thus v 10 forms a frame for the material in vv 4–9, verses which exalt the greatness of Yahweh's majesty and power. At the same time, v 10 makes explicit the themes of Yahweh's kingship and prepares the way for his theophanic coming to judge the earth in vv 11–13, forming another frame or inclusion with v 13.

Vv 11–13 begin with a summons for cosmic rejoicing by the peoples of the nations as they bow in adoration before Yahweh, with the heavens, the earth, the sea, the fields, and the trees: "The elements of creation will join in celebration, just as the 'sons of God' shouted 'Glory!' in 29:10" (Brueggemann, 145). Creation is called to celebrate because the great king is coming to judge the world (v 13). The trees of the forest (in v 12) are singled out to shout for joy at the coming of Yahweh. Perhaps this is only an incidental feature of the natural world, but trees in temples seem to have been important in the ancient world (see *Comment*, Ps 52:10). The courts of the temple in Jerusalem probably had fine olive trees and cedars growing in them (see Pss 52:10; 92:13–15; note the "trees of Yahweh" in Ps 104:16–17; cf. Ps 84:4). In Isa 55:12 the "trees of the field" (עצי השדה) will clap their hands at the new exodus of the Israelites from exile into an Eden-like life (also note, of course, the trees in the garden in Gen 2 and see the description of the great tree in the "garden of God" in Ezek 31:1–9). Is it an accident that the trees will raise the herald's shout when Yahweh comes? Further, the association of trees with the temple and their special emphasis may be an indication that Yahweh's coming is thought of as a coming to the temple (cf. Mal 3:1).

Psalm 97

Bibliography

Jeremias, J. *Das Königtum Gottes in den Psalmen.* Göttingen: Vandenhoeck & Ruprecht, 1987. 136–43. ———. *Theophanie: Die Geschichte einer alttestamentlichen Gattung.* WMANT 10. Neukirchen-Vluyn: Neukirchener Verlag, 1977. 28–29, 192–93. **Kuntz, J. K.** *The Self-Revelation of God.* Philadelphia: Westminster, 1967. 203–14

Translation

1[a]	*Yahweh reigns![b] Let the earth be jubilant;*	(4+3)
	let the many islands[c] rejoice!	
2	*Clouds and darkness surround him;*	(3+4)
	righteousness and justice are the foundation of his throne.	
3	*Fire goes before him*	(3+3)
	and burns up his foes[a] all around.[b]	
4	*His lightning flashes lit up the world;*	(3+3)
	the earth saw and writhed.[a]	
5	*The mountains melted away like wax*	(3+2+3)
	from before[a] Yahweh,[b]	
	from before the Lord of all the earth.	
6	*The heavens proclaimed his righteousness,*	(3+3)
	and all the peoples his glory.	
7	*All who served images were put to shame—*	(3+3+3)
	the ones who boasted in mere idols[a]—	
	even all the gods bowed down to him![b]	
8	*Zion heard and rejoiced,*	(3+3+3)
	the daughters of Judah were jubilant	
	because of your judgments, O Yahweh.	
9	*For you, O Yahweh, are (God) Most High over all the earth,*	(4+3)
	exalted far[a] above all gods.	
10	*You lovers of Yahweh, hate evil![a]*	(4+3+3)
	He[b] protects the lives of his loyal ones;	
	he will deliver them from the hand of the wicked.	
11	*Light shines out[a] for the righteous,*	(3+3)
	and rejoicing for the upright in heart.	
12	*Rejoice, you righteous ones, in Yahweh,*	(3+3)
	and give thanks to his holy name![a]	

Notes

1.a. LXX has a title: Τῷ Δαυιδ, ὅ ὅτε ἡ γη̑ αὐτοῦ καθίσταται, "For David, when his land is established."

1.b. See n. 93:1.a.

1.c. Or, "shores/coastlands." The אײם may have been most directly the islands and shores of the Mediterranean Sea, including the coastland of Europe and Northern Africa. In figurative language, however, the meaning is that of remote areas and nations, distant shores at the limits of the earth (cf. Isa 40:15; 41:5; 49:1; 66:19; Jer 31:10. NEB and REB have "let coasts and islands all rejoice."

3.a. Dahood (II, 361) translates 3b as "and blazes around his back," taking צריו, as cognate to Ugar. zr, "back." Howard (*Structure*, 97) suggests the further possibility that צר might be taken as a preposition (since Ugar. zr can be a preposition, "top/above," with an earlier idea of "the back"): "and blazes round behind him." Howard notes that the parallelism seems to be improved with these suggestions, but refrains from adopting either, recognizing that the parallelism may be supplementary rather than synonymous. Kraus (II, 839) rejects the emendation of Duhm to לצעדיו, "to his steps": "and (fire) blazes about his steps."

3.b. *BHS* indicates minor ms evidence for סביביו, "around him," which would ease the text a bit. As Howard (*Structure*, 97) observes, however, the pronoun is implicit with סביב without a suffix.

4.a. Hiphil impf. from חול, "whirl/writhe in travail," as at birth.

5.a. As noted in n. 96:9.b., there is a difference in nuance, at least, between מלפני and לפני. "Before," with the implication of moving away from Yahweh, should probably be retained, though the difference is slight.

5.b. Kraus' recommendation (II, 839) to omit מלפני יהוה on stichometric grounds should be rejected (cf. Howard, 97–98). The identity of the "Lord of all the earth" is important.

7.a. For אלילים, see n. 96:5.a. LXX has in 97:7 "idols" rather than "demons" (or, "gods").

7.b. The verb השתחוו is usually taken as hithpael impv. (e.g., JB, NEB, NIV, Dahood) rather than as indicative (e.g., NJV; Howard, 98; Delitzsch, III, 95; RSV). The forms of the verb are the same, and the imperative reading may be correct. It would be: "Bow down to him, all you gods." Howard notes that it seems somewhat anomalous for an imperative to appear in the midst of a run of indicative verbs, though it is possible that יבשו in 7a is a jussive (as in Dahood, II, 360; NEB, REB; cf. JB): "Let all who serve images be put to shame." More probably יבשו is indicative, and the point is that all who serve and boast in idols were put to shame because all the gods, including those represented by idols, submitted to Yahweh. LXX reads "all you his angels" rather than "gods"—possibly a change made to avoid the tension between calling the idols and gods "nothings" in 7b and "gods" in 7c (cf. Briggs, II, 306, who does not deal with LXX, however), but more probably as in Ps 8:6 where LXX uses "angels" for אלהים; with little difference between "angels" and "gods" in the generic sense of "divine beings."

9.a. Howard (*Structure*, 99–100) treats מאד as a divine title in direct address: "O Mighty One." Dahood (III, 59, 109, 184, 318, 336) reads מאד, repointed to מָאֵד, as a stative adjective, "the Grand One," in Pss 105:24; 109:30; 119:8, 96, 138; 142:7; 145:3, but he does not in 97:9. Howard notes that a second divine title would argue against deletion of "Yahweh" in 9a (as some propose for metrical reasons; so Kraus, II, 839) because the two would be in parallel. He observes, however, that it could still be argued that the deletion of "Yahweh" would yield balanced colons if each colon is subdivided before the prepositional phrases introduced by על: "For you are the Most High / above all the earth / O Mighty One (מאד) you are exalted / above all gods." Howard retains "Yahweh," however, on the basis of (1) stylistic variation for emphasis and (2) an observation of D. N. Freedman that a pattern of extrametrical occurrence of "Yahweh" is not uncommon (e.g., Lam 5:1a, 19a, 21a). Thus the treating of מאד as a divine title does not really help the metrical situation in v 9. This, plus the repointing required without versional support, combined with no particular difficulty in the usage of מאד as an adverb indicates that it is better not to read it as a divine title and not to delete "Yahweh" (cf. 5.b.).

10.a. Gunkel (426), Kraus (II, 839), and others, insist that the context does not allow the reading, "O lovers of Yahweh, hate evil." They insist that Yahweh must be the subject of the verb "love" and thus change אהבי, "lovers of," to אהב, participle, "one who loves." This necessitates, of course, the change of the imperative שנאו, "hate," to שנאי, "haters of": "Yahweh loves the haters of evil" (as in RSV, etc.; not, however, in KJV, NIV, and NJV). These are relatively minor text changes and they provide a smoother agreement between 10a and the following colons. However, LXX agrees with MT, and MT does not present any extreme difficulty. Howard (*Structure*, 101) retains MT and notes the structural parallel between 10a and 12a, in that both contain imperatives addressed to supporters of Yahweh and Yahweh's name occurs in both, though with different syntactic functions. Vv 10a and 12a form a frame around 10bc and 11ab, and bracket off the final part of the psalm. Yahweh is no longer being addressed in these verses, as in v 9. I suspect that 12b functions as the conclusion to the entire psalm and v 12 may find a parallelistic correspondence to 96:1–3, binding the two psalms together, at least loosely.

10.b. The expected personal pronoun as subject is understood (see GKC 116x).

11.a. Reading זרח for זרע, "is sown," with some ms and versional support (see *BHS*). The imagery of light being "sown" (even "strewn along the life way of the righteous," as in Delitzsch, III, 96) is odd. J. K. Kuntz (*Self-Revelation*, 206, n. 66) notes the lack of any MT parallel in which אור and זרע are connected, while זרח and אור are correlated in such references as Ps 112:4. The change to זרח yields a picture similar to Ps 112:4: "Light dawns / rises in the dark for the upright," a colon which is similar to Isa 58:10 (see Allen, 94, n. 4.a).

Dahood (II, 362, I, 222) proposes an alternative interpretation, reading אור, "light," as "field" (esp. in such passages as Isa 26:19 and Ps 56:14): "A sown field awaits the just." The reading rests on too much conjecture (for critique, see Howard, *Structure*, 102, and Craigie, 292).

12.a. Lit., "for the memorial/remembrance of his holiness," or, "for his holy memorial." The "memorial" (זכר) is frequently taken as equal to "name" (note BDB, 271), as in Exod 3:15; Ps 135:13. B. S. Childs (*Memory and Tradition* [Naperville, IL: Allenson, 1962] 71) argues that שם refers to the name of Yahweh which is spoken while זכר refers to the act of utterance in cultic worship (noting the lack of distinction in meaning in Prov 10:7; Hos 12:6; see also, Allen, 223, n. 13.a; H. Eising, *TDOT*, IV, 76–77;

Job 18:17). This interpretation has been widely adopted by commentators and translations (as in Ps 30:5). For זכר in a wider sense of remembrance or proclamation (Childs, 72; Eising, 77), see Pss 111:4; 145:7.

Comment

This psalm has a hymnic form, setting forth descriptive praise of Yahweh. V 8 suggests that we have a victory song, celebrating a victory by the Divine Warrior-King over those who worship idols and gods. The change of style at v 10 is obvious; the righteous "lovers of Yahweh" are addressed and given assurance in vv 10–12. Vv 1–9 are focused on Yahweh and his majesty. A break may occur in vv 1–9 at v 7, where the subject matter shifts. Howard (*Structure,* 104) proposes a minor break at v 4, because a series of suffixed verbs starts at that point, and there seems to be a temporal distinction between the continued description of Yahweh in vv 1–3 and the theophany described in vv 4–6. Vv 8–9 are addressed directly to Yahweh and can be considered as a separate section of vv 1–9. Thus a fivefold division of the psalm results: 1–3, 4–6, 7, 8–9, 10–12, with v 7 as the central verse. However, this analysis may be too artificial and suggests too much independence for the subsections (Howard, 104). Thus it seems better to work with two main sections: 1–9 and 10–12 (Howard, 105–6, prefers three: 1–6, 7–9, 10–12; Kraus, II, 840, has 1–2, 3–6, 7–9, 10–12; Kuntz, *Self-Revelation,* 206–8, argues for two strophes each of six verses: 1–6, 7–12, with the theophany itself in vv 1–6 and the effects of the theophany in 7–12).

The exaltation of Yahweh's divine kingship (97:1–9). This section of the psalm is focused on the exalted position of Yahweh above the earth and all other gods. He reigns from a great throne sustained by righteousness and justice (vv 1–3). All the world should join in homage and praise of his kingship (Kraus, II, 841). The "islands" or "distant shores" (see note 1.c.) enhance the universal scope of his reign. His throne is supported by those qualities of right order and justice which should characterize the nature of all true kingship (Anderson, II, 687; cf. Ps 89:15 and see *Comment* on this verse; also H. H. Schmid, *Gerechtigkeit als Weltordnung,* BHT 40 [Tübingen: Mohr, 1968] 76, 80). The order which sustains the world is that which supports the throne of Yahweh. Roiling storm clouds surround the divine throne of Yahweh and a vanguard of fire which devours his foes goes before him (v 3). Vv 2 and 3 prepare the reader for the account of theophanic activity which follows in vv 4–5 (cf. Kuntz, 207, 211). For fire in theophanic accounts, see Exod 19:18; 24:17; Pss 18:9, 13, 14; 50:3; Ezek 1:4, 13, 27.

In the account of Yahweh's theophanic activity in vv 4–5 there is a mixture of thunderstorm and earthquake imagery. Lightning flashes light up the world as it writhes, convulsed before the coming presence of the lord of all the earth. The mountains, renowned for stability, melt like wax before the fiery descent of Yahweh. These are characteristic elements of theophanic descriptions: see Exod 19:16–20; 24:10, 16–17; Deut 5:4; 9:10, 15; Pss 18:8–16; 50:3; Hab 3:3–12 (for the burning of foes, see 68:2; 106:18; Isa 42:25; for 4a see 77:19; for 4b see 77:17; Hab 3:10). I take the verbs in vv 4–8 as conveying past tense and as a descriptive account of Yahweh's past theophanic activity rather than being a directly eschatological anticipation of a future theophany (Kraus). There is an eschatological element in the kingship psalms, but it is an implied element: the faithful community of Yahweh waits in expectation of a new coming, or a new extension of the past into the future.

We need not try to fix the action in vv 4–8 in some historical context, though it seems rather evident that the description is most evocative of Exod 19 and Hab 3 (nor should we assume that the primary reference is to a dramatic presentation of Yahweh's appearance in the cult; even if there was such, it was not primary). We should not literalize the highly metaphorical language, nor should we try to reduce the poetry to a banal prose description. The modus operandi of Yahweh's intervention in worldly affairs is being described in high poetic fashion. The portrayal is composite, a mosaic of theophanic history (cf. Nah 1:3–6), and it is doubtful that we should limit it to an extension of Sinaitic imagery (as, e.g., Kuntz, 211–12).

Vv 6–8 describe the results and the response to the theophany in vv 4–5. The heavens became heralds of Yahweh and proclaimed his righteousness and glory to all peoples (v 6). It is well to remember that "righteousness" here refers to divine acts of victory and of putting things in right order (cf. *Explanation*, Ps 71). For "glory," see *Comment*, Ps 96:1–6. Cf. Isa 40:5. The result is a putting to shame of those who boast in "mere idols," leaving exposed the nature of the gods the idols represent. The gods joined the worshipers of Yahweh in bowing before him in homage and adoration (v 7). Cf. Isa 42:17; 45:16. "Yahweh's appearance in glory puts an end to all religious trafficking" (Kraus, *Psalms 60–150*, 260). The verb בוש, "put to shame," connotes humiliation by the failure of a human endeavor, the ridicule or disgrace that follows the failing result of something undertaken. The verb carries ideas of humiliation, ridicule, dishonor, and loss of face. The worshipers of "mere idols" receive no help from the useless gods represented by the idols (see 96:5; cf. Pss 25:3; 37:18–19; Isa 1:29; 44:9–11, 14–20; 45:16; 46:1–7; Jer 10:6–10, 14–16; for 7c, cf. Ps 29:1).

The impact of Yahweh's intervention goes beyond the heavens and the worshipers of other gods. Zion and the towns of Judah (lit., "daughters of Judah," for "daughters of" in the sense of towns, see Josh 15:45 ["Ekron with its towns and villages (lit., "daughters and villages")]; also Josh 15:46, 47; Num 32:42; Josh 17:11, 16; etc.) rejoice because of the "judgments" of Yahweh (cf. Ps 48:12). The "judgments" (משפטים) in v 8 are not defined, but it is safe to assume that the reference is to actions which overthrow hostile powers, deliver, and keep safe the people of Yahweh (cf. Ps 48:12–15). V 9 concludes the first major section of the psalm (vv 1–9) with a direct address to Yahweh which expresses his exaltation above all other gods. The lord of all the earth (v 5) is also the lord of the heavenly realm (note the correlation of 9c with 7c). Yahweh is called the Most High (עליון; see Ps 92:2b).

Encouragement for those devoted to Yahweh (97:10–12). This section is an exhortation, with sermonic-like content addressed to those who worship Yahweh. The speaker is not identified, of course, but one can think of a priest or prophet during festival times, or of a teacher in the wisdom traditions (cf. Howard, *Structure*, 106). Those who are wise and fear God "hate evil" (see Prov 8:13). The righteous are assured that the light of Yahweh shines out (or, is "sown," see note 11.a.) for them in their present darkness. There is reason for rejoicing though they wait for a fuller demonstration of Yahweh's kingship and "they still live in a world in which wickedness and oppression prevail" (Weiser, 635).

The whole psalm finds its raison d'être in these verses; indeed, this includes Ps 96 as well. The exaltation of Yahweh's kingship and the summons to praise are aimed at the strengthening of the worshiping community. Vv 10–12 would have been appropriate in almost any period of Israel's history, but a setting in exilic and post-exilic communities is most persuasive. These were the "lovers of Yahweh," who no longer had the protection of a Davidic king in Jerusalem, but they have the assurance that the "Great King above all Gods" (Ps 95:3) reigns and cares for his own. In my opinion, the universal aspects of these psalms is secondary to their purpose of encouraging and empowering the people of Yahweh. Surrounded by great world powers, the "lovers of Yahweh" may lift up their hearts because he reigns as king over the whole world, and all gods, all peoples, and all created things have been summoned to pay him homage and praise. Let the "lovers of Yahweh" hate evil and sing a new song! (For those who "love" Yahweh, cf. Pss 31:24; 116:1; 119:47, 48, 97, etc.; Deut 6:5; 10:12; 11:13, 22; 19:9; 30:6, 16; Josh 22:5; 23:11). The "lovers of Yahweh" are those who are committed to him in faithfulness and who love his commandments. They are people of pure devotion and genuine obedience (see *Comment*, Ps 69:37).

The question of what sort of actual happenings are reflected in the descriptive language of the theophanic accounts arises repeatedly. Especially, how was theophany enacted in worship? (For discussion, see Kuntz, *Self-Revelation*, 215–31; Kraus, *Psalms 1–59*, 70–71, 490–91; idem, *Theology of the Psalms*, 84–100; Jeremias, *IDBSup*, 896–98). The actual proceedings of theophanic actualization in Israelite worship are not described anywhere in biblical literature and must be inferred from the content of the literature itself (Kuntz, 223). In fact, this is true for most aspects of Israelite worship, though there are bits and pieces of information scattered about in the OT, and there are some analogues in the nonbiblical literature of the ancient Near East, as well as in the history of religion in general. Perhaps it is well to think in terms of theophanic "moments," times of disclosure, when the divine presence was perceived and experienced with special intensity. These "moments" probably occurred on different occasions and in different contexts. The content of OT texts indicates an unpredictable nature regarding the coming and appearances of Yahweh. Kraus (*Psalms 1–59*, 70–71) argues for a charismatic element in theophanic experiences: "The element in the cultus corresponding to Yahweh's freedom is the charisma. A congregation that has to ask for Yahweh's appearances (Pss 80:1; 94:1) does not control the theophany." Thus Yahweh's appearances could not be pre-programmed. However, this does not rule out liturgical action designed to expedite the perception and experience of the divine presence. Yahweh's appearances could not be programmed, but they could be prepared for and anticipated.

The prevalence of meteorological phenomena in theophanic accounts (e.g., Judg 5:4–5; Pss 18:7–15; 97:1–5; 144:5–6; Isa 19:1; 64:1–3; Mic 1:3–4; Nah 1:3–5), such as clouds, thunder, lightning, hail, wind—enhanced by fire and earthquake phenomena—suggest that on some occasions thunderstorms provided theophanic moments (cf. Ps 29). These may have happened in conjunction with historical events, especially during battles, or during festival times. One can imagine the impact of a fierce storm at some climactic moment of a festival. Many scholars have assumed that theophanic moments occurred in connection with the movement of the ark to the temple. If we use our imagination, we can envision people moving in a large procession to the temple area, following the ark, with some ahead and some behind. There would have been singing and chanting of psalms by the people and their leaders, with shouts of exultation, horn blowing, and ecstatic dancing—perhaps with a counter theme of cries of lamentation and woe. With shouts and horn blowing the ark was put in the holy of holies (cf. Ps 47:6–10) and the crowd of worshipers bowed low before the invisible deity enthroned above the cherubim over the ark; surely a theophanic moment.

Theophanic moments are likely to have been provided by various other liturgical procedures. The blowing of the שׁוֹפָר ("ram's horn") was an indicator of the nearness or actual voice of the deity at climactic times during cultic meetings (Kuntz, *Self-Revelation*, 227). The actual killing of an animal during a sacrificial rite was almost certainly an intense event carried out in a charged atmosphere with a sense of being in holy presence (cf. Gen 4:107; 15; Exod 24). The sacrificial moment was always a potential theophanic moment, doubtless enhanced by fire and a column of smoke from the altar and a cloud of incense, accompanied by the blowing of the *shophar* and the chanting of priests and people (cf. Isa 6). Possibly there were dramatic enactments of Yahweh's battles of the Divine Warrior with his foes, followed by victory songs and theophanic testimony.

Two other potential theophanic moments are worth mentioning. First, proclamation of the name of Yahweh and his message by a priest-prophet at a critical point in a service of worship may have activated the reality of divine presence (cf. Weiser, 30–33). Kraus, *Psalms 1–59*, 490, commenting on Pss 50; 81; 95, says, "At the center of things there is always a speech by Yahweh which represents the seriousness and force of a judicial pronouncement." These speeches were doubtless delivered by priest-prophets and are likely to have encompassed more than judicial pronouncements; probably recalling the great saving acts of Yahweh in Israel's history, with his judgments, and including messages of comfort and assurance, depending on the circumstances. Psalms as well were recited. Theophanic moments were doubtless word-events on some occasions at least.

Second, times of silence would have been fertile times of theophany (cf. the famous account of Elijah of 1 Kgs 19:9–14; Hab 2:20; Zeph 1:7; Zech 2:17[13]):

> But Yahweh is in his holy temple;
>> let all the earth keep silence before him.
>>> (Hab 2:20, RSV)

> Be silent before the Lord God!
>> For the day of the LORD is at hand;
> the LORD has prepared a sacrifice
>> and consecrated his guests.
>>> (Zeph 1:7, RSV)

> Be silent, all flesh, before the LORD,
>> for he has roused himself
>> from his holy dwelling.
>>> (Zech 2:17[13], RSV)

All these texts are found in contexts which contain the mention of a theophany. The texts in Hab 2:20; Zeph 1:7; Zech 2:17 seek a completeness and scope of response similar to that in Pss 96–98. One can think of the impact of a time of quiet during festival celebrations, following noisy and exuberant shouting, chanting, and singing of praise. In the stillness which settled across the throng of people near the temple, perhaps called for by the priests with summons like those quoted above, we can imagine the sound of the *shophar* breaking into the silence, followed by Levitical priests and people chanting such psalms as 96–99—

> Yahweh reigns!
> Sing a new song to Yahweh;
> sing to Yahweh, all the earth!

—followed by a prophet speaking as the voice of Yahweh: "This is what Yahweh says, . . ." Then the whole earth must have seemed filled with the glory of God.

Psalm 98

Bibliography

Longman, T., III. "Psalm 98: A Divine Warrior Victory Song." *JETS* 27 (1984) 267–74.

Translation

1   A psalm.[a]
    Sing to Yahweh a new song—   (4+2+3+2)
      for he has done wondrous works;[b]
      his right hand has brought him victory,[c]
      even[d] as has his holy arm.

2   *Yahweh has made known his saving-work;*   (3+2+2)
    to the eyes of the nations,
    he has revealed his righteousness.[a]

3   *He has remembered his loyal-love (for)[a]*   (2[3]+3+3+3)
    and his faithfulness to the house of Israel.
    All the ends of the earth have seen[b]
    the saving-work of our God.

4   *Raise a shout[a] to Yahweh, all the earth;*   (3+3)
    break forth,[b] shout joyfully, sing praise!

5   *Sing praise to Yahweh with the harp,*   (3+3)
    with harp and the sound of song,

6   *with trumpets and the sound of the horn.[a]*   (3+4)
  Raise a shout before the King, Yahweh![b]

7   *Let the sea and all within it resound;*   (3+2)
    the world and those who dwell in it.[a]

8   *Let the rivers[a] clap their hands;[b]*   (3+3)
    let the mountains shout in unison[c]

9   *before Yahweh for he is coming,[a]*   (3+2[3]+3+2)
    (for he is coming) to judge the earth.
  He will judge the world with righteousness
    and its peoples with equity.

Notes

1.a. For מזמור, see n. 51:1.a. LXX adds "to David."

1.b. LXX adds ὁ κύριος, "the Lord," to this colon, which gives it a better balance with the first and third colons.

1.c. Hiphil perf. of ישע, "deliver/save/liberate." The "brought him victory" reflects the divine warrior concept (as in Longman, *JETS* 27 [1984] 268).

1.d. Emphatic *waw* attached to "arm" (Howard, *Structure,* 109; cf. Dahood, III, 401–2). Dahood (II, 365) notes that זרוע, "arm," can share the suffix with ימינו, "his right hand," or function without a suffix as a part of the body, as does כף, "palm(s)/hand(s)" in v 8.

2.a. Reading as tricolon or pivot pattern (Longman, *JETS* 27 [1984] 268). Howard (*Structure,* 109–10) also prefers the three-colon division on the basis of a slightly better syllabic balance and an emphasis on "to the eyes of the nations" as modifying both the preceding and following statements. However, a 3+4 structure would not be seriously out of balance, as, e.g., in RSV.

3.a. LXX adds "for Jacob." Dahood (II, 365) reads the verbs from v 3 to v 6 as imperatives: "Remember . . . see . . . sing, etc." Howard (110) notes that there is nothing in theory to exclude this (except re-vocalizing two verbs and reading a vocative *lamedh* attached to the "house of Israel"), but he argues that the context does not demand a departure from the traditional reading and is supported by LXX. See *Comment.*

3.b. There is some ms and versional support for ראו (see *BHS*): "And (*or,* "Even," if emphatic) all the ends of the earth have seen."

4.a. Hiphil impv. of רוע, "raise a shout" or "shout in praise" (cf. Pss 47:2; 66:1; 81:2; 95:1, 2; 100:1, Isa 44:23). Related to the noun, תרועה, "cultic shout/alarm for war."

4.b. The root פצח always occurs with רנן or רנה, "ringing cry/shout of joy," and means to "break out in a glad song" (Howard; cf. Isa 14:7; 44:23; 49:13; 52:9; 54:1; 55:12.

6.a. The "trumpets" (חצצרות) were metal instruments of either bronze or silver. The tone was probably high with a limited range of four or five notes. See Num 10:2–10; 2 Kgs 12:14; 2 Chr 5:12–13. "Harp," כנור, was more properly a lyre (with equal length strings; unlike a harp), a rectangular or trapezoid-shaped stringed instrument, portable and used to accompany singing. It was a popular instrument throughout the ancient Near East. The "horn" is the widely referred to שׁפר, *shophar,* with a curved, conical shape made from the horns of wild goats or rams, capable of two or three notes and mostly used for signaling (cf., e.g., Judg 3:27; 6:34; Neh 4:18–20; 1 Kgs 1:34; 2 Kgs 9:13; Isa 27:13). Its theophanic use to signal the divine presence is well known from the famous reference in Exod 19:16, 19; see also Ps 47:6; Joel 2:1; Zech 9:14; Zeph 1:14–16.

6.b. "Yahweh" should not be omitted on metrical grounds (as *BHS* suggests). The extrametrical occurrence of "Yahweh" is not uncommon (see Howard's reference to Freedman, 100, and note 97:9.a.

7.a. Some Greek texts have πάντες = כל: "all who dwell . . ." Cf. Ps 24:1. See *BHS;* cf. Craigie, 210, note 1.b.

8.a. The word נהרות is often read as "floods" (which goes back at least to Luther; see Delitzsch, III, 98), with the idea that there is allusion to the primeval waters. Dahood (II, 364) has "ocean currents." Cohen (321) thinks that the colon is "descriptive of the crashing of the waves on the shore," but there is probably no reason to assume anything but rivers and streams. Delitzsch thinks of high waves cast up by rivers flowing into one another like clapping hands.

8.b. The verb מחא, "strike," occurs in qal only here and in Isa 55:12, there with כף ("palm/hand") also: "and all the trees of the field will clap palm(s)." כף appears with תקע, "thrust/clap," in Ps 47:2 and with נכה, "smite/strike," in 2 Kgs 11:12; with ספק / סֹפק, "slap/clap," in Num 24:10 (in anger) and in Job 27:23 (in mockery). The piel of מחא with יד ("hand") is found in Ezek 26:6.

8.c. LXX has the "together" (ἐπὶ τὸ αὐτό) with the clapping of hands by the rivers: "The rivers will clap their hands together." MT uses יחד adverbially with 8b: "unitedly/all together/in unison." Cf. Job 38:7: ברן־יחד כוכבי בקר, "when the morning stars sang together."

9.a. This verse is the same as 96:13, except that כי בא occurs only once and באמונתו, "in his faithfulness" occurs in 96:13 and במישׁרים, "with equity," occurs in 98:9. Codex Alexandrinus has the "he comes" twice and it is often added here (e.g., Kraus, II, 845), explaining its loss by haplography (Howard, *Structure,* 111). The colons are also balanced better with the second כי בא, and Howard calls attention to the stylistic "stairstep" pattern of repetition created by שׁפט שׁפט בא כי בא כי (a pattern he also notes in vv 4b–5b: הריע פצח רנן זמר זמר כנור כנור הצצרות קול שׁופר הריע).

Comment

This psalm is another hymn which praises Yahweh's kingship. It has much in common with Ps 96. The two psalms are close in structure, vocabulary, and thematic elements (Howard, *Structure,* 179). Westermann (*Praise and Lament,* 148) says, "Psalm 98 almost seems to be a variant of Ps 96." The one-word title marks off Pss 98–99 as the second pair of psalms in Pss 96–99.

A call to praise Yahweh and to celebrate his wondrous works (98:1–6). This section seems to have an envelope construction in which the summons to praise is interrupted after 1a and resumed in v 4. Thus 1a and vv 4–6 surround a central core in 1b–3, which provides the basis for the call for a "new song" (for "new song," see *Comment* on 96:1–6). The "new song" should recall Yahweh's saving works, which have revealed his "righteousness" to the nations and his enduring love and faithfulness toward his own people in Israel. An element of Yahweh as the Divine Warrior is revealed in 1cd: he has won victories with his "right hand" and by means of "his holy arm" (see Pss 44:4; 89:14; Isa 52:10). He has not required human assistance, but has done the powerful deeds himself and won his own victories.

Longman contends that Ps 98 is a Divine Warrior victory song, "celebrating the return of Yahweh the commander of the heavenly hosts" (*JETS* 27 [1984] 267). Divine Warrior language is evident and the style of the psalm is that of a hymn of triumph, similar to that of those which follow the successful completion of Yahweh's action in war (cf. Judg 5:4–5; Deut 33:2–5, 26–29; Pss 46:7; 68:8–9; 77:17–20; 114:3–6; Nah 1:2–8; Hab 3:3–15; Jeremias, *IDBSup,* 898). Ps 98 has no specific historical reference, however (as Longman, 272, notes) and should not be forced into the mold of the exodus or the restoration from exile, or any other specific historical context. The psalm encompasses the whole range of Yahweh's victories. The descriptions are characteristic of his actions as the Divine Warrior.

The powerful arm and right hand of Yahweh is a thematic element which may find its earliest expression in OT literature in Exod 15:6, 12, 16; cf. Ps 118:15–16; Deut 33:2; Ps 78:54 (Ollenburger, *Zion,* 89). The victories have been totally Yahweh's:

> Thy right hand, O Lord, glorious in power,
>   thy right hand, O Lord, shatters the enemy. . . .
> Thou didst stretch out thy right hand,
>   the earth swallowed them.
>   (Exod 15:6, 12, rsv)

Yahweh is Israel's great Warrior-King who has done his great works before the whole world (vv 2bc, 3cd). He has "remembered" his commitments and obligations to Israel (v 3); that is, he has been actively involved in the implementation of his commitments (cf. B. S. Childs, *Memory and Tradition in Israel,* SBT 37 [Naperville, IL: Allenson, 1962] 41–42). Childs' summary of remembering on the part of God is found on pp. 33, 34: "Memory is not identical with the action, but it is never divorced from it. . . . God's remembering always implies his movement toward the object of his memory."

Vv 4–6 form a subsection of the larger composition in vv 1–6. The language suggests a congregation at festival time being urged to shout and sing praise to Yahweh accompanied by musical instruments, except that the call is extended to "all the earth" (v 4). The verses call for acclamation before King Yahweh, who is coming in a worldwide manifestation of his salvation and judgment. He has already demonstrated the nature of his work in his saving-work for Israel, which has been carried out before the eyes of the nations (vv 3–4). There is no secret about it, "all the ends of the earth" have already seen it, but the climactic denouement of his works is at hand. The enthusiasm of Israelite worship is illustrated in this passage. Shouts are raised, praises chanted and sung, while musical instruments are played and horns blown. The noise of temple worship was legendary (see 2 Chr 29:25–30; Ezra 3:10–13; 1 Esdr 5:59–66).

A call for nature to acclaim Yahweh, who is coming to judge the world (98:7–9). These verses are very similar to 96:11–13 and function in a similar way in this psalm. The "new song" (v 1) encompasses the coming of Yahweh for a new judgment of the world and those who dwell in it. The reign of Yahweh will establish right order and equity in the world.

Psalm 99

Bibliography

Eaton, J. H. "Proposals in Psalms XCIX and CXIX." *VT* 18 (1968) 555–58. **Jeremias, J.** *Das Königtum Gottes in den Psalmen.* Göttingen: Vandenhoeck & Ruprecht, 1987. 114–21. **Whitley, C. F.** "Psalm 99:8." *ZAW* 85 (1973) 227–30. **Whybray, R. N.** "'Their Wrongdoings' in Psalm 99:8" *ZAW* 81 (1969) 237–39.

Translation

1[a]	*Yahweh reigns!*[b] *Let the people tremble!*	(4+4)
	(Before) the Cherubim-enthroned-One,[c] *let the earth quake!*[d]	
2	*Yahweh in Zion is the Great One,*	(3+3)
	and exalted over all peoples.[a]	
3	*Let them praise your name, O Great and Awesome One*[a] —	(4+2)
	Holy is it![b]—	
4	*and the might of the King who loves justice.*[a]	(4+3+3+2)
	You have established[b] *equity;*	
	(deeds) of justice and (acts of) righteousness[c] *in Jacob*	
	you have done.	
5	*Exalt Yahweh our God;*	(3+3+2)
	bow down at[a] *his footstool*[b]—	
	Holy is he!	
6	*Moses and Aaron were among his priests,*[a]	(3+3+2+2)
	Samuel also was among those who called on his name,	
	they were ones who would call on Yahweh,	
	and he would answer them!	

7   *From^a the pillar of cloud he spoke to them;*   (4+4)
     they obeyed his commands and the decrees he gave them.

8   *O Yahweh our God, you answered them;*   (4+3+3)
     you were a forgiving God to them,
     though punishing their wrongdoings.^a

9   *Exalt Yahweh our God;*   (3+3+3)
     bow down at^a his holy mountain.
     For holy is Yahweh our God.

Notes

1.a. LXX has the title, "a psalm to David," as in the case of Ps 98.

1.b. See n. 93:1.a.

1.c. Most translations understand the statement in v 1b as declarative: e.g., RSV, "He sits enthroned upon the cherubim, . . ." This may be correct, but I have chosen to follow LXX and Howard (*Structure*, 117–18), Johnson (*Sacral Kingship*, 62), and NJV, and understand the expression ישב כרובים as a divine title, which in its complete form would be יהוה ישב כרובים ("Yahweh—who sits-on-Cherubim"). The title is split in 99:1 between 1a and 1b for poetic reasons. Schmid (*ZAW* 67 [1955] 186) refers to ישב כרובים as "*Kerubenthroner*."

1.d. I have translated the verbs in this verse as jussive, which is common. However, they may be indicative and the statements declarative: "Yahweh reigns! The peoples tremble; / he sits [on the] cherubim, the earth quakes" (with Weiser, 640; Kraus, II, 850; Delitzsch, III, 99; NJV). B. C. Ollenburger, *Zion*, 185, n. 158, agrees with Kraus. He also notes that the verb נוט, which is *hapax* in Hebrew, probably has parallels in Ugar., possibly in the restored text of UT 51.7.34–35, "the high places of the earth quaked" (*tttn*), also in the by-form *ntt*, "to wobble," or "leaped/stamped," in dismay or alarm upon receiving news (see Dahood, II, 368; Driver, *Canaanite Myths and Legends* [Edinburgh: Clark, 1956] 157).

2.a. Dahood (II, 368) reads עמים as "the strong ones," a term for pagan deities, but his arguments are rather weak as Howard (*Structure*, 119) observes. Ollenburger (*Zion*, 185, n. 159) adopts the reading אלהים with some mss and versional support (see *BHS*, which also cites Pss 95:3; 96:4; 97:9). "Gods" is an acceptable reading; however, in the three references cited there is a comparative element: Yahweh is greater than all other gods. In 99:2, the matter is positional: he has an exalted position from which he reigns over all the peoples. It is these peoples who are called to praise Yahweh in v 3 (and "peoples" is the subject of the verb [F. Crüsemann, *Studien zur Formgeschichte*, 185, n. 1, who cites Ps 66:3b–4 as similar in content]). Therefore, I prefer to keep "peoples."

3.a. Usually read as attributive adjectives modifying "name": "your great and awesome name," or, more probably: "your name, great and awesome." The translation above treats the words as titles of Yahweh, with Dahood (II, 369) and Howard (120; for different reasons than Dahood's). This treatment strengthens the parallel with 1b (Dahood), the "Cherubim-enthroned-One," and relates well to the second-person address in 4b. For נורא as a divine title, see Exod 15:11; Ps 68:36; cf. Ps 89:8.

3.b. The translation follows Howard (*Structure*, 120–21), assuming that the direct address continues with the pronoun referring to Yahweh's name. The usual preference is to read "Holy is he," as in 5c, where the referent is Yahweh.

4.a. This is a very difficult colon to read with any assurance. Variations in interpretation are too numerous for complete discussion. KJV ("The king's strength also loveth judgment") follows a tradition in LXX, Jerome, Peshitta, and Aquila, but is unlikely to be correct with עז as the subject of the verb אהב (Eaton, *VT* 18 [1968] 555). RSV ("Mighty King, lover of justice") follows Gunkel (431) in transposing (מלך עז) and reading with 3b: "he is holy and a mighty King." Kraus (II, 850) prefers וְעֹז מֶלֶךְ, "a strong one is King (or reigns)! He loves justice!" Eaton (556) seeks refuge in an Arabic root *wa 'aqa*, "he commanded," and thus argues for a rare survival of initial *waw* as a radical, giving the root עוז (cf. BDB, 418), "command." His translation is: "O thou that commandest kingship and lovest just rule" (understanding מלך as "kingship," parallel to משפט). NEB has "he is holy, he is mighty / a king who loves justice" (reading ועז with הוא קדוש in 3b). Howard (*Structure*, 121) maintains that עז is a divine title (similar to Kraus, but without repointing), treating the *waw* as emphatic, with the עז meaning "Strong One" or "Victorious One" (on עז as "victory," see Dahood, I, 180, on Ps 29:11; cf. Craigie, 243, n. 11.a, who translates the עז in 29:11 as "protection," taking it as a homonym from the root עוז and the sense "strength" from the root עזז). Howard translates: "Indeed, the Victorious One is King! He loves justice!" I assume that one could follow Craigie (whose argument seems better for Ps 29:11) and read "Indeed, the Protector is King, he loves justice," or NIV, "The King is mighty, he loves justice." REB has "The King in his might loves justice."

These options are generally acceptable (esp. NEB), but I have preferred to stay close to MT and adopt the approach of taking the governing verb as "let them praise" in v 3a (as in Cohen, 322; rejected out of hand by Eaton, 555), with קדוש הוא as a parenthetical statement (similar to Delitzsch, III, 98) with a relative clause. Two other options are offered in *HOTTP*, 372: (1) "and the might of the king who loves justice, you did (*or*, do) establish it with equity," and (2) "and the might is for the king who loves justice. You have established equity firmly, and. . . ." I assume that in these translations the referent of "king" is the Israelite king. These are possible readings for the psalm in pre-exilic contexts when the monarchy was in existence. The content in the Yahweh-*malak* psalms, however, is focused on the divine king and it would be strange to find a sudden reference to the earthly king.

4.b. Kraus (II, 850) translates the verb כון as "create": "justice and righteousness in Jacob, you have created." This is an acceptable meaning for כון in some contexts: e.g., Pss 8:4; 119:90; Isa 45:18; Prov 8:27. In English, "create" seems somewhat strange with "justice and righteousness." On the other hand, the basic criteria of divine creation in the OT are: (1) the bringing forth of something new, that which has not been before; (2) the production is the work of God by word, action, or process; it cannot be produced by unaided human or natural action. Thus in the light of these criteria, it is possible to think of Yahweh "creating" justice and righteousness in Israel: they are new and they are the work of Yahweh.

4.c. Lit., "justice and righteousness," but actions are implied in these words.

5.a. Understanding the prepositional *lamedh* in a locative sense, which is rare but seems to be present in Ps 132:7 (and possibly 1 Sam 1:28, though the text is uncertain). I assume that the *lamedh* on להר in v 9 ("bow down at his holy mountain") is used in the same way. Ollenburger (*Zion*, 49, 186, n. 164) argues for the meaning of "*to* the footstool" and "*to* the holy mountain," noting that the verb שחה ("bow down," in hithp) when used with the prepositional *lamedh* means "to bow down to" or "to give obeisance to/to venerate" (see Gen 27:29; Exod 32:8; Ps 45:12). When it means "bow down before," it is used with לפני (as in Gen 18:2; 1 Sam 25:41; 2 Chr 32:12); when "bow down at or toward," אל is used, or the simple directive -ה (Pss 5:8; 138:2; Lev 26:1 uses על). Ollenburger maintains that only Pss 99:5 and 132:7 could be locative out of all the uses of השתחוה ל-. However, these two references *may be* locative, and others seem ambiguous because the context is not clear (e.g., Gen 42:6; 2 Sam 12:20; 1 Kgs 1:23; Ps 106:19). Ollenburger (186) makes it clear that he does not intend to say that either the ark or Zion is worshiped, but that they can be "bowed down to" because they represent the presence of Yahweh. He is influenced by Jer 3:16–18 in which it is said that Jerusalem will be called "the throne of Yahweh" (cf. Isa 66:1–2) and Lam 2:1 in which Zion is identified as Yahweh's crown and his footstool (הדם רגליו): "Thus in the exilic period Zion itself could be identified with the throne of Yahweh and could itself symbolize the presence of God" (50; cf. Isa 60:14; 45:15; 49:23). There is no need to question the close association of the ark and of Zion with the presence of Yahweh, but I doubt that it is necessary to assume that the worshipers of Yahweh are to bow down *to* the footstool/ark and *to* Zion.

5.b. For "footstool" in cognate languages, see Dahood, II, 369.

6.a. Johnson (*Sacral Kingship*, 62–63, n. 4) argues strongly that Moses is not included among the priests. He argues that בכהניו involves a *beth essentiae* (GKC, 119i, 124g–i), which means "as," and that the plural "his priests" and "callers on his name" are plurals of excellence (as in Ps 118:7a; for *beth essentiae* with plurals, see Pss 54:5b and 118:7a). The reference is to Moses in a class by himself, according to Johnson, with Aaron and Samuel as priest and prophet par excellence, respectively. His translation is:

> Moses, and Aaron His priest,
> and Samuel as one who calls on His Name
> Would cry to Yahweh, and He would answer them.

The argument is grammatically sound and may be correct, though the Masoretes apparently wanted Moses and Aaron read together (note the *paseq* after Aaron) as does LXX.

7.a. Lit., "in," but the *beth* here probably means "from" (as in Dahood, I, 83; II, 369; Howard, 122; cf. Craigie, 149, n. 2.a, on Ps 15:2).

8.a. This statement has aroused much discussion (see Whybray, *ZAW* 81 [1969] 237–39, and Whitley,

ZAW 85 [1973] 227–30, for surveys of proposed solutions). The basic difficulty arises from what seems to some interpreters to be the strange introduction of the idea of "avenging" or "vengeance" on the part of God in a context which stresses divine forgiveness. Whybray (238) proposes what he calls "a simple solution to the problem" by returning to an old line of interpretation (noted by Delitzsch, III, 103, as going back to Symm and Kimchi, though rejected by Delitzsch) of taking the suffix on עלילותם, "their wrong-doings" as objective genitive, rather than subjective genitive as usually understood: "But also an avenger, on account of the evil deeds done to them." In this reading, Yahweh avenges the actions taken *against* his people by their enemies, and puts the colon in alignment with the mood in v 8.

Whitley (228–29) rejects this solution on the grounds that the passages cited by Whybray to support the objective genitive of the pronominal suffix (Gen 16:5; Obad 10; Jer 51:35; Isa 66:4) are either seriously suspect or else the antecedent is clear (as in Gen 16:5, where the preposition על means "from" rather than "on" [עליך]—Sarah's injury is from Abram, lit., "against you [Abram]"; cf. Whybray, 238; C. Westermann, *Genesis 12–36* [tr. J. J. Soullion (Minneapolis: Augsburg, 1981) 234, n. 5.b], who declares that this sense of על is not possible, and translates: "This outrage to me be upon you!"). Whitley's own solution is to read ונקם as ונקם, a singular active qal ptcp with the plural suffix from the root נקה, with the sense "cleanse" (normally expected in niphal and piel of this verb), thus: "he cleanseth them from (על) their evil deeds." Howard (*Structure*, 123) prefers to treat נקם in the sense of "vindication," denoting "the legitimate exercise of YHWH's executive power against those who do not call on YHWH's name" (following G. Mendenhall, *The Tenth Generation: The Origins of Biblical Traditions* [Baltimore: Johns Hopkins UP, 1973] 70–77, 82–88; see n. 58:11.a.), with על understood in the sense of "despite" (BDB, 754), a rare but not unknown usage (BDB cites Job 10:7 and 34:6): "And One who vindicates (them) despite their evil deeds." This has the advantage of having the entire verse portray Yahweh as acting on behalf of his people. However, I do not find a warning against wrong-doing so out of place in a context dealing with Yahweh's forgiveness, especially in view of the references to Moses, Aaron, Samuel (in v 6) and the wilderness experiences in v 7. These verses would inevitably recall the terrible acts of sin and apostasy by the Israelites, in the past (cf. also Ps 95:8–11; Exod 34:7; Num 14:20–23). Therefore I retain the meaning of punishment of the Israelites' own sins. REB: "Yet you called them to account for their misdeeds."

9.a. See n. 5.a. above.

Comment

Among Pss 96, 97, and 98, Ps 99 is the most anomalous. Kraus (II, 851) argues that unlike Pss 96–98 which are dependent on Deutero-Isaiah, Ps 99 is not dependent on Isa 40–55 at any point. He also contends that nothing speaks against a pre-exilic origin for it, in this regard being like Ps 98 (also Anderson, II, 694). Structurally Ps 99 is more difficult than Pss 96–97, with uneven stanzas and the possibility that the text has suffered some damage (Westermann, *Praise and Lament,* 149). Buttenwieser (321) argues that there is a narrow concern for the welfare of Israel in Pss 95, 99, and 100 which contrasts with broad visions of a universal reign of righteousness in Pss 93 and 96–98. Kraus (*Psalms 60–160,* 211) holds a similar, though milder, position: "In contrast to Psalms 96; 97; and 98, Psalm 99 does not deal with Yahweh's coming to the nations, but is concerned with the meeting with Israel which takes place in the covenant and the justice of God." But Ps 99 begins with the acclamation of Yahweh's kingship (יהוה מלך) and is a hymn of descriptive praise which exalts Yahweh over all peoples (and their gods) and bids the peoples of the world to join with the Israelites in the worship of Yahweh. I would not want to characterize it as expressing narrow concerns, though it lacks some of the broad sweep of Pss 96–98.

Acclamation of Yahweh as king and summons to worship (99:1–5). Vv 5 and 9, almost identical verses, serve to divide the psalm into two major parts (though some interpreters prefer three parts; e.g., Stuhlmueller, *Psalms II,* 92–93). The first part begins with the affirmation of Yahweh's reign as king. He is designated as the "Cherubim-enthroned-One," before whom the peoples and the earth itself are called to quake in respect and submission to his power (v 1). I have chosen to translate the verbs "tremble" and "quake" as jussive, forming a summons to homage as in vv 3, 5, and 9 and reflecting better the acclamatory nature of the verse (see note 1.c.). However, reading the verse as descriptive of a theophany may be correct (as in Weiser, 641). The divine epithet (ישׁב כרובים) refers to Yahweh as the divine king who sits on a cherubim throne, a throne seat visualized as supported by the wings of cherubim (winged creatures who symbolized the power and mobility of the enthroned king; see *Comment* on Ps 80:2). Yahweh is declared to be the "Great and Awesome One" who is located on Mount Zion and is exalted above all peoples (and their gods, see note 2.a.). His name is holy, as he is himself (vv 3 and 5). Yahweh's power and exaltation is used, however, in the service of justice and righteousness; he is "the King who loves justice" (v 4a; cf. Pss 33:5; 37:28). Yahweh is committed to a stable and just order in human society, as he has demonstrated in his actions relating to Israel (v 4bc).

As in other kingship psalms, the peoples are summoned to praise Yahweh (vv 2–3) along with his own people (v 5). I take it that the call in vv 4–5 is less an expression of Israelite superiority and a call for other peoples to submit to *their* (the Israelites') God than it is an appeal based on Yahweh's performance among his own, special people. "Out of this manifestation of God's righteousness, which is more conspicuous, and can be better estimated, within the nation of the history of redemption than elsewhere, grows the call to exalt highly Jahve the God of Israel, and to bow one's self very low at His footstool" (Delitzsch, II, 100). The "footstool" (הדם רגליו) most probably refers to the ark in the sense of it as a box used as a footstool for the enthroned (and invisible) divine king. Kings are depicted in the ancient world as sitting on thrones with their feet on footstools (cf. Solomon's throne in 2 Chr 9:18). For the argument that the "footstool" refers to the whole temple, both here and in Ps 132:7, see M. Haran, *Temple and Temple-Service in Ancient Israel* (Winona Lake: Eisenbrauns, 1985) 256. Isa 60:13 may use "footstool" with reference to the temple; also הדם may refer to the ark itself in 1 Chr 28:2; to Jerusalem in Lam 2:1, and to the whole earth in Isa 66:1; Matt 5:35; see also Ps 110:19. But the ark should not be separated from the cherubim throne (Kraus, II, 853; Weiser, 33–34, 39–40).

The use of the verb רום, "rise/raise up/exalt" in vv 2, 5, and 9 is one of the features which ties the psalm together. Yahweh is exalted (v 2, cf. Isa 6:1) and should be raised up in exaltation (רוממו, polel impv. pl.) by those who praise his name in vv 5 and 9 (for the verb in polel, with Yahweh as the object, see Pss 30:2; 107:32; 118:28; 145:1; Exod 15:2; Isa 25:1). The contexts indicate that the verb means to praise and also to respect and pay homage (as the use of the verb השׁתחוו, "bow down," in vv 5b and 9b indicate). The divine king who merits the homage of all peoples is "our God" (v 5a): Yahweh, who is the great one on Mount Zion.

Encouragement from salvation-history (99:6–9). Moses, Aaron, and Samuel are recalled as people in Israel's history who were powerful in prayer. All three are remembered in the traditions as great intercessors with Yahweh (for Moses, see, e.g., Exod 32–34; for Aaron, see the occasion of the plague in Num 16:44–48; for Samuel, see 1 Sam 7:7–12; 1 Sam 12:6–25; in 1 Sam 12:6 Samuel links himself with Moses and Aaron; also see Jer 15:1). All are powerful priest-prophets in the Israelite traditions. They also heard the voice of Yahweh speaking to them (v 7) and obeyed his commands and decrees.

The "pillar of cloud" recalls the wilderness experiences, of course, and applies directly to Moses and Aaron. Samuel also heard Yahweh speak in the temple at Shiloh (1 Sam 3:1–14). There is no specific mention of a pillar of cloud, but it may be that the column of smoke from the altar in the temple represented the cloud column. Yahweh responded to their prayers with forgiveness, but also held them to account for their wrongdoings. The conjunction of forgiveness and punishment may seem abrupt, but it is amply illustrated in the accounts of the three great priest-prophet-intercessor leaders in Israel's primal traditions. The juxtaposition of the God who forgives and the God who punishes may reflect Exod 34:6–7, where Yahweh is said to be both one who forgives and keeps his loyal-love and the one who punishes sin (Brueggemann, *The Message of the Psalms*, 149; on the coherent manifestation of power, justice, and mercy in Yahweh, see N. K. Gottwald, *The Tribes of Yahweh*. [Maryknoll, NY: Orbis Books, 1979] 685–88).

The recalling of Moses and Aaron, especially, and Samuel in a secondary sense, draws the reader's attention back to the wilderness wanderings and the life of early Israel. This correlates well with Ps 95, which ends (vv 8–11) with a sermonic message from Yahweh which admonishes the people to avoid the behavior of the Israelites at Meribah and Massah in the wilderness, when the ancestors of Israel "tested" Yahweh, though they had seen his works of deliverance. The Moses-wilderness motif provides a fitting conclusion for the first ten psalms in Book IV of the Psalter. Ps 90 is given a title which ascribes it to Moses, and Ps 95 serves as a psalm which frames the first five psalms and functions with Ps 100 to frame the four kingship-of-Yahweh psalms in Pss 96–99.

In fact, Book IV seems to be the "Moses Book" in the Psalter. Moses is mentioned by name in Pss 99:6; 103:7; 105:26; 106:16, 23, 32—six times, plus once in the title of Ps 90:1 (appearing elsewhere in the Psalter only in Ps 77:21). Moses appears with Aaron in Pss 99:6; 105:26, and 106:16, and elsewhere in 77:21 (Aaron appears elsewhere in Pss 115:10, 12; 118:3; 133:3; 135:19). The Moses-wilderness theme in these psalms suggests very strongly that the collection reflects the "wilderness" of the exile and post-exilic periods. The monarchy of David is gone, but Yahweh, who is the great king, above all gods and peoples, reigns and he is coming to judge the world.

The message of Book IV is rather clearly directed to the exiled religious community, as Ps 106:47 indicates (see the treatment of Ps 106 by Allen, 44–56). It is interesting to observe that the internal structure of Book IV is marked off (accidentally? or deliberately?) by Pss 95 and 100: Ps 95 follows five psalms and is followed by four psalms which expound the kingship of Yahweh already brought to focus in Pss 93 and 95. Ps 100 follows four kingship-of-Yahweh psalms and is followed by six psalms which are appropriate for the experience of exile (90–91–92–93–94/95/96–97–98–99/100/101–102–103–104–105–106). The emphasis on the kingship of Yahweh correlates with the Mosaic declaration that the Divine Warrior of Israel, Yahweh, would "reign (as king) forever and ever" (Exod 15:18). The kingship of Yahweh is grounded in the Mosaic traditions, and it is fitting that the largest grouping of psalms that express it be positioned under the Mosaic rubric. (The contention that the notion of the kingship of Yahweh could not have emerged in Israel until the time of the Israelite monarchy was common in the past, but it hardly needs refutation today; for a convenient reference, see Ollenburger, *Zion*, 31, 173, n. 48).

The Moses-wilderness motif in Book IV indicates that the psalms would have been appropriate for the Feast of Tabernacles, which commemorated the wilderness (Kidner, II, 354), and the collection may have been made for use in the celebration of Tabernacles in the second temple after 515 B.C.E. However, we know far too little about the life and worship of the Israelite communities in this period to be dogmatic. In addition to the Feast of Tabernacles, the use of the psalms in sabbath worship must be allowed for, and they may also have been used in family-centered worship and study in the Israelite communities. R. Albertz (*Personliche Frommigkeit und Offizielle Religion* [Stuttgart: Calwer, 1978] 173–90; also, see C. V. Camp, *Wisdom and the Feminine in the Book of Proverbs* [Decatur, GA: Almond, 1985] 243–50) contends that familial piety, the experience of God in the realm of everyday life, maintained social, economic, and religious unity during the time of the exile and was instrumental in protecting official religion during the exilic and post-exilic periods. We do not know how much of our Psalter owes its present form and content to the familial communities of the post-exilic period, but it is most probably a considerable debt.

Explanation

I have argued that Pss 96–99 form a coherent unit in Book IV of the Psalter, with two pairs of "twin" psalms: 96–97 and 98–99. These psalms are at the center of Book IV, and they provide a response to the petition in Ps 94:2–3:

> Rise, O Judge-of-the-Earth
> turn back on the arrogant what they deserve.
> How long will the wicked—O Yahweh—
> how long will the wicked celebrate?

Pss 96–99 give assurance that the Judge-of-the-Earth reigns and is coming to judge the world with equity (96:10, 13; 98:9). Therefore the righteous are encouraged to rejoice and praise Yahweh, anticipating that all peoples and nations will pay him homage and adoration. Those devoted to Yahweh are encouraged to remain true and confident, relying on the commitment of Yahweh to his people (94:12–15; 97:10–12). The hard, stubborn heart and will for rebellion remains a danger of course (95:8–11; 99:8). Wilson (*Editing*, 215) has declared that Book IV (Pss 90–106) is the editorial center of the present form of the Psalter: "As such this grouping stands as the 'answer' to the problem posed in Ps 89 as to the apparent failure of the Davidic covenant with which Books One–Three are primarily concerned."

The response formed by Book IV seems to consist of the following major elements:

1. Long before the monarchy in Israel, Yahweh was the Creator-King, "clothed with majesty and splendor" (Ps 104:1; cf. 96:6): "Before the mountains were brought forth, / and (before) you travailed with earth and world— / from everlasting to everlasting you are God!" (Ps 90:2).

2. Yahweh continues to reign as king over peoples, nations, and all other divine beings. This is, of course, the major direct emphasis of Pss 96–99 (with Pss 93 and 95). "New songs" are still in order (96:1; 98:1), because his works are ever new, and the future will be dominated by him. Pss 96–99 form the center of Book IV (Wilson, *Editing*, 215), and if the

conclusion is correct that Book IV constitutes the central focus of the Psalter, it means that Pss 96–99 form the stackpole for all the psalms. The kingship of Yahweh is associated with his power as creator and owner of the earth and as defender of his people. (For discussion of the exercise of Yahweh's kingship, see, conveniently and competently, Mettinger, *In Search of God*, tr. F. H. Cryer [Philadelphia: Fortress, 1988] 92–157; and Ollenburger, *Zion*, 51–144).

3. Yahweh's reign as king will be manifest with new power in the future. Pss 96–99 anticipate a new theophany, a new song of advent and powerful saving-works; these psalms throb with latent, if not overtly expressed, anticipation of a new coming of Yahweh. He is coming to judge the world: "Sing to Yahweh, bless his name, / proclaim (the news) of his salvation day after day" (Ps 96:2). Let people and nature sing his praise and shout for joy (96:11–12; 98:4–8). Though he tarries, he is still a refuge and a fortress to be trusted (91:2), who can keep his own safe despite pestilence, darkness, and destruction of life in the midst of world powers. The people who trust in him are blessed. "A thousand may fall beside you; / ten thousand on your right, / (but) it will not come near you" (91:7). "He protects the lives of his loyal ones; / he will deliver them from the land of the / wicked" (97:10). "Yahweh's loyal-love stays from age to age upon those who / revere him, and his vindication is for children's / children of those who keep his covenant and are / mindful to perform his charges. / Yahweh has set his throne firmly in heaven / and his kingly power rules over all" (103:17–19, tr. Allen, 17). "For Yahweh will not desert his people, / and his patrimony he will not forsake" (94:14).

The monarchs of Israel are dead and their kingdoms are no more, fallen as all human kingdoms are destined to do, but the Great King above all gods reigns in power and glory, though the full measure of that glory is not yet perceived by the peoples of the world. Nevertheless, it is a time of trembling, of shouting, of singing, and proclaiming. It is a time for Ps 100.

Serve the Lord with Gladness   *(100:1–5)*

Bibliography

Crüsemann, F. *Studien zur Formgeschichte.* 67–69. **Howard, D. M., Jr.** *The Structure of Psalms 93–100.* 129–39, 213–15. **Koch, K.** "'Denn seine Güte wahret ewiglich.'" *EvT* 21 (1961), 531–44. **Lewis, J. O.** "An Asseverative לא in Psalm 100:3?" *JBL* 86 (1967) 216. **Mayes, J. L.** "Worship, World, and Power: An Interpretation of Psalm 100." *Int* 23 (1969) 315–30. **Whitley, C. F.** "Some Remarks on *lu* and *lo*." *ZAW* 87 (1975) 202–4.

Translation

1   A psalm for thanksgiving.[a]
      Raise a shout to Yahweh, all the earth!   (3+3+3)

2   *Serve Yahweh with gladness;*
    come before him with joyful songs.[a]

3   *Acknowledge* [a] *that Yahweh, he is God.*   (4+4+3)
    He made us, and we are indeed [b]
    his people [c] *and the flock he shepherds.* [d]

4   *Enter his gates with thanksgiving,*   (3+2+3)
    his courts with praise;
    give thanks to him, and bless [a] *his name!*

5   *For* [a] *Yahweh is good; his loyal-love is forever,*   (4+3)
    and to generation after generation is his faithfulness.

Notes

1.a. The word תודה (also in v 4) can mean either "thanksgiving praise" or "confession" (Josh 7:19; Ezra 10:11). The root meaning of the verb ידה in hiphil is "to confess/declare/praise": a point strongly emphasized by C. Westermann (*Praise and Lament*, 25–35), who notes that there is no word in Hebrew which properly means "to thank," praise being either declarative, referring to what God has done, or descriptive, referring to what he characteristically does. The word תודה can also mean a "thank offering" or "thank sacrifice" (see the summary in Crüsemann, *Studien zur Formgeschichte*, 282–84). The תודה probably originally was a sacrifice offered in a thanksgiving ceremony and then became a "song of praise" to accompany the sacrifice (Gerstenberger, *Psalms*, 14). I have retained the traditional "thanksgiving," but the double meaning of the word should be remembered. Fortunately, the English "for thanksgiving" has a double nuance of "praise" and the "act of giving thanks" which could involve a worship service and is appropriate for the title (cf. Howard, *Structure*, 130). תודה appears in no other title of a psalm.

2.a. The long form רננה ("joyful songs" or "jubilation") appears here (as in Ps 63:6, in the plural) rather than the usual רנה, perhaps to give the colon a better balance.

3.a. Traditional, "Know that Yahweh is God" (lit., "know that Yahweh, he [indeed] is God") is used in the sense of a summons (1) to learn that Yahweh is God in terms of the "self-involvement in all the demands and responsibilities which the Lordship of Yahweh implies "(Anderson, II, 699), or (2) to be assured, to have no doubt, that Yahweh *is* God (Barnes, II, 472). However, the context seems to favor the idea of "acknowledge/recognize/confess" (as, e.g., Kraus, II, 855; NJV; REB). V 3. seems to be a form of a "recognition formula," which W. Zimmerli has delineated in the Book of Ezekiel, taking his case from the repeated use of the statement "And you (or "you" plural, or "they") shall know that I am Yahweh" (in "Knowledge of God according to the Book of Ezekiel," in *I Am Yahweh*, tr. D. W. Stott [Atlanta: John Knox, (1954) 1982] 30; a full list of the passages in Ezekiel is found on 143, n. 5). The formulaic saying also appears in other contexts (e.g., 1 Kgs 20:13, 28; Exod 6:6–9; 8:20; 16:12; 29:43–46). The freer formulation "know that Yahweh is God" (דעו כי יהוה הוא אלהים) appears to be Deuteronomic (Zimmerli, 51–52; cf. Deut 4:35, 39; 1 Kgs 8:60; 2 Kgs 19:19) and includes Ps 100:3 (Zimmerli, 53). The formula appears in varied forms in other contexts as well (Zimmerli, 53–63). The recognition of Yahweh is an acknowledgment of his identity in terms of his actions.

The pronoun הוא ("he") is added for emphasis (see GKC 141gh; cf. Deut 4:35; 7:9; Josh 4:18; 1 Kgs 18:39): "know that Yahweh, he is God," or even, "Yahweh alone is God" (Rogerson and McKay, II, 230, with special emphasis on 1 Kgs 18:39).

3b. This statement poses a famous question in interpretation. The *ketiv* of MT reads ולא אנחנו, "and not we (ourselves)," but the *qere* reads ולו אנחנו, "and we are his." LXX, Symm, and Syr suggest the "and not we ourselves" reading, but the "and we are his" has good support with some mss, Aquila, Jerome, and Targum (and cf. Ps 95:7; esp. note the variant in *BHS*: cf. Ps 79:13). Also, the Masoretic tradition reckons some fifteen passages in which לא ("not") is written but which should be read as is לו ("to him"; BDB, 520).

The modern translations vary, of course, according to the judgment of the translators. Lewis (*JBL* 86 [1967] 216) argues for an original asseverative ־ל (of the type found in Ugaritic, and vocalized as *lu* in Akkadian), which was either misunderstood or forgotten by the later scribes who wrote the negative לא: "He has made us, and indeed, we are his people." Whitley (*ZAW* 87 [1975] 203) also argues for an emphatic particle concealed behind the MT's לא, possibly לו (normally "would that" but now and then "indeed/verily" as in Gen 23:13; 30:34; probably Deut 17:18), and that in some passages the MT לֹא should be vocalized as לֹו (note 2 Sam 18:12; 19:7; Judg 21–22; Job 9:33; 1 Sam 20:14). Whitley's point is that the לֹא, however vocalized, can have the meaning of "surely/indeed" or a causal "accordingly": "He made us, and accordingly we are his people and the sheep of his pasture." For לֹא as emphatic, Whitley cites such passages as 2 Kgs 5:26; Hos 2:4 (Heb.); Job 13:15 (he does not, but should, list Isa 9:3); for interrogative-affirmative meanings of לֹא he cites such references as Obad 5; Jer 49:9; Job 2:10; Ezek 16:43. Of course, in some cases, the לֹא may be an abbreviated form of אִם־לֹא ("certainly").

Despite its support, the traditional reading of the *ketiv* ("he made us and not we ourselves") is improbable. If adopted, its main appeal is to Ezek 29:3, where the Egyptian Pharaoh claims "I have made myself" (MT). As Howard (*Structure*, 131–32) points out, there is no suggestion of self-creation in the context of Ps 100; the reading "not we ourselves" answers a question that "no one was asking or even thought to ask"—a judgment which is probably too strong, because the scribal tradition knew both readings and neither would have been foreign to their mind-set (cf. Loretz, II, 78). Nevertheless the main issue in Ps 100 is not between Yahweh's creation and Israel's self-creation. The emphasis is on Yahweh as the one who creates, rather than any other god (note the emphatic twofold use of הוּא, "he" in the verse). The reading of the *qere* "and we are his" is acceptable, of course, but it is somewhat tautological in view of the following clause ("his people, his flock, his shepherding"; Whitley, 203).

It seems to me that it is more likely that the לֹא in v 3 is emphatic (or was originally, at least) in the sense of "surely/indeed," and that the colons in 3b and 3c are related by enjambment, which avoids the problems of colon structure which Howard (134) discusses in connection with Lewis' proposal: "Know that Yahweh he is God he made us and indeed we are his people and the sheep of his pasture." The statements in v 3bc are similar to those in Ps 79:13 and 95:7, but the emphatic לֹא is missing in them.

3.c. Howard (*Structure*, 136), influenced by Codex Alexandrinus (which has "And we are his people"), suggests the possibility of adding וַאֲנַחְנוּ ("and we") or אֲנַחְנוּ ("we") at the beginning of the last colon: "It is he who has made us and we are his! / (We are) his people, and the sheep of his pasture." This balances the colons neatly, but is unnecessary because (as Howard notes) the "we are" is present implicitly in any case and MT is to be preferred.

3.d. The Heb. מַרְעִיתוֹ is a fem. sing. noun with a 3rd masc. sing. suffix, which means "his pasturage" or "his grazing place" (as in Jer 25:36). It usually seems, however, to convey the verbal idea of "shepherding" or "pasturing" (so BDB, 945; cf. Jer 23:1; Ezek 34:31; Pss 74:1; 79:13; 95:7). NEB and REB have "the flock which he shepherds"; NAB and NJV, "the flock he tends."

4.a. To "bless God" means to praise him for his deeds and gifts (cf. Pss 16:7, 34:2; 66:8; 68:26; 96:2; 103:1-2; 104:1). The piel forms of the verb "bless" (ברך) are used "to express solemn words that show the appreciation, gratitude, respect, joint relationship, or good will of the speaker, thus promoting . . . respect for the one blessed" (Sharbert, *TDOT*, II, 293). Further, "When God is the object, *brk* in the piel should always be rendered 'praise,' etc." Cf. Tob 12:6.

5.a. Crüsemann (*Studien*, 67) translates 5a as: "Yes, Yahweh is good, his commitment holds good forever," treating the כִּי as emphatic, in keeping with his argument for the force of כִּי in hymns (32–35) as having an emphatic or performance function; i.e., the statements are not primarily motivation or the basis for the praise but the content of the praise. Thus, v 5 could be translated: "How good is Yahweh! His loyal-love is forever, / and to generation after generation is his faithfulness!"

This understanding of the כִּי-statements may be correct in some cases (e.g., Exod 15:19; Pss 118:1b, 3b, 4b), and the translation "for" often appears in some contexts where logical linking to the preceding clause is lacking. However, Crüsemann has not made a very strong case for general application (for a rebuttal of his argument, see A. Aejmelaeus, *The Traditional Prayer in the Psalms*, 78–79). In the case of Ps 100:5, the flow of thought poses no difficulty for the causal force; whereas the causal does not fit in such contexts as Ps 118:2, 3 (though the כִּי there may have the force of introducing a "that" clause; as in the KJV of 118:2, 3, and 4).

Form/Structure/Setting

Ps 100 is almost universally classified as a hymn. In the categories of Crüsemann (adopted by Kraus, *Psalms 1–59*, 43), it is an imperative hymn, a judgment which is sustained by the seven imperative verbs used in vv 1b–4 (eight, if the double-duty verb in 4a is repeated for 4b: "Enter his gates . . . [enter] his courts . . . give thanks . . . bless his name"). The further classification of it as an entry hymn is rather popular (e.g., Gunkel, Oesterley, Kraus, Anderson, Weiser, Dahood). The setting is assumed to be that of a company of worshipers in front of the gates to the sanctuary summoned to enter the courts of the sanctuary with shouts and songs of praise. A thanksgiving service, with a thanksgiving sacrifice, would follow the entry (cf. Lev 7:12–15). A part of the service would be a meal, with the worshipers sharing together in eating part of the meat from the sacrifice. Cf. Ps 107:21–22: "Let them give thanks to Yahweh for his loyal-love, and for his wondrous works for human beings. Let them offer thanksgiving sacrifices, and proclaim his deeds with joyful shouting!"

The language of Ps 100 suggests a setting similar to Ps 95. The relatedness of the two psalms in language is apparent in 95:7 and 100:3. Both psalms open with a cry for shouts of joy (95:1b, 2b; 100:1b), using the verb רוע. Both call for תודה ("thanksgiving") to be given to Yahweh in his presence (95:2; 100:1–4), and Howard (*Structure*, 175) notes that the noun תודה appears only in these two psalms (95:2a; 100:1; 4a) out of all the psalms in Book IV (though the verbal form appears). The liturgical בא ("come/enter") occurs in 95:6a and 100:2a, 4a. Both psalms contain statements which emphasize the close relationship of Yahweh with his people (95:6a–7; 100:3). Of course, Ps 100 is a very short psalm; possibly only a fragment of a longer psalm, which served as an opening hymn "followed by an order of worship including other psalms and acts of worship" (Durham, 372).

The comments above assume a cultic setting for the psalm, which is appropriate. However, it was most probably used apart from occasions of public worship for family and individual use. The language may have been cult-specific in its original formulation, but in the present psalm it is generalized and not restricted to particular specific services of worship. In this regard, it seems wise to consider its placement in the Psalter and in Book IV specifically. Ps 100 is not directly a kingship-of-Yahweh psalm, but its sevenfold summons to give homage and praise to Yahweh forms a suitable sequel to Pss 96–99. The content of vv 1b–4 is that of royal language adapted to the Divine King, Yahweh. The multifold summons is addressed to "all the earth" (100:1b), which accords well with the universal sweep of the perspective in Pss 96–99.

Beyond its suitability as a sequel, the relatedness of the psalm to Ps 95 permits it to form one end of the frame around Pss 96–99 (a point recognized by Howard, 176). Older commentators were not unaware of the suitability of Ps 100 as a sequel to Pss 96–99 or even to 91–99, as, for example, Alexander (II, 349), "these psalms are not thrown together at random," and Perowne (210), who says that Ps 100 "may be regarded as the Doxology which closes the strain" of the "Jehovah is King" psalms in Pss 93–99: "It breathes the same gladness: it is filled with the same hope, that all nations shall bow down before Jehovah, and confess that He is God." Note also, P. Auffret, "Essai sur la structure littéraire du Psaume 94," *BN* 24 (1984) 71–72, who pairs Pss 95 and 100 and arranges Pss 93–101 in the following schema:

	94		
		95	
93			96+97
			98+99
		100	
	101		

Thus Ps 100 is both an appropriate sequel for Pss 96–99, for 93–99, and even for 90–99.

All of Pss 90–100 (and probably all of Book IV: Pss 90–106) respond to the seeming lack of faithfulness on the part of Yahweh in the demise of the Davidic monarchy and the lapse of the great promises which accompanied it as set forth in Ps 89. The last word in Ps 100 (אמונתו) affirms the enduring faithfulness of Yahweh (note the occurrence of אמונה in Ps 89:2, 3, 6, 9, 25, 34, and 50–it is probably of no special significance, but it is interesting to note the sevenfold use of "faithfulness" in Ps 89 and the sevenfold summons to praise Yahweh for his enduring "faithfulness" in Ps 100). Westermann (*Praise and Lament,* 255) says that Ps 100 has been added as a concluding doxology for Pss 93–99, and Stuhmueller, (*Psalms* II, 95) thinks it may conclude Pss 91–99.

The date of Ps 100 is a matter of guesswork. Its general nature and traditional language does not help much. Howard (*Structure,* 137) notes that the psalm is too short (and too lacking in distinctive lexical features) for much help in dating on the basis of lexical criteria, but he considers a pre-exilic date to be "a reasonable guess." V 4 may be used to indicate that it was written while a temple was standing–but which temple? The one before 587 B.C.E. or the one after 515 B.C.E.? I cannot share the confidence of Oesterley (430) who says, "The date is certainly post-exilic" (Kraus too thinks it is post-exilic, although he is more restrained), but the present form of the psalm and its position in the Psalter probably represent the post-exilic period. Its original composition may have been much earlier, or it may be a part of a longer psalm from an earlier date (as is perhaps Ps 93), or it may be a free composition drawn from traditional language and composed for some liturgical purpose in the post-exilic period (possibly for the celebration of Yahweh's kingship in the Festival of Tabernacles).

Comment

Ps 100 requires little comment beyond the discussion above. The language is familiar and the psalm has no difficult structural problems. V 1b–4 constitute an extended call to worship, with the use of seven imperative verbs. As noted above, there is a universal aspect to the call: the summons is given to "all the earth" (1b). Yahweh is assumed to be the lord of all the world and all lands and peoples should come before him with homage and praise (cf. Pss 47:3, 8; 66:1; 96:4–10; 98:2–4; 99:2; also 24:1; 50:12; 74:16; 89:11; 97:5; 115:16). "This is no choir calling only to Israelites within the sound of its voice; the sequence of imperatives reaches out to mankind" (Mays, *Int* 23 [1969] 320). Yahweh is the Great King over all the earth, although this psalm does not say so directly.

The addressees in Ps 100 are urged to "serve (עבד) Yahweh" (v 2). The verb עבד conveys a range of meaning. On one side it means to function as a servant or as a slave; to work for someone: e.g., in military service, Ezek 29:18, or to function as the subjects or agents of rulers, as, e.g., Judg 9:28, 38; 1 Kgs 5:1; Jer 27:7; 28:14. On the other side, the verb is used for worship: "serve a god, worship a god (properly: perform his cult)," (KB, 671). It is frequently used in Deuteronomy for worship of other gods than Yahweh (e.g., Deut 7:4; 8:19; 11:16; 28:36, 64; 30:17) as well as of commitment to and worship of Yahweh (e.g., Deut 6:13; 10:12; 11:13). It is also used of the service in a place of worship of priests and attendants (e.g., Num 3:7, 8; 4:23, 24, 30, 47; 7:5; 16:9; 18:6; Josh 22:27). Beyond the functions of priests and ministers, "you shall serve Yahweh your God" (as in Exod 23:25) is a basic requirement for all Israelites.

Mays (*Int* 23 [1969] 321–22) insists that such "service" of Yahweh has a political dimension, and that the language in Ps 100 has a monarchical frame of reference. "Come before him" in v 2b refers to the entry into a sanctuary and the presence of God (cf. Ps 95:6; Isa 1:12; Exod 34:24), but it is taken from the language for an audience before a human king (as in 2 Sam 14:3, 15; 15:2; Esth 4:11, 16; 8:1). The acclamations of praise called for in Ps 100:1b have their counterpart in the shouts of recognition and acclaim given to a king when he appears in public (cf. 1 Kgs 1:28, 32). The political aspects of "serving" Yahweh are apparent in Ps 2:11, where the kings and judges of the earth are bid to "serve [עבדו] Yahweh with fear" and to give up their rebellion against his divine rule and his anointed king. ("Serve Yahweh," עבדו את־יהוה, appears in Psalms only in 2:11; 100:2, and 106:36; cf. 102:23).

Mays (322) calls attention to the repeated requests of Moses in the exodus traditions for the Israelites to be allowed to leave the domain of the Egyptian Pharaoh to go into the wilderness to "serve Yahweh" (Exod 3:12; 4:23; 7:16; 8:1, 20; 10:26). Pharaoh recognizes that this is a political act as well as a religious one, and offers under duress to allow the Israelites to sacrifice to their God in the land of Egypt (Exod 8:25), or else not far away (Exod 8:28). Thus the summons to serve Yahweh is a call to worship Yahweh, "but its rubrics and movements and responses come from the political life of human society, because it is the recognition by men [*sic*] of the divine locus of power" (Mays, 322). The psalm incorporates a call to opt for the decisive, divine "power structure" in human affairs against the claims of conventional human power structures.

"Acknowledge that Yahweh, he is God" is a "recognition formula" (see note 3.a. above): "The knowledge involved is less cognition than recognition" (Mays, 323). The primary content of the acknowledgment is that "Yahweh is God," a Deuteronomic expression (Kraus, II, 856; Deut 4:35, 39; cf. Josh 24:7; 1 Kgs 18:39). There is a confessional quality to the recognition, because the statement is not a prayer to Yahweh but a statement to others about him. The recognition also involves Yahweh's creative work in the formation of Israel (v 3bc: "He made us"). The verb עשה ("made") is related to Israel's history of redemption (see 1 Sam 12:6; and Israel is the "making/work" of Yahweh (Isa 29:23; 43:7; 44:2; Deut 32:6, 15; Ps 95:6–7). Likewise, the New Israel of the future is to be the work of Yahweh's hands (Isa 60:21; also Isa 64:7). Zimmerli ("Knowledge of God," 64) concludes that the statements of recognition always assume the actions of Yahweh, actions which "precede the recognition, prompt it, and provide it with a basis." He adds: "There is no room here for knowledge emerging darkly from interior human meditation, 'from an existential analysis of human beings and the world, or from speculation.'" His emphasis on the action basis seems well taken, but there is no need to exclude all "human meditation," which seems to be encouraged in vv 3 and 5. Acknowledgment of Yahweh as God stems from an understanding of his deeds, but the understanding involves reflection and meditation.

The shepherd motif in v 3d is a monarchical one, applied to kings and leaders (see Nah 3:17–18; Cyrus in Isa 44:28; David in Ps 78:70–72; also Jer 10:21; 22:22; 23:1–4; 25:34–38; Ezek 34:1–10; Zech 10:3; 11:4–17). For the use of the term "shepherd" for ancient Near Eastern kings, see W. Zimmerli, *Ezekiel 2*, tr. J. D.

Martin (Philadelphia: Fortress, 1983) 213–14; *Ezekiel 1*, 242). Hammurabi refers to himself as "the shepherd who brings salvation and whose staff is righteous." Gods also are designated as shepherds; including such deities as Enlil, Marduk, and Tammuz (cf. Gen 49:24). Yahweh is the shepherd of Israel (Ps 80:1; Ezek 34:11–15; see also 23:1; 28:9; 74:1; 77:21; 78:52–53; 95:7; Isa 40:11; 49:9–10; 31:10; 49:19–20; 50:17–19; Mic 4:6–8; 7:14). The term "flock of his shepherding/pasture" (צאן מרעיתו) is found elsewhere as "the flock of my shepherding" in Jer 23:1 and Ezek 34:31; as "flock of your shepherding" in Ps 44:1; 79:13. The "people of his shepherding and the flock of his hand" is found in Ps 95:7. The image of the divine shepherd is linked to the exodus theme (note Pss 77:20–21; 78:52–52; Isa 60:11–14) which serves to relate this psalm to the Moses-Exodus-Wilderness features in Pss 90–99 (note 95:7–11).

The calls for praise and homage are intensified by v 4 (Mays, 325). Both the noun תודה ("thanksgiving") and the verb הודה (from ידה, "praise/give thanks") appear. As already noted, the תודה may refer to a thanksgiving sacrifice or offering as well as to the praise which constitutes thanksgiving. In the OT generally, praise and thanksgiving are parts of the same whole (P. D. Miller, Jr., "'Enthroned on the Praises of Israel': The Praise of God in Old Testament Theology," *Int* 39 [1985] 10–11). The aim in both praise and thanksgiving is "to exalt and glorify God," and the two belong together. Thanksgiving is more directly focused on what God has done and the experience of the one giving the thanksgiving, but praise also almost always arises from an awareness of what God has done, though it is more generalized and expresses what he *does* (for the mixing of the hymn and thanksgiving in the OT, see H. H. Guthrie, Jr., *Theology as Thanksgiving* [New York: Seabury, 1981] 1–30).

V 5 provides the climactic basis for the repeated calls to praise in vv 1b–4. The threefold qualities of Yahweh set forth in v 5 constitute the primary motivation for his praise: goodness, loyal-love, and faithfulness. V 5 is a variant of a formulaic expression which repeatedly appears in contexts of praising Yahweh (see Pss 106:1; 107:1; 118:1; 29; 131:1 and passim; 1 Chr 16:34; 2 Chr 5:13; 7:3, 6; 20–21; Ezra 3:10–11; Jer 33:11; cf. Pss 25:8; 34:9; 73:1; 86:5; 119:68; 135:3; 145:9). The definitive hymn formulation: "O give thanks to Yahweh, for he is good; / his loyal-love is forever!" may be "the Old Testament paradigm of the song of praise," expressing what the community of the faithful considers to be "its fundamental understanding of God" (Miller, 12). Indeed, the faith of Israel is set forth in this pregnant formulative saying (Koch, *EvT* 21 [1961] 540). Ps 100:5 contains the only form of this expression in the OT which brings together the three aspects of goodness, loyal-love, and faithfulness (for "good," see *Explanation* below; for "loyal-love" (חסד), see note 51:3.a.; for "faithfulness" (אמונה), see *Comment* on Ps 89:6–15).

Explanation

One of the striking features of this psalm is the affirmation that Yahweh is good (v 5). Mays (327) calls attention to the fact that "good" (216) functions in polarity with "evil/bad" (רע). The "good" is that which is not "evil" and the "evil" is that which is not "good." Both are experienced in life, but the satisfactory, happy, and successful life must be dominated by "good." Thus: "To speak of God as good is to affirm that the Lord of Israel is the source of all that makes life possible and worthwhile. It is an all encompassing attribute that catches up everything positive that human beings receive in life and often is experienced specifically in God's deliverance of persons from distress" (Miller, 12). The concept is an active one, of course. Yahweh is "good" because he does good things; acts which give life, which deliver from evil, and which empower the recipient with power.

The goodness of Yahweh is manifest in creation (note the repeated "it is good" in Gen 1). The description of the works of creation as "good" also conveys the sense of their beauty and the joy they evoke. God's works of creation brought forth shouts of joy (the verb is רוע, as in Ps 100:1) from the "sons of God," according to Job 38:7; cf. the exultation of wisdom over the inhabited earth in Prov 8:30–31, and the wish for God to rejoice in his own works in Ps 104:31. C. Westermann (*Creation,* tr. J. J. Scullion [Philadelphia: Fortress, 1974] 60–64) argues that beauty is part of the meaning in Gen 1: "see, it was very beautiful," though he contends that beauty in the OT is not primarily something inherent but is found in the experience with something or someone which brings pleasure and satisfaction. Thus the primary meaning of goodness is that something is good for the purpose for which it was prepared: "Creation is good for that for which God intends it" (61). The created order is intended as a living place for humanity and all of God's creatures, great and small. The goodness of creation lies in its ecological "beauty" and in its potential for life.

The goodness of Yahweh is also demonstrated in the formation and care of his people, which is affirmed in v 3. According to Deuteronomy, he sets before them "life and good" versus "death and evil" (30:15) and urges them to choose life, which is found in obedience to the ways of Yahweh (Deut 30:19–20; "For he is your life and the length of your days").

> Good and upright is the LORD,
>> therefore he instructs sinners in his ways.
> He guides the humble in what is right
>> and teaches them his way.
> All the ways of the LORD are loving and faithful
>> for those who keep the demands of his covenant.
>> (Ps 25:8–10, NIV)

Further, the goodness of Yahweh is manifest in his loyal-love and faithfulness to his people and to his purposes in creation and history. Ezra's successful journey to Jerusalem "because the good hand of Yahweh was upon him" (Ezra 7:9) can serve as a paradigm for Yahweh's good guidance and protection of his people: "The hand of our God is for good upon all that seek him" (Ezra 8:22); see also Ezra 8:18; Nah 2:8, 18; cf. Ezra 7:28; 8:31: "Truly, God is good to Israel" (Ps 73:1). The shepherd of Israel tends his flock so that "goodness and love" (טוב וחסד) pursue his people all the days of their life (Ps 23:6). And Yahweh requires goodness of his people:

> Learn to do good;
> seek justice, correct oppression;
> defend the fatherless, plead for the widow. . . .
> If you are willing and obedient,
> you shall eat the good of the land.
>> (Isa 1:17, 19, RSV)

See also Amos 5:14–15; Mic 3:2; 6:8; Prov 11:27; 12:2. Yahweh expects goodness from all his people, indeed from every human being (Mic 6:8), for he is good and his loyal-love and faithfulness last forever. The goodness of Yahweh is the "unshakable foundation" (Weiser, 647) on which all faith and hope rest. "Bless the Lord, O my soul, / And forget not all his benefits" (Ps 103:2). Yahweh is good, and we can serve him with gladness. He reigns as the Divine King, the Great King above all gods, and he is coming to judge the world. While we wait, we can serve him with gladness and praise his name. We are his family of people and the flock he shepherds. For the "people of Yahweh" as the "family of Yahweh," see N. Lohfink, "The People of God," in *Great Themes from the Old Testament*, tr. R. Walls (Edinburgh: Clark, 1982) 117–33.

Index of Authors Cited

Index of Principal Subjects

Index of Biblical Texts

A. Old Testament

B. New Testament

C. Apocrypha and Pseudipigrapha

D. Dead Sea Scrolls and Related Texts

Index of Key Hebrew Words